International Commercial Law

Shirley Guimarã (handwritten signature)

Third edition

In memory of my father
To my mother

International Commercial Law

Third edition

John Shijian Mo
LLB (Jilin, China), LLB (Mon), LLM (Dalhousie), PhD (Syd)
Barrister of the Supreme Court of Queensland
Barrister and Solicitor of the Supreme Court of Victoria
Professor, Faculty of International Law
Chinese University of Political Science and Law, Beijing
Arbitrator of the China International Economic
and Trade Arbitration Commission

LexisNexis Butterworths
Australia
2003

AUSTRALIA	LexisNexis Australia
	PeopleSoft House, 475–495 Victoria Avenue, CHATSWOOD NSW 2067
	On the internet at: www.lexisnexis.com.au
ARGENTINA	LexisNexis Argentina, BUENOS AIRES
AUSTRIA	LexisNexis ARD Orac GmbH & Co KG, VIENNA
BRAZIL	LexisNexis Latin America, SAO PAULO
CANADA	LexisNexis Butterworths Canada, MARKHAM, ONTARIO
CHILE	LexisNexis Chile Ltda, SANTIAGO
CZECH REPUBLIC	Nakladatelství Orac sro, PRAGUE
FRANCE	Juris-Classeur Groupe LexisNexis, PARIS
GERMANY	LexisNexis Germany, FRANKFURT
HONG KONG	
GREATER CHINA	LexisNexis Butterworths Hong Kong, HONG KONG
HUNGARY	HVG-Orac Publishing Ltd, BUDAPEST
INDIA	LexisNexis India, NEW DELHI
ITALY	Dott Giuffrè Editore SpA, MILAN
JAPAN	LexisNexis Japan, TOKYO
KOREA	LexisNexis Korea, SEOUL
MALAYSIA	Malayan Law Journal Sdn Bhd, KUALA LUMPUR
NEW ZEALAND	LexisNexis Butterworths, WELLINGTON
POLAND	Wydawnictwo Prawnicze LexisNexis, WARSAW
SINGAPORE	LexisNexis Butterworths Singapore, SINGAPORE
SOUTH AFRICA	Butterworths Publishers (Pty) Ltd, DURBAN
SWITZERLAND	Staempfli Verlag AG, BERNE
TAIWAN	LexisNexis, TAIWAN
UNITED KINGDOM	LexisNexis Butterworths Tolley, LONDON, EDINBURGH
USA	LexisNexis Group, NEW YORK
	LexisNexis, MIAMISBURG, OHIO

National Library of Australia Cataloguing-in-Publication entry

---

Mo, John
 International commercial law.

3rd ed. Includes index.
ISBN 0 409 32037 4.

1. Commercial law. 2. International law. I. Title.

341.754

© 2003 Reed International Books Australia Pty Limited

This book is copyright. Except as permitted under the Copyright Act 1968 (Cth), no part of this publication may be reproduced by any process, electronic or otherwise, without the specific written permission of the copyright owner. Neither may information be stored electronically in any form whatsoever without such permission.

Inquiries should be addressed to the publishers
Typeset in Garamond MT, Optima and Gill Sans
Printed in Australia by McPherson's Printing Group
Visit LexisNexis Australia at www.lexisnexis.com.au

Contents

Preface	ix
Table of Cases	xi
Introduction	1

1 International Sale of Goods under Domestic Law — 3

Introduction	3
Conventions relevant to international sale of goods	4
Effect of customs	6
Relevance of domestic law	6
What is an international sale of goods?	8
Application of Incoterms 2000 in international sales	9
Legal framework for international sale of goods in Australia	37
International sale of goods and general contract law	38
International sale of goods and the Australian sale of goods legislation	40
International sale of goods and the Chinese Code of Contract Law	57

2 Contracts of Sale under the CISG — 77

Introduction	77
Application of the Convention	78
Modifying or varying the effect of the provisions of the Convention	85
Formation of a contract	87
Fundamental breach under the Convention	96
Performance of contract	101
Remedies	133
The passing of risk under the Convention	163
Preservation of goods under the Convention	167
Conclusion: potential use of the Convention through modification and interpretation	171
Incorporation of the Convention into Australian law	175
Constitutional implications of the CISG	175

3 Contracts Relating to Intellectual Property — 177

Introduction	177
A brief description of intellectual property	178
Franchising agreements	178
Licensing agreements	192
Distribution agreement	202
Transfer of technology agreements	208
E-commerce	215

4 Contracts for Carriage by Sea, Air and Land — 223

- Introduction to the Law of Carriage — 223
- Carriage of goods by sea — 228
- Contracts for the carriage of goods by air — 296
- Contracts for carriage by land — 329
- Carriage of goods by multimodal transport — 351

5 Means of Payment in International Trade — 358

- Overview — 358
- The major concerns in effecting payment in international trade — 358
- The basic methods of payment in international trade — 359
- International legal framework for payment in international transactions — 360
- Means of payment under domestic law — 363
- Defining terms in effecting payment — 366
- Payment by cash in advance — 371
- Payment by open account — 371
- Payment by collection — 372
- Payment by way of documentary credit — 397
- Means of payment under the UN Conventions — 426

6 Introduction to International Banking and Financing — 438

- Review of international banking and financing system — 438
- International financial centres and international finance — 441
- Issue of bonds and international finance — 442
- International syndicated loans and international finance — 456
- The International Monetary Fund and international finance — 459
- Exchange control and international finance — 461
- Foreign exchange risks — 462
- Factoring in international trade — 470
- Leasing in international trade — 476
- Forfaiting in international trade — 482

7 Marine Insurance, Aviation Insurance and International Trade — 486

- Introduction — 486
- Explaining marine insurance — 487
- General principles for the making of a marine insurance contract — 493
- Making of a cargo insurance contract — 494
- Making of a hull insurance contract — 496
- Legal framework for international marine insurance — 496
- Explaining an insurable interest — 499
- Explaining 'marine risks' — 501
- Categories of marine insurance contracts — 504
- Forms of marine insurance documents — 508
- Assured's duty to disclose the relevant information — 510
- Insurer's duties and inherent vice — 514
- Broker's duties to assured and insurer — 515
- Reinsurance and insurer's liability — 516

Contents

Burden of proof as to the cause of the loss	517
Included and excluded losses	518
Categories of losses	521
Determination of indemnity	523
Assignment of policy	527
Insurer's right of subrogation	527
Aviation insurance	528

8 Foreign Investment Law — 538

Introduction	538
Explaining foreign investment	540
Relationships between foreign investment and host country	541
Forms of foreign investment	543
International legal framework for foreign investment	550
The WTO and foreign investment	564
Selected issues for the regulation of foreign investment	572
Means for protection of foreign investment	574
International Court of Justice and foreign investment	576

9 The World Trade Organisation — 578

Introduction	578
A brief history of the WTO	578
Major functions of the WTO	579
The WTO Agreement and its annexes	581
Structure of the WTO	582
General Agreement on Tariffs and Trade	588
GATT Agreement	590
General Agreement on Trade in Services (GATS)	607
TRIPs Agreement	613
Dispute settlement within the WTO	617
The WTO and competition law	628
The WTO and other international trade organisations	630

10 Regional Trade Organisations — 631

Introduction	631
The European Union	631
Asia Pacific Economic Cooperation (APEC)	644
Association of South East Asian Nations (ASEAN)	648
North America Free Trade Agreement (NAFTA)	652
Australia–New Zealand Closer Economic Relations	657

11 International Commercial Litigation and Conflict of Laws — 660

Defining international trade and commercial disputes	660
Resolving disputes between governments	661
Resolving disputes involving private parties	662
Defining the means of dispute settlement	662
Defining international commercial litigation	664

International Commercial Law

Domestic courts and international commercial litigation	665
Functions of the courts in international commercial litigation	666
Contract disputes and conflict of laws	667
Tortious disputes and conflict of laws	675
Certain exceptions	677
Disputes relating to real estate and conflict of laws	678
Disputes relating to chattels personal and conflict of laws	679
Enforcement of foreign judgment	681
Enforcement of foreign judgments in Australia	684

12 Alternative Means of Settling International Commercial Disputes — 690

Defining alternative means	690
Defining international commercial arbitration	690
Legal framework for international commercial arbitration	693
The Hague Conventions	704
Major international arbitral institutions and their functions	705
Major procedural issues in international commercial arbitration	712
The New York Convention and international commercial arbitration	722
International commercial arbitration and the CISG	729
Other alternative methods of settling international commercial disputes	730

Index — 733

Preface

We are now in the year 2003. So much has happened in the past two years since the second edition of this book was published. China has become a WTO member, the EU has been enlarged to 25 countries, and — far less significantly — I am now working in Beijing. The world has certainly become faster, smaller and better; if we are not at the same time depressed with the war in Iraq, the outbreak of SARS in some 30 countries, and the human rights abuses which continue in many societies today.

Much has also happened to the body of law that we regard as international commercial law. New treaties have been made, cases have been decided and legislation has been passed. The trend of international economic interdependence has grown stronger, and so has that of regional economic cooperation. International commerce and trade has become vital for all countries wishing to achieve a fast and significant economic growth within the legal framework of the WTO, which is effectively developing and shaping a new international economic order across the globe. It is hoped that this new edition can appropriately reflect these changes within, of course, the word limit as set by the publisher.

In order to reflect the new developments of international commercial law and to further rationalise the structure of the book, I have made a number of changes to this edition. In terms of structure, I have merged Ch 8 in the second edition with Chs 7 and 9 respectively of this edition. Presently, the book has 12 chapters, instead of 13 (per the second edition). Recent developments and new cases have been added to all chapters of this edition. The major changes are: the Chinese Code of Contract Law concerning international trade in Ch 1; the addition of new cases concerning the CISG in Ch 2; recent developments and new cases in the area of carriage law and international financial law in Chs 4, 5 and 6; recent developments in foreign investment law and discussions on the new OECD Declaration on International Investment and Multinational Enterprises, as well as the present OECD Guidelines for Multinational Enterprises in Ch 8; recent developments of the WTO in Ch 9; recent developments in regional cooperation and free trade arrangements in Ch 10; and recent developments in the areas of dispute settlement, and the addition of recent information on the China International Economic and Trade Arbitration Commission, in Chs 11 and 12. It is hoped that these changes will ensure that this edition is found to be useful, up-to-date, and also concise and user-friendly.

As usual, in the completion of this new edition, I express my sincere thanks to my publisher, LexisNexis Butterworths, and the friendly staff responsible for the project — in particular, Rowena Oldfield, Susan Gintel and Teresa Vaccaro. I also express my gratitude to the editor of this edition, Andrew Wright, for his efficient editorial assistance.

International Commercial Law

During past years of my teaching and researching in the area of international commercial law, I have benefited greatly from various comments made and challenging questions raised by many of my colleagues and students in Australia, Hong Kong and Mainland China. On this occasion, I express my deep appreciation and sincere thanks to them all. Last, but not least, I thank my wife Catherine Shunyu Liu for her love, understanding and support.

John Shijian Mo
Beijing, PRC
May 2003

Table of Cases

references are to paragraphs; bold references are extracted cases

Abnett v British Airways Plc (Scotland); Sidhu v British Airways Plc (unreported) 4.208, 4.209, 4.259

Accinanto Ltd v A/S Ludwig Mowinskels [1951] 4.79, 4.92

Adhiguna Meranti, The [1987] 11.48

Adler v Dickson [1955] 4.117

Adriano Gardella SpA v Government of the Republic of the Ivory Coast (1993) 8.90

A-G v Times Newspapers [1974] 12.63

AGIP v Congo (1993) **8.89**, 8.90

Agro Air Association Inc v Houston Casualty Co (1997, unreported) 7.105

Air Canada v Demond (1990, unreported) 4.237

Air Separation v Lloyd's of London (1995) 7.104

Akai Pty Ltd v People's Insurance Comp Ltd (1996, unreported) 11.14, 11.30

Allden v Raven (The 'Kylie') [1983] 7.62, 7.65

Altendore Australian Pty Ltd v Parkanson Pty Ltd (1995, unreported) 3.30

Amalgamated Society of Engineers v Adelaide Steamship Co Ltd (1920) 2.310

Amco Asia Corp v Republic of Indonesia (1993) 8.90, **12.30**

American Eagle Insurance Co v John H Thompson (1996, unreported) 7.123

American Network Inc v Access America/Connect Atlanta Inc (unreported) 3.47

American President Lines Ltd v China Mutual Trading Co Ltd [1953] 4.92

Anders Maersk, The [1986] **4.57**

Anthony John Sharp and Roarer Investments Ltd v Sphere Drake Insurance Plc, Minster Insurance Co Ltd and EC Parker & Co Ltd (The 'Moonacre') [1992] **7.32**, 7.34, **7.61**, 7.73, 7.88

Aotearoa International Ltd v Westpac Banking Corp [1984] **5.123**

Apostolos Konstantine Ventouris v Mountain (The 'Italia Express') (No 2) [1992] 7.82

Aqualon (UK) Ltd v Vallana Shipping Corp [1994] **4.305**, 4.322

Arab Bank Ltd v Ross [1952] 5.52

Arcos v EA Ronaasen & Son [1933] 1.75

Argos, The (1873) 4.137

Aronis v Hallett Brick Industries Ltd [1999] 1.11

Ashford Shire Council v Dependable Motor Pty Ltd (1960) 1.77

Ashington Piggeries Ltd v Christoper Hill Ltd [1972] 1.76, 1.77

Asian Century Holdings Inc v Fleuris Pty Ltd [2000] 5.101

Athanasia Comninos, The; and Georges Chr Lemos, The [1990] 4.131

Athens Maritime Enterprises Corp v Hellenic Mutual War Risks Assoc (Bermuda) Ltd (The 'Andreos Lemos') [1983] 7.40

Atlas Air Australia Pty Ltd v Anti-Dumping Authority (1990) 9.32

Audiencia Provincial, Barcelona (1997, unreported) 2.134

Australasian Shipping Commission v Kooragang Cement Pty Ltd [1988] 4.113

Australasian United Steam Navigation Co Ltd v Hiskens (1914) 1.61, 4.90, 4.106, 4.113

Australia and New Zealand v France (1973, unreported) 8.91

Australian Knitting Mills Ltd v Grant (1933) 2.115

Avel Pty Ltd v Multicoin Amusements Pty Ltd (1990) 3.28, **3.36**

Bachmann Pty Ltd v BHP Power New Zealand Ltd [1998] 5.101, 5.102

Bacon v Purcell (1916) 2.85

Balmedie Pty Ltd v Nicola Russo [1997] 8.19

Bank fur Gemeinwirtschaft v City of London Garages [1971] 5.51

Bank Negara Indonesia 1946 v Lariza (Singapore) Private Ltd [1988] **5.110**

Bank of India v Gobindram Naraindas Sadhwani [1988] **11.27**

Bank of Taiwan v Union Syndicate Corp [1981] 5.143

Bankers Trust Co v State Bank of India [1991] **5.127**

Bankinvest AG v Seabrook (1988) 11.50

Banque de L'Indochine ET de Suez SA v JH Rayne (Mincing Lane) Ltd [1983] **5.136**

Baoli Hotel of Yinhai v Mingyue Special Lighting Co Ltd of Inner Mongolia (1994, unreported) **1.100**

Barcelona Traction, Light and Power Company; Belgium v Spain [1970] 8.92

Barclays Bank Ltd v Customs and Excise (1963) 4.63
Bartlett v Sydney Maracas Ltd [1965] 1.76
Base Construction Corporation (Henan) of China Exported Commodities v Foreign Trade Development Co of Shenzhen (1992, unreported) **1.101**
Bedial, SA v Paul Muggenburg and Co GmbH (1995, unreported) 2.282
Beijing Metals & Minerals Import/Export Corp v American Business Centre Inc (1993) 2.307
Bell Bros Pty Ltd v Rathbone (1963) 1.41
Berdero Price (Malyasia) Sdn Bhd v Scheepvaartonderneming Leidesegracht CV [2000] 4.54
Berger & Light Diffusers Pty Ltd v Pollock [1973] 7.52
Berk v Style [1955] 7.67
Bernhard Blumenfeld Kommandit Gesellschaft Auf Aktien v Sheaf Steam Shipping Co Ltd (1938) 4.92, 4.93
Bezirksgericht St Gallen (1997, unreported) 2.20
BHP Trading Asia Ltd v Oceaname Shipping Ltd (1996, unreported) 4.53
Black King Shipping Corp v Massie (The 'Litsion Pride') [1985] 7.63
Bolivinter Oil SA v Chase Manhattan Bank NA [1984] 5.141, 5.145
Boronia Park Properties Pty Ltd v Arramunda Airway Pty Ltd [1995] 1.1
Bowden Brothers & Co Ltd v Robert Little (1907) **1.32**
Boys v Chaplin [1968] 11.48
Braber Equipment Ltd v Fraser Surrey Docks Ltd (1998, unreported) 4.118
Brandt v Liverpool, Brazil and River Plate Steamship Navigation Co [1924] 4.68
Breavington v Godleman (1988) 11.42, 11.47
Bremen, The v Zapata Off-Shore Co (1971) 4.89
Bridge Shipping Pty Ltd v Grand Shipping SA (1991) 1.8
Brinks Ltd v South African Airways (1998, unreported) 4.256
Brown v Craiks Ltd [1970] 1.76
Bundesgerichtshof (1995, unreported) 2.105
— (1995, unreported) 2.175
— (1996, unreported) 2.80
— (1996, unreported) 2.134
— (1997, unreported) 2.250
— (1997, unreported) 2.303
— (1997, unreported) 2.10
Burges v Wickham (1863) 4.83
Burns Philp & Co Ltd v Gillespie Brothers Pty Ltd (1947) 4.92, **4.137**
Burrard Towing Co v Reed Stenhouse Ltd (1996, unreported) 7.81

Business Electronics v Sharp Electronics (1988) 3.34

Cabot Corp v The Mormacscan [1971] 4.25
Cadbury Schweppes Inc v FBI Foods Ltd [1999] 3.27
Calzaturificio Claudia snc v Olivieri Footwear Ltd (1998) **1.15**, 1.16
Cammell v Sewell (1858) 11.56
—v— (1860) 11.56
Canada Inc and Prudential Assurance Co Ltd v Air Canada (1997, unreported) **4.245**
Canastrand Industries Ltd v Ship 'Lara S' (1989, unreported) 4.24
Canton of Ticino: Pretore della giurisdizione di Locarno Campagna (1992, unreported) 2.254
Canusa Systems Ltd v Vessel 'Canmar Ambassador' (1998, unreported) 4.48, 4.322
Cape Asbestos Co Ltd v Lloyd's Bank Ltd [1921] 5.93
Carlos v Fancourt (1794) 5.39
Carlos Federspeil & Co SA v Charles Twigg & Co Ltd [1957] **1.47**
Carragreen Currencies Corp Pty Ltd v Corporate Affairs Commission NSW (1986) 6.90
Carrington Slipways Pty Ltd v Patrick Operations Pty Ltd (1991) 4.23, 4.46, 4.49, **4.51**, 4.85
Catherwood Towing Ltd v Commercial Union Assurance Co (1996, unreported) 7.81
CCR Fishing Ltd v Tomenson Inc (The 'La Pointe') [1989] **7.38**
Century Insurance Co of Canada v Case Existological Laboratories [1984] 7.37
Champanhac & Co Ltd v Waller & Co Ltd [1948] 1.78
Chaplin v Boys [1971] 11.46
Chapman Marine Pty Ltd v Wilhelmsen Lines A/S [1999] 4.91, 4.100, 4.105, 4.120
Charles Goodfellow Lumber Sales Ltd v Verreault, Hovington and Verreault Navigation Inc [1971] 4.93
Chartwell Shipping Ltd v QNS Paper Co Ltd [1989] 4.48
Cheung Yiu-wing v Blooming Textile Ltd (1977) 5.67
China-Schindler Co Ltd North Division v Fung Hing Co Ltd (1991) 1.42
Chloride Industrial Batteries Ltd v FW Freight Ltd [1989] **4.301**
Cicatiello (GL) v Anglo European Shipping Services Ltd [1994] **4.316**
Claude B Fox Pty Ltd v Raynor [1978] 1.77
Comalco Aluminium Ltd v Mogal Freight Services Pty Ltd (1993, unreported) 4.39
Commercial Trading Co Inc v Hartford Fire Insurance Co [1974] 7.82

references are to paragraph numbers; bold references are extracted cases

Table of Cases

Commission v Belgium [1983] 10.12
Compania Maritime Astra, SA v Archdale (The 'Armar') [1954] 7.48
Compania Naviera Santi SA v Indemnity Marine Insurance Co (The Tropaiofaros) [1960] 7.77
Computerland [1989] 3.18
Confecciones Del Atlantico v Lamont Shipping Inc [1982] **11.58**
Consolidated Mining v Straits Towing Ltd [1972] 4.79, 4.92
Consolidated Rutile v China Weal [1998] 1.84
Con-Stan Industries of Australia Pty Ltd v Norwich Winterthur Insurance (Australia) Ltd (1986) 11.16
Continental Shipper, The [1976] 4.92
Continental TV Inc v GTE Sylvania Inc (1977) 3.18
Courage Ltd v Grehan (1999, unreported) 3.18
Craig v Association National Insurance Co Ltd (1983) 7.84
Crayford Freight Services Ltd v Coral Seatel Navigation Co [1998] 4.321
Credit Lyonnais v PT Barnard & Associates Ltd [1976] **6.77**
Curl & Curl v Captain Sturt Marine Pty Ltd (1982) 1.78
Cybersell Inc v Cybersell Inc (1997, unreported) 3.46

Danisches Bettenlager GmbH & Co KG v Forenede Factors A/S (1996, unreported) 2.16
Data Concepts Inc v Digital Consulting (1998, unreported) 3.47
Deaville v Aeroflot Russian International Airlines [1997] 4.261
Delchi Carrier SpA v Rotorex Corp (1994, unreported) 2.269
— (1995, unreported) 2.204
Demby Hamilton Ltd v Barden [1949] 1.57
Demitri v General Accident Indemnity Co (1996, unreported) 7.5
Dennant v Skinner and Collom [1948] **1.45**
DHL International (NZ) Ltd v Richmond Ltd [1993] **4.210**
Direct Acceptance Finance Ltd v Cumberland Furnishing Pty Ltd [1965] 2.66
Discount Records Ltd v Barclays Bank Ltd [1975] 5.120, **5.142**, 5.145
Dixon v Sadler (1839) 4.83
—v— (1841) 4.83
Doak v Weeks (1986) 7.64, 7.70
Dolling-Baker v Merrett [1990] 12.76
Dona Mari, The [1973] **4.65, 4.68**
Dooney, Re [1993] **11.77**
Dora, The [1989] 7.60, 7.63, 7.64, 7.65

Downs Investments Pty Ltd (in vol liq) (formerly known as Wanless Metal Industries Pty Ltd) v Perwaja Steel SDN BHD [2000] 2.152, 5.89
Durham Fancy Goods Ltd v Michael Jackson (Fancy Goods) Ltd [1968] **5.53**

Edward Owen Engineering Ltd v Barclays Bank International Ltd [1978] 5.141
Edward Wong Financial Co Ltd v Infinity Industrial Co Ltd [1977-79] 5.48
Effort Shipping Co Ltd v Linden Management Sa (The 'Giannis Nk') [1994] 4.97, 4.128
Elder Smith Goldsbrough Mort Ltd v McBridge Palmer [1976] 1.75
Elders IXL Ltd v Lindgren (1987) 11.33
Elettronica Sicula SpA ('ELSI') (1989) 8.92, 8.93
Eli Lilly & Co v Apotex Inc (unreported) 3.24
Emery Air Freight Corporation v Merck Sharpe & Dohme (Aust) Pty Ltd [1999] 4.225
Enterprise Alain Veyron v Societe E Ambrosio [1996] 2.77
Esso Australia Resources v Plowman (1995) 12.76, **12.77**
Euro-Diam Ltd v Bathurst [1988] **11.35**, 11.40
Ever Eagle Co Ltd v Kincheng Banking Corp [1993] 5.145
Export Credits Guarantee Department v Universal Oil Products Co, Procon Inc and Procon (Great Britain) Ltd [1983] **5.74**

Fawcett v Smethurst (1914) 1.98
Forestal Mimosa v Oriental Credit Ltd [1986] **5.84**
Four Square Stores (Qld) Ltd v ABE Copiers Pty Ltd (1981) 1.77
Fraser River Pile & Dredge Ltd v Can-Dive Service Ltd (1997, unreported) 7.4
Freight Systems Ltd v Korea Shipping Corp (1990, unreported) 4.48
Furness Withy (Aust) Pty Ltd v Metal Distributors (UK) Ltd (The 'Amazonia') [1990] **12.92**

Gaetano Don v Mario Mantero [1976] 10.13
Gamer's Motor Centre (Newcastle) Pty Ltd v Natwest Wholesale Australia Pty Ltd (1987) 1.61, 2.82
Gatewhite Ltd v Iberia Lineas Aeras de Espena SA [1989] 4.251
—v— [1990] 4.209
Gebruder Metelmann GmbH v NBR (London) Ltd [1984] 1.85
Gee & Garnham Ltd v Whittall [1955] 7.68, 7.82
Gefco UK Ltd v Mason [1998] 4.298, 4.302, 4.308
George Kallis (Manufactures) Ltd v Success Insurance Ltd [1985] **7.17**

references are to paragraph numbers; bold references are extracted cases

George Straith Ltd v Air Canada (1991) 4.251
Gian Singh & Co Ltd v Banque de L'Indochine [1974] 5.99, 5.131
Gibson v Small (1853) 4.83
Godina v Patrick Operations [1984] 4.120
Godley v Perry [1960] 1.78
Golden Acres Ltd v Queensland Estates Pty Ltd [1969] 11.30
Golden Ocean Assurance Ltd and World Mariner Shipping SA v Christopher Julian Martin [1989] **7.76**
Goole and Hull Steam Towing Co Ltd v Ocean Marine Insurance Co Ltd [1928] 7.91
Gosse Millerd v Canadian Government Merchant Marine Ltd [1927] 4.110
GPL Treatment Ltd v Louisiana-Pacific Corp (1996, unreported) 2.6
Grant v Australian Knitting Mills Ltd [1936] 1.76, 1.77
Graves Import Co Ltd v Chilewich Intl Corp (1994, unreported) 2.64
Great China Metal Industries Co Ltd v Malaysian International Shipping Corp [1998] 4.83
Green v Australian Industrial Investment Ltd (1989) 11.29, 11.34, 11.40

Habib Bank Ltd v Bank of South Australia [1977] 5.117
Hadley v Baxendale (1854) 2.72
Halley, The (1868) 11.44
Hamilton, Fraser &Co v Pandorf (1887) 7.36
Hamzeh Malas & Sons v British Imex Industries Ltd [1958] 5.99
Handelsgericht des Kantons Zurich (1995, unreported) 2.217
— (1995, unreported) 2.131
— (1996, unreported) 2.61
— (1997, unreported) 2.248, 2.269
Hardwick Game Farm v Suffolk Agricultural Poultry Producers Asscn [1969] 2.115
Hardy (MW) & Co Inc v AV Pound & Co Ltd [1955] 1.12
Harlow & Jones Ltd v American Express Bank Ltd [1990] 5.21, 5.119
Harper (AC) & Co Ltd v Mackechnie & Co [1925] 7.56
Harris v Plymouth Varnish & Colour Co Ltd (1933) 2.116
Hassneb Insurance v Mew [1993] 12.76
Hellenic Lines Ltd v Chemoleum Corp [1972] 4.85, 4.168
Hellenics Steel Co v Svolamar Shipping Co Ltd (The 'Komninos S') [1990] 4.79, 11.40
Her Majesty the Queen v Purolator Courier Ltd (1997, unreported) 4.19

Herd & Co v Krawill Machinery Corp (1959) 4.115
Hi-Fert Pty Ltd v Kiukiang Maritime Carries Inc [1998] 1.8, 4.54
—v— [2000] 4.35, 4.80
—v United Shipping Adriatic Inc [1998] 1.8
HIH Casualty & General Insurance Ltd v Waterwell Shipping Inc [1998] 7.11, 7.85
Hill & Delamain (Hong Kong) Ltd v Manohar Gangaram Ahuja (t/as Vinamito Trading House) [1994] 4.240
Hines Exports Pty Ltd v Mediterranean Shipping Co [2000] 4.18, 4.35, 4.82
Hing Yip Hing Fat Co Ltd v Daiwa Bank Ltd [1991] **5.129**
Hodge v Club Motor Insurance Agency Pty Ltd and Australian Associated Motor Insurers Ltd (1974) 11.47
Hoeper v Neldner [1931] 1.42
Howe Richardson Scale Co Ltd v Polimex-Cekop and National Westminster Bank Ltd [1978] 5.82
Hoyanger, The [1979] 4.92
Huddart Parker Ltd v Cotter (1942) 4.83
Hunter Grain Pty Ltd v Hyundai Merchant Marine Co Ltd (1993) 4.85

Ian Stach Ltd v Baker Bosley Ltd [1958] 5.106
IBBCO Trading Ltd v HIH Casualty & General Insurance Ltd [2001] 5.22, 7
Indussa Corp v SS Ranborg (1967) 4.89
Industrial Waxes, Inc v Brown [1958] 7.50
Inflatable Toy Company Pty Ltd v State Bank of New South Wales (1994) 5.145, **5.147**
Innsbruck (1994, unreported) 2.135
Inowroclaw, The [1989] 4.79
Integrated Container Service Inc v British Trader's Insurance Co Ltd [1984] 7.98
International Alpaca Management Pty Ltd, Textile Finance Ltd and Coolaroo Alpaca General Partner Pty Ltd v Ben KE Ensor and Garrymere Farms Ltd (1995, unreported) 1.8
International Business Machines Co v Shcherban [1925] 2.115
Interstate Parcel Express Co Pty Ltd v Time-Life International (Nederlands) BV (1977) 3.28, 3.36
Ionides v Pender [1874] 7.60
Islamic Investment 1 SA v Transorient Shipping Ltd and Alfred C Toepfer International Gmbh (1998, unreported) 4.130

Jade International Steel Stahl Und Eisen GmbH & Co KG v Robert Nicholas (Steels) Ltd [1978] 5.44

Table of Cases

Jian Sheng Co Ltd v Great Tempo SA (1997, unreported) 4.35
JK International Pty Ltd v Standard Chartered Bank Australia Ltd [2000] 5.82
John Kaldor Fabricmaker Pty Ltd v Mitchell Cotts Freight (Australia) Ltd (1989) 11.28, **11.31**
John T Bill Co v United States (1939) 9.21
John Weyerhaeuser, The [1975] 4.83, 4.93
Jones v Chatfield [1993] 6.76

Kaleej International Pty Ltd v Gulf Shipping Lines Ltd (1986) 4.48
Kanematsu (F) & Co Ltd v Ship Shahzada (1956) 4.74
Kanematsu Gmbh v Acadia Shipbrokers Ltd and Seanav International Ltd (1999, unreported) 4.48, **4.63**, 4.86, 4.87
Kantonsgericht Nidwalden (1997, unreported) 2.216
Kay Minge v JW Oak Furniture Imports Ltd and William Heinhuis (1998, unreported) **1.10**
Keele v Findley (1990) **11.79**
Kendall v Lillico [1969] 1.76
KH Enterprise (Cargo Owners) v Pioneer Container (Vessel Owners) [1994] **11.41**
Kirkham v Attenborough [1897] 1.53
Kishinchand & Sons (Hong Kong) Ltd v Wellcorp Container Lines Ltd and Wellcorp Express (Canada) Ind (1994, unreported) 4.86, 4.94
Koe Guan Co v Yan On Marine & Fire Insurance Co Ltd [1906] 4.87
Koninklijke Bunge v Compagnie Continentale D'Importation [1973] 4.30, 4.92
Kopitoff v Wilson (1876) 4.83
Korea Exchange Bank v Debenhams (Central Buying) Ltd [1979] **5.28**, 5.29, 5.54
Krasnogrosk, The (1993) 4.169
Kretschmer GmbH & Co KG v Muratori Enzo (1988, unreported) 2.5
Kuebne Nagel (Hong Kong) Ltd v Yuen Fung Metal Works Ltd [1979] 4.38, 4.86
Kwok Wing v Maytex Trading Co (1977) 5.66

Laceys Footwear (Wholesale) Ltd v Bowler International Freight Ltd [1997] 4.313
Laing v Boreal Pacific (1999, unreported) 7.85
Lamb Head Shipping Co Ltd v Jennings (The 'Marel') [1992] 7.77
Landegericht Frankfurt a M (1991, unreported) 2.68
Landgericht Aachen (1989, unreported) 2.254
— (1993, unreported) 2.81
Landgericht Baden-Baden (1991, unreported) 2.113
Landgericht Trier (1995, unreported) 2.111

Law & Bonar Ltd v British American Tobacco Co Ltd [1916] 1.69
Lazarus v Deutsche Lufthansa AG (1985) 11.42
Les Industries Perlite Inc v The Marina Di Alimuri (TD) (1995, unreported) 4.132
Leval v Colonial Steamships [1960] 4.92
Lindsay v Miller [1949] **11.39**
Lloyd v Fleming [1872] 7.99
Lloyd (JJ) Instruments Ltd v Northern Star Insurance Co Ltd [1985] 7.70
Lockwood v Moreira (1998, unreported) 7.93
London General Insurance Co v General Marine Underwriters' Asscn [1921] 7.62
Lucena v Craufurd [1806] 7.31
Lucky Trading Co and Lucky Snow Enterprises (Canada) Ltd v Icicle Seafoods Inc (1998, unreported) 1.76
Lucky Wave, The [1985] 4.92
Lynne Watson and Alessandro Belmann [1976] 10.13
Lyon v Creati (1892) 2.85

Macaura v Northern Assurance Co Ltd [1925] 7.34
MCC-Marble Ceramic Centre, Inc v Ceramica Nuova Dagostino, SpA (1998, unreported) 2.307
McClintock v Union Bank of Australia Ltd (1920) 5.43
McDermid v Nash Dredging & Reclamation Co Ltd [1987] 7.31
McFadden v Blue Star Line [1905] 4.83
McGregor v Huddart Parker (1919) 4.93
McKain v RW Miller & Co (South Australia) Pty Ltd (1991) 11.47
MacKinnon McErlane Booker Pty Ltd v PO Australia Ltd [1988] 7.93
McNeill & Higgins Co v Czarnikow-Reinda Co (1921) 2.116
Magellan International Corp v Salzgitter Handel GmbH (unreported) 2.219
Maharani Woollen Mills Co v Anchor Line [1927] 4.89
Mahkutai, The [1996] 4.121
Malca-Amit Ltd v British Airways Plc (1990, unreported) 4.255
Malik v Bank of Credit; Mahmud v Bank of Credit (1997, unreported) 6.2
Man (ED & F) Ltd v Nigerian Sweets & Confectionery Co Ltd [1977] 5.138, 5.139
Manzel Equipment Pty Ltd v APE Pte Ltd [2000] 5.148
Margaronis Navigation v Henry Peabody [1964] 1.66
Markham Meat Industries Supplier Inc v Air France (1998, unreported) 4.258

references are to paragraph numbers; bold references are extracted cases

Marques Roque, Joaquim v SARL Holding Manin Riviere [1996] 2.68
Marstrand Fishing Co Ltd v Beer (The 'Girl Pat') (1936) 7.88
Matthew Short & Associates Pty Ltd v Riviera Marine (International) Pty Ltd [2001] 1.44, 1.54
Maurice Desgagnes, The [1977] 4.35, 4.38
Maxform SpA v Mariani and Goodville Ltd [1981] 5.36
Mercantile Mutual Insurance (Australia) Ltd v Gibbs [2001] 7.39, 7.40
Merwin Pastoral Co Pty Ltd v Moolpa Pastoral Co Pty Ltd (1933) 11.52
Metro Meat Ltd v Fares Rural Co Pty Ltd [1985] **1.19**, 1.20
Michael Doyle & Associates Ltd v Bank of Montreal (1984) **5.122**
Midland Bank v Seymour [1955] **5.132**
Miller (RW) & Co Pty Ltd v Australian Oil Refining Pty Ltd (1967) 4.96
Mitsui & Co Ltd v Gold Star Line Ltd [1975] 4.54
Monsanto Co v Spray-Rite Service Corp (1984) 3.34
Moore & Co and Landauer & Co, Re [1921] 2.121
Moralice (London) Ltd v ED & F Man [1954] 5.134
Morris v Rayners Enterprises Inc; Morris v Agrichemicals Ltd (1997, unreported) 6.2
Mount Albert Borough Council v Australasian Temperance and General Mutual Life Assurance Society [1937] 11.22
Muirhead v Commonwealth Bank of Australia [1996] 5.66

Nanka Bruce v Commonwealth Trust Ltd [1926] 1.52, 2.156
National Commercial Bank v Wimborne (1979) 11.49
National Semiconductors (UK) Ltd v UPS [1996] 4.313, 4.414
Nauru v Australia (unreported) 8.91
NCNB National Bank v Gonara (HK) Ltd [1984] 5.29
Nederlandse Speciaal Drukkerijen v Bollinger Shipping Agency [1999] 4.22, 4.24
Neuchatel Swiss General Insurance Co Ltd v Vlasons Shipping Inc [2001] 7.18
New Motor Vehicle BD of California v Orrine W Fox Co (1978) 3.10
New Zealand Shipping v Satterthwaite (The 'Eurymedon') [1975] 4.119, 4.120
Niblett Ltd v Confectioners' Materials Co Ltd [1921] 1.74, 2.98, 2.99

Nicaragua v United States (1984, unreported) 8.91
Nikolay Malakhov Shipping Co Ltd v SEAS Sapfor Ltd [1998] 4.78, 4.111
Nippon Yusen Kaisha v Ramjiban Serowgee [1938] 4.64
Nissho Iwai Australia Ltd v Malaysian International Shipping Corporation, Berhad (1988) 2.66, 4.76
— v— (1989) 4.110, 4.111
Nogar Marin, The [1987] 4.54
— [1988] 4.64
North American Speciality Insurance Co v Shirley Myers (1997) 7.111, 7.123
Noten (TM) BV v Harding [1989] 7.67
Novopharm Ltd v Eli Lilly [1998] 3.22, 3.24
NSW v Commonwealth (The Incorporation case) (1990) 1.41
NSW Leather v Vanguard Insurance (1991) 7.31, 7.33, 7.41

Obergericht des Kantons Luzern (1997, unreported) 2.132
Oberlandesgericht Celle (1995, unreported) 2.230
Oberlandesgericht Dusseldorf (1993, unreported) 2.133
— (1994, unreported) 2.229
— (1994, unreported) 2.205, 2.209, 2.215, 2.218
— (1996, unreported) 2.222
Oberlandesgericht Frankfurt a M (1991, unreported) 2.68, 2.216
Oberlandesgericht Hamm (1992, unreported) 2.47, 2.209
— (1995, unreported) 2.221
— (1995, unreported) 2.153, 2.218
Oberlandesgericht Karlsruhe (1997, unreported) 2.130
Oberlandesgericht Koln (1994, unreported) 2.19, 2.48
— (1996, unreported) 2.123
Oberlandesgericht Munchen (1994) 6.87
— (1995, unreported) 2.308
— (1995, unreported) 2.33
— (1995, unreported) 2.131
— (1998, unreported) 2.130
Oberlandesgericht Oldenburg (1995, unreported) 2.240
Oberster Gerishtshof (1997, unreported) 2.18, 2.55
Ocean Shipping Co of Shanghai v Haerbing Chemical Products Import and Export (Dalian) Co (1992, unreported) 4.128
Oceanic Sun Line Special Shipping Co Inc v Fay (1988) 1.32, 11.34

Table of Cases

Oilmes Combustibles SA v Vigan SA S/Ordinario (1991, unreported) 2.5
Osterreichische Landerbank v S'Elite Ltd [1980] 5.51
Overseas Commodities Ltd v Style [1958] 7.68, 7.85

Pacific Composites Pty Ltd v Transpac Container System Ltd (t/as Blue Anchor Line) [1998] 4.81
Pacific Composites Pty Ltd, Lermarne Corp Ltd v Blue Anchor Line, ANL Ltd & United Arab Shipping Co [1997] 1.8, 4.70
Parouth, The [1982] 11.32
Percy v West Bay Boat Builders (1997, unreported) 7.72
Phillips v Eyre (1870) 11.44, 11.46, 11.47, 11.48, 11.50
Phillips Petroleum Co v Cabaneli Naviera SA (The 'Theodegmon') [1990] 4.79, 4.80
Pickersgill v London & Provincial Marine Insurance Co [1912] 7.59
Picturesque Atlas Co Ltd v Searle (1892) 1.67, 2.85
Piesse v Tasmanian Orchardists & Producers Co-operative Assn Ltd (1919) 2.85
Polurrian Steamship v Young [1915] 7.88
Poole v Smith's Car [1962] 1.53
Port Jackson Stevedoring Pty Ltd v Salmond & Spraggon (Australia) Pty Ltd (The 'New York Star') (1978) 4.74, 4.119, 4.120
— v— (1980) 4.120
Power Curber International Ltd v National Bank of Kuwait [1981] 5.120
President of India v Metcalfe Shipping Co [1969] 4.54
Pronuptia de Paris GmnH v Pronuptia de Paris Irmgard Schillgalis [1986] 3.18
— [1989] 3.18

Queen Charlotte Lodge Ltd v Hiway Refrigeration Ltd (1998, unreported) 7.82

Rafsanjan Pistachio Producers Co-operative v Bank Leumi (UK) Plc [1992] 5.141
Randell v Atlantica Insurance Co Ltd (1983) **7.47**, 7.64, 7.70
Rayner (JH) & Oilseeds Trading Co Ltd v Hambros Bank Ltd [1942] 5.134
Razelos v Razelos (No 2) [1970] 11.49
Red Sea Insurance Co Ltd v Bouygues SA [1994] 11.46, **11.48**
Rewia, The [1991] 4.35
Rheinland Versicherungen v srl Atlarex and Allianz Subalphina spa (unreported) 2.28

Rhesa Shipping Co SA v Edmunds (The 'Popi M') [1985] 7.77
Rigby (Nicola) v Decorating Den Systems Ltd (1999, unreported) 3.17
Rocklea Spinning Mills Pty Ltd v Anti-Dumping Authority (1995) **9.32**
Roder Zelt-Und Hallenkonstruktionen GmbH v Rosedown Park Pty Ltd (1995) 1.8, 2.18, 2.278
Rolfe Lubbell & Co v Keith and Greenwood [1979] 5.36
Rosenfeld Hillas & Co Pty Ltd v Ship 'Fort Laramie' (1923) 4.41
Rosenhain v Commonwealth Bank of Australia (1922) **5.39**
Ross v Adelaide Marine Assurance Co [1970] 7.46
Rowland v Divall [1923] 1.74
Rudolph Robinson Steel Co v Nissho Iwai Hong Kong Corp Ltd [1998] 5.21, 5.119
Russell v Canadian General Insurance Co (1999, unreported) 7.83
Rustenberg Platinum Mines Ltd v South African Airways [1977] 4.256
Ryder v Wombwell (1868) 1.98

Sabine Howaldt, The [1970] 4.92, 4.93
Sale Continuation Ltd v Austin Taylor & Co Ltd [1967] 5.138
Samsung Hong Kong Ltd v Keen Time Trading Ltd [1988] 1.75
Sanko Steamship Co Ltd and Grandslam Enterprise Corp v Sumitomo Australia Ltd (1995, unreported) 4.82
SARL Bri Production Bonaventure v Societe Pan Africa Export [1995] 2.306
Saunders v Ansett Industries (1975) 4.252
Schibsby v Westenholz (1870) **11.63**
Schiedsgericht der Hamburger freundschaftlichen Arbitrage (1996, unreported) 2.4
Schiedsgericht der Handelskammer Hamburg (1996, unreported) 2.176
Schureck v McFarlane (1923) 2.85
Scruttons Ltd v Midland Silicones Ltd [1962] 4.118
Shearwater Marine Ltd v Guardian Insurance Co (1998, unreported) 7.88
Shell Chemicals UK Ltd v P & O Roadtanks Ltd [1995] 4.309
Shell International Petroleum v Caryl Antony Vaughan Gibbs (The 'Salem') [1981] 7.40
Ship Agencies Australia Pty Ltd v Fremantle Fishermen's Co-Operative Society Ltd (1991) 1.78, 2.167
Ship 'Marlborough Hill', The [1921] 4.51
Ship 'Mercury Bell' v Amosin (1986) **11.37**
Ship 'Socofl Stream' v CMC [2001] 4.54, 4.86

references are to paragraph numbers; bold references are extracted cases

Shipping Co of Tianjin v China International Engineering and Materials Corp and Tongli Development Co (unreported) 4.135
Shipping Corp of India Ltd v Gamlen Chemical Co (A'asia) Pty Ltd (1980) 4.79, 4.84, 4.151
Siderurgica Mendes Junior SA and Mitsui & Co v Owners of Icepearl (1996, unreported) 4.54
Silbert Sharpe & Bishop Ltd v Geo Wills & Co Ltd [1919] 2.115, 2.121
Simms v West (1961) 1.41
Simms Jones Ltd v Protochem Trading NZ Ltd [1993] 1.77
Skandia Insurance v Skoljarev [1979] **7.78**
Slattery v Mance [1962] 7.84
Smith & Sons v Peninsular & Oriental SN Co (1938) 4.80, 4.83
Societe Calzados Magnanni v SARL Shoes General International (SGI) (1999) 2.4
Societe Camara Agraria Provincial de Guipuzcoa v Andre Margaron [1995] 2.63
Societe Ceramique culinaire de France v Societe Musgrave Ltd (1996, unreported) 2.303
Societe Fauba v Societe Fujitsu [1996] 2.14, 2.59, 2.296
Societe Francaise de Factoring International Factor France v Roger Caiato (1995, unreported) 2.112, 6.98
Societe Isea Industrie SPA v SA Lu (1995, unreported) 2.46
Societe Lorraine des Produits Metallurgiques v Banque Paribas Belgique SA [1995] 2.159
Societe Mode jeune diffusion v Societe Maglificio il Falco di Tiziana Goti e Fabio Goti (1997, unreported) 2.81
Societe Productions SCAP v Roberto Faggioni (1998, unreported) 1.9
Societe Sacovini v SARL Les Fils de Henri Ramel (1996, unreported) 2.7
Societe Termo King v Societe Cigna France (1996, unreported) 2.9, 2.107
Society of Lloyd's v Canadian Imperial Bank of Commerce [1993] 5.145
Soproma SpA v Marine & Animal By-Products Corp [1966] 5.131, 5.137
Southland Rubber Co Ltd v Bank of China [1997] 5.85
Southwark, The (unreported) 4.83
Soya GmbH Kommanditgesellschaft v White [1980] 7.64
—v— [1982] **7.69**
St George Bank Ltd v Heinz Salzberger and Norma Salzberger [2001] 5.131
Standard Bank of Canada v Wildey (1919) 5.56, 5.70
State Auto Mut Ins Co v Babcock (1974) 7.109

Strangemores Electrical Ltd v Insurance Corp of Newfoundland Ltd [1997] 7.80
Suisse Atlantique Societe d'Armement Maritime SA v NV Rotterdamsche Kolen Centrale [1967] 2.66
Sumner Permain & Co v Webb & Co [1922] 2.116
Swell v Burdick (1884) 4.51
Sze Hai Tong Bank Ltd v Rambler Cycle Co Ltd [1959] 4.38, 4.63, 4.86
Sztejn v J Henry Schroder Banking Corp (1941) 5.146

Tanning Research Laboratories Inc v O'Brien (1990) **12.35**
Tasman Express Line Ltd v JI Case (Australia) Pty Ltd (1992) **4.75, 4.101**
Textile Material Co of Huarun Ltd v Shipping Agent Co of Zanijiang (1994, unreported) 4.86, 4.87
Thames & Mersey Marine Insurance Co v Gunford Shipping Co [1911] 7.65
Thomas Cook Group v Air Malta Co Ltd [1997] 4.257
Thomas William v Network Solutions (1999, unreported) 3.47
Thorne v Borthwick (1956) 1.78, 2.119
Thyssen Canada Ltd v Mariana Maritime SA (1999, unreported) **4.171**
Touraine, The (1927) 4.83, 4.92
Trading & General Investment v Gault Armstrong & Kemble (The 'Okeanis') [1986] **7.74**
Trans Western Express v Ouadrant Sales and Imports Inc (1996, unreported) 4.37
Transfield Pty Ltd v Arlo International Ltd (1980) 3.25
Triangle Underwriters Inc v Honeywell Inc (1979) 1.41
Tribunal Cantonal du Valais (1994, unreported) 2.162
Tribunal Supremo (1997, unreported) 2.5
Trishul (UK) Ltd v Winnie Tong t/as Winda Product [1987] **5.149**
Troy v Eastern Co of Warehouses [1921] 4.48
Trustees, Executors & Agency Co Ltd v Margottini [1960] 11.28
Tukan Timber Ltd v Barclays Bank Plc [1987] 5.145
Turner v Manx Line [1990] 7.35

Underwood Ltd v Burgh Castle Brick and Cement Syndicate [1922] 1.51
Union of India v McDonnell Douglas Corp [1993] **12.66**
United City Merchants (Investments) Ltd v Royal Bank of Canada [1982] 5.99, 5.131
—v— [1983] 5.141

Table of Cases

United Dominions Corp Ltd v Brian Pty Ltd (1985) 8.19, 8.23
United Fisheries Ltd v Papasavas & Co [2001] 5.105
United Mills Agencies Ltd v RE Harvey, Bray & Co [1952] 7.16
United States v Iran (1979, unreported) 8.91
United Technologies International Inc v Magyar Legi Kozlekedesi Vallat (Malev Hungarian Airlines) (1992, unreported) 2.36

Van Leer Australia Pty Ltd v Palace Shipping KK (1994) 1.8
Verna Trading Pty Ltd v New India Assurance Co Ltd (1991) 7.98
Victoria Laundry Ltd v Newman Industries Ltd [1969] 2.72
Vimar Seguros Y Reaseguros SA v M/V Sky Reefer (1995, unreported) 4.89
Visscher Enterprises Pty Ltd v Southern Pacific Insurance Co Ltd [1981] 7.64, **7.66**, 7.70
Vita Food Products Inc v Unus Shippings Co [1939] 11.40
Vitol SA v Norelf Ltd [1995] 2.262, 2.263
Viva Vino Import Corp v Farnese Vini srl 2000 (1997) 2.18
Vogel v R & A Kohnstamm Ltd [1973] **11.64**
Voth v Manildra Flour Mills (1990) **11.17**, 11.42

Wait, Re [1927] 1.54
Wayfoong Credit Ltd v Remoco (HK) Ltd [1983] 5.48
Werner v Det Bergenske Dampskibsselskab (1926) 4.79
Westcoast Food Brokers Ltd v Hoyanger and Westfallarsen & Co A/S [1979] 1.34

Westinghouse cases 9.74
Westpac Banking Corp v Royal Tongan Airlines (1996, unreported) 1.11
—v 'Stone Gemini' [1999] 4.38
Westrac Equipment Pty Ltd v 'Assets Venure' [2002] 4.84
Westwood Shipping Lines v Geo International (1998, unreported) 4.72
WFM Motors Pty Ltd v Maydwell [1996] **11.66**
Whybrow v Howard Smith (1913) 4.80
Wilensko v Fenwick [1938] 1.66
William Holyman & Sons Pty Ltd v Foy & Gibson Pty Ltd (1945) 4.90, 4.106
Williams v Society of Lloyd's [1994] 1.8
Wilson v Darling Island Stevedoring and Lighterage Co Ltd (1955) 4.120
Wimble, Sons & Co v Rosenberg [1913] 1.69
Winkenson Impex Co Ltd v Haverton Shipping Ltd [1985] 4.45
Wood v Associated National Insurance Co Ltd [1984] **7.79**
Word Publishing Co Ltd, Re [1992] **11.73**
WŸrttembergische Milchverwertung-SŸdmilch-AG v Salvatore Ugliola [1969] 10.13

X Construction Co v Trading Co of Shuchang (1992, unreported) 1.99

Yeoman Credit Ltd v Gregory [1963] 5.54
Yorkshire Insurance Co Ltd v Nisbet Shipping Co Ltd [1961] 7.100

Zivilgericht des Kantons Basel-Stadt (1997, unreported) 2.159

references are to paragraph numbers; bold references are extracted cases

Introduction

International commercial law or international trade law (defined broadly as a group of loosely connected rules, norms or customs governing trading and commercial activities between states) has developed abreast with international trade and commerce. It is an area of law with growing international importance.

International commerce or trade has long played an essential role in world development. People initially traded within a local region with other people from neighbouring states. As humankind developed the capacity to navigate and fly across continents, people began to trade with people from the other side of the earth. The world has grown closer economically since the end of the Second World War due to the continuous improvements in scientific research, technology, productivity, economic, the social and political environment, international cooperation, and the regulation of international commerce and trade. In particular, international commerce and trade has entered into a new era since 1995, when the World Trade Organisation (WTO) came into existence. The development of international commerce and trade has become vital to all countries of the world, and the development of international commercial and trade law has become crucial for the development of these markets.

This book hopes to provide a concise and yet reasonably comprehensive discussion of major issues of international commercial law within a length deemed reasonable for students. Chapter 1 deals with the international sale of goods under domestic law; Chapter 2 examines contracts of sales under the United Nations Convention on Contracts for the International Sale of Goods (CISG); Chapter 3 concentrates on contracts relating to intellectual property; Chapter 4 investigates contracts for carriage by sea, air and land; Chapter 5 reviews the means of payment in international trade; Chapter 6 provides an introduction to international banking and financing; Chapter 7 discusses marine insurance, aviation insurance and international trade; Chapter 8 relates to foreign investment law; Chapter 9 examines the World Trade Organisation; Chapter 10 discusses the regional trade organisations; Chapter 11 deals with international litigation and conflict of laws; and Chapter 12 is devoted to alternative means of settling international commercial disputes.

This book covers not only those issues of international commercial law that fall under the sphere of 'public' international law, such as the WTO, regional trade organisations and foreign investment, but also those issues falling predominately within the sphere of private law, such as contracts of sale, contracts of carriage, payment in international trade, insurance in international commerce and dispute settlement. All these issues are important, because together they provide a comprehensive navigation chart for anyone venturing into the area of international commercial and trade law.

International Commercial Law

This book represents an effort to study international commercial law from a combined perspective of international and common law. Updated international conventions and documents are examined in most chapters, where relevant. Due to space limitations, howver, a number of international documents have been omitted or only examined briefly. Many legal issues of international trade and commerce, such as E-commerce, E-banking, fair competition in the world market, the relationship between international trade and environmental protection, extraterritorial operation of many domestic commercial laws, conflict of laws rules affecting international trading activities, operation of anti-dumping rules, imposition of countervailing duties, use of safeguard measures within the WTO framework, decisions of WTO panels, international taxation and so on, also cannot be studied in detail in this book because of space limitations. Due to the reality that any study of international law must be based on one or two particular legal systems, Australian law (or the law of a common law jurisdiction) is referred to in most chapters where legal issues are examined in the context of a domestic law. However, it should also be noted that a large quantity of materials on domestic law and case law have been omitted, due to lack of space in this edition.

Chapter One

International Sale of Goods under Domestic Law

Introduction

[1.1] An international sale of goods may be subject to domestic law for at least two reasons. First, the domestic law is supplementary to the relevant international convention or international commercial custom when each covers a different area of the international sale. For example, a contract for the sale of an aircraft is not governed by the United Nations Convention on Contracts for the International Sale of Goods 1980 (CISG);[1] thus, in a situation similar to *Boronia Park Properties Pty Ltd v Arramunda Airway Pty Ltd* [1995] NTSC 16,[2] the relevant domestic law — for example, Australian law — should apply, even if the buyer or seller is a foreign party. Second, the domestic law governs an international sale in the absence of any international convention or international commercial custom. A convention only operates between its members. It is not unusual for an international sale to take place between people from two or more countries (or customs territories)[3] that are not parties to the same convention. Nor is it uncommon for a court to find that a particular piece of domestic law is applicable in an international sale under the rules of conflict of laws adopted by the court. Thus, it can be argued that domestic law is one of the sources of international commercial law. This is why domestic law is relevant to our studies.

[1.2] As we have seen, the substance of international commercial law is not fixed. Nor is the body of laws governing contracts for the international sale of goods. This is because international conventions operate only between countries (or customs territories, if

---

1. CISG, art 2.
2. The case involved the sale of an aircraft located in Darwin. The buyer refused to pay the full price on the ground of misrepresentation. The court found in the seller's favour and granted damages to the seller.
3. 'Customs territory' is an important concept in the present environment for international trade, which is largely regulated by World Trade Organisation (WTO) agreements. Under the present WTO structure, a customs territory can be a member of the WTO and also a party to the WTO agreements, even though it is not a sovereign country — which is a precondition for making many international treaties and conventions. Examples of customs territories within the WTO include Hong Kong, Macau, and Taiwan.

[1.2] applicable) that are parties to those conventions. However, trade and commerce regularly take place between countries that are not parties to the same conventions. In addition, customs vary in different regions and trades. It is naive to assume that the parties to a contract of international sale must have adopted the same system of law and trade customs.

[1.3] The law which may affect a contract for the international sale of goods comes from three sources: international conventions; customs which have received universal recognition, such as International Chamber of Commerce (ICC) rules; and domestic laws applicable to international transactions.

[1.4] This chapter deals with the legal issues arising from international sales of goods in a domestic context. We will first broadly review the international conventions which may affect the international sale of goods. Second, we will examine the meaning of 'international sale of goods'. Third, we will investigate the relevant issues in the context of Australian domestic law and Chinese domestic law. These two countries are chosen for their representation of two different legal traditions, with Australian law following the common law tradition, and Chinese law representing, to some extent, the continental law tradition. 'Incoterms' are international commercial customs, and need to be discussed in the context of a domestic law (in this chapter, Australian law), because their legal effect as binding contractual terms is only derived from an applicable law — either an international convention or a domestic law, as the case may be.

Conventions relevant to international sale of goods

[1.5] The main convention for the international sale of goods is the CISG. As of March 2003, the CISG had 62 member countries.[4] The CISG was intended to replace the 1964 Uniform Law on International Sale of Goods and the 1964 Uniform Law on the Formation of Contracts for the International Sale of Goods, which are referred to collectively as the Hague Conventions on the Uniform Laws on International Sales of 1964.[5] The Hague Conventions on the Uniform Laws on International Sales of 1964 were signed by 12 countries, but ratified by only nine countries: the United Kingdom, San Marino, Belgium, Gambia, Germany, Italy, Israel, Luxembourg and the Netherlands. The Conventions required a minimum of five member countries for them to be operative and came into operation in 1972. Now Belgium, Italy, Germany, Luxembourg and the Netherlands have ratified the CISG, and Israel has denounced them.[6] This means that only the United Kingdom, San Marino, and Gambia remain as members of the Conventions, which are inoperative owing to insufficient members.[7]

---

4. A full list of member countries is available at <http://cisgw3.law.pace.edu/cisg/countries/cntries.html>.
5. For more information, see Schmitthoff, *Schmitthoff's Export Trade*, 9th ed, Stevens & Sons, London, pp 241–9.
6. Israel denounced the 1964 Uniform Law on 16 October 2001 with effect from 16 October 2002. See the UNIDROIT website at <http://www.unidroit.org/>.
7. This information is based on the UN Treaty Services, available at <http://www.un.org./Depts/Treaty> and the UNIDROIT homepage at <http://www.unidroit.org>.

[1.6] There are also other international conventions which are relevant to the international sales of goods. These include:

- the United Nations Convention on the Limitation Period in the International Sale of Goods 1974;[8]
- the UNIDROIT Convention on Agency in the International Sale of Goods 1983;[9]
- the UNCITRAL Model Law on Procurement of Goods, Construction and Services 1994, which has been adopted by a number of countries, including Albania, Azerbaijan, Croatia, Estonia, Kazakhstan, Kenya, Kyrgyzstan, Mauritius, Mongolia, Poland, Slovakia, Tanzania, Uganda, and Uzbekistan;[10]
- the UNCITRAL Model Law on International Credit Transfers 1992, which is also meant to be a model for domestic law-making, and which has been largely adopted by the European Union;[11]
- the United Nations Convention on International Bills of Exchange and International Promissory Notes 1988;[12] and
- the United Nations Convention on Independent Guarantees and Stand-By Letters of Credit 1995.[13]

Although some conventions have received wide acceptance (for example, the CISG), some have little practical significance because very few countries have ratified them. This means that whether a valid convention applies to a particular transaction or not depends on whether the countries involved are members to the convention; or, alternatively, whether the convention becomes applicable under the relevant conflicts rules. Otherwise, customs or other relevant laws apply.

---

8. The convention was concluded in 1974 and came into operation on 1 August 1988. It was amended on 11 April 1980 to ensure its consistency with the CISG. Technically, the convention without the amendment and the convention as amended are two separate regimes or conventions. In 2002, the convention without amendment had 24 members: Argentina, Belarus, Bosnia and Herzegovina, Burundi, Cuba, the Czech Republic, the Dominican Republic, Egypt, Ghana, Guinea, Hungary, Mexico, Norway, Poland, Republic of Moldova, Romania, Slovakia, Slovenia, Uganda, Ukraine, United States of America, Uruguay, Yugoslavia, and Zambia. The convention as amended had 17 members: Argentina, Belarus, Cuba, the Czech Republic, Egypt, Guinea, Hungary, Mexico, Poland, the Republic of Moldova, Romania, Slovakia, Slovenia, Uganda, United States of America, Uruguay, and Zambia. See the United Nations Treaty Collection at <http://untreaty.un.org/>.
9. The convention was adopted in 1983 at Geneva. Ten countries are required for its entry into force. By mid-2002 it had been ratified by Italy and France, while South Africa, Mexico and the Netherlands had acceded to it. Five more countries are needed for its operation. See the UNIDROIT website at <http://www.unidroit.org/>.
10. See the UNCITRAL website at <http://www.uncitral.org/>.
11. Ibid.
12. The convention was concluded in 1988 and has since been open for UN members to approve. A minimum of 10 members are required before it comes into effect. By mid-2002, only Guinea, Honduras and Mexico had ratified or acceded to it. Canada, the Russian Federation and the United States had signed but not yet ratified the convention. See the UNCITRAL website at <http://www.uncitral.org/>.
13. The convention was concluded in 1995 in New York. Five countries have ratified it: Ecuador, El Salvador, Kuwait, Panama and Tunisia. The convention will enter into force on 1 January 2000. Belarus and the United States have signed but not yet ratified the convention.

[1.7]   International Commercial Law

Effect of customs

[1.7] Customs can be regarded as the original source of international commercial law. This is because the original international commercial law was based on customs, and also because international conventions are largely codifications of customs which have been commonly accepted by most countries in the world. Given the diversity of the world's legal systems, customs and their derivative rules are most likely to receive universal recognition for their commercial acceptability. Therefore, where there is no convention governing a particular transaction, customs and commercial practices should apply. The most popular commercial customs so far are the rules codified by the ICC. International commercial terms, or 'Incoterms', are the most popular 'rules' governing sale contracts involving the transport of goods; Incoterms 2000 is the most recent version. The ICC has also published a number of other 'rules' dealing with international trade and commerce.

Relevance of domestic law

[1.8] Domestic law also affects contracts for the international sale of goods. For example, the CISG operates in each Australian state and territory as the law of the relevant state or territory. However, the sale of goods legislation in each state and territory may apply to a contract for international sale as far as its application does not lead to inconsistencies with the Convention. Indeed, certain aspects of sale which are not covered by the Convention, such as passing of property,[14] the validity of contract and the validity of a contractual clause, are governed by the relevant sale of goods legislation.[15]

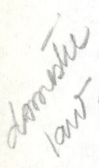

By the same token, in Australia the Corporations Law in each state, the Bills of Exchange Act 1909 (Cth), the Marine Insurance Act 1909 (Cth), the Foreign Acquisitions and Takeovers Act 1975 (Cth), the Securities Industry Act 1980 (Cth), the Carriage of Goods by Sea Act 1991 (Cth), the Banking Act 1959 (Cth), the Civil Aviation (Carriers' Liability) Act 1959 (Cth), Pt X (International Liner Cargo Shipping) of the Trade Practices Act 1974 (Cth), local procedural law,[16] and other provisions of the domestic law, are

---

14. For example, see *International Alpaca Management Pty Ltd, Textile Finance Ltd and Coolaroo Alpaca General Partner Pty Ltd v Ben KE Ensor and Garrymere Farms Ltd* (No G490 of 1995, FED No 1054/95, available at AustLii Databases, <http://www.austlii.edu.au>). That case involved several parties from Chile, New Zealand and Australia who argued about ownership of 100 South American cameloids of the alpaca species. Even though Australia, Chile and New Zealand are members to the CISG, the courts applied Australian sale of goods legislation because the dispute involved passing of property, which is not covered by the CISG.
15. *Roder Zelt-Und Hallenkonstruktionen GmbH v Rosedown Park Pty Ltd* (1995) 17 ACSR 153 was the first Australian case determined under the CISG. The case involved passing of property in an international sale of goods. The issue of whether the German seller retained title in the tents which were in possession of the Australian buyer and its administrator was determined under the sale of goods legislation and general contract law.
16. For example, limitation of time was the issue decided in *Bridge Shipping Pty Ltd v Grand Shipping SA* (1991) 173 CLR 231 and *Van Leer Australia Pty Ltd v Palace Shipping KK and Another* (1994) 180 CLR 337; both are cases involving the carriage of goods by sea.

applicable to contracts for international sales, provided that no inconsistency arises between the application of these domestic laws and the performance of Australia's obligations under any international conventions.[17]

For example, in *Hi-Fert Pty Ltd v United Shipping Adriatic Inc* [1998] FCA 1622, the plaintiff cargo-owner sued the vessel owner, the charterer and the inspection agent for its loss arising from the decision of the Australian Quarantine Inspection Service to prohibit the cargo of urea from entering into Australia, on the ground that the cargo might have been contaminated by a quarantinable disease known as 'karnal bunt'. The plaintiff sued the defendants on various grounds, including a charge against the charterer for misleading or deceptive conduct under the Trade Practices Act 1974 (Cth). Similarly, in *Hi-Fert Pty Ltd v Kiukiang Maritime Carriers Inc* [1998] FCA 1485, a dispute arose from the carriage of a cargo of fertiliser from the United States to Australia. The International Arbitration Act 1991 (Cth) and the Trade Practices Act 1974 (Cth) were applied to determine the rights and obligations of the parties concerned.[18]

[1.9] The relationship between domestic laws affecting international sales and the relevant international conventions or customs are largely similar in other jurisdictions — in particular, common law jurisdictions, such as the United Kingdom, Hong Kong, New Zealand, Canada and the United States. The basic principle is always that the relevant international convention takes priority if the relevant country has ratified and incorporated the convention into the domestic law. Even in countries largely based on a civil-law tradition, such as Japan, France and China, the principle is the same.[19] For example, China is a member of the CISG. It promulgated a Code of Contract of Law in March 1999, which came into operation on 1 October 1999. The code applies to all types of contract, including sales contracts in China. It is supplementary to the CISG in international sales, providing rules for matters not covered by the CISG.[20]

---

17. For example, in *Williams v The Society of Lloyd's* [1994] 1 VR 274, Williams, an anaesthetist practising in Victoria, sued Lloyd's and a number of other defendants in relation to the agreements and trust deeds under which he became an underwriting member of Lloyd's. In doing so, he claimed deceit and negligent misrepresentation, breach of s 52 of the Trade Practices Act, breach of s 11 of the Fair Trading Act 1985 (Vic), and breach of the Companies (Victoria) Code. The action was stayed because the plaintiff failed to satisfy any of the grounds for service of originating process out of Victoria. The case raises issues of conflict of laws, validity of contract, alleged negligence and breach of Australian statutes by foreign parties.
18. See also *Pacific Composites Pty Ltd, Lermarne Corp Ltd v Blue Anchor Line, ANL Ltd & United Arab Shipping Co* [1997] FCA 576.
19. In *Societe Productions SCAP v Roberto Faggioni* (CLOUT Case 312, available at <http://www.uncitral.org>), the French Court of Appeal held in 1998 that, although the CISG applied to the sale, the issue concerning the place of restitution of the price by the seller was governed by the law of the seller, which in that case was Spanish law.
20. For a detailed discussion see J S Mo, 'The Code of Contract Law of the People's Republic of China and the CISG', *American University International Law Review (Am U Int'l L Rev)*, 1999, vol 15, pp 209–70.

> **[1.10]** *Kay Minge v J W Oak Furniture Imports Ltd and William Heinhuis*
>
> 26 February 1998, Supreme Court of British Columbia[1]
>
> *An international sale of a car can be subject to domestic law*
>
> **Facts:** The plaintiff was an antique collector in Norway. The defendants were from Canada. The parties agreed that in 1996 they entered into a contract for the sale of a 1932 Chrysler Imperial Le Baron Roadster by the defendants to the plaintiff for a price of US$124,800. But the defendants argued that the contract of sale also included the sale of a 1976 John Deere Crawler Loader Tractor Model 450 for a price of US$50,000. The plaintiff, who had paid US$124,800 to the defendants, denied the purchase of the tractor. The plaintiff asked the court to order the defendants to deliver up the car to him pending the trial in pursuance of rule 46 of the court. The defendants contended that such an order would deprive them of their right under the Sale of Goods Act (Canada). Whether the court should enforce rule 46 in the present case was the issue to be determined by the court.
>
> **Decision:** The court examined the issue and balanced the interests of the parties solely in the context of Canadian law. The court decided that the plaintiff would be entitled to receive the car pending the trial only if he deposited US$37,400 into the court as security, a sum equivalent to about half of the defendants' counter-claim. In this case, neither Norwegian law, the CISG, nor any other international convention was referred to, even though the dispute obviously involved an international sale. This is not unusual in an international sale for a number of reasons. For example, the sale may be regarded as a consumer sale and thus excluded from the CISG. The parties may prefer to use Canadian law, instead of Norwegian. The court may find Canadian law appropriate to apply. The question before the court may be procedural only, as it was in the present case, and should thus be governed by the local (domestic) law only. In the present case, both Canada and Norway are members of the CISG. If none of the countries is a member of the CISG, the Convention may also be excluded unless it is regarded as being applicable under the relevant conflict of laws rules. Thus, an international sale may be subject to the domestic law of the country where the transaction takes place for several reasons.
>
> ---
>
> 1. Available at <http://www.courts.gov.bc.ca>.

What is an international sale of goods?

[1.11] An international sale of goods is a sale involving parties from different countries. A contract dealing with such a sale or transaction is a contract for the international sale of goods.

There are three essential elements in an international sale of goods:

1. There is a sale, which is different from an exchange of goods, counter-trade or barter as a means of international commerce.[21]
2. The subject matter of the sale is 'goods', which has a different meaning under different laws. For example, 'goods' under the Australian sale of goods legislation (see, for instance, s 5 of the Sale of Goods Act 1923 (NSW)) refers to all chattels personal other than things in action and money. 'Goods' under the Trade Practices

---

21. The use of barter for trade is illustrated by *Aronis v Hallett Brick Industries Ltd* [1999] SASC 92.

Act 1974 (Cth) includes electricity (s 4), which certainly does not fall under the concept of 'chattels personal'. 'Sale of goods' under the CISG does not include the sale of ships, vessels, aircraft (which are, however, covered under the Trade Practices Act and the sale of goods legislation) and electricity: CISG, art 2; see **[2.18]**. If a sale of 'goods' (or anything which is the subject of a sales contract) is not governed by any specific domestic law or convention, the transaction will be subject to the general principles of contract law, unless the transaction is prohibited under the relevant law.

In *Westpac Banking Corp v Royal Tongan Airlines* (5 September 1996, Supreme Court of New South Wales, available at <http://www.Austlii.edu.au>), the Bank of Tonga sold an amount of US currency and New Zealand currency to the Westpac Banking Corporation. The seller actually sent the money by post from Tonga to Sydney, Australia. The money was lost on its way to Sydney. The Supreme Court of New South Wales ordered the third defendant, Qantas Airways Ltd, to pay the buyer, Westpac, for the lost money, together with a sum of estimated interest, on the ground of a breach of the duties of a bailee. Although it was doubtful that the sale itself was subject to the sale of goods legislation in New South Wales, the dispute between the seller and the buyer on the one side, and the carriers who carried the money from Tonga to Sydney on the other, was resolved by applying the law of bailment, which is a particular branch of the domestic law.

3. The sale is effected at an international level, involving various international elements, such as a foreign buyer or seller, foreign origin or destination of the goods, foreign banks or financial institutions, or the application of foreign law and jurisdiction, among others.

The three essential elements remain the same in any jurisdiction or legal tradition. The meaning of 'goods' varies from one jurisdiction to another, because a particular law may have restrictions on what can be sold as goods in a commercial transaction, or on what can be subject to a contract of sale. For example, national restrictions on the export of certain types of high technology to certain countries may make a contract unenforceable or void *ab initio*. On the other hand, refusal to enforce a commercial contract against a government authority may also make the contract concerned unenforceable or void *ab initio*, depending on the relevant domestic law. This is why the CISG does not cover the validity of a contract or a contractual term.

Application of Incoterms 2000 in international sales

What is Incoterms 2000?

[1.12] 'Incoterms' refers to a collection, or a uniform interpretation, of a number of essential trade terms concerning the carriage or delivery of goods. They are compiled by the ICC for the purpose of providing uniform interpretations of the terms and reducing or avoiding potential disputes in their use. The first set of Incoterms was published in 1936. Amendments were made in 1953, 1967, 1976, 1980, 1990 and 1999. 'Incoterms 2000' refers to the current version of the Incoterms, published by the ICC in September 1999. The terms are not binding on any parties before they are incorporated into a

[1.12]   **International Commercial Law**

contract of sale. But they represent the most common commercial practices, usage or customs, which can be voluntarily accepted by the contracting parties. The existence of the ICC's Incoterms means that the 'uncertainties of different interpretations of such terms in different countries can be avoided or at least reduced to a considerable degree'.[22] Indeed, the evolution of the Incoterms themselves proves the truthfulness of this proposition.

For example, in 1955, the Free Alongside Ship (FAS) term (see **[1.18]**) did not specify who was responsible for obtaining an export licence. This omission led to the dispute in *MW Hardy & Co Inc v AV Pound & Co Ltd* [1955] 1 Lloyd's Rep 155 (CA). In that case, the parties concluded an FAS contract for the sale of 300 t of Portuguese turpentine from Lisbon to East Germany. The contract could not be performed because of the Portuguese restriction on exports to East Germany. The contract did not stipulate who was liable for obtaining the export licence. The UK Court of Appeal held that, in the circumstances concerned, the seller was expected to obtain an export licence. If this dispute had taken place today, headings **A2** and **B2** of the FAS term would provide a clear answer. Under the FAS term, the buyer is responsible for obtaining all export permits or licences, but the seller must render necessary assistance to the buyer.

[1.13]   Incoterms 2000 contains 13 terms, which may apply to various modes of transport. The rights and liabilities of the seller and buyer are defined in each term. When a term is incorporated into a contract of sale, the definition of the term — the rights and obligations of the parties — also becomes part of the contract. Wherever a term is accepted in a contract of sale, the parties also undertake a liability to perform the duties specified in the term. This is how the Incoterms operate.

The 13 Incoterms are divided into four groups, largely according to the extent of the seller's responsibilities. As the seller has a number of responsibilities, it is not feasible to use one or two common responsibilities as a uniform criterion for grouping the 13 terms. Incoterms 2000 therefore classifies the 13 terms according to their first letter. There are four groups: E, F, C and D (the order comes from the Incoterms). Although each group of terms is headed by a short title purporting to explain the nature of terms within it, this heading may not always accurately reflect the terms concerned. For example, Group E is headed 'Departure', which does not give any indication of the seller's liability; similarly, Group D is simply headed 'Arrival'. The groups may also be differentiated according to where, when and how the risk in goods passes from the seller to the buyer, as one of the major functions of the Incoterms is to determine the passing of risk.

---

22. ICC, *Incoterms 1990*, ICC Publishing SA, Paris, 1990, p 6.

International Sale of Goods under Domestic Law [1.14]

[1.14] Incoterms 2000 are divided into four groups, as follows:[23]

Group	Description	Terms	See
E-terms — Departure	Risk passes at the seller's premises	EXW — Ex Works	[1.16]
F-terms — Main carriage unpaid	Risk passes when goods are delivered to a named carrier; the seller is not liable for costs after delivery	FCA — Free Carrier	[1.17]
		FAS — Free Alongside Ship	[1.18]
		FOB — Free on Board	[1.21]
C-terms — Main carriage paid	Risk passes when goods are delivered to a carrier contracted by the seller, but the seller is liable for certain costs after delivery	CFR — Cost and Freight	[1.22]
		CIF — Cost, Insurance and Freight	[1.23]
		CPT — Carriage Paid to	[1.24]
		CIP — Carriage and Insurance Paid to	[1.25]
D-terms — Arrival	Risk passes when goods are delivered in the country of the goods' destination	DAF — Delivered at Frontier	[1.26]
		DES — Delivered Ex Ship	[1.27]
		DEQ — Delivered Ex Quay	[1.28]
		DDU — Delivered Duty Unpaid	[1.29]
		DDP — Delivered Duty Paid	[1.30]

The basic meaning of each term under Incoterms 2000 is examined below, using the order and form adopted by Incoterms 2000. Each term consists of 10 headings, or categories, of responsibilities of both the seller and buyer.

The discussion of the Incoterms below does not use the original words of the Incoterms as published by the ICC. However, the obligations of the parties are set out in the same format as they are in the official publication of the ICC.

---

23. ICC, *Incoterms 2000*, ICC Publishing SA, Paris, 1999, p 7.

> **[1.15]** *Calzaturificio Claudia snc v Olivieri Footwear Ltd*
>
> (1998) US Dist Lexis 4586
>
> *The effect of Ex Works is discussed in the context of the CISG*
>
> **Fact:** Calzaturificio Claudia snc, the plaintiff, was a shoe manufacturer set up under Italian law, with its principal place of business in Italy. The defendant, Olivieri Footwear Ltd, was a US company based in New York. The parties had an oral agreement for the sale of shoes by the plaintiff to the defendant. Four transactions had taken place. The plaintiff argued that the shoes were delivered to the defendant Ex Works, which means that the plaintiff was not responsible for any risk occurring after the delivery at the plaintiff's factory. The defendant refused to take part of the delivery in New York and refused to pay the contract price. The plaintiff asked the court to give summary judgment mainly by presenting a number of invoices issued by the plaintiff to the defendant. The invoices contained an 'Ex Works' term.
>
> **Decision:** In the absence of any written contract of sale and corroborating evidence, the court found the plaintiff's argument to be unconvincing, and thus refused to make a summary judgment. When discussing whether or not 'Ex Works' was incorporated into the oral contract of sale, the judge referred to art 19 of the CISG. The court took the view that, if the plaintiff's invoices represented an acceptance, the terms of the acceptance (invoices) must not contain additions, limitations or other modifications stipulated in art 19 of the CISG. The court also referred to art 8 of the CISG, which requires a court to take due consideration of 'all relevant circumstances of the case including the negotiations, any practices which the parties have established between themselves, usages and any subsequent conduct of the parties for determining their intention'. After examining the past dealings of the parties, the court was not satisfied that the argument of the plaintiff was supported by past business dealings. Thus, the court did not accept the plaintiff's argument that the shoes were delivered Ex Works.

EXW — Ex Works

[1.16] 'Ex Works', also known as EXW, means that goods are delivered at the seller's premises, such as a factory, warehouse or place of business. The term normally has no relevance to the means of transport, and is commonly used for the carriage of goods by land or multimodal carriage. It can also be used in the carriage of goods by air and sea. Under the term, the seller is neither responsible for loading goods onto a transportation vehicle or vessel, nor for obtaining export clearance, except for the obligation to assist the buyer to clear customs. The seller is not responsible for the costs and risks involved in taking the goods from the seller's premises. If, however, the parties agree that the seller should undertake the liabilities for loading the goods on departure and bear the risks and costs of loading, they must use explicit words to this effect in the contract of sale. Otherwise the common meaning of EXW prevails. Although risk in the goods passes to the buyer at the seller's premises when delivery takes place, the seller is required to give notice of delivery to the buyer to enable the buyer to make arrangements for such things as shipment, insurance and customs procedures. In *Calzaturificio Claudia snc v Olivieri Footwear Ltd* (1998) US Dist Lexis 4586 (see **[1.15]**), the plaintiff alleged that the goods (shoes) were delivered EXW to the defendant. The court held the argument to be unconvincing because, inter alia, the plaintiff did not notify the defendant as required by the EXW term.

International Sale of Goods under Domestic Law [1.16]

The major responsibilities of the seller and buyer can be summarised as follows:

The Seller	The Buyer
A1 Must provide the goods and documents or equivalent electronic messages in conformity with the contract of sale.	**B1** Must pay the price of the contract.
A2 Must, where applicable, assist the buyer to obtain an export licence or other necessary approval for export.	**B2** Must obtain an export licence or other necessary authorisation for export, import or transit through a third country, as the case may be.
A3 Is under no obligation to make contracts for carriage and insurance.	**B3** Is under no obligation to make contract of carriage.[1]
A4 Must place goods at the disposal of the buyer (similar to 'putting the goods into a deliverable state' under the sale of goods legislation in Australia — see **[1.61]–[1.71]**) at the named place (premises) and at or within the agreed time.	**B4** Must take delivery at the agreed place and time.
A5 Risk passes when goods are placed at the buyer's disposal (delivered) as agreed.	**B5** Must bear risks after goods have been placed at his or her disposal (delivered) as agreed, and bear additional risks caused by his or her failure to give sufficient notice for time and place of delivery (if applicable) when the goods are appropriated or identified according to the contract.
A6 Is liable for costs relating to goods before delivery.	**B6** Is liable for costs after delivery, and additional costs arising from his or her failure to take delivery or to give sufficient notice for the time and place of delivery (if applicable) when goods are appropriated or identified according to the contract, as well as costs for obtaining export, import or transit approval.
A7 Must give adequate notice for delivery to the buyer.	**B7** Must give the seller adequate notice for time and place of taking delivery, if applicable.
A8 Is not liable to provide proof of delivery and transport documents or equivalent electronic messages.	**B8** Must give the seller evidence of having received the goods after delivery.
A9 Is responsible not only for the cost of necessary checking, but also for appropriately marking and packaging goods at his or her own expense in conformity with the contract, unless the usual practice of a particular trade does not require the goods concerned to be packaged. It is expected that the packaging will be adequate for the means of transport made known to the seller before the conclusion of the contract.	**B9** Is responsible for costs of all types of pre-shipment inspection.

13

The Seller	The Buyer
A10 Must assist the buyer in obtaining all necessary documents or equivalent electronic messages for exporting, importing and transporting the goods at the buyer's risk and expense.	**B10** Is responsible for costs of obtaining all necessary documents or equivalent electronic messages.

1. The buyer may have to look into insurance matters because the risk in goods passes to him or her upon delivery EXW.

FCA — Free Carrier

[1.17] This term means that the seller should deliver the goods, cleared for export, to the carrier, who can be any person nominated by the buyer. Accordingly, the risk in the goods passes to the buyer when the seller delivers the goods to a named carrier at a named place. It is suitable for all means of transport, but is usually used for carriage by sea, air or multimodal means. The passing of risk from the seller to the buyer varies depending on the mode of transport. The seller's major obligations include obtaining export clearance at his or her own risk and expense, and providing evidence of delivery to the buyer. In addition, if delivery takes place at the seller's premises, the seller is also responsible for loading. The specific duties of both parties can be summarised as follows:

The Seller	The Buyer
A1 Must provide the goods and documents or equivalent electronic messages in conformity with the contract of sale.	**B1** Must pay the price of the contract.
A2 Must obtain the necessary export licence and, where applicable, customs clearance at his or her own risk and expense.	**B2** Must obtain the necessary import licence and customs clearance, as well as approval for transit through a third country, at his or her own risk and expense.
A3 (i) Is under no obligation to make a contract of carriage, but may do so on the usual terms at the buyer's risk and expense if the buyer so requests or if commercial practice so allows; the seller can refuse the buyer's request by promptly notifying him or her of the refusal. **(ii)** Is under no obligation to insure the goods.	**B3** Must make the contract of carriage or pay costs when the seller arranges the contract.[1]

The Seller	The Buyer
A4 Must deliver goods into the custody of a named (or agreed) carrier (or person) at (or within) the agreed time and in the agreed manner and place. In the absence of an express agreement, the seller may choose one of the available places for delivery and deliver the goods in the manner most suitable to the mode of transport or the goods concerned. Completion of delivery takes two forms: - if the named place of delivery is the seller's premises, the delivery is complete when the goods have been loaded on the means of transport provided by the carrier nominated by the buyer or an authorised person; or - if the named place of delivery is not the seller's premises, the delivery is complete when the goods are placed at the disposal of the carrier or any person appointed by either the seller or the buyer.	**B4** Must take delivery as agreed in the circumstances described in **A4**.
A5 Risk passes at delivery, as the case may be.	**B5** Must bear risk after delivery, and additional risks caused by: - his or her failure to nominate the carrier or another person as agreed; - the failure of the nominated carrier to take delivery as agreed; or - his or her failure to notify the seller or the named person for delivery, named mode of transport, named place or manner for delivery when the goods are duly appropriated according to the contract (that is, clearly set aside or identified according to the contract).
A6 Is liable for costs incurred before delivery and, where applicable, costs for obtaining export clearance.	**B6** Is liable for costs after delivery, and additional costs caused by: - his or her failure to nominate the carrier or another person for delivery; - failure of the nominated party to take delivery; or - his or her failure to give sufficient notice concerning the nominated party, mode of transport, the time and manner of delivery when the goods are duly appropriated according to the contract (that is, set aside or identified according to the contract). Where applicable, the buyer is liable for costs for import, customs formalities or transit through a third country.

[1.17] International Commercial Law

The Seller	The Buyer
A7 Must give sufficient notice to the buyer of the completion, or failure, of the delivery.	**B7** Must give the seller sufficient notice of the name of the carrier, mode of transport, and place, time and manner of delivery, when necessary.
A8 Must give the buyer the usual proof of delivery at the seller's expense and, if necessary, assist the buyer to obtain an adequate transport document suitable to the mode of transport or an equivalent electronic message.	**B8** Must accept the relevant documents and pay for incidental costs of obtaining any document or an equivalent electronic data interchange (EDI) message which is additional to the proof of delivery provided by the seller.
A9 Is responsible not only for the cost of necessary checking, but also for appropriately marking and packaging goods at his or her own expense in conformity with the contract, unless the usual practice of a particular trade does not require the goods concerned to be packaged. It is expected that the packaging be adequate for the means of transport made known to the seller before the conclusion of the contract.	**B9** Is liable to pay costs of pre-shipment inspection, unless such inspection is mandated under the law and regulations of the export country.
A10 Must, at the request, risk and expense of the buyer, assist the buyer in obtaining necessary documents and electronic messages for transporting and importing goods, and necessary information for effecting insurance.	**B10** Must give adequate instructions for assistance of the buyer and pay costs for obtaining the required documents or electronic messages, or for making relevant contracts.

1. The buyer should consider insurance matters because the seller is not liable to insure the goods.

FAS — Free Alongside Ship

[1.18] This term means that the seller should place (deliver) the goods alongside the named ship at the named port of shipment. Under this term, the buyer bears the costs and risks relating to the goods after delivery, but the seller is required to clear the goods for export. FAS is largely a special term of sea carriage or inland water transport, while FCA can be used for other means of transportation, such as railway, road, air, inland waterway or multimodal. The differences are seen mainly in **A4** of each term. The major duties of the seller and buyer are shown in the following table:

International Sale of Goods under Domestic Law [1.18]

The Seller	The Buyer
A1 Must provide goods and documents or equivalent electronic messages in conformity with the contract of sale.	**B1** Must pay the price of the contract.
A2 Must obtain at his or her own risk and expense any export licence or other necessary approval. Where applicable, must complete export customs formalities.	**B2** Is responsible for obtaining an import licence or other necessary approval, and for completing import customs formalities, as well as gaining approval for transit through a third country.
A3 Is under no obligation to make contract of carriage and to insure the goods.	**B3** Is responsible for making contract of carriage.[1]
A4 Must deliver the goods alongside the vessel nominated by the buyer at the named port and at (or within) the agreed time.	**B4** Must take delivery as agreed.
A5 Is responsible for risks before delivery; risks pass at delivery.	**B5** Is liable for risks after delivery, and for additional risks arising from his or her failure to take delivery as agreed or to give sufficient notice for delivery, provided that the goods are duly appropriated, clearly set aside or identified according to the contract.
A6 Is responsible for necessary costs, including the costs of completing customs formalities, where applicable, before delivery.	**B6** Is responsible for costs after delivery and additional costs incurred because of his or her failure to take delivery as agreed or to give sufficient notice for delivery when the goods are duly appropriated, clearly set aside or identified according to the contract. Is also responsible for the cost of completing customs formalities.
A7 Must give the buyer sufficient notice of the completion of the delivery.	**B7** Must give the seller sufficient notice of the vessel name and the place and time of delivery.
A8 Must provide at his or her own expense the usual proof of delivery (which, if agreed by the parties, can be an electronic message) and, where applicable, must assist the buyer in obtaining necessary transport documents or equivalent electronic messages.	**B8** Must accept conforming documents as agreed.
A9 Is responsible not only for the cost of necessary checking, but also for appropriately marking and packaging goods at his or her own expense in conformity with the contract, unless the usual practice of a particular trade does not require the goods to be packaged. It is expected that the packaging be adequate for the means of transport made known to the seller before the conclusion of the contract.	**B9** Is responsible for the costs of pre-shipment inspection, unless such inspection is mandated by the authorities of the export country.

[1.18] International Commercial Law

The Seller	The Buyer
A10 Must, at the request, risk and expense of the buyer, assist the buyer in obtaining necessary documents and electronic messages for transporting and importing goods, and necessary information for effecting insurance.	**B10** Is responsible for the costs of obtaining the relevant documents or electronic messages.

1. The buyer should consider insurance matters because the seller is not liable to insure the goods.

[1.19] *Metro Meat Ltd v Fares Rural Co Pty Ltd*

[1985] 2 Lloyd's Rep 13 (PC)

FAS contract and additional terms — buyer purchases in FAS terms but then sells in CFR terms

Facts: Metro Meat was the appellant and seller in an FAS contract for the sale of lamb, and Fares Rural was the respondent and buyer. The parties agreed orally in July 1979 for the sale of a quantity of lamb in FAS terms at one of two ports in Australia (Adelaide or Fremantle) for shipment to Bandar Shahpour in Iran. The oral agreement was confirmed in writing by several telexes later exchanged between the parties. The seller knew that the buyer bought the goods for the purpose of fulfilling its obligations as a seller under a matching contract in CFR terms to the Iranian Meat Organisation. The quantity of goods in both contracts was 20,000 t, with a tolerance of 10 per cent more or less at the seller's option. Thus, the minimum quantity of goods under the FAS contract was 18,000 t, which was to be delivered in five consecutive instalments. The buyer thus chartered a vessel to carry the goods. Three instalments were delivered as agreed, totalling 10,843 t. The market price of the lamb rose in 1980. The seller refused to deliver the remaining two instalments for a reason which was rejected by the trial court. The court also held that several terms in dispute were consistent with the FAS contract. For example, the quantity of goods was agreed as 20,000 t, with a tolerance of 10 per cent more or less at the seller's option; and the buyer agreed to pay an additional US$125 per t for the purpose of encouraging the seller to perform its obligation to deliver the remaining quantity. The Supreme Court of Western Australia held that the buyer was entitled to accept repudiation of the contract and claim damages. The seller appealed to the Privy Council.

Decision: The Judicial Committee of the Privy Council (consisting of Lord Scarman, Lord Diplock, Lord Roskill, Lord Brightman and Sir Denys Buckley) upheld the finding of the trial judge that the seller's conduct constituted an anticipatory breach, and accordingly dismissed the appeal.

[1.20] In *Metro Meat Ltd v Fares Rural Co Pty Ltd* [1985] 2 Lloyd's Rep 13 (PC), both the trial court and the Privy Council emphasised the fact that, by refusing to deliver the remaining quantity of the lamb, the seller had committed an anticipatory breach of a fundamental term. Because of the anticipatory breach, the buyer was entitled to damages. Alternatively, in light of the FAS term, the seller might have been found in breach of **A1** and **A4**, under which the seller is obliged to deliver goods in the quality, quantity and description agreed, at the time and place agreed. In addition, the increase in the market price, which was the real reason for the seller's anticipatory breach, can be regarded as an issue of risk, which must be borne by the seller under **A5** before delivery. The problem with the operation of **A5** is that the 'risk' under **A5** and **B5** may be limited to the risk of loss of, or damage to, the goods. Thus, a decrease in the market price may not be a relevant loss under those headings. Another feature of this case is that Fares Rural Co Pty Ltd was actually an intermediary which purchased in the FAS term and sold the same goods in CFR terms. Such a combination is possible because, in both situations, Fares Rural was responsible for making the shipping arrangements.

FOB — Free on Board

[1.21] FOB and CIF (cost, insurance and freight, see **[1.23]**) are the most common terms used in contracts for international sale of goods. FOB means that the seller is free from responsibilities and risks once the goods have passed over the rail of a named ship at a named port. In certain types of container shipping, the containers do not pass the ship's rail. In order to avoid confusion relating to the passing of risk, the ICC recommends the use of the FCA term in such cases. FOB usually applies to the carriage of goods by sea or inland water transport. It is often used as a trading term indicating the basis for the price of the goods sold. In this sense, it means that the price quoted by the seller does not include the cost of insurance and freight. Of course, the FOB price is always lower than the CIF price for the same goods. The major difference between FOB and FAS or FCA is that, under the FOB term, the seller's responsibilities do not cease until the goods have passed the ship's rail for loading, while the FAS term requires the seller to place the goods alongside the named vessel, and the FCA term requires the seller to deliver the goods to the named carrier or person. The major duties of the parties under this term are as follows:

The Seller	The Buyer
A1 Must provide goods and documents or equivalent electronic messages in conformity with the contract of sale.	**B1** Must pay the price of the contract.
A2 Is responsible for obtaining an export licence and other necessary export approval, and, where applicable, for completing export customs formalities.	**B2** Is responsible for obtaining the necessary import or transit licence and approval, and, where applicable, for completing import customs formalities.
A3 Is under no obligation to arrange a contract of carriage or to insure the goods.	**B3** Is responsible for making a contract of carriage.[1]
A4 Must deliver the goods to a named vessel at the named port, as agreed (for example, as to the time and manner of delivery).	**B4** Must take delivery, as agreed.
A5 Risk passes to the buyer when the goods have passed the rail of the named ship, as agreed.	**B5** Must bear risks after delivery and additional risks caused by his or her failure to take delivery or to give sufficient notice for details of delivery when the goods are duly appropriated, clearly set aside or identified according to the contract.

The Seller	The Buyer
A6 Is responsible for costs before delivery and the cost of obtaining export approval or completing export customs formalities.	**B6** Is responsible for costs after delivery, including, where applicable, the cost of import customs formalities and additional costs caused by his or her failure to take delivery or to give sufficient notice of details of delivery when goods are duly appropriated, clearly set aside or identified according to the contract. Is also responsible for costs incidental to import or transit approval.
A7 Must give sufficient notice to the buyer of the completion of the delivery.	**B7** Must give sufficient notice to the seller of the vessel name, place and time for delivery.
A8 Must provide, at his or her own expense, the usual proof of delivery (which, if agreed by the parties, can be an electronic message) and, where applicable, assist the buyer in obtaining transport documents or equivalent electronic messages.	**B8** Must accept the usual proof of delivery.
A9 Is responsible not only for the cost of necessary checking, but also for appropriately marking and packaging goods at his or her own expense, in conformity with the contract, unless the usual practice of a particular trade does not require the goods to be packaged. It is expected that the packaging will be adequate for the means of transport made known to the seller before the conclusion of the contract.	**B9** Is responsible for the costs of pre-shipment inspection, unless such inspection is mandated by the authorities of the export country.
A10 Must, at the request, risk and expense of the buyer, assist the buyer in obtaining necessary documents and electronic messages for transporting and importing goods and necessary information for effecting insurance.	**B10** Must pay necessary costs for obtaining the relevant documents or electronic messages.

1. The buyer should consider insurance matters because the seller is not liable to insure the goods.

CFR — Cost and Freight

[1.22] The ICC states that 'CFR' is the correct abbreviation for 'Cost and Freight', although 'C & F' is sometimes used. This term means that the seller is responsible for necessary costs and freight to bring the goods to the named destination under a contract of sale, but risks and additional costs incurred after the goods have been delivered on board the vessel pass to the buyer from the moment when the goods pass the vessel's rail at the named port of shipment. The ICC recommends the use of CPT if the parties do not intend to deliver the goods across the ship's rail. CFR, which is one of the common terms associated with the carriage of goods by sea or inland water transport, differs from

International Sale of Goods under Domestic Law [1.22]

CIF in that CFR does not cover the cost of insurance. The term also indicates the basis of the contract price. The major duties of the parties under the 10 headings are as follows:

The Seller	The Buyer
A1 Must provide goods and documents or equivalent electronic messages in conformity with the contract of sale.	**B1** Must pay the price of the contract.
A2 Is responsible for obtaining an export licence and other necessary export approval and, where applicable, for completing export customs formalities.	**B2** Is responsible for obtaining an import or transit licence and other necessary approval and, where applicable, for completing import customs formalities.
A3 Is responsible for making a contract of carriage on the usual terms with a vessel suitable to carry the goods to the agreed destination by usual route, but is not responsible for insuring the goods.	**B3** Is under no obligation to make a contract of carriage.[1]
A4 Must deliver the goods on board the vessel, as agreed.	**B4** Must accept the delivery, as agreed.
A5 Risk passes to the buyer when the goods have passed the ship's rail, as agreed.	**B5** Must bear risks after delivery and additional risks arising from his or her failure to give sufficient notice for details of delivery when the goods are duly appropriated, clearly set aside or identified according to the contract.
A6 Is responsible for costs incurred before delivery and for costs and freight relating to the contract of carriage (including the cost of loading and unloading payable by the seller under the contract of carriage), as well as for the customs charges for export and transit payable under the contract of carriage.	**B6** Is responsible for: • costs incurred after delivery, except those paid by the seller at the time of the contract; • costs and charges relating to the goods, if they are not payable by the seller under the contract of carriage; • unloading costs not payable by the seller; • additional costs caused by his or her failure to give sufficient notice of details of delivery when the goods are duly appropriated, clearly set aside or identified according to the contract; and • costs for obtaining import or transit approval, or for going through customs formalities.
A7 Must give sufficient notice to the buyer of the completion of the delivery and of other matters to enable him or her to take the goods.	**B7** Must give sufficient notice to the seller of the time and place for delivery or port of destination, when necessary.

The Seller	The Buyer
A8 Must, at his or her own expense, promptly provide the buyer with a full set of the usual transport documents, which must comply with the contract of sale and enable the buyer either to take delivery of the goods at the agreed destination or to sell them in transit. When agreed by the parties, electronic messages may be used.	**B8** Must accept the conforming documents as agreed.
A9 Is responsible for the cost of checking operations, and of packaging and marking the goods as agreed or as deemed adequate in accordance with the relevant commercial practices.	**B9** Is responsible for the cost of pre-shipment inspection when necessary, unless such inspection is mandated by the authorities of export country.
A10 Must, at the request, risk and expense of the buyer, assist the buyer in obtaining necessary documents and electronic messages for transporting and importing goods, and necessary information for effecting insurance.	**A10** Is responsible for the costs of obtaining necessary documents or electronic messages.

1. The buyer should consider insurance matters because the seller is not liable to insure the goods.

CIF — Cost, Insurance and Freight

[1.23] This term means that the seller is responsible for costs, insurance and freight for transporting the goods to the agreed destination, but risks and additional costs incurred after the goods have passed the ship's rail (delivery) are borne by the buyer from the time of delivery. If the parties do not wish to use the ship's rail as the threshold for dividing the risks between them, the ICC recommends the use of the CIP term. As we have seen, this term and FOB (see **[1.21]**) are the most common terms for the carriage of goods by sea. In fact, the ICC recommends the CIF term only for sea or inland water transport. Generally speaking, the CIF price represents the price of the goods on arrival at the destination as agreed in the contract of sale. Compared with CFR (see **[1.22]**), this term imposes a duty upon the seller to insure the goods against risks of transportation. The basic duties of the parties are set out as follows:

The Seller	The Buyer
A1 Must provide goods and documents or equivalent electronic messages in conformity with the contract of sale.	**B1** Must pay the price of the contract.
A2 Is responsible for obtaining an export licence or other necessary export approval and, where applicable, for completing export customs formalities.	**B2** Is responsible for obtaining an import or transit licence and other necessary approval. Where applicable, is responsible for completing import customs formalities.

The Seller	The Buyer
A3 (i) Is responsible for making a contract of carriage with a vessel suitable for transporting the goods concerned on the usual terms to transport the goods to the agreed destination by the usual route. **(ii)** Is responsible for making a contract of insurance which enables the buyer or any person having an insurable interest to make a claim under the policy directly against the insurer. In addition, the insurance contract must satisfy the following requirements: • The insurer must be of good repute. • The contract must, in the absence of an express agreement, be consistent with the minimum cover of the Institute Cargo Clauses (Institute of London Underwriters), or any similar set of clauses. The seller is responsible for insuring additional risks of war, strikes, riots and civil commotion only at the buyer's request and expense. • The contract must cover the whole period before the goods are taken over by the buyer at the place of destination, as agreed. • The contract must cover a minimum value of the contract price plus 10% (that is, 110% of the contract price). It must be pointed out that any person having 'an insurable interest' in the goods (see **[7.31]**–**[7.35]**), and valid evidence of the contract of insurance, can claim directly against the insurer.	**B3** Is under no obligation to make a contract of carriage or of insurance.
A4 Must deliver the goods as agreed.	**B4** Must accept the goods as agreed.
A5 Is responsible for risks until the goods have passed the ship's rail (delivery) as agreed.	**B5** Is responsible for risks after delivery and additional risks caused by his or her failure to give sufficient notice for matters relating to delivery (if applicable) when the goods are duly appropriated, clearly set aside or identified according to the contract.
A6 Is responsible for costs, insurance and freight payable before delivery for transmitting the goods as agreed, and customs charges for export. The seller is also liable for the cost of unloading the goods at the port of discharge if the contract of carriage so stipulates.	**B6** Is responsible for costs incurred after delivery, except those payable by the seller under the contract of carriage. Is also responsible for additional costs caused by his or her own failure to give sufficient notice of matters relating to delivery (if applicable) when the goods are duly appropriated, clearly set aside or identified according to the contract, together with customs charges for import or transit.

[1.23] International Commercial Law

The Seller	The Buyer
A7 Must give sufficient notice to the buyer about the completion of the delivery and other matters to enable him or her to take delivery.	B7 Must give the seller sufficient notice of the place and time for delivery or the port of destination, when necessary.
A8 Must, at his or her own expense, promptly provide the buyer with a full set of the usual transport documents, which must comply with the contract of sale and enable the buyer either to take delivery of the goods at the agreed destination or to sell them in transit. When agreed by the parties, electronic messages may be used.	B8 Must accept the conforming documents as agreed.
A9 Is responsible for the costs of checking operations, and of packaging and marking the goods as agreed, or as deemed adequate in accordance with the relevant commercial practices.	B9 Is responsible for the costs of pre-shipment inspection, unless such inspection is mandated by the authorities of the export country.
A10 Must, at the request, risk and expense of the buyer, assist the buyer in obtaining necessary documents and electronic messages for transporting and importing goods, and necessary information for effecting additional insurance.	B10 Is responsible for costs incurred in obtaining the relevant documents or electronic messages and, at the request of the seller, for providing necessary information on additional insurance.

CPT — Carriage Paid to

[1.24] This term means that the seller pays the freight for the carriage of goods to the named destination, but risks and additional costs incurred after delivery pass to the buyer once the goods have been delivered to the carrier or an authorised person as agreed. The term can be used in any means of transport, in particular for carriage by air or land. The details of this term are as follows:

The Seller	The Buyer
A1 Must provide goods and documents or equivalent electronic messages in conformity with the contract of sale.	B1 Must pay the price of the contract.
A2 Is responsible for obtaining an export licence and other necessary export approval. Where applicable, is responsible for completing export customs formalities.	B2 Is responsible for obtaining an import or transit licence or other necessary approval. Where applicable, is responsible for completing import customs formalities.
A3 Is responsible for making a contract of carriage with a vessel suitable for transporting the goods concerned on the usual terms to transport the goods to the agreed destination by the usual route, but is not responsible for procuring an insurance contract.	B3 Is under no obligation to make a contract of carriage.[1]

24

The Seller	The Buyer
A4 Must deliver goods to the named carrier or the first carrier, as the case may be, at the agreed place and time.	**B4** Must accept the goods as agreed.
A5 Is responsible for risks until the goods have been delivered to the custody of the named carrier.	**B5** Is responsible for risks after delivery and for additional risks arising from his or her failure to give sufficient notice for the time and place of delivery (if applicable) when the goods are duly appropriated, clearly set aside or identified according to the contract.
A6 Is responsible for costs before delivery, and freight and costs incurred after delivery payable by him or her under the contract of carriage, as well as the cost of export approval or clearance.	**B6** Is responsible for costs after delivery except those paid by the seller, and for additional costs caused by his or her own failure to give notice of the time and place of delivery (if applicable) when the goods are duly appropriated, clearly set aside or identified according to the contract, as well as for costs incurred in obtaining import and transit approval or clearance.
A7 Must give the buyer sufficient notice of the completion of the delivery and other matters to enable him or her to take delivery.	**B7** Must give sufficient notice to the seller of the time and destination of the carriage, if necessary.
A8 Must, if customary, provide the usual transport documents or, if agreed by the parties, equivalent electronic messages.	**B8** Must accept the conforming documents.
A9 Is responsible for the costs of checking operations and of packaging and marking the goods as agreed, or as deemed adequate in accordance with the relevant commercial practices.	**B9** Is responsible for the costs of pre-shipment inspection, unless such inspection is mandated by the authorities of the export country.
A10 Must, at the request, risk and expense of the buyer, assist the buyer in obtaining necessary documents and electronic messages for transporting and importing goods, and necessary information for effecting insurance.	**B10** Is responsible for the cost of the relevant documents or equivalent electronic messages.

1. The buyer should consider insurance matters because the seller is not liable to insure the goods.

CIP — Carriage and Insurance Paid to

[1.25] This term means that the seller pays the freight and insurance for the carriage of goods to the agreed destination, but risks (although insured) pass to the buyer after the delivery of the goods to the named carrier. It is suitable for any means of transport, but is more likely to be used for carriage by air and land. In the case of sea carriage, it can avoid the difficulties of determining when risk passes if the ship's rail is not appropriate for this purpose. The term includes the following duties:

The Seller	The Buyer
A1 Must provide goods and documents or equivalent electronic messages in conformity with the contract of sale.	**B1** Must pay the price of the contract.
A2 Must obtain an export licence and other necessary approval for export. Where applicable, must complete export customs formalities.	**B2** Must obtain an import licence and transit approval. Where applicable, must complete import customs formalities.
A3 (i) Is responsible for making a contract of carriage with a vessel suitable for transporting the goods concerned on usual terms, to transport the goods to the agreed destination by the usual route. **(ii)** Is responsible for making a contract of insurance which enables the buyer or any person having an insurable interest to make a claim under the policy directly against the insurer. The insurance contract must satisfy the following requirements: • The insurer must be of good repute. • The contract must, in the absence of an express agreement, be consistent with the minimum cover of the Institute Cargo Clauses (Institute of London Underwriters) or any similar set of clauses. The seller is responsible for insuring additional risks of war, strikes, riots and civil commotion only at the buyer's request and expense. • The contract must cover the whole period before the goods are taken over by the buyer at the place of destination as agreed. • The contract must cover a minimum value of the contract price plus 10% (that is, 110% of the contract price).	**B3** Is under no obligation to make a contract of carriage or of insurance.
A4 Must deliver the goods to the custody of the named carrier.	**B4** Must accept delivery as agreed.
A5 Is responsible for risks before delivery.	**B5** Is responsible for risks after delivery and additional risks arising from his or her failure to give sufficient notice of the time and place of delivery (if applicable) when the goods are duly appropriated, clearly set aside or identified according to the contract.

The Seller	The Buyer
A6 Is responsible for costs before delivery, freight costs, other costs incurred after delivery but payable by the seller under the contract of carriage, and the cost of obtaining export approval or completing export customs formalities.	**B6** Is responsible for costs incurred after delivery except those paid by the seller, together with additional costs arising from his or her failure to give sufficient notice for the time and place of delivery (if applicable) when the goods are duly appropriated, clearly set aside or identified according to the contract. Is also responsible for the cost of obtaining import or transit approval or completing import customs formalities.
A7 Must give the buyer sufficient notice of the completion of delivery and other relevant matters to enable him or her to take delivery.	**B7** Must give the seller sufficient notice of the time and destination of delivery, when necessary.
A8 Must, if customary, provide the usual transport documents or, if agreed by the parties, equivalent electronic messages.	**B8** Must accept the conforming documents.
A9 Is responsible for the costs of checking operations and of packaging and marking the goods as agreed or as deemed adequate in accordance with the relevant commercial practices.	**B9** Is responsible for the costs of pre-shipment inspection, unless such inspection is mandated by the authorities of the export country.
A10 Must, at the request, risk and expense of the buyer, assist the buyer in obtaining the necessary documents and electronic messages for transporting and importing the goods, and necessary information for effecting additional insurance.	**B10** Is responsible for costs incurred in obtaining the relevant documents or electronic messages and, at the request of the seller, in providing necessary information on additional insurance.

DAF — Delivered at Frontier

[1.26] This term means that the seller delivers the goods to the agreed place before the customs line at the frontier of the importing country, or sometimes of the exporting country. Under this term, the seller is liable to clear the goods for export, but not liable to clear the goods for import into the country of destination. Thus, the seller is not usually liable for unloading the goods before delivery. DAF is often used in carriage by land or by inland water. If the parties wish the goods to be delivered in a port, on a quay or on board a vessel, the ICC recommends use of the DES or DEQ terms. The duties of the seller and buyer are summarised in the following table:

The Seller	The Buyer
A1 Must provide goods and documents or equivalent electronic messages in conformity with the contract of sale.	**B1** Must pay the price of the contract.
A2 Is responsible for obtaining an export licence and other approval, as well as approval for transit through a third country. Where applicable, is responsible for completing export customs formalities.	**B2** Is responsible for obtaining an import licence and other necessary approval for import and transport thereafter. Where applicable, is responsible for completing import customs formalities.
A3 (i) Is responsible for making a contract of carriage to transport the goods to the named point or place of delivery on the frontier. In the absence of an express agreement or customary practice, the seller can choose a point on the frontier as the place of delivery. If the buyer requests the seller to deliver to a place beyond the frontier in the importing country, the seller has the option of agreeing to the request or promptly notifying the buyer of his or her refusal to do so. **(ii)** Is under no obligation to insure the goods.[1]	**B3** Is under no obligation to make a contract of carriage.
A4 Must deliver the goods at the disposal of the buyer at the named place on the frontier at or within the agreed time, without unloading them.	**B4** Must take delivery from the seller at the named place on the frontier, as agreed.
A5 Is responsible for risks before delivery.	**B5** Is responsible for risks after delivery, and additional risks arising from his or her failure to give sufficient notice of the time and place of delivery (if applicable) when the goods are duly appropriated, clearly set aside or identified according to the contract.
A6 Is responsible for the costs of transporting and placing the goods at the buyer's disposal at the named place on the frontier, together with the costs of export and transit approval. Where applicable, is responsible for the costs of completing export customs formalities.	**B6** Is responsible for costs after delivery, the costs of import approval or, where applicable, the costs of import customs formalities. Is also responsible for additional costs flowing from his or her failure to give sufficient notice of the time and place of delivery (if applicable) when the goods are duly appropriated, clearly set aside or identified according to the contract.
A7 Must give the buyer sufficient notice of the dispatch of the goods for delivery and other necessary matters to enable him or her to take delivery.	**B7** Must give the seller sufficient notice of the time and place of delivery, when necessary.

The Seller	The Buyer
A8 Must, at his or her expense, provide the usual documents or evidence of delivery, or an equivalent electronic message, as agreed. By agreement of the parties, at the buyer's risk and expense, must obtain a through-document of transport or equivalent electronic message covering the transmission of the goods between the place of dispatch and the named destination on the usual terms.	**B8** Must accept the conforming documents as agreed.
A9 Is responsible for the costs of checking operations, and of packaging and marking the goods as agreed or as deemed adequate for delivering the goods at the frontier or at the named place in the importing country in accordance with the relevant commercial practices.	**B9** Is responsible for the costs of pre-shipment inspection, unless such inspection is mandated by the authorities of the export country.
A10 Must, at the request, risk and expense of the buyer, assist the buyer in obtaining necessary documents and electronic messages for transporting and importing goods, and necessary information for effecting insurance.	**B10** Is responsible for the costs of obtaining the documents or equivalent electronic messages. Where applicable, at the request of the seller but the risk and expense of the buyer, must provide necessary documents of approval to enable the seller to deliver in a place in the importing country beyond the frontier.

1. It is to the seller's benefit to insure the goods against risks of transit before delivery at the named frontier.

DES — Delivered Ex Ship

[1.27] This term means that the seller should make the goods available to the buyer on board the ship uncleared for import at the named port of destination. It requires the seller to put the goods into a deliverable state on board the ship at the named place of destination, but does not require the seller to discharge the goods for import into the named country of destination. If the parties wish the seller to discharge the goods from the vessel, the ICC recommends the use of the DEQ term. Although the expression is 'delivery ex ship', the term is not exclusively for carriage by sea or inland water. For example, the term has been commonly used for carriage by air. To avoid confusion, the ICC recommends this term only for sea, inland water or multimodal carriage. The duties of the seller and buyer are set out in the following table:

The Seller	The Buyer
A1 Must provide goods and documents or equivalent electronic messages in conformity with the contract of sale.	**B1** Must pay the price of the contract.

[1.27] International Commercial Law

The Seller	The Buyer
A2 Is responsible for obtaining approval for export and transit through a third country and, where applicable, for completing export customs formalities.	B2 Is responsible for obtaining approval for import and, where applicable, for completing import customs formalities.
A3 Is responsible for making a contract of carriage to transport the goods to the agreed point of delivery. In the absence of an express agreement or customary practice, the seller may choose a suitable point for delivery at the named port of destination, but is not responsible for insuring the goods.[1]	B3 Is under no obligation to make a contract of carriage or insurance.
A4 Must put goods which are not cleared for import into a deliverable state on board the ship at the usual unloading point[2] which is appropriate for unloading goods of the same nature in the named port of destination, as agreed.	B4 Must take delivery of goods which are placed at his or her disposal, as agreed.
A5 Is responsible for risks before delivery.	B5 Is responsible for risks after delivery, and additional risks caused by his or her failure to give sufficient notice of the time and place of delivery (if applicable) when the goods are duly appropriated, clearly set aside or identified according to the contract.
A6 Is responsible for costs incurred before delivery and the costs of export and transit approval. Where applicable, is responsible for the cost of completing export customs formalities.	B6 Is responsible for costs after delivery, the cost of import approval and, where applicable, for the cost of import customs formalities. Is also responsible for additional costs incurred because of his or her failure to take delivery or to give sufficient notice of the time and place of delivery (if applicable) when the goods are duly appropriated, clearly set aside or identified according to the contract.
A7 Must give the buyer sufficient notice as to the estimated time for delivery and other matters to enable him or her to take delivery.	B7 Must give the seller sufficient notice as to the time and place of delivery, when necessary.
A8 Must, at his or her own expense, provide the delivery order, the usual transport documents or, if agreed by the parties, equivalent electronic messages, to enable the buyer to claim the goods at the agreed destination.	B8 Must accept the conforming documents.
A9 Is responsible for the costs of checking operations and of packaging and marking the goods as agreed or as necessary for the goods concerned.	B9 Is responsible for the costs of pre-shipment inspection, unless such inspection is mandated by the authorities of the export country.

The Seller	The Buyer
A10 Must, at the request, risk and expense of the buyer, assist the buyer in obtaining any documents and electronic messages (other than those covered in **A8**) for transporting and importing the goods, and necessary information for effecting insurance.	**B10** Is responsible for the costs of obtaining necessary documents or equivalent electronic messages under **A10**.

1. The seller may choose to insure the goods, because risks lie with the seller until goods are delivered ex ship.
2. This should be read in conjunction with **A3** duties, under which, in the absence of any express agreement and customs, the seller may choose a suitable point of delivery. It follows that the point chosen by the seller must be one of the usual points for unloading goods of the same nature.

DEQ — Delivered Ex Quay

[1.28] This term means that the seller should place goods which are cleared for importation on a quay (or wharf) of the named port of destination for the buyer to take delivery. Under this term the buyer is responsible for completing customs formalities for imports, unless the parties expressly agree otherwise. This term is suitable for carriage by sea or inland water, or for multimodal carriage, although it is often used in air carriage. The ICC recommends the use of the DDU or DDP terms if the seller is expected to deliver the goods to a point beyond the port of destination. The duties of both parties are set out in the following table:

The Seller	The Buyer
A1 Must provide goods and documents or equivalent electronic messages in conformity with the contract of sale.	**B1** Must pay the price of the contract.
A2 Is responsible for obtaining any licence or other necessary approval for export and transit through a third country and, where applicable, for completing export customs formalities.	**B2** Is responsible for obtaining an import licence and other necessary approval. Where applicable, is responsible for completing import customs formalities.
A3 Is responsible for making a contract of carriage to transport the goods to the agreed quay. In the absence of an express agreement or customary practice, the seller may choose a quay for delivery at the named port, but is not responsible for insuring the goods.[1]	**B3** Is under no obligation to make a contract of carriage or insurance.
A4 Must place the goods at the disposal of the buyer on a quay or wharf of the named port of destination, as agreed.	**B4** Must take delivery when the goods have been placed at his or her disposal, as agreed.

The Seller	The Buyer
A5 Is responsible for risks until goods have been delivered ex quay.	**B5** Is responsible for risks after delivery, and additional risks caused by his or her failure to give sufficient notice for the time and place of delivery (if applicable) when the goods are duly appropriated, clearly set aside or identified pursuant to the contract.
A6 Is responsible for costs before delivery and costs of approval or, where applicable, of customs formalities for export and transit through a third country.	**B6** Is responsible for costs after delivery including, where applicable, costs of customs formalities, and additional costs arising from his or her failure to take delivery or to give sufficient notice of the time and place of delivery (if applicable) when the goods are duly appropriated, clearly set aside or identified pursuant to the contract.
A7 Must give the buyer sufficient notice of the estimated time of delivery and other matters to enable the buyer to take delivery.	**B7** Must give the seller sufficient notice of the time and place of delivery, when necessary.
A8 Must, at his or her own expense, provide the delivery order, the usual transport documents or, if agreed by the parties, equivalent electronic messages, to enable the buyer to take and remove the goods from the agreed quay of delivery.	**B8** Must accept the conforming documents.
A9 Is responsible for the costs of checking operations and of packaging and marking the goods as agreed or as necessary for delivering the goods concerned.	**B9** Is responsible for the costs of pre-shipment inspection, unless such inspection is mandated by the authorities of the export country.
A10 Must, at the request, risk and expense of the buyer, assist the buyer in obtaining any documents and electronic messages (other than those covered in **A8**) for transporting and importing the goods, and necessary information for effecting insurance.	**B10** Is responsible for the costs of obtaining necessary documents or equivalent electronic messages under **A10**.

1. The seller may choose to insure the goods because risks lie with the seller until goods are delivered ex quay.

DDU — Delivered Duty Unpaid

[1.29] This term means that the seller should transport the goods to a named place in the country of importation, but is not liable for import duties or other customs charges for importation, or for unloading the goods from the means of transport. The term is suitable for any means of transport, but is most likely to be used for carriage by air or land. If the delivery is to take place on a vessel or on a quay, the ICC recommends the use of the DES or DEQ terms. The responsibilities of the parties are as follows:

The Seller	The Buyer
A1 Must provide goods and documents or equivalent electronic messages in conformity with the contract of sale.	**B1** Must pay the price of the contract.
A2 Is responsible for obtaining approval for export and transit through a third country and, where applicable, for completing export customs formalities.	**B2** Is responsible for obtaining approval for import and, where applicable, for completing import customs formalities.
A3 Is responsible for making a contract of carriage to transport the goods to the agreed place to delivery. In the absence of an express agreement or customary practice, the seller may choose a point of delivery at the named destination, but is not responsible for insuring the goods.[1]	**B3** Is under no obligation to make a contract of carriage or insurance.
A4 Must place goods which are ready for unloading at the disposal of the buyer or an authorised person, as agreed.	**B4** Must take delivery when the goods have been placed at his or her disposal, as agreed.
A5 Is responsible for risks before delivery.	**B5** Is responsible for risks after delivery, together with additional risks arising from his or her failure to obtain import approval or to give sufficient notice for the time and place of delivery (if applicable) when the goods are duly appropriated, clearly set aside or identified pursuant to the contract.
A6 Is responsible for costs before delivery and the costs of obtaining approval or, where applicable, completing customs formalities for export and transit through a third country.	**B6** Is responsible for costs after delivery and the costs of obtaining import approval or, where applicable, for completing import customs formalities. Is also responsible for additional costs incurred because of his or her failure to obtain import approval, to take delivery or to give sufficient notice of the time and place of delivery (if applicable) when the goods are duly appropriated, clearly set aside or identified pursuant to the contract.
A7 Must give the buyer sufficient notice as to the dispatch of the goods and other necessary matters to enable the buyer to take delivery.	**B7** Must give the seller sufficient notice of the place and time for delivery, when necessary.
A8 Must, at his or her own expense, provide the delivery order, the usual transport documents or, if agreed by the parties, equivalent electronic messages, to enable the buyer to take delivery of the goods, as agreed.	**B8** Must accept the conforming documents or equivalent electronic messages.
A9 Is responsible for the costs of checking operations and of packaging and marking the goods as agreed or as necessary for delivering the goods concerned.	**B9** Is responsible for the costs of pre-shipment inspection, unless such inspection is mandated by the authorities of the export country.

[1.29] International Commercial Law

The Seller	The Buyer
A10 Must, at the request, risk and expense of the buyer, assist the buyer in obtaining any documents and electronic messages (other than those covered in **A8**) for transporting and importing goods, and necessary information for effecting insurance.	**B10** Is responsible for the costs of obtaining necessary documents or equivalent electronic messages under **A10**.

1. The seller should consider insurance matters because risks lie with the seller before delivery at the named place of destination.

DDP — Delivered Duty Paid

[1.30] This term means that the seller should deliver the goods, which are cleared for import, to a named place in the country of importation, being responsible for all costs (including import duty) before delivery. It does not, however, require the seller to unload the goods before delivery. DDP imposes a maximum obligation upon the seller, while EXW imposes a minimum obligation upon the seller. It is a term comparable with DDU, and is also common for all means of transport, in particular carriage of goods by air or land. The details of DDP are set out in the following table:

The Seller	The Buyer
A1 Must provide goods and documents or equivalent electronic messages in conformity with the contract of sale.	**B1** Must pay the price of the contract.
A2 Is responsible for obtaining all approval for export, import and transit through a third country.[1] Where applicable, is responsible for completing all customs formalities.	**B2** Must assist the seller in obtaining approval for import.
A3 Is responsible for making a contract of carriage to transport the goods to the agreed place of delivery. In the absence of an express agreement or commercial practice, the seller is free to choose a point of delivery at the named place of destination, but is not responsible for insuring the goods.[2]	**B3** Is under no obligation to make a contract of carriage or insurance.
A4 Must place the goods, ready for unloading, at the disposal of the buyer for delivery, as agreed.	**B4** Must take delivery of the goods when they have been placed at his or her disposal, as agreed.
A5 Is responsible for risks before delivery.	**B5** Is responsible for risks after delivery, and additional risks caused by his or her failure to give sufficient notice of the time and place of delivery (if applicable) when the goods are duly appropriated, clearly set aside or identified according to the contract.

34

The Seller	The Buyer
A6 Is responsible for all costs before delivery, including the costs of transmission of goods and the costs of obtaining approval for export, import or transit through a third country. Where applicable, is responsible for the cost of completing customs formalities.	**B6** Is responsible for all costs after delivery, and additional costs caused by his or her failure to take delivery or to give sufficient notice for the time and place of delivery (if applicable) when the goods are duly appropriated, clearly set aside or identified according to the contract.
A7 Must give the buyer sufficient notice as to the dispatch of goods and other matters to enable the buyer to take delivery.	**B7** Must give the seller sufficient notice as to the place and time of delivery, when necessary.
A8 Must, at his or her own expense, provide the delivery order, the usual transport documents or, if agreed by the parties, equivalent electronic messages, to enable the buyer to take delivery of the goods as agreed.	**B8** Must accept the conforming documents.
A9 Is responsible for the costs of checking operations and of packaging and marking the goods as agreed or as necessary for delivering the goods concerned.	**B9** Is responsible for costs of pre-shipment inspection, unless such inspection is mandated by the authorities of the export country.
A10 Is responsible for obtaining all necessary documents or equivalent electronic messages for transporting and importing goods to the agreed place of delivery and, at the request of the buyer, providing necessary information for effecting insurance.	**B10** Must, at the request of the seller, assist the seller in obtaining all necessary documents or equivalent electronic messages for transporting the goods to the agreed place of delivery.

1. The parties may, by express agreement, exclude the seller from liability for paying certain costs of import, such as VAT.
2. The seller should consider insurance matters because risks lie with the seller before delivery at the named place of destination.

Summary of Incoterms 2000

[1.31] Incoterms 2000 contains 13 terms, which appear to be complicated; each term contains 10 headings (or categories) of duties. However, the Incoterms can be understood from another perspective — namely, the common elements or considerations of all the terms. After studying the details of each term, we can say that all the terms are based, built upon, or concerned with, the following common elements or considerations:

- **Delivery:**
  - place of delivery;
  - time of delivery; and
  - manner of delivery.
- **Risks:**
  - place for the passing of risk in goods;
  - time for the passing of risk in goods; and
  - manner for the passing of risk in goods.

[1.31]

- **Costs:**
  - responsibility for meeting the costs of loading and unloading the goods;
  - responsibility for meeting the costs of freight;
  - responsibility for meeting incidental costs of transport;
  - responsibility for meeting additional costs incurred because of a party's failure to perform the contract as agreed;
  - responsibility for meeting the costs of approval for export, import and transit through a third country; and
  - responsibility for meeting the costs of export or import customs formalities, where applicable.[24]
- **Approval:**
  - responsibility for obtaining export approval;
  - responsibility for obtaining import approval; and
  - responsibility for obtaining approval for transit through a third country.
- **Carriage:** responsibility for making a contract of carriage.
- **Insurance:** responsibility for making a contract of insurance.
- **Documentation:** responsibility for providing documents or equivalent electronic messages for the transfer of goods.
- **Conformity:** responsibility for ensuring conformity of the goods with the contract of sale.
- **Assistance:** responsibility for assisting the other party in performing the contract of sale.

The terms of each of the Incoterms differ, depending on the variations in the particular duties of the parties. Because of the common considerations of all the terms, it is possible for parties to any contract of international sale to modify or redefine most of them to suit their needs in a given circumstance. However, any modification must be made expressly in writing to avoid possible confusion. In addition, the ICC recommends that the parties choose the term closest to their specific needs to avoid unnecessary departure from the original purposes for which the Incoterms were developed.

---

24. The words 'where applicable' are necessary, as noted by the ICC, because in certain free trade zones or regional trade organisations, such as the EU, formalities are no longer required. See ICC, *Incoterms 2000*, ICC Publishing SA, Paris, 1999, p 21.

Legal framework for international sale of goods in Australia

[1.32] Depending on the meaning of 'goods', the Australian legal framework for the international sale of goods varies. Broadly, any law which may affect an international commercial transaction may be part of the legal framework for the international sale of goods. For example, general contract law is always relevant to any contract of sale, whether domestic, interstate or international.[25] Sale of goods legislation and consumer protection legislation may be relevant, depending on the subject matter involved. In addition, export and import control legislation, law on international banking and intellectual property law, for example, could also be relevant in certain circumstances. In a narrower sense, the legal framework for international sale of goods in Australia includes merely the sale of goods legislation, the relevant provisions of the Trade Practices Act, the CISG, and the common law of contracts and commercial customs (such as Incoterms 2000). This chapter adopts this narrow definition of the legal framework. It emphasises Incoterms 2000 and the sale of goods legislation of Australia. The CISG can also be regarded as part of Australian law, and is examined in detail in **Chapter 2**.

◆

[1.33] *Bowden Brothers and Co Ltd v Robert Little*

(1907) 4 CLR 1364

When both the Incoterms and the sale of goods legislation apply

Facts: Bowden Bros, the plaintiff and appellant, was a joint stock company registered in Queensland. It carried on businesses in Queensland and Japan and had an office branch in Sydney. Robert Little, trading as Robert Little and Co, was the defendant and respondent in the case. He was a merchant carrying on business in Sydney. Under a contract of sale concluded on 14 June 1905, Robert Little agreed to purchase 450 t of Japanese onions from Bowden Bros. The contract of sale was based on the CIF term to Sydney. The buyer found that the onions shipped to Sydney were unmerchantable and refused to accept and pay for them. The seller sued the buyer for the unpaid price of the contract. The buyer argued that the contract meant that the seller was responsible for delivering the onions in Sydney. The seller contended that the contract was intended to deliver the goods at Kobe, Japan. The seller also argued that the condition of the onions was caused by 'marine risks' (for the meaning of this term see **[7.36]**–**[7.37]**), rather than the seller's breach of the implied term as to merchantability under the relevant sale of goods legislation. Under the CIF term, the risk passes to the buyer when the goods have passed over the ship's rail in loading at the named port of shipment (see, for example, **A5** and **B5** of the CIF term, described at **[1.23]**). The parties made claims and cross-claims, and the matter eventually went to the High Court.

---

25. This is illustrated in *Oceanic Sun Line Special Shipping Co Inc v Fay* (1988) 79 ALR 9, where the court discussed not only the general contract law of Australia, but also the Contracts Review Act 1980 (NSW) (referred to by Wilson and Toohey JJ at 24).

> **Decision:** The High Court held that the seller was liable to put the onions on board the ship as agreed and to pay for the costs, freight and insurance under the CIF term. Whether the parties had agreed that the onions must be of merchantable quality at the time of delivery in Sydney, or that the onions should be merchantable only at the time of shipment at Kobe, should be determined in the circumstances involved. The mere fact that the seller knew that the onions were to be shipped to Sydney was not sufficient to establish the guarantee that the onions must be merchantable when delivered in Sydney.

[1.34] This case raises the issue of contract construction when the contract incorporates an Incoterm. It also draws our attention to an uncertain area in the application of the sale of goods legislation to a contract of international sale. The sale of goods legislation in Australia provides that the goods must be merchantable and fit for the purpose for which the goods are acquired, but does not expressly provide rules for ascertaining whether the terms have been complied with in an international sale.[26]

This case also raises the issue of adequacy of remedy in an international sale. We may wonder whether Robert Little should have sued the carrier of the onions on the basis of the 'unseaworthiness' of the ship (see **[4.82]**), rather than refusing to pay the price of the onions to the seller. Depending on the circumstances involved, it might be possible to argue that the carrier did not provide a seaworthy ship which was equipped adequately for carrying the onions from Japan to Sydney. However, if the seaworthiness of the ship is proven, the suitability of the onions for the intended voyage may bring the dispute back to the contract of sale. This is what happened in *Westcoast Food Brokers Ltd v The Hoyanger and Westfallarsen & Co A/S* [1979] 2 Lloyd's Rep 79, where the court decided that, on the balance of probabilities, the over-ripeness of the apples at the time of shipment caused the damage to the apples after the 48-day voyage. The court found that the condition of the apples in this case was not suitable for the contemplated voyage. In such cases, the parties would have to go back to the contract of sale to see what the contract said about the condition of the goods before shipment.

International sale of goods and general contract law

[1.35] General contract law is the basis of the sale of goods legislation in Australia and most common law jurisdictions, in particular the United Kingdom, Hong Kong, Canada and New Zealand. In fact, the legislation contains a modified version of the rules of general contract law. Although in theory it is possible to enter into a contract for international sale merely on the basis of common law, most contracts of international sale would fall under the regime of either the domestic sale of goods legislation or of the CISG. We need to examine general contract law briefly before investigating the relationships between contracts of international sale and sale of goods legislation in Australia.

---

26. It is open to debate whether merchantability in the sale of goods legislation imposes upon the seller an obligation to ensure that the goods are merchantable at the intended destination in an international sale.

[1.36] An international sale of goods is usually effected by a contract of sale. The contract can either be in writing or in oral form. However, although an oral contract is enforceable under general law, the CISG and the sale of goods legislation in most Australian states and territories, an oral contract is not enforceable under the sale of goods legislation in Western Australia (s 4 of the Sale of Goods Act 1895 (WA)), Tasmania (s 9 of the Sale of Goods Act 1896 (Tas)), and the Northern Territory (s 9 of the Sale of Goods Act 1972 (NT)), if the value of the sale exceeds a stipulated sum. In these three jurisdictions, an oral contract is not enforceable if the value of the sale exceeds a fixed amount (10 units in Western Australia and Tasmania, and $50 in the Northern Territory), and certain conditions are not met. The requirement for a written contract can be overridden when the CISG applies in these jurisdictions.

[1.37] In conclusion, in Australia the rules of general contract law apply to any contract of international sale, to the extent that no inconsistency arises between those rules and the provisions of the CISG, or any other convention applicable in the circumstances concerned. Actually, the same can be said about the contract law of all countries, because under the relevant international law a country is obliged to give a prevailing effect to the international conventions ratified by it.

[1.38] The parties to a contract of international sale have a wide liberty to define their rights and obligations, as well as the terms of the contract, by express intention. Parties from different countries often have to define their legal relationships by incorporating commercial usage and customs, such as the Incoterms, into their contract of sale. The common law and sale of goods legislation allow parties to define their rights and duties by way of contract, or to modify the effect of the provisions of the sale of goods legislation unless otherwise prohibited. (For example, certain provisions in Pt IV of the Goods Act 1958 (Vic) and provisions of the Trade Practices Act 1974 (Cth), which deal with consumer protection, cannot be overridden by express agreement of the parties.) The CISG also allows parties to modify or exclude most provisions of the Convention by express agreement: art 6.

[1.39] The Incoterms, which are prepared by the ICC (see **[1.12]**–**[1.31]**), can be incorporated into contracts of international sale under the notion of freedom of contract. As a general rule, the Incoterms are given effect under general contract law. The relevant domestic sale of goods legislation and the CISG allow the incorporation of the Incoterms into a contract of sale. This characteristic of the Incoterms must be noted to avoid a misunderstanding of the status and nature of the Incoterms. Otherwise, parties to an international sale may incorrectly regard an Incoterm as compulsory, inflexible and inviolable, like a rule of law. In fact, Incoterms are standardised and uniform commercial terms, customs or usage.

International sale of goods and the Australian sale of goods legislation

Uniformity of the sale of goods legislation

[1.40] In Australia, contracts for the sale of goods which satisfy the definition of 'goods' under the sale of goods legislation in each state and territory are subject to the relevant sale of goods legislation. The sale of goods legislation is largely uniform — for example, the definition of 'goods' is uniform in each jurisdiction — and is based on the Sale of Goods Act 1893 (UK), which has been replaced by the Sale of Goods Act 1979 (UK). In fact, the sale of goods laws of most major, common law jurisdictions originate from the English Sale of Goods Act 1893. Some uniformity can thus be seen in the domestic sale of goods laws of most major, common law jurisdictions, such as the United Kingdom, Canada, New Zealand and Hong Kong. The emphasis of our study is on the legal implications of contracts of international sale, as opposed to practical activities involving the international sale of goods, such as how to establish business connections and how to market goods in a foreign market. The major legal issues arising from the application of the sale of goods legislation to contracts of international sale are discussed below.

Constitutional implications in Australia

[1.41] Constitutional implications arise from the application of state sale of goods legislation to the international sale of goods. The following three questions are essential:

- Who has power to regulate the international sale of goods in Australia?
- Can state sale of goods legislation apply to a contract for the international sale of goods?
- How does state sale of goods legislation operate in an international sale?

In answer to the first question, the power to regulate the international sale of goods lies with the federal government. But this is a concurrent power, which can also be exercised by a state or territorial parliament, subject to s 109 of the Australian Constitution. The powers of the federal and state governments are divided mainly, though not exclusively, on the basis of s 51 of the Constitution. Many of the heads of power in s 51 are concurrent, and s 109 of the Constitution gives prevailing force to the federal legislation in cases of inconsistency between the federal and state laws. In theory, the federal parliament has power within the territory of the Commonwealth of Australia to regulate:

- interstate and international trade under s 51(i);
- interstate and international banking under s 51(xiii);
- insurance, other than mere state insurance, under s 51(xiv);
- bills of exchange and promissory notes under s 51(xvi); and

- the operation (not the establishment)[27] of financial or trading corporations and foreign companies under s 51(xx).

It also has power to give effect to international treaties under the s 51(xxix) external power.

Nonetheless, the sale of goods is one of the areas where the state parliaments have traditionally exercised their legislative power.[28] Therefore, as far as the international sale of goods is concerned, both the federal and state parliaments can regulate the matter, but the federal legislation prevails wherever inconsistency arises.

The discussion in the preceding paragraph also answers the second question raised above. The sale of goods legislation may apply to any contract for international sale of goods, provided that it is not inconsistent with the relevant federal legislation. Indeed, in circumstances where the CISG applies, the provisions of the sale of goods legislation may be excluded if they are inconsistent with the provisions of the Convention.[29]

This leads us to the third question: how does state sale of goods legislation operate in an international sale? The sale of goods legislation in each state and territory has extra-territorial application. It applies to any contract for the sale of goods which is subject to the law of the state and territory. There are two main conditions for the application of a state's sale of goods legislation to a contract for the international sale of goods:

- the subject matter consists of 'goods' as defined in the sale of goods legislation;[30] and
- the contract is subject to the state law on any of the grounds which make the state law applicable in the circumstances involved; for example, by express intention of the parties, or through any of the conflicts rules adopted in the relevant jurisdiction: see [12.23]–[12.24].

Therefore, state or territorial sale of goods legislation may apply to any contract for the international sale of goods once the above two conditions are satisfied, subject to any express restrictions (if any) of the federal and state law. The mere fact that the CISG applies to a particular contract of international sale does not automatically exclude the operation of the relevant state sale of goods legislation. The state and territorial law is excluded from applying to such a contract only in the case of inconsistency between the Convention and the state law; or, alternatively, by the express intention of the parties to the contract concerned (if such an exclusion is allowed).

Constitutional implications may also arise where the power to regulate trade is divided between the central government and state governments in a federal country. The power

---

27. A federal effort to regulate the incorporation and establishment of financial or trading corporations failed in 1990, in a High Court challenge brought by several state governments: see *New South Wales v Commonwealth (The Incorporation Case)* (1990) 169 CLR 482.
28. Many states had passed their Sale of Goods Act before the establishment of the Commonwealth of Australia in 1901. For example, the Sale of Goods Act 1896 (Qld), Sale of Goods Act 1895 (SA), Sale of Goods Act 1896 (Tas) and Sale of Goods Act 1895 (WA) still operate in these states.
29. The CISG was adopted in each state and territory under a national scheme in 1986–7. The state or territorial statutes which incorporated the Convention provide that the provisions of the Convention prevail in case of any inconsistency between the Convention and the relevant state or territorial laws.
30. For sale of computers, see *Triangle Underwriters Inc v Honeywell Inc* 604 Fed 737 (1979).

to regulate trade can be exercised in different ways, and may interfere with different areas of the economy. For example, in *Bell Bros Pty Ltd v Rathbone* (1963) 109 CLR 225, the appellants appealed to the High Court of Australia against a conviction under the state Transport Co-ordination Act 1933–61 (WA). The appellant was charged for a breach of the said Act for carrying a cargo of timber without licence. The appellant's vehicle was carrying the timber to Fremantle, a sea port in Western Australia, for shipment to Melbourne in Victoria. If the carriage by land is regarded as part of a continuous journey from a place in Western Australia to a place in Victoria, the carriage is subject to s 92 of the Australian Constitution because it involves interstate trade. Accordingly, the prohibition under the said state law would be invalid because of its inconsistency with s 92. In their separate judgments, seven judges of the High Court all held that the appellant was protected by s 92 because the carriage by land was part of the interstate trade.

This case suggests that, in Australia or another country with a similar constitutional arrangement, an act which is part of an international trading activity is not only subject to the relevant state law, but also protected by the relevant provisions of the federal constitution. The general conclusion is that any state legislation which prohibits or restricts interstate or international trade will probably be held to be invalid under the relevant federal constitution.[31] On this point, we can see that the arrangement for implementing the CISG in Australia is more an arrangement of convenience, rather than a constitutional requirement.

Formation of contract under the sale of goods legislation

[1.42] There is no requirement for a formal contract of sale in Australia, except in Western Australia, Tasmania and the Northern Territory. An oral contract for the international sale of goods (although not common) is subject to the requirement of formality in these jurisdictions if it does not fall under the CISG. If a contract is to be enforced in Australia under the sale of goods legislation (as opposed to the CISG), the common law rules of contract, such as the rules on offer and acceptance, must be followed. In general terms, any communication between parties must constitute an offer or acceptance in law before it can be enforced by a court of law. Because of the foreign parties involved, the effect of any offer and acceptance can only be decided under whatever law is regarded as applicable by the court dealing with the issues of validity. Conflict of laws is thus an important issue in these circumstances.

Hoeper v Neldner [1931] SASR 173 demonstrates the relationship between the validity of an international sale contract and the governing law in the context of international commerce. The major point is that the validity of a contract and of an offer or acceptance is affected by the law applicable in the circumstances concerned. This case may be compared with a Chinese case involving similar problems. In *China-Schindler Co Ltd North Division v Fung Hing Co Ltd* (1991) 6 China Law and Practice 1, the parties signed an order confirmation for stainless steel plates on 14 December 1988. According to the confirmation, the seller, Fung Hing Co Ltd, would supply 600 stainless steel plates to the buyer, Schindler. The seller began to perform the contract in the same month the confirmation

---

31. For example, see also *Simms v West* (1961) 107 CLR 157.

was signed. On 19 January 1989, the buyer wrote to the seller, demanding a reduction ⟨ the number of MS-04–type plates ordered from 400 to 200, and requesting a new quote. The seller then sent a new order-confirmation form at a lower price for 200 plates to the buyer on the same day, but the buyer did not confirm this order confirmation. The buyer subsequently refused to perform the original order confirmation, arguing that there was no binding contract because the new order-confirmation form quoting a lower price had not been signed. The buyer argued that the new order-confirmation form suggested that the parties were at the stage of negotiating a contract. The seller sued the buyer for breach of contract on the ground that the original order-confirmation form was signed by both parties and was a binding contract. The Beijing Intermediate Court found that the first order confirmation was a duly signed contract, and that the new order confirmation was not signed by the buyer and therefore did not constitute a valid contract. This case was decided under the 1985 Foreign Economic Contract of China, which was replaced by the Code of Contract Law (or Contract Law) of China in March 1999. The Code of Contract Law came into operation on 1 October 1999. Unlike the 1985 Foreign Economic Contract Law, the written form of contract is no longer compulsory under the Code. The change has reduced the differences between Chinese contract law, the CISG and the contract laws of common law countries.

[1.43] It is interesting to note that, in Germany, 'silence after receiving a commercial letter of confirmation in many circumstances will have legal effect as an acceptance'.[32] In this context, a letter of confirmation is the 'evidence of the formation and the content of the contract'.[33] Although it can be argued that the order forms and order-confirmation forms in the above cases were not the same as 'letters of confirmation', it is possible that German law may not treat a lack of written formality in the same way as Chinese law. Thus, the above Chinese case might have had a different result if it had been dealt with under German law. This suggests that the validity of a contract or the formality of a contract must be examined in the context of a particular law.

Passing of property under the sale of goods legislation

[1.44] Rules for the passing of property in goods are important in any contract of international sale. As we have seen, the Incoterms do not deal with passing of property at all. Nor does the CISG. This territory is reserved for the relevant domestic law. Under the sale of goods legislation of the Australian states and territories, property in goods passes to the buyer pursuant to either the express or implied intention of the parties.[34] An express intention is seen when the parties include provisions in the contract of sale, explicitly stating when and how the property in goods passes to the buyer. Under the sale of goods legislation, the payment for the price of the goods may be regarded as an

---

32. Esser, 'Commercial Letters of Confirmation in International Trade: Austrian, French, German, and Swiss Law and Uniform Law Under the 1980 Sales Convention', *Georgia Journal of International & Comparative Law (GA J Int'l & Comp L)*, 1988, vol 18, p 429.
33. Ibid, p 432.
34. See the Sale of Goods Act 1954 (ACT), s 23; Sale of Goods Act 1923 (NSW), s 23; Sale of Goods Act 1972 (NT), s 23; Sale of Goods Act 1896 (Qld), s 20; Sale of Goods Act 1895 (SA), s 18; Sale of Goods Act 1896 (Tas), s 23; Goods Act 1958 (Vic), s 23; and Sale of Goods Act 1895 (WA), s 18.

[1.44]

indicator of the passing of property if the contracting parties so intend: *Matthew Short & Associates Pty Ltd v Riviera Marine (International) Pty Ltd* [2001] NSWCA 281.

[1.45] *Dennant v Skinner and Collom*

[1948] 2 KB 164

Intention to be ascertained in the circumstances involved

Facts: The seller sold a car at auction to the buyer, who signed a document to the effect that the title to the car was not to pass until full payment was made. The buyer gave a false name and address, as well as a bad cheque, which was subsequently dishonoured. He later sold the car to an innocent third party. The seller sought to recover the car from the third party.

Decision: The court held that in this case both property and risk passed to the buyer at the fall of the hammer at the auction sale. This means that the property passed to the buyer when the parties signed the document in question. In addition, it can be argued that the original seller's right in this case might have been defeated by the innocent third party's right.

[1.46] An implied intention is seen when, reading the contract as a whole, the circumstances of the contract suggest the parties' intention as to when and how to pass the property in goods.

[1.47] *Carlos Federspiel & Co SA v Charles Twigg & Co Ltd*

[1957] 1 Lloyd's Rep 240

Implied intention to pass property on shipment

Facts: Carlos Federspiel, the plaintiff buyer, purchased a quantity of bicycles from Charles Twigg under the FOB term. The buyer paid a sum of money under the contract of sale. The seller went into liquidation before delivering the bicycles according to the contract. The buyer argued that property in the bicycles had passed to it, but the receiver argued that, under the FOB term, property in the bicycles was intended to pass upon shipment.

Decision: The court held that the FOB contract suggested that the parties intended the property to pass to the buyer upon shipment. In addition, there had been no indication of appropriation in relation to the bicycles in question.

[1.48] The sale of goods legislation in the Australian states and territories sets out specific rules for ascertaining the intention of the parties to pass property in goods.[35] These rules are outlined in the following paragraphs.

[1.49] The time and manner in which the property in goods passes should be ascertained according to the rules set out in the sale of goods legislation, unless the parties agree otherwise in the contract of sale.

---

35. Sale of Goods Act 1954 (ACT), s 23; Sale of Goods Act 1923 (NSW), s 23; Sale of Goods Act 1972 (NT), s 23; Sale of Goods Act 1896 (Qld), s 20; Sale of Goods Act 1895 (SA), s 18; Sale of Goods Act 1896 (Tas), s 23; Goods Act 1958 (Vic), s 23; and Sale of Goods Act 1895 (WA), s 18.

[1.50] In an 'unconditional contract' (a contract which does not contain conditions for delivery of goods, passing of property, or for the validity of the contract) which does not reserve the 'right of disposal' (the seller's right under the sale of goods legislation to prohibit the buyer from selling or disposing of the goods concerned before full payment on the goods is made), for the sale of 'specific goods' (goods which are identified, ascertained or distinguished from other similar goods at the time of the conclusion of the contract), which are in a 'deliverable state' (ready for the buyer to take over as agreed in a contract of sale), the property in the goods passes to the buyer at the time of the conclusion of the contract — regardless of the time for payment and delivery. In such a case, the buyer can be the legal owner of the goods even if they are in possession of the seller.

[1.51] In a contract for the sale of specific goods, if the seller is required under the contract to do something to put the goods into a deliverable state (for example, to put a machine onto a railway truck, as was the case in *Underwood Ltd v Burgh Castle Brick and Cement Syndicate* [1922] 1 KB 343),[36] the property in the goods does not pass until the thing is done and the buyer has notice of it.

[1.52] In a contract for the sale of specific goods in a deliverable state, if the seller is required under the contract of sale to do something (for example, to weigh, measure or test), or to ascertain the price of the goods, the property does not pass until the required thing is done and the buyer has notice of it. For example, in *Nanka Bruce v Commonwealth Trust Ltd* [1926] AC 77, the seller and buyer agreed that the buyer was to buy cocoa from the seller at a fixed price. The buyer was to weigh the cocoa at the time of resale, and to pay the total price to the seller according to the buyer's calculation of the quantity of the cocoa. The parties later disagreed as to who was the owner of the unsold cocoa which was in the buyer's possession. The court held that the relevant provision of the Sale of Goods Act 1893 (UK) (equivalent to, for example, s 23(3) of the Sale of Goods Act 1923 (NSW)) required the seller to do something to ascertain the price before the property passed. But this provision did not apply to the present case, where the buyer was bound to do something to ascertain the total price of the goods. The court decided that the property in the cocoa passed to the buyer according to the parties' intention; that is, at the conclusion of the contract of sale.

[1.53] If a contract is based on delivery 'on approval' (which means that a contract is based on the approval of the 'buyer' — the recipient of the goods — to accept the goods delivered) or 'sale or return' (which, in brief, means that the existence of a contract of sale is based on an understanding that the recipient of the goods may either accept the goods delivered by keeping them, or refuse the goods delivered by returning them within a fixed or reasonable time after delivery), the property in the goods passes to the buyer in three ways:

---

36. In that case, the contract said that the seller should put a horizontal condensing machine onto a railway truck. The machine was damaged while being loaded onto the truck. The court held that the property and risk in the machine had not passed to the buyer at the time of the damage and the seller had not fulfilled the requirement to put the machine into the truck in a deliverable state.

[1.53]

- When he or she accepts the goods expressly or implicitly by his or her conduct — for example, by exercising the right of an owner over the goods concerned: see *Kirkham v Attenborough* [1897] 1 QB 201.[37]
- When he or she fails to inform the seller of his or her rejection within the fixed time for return of the goods: see *Poole v Smith's Car* [1962] 1 WLR 744.[38] However, the rule does not apply to consumer transactions under certain circumstances where the Trade Practices Act 1974 (Cth) prohibits the use of particular sales and marketing techniques based on delivery of unsolicited goods: s 65 of the Trade Practices Act.[39]
- When he or she fails to reject the goods delivered within a reasonable period of time, even though no time for returning the goods is fixed.

[1.54] In a contract for the sale of 'unascertained goods' (identical goods that can be replaced by each other for the purpose of meeting a contract description, such as wheat or wool of a particular brand, cars of a particular model, or oil of a particular specification) or 'future goods' (which are to be made or to come into existence in the future) by description, the property in the goods passes to the buyer when the unascertained or future goods are 'appropriated' (which in general means that the goods have been identified, marked and delivered irrevocably to the seller), pursuant to the contract with the assent of the parties: see *Re Wait* [1927] 1 Ch 606.[40] In *Matthew Short & Associates Pty Ltd v Riviera Marine (International) Pty Ltd* [2001] NSWCA 281, the NSW Court of Appeal held that the goods in dispute, a motor cruiser, were future goods, and that property in the goods should pass to the buyer as the parties intended, which was the time when the cruiser was loaded onto the freighter for shipment.

[1.55] These rules can be applied to an international sale of goods when the sale is subject to the law of an Australian state or territory, and no inconsistency arises between the provisions of the CISG and the relevant state or territory law.

The rules can be modified or varied by express intention of the parties. This is evidenced by the use of the Incoterms, which are often an essential part of a contract for

---

37. In that case, Kirkham, the plaintiff, was a manufacturing jeweller who sent a consignment of jewellery to Winter, a retailer, on a 'sale or return' term. Winter pledged the jewellery to Attenborough (the defendant) and disappeared with the money. The plaintiff claimed that he was still the owner of the goods and asked the defendant to return them. The court held that Winter had adopted the transaction by pledging the jewellery to Attenborough and the property in the goods passed to Winter. The plaintiff's remedy was to sue Winter.
38. In that case, the parties agreed that the plaintiff would leave his Vauxhall motor car with the defendants who would sell it and give the plaintiff $325 after the sale. The plaintiff demanded after three months that the defendants either return the car or deliver $325 in three days. The defendants did not return the car until several weeks later and the car was found to be damaged. The court held that the contract was one of sale or return. Since the defendants retained the car beyond a reasonable time, the property in the car passed to the defendants who were then held to be liable to pay the price of the car.
39. A foreign corporation is subject to the Trade Practices Act if it carries out business in Australia. The Trade Practices Act has extra-territorial operation, which may catch certain activities of a foreign corporation carried on outside Australia.
40. In that case, the seller, Wait, sold 500 t of wheat to the buyer out of 1000 t of wheat he was yet to receive. Wait became bankrupt before that 500 t was isolated, identified and appropriated. The buyer had paid for the goods and claimed that he was entitled to the 500 t of wheat yet to be delivered. The court held that the goods were unascertained at the time of bankruptcy, and no property in the goods had passed to the buyer.

the international sale of goods. The CIF or FOB terms (see **[1.23]** and **[1.21]**) are those most commonly used in international sales. If CIF is adopted, the seller's duties are examined in the context of the term. CIF cannot replace the rules for the passing of property because it does not deal with the issue. But the seller's liabilities (for example, the liability to obtain an export licence or authorisation under **A2**, the liability to arrange transportation and marine insurance under **A3**, and the liability to deliver the goods within the agreed time to the agreed place) may be regarded as the things which must be done by the seller before the property in the goods passes to the buyer under the sale of goods legislation, unless the parties expressly agree otherwise (by, for example, passing the property at the time of payment).

Transfer of risks under the sale of goods legislation

[1.56] The transfer of the risk in the goods sold is an important issue in international sales. Risk in an international sale is higher than in a domestic sale, because the sale involves parties from different countries, using various means of transportation. In addition, the sale is also exposed to many natural and political risks, such as political and civil unrest, approval for export, import or transit through a third country, and certain natural disasters, which are not major concerns in a domestic sale. It is necessary to define clearly in any contract of sale when and how the risk in the goods passes from the seller to the buyer.

[1.57] The sale of goods legislation in the Australian states and territories deals with the passing of risk under two basic principles:

- risk and property prima facie pass together;[41] and
- the party which causes delay in delivery is liable for the costs, losses or damages flowing from the delay:[42] see *Demby Hamilton Ltd v Barden* [1949] WN 73.[43]

Under the first principle, the express intention of the parties for the passing of property in the goods, and the rules for ascertaining the intention of the parties for the passing of property, are relevant in determining when and how the risk in the goods has been, or is to be, transferred from the seller to the buyer. Delivery of the goods is not crucial under this principle. In circumstances where the parties' intention is evident, the property and risk in the goods lie with the buyer, even though the goods have not been delivered. Otherwise, the property and risk pass to the buyer at the time of delivery as set out in

---

41. See the Sale of Goods Act 1954 (ACT), s 25; Sale of Goods Act 1923 (NSW), s 25; Sale of Goods Act 1972 (NT), s 25; Sale of Goods Act 1896 (Qld), s 23; Sale of Goods Act 1895 (SA), s 20; Sale of Goods Act 1896 (Tas), s 25; Goods Act 1958 (Vic), s 25; and Sale of Goods Act 1895 (WA), s 20.
42. See the Sale of Goods Act 1954 (ACT), ss 25 and 41; Sale of Goods Act 1923 (NSW), ss 25 and 40; Sale of Goods Act 1972 (NT), ss 25 and 40; Sale of Goods Act 1896 (Qld), ss 23 and 39; Sale of Goods Act 1895 (SA), ss 20 and 37; Sale of Goods Act 1896 (Tas), ss 25 and 42; Goods Act 1958 (Vic), ss 25 and 44; and Sale of Goods Act 1895 (WA), ss 20 and 37.
43. In that case, there was a contract for the sale of apple juice, under which the sellers were to make weekly deliveries. The buyer asked the sellers to hold delivery in January and April 1946, and eventually refused to take more deliveries, despite the fact that the contract was not completed. The remainder of the juice went bad. The sellers sued the buyer for the price of the contract. The court held that, although the property in the goods had not passed to the buyer at the time of deterioration, the risk had nonetheless passed to the buyer because he caused the delay in delivery.

[1.57]

most of the rules mentioned in **[1.44]–[1.54]**. The first principle is consistent with most of the Incoterms, which provide that the risk in goods passes at the time of delivery as agreed in the contract of sale.

The second principle deals with circumstances where the delivery did not take place pursuant to the contract, whereby the property and risk may or may not have passed to the buyer. In such circumstances, the party who normally bears the risk in the goods should not suffer from the fault of the other party in failing to make, or take, delivery of the goods as agreed. Therefore, the party causing delay in delivery is liable for the risk, regardless of who should otherwise bear the risk before delivery. This principle is also consistent with the Incoterms: see **B5** of each term.

[1.58] Passing of risk is subject to specific provisions under the CISG: see **[2.277]–[2.290]**. There should be no conflict between the sale of goods legislation and the Convention in relation to the passing of risk in goods, because the provisions of the Convention will prevail over the principles of the sale of goods legislation in cases of inconsistency. The provisions of the Convention on the passing of risk are sufficient to render the application of the sale of goods legislation unnecessary in most circumstances.

[1.59] When a contract of international sale has incorporated an Incoterm, the rules for the passing of risk in the sale of goods legislation may be overridden by the intention of the parties. The passing of risk in such circumstances is determined by the detailed duties of the parties under the chosen term. The rules for the passing of risk under the sale of goods legislation are relevant to a contract of international sale in circumstances where the parties do not incorporate any Incoterm into the contract, or where the parties have modified the selected term to allow the operation of the sale of goods legislation.

Delivery of goods under the sale of goods legislation

[1.60] The sale of goods legislation sets out a number of detailed rules for delivery.[44] These are listed below.

General rule

[1.61] The place, time and manner of delivery should be determined by the express or implied intention of the parties. This general rule allows the operation of the Incoterm incorporated into a contract of sale. 'Delivery' can be either physical or constructive. This was accepted by Isaacs J in *The Australasian United Steam Navigation Co Ltd v Hiskens* (1914) 18 CLR 646 at 665, in the context of delivery between a carrier and a consignee; and by the majority of the High Court in *Gamer's Motor Centre (Newcastle) Pty Ltd v Natwest Wholesale Australia Pty Ltd* (1987) 163 CLR 236, in the context of a sale by a buyer in possession.

---

44. See the Sale of Goods Act 1954 (ACT), ss 33–41; Sale of Goods Act 1923 (NSW), ss 32–40; Sale of Goods Act 1972 (NT), ss 32–40; Sale of Goods Act 1896 (Qld), ss 31–39; Sale of Goods Act 1895 (SA), ss 29–37; Sale of Goods Act 1896 (Tas), ss 34–42; Goods Act 1958 (Vic), ss 36–44; and Sale of Goods Act 1895 (WA), ss 29–37.

Presumed place of delivery

[1.62] In the absence of an express or implied intention, the place of delivery should be, in order of priority:

1. the place where, to the knowledge of the parties at the time of the contract, the specific goods are located;
2. the seller's place of business; or
3. the seller's place of residence.

Time for delivery

[1.63] The delivery should be made on a fixed day; or, in the absence of a fixed day, within a reasonable time.

Delivery while the goods are in a third party's possession

[1.64] When the goods are in a third party's possession, delivery is not effected until the third party acknowledges to the buyer the buyer's title to the goods concerned. Incoterms 2000 does not deal with this situation.

Incidental costs of delivery

[1.65] The seller bears the incidental costs and expenses of putting the goods into a deliverable state unless the parties agree otherwise.

Delivery of wrong quantity

[1.66] Goods must be delivered in a precise quantity, subject to the *de minimis* rule,[45] as described in a contract. The buyer has an option, subject to the *de minimis* rule, to accept or refuse to accept, wholly or partially, as the case may be, goods delivered in the wrong quantity. Incoterms 2000 does not deal with this issue in such detail.

Instalment deliveries

[1.67] Instalment deliveries are allowed only by the agreement of the parties. Whether or not a breach of the terms of an instalment amounts to a breach of the whole contract must be determined in the context of the whole contract.

In *Picturesque Atlas Co Ltd v Searle* (1892) 18 VLR 633, the plaintiffs, Picturesque Atlas, entered into a contract with the defendant, under which the plaintiffs were to supply a certain publication consisting of several parts. The plaintiffs undertook to deliver the series as soon as possible after its publication. The contract also provided that non-delivery of the publication at any specified date should not release the buyer from his obligation to accept the publication. The first part was delivered and accepted. The second part was published in March 1887 and another part (up to No 20) was published

---

45. This rule means that a departure from the precise terms of a contract concerning quantity may be disregarded by a court of law if the departure is so trivial as to be negligible. A 'trivial departure' must be determined in the circumstances involved, taking into account the nature of the goods, the relevant trade usages and customs, and the practicality of strict compliance with the description of the quantity of the goods. For example, see *Wilensko v Fenwick* [1938] 3 All ER 429; and *Margaronis Navigation v Henry Peabody* [1964] 3 All ER 333.

in December 1887. The plaintiffs put the two parts together and made a delivery in April 1888, but the buyer refused to accept the delivery. The rest of the series was published in December 1888 and November 1889 respectively. The plaintiffs then delivered all parts in March 1890, but the delivery was refused. The plaintiffs sued the defendant for the price of the remaining parts. Whether the time of delivery was reasonable was the central concern. The court held that the plaintiffs did not deliver the parts of the publication within a reasonable time and thus their claim failed.

Seller's duty to make an adequate contract of carriage with a carrier

[1.68] Unless specified otherwise in a contract of sale, the seller is liable under the sale of goods legislation to make an adequate contract of carriage with a carrier when delivering the goods to the carrier pursuant to the contract. The risk in the goods does not pass to the buyer if the seller fails to comply with this requirement.[46]

Seller's duty to notify the buyer of the goods' readiness for insurance

[1.69] Unless otherwise specified by the parties (for example, by a CIF or FOB term in the contract of sale), the seller is obliged to inform the buyer of the shipment of the goods by sea to enable the buyer to insure the goods against marine risks (for the meaning of this term, see **[7.36]–[7.37]**). The risk in the goods does not pass if the seller fails to give such notice. This obligation can be substantially modified in any international sale, where an Incoterm is incorporated into the contract of sale.

In *Law & Bonar Ltd v British American Tobacco Co Ltd* [1916] 2 KB 605, the parties entered into a contract for the sale of hessian under the CIF term in 1914. The seller notified the buyer under s 32 of the Sale of Goods Act 1893 (UK) (the equivalent of, for example, s 35 of the Sale of Goods Act 1923 (NSW)) that the insurance policy taken under the CIF contract did not cover the risk of war. But the buyer did not insure the goods against the war risk. The 1914 war broke out and the goods were lost as a result of the war. The question was whether the seller had performed his duties under s 32. The court held that s 32 did not apply to a contract based on a CIF term, because the CIF term set out the duties of the parties in relation to insurance: see **[1.23]**. In addition, s 32 did not impose any extra duty upon the seller to make sure that the buyer insured the goods against the risk of war.

In *Wimble, Sons & Co v Rosenberg* [1913] 3 KB 743, the parties agreed to sell 200 bags of rice FOB to Antwerp. The buyers named a vessel for the carriage of the goods. The buyers did not request the particulars of the shipment and did not insure the goods. Nor did the seller inform the buyers of the need for insurance under s 32 of the English Sale of Goods Act 1893 (equivalent, for example, to s 35 of the Sale of Goods Act 1923 (NSW)). The vessel was stranded the day after it set out, resulting in a total loss of the rice on board. The buyers relied on s 32 to argue that the sellers were liable for the loss. The court held that the purpose of s 32 was to enable the buyers to insure the goods against marine risks. There was no excuse in the present case for the buyers' failure to insure the

---

46. See the Sale of Goods Act 1954 (ACT), s 36; Sale of Goods Act 1923 (NSW), s 35; Sale of Goods Act 1972 (NT), s 35; Sale of Goods Act 1896 (Qld), s 34; Sale of Goods Act 1895 (SA), s 32; Sale of Goods Act 1896 (Tas), s 37; Goods Act 1958 (Vic), s 39; and Sale of Goods Act 1895 (WA), s 32.

goods against marine risks, because they provided the vessel for the carriage of the goods. The buyers were able to insure the risk without the assistance of the seller, had they intended to do so.

Acceptance of delivery

[1.70] The buyer may accept goods by express statement, or express or implicit conduct of acceptance. An act of acceptance can be established when the buyer exercises the right of an owner over the goods in question, or when he or she fails to reject the goods within a reasonable time after delivery. Acceptance has legal implications under the sale of goods legislation, which are often associated with the performance of contract and the passing of property and risk. This rule may be inconsistent with certain provisions of the CISG, which allow the breaching party to cure defects in the goods regardless of the effect of acceptance. Incoterms 2000 does not define the meaning and legal effect of 'acceptance'.

Buyer's duty in relation to the rejected goods

[1.71] Unless specified otherwise in a contract of sale, a buyer is not obliged to return the rejected goods after he or she has effectively rejected them. But the buyer has a common law duty as a bailee of the goods to mitigate any loss that may occur to the goods. The CISG sets out more detailed rules for the preservation of the rejected goods: see **[2.291]–[2.301]**. This issue is not dealt with in Incoterms 2000.

Application of delivery rules under sale of goods legislation

[1.72] The above rules for delivery may apply to a contract for the international sale of goods on their own, if the CISG does not apply. They may also apply in conjunction with the CISG, if the provisions of the Convention are not sufficient to deal with the issues involved. The Convention prevails only in the case of inconsistency between the Convention and the relevant rules of the sale of goods legislation. It must also be pointed out that the above delivery rules can be overridden or restrained by the incorporation of Incoterms 2000, which provide specific rules of delivery in most circumstances covered by the rules.

Conformity of the goods under sale of goods legislation

[1.73] In any international sale, conformity of the goods with the contract description is always a crucial issue. Sale of goods legislation sets out specific rules to ensure that implied terms as to quality, fitness and conformity of the goods are complied with, and that the goods sold are free from legal claims of another person. These rules can be summarised as follows.[47]

Implied condition that the seller has title to sell

[1.74] Unless the parties expressly or implicitly agree otherwise, the seller has an obligation to guarantee that the goods are free from legal claims by any other parties, that the

---

47. See the Sale of Goods Act 1954 (ACT), ss 17–20; Sale of Goods Act 1923 (NSW), ss 17–20; Sale of Goods Act 1972 (NT), ss 17–20; Sale of Goods Act 1896 (Qld), ss 15–18; Sale of Goods Act 1895 (SA), ss 12–15; Sale of Goods Act 1896 (Tas), ss 17–20; Goods Act 1958 (Vic), ss 17–20; and Sale of Goods Act 1895 (WA), ss 12–15.

buyer should enjoy quiet possession of the goods, and that the goods are not subject to any charge or encumbrance unknown to the buyer at the time of the contract: see *Rowland v Divall* [1923] 2 KB 500 and *Niblett v Confectioners' Materials Co Ltd* [1921] 3 KB 387.[48] This constitutes an implied condition of the contract.[49]

Implied condition that goods conform with the contract description

[1.75] In a contract of 'sale by description' (a contract of sale entered into on the basis of a description of the goods, as opposed to a sale by sample or an auction sale), the seller has an implied duty (implied in the sale of goods legislation) to provide goods which conform with the contract description: see *Elder Smith Goldsbrough Mort Ltd v McBridge Palmer* [1976] 2 NSWLR 631.[50] The buyer has the right to reject non-conforming goods despite the fact that the goods delivered are the commercial equivalent of contracted goods: *Samsung Hong Kong Ltd v Keen Time Trading Ltd* [1988] 2 HKLRD 341. The buyer is also entitled to reject non-conforming goods, even though the goods are merchantable and might have been of a better quality and fit for the purpose for which the contract of sale was made: *Arcos v EA Ronaasen & Son* [1933] AC 470. The rules on conformity with description appear to be too rigid to meet commercial flexibility, and may be overridden by the relevant provisions of the CISG, if the Convention applies.

Implied condition that goods are merchantable

[1.76] In a sale by description, the seller has an implied duty to guarantee that the goods are merchantable, unless the buyer was aware, or ought to have been aware, of the defect affecting merchantability of the goods at the time of the contract or the time of examining the goods. Merchantability is determined in the context of the sale, taking into account the nature of the goods, their price, their marketability at the contract price, the knowledge of the parties and the suitability of the goods for any practical purpose.[51] The seller is liable if the goods are unmerchantable due to a latent defect, but is not liable if the unmerchantability was caused by the fault of the buyer.[52]

---

48. In *Rowland v Divall* [1923] 2 KB 500, the plaintiff, a car dealer, bought a car from the defendant. The car was later found to have been stolen. The court held that the defendant had no right to sell it and the plaintiff was entitled to recover the purchase price. In *Niblett Ltd v Confectioners' Materials Co Ltd* [1921] 3 KB 387, the wrappings on certain tins had the word 'Nissly', which infringed the trademark of the Nestlé company. The offending labels had to be removed. The court held that the sellers breached the implied terms as to title and were liable for the damages.
49. 'Condition' has a special meaning under the sale of goods legislation. If any term is declared a 'condition' in the legislation, a breach of that term will give the innocent party a right to terminate the contract. Such a statutory right to terminate a contract is something the CISG tried to eliminate.
50. In that case, the defendants purchased a bull at an auction sale. The written information described the bull as Midgeon Supreme and a breeding bull. The defendants inspected the bull, which was later proved to be infertile. There was evidence suggesting that the problem in the bull was not detectable without using special tests. The court held that the contract was a sale by description and that the sellers had breached the implied condition that the bull conformed to the description.
51. See, for example, *Kendall v Lillico* [1969] 2 AC 31; *Bartlett v Sydney Maracas Ltd* [1965] 2 All ER 753; *Grant v Australian Knitting Mills Ltd* [1936] AC 85; *Brown v Craiks Ltd* [1970] 1 All ER 823; and *Ashington Piggeries Ltd v Christopher Hill Ltd* [1972] AC 441.

Implied condition that goods are fit for the purpose for which they are acquired

[1.77] In a contract of sale, whether by description or by sample, where the buyer expressly or implicitly makes the purpose or purposes for which the goods are acquired known to the seller and relies on the seller's skill and judgment in entering into the contract of sale, the goods sold must be fit for the purpose or purposes stated by the buyer, unless the seller does not deal with goods of the same nature in his or her usual course of business. In *Ashington Piggeries Ltd v Christopher Hill Ltd* [1972] AC 441, the buyers, Ashington Piggeries, contracted with Christopher Hill to supply mink food known as 'King Size'. The buyers provided the formula for 'King Size' to the sellers, who proposed to replace one ingredient, fish meal, with herring meal, for economic reasons. The sellers were in the business of supplying animal food, but they had not prepared mink food before. The sellers contracted with Norsildmel, a Norwegian firm, to supply herring meal. The mink food supplied by Hill killed Ashington's minks, because the herring meal contained the toxic chemical DMNA, which was later discovered to have caused liver disease in the minks and to be toxic to other animals. Hill sued Ashington for the price of the mink food supplied and Ashington sued Hill for the loss of the minks. The court held that the sellers breached the implied conditions as to fitness for purpose, but did not breach the implied terms as to conformity with description.

In *Simms Jones Ltd v Protochem Trading NZ Ltd* [1993] 3 NZLR 369, Simms Jones was in the business of manufacturing and selling a cleaner called 'Chemico' in New Zealand markets. It intended to develop a liquid cleaner to compete with Jif. The goodwill of Chemico was owned by the County Chemical Company of England (CCC), which produced a formula for developing the new cleaner. BP understood the needs of Simms Jones and supplied the company with an allegedly suitable detergent called 'Gardilene SJ'. Simms Jones obtained approval from CCC for the use of the detergent. The product was unsuccessful, because calcium carbonate, an ingredient of the formula, formed a dense and solid material in a large number of bottles, rendering the cleaner unusable. Simms Jones sued BP for breach of the implied terms. The court held that it was not yet sufficiently established that s 15 of the Sale of Goods Act 1908 (NZ), the sale by sample provision, had been breached. However, the court found that BP had breached the implied term as to merchantable quality and fitness for purpose under s 16.[53]

Implied condition that goods conform with the sample

[1.78] In a sale by sample, in which a contract of sale is entered into on the basis of a sample shown before the conclusion of the contract, the seller has an implied duty to provide goods which are the same as the sample.

---

52. See, for example, *Lucky Trading Co and Lucky Snow Enterprises (Canada) Ltd v Icicle Seafoods Inc* (30 January 1998, Supreme Court of British Columbia, available at <http://www.courts.gov.bc.ca>). In that case, the buyers argued that a large quantity of canned salmon, which showed rust when sold in China, was defective. The court, however, decided that, on the balance of probabilities, the rust was caused by the buyer's bad storage in Hong Kong, because the same product did not show any rust when it was sold in Canada. The same conclusion would be reached by an Australian court in the same circumstances.
53. See also *Grant v Australian Knitting Mills Ltd* [1936] AC 85; *Four Square Stores (Qld) Ltd v ABE Copiers Pty Ltd* (1981) ATPR 40-232; *Claude B Fox Pty Ltd v Raynor* [1978] Qd R 250; and *Ashford Shire Council v Dependable Motor Pty Ltd* (1960) 60 SR (NSW) 27.

In *Thorne v Borthwick* (1956) 56 SR (NSW) 81, there was a contract for the sale of 50 drums of neatsfoot oil. A sample of the oil was shown to the buyer during negotiation, prior to the conclusion of the contract, but the written contract made no reference to the sample. The buyer refused to take delivery on the ground that the goods did not correspond with the sample. The court held that the mere fact that a sample was shown by the seller to the buyer during the course of negotiation leading up to a sale did not necessarily make the contract a sale by sample.

Compare that decision with *Ship Agencies Australia Pty Ltd v Fremantle Fishermen's Co-Operative Society Ltd* (1991) 8 SR (WA) 109, in which Fremantle Fishermen's Co-Operative was the buyer of damaged fishing bait. Ship Agencies was the seller, acting as an agent for a Japanese firm, Tairyo Enterprises, in Fremantle. Tairyo Enterprises delivered three containers of badly damaged fishing bait to Ship Agencies. One of them was not saleable at a discounted price. Ship Agencies made insurance claims on Danzas Wills Pty Ltd on behalf of Tairyo Enterprises. Danzas Wills acted in Fremantle as the agent of the Japanese insurance company, which provided the insurance cover for the fishing bait in question. An agent of Danzas Wills presented two of the best cartons of the damaged bait to Fremantle Fishermen's Co-Operative, which purchased the whole container on the basis of the sample. The payment was made and the goods were transferred to the name of Fremantle Fishermen's Co-Operative before the buyers inspected the whole container. Later, the buyers discovered the true state of the container and requested a refund of the money on the ground of s 15 of the Sale of Goods Act 1895 (SA), alleging that the goods did not correspond with the sample. The court held that the sample was mentioned in the communications which formed the basis of the contract of sale; thus, the contract was a sale by sample, and s 15 was breached.[54]

This condition also implies that the buyer should have a reasonable opportunity to compare the goods and the sample. This implication affects the operation of the rules of acceptance.

Application of conformity rules under sale of goods legislation

[1.79] A common feature of the implied conditions mentioned above is that they can be excluded by an express agreement of the parties to a contract of sale. This is consistent with any warranty or guarantee under the CISG. But this feature is not consistent with the Trade Practices Act or other consumer protection legislation, which does not allow the parties to exclude certain statutory liabilities by express agreement. Consumer sales legislation may be relevant to an international sale when the goods sold fall under the sphere of the Trade Practices Act: see **[2.311]**.

[1.80] Incoterms 2000 does not affect the abovementioned rules substantially, although they require the seller to provide the goods in conformity with the contract of sale. The abovementioned rules apply to any contract which has incorporated Incoterms 2000. In the interpretation of the Incoterms, the implied terms (conditions or guarantees) under

---

54. See also *Champanhac & Co Ltd v Waller & Co Ltd* [1948] 2 All ER 724; *Godley v Perry* [1960] 1 WLR 9; and *Curl & Curl v Captain Sturt Marine Pty Ltd* (1982) ASC 55-190.

the sale of goods legislation can be relied upon to determine whether the goods conform to the contract concerned.

Seller's remedies under the sale of goods legislation

[1.81] A seller needs remedies if the buyer breaches the contract of sale. The sale of goods legislation provides remedies to a seller when the buyer fails to make full payment of the price of the goods, or when the buyer breaches other terms of the contract — for example, by failing to accept delivery as agreed, or failing to send a ship to the named port to take delivery (as required under the FOB term).

The sale of goods legislation in the Australian states and territories provides major remedies to the seller, as follows.[55]

Seller's right to withhold delivery

[1.82] An 'unpaid seller' (a seller who has not been fully paid) who is in possession of the goods may retain, or withhold delivery of, all or part of the goods concerned, if the buyer becomes insolvent before making the full payment as agreed. This rule is based on the presumption that the unpaid seller has a lien (a legal right) in the goods sold.

Seller's right to stop goods in transitu

[1.83] An unpaid seller has a right of stoppage *in transitu* (the unpaid seller may stop the continuous transmission of the goods to the buyer) if the buyer becomes insolvent, in the following circumstances:

- The goods are under the control of a carrier (not being an agent of the buyer) and have not been delivered or taken over by the buyer or his or her agent; nor has the carrier acknowledged the ownership of the buyer expressly to the buyer.
- The goods are currently under control of a carrier (not being an agent of the buyer) and have been rejected by the buyer.

The right of stoppage *in transitu* can be exercised by the seller taking possession of the goods, or notifying the carrier of his or her intention of exercising the right of stoppage.

Seller's right to sue for the unpaid price of the goods

[1.84] An unpaid seller may sue the buyer if the buyer has received the goods, but failed to make the payment according to the contract. On the other hand, a seller is entitled to claim the payment of contract price in pursuance of the terms of contract even before delivery.[56]

---

55. See the Sale of Goods Act 1954 (ACT), ss 42–53 and s 57; Sale of Goods Act 1923 (NSW), ss 41–52 and ss 55–6; Sale of Goods Act 1972 (NT), ss 41–52 and ss 55–6; Sale of Goods Act 1896 (Qld), ss 40–51 and s 55; Sale of Goods Act 1895 (SA), ss 38–49 and s 53; Sale of Goods Act 1896 (Tas), ss 43–54 and s 58; Goods Act 1958 (Vic), ss 45–56 and s 60; and Sale of Goods Act 1895 (WA), ss 38–49 and s 53.
56. For example, in *Consolidated Rutile v China Weal* [1998] QSC 170, the parties agreed in an FOB contract for the sale of zircon that, if the buyer changed the shipping schedule, the seller could invoice the buyer for the quantity of zircon which had not been shipped after the originally agreed shipping date. In such circumstances, the payment was due 28 days after the invoice date. The goods were not shipped within the originally agreed shipping period. The seller claimed the price of the goods against the buyer. White J of the Supreme Court of Queensland held that the seller was entitled to claim the price of the goods in pursuance of the clause concerned and s 50(2) of the Sale of Goods Act (Qld).

[1.85]

Seller's right to claim damages

[1.85] An unpaid seller may claim damages against the buyer if the buyer breaches the contract; for example, by wrongfully failing to pay the price of the goods or accept delivery: see *Gebruder Metelmann GmbH v NBR (London) Ltd* [1984] 1 Lloyd's Rep 614.[57]

Seller's right to claim interest or special damages

[1.86] A seller may claim interest or special damages under law if the buyer breaches the terms of the contract.

Application of seller's remedies under sale of goods legislation

[1.87] The above remedies may operate in conjunction with all the common law remedies available to an innocent party if the contract of international sale is subject to the sale of goods legislation. (Note that not every contract for the international sale of goods involving an Australian party is subject to the CISG.) Some of them may also be supplementary to the provisions of the CISG, in circumstances where the sale of goods legislation does not conflict with the provisions of the Convention.

[1.88] Incoterms 2000 affects the operation of the abovementioned rules only to a limited degree. For example, Incoterms 2000 makes the duty to pay the price of the contract as agreed the number one duty of the buyer (**B1** of each term). However, Incoterms 2000 does not deal with the issue of remedies at all. This means that the abovementioned rules will co-exist with any Incoterm which has been incorporated into a contract of sale.

Buyer's remedies under the sale of goods legislation

[1.89] A buyer needs remedies when the seller breaches the implied terms as to quality of the goods, delivers non-conforming goods, or breaches other terms of the contract. The major remedies available under the sale of goods legislation can be summarised as follows.[58]

Buyer's right to terminate a contract when the seller breaches implied conditions

[1.90] If the seller breaches the implied conditions as to title, conformity of the goods to the description or sample, merchantability of the goods or fitness of the goods for the stated purpose, the buyer is entitled to terminate the contract of sale. This right is inconsistent with several provisions of the CISG (which allows a right of self-cure to either the seller or the buyer) and will likely be overridden by the Convention if it is applicable.

---

57. In that case, Metelmann sold 2000 t of sugar to NBR at a price of $803 per tonne under the FOB term. NBR repudiated the contract of sale before the sugar was shipped. Metelmann sold the sugar at the market price of $673 per tonne, and claimed damages for non-acceptance against NBR. The court held that Metelmann was entitled to the difference between the contract price and the market price. This entitlement was not affected by the fact that, at the time of repudiation, the sugar was not ascertained and appropriated to the contract.
58. See the Sale of Goods Act 1954 (ACT), ss 17–20 and ss 54–7; Sale of Goods Act 1923 (NSW), ss 17–20 and ss 53–6; Sale of Goods Act 1972 (NT), ss 17–20 and ss 53–6; Sale of Goods Act 1896 (Qld), ss 15–18 and ss 52–5; Sale of Goods Act 1895 (SA), ss 12–15 and ss 50–3; Sale of Goods Act 1896 (Tas), ss 17–20 and ss 55–8; Goods Act 1958 (Vic), ss 17–20 and ss 57–60; and Sale of Goods Act 1895 (WA), ss 12–15 and ss 50–3.

Buyer's right to claim damages for non-delivery

[1.91] If the seller fails to deliver the goods as agreed, the buyer may claim damages for the losses flowing from non-delivery. This right is likely to be qualified by the provisions of the CISG in circumstances where the Convention applies, because the Convention encourages the buyer to give the seller a second chance to make delivery: art 37 of the Convention: see **[2.140]**.

Buyer's right to claim damages for breach of warranty by the seller

[1.92] If the seller breaches a contract term which constitutes a warranty, the buyer may claim damages for the breach. Similar rights are provided in the CISG: arts 74–7 of the Convention: see **[2.219]**–**[2.276]**.

Buyer's right to claim interest or special damages

[1.93] In certain circumstances, the buyer is also entitled to claim interest or special damages flowing from the seller's breaches of the contract.

Application of buyer's remedies under sale of goods legislation

[1.94] As we have seen, in certain circumstances the seller's right to terminate a contract of sale upon breach of any implied conditions of the contract may be curtailed by the provisions of the CISG, because one of the underlying principles of the Convention is the preservation of contract. However, if a contract of international sale is exclusively subject to the sale of goods legislation, the rules outlined above will apply.

[1.95] The abovementioned rules do not have a direct relationship with Incoterms 2000, although Incoterms 2000 makes the buyer liable for additional costs when the buyer breaches his or her duties under the terms (see **B6** of each term). These rules will co exist with any Incoterm that has been incorporated into a contract of sale.

International sale of goods and the Chinese Code of Contract Law

Applicability of the Code of Contract Law to international sales

[1.96] The Code of Contract Law (the Code) was promulgated in March 1999 and went into operation on 1 October 1999. The Code is a relatively comprehensive document and is meant to replace a dozen contract laws and regulations made previously. It applies to all types of contracts made for legitimate purposes. It also applies to contracts for the sale of goods, and is supplementary to the CISG in an international sale of goods. Many aspects of a sale may be subject to the Code, while others are subject to the CISG. In addition, a provision of the Code may apply to a sale governed by the CISG if there is no inconsistency between the Code and the CISG. In a situation where the CISG does not apply, the Code becomes the only law governing sales involving parties from mainland China and parties outside mainland China. For example, a contract of sale between a company from mainland China and a company from Hong Kong, Macau or Taiwan may be subject to the Code under the conflict of laws rules of the People's Republic of China. Thus, the Code is important to everyone doing business with China.

Making a contract of sale under the Code

Capacity to contract

[1.97] The capacity to contract under the Code is regulated by arts 2, 9, and 47–50. These provisions are largely supported by the relevant provisions of China's General Principles of Civil Law (GPCL) (see arts 9–19), which regulate the capacity of a natural person, and arts 36–53, which regulate the capacity of a legal person.[59] 'Other organisations', which can be contracting parties under art 2 of the Code, are not defined in the GPCL. Generally speaking, the term 'other organisations' may refer to non-profit organisations or government departments, which may not fully satisfy the legal requirements for a 'legal person' under Chinese law.

The capacity to contract under the Code can be discussed from three perspectives: the capacity of a natural person; the capacity of a legal person; and the capacity of other organisations. Article 2 of the Code states that a contract can be made between these persons or organisations. In the light of the provisions of the Code and the GPCL discussed above, the capacity of the three types of contracting parties can be summarised as follows.

[1.98] Natural persons. A natural person of 18 years of age who does not suffer any mental disability is capable of entering into a contractual relationship of his or her free will: GPCL, art 11; Code, art 9. This age threshold may sometimes drop to 16 years if the person lives on his or her own income: GPCL, art 11. Children of 10 years of age may conclude certain contracts suitable for their age and intelligence: GPCL, art 12. A similar rule underlies the common law principles of contract relating to purchase of necessaries by a minor: see, for example, *Ryder v Wombwell* (1868) LR 4 Ex 32 and *Fawcett v Smethurst* (1914) 84 LJ Ch 473. Children under 10 years of age are deemed to have no capacity to contract. The fixed threshold of 10 years of age distinguishes the Chinese law governing the capacity of a minor from the relevant common law rules, which do not impose a strict threshold of this kind.

A person with limited civil capacity (that is, a person capable of understanding the nature and consequence of only some of his or her own acts) may enter into certain contractual relationships appropriate to his or her mental state: GPCL, art 13. A contract made by such a person is normally subject to retrospective approval by the person's legal agent or guardian, unless the contract is merely beneficial to the person or is appropriate for his or her age, intelligence and mental state: Code, art 47. A natural person who is represented by an agent in the making of a contract is not liable for any act of the agent exceeding the agent's authority, unless the act is supported by an ostensible authority which has been reasonably relied upon by a bona fide third party: Code, arts 48 and 49.[60] The presumption of an ostensible authority in the Code appears to be a step forward from the principles of agent and principal set out in the GPCL, although the presumption

---

59. For a detailed discussion of the civil capacity of a natural or legal person under the GPCL and a general review of the GPCL, see Chapter 4, 'General Principles of Civil Law', in Guiguo Wang and John Mo (eds), *Chinese Law*, London, Kluwer Law International, 1999, pp 95–178.
60. Article 49 of the Code states that an act of an agent that is performed without appropriate authority, falls outside his or her authority, or is performed after the expiry of his or her authority, is valid if it is reasonable for the party dealing with the agent to believe in the existence of a valid authority.

appears to have no basis in the GPCL, which is deemed to be the foundation for all civil and commercial laws in the People's Republic of China. For this reason, an amendment to the GPCL is only a matter of time. Meanwhile, the principles discussed in this paragraph determine whether a contract governed by the CISG has been made by persons with the capacity to contract.

[1.99] Legal persons. A 'legal person' under Chinese law is an organisation which is capable of enjoying and exercising civil rights, as well as undertaking and performing civil liabilities independently: GPCL, art 36. To qualify as a legal person, an organisation must satisfy four requirements: it must be established in pursuance of the law; it must have the necessary property or funds; it must have its own name, organisation and place of business; and it must be capable of undertaking a civil liability independently: GPCL, art 37. A legal person can be a company set up under the relevant law, or an organisation or society that meets these four requirements: GPCL, art 50. A partnership or a joint operation constituting a new economic entity and satisfying the four requirements may also be regarded as a legal person under Chinese law: GPCL, art 51. A legal person may be required to register with the relevant government authority if the law so prescribes.

The capacity of a legal person to contract largely relates to its status as a 'legal person' under Chinese law. A legal person's capacity to contract may be affected by the scope of its business as registered or approved by the relevant authorities. A contract for international sale may be declared void if the Chinese party does not have a so-called 'foreign trading right'.[61] A domestic contract for the sale of goods may also be declared void if the business scope of a party does not cover the goods sold in the contract, or the parties do not have capacity to perform the contract. Such reasoning may appear peculiar to a common law lawyer, but up to now the Chinese courts have still treated the approved scope of business as an issue of capacity, because engaging in a business transaction outside the approved scope of business is regarded as illegal in most circumstances. Similarly, a settlement agreement reached during the mediation process conducted by a court may be set aside by the court if the agreement requires a party to perform an act falling outside its scope of business.[62]

The rules governing contracts made by an agent, discussed above, also apply to contracts where a legal person is the principal. In addition, a legal person is liable in

---

61. For example, in an arbitration case decided by the China International Economic and Trade Arbitration Commission (CIETAC), the tribunal held that a foreign trade contract signed by a Chinese party which did not have a foreign-trading right was void. See Case 2 in Guo Xiaowen (ed), *Case Studies of China International Economic and Trade Arbitration*, Hong Kong, FT Law & Tax Asia Pacific, 1996, pp 7–10.
62. For example, in *X Construction Company v Trading Company of Shuchang*, the defendant sold 300 t of coil steel to the plaintiff in 1991. The defendant delivered only 20 t of coil steel which, however, did not meet the contract description. The court mediated the dispute in 1992, and the defendant agreed to deliver 280 t of coil steel meeting the description. Later, the defendant failed to perform the agreement because it had no goods to deliver. The plaintiff applied to the court for a review of the settlement agreement under the review process of the court. The court set aside the settlement agreement on the ground that the agreement was impossible to perform because the defendant's scope of business did not cover steel products. The case is described (in Chinese) in Lin Zhong, *Settlement of Commercial Disputes in China*, Joint Publishing (HK) Co Ltd, Hong Kong, 1998, pp 203–4.

[1.99] International Commercial Law

contract to a bona fide contracting party who has reasonably relied on an ostensible authority of the legal representative or responsible person of the legal person.[63]

[1.100] *Baoli Hotel of Yinhai v Mingyue Special Lighting Company Ltd of Inner Mongolia*

People's Court, Beijing, 1994[1]

A contract with a Chinese joint venture may be invalid if beyond the scope of the organisation's business

Facts: The plaintiff entered into a contract for the purchase of plywood from the defendant. The defendant was a joint venture between two Hong Kong companies and two inner-Mongolian companies, which never went into operation because of a funding problem. Certain persons from the defendant joint venture signed the contract for the sale of plywood in the name of the venture, but without having any plywood to sell. The plaintiff sued the defendant for breach of contract.

Decision: The trial court and the court of appeal held the contract to be valid and ordered the defendant to pay twice the amount of the deposit to the plaintiff as a penalty for its breach. In the review process, the Provincial Supreme Court held the contract to be invalid because the defendant exceeded the scope of its business in concluding the contract in dispute, and ordered the defendant to return the deposit to the plaintiff and pay appropriate damages to the relevant parties to cover their losses.

---

1. Reported (in Chinese) in Institute for Practical Legal Research of the National Supreme Court, *Selected Cases of the People's Court*, vol 9, Publishing House of the People's Court, Beijing, 1994, pp 124–30.

[1.101] *Base Construction Corporation (Henan) of China Exported Commodities v Foreign Trade Development Company of Shenzhen*

People's Court, Beijing, 1992[1]

A contract with a Chinese company may be unenforceable if the supplier does not hold the necessary licence

Facts: The parties entered into a contract for the purchase of a quantity of mung beans and sesame seeds. The seller's supplier was prohibited from selling the products concerned by the local administration for industry and commerce because the supplier did not have a licence to sell the products. The contract was therefore not performed. The parties accused each other of breach of contract.

Decision: The court of appeal held the contract to be unenforceable because the seller was incapable of performing its obligations under the contract, and ordered the parties to share the losses incurred.

---

1. Reported (in Chinese) in Institute for Practical Legal Research of the National Supreme Court, *Selected Cases of the People's Court*, vol 1, Publishing House of the People's Court, Beijing, 1992, pp 104–8.

---

63. Article 50 of the Code states that a contract made by a legal representative or responsible person of a 'legal person' outside his or her authority is valid, unless the other contracting party knew or ought to have known that the legal representative or the responsible person exceeded his or her authority in making the contract.

[1.102] Other organisations. Article 2 of the Code recognises the right of an organisation which is not a legal person to conclude a contract. This is a new development in the civil law of the People's Republic of China. The GPCL only recognises two types of entities (or persons) who can be the subject of civil rights: natural or legal persons. For example, art 54 of the GPCL defines an 'act of civil law' as a legitimate act of a citizen or a legal person to establish, change and terminate a civil right or obligation. The GPCL implicitly suggests that an organisation which is not a legal person is incapable of performing an 'act of civil law'. When art 2 of the Code permits 'other organisations' besides natural or legal persons to conclude a contract, the meaning of 'organisation' in this context is unclear in Chinese jurisprudence. It is possible that 'organisation' under the Code refers to a government organisation or any other social, political or economic organisation that enters into a commercial contract with another party. The organisation must be allowed to enjoy the relevant right and be required to undertake the relevant liability for the purpose of ensuring stability and fairness in commercial transactions. Article 2 of the Code suggests that a government organisation or department engaged in a commercial activity may be liable to the other contracting party,[64] even though this proposition has no basis in the GPCL. Consequently, the Code provides guidance for ascertaining the legality of contracts made by organisations that are not legal persons.

Negotiation of contract

[1.103] 'Negotiation of contract' refers to the whole negotiation process leading to the conclusion of a contract. This always starts with an offer, or invitation to treat, which will be followed by acceptance or counter-offer, finally ending with a concluded contract. Articles 10–34 of the Code deal with the formalities of offer and acceptance. Generally speaking, these provisions are similar to the relevant provisions of the CISG. It must be emphasised, however, that art 10 of the Code has adopted the same position as art 11 of the CISG, giving effect to an oral contract which may or may not be supported by written evidence. Article 10 of the Code states that a contract can be made between parties in writing, orally or in any other form. Under this provision, the written form is necessary only when expressly required by the relevant law or by an agreement between the parties.

This represents a crucial change in Chinese contract law. China made a reservation when it ratified the CISG to deny the effect of an oral contract. The passing of the Code means that this reservation should be amended. The recognition of oral contracts increases flexibility in commercial transactions and makes the use of oral evidence possible in a dispute arising from a contract in the People's Republic of China. This change also reduces the differences between common law contract rules, such as those practised in Australia and Hong Kong, and the contract rules of mainland China.

The similarities between the Code and the CISG reflect a consistency between the two legal regimes which may be applicable to contracts of international sale in China. However, there are differences between them, including both direct and indirect inconsistencies; the latter may not always be resolved by the prevalence of the CISG. The major

---

64. The meaning of 'commercial activity' is unclear in Chinese law. Article 38 of the Code appears to regard most government contracts as a special type of contract; however, the article also subjects some aspects of this type of contract, such as contract formation, to the provisions of the Code.

[1.103] differences between the Code and Convention relating to the formation of contract can be summarised as follows.

[1.104] Oral contracts. Article 10 of the Code recognises the effect of a contract entirely or partly made in oral form. If other relevant laws and regulations require a special contract to be concluded in writing or the parties so agree, the contract must be made in writing. Article 11 of the CISG states that a 'contract of sale need not be concluded in or evidenced by writing and is not subject to any other requirement as to form'. Since art 10 of the Code makes an exception for contracts subject to special legislative requirements or the parties' preference for the written form, the two provisions are not consistent on this particular point. The Chinese reservation on art 11 of the CISG, which is a blind refusal of all forms of oral contract, should be amended to reflect the present inconsistency between art 10 of the Code and art 11 of the CISG. In case of inconsistency between the CISG and the Code, the reservation (whose substance is yet to be clarified) prevails over the relevant provision of the CISG.

[1.105] Forms of communication. Article 11 of the Code expressly recognises the use of EDI, e-mail, written contracts, postal letters, telegram, telex and fax as forms of writing, but the CISG only specifically refers to telegram and telex, as well as written contracts and postal letters: CISG, arts 13 and 20(1).[65] Thus, the Code has included specific forms of electronic data transmission or other means of modern communications which were not available when the CISG was drafted. A wide interpretation of the relevant provisions of the CISG should be capable of extending the CISG to such means of communication. Consequently, the superficial differences between the Code and the CISG regarding this point suggest that the Code is supplementary to the CISG for the purpose of ascertaining the formation of a particular contract in writing. In particular, art 16 of the Code, which regulates the arrival time of an offer or acceptance via EDI or internet, may be supplementary to the CISG, which does not regulate such matters.

[1.106] Offers and invitations. When one party sends a proposal to another, art 15 of the Code uses the intention of the party sending the proposal as the main criterion in determining whether the proposal is an offer or an invitation to treat. The CISG, in contrast, resolves the same question by considering whether the proposal was sent to one or several specific persons: CISG, art 14(1). The difference between them suggests that a proposal to the public may be regarded as an offer under the Code, but an invitation to treat under the CISG. Where such an inconsistency arises, the CISG prevails.

[1.107] Revocation of offers. Article 20(2) of the Code permits an offer to be revoked in pursuance of the relevant law, presumably regardless of whether it has been accepted by the offeree. There is no compatible provision under the CISG. There is thus an indirect conflict between the Code and the CISG. Consequently, an acceptance which is regarded as valid under the CISG may be regarded as invalid under the Code because of a revocation by the offeror in pursuance of law. Since the conflict does not fall under a

---

65. In a case arbitrated by the CIETAC, the tribunal held that a contract partly concluded in fax was made in writing, despite the fact that the contract was said to be subject to the CISG. See Case 1, Guo Xiaowen (ed), *Case Studies of China International Economic and Trade Arbitration*, Hong Kong, FT Law & Tax Asia Pacific, 1996, pp 1–6.

reservation made by China when ratifying the CISG, the relevant provisions of the CISG prevail where different consequences flow from the relevant provisions of the Code and the CISG.

[1.108] Resolving inconsistencies. These are the major differences between the Code and the CISG relating to the formation of contract. As we have seen, although the provisions of the CISG prevail in most circumstances, certain provisions of the Code are supplementary to the CISG because of the absence of any directly inconsistent rules in the CISG concerning the matters covered by these provisions. Where oral contracts are concerned, the Code still denies their validity in special but much-reduced circumstances. This inconsistency with the CISG can be justified by the reservation made by China when ratifying the CISG. However, the reservation should be amended to reflect the present position of Chinese law accurately.

Validity of contract

[1.109] Validity of contract is not regulated by the CISG. In an international sale of goods in China, the issue is determined under the relevant provisions of the Code, which sets out the following rules:

- A standard-form contract is concluded when the parties sign or seal it: art 32.[66]
- A contract made by way of postal letters, EDI or similar means is regarded as having been concluded when a letter of confirmation is signed: art 33.[67]
- The place of contract is the place where the "acceptance" concerned becomes effective: art 35.[68] Where a contract is concluded by EDI, the recipient's principal place of business or permanent residence is regarded as the place of contract: art 34.
- The place of a standard-form contract is the place where the contract is signed or sealed: art 35.
- An exclusion clause may be used in a standard-form contract, but the party inserting the clause needs to draw the other party's attention to the clause in a reasonable manner: art 39.
- A standard exclusion clause is invalid if it excludes the liability of the party drafting the clause, increases the other party's liability and excludes the main right of the other party: art 40.[69]

---

66. Articles 25 and 32 appear to be inconsistent on this point.
67. It must be pointed out that art 33 of the Code is ambiguous. Its meaning appears to be that, if the parties intend to make a contract by way of postal letters or any means of modern communications, they can sign a confirmation letter to evidence the conclusion of the contract. Signing the confirmation letter represents the conclusion of the contract. However, on its current wording art 33 is difficult to follow; it needs to be rephrased.
68. This rule may contradict art 32, which provides that a written contract is concluded when the parties sign or seal it — but the contradiction may be overridden by art 35, which regards the place of signature or seal as the place of a written contract.
69. The meaning of this provision is unclear in the Chinese original, so that it is uncertain whether the three conditions are conjunctive or alternative in determining the validity of a clause. Nor is it clear whether the provision really means that the party drafting the standard exclusion clause is not allowed to exempt his or her liability at all. However, art 53 provides some assistance in determining the validity of an exclusion clause.

[1.109] International Commercial Law

- An exclusion clause purporting to exempt a liability arising from a personal injury claim or property damages caused by an intentional or reckless act is invalid: art 53.
- Under art 52, a contract is invalid if it is:
  1. made under fraud or duress, or in contravention of the state interest;
  2. a result of a conspiracy to harm the interest of the state, the collective or a third party;
  3. used to disguise an illegitimate purpose;
  4. harmful to public interest; or
  5. in contravention of law, regulations and compulsory measures.

Some of the abovementioned rules are compatible with the relevant contract rules of common law, and some are not.

Performance of contracts

Transfer of property

[1.110] Transfer of property is not regulated by the CISG. Thus, in a contract for international sale of goods involving a Chinese party or a Chinese connection,[70] the transfer of property is determined according to the relevant rules of the Code. The major rules of the Code governing the transfer of property are as follows:

- the seller must have title in the goods to be sold, or the right to sell that title: art 132;
- unless stipulated by law, or unless the buyer knew or ought to have known of the existence of a third party's interest in the goods sold, the seller is obliged to guarantee that no third party will claim his or her right against the buyer over the goods sold: arts 150 and 151;[71]
- unless stipulated in law or otherwise agreed by the parties, the property in the goods sold passes to the buyer with the delivery of the goods: art 133;
- in a barter contract, the property in the goods bartered transfers to each party according to the terms of contract: art 175; and
- the parties may agree that the seller retains the property in the goods sold until the buyer has paid the price of the goods or complied with other obligations: art 134.

These rules suggest that the property in goods sold normally transfers from the seller to the buyer according to the parties' agreement. These rules are largely consistent with the relevant rules of common law jurisdictions, except for the distinction between specific goods and 'unascertained goods' (generic goods or goods capable of being replaced by each other) used in the common law. There appears to be no equivalent concept in the Code.

---

70. The Code may also apply to a contract of sale which does not involve any Chinese party under the rules of conflict of laws adopted by the court handling a dispute arising from the contract.
71. Article 41 of the CISG is largely identical to art 150 of the Code. This issue appears to fall within either the category of property in goods or the category of delivery.

Transfer of risk

[1.111] Transfer of risk in a contract for the sale of goods is regulated by arts 142–9 of the Code and arts 66–70 of the CISG. The major similarities between the two laws are:

- The Code expressly states that, unless stipulated by law or agreed otherwise by the parties, the risk in the subject matter sold (the goods) is borne by the seller before delivery and the buyer after delivery: Code, art 142. A similar rule is implied in the CISG: CISG, art 67(1).
- Both state that the risk passes to the buyer, as agreed, if the buyer fails to take delivery according to the contract: Code, arts 143 and 146; CISG, art 69(1) and (2).
- Both take the position that, unless otherwise agreed, the risk in the goods sold in transit transfers to the buyer at the conclusion of the contract: Code, art 144; CISG, art 68.
- Both provide that, in the absence of agreement, the risk passes to the buyer when the seller delivers the goods to the first carrier: Code, art 145; CISG, art 67.

[1.112] There are also differences between the Code and the CISG in this area. Where there is a direct inconsistency between the Code and the CISG, the CISG applies. Where the CISG is silent or there is an indirect inconsistency between the two, then, depending on the meaning of the inconsistency, the rules of the Code may be supplementary to the CISG. The major differences between the Code and the CISG relating to the passing of risk are as follows:

- the Code does not differentiate between specific goods and unascertained goods, and has no specific rule governing the transfer of risk in unascertained goods, while the CISG does: CISG, arts 67(2) and 69(3);
- the Code expressly states that a failure by the seller in passing the relevant documents and information to the buyer does not affect the transfer of risk (Code, art 147), but there is no compatible provision in the CISG;
- the Code holds the seller liable for risk if the buyer chooses to terminate the contract on the ground that the goods do not conform with the contract (Code, art 148), but there is no compatible provision in the CISG; and
- the Code states that the transfer of risk to the buyer does not affect the obligation of the seller to compensate the buyer for a loss caused by the seller's breach (Code, art 149), but the CISG states that loss of or damage 'to the goods after the risk has passed to the buyer does not discharge him from his obligation to pay the price unless the loss or damage is due to an act or omission of the seller': CISG, art 66.

[1.113] These differences may have different consequences. In the case of unascertained goods, the absence of any rule in the Code means that the relevant rules of the CISG should be followed where a contract of international sale is involved. But art 147 of the Code appears to be supplementary to the relevant provisions of the CISG, because of a lack of direct or indirect inconsistency between them. Generally speaking, the passing of relevant documents, such as a document of title, may affect the transfer of property, but the transfer of property and transfer of risk are usually separate in international transactions. Article 148 of the Code, which holds the seller liable for risk if the buyer terminates

[1.113]

the contract on the ground of non-conformity of goods, may cause disputes in international and domestic sales. This is because, technically, the risk has passed to the buyer in pursuance of the contract before the buyer decides to terminate the contract. A more logical rule would be that the buyer remains liable for the risk until the contract is terminated, and can claim compensation against the seller if he or she has suffered any loss. Such a rule would impose an obligation upon the buyer to take care of the goods in a reasonable manner. Article 148 of the Code may be abused by a buyer to cause aggravated damage to the goods concerned, because the risk will eventually be borne by the seller. Therefore, it can be argued that, if art 148 remains unchanged, there should be an express qualification to art 148 to the effect that the seller is entitled to seek contribution from a buyer who has caused further damage to the returned goods. As art 148 stands, there may be an indirect inconsistency flowing from the application of the Code and the CISG to some cases. Whether or not such an inconsistency is covered by art 142 of the GPCL, which gives prevalence to the CISG, is unsettled in Chinese law.

Conformity of goods

[1.114] Conformity is always an important issue in the sale of goods. The CISG is compatible with the common law practice concerning conformity. The Code has reduced the differences between Chinese practice and the relevant rules of the common law by addressing certain common issues concerning conformity and providing more specific rules for dealing with them. However, the Code has not adopted the concepts of 'fitness for purpose' and 'merchantable quality' used by its counterparts in common law jurisdictions, although the concept of 'quality' in the Code appears to overlap to some extent with the concept of merchantable quality.[72]

For purposes of comparison, the similarities between the Code and the relevant provisions of the CISG are as follows:

- Both require the seller to provide goods conforming with the contract or specific description: Code, art 153; CISG, art 35.
- In the absence of a specific agreement, both require the goods to meet the general purposes or standards that goods of the same description are expected to meet: Code, art 62(1); CISG, art 35(2)(a).
- In a sale by sample, both require the goods to be the same as the sample: Code, art 168; CISG, art 35(2)(c).
- In the absence of an express agreement, both require the goods to be packaged or contained in a manner suitable for protecting or preserving the goods: Code, art 156; CISG, art 35(2)(d).

---

72. Article 62(1) of the Code states that, in the absence of an agreement, the quality of the goods is to be determined according to the relevant national standard, professional standard, ordinary standard or the special standard of the contract, as the case may be.

[1.115] Also for comparison, the major differences between the Code and the CISG in relation to conformity are:

- The Code does not regard fitness of the goods as an issue of conformity, but the CISG treats fitness for 'special purpose' as one of the issues of conformity: CISG, art 35(2)(b).
- In the absence of an express agreement, the Code sets out an order of priority among applicable standards for ascertaining the quality or conformity of the goods, as follows: the national standard, the professional standard, the ordinary standard and a special standard meeting the purpose of the contract: Code, art 62(1). There is no compatible provision in the CISG.
- The Code specifically states that, in a sale by sample, where the sample has a latent defect unknown to the buyer, the goods must not only meet the quality of the sample but must also have the ordinary quality expected in goods of the same nature: Code, art 169. There is no compatible provision in the CISG.

[1.116] These differences may or may not lead to inconsistencies between the Code and the CISG, depending on the circumstances. For example, in an international sale of goods governed by the CISG, the provisions of the CISG governing fitness for purpose will apply, even though there is no compatible provision in the Code. Similarly, the order of priority among the applicable standards for the determination of the goods' quality may be used as an illustration of art 35(2)(a) of the CISG, which requires the goods sold to be merchantable. Since the CISG does not prohibit the determination of merchantability in such a manner, there may be no inconsistency if art 62(1) of the Code is relied upon for the purpose of providing assistance in the application of art 35(2)(a) of the CISG in China. The requirement in art 169 of the Code that goods sold under a contract based on a sale by sample must also have the ordinary quality expected in goods of the same nature may sometimes cause inconsistency between the Code and the CISG, because art 35(2)(c) of the CISG only requires the goods sold to 'possess the qualities of goods which the seller has held out to the buyer as a sample or model'. If a court decides that the meaning of 'qualities' under art 35(2)(c) does not include 'latent defect' because the defect is not a 'quality' known to the buyer, there is no inconsistency between the Code and the CISG. On the other hand, if a court considers the meaning of 'qualities' to be 'the sample as it is', the seller will not be liable for the latent defect in the goods. In that case, an inconsistency arises between the Code and the CISG. Where an inconsistency arises, art 35(2)(c) of the CISG prevails.

Delivery

[1.117] Chinese law had not formulated specific rules on delivery until the Code was promulgated. Delivery is relevant to the passing of property and risk between the seller and the buyer, and to determining the performance of the parties. Inspection of the goods delivered and notice of defects in the goods are also regulated in the rules of delivery. The CISG and the Code set out largely similar rules governing delivery, as follows:

- Both state that the seller should deliver the goods to the buyer on the agreed date or within the agreed period of time: Code, art 138; CISG, art 33(1) and (2).

- Both require the seller to deliver the goods at the agreed place of delivery: Code, art 141; CISG, art 34.
- In the absence of an agreed place of delivery, both adopt the same criteria for determining the place of delivery: Code, art 141; CISG, art 31.
- Both require the buyer to examine the goods received in pursuance of the relevant agreement, or within a reasonable period of time, as the case may be: Code, art 157; CISG, art 38.
- Both take the position that the buyer loses the right to rely on a lack of conformity if he or she does not inform the seller of the non-conformity within a reasonable time: Code, art 158; CISG, art 39(1).
- Both adopt a two-year limitation period in which the buyer can notify the seller of the non-conformity of the goods received: Code, art 158; CISG, art 39(2).
- Where the goods delivered exceed the agreed quantity, both take the position that the buyer has the option of deciding whether or not to accept the excess: Code, art 162; CISG, art 52(2).[73]
- Both adopt identical rules dealing with instalment delivery, including the termination of the contract relating to a particular instalment and the termination of the whole contract for a breach committed in delivery of one of the instalments: Code, art 166; CISG, art 73.

There do not appear to be any significant differences between the Code and the CISG in relation to delivery. In fact, the rules governing delivery set out in the Code are largely identical to the relevant provisions of the CISG, except for the rules affecting the passing of risk, discussed earlier. The similarities we have seen suggest that this part of the Code was modelled on the relevant provisions of the CISG.

Payment of price

[1.118] Payment of price is the major obligation of the buyer and the major concern of the seller in a sale of goods. Generally speaking, in an international sale the seller aims to control the goods to secure payment against them, while the buyer tries to control the payment to ensure that the goods conform to the terms of contract. Thus, a contract of sale often contains a clause permitting the unpaid seller to have a lien on the goods sold until full payment has been made. The issue of payment is regulated in the CISG, the sale of goods law (in common law jurisdictions) and also in the Code. Similarities between the Code and the CISG are as follows:

- Both state that the buyer is obliged to pay the price of contract as agreed: Code, art 159; CISG, arts 53 and 54.
- Both (directly or indirectly) require the buyer to make payment according to the agreed time: Code, art 161; CISG, arts 53 and 54.

---

73. If the buyer accepts the excess, he or she must pay for the goods according to the contract price.

- In the absence of any agreement on the time of payment, both state that the buyer should pay the price at the time of receiving the goods or the document of title concerning the goods: Code, art 161; CISG, art 58(1).
- Both adopt identical wording in stating that, in the absence of any agreement on the place of payment, the place of payment should be the seller's place of business, or the place where the goods or relevant document of title are to be handed over to the buyer: Code, art 160; CISG, art 57.[74]

[1.119] On the other hand, the Code has adopted a number of rules relating to the payment of price which are dissimilar to the CISG. The major differences between the Code and the CISG are:

- In the absence of any agreement on the price, the Code requires the parties to fix the price either by a subsequent agreement, or according to:
  - the relevant contractual terms;
  - the relevant trading usage;
  - the market price of the goods at the place of performance; or
  - the relevant directives or guidance of the government, as the case may be: Code, arts 61, 62 and 159.

  In contrast, subject to any agreement otherwise, the CISG requires the price to be determined by reference to the market price of the goods at the time of the conclusion of the contract: CISG, art 55.

- In the absence of any agreement on the time or place of payment, besides the provisions discussed above, the Code requires the parties to fix a time or place by negotiation and permits the court to fix a time or place according to the terms of the contract or the relevant commercial usage: Code, arts 61 and 161.
- The Code specifically states that, if the buyer fails to pay an instalment that has fallen due, amounting to one-fifth of the total price of the contract, the seller may either demand the payment of the full price or terminate the contract: Code, art 167. There is no compatible provision in the CISG.

These differences may or may not lead to conflicts or inconsistencies between the Code and the CISG, depending on the interpretation of the CISG. The Code provides additional rules for determining the sum, place or time of payment. If the relevant provisions of the CISG are regarded as exhaustive or exclusive, there is no scope for the operation of these rules of the Code. Otherwise, these rules may be regarded as supplementary to the provisions of the CISG. In addition, the payment of price in an instalment contract is not specifically regulated by the CISG. It can thus be argued that the Code supplements the CISG in this regard. Consequently, it is likely that there is no direct or indirect conflict between art 167 of the Code and the CISG. Of course, this statement is subject to a reasonable and narrow interpretation of the provisions of the CISG.

---

74. It appears that art 160 of the Code is a translation of art 57 of the CISG.

Remedies for breach of contract under the Code

Suspension of contract

[1.120] Suspension of contract performance is a temporary measure to relieve an innocent party from performing his or her obligations under a contract. It is different from rescission or termination of a contract because the performance may be resumed if the situation justifying the suspension ceases to exist, or if the condition stipulated in law for resuming performance occurs. It is also different from the termination or rescission of a contract in the sense that it is often based on evidence suggesting the probability of a future breach or used to prevent damages likely to be caused by a party's future breach. The right of suspension is fair to the innocent party because the other party has shown some evidence of his or her inability to perform contractual obligations in the future.

[1.121] The Code permits a party who is obliged to perform a certain obligation under the contract ahead of the other party's performance to suspend his or her own performance if the other party appears to be unable to perform his or her obligation: art 68. This rule has a strong flavour of the continental-law tradition, in the sense that it assumes the existence of an order of priority between the parties' obligations to perform a contract, implying the existence of an obligation and right in the order of performance. It appears that the right to suspend a contract is a right to be exercised by the party who is obliged to perform certain contractual obligations before the performance of the other party. In this sense, the rule of anticipatory breach in a common law jurisdiction may be similar to this rule of suspension in Chinese law. Article 68 of the Code permits an obligor to suspend performance of his or her obligations in any of the following situations:

- the other party's state of business has seriously deteriorated;
- the other party has transferred or moved his or her property or money for the purpose of avoiding his or her obligations and debts;
- the other party has lost his or her business reputation; or
- there is any other possibility of the other party losing or becoming likely to lose the ability to perform his or her obligation.

The party intending to exercise the right of suspension is obliged to provide evidence. Otherwise, the party suspending the performance is liable to the other party for breach of contract.

[1.122] If a party intends to exercise the right of suspension under art 68 of the Code, he or she must inform the other party of the decision promptly: art 69. If the other party provides adequate security for performance, the suspending party should resume his or her performance. The suspension is a transitional stage for the suspending party to rescind the contract. Under art 69 of the Code, if the other party is not only unable to regain the ability to perform, but also fails to provide an adequate security for performance, the suspending party is entitled to avoid the contract concerned. It appears that art 69 does not permit a party to avoid a contract if the other party has provided an adequate security, regardless of whether the latter has shown an ability to perform.

Termination of contract

[1.123] Termination of contract is one of the basic remedies in contract law. The rights and obligations of the contracting parties under the contract, which are reciprocal and correspondent, cease to exist after termination. If one party breaches the essential terms of a contract, or fails in or is unable to perform his or her essential obligations, it would be unfair to the innocent party to compel him or her to perform his or her obligations under the contract unilaterally. Thus, termination of the contract is one of the options available to ensure fairness in commercial relationships. Sometimes a contract cannot be realistically performed as the parties intended because of some reason beyond their control; in that case, termination of the contract appears to be the only fair and reasonable solution to relieve the parties from their obligations to each other. This is also necessary to ensure the stability of commercial relationships and the dignity of the law governing contracts.

[1.124] Article 94 of the Code states that a party is entitled to terminate a contract in any of the following situations:

1. the purpose of the contract cannot be realised due to *force majeure*;
2. before the expiration of the time for performance, a party has stated expressly or by conduct an intention not to perform his or her major obligations;
3. a party has not only failed to perform his or her major obligations within the agreed time, but has also refused to perform them within a reasonable time after the other party's notice to urge the performance;
4. the purpose of the contract cannot be realised due to a party's delay in performing his or her obligations, or due to another breaching act; or
5. any other situations stipulated in law.

It must be pointed out that the Code regards the option of terminating a contract as a 'right'. Article 93 of the Code actually uses the expression 'holder of the right of termination'. Such a treatment of termination reflects one of the underlying notions, if not *the* underlying notion, of the Code: a contract is largely based on the dichotomy of right and obligation. In other words, a contract is by nature an obligation.

[1.125] The first ground for the termination of a contract is commonly accepted across the world. Usually it refers to any natural cause, any reason beyond the control of the contracting parties or any reason for which neither contracting party is liable. It must be pointed out that, under the Code, the change of the party's name or title, or any personnel change involving the appointment or resignation of the legal representative, director or responsible person of a contracting party does not constitute *force majeure* and thus does not affect the party's obligations under the contract concerned: Code, art 76. This provision is included in the Code largely because of the malpractice of many Chinese companies, in particular those owned by the state or by collectives, designed to avoid their contractual obligations on the ground that their managerial structure or their identity has been changed.

[1.126] In the second and third grounds for termination, the Code appears to have adopted something similar to what is known as 'fundamental breach' under the CISG or a 'breach of fundamental terms' in the common law tradition. These grounds both refer to a 'breach of major obligations'. As we have seen, the second ground allows a party to terminate a contract on the ground that the other party has shown an intention to refuse to perform the latter's 'major obligations'. The relevant words in Chinese may also be translated as 'main obligations', 'principal obligations' or, very arguably, 'fundamental obligations'. The third ground uses the same expression, 'major obligations', and allows a party to terminate a contract if the other party fails to perform his or her major obligations even after the first party has given an extension for performance and urged the latter to perform. The meaning of 'major obligations' is unclear, but can be assumed to be similar to 'fundamental breach' or 'breach of fundamental terms'. However, different judicial interpretations of these concepts can be expected. 'Major obligations' implies that a party cannot terminate a contract on the second or third ground if the other party has not breached or has not refused to perform any 'major obligation'.

The differences between the second ground and third ground in art 94 are not clear. The second ground permits a party to terminate a contract if the other party has shown an intention by conduct not to perform his or her major obligations. But the third ground appears to request a party to give a warning or notice to urge the other party, who has failed to perform his or her obligations within the time stipulated by the contract, before the first party can terminate a contract. The second and third grounds are inconsistent in the sense that the second ground appears to suggest that non-performance is itself an indication of a party's intention to breach his or her major obligations, but non-performance within the stipulated time for performance is insufficient for a party to terminate a contract on the third ground. If such an interpretation is correct, who would bother to rely on the third ground for termination? The co-existence of the second and third grounds may perhaps be explained by two reasons: first, a party's non-performance within the stipulated time may not, per se, be an indication of an intention to breach his or her major obligations; and, second, the third ground is intended to have the same function as arts 47, 49, 63 and 64 of the CISG — that of encouraging the use of a grace period to facilitate the performance of a contract. However, the first reason may be challenged on the ground that, if the delay in performing a party's major obligations is not the party's fault, the party is not liable. Why should the party be penalised later in an additional period for performance by giving the other party a right to terminate the contract, while the first party is probably entitled to declare a contract avoided on the ground of *force majeure*? In addition, it is arguable that certain non-performance without justification always constitutes a breach of major obligations.

The third ground of art 94 appears to be similar to what is known as the 'grace period' set out in arts 47 and 63 of the CISG and the right to terminate a contract at the end of a grace period, as set out in arts 49(1)(b) and 64(1)(b) of the CISG. Articles 47 and 49 apply to the buyer, and arts 63 and 64 apply to the seller. The rights and obligations of the buyer and the seller are parallel to, or correspond with, each other.

[1.127] The fourth ground under art 94 does not refer to 'major obligations'. It focuses on the issue of whether or not a party's breach of contract has made the realisation of the goal of the contract impossible. Is this ground closer to the meaning of 'fundamental breach' under the CISG and 'breach of fundamental terms' under the common law tradition than the previous grounds referring to 'major obligations'? The answer lies in the hands of the court, because all of the grounds are capable of covering the same issues, also covered by the concepts of 'fundamental breach' and 'breach of fundamental terms'. It appears that all of the grounds are supplementary to each other, providing a basis for the termination of a contract whenever it is necessary and justified.

[1.128] Article 166 of the Code provides that, on the ground that the purpose or object of the contract cannot be fulfilled due to a breach in any instalment, the buyer may terminate the relevant part of the contract, the future part of the contract or the whole contract, including the part already performed. It appears that art 166 of the Code is modelled on art 73 of the CISG.

Damages

[1.129] Damages are one of the feasible ways recognised by law to compensate an innocent party for losses sustained as a result of the breaching party's act. They should reflect a fair assessment of the loss sustained by the innocent party. Sometimes a reasonable sum of penalty against the breaching party may arguably be implied in the sum of damages granted. Although a common law court may be reluctant to grant punitive damages in a contractual dispute,[75] art 114 of the Code expressly permits the court or an arbitration tribunal to fix the sum of a fine or penalty according to the method of calculation agreed by the parties in a contract. The discussion that follows uses 'damages' in a broad sense, covering all forms of monetary compensation that a court may grant to an innocent party under the Code and the CISG.

[1.130] The major provisions of the Code regulating damages are arts 107 and 112–16. Article 107 states the breaching party's obligation to remedy his or her breach by remedial acts or by compensation. Article 112 states the right of an innocent party to seek damages if the remedial act of the breaching party has not cured or remedied all the losses sustained by the innocent party. Article 112 of the Code is compatible with arts 45(2) and 61(2) of the CISG. Article 113 of the Code states that the sum of compensation should be equivalent to the loss caused by the breach, including the expected profit which might have been gained if the contract had been performed, but cannot exceed the sum of loss foreseen or foreseeable by the breaching party at the time of the conclusion of the contract. This provision is largely identical to art 74 of the CISG, suggesting that art 74 has strongly influenced the drafting of art 113 of the Code.

Art 114 of the Code regulates the use of a fine or penalty in a contract. Under that provision, parties may agree the sum of the fine or penalty in case of a breach by any party; they may also agree the method for calculating the fine or penalty. The relevant Chinese word in art 114 can be translated as either 'fine' or 'penalty'. If the fine or penalty fixed in a contract is lower or excessively higher than the actual loss, a party may ask the court or the relevant arbitration authority to increase or decrease the sum accordingly. If a fine or penalty is imposed for late performance, the payment of the fine or penalty does not relieve the obligor from the obligation to perform the obligation.

---

75. See, for example, G H Treitel, *The Law of Contract*, 9th ed, Sweet & Maxwell, London, 1995, p 845.

[1.130]   In the light of art 114, it appears that a fine or penalty is proportionate to the actual loss caused by the breaching act concerned. In practice, the application of art 114 may be problematic. In a case of late performance, the loss is restricted to the loss caused by the late performance. In comparison, where a contract is terminated due to non-performance, the loss includes the loss caused by the termination of the contract. If the loss is assessed in this way, what is the difference between a fine or penalty under art 114 and damages under art 113? It appears that some clarification of art 114 by the court may be necessary. The CISG does not have any equivalent provision concerning the use of a fine or penalty in a contract.

[1.131]   Article 115 of the Code regulates the use of a deposit. This provision states that the parties may, in pursuance of the Law of Guarantee of the People's Republic of China, agree on the payment of a deposit as a guarantee. If the party paying the deposit has performed his or her obligation, the deposit may be converted to the payment of price or be returned to him or her. If the party paying the deposit fails to perform his or her obligation, he or she is not entitled to demand the return of the deposit. On the other hand, if the party taking the deposit fails to perform his or her obligation, he or she must pay the party that paid the deposit a sum twice that of the amount of the deposit. The punitive nature of such a deposit is clear. There is no compatible provision in the CISG.

It appears that both a fine and a deposit may not be applied in the same contract. Article 116 provides that, if parties have incorporated both fine and deposit clauses in a contract, the innocent party may choose one of the clauses, suggesting that the two forms of punitive remedy are not available in the same contract. Generally speaking, the provisions of the Code concerning damages show a strong tendency to provide remedies to penalise the breaching party; in comparison, the provisions of the CISG focus more on compensating the innocent party for loss.

[1.132]   Mitigation of loss is an important aspect of damages. The innocent party has an obligation to mitigate losses incurred and to prevent as much as possible the aggravation of losses. This is rational and sound in economics, as well as sensible and fair to the party breaching a contract. Both the Code and the CISG require the parties to mitigate losses whenever possible. Article 119 of the Code provides that the innocent party should adopt adequate measures to prevent the aggravation of the loss caused by the breaching party. If the innocent party fails to mitigate the loss concerned, he or she is not entitled to claim damages for the aggravated damage caused by his or her failure. The cost for mitigating losses is borne by the breaching party. A similar position has been taken by art 77 of the CISG. Although the wording of these provisions differs, they appear to be capable of reaching the same result in the same circumstance.

Specific performance

[1.133]   Specific performance means that the court directs a party to perform a specific act in pursuance of the contract concerned. As a remedy, it appears to be tough on the breaching party in the sense that, in certain circumstances, the breaching party may be willing to pay damages rather than to perform the contract. On the other hand, it appears to be fair and just to the innocent party where that party's loss cannot be assessed adequately by financial compensation or cannot be compensated by damages at all.

However, whether or not a particular situation justifies the grant of specific performance is totally subject to the discretion of the court. This may lead to some degree of unpredictabililty in the decision of the court. This is probably one of the reasons for the reluctance of courts in common law jurisdictions to grant specific performance.

[1.134] Articles 109–11 of the Code regulate specific performance. Article 110 is the principal provision; arts 109 and 111 supplement art 110. It appears that the Code has adopted a generous attitude to the use of specific performance. Article 110 states that, if a party does not perform his or her obligation and that obligation is not a financial obligation, or does not perform the obligation properly according to the contract, the other party may request the first party to perform the obligation concerned, unless one of the following situations arises:

- performance is impossible in law or in practice;
- the subject of the obligation is not suitable for performance, or the cost of performance is too high; or
- the obligee has not requested performance within a reasonable time.

This provision suggests that specific performance is generally available unless the obligor establishes that one of the situations prescribed in art 110 exists. Article 110 supports either a request by the innocent party made directly to the breaching party or an action brought by the innocent party to request a court to order specific performance.

[1.135] Article 110 does not cover all situations where specific performance may be adequate to remedy the loss of the innocent party. For example, the buyer's failure to pay the price of contract is not covered by art 110. Thus, art 109 provides that, if a party has not paid money or other rewards in compliance with the contract, the other party may request the first party to do so. Of course, if the breaching party refuses to comply with the innocent party's request, the court will force him or her to pay the innocent party under art 109.

[1.136] Article 111 deals with a different type of specific performance. This provision states that, where the subject matter of the contract (including goods) does not conform with the contract, and in the absence of an agreement on quality, the innocent party may choose to:

- request the breaching party to repair, substitute or remake the subject matter;
- return the non-conforming subject matter to the breaching party; or
- reduce the price or reward for the non-conforming subject matter.

Because art 111 applies to all types of contract — including, for example, service and processing contracts — the 'subject matter' concerned may not necessarily be goods. This type of specific performance is different from the specific performance under art 110, in the sense that it largely involves an act to make the non-conforming goods conform by various, feasible means. In addition, art 111 applies only to disputes on quality where no other means of resolution has been stipulated by the contract, fixed by the agreement of the parties or established by relevant commercial usage. Thus, the right of the innocent party to seek specific performance under art 111 depends on the nature of the subject matter or the goods involved, and the extent of damage to them.

General operation of the Code

[1.137] In summary, it can be said that all types of commercial contracts made in China or with a Chinese party (such as service contracts, loan agreements or transfer-of-technology contracts) may be subject to the Code. Contracts for the establishment of foreign investment enterprises are not regulated by specific provisions of the Code. Thus, we can expect to apply the general principles of the Code to such contracts. In the absence of specific rules, it is possible that a foreign investor investing in China also needs to consider the relevant foreign investment law. The precise boundary between the Code and the relevant foreign investment law in relation to a contract for the establishment of foreign investment enterprise is yet to be ascertained by a court. In this sense, the outer limits of the Code have yet to be demarcated by a court or by the Standing Committee of the National People's Congress (NPC).

Finally, it can be said that the passing of the Code is good news for foreign companies and those who deal extensively with Chinese companies and business-people. Contractual principles and specific rules are transparent and ascertainable under the Code, reducing and preventing the abuse of judicial discretion in handling disputes arising from contracts. Although the Code is not yet perfect or fully comprehensive, it is an important step for the People's Republic of China in its movement towards the rule of law. The Code offers a certain theoretical basis for developing contractual rules relating to many other types of contract which it does not specifically address. Of course, the application and the efficacy of the Code are yet to be tested. It remains to be seen how it works in practice, and amendments may be expected in the future.

Chapter Two

Contracts of Sale under the CISG

Introduction

[2.1] The United Nations Convention on Contracts for the International Sale of Goods (CISG) was adopted by the United Nations Conference on Contracts for the International Sale of Goods on 11 April 1980 in Vienna, and entered into force on 1 January 1988. The Convention was intended to replace the 1964 Hague Convention relating to a Uniform Law on International Sale of Goods and the 1964 Hague Convention relating to a Uniform Law on the Formation of Contracts for the International Sale of Goods (see art 99 of the CISG). Both were formed on 1 July 1964 in The Hague. The CISG replaces the Hague Conventions among the contracting members to the new convention.

[2.2] There are 62 contracting countries to the CISG, as follows:[1]

Argentina	Georgia	Norway
Australia	Germany	Peru
Austria	Greece	Poland
Belarus	Guinea	Romania
Belgium	Honduras	The Russian Federation
Bosnia and Herzegovina	Hungary	Saint Vincent and the Grenadines
Bulgaria	Iceland	Singapore
Burundi	Iraq	Slovakia
Canada	Israel	Slovenia
Chile	Italy	Spain
China	Kyrgyzstan	Sweden
Columbia	Latvia	Switzerland
Croatia	Lesotho	The Syrian Arab Republic
Cuba	Lithuania	Uganda
Czech Republic	Luxembourg	Ukraine
Denmark	Mauritania	The United States of America
Ecuador	Mexico	Uruguay
Egypt	Moldova	Uzbekistan
Estonia	Mongolia	Yugoslavia
Finland	The Netherlands	Zambia
France	New Zealand	

---

1. An up-to-date list is available from the Pace University Law School CISG website at <http://cisgw3.law.pace.edu/cisg/countries/cntries.html>.

[2.3] Member countries of the CISG are allowed to make reservations to most provisions of the Convention. If a member country has made a reservation to a particular provision, this provision will not apply to a contract involving a party having a place of business in the member country; alternatively, the provision will operate in a contract involving the member country in the manner as intended in the reservation.

Application of the Convention

An overview

[2.4] There are seven main provisions which determine the application of the CISG in particular circumstances: arts 1–6 and art 10.

Three essential criteria determine whether the Convention applies to a contract of sale. The Convention applies if:

- the parties to the contract have their places of business in different countries;
- either both parties to the contract have their places of business in countries that are members of the Convention,[2] or the Convention is applicable as a result of the operation of conflicts rules,[3] even though one party may come from a country which is not a member;[4] and
- the subject matter of the contract, or the particular issue to be dealt with by a court of law, does not fall under one of the exceptions to the application of the Convention, such as those stated in arts 3–5.

The time of contracting is also relevant for the application of the Convention under art 1. The time factor is addressed in art 100, which provides as follows:

    (1) This Convention applies to the formation of a contract only when the proposal for concluding the contract is made on or after the date when the Convention enters into force in respect of the Contracting States referred to in subparagraph (1)(a) or the Contracting State referred to in subparagraph (1)(b) of article 1.

    (2) This Convention applies only to contracts concluded on or after the date when the Convention enters into force in respect of the Contracting States referred to in subparagraph (1)(a) or the Contracting State referred to in subparagraph (1)(b) of article 1.

[2.5] In the light of arts 1 and 100, it can be said that, even if the Convention is applicable under the relevant conflict of laws rules of a country, it is also necessary that the country whose law becomes the governing law of the contract under those rules is a member of the Convention at the time of contract.[5] Otherwise, the Convention will not

---

2. See, for example, *Societe Calzados Magnanni v SARL Shoes General International (SGI)*, decided in October 1999 by a French court. An abstract of it is available as CLOUT Case 313. The CLOUT cases cited in this chapter are reported in abstract at <http://www.uncitral.org>.
3. For example, in a dispute between a German buyer and a Czech seller, the arbitration tribunal held that, in the absence of an express agreement on the governing law, German law was applicable because the parties had chosen Germany as the place of arbitration. Accordingly, the CISG was applicable as part of German law. See *Schiedsgericht der Hamburger freundschaftlichen Arbitrage* (CLOUT Case 293).
4. In a Spanish case (CLOUT Case 394), the court decided that the CISG applied even though the buyers were from the United Kingdom, which is not a member of the Convention.
5. The operation of art 100 is illustrated by a French case decided in January 2001: see CLOUT Case 399.

have been a law of the country whose law should govern the contract in question. Thus, the Convention may not apply to a contract made when none of the countries of the contracting parties was a member of the Convention, or where the governing law of the contract did not include the Convention when the contract was concluded.[6]

This issue was examined in a case involving an Egyptian party and a Yugoslavian party. The arbitration tribunal took the view that the Convention did not apply to the dispute, because none of the countries concerned was a member of the Convention at the time of the conclusion of the contract.[7] Similarly, in a Spanish case, *Tribunal Supremo* (3 March 1997, CLOUT Case 188), the Spanish court held that an FOB contract for the sale of lemons between a Spanish seller and a US buyer was not subject to the Convention because Spain, whose law was deemed to be the governing law by the Spanish court, was not a member of the Convention when the contract was concluded.

[2.6] Whether or not the application of the Convention is compulsory in a member country, once the conditions for its application are satisfied, is an issue subject to debate. On one hand, provisions of the Convention imply that the application of the Convention is compulsory, unless any restriction or deviation from whole or part of the Convention has been agreed expressly by the parties to a contract, in pursuance of art 6 of the Convention. On the other hand, there is nothing in the Convention stating expressly what the consequence is if a court of a member country decides that the Convention is not applicable, for whatever reasons justified under the relevant domestic law.

In *GPL Treatment Ltd v Louisiana-Pacific Corp* 914 Pacific Reports (2d Series) 682; 323 Oregon Reports 116; CLOUT Case 137 the Canadian seller sued the US buyer for breach of the contract for the sale of cedar shakes. The sellers commenced their case under the Uniform Commercial Code (UCC) of the United States. During the trial, the sellers attempted to raise the issue of whether the Convention, rather than the UCC, should apply. The trial judge denied the motion on the ground that it was too late for the sellers to rely on the Convention to proceed with their case. The sellers won their case all the way against the buyer, and thus the question of whether the Convention should apply appeared to be only a technical question. A dissenting judge of the intermediate appellate court questioned the rationale of the trial judge in denying that the Convention applied, but the Supreme Court did not address this issue at all.

Though this case was decided largely on the basis of the UCC, it may suggest that the application of the Convention may be denied by the implied agreement of the parties, which can be inferred from the acquiescence of the parties to undertake proceedings at the beginning of a trial without raising the issue of Convention. This proposition, if it accurately expresses the trial judge's meaning in *GPL Treatment Ltd v Louisiana-Pacific Corp*, is inconsistent with art 6 of the Convention. In addition, the court of each member of the Convention must answer the question as to whether or not its country has an

---

6. For example, in the Italian case of *Kretschmer GmbH & Co KG v Muratori Enzo*, Corte Suprema Di Cassazione (No 5739, 3 March 1988, as CLOUT Case 8), the court denied the application of the Convention because Italy was not a member of the Convention when the contract was concluded. See also *Oilmes Combustibles SA v Vigan SA S/Ordinario* (Argentina, 15 March 1991, CLOUT Case 22).
7. Case 102, available in the *Yearbook of Commercial Arbitration*, vol XV, no 83, 1990, at <http://www.uncitral.org>.

international obligation to implement the Convention within its own territory. In light of these arguments, the scales will lean heavily towards the conclusion that the court of a member of the Convention probably has an obligation to apply the Convention, once the conditions for its application have been established, and its application has not been excluded in pursuance of the provisions of the Convention.

[2.7] The application of the Convention in any particular circumstance has been inevitably affected by the legal tradition concerned. In a French case, *Societe Sacovini v SARL Les Fils de Henri Ramel* (23 January 1996, Court of Cassation (1st Civil Division), CLOUT Case 150), the Montpellier Court of Appeal of France applied the Convention, in particular art 35, to dismiss an appeal by the Italian wine seller against a decision of the Sete Commercial Court in favour of the French buyers, despite the fact that the trial court did not apply the Convention to adjudicate the dispute in the first instance. This case is interesting, in the sense that at the trial the dispute was settled under the French domestic law, but at the appeal the Court of Appeal brought in the Convention by its own initiative to dismiss a claim formulated on the basis of the French domestic law.

[2.8] The application of the provisions of the Convention to a severable part of a contract is possible, and is also implicitly allowed under the Convention. In current international commercial transactions, more and more parties are engaged in complicated business relationships, by virtue of combining contracts of sale with contracts of service, licensing agreements, distribution agreements or franchising agreements, among others. It is reasonable to apply the Convention to part of a comprehensive agreement between parties from different countries concerning international sale of goods. It is also reasonable to apply the Convention to a sub-contract under a principal contract, or to one of the contracts in a series of contracts, as long as the particular contract concerned is a contract for the international sale of goods.

[2.9] In *Societe Termo King v Societe Cigna France* (15 May 1996, Court of Appeal of Grenoble (Commercial Division), CLOUT Case 204), the French court held that a franchise contract between the parties was subject to the chosen law of the contract (that is, the law of Monnesta); but the contract for the sale of a refrigeration unit, which was incidental to the franchise contract, was subject to the Convention.

[2.10] Similarly, in a German case, *Bundesgerichtshof* (VIII ZR 134/96, 23 July 1997, CLOUT Case 236), the court held that a franchise agreement between an Italian seller and a German buyer was subject to the German anti-trust law, while the supply contract under the franchise agreement was subject to the Convention. Consequently, the invalidity of the franchise agreement did not affect the validity of the supply contract.

Place of business

[2.11] Articles 1 and 10 are relevant to the determination of the parties' places of business. These provisions set out the following rules for determining or ascertaining whether the parties to a contract have places of business in different countries:
- the place of business must be determined on the basis of information revealed in the contract or dealings of the parties prior to the conclusion of the contract, and any

Contracts of Sale under the CISG [2.14]

inference implying a place of business but having no basis in the contract or any fact unknown to the parties prior to the conclusion of the contract must be disregarded for the purpose of determining the parties' places of business: art 1(2);

- the place of business is not determined by the nationality of the parties or the civil or commercial character of the parties or of the contract, which may otherwise expressly or implicitly suggest the places of business of the parties: art 1(3);[8]
- if a party has more than one place of business, the place of business should be the one which has the closest relationship to the 'contract and its performance': art 10(a);[9] and
- if the party does not have a nominal place of business, the 'place of business' should be the party's habitual residence: art 10(b).

[2.12] The place of the business is crucial for determining the international nature of a contract of sale. It is one of the prerequisites for the application of the Convention that the contract of sale must be of an international nature. In determining that a sale is of an international nature, the mere movement of goods and payments across the national borders of two countries is not sufficient to meet the implied definition of international sales contract as suggested by art 1 of the Convention. This is why the parties' places of business are crucial for determining the international nature of the contract concerned.

[2.13] The place of business is relevant for the application of the Convention, because it not only determines the international nature of the contract, but also serves as a link between the Convention and a contract. As we can see from art 1 of the Convention, the Convention may apply to a contract if one of the parties is from a member country of the Convention. In a dispute involving a Bulgarian buyer and an Austrian seller, arbitrated by the International Court of Arbitration in 1993 (Case No 7197, CLOUT Case 104), the tribunal held that, in the absence of any express choice by the parties, the Convention was applicable because it had been incorporated into the Austrian law at the time of the contract. The tribunal considered it to be immaterial that Bulgaria was not a party to the Convention at the time when the contract was concluded.

[2.14] Sometimes, the ascertainment of a party's place of business is an issue which must be decided by the court hearing the case. In *Societe Fauba v Societe Fujitsu* [1996] UNLEX (22 April 1992, Court of Appeal of Paris (15th Division), CLOUT Case 158), a French buyer bought several batches of electronic components from a German seller, though the seller's liaison office was in France. When determining whether the Convention should apply, the court held that the seller's liaison office in France did not have due legal personality, and thus that it could not have made a contract of sale at all. On the basis of this finding, the court held that the contract of sale was formed between the

---

8. In other words, we cannot determine the places of business by the nationality of the parties, or assume that certain types of contract can only be concluded by parties from different countries.
9. It is unclear what the relationship is between a 'contract' and 'its performance' in art 10(a). It is quite likely that a place of business which has the closest relationship to the 'conclusion' or 'formation' of the contract will not have the closest relationship to the performance of the contract. By the same token, a place of business which has the closest relationship to the delivery of the goods may not be the same place where the price of the goods is paid. It is unclear how to prioritise the places of performance if a party's performance involves several places.

[2.14] **International Commercial Law**

French buyer and the German seller, and that the contract was subject to the Convention because both France and Germany were members of the Convention.

The Convention is silent on ascertaining the nature of a representative office. Although the decision of the French court may be justified by art 4(2) of the Convention on the ground that the issue relates to the capacity of a party to make a contract, the finding of the French court in this case (which is regarded as reasonable in countries adopting the civil law tradition, such as Germany, Japan and China), may not be easily reconciled with the agent–principal rules adopted by the common law tradition. This is because the dual legal personality is not an issue in the common law tradition. Possible differences in the understanding of the meaning of 'place of business' between different countries reflect one of the practical difficulties in adopting any universal rules for countries whose laws are based on various legal traditions.

Rules governing the operation of the Convention

[2.15] The Convention does not apply to all contracts which involve parties from different countries. In fact, it applies only to the sale of goods across national frontiers. A distribution agreement which is a severable part of a contract for international sale of goods is not subject to the Convention because it is not a contract of sale directly.[10] Therefore, after the determination of the parties' places of business, it is necessary to decide whether the Convention is applicable to the particular contract.

[2.16] The Convention becomes applicable under one of the two following rules:

- the countries where the parties to a contract have their respective places of business are members of the CISG: art 1(1)(a); or
- by virtue of the operation of the conflicts rules adopted by the forum — where the rules determine that the law of a member country is the proper law of the contract, or where both parties choose the CISG as the governing law — and the contract involves parties from different countries,[11] regardless of whether the countries where the parties have their respective places of business are members of the Convention: art 1(1)(b).[12]

[2.17] The operation of art 1 is illustrated by a case arbitrated by the International Court of Arbitration of the International Chamber of Commerce in 1993 (Case No 6653, CLOUT Case 103). In that dispute, the parties chose French law as the governing law. French law had incorporated the Convention at the time of contract. The buyer was located in Syria, which was a member of the Convention when the contract was

---

10. For example, see CLOUT Case 126, decided on 19 March 1996 by the Metropolitan Court of Hungary.
11. For example, in *Danisches Bettenlager GmbH & Co KG v Forenede Factors A/S* (22 January 1996, CLOUT Case 161), the Danish court applied art 5(1) of the 1968 EU (Brussels) Convention on Jurisdiction and Enforcement of Judgements in Civil and Commercial Matters, deciding that the Convention was applicable as the domestic law of either Denmark or Germany and that the German court had the appropriate jurisdiction to hear the case.
12. There may be unpredictability in the operation of art 1(1)(b), because little connection is needed between the country where a party has a place of business and the CISG. This is probably why China and the United States have made reservations to this provision.

concluded. The seller was located in Germany, which became a member of the Convention after the conclusion of the contract. The tribunal found that the contract was an international sales contract because its performance assumed a movement of goods and payment across frontiers. The tribunal decided that the Convention was probably applicable on several grounds, including:

1. the Convention was part of the French law;
2. the parties were from two countries;
3. the sale was international;
4. the goods were not excluded goods under art 2 of the Convention;
5. the sale was not an excluded sale under art 2 of the Convention; and
6. the issues in dispute were governed by the provisions of the Convention.

This dispute demonstrates the relevant factors which should be taken into account when determining the application of the Convention.

Restrictions on the application of the Convention

[2.18] The Convention does not apply to all contracts which involve parties from different countries.[13] Nor does it apply to all contracts which may otherwise be subject to the Convention by virtue of art 1(1). Its application is restricted by a number of provisions. In particular, the Convention does not apply to:

- A sale of consumer goods (goods bought for personal, domestic or household use) if the seller knew or ought to have known that the goods were purchased as consumer goods: art 2(a).[14] This provision was applied in an Austrian case, *Oberster Gerichtshof* (10 Ob 1506/94, CLOUT Case 190), to dismiss an action brought by a Swiss buyer of a Lamborghini Countach against an Austrian seller under the Convention.
- A sale at an auction or any sale based on authority of law, such as a sale in execution of a court order: art 2(b) and (c).
- Sales of stocks, shares, investment securities, negotiable instruments, money, ships, vessels, hovercraft, aircraft or electricity: art 2(d), (e) and (f).
- Any contract for the processing of goods, or contract for the supply of skills, labour or services: art 3.[15]
- Any legal issue concerning the validity of a contract or of its terms, even if the Convention may govern the contract concerned: art 4(a).

---

13. For example, a US court held that a distribution agreement between a US company and an Italian company was not governed by the CISG. See *Viva Vino Import Corp v Farnese Vini srl* 2000 (WL 1224903, CLOUT Case 420).
14. In other words, the Convention applies to a consumer sale if the seller did not know or ought not to have known of the nature of the sale. This exclusion is probably necessary for the purpose of maintaining the integrity of the consumer protection law of each member country.
15. Article 3(1) provides that contracts for the supply of goods to be manufactured or produced are to be considered sales unless the party who orders the goods undertakes to supply a substantial part of the materials necessary for such manufacture or production.

[2.18] International Commercial Law

- Any legal issue concerning the effect of passing of property under a contract, even though the Convention may govern the contract concerned: art 4(b).[16]
- The liability of the seller for death or personal injury caused by goods which are sold under a contract governed by the Convention: art 5.[17]
- Any contracts or issues if the parties have excluded the application of the Convention under art 6 of the CISG.

[2.19] A consulting contract falls under art 3, because it involves the provision of skills and labour. It is by nature a service contract.

A German case, *Oberlandesgericht Koln* (19 U 282/93, decided on 26 August 1994, CLOUT Case 122), examined the question of whether a contract for the production of a research paper can be subject to the Convention from a rather interesting perspective. In that case, a Swiss market research institute contracted with a German company to write a market report for the company. The Swiss company submitted the report to the German company, which refused to pay for the report on the ground that the report did not meet the conditions of the contract.

The court decided that the Convention did not apply to the contract because it was not a contract for the sale of goods. In answering the question of whether a report can be a subject of sale, the court observed that the sale of goods was characterised by the transfer of property in the article sold. The court further commented that, when the report was handed over to the German company, the major concern of the parties was to transfer the right to use the ideas contained in the report, instead of passing the property in the report itself to the German company. Thus, the report itself was not a subject of sale in the contract concerned.

The distinction drawn by the court between a sale of a report (or a book or paper), and a sale of ideas is undoubtedly correct, although a court in a common law jurisdiction may express a similar view from a different perspective.

---

16. The first Australian case determined under the CISG is *Roder Zelt-Und Hallenkonstruktionen GmbH v Rosedown Park Pty Ltd* (1995) 13 ACLA 776. In that case, Roder was a major German manufacturer and supplier of large tents and party marquees. Rosedown was incorporated in Victoria and provided hire services for major events throughout Australia. Rosedown contracted with Roder to purchase a number of large tents to be used for the 1992 Australian Grand Prix in South Australia. The goods were to be paid for by a deposit and five instalments as agreed by the contracting parties. The evidence suggested that the seller would retain title in the goods until the full price had been paid. The buyer defaulted in making the first and second instalment payments and came under administration under Pt 5.3A of the Corporations Law in October 1993. The administrator refused to recognise the seller's title in the tents. The seller sued Rosedown and the administrator for the return of the goods. The evidence of communications between the parties prior to the conclusion of the contract of sale suggested that Roder intended to retain title in the goods until the full price of the goods had been paid. There was also a declaration signed by both parties to evidence the same intention. Von Doussa J held that the buyer had breached the contract and the seller was entitled to repossess the goods or to seek appropriate remedies in pursuance of the relevant provisions of the CISG.
17. This means that there will be no inconsistency as far as personal injury and death are concerned between the provisions of Pt VA of the Trade Practices Act, which deals with the liability of manufacturers and importers for defective goods that caused personal injury or death to consumers, and the provisions of the Convention.

[2.20] Article 3 appears to be one of the controversial provisions of the Convention. Its sphere of operation is yet to be settled in practice.

In a Swiss case, *Bezirksgericht St Gallen* (3PZ97/18, on 3 July 1997, CLOUT Case 215) a Dutch party and a Swiss party concluded a contract for the sale of goods which were based on the raw materials provided by the Dutch party. On the basis of this fact, art 3(1) would probably deny the operation of the Convention, unless the materials used did not constitute a substantial part of the materials necessary for the manufacture of the goods concerned. What happened in this case was rather interesting. The Swiss party used about 10 per cent of the materials supplied by the Dutch party, then returned the unused materials back to the Dutch party and broke off their relationship. The Dutch party demanded payment for all the materials as the seller of the materials, even though, under the original contract, the Dutch party was meant to be the buyer of the goods to be manufactured using the materials provided by it. The Swiss court decided that the parties were in a sales relationship as far as the materials were concerned, and ordered the Swiss party to pay for all the materials, 90 per cent of which had been returned back to the Dutch party.

The problem with this decision is that, while the arrangement to supply materials by the Dutch party to the Swiss party was capable of making the contract a contract of processing instead of a contract of sale, the use of the materials by the Swiss party was regarded as a separate contract, independent of the contract for the sale of the end-products. Whether or not the Swiss court was correct in reaching the decision concerned depends on whether the materials supplied by the Dutch party constituted a substantial part of the materials necessary for manufacturing the goods to be bought by the Dutch party. The court did not answer this question clearly.

Modifying or varying the effect of the provisions of the Convention

[2.21] Before we discuss the application of the CISG in detail, it is paramount to examine the provisions of the Convention which allow parties to modify or vary the effect of its provisions. Parties have autonomy to tailor the provisions of the Convention according to their needs, and to override the effect of those provisions which a party does not favour. The major provisions which deal with the parties' right to vary or modify the effect of the provisions of the Convention are arts 6, 12, 92, and 94–6.

[2.22] The most important provision concerning the modification or variation of the effect of the provisions of the Convention is art 6, which states as follows:

> The parties may exclude the application of this Convention or, subject to article 12, derogate from or vary the effect of any of its provisions.

Article 12 ensures that arts 11 and 29, and Pt II of the Convention, which deal with formation of contract, do not apply to a contract where a party has its place of business in a contracting state that has made reservations under art 96 to these provisions. The reservations made by the contracting state cannot be circumvented by the parties to the contract under art 6 by modifying or varying the effect of arts 11, 29 or 96, or Part II of

[2.22]

the Convention. This provision ensures that the intention of the members which adopted the Convention under specified conditions is fully respected.

[2.23] Subject to the preceding paragraph, if the parties are not happy about any provision, or any effect of a provision, they can change it by express agreement under art 6. This right enables the parties to overcome many 'barriers' — such as the preconditions for avoiding a contract and the requirements for allowing self-cure to the other party under arts 37, 48 or 63 — which may be unfamiliar to common law lawyers. Article 6 allows the contracting parties to have better control of their obligations under the contract.

[2.24] Article 94 allows contracting states which share the same or similar legal traditions to modify the effect of the provisions of the Convention between them. Any modification made under art 94 is effective only between states which meet the description of art 94, and which have made declarations under that article.

[2.25] Article 92 empowers a contracting state to declare that it will not be bound by Pts II or III of the Convention. This provision appears to authorise a contracting state to exclude the whole of Pts II or III, rather than certain provisions of them.

[2.26] Article 95 permits a state to exclude the operation of art 1(1)(b), which makes the Convention applicable under conflicts rules.

[2.27] Article 96 allows a state to exclude the operation of arts 11 or 29, or Pt II, which do not require a contract to be made or evidenced in writing. If a state makes a declaration under art 96, the relevant provisions requiring a contract to be made or evidenced in writing do not apply to a contract which is governed by the law of that state. However, it must be pointed out that such a reservation only affects the validity of a contract made by a contracting party whose place of business is in the state making the reservation where the law of that state applies to the contract: see **[2.15]–[2.16]**. The reservation does not automatically affect the validity of a contract concluded by a party having a place of business in the state, if the law of that state does not govern the contract in question.

[2.28] Parties to a contract of international sale, or a contracting state may, under the above provisions, modify, vary or exclude the effect of most provisions of the CISG. It must be pointed out that any parties intending to rely on these provisions must comply with the procedural requirements under these provisions (if any) for varying the effect of the relevant provisions. In an Italian case, *Rheinland Versicherungen v srl Atlarex and Allianz Subalphina spa* (CLOUT Case 378), the court took the view that, while the parties are free to exclude the application of the CISG either expressly or implicitly, a mere reference to domestic law is not itself sufficient to exclude CISG. This means that, for art 6 to operate, the parties must first be aware that the CISG would apply and then intend to exclude its application.

Formation of a contract

Formality of contract

[2.29] Formality of contract involves the form in which a contract is made and the procedures through which it can be entered into. Whether or not a contract must be made in writing is an issue of formality, which is regulated by art 11. The other issues of formality (such as offer, acceptance and counter-offer), are regulated in Pt II, arts 14–24. Article 12 of the Convention permits a country to make a reservation against arts 11 and 29, and Pt II of the Convention at the time of acceding to or ratifying it. The reservation may partially or entirely exclude the application of the relevant provision in the territory of the country making the reservation.

[2.30] One of the most controversial provisions of the Convention is art 11, which deals with the written formality of contract. This provision states that a contract of sale need not be concluded in, or evidenced by, writing and is not subject to any other requirement as to form. It may be proved by any means, including witnesses. A number of contracting countries made reservations to exclude the effect of this provision.[18] Thus, it is necessary in an international sale to ascertain whether a particular contracting state has declared that this provision and other provisions relating to it are inapplicable within that state. If the Convention applies as part of the law of a country which has made reservation against art 11, it should apply without art 11 and other provisions (or the effect of the provisions) which are based on or related to art 11.

[2.31] In a country which has approved art 11, it is yet to be seen whether this provision can sit comfortably with the relevant domestic law. For example, although Australia did not make any reservation at the time of ratification, the application of art 11 may have some uncertainty. The potential uncertainty is seen in the second limb of art 11, which says that a contract can be 'proven' by any means, including witnesses. However, under Australian common law, not every oral contract can be proven by witnesses alone, or 'any means'. In addition, the enforcement of an oral contract is subject to special rules at common law. Will these rules be overridden by the Convention?

By virtue of the Convention's prevalence, these rules are likely to be overridden. But it is yet to be seen how this will be done in certain cases where a judge has discretion to decide the enforcement of an oral contract on several alternative grounds.

[2.32] The purpose of a reservation is to exclude partially or entirely from the text of the Convention the provision against which the reservation has been made; thus the Convention can be incorporated into the domestic law of the country without that provision. While a reservation will be enforced by the country making it, its effect outside the country depends on the attitude of the foreign court hearing a case.

[2.33] The effect of a reservation against Pt II was tested in a German case involving the sale of 3000 t of electrolytic nickel–copper cathodes between a Finnish seller and a German buyer: *Oberlandesgericht Munchen* (7U 5460/94, 8 March 1995, CLOUT Case 134).

---

18. See <http://www.un.org/Depts/Treaty> for details.

In that case, the buyer signed a standard form of contract. The seller did not sign it, but delivered the metal to the buyer. The seller later assigned the right to claim payment from the buyer to a third party, who sued the buyer after the buyer refused to pay. Finland declared that it was not bound by Pt II at the time of ratification. This meant that the formality for the making of the contract, as set out in arts 14–24, was not part of Finnish law. The German court found the Convention to be applicable nevertheless, because, in the view of the court, refusing to be bound by arts 14–24 did not mean that a contract concerning a Finnish seller could not be formed by agreement of the parties, which might or might not be subject to arts 14–24.

On the basis of this finding, the court permitted the third party to claim payment directly from the buyer under art 53 of the Convention, which imposes an obligation to pay upon the buyer. In this case, the court would have reached a similar decision on the validity of the contract if it had found German law to be the governing law. However, in holding the contract to be valid, the court was reluctant to ignore the intention of Finland in making the reservation, without either excluding the application of the Finnish law or answering the issue of whether the contract was valid under the relevant Finnish law, since these were the only logical ways to recognise the effect of the reservation made by Finland. In addition, the extension of art 53 to justify the right of assignment, without looking at the terms of the contract, was a huge step, which a court of common law jurisdiction in ordinary circumstances may be reluctant to take.

[2.34] In comparison, the Hungarian court has taken a more reasonable approach than the German court, in a case similar to the one referred to above. In this case, decided by the Metropolitan Court of Hungary (CLOUT Case 143), the Swedish seller sued the Hungarian buyer for the unpaid price of the goods delivered. The buyer contested the existence of a valid contract of sale. The court noted that Sweden had made a reservation against Pt II at the time of ratification, and thus applied the conflict of laws rules adopted by the Hungarian court in order to determine the governing law of the case. Subsequently, the court found that the Swedish law was applicable with regard to the formation of the contract in dispute. Under the Swedish Act No 28 of 1915, a contract must be concluded in writing. The court found that the contract in question had, in fact, been concluded in writing, and thus was valid under Swedish law. On that basis, the court applied the Convention to find the buyer liable for the unpaid price of the contract. This approach is reasonable, because it gives due respect to the reservation made by Sweden against Pt II.

Meaning of an 'offer' under the Convention

[2.35] Under art 14(1) of the Convention, an offer is a 'proposal for concluding a contract addressed to one or more specific persons'. It must be 'sufficiently definite and indicate the intention of the offeror to be bound in case of acceptance'. Whether it is 'sufficiently definite' is determined by a consideration of the following three indicators:

- the description of the goods;
- their quantity or determinable quantity; and
- their price or determinable price.

[2.36] This means that if a proposal clearly describes the goods and expressly or implicitly refers to the quantity and price of the goods (for example, making provision for determining the quantity and price of the goods), the proposal would be sufficient to be an offer under the Convention if it suggests that the person intends to be bound by it in case of acceptance. On the other hand, a reference to the specifications of a product alone does not constitute a valid offer.[19] In addition, a late agreement to determine the price of goods of special quality in the future may not make an earlier offer which did not contain any information on the price of the goods definite or sufficient for the purpose of art 14. In a case arbitrated by the Russian Federation Chamber of Commerce and Industry (Case No 309/1993, 3 March 1995, CLOUT Case 139) the arbitration tribunal denied the existence of any contract of sale between an Austrian company (the alleged buyer) and a Ukrainian company (the alleged seller), on the ground that the original offer, made in the form of a telex from the Ukrainian company, did not contain any information on the price of the goods.

The parties later agreed by telex that the price of the goods should be decided 10 days prior to the beginning of the New Year, but the agreement neither fixed a price nor provided any rules for determining the price. In addition, the tribunal held that art 55 of the Convention, which permits the price of the goods to be determined according to the relevant market price unless the parties have agreed otherwise, to be inapplicable because, in the view of the tribunal, the agreement to determine the price at a later time indicated the parties' objection to the operation of art 55.

[2.37] Article 14(2) distinguishes between an offer and an invitation to make an offer by examining whether the proposal is addressed to one or more 'specific persons'. A proposal can be an offer if it is directed to a specific person or persons; it cannot be an offer if it is directed to the general public, unless the person making the proposal expressly states otherwise in the proposal. This effect was intended by the majority delegates to the drafting of the Convention.[20] The restriction in art 14 on the use of 'offer to the public' does not have a substantial impact upon international sales because, in most circumstances, an offeror does not realistically expect to do international business by making an offer to the public at large within a particular country, or throughout the world.

Meaning of an 'effective offer'

[2.38] Article 15(1) provides that the time that an offer becomes effective is the time when the offer reaches the offeree. It follows that art 15(2) allows the offeror to withdraw any offer, as long as the withdrawal reaches the offeree before or at the same time as the offer. Article 15 should be read together with art 24, which allows the parties to use any

---

19. For example, in *United Technologies International Inc v Magyar Legi Kozlekedesi Vallat (Malev Hungarian Airlines)* (25 September 1992, Supreme Court of Hungary, CLOUT Case 53), the US seller offered two types of engine without quoting the prices. The Hungarian buyer chose one from the two. The court held that no contract had been concluded under art 14 because there was neither a price nor agreement on the determination of the price of the engine.
20. See Bianca and Bonell (eds), *Commentary on the International Sales Law — the 1980 Vienna Sales Convention*, Giuffré, Milan, 1987, pp 135–6.

means of communication to make or to accept an offer. An offer will not become effective if made by a letter but withdrawn by a fax or oral statement which reaches the offeree before or at the same time as the offer arrives.

[2.39] Article 15 suggests that the time at which the offeree receives an offer, rather than the time at which the offeror dispatches the offer, is crucial. The offeror has no legal liability under an irrevocable offer until the offer reaches the offeree. This rule gives more time for the offeror to respond to any change in circumstances that may affect his or her offer between the time at which the offer is dispatched and the time at which it is received. The offeree is not disadvantaged by this rule because he or she does not know the terms of the offer until it has reached (or has been communicated to) him or her.

Revocation of an offer

[2.40] Under art 15, an offeror can change his or her mind and withdraw an offer before the offer reaches the offeree. Under art 16, the offeror can also change his or her mind and revoke an offer before it is accepted. The general rule for revocation of an offer under art 16 is that a revocable offer can be revoked at any time before acceptance, but the revocation must reach the offeree before the offeree dispatches an acceptance. Article 24, which allows the use of any means of communication, is also relevant to art 16.

[2.41] The general rule of revocation does not apply to an irrevocable offer. Under art 16(2), an offer can be irrevocable either expressly or by implication. An expressly irrevocable offer contains terms which suggest a fixed time for acceptance or an undertaking not to revoke the offer before a fixed or determinable time. An implicitly irrevocable offer is established by an inference of irrevocability drawn from the circumstances involved; the offeree must have reasonably relied on this inference.

[2.42] If an offer is revoked, the offeror is not bound by it. If an offer is irrevocable, the offeror is bound by the offer until such time as the offeree has done something which is not consistent with the offeree's rights under the offer, the offer has been rejected, the offer has lapsed, or no contract is formed on the basis of the offer, for whatever reasons.

Rejection of offer

[2.43] A rejection is an indication by the offeree that he or she will not accept the offer. It can be an express indication of the offeree's intention to reject the offer; any reply to an offer which contains terms substantially different from the offer also constitutes a rejection to the original offer under art 19.

An effective rejection

[2.44] An offer is terminated when it is rejected. Article 17 provides that a rejection becomes effective when the rejection reaches the offeror. This implies that the offeree is able to accept the offer or withdraw the rejection if the acceptance or withdrawal of the rejection reaches the offeror before the rejection.

Meaning of acceptance under the Convention

[2.45] Two issues are involved: the manner of acceptance and the time of acceptance. The manner of acceptance is defined in art 18(1) and (3) of the Convention. Under art 18, an acceptance can be either a statement or an act of the offeree 'indicating assent to an offer'. Article 18 expressly says that silence or inactivity 'does not in itself amount to acceptance'. The expression 'in itself' in this provision means that silence or inactivity alone does not amount to acceptance, unless the circumstances described in art 18(3) occur.

[2.46] Article 18(1) implies that an offer which provides that the offeree is deemed to have accepted the offer if no rejection is received within a fixed time would not be allowed under the Convention, unless the parties have adopted this practice in their prior dealings.

This construction is indirectly reinforced by art 18(2), which clearly states that an acceptance becomes effective only when the indication of the statement or conduct was received by the offeror either within a fixed time or a reasonable time. In *Societe Isea Industrie spa v SA Lu* (13 December 1995, Court of Appeal of Paris, CLOUT Case 203), the French court applied art 18(2) to confirm its jurisdiction to hear the case, on the ground that the French buyer's order (which chose the French court as the court of forum) was returned to the buyer by the Italian seller, with the signature of the seller's representative. Accordingly, the court rejected the validity of a choice-of-forum clause, contained in a confirmation letter sent by the Italian seller to the French buyer 10 days after the return of the buyer's order, nominating the Court of Tortona as the court of forum.

[2.47] The manner of acceptance under art 18(1) is subject to the established practice between the parties, or the usage accepted in their course of business dealings. This means that an offer can be accepted without communicating directly to the offeror as required by art 18(1), if this has been the established practice of the parties. However, art 18(3) appears to be based on an act done by the offeree, rather than mere silence or inactivity. This seems to reinforce art 18(1) — silence or inactivity 'does not in itself amount to acceptance'. Article 18(3) is illustrated by a German decision, *Oberlandesgericht Hamm* (19U 97/91, 22 September 1992, CLOUT Case 227). In that case, a German buyer offered to purchase a specific type of bacon from an Italian seller, who responded to the buyer's offer by agreeing to sell a different type of bacon. The buyer did not object to the change. After having accepted four consignments of goods, the buyer refused to take further deliveries. The court held that, under art 18(3) of the Convention, a valid contract of sale had been concluded between the parties.

[2.48] Article 18 was applied in an interesting manner in a German case decided by a German court on 22 February 1994, *Oberlandesgericht Koln* (29 U 202/93, CLOUT Case 120).

In that case, the German buyer refused to pay the contract price for a sale of rare wood, on the ground that the wood was of inferior quality. The trial court ordered the buyer to pay and the buyer appealed against the decision. The Court of Appeal found that the buyer had lost the right to declare the contract void under art 49(1)(b) of the Convention,

[2.48] because it had failed to fix an additional period of time for performance. On the other hand, the court found that the contract had been terminated under art 29, by agreement of the parties in a manner prescribed in art 18. The court reviewed the facts of the case and discovered that the seller had examined the wood and offered to take it back for resale. The buyer neither refused this offer nor claimed damage or replacement of the defective wood. The court held that the buyer, by its inactivity, had accepted the offer to terminate the contract. Discussing art 18(1), which provides that silence or inactivity does not in itself amount to acceptance, the court stated that silence could be interpreted as a declaration of acceptance in certain circumstances. Accordingly, the Court of Appeal set aside the decision of the trial court and decided that the seller had the right to claim payment, as the contract had been terminated by agreement.

This case may appear to be strange to a common law lawyer, for at least two reasons. First, it appears somehow difficult to treat a suggestion to take the goods back as an offer to terminate a contract, without either an express or implied intention to support the suggestion. Second, the mere proposition that silence may be interpreted as a declaration of acceptance is not convincing unless it is substantiated by sufficient reasons. In addition, to apply the rules on the making of a contract for the purpose of terminating a contract is an interesting approach, although nothing appears to be fundamentally unfair or unjust about it.

[2.49] The time of acceptance is set out in arts 18(2) and (3). Under art 18(2), notice of acceptance must reach the offeror within a fixed time or a reasonable time. 'Reasonable time' should be determined by taking into account the circumstances of the transaction, and the means of communication employed by the offeror (only). This requires the offeree to respond to the offer in a manner and at a speed similar to that with which the offer is made. But a late acceptance may be accepted at the offeror's option under art 21.

[2.50] An acceptance can be withdrawn under art 22 at any time before the acceptance reaches the offeror. This article is similar to art 15, providing that an acceptance is regarded as withdrawn if the withdrawal reaches the offeror at the same time as the acceptance.

Rules for calculating the time for acceptance

[2.51] If a fixed period for acceptance is specified in the offer, art 20 sets out these two rules for determining when that period begins:

- if an offer is made in the form of a letter or a telegram, the period begins from the date of dispatch; but,
- if an offer is made by any means of instantaneous communication, the period begins from the moment the offer reaches the offeree.

[2.52] The first rule is inconsistent with the rule for determining when and where an offer or acceptance becomes effective adopted in most provisions of the Convention. For example, art 15 provides that an offer becomes effective when it *reaches* the offeree; art 17 states that a rejection becomes effective when it *reaches* the offeror; and art 18(2) says that an acceptance becomes effective when it *reaches* the offeror. However, art 20 says that a fixed time for the offeree to accept an offer made in a letter or a telegram begins to run from the 'moment the telegram is handed in for dispatch or from the date shown on the letter or, if no such date is shown, from the date shown on the envelope'. This means that, under art 15, the fixed time for reply begins even before the offer becomes effective (that is, before it reaches the offeree). This rule is perhaps designed to give the offeror better control and a clearer understanding of the period within which the offeree is required to respond to the letter or telegram.

The second rule is consistent with most provisions which decide when and where an offer or an acceptance becomes effective.

[2.53] For the purpose of calculating the time for acceptance, art 20(2) does not exclude any official holidays or non-business days, unless the last day of the fixed period is an official holiday or non-business day. This makes sense when the number and date of official holidays or non-business days varies from country to country.

Counter-offer and modified acceptance

[2.54] Under the Convention, an offeree can respond to an offer in five different ways. The offeree can respond with:

- an acceptance;
- a modified acceptance (an acceptance with modifications which are not materially different from the terms of the offer);
- a counter-offer;
- a rejection; or
- silence (no response), which amounts to rejection in most circumstances but may be regarded as acceptance in special circumstances.

While an acceptance indicates the formation of a contract, rejection terminates the offer and silence would normally render the offer ineffective. The meaning of these terms is largely self-evident.

[2.55] Article 19 distinguishes between a counter-offer and a modified acceptance. A counter-offer is a reply which 'contains additions, limitations or other modifications' to the terms relating to the price, quality or quantity of the goods, the place and time for delivery, and the liabilities of the parties. If the terms of the offer have been materially changed, the reply amounts to a counter-offer. By contrast, a modified acceptance is a reply containing additions or limitations which do not materially alter the terms of the offer. In an Austrian case, *Oberster Gerichtshof* (2 Ob 68/97m, 20 March 1997, CLOUT Case 188), the Austrian Supreme Court sent a case back to the court of first instance for a retrial and directed the court to consider whether an alteration of the offer should be considered material if it was merely in favour of the offeror. Perhaps in anticipation of the difficulties of differentiating between the legal effect of a counter-offer and a modified acceptance, art 19(2) gives the offeror an option to reject any additions or limitations immediately, or to accept them by raising no objection.

Effect of late acceptance

[2.56] The Convention does not make a late acceptance ineffective merely because it is late. Article 21(1) gives the offeror an opportunity to accept a late acceptance, either by informing the offeree orally of such an intention, or by giving the offeree immediate notice in writing, to the effect that he or she regards the late acceptance as effective. This provision implies that a late acceptance will be ineffective if the offeror chooses not to accept it by these means. Under art 21(1), there is a rebuttable presumption that a late acceptance is ineffective, which remains in place unless rebutted by the offeror. It appears that art 21(1) is based on the presumption that the offeree knows or ought to know that the acceptance is late. Article 21(1) does not take into account whether or not the offeree is aware of the ineffectiveness of a late acceptance, and whether or not the offeree's lack of awareness has resulted in any act or omission on his or her part. It appears that the offeree would bear the loss arising from his or her negligence in failing to ascertain whether a late acceptance has been accepted by the offeror, if the offeree sustained the loss as a result of his or her act or omission by acting under the presumption that a late acceptance was effective by virtue of the offeror's silence.

[2.57] In contrast, art 21(2) provides a rebuttable presumption of a different kind. It says that an acceptance which has been delayed by errors in transmission is nevertheless effective, unless the offeror informs the offeree immediately that the late acceptance is ineffective. This means that an acceptance which reaches the offeror after the lapse of the specified time for acceptance because of an error in transmission is presumed to be effective, unless a contrary intention has been expressed immediately by the offeror.

Article 21(2) appears to be based on the presumption that both the offeror and offeree knew or ought to have known that the error in transmission had caused delay in acceptance, by observing the facts shown in the late acceptance. However, this presumption may cause uncertainty in practice. For example, if the offeror did not think that the delay was caused by an error in transmission and treated the late acceptance as one described in art 21(1), and did not want to accept the late acceptance, he or she would not give any notice to the offeree. This is because art 21(1) requires only an offeror who *accepts* a late acceptance to inform the offeree of such intention. This omission of the offeror will, however, be regarded as accepting the late acceptance under art 21(2) if the lateness was indeed caused by an error in transmission. Therefore, a misunderstanding and an innocent omission by the offeror in this hypothetical situation would lead him or her to a liability that he or she would not otherwise be obliged to undertake.

[2.58] The key point for resolving the uncertainty raised in the preceding paragraph is the sentence in art 21(2) which refers to 'a letter or other writing containing a late acceptance [which] shows that it has been sent in such circumstances that if its transmission had been normal it would have reached the offeror in due time'. The sentence puts the burden of proof upon the offeror who fails to comply with art 21(2) to prove that there is no reasonable inference in the late acceptance that its delay in arrival was caused by an error in transmission. If the offeror ought to have known that an error in transmission caused the delay, but failed to comply with art 21(2), he or she will be held liable under a contract formed on the basis of the offer and late acceptance, regardless of whether the offeror intended to be bound by the late acceptance. This appears to be a penalty the offeror has to pay for his or her failure to discharge the burden of proof adequately under art 21(2). This is perhaps the reason for the existence of the contrary presumptions under art 21(1) and (2).

Conclusion of contract

[2.59] Under art 23, a contract is concluded at the moment when the acceptance of an offer becomes effective in accordance with arts 18, 19(2) and 21. In *Societe Fauba v Societe Fujitsu* [1996] UNLEX (22 April 1992, Court of Appeal of Paris (15th Division), CLOUT Case 158), the court held that the contract of sale between the French buyer and the German seller was concluded under art 23 when the buyer received the seller's notice that the seller had accepted the buyer's order for electronic components.

[2.60] After the formation of a contract, art 4 of the Convention becomes relevant. This provision states that the 'Convention governs only the formation of the contract of sale and the rights and obligations of the seller and the buyer arising from such a contract'. The Convention is not concerned with the validity of the contract or of any of its terms. Nor is it concerned with passing of property under the contract of sale. This means that the formation of a contract under the Convention does not necessarily lead to enforcement of the contract, if the validity of the contract or its terms are questionable under the relevant domestic law. For example, a contract appropriately formed under the Convention may be unenforceable under Australian law or Canadian law because it contravenes the public interest. Similarly, it may also be unenforceable under Chinese law for non-compliance with the requirement for contract approval and registration.

Modification or termination of contact

[2.61] After the conclusion of a contract, the parties may wish to modify the terms or terminate the contract by agreement. This frequently takes place in commercial transactions. For example, in a Swiss case involving the sale of printed chips between a German seller and a Swiss buyer, the seller sought to increase the sale price after the conclusion of the sales contract because it had realised that the production of the chips would be more costly than it expected: *Handelsgericht des Kantons Zurich* (HG 940513, 10 July 1996, CLOUT Case 193). The court disallowed the seller's action for claim for payment based on the increased price, on the ground that the seller's act amounted to a counter-offer, which had never been accepted by the buyer. What the seller did in this case was to change the original terms of the contract, which is more appropriately regarded as an offer to make a new contract rather than a counter-offer. At the time of the request, a contract of sale had been made between the seller and the buyer, which is not the situation covered by art 18 and its regulation of acceptance and counter-offers.

[2.62] The right of the parties to modify or terminate a contract is consistent with the principle of freedom of contract, and is expressly set out in art 29, which provides:
> (1) A contract may be modified or terminated by the mere agreement of the parties.
> (2) A contract in writing which contains a provision requiring any modification or termination by agreement to be in writing may not be otherwise modified or terminated by agreement. However, a

[2.62]

party may be precluded by his conduct from asserting such a provision to the extent that the other party has relied on that conduct.

[2.63] 'Mere agreement' appears to include 'agreement' in any form under this provision. However, the existence of an agreement must be determined by the court of law adjudicating the case.

In *Societe Camara Agraria Provincial de Guipuzcoa v Andre Margaron* [1995] UNLEX, (29 March 1995, Court of Appeal of Grenoble (Commercial Division), CLOUT Case 153), the Spanish buyer alleged that the parties had met after the conclusion of the contract to agree on the reduction of the contract price. The court held that the parties had met, but no agreement on the reduction of the price was made during the meeting. Accordingly, the court ordered the buyer to pay the French seller of maize the unpaid price plus interest on the sum. Interestingly, in this case at first instance, the trial court decided in the seller's favour purely under French domestic law; however, it refused to grant any interest to the seller, because no basis for such a grant existed in the relevant French law. The buyer appealed against the decision by challenging the jurisdiction of the trial court under the Convention. The Court of Appeal accepted the applicability of the Convention, but still found in the seller's favour. Consequently, the Court of Appeal added the interest payment to the compensation the seller was entitled to claim.

[2.64] Article 29(2) purports to regulate the formalities for the modification and termination of a contract. It also appears to allow a party to prove the existence of an 'agreement' on the basis of misrepresentation, 'estoppel' or 'unconscionable conduct', for the purpose of modifying or terminating a contract orally or by conduct, despite the fact that the contract specifies that the contract can only be modified or terminated in writing. However, the use of art 29(2) for this purpose is difficult.

In *Graves Import Co Ltd v Chilewich Intl Corp* 1994 US Dist Lexis 13393, decided on 22 September 1994, the US buyer attempted to argue the oral amendment to the written contract under art 29(2). However, the court held that the buyer had been precluded from asserting the existence of an oral modification under art 29(2) because the contract expressly required any amendment to be made in writing.

Fundamental breach under the Convention

Flexible meaning of 'fundamental breach'

[2.65] The meaning of 'fundamental breach' under the Convention can be understood in two ways:

- First, as in most provisions of the Convention, the parties are able to define the meaning of 'fundamental breach' in their contract. This can be done by defining a situation in which a contract can be avoided as a result of the other party's breach, or by defining a situation in which the breach of a term will give the innocent party the right to terminate the contract.

- Second, in the absence of the parties' own definition of a 'fundamental breach', art 25 of the Convention applies. In such cases, the definition of a 'fundamental breach' will be relied upon to determine the operation of arts 49 and 64, which allow the innocent party to avoid a contract on the ground of a fundamental breach.

We will examine the meaning of a fundamental breach under art 25 below.

Fundamental breach under art 25

[2.66] 'Fundamental breach' is not a new term at common law,[21] although the case law has not shown a great deal of consistency in the use of this expression.[22] In general, we can say that a fundamental breach at common law means a breach of a fundamental term. 'Fundamental terms' are terms of fundamental significance to the validity of a contract and the obligations of the parties. A breach of such terms will give the innocent party the right to terminate the contract. On the other hand, 'fundamental breach' may be given a totally different meaning by a person trained in the civil law tradition.

For example, in a case arbitrated by the Russian Federation Chamber of Commerce and Industry (Case No 123/1992, 17 October 1995, CLOUT Case 142), the Russian buyer raised an argument of fundamental breach on the ground that the Swiss seller delivered the goods (chocolate confectionery products) to the buyer before the buyer transmitted the bank's guarantee to the seller as agreed by the parties. The bank's guarantee against the buyer's performance was provided in favour of the seller. In the view of someone trained in the common law tradition, a breach of this term by the seller could hardly be described as a fundamental breach, because it is virtually impossible for the buyer to claim any damage for such breach. However, the Russian tribunal did not question the rationale of this argument. Instead, it held that the buyer could not rely on the alleged breach because it had taken delivery of the chocolates. In addition, the tribunal observed that the buyer had not suffered any loss or damage from the alleged breach. Consequently, the tribunal ordered the buyer to pay for the chocolates.

This case illustrates the difficulties for the interpretation of art 25 in different countries, or under different legal traditions. Another tribunal in the same circumstances might have disposed of the allegation of fundamental breach by pointing out that, first, the buyer needs to prove the substantial detriment caused by the alleged breach; and, second, the buyer needs to know that the term concerned is fundamental to the interest of the seller in most cases, and that it should not be relied on by the buyer unless its fundamental interest to the buyer can be established.

[2.67] 'Fundamental breach' is defined in art 25 of the Convention, which provides as follows:

> A breach of contract committed by one of the parties is fundamental if it results in such detriment to the other party as substantially to deprive him of what he is entitled to expect under the contract,

---

21. In *Nissho Iwai Australia Ltd v Malaysian International Shipping Corporation* (1988) 12 NSWLR 730 at 734–6, Kirby P briefly reviewed the history of the 'doctrine of fundamental breach' (whatever it means) at common law and concluded (at 734) that 'there was no overt dispute that the flirtation of the common law with the so-called "doctrine" of "fundamental breach" of contract is now over'.
22. For example, in *Suisse Atlantique Société d'Armement Maritime SA v NV Rotterdamsche Kolen Centrale* [1967] 1 AC 361, the expression describes a breach that gives rise to a right to terminate a contract; but in *Direct Acceptance Finance Ltd v Cumberland Furnishing Pty Ltd* [1965] NSWR 1504, the expression is applied to a breach of an intermediate term, a breach of which does not always give rise to a right to terminate a contract.

unless the party in breach did not foresee and a reasonable person of the same kind in the same circumstances would not have foreseen such a result.

[2.68] This provision tells us at least three things about the meaning of 'fundamental breach' as defined in the Convention:

- First, a fundamental breach is determined by looking at the result of the breach, rather than the nature of the term breached. There is no need to distinguish a 'fundamental term' from, for example, an 'intermediate term', a 'definitional term', a 'procedural term', or a 'warranty'. A fundamental breach should be determined under art 25 by examining whether the innocent party has been 'substantially' deprived of interests and rights which he or she can legitimately expect to have under the contract concerned. This means that an objective test, rather than a subjective test, must be adopted to establish a fundamental breach under the Convention. However, it is yet to be seen what amounts to a 'substantial deprivation' of the innocent party's contractual interest and benefit in the application of art 25.

    For example, in *Marques Roque, Ioaquim v SARL Holding Manin Riviere* [1996] UNLEX, (26 April 1995, Court of Appeal of Grenoble (Commercial Division), CLOUT Case 152), the court agreed that part of the metal elements of a dismantled warehouse were not fit for the specific purpose of re-assembling the warehouse in Portugal, a purpose expressly made known to the French seller by the Portuguese buyer. However, the court held that the defect in the metal elements could be repaired, and that, accordingly, there was no fundamental breach under art 25. In a German case, *Oberlandesgericht Frankfurt a M* (5 U164/90, 17 September 1991, CLOUT Case 2), the court held that the Italian seller's breach of an obligation to supply specific shoes to the German buyer had amounted to a fundamental breach under art 25. This decision can be compared to another German case, *Landegericht Frankfurt a M* (3/11 O 3/91, 16 September 1991, CLOUT Case 6). In that case, the German buyer discovered that it was not the exclusive retailer of the shoes known as 'Esclusiva su B', and returned the remaining 100 pairs to the Italian seller after having sold 20 pairs. The court held that the buyer was not entitled to avoid the contract on the ground of the seller's breach of the term on exclusive dealing, because the seller did not have knowledge of the act of its business partner and commercial agent, who was not in a close relationship with the seller. The rationale of this decision is questionable, in the sense that it reduces the level of the seller's responsibility in honouring contractual obligations.

- Second, the definition of 'fundamental breach' under art 25 is qualified by the requirement that the detrimental effect of the breach must be foreseeable by the breaching party. This means that a substantial deprivation of the innocent party's interest and benefit under the contract does not amount to a fundamental breach if the party in breach did not foresee or ought not to have foreseen the potentially detrimental effect of the breach at the time it was committed (or, arguably, at the time of contract). This qualification introduces a mental element into the concept of fundamental breach under the Convention. This suggests that art 25 is 'guilt-based', and the right to terminate a contract on the ground of the art 25 definition is available only when the extent of the detriment was foreseen or foreseeable by the breaching party at the time of the breach (or of the contract).

- Third, art 25 appears to require an ability to foresee the extent of the detriment flowing from a breach. It follows that a party might deliberately breach a contract, but nevertheless not be able to foresee, or ought not to be able to foresee, the extent of the damage, because the term breached is not 'fundamental' or 'essential'. There is a possibility that a party might deliberately breach a non-fundamental term of the contract, expecting the other party to suffer only insignificantly, because of the nature of the terms breached; however, the effect might turn out to be so serious that the other party suffers substantially as a result of circumstances that the party in breach did not foresee or ought not to have reasonably foreseen. The fundamental breach will not be established in such circumstances, even if the innocent party has been substantially deprived of his or her interest and right under the contract. This possibility raises a doubt about the rationale underlying the requirement for 'foreseeability' under art 25.

[2.69] Article 25 does not expressly state the time at which this requirement of foreseeability applies. It is not clear whether it refers to what the breaching party foresaw or ought to have foreseen at the time of the conclusion of the contract, or to what was foreseen or ought to have been foreseen by the breaching party at the time of the breach. It is not yet clear whether the expression 'a reasonable person of the same kind in the same circumstances' is capable of being applied both to foreseeability when the contract was made, and to foreseeability when the breach was committed.

History of art 25

[2.70] The concept of fundamental breach in the Convention was based on a proposal from Denmark in 1951.[23] The expression 'fundamental breach of an obligation' was intended to replace the expression 'breach of a fundamental obligation' for the purpose of preserving the contract where the term breached is fundamental, but the damage is nominal. This explains why the seriousness of the breach, rather than the nature of the term breached, is the key to the interpretation of 'fundamental breach' in art 25.

[2.71] The concept of 'detriment' and, in particular, of 'substantial detriment', was proposed by the Mexicans in 1975 for the purpose of seeking a more objective, rather than subjective, test for determining the severity of a breach.[24] The concept was developed into the present form of art 25, which particularises 'such detriment' as substantially depriving the innocent party of 'what he is entitled to expect under the contract'. This is why we say that a fundamental breach under art 25 is determined by the degree of the damage (detriment) incurred, rather than the nature of the term which itself indicates the 'severity' of its breach.

Foreseeability and the reasonable person test

[2.72] Foreseeability, or the mental requirement for a fundamental breach in art 25, can only be explained as a mysterious and puzzling compromise between the common law tradition and other legal traditions. Foreseeability is a common law concept. Common law appears to say that foreseeability is the foreseeability of damage at the time when the

---

23. Bianca and Bonell, 1987, p 206.
24. Ibid, p 208.

[2.72] contract is made: see *Hadley and Baxendale* (1854) 9 Exch 341 per Alderson B at 355; and *Victoria Laundry Ltd v Newman Industries Ltd* [1969] 1 AC 350 per Asquith J at 539. This point is unsettled in art 25.

[2.73] Foreseeability under art 25 can exist in two forms: actual foreseeability and presumed foreseeability. Actual foreseeability is the damage the breaching party foresaw. Presumed foreseeability is the damage the breaching party ought to have foreseen as 'a reasonable person of the same kind in the same circumstances' would have. The reasonable person test was introduced into art 25 for the purpose of developing a more objective criterion for determining the detriment of a fundamental breach.[25] However, the irony is that the application of this test involves more subjective than objective considerations. While foreseeability is supposed to reflect the mental state of the party in breach, it is not always able to reflect his or her real mental state. It is argued that, in the application of art 25, the question of whether 'the breaching party actually failed to foresee that result will have to be evaluated like in the context of Article 74 of the Convention, "in the light of the facts and matters of which he then knew" '.[26]

In addition, the identification of a reasonable person of the 'same kind' in the 'same circumstances' would require the adjudicating authority to exercise a value judgment assessing the similarity of the breaching party to the 'reasonable person', and the similarity between the event relating to the breach and the circumstances in which the reasonable person of the same kind operates. This makes the choice of a reasonable person of the same kind in the same circumstances a subjective test, rather than an objective test, as was intended by the incorporation of the detrimental result provision in art 25.

[2.74] There is uncertainty in applying facts and matters which can be seen or can be reasonably assumed by others to the determination of the breaching party's ability to foresee the detriment. The mental state of the breaching party is something no other person can really see, although it has been argued that foreseeability depends on the breaching party's knowledge of the relevant circumstances.[27] It can be argued that the purpose for which the reasonable person test is brought into art 25 will probably never be satisfied, because a person's knowledge of circumstances may have been deficient for various reasons. For example:

> He himself may have been ignorant, lacking perception, experience or talent, and there may have been other personal or organisational shortcomings within his sphere of influence and responsibility. On the other hand the aggrieved party may, willing or not, have omitted to communicate his expectations or any other sensitive piece of information. Third persons may have neglected to observe and transmit crucial occurrences: information dispatched may not have arrived as in the case of a message lost in the mail. Or, even if all the necessary information has been furnished, he may have been unable to assemble the pieces, interpret and evaluate them correctly and may thus have failed to draw the proper conclusions. Whatever the reason, whoever the culprit — he simply did not know, he did not foresee![28]

---

25. Ibid, p 207.
26. Ibid, p 217.
27. Ibid.
28. Ibid.

[2.75] A dilemma has been created by the puzzling compromise between the subjective and objective tests. While a breach may be substantially detrimental, it is not a fundamental breach in art 25 if the breaching party fails to foresee the result of the breach. The dilemma is that, while a party may have been acting intentionally or negligently in carrying out the act of breach, he or she may have been unable in the circumstances to foresee the result of the breach. By the same token, while the circumstances (facts or matters) appear to be objective, the interpretation of these circumstances is subjective. Indeed, the incorporation of the reasonable person and foreseeability tests into art 25 makes the establishment of fundamental breach one of the most difficult tasks under the Convention. The onus of proof for foreseeability lies on the breaching party, whose evidence will be assessed by a court of law. This imposes the ultimate task of construing and determining the existence of a presumed foreseeability in the hands of the court.

Performance of contract

Defining performance of contract under the Convention

[2.76] Performance of a contract for the international sale of goods involves the same issues as performance of a contract for domestic sale. We have to deal with the duties and rights of the buyer and seller, the delivery of goods and the passing of property and risk, among other issues. However, in an international sale, the interests of third parties such as carriers, agents and 'sub-buyers' (persons who obtain a document of title, bill of lading or delivery order from the original buyer to the contract, such as endorsees or consignees) may be involved. For example, a seller and a buyer may enter into a contract for the sale of goods under a CIF term. The seller (shipper) will then enter into a contract for the carriage of the goods with a carrier for the purpose of transporting the goods to the buyer. The carrier will issue a bill of lading to the shipper after the goods are placed on board the specified vessel. The bill of lading evidences the existence of a 'contract of carriage' between the shipper and the carrier, but may not itself be a contract between them. The seller will then indorse the bill of lading and send it to the buyer. When the buyer presents the bill of lading to the carrier, the bill of lading becomes a contract of carriage between the carrier and the buyer, although they themselves have not directly and voluntarily entered into any contract. The performance of the original contract of sale between the seller and buyer is dependent upon the performance of the contract of carriage between the buyer and the carrier. This is why we sometimes have to examine the relevant interests of third parties in determining the performance of an international contract.

If we look carefully at the above example, we can see that we are talking about 'contracts' rather than 'contract'. The whole transaction involves several, separate but interdependent contracts, and the duties and rights of contracting parties to one particular contract may be affected by the performance of contractual obligations under another contract, although the rights and duties of the parties can only be enforced under the respective contracts. Accordingly, we must bear in mind that, when we talk about the performance of a contract in this chapter, we are referring to the performance of the

[2.76] contract between the original seller and the original buyer. The related contracts — such as the contract between the seller or buyer and their agents (if there are agents), the contract between the seller and carrier, the contracts between the buyer and subsequent buyers, and the contract between an insurer and an insured — are relevant to the performance of the main contract.

[2.77] Such a mixed contractual relationship is seen in a French case, *Enterprise Alain Veyron v Societe E Ambrosio* [1996] UNLEX (26 April 1995, CLOUT Case 151).

In that case, an Italian company and a French individual had a commercial collaboration contract, under which the French individual was the sole representative and importer of confectionery exported to France by the Italian company. The Italian company broke off the agreement. The French individual sued under the Convention for a breach of contract. The Court of Appeal found that the agreement consisted of two parts — the sale of confectionery and arrangements on representation — and held that the part of the agreement on sale was subject to the Convention. Furthermore, the court discovered the existence of a contractual clause which stated that the contract was revocable at will by the Italian company, and held that the Italian company was entitled to break the contract. This case illustrates two points: first, the Convention may apply to a severable part of a contract which pertains to an international sale falling under the scope of the Convention; and, second, a contract may define the right of the parties to exclude the operation of art 25. Otherwise, the French party in this case would have been able to rely on art 25 to establish a fundamental breach on the part of the Italian party.

[2.78] The CISG only deals with contracts between buyers and sellers from two different countries. The provisions concerning performance of contracts under the Convention deal only with the performance of contracts by the buyer or seller. Therefore, if a contract of sale incorporates Incoterms 2000, the liabilities of the parties under such a contract must be interpreted in the combined light of the Incoterms and the relevant provisions of the Convention. In the case of inconsistency between Incoterms 2000 and the provisions of the Convention, the Incoterms will prevail because the incorporation of an Incoterm should be treated as an express agreement of the parties to modify the effect of the relevant provisions of the Convention.

Performance of the seller's obligations

What are the seller's obligations?

[2.79] The seller has two basic obligations under the Convention:

- to deliver the goods and documents in accordance with the contract: arts 30–4; and
- to guarantee the conformity of the goods with the contract: arts 35–44.

For both obligations, the terms of the contract form the basis for assessing whether the obligation has been appropriately performed. However, certain provisions of the Convention do impose implied obligations which can be incorporated into a contract of sale automatically, unless expressly excluded by the parties. That is why art 30 states that the 'seller must deliver the goods, hand over any documents relating to them and transfer the property in the goods, as required by the contract and this Convention'; and art 35 provides that the 'seller must deliver goods which are of the quantity, quality and description required by the contract and which are contained or packaged in the manner required by the contract'.

[2.80] The seller's obligations under various provisions of the Convention are sometimes balanced by the court adjudicating a dispute, resulting in variations in the interpretation of certain provisions of the Convention.

For example, in a German case, *Bundesgerichtshof* (VIII ZR 51/95, 3 April 1996, CLOUT Case 171), the Dutch seller and the German buyer agreed in their contract that the goods, cobalt sulphate, should be of British origin and accompanied by certificates of origin and quality. The buyer avoided the contract on the ground that the cobalt sulphate was made in South Africa and that the certificate was wrong. In addition, the buyer alleged that the quality of the goods was inferior to that agreed in the contract. If the buyer could prove these allegations, the seller should be found to have breached its obligations under arts 30 and 35 of the Convention. However, the German court did not pay much attention to the terms of the contract. Instead, it examined the buyer's right to avoid the contract under art 49(1), and concluded that the buyer was not entitled to avoid the contract under art 49(1) because the alleged breaches were not fundamental under art 25.

The court took the view that the buyer had not established that it was substantially deprived of any right by the delivery of cobalt sulphate of South African origin. In addition, the court held that the delivery of the wrong certificate might be remedied by the seller, by delivering the correct one. The court's interpretation of a fundamental breach in this case was rather narrow because, if the buyer's allegations were true, the seller had obviously breached art 35(2)(b), which requires the supply of particular goods to be fit for a specific purpose. In addition, the court's understanding of the defect in the certificate was dubious, in the sense that the contract was intended to require the seller to provide a certificate to prove the British origin of the cobalt sulphate. If the cobalt sulphate was not made in the UK, any certificate indicating that it was made in the UK would amount to a fraud. On the other hand, if the certificate had indicated that the cobalt sulphate was made in South Africa, it would amount to a breach of the express term of the contract. This case suggests that sometimes the preference given by a court to a particular provision may substantially affect the result of a dispute.

The seller's obligations concerning the place of delivery

[2.81] The place of delivery is essential to effect a delivery: it is the location where property and risk in the goods may pass to the buyer (although the Convention does not deal with passing of property). The place of delivery is sometimes regarded as the principal place of performance, which is important for determining the appropriate jurisdiction of the court under art 5(1) of the Brussels Convention.[29] The place for delivery must be

---

29. For example, in *Societe Mode jeune diffusion v Societe Maglificio il Falco di Tiziana Goti e Fabio Goti and Others*, (2 December 1997, Court of Cassation (1st Civil Division), CLOUT Case 207), the French buyer relied on the choice-of-forum clause in the order to submit the dispute to the French court, while the Italian seller relied on the choice-of-forum clause in the invoices to deny the jurisdiction of the French court in favour of the Italian court. The French court applied art 5(1) of the Brussels Convention and art 31 of the Convention to move the matter to the Italian court.

[2.81] International Commercial Law

unambiguous and acceptable to both parties. While the parties can always define the place for delivery in the contract of sale (for example, by adopting an Incoterm), art 31 sets out the following rules for ascertaining the place of delivery:

- First, if the contract of sale involves the carriage of goods by sea, land or air, in the absence of any express agreement the seller is obliged to deliver the goods only to the first carrier. This means that if the buyer intends to change the effect of art 67, which governs the transfer of risk in goods, he or she must enter an agreement with the seller to specify the place for delivery — which has a direct impact upon the transfer of risk under the Convention. In addition, the parties must agree expressly if they intend the property and risk in goods to pass to the buyer at a particular place.

- Second, if the contract of sale involves specific goods (including specific goods to be manufactured in the future and goods yet to be identified from specific stock), in the absence of any express agreement otherwise, the place of delivery is the place where, to the knowledge of the parties, the goods were or will be. This presumed place of delivery is qualified by the knowledge of the parties at the time of the contract, which means that both parties must have known of the place of the specific goods at the time of the contract. Under art 31(b), the seller's obligation to deliver is an obligation to place the goods at the buyer's disposal, at the location where the goods are to be manufactured, unless the parties agree otherwise. This suggests that art 31(b) is based on a presumption that, by omission (omitting to specify a place for delivery), the parties intend to let the buyer take delivery of the goods at the place where the goods were kept (or, as known to the parties, will be kept) at the time of the conclusion of the contract. In a German case, *Landgericht Aachen* (43 0 136/92, 14 May 1993, CLOUT Case 47), the court applied art 31 and decided that Aachen, where the goods had been manufactured, was the place where the seller was obliged to deliver the goods concerned.

- Third, in cases which do not fall into the above two situations, in the absence of any express agreement otherwise, the place of delivery is the place where the seller had his or her place of business at the time when the contract was made. Under art 31(3), the buyer is required to take delivery of the goods from the place where the seller's place of business is located, unless the parties specify another place for delivery. It must be pointed out that, under art 31(3), if the seller changes the place of business after the conclusion of the contract, the place of delivery is the place where the seller's business was at the time when the contract was made. The seller's place of business is determined by arts 1(3) and 10.

[2.82] Although it is likely that the expression 'delivery' would be construed as physical delivery of goods under the Convention, there is a possibility that delivery may be given a different meaning by a court where the Convention is silent. For example, in *Gamer's Motor Centre (Newcastle) Pty Ltd v Natwest Wholesale Australia Pty Ltd* (1987) 163 CLR 236; 72 ALR 321, the High Court of Australia was divided 4:1 as to whether delivery under s 28 of the Sale of Goods Act 1923 (NSW) includes 'constructive delivery'.

This case also raised the question as to whether 'delivery' in other sections of the Act could also be 'constructive'. The argument against the extension of *Gamer's* case to a situation in which the seller sells the goods to the buyer is that a change of physical possession of the goods is what the parties really intended. By contrast, we may perhaps argue that, legalistically, there is no reason to say that constructive delivery can apply to a transfer of goods by a non-owner on the one hand, but not to a transfer of goods by a true owner on the other. This is because in both cases the buyer does not always want to have physical possession of the goods immediately (for example, a sale of goods in transit under art 38 of the Convention), and constructive delivery thus becomes necessary.

The seller's obligations concerning the time for delivery

[2.83] Time for delivery determines when the goods pass from the seller to the buyer. The property and risk in the goods usually pass from the seller to the buyer at the time of delivery.

[2.84] Article 33 of the Convention sets out rules for determining the time of delivery. Three conditions are stipulated:

- First, if a particular date is fixed by, or determinable from, the contract of sale, the goods must be delivered on that date.

- Second, if a period of time is fixed by, or determinable from, the contract, the goods can be delivered at any time within that period, unless 'circumstances' indicate that the buyer is to choose a date within that period of time. The term 'circumstances' is not defined in the Convention. It certainly includes the intention of the parties and the terms of the contract, and probably extends to the usage, customs and practices established in the trade or the course of dealings between the parties. It also possibly extends to any indication or facts which may suggest the parties' intention to allow the buyer to choose a date. Article 33(b) must be read together with art 37, which allows the seller to remedy any defects in the goods before the date for delivery.

- Third, if a date or a period of time is neither fixed nor determinable in the contract, the goods must be delivered within a reasonable time after the conclusion of the contract. What constitutes a 'reasonable time' is to be determined in the circumstances involved, taking into account the nature of the goods and the customs, usage and practices established in the trade and by the course of dealings between the parties. Although there is certainly a possibility that the meaning of 'reasonable time' may vary from one legal tradition to another, any such variation would be affected by and based on the relevant local customs and usage. This suggests a certain degree of predictability and stability in determining the reasonableness of the time for delivery under art 33.

[2.85] In a common law jurisdiction, the common law determines what is considered a reasonable time for delivery. Factors or considerations which may be taken into account are, inter alia:

- the terms of a contract in relation to delivery: see *Picturesque Atlas Co Ltd v Searle* (1892) 18 VLR 633 (discussed in **[1.67]**), and *Schureck v McFarlane* (1923) 41 WN (NSW) 3;

- the necessary time and manner in which the goods can be produced and delivered: see *Lyon v Creati* (1892) 18 VLR 629 and *Bacon v Purcell* (1916) 22 CLR 307; and

[2.85]

- if there is a delay, whether the parties knew the cause of the delay and whether the seller has been diligent in overcoming the cause of delay: see *Piesse v Tasmanian Orchardists and Producers Co-operative Association Ltd* (1919) 15 Tas LR 67.

[2.86] Given the indefinite nature of the circumstances where deliveries occur, 'reasonable time' boils down to the meaning of 'reasonableness' in any given case. This often involves the so-called 'reasonable person test'; namely, what a reasonable person would do or would consider to be adequate and reasonable in the same circumstances.

The seller's obligation to give notice on consignment of goods

[2.87] The Convention does not distinguish between specific goods and unascertained goods in the same way as the sale of goods legislation in Australia, Canada, Hong Kong, New Zealand or the UK. This is because the Convention is not concerned with the passing of property in the goods.

Although art 32(1) does not require the seller to identify or ascertain the goods for the purpose of delivery, the combined effect of arts 32(1) and 67(2) (which provides that risk in goods does not pass to the buyer unless the seller has done something to enable the buyer to identify the goods) suggests that the seller will have to identify the goods sufficiently under the Convention for the purpose of making a delivery. It follows that, under art 32(1), the seller has the option of either identifying or marking the goods clearly according to the contract, or giving 'the buyer notice of the consignment specifying the goods', if he or she has not marked the goods physically or identified them specifically in the shipping documents. The provision may apply to a situation where non-specific or identical goods (such as rice of a certain description) are shipped on board a vessel for several buyers who will receive different (or the same) quantities of the rice on board the vessel. In such a case, a written note specifying the quantity of the goods will be sufficient to effect the delivery.

[2.88] Under art 67(2), giving notice to the buyer to specify the consignment of the goods is regarded as having the same effect as clearly marking the goods or describing the goods in shipping documents for the passing of risk. This means that art 32(1) imposes a general duty upon the seller to identify or mark the goods clearly, or to describe the goods clearly in the shipping documents or in the notice to the buyer. The purpose of these acts is to enable the buyer to identify the goods upon delivery.

The seller's obligation to enter a contract of carriage

[2.89] Article 32(2) provides that if the seller is liable to arrange for carriage of the goods, as is the case in a contract of sale based on the CIF, CPT, or CIP terms (see **[1.23]–[1.25]**), the seller has an obligation to make a contract of carriage. The contract of carriage must be in such terms as are appropriate for transporting the goods to the agreed destination. This means that the seller is responsible for choosing the most suitable means and route of transport, and for the price for transporting the goods to the buyer, although the delivery is deemed to take place according to the relevant Incoterm. Whether a contract of sale arranged by the seller is 'appropriate' should be determined in the circumstances concerned, taking into account the nature of the goods, relevant trade usage, previous dealings between the parties, the distance of transport and, in some circumstances, the market demand for the goods.

[2.90] Article 32(2) will often be modified or overridden if any of the Incoterms is adopted in the contract of sale, because they set out in detail, when necessary, the seller's duty to make a contract of carriage.

Article 32(2) is similar to the seller's duty to make an adequate contract of carriage under the sale of goods legislation: see **[1.68]**.

The seller's obligation to facilitate insurance

[2.91] Insurance of the goods in transit is very important for international sales of goods. All the Incoterms state clearly (whenever applicable) which party has an obligation to insure the goods. Article 32(3) requires the seller to assist the buyer in insuring the goods, even though the seller is not obliged to insure the goods under the contract of sale. This provision states that if the seller does not have an obligation to insure the goods, as is the case in a contract based on the FCA or FOB terms (see **[1.17]** and **[1.21]**), the seller still has an obligation to provide the necessary information about insurance if the buyer so requests, unless the incorporation of the terms can be regarded as a modification of art 32(3).[30] It must be pointed out that the seller's obligation to provide such information is subject to the buyer's request. Therefore, the seller has not breached art 32(3) if the uninsured goods are lost or damaged because the buyer, who has not requested the seller to provide the necessary information, failed to insure them.

Incoterms 2000 will override this provision if the term incorporated into the contract sets out detailed rules for insurance.

[2.92] Article 32(3) can be compared with a similar provision under the sale of goods legislation: see **[1.69]**. The seller's obligation to provide the buyer with information about the goods for insurance purposes is not subject to the buyer's request under the sale of goods legislation.

The seller's obligations to deliver documents

[2.93] The delivery of documents differs from the delivery of goods, because, in most international sales, goods and documents are delivered separately: see **[5.22]**. The delivery of documents is often part of the process of the payment of the price. Article 34 of the Convention specifically deals with the delivery of documents.

[2.94] Article 34 states that if the seller is liable to 'hand over documents relating to the goods, he must hand them over at the time and place and in the form required by the contract'. It must be pointed out that the expression 'hand over', rather than 'deliver', is used in this provision. This suggests that delivery of documents under art 34 refers to physical delivery, because the phrase 'hand them over' may not be capable of including constructive delivery.

---

30. It is arguable whether the seller can avoid his or her liability under art 32(3) on the ground of the Incoterms adopted. This is because the relevant terms may simply say that the seller has no obligation to insure the goods. This may not be construed as saying that the seller is not liable to provide information because he or she is not liable to insure the goods.

[2.95] Article 34 sets out the requirements for handing documents over, requiring the seller to hand the documents over 'at the time and place and in the form required by the contract'. It may be argued that if the contract of sale does not clearly specify the time or place for handing over the documents, the seller should have an implied obligation to hand the documents over at a time and place appropriate to the terms of the contract. For example, if the method of payment under the contract of sale is a 'bill of exchange' (see **[5.27]**), the place would probably be the place where the bill of exchange is paid and the time would probably be the time at which the bill is paid. Similarly, if the method of payment is a 'letter of credit' (see **[5.8]**), the place would probably be the buyer's place of business and the time would probably be a time immediately after the shipment of the goods.

[2.96] Article 34 allows the seller to cure any defect in the documents already delivered before the agreed time for delivery. The buyer is obliged to allow the seller to do so unless the exercise of this right by the seller would cause the buyer 'unreasonable inconvenience or unreasonable expense'. This is the standard term for the exercise of the right to self-cure under the Convention: see art 37. The right to cure defects in the documents will effectively take away the buyer's right to terminate the contract of sale on the ground of non-conformity of the documents, in certain circumstances. But the right to cure defects in any document benefits the buyer more than it does the seller. This is because, in an international transaction, the documents of title are usually delivered (or handed over) against payment of the price. This means that, at the time when the defect in a document is discovered, the buyer would probably have paid, or have undertaken a liability to pay, for the document.[31] If the defect is not cured, the buyer would have practical difficulties in claiming the goods under the document. The buyer would be better off allowing the seller to remedy any defect in the document.

[2.97] Under art 34, regardless of whether or not the buyer allows the seller to cure the defect in the document delivered, he or she is entitled to claim damages for any losses incurred because of the defective document. The same rule is adopted in all the provisions which recognise the right of self-cure.

The seller's obligation and title to sell in general

[2.98] The Convention does not clearly address the *nemo dat* rule (the rule that, in brief, no-one can sell or give what he or she does not own), although the rule can reasonably be assumed to be universal. Article 41 imposes a general duty that goods delivered must be 'free from any right or claim of third party' upon the seller. It can be assumed that 'a title to sell' in this context is the same as that in a common law jurisdiction, such as Australia, including a right to sell, a right to enjoy quiet possession and a right to receive the goods free from unknown charges or encumbrance on the goods: see *Niblett Ltd v Confectioners' Materials Co Ltd* [1921] 3 KB 387 and **[1.74]**. Under art 41, the buyer may waive his or her right to receive goods which are free from any right or claim of a third party, by agreeing to take the goods subject to the existing right or claim. Such consent

---

31. It is rare in an international sale for a buyer to be allowed to have possession of the documents of title without having paid or undertaken to pay the price of the goods.

can be given at the time when the contract is concluded or at any time before or after the goods are delivered.

The seller's obligation and title to sell intellectual property

[2.99] The Convention sets out special rules dealing with the seller's title with respect to intellectual property. Article 42 provides the following rules:

- The seller must guarantee the goods to be free from any third party's claim based on industrial or intellectual property. (*Niblett Ltd v Confectioners' Materials Co Ltd* [1921] 3 KB 387 would have fallen under this provision if it had been subject to the Convention.)
- This obligation is based on either an actual or a presumed knowledge of the seller at the time when the contract is made. This means the seller does not breach art 42 if he or she can prove that, at the time of the conclusion of the contract, he or she neither knew nor ought to have known of the possibility of the third party's claim.
- The third party's claim under art 42 should be a claim under the law of the state where the goods were contemplated to be sold or to be used at the time when the contract was concluded.
- The third party's claim under art 42 can also be a claim under the law of the state where the buyer has his or her place of business.
- Article 42 is not breached if the buyer knew or ought to have known of the possibility of the claim at the time of the conclusion of the contract.
- Article 42 is not breached if the claim 'results from the seller's compliance with technical drawings, designs, formulae or other such specifications furnished by the buyer'.

[2.100] This provision specifies that any third party's claim under art 42 must be a claim made under the law of the state for which the goods are destined or where the buyer has his or her place of business. It holds the seller liable for any breach of a law governing intellectual property in the place where the goods are sold or used. Such a specification is necessary because of the differences between, and territorial operation of, the laws on industrial or intellectual property in different countries. In general, art 42 requires the seller to ensure that the buyer's right to sell or to use the goods will not be disturbed or restrained, without the knowledge of the buyer, by any claim based on industrial or intellectual property under the law of the state within which the goods are intended to be sold or used.

Limitation on action based on breach of title

[2.101] In order to encourage commercial expedience and speedy performance of a contract of sale, art 43, like art 39, requires the buyer to notify the seller as soon as possible of any breach of title to sell under arts 41 and 42. Article 43 sets out time limitations on the buyer's right to rely on arts 41 and 42. Article 43 has the following elements:

- the buyer must give notice to the seller within a reasonable time after the buyer knows or ought to have known of the existence of a third party's claim based on industrial or intellectual property in the goods sold;[32]

[2.101]

- the notice must specify the nature of the third party's claim or right;
- there is no maximum limitation period of two years for making a claim against the seller, as set out in art 39(2); but
- there is a proviso that the seller cannot rely on the benefit of the limitation under art 43 if he or she knew or ought to have known of both the possibility and the nature of the third party's claim.[33]

[2.102] 'Reasonable time' is not defined in this provision. Again, the circumstances of the case — such as the nature of the claim, the likely success of the claim, the requirements of domestic law for dealing with such a claim, any trade usage, any previous dealings between the parties and the reliability of the communications between the parties, among other factors — should be taken into consideration.

Meaning of 'conformity of the goods' under the Convention

[2.103] 'Conformity of the goods' does not always mean conformity with the express terms of a contract, because the Convention imposes a general duty upon the seller (effectively imposing implied terms on the contract) as to the fitness, quality, quantity and conformity of the goods with the description or sample, unless the parties have expressly agreed otherwise. Conformity of the goods means not only conformity with the explicit or implicit terms of a contract, but also conformity with the 'implied terms' of art 35 (although the Convention has not adopted this expression).

[2.104] Unlike the sale of goods legislation in Australia, England, New Zealand and Hong Kong, the Convention does not clearly distinguish between fitness for purpose, merchantable quality, conformity with description or sample, and conformity with contract quantity. It appears that, in the absence of an express description in the contract or the Convention, the domestic constructions of 'merchantable quality', 'fitness for purpose', 'correspondence with description' and 'conformity with sample' should be taken into account in the application of art 35 in common law jurisdictions.

[2.105] The German Supreme Court was asked in 1995 to determine a case involving the sale of New Zealand mussels by a Swiss seller to a German buyer: *Bundesgerichtshof* (VIII ZR 159/94, 4 March 1995, CLOUT Case 123). The mussels could be sold in many other countries, but could not be sold in Germany because their cadmium concentration exceeded the limit recommended by the German health authority. The buyer alleged that the existence of a higher level of cadmium concentration constituted a breach of art 35 on the ground of non-conformity. The court took the view that the cadmium concentration

---

32. Article 43 does not make it clear whether the reasonable time begins to run from the time when the buyer knew or ought to have known of the existence of the claim, or from the time when the claim is made. It appears to be more reasonable that the time should begin to run from the time when the buyer realised or ought to have realised the existence of the claim.
33. It is unclear whether art 43(2) requires the seller to know of the possibility of the claim or the existence of the claim. There is a difference between possibility and existence. Given the purpose of the proviso, it seems reasonable to hold the seller liable even if he or she only knew or ought to have known of the possibility of the claim. However, the possibility in this context must be a real possibility, as opposed to a far-fetched or fanciful possibility.

itself did not make the mussels non-conforming goods under art 35, because they were edible and marketable outside Germany.

In addition, the court held that art 35 does not implicitly impose upon the seller an obligation to ensure the goods conform to all statutory or public standards of the buyer's country. According to the view of the court, the seller is obliged to comply with the special requirements of the importing country only when:

- the same requirements exist in the exporting country;
- the buyer has made the requirements known to the seller;
- the buyer has expressly relied on the special knowledge of the seller; or
- the seller has knowledge of the requirements due to the special circumstances of the case.

The views expressed by the German court in this case are quite similar to those expressed by courts of common law countries in similar circumstances.

[2.106] 'Conformity of the goods' has two meanings under art 35. Under art 35(1), when the parties to a contract expressly describe the quality, quantity, fitness and the manner or standard of packaging, 'conformity of the goods' means conformity with the terms of the contract.

Under art 35(2), when the parties have not expressly agreed on the matters set out in art 35(1), or expressly excluded guarantees of the matters specified in art 35(2), there are implied terms in the Convention to the effect that the goods must be fit for the purpose for which the goods are acquired; of such a quality as 'goods of the same description would ordinarily' be expected to be; of the same quality as the sample, if there was a sample; and packed in a reasonable manner adequate for preserving and protecting the goods. Article 35(2) imposes the implied terms as to fitness, quality, conformity with sample and adequate packaging upon the seller.

[2.107] The Convention does not set out rules on the burden of proof for establishing the conformity or non-conformity of the goods. Generally speaking, most domestic laws expect a party making an allegation or claiming a particular right to bear the burden of proof, except where a law has made a presumption to permit a party to rely on the presumption under specific conditions. The party challenging the presumption should have the burden of proof in such circumstances. In a case arbitrated by the International Court of Arbitration of the International Chamber of Commerce, the tribunal decided to search the rules on burden of proof in the relevant domestic law applicable to the dispute, which was French law.[34]

The tribunal took the view that, under art 1315 of the French Civil Code and general principles of international trade, the party alleging a lack of conformity under the Convention should bear the burden of proof. The application of the relevant domestic law, where gaps are left by the Convention, is anticipated by art 7(2).[35]

---

34. The case was decided in 1993 by the International Court of Arbitration as Case 6653; an abstract of the case is available as CLOUT Case 103 at <http://www.uncitral.org>.

[2.107] In a decision largely consistent with this case, *Societe Termo King v Societe Cigna France* (15 May 1996, Court of Appeal of Grenoble (Commercial Division), CLOUT Case 204), the French court held that a refrigeration unit had broken down within a short period of time after delivery, and thus there was a reasonable presumption that art 35 had been breached by the seller. Accordingly, the court asked the seller to prove that it was not responsible for the defect complained of. It seems that in this case the court was suggesting that, since the buyer had proven the defect of the goods, the seller had the burden of discharging its liability under art 35.

The seller's obligation and fitness for purpose

[2.108] Article 35(2)(b) imposes an implied term as to fitness for purpose upon the seller. This provision states that, in the absence of any express agreement, the seller is liable to provide goods which 'are fit for any particular purpose expressly or impliedly made known to the seller at the time of the conclusion of the contract'. The existence of this obligation under art 35(2)(b) is subject to the seller's rebuttal that 'the buyer did not rely, or that it was unreasonable for him to rely, on the seller's skill and judgment' in the circumstances concerned. This means that if the seller can prove that the buyer did not or ought not to have relied on his or her skill or judgment, the implied term as to fitness for purpose will not operate in the circumstances concerned.

[2.109] It must be pointed out that art 35(2)(b) requires the goods to be fit for the particular purpose made known to the seller. It can be argued that if any particular purpose has been communicated expressly or implicitly to the seller, the seller is liable for guaranteeing the fitness of the goods for that purpose only. It follows that art 35(2)(b) is not breached if the goods supplied are not fit for purposes which have not been expressly or implicitly made known to the seller, even if a reasonable person in the same circumstances would expect the goods to be fit for these purposes. However, contrary arguments may arise from the construction of an implicit communication of the purpose. The notion that the expectation of a reasonable person in the same circumstances can be regarded as being implied in the contract or communication between the seller and buyer, while arguable, is uncertain. The argument will have to be dealt with in the circumstances concerned, taking into account any trade usage or customs, and the business relationships established in any previous dealings between the parties.

[2.110] There are similarities between art 35(2)(b) and the relevant provisions of the consumer sales legislation in Australia, such as s 90 of the Goods Act 1958 (Vic) and s 71(2) of the Trade Practices Act 1974 (Cth). Both s 90 and s 71(2) impose a burden of proof upon the seller, requiring him or her to prove that in the circumstances concerned the buyer did not rely, or that it was unreasonable for him or her to rely, on the skill or judgment of the seller. This suggests that art (2)(b) may be construed in the light of these similar provisions in the domestic law.

---

35. Article 7(2) states that 'questions concerning matters governed by this Convention which are not expressly settled in it are to be settled in conformity with the general principles on which it is based or, in the absence of such principles, in conformity with the law applicable by virtue of the rules of private international law'.

The seller's obligation and merchantability of the goods

[2.111] Article 35(1) states that the seller must provide goods which are of the quality required by the contract. 'Quality' in this context means 'merchantable quality'. In a German case, *Landgericht Trier* (7 HO 78/95, 12 October 1995, CLOUT Case 170), the German buyer counter-claimed that a quantity of the wine provided by the Italian seller was unmerchantable, because it was mixed with 9 per cent water. As a result, the bottles containing the unmerchantable wine were seized and destroyed by the German authorities and the German buyer was charged for the costs incurred. The court held that the seller had breached art 35 in the supply of unmerchantable wine, and permitted the buyer to set off against the unpaid price of the contract.

[2.112] *Societe Française de Factoring International Factor France v Roger Caiato* (December 1995, Court of Appeal of Grenoble (Commercial Division), CLOUT Case 202), is a French case illustrating merchantable quality. In this case, the court held that the seller's failure to mark the composition of the goods on the package had rendered the goods unmerchantable under art 35.

[2.113] Article 35(2) does not expressly deal with the issue of merchantable quality. But art 35(2)(a) in fact imposes an obligation upon the seller to guarantee the merchantable quality of the goods by stating that the goods delivered must be 'fit for the purposes for which goods of the same description would ordinarily be used'. This provision was applied in a German case, *Landgericht Baden-Baden* (4 0 113/90, 14 August 1991, CLOUT Case 50), where the court held that the goods were not fit for the purpose for which goods of the same description would ordinarily be used.

It can be argued that this provision does not deal with the issue of fitness for purpose, because fitness for purpose is dealt with expressly in art 35(2)(b). Article 35(2)(a) effectively sets out the *meaning* of merchantable quality in the Convention. However, it avoids the use of the expression 'merchantable quality', which has never been given a uniform and satisfactory meaning at common law, despite the fact that the sale of goods legislation in common law countries, such as Australia, Canada, Hong Kong, New Zealand, the United Kingdom and the United States, have applied the expression for years.

[2.114] The similarity between art 35(2)(a) and the implied term as to merchantable quality at common law has been discussed by Honnold, who observes as follows:

> ... [the] basic standard in paragraph (2)(a) is similar to the warranty of 'merchantable quality' developed in early English case law incorporated in the Sale of Goods Act (1893). However, the meaning of 'merchantable quality' was left to case law. The basic ideas developed by the cases were used by the (USA) Uniform Commercial Code in defining 'merchantable quality'. Under Section 2-314(2), 'goods to be merchantable' must be '(a) pass without objection in the trade under the contract *description*' and '(c) are fit for the ordinary purposes for which *such* goods are used'.[36]

---

36. Honnold, *Uniform Law for International Sales under the 1980 United Nations Convention*, 2nd ed, Kluwer, Deventer, 1991, pp 304–5.

[2.115] It appears that art 35(2)(a) is narrower than the implied term as to merchantable quality at common law, which will hold goods unmerchantable if:

- they lack an adequate warning as to their danger to potential customers: see *Hardwick Game Farm v Suffolk Agricultural Poultry Producers Association* [1969] 2 AC 31;
- their appearance is damaged: see *International Business Machines Co v Shcherban* [1925] 1 DLR 864 and *Silbert Sharpe & Bishop Ltd v George Wills & Co Ltd* [1919] SALR 114; or
- they satisfy some purpose for which the goods can be used but the buyer is willing to pay only a discounted price for them because of the defect in them: see *Australian Knitting Mills Ltd v Grant* (1933) 50 CLR 387.

In contrast, the seller will be regarded as having fulfilled his or her obligation under art 35(2)(a) if the goods delivered 'are fit for the purposes for which goods of the same description would ordinarily be used'.

[2.116] It is unclear under art 35(2)(a) whether the goods must be fit for 'all the purposes' or only one or some of the purposes for which the goods of the same description are normally used. If the goods are required to be fit for one or some of the purposes only, the test of art 35(2)(a) will certainly be lower than the requirement that the goods must be fit for all the purposes. In light of common law practices, the matter must be determined by referring to the contract description concerned. The goods may be found to be merchantable under a contract description even if they do not satisfy all the purposes for which the goods were acquired: see *Sumner Permain & Co v Webb & Co* [1922] 1 KB 55, where tonic water was saleable but for the contravention of an Argentine law which, unknown to both the seller and the buyer, prohibited the use of a substance in the tonic water. On the other hand, the common law holds that a buyer is entitled to expect the goods delivered to be fit for *all* purposes for which the goods of the contract description are expected to be used: see *McNeill & Higgins Co v Czarnikow-Rienda Co* (1921) 274 F 397 and *Harris v Plymouth Varnish & Colour Co Ltd* (1933) 49 TLR 521.

[2.117] There is also another possible disagreement about the interpretation of the meaning of the term 'purposes' in art 35(2)(a). The question is whether the purposes for which the goods are acquired should be assessed by reference to the purposes which are acceptable in the seller's place of business, or the purposes which are acceptable in the buyer's place of business, or in the place where the goods are destined to be used.[37] The purposes for which the goods are acquired may differ in the seller's and buyer's countries. The argument supporting the seller's place of business is based on the proposition that it is not reasonable to require the seller to know the purposes for which the goods are acquired in another country.[38] The argument in favour of the buyer's place of distribution may be based on the proposition that the fact that the buyer is in a particular country requires the seller to provide goods which are fit for the purposes in that country. Bearing in mind the existence of art 35(2)(b), it seems reasonable to assume that the ordinary purposes are the purposes established in the seller's place of business, because the buyer could be protected in art 35(2)(b) by making the 'purpose' in a particular country known

---

37. Bianca and Bonell, 1987, pp 274–5.
38. Ibid, p 274.

to the seller. Of course, the parties can always define their requirements and understanding of the quality of the goods in the contract of sale to avoid possible disagreements in the construction of art 35(2)(a).

The seller's obligation concerning conformity of the goods with a sample

[2.118] Under art 35(2)(c), conformity with a sample actually means that the goods must 'possess the qualities of goods which the seller has held out to the buyer as a sample or model'. The meaning of 'the qualities' is, however, unclear. Does this expression refer only to 'merchantable quality'; or does it also extend to the implied condition set out, for example, in s 20(2)(c) of the Sale of Goods Act 1923 (NSW), that 'the goods shall be free from any defect rendering them unmerchantable which would not be apparent on reasonable examination of the sample'? In other words, for the application of art 35(2)(c), it is unclear whether we have to characterise any non-conformity as an issue of 'quality' or an issue irrelevant to 'quality'. Since art 35(2)(c) applies to 'qualities' only, a certain type of non-conformity, such as inconsistency between the package or appearance of the goods and sample, may not fall under art 35(2)(c) if it has been characterised as an issue irrelevant to 'qualities'. This construction of art 35(2)(c) appears to be questionable, given the ordinary meaning of 'conformity with sample' to a reasonable person. But it seems to be a legalistic interpretation of art 35(2)(c).

[2.119] Unlike the provision of the sale of goods legislation in Australia, which requires a sample to be expressly or implicitly incorporated into the contract of sale (see *Thorne v Borthwick* (1956) 56 SR (NSW) 81, discussed in **[1.78]**), art 35(2)(c) does not expressly define the meaning of a sale by sample. In fact, art 35(2)(c) appears to suggest that, in order to hold the seller liable to deliver goods which correspond with a sample, there is no need to establish that the contract is a sale by sample. Article 35(2)(c) will apply so long as there was a sample or model which was shown to the buyer before the conclusion of the contract. This position is similar to s 88 of the Goods Act 1958 (Vic), which does not require a sample to be expressly or implicitly incorporated into a contract of sale.

The seller's obligation concerning a reasonable manner of packaging

[2.120] Article 35(2)(d) requires goods to be contained or packed in a reasonable manner. The reasonableness of the packaging is determined by comparing it with the common commercial practice for packing goods of the same nature. In the absence of an established practice, the reasonableness of the packaging is determined by considering whether the packaging is adequate for the purpose of preserving and protecting the goods concerned.

[2.121] Under the sale of goods legislation, the issue of packaging is usually dealt with under the implied terms as to correspondence with description: see *Re Moore & Co and Landauer & Co* [1921] 2 KB 519. Alternatively, an action may be taken on the ground of merchantable quality, if the packaging of the goods adversely affects the marketability of the goods or damage arises from defects in packaging: see *Silbert Sharpe & Bishop Ltd v George Wills & Co Ltd* [1919] SALR 114. It is probably due to the fact that the Convention neglects both the concept of 'merchantable quality' and the concept of 'correspondence with description' that the manner of packing the goods arises as an

[2.121] independent issue under the Convention. It is interesting to note that the requirements relating to the manner and standards of packaging are based on a proposal made by the Australian delegation in 1974.[39]

The seller's obligation and provisos relating to implied terms

[2.122] Article 35(3) contains a proviso that the seller is not liable under art 35(2) for any lack of conformity, 'if at the time of the conclusion of the contract the buyer knew or could not have been unaware of such lack of conformity'. This proviso negates the obligations of the seller under art 35(2) on the ground of the buyer's actual, or presumed, knowledge of the non-conformity. The rationale of this proviso is that if the buyer knew or ought to have known of the existence of non-conformity, he or she would be regarded as having entered into the contract of sale voluntarily.

[2.123] Article 35(3) was discussed in a German case, *Oberlandesgericht Koln* (22 U 4/96, 21 May 1996, CLOUT Case 168). The dispute involved the sale of a used car between two car dealers. The seller misrepresented the age and the mileage of the car to the buyer. The contract of sale contained an exclusion clause. The buyer sold the car to its customer, who discovered the misrepresentations. The seller sought to rely on the argument that the buyer should have known the age and mileage of the car because it was a professional car dealer.

The court held that art 35(3) could not be relied on by a fraudulent seller because art 40 of the Convention states that the seller is not entitled to rely on the provisions of arts 38 and 39, 'if the lack of conformity relates to facts of which he knew or could not have been unaware, and which he did not disclose to the buyer'. Article 7 of the Convention sets out the principle of good faith. It appears that the court took upon itself the task of balancing the interests of an allegedly negligent buyer, and of a proven fraudulent seller, and concluded that the negligent buyer deserved more protection than the fraudulent seller. The court's conclusion explains why the court applied arts 7 and 40 to the interpretation of art 35(3), even though none of these provisions is directly related to art 35(3). In relation to the exclusion clause, the court held that, although parties may conclude any clause to vary the effect of any provisions of the Convention in pursuance of art 6 of the Convention, the exclusion clause was denied under the German domestic law which invalidated an exclusion clause on the ground of the fraudulent act of a contracting party. Since the contract in question did not change the effect of art 4 of the Convention, the German court's finding on the validity of the exclusion clause is justified by that article, which provides that the validity of a contract or a contractual clause is not subject to the provisions of the Convention.

[2.124] This proviso appears to be based on the notion of freedom of contract. Supposing that a buyer knew and ought to have known of the lack of conformity at the conclusion of the contract, the buyer would then have had an opportunity of addressing the lack of conformity in the contract or refusing to enter into the contract. The fact that the buyer entered into the contract with actual or presumed knowledge of the lack of conformity would be an indication of the buyer's intention to accept the goods as they

---

39. Ibid, p 271.

were or as they would be. However, the real difficulty with this proviso is the presumed knowledge of the buyer as to the lack of conformity. The rules of conflict of laws will certainly result in variations in the application of this proviso.

The seller's obligations concerning latent defect

[2.125] Article 36(1) holds the seller liable for latent non-conformity (which means any non-conformity that cannot be discovered at, for example, the time of delivery, by a reasonable person in the circumstances concerned). This provision states that the seller is liable under the contract or the Convention 'for any lack of conformity which exists at the time when the risk passes to the buyer, even though the lack of conformity becomes apparent only after that time'. This provision has the following requirements:

- the lack of conformity must exist at the time when the risk passes under arts 67–9;
- the lack of conformity is usually latent at the time when the risk passes; and
- there is an implied proviso that art 36(1) does not apply if the seller can prove that the non-conformity did not exist at the time when the risk passed.

[2.126] Article 36(1) can be compared with ss 19 and 20 of the Sale of Goods Act 1923 (NSW), which also hold the seller responsible for any latent defect in the goods after delivery. The period of time during which the latent non-conformity is revealed does not appear to be crucial under art 36(1), so long as the latent non-conformity exists at the time at which the risk passes to the buyer. However, it can be reasonably expected that any lack of conformity in the goods which existed at the time at which the risk passed would be likely to emerge, or be detected, within a reasonable time. The reasonableness of the time should be considered by taking into account the nature of the goods, the purpose for which the goods are used and the general trade practice for detecting the non-conformity in question.

The seller's obligations to ensure conformity after delivery

[2.127] Article 36(2) provides that the seller remains responsible for any lack of conformity which occurs after the passing of the risk, so long as the lack of conformity is the result of a breach of the seller's of any kind. 'Lack of conformity' in art 36 means any defect in the goods which has not been expressly or implicitly accepted by the parties to the contract. This obviously extends to 'a breach of any guarantee that for a period of time the goods will remain fit for their ordinary purpose or for some particular purpose or will retain specified qualities or characteristics'.

[2.128] The element of time does not appear to be important under art 36(2), because the non-conformity under this provision refers to those defects which are caused by the seller's breaches of his or her obligations under the contract or Convention. This suggests that if the seller has guaranteed that the goods would remain fit, or retain certain qualities or characteristics, for a period of time, a breach of those guarantees will amount to a breach of art 36(2). If the seller has not made such express guarantees, he or she may be found to have breached art 36(2) if the defect is caused by a breach of his or her obligations under the contract or the Convention. The obligations themselves may imply a certain time element; for example, 'fitness for a particular purpose' would imply

[2.128] a requirement that the goods remain fit for that purpose for a period of time for which goods of the same nature in the same circumstances would be expected to last.

The seller's obligations and the buyer's right of examination

[2.129] In order to determine whether the goods conform to the contract or the Convention, the Convention gives the buyer a right to have a fair opportunity to examine the goods. Article 38 sets out the following rules for examining the goods:

- the buyer is obliged to examine the goods as soon as practicable after the goods are at his or her disposal in the circumstances concerned: art 38(1);
- when the sale involves the carriage of goods by sea, land or air, the buyer should examine the goods as soon as practicable after the goods have arrived at their destination: art 38(2); and
- when the goods have to be redirected or re-dispatched before the buyer is able to examine them and the seller knew or ought to have known of this, the buyer should examine the goods as soon as practicable after the goods have arrived at the new destination: art 38(3).

[2.130] The opportunity to examine the goods is important because the buyer is expected to discover any non-conformity pursuant to art 35 at the time of examination. If the buyer fails to discover defects in the goods which should have been discovered, he or she will be likely to lose the right to rely on a lack of conformity under art 39, which requires the buyer to give adequate notice of the non-conformity within a reasonable time after the buyer ought to have discovered the defect.[40] However, a buyer who has failed to discover any detectable non-conformity may still be able to make out a case of breach under art 36(2), which holds the seller liable for a breach of his or her obligations under the contract and the Convention. In addition, the buyer may also rely on art 40 after having failed to discover any detectable non-conformity at the time of examination. Article 40 deprives the seller of his or her right to rely on arts 38 and 39, if the seller knew or ought to have known of the existence of the non-conformity complained of.

In a case arbitrated by the Arbitration Institute of the Stockholm Chamber of Commerce (5 June 1998, CLOUT Case 237), the Chinese buyer of a press sued the US seller for non-conformity under art 35 four years after the delivery of the press. The tribunal held that the seller could not rely on arts 38 and 39 to deny the buyer's right to claim non-conformity, because the seller knowingly supplied a lock-plate to the buyer that was inconsistent with the contractual description, without informing the buyer of the requirements for installing the lock-plate. It appears that, in the view of the tribunal, had the seller supplied a conforming lock-plate, or had it advised the buyer of the differences in the substituted lock-plate, the damage to the press would have been avoided. This is probably why the tribunal deprived the seller of the benefits of arts 38 and 39 under art 40.

---

40. Adequacy of notice was raised as an issue in a German case, where the court took the view that the statement that 'the truffles are soft' was too general to describe the nature of the non-conformity: CLOUT Case 411.

However, the operation of art 40 may not be easy to determine. In a German case, *Oberlandesgericht Karlsruhe* (I U 280/96, 25 June 1997, CLOUT Case 230) the court held that it was insufficient to prove that the seller had knowledge of a particular feature of the goods, and that the buyer must prove that the seller knew the feature would constitute a lack of conformity under the contract.

While granting the buyer a right to examine the goods, art 38 also imposes on the buyer an obligation to examine the goods as soon as possible. The length of the reasonable time for examination may vary depending on the circumstances involved. In *Oberlandesgericht Karlsruhe*, the Austrian buyer alleged that the surface-protective film supplied by the German seller was defective, because it left residues of glue on the surface of high-grade steel products. Written notice was given to the seller 24 days after the delivery of the film, one day after the buyer discovered the defect. The court took the view that, for durable goods, a reasonable period for examination was three to four days after delivery, and accordingly a reasonable period for notification in the case of durable goods was eight days after the end of the examination period. The court held that the buyer had not given the notice of defect within a reasonable time.

In another German case, *Oberlandesgericht Munchen* (7 U 4427/97, 11 March 1998), the court held that, since the parties had incorporated the Standard Conditions of the German Textile and Clothing Industry into their contract, the examination period was two weeks, as set out in the Standard Conditions.

[2.131] Under art 38, if a buyer fails to examine the goods as soon as practicable, the seller may argue that the buyer has failed to give notice within a reasonable time under art 39, leading to the loss of the buyer's right to rely on the lack of conformity in question. This is what happened in a German case, *Oberlandesgericht Munchen* (7 U 3758/94, 8 February 1995, CLOUT Case 167). The case involved a sub-sale between the buyer and a sub-buyer. A German seller sold goods to an Austrian buyer, which sold them to a Danish sub-buyer without examining them. The Danish sub-buyer examined the goods and informed the Austrian buyer of the non-conformity. The Austrian buyer did not notify the German seller of the non-conformity. Instead, it claimed insurance against an insurance policy and assigned its right of claim to the insurer.

The court dismissed the insurer's action against the German seller, mainly on two grounds: first, neither the Austrian buyer nor the Danish sub-buyer had given notice to the German seller specifying the non-conformity within a reasonable time under arts 38 and 39; and, second, the notice given by the Danish sub-buyer to the Austrian buyer, and in turn to the insurer, was not given within a reasonable period of time under arts 38 and 39, because three months had passed since the delivery.

Similarly, in a Swiss case where a German buyer purchased a floating house (which used a container filled with salt water for weightless floating) from a Swiss seller, the buyer's failure to give notice under art 39 resulted in the loss of the right to avoid the contract and claim damages: *Handelsgericht des Kantons Zurich* (HG 920670, 16 April 1995,

[2.131]

CLOUT Case 196).[41] By the same token, a German buyer's failure to give notice under art 39 to an Italian seller led to the loss of its right to claim non-conformity against the seller: CLOUT Case 409.[42]

[2.132] The length of the reasonable period of time under arts 38 and 39 may vary depending on the court adjudicating the case. In a Swiss case, *Obergericht des Kantons Luzern* (11 95 123/357, 8 January 1997, CLOUT Case 192), the court observed that the German cases appeared to be restrictive and that the American and Dutch cases appeared to be liberal in determining the reasonable period of time under arts 38 and 39. In that case, the court expressed a view that a period of 10 days after delivery was appropriate for the purpose of art 38, and an average period of one month was appropriate for the purpose of art 39. Of course, the Swiss court's view only represents its own understanding of the meaning of 'reasonable time' under these provisions.

[2.133] It may be argued that, under art 38(3), the original buyer's right of examination should extend to the ultimate buyer or sub-buyer who received the goods from the original buyer. This is because it would be unrealistic to expect the original buyer always to go to the ultimate destination of the goods to examine them. The reasonable time for the buyer to exercise his or her right of examination would certainly be longer under art 38(3) than under art 38(1) and (2). However, whether or not a particular case falls under art 38(1), (2) or (3) needs to be determined by the court of law concerned. In a German case, *Oberlandesgericht Dusseldorf* (17 U 82/93, 8 January 1993, CLOUT Case 48), the goods were first delivered in Turkey and later carried to Germany, where the alleged non-conformity was revealed. The court held that the German buyer had lost the right to claim non-conformity against the Turkish seller because it gave the notice of non-conformity when the goods arrived in Germany, which was seven days after the buyer had the opportunity to examine the goods in Turkey. Obviously the court regarded the dispute as falling under art 38(1) in this case.

The seller's obligations and notice of non-conformity

[2.134] Article 39(1) requires the buyer to 'give notice to the seller specifying the nature of the lack of conformity within a reasonable time after he has discovered it or ought to have discovered it'. This provision contains the following requirements:

- the buyer must give notice of the discovery of the non-conformity;
- the notice must specify the nature of the non-conformity;[43]

---

41. In this case, the buyer alleged that the floating house was leaking and the house was damaged by the water. The buyer declared that the contract was avoided under art 49 and refused to pay the balance of the purchase price. The court held that the buyer had lost its right to avoid the contract under art 49 because it had failed to notify the seller of the non-conformity as requested by art 39. In addition, the court held that the buyer had lost its right to claim damages under art 74 because of its failure to comply with art 39. The importance of art 39 to the interest of the buyer is illustrated by such cases.
42. In that case, the German court held that the buyer failed to meet the notice requirement under art 39 by giving a notice of non-conformity to a self-employed broker who was not the agent of the seller.

- the notice must be given within a reasonable time after the buyer actually discovered, or ought to have discovered, the non-conformity; and
- the reasonable time is determined in the circumstances concerned, by taking into account arts 36 and 38,[44] any common business practices and any previous dealings between the parties.

In a Spanish case, *Audiencia Provincial, Barcelona* (20 June 1997, CLOUT Case 210), the court expressed several interesting views on the operation of art 39. First, it was held to be unreasonable for the buyer, who had received a complaint about the non-conformity of the goods from the sub-buyer, to say nothing about the non-conformity to the seller. Second, it was unreasonable for the buyer not to give notice of the non-conformity to the seller until the seller sought payment. Third, it was reasonable for the buyer to give a notice of non-conformity to the seller as soon as the buyer knew the non-conformity complained of by a third party. It must be noted that the Spanish court seemed to place more emphasis on the response of the buyer to the notice given by the third party, instead of the time elapsed before the buyer's response.

[2.135] A failure to comply with art 39(1) may lead to the buyer losing his or her right to rely on a lack of conformity. This means that the buyer will lose the right to terminate the contract or to claim remedies. In an Austrian case, *Innsbruck* (4R 161/94, Court of Appeal, CLOUT Case 107), the Austrian buyer refused to pay the full price of the flowers sold by a Danish seller, on the ground that some of the flowers did not conform to the description in the contract under art 36 of the Convention.

At first instance, the court found that art 39(1) is similar to art 377 of the Austrian Commercial Code and held that the buyer had lost the right to rely on art 36, because it failed to give a notice of non-conformity within a reasonable period of two months after the delivery. The period of two months was regarded as reasonable by the court for the buyer to act under art 39. The finding was affirmed by the Court of Appeal.

For comparison, in a German case involving an alleged non-conformity of the mussels sold by a Swiss seller to a German buyer, the German Supreme Court held that the buyer did not act within a reasonable time to notify the seller of the alleged non-conformity under art 39, because it had waited for more than one month before giving such notice. It appears that, in the event of a failure by the buyer to comply with art 39(1), the only hope of the buyer would be to prove the seller's knowledge or presumed knowledge of the defect under art 40.

---

43. In a German case, *Bundesgerichtshof* (VIII ZR 306/95, 4 December 1996, CLOUT Case 229), the Austrian buyer sent a written notice to the German seller about eight deficiencies in the computer printing system provided by the seller. One of the deficiencies related to the absence of documentation concerning the printer. The seller subsequently sent to the buyer the documentation concerning the printer only. The buyer declared the contract avoided.
44. It can be argued that the mere fact that the latent defects are not detectable for a period of time does not deprive the buyer of his or her entitlement to rely on a lack of conformity. Similarly, the reasonable time would be longer if transit of goods over a long distance or a redirection of the goods is involved.

The seller's obligations and the limitation period under the Convention

[2.136] Article 39(2) of the Convention sets out a 'statutory' limitation period for a buyer to take legal action on the ground of non-conformity of the goods. This provision states as follows:

> In any event, the buyer loses the right to rely on a lack of conformity of the goods if he does not give the seller notice thereof at the latest within a period of two years from the date on which the goods were actually handed over to the buyer, unless this time-limit is inconsistent with a contractual period of guarantee.

This provision suggests that the two-year limitation is subject only to an express guarantee of a longer time under the contract. It means that the two-year limitation will be the maximum time a buyer can rely on for bringing an action on non-conformity in most circumstances.

[2.137] There is uncertainty in the interpretation of the expression 'the date on which the goods were actually handed over to the buyer'. In a situation where art 38(3) applies, the goods might actually have been handed over to the buyer for the purpose of re-dispatching them. However, under these circumstances, because of a lack of reasonable opportunity for examination, the buyer is not required to examine the goods until they have arrived at the ultimate destination. If the two-year limitation begins to run from the date on which the goods are actually handed over to the buyer for re-dispatch, it will be some time before the buyer or sub-buyer is able to examine the goods under art 38(3).

It appears to be unfair to have a time limitation run against a party who is not legally required to exercise his or her right of examination under the Convention in the circumstances concerned. Similarly, the original buyer would be put in an awkward situation in a case of re-dispatch or sale of goods in transit, where there are two separate contracts in relation to the same goods which are defective. The time begins to run against the original buyer from the date on which the goods were actually handed over to him or her. But the time does not run against the sub-buyer (in a subsequent contract between the original buyer and the sub-buyer) until the goods are actually handed over to the sub-buyer at the ultimate destination of the goods. Hypothetically, there could be a situation where the original buyer has lost any rights of redress against the original seller under art 39(2), but would still be liable to the sub-buyer under art 39(2), because the time limitation against the original seller under the first contract has elapsed, but the time limitation against the original buyer under the subsequent contract has not.

[2.138] It must be pointed out that the limitation period does not operate in cases where the seller knew or ought to have known of the existence of the defect or non-conformity, according to art 40. This provision requires the seller to disclose to the buyer any facts which relate to the lack of conformity which are known or ought to have been known to the seller. The seller is deprived of the right to benefit from arts 38 and 39 if he or she fails to disclose the said facts to the buyer. It should be noted that, under art 40, the seller is obliged to disclose not only the existence of any non-conformity, but also any facts relating to the non-conformity which are known or ought to be known to him or her. Given the wider meaning of 'facts' relating to non-conformity,[45] there appears to be a reasonable opportunity for the buyer to overcome the effect of arts 38 and 39 by proving the seller's failure to disclose the relevant facts.

The seller's obligations and the self-cure remedy before date for delivery

[2.139] For the purpose of preserving the contract, the Convention grants in several provisions a right of self-cure to both the seller and the buyer, enabling them to remedy any lack of conformity in their performance under specified conditions. Article 37 is one of these provisions. This provision states as follows:

> If the seller has delivered goods before the date for delivery, he may, up to that date, deliver any missing part or make up any deficiency in the quantity of the goods delivered, or deliver goods in replacement of any non-conforming goods delivered or remedy any lack of conformity in the goods delivered, provided that the exercise of this right does not cause the buyer unreasonable inconvenience or unreasonable expense. However, the buyer retains any right to claim damages as provided for in this Convention.

This provision creates a right for the breaching party to remedy his or her own breaches, when the non-conforming goods have been accepted by the buyer. It does not have a direct root in the civil law tradition.[46] Nor is there any precedent for this in the common law tradition.

[2.140] The major points of this provision can be summarised as follows:

- self-cure is a right of the seller, which arises once the buyer has accepted the early delivery;
- the right can be exercised under art 37 at any time before the fixed date for delivery;
- the right can be exercised to remedy or cure any non-conformity, such as short delivery (delivery of the wrong quantity), delivery of unmerchantable or unfit goods, delivery of goods inconsistent with the description or sample, or inadequate packaging, among others;
- the right of self-cure is subject to the proviso that 'the exercise of this right does not cause the buyer unreasonable inconvenience or unreasonable expense'; and
- the buyer is entitled to claim damages against the original lack of conformity and any inadequate exercise of the right of self-cure by the seller under art 37.

[2.141] The proviso in art 37 appears to have placed the burden of proof against the exercise of the seller's right of self-cure upon the buyer. This means that, although the seller has an obligation (probably moral)[47] not to exercise the right of self-cure at the expense of the buyer's convenience and cost, the seller appears to be able to resort to this right in most circumstances unless the buyer can refuse the exercise of this right on the proven ground of unreasonable inconvenience or expense. Of course, if the buyer wrongfully refuses the seller the exercise of the right of self-cure under art 37, his or her

---

45. The term 'facts' includes information which may or may not directly evidence the existence of non-conformity, but which may imply the existence of, or lead to the discovery of, non-conformity.
46. Bianca and Bonell, 1987, p 291.
47. This is because the seller can always argue that, in his or her honest belief, the exercise of self-cure in the circumstances concerned does not cause the buyer unreasonable inconvenience or expense.

[2.141]

claims for damages will be reduced proportionally under art 77, which requires the innocent party to take reasonable measures to mitigate loss.

[2.142] On the other hand, the wording of art 37 does not make an exercise of the right of self-cure a wrongdoing, even if the seller's self-cure act has caused the buyer unreasonable inconvenience or expense in the circumstances concerned. If this is the case, the buyer who has not been able to refuse the seller's exercise of self-cure, for whatever reasons, would be able to claim damages against the seller. This is probably why there is no need to provide a special ground for damages claims against the seller's improper use of the right of self-cure under art 37.

[2.143] The important, but as yet unsettled, issues in the interpretation of art 37 are the meaning of 'date for delivery' and 'unreasonable inconvenience or unreasonable expense'. The provision operates under the presumption that all contracts stipulate or imply a date for delivery. It can be argued, however, that if the goods are delivered 'within a reasonable time' under art 33(c), the interpretation of art 37 may cause disagreement. This is because under art 33(c) the date for delivery may not be readily agreeable between the parties in dispute, and 'a reasonable time' does not always yield a determinable date for delivery. But this is not to say that the seller will have no right of self-cure if the date of delivery is not fixed or implied in the contract.

Similarly, what constitutes the 'unreasonableness' of inconvenience or expense in any given situation is invariably open to debate, and therefore must be determined on a case-by-case basis. It can be expected that, in many cases, the seller and buyer would disagree as to whether the exercise of the self-cure remedy would cause unreasonable inconvenience or expense to the buyer. In addition, we should bear in mind that our legal reasoning is affected by the Australian common law principles with which we are familiar, and that there is always a possibility of disagreement if the principles of another legal tradition with which we are less conversant apply in construing the meaning of 'unreasonable inconvenience or unreasonable expense' in a given situation. In any case where a party suffers from an unfavourable construction of 'unreasonable inconvenience or unreasonable expense' by the other party, a damages claim is an effective remedy by which injustice can be redressed.

The seller's obligation and the self-cure remedy after the date for delivery

[2.144] The seller may also wish to exercise the right to the self-cure remedy after the fixed date for delivery. This right is given by art 48. The major points of this provision are as follows:

- when the buyer is not entitled, or does not intend, to avoid the contract under art 49, the seller may request a cure for any lack of conformity at his or her own expense, provided that this will not cause unreasonable delay or unreasonable inconvenience to the buyer, or cause any uncertainty of reimbursement by the seller of expenses advanced by the buyer;
- the seller should make a request to the buyer to exercise the self-cure remedy if he or she intends to rely on art 48;

- the request so made implies a demand for the buyer's response within a reasonable time;
- the request becomes effective when it reaches the buyer;
- the seller has a presumed right to self-cure if the buyer fails to respond to the seller's request within a reasonable time; and
- the seller's presumed right, once applicable, will prohibit the buyer from resorting to any remedy inconsistent with the seller's right to self-cure within the requested period of time for performance.

[2.145] Article 48 gives rise to a rebuttable presumption that the seller is entitled to cure any lack of conformity after the date for delivery. This presumption can be rebutted if the buyer can prove that so doing will cause him or her 'unreasonable inconvenience' or 'unreasonable delay', or cause 'uncertainty of reimbursement by the seller of expenses advanced by the buyer'. If the buyer intends to rebut the presumption, he or she must do so within a reasonable time after the seller's request to cure the non-conformity reaches him or her. In the context of the whole of art 48, the buyer must refuse the request of the seller on one of the specified grounds, even though art 48(2) does not state so expressly.

[2.146] The seller may also request to exercise the self-cure remedy in relation to part delivery or to non-conformity in part of the goods under art 51. This right is based on the presumption that the performance of the contract or the goods under the contract are severable.

The seller's obligations and exemptions

[2.147] Under art 79(1), a seller in breach (or a buyer, as the case may be) can be excused if he or she can prove that the breach was 'due to an impediment beyond his control'. But the seller must also prove either that the impediment was not reasonably foreseeable at the time of the conclusion of the contract, or that it was not reasonable to expect him or her to avoid or overcome the impediment or its consequences. This is similar to what we know as *force majeure* at common law.

Article 79(1) was considered in a dispute between an Egyptian party and a Yugoslavian party: International Chamber of Commerce Case No 6281 (reported in the *Yearbook of Commercial Arbitration*, vol XV, 1990, p 83, and in abstract as CLOUT Case 102). The parties concluded a contract for the sale of steel. The contract contained an option for the buyer to purchase a further quantity of steel at the contract price. The buyer exercised the right to buy, but the seller refused because the market price had gone up. The parties submitted the matter for arbitration. Although the arbitration tribunal took the view that the CISG did not apply to the dispute because the countries of the buyer and the seller were not members of the Convention at the time of the conclusion of the contract, it nevertheless applied art 79(1) to the case. In the view of the tribunal, art 79(1) could only have relieved the seller of the obligation to deliver the steel at the contract price in case of frustration, or if some sudden, substantial and unforeseeable event had taken place. An increase in market price was not regarded as unforeseeable. The tribunal also took the view that a price adjustment clause in the contract in dispute would have relieved the seller of the obligation to sell more at the contract price.

[2.148] Under art 79(3), a seller can claim exemption under art 79(1) only for the period during which the impediment exists. While 'the period during which the impediment exists' may naturally extend to the period during which the inevitable consequence of the impediment exists, art 79(3) will not excuse the seller (or the buyer, as the case may be) for the part of a breach that continues after the disappearance of the impediment and its consequence, if the breach should have reasonably been discontinued in the circumstances concerned. Article 79(3) does not set out clear rules for the construction of 'the period during which the impediment exists'. Nor does it provide guidance for distinguishing an exempt breach from a non-exempt breach. It appears that the interpretation of art 79(3) will largely depend on the domestic law of the court applying this provision.

[2.149] Article 79(2) allows the seller (or buyer, as the case may be) to claim exemption under art 79(1) if his or her breach is due to a breach by a subcontractor who claims *force majeure*. In such circumstances, art 79(2) requires both the seller and the subcontractor to prove that they can be exempted under art 79(1). In a case arbitrated by the Russian Federation Chamber of Commerce, (Case No 155/1994, 16 March 1995, CLOUT Case 140) the seller sought to rely on art 79 by arguing that it was unable to supply the goods, chemicals, as agreed because of an emergency production stoppage at the plant manufacturing the chemicals. The tribunal refused to accept the argument on the ground that a mere refusal on the part of the manufacturer to supply the chemicals did not satisfy the requirements of art 79. In addition, the tribunal took the view that the seller had not discharged its liability to prove the unforeseeability of the emergency claimed.

[2.150] Article 79(4) requires the party in breach to notify the innocent party of the impediment and its effect on his or her ability to perform. This requirement is compulsory. If the seller fails to give the requisite notice, or such notice did not reach the buyer within a reasonable time after the seller knew or ought to have known of the impediment, the seller cannot rely on art 79(1). However, it is uncertain in the words of art 79(4) whether the seller is totally deprived of the right to rely on art 79(1) because the buyer did not receive the notice within a reasonable time, or whether the seller is deprived of the right to rely on art 79(1) proportionally to the lateness of the notice in reaching the buyer. It may be argued that the buyer may receive the notice after the lapse of a reasonable time, and that in such a case he or she may still be able to mitigate his or her loss to some extent.

Bianca and Bonell imply that there is a difference in the sum of damages between non-compliance with art 79(4) and non-performance of the contract (when art 79(1) is unavailable). They observe as follows:

> If the notice has not been given or received within a reasonable time, the defaulting party is liable for damages. It should be noted that the damages for which the latter is liable are only those which result from the failure to give notice as opposed to those which follow from the non-performance of the contract. The former will, in effect, often constitute an additional charge for the defaulting party, as the other party will have been unable to take the steps necessary to alleviate the consequences of non-performance.[48]

---

48. Bianca and Bonell, 1987, p 587.

However, it is yet to be seen how a court of law is to construe the words 'such non-receipt' in art 79(4), in the absence of any express guidance in this provision.

Performance of the buyer's obligations

What are the buyer's obligations?

[2.151] The buyer under the Convention has two basic obligations:

- to pay the price of the goods; and
- to take delivery of the goods.

Article 53 states that the 'buyer must pay the price for the goods and take delivery of them as required by the contract and this Convention'. Any breach by the buyer will be related to these two basic obligations.

The buyer's obligation to pay the price

[2.152] Article 54 provides that the buyer's obligation to pay the price of the goods includes an obligation to take such steps or comply with such formalities as are required by the contract, and any laws and regulations to enable the payment to be made. These laws and regulations include the relevant international conventions governing financial transactions, such as the 1930 Geneva Convention Providing a Uniform Law for Bills of Exchange and Promissory Notes, and the 1988 UN Convention on International Bills of Exchange and International Promissory Notes; customs and usage, such as UCP[49] 500; and relevant domestic law governing, for example, export, foreign exchange and transfer of funds. These matters may not have been stipulated in a contract but are implied in international transactions of such a nature. Article 54 imposes upon the seller an obligation to take active measures to enable or facilitate the payment of the price. In *Downs Investments Pty Ltd (in vol liq) (formerly known as Wanless Metal Industries Pty Ltd) v Perwaja Steel SDN BHD* [2000] QSC 421 (available at <http://www.butterworthsonline.com>), the Supreme Court of Queensland held that the buyer's failure to issue a letter of credit as agreed in the contract of sale amounted to a breach of art 54, as well as arts 25 and 64 of the CISG.

[2.153] Articles 53 and 54 jointly impose an obligation to make payment under a contract of sale. How far this obligation can be extended is an issue yet to be decided by the courts of the members of the Convention. In a German case *Oberlandesgericht Hamm* (11 U 206/93, 8 February 1995, CLOUT Case 132), the court held that the buyer was obliged to pay the contract price a second time. The German buyer originally paid the contract price to the Italian seller, which subsequently became bankrupt. This payment was made, however, after the buyer had received a notice of assignment (of the seller's right to claim the contract price) in favour of an Italian bank. The bank was therefore entitled to recover the contract price from the buyer.

The major issue of this case was whether the seller was entitled to assign its right to receive the payments to another party under the contract of sale concerned. There were

---

49. The Uniform Customs and Practice for Documentary Credits (UCP) is discussed further in Chapter 5.

[2.153]   **International Commercial Law**

four contracts concluded in Italian language for the sale of a large quantity of socks. The Italian seller assigned its right to claim the payments under the contract to the Italian bank, and gave an assignment notice in French and English to the German buyer, who later claimed to know very little English and French. Probably as a result of this language difficulty, the buyer paid the contract prices directly to the Italian seller. When the bank was unable to recover these moneys from the seller, which had gone into bankruptcy, the bank sued the buyer under the assignment notice.

The court found that the Convention did not provide any specific rules on the assignment of rights, and applied the Italian law — which was determined to be the governing law — to resolve the claim. The court held that the alleged language risk or difficulty was not a recognised defence under the Italian law for the assignment of rights, and thus ordered the German buyer to pay (a second time) the contract price to the bank.

The court's decision was largely based on a presumption that the Italian seller was entitled to assign its right under the contracts of sale and under the Convention. While the court concluded that the Convention did not apply to the issue expressly, it did not answer the question as to whether the contracts of sale permitted such an assignment. Instead, the court relied heavily on art 53 of the Convention, which states that the buyer has an obligation to pay the price of the goods. Accordingly, it could be argued that the court's decision is questionable — that the buyer had no obligation to accept the assignment notice, on the basis that the Convention heavily emphasises that it is the terms of the contract and the intention of the parties as evidenced by the contract which are determinative.

The buyer's obligation and determination of the price

[2.154]   Article 55 sets out rules for determining the price of the goods when the contract fails to fix the price, or to make a provision expressly or implicitly for the determination of the price. Article 55 provides a presumed intention of the parties to contract at 'the price generally charged at the time of the conclusion of the contract for such goods sold under comparable circumstances in the trade concerned', unless the parties have agreed otherwise. In a case arbitrated by the Russian Federation Chamber of Commerce and Industry (Case No 309/1993, 3 March 1995, CLOUT Case 139), the arbitration tribunal decided that art 55 was not applicable because the parties had agreed that the price of the goods was to be determined 10 days prior to the New Year. The said agreement to fix the price of the goods in future was regarded by the tribunal as an intention not to use the market price to fix the price of the goods under art 55.

[2.155]   Under art 55, there are four considerations which must be taken into account in determining the price:

- First, the price should be the one which is generally charged. This rule is qualified by certain considerations, such as the time at which the contract was made, the compatibility of the goods whose price is referred to, and the circumstances in which the goods are sold. In circumstances qualified by these variables, the presumed price under art 55 would be the one which is generally charged. In the absence of such a price, the average price of the prices of the same or compatible goods would be a rational substitution.

128

- Second, the price of the compatible goods must be the one which existed at the time of the contract. This requirement avoids the impact of market fluctuation upon the ascertainment of the reasonable price.
- Third, the goods whose price is under consideration must be goods of the same description. It is yet to be seen whether 'such goods' under art 55 may extend to compatible goods in circumstances where there is no price for goods of the same description.
- Fourth, the circumstances in which the sample price is taken must be comparable with the circumstances in which the contract in question was made. Article 55 requires the parties to the present contract to take into account the 'trade' in which they are engaged and the 'trade' in the comparable circumstances in which the sample price is taken. However, it is yet to be seen how the word 'trade' in art 55 will be construed by a court of law. Is this a matter of characterisation? If the seller and buyer are not engaged in the same type of 'trade', how do we characterise the 'trade' of the seller and buyer respectively under the contract of sale? How do we determine the compatibility of the 'trade' in comparable circumstances in which the sample price is taken with the 'trade' as represented by the contract of sale in question? These questions are not answered in art 55.

Article 55 was tested in a case decided by the Austrian Supreme Court in 1994 (Case No 2 Ob 547/93, 10 November 1994, CLOUT Case 106). In that case, the Austrian buyer bought a large quantity of chinchilla pelts of middle or better quality at a price of between 35 and 65DM (German Marks) per piece. The buyer sold the goods to an Italian sub-buyer without examining them; the sub-buyer later returned 13 pelts to the Austrian buyer on the ground of defective goods. The Austrian buyer returned the goods to the German seller and refused to pay for them on the ground that it acted as the agent of the seller to sell the goods to the Italian sub-buyer. The trial court found that a contract of sale existed between the Austrian buyer and the German seller, and ordered the Austrian buyer to pay the German seller for the pelts alleged to be defective at the price of 50DM per pelt. The price of 50DM was decided using the market price for a pelt of middle or better quality. The Court of Appeal affirmed this decision. The Supreme Court of Austria affirmed the price decided by the trial court on the basis of the contract, which set out a price range between 35 to 65DM for pelts of middle or better quality. The Supreme Court of Austria took the view that the contract was sufficient to determine the price of the pelt in dispute, and thus there was no need to apply art 55 of the Convention.

[2.156] The price of goods may also be affected by their weight in certain circumstances in which the price of the goods is calculated on the basis of their weight: see *Nanka Bruce v Commonwealth Trust Ltd* [1926] AC 77, discussed at **[1.52]**. Article 56 states that, where the parties disagree because of a lack of express or implied intention in the contract of sale, the net weight of the goods will be the basis for determining the price of the goods. This provision does not deal with the situation in which the price can be calculated by other means, such as the size of the goods or using a price per unit of the goods. This is probably because the other methods of calculation will not normally cause disagreement between the parties.

The buyer's obligation concerning place of payment

[2.157] The place of payment is central to the buyer's obligation to pay the contract price. If the buyer does not make payment at the place agreed, he or she breaches art 57.

[2.158] Article 57 sets out the following rules for determining the place of payment:
- the parties can determine the place of payment in the contract;
- in the absence of any agreement, the place of payment is the seller's place of business;
- if payment is made against the handing over of the goods, the place of payment is the place where the goods are handed over to the buyer;
- if the payment is made against the handing over of the documents, the place of payment is the place where the documents are handed over to the buyer, or his or her agent; and
- if the seller's place of business is chosen as the place of payment either by the parties' express intention or their omission, and the seller has changed his or her place of business after the conclusion of the contract, the seller is liable for the additional costs of making the payment at his or her present place of business.

[2.159] It must be pointed out that the incorporation of any term dealing with the means of payment in a contract will exclude or alter the effect of this provision. For example, if the parties choose to make the payment on the basis of a letter of credit, the trade customs governing the use of a letter of credit of the same nature will override or modify the effect of art 57. Therefore, art 57 applies only to a situation in which no express or implied agreement on the place of payment has been reached between the parties concerned. This provision was applied in *Societe Lorraine des Produits Metallurgiques v Banque Paribas Belgique SA* [1995] UNLEX D93-23 (Court of Appeal of Paris (1st Division, Urgent Proceedings Section), CLOUT Case 156). In that case, the court held that, in the absence of any express agreement, the purchase price of metal sheets was payable by the Belgian buyer at the place of business of the French seller.

For comparison, in a Swiss case, *Zivilgericht des Kantons Basel-Stadt* (P4 1996/00448, 3 December 1997, CLOUT Case 221) the court held that it was not necessary for art 57(1)(a) and (b) to apply because the contract of sale stipulated that the payment was to be made 30 days after the delivery of a bill of lading and several other documents.

The buyer's obligation concerning time of payment

[2.160] Compliance with the time for payment is one of the fundamental obligations of the buyer under the Convention. This obligation is set out in arts 58 and 59. Article 59 says that the buyer 'must pay the price on the date fixed by or determinable from the contract and this Convention without the need for any request or compliance with any formality on the part of the seller'. The use of the word 'must' indicates the importance of complying with the time for payment under the Convention.

[2.161] The obligation to pay the price on the date fixed or implied in the contract is absolute. This appears to suggest that if there is a date for payment in the contract, the buyer will have an obligation to pay the price on that date even if the contract does not require the seller to deliver the goods or documents before or on the date of payment. However, if the contract requires the seller to deliver the goods or documents before or on the date of payment, and the seller has failed to do so, the buyer is entitled (if he or she chooses to do so) to suspend his or her performance under art 71, or terminate the contract under arts 49 and 72, as the case may be. This means that the buyer's obligation to pay at the time agreed in the contract is dependent upon the terms of the contract and performance of the seller.

[2.162] Article 58 sets out the following rules for ascertaining the time of payment, which are applicable in the absence of a contrary intention of the parties to the contract:

- if the buyer is not bound to pay the price at a fixed time, he or she must pay it at the time when the seller places the goods or documents (whichever is earlier[50]) at the buyer's disposal in accordance with the contract or the Convention;[51]
- if the sale involves carriage of the goods by sea, land or air, the seller is entitled to require the buyer to pay the price of the goods against the handing over of the goods or documents to the buyer or his or her agent;[52] and
- in the absence of an agreement between the parties, the buyer is entitled to have an opportunity to examine the goods under art 38 and is not obliged to pay the price until the time of examination.

[2.163] As suggested by art 58, this provision does not expressly set out the time of payment. Instead, it describes the occasion when the payment should be made. Whether or not the buyer has complied with art 53 in making the payment on time must be determined in the circumstances concerned. The buyer can deny an obligation to pay after delivery on the ground of the right of examination only in a rare situation where the seller and buyer deal with each other directly in making both the delivery of the goods and payment of the price.

The buyer's obligation to take delivery

[2.164] The buyer's obligation to take delivery is an obligation to accept the goods. The actual delivery can take several forms; for example, the seller can deliver to the agreed place of delivery (see the DAF term, discussed at **[1.26]**) or the buyer can take the goods over from the seller's place of business, or from the place where the goods are manufactured or stored (see the EXW term, discussed at **[1.16]**). This suggests an obligation to take possession of the goods in accordance with the terms of the contract or the Convention.

[2.165] Article 60 sets out the buyer's obligation to take delivery as follows:

- the buyer is obliged to take over the goods in accordance with the contract and the Convention; and

---

50. Article 58 does not expressly so state. However, if the buyer 'must' pay in either of the situations, he or she would have to pay the price at whichever of the occasions which occurs first.
51. Article 58(1) was applied in a Swiss case, *Tribunal cantonal du Valais* (20 December 1994, CLOUT Case 197).
52. This requirement coincides in effect with art 57(1)(b), which requires the payment be made at the place where the goods and documents are handed over to the buyer.

[2.165]

- the buyer is obliged to do all the acts which he or she is reasonably expected to do for the purpose of enabling the seller to make delivery in accordance with the contract and the Convention.

[2.166] It is unclear from the language of art 60 how to determine the reasonableness of the expectation. However, it can be assumed that the expectation should be based on the nature of the goods, trade customs and usage in dealing with goods of the same nature and description, the established practices between the parties, and the circumstances in which the goods are to be delivered. If any of the Incoterms is incorporated into the contract of sale, the buyer's obligation to take over the goods under art 60 should be construed in the light of the term concerned.

[2.167] It is also unclear under art 60 whether 'taking over the goods' includes both physical and constructive delivery. The purpose of art 60 is to ensure a smooth and expedient transaction of goods from the seller to the buyer. It can be argued that art 60 is fulfilled so long as the goods, or the property in the goods, can be transferred from the seller to the buyer with certainty and expediency. 'Taking over the goods' under art 60 can thus be both physical and constructive. The circumstances in which constructive delivery can take place will be fairly limited in international sales. However, this is possible in some circumstances; for example, where the goods are sold while being stored in a warehouse, as occurred in *Ship Agencies Australia Pty Ltd v Fremantle Fishermen's Co-Operative Society Ltd* (1991) SR (WA) 109 discussed at **[1.78]**.

[2.168] The buyer's obligation to take delivery is subject to the seller's adequate performance of the contract. For example, art 52 provides that if 'the seller delivers the goods before the date fixed, the buyer may take delivery or refuse to take delivery'. In this case, the obligation to take delivery does not arise because the seller has not performed his or her obligations adequately. By the same token, the buyer has no obligation to take delivery when the seller delivers the wrong quantity of goods. The only obligation in such circumstances is to pay for the goods received, if the buyer decides to take all or part of the goods delivered.

The buyer's obligation and exemptions

[2.169] Under art 79(1), if a buyer can prove that his or her failure to perform a particular obligation was 'due to an impediment beyond his control and that he could not reasonably be expected to have taken the impediment into account at the time of the conclusion of the contract', he or she is not liable for the breach. Similarly, if the buyer can prove that in the circumstances concerned it was unreasonable to expect him or her 'to have avoided or overcome' the impediment or its consequences, the buyer is not liable for the breach.

However, it must be pointed out that only a breach arising during the period in which the impediment exists can be exempted under art 79(3). This provision is based on the concept of *force majeure*, which, however, may have different interpretations in different legal systems.[53] In a case arbitrated by the Hungarian Chamber of Commerce and Industry

---

53. See Bianca and Bonell, 1987, p 573.

(Case No VB/96074, 10 December 1996, CLOUT Case 163), a Hungarian buyer of caviar argued that it was unable to pay the Yugoslav seller because the UN embargo against Yugoslavia was in force. The tribunal held that the seller had assigned its right of claim to a party in Cyprus, and that the UN embargo did not constitute a *force majeure* preventing the buyer from performing its obligation to make the payment to the assignee.

[2.170] The exemption under art 79(1) may extend to a breach by the buyer caused by a breach by a third party, whose services were engaged by the buyer to perform part or the whole of the contract. However, if the buyer seeks to rely on the exemption in such cases, her or she must prove that both himself or herself and the third party would have been exempt under art 79(1) had they both been dealt with under that provision. This means that *both* the buyer and his or her subcontractor must prove that the impediment was beyond their control. It follows that if this was the case they could not be reasonably expected to have taken the impediment into account at the time of the conclusion of the respective contracts, or to have avoided or overcome the impediment or its consequences.

[2.171] Article 79(4) requires a buyer who is exempt to give notice to the other party, specifying the nature and effect of the impediment. This obligation appears to be absolute, because the exempt party may be held liable for damages caused by his or her failure to give notice, even though he or she would have been exempt had the notice reached the seller on time.

Remedies

The seller's remedies under the Convention

Categories of the seller's remedies

[2.172] The expression 'categories of remedies' is based on the concepts of common law, as seen in the sale of goods legislation in many common law jurisdictions, such as Australia, Canada, Hong Kong, New Zealand and the UK. Under the sale of goods legislation, remedies can be divided into two categories: those relating to a breach of a condition; and those to a breach of warranty. Bearing in mind that any categories of this nature will inevitably be artificial creations, we may divide the seller's remedies under the Convention into the following categories:

- requesting the buyer to perform his or her contractual obligations under art 62;
- fixing an additional period of time for the buyer to perform (*nachfrist*) under art 63;
- requesting 'specific performance' under arts 28 and 62;[54]
- declaring the contract avoided under art 64;
- suspending the performance of the contract under art 71;

---

54. 'Specific performance' here is used in a broad sense, referring to the remedy of specific performance as ordered by a court of law and the right to request the other party to perform specific duties under the Convention.

[2.172] International Commercial Law

- avoiding the contract on the ground of an anticipatory breach under art 72; and
- claiming damages under arts 74–78.

These remedies will be examined in turn.

The seller's right and the proviso of no-fault

[2.173] Article 80 is a proviso which says that a seller (or a buyer, as the case may be) may not rely on the other's breach if the breach is caused by the party's own act or omission. Under this provision, the seller's right to rely on the buyer's breach can be restricted in proportion to the impact of the seller's act or omission upon the buyer's breach. This provision is consistent with one of the basic principles of common law — that one is not allowed to benefit from one's own mistake or misconduct.

The seller's right to request performance

[2.174] Article 62 says that the 'seller may require the buyer to pay the price, take delivery or perform his other obligations, unless the seller has resorted to a remedy which is inconsistent with this requirement'. This provision is compatible with art 46(1), which allows the buyer to request the seller to perform his or her contractual obligations.

Article 62 simply declares that the seller is entitled to request the buyer to perform his or her obligations if the seller chooses to make such a request. But art 62 does not itself lay down any specific penalty if the buyer refuses the seller's request. It appears that if the buyer refuses to comply with the seller's request, the seller may have to resort to either an arbitration tribunal or a court of law to enforce the rights provided in art 62 — if the seller still prefers to use the remedies provided in art 62. In a case arbitrated in 1993 (Case No 7197, CLOUT Case 104), the International Court of Arbitration took the view that the Austrian seller was entitled to request the Bulgarian buyer to offer a documentary credit as stipulated by the contract, and also to claim compensation in pursuance of the relevant provisions of the Convention.

[2.175] In a dispute involving an unpaid seller, the seller's right to request the buyer to perform the contract (by, for example, paying the contract price) may be balanced against the buyer's right to avoid the contract, because, more often than not, the buyer's failure to perform his or her obligation is related to the alleged breach of contract by the seller.

In a case decided by the German Supreme Court, *Bundesgerichtshof* (VII ZR 18/94, 15 February 1995, CLOUT Case 124) the unpaid seller's right to request the buyer to pay the contract price was examined from the perspective of the buyer's right to terminate the contract, rather than the seller's right to demand payment. In 1991, the German seller sold a key-stamping machine, which was to be manufactured by another German company, to the Swiss buyer, and the contract of sale stipulated that the payment was to be effected by three instalments. The parties agreed that the seller would remain the owner of the machine until full payment of the price. The buyer paid the first instalment. For some unknown reason, the manufacturer of the machine refused to deliver the machine to the seller. Instead, in October 1991, the manufacturer delivered the machine directly to the buyer, who later refused to pay the remaining two instalments to the seller on the ground that the seller could not pass the property in the machine to it.

The trial court ordered the buyer to pay the remaining two instalments to the seller, but the court of appeal decided that the buyer was not obliged to pay the remaining price to the seller. The seller appealed to the German Supreme Court. The court did not look at the alleged breach of the seller. Nor did the court look at the seller's remedies under arts 28 and 62 for specific performance. Instead, the court examined the buyer's right to avoid the contract under art 72, implying that the buyer should have avoided the contract when the manufacturer refused to deliver the machine to the seller. The court considered that the buyer's act in accepting the machine directly from the manufacturer was performed in pursuance of the original contract between the seller and the buyer. Consequently, the Supreme Court held that the buyer must pay the seller the remaining price of the machine.

If in this case the court had looked at the unpaid seller's right to demand specific performance, the court would probably have had to answer the question whether or not the seller had breached its obligation to deliver the machine and pass the title in the machine to the buyer upon the full payment of the price. If the seller was unable to perform its side of the contract because the manufacturer refused to deal with it, the court would probably have had to find the existence of a new contract between the manufacturer and the buyer, or a modification of the terms of the original contract by virtue of the manufacturer's direct delivery of the machine to the buyer. If the buyer has not paid the price of the machine to anyone yet, it will have to pay it to someone for the sake of fairness and justice, no matter what legal ground is used. On the other hand, if the buyer has paid the money to the manufacturer and is required to pay to the seller again, the decision of the German Court would appear to be unfair to the buyer.

The seller's right to fix an additional period for performance (nachfrist)

[2.176] *Nachfrist* is a German term describing the situation in which the innocent party sends a final notice to the breaching party requesting him or her to perform the contractual obligation within a specified period of time. Article 63 serves the same purpose. This provision encourages the seller to give a second opportunity to the buyer for the purpose of ensuring the performance of the contract by the parties themselves. While the meaning and legal effect of art 63 under the Convention is open for discussion by courts of different countries, a German arbitration tribunal appeared to have an interesting interpretation of that article in a case involving an alleged breach of contract between a Hong Kong seller and a German buyer: *Schiedsgericht der Handelskammer Hamburg* (decided on 21 March 1996 for substantive issues and 21 June 1996 for the cost of proceedings respectively, CLOUT Case 166). In that case, the tribunal awarded the cost of proceedings to the seller, and further stated that if the buyer refused to pay the cost as ordered, the seller was not obliged to fix an additional period of time for performance under art 63. The application of art 63 to such a situation, and even the reference to art 63, would appear unnecessary from the viewpoint of someone trained in the common law tradition. However, since *nachfrist* comes from German law, whether or not the tribunal's interpretation of the potential use of art 63 accords with the intended meanings of art 63 is subject to further discussion.

[2.177] Article 63(1) provides that the 'seller may fix an additional period of time of reasonable length for performance by the buyer of his obligations'. This provision appears to give the seller an option, which means that the seller does not have to give an additional time for performance to the buyer if the seller does not opt to do so under art 63(1).

[2.178] The reasonable length of time for performance should be determined in the light of the circumstances concerned, taking into account relevant commercial practices, the reason for the buyer's failure to perform, the effect of late performance on the seller's interest, the buyer's ability to perform within the additional time, and so on. It is yet to be seen to what extent the construction of 'reasonable length' will affect the application of art 63(1). It must be borne in mind that the seller has no obligation to give additional time. It would be unfair and discouraging if a seller were more likely to be found in breach of the requirement for 'reasonable length' if he or she chose to give additional time for the purpose of preserving and promoting the contract.

[2.179] Article 63(2) restrains the seller from resorting to other remedies during the additional time, if the seller has opted to give an additional period of time to the buyer. This provision says that if the seller gives additional time to the buyer, the seller must not during that time resort to any other remedy unless he or she receives notice from the buyer refusing to perform the contractual obligations within the additional period. Two things should be emphasised in this provision:

- since the notice by the buyer is not effective until it reaches the seller, evidence of the buyer sending the notice does not relieve the seller from the burden of proof under art 63(2); but
- the seller is entitled to claim damages under other provisions of the Convention, even though he or she is not entitled to resort to other remedies during the additional time.[55]

[2.180] Although art 63 appears to be compatible with art 47, it does not have a close relationship with art 64 (which allows a contract to be avoided) in the same way as art 47 does with art 49. This is because the reference in art 64 to art 63 does not appear to make art 63 compulsory in the same way as art 49 does with art 47: see **[2.240]–[2.241]**.

The seller's remedy of specific performance

[2.181] Articles 62 and 63 appear to give the seller a right to request specific performance. Indeed, the seller may do so if the buyer refuses to cooperate under art 62. However, if the seller seeks assistance from a court of law for specific performance pursuant to art 28, then the enforcement of his or her right will be subject to the relevant domestic law. Consequently, whether the seller is entitled to request the buyer's 'specific

---

55. Article 63(2) provides that 'the seller is not deprived thereby of any right he may have to claim damages for delay in performance'. Although art 63(2) mentions only the 'damages for delay in performance', the seller is entitled under other provisions, such as arts 61 and 74–8, to claim any damages resulting from the buyer's breach. The buyer may fail to perform the obligations totally (as opposed to late performance) in certain circumstances, and art 63(2) cannot be regarded as a provision which limits the damages claim of the seller to the extent of the damages recoverable from the delay in performance only.

performance' under art 62 is an irrelevant issue. It is likely that the seller will not be able to enforce his or her right if the domestic law does not allow specific performance in such circumstances. The seller should explore the possibility of making a request to the buyer directly under art 62 before asking a court to order specific performance.

The seller's right to avoid a contract in general

[2.182] A seller is entitled to avoid a contract if the buyer has performed one of the acts described in art 64. However, this is different from saying that the seller can avoid the contract on the grounds of a fundamental breach or a breach of a fundamental term as understood at common law. In fact, the right to avoid a contract under the Convention is not based on the notion of fundamental breach nor breach of a fundamental term, as it is at common law.

[2.183] Article 64 contains two sets of rules for avoiding a contract. The difference between these sets of rules is whether or not the buyer has paid the price of the contract.

[2.184] Article 64(1) deals with a situation in which the buyer has failed to pay the price of the contract. It allows the seller to declare the contract void in the following circumstances:

- when the buyer has committed a fundamental breach as defined by the parties or in art 25 ('fundamental breach' as defined by the parties and 'fundamental breach' at common law are different concepts); or
- when the buyer refuses, or gives notice of refusal, to perform his or her obligations within an additional period of time fixed by the seller under art 63(1).

[2.185] These two grounds for avoiding the contract are alternatives. The second ground (art 64(1)(b)) suggests that the seller is entitled to avoid the contract when the buyer fails to perform within the additional time period. The seller is not expressly required to establish a fundamental breach under art 64(1)(b) for the purpose of avoiding a contract. Thus, it can be argued that a fundamental breach, as defined in art 25, is irrelevant for the seller wishing to avoid a contract under art 64(1)(b). If the seller is not able to prove the existence of a fundamental breach, he or she may instead fix an additional period of time for performance under art 63(1). If the buyer fails to perform his or her obligations within that time, the seller is then entitled to declare the contract avoided, without the need to prove the nature of the buyer's breach.

[2.186] Article 64(2) provides the second set of rules for avoidance. It deals with situations in which the buyer has paid the price of the goods. Although the seller is not normally allowed to avoid the contract after the price has been paid, he or she may do so in the following circumstances:

- the seller may avoid the contract before he or she has become aware that the buyer has rendered late performance (that is, made late payment of the price);

[2.186]

- the seller may avoid a contract on the ground of a breach (other than late performance), provided that he or she does so within a reasonable time after he or she knew or ought to have known of the breach;[56] and

- the seller may avoid a contract regardless of the nature of the breach if the buyer fails or refuses to perform his or her obligations within the additional time period fixed under art 63(1).

[2.187] It appears that art 64(2)(b)(ii) repeats what is said in art 64(1)(b), allowing the seller to avoid a contract after art 63(1) has been complied with. These provisions suggest that the nature of the breach which the seller required the buyer to remedy under art 63(1) is irrelevant to a seller who wishes to avoid the contract under these provisions, so long as the buyer has been given additional time and failed to perform within that time.

The seller's right to supply specifications

[2.188] This is not what we normally call a right of the seller. However, art 65 does give the seller a 'right' to supply his or her own specifications for the purpose of facilitating contract performance when the buyer fails to do so in accordance with the contract or the Convention. It is a 'right' in the sense that the seller is entitled to do something which should otherwise be performed by the buyer.

[2.189] Article 65(1) provides as follows:

> If under the contract the buyer is to specify the form, measurement or other features of the goods and he fails to make such specification either on the date agreed upon or within a reasonable time after receipt of the request from the seller, the seller may, without prejudice to any other rights he may have, make the specification himself in accordance with the requirements of the buyer that may be known to him.

Obviously, the provision is based on the notion of contract preservation and promotion. Otherwise, the seller may avoid the contract on the ground of a fundamental breach (if the failure to provide specification is defined as a fundamental breach), or of art 63(1) (when the buyer fails to provide specifications within the additional time). Rather than allowing the seller to avoid the contract in the case of the buyer's failure to perform, art 65 provides the seller with a right to use his or her own specification for the purpose of preserving the existing contract. It is a 'right' of the seller, because the seller has no obligation to do so under art 65. This means that the seller is entitled to resort to other remedies in the Convention, if he or she wishes.

[2.190] Article 65(2) imposes specific obligations upon the seller and buyer, if the seller chooses to exercise the right under art 65(1). The seller's obligation is to notify the buyer of the detail of the specification and request the buyer to make any objections to the specification within a fixed time of reasonable length. The buyer's obligation is to accept the specification if he or she fails to object to it within the fixed time. This provision is necessary in order to ensure a fair and smooth performance of the contract.

---

56. Article 64(2) does not expressly say that the 'breach' must be a fundamental breach. However, it would appear to be strange if the seller must establish a fundamental breach under art 64(1)(a), but can avoid a contract on the ground of any breach under art 64(2)(b).

The seller's right to suspend the contract

[2.191] Article 71 allows the seller (or the buyer, as the case may be) to suspend the performance of a contract if the buyer appears to be unable to perform a substantial part of his or her obligations. However, the buyer's inability to perform must be supported by one of the following grounds:

- the existence of a serious deficiency in his or her ability to perform;
- the existence of a serious deficiency in his or her creditworthiness;
- the conduct of the buyer in preparing to perform; or
- the conduct of the buyer in performing the contract.

The above grounds suggest that the tests for determining the reasonableness of a suspension are based on the ground of an anticipatory breach under the Convention.

[2.192] Article 71(3) requires the seller suspending a contract (or the buyer, as the case may be) to give notice of the suspension to the other party immediately after the suspension. A failure to comply with this may deprive the seller of his or her right to rely on art 71(1). Although art 71(3) does not expressly state this, the use of the word 'must' emphasises the importance of the notice.

[2.193] Article 71(3) also restricts the right of the seller (or the buyer, as the case may be) to suspend a contract by requiring him or her to stop suspension 'if the other party provides adequate assurance of his performance'. The adequacy of the assurance must be assessed against the four grounds of suspension set out in art 71(1), and must be determined by examining whether the ground for suspension under art 71(1) has been changed or eliminated by the assurance of the buyer in the circumstances involved. The seller's duty to resume contract performance after the buyer's adequate assurance also illustrates the need for the seller to give timely notice of suspension to the buyer, so that the buyer is given an appropriate opportunity to provide an adequate assurance.

The seller's right to stop delivery after suspension

[2.194] The Convention does not give the unpaid seller a right of stoppage in the same way as the sale of goods legislation in Australia, Hong Kong, New Zealand or the UK does. However, art 71(2) allows the seller suspending the contract to prevent the goods from being delivered to the buyer, even if the buyer holds a document of title over the goods. (For example, the document of title may be given to the buyer under a sight bill, which will be honoured 60 days after the presentation of the bill of exchange.) This means that a seller who has suspended the performance of a contract is entitled to stop the delivery of the goods to the buyer, provided that it is still possible (provided, that is, that the seller is able to control the movement of the goods at that stage). It is yet to be seen whether the right of the seller under art 71(2) can be used against a bailee who is not the agent of either the buyer or the seller.

[2.195] It must be pointed out that the seller's right to stop delivery under art 71(2) cannot be exercised against a third party who has received property in the goods. This rule is consistent with the common law principle that a bona fide, third party purchaser for value should be given good title against the original owner of the goods who makes a claim after the third party has received property in the goods.

The seller's right to avoid a contract on the ground of anticipated fundamental breach

[2.196] Article 72 provides an alternative to art 64, enabling the seller to avoid a contract. It allows the seller to avoid a contract on the ground of an anticipated fundamental breach. This provision sets out the following rules for effecting avoidance:

- the ground for avoidance under art 72 is an anticipated 'fundamental breach' only;
- the anticipated fundamental breach must be certain in the sense that the buyer will definitely commit it;[57]
- the seller (or the buyer, as the case may be) is obliged to notify the other party of the avoidance only when 'time allows';
- if the buyer (or the seller, as the case may be) provides an adequate assurance, the other party will not be able to rely on art 72(1);[58] but,
- the requirement for notice does not apply if the buyer (or the seller, as the case may be) 'has declared that he will not perform his obligations'.

[2.197] Article 72 does not set out clear rules for determining the certainty of an anticipated fundamental breach; this can nonetheless be defined by the parties or pursuant to art 25. The normal standard of a 'reasonable person' test appears to be appropriate for this purpose. In addition, value judgments may also be needed to determine the adequacy of the assurance under art 72(2) against the certainty of the anticipated fundamental breach.

[2.198] It must be pointed out that the freedom of the parties under art 6 to define a fundamental breach may make arts 71 and 72 overlap to some extent. For example, if the parties define that a failure to maintain creditworthiness by the buyer amounts to a fundamental breach, a proven lack of creditworthiness in the buyer will allow the seller to act under both art 71 and art 72. By the same token, the parties may also define that a failure to carry out any conduct or performance constitutes a fundamental breach. The seller (or the buyer, as the case may be) might have an option to suspend or avoid a contract in the event of a failure by the other party to perform the defined conduct.

The seller's right to avoid contract and instalment deliveries

[2.199] For the purpose of preserving a contract, art 73(1) allows the seller (or the buyer, as the case may be) to avoid a contract in relation to a particular instalment on the ground of a fundamental breach. This means that if the buyer has committed a fundamental breach in relation to a particular instalment, the seller should avoid only that part of the contract concerning the instalment. Although art 73(1) does not adopt the word 'must', a failure of the seller (or the buyer) to preserve a contract in certain circumstances may affect his or her right to claim damages under arts 74–8. Alternatively, the seller (or

---

57. This rule appears to require the seller to establish his or her honest and reasonable belief that the buyer will commit a fundamental breach.
58. This conclusion can be drawn from the combined effect of art 71(2) and (3).

the buyer) may be found to have failed to mitigate the loss under art 77, if he or she has failed to comply with art 73(1).

[2.200] Article 73(2) allows the seller (or the buyer, as the case may be) to avoid a contract concerning future instalments, if the failure of the buyer to perform his or her obligation in relation to a particular instalment gives the seller 'good grounds to conclude that a fundamental breach of the contract will occur with respect to future instalments'.

The main function of this provision is to preserve the part of the contract that has been performed satisfactorily. 'Good grounds' is not defined in art 73(2). Since the ground for avoiding the contract with respect to future instalments is an anticipated fundamental breach, arts 71 and 72 should be relied upon in the construction of art 73(2). The interpretation of art 73(2) is not as easy as it looks.

[2.201] In a case decided in the Supreme Court of Austria (2 Ob 328/97t, 12 February 1998, CLOUT Case 238) the Austrian buyer failed to make payments to the Czech seller for instalments of umbrellas delivered, and also defrauded the seller by showing a copy of a bank payment order to the seller and later cancelling it. The seller avoided the contract for future deliveries. The court held that neither the buyer's failure to make payments, nor the cancellation of the bank payment order indicated with a sufficient degree of probability a serious deficiency in the buyer's ability to perform the contract in the future, or in its creditworthiness under arts 71 and 73. Accordingly, the court denied the seller's right to avoid the contract under art 73. Although the decision is in favour of the continuation of the contract for instalment deliveries, is it fair to the seller? Is it a reasonable interpretation of art 73?

[2.202] Article 73(3) carries the matter a step further and allows the seller (or the buyer) to declare that any deliveries already made are avoided. It virtually allows the seller (or the buyer) to avoid the whole contract if the previous and future deliveries are not severable from the instalment in question. The severability of the deliveries or the goods delivered is determined by the interdependence between them. 'Interdependence' may be assessed by examining whether the goods delivered can be used independently for the purpose contemplated in the contract.

[2.203] The order of the three paragraphs in art 73 suggests that the Convention intends to limit as much as possible the exercise of the right to avoid a contract. Again, the notion of contract preservation must be the underlying rationale.

The seller's right to claim damages and foreseeability

[2.204] The seller has a right to claim damages as a remedy under arts 74–8. Article 74 has two functions — defining the meaning of 'damage' and setting out the requirement of foreseeability, as follows:
- damages 'consist of a sum equal to the loss, including loss of profit', which may include shipping or customs charges arising from the return of non-conforming

[2.204]

goods, and the costs of purchasing special materials or tools which have become obsolete due to the return of non-conforming goods of a specific description;[59] and

- the sum of damages is restricted by foreseeability, which means that the sum should not exceed 'the loss which the party in breach foresaw or ought to have foreseen at the time of the conclusion of the contract'.

[2.205] Article 74 requires the damage to be the loss suffered by the claimant. Otherwise, there is no damage at all. This part of art 74 is illustrated by a German case, *Oberlandesgericht Dusseldorf* (17 U 146/93, 14 January 1994, CLOUT Case 130). In that case, the Italian seller avoided the contract for the sale of 140 pairs of shoes it had manufactured, because the German buyer failed to provide any security or make payment for the delivery of the shoes. After the avoidance, the seller sold the shoes on the market and suffered a loss because most shoes were sold at lower prices. The court permitted the seller to claim the difference between the contract price and resale price of the shoes, together with interest on the sum due. But the court rejected the seller's claim for legal costs, and for the loss arising from the exchange rate between the Italian Lira and the German Deutsche Mark. The court rejected the claim for the lawyer's fee because the lawyer had made a separate application to fix his cost. The court rejected the loss in exchange rate because it took the view that exchanging between the two currencies was neither a common commercial practice, nor an established practice between the parties. Thus, the court held that the alleged loss in exchange rate was groundless.

[2.206] In determining whether the party in breach ought to have foreseen the breach, art 74 requires consideration of the facts and matters which the party in breach ought to have known to be possible consequences of the breach, at the time when the contract was made. It can be argued that presumed foreseeability is the foreseeability of possible facts and matters which will flow from the breach. The requirement of foreseeability is based on the 'well-known theory of so-called adequate causality', which means 'that having regard to all circumstances of the given case, the party in breach is not liable for a loss he could not foresee'.[60]

[2.207] Attention should be paid to the difference between foreseeability under art 74 and foreseeability under art 25 for fundamental breach. Article 25 does not expressly state the time of foreseeability; namely, whether it should be at the time when the contract is made, or at the time of breach. In contrast, art 74 clearly states that 'foreseeability' means foreseeability at the time of the conclusion of the contract. It is yet to be seen whether this difference will have any significant impact upon the operation of the two provisions.

The seller's damages claim and resale of goods

[2.208] Article 75 deals with a particular instance of damages claim. This provision states that if the seller has resold the goods, the damages claimable consist of the difference between the contract price and the resale price, as well as any further damages recoverable under art 74.[61]

---

59. See *Delchi Carrier SpA v Rotorex Corp* 10 Federal Reporter (3rd series) 1024 (6 December 1995, US Court of Appeal (Second Circuit), CLOUT Case 138).
60. Bianca and Bonell, 1987, p 541.

[2.209] Article 75 requires the seller to resell the goods in a reasonable manner and within a reasonable time after avoidance. This is probably for the purpose of ensuring that the goods will be sold at the best price in the circumstances. It appears that if the seller has not resold the goods in a reasonable manner and within a reasonable time, he or she cannot rely on art 75. It follows that the seller may also be found to have breached art 77, which requires the innocent party to mitigate the loss. Therefore, it can be argued that art 75 in fact requires the seller (or buyer, as the case may be) to resell the goods in a reasonable manner (or, in the words of a German court, 'to undertake a profitable resale')[62] and within a reasonable time if the seller intends to claim the maximum damages recoverable under the Convention.

The length of time considered reasonable can only be determined by a court in the circumstances concerned. In a German case, *Oberlandesgericht Dusseldorf* (17 U 146/93, 14 January 1994, CLOUT Case 130), the seller (who was also the manufacturer of the shoes sold under a contract with the German buyer) sold the shoes on the market nearly two months after the avoidance of the contract. Avoidance took place on 7 August and resale on 6 and 15 October respectively. The court held that, in the circumstances, the seller acted within a reasonable time under arts 75 and 77 of the Convention.

[2.210] It can be assumed that if the resale price is higher than the contract price, the damages claimable by the seller (if there are any) will be reduced in proportion under art 74, probably against the claim for loss of profit.

The seller's damages claim and market price of the goods

[2.211] Article 76 extends the principles under art 75 to a situation in which the seller has not resold the goods after the avoidance. Article 76 is based on the presumption that the seller (or the buyer, as the case may be) will normally resell the goods (or purchase the substitute) after the avoidance, and thus the recoverable damages should be based on the difference between the market price of the goods and the contract price if the goods were not resold within a reasonable time.[63]

[2.212] Article 76 sets out the following rules:
- if the goods are not resold, the seller should claim the difference between the market price for the same goods and the contract price of the goods, in addition to other damages recoverable under art 74;
- the market price should be the current price at the time of the avoidance;

---

61. The operation of arts 74 and 75 is illustrated by a Spanish case, decided in January 2000, and available in abstract as CLOUT Case 395.
62. The quote comes from *Oberlandesgericht Hamm* (19U 97/91, 22 September 1992, CLOUT Case 227), in which the German buyer refused to accept more deliveries of bacon from the Italian seller, who later sold the bacon at a price lower than both the contract price and the prevailing market price. The court decided that the seller was obliged by arts 75 and 77 to undertake a profitable resale of the goods on the relevant market.
63. Bianca and Bonell, 1987, p 553.

[2.212]

- alternatively, if the seller avoided the contract after taking over the goods, the market price should be the current price at the time when the goods were taken over by the seller;[64]
- the current price should be 'the price prevailing at the place where delivery of the goods should have been made'; or
- in the absence of such a price, the current price should be 'the price at such other place as serves as a reasonable substitute, making due allowance for differences in the cost of transporting the goods'.

[2.213] It can be argued that arts 75 and 76 set out rules which compel the seller (or the buyer, as the case may be) to mitigate the loss by reselling the goods (or purchasing a substitute). Although art 75 appears to say that the 'current price' is an option for determining the seller's loss if the seller has not resold the goods, the combined effect of arts 75 and 76 is that the seller would be forced by economic considerations in certain circumstances to resell the goods at the market price in a reasonable manner, and within a reasonable time in order to avoid the use of the current price for determining his or her loss.

If the seller is better off under the actual resale price, he or she would prefer to resell the goods under art 75; and if the seller is better off under the current price, rather than the resale price, he or she has the option of resorting to art 76 by inaction. The matter will eventually be redressed by art 77, which imposes an obligation upon the innocent party to mitigate the loss. Therefore, it can be further argued that arts 75–77 operate together to ensure that the innocent party has preserved the contract and mitigated the loss to the maximum extent that he or she ought to in the circumstances concerned.

The seller's claim and mitigation of loss

[2.214] The innocent party's obligation to mitigate losses, which has also been regarded as a right,[65] is enunciated in art 77. This provision states as follows:

> A party who relies on a breach of contract must take such measures as are reasonable in the circumstances to mitigate the loss, including loss of profit, resulting from the breach. If he fails to take such measures, the party in breach may claim a reduction in the damages in the amount by which the loss should have been mitigated.

[2.215] The scope of art 77 goes beyond arts 75 and 76. A seller under art 77 must not only resell the goods in a reasonable manner and within a reasonable time, but also preserve and protect the goods in a reasonable manner. The reasonableness of the measures adopted by the seller must be assessed according to the circumstances involved. For example, in a German case, *Oberlandesgericht Dusseldorf* (17 U 146/93, 14 January 1994,

---

64. Honnold comments as follows (Honnold, 1991, pp 510–11):

    Avoidance by a seller usually occurs while the seller still has possession of the goods … However, in these cases, the second sentence does not apply since avoidance will occur *before* rather than '*after* taking over the goods'.

    It can be argued, however, that in a case of an unpaid seller exercising the right of stoppage under the Australian sale of goods legislation (see [1.83]), which is possible for a lack of contrary rules under the Convention, an unpaid seller may take over the goods before avoiding the contract.

65. See a case arbitrated by the Internationales Schiedsgericht der Bundeskammer der gewerblichen Wirtschaft-Wien, SCH-4366, [1995] UNLEX D 94-12 (15 June 1994, CLOUT Case 93).

CLOUT Case 130), the court considered the lower prices at which the shoes were sold were reasonable, because, in the Italian market, most retailers had filled their stock in August for the coming season, and the demand for winter shoes was lower than the time when the contract was made. This means that the nature of the goods, the market needs, the established commercial practice in reselling or preserving the goods of the same nature, the buyer's cooperation in resolving the dispute, and the seller's capacity to control and preserve the goods in the circumstances concerned, among other factors, must be taken into account. The notion of contract promotion and preservation will certainly be a consideration under art 77.

The seller's right to claim interest

[2.216] Article 78 allows the innocent party to claim interest on any payment that is in arrears. This provision does not expressly state how to calculate interest, failing to stipulate such matters as the time when the interest begins to accrue and when it stops accruing. It can be argued, however, that interest should begin to accrue from the date when the payment becomes due and should keep accumulating until the date when the payment is made. In the absence of specific rules in the Convention, the determination of the interest rate and calculation of the interest payment are totally subject to the law of the court determining the dispute. In a German case, *Oberlandesgericht Frankfurt a M* (5 U 261/90, 13 June 1991, CLOUT Case 1), the court noted that, for the purpose of determining the interest rate, the prevailing view was that the law of the creditor's country should apply, and the minority view was that the law of the debtor's country should apply.

As we can see in the cases referred to below, the courts have determined the applicable interest rate under the relevant domestic law, without necessarily deciding whether to give preference to the law of the creditor's country or the law of the debtor's country. Due to the belief that either the law of the creditor's country or the law of the debtor's country should apply to the determination of interest rate, a national court may thus determine the interest rate under a foreign law.

In a Swiss case involving a dispute between an Italian seller of furniture and a Swiss buyer, *Kantonsgericht Nidwalden* (15/96 Z, 3 December 1997, CLOUT Case 220), the court adjudicated the case on the basis of the Swiss law (which had incorporated the Convention), but determined the interest rate on the basis of the Italian law, probably because the seller was Italian. When the court decided the period for which the buyer had to pay the interest, it moved back to Swiss law for that purpose. Thus, in this case the court actually applied the Convention, Swiss law and Italian law to determine the dispute.

[2.217] It must be noted that, under art 78, interest is payable on any sum of payment which is in arrears. This includes the payment which became due before the contract was avoided, or before a particular breach (rather than late payment) took place. This also includes the refund of a payment in advance which the seller should have returned to the buyer in pursuance of the contract, or due to the seller's breach or inability to perform.

For example, a buyer who has failed to open a documentary credit within the time agreed in the contract is liable to pay interest on the principal due. In the absence of any specific rules on the determination of interest in art 78, the International Court of

Arbitration, when arbitrating a dispute between a Bulgarian buyer and an Austrian seller, decided that the payment of interest should be determined by the relevant rules of Austrian law, which was the applicable law of the contract: CLOUT Case 104.[66] In that case, the seller established that it had to borrow credit at the rate of 12 per cent to replace the funds which could have been available to the seller if the documentary credit had been opened as agreed. The tribunal granted a sum of interest at the rate of 12 per cent on the principal due under the documentary credit against the buyer, even though the rate appeared to be higher than that normally accepted under the Austrian law.

[2.218] Similarly, in a German case, *Oberlandesgericht Dusseldorf* (17 U 146/93, 14 January 1994, CLOUT Case 130) the court allowed the seller to claim an interest rate of 16.5 per cent, on the ground that this was the actual rate of the bank loan taken out by the seller to cover the cost of the shoes which should have been paid by the buyer. The court's decision in this case was supported by art 287 of the German Civil Code.

The decisions in both of these cases were based on the finding that the claimants had established the existence of a high interest rate on loans taken out as a result of the other party's breach. In the absence of such a finding, the court will grant a lower interest rate. In another German case, *Oberlandesgericht Hamm* (11 U 206/93, 8 February 1995, CLOUT Case 132) the court refused the claim for a 14 per cent interest rate by a bank, and allowed a moderate rate of 10 per cent, as permitted by the relevant Italian law (art 1284 of the Codice Civile).

The buyer's remedies under the Convention

Categories of remedies

[2.219] Under the Convention, the remedies available to the buyer can be divided into the following categories:

- requesting the seller to perform his or her contractual obligations under art 46;
- fixing an additional period of time for the seller to perform (*nachfrist*) under art 47;
- requesting a court to order specific performance under arts 28 and 46;[67]
- declaring the contract avoided under art 49;
- reducing the price of the non-conforming goods under art 50;
- refusing to take an earlier delivery under art 51;
- refusing to take delivery of a greater (or lesser) quantity under art 52;[68]
- suspending the performance of a contract under art 71;

---

66. A similar position was adopted by a Swiss court in *Handelsgericht des Kantons Zurich* (HG 930476, 21 September 1995, CLOUT Case 195). The court decided that the interest rate should be determined by the governing law, which was Austrian law.
67. Again it must be noted that 'specific performance' under art 28 is a different remedy from the right to request the seller to perform a specific obligation under art 46. 'Specific performance' is used here as a broad term. In a US case, the court expressed the view that if a buyer could prove alleged facts, that buyer would be entitled to claim specific performance under both art 46 and the relevant US law: *Magellan International Corp v Salzgitter Handel GmbH*, 76 Federal Supplement (2d series) 919; CLOUT Case 417.

- avoiding a contract on the ground of an anticipated fundamental breach under art 72;
- avoiding a contract in proportion to the defective instalments under art 73; and
- claiming damages and interest under arts 74–78.

[2.220] The right to claim damages forms a special category of remedy under the Convention. It is special in the sense that it is always available, even if the buyer has resorted to other remedies. For example, a buyer may request or allow a seller to cure any lack of conformity in the goods delivered under arts 37, 46, 47 and 48, but this does not deprive the buyer of his or her right to claim damages under arts 74–8. This is why art 45(2) states that the 'buyer is not deprived of any right he may have to claim damages by exercising his right to other remedies'.

[2.221] Set-off is a remedy available to a contracting party in most countries, but the Convention does not provide such a remedy. Thus, whether or not a buyer has the right to set-off against the claim of the seller is a grey area of the Convention. In a German case, *Oberlandesgericht Hamm* (11 U 1991/94, 9 June 1995, CLOUT Case 125), the court was asked to decide the buyer's right of set-off. The Italian seller sold 19 windows to the German buyer. Some of the windows delivered were defective. The seller subsequently replaced the defective ones with new ones, in pursuance of the agreement with the buyer. The buyer refused to pay the full price of the contract on the ground that the balance should be set off against the cost incurred in replacing the defective windows.

In the absence of a specific provision on set-off in the Convention, the court decided that German law, which had been chosen as the governing law by the parties, should apply. Under art 387 of the German Civil Code, the right to set-off rests on the existence of a counter-claim — which, however, in the present case, would be determined by the relevant provisions of the Convention. The court found that art 48(1) of the Convention, which permits self-cure by the seller after delivery of the defective goods, also imposes an obligation upon the seller to bear the cost arising from the act of self-cure. Accordingly, the buyer had a right under art 48(1) to raise a counter-claim, and the claim was set-off against the seller's claim under art 387 of the German Civil Code. In addition, the court also applied art 478 of the German Civil Code to extend the limitation period of the buyer's set-off claim, which would have been time-barred under the relevant provisions of German law — but for the fact that the buyer had given a notice to the seller under art 487, in the exercise of the right to set-off.

This case has general implications for the operation of the Convention, in the sense that a domestic court has a certain discretion in determining whether to apply domestic law to fill in gaps in the Convention. The court's power is discretionary, because certain gaps or omissions of the Convention may be regarded as a prohibition by a court in certain circumstances, depending on the approach that the court adopts. Of course, this

---

68. The Convention does not expressly allow the buyer to refuse to take delivery of a quantity less than the contract quantity. However, the seller is obliged to deliver the right quantity of goods under art 35. Therefore, it can be argued that if the seller delivers a quantity less than the contract quantity on a date earlier than agreed, the buyer has the option of either accepting or refusing the delivery under art 52. If the seller delivers a quantity less than the contract quantity on the fixed date, the buyer is entitled, if he or she chooses to do so, to reject the delivery on the ground of art 35, probably by arguing a fundamental breach.

proposition does not apply to provisions of the Convention which have expressly permitted the application of the relevant domestic law, such as arts 4, 6 and 28.

[2.222] It must be emphasised that even though the buyer may be granted a right of set-off under a domestic law, the right can only be exercised against a claim arising from a contract for the international sale of goods. Thus, in another German case involving a German seller and an Italian buyer, the court held that the buyer's set-off claim must be disallowed, because it was based on a distribution agreement serving as the umbrella agreement for a number of sales contracts between the parties: *Oberlandesgericht Dusseldorf* (6 U 152/95, 11 July 1996, CLOUT Case 169).

The buyer's right and the proviso of no-fault

[2.223] Article 80 is a proviso which says that a buyer (or a seller, as the case may be) may not rely on the breach of the other party if the breach is caused by his or her own act or omission. Under this provision, the buyer's right to rely on the seller's breach can be quantified in proportion to the impact of the buyer's act or omission upon that breach. This provision is consistent with one of the basic principles of common law, that one is not allowed to benefit from one's own mistake or misconduct.

The buyer's right to require performance

[2.224] Article 46 gives the buyer a right to require the seller to perform his or her obligations under the contract or the Convention. This right is different from specific performance under art 28, because art 46 allows the buyer to make a request to the seller directly.

[2.225] Article 46 provides the following rights to the buyer:

- If a lack of conformity constitutes a fundamental breach of contract, the buyer may require the seller to deliver substitute goods. The request must be made in compliance with the requirement for giving notice under art 39, or within a reasonable time after the discovery of the lack of conformity.[69]

- If a lack of conformity does not amount to a fundamental breach, the buyer may require the seller to repair the lack of conformity. The request must be made in compliance with the requirement for giving notice under art 39, or within a reasonable time after the discovery of the lack of conformity.[70] The request must not be unreasonable in the circumstances concerned.

- The buyer has a general right to require the seller to perform his or her contractual obligations, unless the buyer has resorted to a remedy (such as a suspension or termination of the contract) which is inconsistent with the exercise of this right.

---

69. Article 46(2) provides that the request for substitute goods should be made either under art 39 or 'within a reasonable time *thereafter*' (italics added). The meaning of 'thereafter' in this provision is unclear. A reasonable interpretation appears to be 'after the discovery of the lack of non-conformity'.
70. Like art 46(2), art 46(3) provides that the request for repairing goods should be made either under art 39 or 'within a reasonable time thereafter'. As before, a reasonable interpretation of 'thereafter' would be 'after the discovery of the lack of non-conformity'.

[2.226] The seller does not appear to have an obligation to respond to the buyer's request under art 46. However, it may be assumed that a seller who rejects the buyer's request under art 46 will have to face the consequences of the rejection when the buyer makes damages claims against him or her.

[2.227] The right to request performance can be exercised in response to part delivery, or non-conformity in part of the goods delivered: art 51. This provision restates the notion of contract promotion and preservation underlying the Convention; the parties are encouraged to separate part of the goods or the contract performance in dispute from the rest of the goods or contract performance, wherever this is possible.

The buyer's right to fix an additional period of time for performance (nachfrist)

[2.228] Article 47 gives the buyer a right to offer an additional period of time for the seller to perform his or her obligations. This is a right because the buyer is at liberty to do so: the 'buyer may fix an additional period of time of reasonable length for performance by the seller of his obligations'.

[2.229] However, in the exercise of this right, the buyer has undertaken the following two implied obligations:

- the buyer must fix a period of 'reasonable length', which means that the buyer may breach art 47 in the exercise of his or her right if the length of the grace period is unreasonably short; and
- the buyer has also undertaken an obligation not to resort to other remedies during the period of grace, even though the buyer is still entitled to claim damages after the elapse of the additional period of time for performance.

These two obligations suggest that art 47 is not what we call a 'buyer's remedy' in the traditional sense.[71] It is an option and remedy for a buyer who wishes to resolve the dispute in a non-adversarial manner. However, this right of the buyer is provided for the common interest of both the buyer and seller, rather than for the sole benefit of the buyer (as most buyer's remedies at common law are).

[2.230] It must also be pointed out that when a buyer intends to avoid a contract under art 49(1)(b) (that is, when non-delivery is the sole ground for avoidance), the buyer may arguably have an 'obligation', rather than a 'right', to give a grace period for delivery to the seller, under art 47(1).

This is because, arguably, art 49(1)(b) has made the granting of a grace period under art 47(1) a prerequisite for declaring a contract avoided on the ground of non-delivery. However, it must also be pointed out that art 49(1)(b) is only one of the available grounds for avoiding a contract. This means that the buyer is not 'obliged' to consider art 47, if he or she relies on the ground of fundamental breach set out in art 49(1)(a). Neither art 47 nor art 49 prescribes the length of the additional period for performance. In a German

---

71. In a German case, *Oberlandesgericht Dusseldorf* (6 U 119/93, 10 February 1994, CLOUT Case 82), the German buyer was denied the right granted in arts 46–50 of the Convention on the ground that it had failed to fix an additional period of performance for the Italian seller as requested by arts 47(2) and 49(1)(b).

[2.230]

case, *Oberlandesgericht Celle* (20 U 76/94, 24 May 1995, CLOUT Case 136), the court held that a period of two weeks for the seller to deliver used printing machines was sufficient for the purposes of arts 47 and 49.

[2.231] Article 47 is also applicable to non-conformity in part of the goods or part performance of the contract by virtue of art 51.

The buyer's right to request substitute goods and restitution

[2.232] The buyer is entitled to request the seller to deliver substitute goods under arts 46 and 47. However, under art 82(1), the buyer's right to do so is subject to his or her ability to 'make restitution of the goods substantially in the condition in which he received them'. This means that if the buyer is unable to make restitution of the goods received, he or she will lose the right to request the delivery of substitute goods. However, the buyer can still claim damages under art 74, even though he or she cannot make restitution of goods: art 83.

[2.233] The restrictive effect of art 82(1) upon the buyer's right to request substitute goods is qualified in art 82(2) in the following circumstances:

- the buyer does not lose the right if the impossibility of making restitution of the goods delivered was not due to his or her act or omission;
- the buyer does not lose the right if the goods or part of the goods 'have perished or deteriorated as a result of the examination provided for in article 38';
- the buyer does not lose the right if 'the goods have been sold in the normal course of business' before the buyer discovered or ought to have discovered the lack of conformity; and
- the buyer does not lose the right if the goods 'have been consumed or transformed by the buyer in the course of normal use before he discovered or ought to have discovered the lack of conformity'.

[2.234] Article 82 suggests that the seller may rely on this provision to refuse the buyer's request for delivery of substitute goods in circumstances in which the buyer is unable to make restitution of the goods delivered. The burden of proof is on the buyer to prove that the inability to make restitution falls under one of the heads in art 82(2).

[2.235] When the buyer is liable to make restitution, art 84(2) requires the buyer to 'account to the seller for all benefit which he [or she] has derived from the goods or part of them', regardless of whether the buyer is exempt under art 82(2). This means that the buyer is liable to return all benefit he or she has received from the use, control or possession of the goods delivered to him or her, if the buyer avoids the contract or requests the seller to deliver substitute goods.

The buyer's remedy of specific performance

[2.236] Articles 46 and 47 allow the buyer to request the seller to perform his or her obligations under the contract or the Convention. The buyer has a 'right' to do so under these provisions. However, the right cannot be translated directly into a right to request a court of law to order specific performance under the Convention. This is because art 28 of the

Convention makes specific performance by the order of the court a matter of domestic law. This means that the buyer should explore the potential of arts 46 and 47 fully if he or she prefers to enforce the contractual obligations against the seller specifically.

The buyer's right to avoid contracts in general

[2.237] The termination of a contract is the most serious remedy to which a party can resort under the Convention, although it is not the last remedy the party can take in relation to the contract. This is suggested in art 81, which states that avoidance of the contract 'releases both parties from their obligations under it, subject to any damages which may be due'. Similarly, art 51 requires the buyer to avoid a contract against part delivery or part of the goods, wherever the deliveries and goods are severable under the contract. This is for the purpose of preserving and promoting the contract to the maximum extent which is fair to the parties concerned. By the same token, if the contract or the goods are not severable, art 51(2) allows the contract to be avoided 'in its entirety only if the failure to make delivery completely or [failure to make delivery] in conformity with the contract amounts to a fundamental breach'.

[2.238] Article 49 does not allow the buyer to avoid the contract lightly. It provides two sets of rules for the avoidance of a contract. The first set of rules, which is found under art 49(1), deals with situations in which the goods have not been delivered. The second set of rules, which is included under art 49(2), deals with situations in which the goods have been delivered.

[2.239] Article 49(1) contains the following rules:

- the buyer may avoid the contract if the seller's breach has amounted to a fundamental breach, which can be defined by the parties themselves or based on art 25; or
- the buyer can avoid a contract on the ground of non-delivery after the seller has failed, or refused, to deliver the goods within the additional time given by the buyer under art 47(1).

[2.240] The construction of art 49(1) is a difficult task for the following reasons:

- First, art 49(1)(a), which allows a contract to be avoided on the ground of a fundamental breach, and art 49(1)(b), which allows a contract to be avoided on the ground of non-delivery after the buyer has complied with *nachfrist* procedures under art 47(1), are parallel. This means that art 49(1)(b) can be understood as merely optional and supplementary to art 49(1)(a), which may have included non-delivery as a fundamental breach. It follows that there is no connection, contrary to the arguments in the next paragraph, between art 49(1)(b) and art 47(1).
- Second, contrary to the first construction, it can be argued that the parallel structure or equal relationship between art 49(1)(a) and art 49(1)(b) suggests that art 49(1)(b) sets out specific rules for avoiding a contract on the ground of non-delivery. This argument is based on the language of art 49(1)(b), which specifically refers to 'in case of non-delivery'. This reference may be interpreted as saying 'in case of non-delivery, the following rules apply'. If so, art 49(1)(b) would make it compulsory in the case of non-delivery for the buyer to give additional time as provided in art 47(1). This

[2.240] controversial construction of art 49(1)(b) can be avoided by the parties expressly defining a fundamental breach, thus unambiguously making non-delivery a fundamental breach under art 49(1)(a).

- Third, it can be argued that art 49(1)(b) makes compliance with art 47(1) procedures compulsory only when the buyer has chosen to rely on 'non-delivery' as the ground of avoidance under art 49(1)(b). This may be the case either because the buyer is not able, or fails, to rely on any other grounds for avoidance in art 49, or because the buyer prefers to resort to art 49(1)(b). It can be argued that if art 49(1)(b) is relied upon, the provision would impose an obligation upon the buyer to give an additional time for delivery to the seller, although art 47(1) has given the buyer a mere option to allow a period of grace to the seller. It can be further argued that the combined effect of arts 49(1)(b) and 47(1) means that if the buyer intends to avoid the contract on the ground of non-delivery (which is not defined expressly by the parties as a fundamental breach), he or she must give the seller a period of grace under art 47(1) before so doing. In a German case, *Oberlandesgericht Oldenburg* (11 U 64/94, 1 February 1995, CLOUT Case 165), the court held that, under art 49, the German buyer was entitled to avoid the contract for the sale of furniture because the Austrian seller had failed to make the furniture conform to the contract after it was given an opportunity to fix it. In addition, the court also took the view that the non-conformity of the furniture amounted to a fundamental breach under art 25 of the Convention.

[2.241] It appears that the third construction of art 49(1) would be more logical, in the sense that art 47(1) becomes compulsory only when the buyer has chosen to rely on art 49(1)(b). This construction coincides with the first construction, in that art 49(1)(b) is optional. However, it is inconsistent with the first construction in the sense that sometimes the seller may have no option but to rely on art 49(1)(b). For example, a buyer cannot rely on art 49(1)(a) if a fundamental breach has not been proven, and cannot rely on art 49(2) if the goods have not been delivered.

[2.242] Article 49(2) includes the following rules for avoiding a contract where the goods have been delivered:

- if a late delivery has been made in breach of the contract, the buyer may avoid the contract on the ground of the late delivery only when he or she does so within a reasonable time after becoming aware of the late delivery;
- if any breach has been committed,[72] the buyer may avoid the contract on the ground of the breach only when he or she does so within a reasonable time after he or she knows or ought to know of the breach;
- where the buyer has given the seller an additional period of time for performance under art 47(1), he or she can avoid the contract if the seller has failed or refused to cure 'any breach' within the additional time period, provided that the buyer avoids the

---

72. Article 49(2)(b)(i) does not expressly say that 'any breach' must be a 'fundamental' breach. However, it can be assumed in the context of the whole Convention that only a 'fundamental breach' can reasonably fit in the context of art 49(2)(b)(i).

contract within a reasonable time after the expiration of the grace period or the receipt of the seller's refusal; and

- where the seller has requested a grace period for performance under art 48(2), the buyer can avoid the contract on two grounds:
  - if the buyer failed to refuse the request, he or she can avoid the contract only if he or she does so within a reasonable time after the expiration of the additional period in which the seller failed to cure the 'breach'; or
  - if the buyer refused the request, he or she can avoid the contract only if he or she does so within a reasonable time after his or her refusal.[73]

[2.243] Article 49(2)(b)(ii) applies to the situation where an additional period for performance has been given to the seller under art 47. When art 49(2)(b)(ii) is relied upon, the additional period for performance appears to be a de facto requirement for the buyer to avoid a contract. If the buyer is unable, or fails, to comply with art 49(2)(b)(i) and (iii) for the purpose of avoiding a contract in circumstances where a breach, rather than late delivery, has occurred, he or she has to give a grace period to the seller (under art 47) before being able to rely on art 49(2)(b)(ii) to avoid the contract. In contrast, if the seller requests a grace period under art 48, the buyer has an option to refuse the request, and to avoid the contract within a reasonable time after such refusal.

[2.244] Article 49(2)(b)(ii) shows an inconsistency with the effect of art 47, under which the granting of a grace period to the seller is merely an option for the buyer. There is no pressure in this provision for the buyer to give additional time for performance. Nor is there any need for the buyer to justify his or her decision not to give additional time to the seller. However, in the context of art 49(2)(b)(ii), the buyer appears to be obliged to 'opt' to give an additional period under art 47(1) for the seller to cure non-conformity in the goods already delivered if the buyer cannot rely on other grounds for avoiding a contract under art 49.

[2.245] Article 49(2)(b)(iii) provides another ground for avoidance. If the buyer chooses to rely on this ground, he or she must either await the expiration of the additional period requested by the seller under art 48(2), or refuse the seller's request in compliance with art 48(1), before avoiding the contract.

This means that if the buyer cannot justify his or her refusal to allow the seller's self-cure on one of the grounds set out in art 48(1), he or she will not be able to avoid the contract under art 49(2)(b)(iii) before the expiration of the additional period requested by the seller. The combined effect of arts 49(2)(b)(iii) and 48 suggests that when the buyer intends to rely on art 49(2)(b)(iii) for avoidance, he or she is obliged to comply with art 48 before declaring the contract avoided. Again, we may argue that art 49(2)(b)(iii) has made

---

73. Article 49(2)(b)(iii) does not expressly state that the buyer's refusal to give a grace period under art 48(2) must be based on any of the grounds set out in art 48(1). However, it can be inferred from the whole context of art 48 that the buyer can only do so on one of the specified grounds set out in art 48(1). This is because art 48(1) makes the seller's self-cure after the date for delivery a de facto right of the seller subject to the grounds for refusal set out in this provision.

[2.245]

art 48, which is otherwise less compelling, a compulsory provision which must be followed if the buyer relies on art 49(2)(b)(iii) for avoidance.

[2.246] The effect of avoiding a contract is defined in art 81. This provision states that avoidance of the contract 'releases both parties from their obligations under it'. But the innocent party is able to claim damages after the avoidance. Article 81 also emphasises that avoidance of the contract does not affect the provisions of the contract that were designed to deal with the relationships of the parties after the termination of the contract. Article 81 enables the innocent party to seek compensation after the termination of a contract, whether it is terminated by the agreement of the parties or following a breach by one of the parties.

This provision is necessary in the sense that, technically, the parties' contractual relationship ceases to exist after termination, but art 81 gives the innocent party a right to claim damages even if the contract had been terminated by an earlier event. In a German case, *Oberlandesgericht Celle* (20 U 76/94, 24 May 1995, CLOUT Case 136), the court held that an oral contract for the sale of secondhand printing machines between an Egyptian buyer and a German seller was avoided when the seller failed to deliver three machines, which should have been delivered earlier, after the expiration of the grace period of two weeks allowed by the buyer. The court held that, under art 81, the buyer was entitled to claim the refund of the prepaid price of the machines, and also the interest on the sum due. Since the buyer failed to justify a higher rate of interest, the court fixed an interest rate of 4 per cent, pursuant to art 288 of the German Civil Code.

The buyer's right to avoid a contract and restitution

[2.247] Rules regarding restitution are set out in art 81(2) of the Convention, which states:

> A party who has performed the contract either wholly or in part may claim restitution from the other party of whatever the first party has supplied or paid under the contract. If both parties are bound to make restitution, they must do so concurrently.

[2.248] This provision requires the parties to compensate each other for the work already performed under the avoided contract. Article 81(2) was applied in a Swiss case, *Handelsgericht des Kantons Zurich* (HG 950347, 5 February 1997, CLOUT Case 213). In that case, the German buyer demanded a restitution of the first instalment paid to the French seller, who had failed to perform the contract totally. The court held that the seller must refund the buyer the money already paid; in addition, the court ordered the seller to compensate the buyer for the loss of profit under art 74.

[2.249] Restitution is also a prerequisite for the buyer to declare a contract avoided. This requirement is set out in art 82(1), which says that the buyer loses the right to avoid a contract if he or she is unable to make restitution of the goods delivered. However, art 83 allows the buyer to claim damages under art 74, regardless of whether he or she has lost the right to avoid the contract.

[2.250] Similarly, art 82(2) sets out exemptions to the above general rule:
- the buyer is still entitled to avoid the contract if he or she can prove that the impossibility of making restitution is not due to his or her act or omission;

- the buyer is still entitled to avoid the contract if he or she can prove that the 'goods or part of the goods have perished or deteriorated as a result of the examination provided for in article 38';
- the buyer is still entitled to avoid the contract if he or she can prove that the 'goods or part of the goods have been sold in the normal course of business' before he or she discovered or ought to have discovered the lack of conformity; or
- the buyer is still entitled to avoid the contract if he or she can prove that the goods or part of the goods 'have been consumed or transformed by the buyer in the course of normal use before he discovered or ought to have discovered the lack of conformity'.[74]

[2.251] Again, art 82(2) imposes the burden of proof upon the buyer if he or she cannot make restitution of the goods delivered owing to one of the reasons set out in this provision.

[2.252] Under art 84(2), the buyer is required to 'account to the seller all benefits he has derived from the goods or part of them'. This obligation extends to the situation in which the buyer cannot make restitution of the goods delivered because of any of the reasons set out in art 82(2), but he or she has nevertheless benefited from partial or full use of the goods delivered, as long as the buyer has declared the contract avoided or required the delivery of substitute goods.

The buyer's right to reduce price

[2.253] The buyer's right to reduce the price of the goods in proportion to the degree of non-conformity or defect in the goods is a special remedy available to the buyer under art 50. It is different to damages enforced by a court of law because a buyer is entitled to reduce the price pursuant to art 50 without the assistance of a court.

[2.254] Article 50 sets out the following rules for a buyer exercising the right to reduce the price:
- the buyer may reduce the price of the goods when the goods do not conform with the contract;[75]
- the extent of the reduction should be in proportion to the difference between the actual value of the non-conforming goods and the expected value of the conforming goods;
- the difference in the values should be determined on the basis of the market values of the non-conforming and conforming goods at the time of delivery;[76] and

---

74. In a German case, *Bundesgerichtshof* (VIII ZR 300/96, 25 June 1997, CLOUT Case 235), a Swiss buyer avoided a contract for the sale of stainless steel wire by a German seller on the ground of non-conformity of the goods. The court held that the contract had been avoided, even though the buyer was unable to restore the goods to their original condition. The court noted that both parties knew the fact that the non-conformity could be discovered only after the goods had been processed.
75. This includes non-compliance with art 35(2), which reads certain implied terms into a contract in the absence of a contrary intention of the parties.
76. Article 50 does not specifically refer to 'market value'. However, it is reasonable to use market value in most circumstances, rather than any other 'value' — although this is not to say that in special circumstances an agreed 'value' other than market value may be more appropriate.

[2.254]

- there is a proviso which states that the right to reduce the price is not available if the seller has cured the non-conformity pursuant to arts 37 and 48, or if the buyer has refused to allow the seller to cure the non-conformity under arts 37 and 48.

Article 50 was applied in a German case, *Landgericht Aachen* (41 0 198/89, 3 April 1989, CLOUT Case 46). In a Swiss case, *Canton of Ticino: Pretore della giurisdizione di Locarno Campagna* (27 April 1992, CLOUT Case 55), the court stated that art 50 is not intended to provide for restitution which enables the seller to pay for the repair cost, but to offer a remedy of reduction in the purchase price to the buyer, in the same proportion as the difference between the value of the goods delivered and the value of conforming goods under the contract.

[2.255] The proviso is an interesting one. Its function is twofold: to restrict the use of the right to reduce the price, and to encourage the use of self-cure measures under arts 37 and 48. While it appears to be reasonable that if the seller cures the lack of conformity in the goods there is no ground for reducing their price, it does not appear to be fair that the buyer loses his or her right to reduce the price for a refusal to allow self-cure for unreasonable inconvenience, unreasonable expense, unreasonable delay and uncertainty of reimbursement by the seller of expenses advanced by the buyer. All of these are legitimate grounds for refusal under arts 37 and 48. This doubt may perhaps be explained by the difficulty of reaching a mutually acceptable understanding of 'unreasonable inconvenience', 'unreasonable expenses' and so on, in most cases.

In order to avoid any disagreement with respect to the existence of any of the grounds for refusal under arts 37 and 48, art 50 prevents a buyer from exercising the right to reduce the price if a possibility of such a disagreement arises. In addition, art 50 appears to be phrased in a way which discourages the buyer from exercising his or her discretion to reduce the price in cases where the exercise of this discretion can be avoided (that is, in situations where arts 37 and 48 apply).

It must be pointed out that the proviso does not apply to the situation where the seller has exercised the right of self-cure under arts 37 and 48, but the non-conformity in the goods has not been fully cured. The buyer may reduce the price of the goods if the seller fails to remedy the non-conformity through the procedures set out in arts 37 and 48.

[2.256] It must also be pointed out that the right to reduce the price can be exercised against non-conformity in part of the goods if the goods delivered are severable. This is emphasised in art 51, which requires the buyer to limit the exercise of his or her right to the non-conforming part of the goods whenever it is possible.

The buyer's limited right to refuse delivery

[2.257] Article 52(1) allows the buyer to refuse to take delivery if the goods are delivered before the agreed date. This provision gives the buyer an option either to accept or refuse an early delivery. Article 52(1) provides only one specific ground for refusing to take delivery, which is delivery before the fixed date. It can thus be argued that if the seller delivers goods in a lesser quantity than the contract quantity on the date fixed, the buyer cannot rely on art 52(1) to refuse to take the delivery, even though the buyer has a right to require the seller to deliver goods in the correct quantity under art 35(1). In such a case, the buyer's option would lie in arts 49(1)(a) and 51(2) (avoidance of the contract), art 47 (giving an additional time for performance), art 48 (allowing the seller to request additional time) and arts 74–8 (claiming damages). There is no express right to refuse to take delivery on the ground of lesser quantity in art 52. Therefore, the relevant provisions of a domestic law, such as the Australian sale of goods legislation, can be distinguished on this ground.

[2.258] If the seller delivers a quantity which is greater than the contract quantity, art 51(2) gives the buyer the option of either taking delivery and paying for the excess quantity at the contract rate, or refusing to take the part which exceeds the contract quantity. This provision is based on a presumption that the goods are severable — otherwise, it would be impossible for the seller to reject only the part exceeding the contract quantity. It must be pointed out that art 51(2) does not give the buyer a right to refuse to take the whole delivery on the ground that the quantity is greater than the contract description. In a case where the goods are not severable and the quantity of the goods is greater than the contract description, the buyer would have to look at arts 35(1), 49(1)(a), 49(2)(b), 51(2), 47, 48 and 74–8 for an adequate remedy. This is different from the relevant provisions of the sale of goods legislation in Australia (see **[1.89]–[1.95]**); the buyer's right to refuse to take delivery is limited under the Convention.

[2.259] The policy underlying art 52 is again the notion of contract promotion and preservation. This notion requires the parties to seek a way of compromise or cooperation for the purpose of performing a contract, rather than simply refusing the whole delivery.

The buyer's right to suspend contract

[2.260] Both the buyer and the seller are allowed, under art 71, to suspend the performance of a contract on the ground of an anticipatory breach. Although, in principle, a buyer may suspend the performance of his or her obligations if 'it becomes apparent that the other party will not perform a substantial part of his [or her] obligations', in practice, the buyer must rely on one of the following grounds for the suspension of a contract:

- the seller has shown a serious deficiency in his or her ability to perform the contract;
- the seller has a serious deficiency in his or her creditworthiness (for example, the seller is insolvent);
- the seller's conduct in preparing to perform the contract suggests that he or she is not able to perform at least a substantial part of the contract; or
- the seller's act in performing the contract suggests that he or she is not able to perform at least a substantial part of the contract.

In other words, the buyer must prove an anticipatory breach on the part of the seller on one of the specified grounds before he or she is entitled to suspend his or her own performance of the contract.

[2.261] Article 71(3) requires that the buyer suspending the contract give notice of the suspension to the seller. The notice must be given immediately after the suspension. The buyer is obliged to resume the performance of the contract after the seller has provided an adequate assurance which would reasonably eliminate or change the ground of

[2.261]

suspension. An adequate assurance is one that would be adequate and sufficient in the eyes of a reasonable person to remove the ground for suspension.

[2.262] Article 71 permits a party, either the buyer or the seller, to suspend his or her performance in view of the other party's anticipatory breach. It is a right granted to the party alleging anticipatory breach by the other. Exercise of the right to suspend performance under art 71, and also art 72 (discussed at **[2.264]–[2.266]**), is not subject to acceptance or response by the other party. As far as the anticipatory breach or repudiation is concerned, the application of arts 71 and 72 of the CISG may lead to different results from the relevant common law rules.

Under the common law rules, the right to suspend one's performance on the ground of another's anticipatory breach is subject to the innocent party's express acceptance of the anticipatory breach. For example, in *Vitol SA v Norelf Ltd* [1995] 2 Lloyd's Rep 128, the UK Court of Appeal took the view that, as a matter of principle, the innocent party must communicate his or her intention to accept the other party's anticipatory breach or repudiation unequivocally.

[2.263] Articles 71 and 72 of the CISG require the innocent party suspending his or her performance to give a notice of suspension to the party who has allegedly committed an anticipatory breach. However, under the common law, an innocent party in this situation is required to communicate acceptance of the other party's anticipatory breach unequivocally. Taken together, these two sets of rules may lead to totally different consequences when applied to the same facts.

In *Vitol SA v Norelf Ltd* [1995] 2 Lloyd's Rep 128, for example, the contract stipulated that the loading period was between 1 March and 7 March 1991. The seller admitted to the buyer on or about 7 March that it was unable to complete loading until 9 March. This admission would have amounted to an anticipatory breach under art 71 of the CISG.

If the Convention applied, the buyer might have simply followed the requirement for notifying the seller of its intention to suspend or to terminate the contract. Indeed, the buyer sent a telex to the seller on 8 March to inform the seller of its intention to reject the cargo, and to repudiate the contract on the basis of the seller's admission. However, the case was not subject to the Convention, and thus the contract was not legally terminated by the telex. In this case, the buyer's telex, instead of the seller's admission, was regarded as an anticipatory breach, which required unambiguous acceptance by the seller. The seller failed to respond to the said telex unambiguously (in a way demonstrating an intention to accept the anticipatory breach). Although the arbitrator held that the seller was entitled to claim the difference between the contract price and the resale price of the cargo concerned, the Court of Appeal held that, as a matter of legal principle, the seller's inactivity when faced with the buyer's telex of 8 March did not constitute a valid acceptance of the buyer's anticipatory breach. The seller, impliedly, had breached its contractual obligations by its inaction.

The potential differences between arts 71 and 72 of the CISG and the relevant contract rules of common law are well illustrated by this case. In a way, the determination that the anticipatory breach was the buyer's telex, rather than the seller's admission of inability to

The buyer's right to avoid a contract on the ground of anticipated fundamental breach

[2.264] A buyer may avoid a contract on the ground of an anticipated fundamental breach under art 72. It must be pointed out that art 71 allows a contract to be suspended when one party appears to be unable to perform a substantial part of his or her obligations, but art 72 allows a contract to be avoided only when there will be a fundamental breach. In other words, while a breach under art 71 will probably amount to a fundamental breach in most cases because of one party's inability to perform a substantial part of the contract, a breach under art 72 *must* be a 'fundamental breach' as defined either by the parties or in art 25. The breaches in the two provisions may overlap if the definition of a fundamental breach under art 25 applies. However, a fundamental breach in art 72 could be less serious than an anticipatory breach of substantial obligations under art 71, if a fundamental breach was so defined by the parties themselves (using their freedom under art 6 to define the terms and vary the effect of provisions of the Convention). Hopefully, the common sense of the parties will not allow avoidance of a contract to be simpler than suspension of a contract.

[2.265] Article 72 allows the buyer (or the seller) to avoid a contract on the ground of an anticipated fundamental breach under the following rules:

- it must be clear that the other party will commit a fundamental breach;
- the buyer is obliged to give reasonable notice to the seller before avoidance only if time allows;[77] and
- the buyer is not required to give notice to the seller if the seller has declared that he or she will not perform the obligations.

[2.266] Whether the seller will commit a fundamental breach can only be determined in the particular circumstances concerned. The buyer needs to establish with certainty, as a reasonable person would in the same circumstances, that the seller will commit a fundamental breach. It is insufficient for the buyer to prove only that a fundamental breach is *likely* to occur. The buyer (or the seller) must also prove that his or her belief that the anticipated fundamental breach 'will' occur is reasonable.

The buyer's damages claim and instalment deliveries

[2.267] A buyer can claim damages in the case of a seller breaching the terms for instalment delivery. Article 73 deals with the following three situations in which a breach in instalment delivery can occur:

- First, art 73(1) says that if a seller commits a fundamental breach in relation to an instalment, the buyer may declare the contract avoided with respect to that instalment. This rule is based on the presumption that the instalment deliveries are independent of

---

77. When the seller provides an assurance in response to the buyer's notice, the buyer cannot avoid the contract if the assurance is adequate for removing the ground evidencing the anticipated fundamental breach.

each other. Avoidance of the contract with respect to one instalment delivery does not affect the performance of the contract with respect to other instalments.

- Second, art 73(2) states that if the buyer can prove on 'good grounds' that a fundamental breach in one instalment delivery will lead to a fundamental breach in future instalment deliveries, the buyer may, within a reasonable time (after he or she knows or ought to know of the anticipated fundamental breach),[78] declare the contract avoided for the future instalments. It must be pointed out that, as in art 72, the buyer must prove and believe that a fundamental breach 'will' occur, rather than merely establish that it is highly probable.[79]

- Third, art 73(3) allows the buyer to avoid the whole contract, including the instalments already made and future instalments. This provision states that if the instalments or the goods are not severable — if 'by reason of their interdependence, those deliveries could not be used for the purpose contemplated by the parties at the time of the conclusion of the contract' — the buyer (or the seller) may declare the whole contract avoided on the ground of a fundamental breach in one instalment. The key point under art 73(3) is that the avoidance of the contract with respect to a particular instalment will render the instalments already made and future deliveries unfit for the purpose for which the goods were acquired. This provision may only apply to cases in which a fundamental breach, either as defined by the parties or by art 25, has been committed. Otherwise, the seller may be able to cure the defect in the instalment under arts 37, 46, 47 or 48.

The buyer's damages claim and foreseeability

[2.268] Both the buyer and seller can claim damages under arts 74–8. As we have seen in the case of the seller's claim, the sum of damages is restricted by the breaching party's ability to foresee the extent of the damage at the time when the contract was concluded. The same rule applies to the buyer's claim.

[2.269] Article 74 deals with the buyer's damages claim in the following ways:

- 'damages' under the Convention is defined as consisting of all losses (including the loss of profit) that flow from the breach;

- the sum of the damages is limited to the extent which was foreseen or ought to have been foreseen by the seller at the time when the contract was made; and

- the seller's ability to foresee should be determined by taking into account natural and inevitable consequences of the breach which the seller knew or ought to have known at the time of the conclusion of the contract.

Article 74 sets out general principles for assessing damages under the Convention. This provision is the basis for the application of other rules relating to damages claims under the Convention. However, the interpretation of art 74 is subject to the relevant domestic

---

78. Article 73(2) does not expressly say so.
79. It must be admitted, however, that the difference between a certainty represented by the word 'will' and the high probability of an event is more often than not merely a matter of value judgment as mastered and developed incomprehensibly by lawyers and courts.

law of the court hearing a dispute. For example, in a Swiss case, *Handelsgericht des Kantons Zurich* (HG950347, 5 February 1997, CLOUT Case 214), the court held that a loss arising from the fluctuation in the exchange rates could not be allowed under one of the general principles of the Swiss tort law, that damages for future losses can only be awarded when the amount can at least be estimated at the time of the commission of the tort. Similarly, in *Delchi Carrier SpA v Rotorex Corp* 1994 US Dist Lexis 12829 (9 September 1994, CLOUT Case 85), the court granted the following damages under art 74:

- expenses incurred for remedying the non-conformity in the goods;
- the cost of shipping the goods from a third party for the purpose of mitigating the loss;
- the costs of handling and storing the non-conforming goods; and
- loss of profit resulting from a diminished volume of sales.

The buyer's damages claim and purchase of substitute goods

[2.270] Article 75 allows the buyer to purchase substitute goods in a reasonable manner and within a reasonable time after avoidance. If the buyer does so, he or she is entitled to recover the difference between the contract price and the price of the substitute goods, as well as other recoverable damages under art 74. In pursuance of this provision, the Russian Federation Chamber of Commerce and Industry, in an arbitrated case, allowed the buyer to claim the difference between the contract price and the replacement purchase price, since the seller failed to deliver the goods after the buyer had given an extension of about four months for delivery: Case No 155/1994 (16 March 1995, CLOUT Case 140).

[2.271] Under art 75, the substitute goods must be purchased in a reasonable manner and within a reasonable time after avoidance. The substitute goods must be reasonably similar in quality, quantity and fitness to the goods under the avoided contract. The price of the substitute goods must be reasonable, representing the market price of the conforming goods as described in the avoided contract at a reasonable time after avoidance.

[2.272] This provision appears to provide a right to the buyer (or the seller, as the case may be) by giving him or her the option of choosing whether to comply with art 75. However, the combined effect of arts 75 and 77 (which requires the innocent party to mitigate the loss), suggests that the buyer (or the seller) is obliged to do so if this is a reasonable thing to do for the purpose of mitigating the loss.

The buyer's damages claim and market price

[2.273] Article 76 gives the buyer (or the seller, as the case may be) an option to claim the difference between the market price of the goods (as opposed to the actual price of the substitute goods under art 75) and the contract price. In detail, art 76 states as follows:

- after avoidance, the buyer who has not purchased substitute goods may claim the difference between the market price for purchasing the substitute goods and the contract price;

[2.273]   **International Commercial Law**

- the market price should be the price at the time of avoidance;
- if the contract was avoided after the buyer had taken over the goods, the market price should be the price at the time of taking over the goods;
- the market price should be the price where the goods are to be delivered;
- in the absence of a market price at the place of delivery, the market price should be the price found in a place which serves as a reasonable substitute for the place of delivery, 'making due allowance for differences in the cost of transporting the goods'; and
- the claim under art 76 does not affect the buyer's right to other remedies under art 74.

In light of the above rules, it is clear that the market price of goods under art 76 is qualified by two crucial elements: time and place. The reasonableness of the market price is determined by looking at the time when the price exists and the place where the price is taken. Article 76 cannot be used by either the buyer or the seller to his or her advantage without complying with the requirements set out above.

The buyer's remedy and mitigation of loss

[2.274] Article 77 provides as follows:

> A party who relies on a breach of contract must take such measures as are reasonable in the circumstances to mitigate the loss, including loss of profit, resulting from the breach. If he fails to take such measures, the party in breach may claim a reduction in the damages in the amount by which the loss should have been mitigated.

This provision imposes a general obligation upon the buyer to mitigate the loss in a reasonable and appropriate manner in the circumstances concerned. This requires us to read arts 75 and 76 in conjunction with art 77 for the purpose of determining the reasonableness of the buyer's conduct in mitigating the loss. It implies that while a buyer has an option to take advantage (if there is any) of arts 75 and 76, he or she is also obliged to comply with either art 75 or art 76, if it is proved to be the reasonable thing to do in the particular circumstances.

The buyer's right to claim interest

[2.275] Article 78 allows a buyer (or a seller, as the case may be) to claim interest on any sum 'that is in arrears' under the contract. This right is independent of the buyer's (or seller's) right to claim damages under art 74. Even if a contract has been performed, the buyer (or the seller) may still be entitled to claim interest on the sum which became due before the contract had been performed. We may conclude that he or she may claim interest not only on any debt covered under a damage claim, but also on any sum which became due before the seller paid the buyer (for example, a reimbursement of the buyer's expenses). The sum in this context will be most likely to consist of incidental costs associated with the seller's performance of his or her obligations. For example, under a DDP term (see **[1.30]**), the seller is liable to pay for an import licence and customs, but the buyer is required to assist the seller. If the buyer has paid on behalf of the seller to obtain an import licence, the seller is liable to reimburse the buyer. Article 78 becomes applicable if the seller is late in reimbursing the buyer for such assistance and interest on the late payment accrues.

[2.276] The buyer's right to claim interest on a refund from the seller is dealt with in art 84(1). This provision states that if 'the seller is bound to refund the price, he must also pay interest on it, from the date on which the price was paid'. This provision was applied in a case arbitrated by the International Court of Arbitration in 1993, Case No 6653 (CLOUT Case 103). The tribunal decided that in the absence of detailed rules on the calculation of interest in the Convention, art 1151–1 of the French Civil Code should be applied to determine the payment of interest. Under the relevant provisions of the French law, the tribunal referred to the rate commonly applied to Eurodollar settlements between operators in international trade; that is, the one-year London Interbank Offered Rate (LIBOR), to calculate the sum of interest payable.

The passing of risk under the Convention

Determining the passing of risk under the Convention

[2.277] The passing of risk is a vital issue in the sale of goods. It determines which of the parties involved in a contract of sale is liable for losses incurred before the completion of the contract. At common law, as far as the sale of goods is concerned, the passing of risk and property are related, although not inseparable, concepts. However, the Convention does not deal with the issue of property at all. This means that although the property in the goods in any international sale invariably passes to the buyer, art 4(b) leaves the passing of property to the relevant domestic law. This is because the property laws of the contracting countries are too complex to be adequately dealt with under the Convention.

[2.278] The absence of rules governing the passing of property in the Convention gives rise to a need for a different approach to the construction of the Convention's rules on passing of risk. We must free ourselves from the established doctrine of common law that risk and property normally pass together. Thus, the rules for the passing of risk under the Convention may or may not have implications for the passing of property under the relevant domestic law; for example, under the Australian sale of goods legislation.[80]

Passing of risk and buyer's duty to pay the price

[2.279] Article 66 deals with the buyer's duty to pay the price of the contract after the risk has passed to the buyer. It provides that a buyer who has received the risk in the goods is liable to pay the contract price even though the goods have been damaged or lost, 'unless the loss or damage is due to an act or omission of the seller'. This provision is consistent with the common law understanding of risk. The buyer is liable to pay the

---

80. For example, in *Roder Zelt-Und Hallenkonstruktionen GmbH v Rosedown Park Pty Ltd* (1995) 13 ACLA 776, Von Doussa J examined the evidence on the passing of property in the goods sold under German law and s 24 of the Goods Act 1958 (Vic). His Honour then found the intention of the parties as shown in the contract of sale indicated that the property in the tents and their accessories would remain with the German seller until the full price of the goods had been paid.

[2.279]

price of the goods, because he or she is liable for the risk in the goods. We may argue that art 66 has the following two functions:

- to hold the buyer liable for the loss or damage after the risk has passed to him or her; and
- to allow the buyer to claim the return of the price paid or to refuse to make the payment, as the case may be, if the loss or damage to the goods has been caused by the seller's act or omission, regardless of whether the property has passed to the buyer.

[2.280] The first function is self-explanatory. The second function can be illustrated by a hypothetical situation in which the goods have been properly delivered and the risk passed to the buyer, but the seller has done something either deliberately or negligently, resulting in the loss of the goods or damage to them. In this case, under art 66, the buyer would be discharged from his or her obligation to pay the price, because the seller has breached his or her contractual obligations. The buyer would either be entitled to claim the return of the money if the price had been paid, or to refuse to pay the price if the price had not been paid. Therefore, art 66 in fact gives the buyer a right to claim a refund of the payment, if the seller has by act or omission caused the loss of, or damage to, the goods.

Passing of risk in goods to be transported by carrier

[2.281] Article 67(1) sets out the following rules for passing of risk in the goods to be transported by a carrier:

- if the contract does not expressly specify a place of delivery, the risk in goods passes to the first carrier for transmission of the goods to the buyer pursuant to the contract;
- if the contract specifies a place of delivery, the risk in goods passes to the buyer when the goods are 'handed over' to the carrier at that place;[81] and
- the passing of risk is irrelevant to the seller's ability to control the disposition of the goods by holding the document of title over the goods.

[2.282] It must be pointed out that the above rules can be overridden by the parties concerned, and that they will certainly be overridden if any of the Incoterms are incorporated into the contract of sale. Article 67 was applied by an Argentine court in a case involving the sale of dried mushrooms by a German seller to an Argentine buyer under the CFR term: *Bedial, SA v Paul Muggenburg and Co GmbH* (31 October 1995, Camara Nacional de Apelaciones en lo Comercial, CLOUT Case 191). In that case, the cargo of dried mushrooms had deteriorated during the carriage to Buenos Aires. The court applied art 67 and decided that the risk in the cargo had passed to the buyer when the cargo was delivered to the first carrier. While the court's finding that the risk had passed to the buyer was correct, its finding that the risk had passed under art 67 was questionable, because the

---

81. While the word 'delivery' may include 'constructive delivery', the expression 'hand over' is likely to refer to the physical exchange of possession of the goods only. Thus, art 67(1) is likely to require the seller to hand the goods over physically to the carrier for the purpose of passing the risk in goods. This effect of art 67(1), if this interpretation is correct, will be overridden by certain of the Incoterms, because the terms may require the seller to place the goods at the carrier's 'disposal' or 'custody' for the purpose of passing the risk in goods. For example, see the CPT term (discussed at **[1.24]**) and the DDU term (discussed at **[1.29]**).

CFR term has provisions to deal with the passing of risk; on this particular point, the court incorrectly held that the CFR term does not affect the passing of risk. In addition, the court incorrectly applied art 67 in a contract incorporating an Incoterm, because art 67 is meant to operate only when there is no specific term concerning delivery and passing of risk between the parties.

[2.283] It should also be pointed out that art 67(1) applies to delivery through carriage of goods only. This means that if a contract of sale does not involve carriage of goods by sea, air or land (although this is not likely in most international sales) the risk will pass to the buyer under art 69, which is based on the agreed place and time for delivery.

Passing of risk in unascertained goods

[2.284] Under the sale of goods legislation of a common law jurisdiction, such as Australia or the UK, risk in unascertained goods does not pass until the goods are 'ascertained': see **[1.54]–[1.59]**.[82] Under art 67(2), goods can be ascertained when the seller marks the goods, specifies them in shipping documents or gives notice of them to the buyer. However, the mere fact of ascertaining goods alone may not pass the risk to the buyer, because art 67(1) clearly states that the risk passes through delivery. This means that art 67(2) and (1) must be read together for the purpose of determining whether the risk has passed.

Passing of risk in goods sold in transit

[2.285] There are special rules governing the transfer of risk in goods sold in transit. In international sales, goods are often sold in transit by the owner of the goods to buyers (or consignees) who may or may not have places of business in the country of the goods' destination. In order to facilitate such transactions, art 68 sets out the following rules:

- the risk in the goods sold in transit passes to the buyer from the time when the contract of sale is made;
- the risk in the goods sold in transit may pass to the buyer at the time when the goods are handed over to the carrier 'who issued the documents embodying the contract of carriage', if the circumstances so indicate; but
- the risk in the goods sold in transit does not pass to the buyer if at the time of the conclusion of the contract the seller knew or ought to have known of the loss or damage to the goods but did not disclose this to the buyer.

[2.286] It is not clear exactly how to identify whether the buyer assumes the risk at the time when the goods are delivered to the carrier. If the goods, sold in transit, are actually loaded onto a ship controlled by the potential or real buyer before the contract of sale is made, the buyer should be liable for the risk from the moment at which the goods are handed over to the carrier who issues the bill of lading concerned. It is also possible that goods sold in transit might be transferred to another carrier after the conclusion of the contract and this carrier issues 'the documents embodying the contract of carriage'.

---

82. 'Ascertained' is a term borrowed from the Australian sale of goods legislation (see **[1.54]**). It does not have the same meaning in the Convention as in the sale of goods legislation.

[2.286] Whether the risk in goods should pass at the time when the goods are delivered to a carrier, rather than at the time of the conclusion of the contract, is to a large extent determined by whether the carrier in question is the one 'who issued the documents embodying the contract of carriage'. The parties should ascertain the issuer of the bill of lading in question before attempting to prove that under art 68 the risk passed to the buyer when the goods were handed over to the carrier.

[2.287] It appears that risk in goods before the conclusion of the contract between the seller and buyer may pass to the buyer by his or her voluntary acceptance. This is implied by art 68, which deprives the seller of the right to rely on the provisions for passing of risk in goods sold in transit if he or she did not disclose an existing loss of, or damages to, the goods which he or she knew or ought to have known of at the time of the conclusion of the contract. It can be argued that if the seller had disclosed this and the buyer had not rejected the goods, the risk in the goods might still pass to the buyer.

Passing of risk through delivery

[2.288] Article 69 deals with passing of risk in goods which are neither delivered to a carrier nor sold in transit. This provision states the following rules:

- the risk passes to the buyer when he or she takes over the goods from the seller;
- the risk passes to the buyer when the goods are 'placed at his disposal' (in a deliverable state) in accordance with the contract or the Convention, but he or she fails to take over the goods as required;[83]
- the risk passes to the buyer at the agreed place 'when delivery is due and the buyer is aware of the fact that the goods are placed at his disposal at that place', regardless of whether the buyer has taken over the goods as agreed; and
- the risk in unascertained goods does not pass to the buyer until 'they are clearly identified to the contract' and placed at the disposal of the buyer as agreed.[84]

It appears that art 69 is based on the principle that the risk in goods should pass to the buyer at an agreed place and time and in an agreed manner. The risk in goods passes to the buyer when the goods are put into a deliverable state in accordance with the contract at the agreed place and time, regardless of whether the buyer has actually taken over the goods. This can be compared with a similar provision under the Australian sale of goods legislation, which holds the party causing delay in delivery liable for the loss flowing from the delay: see **[1.57]**.

---

83. The word 'disposal' in art 69 describes a state where the goods are delivered but not taken over by the buyer. Such use of 'disposal' implies that the expression 'hand over' (eg in art 67) means physically handing the goods over to the buyer.
84. Whether the goods have been placed at the buyer's disposal should be determined under the terms of the contract. The expression 'goods are placed at the buyer's disposal' is similar to 'goods are in a deliverable state' under the Australian sale of goods legislation: see **[1.51]–[1.52]**.

Passing of risk and seller's fundamental breach

[2.289] This issue is expressly raised in the Convention. Article 70 provides that if the seller has committed a fundamental breach, the fact that the risk lies in the buyer does not 'impair the remedies available to the buyer on account of the breach'. This means that after the occurrence of the seller's fundamental breach, the buyer is entitled to resort to remedies under the Convention, regardless of whether he or she is liable for the risk in the goods. It follows that the buyer may avoid the contract on the ground of fundamental breach and claim damages under arts 74–78 and 81 (which expressly says that avoidance of a contract does not affect the innocent party's claim to damages). Alternatively, the seller may resort to provisions such as arts 46 and 47 which allow the buyer to request the seller to perform his or her obligations, and claim damages under arts 74–77 and 81.

[2.290] Article 70 appears to be based on a presumption that the seller's fundamental breach will entitle the buyer to avoid the contract and that such avoidance will release 'both parties from their obligations' under the contract, as provided in art 81. Therefore, whether the buyer is liable for the risk in goods is irrelevant when the seller has committed a fundamental breach. However, the buyer's liability for the risk may be taken into account in determining the reasonableness of a measure under art 77, which requires the innocent party to take reasonable measures to mitigate the loss of, or damage to, goods.

Preservation of goods under the Convention

Dealing with preservation of goods under the Convention

[2.291] The Convention has special provisions (arts 85–8) for dealing with the preservation of goods. The preservation of goods arises as an issue when one party breaches the terms of the contract or the Convention and the other party is in possession of the goods after the breach. Preservation of the goods is consistent with the general duty of an innocent party to mitigate the loss in art 77. However, art 85 appears to have gone further than art 77 by allowing the seller (or the buyer) to hold the goods as security until the other party has paid reasonable expenses for preservation. The Convention has set out detailed rules for dealing with issues arising from, or associated with, preservation of goods.

Seller's duty and right in preserving goods

[2.292] Article 85 deals with the situation in which the buyer has breached his or her obligation to take delivery of the goods as agreed, or to make payment of the price as agreed at the time of taking delivery. In the former case, the seller who is either in possession of the goods or able to control the disposition of the goods as holder of the document of title will be forced to continue in possession of the goods. In the latter case, the seller has the option of letting the buyer take over the goods before payment (although this is usually not the preferred option), or holding the goods until the payment is made. If the seller chooses to hold the goods, he or she is obliged to preserve the goods under art 85.

[2.293] Article 85 sets out the seller's duty and right in these circumstances as follows:

- 'the seller must take such steps as are reasonable in the circumstances to preserve' the goods; but
- the seller is 'entitled to retain them until he has been reimbursed his reasonable expense by the buyer'.

[2.294] Article 85 gives the seller a right to retain the goods until he or she is reimbursed. However, this right is subject to two implied qualifications:

- the reimbursable expense must be 'reasonable'; and
- the seller is obliged to preserve the goods continuously, subject to art 88, if the parties disagree as to the reasonable sum of reimbursement.

This means that the seller's right to hold the goods as security against reimbursement for reasonable expenses must be exercised and read in conjunction with other relevant provisions, such as art 77 (mitigation of loss), art 87 (entrusting goods to a third party for preservation), and art 88 (sale of the goods under preservation). The conduct of the seller under art 85 will be assessed in the light of the other relevant provisions.

Buyer's duty and right in preserving goods

[2.295] Article 86 deals with a situation where a buyer who is in possession of the goods, or able to control their disposition, intends to reject them. The buyer may reject the goods without necessarily avoiding the whole contract — under, for example, art 51 (non-conformity in part of the goods delivered), art 52 (delivery before the fixed date), and art 73 (instalment deliveries).

[2.296] Article 86 provides the following rules:

- if the buyer intends to reject goods already in his or her possession, the buyer must take such steps to preserve the goods as are reasonable in the circumstances;
- if the buyer intends to reject the goods which are being delivered to him or her, he or she 'must take possession of them on behalf of the seller, provided that this can be done without payment of the price and without unreasonable inconvenience or unreasonable expense';
- the buyer rejecting the goods delivered to him or her is not required to preserve them 'if the seller or a person authorised to take charge of the goods' on the seller's behalf is present at the destination; and
- if the buyer has preserved the goods, he or she is entitled to retain the goods until the seller has reimbursed him or her for reasonable expenses.

In *Societe Fauba v Societe Fujitsu* [1996] UNLEX, (4 January 1995, Court of Cassation (1st Civil Division), CLOUT Case 155), the French court suggested that, while the buyer was entitled to retain possession of the rejected goods for reasonable reimbursement of the cost of preservation, it must have claimed for incurring such a cost. Perhaps in this case, the court regarded the making of a claim as the evidence of the existence of such a cost.

[2.297] The above rules suggest that a buyer rejecting goods which are being delivered to him or her is liable to preserve them only when so doing does not impose upon him or her an obligation to pay the price and does not cause him or her unreasonable inconvenience or expense. While it is understandable that a buyer should be exempt from liability to preserve goods where this would impose a duty on him or her to pay the price of those goods,[85] the fact that the buyer can refuse to preserve goods on the ground of unreasonable inconvenience or expense may be questionable, as the buyer is always entitled to claim reimbursement from the seller for reasonable expenses incurred in preserving the goods.

Of course, if the preservation of the rejected goods causes great inconvenience to the buyer, it would be unfair to put the buyer to such inconvenience because of the seller's fault. But if the inconvenience is within limits which can be compensated by the seller in monetary terms, there is no compelling reason why the buyer should not have to preserve the goods, unless the cost of preservation is higher than the value of the goods. Therefore, art 86(2), which exempts the buyer from the duty to preserve the goods on the ground of unreasonable inconvenience and unreasonable expense, may create a situation where the buyer may refuse to preserve the goods, even if the inconvenience and expense can later be reasonably compensated by the seller. Alternatively, it is also arguable that, as a matter of construction, the expressions 'unreasonable inconvenience' and 'unreasonable expense' may restrain the buyer from discharging his or her duty to preserve the goods lightly.

Preservation of the goods by third party

[2.298] Article 87 provides as follows:
> A party who is bound to take steps to preserve the goods may deposit them in a warehouse of a third person at the expense of the other party provided that the expense incurred is not unreasonable.

This provision allows a seller or buyer to leave the goods in a third party's custody for the purpose of preserving them. The breaching party is liable for the cost involved. The rule under arts 85 and 86, stating that the innocent party is entitled to retain the goods until the breaching party has reimbursed reasonable expenses for their preservation, also applies to goods in a third party's custody. However, it can be argued that the language of art 87 suggests that the burden of proving the unreasonableness of the expense normally lies with the breaching party, because the innocent party can always claim reimbursement by virtue of his or her control of the goods, and the breaching party has to prove that the sum incurred is unreasonable in the circumstances concerned.

---

85. This is understandable because the buyer should not be forced to undertake a liability to pay after the seller has breached his or her obligation to provide conforming goods or to deliver as agreed.

[2.299]

Preservation and sale of the goods

[2.299] Article 88 allows the party preserving the goods to sell them in the following circumstances:

- the buyer is entitled to sell the rejected goods by 'any appropriate means' if the seller has failed to take them back within a reasonable time after rejection, provided that the buyer has given the seller reasonable notice of his or her intention to sell;
- the seller is entitled to resell the goods by 'any appropriate means' if the buyer has again failed to pay the price within a reasonable time after having already failed to pay the price as agreed in the contract, provided that the seller has given the buyer reasonable notice of his or her intention to sell;
- in general, the party preserving the goods is entitled to sell them by 'any appropriate means' if the other party has failed to take over the goods within a reasonable time after the first party had taken over the goods for preservation, provided that the innocent party has given the breaching party reasonable notice of his or her intention to sell;
- in general, the party preserving the goods is entitled to sell them by 'any appropriate means' if the breaching party has failed to pay the reasonable cost of preservation within a reasonable time after the occurrence of an unreasonable delay in paying the reasonable cost, provided that the innocent party has given the breaching party reasonable notice of his or her intention to sell;[86]
- if the goods are deteriorating or the preservation of the goods involves unreasonable expense (for instance, if the cost of preservation is higher than the value of the goods), the innocent party 'must take reasonable measures to sell them', and give the breaching party notice of sale if possible;[87] and
- the party selling the goods is entitled to deduct from the proceeds of sale a sum equal to the reasonable expense of preservation and cost of sale, but he or she must pay the other party the balance of the proceeds.

[2.300] Article 88 must be read in conjunction with arts 85 and 86. For example, art 86 says that a buyer does not have to take over the goods if so doing imposes a liability to pay the price upon him or her, or incurs unreasonable inconvenience or expense. Article 86 should be construed in the light of the right to sell under art 88. It can be argued that the buyer's right to refuse to take over the goods for preservation under art 86 is qualified and restricted by the right to sell under art 88, because the buyer can always take over the goods and sell them later under art 88 if the cost for preservation is not justified. Such restriction is necessary to avoid a situation where the goods are lost or damaged unnecessarily because no one takes responsibility for them. This proposition is

---

86. This conclusion can be inferred from art 88(1). 'Unreasonable delay' in case of a failure to pay the cost of preservation should begin to accrue from the moment at which the payment of the cost is the main reason for the breaching party's failure to take over the goods. In other words, if the payment of the cost is not the main reason, the innocent party should rely on other grounds for the sale of the goods.
87. It must be pointed out that the innocent party is required to give notice of sale in this case only when it is possible for him or her to do so.

based on art 77, which requires both parties to do their best to mitigate the loss and damage to the goods.

[2.301] The application of art 88 depends to a large extent on the value judgment of the party preserving the goods. The reasonableness of the parties' acts would be the focus of argument. For the purpose of determining the reasonableness of an act, the general principles of art 77 and the notion of contract preservation and promotion underlying the Convention should be taken into account.

Conclusion: potential use of the Convention through modification and interpretation

[2.302] In concluding our study of the CISG, we should emphasise the following two fundamental issues:

- the provisions of the Convention can be, and often are, modified or excluded expressly or implicitly by the parties to a contract; and
- the provisions of the Convention must be interpreted in the context of the Convention as a whole.

The potential use of the Convention through modification and interpretation of its provisions is yet to be fully explored by the members of the Convention. As we have seen from a number of cases referred to in this chapter, many of the provisions of the Convention and the interconnections between them are capable of resulting in consequences which may not be easily ascertained from, or reconciled with, the wording of the provisions by a person who does not share the same legal tradition as the court interpreting the provisions. This reflects one of the inherent dilemmas of the Convention, which is largely a compromise between the civil law and common law traditions. The language of the Convention comes to life through the interpretation of the contracting parties and the courts of law from all member countries across the world. Such interpretation is inevitably affected by the legal tradition to which the person making the interpretation belongs, together with their social and economic conditions. Thus the scope of the potential operation of the Convention is something which deserves more attention from the members of the Convention, during the years to come.

[2.303] Modification and variation of the effect of the provisions are explicitly allowed in art 6 of the Convention. For example, in a German case, *Bundesgerichtshof* (VIII ZR 130/ 96, 23 July 1997, CLOUT Case 231), the court held that the parties had chosen the application of German law to the exclusion of the Convention under art 6. Such changes can be made either through an express agreement between the parties, or by implication, as seen in their conduct and the terms of the contract.[88]

This suggests that the Convention gives priority to the intention of the parties and allows them to define the contract to the extent they wish. Provisions of the Convention provide supplementary rules when the parties have omitted their own rules or when the

---

88. It can be argued that art 6 does not require modifications to be made by express words only.

[2.303] parties choose to be bound by the Convention. In *Societe Ceramique culinaire de France v Societe Musgrave Ltd* (17 December 1996, Court of Cassation (Commercial Division), CLOUT Case 206), the French seller and the Irish buyer disagreed on the quality of the ceramic ovenware sold. The contract chose French law as the governing law. On appeal, the Court of Appeal of Colmar took the view that the choice-of-law clause and the act of the Irish buyer in seeking remedies under French law indicated the intention of the parties to waive or exclude the operation of the Convention in pursuance of art 6, thus denying its application.

The decision of the court did not enunciate the rules for determining whether the parties had effectively invoked art 6 to override the application of part or the whole of the Convention. The Court of Cassation expressed reservations on the finding of the Court of Appeal of Colmar on the applicability of the Convention, but nevertheless decided the issue in dispute under art 1641 of the Civil Code, instead of the Convention. This case can be criticised for its failure to differentiate between the operation of art 1 (which leads to the operation of the Convention under the relevant conflict of laws rules), and art 6 (which excludes partially or wholly the operation of the Convention by agreement of the parties).

[2.304] The provisions of the Convention must be construed in the broad context of the circumstances involved, taking into account the notion of contract preservation and promotion which underlies the Convention. As stated in art 7(1), in 'the interpretation of this Convention, regard is to be had to its international character and to the need to promote uniformity in its application and the observance of good faith in international trade'. Thus the provisions of the Convention should be construed in the light of the terms of the contract and intention of the parties as seen in the contract concerned. This requires the parties to a contract and the court dealing with a dispute to give appropriate consideration to the modifications made by the parties with respect to the effect of a particular provision. In the presence of gaps in the Convention, art 7(2) requires the parties and the court to consider the general principles on which a particular legal relationship is based and to make a choice between such principles under the relevant conflicts rules. This gives rise to a possibility that the same provision of the Convention may be given a different interpretation in different circumstances and by different courts of law. This characteristic of the interpretation of the Convention must be noted.

[2.305] Besides art 7, art 8 also sets out principles for the interpretation of the terms of contract or the conduct of the parties for the purpose of the Convention. This provision states as follows:

   (1) For the purposes of this Convention statements made by and other conduct of a party are to be interpreted according to his intent where the other party knew or could not have been unaware what that intent was.
   (2) If the preceding paragraph is not applicable, statements made by and other conduct of a party are to be interpreted according to the understanding that a reasonable person of the same kind as the other party would have had in the same circumstances.
   (3) In determining the intent of a party or the understanding a reasonable person would have had, due consideration is to be given to all relevant circumstances of the case including the negotiations, any practices which the parties have established between themselves, usage and any subsequent conduct of the parties.

[2.306] Even though art 8 appears to be related to the technique or considerations which should be taken into account when interpreting the agreement, conduct, and intention of the parties under the Convention, it may be applied for some purpose which results in certain consequences beyond the technique of interpretation. In *SARL Bri Production Bonaventure v Societe Pan Africa Export* [1995] UNLEX D 95-1 (22 February 1995, Court of Appeal of Grenoble (Commercial Division), CLOUT Case 154), a French seller of jeans expressly and repeatedly made known to the US buyer that it wished to know the destination of the goods. The buyer informed the seller that the goods were to be shipped to South America and Africa. It turned out later that the jeans were shipped to Spain. The seller refused to trade with the buyer, which sued the seller for the breach of contract. The court referred to art 8 and concluded that the US buyer had not respected the wish of the French seller to know the real destination of the goods. Further, the court held that the attitude of the US buyer constituted a fundamental breach of contract within the meaning of art 25. In addition, the court also found the US buyer to have violated the principle of good faith set out in art 7 of the Convention in abusing the legal process, and ordered the US buyer to pay the seller a sum of 10,000 French francs as damages. The application of art 8 by the French court for the purpose of establishing a fundamental breach under art 25 is an interesting approach. It appears that even though the misrepresentation by the US buyer, if proven, may amount to a fundamental breach under art 25, art 8 itself is incapable of leading to any breach because art 8 only sets out the principles or rules for construing intention or conduct of the parties. In other words, art 8 per se cannot be violated or breached by any party, no matter what the party has done or not done.

[2.307] Article 8 was also considered in a US case, *MCC-Marble Ceramic Centre Inc v Ceramica Nuova DAgostino SpA*, 1998 US App Lexis 14782 (29 June 1998, US Court of Appeals (11th Circuit), CLOUT Case 222), in which the court held that the domestic parole evidence rule did not apply to a contract subject to the Convention because of art 8.

In that case, a standard contract for the sale of ceramic tiles was concluded in Italian between a US buyer and an Italian seller. The contract contained a statement in Italian that the buyer was aware of the conditions and terms printed on the reverse side of the contract. On that side there was a clause permitting the seller to stop delivery if the buyer failed to pay for the goods as agreed. The buyer presented affidavits to prove that the terms of the contract did not represent the true intention of the parties. The parole evidence rule excludes evidence of oral agreement which contradicts or varies the terms of a subsequent or contemporaneous written contract. The court's decision in this case opened the door for the buyer to challenge the terms of the written contract in the Italian language. Whether or not the court's interpretation of art 8 in this case is reasonable and productive is subject to debate.

This case forms a contrast with *Beijing Metals & Minerals Import/Export Corp v American Business Centre Inc* 993 Federal Reports 2d 1178 (1993) (15 June 1993, CLOUT Case 24), in which the court held that the parole evidence rule applied whether or not the Convention also applied.

[2.308] Even though the Convention sets out the general principles of its interpretation, the particular interpretations given to it by the courts of a member country are inevitably affected by the legal tradition of that country. This can be seen in many cases decided by the courts following the civil law tradition, such as the German and Austrian courts. This feature of the interpretation of the Convention can be illustrated by a German case involving the use of a bank guarantee, *Oberlandesgericht Munchen* (7 U 1720/94, 8 February 1995, CLOUT Case 133). That case involve the sale of 11 German cars by a German seller to an Italian buyer. The contract stipulated a total price of 400,000 Deutsche Marks. The buyer provided a bank guarantee in the amount of 55,000 Deutsche Marks at the request of the seller. The seller delivered five cars in August and informed the buyer in October that six cars were ready for delivery. The buyer repudiated the contract for the remaining six cars on the ground that the fluctuations in the exchange rate between the Lira and Mark had made the purchase impossible under the price stipulated in the contract. The seller subsequently claimed the sum of DM55,000 under the bank guarantee.

What the seller did would probably be regarded as normal from a common law perspective. However, when the buyer sued the seller to recover the payment under the bank guarantee, the German court found the seller had obtained unjustified enrichment under art 812(1) of the German Civil Code for obtaining the payment of the bank guarantee without any legal ground. What the court meant to say appeared to be that the seller had not proven its entitlement under art 812(1) to claim payment under the bank guarantee. From a common law perspective, the bank guarantee must contain the condition under which the beneficiary can make a claim. In addition, the buyer's breach would be a ground per se for the seller to claim compensation under the bank guarantee. The different approaches to the interpretation of the bank guarantee reflects the difference between the civil law tradition and the common law tradition.

In this case, the court went back to the original contract of sale to identify the rights of the parties, even though two-and-a-half years had passed since the repudiation of the contract by the buyer. The court found that the seller was originally entitled to claim damages or termination of the contract under art 61 of the Convention, but had lost the right to claim damages because of its failure to avoid the contract and to mitigate the loss under art 77. A common law lawyer would wonder why a failure to mitigate the loss could deprive the seller of the right to claim damages, even though the failure to mitigate would affect the sum claimable by the seller. Again, different approaches can be taken in interpreting the relationships between art 61 and art 77.

Also, in this case, the buyer claimed a right to avoid the contract on the ground that the seller had not delivered the car as stipulated in the contract of sale. A common law lawyer might answer the claim by pointing out that the seller had accepted the buyer's breach and claimed damages under the bank guarantee; therefore, the buyer's right to terminate the original contract was no longer an issue because the contract was no longer in existence. However, the German court examined the claim from a different perspective. It observed that the buyer had lost the right to avoid the contract after two-and-a-half years, since the seller claimed the payment under the bank guarantee and disallowed the buyer's claim largely on the ground of art 7(1) of the Convention, which sets out the principle of good faith. In other words, the German court considered the lack of any prescribed activity by the seller in pursuance of the relevant provisions of the Convention, such as arts 53, 61 and 77, had given rise to a presumption that the original contract of sale had not been terminated formally. In drawing this conclusion, the court did not consider the act of the seller claiming payment under the bank guarantee as in any way accepting the buyer's repudiation or termination of the original contract.

In the light of *Oberlandesgericht Munchen*, it may be concluded that the German court is very serious about compliance with the formalities set out in the Convention. In addition, as is common under the civil law tradition, the court places a strong emphasis on the legal basis of a party's right to act or not to act in the statute. For comparison, the court of a common law jurisdiction will rely heavily on the contractual basis of a party's right in the contract itself, instead of the statute.

Incorporation of the Convention into Australian law

[2.309] The CISG became part of the law of each Australian state and territory in April 1989 under a uniform scheme agreed upon by the federal and state governments. Under this scheme, each state adopted the CISG through its own legislation, which was based on a uniform model. New South Wales, Queensland, South Australia and Western Australia incorporated the Convention into their laws through their own Sale of Goods (Vienna Convention) Act 1986; and Victoria, Tasmania, the Northern Territory and the Australian Capital Territory adopted the Convention through their own Sale of Goods (Vienna Convention) Act 1987. It must be pointed out, however, that although the Convention exists in Australia as part of the law of each state or territory, the laws applicable to the international sale of goods are uniform throughout Australia. The uniformity of Australian law governing the international sale of goods is also evidenced by the fact that the sale of goods legislation in all states or territories (excluding the Convention)[89] is largely uniform, being based on the United Kingdom Sale of Goods Act 1893 (which has since been replaced by the Sale of Goods Act 1979).

Constitutional implications of the CISG

[2.310] The manner in which the CISG was adopted in Australia reflects particular features of the Australian Constitution. Under the Australian Constitution, the legislative powers of the federal and state governments are divided mainly, though not exclusively, on the basis of s 51 of the Constitution. Many of the heads of power in s 51 are concurrent, and s 109 of the Constitution gives prevalence to the federal legislation in case of inconsistency between the federal and state laws. The power to regulate the sale of goods falls under the category of concurrent power: see **[1.41]**.[90]

---

89. The Convention has become part of Australian sale of goods legislation by virtue of the state's enabling statute to incorporate the Convention into the relevant state law. However, in this chapter, the expression 'Australian sale of goods legislation' does not include the Convention, unless otherwise specified.

[2.310]

The way in which the CISG has been adopted in Australia is not a recognition of state power to regulate contracts for the international sale of goods, because the 'reserved state power' theory under the Constitution has long been rejected by the High Court of Australia: *Amalgamated Society of Engineers v Adelaide Steamship Co Ltd* (1920) 28 CLR 129. Rather, the uniform scheme for incorporating the CISG into Australian law appears to be a compromise between the federal and state governments for administrative convenience. This proposition is supported by the fact that most sales carried out under the state sale of goods legislation certainly fall under federal powers, such as the power to regulate interstate and international trade, and the power to regulate the operation of financial or trading corporations. The federal parliament has not attempted to replace the existing state laws with the relevant federal sale of goods legislation, although the federal and state laws overlap in the area of consumer protection relating to supply of goods and services.

[2.311] The provisions of the Convention prevail over Australian law in cases of inconsistency. At the state level, the Act of each Australian state or territory enacting the CISG in the relevant state and territory contains the same provision, which states that the 'provisions of the Convention prevail over any other law in force', 'to the extent of any inconsistency'. At the federal level, s 66A of the Trade Practices Act 1974 (Cth) provides that the provisions of the CISG 'prevail over the provisions' of Div 2 of the Trade Practices Act. It is yet to be seen whether the Convention will also prevail over the provisions of Div 2A of the Trade Practices Act (and, to some extent, Pt VA), in the case of inconsistency. The federal government has yet to take the legislative initiative to resolve this uncertainty.

---

90. Many states had passed their Sale of Goods Act before the establishment of the Commonwealth of Australia in 1901. For example, the Sale of Goods Act 1896 (Qld), Sale of Goods Act 1895 (SA), Sale of Goods Act 1896 (Tas) and Sale of Goods Act 1895 (WA) still operate in these states.

Chapter Three

Contracts Relating to Intellectual Property

Introduction

[3.1] When GATT was concluded in 1947, what the drafters of the convention had in mind was the sale of goods only. Sale of goods was then regarded as the most important, if not the only, means of international trade. More than 50 years have passed since GATT came into operation in 1948. International trade and commerce have experienced tremendous changes during these years. The establishment of the WTO in 1995 was a response to the rapid development of international trade and commerce. The WTO Agreement, which includes dozens of sub-agreements, covers many areas which were not covered by GATT 1947 (GATT incorporating amendments made up to the Uruguay Round negotiations). These new areas, such as intellectual property, services and investment, reflect the changes in the scope, nature, means and complexity of trading and commercial activities in the past 50 years. This chapter discusses several forms or means of international trading and commercial activities or arrangements which fall outside the conventional mode of trade, that is, sale of goods.

Nine types of international commercial activities or arrangements — franchising, licensing distribution arrangements, transfer of technology, e-commerce, international construction contracts, international oil and gas exploration and exploitation contracts, international mineral development agreements, and international countertrade agreements — are discussed in this chapter. The common bond between the first five types of commercial transactions or activities is that they are all related to intellectual property. Most of the five, such as licensing, franchising, distributions and transfer of technology, have intellectual property as the subject matter of transactions or agreements. As we will see later in this chapter, these activities or arrangements have been subject largely to contract law and intellectual property law across the world. E-commerce is a new domain of international trade and commerce, built entirely on the development of technology and intellectual property. E-commerce has not only substantially changed the ways people carry on conventional types of business, but also created a new territory and world of commerce. It is both related to and different from the other types of commercial activities to be covered in this chapter. The last four types of international commercial agreements are common forms of trade and investment; they may or may not be related to transfer of technology. In the case of joint ventures, arrangements relating to the transfer of technology will often be made to enable the joint venture to perform the project it purports to do. In the case of a sole foreign investment or foreign company carrying out these projects, a transfer of technology may not be necessary. This chapter purports only to give some basic introductions to all these forms of commercial activities.

A brief description of intellectual property

[3.2] The meaning of 'intellectual property' (IP) may vary under different domestic laws and international conventions, but there appears to be some common understanding of its meaning throughout the world. In broad terms, 'intellectual property' refers to a range of intangible property rights, which are based on the intellectual achievements of humans as recognised or protected by law. In most cases, IP can be divided into several categories of rights, including patents, industrial designs, copyrights and related rights, trademarks and trade names, geographical indications, layout-designs (topographies) of integrated circuits, and confidential information.[1] Sometimes, fair competition issue is also related to IP protection.[2] For example, the Agreement on Trade-Related Aspects of Intellectual Property Rights (Agreement on TRIPs) sets out rules to control the use of anti-competitive practices in contractual licences pertaining to IPs: art 40. It could be said that there are two characteristics common to all IP rights: first, all are related to a form of intellectual achievement or activitiy; and second, all are rights as recognised and protected by a particular law. These common characteristics are crucial for understanding the rules for protecting intellectual property rights.

Franchising agreements

Definitions of franchising

Lack of universal definition

[3.3] The formulation of a universal definition of franchising is not an easy task. *Black's Law Dictionary* defines 'franchise' as an arrangement for the grant of the sole right to engage in a certain business, or in a business using a particular trademark, in a certain area.[3] This description of 'franchising' is very broad, and is capable of a wide application in many areas of commercial operation. In practice, different legal or commercial definitions of franchising have been offered by lawyers and business people from different countries, in different times. Some of these examples are examined below.

---

1. For detailed discussions on most of these rights, see W R Cornish, *Intellectual Property: Patents, Copyright, Trade Marks and Allied Rights*, 4th ed, London, Sweet & Maxwell, 1999.
2. See for example *Black's Law Dictionary*, 7th ed, St Paul Minn, West Group, 1999.
3. *Black's Law Dictionary*, 7th ed, St Paul Minn, West Group, 1999.

Early English legal definition

[3.4] In 1982, David Shannon, in his book *Franchising in Australia*, described franchising as a grant of right or a grant of freedom to do something or to use something in certain places.[4] He observed that:

> ... the concept of franchising has existed in English common law for several centuries. It was originally synonymous with liberty, granted by the Crown 'a royal privilege, or branch of the King's prerogative, subsisting in the hands of the subject'.[5]

Shannon then referred to *Blackson's Commentaries* (1769) as an authority on the use of franchising in the history of English common law. Part of this quote follows:[6]

> To be a county palatine is a franchise, vested in a number of persons. It is likewise a franchise for a number of persons to be incorporated, and subsist as a body politic, with a power to maintain perpetual succession and do other corporate acts: and each individual member of such corporation is also said to have a franchise or freedom. Other franchises are, to hold a court leet: to have a manor or lordship; or, at least, to have a lordship paramount: to have waifs, wrecks, estrays, treasure-trove, royal fish, forfeitures, and deodands: to have a court of one's own, or liberty of holding pleas, and trying causes: to have the cognisance of pleas; which is a still greater liberty, being an exclusive right, so that no other court shall try causes arising within that jurisdiction: to have a bailiwick, or liberty exempt from the sheriff of the county, wherein the grantee only, and his officers, are to execute all processes: and to have a fair or market; with the right of taking toll, either there or at any other public places, as at bridges, wharfs, and the like; which tolls must have a reasonable cause of commencement, (as in consideration of repairs, or the like) else the franchise is illegal and void: or, lastly, to have a forest, chase, park, warren, or fishery, endowed with privileges of royalty (2Bl. Comm. 4th edn, 37, 38).

The meaning of 'franchise' in early English common law is interesting. The word is still the same today, but does it have the same meaning as in the quote above? Perhaps the most important aspect of this early definition of franchising is that a person who has a right or power may 'franchise' the right or power to another person under specific conditions and terms. As we will see, this characteristic of franchising has remained more or less the same through history.

Definition in Californian law

[3.5] Another definition of franchising is given in the California Franchise Investment Law 1970, which is referred to by Dennis Campbell in *International Franchising: An In-Depth Treatment of Business and Legal Techniques*.[7] Section 315005(a) stated as follows:

(1) a franchisee is granted the right to engage in the business of offering, selling or distributing goods or services under a marketing plan or system prescribed in substantial part by a franchisor; and

(2) the operation of the franchisee's business pursuance to such plan or system is substantially associated with the franchisor's trademark, service mark, trade name, logotype, advertising or other commercial symbol designating the franchisor or its affiliate; and

(3) the franchisee is required to pay, directly or indirectly, a franchise fee.

---

4. Shannon, *Franchising in Australia,* Law Book Company, Sydney, 1982, p 3.
5. Ibid.
6. Ibid.
7. D Campbell, 'Introduction' in Gramatidis and Campbell (eds), *International Franchising: An In-Depth Treatment of Business and Legal Techniques*, Kluwer, Deventer, 1991, pp 1–9.

This statutory definition of franchising is closer to the commercial reality of today. Franchising here is regarded as a way to organise a business operation and is a bond linking franchisor and franchisees. But it should also be pointed out that franchising is in itself a business and a way of making money. The sale of goods or services or the use of trademarks, etc are the raw materials which make up a franchising system.

Definition in the Block Exemption Regulation of the EU

[3.6] The Block Exemption Regulation purports to exempt certain franchising arrangements from the operation of art 85 of the EU Treaty. It also offers a definition of franchise and a definition of a franchising agreement. Under the regulation, franchise means:

> ... a package of industrial or intellectual property rights relating to trade marks, trade names, shop signs, utility models, designs, copyrights, know-how or patents, to be exploited for the resale of goods or the provision of services to the end users.[8]

Under the same regulation, franchising agreement is defined as follows:[9]

> Franchise agreement means an agreement whereby one undertaking, the franchisor, grants the other, the franchisee, in exchange for direct or indirect financial consideration, the right to exploit a franchise for the purpose of marketing specified types of goods and/or services; it includes at least obligations relating to:
> - the use of common name or shop sign and a uniform presentation of contract premises and/or means of transport;
> - the communication by the franchisor to the franchisee of know-how; or
> - the continuing provision by the franchisor to the franchisee of commercial or technical assistance during the life of the arrangement.

The definitions adopted in the Block Exemption Regulation were apparently based on the views of the European Court of Justice (ECJ) in the *Pronuptia* case, where the court identified three types of franchising:[10]

- service franchising, under which the franchisee offers a service under the sign, trade name or trademark of the franchisor, and conforms with the requirements of the latter;
- production franchising, under which the franchisee him/herself manufactures, in accordance with the franchisor's directions, the goods which he or she sells under the latter's trademark; and
- distribution franchising, under which the franchisee undertakes to sell certain goods in a shop which carries the franchisor's sign.

The definitions of franchise and franchising agreement offered by the Block Exemption Regulation are more concise than those offered by business people. Their function is to qualify transactions which might otherwise be subject to the block exemption under the regulation. Whether or not that purpose has affected the said definitions is yet to be proven.

---

8. The definition is cited in Mendelsohn and Bynoe, *Franchising*, FT Law & Tax, London, 1995, p 276.
9. Ibid.
10. See discussions in J Nelson-Jones, 'An Introduction to International Franchising' in Campbell and Pombo (eds), *Penetrating International Markets: From Sales and Licensings to Subsidiaries and Acquisitions*, Kluwer, Deventer, 1991, p 69.

Definition by the International Franchise Association (IFA)

[3.7] The IFA is a self-regulatory organisation established in the United States. It has adopted the following definition of franchising:[11]

> A franchising operation is a contractual relationship between the franchisor and franchisee in which the franchisor offers or is obliged to maintain a continuing interest in the business of the franchisee in such areas as know-how and training; wherein the franchisee operates under a common trade name, format and/or procedure owned or controlled by the franchisor, and in which the franchisee has or will make a substantial capital investment in his business from his own resources.

This definition describes what is known as business format franchising. It refers to the form or format of business operation, and the specific manner in which a franchise is arranged is no longer important. This definition is more general than that adopted by Californian law: see **[3.5]**. The emphasis appears to be on the fact that franchising is a format or a way to carry on business.

Definition by the European Franchise Federation (EFF)

[3.8] The EFF, which is sometimes referred to as the European Franchise Association, is a self-regulatory organisation established in 1972. Membership is open to national franchise associations or federations established in Europe. It offers associate membership to non-European national franchise associations. It has formulated its own Code of Ethics, in which franchising is described in the following words:[12]

> Franchising is a system of marketing goods and/or services and/or technology, which is based upon a close and ongoing collaboration between legally and financially separate and independent undertakings, the franchisor and its individual franchisees, whereby the franchisor grants to its individual franchisees the right, and imposes the obligations, to conduct a business in accordance with the franchisor's concept. The right entitles and compels the individual franchisee, in exchange for direct and indirect financial consideration, to use the franchisor's trade name, and/or trade mark and/or service mark, know-how, business and technical methods, procedural system, and other industrial and/or intellectual property rights, supported by continuing provision of commercial and technical assistance, within the framework and for the term of a written franchise agreement, concluded between the parties for that purpose.

This definition is similar to that adopted by the IFA in that both emphasise the operation of a franchise as a vehicle, system or format of business. But the EFF definition is more detailed in describing the manner in which a franchising system operates.

Summarising definitions of franchising

[3.9] As we have seen, different definitions of franchising have developed across the world. Commercial definitions and legal definitions of franchising differ. Commercial definitions aim to make business people understand the operation of franchising, whereas legal definitions are designed to improve certainty, transparency and predictability in law for the purpose of determining the rights and obligations of the parties to a franchising arrangement. Thus, a legal definition emphasises the legal nature of the rights and obligations of the parties and the connections between franchising and other branches of law.

---

11. From Adams et al, *Franchising: Practice and Precedents in Business Format Franchising*, 4th ed, Butterworths, London, 1997, p 22.
12. Ibid.

[3.9]

Bearing in mind the differences between commercial and legal definitions, the legal definition of franchising can be summarised as follows.

First, the idea of franchising originates from the common law concept of 'franchise', which referred to a grant or delegation of power, privilege or right by the Crown, King or sovereign to a person or a group of persons. Franchising of this nature was common in many countries, particularly in the 1950s and 1960s; a government might, for example, grant an exclusive right, privilege or licence to operate telecommunication services, railway services or airline services, to one or several companies in a country or jurisdiction, or it might grant a franchise to one or several companies to develop specific natural resources. This was the case for Australia's uranium industry.

Second, franchising is a format, a system or a particular way of doing business, in which a person holding a right, privilege, secret information, skill, process or anything which is subject to legal protection or capable of claiming legal protection under a specific law may franchise (grant) the right, privilege, secret information, etc to another person or persons for commercial purposes. The right to franchise is based on the legal protection vested in the subject matter of the franchise.

Third, franchising differs from conventional sale of goods and services, or the normal assignment of intellectual property rights in the sense that it is an ongoing operation. The franchisor and franchisee(s) are locked into an arrangement under which the franchisor ensures a continuous growth of the business and returns of profit for the grant of the franchise to the franchisee(s). Most franchising arrangements are organised in such a manner that the franchisor retains a certain level of control over the operation of the franchisee's business, which is generally invested in by the franchisee alone; he or she adopts the successful business format, model, technique or trademark, etc under the franchising arrangement in order to maximise return on this investment.

Fourth, a franchising arrangement is largely based on contract. The rights and obligations of the franchisor and franchisee are defined by the relevant contract, which may be a combination of sale of goods, supply of services, agency arrangement, distribution agreement, licensing agreement, transfer of technology, assignment of intellectual property rights, etc.[13] Thus, the contract is not only subject to general contract law, but also subject to many other types of law which affect the subject matter of the contract(s). In most cases, a franchisor relies heavily on the protection of the intellectual property laws of the relevant country.

Last, a franchising arrangement is extremely flexible because there is no legal limit on its operation in most countries and jurisdictions across the world. However, depending on the particular format adopted in a franchising arrangement, a relevant law may impose restrictions on its operation or organisation. Since franchising creates a special relationship between the franchisor and franchisees, as well as between the franchisees, the competition law, anti-trust law or restrictive trade practices law of the relevant country may impose restrictions on the arrangement. For example, s 51ACA of the

---

13. For a sample contract, see *Australian Encyclopaedia of Forms and Precedents*, Section 40.1: Franchising agreement, available at <http://www.butterworthsonline.com/>.

Trade Practices Act 1974 (Cth) declares that franchising is an industry covered by the Act, making the Act applicable to the restrictive practices of a franchising arrangement. Similarly, the EU competition law has implications for franchising within the EU.[14] The effects of other laws on franchising arrangements are very important to international franchising because legal systems vary from one country to another, and so do the conflict of laws rules adopted by each court. Investigating all laws relevant to a franchising arrangement is the key to protecting the interests of both franchisor and franchisee in any international franchising agreement.

Legal framework for franchising

Regulation by domestic law

[3.10] There is no international convention on franchising. Although franchising is subject to domestic regulation, there are in fact only about 15 jurisdictions which are known to have passed domestic laws regulating franchising specifically.[15] In the jurisdictions where special legislation has been passed, franchising must comply with the relevant requirements.[16] For example, in California, the California Automobile Franchise Act regulates franchising in the automobile industry. Under this Act, an automobile manufacturer which intends to open or relocate a retail dealership within the market area of an existing franchisee needs to negotiate with the franchisee first. If the franchisee disagrees, the manufacturer must seek approval from the California New Motor Vehicle Board before opening or relocating a new retail dealership. Whether or not the decision process of the board under the Act was subject to the principle of due process was argued in *New Motor Vehicle BD of California v Orrine W Fox Co* 439 US 96 (1978). In this case, the US Supreme Court by majority held that the Act, which did not require a prior hearing before the board makes a decision, did not violate due process. This case reflects some of the difficulties in the regulation of franchising. As observed by Brennan J at 443, the Act was designed to displace unfettered business freedom in the matter of the establishment and relocation of automobile dealerships and to balance the unequal bargaining powers of the franchisor and the franchisees. This case also illustrates that fair competition is one of the major concerns of statutes regulating franchising. This feature of a statute on franchising is also seen in the Alberta Franchises Act 1971 which sets out the registration and disclosure requirements for franchisors. The Act stipulates such requirements because the franchisor is in a less risky position than the franchisee in any franchising arrangement where the franchisee is the one who invested the capital in the business established under that arrangement.

---

14. For discussion, see Adams et al, note 11 above, pp 57–92.
15. See M Cohen, 'Franchising in Canada' in Campbell (ed), *The Comparative Law Yearbook of International Business*, vol 16, 1994, p 190; and Annex 3 to the UNIDROIT *Guide to International Franchise Arrangements*, available at <http://www.unidroit.org/>.
16. For discussion on franchising law in certain countries, see B K Hammer, 'Franchising in Mexico: Paving the New Frontier' (1992) 27(3) *Texas International Law Journal* pp 795–835; C M Wissels, 'The Russian Civil code: Will It Boost or Bust Franchising in Russia' (1996) 22(5) *Review of Central and East European Law*, pp 495–519; M Cohen, 'Franchising in Canada' in Gramatidis and Campbell, note 7 above, pp 179–217; G Ulloa, 'Franchising in Spain' in Gramatidis and Campbell, note 7 above, pp 69–73.

As we have seen, franchising involves many legal issues, subject to different branches of existing laws. Would it be useful to create specific franchising legislation which might overlap with many existing laws? In addition, if we adopt the notion of a free market economy, what is the justification for regulating franchising? For these reasons, franchising will probably not be regulated by any international convention detailing the specific rights and obligations of the parties. However, an international convention may be developed for the purpose of unifying the basic commercial practices of franchising internationally or to offer minimum standards of legal protection to the franchisor and the franchisee. The need for such an international agreement will arise only when franchising has achieved a certain level of commercial significance internationally.

Self-regulation

[3.11] Besides domestic statutes, self-regulation is the only method by which franchising is regulated in most countries and jurisdictions. Self-regulation is supposedly carried out by national and international franchise associations in most jurisdictions. A large number of national franchise associations have been established, and there are also two international franchise associations — the European Franchise Federation and the World Franchise Association. Some of these associations have published their own codes of conduct or codes of ethics. In addition, certain associations, such as the BFA and the HKFA, have made compliance with certain ethical standards a precondition for joining. Such self-regulatory efforts by the industry may provide a certain redress to the inequality of bargaining power between the franchisor and the franchisee.

The present state of the regulation of franchising in a domestic context may be illustrated by the case of Hong Kong. In general terms, Hong Kong is a free city which has little control over imports, exports and foreign investment. Franchising in Hong Kong is not subject to any exchange control, competition law, or foreign equity participation or local management participation regulations. Disputes arising from franchise agreements are subject to the relevant common law, in particular, the principles of contract law, and to the legislation relating to the registration, licensing and protection of intellectual property rights, such as the Trade Marks Ordinance (Cap 43), the Trade Descriptions Ordinance (Cap 362), the Copyright Ordinance (Cap 528), the Registered Designs Ordinance (Cap 522), and the Patents Ordinance (Cap 514). In the absence of any formal regulation, the HKFA has formulated its own code of ethics to regulate the industry.

This self-regulation is necessary because Hong Kong does not have any specific legislation relating to franchising. Nor does it have any competition law, which functions as a powerful restriction on franchising agreements in many jurisdictions.[17] The effectiveness of the HKFA code is yet to be seen, because franchising in Hong Kong is still relatively new. As at July 2002, there had been about 106 franchise operations in Hong Kong. Half of them were local franchises. Three-quarters of the operations were also involved in sub-franchising arrangements. The development of franchising in Hong Kong is limited by its

---

17. For a review of franchising in Hong Kong, see E Cheong, 'Franchising in Hong Kong' (1992) 20 *IBL*, pp 13–46.

physical size, but development franchising in mainland China through connections in Hong Kong presents an opportunity for many multinational companies.

Self-regulation is a matter of self-interest and survival for the franchise industry worldwide. If it proves unable to govern itself, governments will step in; thus, the development of an international code of ethics or conduct for the franchising industry is in the long-term interests of the industry itself.

Format of franchising arrangements

Problems arising from classification of formats

[3.12] Franchising arrangements can be made in various forms. Konigsberg QC has classified international franchising arrangements into three categories: direct franchising, master franchising and joint venture arrangements.[18] Mendelsohn divided franchising arrangements into three types: franchise agreements, master franchise agreements and development agreements.[19] Lerner has classified franchising arrangements by examining the relationships between the franchisor and the franchisee: single location franchise agreement, area development agreement, sub-franchising, master franchisee arrangement, conversion agreement, and multiple franchise operation;[20] while Petroff divided franchising into two major categories: product or trade name franchising which is identified with the supplier; and business format or package franchising which is characterised by established standards for the operation of the business.[21] These writers have emphasised different aspects of franchising arrangements and applied different criteria for classification. Bearing in mind that the formats in which a franchising arrangement can be made are inexhaustible and that the purpose of studying the format of franchising arrangements is to understand their operation in international commerce, the categories adopted by Konigsberg will be relied on in this section of the book.

Direct franchising

[3.13] Direct franchising means that:

> [the] franchisor franchises directly to franchisees situated in the foreign country without the intervention of a third party. In other words, there is a direct contractual relationship between the franchisor and the foreign franchisee which permits the latter to establish a franchise outlet in the foreign country pursuant to a unit franchise agreement entered into between the franchisor and the franchisee.[22]

---

18. A S Konigsberg, QC, 'The Structure of International Franchising Agreements', paper delivered at the American Bar Association Annual Meeting Fundamentals of International Franchising, available at <http:/www.lapros.qc.ca/frana/internat-franchis.html>. See also A S Konigsberg, 'Analysing the International Franchising Opportunity' in Gramatidis and Campbell, note 7 above, pp 11–34.
19. Mendelsohn and Bynoe, note 8 above, pp 63–4.
20. Berner, 'Current Trades in Franchising' in Gramatidis and Campbell, note 7 above, pp 133–40.
21. Petroff, 'Franchising' in Campbell and Pombo, note 10 above, p 83.
22. Konigsberg, note 18 above.

Direct franchising can be arranged through three methods: making a franchising agreement directly with a foreign party, establishing a branch office or foreign subsidiary to promote franchising, or entering into a development agreement for the purpose of franchising.

Making a franchising agreement directly with a foreign party is the simplest form of franchising. Its major advantages are the low cost and the direct contact between the franchisor and the franchisee, but its major disadvantages are the loss of certain tax benefits, which are available only to local companies in certain foreign countries, and the difficulty of monitoring the franchisee's operation.

The major advantages of this method are tax advantages under certain foreign laws, better supervision of the franchisees' operations and possible discovery of more opportunities in that foreign country. The major disadvantages are cost and possible local restrictions on foreign investment.

A development agreement is a combination of a direct franchising agreement and an agreement on exclusive dealership within a specific territory. It is not an ordinary exclusive right to do something in the sense that there is no sub-franchising in the area concerned even though there is more than one outlet within the agreed area. It has similar advantages and disadvantages to a direct agreement with a foreign party. It may provide better foreseeability or certainty to the franchisor for the development of outlets within a particular territory because of the obligation undertaken by the franchisee in the development contract.

Master franchising

[3.14] Master franchising is an arrangement under which:

> [the] franchisor enters into a master franchise agreement directly with a sub-franchisor, usually a foreign national, pursuant to which the sub-franchisor himself develops and owns franchise outlets in addition to sub-franchising outlets to sub-franchisees in the foreign country. Thus, the entering into of a master franchise agreement involves sub-franchising directly from the sub-franchisor to sub-franchisees and accordingly, it is the sub-franchisor who enters into a unit franchise agreement with a sub-franchisee for each franchise outlet to be established in the foreign country.[23]

This definition can be compared with that given in the Block Exemption Regulation of the EU, where a master franchising agreement is defined as an:

> ... agreement whereby the one undertaking, the franchisor, grants the other, the master franchisee, in exchange for direct or indirect financial consideration, the right to exploit a franchise for the purposes of concluding a franchising agreement with third parties, the franchisees.[24]

The two definitions together offer a more comprehensive description of master franchising.

When a master franchisee is allowed to grant a sub-franchise, the concept of 'area franchise' becomes relevant. According to the New York Franchise Act, an area franchise:

> ... means a contract or agreement between a franchisor and sub-franchisor whereby the sub-franchisor is granted the right, for consideration given in whole or in part for such right, to sell or

---

23. Ibid.
24. Mendelsohn and Bynoe, note 8 above, p 276.

negotiate the sale of franchises in the name or on behalf of the franchisor, unless specifically stated otherwise.

A master franchise by implication permits the use of area franchises and has the following characteristics:

- it enables the franchisor to introduce his or her system into the target country at minimum cost;
- it permits the franchisee to become a sub-franchisor in that target country;
- it encourages maximum growth of the franchisor's operations in the target country; and
- it allows the franchisor to have certain control over the growth of the franchising in the target country.

The master franchising agreement has both advantages and disadvantages, of course. The major advantages are the relatively low cost and relatively high return for the franchisor, because the franchisor takes royalties on each outlet developed by the master franchisee. Its major disadvantages are the loss of direct control over sub-outlets franchised by the master franchisee and the complexity arising from the chain of franchising agreements concluded by the master franchisee.

The major feature of master franchising is the delegated authority vested in the franchisee under the master franchising agreement. The master franchisee has an exclusive right to develop sub-outlets within a designated area: this protects his or her interests. However, most master franchising agreements also contain clauses which compel the master franchisee to develop sub-franchising at a minimum speed. This is a financial obligation on the part of the master franchisee. If no sub-franchisee is available within a particular period of time, the master franchisee has to commit his or her own capital to develop new outlets in pursuance of the terms of the master franchising agreement. This obligation counter-balances the master franchisee's exclusive right to develop a particular franchise within a specified area. Many versions of standard master franchising agreements, and other types of franchising agreements also, have been developed by lawyers and business people across the world. The standard contracts provide guidance for the common issues which should be covered in a master franchising agreement.

Joint venture agreements

[3.15] A joint venture agreement for the purpose of franchising refers to an arrangement under which:

> [the] franchisor enters into a joint venture agreement with a joint venture partner who is usually a national of the foreign country, pursuant to which the parties agree to establish what is usually a joint venture company but which may sometimes take the form of a partnership or a trust. The joint venture company, partnership or trust then enters into either a development agreement or, more typically, a master franchise agreement with the franchisor.[25]

The joint venture agreement is different from any other formats for franchising already discussed. It is a mixture of establishing a subsidiary and master franchising. The joint venture is partially invested in by the franchisor, but the joint venture is the master

---

25. Konigsberg, note 18 above.

franchisee under the master franchising agreement which is signed after the establishment of the joint venture between the franchisor and the venture. The arrangement makes sense as each legal person has its own legal status and limited liability. It is also necessary to circumvent certain local regulations on foreign investment or foreign trade, because the joint venture invested in by the franchisor is a local legal person.

The advantages and disadvantages of this type of arrangement must be assessed in context. Generally speaking, the franchisor takes more risk and incurs higher costs for investing in a joint venture in a foreign country. However, if this is the only way or the most efficient way to develop franchising in a particular country or jurisdiction, it may be the best option for the franchisor. The major advantage of such an arrangement is that it allows the franchisor to take advantage of local company law, tax law and foreign investment law. In addition, a joint venture permits the franchisor to have closer control over local outlets than a master franchising agreement. The major disadvantages are the higher costs and greater risks the franchisor has to bear when entering into the joint venture agreement.

Major considerations of franchising arrangements

[3.16] Franchising can take various forms, which can be continuously modified and created. The major considerations which decide the formality of a franchising arrangement are its feasibility, profitability and certainty. Both the franchisor and the franchisee are in business ventures. They are after maximum profit and minimum risk in the same deal. Thus, their interests may be in conflict to some extent or in certain circumstances. Their agreement on how to share the risk and profit in a particular transaction determines the format the transaction will take. Since the franchisor and the franchisee operate in different social contexts, the benefit and risk to each are assessed differently. A risk to the franchisor may not be a risk to the franchisee. To take one example, if the franchisor has sufficient funds and the investment risk in a target country is low, he or she will probably set up a local subsidiary to develop franchising in the target country, rather than signing a master franchising agreement to share the market with the master franchisee. On the other hand, if the franchisor does not have sufficient capital or does not wish to take any investment risks, the rational option would be to make a master franchising agreement. Similarly, if a joint venture gives the franchisor some advantage in local investment concessions or tax benefits, he or she should of course pursue a joint venture development, instead of a solely owned local subsidiary. These commercial, practical and legal considerations determine the particular form which a franchising arrangement will take.[26]

---

26. For a discussion on international franchising, see M G Brennan and D Mendelsohn, 'Launching an International Franchising Program' in Gramatidis and Campbell, note 7 above, pp 35–51; and P Arendorff, 'Franchising as a Vehicle for International Expansion' in Gramatidis and Campbell, note 7 above, pp 53–5.

Major legal issues of franchising

Contract law

[3.17] A franchising arrangement is a contract. The franchisor and the franchisee are in a contractual relationship with each other, no matter what name or format the franchising arrangement takes. For example, in a standard master franchising agreement[27] there are clauses stating that the franchisor is obliged to permit the franchisee to operate the business under the permitted trade name, to use a particular trademark or to carry on the business in a particular style; and not to derogate from his or her promises given to the franchisee. There are also clauses concerning the parties' obligations to advertise the business, the franchisor's obligation to provide training to the franchisee and his or her staff, and the franchisor's obligation to supply essential materials for the operation of the business. There are also clauses on the obligations of the franchisee, such as payment, continuous development of business, confidentiality clauses, etc. The right of the franchisee to develop franchising in the designated area, governing law issues and the forum for litigation are also set out in the agreement. It can be concluded that, whatever its particular features, a franchising agreement is a contract. Misrepresentation and fraud inducing the making of a franchising agreement were argued in the same way as misrepresentation and fraud in contract law in *Rigby (Nicola) v Decorating Den Systems Ltd*, decided on 15 March 1999 by the Court of Appeal of the High Court of the UK.[28] The parties' rights and obligations must be defined in the contract and the parties are connected to each other on the basis of the contract. Thus, protecting the parties' interests under the franchising agreement is the most essential legal issue of any franchising arrangement.

Generally speaking, a franchising agreement should contain a number of common terms. For example, the identity of the parties; the rights to be granted; the territory within which the franchisee may exercise the rights; the exclusivity of the rights; the performance schedule, which requires the franchisee and the franchisor to perform their obligations in accordance with the agreed schedule; franchising fees, such as the initial fee, continuing fee, and other payments; the arrangement on the payment of withholding taxes (if applicable); training of the franchisee's staff; protection and use of trademarks and other intellectual property rights, including arrangements relating to improvements made by the franchisee on the intellectual property and new developments made by the franchisor; transfer of business between the parties (if applicable), or to a third party; termination of contract, which should set out the grounds for avoiding the contract by the innocent party in case of the other's breach;[29] and dispute settlement, which should include an arbitration clause or a choice of law and choice of forum clause.[30] These terms are essential for the protection of both parties' interests. In most cases, the franchisee is required to make a financial commitment under a franchising agreement. Thus, the franchisee must be very

---

27. A sample copy of the master franchising agreement is collected in Adams et al, note 11 above, pp 335–88.
28. The case is available at <http://www.casetrack.com/casetrack_frame.htm>.
29. For relevant discussions, see M Abell, 'Termination of an International Franchise Agreement' in Gramatidis and Campbell, note 7 above, pp 131–7.
30. For discussion, see A Powles, 'Alternative Commercial Dispute Resolution: A Contemporary Australian Experiment' in Gramatidis and Campbell, note 7 above, pp 125–30.

careful about his or her obligations under the contract. For example, a normal franchising agreement does not permit the franchisee to make arrangements for sub-franchising, but a master franchising agreement does. Similarly, a franchising agreement may promise that the franchisee will be the sole franchisee within a particular territory in relation to a particular type of franchising arrangement. The franchisee must ascertain the exact meaning to protect his or her exclusive right. The franchisor, on the other hand, must protect his or her interests by incorporating confidentiality clauses into the franchising agreement. A franchising agreement often contains a clause which requires the franchisee not only to maintain confidentiality of the information or technology granted under the agreement during the term of the agreement, but also to undertake not to use the information or technology obtained under the contract for a number of years after the termination of the agreement.

Competition law

[3.18] Competition law is known as anti-trust legislation in the United States, trade practices law in the United Kingdom and Australia, and competition law in most continental law countries. Sometimes it is also known as fair competition law and law against unfair competition.

Competition law is relevant to franchising because franchising is a system of business operation,[31] and may therefore result in unfair business practices, create a monopoly prohibited by law, or engage in exclusive dealing or any other business activities which are prohibited by law. Therefore, a franchising arrangement must comply with the relevant competition law applicable to the arrangement. However, it must be pointed out that a franchising agreement or a clause of the agreement is prohibited by law only when it falls under the scope of the relevant provisions of the law. In *Continental TV Inc v GTE Sylvania Inc* 433 US 36 (1977), the franchising agreement in dispute contained a clause which barred the franchisee from selling franchised products from locations other than those specified in the agreement. The franchisee intended to develop its business by establishing outlets in other cities. The franchisor refused to continue with the franchising agreement. The franchisee alleged that the said clause violated the Sherman Act, the US anti-trust legislation. The jury found that the clause violated the Sherman Act. The Court of Appeal reversed the decision, holding that the clause should be judged under the 'rule of reason', instead of the Sherman Act. The US Supreme Court affirmed the decision and held that the clause did not have a pernicious effect on competition.

The EU competition law may illustrate the relationship between a franchising arrangement and a competition law. Article 85 of the EC Treaty prohibits any agreements which have a negative impact on the free trade policy of the EU. In particular, art 85(1) prohibits any agreements, decisions, associations or practices which are incompatible with the common market within the EU, or which have restrictive or distorting impacts on competition within the EU. Arrangements involving the sale of goods and services, control of business operations or markets, restriction on technical development or investment, and

---

31. For discussion, see M Mendelsohn, 'Competition Laws: Their Applicability and Their Impact' in Gramatidis and Campbell, note 7 above, pp 81–3.

imposition of conditions on trading activities or commercial activities may fall under art 85(1). A franchising agreement may be caught by art 85 because of the parties' business arrangements in the agreement. For example, *Pronuptia de Paris GmnH v Pronuptia de Paris Irmgard Schillgalis* was decided by the European Court of Justice,[32] and *Pronuptia*,[33] and *Computerland* were examined by the European Commission.[34] These cases caused debate on the operation of art 85, leading to the making of the Block Exemption Regulation,[35] which exempts certain types of franchising arrangements and also some other types of agreements from the operation of art 85.[36]

In conclusion, competition law has implications for franchising arrangements. Most countries and jurisdictions have some sort of competition law, although there is no uniform international competition law except the EU competition law which applies within the EU. Due to the differences between the competition laws of most countries, it is necessary to examine the law of the relevant country to ensure a particular franchising arrangement is legal under that law. This is an issue of conflict of laws. The parties may be able to choose a particular law in a franchising agreement to ensure the validity of the agreement. However, under the general principles of conflict of laws, the choice of law clause may be denied in certain circumstances by a court of law on the ground of illegality under local law or public interest considerations. Thus, a choice of law clause is one of the methods of avoiding the application of an unfavourable law, but the power eventually lies in the hands of the court adjudicating the validity of the clause in the case of a dispute.

Tax law

[3.19] Tax law is relevant to franchising arrangements. In most cases, the franchisor is subject to withholding tax on the royalties received under a franchising agreement. Depending on the nature of the franchise, value added tax may also apply to the franchising agreement or to the product or activities covered by the agreement. Similarly, other types of taxes, such as company tax or other levies, may also apply to a franchising agreement.[37] Often a franchising arrangement is modified to maximise the franchisor's tax benefit.

Intellectual property law

[3.20] Intellectual property law has wide implications for franchising arrangements, because most franchising arrangements are based on intellectual property of some sort.[38]

---

32. Case 161/84 [1986] ECR 353; [1986] 1 CMLR 414, ECJ; see discussions in Adams et al, note 11 above, p 57.
33. OJ 1987 L 13/39; [1989] 4 CMLR 355; see Adams et al, note 11 above, p 57.
34. OJ 1987 L222/12; [1989] 4 CMLR 259; see Adams et al, ibid.
35. Council Regulation (EEC) 4087/88 (OJ 1988 L359/46).
36. For discussion on the operation of the Block Exemption Regulation, see Adams et al, note 11 above, pp 60–1; and Mendelsohn and Bynoe, note 8 above, pp 376–84; Byrne, *Licensing Technology*, 2nd ed, Jordans, Bristol, 1998, pp 157–8; and see also discussions in *Courage Ltd v Grehan*, decided on 25 May 1999, Court of Appeal of High Court of UK, the case is available at <http://www.casetrack.com>.
37. For discussion, see Saleh, 'Franchising and International Taxation Considerations' in Gramatidis and Campbell, note 7 above, pp 75–80.
38. For discussion, see Kroman, 'International Intellectual Property Aspects of Franchising' in Gramatidis and Campbell, note 7 above, pp 85–99.

Trade names, trademarks, copyrights, designs, know-how, goodwill and patents are protected by intellectual property law. Commercial secrets and confidential information may also be protected by the laws of certain countries. For international franchising, it is necessary to find out whether or not the target country is a member of any international conventions on copyright protection. The major international intellectual property conventions are set out later in this chapter in the subsection on the transfer of intellectual property: see **[3.38]**.

The international conventions regulate different aspects of intellectual property rights. As a general principle of international law, a convention binds only the countries which have ratified it. Thus, it is necessary for a franchisor to ascertain whether a target country has ratified a particular convention and what the intellectual property laws of that country are. It is also necessary for the franchisee to ensure that the franchisor has the rights he or she claims to have under the relevant law, which is the law of the franchisor's country in most cases.

Licensing agreements

Meaning of licensing

[3.21] The meaning of licensing is not as controversial, ambiguous or flexible as the definition of franchising. Licensing comes from 'licence'; that is, a permit to do something which is otherwise illegal or an authority to exercise a specific privilege or right which is not available to any unauthorised person. For example, it has been argued that a 'licence is simply a permission given to someone (licensee) to do something which someone else (licensor) otherwise has the right or power to stop him doing'.[39] A licence is based on the legal rights of the licensor. Because the licensor has legal rights to carry on certain activities, to authorise certain activities, or to receive certain benefits, the licensor may in accordance with law transfer his or her legal rights under a licence to a licensee. While the particular right or activity could be anything which is capable of being licensed in law, in international commercial law most licences relate to the transfer of industrial or intellectual property (such as copyright, patent, know-how, or trademark), and of exclusive or non-exclusive rights (franchises) to engage in certain business activities in a particular market, for example, an exclusive or non-exclusive right to sell a patented product or use a trade name.[40]

Licensing in international commercial law is the same as licensing in a domestic context. Licensing is a concept common to the domestic law of all countries. Governments have the power to issue licences to various people to do different things. The freer a system is, the fewer licences required in the daily operation of that society. But all governments must maintain some control over certain professions, industries or sectors of the economy for the sake of achieving certain social, political and economic aims. Licences are issued or granted by the government to allocate power, privilege, control

---

39. Brown, 'Licensing Technology' in Campbell and Pombo, note 10 above, p 119.
40. For discussion, see Fox, *International Commercial Agreements*, 2nd ed, Kluwer, Deventer, 1992, pp 76–7.

and order as deemed necessary by that government. To put it another way, the government has created certain artificial powers and restrictions and then administers the use of this power and the enforcement of the restrictions by way of licensing. Broadcasting licences, air carrier's licences, development licences and liquor licences are examples of domestic licensing.[41]

Commercial licensing and international commercial licensing are similar to government licensing in a domestic context in the sense that they are all based on the existence of special rights or powers protected or recognised in law, which become the subject matter of licensing. They are different from each other in that commercial licensing and international commercial licensing are based on the private rights of the licensor (the person granting the licence), but government licensing is based on the government's power or public power. The existence of a private right vested by law in a particular person, either natural or legal, is the prerequisite for commercial licensing. Commercial licensing is closely related to intellectual property rights, artificial rights created by law. That these rights are artificial can be seen from the fact that in countries or jurisidictions which have not ratified the relevant international convention, or passed specific domestic laws, these rights are not protected.

Licensing in a commercial transaction can be understood as an arrangement under which the person holding a particular right or privilege grants part of the right or privilege to another person under specific terms and conditions for commercial purposes. The person granting the right is the licensor, and the person receiving the right is the licensee. The agreement giving legal effect to the arrangement is the licensing or licence agreement.

Definition of licensing agreement

[3.22] Most licensing agreements are related to the transfer of intellectual property rights. A licensing agreement can be defined as a contract or arrangement under which the licensor, who is entitled to transfer the right to use a particular intellectual property right, licenses the intellectual property concerned to the licensee under agreed terms and conditions. Thus, a licensing agreement is also known as the licensing of intellectual property.

A licensing or licence agreement can be defined in a number of ways. It may be described as:

> ... a contractual arrangement pursuant to which a party, commonly known as a licensor, grants unto another party, the licensee, the right to use the licensor's patents, know-how and/or trademarks in connection with the manufacturing and/or distribution of a certain product.[42]

A licensing agreement has also been described as being 'concerned with the transfer of technology for profit, or at least in the expectation of profit where the money consideration

---

41. For discussion on domestic licensing, see Phillips, *Licensing Law Guide*, 2nd ed, Butterworths, London, 1998.
42. Description provided by Konigberg, cited in W A Scott, 'Technology Transfer Laws and International Franchising' (1994) 22 *IBL* 256.

for a licence is a running royalty on sales'.[43] Or it may be simply understood as a 'transfer of technology from its owner to another party'.[44]

The legal effect of a licence or a licensing agreement is described by the Canadian Supreme Court in *Novopharm Ltd v Eli Lilly* [1998] 2 SCR 129. The court observed as follows (para 49):

> A licence, even though exclusive, does not give the licensee all the rights of the patentee. A licence does not set up rights as between the licensee and the public, but only permits him to do acts that he would otherwise be prohibited from doing. He obtains merely a right of user. But a licence is a grant of a right and does not merely confer upon the licensee a mere interest in equity. A licence is the transfer of a beneficial interest to a limited extent, whereby the transferee acquires an equitable right in the patent. *A licence prevents that from being unlawful which, but for the licence, would be unlawful; it is a consent by an owner of a right that another person should commit an act which, but for that licence, would be an infringement of the right of the person who gives the licence. A licence gives no more than the right to do the thing actually licensed to be done.* [original emphasis]
>
> In other words, by the grant of a licence, the patentee grants to the licensee the right to act in a certain way vis à vis the patented article, a right which, but for the licence, the licensee would not enjoy. The licensee's rights, however, are not necessarily equivalent to those of the patentee; rather, they are limited to, and qualified by, the express terms of the licence.

The observation of the court emphasises strongly the authority to act as granted under the licensing agreement. The authority to do a specified act or to use the subject matter in a particular manner is the key to a licence or a licensing agreement.

Legal framework for licensing

International convention

[3.23] There is no international convention regulating licensing agreements. However, the Agreement on TRIPs, which is an integral part of the WTO Agreement (all WTO members must comply with it), has provisions affecting certain aspects of licensing agreements. Broadly speaking, arts 21 and 40 of the Agreement on TRIPs are relevant to international licensing of intellectual property rights. Article 21 provides as follow:

> Members may determine conditions on the licensing and assignment of trademarks, it being understood that the compulsory licensing of trademarks shall not be permitted and that the owner of a registered trademark shall have the right to assign the trademark with or without the transfer of the business to which the trademark belongs.

This provision appears to be related to the right to assign or license registered trademarks. It purports to restrict governmental interference with private rights to transfer and to use registered trademarks.

Article 40 of the Agreement on TRIPs is concerned with licensing of intellectual property and competition. This article states as follows:

1. Members agree that some licensing practices or conditions pertaining to intellectual property rights which restrain competition may have adverse effects on trade and may impede the transfer and dissemination of technology.
2. Nothing in this Agreement shall prevent Members from specifying in their legislation licensing practices or conditions that may in particular cases constitute an abuse of intellectual property

---

43. Byrne, note 36 above, p 4.
44. Ehrbar, *Business International's Guide to International Licensing*, McGraw-Hill Inc, New York, 1993, p xvi.

rights having an adverse effect on competition in the relevant market. As provided above, a Member may adopt, consistently with the other provisions of this Agreement, appropriate measures to prevent or control such practices, which may include for example exclusive grant-back conditions, conditions preventing challenges to validity and coercive package licensing, in the light of the relevant laws and regulations of that Member.

This provision permits WTO members to regulate licensing agreements to ensure fair competition. It balances the need to protect IP rights and the need to ensure fair competition in a given market. The Agreement on TRIPs is the only international convention that has an impact on international licensing agreements generally. The existing international conventions on intellectual property protection have implications for the subject matters covered by licensing agreements, rather than the agreements themselves.

Domestic law

[3.24] Licensing agreements are subject to domestic contract law, intellectual property law, agency law, competition law and any other laws which may be relevant, depending on the subject matter of the licensing agreement. For example, in *Novopharm Ltd v Eli Lilly* [1998] 2 SCR 129, a compulsory licence under the Patent Act (Canada) was involved. In this case, Eli Lilly and Co (Eli Lilly), the licensor, owned the Canadian patents for nizatidine and for its manufacturing process. It alone held a notice of compliance (NOC) to produce and market certain final-dosage forms of the medicine. Novopharm held a compulsory licence, obtained under the Patent Act as it existed prior to February 1993, which permitted it to use the patented process to make nizatidine for the preparation or production of medicine and to import and/or sell medicine made by the process. The licence stipulated that it was non-transferable, prohibiting Novopharm from granting any sub-licence, and providing Eli Lilly with the option to terminate the licence upon any breach of its terms.

The system of compulsory licence was abolished in 1993. Before the abolition, Novopharm and Apotex entered a 'supply agreement', which provided that, where one party held a licence for a patented medicine for which the other did not, the licensed party would obtain, at the request and direction of the unlicensed party, specified quantities of that medicine, and supply it to the unlicensed party at cost plus a 4 per cent royalty. In April 1993, Apotex commenced efforts to obtain an NOC for certain final-dosage forms of nizatidine, and issued a notice of allegation (NOA) alleging that no claim for nizatidine or for its use would be infringed. In support of this allegation, Apotex relied upon the licence issued to Novopharm and the 'mutual understanding' with Novopharm. At the same time, Apotex notified Novopharm of its intention to request Novopharm to supply it with nizatidine. However, Apotex also indicated that, because it did not yet have an NOC to permit it to market nizatidine in Canada, it could not provide Novopharm with any specifics as to its requirements, but that it would advise in due course as to the required quantity and the manufacturer from whom the nizatidine should be purchased. Eli Lilly and Eli Lilly Canada Inc brought an application (*Eli Lilly and Co v Apotex Inc* (SCC, No 25348)), under s 6(1) of the Patented Medicines (Notice of Compliance) Regulations, for an order prohibiting the Minister from issuing an NOC to Apotex at all or, alternatively, until after 31 December 1997, 10 years after the issuance of the NOC to Eli Lilly Canada, which, under the amended Patent Act, would be the first date on which

[3.24]

Apotex, without an NOC, would be entitled to import nizatidine for consumption in Canada. On 15 July 1993, Eli Lilly purported to exercise its option to terminate Novopharm's compulsory licence, alleging that Novopharm had breached the terms of the licence by granting a sub-licence to Apotex. Novopharm denied this allegation, stating that the commercial agreement into which it had entered with Apotex did not constitute a sub-licence or any transfer of rights under the licence.

Legislation relevant to this dispute was the Patent Act, the contract law which governed the nature of the supply agreement between Novopharm and Apotex and the administrative law which applied to the Minister's power to issue an NOC under the relevant law. The trial court found that the supply agreement between Novopharm and Apotex did not constitute a sub-licence but nonetheless granted the prohibition order on the grounds that, because the reformulation of nizatidine for consumption in Canada would infringe Eli Lilly's patent, the NOA was not justified. The Federal Court of Appeal dismissed Apotex's appeal, but on the grounds that the agreement did constitute a sub-licence. Novopharm appealed to the Canadian Supreme Court. Whether or not the supply agreement constituted a grant of a sub-licence in contravention of the terms of the compulsory licence was the major issue in dispute. If it were, the licensor would be entitled to terminate the licence. The Supreme Court commented on the meaning of sub-licence as follows (at para 48):

> As a general matter, a sublicense amounts to a grant by a licensee of certain licensed rights to a third party, the sublicensee. That is, the licensee in effect transfers or licenses some or all of his or her rights to the sublicensee, which means that the sublicense has similar incidents to the primary license, including the right to exercise independently certain rights enjoyed by the licensee pursuant to its license. It has been said, in fact, that 'a sublicense is simply another name for the indirect granting of a license': see Leslie W. Melville, *Forms and Agreements on Intellectual Property and International Licensing*, vol 1 (3rd ed rev 1997 (loose-leaf)) at ¶3.18.

Largely because the Supreme Court did not consider the supply agreement had transferred the licensee's right to the third party, it allowed the appeal by the licensee against the decisions of the lower courts to prohibit the issue of the NOA to Apotex by the minister.

[3.25] A licensing agreement under domestic law can also be illustrated by an Australian case, *Transfield Pty Ltd v Arlo International Ltd* (1980) 144 CLR 83. This case involved the alleged breach of a licensing agreement by the licensee failing to promote the use of the licensed products in Australia. In this case, Arlo International Ltd (the respondent) was the licensee from Arlo Incorporated, the owners of letters patent to a process for the manufacture and erection of steel poles for use in the construction of electricity transmission lines. By a deed dated 27 June 1973, the respondent, then known as Andromeda Co Ltd, granted to Transfield Pty Ltd (the appellant), which was one of the major contractors for building electricity transmission lines in Australia, an exclusive sub-licence for the Commonwealth of Australia, its territories and protectorates, including the Territory of Papua New Guinea. Under the sub-licence, the licensee was required to make, use, exercise and vend the patented process for the purpose of electricity transmission lines, poles and any non-loadbearing poles of a like nature. The sub-licensee experienced some difficulties in the use of the patented product known as Arlo poles. In 1975, the sub-licensee did not specify the use of Arlo poles in its tender for the construction of a power line in

New South Wales. There was evidence to suggest that the Electricity Commission had some reservations on the suitability of Arlo poles. By the end, the sub-licensee won the project under the condition that it would use its own poles, instead of the Arlo poles. The sub-licensor sued the sub-licensee for a breach of the sub-licensing agreement. The trial court found in favour of the sub-licensor. The sub-licensee appealed to the Court of Appeal of the Supreme Court of New South Wales, which dismissed the appeal. The sub-licensee appealed to the High Court of Australia, which by majority dismissed the appeal.

The major reason for the failure of the sub-licensee's appeal was clause 7 of the sub-licence agreement, which provided as follows:

> The Licensee covenants during the period of the Power Transmission Line Licence at all times to use its best endeavours in and towards the design fabrication installation and selling of the ARLO PTL pole throughout the licensed territory and to energetically promote and develop the greatest possible market for the ARLO PTL pole.

The sub-licensee's major argument was that clause 7 restricted competition and was prohibited by s 112 of the Patents Act 1952 (Cth). The majority of the High Court refused to accept that argument. Mason J (as his Honour then was) observed (at 102) as follows:

> I can see no adequate basis for importing into this positive obligation a negative implication that the appellant will not use or for that matter sell a pole which competes with the ARLO pole, whether that pole be manufactured by the appellant or by another. It is significant that the Agreement contains no express prohibition against the appellant's use of competing poles or products. However, to conclude that there is no implied prohibition may not be decisive of the question which arises. Section 112 makes the 'effect' of the provision the all important consideration (see the Tool Metal Co. Case; cf. Thomas Hunter Ltd's Patent). But I do not think that the practical effect of the clause is to prevent use or sale of another pole. There is no necessary inconsistency between the appellant's compliance with its obligations under cl. 7, as I understand them, and its use and sale of a competing pole. The appellant may do all that is within its power to comply with cl. 7 yet find that it has no practical alternative but to use or sell a competing pole. The clause does not prohibit or prevent such use or sale.
>
> As I have shown, cl. 7 is readily susceptible of an interpretation which preserves its validity by not bringing it into conflict with s. 112. This is the interpretation which should be given to it.

Relevant to this case were the Restrictive Trade Practices Act 1974 (Cth), the Patents Act 1952 (Cth), and principles for contract construction. As can be seen, different branches of domestic law may have implications for a licensing agreement, depending on the terms and conditions of that agreement.[45]

Forms of licensing agreements

[3.26] Licensing agreements can be made in various forms. There is no uniform rule for the classification of licensing agreements. In practice, agreements are categorised according to their function or the matter or right subject to the licence. These categories are for commercial convenience only. For example, under the model EEC patent licensing agreement, licensing agreements were divided into licensed patents, licensed

---

45. For discussions on licensing in a number of selected countries, see Ehrbar, ibid; Scott, note 42 above, pp 256–68; and also H L Christiansen, 'The Nordic Licensing Systems — Extended Collective Agreement Licensing' [1991] *EIPR* 346.

know-how, licensed invention, licensed product and licensed territory.[46] Licence agreements can also be classified into the following four categories:[47]

- **technology transfer agreements:** the major feature of this type of agreement is that under its terms a licensee is granted the right to establish a manufacturing facility to produce a product by using the licensor's technology;
- **trademark licence agreements:** the major feature of this type of agreement is that under its terms the licensee is granted the right to use the licensor's trademark in distributing products or performing services;
- **celebrity licence agreements:** the major feature of this type of agreement is that under its terms the licensee is granted the right to use the name or likeness of a celebrity; and
- **character licence agreements:** the major feature of this type of agreement is that under its terms the licensee is granted the right to use the name and likeness of a character, such as Mickey Mouse, in connection with the distribution of a product or the performance of a service.

The differences between these categories are determined on the basis of the licensed matter or right. This is not a particularly efficient way of categorising agreements, because the last two categories are similar to the second category, being essentially related to trademarks or service marks. A logical way to categorise licensing agreements is to place them into several major groups identified by generic terms. Since licensing agreements mainly involve the transfer of certain property rights, the nature of the property right is used as the basis of categorisation:

- licensing of patent rights;
- licensing of trademarks or service marks;
- licensing of copyright;
- licensing of utility models;
- licensing of plant variety rights;
- licensing of design rights;
- licensing of know-how;
- licensing of trade secrets;
- licensing of a system to operate (a system may involve several elements of intellectual property rights) or a process;
- licensing of a privilege protected or granted by law;
- licensing of a mixed right, which may include several types of intellectual property or rights or privileges protected or granted by law; or
- licensing of any subject matter, right or privilege which has commercial value to the licensee and the licensor.

---

46. H Lutz and T R Broderick, 'A Model EEC Patent Licensing Agreement' (1985) 13 *IBL*, p 161.
47. Scott, note 42 above, p 256.

We need to return to the original meaning of licence or licensing as discussed in **[3.21]**. A licence is a permit or authority granted by the licensor to the licensee under agreed terms and conditions. A licence is a form of commercial operation. As long as the parties to the transaction wish to conclude a contract by way of licensing agreement to define the rights and obligations between them, they are entitled to do so, except in circumstances where prohibition has been expressly stipulated in law. There is no limit on what can be the subject of licensing, although the law protects only those things which have positive value to society and the economy. For example, the internet has created a new form of intellectual property. Whenever it is commercially viable and technically feasible, licensing agreements will be made on the many rights and privileges developed by the internet industry. There will no doubt be interesting developments in this area in the future.

Major legal issues of licensing agreements

Protection of intellectual property

[3.27] Protection of intellectual property is the major concern of most licensing agreements. In order to protect the licensor's intellectual property rights, the rights and obligations of the parties must be clearly defined in the agreement, as must the nature and scope of the right concerned. Different types of intellectual property rights are subject to different laws. It is necessary to ensure that a contract clause purporting to protect a particular intellectual property right is valid under laws governing the agreement concerned. Whether the home country of the licensor and the licensee is a member of a particular international convention, and what laws have been passed by each of the two countries for the protection of intellectual property are relevant considerations. A licensing agreement may be part of a franchising arrangement: the parties must ensure consistency between the protection offered by the franchising agreement and the licensing agreement, if they are separate. Protection of intellectual property in a licensing agreement is illustrated in *Cadbury Schweppes Inc v FBI Foods Ltd* [1999] 1 SCR 142.

Contract law

[3.28] As we have seen in the discussion concerning the regulation of licensing agreements under domestic law, contract law is the most important for licensing agreements. The relationship between the licensor and the licensee can be defined in contract, no matter how complicated the relationship. Licensing agreements are often used as a method to organise franchising arrangements, the structures of which are based on contract. Also, if a licensing agreement is tied up with other arrangements, such as the supply of certain goods or services between the licensor and the licensee, or distribution of the products manufactured under the licensing agreement, or improvement of the licensed technology, etc, the arrangements and relationships between them must be defined clearly and efficiently in the contracts concerned. In the area of international investment, parties may organise a joint venture by incorporating a licensing agreement. A joint venture agreement is different from a licensing agreement; the licensing agreement regulates the transfer of a particular intellectual property right between the parties, constituting the basis of the joint venture operation.

There are a number of common terms or issues a licensing agreement should cover. These include the identity of the licensor and the licensee, a sufficient description of the licensed right, the scope of the right granted to the licensee, exclusivity or non-exclusivity, whether it is a sole licence, the duration of the licence, quality control of the licensed product or services, quantity restrictions (if any), royalties, the right of the licensee to use the licensed right or technology or information after the termination of the licensing agreement, a confidentiality clause, access of both parties to the technological improvement of the licensed right, breach of contract, remedies, governing law, an arbitration clause or choice of forum clause (if applicable).

It is necessary to distinguish between exclusive, non-exclusive and sole licences. An exclusive licence permits the licensee to be the only licensee for the exercise of the licensed right within a designated territory and within the terms of the licence. It excludes participation by the licensor in the designated territory within the terms of the licence. This is an undertaking of the licensor. A non-exclusive licence permits the licensor to license more licensees within the designated territory as he or she wishes. The licensee may face competition from other licensees subsequently licensed. A sole licence is a limited undertaking by the licensor, who promises not to issue more licences within the designated area but reserves the right to use the licensed right him or herself. Thus, a sole licensee may face competition from the licensor in the future. The terms represent different levels of rights and liabilities for the licensor and the licensee, and the licensee is usually expected to pay more for a more exclusive right.

An exclusive licence means that the licensee is the exclusive dealer and user of the licensed right. This binds both the licensor and the licensee. It also has implications for the market in the designated territory. But can the term provide protection to the licensee against a third party who is not a party to the licence agreement? The right of the licensee against a third party was tested in an Australian case, *Interstate Parcel Express Co Pty Ltd v Time-Life International (Nederlands) BV* (1977) 138 CLR 534. In this case, Time-Life International was an exclusive licensee under a licence agreement with Time Incorporated of the United States. The licence agreement granted Time-Life the exclusive right to publish books owned by Time Incorporated throughout the world other than in North America. Accordingly, Time-Life had the exclusive right to publish and market Time Incorporated books in Australia. Interstate Parcel Express was a retail bookseller, operating under the business name of Angus & Robertson Bookshops. In 1976, it imported directly from a book wholesaler in the United States a quantity of cookery books published by Time Incorporated because the cost for such importation was lower than purchasing books from Time-Life. Time-Life and Time Incorporated sought a court declaration against Interstate Parcel for such importation and other relief under the Copyright Act 1968 (Cth) and other relevant law. The trial court granted the order sought and certain relief was also granted. Interstate Parcel appealed to the High Court of Australia after its appeal to the Court of Appeal of the New South Wales Supreme Court failed. One of the major arguments presented by Interstate Parcel was that the exclusive licence of Time-Life, which was justified under the Copyright Act 1968 (Cth), had nothing to do with the importation, and that the Copyright Act did not apply to the situation in dispute. Interstate Parcel also argued that by selling the books to the public in the United States, the copyright holder, Time Incorporated, had granted a licence to use and sell the books somewhere else by the buyer. The High Court unanimously dismissed the appeal. In reaching their decisions, most judges relied heavily on ss 37 and 38 of the Copyright Act 1968 (Cth). The relevant parts of these two provisions are set out below:

> Section 37: The copyright in a literary, dramatic, musical or artistic work is infringed by a person who, without the licence of the owner of the copyright, imports an article into Australia for the purpose of:
> (a) selling, letting for hire, or by way of trade offering or exposing for sale or hire, the article;
> ...
> Section 38: (1) The copyright in a literary, dramatic, musical or artistic work is infringed by a person who, in Australia, and without the licence of the owner of the copyright:
> (a) sells, lets for hire, or by way of trade offers or exposes for sale or hire, an article; or
> (b) by way of trade exhibits an article in public, where, to his knowledge, the making of the article constituted an infringement of the copyright or, in the case of an imported article, would, if the article had been made in Australia by the importer, have constituted such an infringement.

Murphy J also considered the effect of the Trade Practices Act 1974 (Cth). His Honour referred to s 46(1) of the Trade Practices Act 1974, which is set out as follows:

> A corporation that is in a position substantially to control a market for goods or services shall not take advantage of the power in relation to that market that it has by virtue of being in that position —
> (a) to eliminate or substantially to damage a competitor in that market or in another market;
> (b) to prevent the entry of a person into that market or into another market; or
> (c) to deter or prevent a person from engaging in competitive behaviour in that market or in another market.

In addition, his Honour noted that s 48 of the Trade Practices Act prohibited resale price maintenance, and the possibility that Time-Life and Time Incorporated might have breached the Trade Practices Act by establishing a monopoly in the Australian market under the exclusive licence. This case suggests that the effect of an exclusive licence to competition in a local market may sometimes be examined by a local court. This case can be contrasted with *Avel Pty Ltd v Multicoin Amusements Pty Ltd* (1990) 171 CLR 88, which involved a distribution agreement and is discussed in **[3.36]**. Its facts were similar to those of *Interstate Parcel Express Co Pty Ltd v Time-Life International (Nederlands) BV* in that the Australian exclusive distributor sought to rely on ss 38 and 39 of the Copyright Act to prohibit the direct import by a third party of game machines manufactured by the supplier in the United States. However, in *Avel* the distributor failed.

For any international licensing agreement, conflict of laws must always be considered by the parties. The validity of the agreement, the validity of a contract clause, or the enforcement of a particular right or obligation may vary depending on which domestic law applies. While parties or a party may be able to avoid or minimise disputes by deliberately and expressly designing a transaction and agreement under the commonly accepted principles of conflict of laws rules, the court which ultimately makes a decision may sometimes deny or disregard the intention of the parties or party on the ground of illegality under local law or public interest considerations.

There are several basic issues which a lawyer involved in an international licensing contract should pay attention to:

- the laws of the licensee's and licensor's countries in relation to industrial property and international treaties applicable in the circumstances concerned;
- the meaning and nature of industrial property and other relevant concepts relating to the rights and obligations of the parties as defined in the underlying agreement;
- the scope of the right or privilege, including the rights and obligations of the licensee and licensor, the territorial limits of the right or privilege licensed, conditions attached to the licence, method of payment, supervision of the use of the licence, and duration of the contract;
- whether the licensee is liable to disclose improvements to the licensor and how much the licensor should pay to the licensee for such disclosure;
- the necessity to define the duty of confidentiality in order to prevent unauthorised disclosure or use of the licensed rights, technology and privilege;
- the method and procedure for terminating the contract, either at the end of the contract or at the occurrence of a prescribed event; and
- the method, procedure and governing law for settling disputes arising from the contract, including consultation, mediation, arbitration and litigation.

Competition law

[3.29] Licensing agreements are subject to competition law, because most licensing agreements contain conditions and restrictions on the licensee's right to use the licensed right or product. If a licensing agreement imposes certain obligations upon the licensee, resulting in certain prohibited marketing arrangements, price-fixing, monopoly or quantity restriction which amounts to a restriction on competition or unreasonable restraint of trade, or any unfair business arrangements prohibited by the relevant competition law, the part of the obligation contravening the provisions of the competition law may be found invalid by the court adjudicating a dispute. The particular rules of competition law adopted by each country may differ to some extent.[48] It is necessary to examine the law that governs or may be applicable to the licensing agreement in question.

Distribution agreement

Definition of distribution agreement

[3.30] A distribution agreement is a market arrangement. It relates to the sale of goods or supply of services, but it is not a sale of goods or services contract.[49] A distribution

---

48. For detailed discussions on EU competition law and competition laws in the US, Canada, the UK, Australia and Japan, see Byrne, note 36 above, pp 129–62 and 367–422; and H W Gogt Jr and I K Gotts, 'The Antitrust and Technology Transfer Licensing Interface: A Comparative Analysis of Current Developments' (1995) 13 *International Tax and Business Law*, pp 1–45.
49. For further discussion, see Schmitthoff, *Schmitthoff's Export Trade: the Law and Practice of International Trade*, 9th ed, Sweet & Maxwell, London, 1993, pp 260–2.

agreement is a contract or arrangement between a supplier and a distributor made for the purpose of distributing (selling), supplying or marketing a particular product or products within a particular geographical area. A distribution agreement 'covers a whole range of vertical agreements between a vendor and a seller or distributor who are situated at different levels of economic transactions'.[50]

Under Spanish law, a distribution agreement may be understood as:

> [an] agreement by which the entrepreneur (distributor) places his network at the service of another entrepreneur, industrialist, or merchant (supplier), to distribute, for an indefinite or definite period, in a specific geographical area, and under the supervision of the supplier, even though acting in his own name and on his own account, the products whose exclusive resale is granted under predetermined conditions.[51]

Different emphasis has been placed on this definition of distribution agreement. This reflects the differences between the common law tradition and the civil law tradition.

Distribution agreements are often discussed with agency agreements,[52] but a distribution agreement is not an agency agreement, although the distribution agreement may overlap with the agency agreement to some extent. The distributor is not an agent of the supplier, in the sense that *the distributor* acts in *his or her own capacity* to market the products of the supplier. It should be noted that in a distribution agreement, the two parties stand on an equal footing for the purpose of distributing a particular product. The distributor may be asked by the supplier to distribute the supplier's products only. The distributor may ask the supplier to grant him or her an exclusive right to distribute a particular product within a designated territory. But these arrangements do not make the supplier and the distributor an agent and principal. When a distributor acts as the sole or exclusive dealer for the product of a supplier, it simply means that the distributor does not have a competitor selling the same product within the designated territory; but the distributor may act as the sole distributor for several suppliers whose products may be directly or indirectly in competition with each other in a particular market. If a supplier attempts to restrict the distributor's freedom to sell competitive products, he or she runs the risk of contravening competition law in some jurisdictions where such arrangements are prohibited. In jurisdictions which have not adopted formal competition law, the issue may be subject to the relevant competition policy, which is in most cases more tolerant to acts which have a negative impact on competition in the local market. Hong Kong is one of the minority of jurisdictions which have not adopted any formal competition law.

A distribution agreement often operates in conjunction with a franchising arrangement.[53] A franchising agreement may consist of several agreements of different nature, such as a licensing agreement, a supply of goods or services agreement and a distribution agreement. The different agreements may become different clauses of a large and comprehensive franchising agreement. Noting the connections between a franchising agreement and a licensing agreement or distribution agreement can help us to understand the various

---

50. J Feenstra, 'Distribution and Commercial Agency and EEC Law' in Weijer, ed, *Commercial Agency and Distribution Agreements: Law and Practices in the Member States of the European Community*, Graham & Trotman, London, 1991, p 21.
51. See R A Dregi et al, 'Spain' in Weijer, ibid, p 250.
52. For example, Schmitthoff, note 49 above, pp 259–62.
53. For discussion, see Bogaert et al, 'Belgium' in Weijer, note 50 above, pp 130–4.

arrangements for the operation of a distribution agreement; for example, in *Altendore Australian Pty Ltd v Parkanson Pty Ltd* (26 April 1995, NG493 of 1991, Fed No 252/95),[54] the parties concluded a distribution agreement and in conjunction with the agreement, the parties also made a licensing agreement to allow the distributor/licensee to use a particular trade name associated with the products marketed.

Forms of distribution agreement

Exclusive distribution agreement versus non-exclusive distribution agreement

[3.31] Distribution agreements are usually categorised according to the right of the distributor, who may have either an exclusive or a non-exclusive right to distribute the product concerned. An exclusive right means that the distributor is the *only* distributor (the supplier itself is also excluded from distribution), within a designated territory and sometimes within a specified period of time. The supplier undertakes not to create competitors for the distribution of the same product within the designated area. The essence of the right is its exclusivity. A non-exclusive right means that the distributor may face competitors for the sale of the same product subject to the distribution agreement. There is no guarantee on the part of the supplier not to create competitors for the distributor. A contract with an exclusive right is known as the exclusive distribution agreement, or 'an agreement by which the supplier agrees to deliver certain products only to the distributor for resale within a certain area'.[55] A contract with a non-exclusive right is known as a non-exclusive distribution agreement.

The nature of a distribution agreement may be affected by several considerations. For example, the bargaining powers of the parties to a distribution agreement, the strategic development plans of the supplier and the distributor, and the cost for granting an exclusive right or a non-exclusive right are all relevant factors. Generally speaking, an exclusive agreement costs more for the distributor, but a non-exclusive agreement attaches fewer conditions on the distributor's rights under the agreement.

Exclusive distribution agreement v sole distribution agreement

[3.32] The meaning of exclusive distribution agreement is discussed above. A sole distribution agreement means that the distributor is the sole 'distributor' within a designated territory. Thus, a sole distribution agreement prohibits the supplier from granting a distribution agreement to any other distributors within the designated territory, but does not deprive the supplier of his or her own right to distribute goods, products or services within that area. This is the major difference between an exclusive distribution agreement and a sole distribution agreement. Schmitthoff regards distribution as a right of 'representation' and observes that if the representation is sole, 'the principal himself may undertake sales in the territory of the representative on his own account without any liability to the representative'.[56] The use of the expressions 'representation' and 'representative' suggest that he regards a distribution agreement to be similar to an agency agreement.

---

54. The case is available at <http://www.austlii.edu.au>.
55. Feenstra, note 50 above, p 21.
56. Schmitthoff, note 49 above, p 260.

Exclusive purchase agreements

[3.33] An exclusive purchase agreement is regarded as a form of distribution agreement, particularly in Europe. An exclusive purchase agreement is 'an agreement by which the reseller agrees with the supplier to purchase certain goods for resale only from the supplier'.[57] In other words, under an exclusive purchasing agreement, the distributor undertakes to purchase specific product(s) from the supplier only. This is the sort of exclusive dealing agreement which may be caught by the competition law of certain countries. The EU Commission in its *Seventh Report on Competition Policy* (para 9) noted that 'exclusive purchasing agreements may endanger competition, because they limit the purchaser's freedom of choice and therefore at least potentially restrict the sales outlets open to other suppliers'. Whether or not an exclusive purchasing agreement or arrangement falls under a competition law depends on the terms of the agreement and the wording of the law concerned. The competition law of different countries may set out different criteria for prohibiting activities and arrangements which may have harmful, negative or restrictive effects on competition.

Legal framework for distribution agreements

[3.34] There is no international convention on distribution agreements. The matter is largely subject to the relevant domestic law, although in the EU certain regulations have been passed to deal with distribution agreements. For example, Commission Regulation (EEC) 1983/83 has been made to deal with the application of art 85 of the EU Treaty to distribution agreements; and Commission Regulation (EEC) 1984/83 has been made to deal with the application of art 85 to exclusive purchasing agreements, which are regarded as a form of distribution agreement.[58] The WTO Agreement may have some relevance to issues of competition and market access in relation to distribution agreements in a particular country, but this is yet to be seen. In 1998, the US Government resorted to panel proceedings with the WTO against the Japanese Government, alleging that certain Japanese Government measures denied US colour photographic materials access to the Japanese market. The case is known as the *Kodak-Fuji Film* dispute.[59] The panel refused the US arguments largely on the grounds that the arrangements complained of had nothing to do with the Japanese Government. This dispute illustrates the connection between distribution agreements and competition or market access in international trade. Market access to domestic markets for goods and services is guaranteed by the WTO Agreement.

Domestic law regulates distribution agreements through contract and competition law. Distribution agreements are contractual arrangements establishing certain relationships between supplier and distributor and thus the basic principles of contract law apply. Distribution agreements are also market arrangements, which brings them into the sphere of competition law. In *Business Electronics v Sharp Electronics* 485 US 717 (1988), a former

---

57. Feenstra, note 50 above, p 21.
58. For discussion, see Goyder, *EC Distribution Law*, London, Chancery Law Publishing, 1992.
59. For relevant discussion, see N Komuro, 'Kodak–Fuji Film Dispute and the WTO Panel Ruling' (1998) 32:5 *Journal of World Trade* pp 161–217.

distributor sued the supplier, who had terminated the distribution agreement in accordance with the terms of the agreement, on the ground that the supplier terminated the agreement because it had entered another agreement with a third party for the purpose of vertical price-fixing. The Supreme Court of the US held that 'price-fixing' and 'restraint of trade' must be examined in the light of their impact on trade and competition in the market. In *Monsanto Co v Spray-Rite Service Corp* 465 US 752 (1984), a former distributor succeeded in suing the supplier on the ground that its contract was terminated by the supplier for the purpose of furthering a conspiracy to fix prices. The trial court found evidence of price-fixing as prohibited by the Sherman Act. The Court of Appeal affirmed the finding. The Supreme Court of the US also affirmed the decisions of the lower courts.

Major legal issues of distribution agreements

[3.35] A distribution agreement regulates the rights and obligations of the supplier and the distributor. The rights and obligations vary in different types of agreements; exclusive, non-exclusive, sole or sometimes purchasing agreement. In general terms, a distribution agreement should cover a number of basic legal issues, including the identity of the supplier and the distributor, the nature of the distributor's right, the scope of the supplier's rights and obligations, the scope of the distributor's rights and obligations, the product(s) covered by the agreement, a description of the area of distribution, the duration of the agreement, product liability, grounds for termination, remedies, governing law, arbitration clause, and choice of jurisdiction clause (if applicable).

When involved in the preparation of an international distribution contract, a lawyer should pay attention to the following matters:

- the laws of the supplier's and distributor's countries governing restrictive trade practices and import and export control, particularly arrangements such as 'tie-ins' (where the distributor is forced to purchase certain products or goods together), or 'price restraints' and 'discriminatory prices' based on the volume of sale, because these arrangements are prohibited in many countries;
- definitions of the terms used in the contract;
- the nature and specification of the industrial property rights if the contract involves such rights;
- the rights and obligations of both parties, including the exclusivity of the distributorship, its territorial limit, its duration, the warranty of the products or goods, the power of the supplier to interfere with the performance of the contract and the conditions attached to the distributorship;
- the legal relationship between the supplier and distributor, indicating that there is only a contractual relationship — as opposed to, for example, the relationship between a parent company and a subsidiary — between them;
- matters relating to the termination of the contract, including *force majeure* clauses and requirement for minimum sales (if applicable); and
- the governing law of the contract and measures relating to dispute resolution.

As we have seen, relationships between the parties are regulated by contract. If the agreement has been drafted properly, its enforcement is not a problem in most countries. The enforcement of the agreement and the obligations of the parties may be subject to the relevant competition law. When a distribution agreement, which is meant to be a marketing arrangement between parties, results in certain arrangements which are prohibited under the relevant competition law, the arrangement and the obligations arising from the arrangement will often be invalidated by a court of law. When a distribution agreement is tied in with a franchising agreement, the possible impact on competition in a local market will be examined closely by the country concerned.

♦

[3.36] *Avel Pty Ltd v Multicoin Amusements Pty Ltd*

(1990) 171 CLR 88

Exclusive and sole distributor, right to prohibit direct import from overseas, knowledge of the copyright owner, in contrast with Interstate Parcel Express Co Pty Ltd v Time-Life International (Nederlands) BV *(1977) 138 CLR 534*

Facts: Avel Pty Ltd was the appellant and the distributor under the distribution agreement in question. Multicoin Amusements Pty Ltd was the respondent and the prospective importer of the game machines allegedly covered by the distribution agreement. In 1986, the distributor entered into a sole and exclusive distribution agreement with Williams Electronics Games Inc ('Williams'), a US manufacturer of amusement machines. The agreement, which was dated 1 May 1986, was for one year, but was subject to extension. The agreement gave the distributor exclusive selling and distribution rights in respect of two models of pinball machine, the 'Williams Grand Lizard' and 'Williams Road King' machines, and contemplated that, from time to time, Williams and the distributor might apply the terms of the agreement to other models. But the precise rights which the distributor obtained under this agreement were later debated by the parties. In 1987, Multicoin Amusements Pty Ltd intended to import used Williams 'Hi-Speed' machines and 'Pin-Bot' machines from two American dealers. The distributor threatened to take legal action for breach of copyright if the importers imported any Williams' machines. On 22 June 1988, the importers instituted proceedings against the distributor in the Supreme Court of Queensland, alleging that the threats made by the distributor were unjustifiable within the meaning of s 202 of the Copyright Act 1968 (Cth). They also sought an injunction to restrain the distributor from threatening them with any legal proceedings for infringement of copyright for importing secondhand Williams amusement games and any new Williams games, apart from games known as 'Grand Lizard', 'Road King' and 'Pin-Bot'. The distributor counter-claimed for a declaration that its conduct was justifiable in protection of its rights as an exclusive licensee of Williams.

It also sought an injunction restraining the importers from infringing copyright in Williams 'games' and otherwise acting in contravention of the distributor's rights under its exclusive distribution agreement. The trial judge found in favour of the distributor. The Full Court of the Federal Court of Australia unanimously held that the distributor was not an 'exclusive licensee' within the meaning of the Act and that the distributor had no standing to restrain any infringement by the importers of Williams' rights. Their Honours said that the distributor had also failed to demonstrate any infringement by the importers of Williams' copyright. The Full Court held that the onus was on the distributor to prove that the machines were to be imported 'without the licence of the owner of the copyright' and stated that 'there was no evidence before the trial Judge that Williams had not consented to the importation'. The distributor appealed to the High Court of Australia against the decision of the Federal Court.

> **Decision:** The High Court by a 4:1 majority dismissed the appeal. Mason CJ, Deane and Gaudron JJ held (at 93) that the:
>> ... distribution agreement did not make the distributor an 'exclusive licensee' of the copyright in the artwork or the computer programs of the particular models. The exclusive rights of local sale conferred upon the distributor in respect of machines of those models did not encompass exclusive rights of first or other publication. In particular, Williams, as owner of the copyright, remained entitled to publish, and to authorise another to publish, the artwork and computer programs incorporated in machines of those models.
>
> Dawson J observed (at 108) that, clearly, 'Williams adopted the attitude that it did not seek to control the distribution of used machines' and concluded that Avel had not 'established any such defence, being unable to prove that the importation of used machines would be without the licence of Williams'.

♦

Transfer of technology agreements

Defining transfer of technology agreements

[3.37] Transfer of technology is a generic term capable of embracing the three types of contracts (franchising, licensing and distribution) which have been examined in this chapter, although it may be claimed that a simple distribution agreement does not really involve a transfer of technology. But the meaning of technology is so wide that it could be argued that a distribution agreement, with or without the co-existence of a franchising or licensing agreement, must involve some transfer of technology. Technology is 'a rich and multi-faceted concept which does not admit of simple definition'.[60] It has been defined as: 'the skills, knowledge and procedures for making, using and doing useful things', or as 'the means and capacity to perform a particular activity'. In its commercial context technology is taken to embrace the 'knowledge of how to make use of factors of production to produce goods or services for which there is an economic demand'. Most definitions of technology attempt no more than to describe one or more of the combinations of skills or rights embodied within the notion.[61]

A comprehensive definition of technology was provided in the Licensing Guide for Developing Countries prepared by the World Intellectual Property Organisation, as follows:[62]

> Technology means systematic knowledge for the manufacture of a product, the application of a process or the rendering of a service, whether that knowledge be reflected in an invention, an industrial design, a utility model, or a new plant variety, or in technical information or skills, or in the services and assistance provided by experts for the design, installation, operation or maintenance of an industrial plant or for the management of an industrial or commercial enterprise or its activities.

---

60. Blakeney, *Legal Aspects of the Transfer of Technology to Developing Countries*, ESC Publishing, Oxford, 1989, p 1.
61. Ibid.
62. WIPO, *Licensing Guide for Developing Countries*, Geneva, 1977, p 28.

This definition is comprehensive, including both the broad approach and the narrow approach referred to above. If we accept this definition, a distribution agreement may involve the transfer of technology in the form of technical information and skills.

A transfer of technology agreement therefore means a contract or an arrangement through which a party who owns or holds a proprietary right over the technology concerned transfers certain rights to use or to own the technology to another party under agreed terms and conditions. 'Transfer' includes not only franchising arrangements, licensing agreements, distribution agreements, mixed arrangements of some or all of these three forms, but also sale of the technology and grant of the technology free of charge. As a generic term, then, transfer of technology is wider than the combination of franchising, licensing and distribution agreements, because it includes sale and giving away by the owner or legal holder of the technology.

Legal framework for international transfer of technology

International legal framework

[3.38] There is no formal international convention on the transfer of technology. However, there are a number of international instruments, not necessarily treaties, concerning the international transfer of technology. Existing international conventions on intellectual property are also relevant to the protection of certain types of technology transfer. In broad terms, the international legal framework for the transfer of technology consists of the following major conventions and instruments:

- the 1883 Paris Convention for the Protection of Industry Property, signed on 20 March 1883 in Paris and last amended on 14 July 1967 in Stockholm;
- the 1886 Bern Convention for the Protection of Literary and Artistic Work;
- the 1891 Madrid Agreement concerning the International Registration of Marks, signed on 14 April 1891 in Madrid, last amended on 14 July 1967 in Stockholm;
- the 1952 Universal Copyright Convention, signed on 6 September 1952 in Geneva, last amended on 24 July 1971 in Paris;
- the 1961 International Convention for the Protection of Performers, Producers of Phonograms and Broadcasting Organisations (Rome Convention);
- the 1967 Convention Establishing World Intellectual Property Organisation, concluded on 14 July 1967 in Stockholm;
- the 1970 Patent Cooperation Treaty, signed on 19 June 1970 in Washington;
- the 1971 Strasbourg Convention on the Unification of Certain Points of Substantive Patent Law, signed on 24 March 1971 in Strasbourg;
- the 1973 European Patent Convention;
- the Treaty on Intellectual Property in Respect of Integrated Circuits (opened for signature in 1989 in Washington);
- the 1993 Agreement on Trade Related Intellectual Property Rights;

[3.38] International Commercial Law

- the International Code of Conduct on the Transfer of Technology (TOT Code), prepared by UNCTAD in the 1970s and 1980s;
- the EU Regulation on Technology Transfer Agreements, effective on 1 April 1996;[64] and
- the 1996 WTO Ministerial Declaration on Trade in Information Technology Products.[65]

Most of these conventions were made for the protection of a specific type of IP or a specific aspect of IP. Only the TOT Code and the EU Regulation on the Transfer of Technology have direct relevance to the transfer of technology. But the TOT Code has not been formally adopted by the UN, and the EU Regulation applies only to EU countries or transactions taking place within the EU. These two instruments are examined below.

International Code of Conduct on the Transfer of Technology

[3.39] The establishment of a code of conduct by the UN is difficult. Since a code imposes specific obligations upon its members, most countries are reluctant to ratify it for fear of being placed in a disadvantageous position. This was the case for the TOT Code, with views on the code so divergent that it was impossible to reconcile them.[66] Even though the TOT Code is not a formal international instrument, it may still provide some ideas about the regulation of technology transfers from an international perspective. The major features of the code can be summarised as follows:[67]

- **Definition of technology transfer:** Transfer of technology is defined as a transfer of systematic knowledge for the manufacture of a product, for the application of a process or for the rendering of a service and does not extend to transactions involving a mere sale or mere lease of goods. Technology can be transferred by way of assignment, sale or licensing of intellectual property; the provision of know-how and technical expertise; the provision of technological knowledge necessary for the installation, operation and functioning of plant and equipment, and turn-key projects; the provision of technological knowledge necessary to acquire, install and use machinery, equipment, intermediate goods and/or certain raw materials; and the provision of technological contents of industrial and technical cooperation agreements.

- **Principles of national regulation of technology transfer:** Chapter 3 of the code sets out a number of principles guiding the national regulation of technology transfers,

---

64. Commission Regulation No 240/96 on the application of Article 85(3) of the Treaty to certain categories of technology transfer agreement, OJ No L31/2.
65. The declaration was made in Singapore between more than 20 WTO members. Taiwan, which intends to join the WTO, also signed the declaration. WTO members which have signed the declaration include Australia, Japan, Canada, Korea, Norway, the European Community, Singapore, Hong Kong, Switzerland, Iceland, Turkey, Indonesia and the United States. The declaration lists types of information technology products and requires the members to reduce and eliminate tariffs and other trade barriers for the transfer of information technology products.
66. For relevant discussion, see Blakeney, note 61 above, pp 131–5.
67. The summary is based on the information supplied in Blakeney, note 61 above, pp 134–61.

requesting members to take into account the equitable and legitimate interests of the parties and to comply with their international obligations.

- **Restrictive trade practices:** Chapter 4 regulates restrictive trade or business practices, setting out criteria for the determination of exclusive dealing, restrictions on research, export restrictions and other unlawful practices.

- **Rights and obligations of the parties:** Chapter 5 deals with the rights and obligations of the parties, covering access to improvements, confidentiality, dispute settlement, description of technology, quality, performance guarantee, transmission of documents, training and liability.

- **Special provisions for developing countries:** Chapter 6 addresses the needs of developing countries for technology and states a number of moral principles which should be taken into account by a developed country when making its domestic law on technology transfer.

- **International collation:** Chapter 7 emphasises the need for government cooperation in the development of technology and encourages such activities.

- **International institutional machinery:** Chapter 8 promotes the idea of setting up international institutional machinery for the purpose of monitoring or administering international transfer of technology.

- **Settlement of disputes:** Chapter 9 deals with conflict of laws issues, such as the applicable law and recommended methods for resolving disputes.

The TOT Code is drafted in a style which was acceptable in the 1970s, when the transfer of technology was still a relatively new concept and the forms in which technology could be transferred were not as complicated as they are today. It appears that making an international convention that is intended to impose concrete obligations to deal with sensitive issues of international trade and commerce is not feasible, given the diversity in the interests of the countries. A model law is more feasible because it does not impose specific obligations upon any country. An agreement made in a style similar to most WTO agreements may also be feasible if it sets out the general principles only, leaving the details to be worked out by the countries concerned.

The EU Regulation on Technology Transfer Agreements

[3.40] The EU Regulation on Technology Transfer Agreements is another example of international regulation of technology transfers. Its major purpose is to exempt qualified arrangements from the prohibitions against restrictions of competition in art 85 of the EU Treaty. It applies to patent and know-how licensing agreements and replaced and consolidated earlier regulations on the same matters. It applies to licensing agreements for the transfer of patent and know-how or a mixture of both, excluding the transfer of other types of intellectual property. It is perhaps the only formal regulation of technology transfer at an international level.[68]

---

68. See T R Broderick, 'EC Regulation for Technology Transfer Agreements' (1996) 24 *IBL* 403.

Domestic regulation of technology transfers

[3.41] Transfer of technology as a generic concept has become a common vehicle of international trade and investment.[69] As suggested by the TOT Code, provision or supply of technical assistance or consultancy has become an important part of international transfers of technology between developed and developing countries. Different stages of technological development have made it desirable to transfer technology from industrialised to developing countries, and technology transfers have developed significantly in the last 30 years. Countries and jurisdictions wishing to attract more foreign investment and foreign technology have passed their own domestic laws on technology transfer. China is one of those countries which have passed special technology transfer laws to attract foreign investment.

The Chinese law governing the transfer of technology is the Code of Contract Law (or Contract Law), which came into effect on 1 October 1999.[70] This code replaced the earlier Economic Contract Law and Foreign Economic Contract Law. It provides basic contract rules for the making of technology transfer agreements. The major restrictions or rules on the control of technology transfer are set out in the Detailed Rules. The list that follows includes the most significant rules from both instruments:

- These laws apply to technology transfer agreements under which at least one party is situated in China.

- A technology transfer contract should be concluded in writing and be approved by the relevant government authority.

- Technological transfer agreements include assignment or licensing of patent or other intellectual property rights;[71] transfer of proprietary technology;[72] and provision of technical services.[73]

---

69. For discussion, see Kasto, *International Law of Technology*, London Print Centre, published by the author, 1992; Wallerstein et al, eds, *Global Dimensions of Intellectual Property Rights in Science and Technology*, Washington, National Academy Press, 1993; and OECD, *Intellectual Property, Technology Transfer and Generic Resources*, OECD, Paris, 1993.
70. For relevant discussions, see John Mo, 'The Code of Contract Law of the People's Republic of China and the Vienna Sales Convention', (1999) 15(1) *Am U Int'L Rev* 209–70.
71. A contract for the assignment or licensing of intellectual property rights includes the assignment or licensing of an invention patent, a patent for usage rights to a new pattern, an exterior design patent, or a trademark.
72. A contract for the licensing of proprietary technology includes providing or imparting technical knowledge on the manufacturing of a certain product or the use of a certain area of technology, as well as information on product design, technological processes, formulas, quality control, management skills, etc, which has yet to be made public or has yet to receive the protection of intellectual property laws.
73. A technical service contract refers to a contract whereby the supplier uses certain technology to provide a service or consultancy to the recipient in order to achieve a specific target. It includes contracts in which the recipient engages the supplier or cooperates with the supplier to carry out a feasibility study or engineering design for a project, or employs a foreign geologic prospecting team or a construction team to provide technical services, or engages the supplier to carry out technological transformation on an enterprise, or improve production technology, product design or quality control or provide technical services or consultancy with regard to enterprise management.

- The technology transferred to China must be advanced and satisfy one of the following requirements:
  - capable of developing and producing new products;
  - capable of improving quality and performance of products, reducing production costs and lowering consumption of energy or raw materials;
  - favourable to maximum utilisation of local resources;
  - capable of expanding product export and increasing earning of foreign currencies;
  - favourable to environmental protection;
  - favourable to production safety;
  - favourable to improvement of management; or
  - contributing to advancement of scientific and technical levels.
- The supplier is required to guarantee his or her right to assign or license the right or product concerned.
- The transferee or licensee is obliged to keep the right, technology or information received confidential as agreed in the contract.
- A contract cannot contain unreasonable restrictions, which are listed as follows:
  - requiring the transferee to accept additional conditions which are not related to the technology to be imported, such as requiring the transferee to purchase unnecessary technology, technical services, raw materials, equipment or products;
  - restricting the freedom of choice of the transferee to obtain raw materials, parts and components or equipment from other sources;
  - restricting the development and improvement by the transferee over the imported technology;
  - restricting the acquisition by the transferee of similar or competing technology from other sources;
  - unilateral restrictions on transferees' access to improvements of the imported technology;
  - restricting the quantity, variety and sales price of products to be manufactured by the transferee with the imported technology;
  - unreasonably restricting the sales channels and export markets of the transferee;
  - forbidding use by the transferee of the imported technology after the expiration of the contract; or
  - requiring the transferee to pay for or to undertake obligations for patents which are unused or no longer effective.

These are the major rules governing transfer of technology to a party situated in China, which may be a Chinese-owned company, a Sino–foreign venture or a sole foreign investment company. The prohibition on the use of restrictive clauses depriving the transferee of the right to use the licensed right or technology after the termination of the contract shows the substantial differences between Chinese law and the common practices of

[3.41]

industrialised countries; these differences demonstrate the need to examine the law of the country concerned when preparing a contract for a technology transfer. Otherwise, a clause in the contract may later be invalidated.

Forms of technology transfer

[3.42] Forms of technology transfer change depending on the purpose of the transfer. The purpose can be viewed from different perspectives: commercial or non-commercial, transfer of ownership or transfer of part of the proprietary rights, for investment or for royalties, and so on. The forms will also differ depending on the nature of the proprietary right, the type of proprietary right and the status of the transferor. For commercial transactions, transfers of technology are usually classified into six categories: transfer of patent or similar rights; transfer of know-how or similar rights; transfer of proprietary information or commercial secrets; computer software licence which is different due to the subject matter of the transfer; trademark licence; and technical services contracts. Technology transfers may take the form of franchising and/or licensing agreements as discussed above, but these are not the only forms available.

Major legal issues of technology transfer

[3.43] As we have seen in the previous discussion on the TOT Code, the EU Regulation for Technology Transfer Agreements, and the Chinese law on technology transfers, many issues may arise under a contract for the transfer of technology. We need to emphasise, however, that the major legal issues will be determined by the purpose for which the contract for the transfer of technology is made. For example, transfers of technology can be used as a means of foreign investment. In such cases, the arrangements concerning the investment are, in addition to the issues arising from the contract of technology transfer or licensing itself,[74] the major issues to be considered. If a contract of technology transfer is tied up with an arrangement of countertrade, BOT project or compensation, these arrangements must be considered carefully with the contract for the transfer of technology.[75] The following major issues are common in most transfer of technology agreements:

- nature of the arrangement, for example, licensing, assignment or provision of technical services;
- nature of the technology;
- identity of the parties;
- right of the transferor to transfer;
- means and sum of payment;

---

74. For discussion on the use of licensing agreements in developing countries, see the UN Centre on Transnational Corporations, *Licence Agreements in Developing Countries*, UN, New York, 1987.
75. For discussion in specific contexts, see I Govaere, 'The Impact of Intellectual Property Protection on Technology Transfer between the EC and the Central and Eastern European Countries' (1991) 25 *Journal of World Trade* pp 57–76; and H A Kown, 'Patent Protection and Technology Transfer in the Developing World: The Thailand Experience' (1995) 28:3 *The George Washington Journal of International Law and Economics* pp 567–605.

Contracts Relating to Intellectual Property [3.45]

- rights of the transferee to use the technology;
- protection of the technology concerned;
- restrictive trade practices legislation;[76]
- quality issues;
- access to improvements of the technology; and
- dispute settlement.

Most of the earlier discussion on franchising, licensing and distribution agreements is also relevant to the transfer of technology. Technology transfers overlap with franchising, licensing and to some extent distribution agreements as means of international trade and commerce. The differences among these do not have any legal significance. They may be subject to a particular law or treaty because of the particular issues covered by each agreement, not because of the descriptive names or categories we artificially apply to them.

E-commerce

Defining e-commerce

[3.44] One of the commonly accepted and also one of the few available definitions of e-commerce is offered by the OECD, one of the pioneers in the development and regulation of e-commerce, as the working definition of e-commerce. 'The definition includes the networks over which e-commerce activities are carried out (Internet or others), the specific business process related to e-commerce and the different actors involved (business, households or Governments).'[77] This definition is fairly wide, emphasising activities which may be carried out via the internet or similar for commercial purposes.

[3.45] A different definition of e-commerce was attempted in a research paper published by WTO, where the term 'e-commerce' or 'electronic commerce' refers to the production, advertising, sale and distribution of products via telecommunications networks. This chapter further divides e-commerce into three broad categories for the purposes of policy discussion:[78]

- the searching stage where producers and consumers, or buyers and sellers, first interact;
- the ordering and payment stage once a transaction has been agreed upon; and
- the delivery stage.

The definition is pragmatic and functional, and may not cover all possible forms of e-commerce. This definition appears to be primarily intended to entertain the conventional form of trade — that is, sale of goods. It needs to be extended if it is to apply to

---

76. For discussion on the relationships between transfer of technology and competition law, see Anderson, *Technology: The Law of Exploitation and Transfer*, Butterworths, London, 1996.
77. This definition is referred to in UNCITRAL, *E-Commerce and Development Report 2001*, p xxvi.
78. Rosa Pérez-Esteve and Ludger Schuknecht, 'A Quantitative Assessment of Electronic Commerce', Staff Working Paper ERAD-99-01, available at WTO website: <http://www.wot.org/>.

various new forms of trade, such as e-banking, securities transactions over the internet and web-advertising. In addition, the provision of web services is a form of e-commerce, which should be duly acknowledged in any definition of e-commerce.

In the Policy Paper adopted by the European Commission on 16 April 1997, e-commerce was described as follows:[79]

> Electronic commerce is about doing business electronically. It is based on the electronic processing and transmission of data, including text, sound and video. It encompasses many diverse activities including electronic trading of goods and services, online delivery of digital content, electronic fund transfers, electronic share trading, electronic bills of lading, commercial auctions, collaborative design and engineering, online sourcing, public procurement, direct consumer marketing, and after-sales service. It involves both products (eg consumer goods, specialised medical equipment) and services (eg information services, financial and legal services); traditional activities (eg healthcare, education) and new activities (eg virtual malls).

This description is more thorough than the one attempted by the WTO research paper (above), and appears to be similar in approach to the OECD definition.

E-commerce can be understood as a term describing a new era and new dimension of commerce. It is based on telecommunications networks, including the internet and other forms of electronic and telecommunications techniques. It has not only provided new means of carrying on conventional commercial activities, such as sales, advertising, supply of services, distribution of goods and services, etc, but also created a new form of commerce itself. E-commerce is itself, particularly the internet, a commercial enterprise. Yahoo (or any other similar service provider) is a good example of a commercial activity or form created by e-commerce. The internet has created its own business model, and a community running the models. Thus, we may conclude that e-commerce is a broad concept referring to all commercial activities, conventional or innovational, carried out via or with the assistance of the internet or telecommunications networks, including commercial activities which make the internet and telecommunications networks commercially viable.

According to the EU's policy paper on the subject, e-commerce:

> covers mainly two types of activities: indirect electronic commerce — the electronic ordering of tangible goods, which still must be physically delivered using traditional channels such as postal services or commercial couriers; and direct electronic commerce — the online ordering, payment and delivery of intangible goods and services such as computer software, entertainment content, or information services on a global scale. Both direct and indirect electronic commerce offer specific opportunities. Both are often undertaken by the same companies who, for example, sell software online as well as off the shelf.[80]

Recent developments of e-commerce

[3.46] As described by the EU's policy paper:

> Electronic commerce is not a new phenomenon. For many years companies have exchanged business data over a variety of communication networks. But there is now accelerated expansion and radical changes, driven by the exponential growth of the Internet. Until recently no more than a business-to-business activity on closed proprietary networks, electronic commerce is now rapidly

---

79. The Policy Paper, para 5, available at <http://www.cordis.lu/esprit/src/ecomcom.htm>.
80. The Policy Paper 1997, EU Commission, para 7, available at <http://www.cordis.lu/esprit/src/ecomcom.htm>.

expanding into a complex web of commercial activities transacted on a global scale between an ever-increasing number of participants, corporate and individual, known and unknown, on global open networks such as the Internet.[81]

One of the major difficulties created by e-commerce over the internet is the jurisdiction issue. Which court has appropriate jurisdiction over a dispute involving two parties from two ends of the world who have never met? In *Cybersell Inc v Cybersell Inc* decided on 2 December 1997 by the US 9th Circuit Court of Appeals,[82] the court observed that:

> [We] are asked to hold that the allegedly infringing use of a service mark in a home page on the World Wide Web suffices for personal jurisdiction in the state where the holder of the mark has its principal place of business. Cybersell, Inc., an Arizona corporation that advertises for commercial services over the Internet, claims that Cybersell, Inc., a Florida corporation that offers web page construction services over the Internet, infringed its federally registered mark and should be amenable to suit in Arizona because cyberspace is without borders and a web site which advertises a product or service is necessarily intended for use on a world wide basis. The district court disagreed, and so do we.

E-commerce has become a commercial reality only in recent years. As noted by Robert Verrue, Director General, Directorate General XIII — European Commission:

> Europeans are growing rapidly as a proportion of the world Internet population. One fifth of Internet users are in Europe (33 million out of 150 million). But the USA and Canada account for two-thirds of Internet users. The high cost of Internet access in Europe (especially the lack of flat-rates) continues to be a key obstacle. Nordic countries are ahead of the pack: Some estimates (e.g. Gallup) show that over 30% of the Finnish and Swedish populations are online, Denmark 22% and 16% in the UK. The number of Internet users in some Southern countries is growing rapidly: e.g. in Spain from 2% (1997) to 7% (1998), in Italy from 1% (1997) to 4% (1998).[83]

It is estimated that approximately 16 million Europeans make purchases over the internet; in 1998 electronic commerce generated around 165 million euros in revenue in the EU.[84] E-commerce has significantly increased in recent years. It was reported that in the last quarter of 1999, e-commerce sales in the US were estimated to be 0.7 per cent of total sales. But in 2002, the figure representing e-commerce sales reportedly rose to 1.3 per cent of total sales.[85] A study estimated in July 2002 that in the US interactive e-commerce sales rose 12.1 per cent in 2001 to US$31.4 billion from US$28 billion in 2000.[86] In the United Kingdom, annual e-commerce sales in 2001, excluding travels and tickets, reached about 3.3 billion pounds, accounting for 1.5 per cent of the retail sales of the year. This was an increase of 142 per cent on the figure of 1.3 billion pounds for 2000.[87] The growth of e-commerce is a worldwide phenomenon. For example, in China, the total sales of e-commerce reached about US$9.3 billion in 2000.[88] It is estimated that in 2004 or 2005,

---

81. Policy Paper 1997, EU Commission, para 6, available at <http://www.cordis.lu/esprit/src/ecomcom.htm>.
82. The case is available at <http://laws.findlaw.com/9th/9617087.html>.
83. R Verrue, 'Electronic Commerce In Europe: The Present Situation', available at <http://europa.eu.int/comm/dg13/ecie.htm>.
84. Verrue, ibid.
85. 'Market in Asia Still Hot After Dotcom B', 3 June 2002, *Xinhua Economic News Services*, available at <http://web.lexis-nexis.com/>.
86. 'The DMA Forecasts Interactive/Electronic Commerce Sales to Reach US$36 Billion in 2002', 25 July 2002, *PR Newswire*, available at <http://web.lexis-nexis.com/>.
87. 'Wary Along the High Street', 14 September 2002, *Estate Gazette*, available at <http://web.lexis-nexis.com/>.
88. UNCITRAL, *E-Commerce and Development Report 2001*, p xl.

[3.46] International Commercial Law

sales in China may reach a sum higher than US$16 billion.[89] If so, China will become one of the largest national markets for e-commerce after the United States. In Japan, it was estimated that in 2001 about 10.5 per cent of Japanese companies used e-commerce systems, and about 80 per cent of those using e-commerce used the internet.[90]

The recent development of e-commerce in OECD countries was noted in the *Report on the Economic and Social Impacts of Electronic Commerce: Preliminary Findings and Research Agenda* released in 1999. The report observed that:

> [the] promise of significant economic growth places electronic commerce (see Box 1.1) high on many public and private sector agendas. And to date, the growth has been impressive. Starting from basically zero in 1995, total electronic commerce is estimated at some $26 billion for 1997; it is predicted to reach $330 billion in 2001–02 (near term) and $1 trillion in 2003–05 (future). These estimates are very speculative and rank among the highest of the dozen estimates generated by various management consultancy or market research firms (Table 1.1). They are adopted so as to ensure complete geographical (world) and product (business-to-business and business-to-consumer) coverage and because recent reports of sales by leading e-commerce merchants (Table 1.2) suggest that the growth rate may be faster than expected. To put these estimates into a broader context, four benchmarks are selected for comparison: US catalogue sales, purchases made on credit cards in the United States, total sales generated by direct marketing in the United States, and retail sales summed across seven OECD countries. Electronic commerce in 1995–97 is the equivalent of 37 per cent of US mail order catalogue shopping, 3 per cent of US purchases using credit/debit cards, and 0.5 per cent of the retail sales of the seven OECD economies (Table 1.3). The near-term estimate suggests that e-commerce will quickly overwhelm US catalogue shopping. If the optimistic future forecast (2003–05) is realised, OECD-wide e-commerce will be the equivalent of 15 per cent of the total retail sales of seven OECD countries. While significant, this level of activity is less than current sales generated by direct marketing in the United States through mail, telephone and newspapers (Direct Marketing Association, 1998).[91]

These studies and research by major international organisations reflect recent trends in the development of e-commerce. The growth of e-commerce and the potential legal issues associated with its expanded development are pressing problems facing the international community today. E-commerce's unique features have created a new area of international commerce requiring regulation.

Major legal issues arising from e-commerce

[3.47] E-commerce has launched a full-scale attack on conventional ways of doing business. In some areas this has created an urgent need for regulation, while in others dominant forms of commerce remain essentially unchanged. Regardless of its impact on specific areas, e-commerce has raised many issues of international commercial law.[92] One issue

---

89. 'Market in Asia Still Hot After Dotcom B', 3 June 2002, *Xinhua Economic News Services*, available at <http://web.lexis-nexis.com/>.
90. '10.5% of Japanese firms use e-commerce systems: survey' 23 April 2002, *Japan Economic Newswire*, available at <http://web.lexis-nexis.com/>.
91. Available at <http://www.oecd.org/dsti/sti/it/ec/index.htm>.
92. For example, on an alleged trademark infringement, see *Data Concepts Inc v Digital Consulting*, 1998 FED App. 0241P (6th Cir.), available at <http://laws.findlaw.com/6th/980241p.html>; for a claim of unfair competition, see *American Network Inc v Access America/Connect Atlanta Inc*, 96 Civ 6823 (LLS), available at <http://www.bna.com/e-law>; and for a complaint about a breach of antitrust law, see *Thomas William V Network Solutions*, decided on 14 May 1999 by the United States Court of Appeals for the District Of Columbia Circuit, available at <http://caselaw.findlaw.com>.

which has been settled is the acceptance of electronic data or digital signatures as having the same effect as written evidence for many legal documents, particularly contracts.

The WTO's Seminar on Electronic Commerce and Development made the following points:

> Trade and business communications through electronic means give rise to a number of legal issues. For instance if a service was sold over the Internet across countries in which geographical location can the transaction be deemed to have occurred? This question may be important from the point of view of consumer protection and establishing the jurisdiction. Furthermore electronic transactions require electronic contracts and electronic signatures which have not been provided for in the contract laws of many countries. Most developing countries that wished to participate in electronic commerce needed to undertake major legislative reforms in this regard.[93]

E-commerce, as a new model of business operation, has created a lot of problems and difficulties in law. For example, when parties communicate with each other via the internet, the issue of identification is raised. How do we know that the other party is what he or she claims to be? Contractual liability arises from the identity of the parties. Privacy is another sensitive issue. Other issues include free speech (less of a commercial concern) and intellectual property protection. The duty of care for parties engaged in internet banking or stockbroking is an issue that will have to be faced sooner or later. The reliability of evidence kept as electronic data will also create problems for courts, as these forms of storage are vulnerable to forgery or may be so complex as to make their credibility difficult to establish. There is also a problem of jurisdiction in cases of both contractual and non-contractual disputes. Applicable law is often a problem in international tranactions carried out online, because the identity of the parties, the place of contract, the place of delivery and place of damage, etc, are all regarded as connections and indicators for determining the applicable law in the absence of a chosen law. Taxation on electronic transactions has caused serious concerns for many national governments, who are unwilling to see the loss of revenue on such transactions, yet cannot agree on how to tax B2C sales across national borders. In addition, the settlement of e-commerce disputes must take account of certain features of e-commerce, such as promptness and instantaneousness. All these problems, and any other new ones which may arise from further developments in e-commerce worldwide, demand adequate response from national governments and relevant international organisations.

As is often the case, the rapid development of economy and technology, including e-commerce, has compelled national legislatures and regulators to make adequate response to the changing situation. Although various issues arising from e-commerce transactions could be dealt with to differing degrees of satisfaction by the existing law, which has not been designed specifically for e-commerce, many countries and local governments have felt the need to adopt special laws and regulations. For example, Australia passed the Electronic Transactions Act in December 1999; the UK passed the Electronic Communications Act in May 2000; the US passed the Electronic Signatures in Global and National Commerce Act in June 2000, and recommended the Uniform Electronic Transactions Act and the Uniform Computer Transaction Act in 1999 by the

---

93. WTO, Seminar on Electronic Commerce and Development, 19 February 1999, available at <http://www.wto.org>.

National Conference of Commissioners on Uniform State Laws (both have been adopted by a number of states in the US); Canada passed the Electronic Transactions Act in April 2001, and the Personal Information Protection and Electronic Documents Act in April 2002; Hong Kong passed the Electronic Transactions Ordinance in April 2000; and Japan passed the Law Concerning Electronic Signatures and Certification Services in April 2001. Many other countries and jurisdictions, such as New Zealand, India and a number of other countries,[94] have also prepared for the introduction of e-commerce legislation. These practices suggest a trend towards the acceptance of e-commerce as a special form of business transaction, deserving of special attention from legislatures and regulators across the world.

Recent international efforts to regulate e-commerce

Recent developments

[3.48] E-commerce has become a part of international commercial activities. Both the supply of internet access services and many of the products delivered over the internet fall within the ambit of GATS. It is necessary to clarify how far particular activities are covered by WTO members' market-access commitments. The WTO Declaration on Global Electronic Commerce was adopted on 20 May 1998. This declaration stated that the WTO ministers recognised the continuing growth of global e-commerce and the new commercial opportunities created by e-commerce. The WTO ministers met in the fourth Ministerial Conference in Doha in November 2001. The Doha Declaration made the following statement concerning e-commerce:[95]

> **34.** We take note of the work which has been done in the General Council and other relevant bodies since the Ministerial Declaration of 20 May 1998 and agree to continue the Work Programme on Electronic Commerce. The work to date demonstrates that electronic commerce creates new challenges and opportunities for trade for members at all stages of development, and we recognize the importance of creating and maintaining an environment which is favourable to the future development of electronic commerce. We instruct the General Council to consider the most appropriate institutional arrangements for handling the Work Programme, and to report on further progress to the Fifth Session of the Ministerial Conference. We declare that members will maintain their current practice of not imposing customs duties on electronic transmissions until the Fifth Session.

Since 1998, e-commerce has become one of the topics studied by the WTO. Thus far, however, the WTO has not developed any particular legal instrument to regulate e-commerce. It appears that the WTO needs to find a position or leverage from which e-commerce can be regulated adequately and effectively. Currently, the legal framework of the WTO and the scope of its powers of regulation are defined by those agreements covered by the WTO Agreement.

The UN, in particular, the United Nations Commission on International Trade Law (UNCITRAL) has done a lot of work in the development of uniform rules for

---

94. See for example the relevant information provided in WorldLII at <http://www.worldlii.org/catalog/53106.htm>, and UNCITRAL, Press Release GA/L/3143, available at <http://www.uncitral.org/en-index.htm>.
95. Available at <http://www.wto.org/>.

Contracts Relating to Intellectual Property [3.49]

e-commerce. Up to 2002, UNCITRAL had carried out the following major activities concerning e-commerce:

- the UNCITRAL Recommendations on the Legal Value of Computer Records (1985);[96]
- the UNCITRAL Model Law on Electronic Commerce, adopted in 1996 by the UN and amended in 1998;
- the UNCITRAL Model Law on Electronic Signatures, presented for discussion at the 35th session of UNCITRAL in Vienna on 6–17 September 1999, and adopted in 2001;
- the United Nations Rules for Electronic Data Interchange for Administration, Commerce and Transport (UN/EDIFACT Standards);[97] and
- the Trade Facilitation Information Exchange (TraFix).[98]

These provide certain rules and assistance for the use of e-commerce in international commerce. Although some developments have been made in the regulation of e-commerce, it must be noted that none of these is in the form of an international convention. The UNCITRAL Uniform Rules on Electronic Signature is the first proposed international document which will become an international convention if adopted in the future.

UNCITRAL Model Law on Electronic Commerce

[3.49] The Model Law was adopted by UN General Assembly Resolution 51/162 of 16 December 1996 as a response to an increasing number of transactions in international trade, which are carried out by means of electronic data interchange and other means of communication, commonly referred to as 'electronic commerce', that involves the use of alternatives to paper-based methods of communication and storage of information. The objectives of the Model Law are to enable and facilitate the use of e-commerce and provide equal treatment to users of paper-based documentation and to users of computer-based information. These objectives are essential for fostering economy and efficiency in international trade. In 1998, it was amended by adding a provision, art 5*bis*, to the original text. UNCITRAL hopes that a country would create a media-neutral environment by incorporating the procedures and rules prescribed in the Model Law in its national legislation for the regulation of e-commerce in that country.

The Model Law has two parts, which are divided into four chapters and 17 articles. Since art 5*bis* was added to the Model Law in 1998, there should be 18 articles in total. Part One deals with electronic commerce in general, covering issues such as sphere of application, definition, variation by agreement, legal recognition of data messages, incorporation of information omitted in a data message, the legal effect of a data message as a

---

96. At its 18th session (1985), the commission adopted the 'Legal Value of Computer Records' (A/CN.9/265).
97. UN/EDIFACT Standards comprise a set of internationally agreed standards, directories and guidelines for the electronic interchange of structured data, and in particular that related to trade in goods and services between independent, computerised information systems.
98. Trade facilitation is a systematic approach to improving the efficiency and effectiveness of procedures, documentation and data exchange used in international trade transactions.

written document, digital signature, original message, admissibility of data messages as evidence, retention of messages, the legal effect of communications between parties carried out in the form of data messages, formation of contract, time and place of dispatch and receipt of data messages, etc. Part Two is entitled 'electronic commerce in specific areas' but has only one chapter and two articles which deal with transport documents. For whatever reasons, Part Two appears to be incomplete and leaves all the specific rules to be fixed by countries adopting the Model Law. Such an arrangement reflects the difficulty of achieving uniformity in the regulation of specific issues of international trade and commerce, and does not lead to uniformity in the regulation of e-commerce internationally.

The Model Law is a very brief document for the enormous area that is e-commerce. It does not provide rules for e-commerce in general. Instead, it provides rules for the use of electronic data or messages only, in particular the legal effect of any documents and communications carried out in electronic form. The Model Law relates specifically to the determination of the legal effect of electronic data used in commercial activities; its name is really a misnomer given the wide meaning of e-commerce today. As at October 2002, legislation based on the Model Law had been adopted in Australia, Bermuda, Columbia, Ecuador, France, Hong Kong, India, Ireland, Philippines, Korea, Singapore, Slovenia, the states of Jersey and the US state of Illinois.[99] In addition, the principles of the Model Law had been incorporated into the relevant laws in Canada and the US.[100] The Model Law may become a real model for e-commerce after Part Two has been substantially developed. For the purpose of promoting the use of the Model Law, the UNCITRAL has published the *Guide to Enactment of the UNCITRAL Model Law on Electronic Commerce.*[101]

---

99. UNCITRAL, *Status of Conventions and Model Laws*, updated on 15 October 2002, available at <http://www.uncitral.org/>.
100. Ibid.
101. Available at <http://www.uncitral.org/>.

Chapter Four

Contracts for Carriage by Sea, Air and Land

Introduction to the Law of Carriage

Modes of international transport

[4.1] International sales of goods often involve the transport of goods from one country to another by sea, air or land. Incoterms 2000, which is examined in **Chapter 1**, deals with the responsibilities of parties performing a contract of international sale based on carriage by sea, air or land, or a combination of these means. When carriage of goods involves only one mode, it is called 'unimodal transport'. When it involves two or more modes, it is regarded as 'multimodal transport'.

[4.2] The difference between unimodal and multimodal transport is a matter of classification or characterisation. For example, an international sale between Australia and a European country may involve carriage by sea, air and land at different stages of the carriage. If the seller is only responsible for delivering the goods to the first carrier, such as under EXW (see **[1.16]**) or FCA (see **[1.17]**), it is immaterial to the seller whether the subsequent transport involves other modes. In this case, there is no need to distinguish unimodal transport from multimodal transport. On the other hand, if the seller is responsible for delivering the goods to an agreed destination by whatever means necessary, such as DDU (see **[1.29]**) and DDP (see **[1.30]**), the seller is liable to arrange multimodal transport if so agreed. In this case, the seller's responsibility can be affected by the modes of the transport involved.

[4.3] The difference between unimodal and multimodal transport is of significance in two ways: first, it indicates the complexity of modes of transport used in any particular contract of sale; and second, the parties' responsibilities differ depending on the mode of transport. In addition, different modes of transport are subject to different international conventions and customs. In the absence of an accepted international convention or custom, the relevant domestic laws, when available, may apply to different modes of transport.

[4.4] The modes of transport can be classified as follows:

- carriage of goods by sea;
- carriage of goods by air;
- carriage of goods by land;
- carriage of goods by inland water; and
- multimodal transport of goods.

Legal framework for carriage by sea

[4.5] The carriage of goods by sea is presently regulated by both international conventions and domestic laws. While the domestic laws vary between countries, the following international conventions purport to bring uniformity in the carriage of goods by sea law across the world:

- the International Convention for the Unification of Certain Rules of Law Relating to Bills of Lading 1924 (the Hague Rules);[1]
- the Brussels Protocol Amending the Hague Rules Relating to Bills of Lading 1968 (the Hague-Visby Rules);[2]
- the Convention on the Carriage of Goods by Sea 1978 (Hamburg Rules);[3]
- the United Nations Convention on International Multimodal Transport of Goods 1980;[4]
- the United Nations Convention on the Liability of Operators of Transport Terminals in International Trade 1991.[5]

---

1. The Hague Rules were made on 25 August 1924, and were put into operation on 2 June 1931. In 2002, about 50 countries had adopted the Hague Rules. These were: Algeria, Angola, Antigua and Barbuda, Agentia, Bahamas, Barbados, Belize, Bolivia, Bosnia, Congo, Croatia, Cuba, Cyprus, Fiji, Gambia, Ghana, Grenada, Guyana, Iran, Ireland, Israel, Ivory Coast, Jamaica, Kenya, Kiribati, Kuwait, Macedonia, Madagascar, Mauritius, Monaco, Nauru, the Netherlands, Nigeria, Papua-New Guinea, Paraguay, Peru, Portugal, St Kitts-Nevis, St Lucia, St Vincent, Solomon Island, Seycelles, Slovenia, Somalia, Trinidad & Tobago, Turkey, Tuvalu, the United States and Yugoslavia. See Internationale Konventionen, at <http://informare.it/dbase/convde.htm>.
2. The Hague Rules were amended in 1968; the amended rules are known as the Hague-Visby Rules. In 2002, about 25 countries had adopted the Hague-Visby Rules. These were: Australia, Belgium, Canada, Denmark, Ecuador, Finland, France, Greece, Italy, Japan, Latvia, Luxembourg, the Netherlands, New Zealand, Norway, Poland, Singapore, Spain, Sri Lanka, Sweden, Switzerland, Syria, Tonga, and the United Kingdom. See Internationale Konventionen, at <http://informare.it/dbase/convde.htm>. Hong Kong continues to apply the Hague-Visby Rules after 1 July 1997, in pursuance of art 153 of the Basic Law of Hong Kong Special Administrative Region of PRC, despite the fact that the PRC has not adopted the Hague-Visby Rules.
3. The Hamburg Rules were made in 1978. They came into operation in 1992. In October 2002 28 countries had ratified or acceded to the Hamburg Rules. These were Austria, Barbados, Botswana, BurkinaFaso, Burundi, Cameroon, Chile, Czech Republic, Egypt, Gambia, Georgia, Guinea, Hungary, Jordan, Kenya, Lebanon, Lesotho, Malawi, Morocco, Nigeria, Romania, Saint Vincent and the Grenadines, Senegal, Sierra Leone, Tunisia, Uganda, United Republic of Tanzania, and Zambia.
4. The convention was concluded in 1980, and has not yet entered into force by July 2002. Ten countries, Burundi, Chile, Georgia, Lebanon, Malawi, Mexico, Morocco, Rwanda, Senegal, and Zambia, have ratified it.

Legal framework for carriage by air

[4.6] The international air transportation is largely regulated by international conventions, which are normally regarded as being divided into two systems: the Chicago System and the Warsaw System. Both systems are relevant to the carriage by air, but to different degrees. The Chicago System regulates international civil aviation by maintaining the order and peace in international civil aviation. It sets out the uniform rules for the share, use and control of national air space for the purpose of international civil aviation. In fact, it largely deals with the relationships between governments. The Warsaw System largely regulates carriers' liability in the carriage of cargoes and passengers by air, which is the major concern of this book. However, the structure and operation of the Chicago System will be examined further later in this chapter to provide a full picture of carriage by air across the world today. In this chapter, the two systems are to be introduced separately.

[4.7] The Chicago System mainly consists of the following international conventions:

- the Chicago Convention on International Civil Aviation (the Chicago Convention), signed at Chicago on 7 December 1944;[6]
- the International Air Services Transit Agreement (the Transit Agreement), signed at Chicago on 7 December 1944;[7]
- the International Air Transport Agreement (the Transport Agreement), signed at Chicago on 7 December 1944;
- the Protocol on the Authentic Trilingual Text of the Convention on International Civil Aviation, signed at Buenos Aires on 2 September 1968;
- the Protocol relating to an Amendment to the Convention on International Civil Aviation signed at Montreal on 30 September 1977; and
- the Protocol relating to an Amendment to the Convention on International Civil Aviation (art 83bis), signed in Montreal on 6 October 1980.[8]

[4.8] In comparison, the Warsaw System mainly consists of the following conventions:[9]

- the Convention for the Unification of Certain Rules relating to International Carriage by Air (the Warsaw Convention), signed at Warsaw on 12 October 1929;[10]

---

5. The convention was concluded in 1991 in Vienna. Five actions are required for entry into force. As at October 2002, only Egypt and Georgia had ratified it, and France, Mexico, the Philippines, Spain and the United States had signed but not yet ratified the convention.
6. The Chicago Convention is truly international. As at June 2002, it had 188 members. See <http://www.icao.int/icao/en/members.htm>. Australia is a member of the Chicago Convention. The Air Navigation Act 1920 (Cth) incorporates the Chicago Convention.
7. The Agreement had 119 members in 2002. See <http://www.jurisint.org/>. Australia has ratified the Transit Agreement and incorporated it into the Air Navigation Act 1920 (Cth).
8. There were 121 members to the protocol in 2002. See <http://www.jurisint.org/>.
9. It should be noted that the Convention for the Unification of Certain Rules for International Carriage by Air was concluded on 28 May 1999 for the purpose of replacing the Warsaw Convention and a number of protocols. The 1999 Convention requires a minimum 13 countries to give it effect. It was not effective as at July 2002.
10. As at December 2000, the convention had 148 members. Australia is a member of the convention and has incorporated the convention in the Civil Aviation (Carrier's Liability) Act 1959: see Schedule. New Zealand has incorporated the convention into the Carriage by Air Act 1967 (NZ).

[4.8]   International Commercial Law

- the Hague Protocol to Amend the Convention for the Unification of Certain Rules relating to International Carriage by Air (the Hague Protocol 1955), signed at The Hague on 28 September 1955;[11]
- the Convention Supplementary to the Warsaw Convention, for the Unification of Certain Rules relating to International Carriage by Air Performed by a Person other than the Contracting Carrier (the Guadalajara Convention 1961), signed in Guadalajara on 18 September 1961;[12]
- the Protocol to Amend the Convention for the Unification of Certain Rules relating to International Carriage by Air as amended by The Hague Protocol 1955 (the Guatemala City Protocol 1971), signed at Guatemala City on 8 March 1971;
- the Additional Protocol No 1 to Amend the Convention for the Unification of Certain Rules relating to International Carriage by Air, (the Additional Protocol No 1), signed at Montreal on 25 September 1975;
- the Additional Protocol No 2 to Amend the Convention for the Unification of Certain Rules relating to International Carriage by Air as amended by The Hague Protocol 1955 (the Additional Protocol No 2), signed at Montreal on 25 September 1975;
- the Additional Protocol No 3 to Amend the Convention for the Unification of Certain Rules relating to International Carriage by Air as amended by The Hague Protocol 1955 and the Guatemala City Protocol 1971 (the Additional Protocol No 3), signed at Montreal on 25 September 1975; and
- the Montreal Protocol No 4 to Amend the Convention for the Unification of Certain Rules Relating to International Carriage by Air as amended by The Hague Protocol 1955 (the Additional Protocol No 4), signed at Montreal on 25 September 1975.

[4.9] Both the Chicago System and the Warsaw System are international conventions and operate under the same principles affecting the operation of international conventions. Each convention forms an independent regime of law. Each amended convention also forms an independent regime separated from the unamended convention, unless the members of the original convention agree that the acceptance of the amendment is compulsory for any member to remain in the legal framework based on the convention.

This is why, for example, there are four additional protocols under the Warsaw Convention, adopted at Montreal on the same day. Each additional protocol and the original convention it amends forms a distinctive regime within the legal framework of the Warsaw Convention. The members of the original Warsaw Convention have an option to determine which protocol to ratify for the purpose of accepting further rules added to the Warsaw Convention. Thus, the different combinations between the Warsaw Convention and one or more protocols result in the co-existence of several versions of the Warsaw Convention within the Warsaw System. Each version binds only the countries which

---

11. In December 2000, the protocol had 130 members. Australia has ratified the protocol and incorporated it into the Civil Aviation (Carriers Liability) Act 1959 (Cth): see Schedule 2. New Zealand has incorporated it into the Carriage by Air Act 1967 (NZ).
12. This convention has been adopted in Australia through the Civil Aviation (Carrier's Liability) Act 1959 (Cth): see Schedule 3.

Contracts for Carriage by Sea, Air and Land [4.11]

have ratified the version. The Warsaw System will be examined in detail later in this chapter: see **[4.191]–[4.198]**.

Legal framework for carriage by land

[4.10] The carriage of goods by land is presently subject to the following international conventions:

- the Convention concerning International Carriage by Rail (COTIF), incorporating the Uniform Rules concerning the Contract for International Carriage of Goods by Rail (CIM),[13] and the International Convention concerning the Carriage of Passengers and Luggage by Rail (CIV), signed in Berne on 9 May 1980 and entered into force on 1 May 1985;[14]

- the International Convention to Facilitate the Crossing of Frontiers for Goods Carried by Rail, concluded at Geneva on 10 January 1952 and entered into force on 1 April 1953;[15]

- the Convention on the Contract for the International Carriage of Goods by Road (CMR),[16] adopted on 19 May 1956 and entered into force on 2 July 1956;[17] and

- the Protocol to the Convention on the Contract for the International Carriage of Goods by Road, concluded at Geneva on 5 July 1978 and entered into force on 28 December 1980.[18]

There is also the Convention on the Contract for the International Carriage of Passengers and Luggage by Road (CVR), which was concluded at Geneva on 1 March 1973 and entered into force on 12 April 1994. As at July 2002, it had six members, including Bosnia, Croatia, Czech Republic, Latvia, Slovakia and Yugoslavia. Germany and Luxembourg have signed but not ratified it. The convention will not be discussed in this book because of its limited application to the carriage of passengers.

Legal framework for multimodal carriage

[4.11] The carriage of goods by multimodal means will be subject to the United Nations Convention on International Multimodal Transport of Goods, which was adopted at Geneva on 24 May 1980. As at July 1999, the convention had nine members and had not yet come into effect. There are six more countries which have signed but not ratified the convention. In relation to multimodal transport, the European Agreement on Important

---

13. COTIF stands for *Convention relative aux transports internationaux ferroviaires*. CIM stands for *Convention internationale concernant le transport des marchandises par chemin de fer*. CIM was originally adopted as the 1893 International Convention concerning the Carriage of Goods by Rail and had been amended in several conferences before being incorporated into Appendix B of the 1980 Berne Convention concerning International Carriage by Rail (COTIF). Australia is not a party to the convention.
14. As at February 2001, the convention had 40 members.
15. As at December 2000, it had 10 European members.
16. CMR stands for *Convention relative au contrat de transport international des marchandises par route*. Australia is not a party to the convention.
17. As at November 2000, the convention had 44 members.
18. As at November 2000, 30 members had ratified the protocol. It operates as an amendment to CMR to those countries which have ratified it.

[4.11] International Combined Transport Lines and Related Installations (AGTC) should be mentioned. The agreement was concluded at Geneva on 1 February 1991 and entered into force on 20 October 1993. As at July 1999, it had 22 European members.

[4.12] In addition, the United Nations Convention on the Liability of Operators of Transport Terminals in International Trade, which was concluded at Geneva on 19 April 1991, may have implications to all types of transport, including multimodal transport. As at July 1999, only Egypt and George have ratified it. Five countries, France, Mexico, the Philippines, Spain and the United States, have signed but not ratified it. Thus, the convention is not yet in force.

Each mode of transport and the relevant international conventions will be examined in turn.

Carriage of goods by sea

The Hague Rules

[4.13] The Hague Rules 1924 were adopted in Brussels on 25 August 1924 as an 'international convention' on the carriage of goods by sea and entered into force on 2 June 1931. There are 16 articles in total. Ten of them deal with legal issues relating to bills of lading and the rest are concerned with procedural issues relating to the operation of the Rules. Many jurisdictions have formally incorporated the Hague Rules into their domestic laws, while a few others have adopted the Hague Rules without having formally adopted them.[19]

The purpose of the Hague Rules was to unify the rules governing the liability of a carrier. Under the Hague Rules a carrier has a general liability to provide a seaworthy ship and to handle the goods with care. However, the Hague Rules also list several exceptions, such as fault of the master of the ship or pilot in the navigation or management of the ship, act of God, act of war, riots, strikes, saving life or property at sea, and others, to restrict the liability of the carrier.

These exceptions remain the same under the Hague-Visby Rules (see **[4.92]**), which amended the Hague Rules. The liability of a carrier under the Hague Rules was limited to £100 sterling per package or unit, unless the parties had agreed to a higher value. This was considered to be too low and unfair to the shippers. The limit of liability is increased in the Hague-Visby Rules. Since the Hague Rules and the Hague-Visby Rules are largely similar — except for the limits on liability and a few other provisions, and the Hague-Visby Rules' incorporation of amendments to the Hague Rules — only the Hague-Visby Rules will be discussed in the book.

---

19. These are Pakistan, Panama, Philippines, Sabah, St Martin and Taiwan. See Richardson, *The Hague and Hague-Visby Rules*, 4th ed, London, LLP, 1998, p 108.

The Hague-Visby Rules

[4.14] The Hague-Visby Rules are based on the 1968 Brussels Protocol to Amend the International Convention for the Unification of Certain Rules of Law Relating to Bills of Lading. The protocol was adopted in Brussels in February 1968 and entered into force on 23 February 1968. The amended Hague Rules (the Hague-Visby Rules) have 16 articles in total. While about 25 jurisdictions have formally incorporated the Hague-Visby Rules in their domestic laws,[20] about seven jurisdictions have adopted the Hague-Visby Rules without having formally acknowledged them.[21]

Australia is now a party to the Hague-Visby Rules, and the Carriage of Goods by Sea Act 1991 (Cth) incorporates arts 1–10 of the Hague-Visby Rules. The Hague-Visby Rules operate in those countries or jurisdictions which have ratified the protocol, and were intended to redress the unfairness to the shipper in the Hague Rules. The exceptions are the same under the two conventions; however, the Hague-Visby Rules set out the limitation of the liability as 666.67 units of account per package, or two units of account per kilogram of the gross weight of the goods, whichever is higher, unless the parties have agreed on a higher value. These amendments are still regarded by many developing countries and cargo-owners' countries as being unfair to shippers: thus the creation of the Hamburg Rules in 1978.

The Hamburg Rules

[4.15] The Hamburg Rules were adopted by the United Nations in Hamburg on 30 March 1978. There are 34 articles in total. Twenty-six articles deal with substantial legal issues and eight deal with procedural issues. Having been ratified by 27 countries,[22] the Hamburg Rules entered into force on 2 November 1992.

The Hamburg Rules impose wider liabilities upon the carrier and are relatively even-handed in comparison with the Hague Rules or the Hague-Visby Rules. Australia has not ratified the Hamburg Rules, although arts 1–26 of the Hamburg Rules have been incorporated into Schedule 2 of the Carriage of Goods by Sea Act 1991 (Cth). Under the Hamburg Rules, the carrier is liable for the risk in goods from the moment the goods are put under his or her care until the time they are delivered as agreed. Depending on the construction of the expression 'the carrier is in charge of the goods' in art 4(1), the carrier could be liable for any losses of or damage to goods under his or her care, regardless of whether the goods are on board a vessel.

Under the Hague Rules or Hague-Visby Rules, the carrier is only liable for the risk in goods during the 'carriage of goods' — the period after the goods pass the ship's rail for loading and before the goods pass the ship's rail for discharge.

---

20. See note 2 above.
21. These are Germany, Iceland, India, Israel, Oman, South Africa and Vietnam. See Richardson, note 19 above, pp 108–9.
22. See note 3 above.

Defining a contract of carriage by sea

[4.16] A contract of carriage by sea is a contract entered into between a shipper (who may be a seller, a buyer, or an agent of the seller or the buyer), and the carrier (who could be a shipowner, a charterer of a vessel, or their agent or a freight forwarder), for the purpose of transporting goods from one place to another by sea. Such a contract has the following characteristics:

- it is made between a 'shipper' (see **[4.27]**) and a 'carrier' (see **[4.20]**);
- it is a contract for providing the services of transporting goods;
- it involves transmission of goods by sea either partly or entirely; and
- it often involves transport of goods from one country to another, although in Australia interstate carriage of goods by sea is subject to the same law as international carriage of goods by sea.

[4.17] A contract of carriage stipulates matters relating to safe conveyance of goods from one designated place to another designated place. The purpose of the contract is to ensure that the goods are carried in a safe and timely manner by the carrier. The rights and duties of the contracting parties are defined on this basis. Generally speaking, the parties should agree on the time and place of shipment and delivery, the route of voyage, the payment of freight, the liabilities of the parties in performing the necessary task of transmitting the goods from the agreed place to their destination, transhipment, liability of the carrier's servants or agents, choice of law, choice of forum or arbitration, incorporation of charterparty clauses (if applicable), and any other matters which may affect the rights and liability of the parties.

The agreement on the route of the voyage is important, in order to avoid unnecessary risks, and to ascertain the scope of the carrier's liability when losses or damages arise from unauthorised stopovers. The agreed route of the voyage is also important in practice, in the sense that a certain type of cargo, such as fruits, may only stand a relatively short period of carriage before turning bad, or that the market for a certain type of product is too volatile to stand a long period of carriage. The liabilities of the carrier and shipper will be discussed in detail in the sections dealing with their liabilities under the Hague-Visby Rules and the Hamburg Rules.

[4.18] A contract of carriage can be made orally or in writing.[23] Although the existence of a contract of carriage is often represented by a bill of lading, a voyage charterparty, or a similar document, such as a sea waybill, consignment note or a mate's receipt, the contract can exist independently of the bill of lading, the voyage charterparty or similar document.

In other words, the parties have an option either to conclude a written contract of carriage in addition to the bill of lading issued by the carrier, or to rely on the bill of lading to be the evidence of any prior existent oral contract. For example, art 1(b) of the Hague-Visby Rules extends the meaning of a contract of carriage to any document issued or

---

23. For example, an oral contract of sea carriage was found to have existed before the beginning of loading in *Hines Exports Pty Ltd v Mediterranean Shipping Co* [2000] SADC 71.

made for the purpose of carriage; and art 1(6) of the Hamburg Rules defines a 'contract of carriage' as 'any contract whereby the carrier undertakes against payment of freight to carry goods by sea from one port to another'.

Under the Carriage of Goods by Sea Act 1991 (Cth), a contract of carriage 'means a contract of carriage covered by a sea carriage document (to the extent that the document relates to the carriage of goods by sea), and includes a negotiable sea carriage document issued under a charterparty from the moment at which that document regulates the relations between its holder and the carrier concerned'.[24] The meaning of 'sea carriage document' is also defined in art 1(1) of the modified Hague-Visby Rules, incorporated into Schedule 1 and 1A of the Carriage of Goods by Sea Act 1991 (Cth). Therefore, it is necessary to remember that a contract of carriage means more than a bill of lading.

[4.19] The meaning of a contract of carriage is flexible, depending on the circumstances and the relevant law applicable. Its flexibility is illustrated by a Canadian case, *Her Majesty the Queen v Purolator Courier Ltd*, decided on 7 January 1997 in the Supreme Court of British Columbia.[25]

In this case, the Crown charged the respondent for breaches of the Transportation of Dangerous Goods Act and the Transportation of Dangerous Goods Regulations. The Crown alleged that dangerous materials were found in 1995 in two separate sites in the goods belonging to the respondent. The Crown sought to establish the alleged breaches by referring to the waybills and packing slips found with the goods. The technical argument was whether the waybills and packing slips constituted shipping documents or prescribed documents under the relevant law.

The court took the view that the shipping document under the relevant law requires the document has legibly and indelibly printed on it a shipping document identification number and the name of the consignor. Such information was missing from the waybills and packing slips in question. Accordingly, the court held that the waybills and packing slips concerned did not constitute the shipping document required by the relevant law. On this technical ground, the Crown failed. This case suggests that the meaning of similar documents may vary depending on the circumstances and the relevant law which is applicable to the document in question.

Meaning of carrier

General meaning of carrier

[4.20] A carrier is a person (either natural or legal) who undertakes the responsibility of transporting goods from one place to another under a contract of carriage, against the payment of freight. It is crucial, for the purpose of determining the responsibilities of the parties to a contract of carriage, that the carrier is the person who is the named party under the contract of carriage. This is because the contract forms the basis of the parties' responsibilities, although the relevant international conventions, such as the Hague-Visby

---

24. See art 1(1)(b) of the modified Hague-Visby Rules which are incorporated into Schedule 1A of the Carriage of Goods by Sea Act 1991 (Cth).
25. Canadian Cases — available at <http://www.courts.gov.bc.ca>.

[4.20]

Rules and the Hamburg Rules, stipulate the parties' duties under a contract of carriage falling under the conventions.

[4.21] The meaning of carrier may vary in different countries, depending on the relevant provisions of law. The Australian Carriage of Goods by Sea Act 1991 (Cth) incorporates the Hague-Visby Rules, and also the definition of carrier as adopted in the Hague-Visby Rules. The Chinese Maritime Law does not expressly incorporate any international convention on the carriage of goods by sea, and thus has to provide its own definition of carrier. Article 42 of the Maritime Law defines the meaning of 'carrier' and 'actual carrier', which appears to be similar to the meaning of 'carrier' and 'actual carrier' under art 1 of the Hamburg Rules.[26] New Zealand has also adopted the Hague-Visby Rules, but the Carriage of Goods Act 1979 (NZ) also provides its own definition of carrier. Article 2 of the Carriage of Goods Act 1979 (NZ) defines carrier as a person in the ordinary course of business who carries or procures to be carried goods owned by another person, including a person who performs any 'incidental service' in respect of the goods to be carried. This extends the definition of carrier to include persons, such as consolidators, packers, stevedores, and warehouse workers, who perform services which are undertaken to facilitate the carriage of goods pursuant to the contract of carriage.

[4.22] The wording of the said provision covers a person performing certain works prior or subsequent to the loading or unloading of the cargo from the vessel. This definition of 'carrier' is much wider than that which is adopted in Australia, which is a member of the Hague-Visby Rules, or China, which has not ratified any of the three conventions on the carriage of goods by sea.

In *Nederlandse Speciaal Drukkerijen v Bollinger Shipping Agency* [1999] NSWSC 200, a case involving a shipping company based in Australia and two companies providing packing services in New Zealand, the owner of the printing press which was damaged in the course of shipment from Auckland, New Zealand to Delft, Holland sued in Australia the carrier, and one of the companies packing the printing press. The Supreme Court of New South Wales noted the differences between the meanings of carrier under Australian law and New Zealand law, and the fact that the carriage involved a port in New Zealand and a port in Holland. It decided that the action against the New Zealand company should be stayed in favour of an action in the New Zealand court, and implied that the whole action may as well be tried in New Zealand. The case suggests that the meaning of carrier under different laws certainly affects the liability of a person, in the sense that the person may be held to be a carrier under one law, but as an agent or sub-contractor of the carrier under another law.

Meaning of carrier under the Hague-Visby Rules

[4.23] The Hague-Visby Rules adopt a narrower definition of 'carrier' than the Hamburg Rules. Under the Hague-Visby Rules, a carrier 'includes the owner or the charterer who enters into a contract of carriage with a shipper'. An agent of the shipowner or charterer is not a 'carrier' under the Hague-Visby Rules, even if the agent might have

---

26. For the relevant discussions, see John Mo, *Shipping Law in China*, Hong Kong, Sweet & Maxwell, 1999, pp 65–67.

issued and signed a bill of lading.[27] In contrast, the Hamburg Rules define the meaning of a 'carrier' broadly as referring to 'any person by whom or in whose name a contract of carriage of goods by sea has been concluded with a shipper'.

The freight forwarder in *Carrington Slipways Pty Ltd v Patrick Operations Pty Ltd* (1991) 24 NSWLR 745 would be a 'carrier' under the Hamburg Rules, had the Hamburg Rules been applicable. The house bill in this case might fall under the meaning of 'bill of lading' in arts 1 and 14 of the Hamburg Rules, if the bill contains an undertaking to ship the goods. This difference between the Hague-Visby Rules and the Hamburg Rules affects the interests of the parties substantially, depending on which of them apply.

[4.24] Sometimes a domestic law may affect the meaning of carrier under the Hague-Visby Rules. For example, Canada adopts the Hague-Visby Rules. But under Canadian law, 'the shipowner would be liable as a carrier since the vessel was not under a demise charter and the bills of lading were signed on behalf of the master. Carriage of goods is a joint venture of owners and charterers who should therefore be held jointly and severally responsible as carrier'.[28] This position of the court is more certain in comparison with the position of the Australian law in similar circumstances, because, for example, arts 10(6) and (7) of the modified Hague-Visby Rules as incorporated into Schedule 1A of the Carriage of Goods by Sea Act 1991 (Cth) make the modified Hague-Visby Rules apply on the basis of a negotiable sea carriage document rather than impose a joint venture between the shipowner and the charterer. Another example is the Carriage of Goods Act 1979 (NZ), which also incorporates the Hague-Visby Rules. However, the meaning of 'carrier' under the said law may extend to a person engaged in the packing of the cargo prior to its shipment.[29]

Defining carrier in the contract

[4.25] Parties may define the meaning of 'carrier' themselves in a contract of carriage or a bill of lading. For example, in *Cabot Corp v The Mormacscan* [1971] 2 Lloyd's Rep 351, the bill of lading defined the word 'carrier' as including 'the ship, her owner, operator, demise charterer, time charterer, master and any substituted carrier, whether acting as carrier or bailee, and all persons rendering services in connection with the performance' of the contract of carriage evidenced by the bill of lading.

This means that as far as the contract of carriage (or the bill of lading) was concerned the parties agreed that the word 'carrier' should be understood and used as defined. In this case, the stevedoring company negligently damaged the goods of the shipper in the process of loading the cargo belonging to another shipper but sought to rely on the

---

27. For example, in *Carrington Slipways Pty Ltd v Patrick Operations Pty Ltd* (1991) 24 NSWLR 745; **[4.51]**, two bills of lading were issued with respect to the same cargo. One was a 'house bill' issued by a freight forwarder. The other was an 'ocean bill' or 'shipped bill' issued by the actual carrier. The parties disagreed as to which bill was applicable for the purpose of determining the liability of the stevedoring company. The first bill may be excluded from the Hague-Visby Rules on the ground of art 1(a) of the Hague-Visby Rules. However, the court found the house bill was merely a receipt of the goods.
28. *Canastrand Industries Ltd v The Ship 'Lara S' and Others*, decided on 1 May 1989 by the Federal Court of Canada, see Canadian Cases, available at <http://www.fja-cmf.gc.ca>, per Reed J.
29. See *Nederlandse Speciaal Drukkerijen v Bollinger Shipping Agency* [1999] NSWSC 200, discussed in **[4.22]**.

definition of carrier to limit its liability under the bill of lading. The United States District Court held that the stevedoring company was not a 'carrier' in relation to the contract of carriage with the shipper, because at the time of the damage it was loading goods belonging to another shipper. Therefore, the stevedoring company was not entitled to rely on the bill of lading to limit its liability. This decision was affirmed by the Court of Appeal. This case suggests that had the stevedoring company been rendering services in connection with the contract of carriage with the shipper, it would have been eligible as a 'carrier' under the bill to limit its liability.

'Actual carrier' and 'carrier'

[4.26] The Hamburg Rules distinguish a 'carrier' from an 'actual carrier', who performs part or the whole of the contract of carriage concluded between the shipper and the 'carrier'. Under art 1(2) of the Hamburg Rules, an actual carrier is 'any person to whom the performance of the carriage of the goods, or of part of the carriage, has been entrusted by the carrier, and includes any other person to whom such performance has been entrusted'. The purpose of distinguishing a carrier from an actual carrier, or alternatively, of defining the legal concept of an 'actual carrier', is to enforce the contract of carriage against the carrier who undertakes to carry the goods to the agreed destination, even though he or she has to engage the services of other carriers to perform the whole or part of the contract.

Meaning of shipper

Meaning of shipper under the Hague-Visby Rules

[4.27] A shipper is a person (whether legal or natural) who is a party to a contract of carriage with a carrier. The Hague-Visby Rules (and the Hague Rules also) do not define the meaning of 'shipper', although the word 'shipper' is used in these conventions. Under the Hague-Visby Rules, 'shipper' has its ordinary meaning, referring to anyone whose name appears as party to a contract of carriage with a carrier.

Meaning of shipper under the Hamburg Rules

[4.28] Under art 1(3) of the Hamburg Rules, 'shipper' is clearly defined as follows:

'Shipper' means any person by whom or in whose name or on whose behalf a contract of carriage by sea has been concluded with a carrier, or any person by whom or in whose name or on whose behalf the goods are actually delivered to the carrier in relation to the contract of carriage by sea.

[4.29] It appears that the word 'shipper' was intended to have a wider meaning than the word 'carrier' under the Hamburg Rules. For example, art 1(1) of the Hamburg Rules states that a 'carrier' is a person who contracts (either by him- or herself or in his or her name) with the shipper as the carrier under the contract of carriage. A person will not be a 'carrier' under the Hamburg Rules as long as he or she is not a party to the contract of carriage, even though he or she might have rendered the services of carriage (that is, may have been an 'actual carrier'). The narrow definition of 'carrier' under the Hamburg Rules does not mean that the carrier's liability is narrow, because art 1(2) creates a definition of 'actual carrier' and art 10 makes a 'carrier' accountable for the acts of an 'actual carrier'. In comparison with the definition of 'carrier', art 1(3) of the Hamburg Rules makes a person 'by whom or in whose name or on whose behalf the goods are actually delivered to the carrier' a shipper for the purpose of the contract of carriage. This definition raises the following possible interpretation of the meaning of 'shipper' under the Hamburg Rules:

- a shipper is a person who enters into a contract of carriage with a carrier;
- a shipper may also be a person who delivers the goods to the carrier regardless of whether he or she is expressly or directly a party to the contract of carriage; and
- there is a possibility that there may be more than one shipper in relation to the same contract of carriage and the same goods.[30]

[4.30] In cases where the Hamburg Rules do not apply, the meaning of 'shipper' should be determined in the circumstances concerned and according to the intention of the parties as shown in a bill of lading or a contract of carriage. For example, in *Koninklijke Bunge v Compagnie Continentale D'Importation* [1973] 2 Lloyd's Rep 44, the contract of sale based on the CIF term incorporated the London Corn Trade Association contract form No 30.

Clause 20 of the contract adopted the word 'shipper'. Kerr J of the Queen's Bench Division (Commercial Court) held (at 49) that 'the word "shipper" is clearly wider than to denote the person or body responsible for carrying out, or paying for, or procuring the physical operations of putting goods on board a ship, such as stevedoring companies or an elevator company or other concerns owning or operating storage and loading facilities'. The judge held that the word 'shipper' means a 'person who, whether or not he has the title to the goods, causes them to be shipped' (at 50). This reasoning suggests that in other cases the word 'shipper' may be given a narrower or wider meaning, depending on the intention of the parties and terms of the contract (or bill of lading).

Meaning of consignee

[4.31] A 'consignee' is, generally speaking, a person who is specified as the recipient of the goods in a bill of lading or a similar document which may not be negotiable, but must evidence the carriage of the cargo concerned and satisfy the requirements for a 'similar document' or a 'shipping document' as set out in the relevant statute, if any, or the common law. Sometimes the goods can be transported or transferred without there necessarily being a negotiable document (for example, by holding a non-negotiable bill of lading or by presenting a delivery order). This is probably why art 1(4) of the Hamburg Rules defines a 'consignee' as 'the person entitled to take delivery of the goods'. This definition is capable of including a situation where a person is entitled to take delivery under any contractual arrangement between the shipper and carrier.

[4.32] The Australian sale of goods legislation does not define the meaning of 'consignee'. However, s 50A of the Sale of Goods Act 1923 (NSW) and s 73 of the Goods Act 1958 (Vic) allow a consignee or indorsee (interchangeable with 'consignee' in

---

30. This is because the person who delivers the goods (or in whose name the goods are delivered) may not be the person whose name appears as the shipper in the contract of carriage under which the goods are delivered. Article 1(3) of the Hamburg Rules does not make the existence of a 'shipper' by virtue of the contract of carriage, and the existence of a 'shipper' by virtue of delivery, mutually exclusive.

this context) to have all the rights of a legal owner of the goods. In addition, s 66 of the Goods Act 1958 (Vic) allows a consignee who is bona fide for value to receive a good title against the original owner, even though the consignor (who is not the true owner of the goods) does not have authority to sell. These provisions are relevant for the determination of a consignee's rights in certain circumstances.

Meaning of consignor

[4.33] A 'consignor' is a person who indorses or transfers the goods under a bill of lading or similar document to a consignee. Since most bills of lading are negotiable, a legal holder of a bill of lading is able to sign his or her name on the bill and to name another person as the consignee under it. The word 'consignor' is not defined in the Hague-Visby Rules and the Hamburg Rules, because the conventions are concerned with the carriage of goods by sea only. However, the word 'consignor' is important to a student of international commercial law, because a bill of lading is in most circumstances a document of title which can be transferred (sold) from one party to another. In such cases, the word 'consignor' indicates the legal status and responsibility of the person who passes the bill (or similar document) to a buyer of the goods covered by the bill.

Indorsee and indorser

[4.34] These words are not normally relevant to a contract of carriage. However, as far as the negotiability of a bill of lading is concerned, these words have similar meanings to 'consignee' and 'consignor'. The words 'indorsee' and 'indorser' will become more important in **Chapter 5** when we study bills of exchange.

Bill of lading

Defining a bill of lading

[4.35] A 'bill of lading' is a document signed and issued by a carrier, or his or her agent, to a shipper, or his or her agent, to acknowledge the receipt of goods by the carrier or his or her agent in the condition stated and to set out the terms under which the goods are carried.[31] It represents or evidences the existence of a contract of carriage between the carrier and the shipper.[32] It often forms the basis for, or exists as, a contract of carriage. However, it is not necessarily the same as a contract of carriage: in a carriage of goods by sea, a contract of carriage and a bill of lading may co-exist.[33]

This is why the Hamburg Rules define 'contract of carriage by sea' and 'bill of lading' separately. In cases where they co-exist, the two documents must be read together in

---

31. It should be noted that in *Hi-Fert Pty Ltd v Kiukiang Maritime Carriers Inc* [2000] FCA 660, the defendant unsuccessfully argued that the bill of lading in dispute was merely a receipt, instead of evidence of the contract of carriage. The court found that the bill of lading also amounted to evidence of the terms of contract between the parties.
32. Various definitions of bill of lading are discussed in *The Maurice Desgagnes* [1977] 1 Lloyd's Rep 290.
33. For example, in *Hines Exports Pty Ltd v Mediterranean Shipping Co* [2000] SADC 71, the court held that an oral contract for the carriage of goods was made between the parties before 22 March 1995, and the carrier failed to prove that the bill of lading issued on 1 April 1995 contained the same terms as the oral contract.

accordance with the intention of the parties as shown in the documents, if any inconsistency arises between them. On the other hand, in cases of inconsistency, there may sometimes be a necessity to read them separately to identify the parties to the contract of carriage, and the parties to the bill of lading, respectively.

In *Jian Sheng Co Ltd v Great Tempo SA*,[34] the booking note specified Sinotrans Canada Inc as the carrier, and contained an arbitration clause to submit all disputes arising from the booking note to the Vancouver Maritime Arbitrators Association, while the bill of lading issued by Sinotrans Canada Inc stated that Sinotrans Canada Inc was the agent for the carrier, *Trans Aspiration,* which was the name of the vessel carrying the cargo concerned. The bill of lading also contained a choice of jurisdiction clause stating that all disputes should be tried in the country of the carrier's principal place of business. In dealing with such inconsistency, the court took a view that the booking note was a contract of carriage, but the bill of lading evidenced another contract of carriage. Thus, the conclusion is that the parties to the contract of carriage and to the bill of lading should be examined respectively according to the nature of the dispute, if the contract and the bill are not consistent.[35]

[4.36] Article 1(7) of the Hamburg Rules defines 'bill of lading' as follows:

[The expression] means a document which evidences a contract of carriage by sea and the taking over or loading of the goods by the carrier, and by which the carrier undertakes to deliver the goods against surrender of the document. A provision in the document that the goods are to be delivered to the order of a named person, or to order, or to bearer, constitutes such an undertaking.

[4.37] Occasionally, we may see people using 'bill of lading' in a very informal way, referring to a contract of carriage between the parties. For example, in *Trans Western Express v Quadrant Sales and Imports Inc*, decided on 19 November 1996 by the Supreme Court of British Columbia,[36] a bill of lading was issued by the defendant (appellant) carrier for the purpose of carrying a cargo for exhibition to Montreal by rail. Nevertheless, the carrier issued a 'bill of lading' to the shipper and the 'bill' so issued formed the basis for the court to hold the carrier liable for the shipper's economic loss, arising from the delay in delivery caused by bad weather. In this case, the use of the term 'bill of lading' was not questioned and the court regarded it as a contract of carriage between the parties. In such a case, of course, the 'bill of lading' is not the same as we understand for the sea carriage or multimodal carriage.

Characteristics and functions of a bill of lading

[4.38] Under both common law[37] and the Hamburg Rules, a bill of lading has the following characteristics or functions:

---

34. Decided on 4 June 1997 by the Federal Court of Canada, available at <http://www.fja-cmf.gc.ca>.
35. See also *The Rewia* [1991] 2 Lloyd's Rep 325 (CA).
36. Available at <http://www.courts.gov.bc.ca>.
37. For example, in *The Maurice Desgagnes* [1977] 1 Lloyd's Rep 290, Dube J of the Canadian Federal Court (Trial Division) examined various definitions of bill of lading.

- it is a document of title, which allows its legal holder to claim the goods,[38] and delivery of goods without requesting the production of the bill of lading may amount to a fundamental breach of contract;[39]
- it is usually, but not exclusively, issued by the master of a ship;
- it evidences the receipt of the goods concerned;
- it evidences the existence of a contract of carriage between the carrier and the shipper;
- it constitutes an undertaking by the carrier to deliver the goods to the destination specified;
- it evidences the condition of the goods at the time of receipt;
- it constitutes an undertaking by the carrier to deliver the goods in the same condition as they were received by him or her;
- it evidences the terms under which the goods are carried;
- it forms the contract of carriage between the consignee and the carrier;[40] and
- it can be either negotiable (transferable) or non-negotiable.[41]

These characteristics and functions will be discussed further in the relevant sections.

[4.39] The characteristics or functions of the bill of lading are crucial for determining whether a sea transport document is a bill of lading. It is also important for determining whether a document or contract of transportation involving partly the carriage by sea is a bill of lading.

In *Comalco Aluminium Ltd v Mogal Freight Services Pty Ltd*,[42] a document known as a consignment note evidenced the contract between Comalco as the cargo-owner and Mogal as the carrier, or freight forwarder. According to the contract between them, Mogal undertook in 1990 to transport 46 aluminium coils from Comalco's premises in a suburb of Sydney, to New Zealand Cans' premises in New Zealand. The transaction consisted of both carriage by road in Australia and New Zealand respectively, and carriage by sea from Sydney to Auckland. A number of coils were damaged during the whole carriage. Comalco sued Mogal for damage, and alleged that the consignment note was, inter alia, a bill of lading under the Carriage of Goods by Sea Act 1991 (Cth).

Sheppard J held that the consignment note bore three essential elements of a bill of lading, namely, its being a receipt for the goods, evidence of the contract of affreightment, and a document of title; thus, it was a bill of lading for the purpose of the Carriage

---

38. For example, in *Westpac Banking Corp v 'Stone Gemini'* [1999] FCA 434, the court allowed the legal holder of the bill of lading to claim compensation against the carrier who had delivered the goods covered by the bill without the presentation of the bill.
39. *Sze Hai Tong Bank Ltd v Rambler Cycle Co Ltd* [1959] AC 576; and *Kuehne Nagel (Hong Kong) Ltd v Yuen Fung Metal Works Ltd* [1979] HKLR 526.
40. This means that, regardless of the terms of the contract of carriage between the carrier and the shipper, the consignee of the bill can enforce its terms against the carrier as if it is a contract of carriage between them. By the same token, the consignee is bound also by the terms of the bill.
41. For discussion on the negotiability of a bill of lading, see Schmitthoff, *Schmitthoff's Export Trade*, 9th ed, Stevens & Sons, London, 1990, pp 571–3.
42. Decided by the Federal Court of Australia on 18 March 1993, available at <http://www.austlii.edu.au>.

of Goods by Sea Act 1991 (Cth). However, in his Honour's view, since it was a bill of lading, the consignment note did not help the plaintiff's position, because the damage was caused by the negligence of the carrier — committed prior to the loading of the cargo — and thus the Hague Rules did not apply to such negligence. In this case, the consignment note concerned looked more like a transport document for multimodal carriage. It bore some resemblance to a forwarder's bill of lading, or a 'received for shipment' bill or a house bill, and was certainly more than a bill of lading. Therefore, it was arguable either way, as implicitly admitted by Sheppard J (at para 97), as to whether or not this was strictly a bill of lading, since it contained not only the basic elements of a bill of lading, but also some other features not usually found within a bill of lading.

Historical perspective of the bill of lading

[4.40] The bill of lading originated around the 14th century as a non-negotiable receipt issued by a shipowner, for cargo received, to a merchant who did not intend to travel with his goods. It contained statements as to the type and quantity of goods shipped and the condition in which they were received. Subsequent experience led to the incorporation into the document of the terms of the contract of carriage in order to resolve disputes which inevitably arose between cargo-owners and carriers.

By the 18th century, the bill of lading had acquired its third characteristic, that of being negotiable by indorsement in order to meet the needs of those merchants who wished to dispose of their goods before the vessel reached its destination.[43]

Bills of lading under the Hague-Visby Rules

[4.41] The Hague-Visby Rules do not expressly define a bill of lading, but they incorporate the following basic features of the bill of lading at common law:

- First, the carrier, or the master of the ship or an agent of the carrier, is required under art 3(3) of the Hague-Visby Rules, on demand of the shipper, to issue a bill of lading. The bill of lading can be either a clean bill of lading which contains such words as 'goods shipped in good order and condition', or a claused bill of lading which contains words describing the defects in the goods or package. If the carrier issues a clean bill of lading on the basis of the information (such as marks, quantity and weight of the goods) provided by the shipper, the shipper is obliged under art 3(5) of the Hague-Visby Rules to indemnify the carrier against any claims or expenses arising from inaccuracies in the information.

- Second, art 3(4) of the Hague-Visby Rules provides that 'a bill of lading shall be prima facie evidence of the receipt by the carrier of the goods as therein described in accordance with paragraph 3(a), (b) and (c)'. But this provision also implicitly allows the parties to rebut the prima facie evidence by contrary proof.[44] This provision can be compared with the effect of a bill of lading at common law as seen in *Rosenfeld Hillas &*

---

43. Wilson, *Carriage of Goods by Sea*, 2nd ed, Pitman Publishing, London, 1993, p 123.
44. Article 3(4) implicitly allows so because it only states that 'proof of the contrary shall not be admissible when the bill of lading has been transferred to a third party acting in good faith'. This means that the contrary proof can be used against the shipper.

[4.41]   **International Commercial Law**

Co Pty Ltd v The Ship Fort Laramie (1923) 32 CLR 25, and with the relevant provision of the sale of goods legislation.

[4.42] The Hague-Visby Rules (or the Hague Rules) are not well drafted in terms of the rationalising of the relationships between the rules and the bill of lading. For example, art 3(4) of the Hague-Visby Rules defines the bill of lading as prima facie evidence of the receipt of the goods, only implying that the carrier should also deliver the goods concerned because he or she has received them. But the primary function of art 3(4) is to permit the carrier to rebut the evidence of the bill of lading on the condition, state, nature or quantity of the goods in dispute. Another neglected aspect of the bill of lading in the Hague-Visby Rules (or the Hague Rules) is the use of exclusion clauses in the bill. Carriers have attempted to exclude theirs and their agents' (including the independent contractors') liability to the goods under the bill of lading.

Disagreements often arise when goods are damaged after discharge from the vessel but before delivery to the consignee. There is even a contradiction in the case of non-delivery for whatever reason. The contradiction is seen in the fact that if the consignee sues the carrier for failing to look after the goods appropriately after they have been discharged from the vessel, the court may have to accept the argument that the liability to look after the goods appropriately under art 3(1) does not extend to the period after the goods have been discharged from the vessel. On the other hand, in the same scenario, the court often permits the carrier to rely on art 4(5) of the Hague-Visby Rules (or the equivalent of the Hague Rules) to claim limited liability if the carrier has to compensate the loss of the consignee. Is there an issue of double standards in dealing with the carrier's liability outside the period of carriage as defined in the Hague-Visby Rules or the Hague Rules?

Bills of lading under the Hamburg Rules

[4.43] The Hamburg Rules expressly define the meaning of bill of lading in art 1(7): see Appendix 2. This definition suggests that a bill of lading has similar functions under the Hamburg Rules as under the Hague-Visby Rules: for example, it evidences the receipt of the goods. Although the Hamburg Rules do not use the expression 'receipt', art 14 requires the carrier, on demand of the shipper, to issue a bill of lading after the carrier has taken the goods into his or her charge. Similarly, under art 16, a bill of lading is prima facie evidence that the carrier has received the goods as described in the bill, unless contrary evidence is established. The details of the Hamburg Rules will be discussed in the relevant sections below.

Issuance of the bill of lading

[4.44] There is no law governing the procedure for the issue of a bill of lading. Generally speaking, the shipper or shipper's agent should provide details of the shipper, notify the party and the goods as requested by the bill of lading concerned, and the carrier or his or her agent (in particular, the master of the ship) should examine the goods and sign the bill of lading after having taken over the goods. The bill of lading signed appropriately by the carrier should be issued to the shipper or his or her agent. Sometimes, a bill of lading may be issued separately from the taking of goods by the shipmaster or an agent of the carrier. For example, the shipper may deliver the goods to the shipmaster, who may issue a mate's receipt; and the shipper may exchange the mate's receipt for a formal bill of lading later on by presenting the mate's receipt to the carrier or the agent of the carrier. Sometimes, an arrangement may be made between the parties, under which the shipper delivers the goods to a vessel first and receives a bill of lading later from the carrier or a forwarder.

[4.45] The bill of lading should accurately reflect the condition of the goods. The carrier or his or her agent is not bound to issue a clean bill of lading, or state the goods to be in any particular condition, if he or she has no reasonable means of verifying the goods, but has reasonable ground for believing the existence of an inconsistency between the goods and the information provided by the shipper.

The carrier is not liable for the accuracy of the contents of a container or package if the carrier has expressly disclaimed his or her responsibility for the accuracy of such information in the bill of lading. In *Winkenson Impex Co Ltd v Haverton Shipping Ltd*,[45] the shipper packed and sealed the container allegedly packaged with baby carriers. The carrier noted on the bill of lading the words 'Shippers load and count'. The bill concerned also contained a disclaimer in small print to the effect that the carrier was not responsible for the description of the cargo in the bill of lading and the contents of the container. The container was lost after it was discharged from the vessel and before it arrived at the bonded warehouse for storage. As far as the contents of the container were concerned, the court held that the carrier was not responsible for any claims arising from the accuracy of the contents of the container. Accordingly, the shipper's claim based on the contents of the container failed.

[4.46] Bills of lading issued by different persons may have different effects. For example, a freight forwarder may issue a bill of lading to evidence receipt of the goods by him or her. Such a bill is often called a 'house bill': see *Carrington Slipways Pty Ltd v Patrick Operations Pty Ltd* (1991) 24 NSWLR 745; **[4.51]**. The master of a vessel may issue a bill of lading after the goods have been loaded on board. Such a bill is often called a 'marine bill' or 'ocean bill', or in the words of art 3(7) of the Hague-Visby Rules and art 15(2) of the Hamburg Rules, a 'shipped bill'. A house bill does not prove that the goods concerned have been shipped, but an ocean bill evidences that the goods have been shipped in the conditions stated in the bill. This practical difference between bills issued by different persons should be noted.

Classification of bills of lading

[4.47] Bills of lading can be categorised; however, the differentiations are not necessarily exclusive. Following are some examples of categories of bills of lading.[46]

[4.48] Forwarder's bill: A forwarder's bill of lading is issued by a freight forwarder who can be either a vessel owner, or a broker having no direct control of the vessel at all. 'Forwarder's bill' is a term of convenience and its use has become more and more popular

---

45. [1985] HKLR 141.
46. For relevant discussions, see Schmitthoff, note 41 above, pp 569–82; Burnett, *The Law of International Business Transactions*, Federation Press, Sydney, 1994, pp 74–102; and Todd, *Modern Bills of Lading*, 2nd ed, Blackwell Law, Oxford, 1990, pp 15–16.

[4.48]

in shipping practice.[47] The terminology implies an inherent contradiction: logically, a 'forwarder' receives cargo for the purposes of on-shipment, but a bill of lading usually means that the cargo has already been shipped. Sometimes, a common law court may have difficulties in determining whether a forwarder's bill is a bill of lading under either the Hague Rules or the Hague-Visby Rules, because the forwarder is neither a vessel owner nor a charterer, or alternatively, because the bill is not a shipped bill.

In broad terms, if the forwarder is a vessel owner or a charterer, the bill issued by the forwarder is the same as a bill of lading issued by a carrier. If the forwarder is merely an agent or middle person who assists his or her clients to make shipping arrangements, the bill issued by such person may not be regarded as a bill of lading under the Hague Rules or the Hague-Visby Rules. However, the same bill can be regarded as a bill of lading under the Hamburg Rules.

In cases where a forwarder's bill is involved, the court usually tries to determine the rights and obligations of the parties on the basis of contract, either a contract of carriage or a contract of agency. Accordingly, the general law of contract becomes relevant. For example, in *Troy v The Eastern Company of Warehouses*,[48] the court held that the through bill of lading issued by the forwarder was a contract between the forwarder and the shipper, and thus the forwarder was allowed to keep the prepaid freight even though the shipper took possession of the goods before they reached the original destination. In *Kaleej International Pty Ltd v Gulf Shipping Lines Ltd*,[49] the court held that the forwarder issued the bill of lading on behalf of the vessel owner because the bill contained a statement to such effect.

Sometimes, a court may enforce the bill of lading issued by the forwarder against him or her on the ground that the forwarder has undertaken specified liability as a forwarder under the bill of lading concerned. For example, in *Canusa Systems Ltd v The Vessel Canmar Ambassador*,[50] the combined transport bill of lading expressly stated that the freight forwarder was liable for loss of or damage to the goods occurring when the goods were under control of the forwarder. The goods of heat shrunk tubing were damaged on arrival at Chicago. The court held the forwarder to be liable under the bill of lading to the consignor and consignee, while the court accepted that the forwarder might have a cause of action against the vessel owner and charterer who performed the carriage concerned.

In summary, it can be concluded that a forwarder's bill of lading is not technically a category of bill of lading in law, at least in jurisdictions which are members of the Hague Rules or the Hague-Visby Rules. A forwarder's bill is regarded as a bill of lading (instead of a forwarder's bill) in jurisdictions which have ratified the Hamburg Rules.

In the jurisdictions adopting the Hague Rules or the Hague-Visby Rules, the forwarder's bill is dealt with on a case-by-case basis. The forwarder may thus be held liable as a carrier, an independent contractor or an agent of the carrier, as the case may be.

---

47. For a detailed discussion, see Mo, 'Forwarder's Bill and Bill of Lading' (1997) vol 2 *Asia Pacific Law Review*, pp 96–110.
48. [1921] 8 Ll L Rep 17.
49. (1986) 6 NSWLR 569 (Sup Court of NSW).
50. Decided on 16 February 1998 by the Federal Court of Canada, available at <http://www.fja-cmf.gc.ca>.

A forwarder may often act as the agent of the shipper or the carrier. In such cases, the disclosure of the true identity of the principal may or may not be crucial for the forwarder relying on the agent–principal relationship as a defence, depending on the domestic law concerned.[51] However, if a bill of lading has been issued by the forwarder in whatever capacity, the forwarder cannot be held to have acted as the agent of the shipper in issuing the bill of lading to the shipper.[52] On the other hand, if a forwarder has procured a bill of lading on behalf of the shipper from the carrier, the forwarder may be not allowed to sue the carrier as the shipper because he or she only acts as an agent of the shipper.[53]

[4.49] **House or received bills:** A 'house bill' can be issued by a freight forwarder (or forwarding agent) or an agent of the carrier. Sometimes, it can be issued by the carrier who will later on carry the goods by his or her own vessel. It evidences that the goods have been received by the freight forwarder or the agent and will be forwarded to the vessel as agreed. Similarly, if the goods have been delivered to a carrier or his or her agent, he or she may issue a 'received bill', which means that the goods have been received for shipment. There is no legal distinction between a 'house bill' and a 'received bill'. Indeed, the expressions were used interchangeably by Handley JA in *Carrington Slipways v Patrick Operations* (1991) 24 NSWLR 745 at 752–3. A house or received bill does not prove that the goods have been loaded on board a vessel. This is the fundamental difference between a 'house (or received) bill' and an 'ocean (or marine/shipped) bill'.

At common law, a 'house bill' is not regarded as a 'bill of lading'. This is because, by definition, a bill of lading is a document issued after the goods have been shipped. However, a house bill or a received bill may become a 'bill of lading' (or a shipped/marine/ocean bill) by the indorsement of the carrier after the goods have been shipped. Article 3(7) of the Hague-Visby Rules and art 15(2) of the Hamburg Rules grant the carrier or his or her agent an option to indorse on a previously issued 'document of title' (such as a house or received bill) the detail of the shipment, and turn the document into a 'shipped bill'. This means that a house or received bill may become a 'bill of lading' through the indorsement of the carrier or his or her agent who has shipped the goods.

---

51. For example, in *Chartwell Shipping Ltd v QNS Paper Co Ltd* [1989] 2 SCR 683, the Superior Court of Quebec decided that it was not necessary for the agent to disclose the identity of the principal if the agent intended to claim to be an agent. The Court of Appeal of Quebec reserved the decision. The Supreme Court of Canada reinstated the decision of the Superior Court of Quebec.
52. For example, in *Kanematsu Gmbh v Acadia Shipbrokers Ltd and Seanav International Ltd*, decided on 18 February 1999 available at <http://www.fja-cmf.gc.ca>, Seagual Maritime Ltd of Piraeus was the agent of Ironimpex which was both the voyage charterer and the shipper. It issued a number of bills of lading on behalf of the vessel owners to Ironimpex. The court held the vessel owners to be liable as the carrier under the bills of lading concerned. Thus, the forwarder in such circumstances is held to be the agent of the carrier, not the shipper.
53. In *Freight Systems Ltd v Korea Shipping Corp*, (CL No 174 of 1988, 21 November 1990, High Court of Hong Kong, unreported), the plaintiff, a freight forwarder, compensated part of the loss sustained by a cargo of mushrooms carried from Hong Kong to Seattle and then sued the carrier under the bill of lading, which described the shipper as 'Freight Systems Ltd o/b of the cargo owner'. It was agreed that o/b stands for 'on behalf of'. The court held that the bill of lading suggested the forwarder to be the agent of the shipper, but not the shipper. The forwarder's action against the carrier failed.

[4.50] International Commercial Law

[4.50] Shipped or ocean (marine) bills: A shipped bill is often issued by the master of a vessel. It evidences that the goods have been received and loaded on board the vessel in the condition stated in the bill. It may be either clean or claused, or negotiable or non-negotiable, but it must prove that the goods have been shipped. This characteristic of the shipped bill distinguishes it from a house or received bill. A 'shipped bill' can also be called a 'marine or ocean bill'.

♦

[4.51] *Carrington Slipways Pty Ltd v Patrick Operations Pty Ltd*

(1991) 24 NSWLR 745

Distinction between a 'house bill' and an 'ocean bill'

Facts: Carrington Slipways, the plaintiff and appellant, was the purchaser of two Daihatsu diesel engines from Nissho Iwai Corp in Japan. Patrick Operations, co-defendant and respondent, was the stevedoring company, which negligently damaged one of the engines in the process of unloading. Two bills of lading were issued with respect to the same engines. The first was issued by Pacific East Asian Container Express Line, which was controlled by Pacific Australia Pty Ltd, the forwarding agent acting on behalf of the plaintiff to transport the engines to Australia. This bill was signed by the Japanese agent of Pacific Australia and was called the Peace Line bill in this case. But the Pacific East Asian Container Express Line did not carry the engines to Australia. Instead, the Japanese agent of Pacific Australia engaged the time charterer (a charterer who charters a vessel on the basis of time, as opposed to a voyage charter) Simsmetal, to carry the engines to Sydney.

Hong Kong and Eastern (Japan) Ltd, which is a subsidiary of Simsmetal, issued a bill of lading to the Japanese agent of Pacific Australia. This bill was called the Simsmetal bill. Both bills contained the Himalaya clause (see **[4.116]–[4.122]**), which limits the liability of any persons engaged by the carrier for performing the contract of carriage to the same extent as the carrier's liability. But Carrington Slipways did not know of the existence of the Simsmetal bill until the occurrence of the dispute, because it paid the price of the engines on the basis of the Peace Line bill. The trial judge allowed the stevedoring company to rely on the Himalaya clause in the Peace Line bill. The plaintiff appealed against this decision. The stevedoring company then sought to rely on the Simsmetal bill. The Court of Appeal of the Supreme Court of New South Wales had to determine which bill applied.

Decision: The court unanimously decided that the stevedoring company was entitled to rely on the Himalaya clause in the Simsmetal bill, because it is a shipped or ocean bill.

Handley JA observed as follows:

<751> [The Peace Line bill is not related to the actual carriage of the engines, because the issuer of the Peace Line bill was not directly involved in the carriage.[1]] Pacific [Pacific East Asian Container Express Line] neither owned nor operated the 'Cape Comorin' [which carried the engines] nor had it contracted for its services by time charter [because Simsmetal's services were engaged by the Japanese agent of Pacific Australia, rather than by the Pacific]. Pacific by issuing the Peace Line bill had not secured space on the vessel, or obtained a bill of lading which would enable the appellant to clear the goods in Sydney.

...

A document is not a bill of lading merely because that is what the parties have called it.

<752> In my opinion, the Peace Line bill was not a bill of lading, and in particular was not an on board ocean bill. It is not within the definition of a bill of lading contained in Scrutton [*Scrutton on Charterparties and Bills of Lading* (19th ed, London, Sweet and Maxwell, 1984)], *Swell v Burdick* [(1884) 10 App Cas 74], or in *The Ship 'Marlborough Hill'* [[1921] 1 AC 444].

<753> ... The Peace Line bill, on its face, was an ocean bill. It was a house bill in fact but its true character was concealed. Nevertheless I have derived considerable assistance from the statement by the editor of the 19th edition of Scrutton (at 384):

> 'A "house bill of lading" issued by a forwarding agent acting solely in the capacity of an agent to arrange carriage is not a bill of lading at all, but at most a receipt for the goods coupled with an authority to enter into a contract of carriage on behalf of the shipper. It is not a document of title, nor within the Bills of Lading Act, 1855, and it is unlikely that it would ever be regarded as a good tender under a CIF contract.'

1. In this analysis, his Honour distinguished the parties involved on the basis of their corporate identity, even though Pacific Australia controlled Pacific East Asian Container Express Line (in whose name the Peace Line bill was issued), and Pacific Australia's Japanese agent signed the Peace Line bill and later obtained the Simsmetal bill from Hong Kong and Eastern (Japan) Ltd. In other words, what Pacific Australia did in this case was to instruct its Japanese agent to issue a bill of lading on behalf of a carrier controlled by it, but then engaged the services of another carrier to carry the engines.

♦

[4.52] Clean or claused bills: After goods have been shipped or loaded on board a vessel the shipper can ask the carrier, the master of the vessel, or other agent of the carrier (if relevant), to issue a shipped/marine/ocean bill. This may be either a 'clean bill' or a 'claused bill'. A 'clean bill' is a bill which states that the goods have been shipped in good condition and order. A 'claused bill' is one which states that the goods have been shipped with noted defects or damages in goods or package. Article 3(3) of the Hague-Visby Rules and art 16 of the Hamburg Rules allow a carrier to issue either a clean bill or a claused bill to reflect the true condition of the goods shipped.

[4.53] Negotiable or non-negotiable bills: A bill of lading is a document of title. As a document of title, it should be transferable or negotiable. The negotiability of the bill of lading facilitates commercial transactions. This is why s 50A of the Sale of Goods Act 1923 (NSW) and s 73 of the Goods Act 1958 (Vic) provide that a consignee of a bill has the same right and liability as the consignor of the bill; and s 66 of the Goods Act 1958 (Vic) allows a third party who obtains a bill of lading to have a good title in relation to the goods covered under the bill, provided that the third party is bona fide for value.

The negotiability of a bill of lading is determined in a similar way as the negotiability of a normal negotiable instrument (such as a cheque or a bill of exchange).[54] Common law treats a bill of lading as a contract and a document of title. As a contract, the negotiability of a bill of lading is determined under the bill's terms.

For example, if a bill specifies the name of a consignee, the specified consignee will be the person who is entitled to receive the goods from the carrier. On the other hand, if the bill of lading allows the holder of the bill or a person indorsed by the shipper or consignee (for example, with the words 'by order of the consignee') to claim the goods, the bill is negotiable.[55] Thus, in *BHP Trading Asia Ltd v Oceaname*

---

54. Schmitthoff opines that the negotiability of a bill of lading is much narrower than that of a bill of exchange. See note 41 above, pp 572–3.
55. Certain bills of lading are negotiable by the intention shown in the bills. For example, a sample bill of lading collected in Wilson, note 43 above, pp 446–55, contains a definition of 'holder' which suggests that the bill is meant to be negotiable unless a contrary intention is expressed in the bill.

Shipping Ltd,[56] Hill J at para 55 of the judgment stated there must be something on the face of the bill which indicates that the bill is transferable before it will be correct to treat the bill as negotiable. As a document of title, the negotiability of a bill of lading improves commercial expediency, although a bill of lading does not require the same degree of negotiability as a bill of exchange for fulfilling its role in commercial transactions.

The negotiability of a bill of lading has been accepted in s 50A of the Sale of Goods Act 1923 (NSW) and s 73 of the Goods Act 1958 (Vic), which appear to have given a presumed negotiability to a bill of lading, unless a contrary intention is shown in the bill. Similarly, art 1(7) of the Hamburg Rules also envisages the negotiability of a bill of lading. This provision states that one of the basic features of a bill of lading is that the carrier undertakes to deliver the goods to 'the order of a named person, or to order, or to bearer'.

The negotiability of a bill of lading should be ascertained in the terms of the bill,[57] although a bill may not be prima facie negotiable in the same sense as a bill of exchange.[58]

[4.54] Charterparty bills of lading: This expression refers to a bill of lading issued pursuant to a charterparty, or a bill which has incorporated the terms of a charterparty. 'Charterparty' means a contract for the hire of a ship made between a shipowner and a charterer: see **[4.61]**. A charterparty bill is issued by the shipowner or his or her agent in the case of a time or voyage charter,[59] and by a charterer in the case of a demise or bareboat charter: see **[4.61]**. A shipowner under a time or voyage charter may incorporate some or all of the terms of the charterparty into the bill of lading issued while the ship is under the charterparty to restrict his or her liability to the shipper to the same extent as defined in the charterparty.

On the other hand, a charterer may for some reason issue a bill of lading which may subject the vessel owner to certain liability or risk which has not been set out in the charterparty between the vessel owner and charterer. In such cases, the court may impose an implied undertaking upon the charterer to indemnify the vessel owner for the loss arising from such inconsistency between the terms of the charterparty and the bill of lading concerned.[60] If a charterer does not wish to take any responsibility for the carriage done by the vessel owner or another charterer, he or she may perhaps expressly disclaim all liabilities in the bill of lading concerned. In *Mitsui & Co Ltd v Gold Star Line Ltd*,[61] the time charterer issued a bill of lading which contained a clause stating that a charterer who

---

56. Decided on 24 April 1996 by the Federal Court of Australia, available at <http://www.austlii.edu.au>.
57. For example, the sample of a 'Common Short Form Bill of Lading' in Wilson, note 43 above, pp 456–9, bears the words 'Consignee (if "order" state Notify Party and Address)', implying the negotiability of the bill; and the sample of 'Non-Negotiable Sea Waybill' in Wilson, note 43 above, pp 464–7, makes it clear that the bill is non-negotiable by its title. It must be pointed out that a 'sea waybill', by definition, is treated as a form of non-negotiable document: see **[4.55]**.
58. While it might be that the negotiability of a bill of lading is not as wide as that of a bill of exchange, it is submitted that Schmitthoff's commentary on negotiability (see note 41 above, pp 572–3) is too dogmatic to illustrate the true state of affairs in respect of bills of lading.
59. For example, in *Hi-Fert Pty Ltd v United Shipping Adriatic Inc* [1998] FCA 1622, the shipmaster issued a bill of lading on behalf of the shipowner while the ship was under a voyage charterparty.
60. For example, *The 'Nogar Marin'* [1987] 1 Lloyd's Rep 456.
61. [1975] HKLR 74.

was neither the vessel owner nor the demise charterer issued the bill of lading as the agent for the vessel owner or the demise charterer only. The court held that the clause was effective to exclude the time charterer from any action against the carrier under the bill of lading concerned. The same technique may be employed by any charterer who issues a bill of lading on behalf of the party actually carrying the goods concerned. For comparison, in *Berdero Price (Malaysia) Sdn Bhd v Scheepvaartonderneming Leidsegracht CV* [2000] WASC 263, the court held that the defendants, who signed a sea-freighting contract with the shipper on 9 May 1996, was liable for the damages to the cargo under the two bills of lading dated 28 May 1996, even though the defendants chartered the vessel concerned from the shipowner under a charterparty on 14 May 1996. In the present case, the court considered the shipowner to be the subcontractor of the defendants who had presented themselves as the carriers to the shipper, and thus excluded the operation of the charterparty. The fact that parties to the bill of lading and the charterparty concerned are different is one of the major reasons for the court to give priority to the terms of the bills of lading in dispute.[62] It was not clear, however, who appeared as the 'carrier' in the two bills of lading in dispute, because the charterparty appeared to be a voyage charterparty and in such cases the bills of lading might have been issued by the shipowner. If so, the case should have perhaps been examined from this perspective.

Traditional banking practice has been to refuse to accept a charterparty bill as good tender unless the bank is instructed otherwise.[63] This was reflected in the language of the ICC 1983 Uniform Customs and Practice for Documentary Credits (UCP 400). For example, art 25(c) of UCP 400 provided that unless 'otherwise stipulated in the credit in the case of carriage by sea' banks will reject a charterparty bill. This practice continues today, but it has been relaxed. This change is seen in the ICC 1993 Uniform Customs and Practice for Documentary Credits (UCP 500), art 26 of which states that if 'a Credit calls for or permits a charter party bill of lading, banks will, unless otherwise stipulated in the Credit' accept a charterparty bill. The difference between the two compatible provisions is important. Under UCP 400, a bank will reject a charterparty unless expressly authorised to accept it. However, under UCP 500 a bank may infer a 'call for or permission of' the acceptance of a charterparty bill from a credit and accept the bill accordingly, unless the credit expressly prohibits so doing. This difference reflects present commercial practice. It implies that the traditional attitude to a charterparty bill has not been abandoned, but has definitely been softened.

The inconsistency between the terms of the charterparty and the relevant bill of lading and the implications arising from the inconsistency have always been an issue for lawyers and courts across the world. Besides the extra liability the vessel owner may be facing, there may be some other implications arising from such inconsistency. For example, in *President of India v Metcalfe Shipping Co* [1969] 2 All ER 1549 (CA), the court held that the charterparty governed the relationship between the shipowners and the charterers who had also taken the goods as indorsee of the bill of lading.

---

62. A similar line of reasoning was also followed in *The Ship 'Socofl Stream' v CMC* [2001] FCA 961.
63. For example, see Schmitthoff, note see note 41 above, p 574; and Todd, *Contracts for the Carriage of Goods by Sea*, BSP Professional Books, Oxford, 1988, p 187.

[4.54]

This means that as far as the relationship is concerned, the charterparty prevails. The same logic was applied in *Siderurgica Mendes Junior SA and Mitsui & Co v The Owners of Icepearl*, decided on 31 January 1996, in the Supreme Court of British Columbia.[64] In this case, the parties had a charterparty, which contained an arbitration clause to submit all disputes between them to an arbitrator in New York. But the bill of lading endorsed to Mitsui & Co contained a clause superseding the terms of the charterparty which are relevant to the bill of lading. The court held that the arbitration clause of the charterparty was not superseded by the bill of lading, because the arbitration clause was concerned with a number of aspects which were not covered by the bill of lading. Thus, the court enforced the arbitration clause in the charterparty. This case reflects to some extent the issues which may arise from the inconsistency between a charterparty, on the one hand, and the bill of lading issued by or to a party to that charterparty, on the other.

[4.55] Non-negotiable sea waybills: These bills form a special category of bill of lading. The word 'waybill' refers to a non-negotiable receipt, which is issued to the consignor to prove the receipt of goods by the carrier in the condition as stated in the bill. The consignor keeps the waybill as his or her evidence of the carriage. The consignee can be notified of the content of the waybill. But he or she only needs to identify him- or herself to the carrier for the purpose of taking delivery of the goods. This is why a 'waybill' is not a document of title. 'These documents were first developed for use in land and air transport in which negotiable documents of title were not required, since the journeys involved were normally so brief that little opportunity was provided for the consignee to sell the goods in transit.'[65] The word 'sea' in front of 'waybill' simply means that the waybill is used in sea carriage.

Since a sea waybill is neither negotiable, nor a document of title, banks have been reluctant to treat it as a 'document' for the purpose of financing international sales. UCP 400 did not have any provision dealing with a non-negotiable sea waybill. This has been changed by art 24 of UCP 500, which provides that if 'a Credit calls for a non-negotiable sea waybill covering a port-to-port shipment, banks will, unless otherwise stipulated in the Credit', accept a non-negotiable sea waybill. A sea waybill under art 24 is not a document of title, but a document which evidences the terms of the contract of carriage between the consignor and the carrier, the receipt of the goods, the condition of the goods and details for delivery of the goods.

Article 24 requires a sea waybill to provide sufficient detail about time and place of loading the goods onto the vessel and of delivering them to the consignee. Under this provision, a sea waybill must be a shipped bill, which means that the goods covered under the waybill must have been loaded on board a named ship. This provision also requires the consignor to provide either the sole copy or the full set of the sea waybill, as the case may be. In addition, an acceptable sea waybill must not be a charterparty bill, nor a bill which suggests that 'the carrying vessel is propelled by sail only'. These conditions must be satisfied before a bank can treat a sea waybill as a 'document' under art 24 of UCP 500.

---

64. Available at <http://www.courts.gov.bc.ca>.
65. Wilson, note 43 above, p 163.

[4.56] Through bills of lading: This expression refers to bills of lading which may involve the carriage of goods either by several carriers or several modes of transport. In other words, a 'through bill of lading' means the carrier issues a bill of lading to the shipper and undertakes to deliver the goods at the agreed destination, regardless of whether or not the carrier has to engage the services of other carriers for the purpose of carrying the goods to that destination.

Through bills of lading may sometimes be similar to forwarder's bills of lading where the forwarder undertakes to carry the goods to the agreed destination by employing the service of one or more actual carriers. The two types of bills of lading have different emphasis. The through bill bears the characteristic that the carriage involves several sub-carriages, but the forwarder's bill emphasises the aspect that the bill is issued by a forwarder, who may carry the cargo him- or herself, or contract someone else to carry the goods concerned. 'Through' in this context means that 'throughout' the process of transporting the goods, there is only one bill of lading as far as the shipper or the consignee is concerned. This process of carriage can be compared with a contract where the contractor has to engage the services of sub-contractors for the purpose of performing his or her contractual obligations. The liability of each carrier under the bill should be ascertained under the general principles of contract, unless statute, conventions (such as the Hague Rules, the Hague-Visby Rules or the Hamburg Rules) or customs state otherwise.

The definitions of 'carrier' and 'actual carrier' under art 1 of the Hamburg Rules are relevant to a through bill of lading. The shipper under a through bill of lading is able to hold the carrier liable for any damage to the goods caused by the act or omission of any sub-carriers engaged by the carrier. However, the responsibilities of the carrier and the sub-carriers (if applicable) under the Hague-Visby Rules will have to be dealt with under arts 3 and 4, which set out the liabilities of the carrier and his or her agents and exceptions to, or limitations of, the liabilities.

[4.57] *The Anders Maersk*

[1986] 1 Lloyd's Rep 483

Liability of a carrier for damages caused by a sub-carrier under a through bill

Facts: The shippers engaged the services of the carrier to ship two large steam boilers from Baltimore, United States, to Shanghai, China, in 1981 under a through bill of lading. The boilers had to be transhipped in Hong Kong, which was arranged by the carrier. The ship carrying the boilers from Hong Kong to Shanghai encountered heavy weather. One boiler fell into the sea and the other was damaged. The through bill incorporated the Carriage of Goods by Sea Act 1936 (US) (COGSA). This Act limited the liability of the carrier to $US500 per package. The holders of the bill of lading argued that the boilers were transhipped in Hong Kong and accordingly, the Carriage of Goods by Sea (Hong Kong) Order 1508 of 1980 was applicable. This Order gave effect to the Hague-Visby Rules. The holders of the bill argued that they were entitled to recover substantial damages under the Hague-Visby Rules.

Decision: Mayo J of the High Court of Hong Kong, being aware that there had been no precedent in Hong Kong and the United States on the legal issue in dispute since the introduction of the Hague-Visby Rules (at 485), held that COGSA governed the through bill of lading.

[4.57]   UCP 500 sets out special rules for dealing with a through bill of lading, found in arts 23 and 24. Article 23 deals with marine/ocean bills; art 24 deals with non-negotiable sea waybills. Both provisions contain the same rules dealing with a situation where a through bill is involved. These provisions allow a bank to accept a through bill which involves transhipment unless the credit concerned specifies otherwise. They even allow a bank to accept a through bill involving transhipment regardless of the instruction in the credit, under the conditions that the goods are shipped in a container or by similar means, or that the carrier has the right to determine transhipment under the contract of carriage.

[4.58]   Liner bills of lading: This expression refers to the standard bills used by a liner, who is a shipowner or a charterer providing regular services of carriage by sea. The term does not have any legal implication unless it indicates that the bills are those used in liner trade or by a liner. In commercial practices, a 'liner bill of lading' usually represents the common conditions and terms for carriage by a liner in a particular country or place. This will be taken into account in the construction of the terms of a liner bill.

[4.59]   Electronic bills of lading: 'Electronic bill of lading' describes a type of bill of lading based on computer or electronic technology, such as Electronic Data Interchange (EDI, which is an acceptable form of documentation under Incoterms 2000). Since an electronic bill of lading is based on computer technology, its use as a document of title raises many legal issues (none of which arises in the case of written bills of lading), such as: the form in which an electronic bill exists and is transferred, the identity of the issuer or consignor, and the authenticity of the message.

These issues are yet to be thoroughly explored and satisfactorily resolved. The International Maritime Committee (CMI) proposed the Rules for Electronic Bills of Lading in 1990, which can be used by agreement of the parties.[66] At present, the use of electronic bills of lading is still limited. However, this form of communication will receive wider recognition in the future: such change can be seen in the use of various electronic banking programs in international banking today.[67] This is why Incoterms 2000 accepts electronic messages as a form of documentation where applicable. Electronic bills of lading are also envisaged by art 14(3) of the Hamburg Rules, which allows the signature on a bill to be made by mechanical or electronic means.[68]

Bills of lading and charterparty

[4.60]   Attention should be drawn to the distinction between a bill of lading and a charterparty. As we have seen, a bill of lading is a document of title, which allows a holder or specified person to claim the goods described in the bill from the carrier issuing it.

---

66. For discussion, see Burnett, note 46 above, pp 84–90, and Kelly, 'The CMI Charts a Course on the Sea of Electronic Data Interchange: Rules for Electronic Bills of Lading' (1992) vol 16 *Tulane Maritime Law Journal*, p 349.
67. For example, see Busto (ed), *Funds Transfer in International Banking*, ICC Publishing SA, Paris, 1992; and Kozolchyk, 'Evolution and Present State of the Ocean Bills of Lading from a Banking Law Perspective' (1992) 23 *Journal of Maritime Law and Commerce*, p 161.
68. Although art 14(3) deals with 'signature' only, it can be argued that in the absence of any requirement for the formality of a bill of lading under the Hamburg Rules, art 14(3) implies that a bill of lading can be made in an electronic form.

A charterparty, in brief, is a contract for the hire of a vessel for a specified period of time or a specified voyage.

[4.61] The main types of charterparty are as follows:[69]

- a demise or bareboat charterparty refers to an arrangement under which the charterer leases or hires a ship completely for an agreed period of time or an agreed voyage, while acting in the capacity of the owner to third parties during the period of charterparty;
- a voyage charterparty refers to an arrangement under which a charterer hires a ship for a specified voyage, but the shipowner is entitled to control the ship and is responsible for supplying and equipping the ship; and
- a time charterparty refers to an arrangement under which the charterer hires a ship for a specified period of time, but the shipowner is entitled to control the ship and is responsible for supplying and equipping the ship.

The differences between these three types of charterparty relate to two issues: the responsibility of the shipowner and the basis of the charterparty. The shipowner is not involved in the operation of a ship under a demise or bareboat charterparty, but is responsible for it under a time or voyage charterparty. Depending on the terms of a contract of carriage, a shipowner under a time or voyage charterparty may be found liable for unseaworthiness of the ship. As the terms imply, the elements of 'time' and 'voyage' form the basis of distinction between a time charterparty and a voyage charterparty.

A slot charterparty has become more and more common in shipping practice. It refers to a charterparty for hiring part of the vessel, which is usually under another charterparty, probably a voyage charterparty. Slot charterparties are the result of commercial reality, and the need for flexibility. For practical reasons, many shipping companies need to charter vessels from other companies during a particular period of time or for a specific purpose. The demand for and supply of a vessel or some space on the vessel are often matched by intermediate parties playing the double role of charterer and lessor in relation to the different arrangements concerning the same vessel.

A party may charter a vessel under a demise charterparty from the vessel owner, and later lease to another party under a time or voyage charterparty. The time charterer or the voyage charterer may in turn lease the vessel to another party under a voyage charterparty, who may in turn lease part of the vessel under a slot charterparty to another party, who may or may not act as a carrier during the duration of the slot charterparty. This is the commercial reality and in fact, charterparty has become a business for many companies which have the resources and connections in matching the demand and supply in a particular place and specific time.

[4.62] A charterparty is not subject to the Hague-Visby Rules or the Hamburg Rules, because it is not a 'bill of lading' as defined in the conventions. However, parties to a charterparty may expressly incorporate the Hague Rules, the Hague-Visby Rules or the Hamburg Rules, or any other laws and customs into the charterparty to make them part

---

69. For a discussion, see Butler and Duncan, *Maritime Law in Australia*, Legal Books, Sydney, 1992, p 131.

of the contract for the hire of the vessel when necessary. Bills of lading are issued while the ship is under a charterparty. If a bill so issued incorporates part or all of the terms of the charterparty, it is called a 'charterparty bill of lading': see **[4.54]**.

[4.63] *Kanematsu Gmbh v Acadia Shipbrokers Ltd and Seanav International Ltd*

18 February 1999, Federal Court of Canada, <http://www.fja-cmf.gc.ca>

The vessel owner released the cargo without presentation of a bill of lading, but under the letter of indemnity offered by the charterers; carriage involved several charterparties in a chain transaction

Facts: Kanematsu was the cargo owner and the holder of the bills of lading issued by the cargo-owner. The first defendant (Acadia) was the time charterer. The second defendant (Seanav) time chartered the vessel which had a Maltese flag from Acadia, and let it under a voyage charterparty to Ironimpex of Basel, Switzerland. Ironimpex sold the cargoes concerned to Kanematsu.

The bills of lading were issued by Ironimpex's agent (not the defendant's agent) on behalf of the vessel owners to Ironimpex. The cargoes consisted of 6,368,200 t of steel billets carried from Odessa to Thailand and India in 1995. Nicco in Bangkok was nominated as the notify addressee in two of the bills of lading. Nicco did not have the bills of lading for taking delivery of the cargoes concerned. The first and second defendants obtained a letter of indemnity from Ironimpex, which was the voyage charterer and the nominated shipper of the bills of lading, and offered their own letters of indemnity to the vessel owner and asked the vessel owners to release the cargoes without bills of lading to Nicco, which had also offered a letter of indemnity to the vessel owner.

The vessel owners released the cargoes as requested, but Kanematsu was the holder of the two bills of lading covering the cargoes released. It appeared that Kanematsu sued the Maltese vessel owner at the Maltese court and sued the two defendants at the Federal Court of Canada on the ground that the defendants had induced the vessel owner to release the cargoes concerned without the bills of lading. The defendants did not argue that they were not the carriers. Instead, they built their defence on the ground that Kanematsu had acquiesced in Nicco's ownership of the cargoes in question.

Decision: The court delivered a summary judgment in favour of Kanematsu. The judgment of the court appeared to be largely based on the proposition that the defendants were the carriers and issued the bills of lading concerned as the vessel owners. Thus, the defendants must be liable to Kanematsu, who was the holder of the two bills of lading covering the cargoes delivered without the bills.

This finding of the court appears to be questionable given that the shipmaster and staff were obviously employed by the Maltese vessel owner. If this finding of the court was unsound, the court also found that the defendants had induced the vessel owners to release the cargoes in question without requiring the presentation of the bills of lading held by Kanematsu. Thus, on either ground, the defendants were liable as charged. Even relying on the second ground, the court placed a heavy emphasis on the general rule that the carrier is obliged to deliver the cargo to the legitimate holder of the bill of lading as set out in *Sze Hai Tong Bank Ltd v Rambler Cycle Co Ltd* [1959] AC 576 (HL) per Lord Denning at 586; and *Barclays Bank Ltd v Customs and Excise* (1963) 11 Lloyd's Rep 81 (QBD), per Lord Diplock, at 88–9.

Bills of lading and mate's receipts

[4.64] A mate's receipt is an acknowledgement issued by the carrier or his or her agent, before the issue of a bill of lading, to evidence the receipt of the goods by the carrier or his or her agent. For example, when the goods have been delivered to a dock but cannot be loaded onto a ship immediately, the carrier or his or her agent may issue a receipt to the shipper to evidence the receipt of the goods and their condition at the time of receipt. A mate's receipt is not usually regarded as a document of title in an international sale, although the expression 'document of title to goods' as defined under s 65(1) of the Goods Act 1958 (Vic) seems to apply to a mate's receipt. The mate's receipt entitles the holder to receive a bill of lading which, unless contrary evidence is available, states the quantity and condition of the goods in the same way as the mate's receipt.[70]

[4.65] *The Dona Mari*

[1973] 2 Lloyd's Rep 366

Discrepancy between the mate's receipt and the bill of lading in relation to the condition of the goods

Facts: The consignee was the buyer of broken tapioca roots under a CIF contract from the seller in Thailand. Under the CIF contract, the seller was responsible for making the contract of carriage. The seller delivered two lots of tapioca roots for shipment to the carrier, who issued two mate's receipts. The mate's receipts stated the condition of the goods as 'not quite dry' and 'not quite dried'. But the two bills of lading issued subsequently stated the condition of the goods as 'shipped in good order and condition'. The consignee accepted the bills of lading and other documents, including two inspection certificates which also indicated the moisture content of the tapioca roots. On arrival, the tapioca roots were found to have been damaged because they had been shipped in a moist condition. The consignee claimed damages against the carrier, who, however, argued that the damage was caused by the pre-shipment condition.

Decision: Kerr J of the Queen's Bench (Commercial Court) held that the carrier was estopped by the statement of the bills of lading that the goods were shipped in good order and condition, because the consignee relied on that statement in accepting the shipping documents. His Honour was of the opinion that the mate's receipts were irrelevant, because the consignee accepted the documents in reliance on the bills of lading. His Honour also held that the inspection certificates which might have suggested the high moisture content of the goods were immaterial, because they formed part of the contract of sale between the consignee and the seller, which was, however, not a concern of the carrier.

Bills of lading and delivery orders

[4.66] A 'delivery order' is a document which is created to deal with a situation where the bill of lading issued does not meet the needs of commercial transactions. For example, a seller (who is also a shipper) may ship the goods in one consignment and later sell them to several buyers. The carrier may issue one bill of lading for the whole consignment.

---

70. For example, see *Nippon Yusen Kaisha v Ramjiban Serowgee* [1938] AC 429; and *The Nogar Marin* [1988] 1 Lloyd's Rep 412.

[4.66]   In this case, the contract of carriage may include a clause which allows the shipper to issue a delivery order to direct the carrier to release part of the goods to the holder of the order. Similarly, a shipper may ship the whole consignment under one bill of lading to his or her agent at the place of discharge and later direct the agent to release the goods as instructed in a delivery order to its holder. In this case, the agent is obliged to honour the delivery order issued by the shipper, because of the existence of the agent–principal relationship. Sometimes a carrier may issue a delivery order as a 'ship's delivery order' and undertake to deliver the goods specified in the order to its holder. This is necessary when, for whatever reasons, the bill of lading issued does not meet the needs of a particular transaction. A delivery order is a supplementary means, added to a bill of lading or contract of sale, which enables the issuer of the order to complete his or her obligations under the relevant contract of carriage or contract of sale.

[4.67]   A bill of lading and a delivery order have differences as well as similarities. A bill of lading evidences the existence of a contract of carriage, but a delivery order represents an entitlement to claim the goods described from the addressee (to whom the delivery order is directed). A delivery order does not evidence a contract of carriage, although it reflects a contractual relationship between the issuer and the beneficiary of the order (the recipient of the goods specified in the order). A bill of lading is issued by a carrier, but a delivery order can be issued by the owner of the goods, who can be either a shipper or a consignee, although if the goods are claimable directly from a carrier the delivery order is usually issued by the carrier. There is no jurisprudential difficulty for any person in possession of the goods to issue delivery orders to specified persons for the purpose of performing his or her contractual obligations relating to the delivery of the goods. A similarity between bills of lading and delivery orders is that they can both be documents of title.[71]

[4.68]   *The Dona Mari*

[1973] 2 Lloyd's Rep 366

A situation where ship's delivery orders were issued

Facts: The facts of this case were discussed in **[4.65]**. In addition to the difference between mate's receipts and bills of lading, this case also illustrates a situation where a delivery order was used by the carrier. The consignee in this case surrendered one of the bills of lading to the carrier in exchange for two delivery orders. He then sold a quantity of tapioca roots under the other bill of lading and one delivery order to a sub-buyer before the shipment arrived. Delivery orders were requested in this case for the convenience of reselling the tapioca roots to another buyer. The tapioca roots were damaged because they had been shipped in a moist condition. Both the consignee and the sub-buyer claimed damages against the carrier.

Decision: Kerr J of the Queen's Bench (Commercial Court) decided as follows.
- The sub-buyer was entitled to sue the carrier for breach of the contract of carriage under the bill of lading; and

---

71. For example, s 65 of the Goods Act 1958 (Vic) treats, inter alia, bills of lading and delivery orders as documents of title.

> - The holders of the ship's delivery orders (both the consignee and the sub-buyer) in this case were entitled to sue the carrier for breach of the contract of carriage, because the relationships between the holders of the delivery orders and the carrier were very much the same as those under the bill of lading.
>
> His Honour examined the effect of a ship's delivery order (at 371–2) and referred particularly to *Brandt v Liverpool, Brazil and River Plate Steamship Navigation Co* [1924] 1 KB 575 (at 371).

Bill of lading and fraud

[4.69] Fraud is one of the issues relating to the carrier's liability arising from a bill of lading. In practice, a bill of lading may be backdated to meet the request of a shipper who must show the shipment of a cargo before a specified date under a documentary credit for the purpose of negotiating the credit. Sometimes a bill of lading may be changed after it is issued for whatever purpose deemed necessary by the party (who may be the carrier, forwarder or the holder of the bill) making the change. Use of a forged bill of lading to negotiate payment under a documentary credit is not unheard of.[72] So is the claim of delivery without presentation of the full set of the bill of lading. The common law has not established uniform standards for determining the existence of a fraud, although the fraudulent act and intention to defraud someone are considered to be essential for ascertaining the existence of a fraud.

[4.70] In *Pacific Composites Pty Ltd, Lermarne Corp Ltd v Blue Anchor Line, ANL Ltd & United Arab Shipping Co* [1997] FCA 576, the plaintiff alleged that the carrier committed a fraud when its employee changed the statement of the bill of lading after the bill was issued. Commenting on the establishment of a fraud under Australian law, Tamberlin J of the Federal Court stated as follows:

> There was no evidence that Ms Yang, the person who amended the Blue Anchor Line Bill, had any fraudulent intent. There may be some possibility of a negligence claim arising on the material but the evidence does not rise to a level capable of supporting an allegation of fraud. The mere fact of alteration to the Bill after discussion with a representative of Sunkyong is not of itself indicative of fraud. As pointed out by counsel for Blue Anchor, Sunkyong is the shipper nominated in the Bill and might reasonably have been expected by Ms Yang to have known the details of the storage including the type of container.

[4.71] This observation reflects certain important features of fraud, such as the intent and the circumstances in which the alleged fraud is committed.

[4.72] Sometimes, a dispute involving an alleged fraud may be resolved without a determination on the issue of fraud. In *Westwood Shipping Lines v Geo International*,[73] the notify party under a bill of lading obtained goods from the carrier by misrepresenting that the original bills of lading had been surrendered by the shipper. The shipper who was the holder of the original bills of lading sued the carrier and won. The carrier sued the notify party for fraudulent misrepresentation. The court found the notify party's act of taking

---

72. For example, several cases involving the use of a forged bill of lading to defraud the buyer payment under a documentary credit are reported in Yuchui Meng and Zhenyi Chen, *Maritime Fraud and Legal Remedies* (in Chinese), Beijing, People's Court Press, 1999, pp 365–411.
73. 24 June 1998, No T-359-98, FCTD; available at <http://www.admiraltylaw.com>.

over the goods without payment to the shipper amounted to conversion. The dispute was resolved without determining the issue of fraud.

Carrier's liabilities under the Hague-Visby Rules

Carrier's liability and the meaning of 'carriage of goods'

[4.73] Under the Hague-Visby Rules, a carrier is liable for the risk arising from the 'carriage of goods'. The expression 'carriage of goods' is defined in art 1(e) of the Hague-Visby Rules. It refers to the period of time in which goods are carried by a carrier. The period (the carriage) commences from 'the time when the goods are loaded on to the time they are discharged from the ship'. Although the definition of carriage of goods in art 1(e) implies that the Hague-Visby Rules intend to limit the carrier's liability under the rules to the period when the goods are on board a vessel, the period of the carrier's liability can also be determined by the terms of the bill of lading or contract of carriage.

[4.74] This is illustrated by *Port Jackson Stevedoring Pty Ltd v Salmond & Spraggon (Australia) Pty Ltd* (1977–1978) 139 CLR 231. In this case, the majority of the High Court (Stephen, Mason, Jacobs and Murphy JJ) held that the terms of the bill of lading suggested that the carrier's liability ceased when the goods passed the ship's rail.

By reading the relevant provisions of the Hague-Visby Rules (or the Hague Rules, as the case may be), and the relevant provisions of a bill of lading, we can argue that the carrier's liability within the period of carriage as defined in the Hague-Visby Rules cannot be reduced by the bill of lading, but can be extended by it. The carrier may be liable for the safety of the goods prior to the loading and after the discharge if the contract of carriage so stipulates. But the liability of the carrier in such a case is defined by the terms of the contract, rather than the provisions of the Hague-Visby Rules, because the Hague-Visby Rules normally cover only the period of time defined as 'carriage of goods'. In conclusion, we may argue that the meaning of 'carriage of goods' in the Hague-Visby Rules implies that the carrier has the benefits and liabilities of the Hague-Visby Rules during the 'carriage of goods' period; but the carrier may have a contractual liability to the goods during the time which is outside the 'carriage of goods'.[74]

---

74. For example, in *F Kanematsu & Co Ltd v The Ship Shahzada* (1956) 96 CLR 477, the cargo-owner sought to hold the carrier liable for the loss arising from the discounted sale of its cargo of cattle hides, which could not be shipped out on time because the vessel carrying the cargo collided with another vessel on its way to leave the harbour. The cargo was unloaded from the vessel after the collision to enable the vessel to be repaired. The cargo-owner decided to sell the cargo locally because it appeared to be in a deteriorated state. Taylor J (HCA) took the view that the matter concerned was governed by the contract or arrangement made between the parties after the unloading of the cargo. Given the lack of evidence to substantiate the cargo-owner's allegation against the carrier, the court dismissed the action. But the case suggests that once the cargo has been unloaded from the vessel for repair or any other reason, the cargo owner enforcing a claim may have to rely on the contractual terms between him or her and the carrier, rather than on the Hague-Visby Rules or the Hague Rules.

> **[4.75]** *Tasman Express Line Ltd v JI Case (Australia) Pty Ltd*
>
> (1992) 111 FLR 108
>
> *A contract clause exempting the carrier from all liability arising from the carriage of cargo on a deck, was upheld*
>
> **Facts:** Tasman Express Line was the carrier, and JI Case (Australia) was the shipper. The parties orally agreed that the cargo of two combine harvesters was to be carried on deck at the shipper's risk from New Zealand to Sydney. This agreement was later inserted into the bill of lading by the order of the trial judge when the matter was being tried at the Admiralty Division of the Supreme Court of New South Wales. The bill of lading contained a clause which stated that the carrier was not liable for any damage to or loss of the goods carried on deck however caused. One of the harvesters was damaged in the process of discharging in Sydney because of the stevedores' negligence. The trial judge held that the method of discharging the machine amounted to a 'deviation' because the method adopted was not the method contemplated and, therefore, the carrier was not entitled to rely on the exclusion clause. The carrier appealed.
>
> **Decision:** The Court of Appeal of the Supreme Court of New South Wales held that the 'deviation' was not established because the method adopted for discharging the machine did not necessarily amount to a radical departure from the carrier's obligation under the bill of lading. Therefore, the carrier was allowed to rely on the exclusion clause.
>
> **Note:** This case suggests the following two points.
> - The Hague Rules and Hague-Visby Rules do not apply to cargo carried on deck by virtue of the definition of 'goods' under the rules;
> - A valid clause excluding the carrier from liabilities in relation to the cargo carried on deck may exempt the carrier from not only the liabilities under the Hague Rules or Hague-Visby Rules, but also contractual or tortious liabilities which are not covered by the Rules.

[4.76] There appears to be a dilemma in the carrier's liability under the bill of lading and the Hague-Visby Rules or the Hague Rules. On the one hand, the carrier's liability to perform the obligations set out in the Hague-Visby Rules or the Hague Rules is largely limited to the period of carriage, that is, the tackle to tackle rule.

For example, in *Nissho Iwai Australia Ltd v Malaysian International Shipping Corp* (1988) 12 NSWLR 730, the trial judge (Yeldham J) decided that the Hague Rules did not apply to the dispute (which involved an alleged misdelivery or non-delivery against the carrier), because the cause of misdelivery or non-delivery had likely taken place after the goods had been discharged from the ship. In other words, it did not occur during the 'carriage of goods' under the Hague Rules (or the Hague-Visby Rules). This finding was affirmed by the Court of Appeal (consisting of Kirby P, Hope and Clarke JJA) of the Supreme Court of New South Wales.

[4.77] On the other hand, the carrier is obliged to deliver the goods in the same state, condition and quantity to the consignee under the bill of lading. This obligation is implied in the Hague-Visby Rules (or the Hague Rules) and the common law in common law jurisdictions. The dilemma is: can a carrier avoid his or her liability to deliver the goods safely to the consignee after the goods have been discharged from the vessel by an exclusion clause in the bill of lading?

[4.78] Exclusion of liability within the period of carriage is prohibited by art 3(8) of the Hague-Visby Rules or the Hague Rules, but exclusion of liability outside the period of carriage may not be caught by the said art 3(8). Sheller JA of the Supreme Court of New South Wales in *Nikolay Malakhov Shipping Co Ltd v SEAS Sapfor Ltd* [1998] NSWSC 65, at 75, observed that art 3(8) arguably made the exclusion clause which provided that the carrier was not liable for damage to the goods 'after the goods leave the ship's deck in discharging port' null and void:

> ... since the carrier's responsibility for discharge of the goods, consistent with its agreement to transport them to the port of discharge there to be delivered, extends to the moment when they cross the ship's rail or are delivered from the ship's tackle, depending upon whether shore tackle or the ship's tackle is used.

In this statement, his Honour brings in a concept of 'shore tackle' to extend the carrier's liability to deliver the goods beyond the ship's tackle. This statement reflects the said dilemma because shore tackle has no basis under the Hague-Visby Rules or the Hague Rules. If we apply the concept of period of carriage strictly as defined in the Hague-Visby Rules or the Hague Rules, the carrier would be able to avoid most liabilities under these rules by excluding or limiting them expressly in the bill of lading after the goods have passed the ship's rail in unloading. If we extend the period of carriage beyond the ship's rail, we are running the risk of violating the principle of the rule of law.

In such a dilemma, the best choice of the consignee appears to be taking over goods immediately after they are discharged from the ship. But, in reality most consignees are unable to do this. The courts of the countries which are members of the Hague Rules or the Hague-Visby Rules have to deal with such dilemmas from time to time. For comparison, the courts of Hamburg Rules members do not have such dilemmas because the Hamburg Rules require the carrier to be liable during the period when the goods are under the carrier's control.

Carrier's liabilities under Article 3

[4.79] The general duty of due diligence: The carrier's responsibilities are set out in art 3(1) of the Hague-Visby Rules. This provision provides the following responsibilities:

- to make the ship seaworthy;[75]
- to staff, equip and supply the ship properly;[76] and
- to make the holds, refrigerating and cool chambers, and all other parts of the ship in which goods are carried, fit for their reception, carriage and preservation.[77]

[4.80] There are two qualifications to the above responsibilities: 'due diligence' and seaworthiness of the ship at the 'commencement of the voyage'. Under the Hague-Visby Rules (and the Hague Rules), a carrier does not have an obligation to make the

---

75. For example, see *Phillips Petroleum Co v Cabaneli Naviera SA (The Theodegmon)* [1990] 1 Lloyd's Rep 52; *Werner v Det Bergenske Dampskibsselskab* (1926) 24 Ll L Rep 75; *Accinanto Ltd v A/S Ludwig Mowinckels* [1951] 2 Lloyd's Rep 285; and *Hellenics Steel Co v Svolamar Shipping Co Ltd ('The Komninos S')* [1990] 1 Lloyd's Rep 541.
76. For example, see *Consolidated Mining v Straits Towing Ltd* [1972] 2 Lloyd's Rep 497 and *The Shipping Corp of India Ltd v Gamlen Chemical Co (A'Asia) Pty Ltd* (1980) 147 CLR 142; (1980) 32 ALR 609.
77. For example, see *The Inowroclaw* [1989] 1 Lloyd's Rep 498.

ship absolutely seaworthy or fit and safe for carrying the goods concerned. He or she, however, has an obligation to exercise 'due diligence' to make the ship seaworthy and fit for carrying the goods concerned. The duty to provide a seaworthy vessel is not discharged merely because of the existence of a certificate of seaworthiness issued by a firm of surveyors.[78] By the same token, the carrier's duty to 'man, equip or supply the ship' properly is not absolute. In addition, the carrier's duty to exercise due diligence to make the ship seaworthy is limited to the 'commencement of the voyage'.[79] These qualifications are necessary because perils at sea can be unavoidable and unpredictable. Therefore, it would be unreasonable and unrealistic to require a shipowner to guarantee the ship to be absolutely seaworthy to stand all perils at sea. The distinction between losses caused by the unseaworthiness of a ship and by perils at sea is illustrated by *Phillips Petroleum Co v Cabaneli Naviera SA (The Theodegmon)* [1990] 1 Lloyd's Rep 52.

[4.81] The carrier's liability under art 3(1) of the Hague-Visby Rules is sometimes mixed and interchangeable. For example, making the vessel fit to carry the goods concerned is one of the obligations to make the vessel seaworthy. On the other hand, it may stand on its own to impose upon the carrier a specific obligation to provide refrigeration to the goods carried, if the contract of carriage or the bill of lading expressly so states. In *Pacific Composites Pty Ltd v Transpac Container System Ltd (t/as Blue Anchor Line)* [1998] FCA 496, the bill of lading expressly stated that the goods were refrigerated, but in fact they were not refrigerated during carriage. The court held that the carrier had breached this clause of the contract, and also its obligation to provide refrigeration under art 3(1) of the Hague-Visby Rules. The carrier was ordered to compensate the cargo-owner under the relevant provision of the Hague-Visby Rules. In this case, the carrier might have also been found to have breached the duty of providing a seaworthy vessel in the circumstances concerned.

[4.82] The seaworthiness of a vessel has wide meanings. A vessel is unseaworthy if it is not fit to carry the particular cargo concerned. A vessel is also unseaworthy if it is not properly manned by a qualified shipmaster and staff. A vessel can be unseaworthy if it is not equipped with an adequate chart for the areas it is meant to sail.

---

78. For example, in *Hi-Fert Pty Ltd v Kiukiang Maritime Carriers Inc* [2000] FCA 660, the defendant carriers obtained a certificate of seaworthiness issued by a firm of surveyors before the loading of the fertiliser in dispute in 1996. The Australian Quarantine Inspection Service found wheat residues in the holds carrying the fertiliser, and refused to allow the fertiliser to be unloaded because the wheat residues contained a quarantined disease known as 'Karnal Bunt'. Accordingly, the court found the defendants liable for the loss suffered by the plaintiff shipper.
79. The expression 'beginning of the voyage' was discussed in *Whybrow v Howard Smith* (1913) 17 CLR 1. In this case, a ship and its cargo were damaged in the process of unmooring and moving out of the harbour. The shipper sued the carrier on the ground of unseaworthiness of the ship. The High Court of Australia was of the opinion that the shipper had failed to prove that the damage occurred (namely the unseaworthiness of the ship existed) before the commencement of the voyage. In other words, the court held that the ship was probably damaged after having commenced the contemplated voyage, even though the ship had likely sustained the damage before it fully disconnected with the mooring place. See also *Smith & Sons v Peninsular & Oriental S N Co* (1938) 60 Ll L Rep 419.

[4.82]

In *The Sanko Steamship Co Ltd and Grandslam Enterprise Corp v Sumitomo Australia Ltd*, No G082 of 1991 Fed No 962/95,[80] Sheppard J held that the plaintiffs' vessel which was sailing on incorrect charts was unseaworthy.

Container shipping has perhaps raised new issues for the carrier's duty to provide a seaworthy vessel. Should a carrier who provides a container also be subject to the duty of seaworthiness — given that a carrier is obliged to ensure that the chamber, or hold of a vessel, is fit to carry the particular cargo concerned? In *Hines Exports Pty Ltd v Mediterranean Shipping Co* [2000] SADC 71, the carrier provided refrigerated containers in March 1995 to carry a cargo of frozen mutton from Australia to South Africa. The cargo of mutton in one of the containers was found to have thawed, and to be unfit for human consumption on arrival, and so was destroyed. The container was found to be unfit for carrying the frozen mutton because its lower door seal was missing and it was in a generally poor condition. The court found that the carrier was negligent in tort in providing a unfit container to the shipper, even though the court eventually refused to grant damage to the shipper on the ground that the shipper had failed to prove its loss. This case raised an interesting question: can the container supplied by the carrier be regarded as 'part' of the carrier's vessel (see art 3(1) of the Hague-Visby Rules) and be governed by the duty of seaworthiness? If this point is pursued, the meaning of 'carriage of goods' under art 1 of the Hague-Visby Rules needs to be reinterpreted.[81] If not, the approach taken in the present case would be one of the possible ways to deal with such disputes arising from container shipping.

[4.83] The carrier's duty to provide a seaworthy ship is not absolute, and is qualified by his or her exercise of due diligence. In *The John Weyerhaeuser* [1975] 2 Lloyd's Rep 439, the carriers were found to have breached this duty. In *Smith & Sons v Peninsular & Oriental S N Co* (1938) 60 Lloyd's List Law Reports 419, the carriers were found to have exercised due diligence in maintaining the ship seaworthy, even though it had sustained water damage because of a broken bolt. This is because the bolt had been maintained before the voyage by reputable ship repairers and it was broken by a water blow during the voyage. However, in the same case, the carriers were found to have failed to exercise due diligence in controlling the water damage during the voyage.

For a lack of want of due diligence, in *The Touraine* (1927) 29 Lloyd's List Law Reports 265, the court found the ship seaworthy, even though sea water, which had unexpectedly got into the vessel through a hole in a waste pipe from the crew's washhouse, had damaged the opossum skins carried on board. Thus, in *Great China Metal Industries Co Ltd v Malaysian International Shipping Corp* [1998] HCA 65, Gaudron, Gummow and Hayne JJ observed (at para 27) that the duty to make the ship seaworthy includes the following three aspects (footnotes edited):

> First, it fixes the time at which the obligation operates as before and at the beginning of the voyage. It therefore resolves the dispute that had been litigated in relation to time policies and voyage policies of marine insurance about whether a warranty of seaworthiness implied in such a policy was a warranty about the condition of the vessel at the time of sailing, or at the commencement of each

---

80. AustLII databases, available at <http://www.austlii.edu.au>.
81. In the present case, the court held that the contract of carriage only began when the cargo was loaded onto the ship.

of several distinct and difference parts of a voyage, or was a warranty extending to the whole of the period of the policy (*Dixon v Sadler* (1839) 5 M & W 405 at 414 151 ER 172; affd (1841) 8 M & W 895, 151 ER 1303; and *Gibson v Small* (1853) 4 HLC 353, 10 ER 499). Secondly, it is not an absolute warranty; the obligation is to exercise due diligence (*Dixon v Sadler* (1839) 5 M & W 405 at 414, 151 ER 172; *McFadden v Blue Star Line* [1905] 1 KB 697). In cases where loss or damage has resulted from unseaworthiness, the burden of proving the exercise of due diligence is on the carrier. Thirdly, however, seaworthiness is to be assessed according to the voyage under consideration; there is no single standard of fitness which a vessel must meet (*Burges v Wickham* (1863) 3 B & S 669, 122 ER 251; *Kopitoff v Wilson* (1876) 1 QBD 377; *Gibson v Small* (1853) 1 HLC 353, 10 ER 499). Thus, seaworthiness is judged having regard to the conditions the vessel will encounter (*Huddart Parker Ltd v Cotter* (1942) 66 CLR 624; *McFadden v Blue Star Line* [1905] 1 KB 697; *The Southwark* 191 US 1). The vessel may be seaworthy for a coastal voyage in a season of light weather but not for a voyage in the North Atlantic in mid winter.

[4.84] A duty of properly and carefully dealing with goods: This duty is set out in art 3(2) of the Hague-Visby Rules. This provision states that 'the carrier shall properly and carefully load, handle, stow, carry, keep, care for, and discharge the goods carried'. The meaning of this provision is explained by Mason and Wilson JJ in *Shipping Corp of India Ltd v Gamlen Chemical Co (A'asia) Pty Ltd* (1980) 147 CLR 142; 32 ALR 609 at 621–2. This provision requires the carrier to handle and carry goods in a proper and careful manner. The 'propriety' and 'carefulness' of the carrier's act must be construed in the circumstances concerned, taking into account the nature of the goods, established commercial practices, the contract terms, and the reasonableness of the carrier in loading, handling, stowing, carrying, keeping and discharging the goods. Stephen J observed in *Shipping Corp v Gamlen Chemical* (1980) 147 CLR 142 at 144, that the meaning of property stowage depends 'on all the circumstances, including the nature of the particular goods and the conditions of the weather and of sea likely to be encountered on the voyage'. In *Westrac Equipment Pty Ltd v 'Assets Venture'* [2002] FCA 404, the court held the defendants liable for the loss of the cargo, a Caterpillar bulldozer, carried on deck by the decision of the defendants, as the bulldozer was not secured adequately on deck to endure rough seas. It must be pointed out, however, that while the carriers had apparently breached their obligation under art 3(2), the court held them to be liable largely under the law of tort in the present case.

[4.85] Carrier's liability and issue of bill of lading: A carrier is obliged to issue a bill of lading, on demand of the shipper, after the carrier has taken over the goods. This obligation is set out in art 3(3) of the Hague-Visby Rules. This provision does not say that the goods must have been loaded on board a vessel before a bill of lading can be issued: a 'received for shipment bill of lading' or a 'house bill' can be issued as long as its issue is authorised by the carrier (as opposed to a bill issued by a freight forwarder without authority from the carrier; in such a case, the bill is not a contract of carriage between the holder and the carrier). However, a 'received bill of lading' or a 'house bill of lading' must be indorsed by the carrier under art 3(7) of the Hague-Visby Rules as a 'shipped bill' after the goods have been loaded on board a vessel, before it can be regarded as a 'bill of lading' under the convention. This is why in *Carrington Slipways Pty Ltd v Patrick Operations Pty Ltd* (1991) 24 NSWLR 745; **[4.51]**, the house bill was not regarded as a 'bill of lading'.

The carrier is obliged to record the true condition, marks, labels, quantity or weight of the goods shipped. The shipper is obliged, where applicable, to furnish the correct

[4.85]

information which is necessary for filling in the bill of lading. Article 3(3) exempts the carrier from restating the information supplied by the shipper if the carrier has reasonable grounds for suspecting the accuracy of the information and has no reasonable means of verifying it.

The shipper's obligation to supply accurate information is further enforced in art 3(5), which requires a shipper who has furnished inaccurate or false information to the carrier to indemnify any loss, damage, or expense arising from the information. This requirement is necessary for the protection of the carrier, who, under a bill of lading, could be liable to any holder of the bill for any loss or damage resulting from the discrepancy between the bill and the goods. However, the carrier and shipper are not allowed to enter into an arrangement to defraud the consignee or any third party through issuing a bill of lading providing false information on goods, whether or not the shipper undertakes to indemnify the carrier for so doing: see *Hellenic Lines Ltd v Chemoleum Corp* [1972] 1 Lloyd's Rep 350; and *Hunter Grain Pty Ltd v Hyundai Merchant Marine Co Ltd* (1993) 117 ALR 507.

Carrier's liability to deliver the goods

[4.86] The obligation to deliver the goods in the condition and state as noted in the bill of lading to the consignee or the holder of the bill of lading is an implied term of the contract of carriage. It is thus an implied obligation of the carrier under the Hague Rules or the Hague-Visby Rules to deliver the goods with reasonable dispatch.[82] Failure to deliver the goods to the holder of the bill of lading constitutes a fundamental breach of the contract of carriage.[83] So is the delivery of goods to a party who cannot produce the bill of lading.[84] In *Kishinchand & Sons (Hong Kong) Ltd v Wellcorp Container Lines Ltd and Wellcorp Express (Canada) Inc*,[85] the court held the carrier to be liable for delivery without surrender of the bill of lading even though the delivery was allegedly made by an unauthorised act of the carrier's employee.

In commercial practice, it is common that the carrier may deliver goods to a party who does not have a bill of lading against a letter of indemnity from the party, the shipper or another party. This is what happened in *Kanematsu Gmbh v Acadia Shipbrokers Ltd and Seanav International Ltd*;[86] see **[4.63]**. This is also what happened in a Chinese case, *Textile Material Co of Huarun Ltd v Shipping Agent Co of Zanjiang*.[87] However, such commercial practice may not exempt the carrier from the liability to deliver the goods against the presentation of the bill of lading.

---

82. For example, in *The Ship 'Socofl Stream' v CMC* [2001] FCA 961, the court held that the carrier breached its duty to deliver the goods with reasonable dispatch because its own conduct caused the vessel's arrest, which led to the delay in delivery.
83. *Kishinchand & Sons (Hong Kong) Ltd v Wellcorp Container Lines Ltd and Wellcorp Express (Canada) Inc*, decided 14 December 1994 by the Federal Court of Canada.
84. *Sze Hai Tong Bank Ltd v Rambler Cycle Co Ltd* (1959) AC 576, and *Kuehne Nagel (Hong Kong) Ltd v Yuen Fung Metal Works Ltd* [1979] HKLR 526.
85. Decided 14 December 1994 by the Federal Court of Canada.
86. Decided on 18 February 1999 by the Federal Court of Canada, available at <http://www.fja-cmf.gc.ca>.
87. The Institute for Practical Legal Research of the National Supreme Court (ed), *Selected Cases of the People's Court* (in Chinese), vol 10, Publishing House of the People's Court, Beijing, 1994, pp 139–44. For discussion, see Mo, *Shipping Law in China*, Hong Kong, Sweet & Maxwell Asia, 1999, pp 80–1.

[4.87] It did not do so in *The Koe Guan Co v The Yan On Marine & Fire Insurance Co Ltd*,[88] a Hong Kong case decided in 1907, and it did not do so in *Kanematsu Gmbh v Acadia Shipbrokers Ltd and Seanav International Ltd*,[89] a Canadian case decided in 1999. In a Chinese case, *Textile Material Company of Huarun Ltd v Shipping Agent Company of Zanjiang*,[90] the court held that the delivery without requesting the production of a bill of lading did not amount to a breach of contract, because the holder of the bill had later acquiesced to the delivery by its conduct. Legally speaking, the Chinese case does not endorse the exemption of the carrier from the liability to deliver the goods against the bill of lading either, because the court merely found that the holder had lost its right to sue on the ground of estoppel. Therefore, the carrier is obliged to deliver the goods against the production of the bill of lading under the relevant international conventions or the relevant domestic law. If the carrier is found to be liable to the holder of the bill for misdelivery, he or she may always seek compensation from the party offering the letter of indemnity. This is why delivery against a letter of indemnity is a common commercial practice today.

[4.88] Carrier's liability and exclusion clause: Article 3(8) of the Hague-Visby Rules prohibits a carrier from excluding or limiting his or her liability under the rules. This provision states as follows:

> Any clause, covenant, or agreement in a contract of carriage relieving the carrier or the ship from liability for loss or damage to, or in connexion with, goods arising from negligence, fault, or failure in the duties and obligations provided in this article or lessening such liability otherwise than as provided in this convention, shall be null and void and of no effect. A benefit of insurance in favour of the carrier or similar clause shall be deemed to be a clause relieving the carrier from liability.

The provision indicates that a carrier is not allowed to limit, lessen or avoid his or her obligations imposed in the Hague-Visby Rules on grounds other than those specified in the convention, particularly in art 4. This provision is doubly qualified: first, only a clause which lessens or avoids the carrier's liability under the Hague-Visby Rules falls under this provision; second, only a clause which lessens and avoids the carrier's liability as specified in the convention falls under this provision. Thus, a bill of lading may not exempt the carrier from the liability of due diligence to make the ship seaworthy, but may state that the carrier is not liable for damages to goods arising from the buyer's failure to obtain an import licence (this would fall under the exceptions in art 4 of the Hague-Visby Rules).

[4.89] Article 3(8) has been litigated in the United States to determine the validity of the choice of forum clause, including an arbitration clause. For example, in *Indussa Corp v SS Ranborg* 377 F 2d 200 (2d Cir 1967), the court struck down a choice of forum clause on the ground that the clause might lead to the lessening of the carrier's liability under the US Carriage of Goods by Sea Act 1936. In contrast, the English case *Maharani Woollen Mills Co v Anchor Line* [1927] 29 Lloyd's List L Rep 169 (CA) held that a choice of forum clause per se did not lessen the carrier's liability.

---

88. [1906–7] HKLR 95.
89. Decided on 18 February 1999 by the Federal Court of Canada, available at <http://www.fja-cmf.gc.ca>.
90. *Selected Cases of the People's Court*, note 87 above, pp 139–44. For discussion, see Mo, note 87 above, pp 80–1.

[4.89] The reasoning of the *Indussa* case has been abandoned by the US court. For example, in *The Bremen v Zapata Off-Shore Co* (1971) 407 US 1, the court recognised the effect of the choice of forum clause because it did not lessen the carrier's liability. Similarly, in *Vimar Seguros Y Reaseguros SA v M/V Sky Reefer*,[91] the Supreme Court of the United States decided that a choice of law clause which chose the Japanese law as the governing law, and an arbitration clause which submitted disputes arising from the bill of lading to arbitration in Tokyo, did not contravene art 3(8) of the Hague Rules as adopted by the Carriage of Goods by Sea Act 1936 (US). In the view of the court, a choice of forum clause or an arbitration clause does not lessen the carrier's liability under the Hague Rules or the Hague-Visby Rules per se. Such a clause contravenes art 3(8) of the Hague Rules or the Hague-Visby Rules only when the application of the clause results in the consequence of lessening the carrier's liability as set out in the relevant rules.

[4.90] Article 3(8) has been litigated in Australia to determine the validity of clauses fixing a ceiling on the carrier's liability lower than those stipulated in the Hague Rules (note: art 3(8) is the same under both the Hague Rules and the Hague-Visby Rules). However, the High Court was of the opinion that a clause fixing a lower ceiling on the carrier's financial liability did not offend art 3(8).

For example, in *The Australasian United Steam Navigation Co Ltd v Hiskens* (1914) 18 CLR 646, Griffith CJ, Isaacs and Powers JJ held that the clause which fixed the amount of the carrier's liability at £10 per package, unless the shipper declared a higher value, did not contravene art 3(8), because the shipper had an option under the bill to declare a higher value. The principle of freedom of contract appears to be the basis of this conclusion. Similarly, in *William Holyman & Sons Pty Ltd v Foy & Gibson Pty Ltd* (1945) 73 CLR 622, Appendix 2, the High Court accepted the construction of art 3(8) in the *Hiskens* case, but held a clause which set a ceiling on the carrier's financial liability lower than the Hague Rules as contravening art 4(5). The *Gibson* case represents an effort by the High Court to redefine the implications of the *Hiskens* case.

[4.91] A recent case concerning art 3(8) of the Hague-Visby Rules is *Chapman Marine Pty Ltd v Wilhelmsen Lines A/S* [1999] FCA 178. In this case, the plaintiff who was the owner of a damaged Martinique cruiser sued the carrier and the stevedoring company for damages. The bill of lading was subject to the Carriage of Goods by Sea Act 1936 (US), which adopts the Hague Rules. Article 3(8) of the Hague Rules and art 3(8) of the Hague-Visby Rules are identical. The defendants sought to rely on the limitation of liability set out in the Act to limit their liability to US$500 per package. The stevedoring company relied on the Himalaya clause to limit its liability in tort. The plaintiff attempted to argue that the carrier contravened art 3(8) of the Hague Rules by relying on cl 6(b) of the bill of lading to relieve its liability (possibly) arising from the stevedoring company's cross-claim. Although this argument may or may not have assisted the plaintiff's case, the court held that art 3(8) applies only between the carrier and cargo-owner. In the words of Emmett J, art 3(8) 'is concerned with provisions which limit the direct liability of the carrier to the owner of cargo'. Thus, it is not concerned with any arrangement

---

91. Decided on 19 June 1995 by the Supreme Court of the United States, available at <http://supct.law.cornell.edu>.

concerning liability of the carrier to a third party. This case illustrates the operation of art 3(8) of the Hague-Visby Rules.

Carrier's liability and exceptions under Article 4

[4.92] **General exceptions:** Article 4(2) declares the exceptions where a carrier is not liable for the loss of or damage to the goods. This means that if the carrier can prove that the loss or damage to goods was caused by one of the exceptions under art 4, the carrier will be exempt from any liability. The purpose of the exceptions is to protect the carrier and exclude the carrier's liability in the circumstances where the loss or damage is caused by something outside the carrier's control, or by something which cannot be attributed to the carrier's fault. The major exceptions under art 4 are as follows:

- an act, neglect or default of the master, mariner, pilot or the servants of the carrier in the navigation or management of the ship;[92]
- fire which is not caused by the carrier's fault;[93]
- perils, dangers and accidents of sea or other navigable waters;[94]
- an act of God;
- an act of war;[95]
- an act of public enemies;
- arrest or restraint of governments or people, or seizure under legal process;[96]
- quarantine restrictions;
- an act or omission of the shipper or owner of the goods, his or her agent or representative;
- a strike, lock-out, stoppage or restraint of labour;[97]
- riots and civil commotion;
- saving or attempting to save life or property at sea;

---

92. For example, *The Touraine* (1927) 29 Ll L Rep 265; and *Leval v Colonial Steamships* [1960] 2 Lloyd's Rep 198.
93. See *Accinanto Ltd v A/S Ludwig Mowinckels* [1951] 2 Lloyd's List Law Reports 28.
94. For example, see *Consolidated Mining v Straits Towing Ltd* [1972] 2 Lloyd's Rep 497; *Bernhard Blumenfeld Kommandit Gesellschaft Auf Aktien v Sheaf Steam Shipping Co Ltd* (1938) 62 Ll L Rep 175; and *The Sabine Howaldt* [1970] 1 Lloyd's Rep 185.
95. For example, *Burns Philp v Gillespie Brothers* (1946–7) 74 CLR 149. This case deals with not only the exception of war, but also the freight arising from the preservation of the goods in an act of war.
96. The jurisdiction of the government in arresting or restraining the goods concerned may sometimes arise as an issue in applying for exemption under this rule. In *American President Lines Ltd v China Mutual Trading Co Ltd* [1953] HKLR 111, the carrier refused to deliver goods to the consignee in the United States. The carrier was sued in Hong Kong. It forwarded a defence of the restraint of prices and argued that the delivery of the goods was prohibited by the order of the US Government. The High Court of Hong Kong took the view that the US Government did not have the jurisdiction to prohibit the delivery of the goods in question. This decision raises the issue of conflict of laws and also the issue of statutory interpretation.
97. For example, *Koninklijke Bunge v Compagnie Continetale D'Importation* [1973] 2 Lloyd's Rep 44.

[4.92] **International Commercial Law**

- loss or damage arising from inherent defect, quality, or vice of the goods;[98]
- insufficiency of packing;[99]
- insufficiency or inadequacy of marks;
- latent defects; and
- any other causes arising without the actual fault or privity of the carrier or without the fault or neglect of the agents or servants of the carrier.[100]

[4.93] These exceptions should be read together with art 4(1), which states in general that a carrier is only liable for losses or damages arising from want of due diligence on the part of the carrier in complying with art 3(1).[101] In a sense, art 4(1) repeats art 3(1), which makes it clear that the carrier's duty to make the ship seaworthy, to staff, equip and supply the ship properly and to make the ship fit for carrying the goods concerned is fulfilled as far as the carrier has exercised 'due diligence'.

However, art 4(1) imposes a burden of proof upon the carrier to prove that he or she has exercised 'due diligence' if the carrier intends to rely on the exemptions under art 4(1).[102] If the carrier intends to rely on one of the exceptions under art 4(2), he or she has to prove that the ship was seaworthy and the loss or damage was caused or was likely to have been caused by one of the exceptions. In certain circumstances, a court of law may find the existence of a presumption that the loss or damage was caused by perils of sea once the carrier established that the ship was seaworthy at the commencement of the voyage.[103] The burden of proof (except the burden to prove the seaworthiness of the ship) appears to rest on the party making an allegation.

---

98. In *The Hoyanger* [1979] 2 Lloyd's Rep 79, a cargo of apples was carried by the vessel *Hoyanger* from Buenos Aires, to Vancouver, Canada. The voyage took about 45 days. The owners of the apples found them to be unmerchantable on arrival. They sued the carriers for damages. The carriers claimed inherent vice. The Federal Court of Canada held that the carriers had established that they had properly stowed and kept the apples on board. The apples were overripe when loaded on board the vessel in Argentina. The court held that the carriers should not be expected to have the knowledge and expertise to determine whether the apples were suitable for the 45-day voyage. Thus, the loss was caused by inherent vice in the apples. Similarly, in *The Continental Shipper* [1976] 2 Lloyd's Rep 234, the vessel carried 321 new cars to Montreal. The cars were uncrated, which is an acceptable practice. On arrival, 174 cars were found to bear scratches and dents to various degrees. The carrier admitted liability in relation to the major damages, but claimed the defence of inherent vice under art 4(2)(m) in relation to the rest. The Canadian Federal Court of Appeal held that the scratches and dents were caused by improper stowing and handling by the carrier, and that inherent vice was not established.
99. In *The Continental Shipper* [1976] 2 Lloyd's Rep 234, the carrier also relied on the defence of insufficient packing. The court held that carrying cars uncrated was an acceptable practice to both parties and thus an art 4(2)(n) exception was not established. See also *Lucky Wave* [1985] 1 Lloyd's Rep 80.
100. It must be pointed out that under this exception, the involvement of the carrier must be based on an 'actual fault', but the involvement of the carrier's agents or servants can be based on 'fault' and 'neglect'. In other words, the neglect of the carrier is not relevant.
101. For example, *The Sabine Howaldt* [1970] 1 Lloyd's Rep 185.
102. For example, see *McGregor v Huddart Parker* (1919) 26 CLR 336; *The John Weyerhaeuser* [1975] 2 Lloyd's Rep 439; and *Charles Goodfellow Lumber Sales Ltd v Verreault, Hovington and Verreault Navigation Inc* [1971] 1 Lloyd's Rep 185.
103. For example, *Bernhard Blumenfeld Kommandit Gesellschaft Auf Aktien v Sheaf Steam Shipping Co Ltd* (1938) 62 Ll L Reports 175.

[4.94] It should be noted that sometimes a court may interpret the meaning of loss of or damage to goods in an interesting manner. In *Kishinchand & Sons v Wellcorp Container Lines and Wellcorp Express (Canada) Inc*,[104] a limitation clause in the bill of lading contained the words loss of or damage to goods. The court held that the alleged misdelivery in the case did not amount to the loss of or damage to the goods in question, because the goods were not lost or damaged by the misdelivery. Consequently, the limitation clause was not applicable.

[4.95] A carrier is also exempt from any liability under art 4(5)(h). This provision states that the carrier is not liable for any loss or damage to goods if the nature and value of the goods has been knowingly misstated by the shipper in the bill of lading. The shipper must have utmost good faith in furnishing information about the goods to the carrier. This provision gives additional protection to the carrier, who has been protected under art 4(5)(f) which allows the carrier to rebut the declared value of the goods in a bill of lading by contrary evidence, and art 4(6) which allows the carrier to seek indemnity from the shipper for failing to disclose the dangerous nature of the goods.

[4.96] The exemptions under the Hague-Visby Rules apply only to a bill of lading or a similar document. The meaning of similar document may sometimes result in disagreement. *R W Miller & Co Pty Ltd v Australian Oil Refining Pty Ltd* (1967) 117 CLR 288 appears to be an interesting illustration of the relationship between the exempted liability of the Hague-Visby Rules (or the Hague Rules) and the nature of the document concerned. This case involved a claim arising from damages to the wharf for loading oil in Botany Bay. Australian Oil Refining, the plaintiff at trial and the respondent in the appeal to the High Court of Australia, was the charterer of the vessel provided by R W Miller, the appellant and defendant at trial. Australian Oil Refining was also the lessee and occupier of the wharf damaged by R W Miller's vessel.

The Supreme Court of Victoria found in the plaintiff's favour largely on the ground that the relevant clauses of the charterparty (intended to exempt the vessel owner from liability for loss or damage caused by the negligent act or omission of the master mariner, pilot or servants of the vessel owner done in the navigation or management of the vessel), only covered loss of or damage to goods.

The High Court was divided on the interpretation of the nature of the charterparty concerned, and allowed the appeal on a 3:2 majority. The majority took the view that the charterparty was not a bill of lading and was not limited to the loss or damage to goods. It appears that the majority of the High Court regarded the charterparty as a contract and thus interpreted the exemptions under the terms of the charterparty itself, instead of in the context of art 4(2) of the Hague Rules, which appeared to be identical to cl 15 of the charterparty relied upon by the vessel owner. This case is interesting. Clause 15 of the charterparty was identical to art 4(2) of the Hague Rules. However, if we link these two provisions together, the vessel owner would be deprived of the benefit of exempted liability because the damage was done to the wharf instead of the goods. The present case

---

104. Decided on 14 December 1994 by the Federal Court of Canada, available at <http://www.fja-cmf.gc.ca>.

suggests that, at least in the present circumstances, a charterparty may not be regarded as a similar document for the purpose of the Hague-Visby Rules.

[4.97] Carrier's right of indemnity: A shipper has an obligation to indemnify the carrier in certain circumstances under the Hague-Visby Rules. Article 3(5) requires a shipper to indemnify a carrier for his or her losses arising from the use of inaccurate information provided by the shipper: see **[4.124]**. Article 4(6) requires the shipper to disclose to the carrier the nature of the goods, in particular, goods of inflammable, explosive and dangerous nature: see **[4.126]**. The shipper is liable to indemnify the carrier for consequential or incidental costs arising from his or her failure to comply with this requirement.

For example, in *Effort Shipping Co Ltd v Linden Management Sa (The 'Giannis Nk')* [1994] 2 Lloyd's Rep 171, the shippers contracted with the carrier in 1990 to carry a cargo of ground-nut extraction meal from the port of Daker to Rio Haina in the Dominican Republic. On the balance of probabilities, the cargo carried with it Khapra beetle, which later contaminated other cargoes on board the vessel. The vessel was ordered to leave the Dominican Republic without discharging the cargoes because of the infestation of Khapra beetle. The vessel was subsequently ordered by the US Department of Agriculture at San Juan either to carry the cargoes back to their countries of origin or dump them 25 miles off the coast of San Juan. The carrier dumped the cargoes off the US coast and later sued the shipper of the ground-nut extraction meal for the costs and expenses arising from the incident. The court held that the cargo was of a dangerous nature in the sense that it contaminated other cargoes on board the vessel and held that the shipper was liable for the costs and expenses incurred.

In addition, under general contract law the shipper is also liable for any loss sustained by the carrier because of any act or omission of the shipper or his or her agents.

[4.98] Article 4(3) is intended to qualify the duty of the shipper to indemnify the carrier. The provision states that the 'shipper shall not be responsible for loss or damage sustained by the carrier or the ship arising or resulting from any cause without the act, fault or neglect of the shipper, his agent or his servants'. This provision suggests that the shipper's duty to indemnify the carrier is fault-based. This can be compared with the duty of the carrier to the shipper. As we have seen, under the Hague-Visby Rules the carrier is not liable for losses arising from the unseaworthiness of the ship unless want of due diligence is established. The carrier is responsible for providing a seaworthy ship at the commencement of the voyage and for guaranteeing the fitness of the ship to the cargo under the contract of carriage.

[4.99] Carrier's duty and necessary or reasonable deviation: Deviation normally means that the ship departs from the route of voyage as agreed in the contract of carriage. The shipper and carrier often agree on the route for the purpose of defining and dividing responsibilities between them. The shipper undertakes the risk of perils at sea within the agreed route, but the carrier is liable for perils at sea if the ship deviates from the agreed or reasonable route, because he or she breaches the contract of carriage by making the deviation. Article 4(4) exempts the carrier from any liability arising from the breach if the deviation is necessary for saving life and property at sea. The carrier is also allowed to deviate from the agreed or normal route if he or she can prove that the deviation is reasonable and necessary. The burden of proof lies on the carrier.

[4.100] Deviation is sometimes used to refer to an act of the carrier, which has deviated or departed from the terms of the original contract or general shipping and commercial practice. In *Chapman Marine Pty Ltd v Wilhelmsen Lines A/S* [1999] FCA 178, the plaintiff forwarded an argument of 'deviation' and alleged that the defendant carrier had carried the damaged boat on deck without authority, amounting to a deviation which had deprived the carrier of the limited liability under COGSA 1936 (US). Emmett J examined cl 22 of the bill of lading and s 1(c) of COGSA, and concluded that in the circumstances concerned there was neither an express prohibition nor an implied prohibition that the boat in question could not be carried on deck, holding that there was no deviation which had deprived the carrier of the limited liability under COGSA.

[4.101] *Tasman Express Line Ltd v JI Case (Australia) Pty Ltd*

(1992) 111 FLR 108

Deviation may occur in a non-geographical sense — the carrier's conduct amounts to a radical transgression similar to the transgressions usually regarded as deviations

Facts: Tasman Express Line carried two combine harvesters on deck from New Zealand to Sydney. JI Case (Australia) was the shipper. The bill of lading contained an exclusion clause which exempted the carrier from any responsibility for the harvesters carried on deck. One of the harvesters was negligently damaged by the stevedores in the process of unloading in Sydney. The trial judge found that there was a deviation in the sense that the carrier allowed the stevedores to employ a discharging method which was not contemplated in the contract of carriage. The carrier was not allowed to rely on the exclusion clause. The carrier appealed.

Decision: The Court of Appeal of the Supreme Court of New South Wales did not question the proposition that a deviation may occur in a non-geographical sense, but held that the discharging method did not amount to a deviation. Accordingly, the court held that the carrier was entitled to rely on the exclusion clause.

[4.102] Limits of carrier's financial liability: One of the basic differences between the Hague Rules and the Hague-Visby Rules is the limits of the carrier's financial liability in case of loss of or damage to goods. The Hague-Visby Rules adopt a higher ceiling for compensation than the Hague Rules. Under art 4(5) of the Hague Rules, a carrier is not liable for any loss or damage to or in connection with goods in an amount exceeding £100 sterling per package or unit, unless the nature and value of the goods has been declared before the shipment, and inserted in the bill of lading. In contrast, under art 4(5)(a) of the Hague-Visby Rules, a carrier is not liable for any loss or damage to or in connection with goods in an amount exceeding 666.67 units of account per package or unit, or two units of account per kilogram of gross weight of the goods, whichever is the higher. The maximum limit of compensation can be increased if the nature and value of the goods have been declared before the shipment and inserted in the bill of lading. Under art 4(5)(f), the declared value of goods in a bill of lading is prima facie evidence of

[4.102] the true value of the goods, but the carrier is entitled to rebut the declaration by providing contrary evidence of the true value of the goods.

[4.103] The expression 'unit of account' refers to the Special Drawing Right (SDR),[105] an artificially created 'instrument' which is the substitute for the 'currency' of any particular country in international trade and commerce. The real value of a 'unit of account' in terms of gold or any currency is determined by the particular method of valuation adopted by the persons, countries or organisations applying the 'unit of account'. This means that any international convention establishing a particular fund may adopt its own method of valuation for determining the 'unit of account' applicable for the purpose of the convention, and any regional economic community is able to define the value of its own 'unit of account' if necessary. The Hague-Visby Rules adopt the method of valuation defined by the International Monetary Fund (IMF).

[4.104] The Hague-Visby Rules also define the value of the 'unit of account' for those members who are not able to adopt the SDR as defined by the IMF. Under art 4(5)(d), a carrier from such a country is not liable for loss or damage to or in connection with goods in an amount exceeding 10,000 'monetary units' or 30 'monetary units' per kilogram of gross weight of the goods, whichever is the higher. One 'monetary unit' under the Hague-Visby Rules contains 65.5 mg of gold of millesimal fineness 900. Gold is the basis for converting the 'monetary unit' into any currency payable to the shipper.

[4.105] If a container, pallet or similar article of transport is used for carrying goods, the carrier is liable to compensate the shipper on the basis of the number of packages or units of goods in each container, pallet or similar article as recorded in the bill of lading. If the shipper fails to declare the number of packages or units of goods in a container, pallet or similar article, the container, pallet or similar article will be treated as one package or unit. It is therefore crucial for a shipper to declare the number of packages or units within a container, pallet or similar article, if there is more than one package or unit of goods in it.

In *Chapman Marine Pty Ltd v Wilhelmsen Lines A/S* [1999] FCA 178, a cruiser was damaged during a carriage from the United States to Australia. For the purpose of determining the carrier's liability, the court accepted the defendants' argument that a cruiser should be regarded as one 'package', 'unit' or 'piece' of cargo for which the carrier's liability was limited to US$500 per package. The size of the cruiser as recorded in the bill of lading was considered to be irrelevant for determining compensation to the shipper in the present case.

[4.106] Illegality of fixing a lower ceiling of liability: Article 4(5)(g) makes it clear that a carrier is not allowed to fix a maximum amount for compensation which is lower than the sum of 666.67 units of account per package, or two units of account per kilogram of gross weight of the goods, as set out in art 4(5)(a). This means that had *The Australasian United Steam Navigation Co Ltd v Hiskens* (1914) 18 CLR 646 and *William*

---

105. The expression Special Drawing Right (SDR) refers to a monetary 'unit' defined by the International Monetary Fund (IMF). Presently, the IMF adopts a method of valuation based on a 'basket of currencies' which includes the US dollar, the Deutschemark, the UK sterling, the French franc and the Japanese yen. This means the actual 'value' of a unit of account as expressed in a particular currency may vary depending on the change of value in the currencies within the basket.

Holyman & Sons Pty Ltd v Foy & Gibson Pty Ltd (1945) 73 CLR 622 been dealt with under the Hague-Visby Rules, the dicta of the cases might have been clearer. It must be emphasised that art 4(5)(g) allows parties to a bill of lading to *increase* the carrier's maximum liability. This is consistent with art 4(5)(a), and not prohibited under art 3(8).

[4.107] Loss of the benefit of the limitation: The maximum amount of liability is a benefit for the carrier, as it exempts the carrier from liability beyond that amount. Article 4(5)(e) imposes a duty upon the carrier not to contribute to the loss or damage either by act or omission. This provision states that the carrier is not allowed to rely on the limitation of the liability if he or she has intentionally or negligently caused the loss of or damage to goods, or if he or she has acted or failed to act with knowledge that the act or omission would probably result in damage to the goods. This provision is consistent with art 3 which requires the carrier to exercise due diligence in making the ship seaworthy and in handling and carrying the goods.

[4.108] Alteration of the carrier's liability relating to 'carriage of goods': The parties to a bill of lading are free to make any arrangements in relation to the carriage of goods. The carrier is also free to waive any defences and limits of liability which are otherwise available under the Hague-Visby Rules. However, the freedom of contract to alter the effect of the provisions of the Hague-Visby Rules is qualified, in particular under arts 5 and 6, by the following restrictions:

- the carrier is not allowed to fix a maximum liability lower than art 4(5)(a);
- the alteration must not be contrary to public policy;
- the alteration must not be inconsistent with the duty of due diligence of the carrier and his or her agents or servants; and
- the alteration is contained in a non-negotiable document and marked as such.

The last restriction is necessary to avoid any bill of lading or similar document containing alterations to the provision of the convention being forced upon a third party, who has accepted the bill under the assumption that the bill is subject to the standard provisions of the Hague-Visby Rules.

Freedom to contract outside 'carriage of goods'

[4.109] The Hague-Visby Rules regulate the liabilities of the carrier and shipper in relation to the 'carriage of goods'. The parties can, subject to the relevant provisions of the Hague-Visby Rules (or any other relevant law as the case may be), alter the effect of the provisions which apply to the carriage of goods within the specified restrictions: see **[4.108]**. The parties are free to contract in any terms in relation to their responsibilities to goods prior to the loading and subsequent to the discharge of the goods from the ship, because these periods do not fall under the meaning of 'carriage of goods'. Under art 7 of the Hague-Visby Rules, the parties can define the carrier's liability in relation to goods during the time prior or subsequent to the carriage. If the parties agree in a contract of carriage that the carrier is liable to take care of the goods after their discharge and before the shipper or consignee takes over, the carrier has a contractual obligation to exercise due diligence in relation to the goods even though the Hague-Visby Rules do not so require.

[4.110] There appears to be a dilemma in a bill of lading which contains an exclusion clause in favour of the carrier during the period of time outside 'carriage of goods' as defined in the Hague-Visby Rules or the Hague Rules. Article 1(d) of the Hague-Visby Rules defines the 'carriage of goods' as 'the period from the time when the goods are loaded on to the time they are discharged from the ship'. Therefore, the carrier is subject to the obligations contained in the Hague-Visby Rules, or the Hague Rules (if applicable), from the time the goods are loaded on to the vessel until they are discharged.[106] 'Otherwise, the obligations of the carrier depended upon the terms of the bill of lading' and not the Hague-Visby Rules or the Hague Rules.[107] Such a regime of the carrier's liability results in a dilemma in the sense that under the Hague-Visby Rules or the Hague Rules, the carrier is obliged to deliver the goods to the consignee in the state in which the carrier received them at the port of shipment, but on the other hand, the provisions of the Hague-Visby Rules or the Hague Rules do not apply to the carrier after the goods have been unloaded from the vessel carrying the goods.

[4.111] There is a grey area where the liability of the carrier becomes uncertain: after the goods have been discharged but before they are delivered to the consignee. If the carrier is not bound by the provisions of the relevant convention, that is, the Hague-Visby Rules or the Hague Rules, the meaning and functions of a bill of lading, which have been defined in the Hague-Visby Rules or the Hague Rules, are qualified or restricted by the specific terms of the bill of lading dealing with such a situation and the general contract law. The shipper, consignor or consignee are not eligible to the protection provided by the Hague-Visby Rules and the Hague Rules.

This is the finding in *Nissho Iwai Australia Ltd v Malaysian International Shipping Corp, Berhad* (1989) 167 CLR 219 by the Supreme Court of the New South Wales, the Court of Appeal of the Supreme Court of New South Wales and the High Court of Australia. In the light of this case, the liability of the carrier for the period after the discharge of the goods from the vessel and before the delivery of them to the consignee is contractual and tortious. A similar conclusion was reached by the majority judges in *Nikolay Malakhov Shipping Co Ltd v SEAS Sapfor Ltd* [1998] NSWSC 65. Technically, the findings of these courts are correct. An inevitable consequence from this case is that a carefully drafted bill of lading is able to circumvent the carrier's statutory liability as set out in either the Hague-Visby Rules or the Hague Rules. In comparison, the Hamburg Rules are much more favourable to the shipper because the carrier's liability 'covers the period during which the carrier is in charge of the goods at the port of loading, during the carriage or at the port of discharge'.[108]

Carrier's liability and notice of loss

[4.112] The Hague-Visby Rules require a shipper or consignee who claims loss of or damage to goods to give written notice to the carrier or his or her agents specifying the nature of the loss or damage. Article 3(6) requires the shipper or consignee to give notice

---

106. *Gosse Millerd v Canadian Government Merchant Marine Ltd* [1927] 2 KB 432 at 434 per Wright J.
107. *Nissho Iwai Australia Ltd v Malaysian International Shipping Corp, Berhad* (1989) 167 CLR 219 at 219 per Mason CJ, Brennan, Deane, Gaudron and McHugh JJ.
108. The Hamburg Rules, art 4(1).

at the time when the goods are delivered to him or her, or to his or her agents, pursuant to the contract of carriage. If the loss or damage is not apparent, the shipper or consignee should give notice within three days after the delivery.

The Hague-Visby Rules also require the parties to a contract of carriage (carrier and shipper or consignee) to assist each other in inspecting the alleged loss or damage. This rule applies not only to circumstances where the shipper or consignee claims loss or damage, but also to a situation where the goods are lost or damaged while under the care of the carrier.

Carrier's liability and limitation of time

[4.113] Article 3(6) of the Hague-Visby Rules sets out a limitation period of one year for the shipper or consignee to claim loss or damage. This is the same under the Hague Rules. A shipper or consignee who claims loss or damage against a carrier under a bill of lading must commence the action within one year of the date of delivery (if the goods have been delivered), or of the date on which the goods ought to be delivered (if the goods have not been delivered). 'Delivery' can be either actual delivery or constructive delivery: see *The Australasian United Steam Navigation Co Ltd v Hiskens* (1914) 18 CLR 646 per Griffith CJ at 656. This is important for the calculation of the running of the time.

The one-year limitation can be extended by agreement between the parties. It may also be extended under relevant domestic law in certain circumstances. For example, in *Australian Shipping Commission v Kooragang Cement Pty Ltd* [1988] VR 29, the plaintiff, who was the owner of the damaged cargo, chartered a vessel from the shipowner in 1984 for the carriage of the cargo of cement clinker from Adelaide to Newcastle. The cargo was damaged by sea water during the voyage. The plaintiff sued the shipowner for damages. The trial judge allowed the plaintiff to commence arbitration proceedings even though the one-year limitation period had elapsed. This decision was affirmed by the Full Court of the Supreme Court of Victoria on the ground that the court has a discretion to do so under s 48 of the Commercial Arbitration Act 1984 (Cth).

[4.114] Article 3*bis*(6) provides that the one-year limitation does not apply to an action for indemnity against a third party, unless it is prohibited by the law of the court dealing with the action. This means that an action against a third party is subject to the relevant domestic law. In Australia, the matter is governed by the law of torts, and the relevant statute of limitation in each state and territory applies. Although this provision suggests that a shipper is able to sue an independent contractor in connection with the carriage of goods, a stevedoring company and other agents of the carrier (who do not fall under art 4*bis*(2) of the Hague-Visby Rules) may rely on the one-year limitation against the shipper's tortious claims under the Himalaya clause: see **[4.116]–[4.122]**. Article 3*bis*(6) may be qualified by the contract of carriage between the carrier and shipper. Courts of law have not treated any modification of art 3*bis*(6) as contravening art 3(8).

Liability of carrier's servants and agents

[4.115] **Liability of servants and agents under Article 4*bis*:** Article 4*bis*(2) of the Hague-Visby Rules expressly extends the defences and limits of liability available to a carrier to the servants or agents of the carrier. The meaning of the carrier's servants and

[4.115]

agents does not include independent contractors, such as the persons who perform works relating to or in connection with a contract of carriage under independent contracts (other than employment contracts or agent–principal contracts). Generally speaking, stevedoring companies and warehouse operators fall under the category of independent contractors. This provision applies to any actions, either in contract or in torts, against the servants or agents of the carrier.

It must be pointed out that under art 4*bis*(3) the maximum amount in aggregation a shipper can recover from the carrier and his or her agents and servants is limited by art 4(5)(a). This limitation in most circumstances makes actions against the servants and agents pointless.

The right of a servant or agent to avail him- or herself of the abovementioned defences and limits is subject to the same qualification as the carrier's entitlement under art 4(5)(e). This means that an agent or servant cannot rely on the defences and limits if he or she has intentionally or recklessly caused the damage, or has acted or failed to act with knowledge that damage would probably result. The burden of proof lies on the shipper or consignee to prove that the agent or servant should not be allowed under art 4*bis*(4) to rely on the defences and limits available to the carrier in the circumstances concerned.

Under the Hague-Visby Rules, the Hague Rules do not extend the limited liability to the servants and agents of the carrier. The United States is still a member of the Hague Rules. Thus, in *Herd & Co v Krawill Machinery Corp*,[109] the stevedoring company which attempted to rely on the limited liability of US$500 per package under the Carriage of Goods By Sea Act 1936 (US) was denied the right to do so under s 4(5) of the Act. The situation is the same in any other countries which are members of the Hague Rules.

[4.116] Liability of independent contractors and the Himalaya clause: As we have seen, art 4*bis* does not protect independent contractors, but a carrier from time to time has to rely on independent contractors to perform part of the contract of carriage in order to fulfil his or her own obligations. An independent contractor would seek certain immunity, indemnity or exclusion from the carrier for the purpose of protecting him- or herself against possible claims of cargo-owners. This has led to the use of a mechanism known as the 'Himalaya clause' in circumstances where the carrier has to engage the services of an independent contractor and the independent contractor is liable in torts to the owner of the goods. This mechanism is intended to relieve the independent contractor from, or limit his or her tortious liability to the cargo-owner by incorporating a clause purporting to protect the independent contractor engaged by the carrier into the bill of lading or contract of carriage between the carrier and the cargo-owner (either a shipper or a consignee).

[4.117] The term 'Himalaya clause' came from the case *Adler v Dickson* [1955] 1 QB 158. The *Himalaya* was the name of the ship in dispute. In this case a passenger was injured while on board the *Himalaya* and sued the master of the ship. The master sought to rely on an exclusion clause contained in the passenger's ticket, but the ticket is a contract of carriage between the carrier and the passenger. In construing the words of the exclusion

---

109. 359 US 297 (1959).

clause, the court held that the benefit of the clause could not be extended to the master. However, the court was of the opinion that a clause which was drafted differently could be capable of extending the exemption to the master or other servants of the carrier. This was the beginning of the search for a validly drafted Himalaya clause.

[4.118] In *Scruttons Ltd v Midland Silicones Ltd* [1962] AC 446 at 474, Lord Reid proposed the following formula for determining the validity of a Himalaya clause:

- the bill of lading makes it clear that the carrier intends to protect the stevedore;
- the carrier contracts with the cargo-owner for the protection of him- or herself as well as the stevedore;
- the authority of the carrier to act in this way, either antecedently or by ratification, is established; and
- any difficulties about considerations moving from the stevedore have been overcome.

Under this formula, the validity of an exclusion clause is difficult to establish, but the formula suggests the possibility of making such an exclusion clause. In *Braber Equipment Ltd v Fraser Surrey Docks Ltd*,[110] a container of equipment was damaged by the negligence of the terminal operator, who sought to limit its liability under the Himalaya clause incorporated in the bill of lading. The court denied the defence of the Himalaya clause on the ground that the terminal operator failed to establish that the carrier had authority from the terminal operator to conclude the Himalaya clause in question.

[4.119] *New Zealand Shipping v Satterthwaite ('The Eurymedon')* [1975] AC 154 set a new milestone for the Himalaya clause in common law countries. The majority of the Privy Council recognised the ability of a Himalaya clause to extend benefits under a bill of lading to independent contractors. In this case, the clause stated that for the purpose of certain provisions, the agents, servants and independent contractors of the carrier were deemed to be parties to the contract, and thus the benefits of the provisions were extended to them. The majority judges gave weight to the commercial reality of such a clause and the shipper's (or cargo-owner's) knowledge of such commercial reality. They overcame the issue of privity of the contract by imposing a quasi-contract (arrangement, understanding or bargain) between the cargo-owner and the independent contractor who had been presumably represented all the way by the carrier. This approach was criticised by Murphy J in *Port Jackson Stevedoring Pty Ltd v Salmond and Spraggon (Australia) Pty Ltd ('The New York Star')* (1978) 139 CLR 231.

[4.120] In Australia the proposition that a Himalaya clause is capable of protecting a third party has now been accepted. In *Wilson v Darling Island Stevedoring and Lighterage Co Ltd* (1955) 95 CLR 43, the majority of the High Court refused to extend an exclusion clause under the bill of lading to the stevedoring company on the ground that the stevedoring company was not a party to the bill of lading. The stevedoring company was consequently not allowed to rely on the exclusion clause of the bill to avoid tortious liability to the cargo-owner.

---

110. 10 October 1998, Vancouver Registry No C961205, BCSC, available at <http://www.admiraltylaw.com>.

[4.120]

In *Port Jackson Stevedoring Pty Ltd v Salmond & Spraggon (Aust) Pty Ltd* ('*The New York Star*') (1978) 139 CLR 231, the High Court was divided as to whether '*The Eurymedon*' should be followed. However, as a matter of construction, the majority of the High Court held that the exclusion clause did not apply to the case involved by virtue of the fact that at the time of the damage the carrier had discharged all liability under the contract of carriage and that the bill of lading could not cover the act or omission of the stevedoring company after the discharge. The clause was reinterpreted by the Privy Council (see (1980) 144 CLR 300 (PC)), which held that the exclusion clause effectively applied to the stevedoring company under the principle of '*The Eurymedon*'. The present position of the Australian courts is represented by *Godina v Patrick Operations* [1984] 1 Lloyd's Rep 333, where the Court of Appeal of the Supreme Court of New South Wales recognised the effect of a Himalaya clause in similar circumstances to '*The New York Star*'. Recently, in *Chapman Marine Pty Ltd v Wilhelmsen Lines A/S* [1999] FCA 178, the Federal Court allowed the stevedoring company to rely on the Himalaya clause to limit its liability to the owner of a damaged cruiser.

[4.121] Himalaya clauses are intended to extend the benefit of limited or excluded liability enjoyed by the carrier under the relevant law to his or her agents and servants. The clause may also expressly extend to an independent contractor dealing with the carrier. But, it may not extend the exclusive jurisdiction clause relied on by the carrier to the agents, servants and sub-contractors, if the intention to do so is not expressed in the contract of carriage concerned. This is the view expressly adopted by the Privy Council in a Hong Kong case, *The Mahkutai*,[111] which was a carriage of goods dispute involving a vessel with an Indonesian flag.

This case appears to suggest that if the contract of carriage or the bill of lading specifically or expressly extends the benefit of exclusive jurisdiction to agents, servant or sub-contractors, the agents, servants or sub-contractors may be allowed to rely on the benefit of exclusive jurisdiction. However, even if a contract or bill has expressly so stated, the issue falls within the territory of conflict of laws. A court may actually deny a choice of jurisdiction clause or a choice of law clause on the ground of illegality, public interest consideration, the *forum non conveniens* doctrine or clearly inappropriate forum principle. This is possible because it would appear to be unreasonable or unfair if a local sub-contractor or agent cannot be sued for negligence by a local consignee. It would also appear strange if both local parties had to take legal actions at a foreign court for something done locally, merely because of the exclusive jurisdiction clause in a bill of lading or contract of carriage — which was originally designed to protect the interest of the foreign carrier.

[4.122] The United Nations Convention on the Liability of Operators of Transport Terminals in International Trade (known as the OTT Convention) was adopted in Vienna on 19 April 1991. It deals with the liability of terminal operators, including stevedoring companies, in international carriage. If this convention is adopted by a country, the Himalaya clause will be construed in the light of the convention in that country, if the

---

111. [1996] 2 HKLR 199.

law of that country applies. The convention needs to be ratified by five states before becoming effective.

Shipper's liability under the Hague-Visby Rules or the Hague Rules

An overview

[4.123] As far as the shipper's liability is concerned, the Hague-Visby Rules and the Hague Rules are identical. Thus, the shipper's liability under each of these conventions will be discussed together. Whenever a reference is made to the Hague-Visby Rules, the reference also applies to the Hague Rules, unless stated otherwise.

The Hague-Visby Rules do not expressly separate the carrier's liability from the shipper's liability in the sense that they are regulated together within the same Article (heading). In fact, arts 3 and 4 of the Hague-Visby Rules deal with both the carrier's liability and the shipper's liability, although the carrier's liability appears to be the major concern of these provisions. In the light of the said two provisions, the shipper's liability can be divided into three categories: the obligation to provide accurate information on the goods to the carrier, to give appropriate warning and instructions to the carrier for the carriage of dangerous cargo, and to be responsible for the carrier's loss or damage which is caused by the act, fault or neglect of the shipper, his or her agents or servants. In addition, the shipper is obliged to pay the freight to the carrier unless the bill of lading states otherwise. This is not stated anywhere in the Hague-Visby Rules, but it is one of the fundamental duties of the shipper because earning freight is the reason for the carrier to undertake the liability to carry the cargo in a normal commercial transaction.

Obligation to provide accurate information

[4.124] When the carrier or his or her agent issues a bill of lading, the shipper is supposed to provide the relevant information about the goods concerned to the carrier. The bill of lading which contains the information provided by the shipper subsequently becomes an undertaking of the carrier to deliver the goods in the state and quantity as recorded in the bill to the consignee or holder of the bill.

Since it is often impossible for the carrier to examine the goods or to collect all the information about the goods him- or herself, the carrier has to rely to some extent on the information furnished by the shipper. In order to protect the interest of the carrier, art 3(4) of the Hague-Visby Rules makes the bill of lading prima facie evidence of the goods concerned, subject to the contrary evidence provided by the carrier. In addition art 3(5) states expressly as follows:

> The shipper shall be deemed to have guaranteed to the carrier the accuracy at the time of shipment of the marks, number, quantity and weight, as furnished by him, and the shipper shall indemnify the carrier against all loss, damages and expenses arising or resulting from inaccuracies in such particulars. The right of the carrier to such indemnity shall in no way limit his responsibility and liability under the contract of carriage to any person other than the shipper.

[4.125] Article 3(5) is the major provision regulating the shipper's liability to provide accurate information to the carrier. The provision has the following meanings:

- It imposes an obligation to furnish accurate information about the goods to be carried upon the shipper only, and the carrier cannot rely on this provision to discharge his or her obligations under the Hague-Visby Rules to the consignee or holder of the bill of lading.

- The provision presumes the existence of a shipper's guarantee in relation to the information concerning the marks, number, quantity and weight of the goods to be carried — thus, although a fraud involving falsely declared goods may not be caught by this provision, no court is generally prepared to let a swindler go unpunished in such circumstances.

- Technically, the provision applies only to the information furnished by the shipper at the time of shipment, and may exclude the representation made by the shipper prior to the time of shipment.

- The provision applies only to the loss, damages or expenses directly arising or resulting from the inaccurate information provided by the shipper at the time of shipment in relation to the marks, number, quantity and weight of the goods carried, excluding any loss, damages or expenses which are not caused by the said information.[112]

Obligation in relation to the dangerous goods

[4.126] The shipper must furnish accurate information on the goods to be carried with the carrier. From this obligation, the shipper must advise the carrier appropriately on the dangerous nature of any goods to be carried. The Hague-Visby Rules do not expressly require the shipper to warn the carrier appropriately about the danger, but art 4(6) of the Hague-Visby Rules which permits the carrier to unload, destroy or render innocuous the dangerous cargo, suggests an implied obligation on the shipper to do so. Article 4(6) of the Hague-Visby Rules is the major provision regulating the shipper's obligation relating to the dangerous goods. It provides as follows:

> Goods of an inflammable, explosive or dangerous nature to the shipment whereof the carrier, master or agent of the carrier has not consented with knowledge of their nature and character, may at any time before discharge be landed at any place, or destroyed or rendered innocuous by the carrier without compensation and the shipper of such goods shall be liable for all damages and expenses directly or indirectly arising out of or resulting from such shipment. If any such goods shipped with such knowledge and consent shall become a danger to the ship or cargo, they may in like manner be landed at any place, or destroyed or rendered innocuous by the carrier without liability on the part of the carrier except to general average, if any.

[4.127] Besides art 4(6), art 4(3) of the Hague-Visby Rules (which will be discussed in **[4.133]**), is also relevant to the shipper's liability relating to dangerous goods.

As far as the shipper's liability is concerned, art 4(6) has the following meanings:

- The shipper is obliged to obtain consent from the carrier for the shipment of dangerous goods, which include inflammable, explosive, contaminative goods and

---

112. Article 3(5) does not differentiate between direct loss or damages from indirect loss or damages, but in the context of the whole provision, it is more likely that it covers only the direct loss or damages.

goods of any other characteristics which are regarded as dangerous by the relevant countries which the vessel must visit during a particular voyage.[113]

- If the carrier has given consent, the carrier can unload, destroy or render innocuous the dangerous goods as the carrier considers appropriate; in such a situation, the carrier and shipper are not liable to each other unless general average is an issue.
- If the shipper has not obtained the consent of the carrier, the carrier can unload, destroy or render innocuous the dangerous goods as the carrier considers appropriate, but the shipper is liable for any damages, cost and expenses arising from the shipment of the dangerous goods.

[4.128] The shipper's liability under art 4(6) of the Hague-Visby Rules may be illustrated by a Chinese case determined under art 70 of the Chinese Maritime Law, which has adopted similar rules as art 4(6). In *Ocean Shipping Co of Shanghai v Haerbing Chemical Products Import and Export (Dalian) Co*,[114] the defendant shipper, Haerbing Chemical Products Import and Export (Dalian) Co, contracted the plaintiff carrier to ship 29 containers of glacial acetic acid from the Port of Dalian to Japan in August 1991.

Many barrels containing the chemical were defective. Several containers containing the barrels showed a serious leakage of glacial acetic acid when the vessel arrived at the Port of Kobe. The local stevedore refused to unload the containers containing the chemical. The carrier informed the shipper of the incident and the shipper instructed the carrier to bring the containers back to the Port of Dalian. The vessel visited the Port of Nagoya to discharge other cargoes on board. The Japanese Maritime Safety Bureau discovered the leakage of the dangerous chemical and banned the vessel from stopping at any Japanese port. The vessel sailed back to the Port of Dalian with the 29 containers containing the chemical and the other 95 containers that should have been unloaded at the Port of Yokohama. The vessel had to cancel its plan to bring 71 containers from Japan to China because of its inability to discharge the containers in Japan. The carrier claimed compensations for the return freights concerning the 29 containers containing the chemical, and the 95 containers that were not allowed to be unloaded in Japan because of the leakage of the chemical, the cost for shipping the 95 containers again from Dalian to Yokohama, and the loss of freight arising from the loss of the next scheduled voyage.

In March 1992, the Maritime Court of Dalian allowed the carrier to claim the losses arising from the return carriage of 29 containers, the loss of freight arising from the loss of the next scheduled voyage, the costs for inspecting and repairing the containers and the vessel, the cost for inspecting the containers in Japan, and the cost for storing the containers in the Dalian Port. Interest on the losses and costs claimed was also granted. The Court of Appeal disallowed the claim for the loss of the next scheduled voyage

---

113. *Effort Shipping Co Ltd v Linden Management Sa (The 'Giannis Nk')* [1994] 2 Lloyd's Rep 171: see **[4.97]**. In this case, the vessel owner sued the charterer and the shipper for the cost and expenses arising from fumigation of the vessel which was infested with Khapra beetle brought on board the vessel by the cargo of groundnut. The infested groundnut was regarded as a dangerous cargo because the customs of the US Department of Agriculture refused to give permission to the vessel to enter into the US ports. The Court of Appeal of the UK found in favour of the carrier. The shipper appealed to the House of Lords, which unanimously dismissed the appeal. The House of Lords decision is available at <http://www.elevennewsquare.demon.co.uk>.

114. *Selected Cases of the People's Court*, note 87 above, pp 152–60.

[4.128]

because the carrier had arranged another vessel to carry the containers concerned. The Court of Appeal also reduced the costs for inspection in China, for repairing the containers and vessel and for storage of the containers because the carrier was held to be partially liable for the costs incurred.

This case involved the occurrence of indirect loss to the shipment of a dangerous cargo. The cargo was carried with the knowledge of the carrier. The insufficiency of the containers containing the dangerous chemical may not be detectable by the carrier. If this case were determined under the Hague-Visby Rules, the carrier may perhaps rely on art 4(3) to allege that the loss concerned was caused by the fault or negligence of the shipper.

[4.129] Disputes may sometimes arise between the carrier and shipper in relation to the cause for the damage to certain common goods which are nevertheless regarded as dangerous. The shipper may rely on the relevant rules governing the carrier's responsibilities in carrying the goods safely to the agreed destination to hold the carrier liable for the loss.

On the other hand, the carrier may argue that the damage was caused by the dangerous nature of the goods to avoid liability. Fishmeal is one of the goods which is usually regarded as dangerous because it contains some highly unsaturated fat that is vulnerable to heating, combustion and fire. Since the nature of the goods is expressly known to the carrier before shipment, the carrier is obliged to provide a vessel suitable to carry such goods and also to carry them carefully and adequately. The burden to prove such compliance is on the carrier.

[4.130] *Islamic Investment 1 SA v Transorient Shipping Ltd and Alfred C Toepfer International Gmbh*[115] was a case involving disputes on liabilities arising from deviation and damage to the goods carried between the vessel owner, time charterer and sub-charterer which chartered the vessel from the time charterer under a voyage charterparty. The carrier's liability to the cargo-owner for damage to the Peruvian fishmeal carried from Peru to Kaohsiung in Taiwan arose as an issue. The charterers were held liable for the damage to the fishmeal which suffered from heating, combustion, fire and water damage, and appealed to the Court of Appeal. The Court of Appeal referred to the relevant IMO regulations setting out the safety standards for the carriage of fishmeal, and found that the damaged fishmeal complied with the standards before the shipment. Thus, the charterers were again found to be liable because they had failed to establish that the damage occurred after they had performed their duties under the relevant charterparties or the relevant international convention. This case suggests that the carriage of common goods of a dangerous nature may be subject to the relevant conventions or commercial customs if the parties have expressly or implicitly agreed.

[4.131] Sometimes a cargo is dangerous in certain circumstances, but neither the shipper nor the carrier had knowledge of the dangerous nature of the cargo. Whether or not the shipper breaches his or her obligation under art 4(6) may be subject to debate, although the courts in common law jurisdictions are in favour of imposing an implied obligation upon the shipper in such circumstances.

---

115. Decided by the Court of Appeal of the High Court (UK) on 24 July 1998, available at Casetrack, <http://www.casetrack.com>.

In *The Athanasia Comninos and Georges Chr Lemos* [1990] 1 Lloyd's Rep 277, Mustill J (as his Lordship then was) at 282, noted the different views on the shipper's absolute liability or qualified liability in relation to the obligation to disclose the dangerous nature of a cargo unknown to the shipper. Although in favour of an absolute obligation, Mustill J found the shipper liable for the explosion caused by the coal carried on a vessel, on the ground that it misrepresented to the carrier before the shipment that a dangerous cargo (which was excessively gassy), was coal.

[4.132] The knowledge of the shipper was discussed in a Canadian case, *Les Industries Perlite Inc v The Marina Di Alimuri (TD)*.[116] In this case, a cargo of peat moss was involved. The shipper had guaranteed a maximum stowage factor before loading. The stowage factor became much lower after heavy rain. The shipper advised the shipmaster of the change and the stowage plan was modified. However, during loading a bulkhead of the vessel collapsed. The cargo was discharged onto a gravel surface.

The shipper claimed damages against the carrier on the ground of a breach of art 3(2) of the Hague-Visby Rules for bad stowage. The Federal Court of Canada found that the peat moss became a dangerous cargo when its moisture content exceeded 90 per cent of the flow moisture point. The peat moss caused damage to the structure of the vessel. The shipmaster did not know the dangerous nature of the cargo until the loading had begun. On the other hand, the shipper ought to have known the characteristics of its cargo and should have informed the shipmaster of the dangerous nature of the cargo prior to the loading. Although neither the shipper nor the carrier was aware of the dangerous nature of the peat moss, the shipper had an implied obligation at common law to warn the carrier of the special characteristics of the cargo to be shipped. On the basis of the implied obligation, the court held the shipper liable for the loss of the carrier, who nevertheless was not liable for the loss of the shipper.

Liability arising from fault or negligence of the shipper

[4.133] It appears that the shipper has a general liability to the carrier for any loss or damage caused by the act, fault or neglect of the shipper, his or her agents or servants.[117] The liability is set out in a negative way in art 4(3) of the Hague-Visby Rules, which provides that the shipper is not 'responsible for loss or damage by the carrier or the ship arising or resulting from any cause without the act, fault or neglect of the shipper, his agents or servants'. The general liability of the shipper is seen in this provision in the sense that the shipper is liable for the carrier's loss or damages, if they are caused by the fault or negligence of the shipper, including the fault or negligence of the shipper's agents and servants.

Article 4(3) appears to be a catch-all clause. It has two major functions. First, it imposes a general liability upon the shipper. Second, it provides a defence to the shipper, on which the shipper may deny any liability if there is a lack of fault or negligence on the part of the shipper, his or her agents or servants. Since the shipper's liability under the Hague-Visby

---

116. Decided by the Federal Court of Canada on 8 December 1995, available at <http://www.fja-cmf.gc.ca>.
117. The Hague-Visby Rules, art 4(3).

Rules is set out specifically in arts 3(5) and 4(6) respectively, art 4(3) appears to give more protection than liability to the shipper. However, in the letter of the law, art 4(3) does imply a general liability on the part of the shipper.

Liability to pay freight

[4.134] The liability to pay freight is the basic obligation of the shipper. The payment is always part of any contract of carriage, although sometimes the shipper and carrier may agree that the freight is to be paid by the consignee after the completion of the carriage. In such cases, the risk in freight transfers to the carrier. This means that the risk of losing the freight for whatever reason is borne by the carrier. But in most cases, the shipper must pay freight in advance before the carrier accepts the goods for carriage.

[4.135] The Hague-Visby Rules do not have specific rules on the payment of freight. In practice, the unpaid carrier has a lien in the goods carried by him or her before the payment of freight. The unpaid carrier may also sue the shipper in contract to recover the unpaid freight. Such contractual right can be illustrated by a Chinese case of shipping law. In *Shipping Co of Tianjin v China International Engineering and Materials Corp and Tongli Development Co*,[118] the plaintiff, the Shipping Company of Tianjin, sued the two defendants for unpaid freight under a contract of carriage signed by Tongli Development Company on behalf of Tongli and China International Engineering.

The two defendants were partners in a contract for the sale of timber to a Japanese buyer. The contract of carriage was concluded by an employee of Tongli in the name of China International Engineering. The Japanese buyer was unhappy about the quality of the timber. The two defendants disagreed on who should be responsible for the loss incurred, and neither was willing to pay the freight due. The Maritime Court of Dalian noted that the contract of carriage was concluded by an employee of Tongli in the name of China International Engineering, and held that the contract was concluded by China International Engineering and that the employee of Tongli acted as the agent of China International Engineering. Subsequently, China International Engineering was ordered to pay the freight of US$133,428 to the plaintiff. China International Engineering's appeal to the Provincial Supreme Court failed. The major basis for the court's decision in this case is the fact that the contract of carriage was concluded in the name of China International Engineering. The court affirmed the existence of an agent and principal relationship between the employees of Tongli and China International Engineering.

[4.136] Back freight, which means the freight incurred from carrying the undelivered goods back to the shipper, is an issue which may sometimes arise from a contract of carriage between the carrier and the shipper. Whether or not the shipper is obliged to pay for the back freight can only be determined in the circumstances concerned, and is often subject to debate, unless the bill of lading has expressly incorporated a clause on back freight.

In the absence of any agreement, the shipper and carrier may disagree on whether the payment of back freight is reasonable. The shipper may argue that the carrier is obliged to carry the goods to the agreed port. Thus, in the case of non-delivery at the agreed port,

---

118. *Selected Cases of the People's Court*, note 87 above, pp 142–9.

the carrier is liable for all the loss unless the non-delivery is caused by the fault of the shipper. The carrier may argue that the non-delivery is not caused by the carrier's fault, and therefore the shipper must pay the carrier back freight for looking after and bringing back the goods. The major point of argument is the basis on which the carrier is entitled to claim back freight or the shipper is obliged to pay back freight. Is the obligation based on contract or equity? If in contract, there must be a contractual term to give rise to such obligation. If in equity, there must be an equitable principle which requires the shipper to compensate the carrier for the service voluntarily rendered by the carrier. Since the Hague-Visby Rules or the Hague Rules do not deal with the payment of freight at all, the issue of back freight is entirely subject to the relevant domestic law governing the dispute.

[4.137] *Burns Philp and Co Ltd v Gillespie Brothers Pty Ltd*

(1947) 74 CLR 148

Non-delivery caused by a state of war, whether back freight is payable

Facts: The appellant was the carrier, and the respondent was the cargo-owner. In 1941, the carrier carried a cargo of flour for the shipper from Australia to Singapore. The vessel reached Batavia, but could not reach Singapore for fear of being captured by the Japanese forces. The vessel returned to Fremantle, Australia with the undelivered cargo, and the carrier eventually delivered the cargo to the shipper at Sydney. The carrier demanded back freight from the shipper, who paid about £795 under protest in order to take possession of the cargo. The carrier's claim was based on the allegation that the ship was the cargo-owner's agent of necessity, and thus the cargo-owner should compensate the carrier for the reasonable and proper act to bring the cargo back to Australia. The cargo-owner subsequently sued the carrier in the Supreme Court of New South Wales and won the case. The carrier appealed to the High Court of Australia.

Decision: The High Court by a 4:1 majority dismissed the appeal. Latham CJ as the dissenting judge allowed the appeal. As to the crucial issue relating to the basis of the carrier's claim for back freight, his Honour observed (at 177) as follows:

> When an emergency threatening the loss or destruction of cargo occurs, and no term of the contract is applicable to the circumstances, there are three possible views of the position of the master of the ship — (1) the master has no right (and *a fortiori* no duty) to do anything with respect to the cargo *unless*: it is required or at least authorised by some provision, express or implied, to be found in the terms of the contract between the shipowner and the cargo owner; or is justifiable under an authority subsequently given (eg, in reply to a communication from the master to a cargo-owner asking for instructions); (2) the master is entitled, but not bound, to take any reasonable and prudent, though uncovenanted, action in order to preserve the cargo; (3) the master is under a duty to act in the interest of the cargo-owner and therefore to take active steps to preserve the cargo. If he does not so act, the shipowner will be liable in damage.

Subsequently, his Honour dismissed the first and second views for their inconsistency with the relevant case law, and upheld the third view, which supported his Honour's conclusion that the carrier was entitled to receive the back freight for bring the cargo to the nearest safe port.

The majority judges (Rich, Starke, Dixon and McTiernan JJ) delivered separate judgments. Rich J largely based his decision on the combined ground that there was neither a contractual right nor any right in the case law to claim back freight. Starke, Dixon and McTiernan JJ denied the appeal largely on the ground that returning to Australia with the cargo was a measure to avoid a common danger faced by the vessel and the cargo. In the absence of general average, the carrier was not entitled to claim back freight from the cargo-owner for avoiding the common risk. The majority also denied *The 'Argos'* case (1873) LR 5 PC 134 to be a general authority for the carrier's entitlement to claim back freight.

Carrier's liability under the Hamburg Rules

Carrier's basic liability

[4.138] While the Hague-Visby Rules specify the duty of 'due diligence' to make the ship seaworthy and fit for carrying goods, of properly staffing, equipping and supplying the ship and of carefully handling goods, the Hamburg Rules impose a general duty upon the carrier to guarantee the safety of the goods when the goods are under the carrier's care or custody. For example, art 5(1) of the Hamburg Rules states that the:

> ... carrier is liable for loss resulting from loss of or damage to the goods, as well as from delay in delivery, if the occurrence which caused the loss, damage or delay took place while the goods were in his charge as defined in article 4, unless the carrier proves that he, his servants or agents took all measures that could reasonably be required to avoid the occurrence and its consequences.

This provision imposes a general duty of reasonable care upon the carrier to take care of the goods and to deliver them on time.

[4.139] Under art 5 of the Hamburg Rules, a carrier is liable:

- subject to the exercise of reasonable care, for loss of or damage to goods which are under his or her care;
- subject to the exercise of reasonable care, for delay in delivery as agreed in the contract; and
- for loss of or damage to goods in a fire caused by the fault or neglect of the carrier or his or her servants or agents.

The above duties can be further simplified into two main duties: a duty to take reasonable care of the goods, and a duty to deliver the goods pursuant to contract, as the fault or neglect of the carrier, or of his or her agents or servants, in causing a fire will result in either a breach of the duty to take reasonable care of the goods, or a breach of the duty to deliver the goods on time.

Carrier's duty to take care of goods

[4.140] Under art 5(1), a carrier is prima facie liable for any loss of or damage to the goods resulting from any cause while the goods are under his or her custody or care. Two points are important under this duty:

- the cause which results in the loss or damage occurs when the goods are under the custody, care or charge of the carrier; and
- the period of the carrier's responsibility for the goods (see **[4.73]**) is not limited to 'tackle to tackle', such as is defined as 'carriage of goods' in art 1(e) of the Hague-Visby Rules.

[4.141] There is a rebuttable presumption that the carrier is liable for loss of or damage to the goods while the goods are in his or her charge. This means that under art 5(1) of the Hamburg Rules the carrier is liable for the loss of or damage to the goods under his or her care, unless the carrier proves that he or she, or his or her servants or agents, has taken all reasonable measures 'that could reasonably be required to avoid the occurrence [of the cause] and its consequences'. The burden of proof lies on the carrier to establish that he or she has done everything he or she was reasonably expected to do for the purpose of avoiding the loss or damage or its consequences; or alternatively, that the loss or damage was caused by *force majeure*.

Carrier's duty to deliver goods on time

[4.142] A carrier is prima facie liable for delay in delivery under art 5(1). This presumption can be rebutted by the carrier proving that the cause for the delay is beyond his or her control, and he or she has done everything reasonable to avoid delay.

Article 5(2) defines the meaning of 'delay'. Under the Hamburg Rules 'delay' occurs in the following circumstances:

- where the carrier fails to deliver the goods at the agreed port within the agreed time; and
- where, in the absence of an agreed time, the carrier fails to deliver the goods at the agreed port within a reasonable time within which a diligent carrier is expected to deliver.

[4.143] The carrier's failure to deliver as agreed may amount to a presumed loss of the goods in question. Under art 5(3) a shipper is entitled to treat non-delivery as a total loss of the goods after 60 consecutive days following the expiry of the agreed or reasonable time for delivery under the contract of carriage. A carrier who intends to avoid liability must prove that the cause for delay or loss is beyond his or her control.

Carrier's duty and acts of agents

[4.144] Under the Hamburg Rules, the carrier's duty extends to his or her agents or servants. The carrier is fully responsible for any act or omission of his or her servants and agents and a breach of contract by an agent or servant of the carrier is regarded as a breach by the carrier him- or herself. The same rule applies to the actual carrier and his or her servants and agents. It follows that a servant or agent is entitled to avail him- or herself of the defences or limits of liability available to the carrier for the act or omission carried out within the scope of his or her employment. The aggregate of the amounts recoverable from the carrier and his or her servants or agents for any act or omission, either in contract or in torts, is limited to the maximum limits of liability under art 6 of the Hamburg Rules.

Carrier's duty and acts of actual carrier

[4.145] The Hamburg Rules distinguish a 'carrier' from an 'actual carrier'. A carrier is the person who enters into a contract of carriage as 'carrier' with the shipper. An actual carrier is the person whose services are engaged by the carrier for the purpose of performing part of or the whole contract of carriage. There is no contractual relationship between an actual carrier and the shipper. This means that generally speaking, there is no redress in contract for the shipper to hold the actual carrier accountable. In order to deal with this issue, art 10(1) of the Hamburg Rules provides that the 'carrier' is liable for any act or omission of the 'actual carrier' or his or her agents or servants in the performance of the contract of carriage. The shipper has redress against the carrier for any loss of or damage to goods caused by an act or omission of the actual carrier or his or her agents.

[4.146] Article 10 also sets out the following rules for defining and clarifying the relationships and liabilities of the carrier and actual carrier:

- the actual carrier is subject to the same duties as the carrier in performing the contract of carriage as authorised by the carrier;
- the actual carrier is prima facie entitled to rely on the provisions of the Hamburg Rules and is not bound by any agreement between the shipper and carrier altering the effect of the provisions unless the actual carrier expressly accepts otherwise;
- the carrier is not exempt from any undertaking in contract with the shipper regardless of whether the actual carrier accepts or not;
- where and to the extent that both the carrier and actual carrier are liable, their liability is joint or several;
- the aggregate of the amounts recoverable from the carrier, the actual carrier and their servants and agents are subject to the maximum limits of liability of the carrier under art 6; and
- the carrier and actual carrier have a right of recourse against each other.

[4.147] The carrier and actual carrier may be regarded as the same person (or party) for the purpose of certain provisions under the Hamburg Rules. For example, art 19(6) provides that if the goods have been delivered by an actual carrier, any written notice claiming loss, damage or delay in delivery can be given either to the actual carrier or the carrier and it should be deemed to have been received by both of them. This rule avoids the legal technicality as to whether one of them has knowledge of the claim.

Period of carrier's liability

[4.148] The carrier is responsible for the safety of goods for a much longer time under the Hamburg Rules than under the Hague-Visby Rules. Under the Hague-Visby Rules, the parties to a contract of carriage can by agreement extend the carrier's responsibility over goods to the period prior and subsequent to the loading and unloading of the goods. In the absence of such agreement, the carrier is responsible for the safety of the goods from 'tackle to tackle', which means when the goods are within the ship's rails after their loading and before their unloading. Under the Hamburg Rules, the responsibility of the carrier 'covers the period during which the carrier is in charge of the goods at the port of loading, during the carriage and at the port of discharge'.

[4.149] Under art 4(2) 'the carrier is deemed to be in charge of the goods' in the following circumstances:

- from the time the carrier takes over the goods from a shipper or his or her agents until the goods have been handed over to the consignee, or placed at the disposal of the consignee pursuant to contract or trade usage, or handed over to a port authority or person as required by law at the port of discharge; and
- from the time the carrier takes over the goods from a port authority or any person who has authority under law to take possession of the goods before shipment until the goods have been handed over to the consignee, or placed at the disposal of the

consignee pursuant to contract or trade usage, or handed over to a port authority or person as required by law at the port of discharge.

Carrier's duty and live animals

[4.150] The carrier's liability for live animals is qualified in art 5(5) of the Hamburg Rules. This provision states that 'the carrier is not liable for loss, damage or delay in delivery resulting from any special risks inherent in that kind of carriage'. The onus of proof is on the carrier to establish that any loss, damage or delay in delivery is caused by an inherent vice in the animals or inherent risk in the carrying of the animals. In the case of loss of or damage to, or delay in delivery of, live animals, the carrier does not have to prove the exercise of reasonable care, but he or she must prove that he or she has complied with any special instructions from the shipper. Once the carrier establishes the existence of inherent risk and compliance with the shipper's instructions, it is the duty of the shipper to prove that the loss, damage or delay was caused by the fault or neglect of the carrier or his or her agents or servants, if the shipper intends to sue the carrier for breach of contract.

Carrier's breach as a concurrent cause

[4.151] The Hamburg Rules hold the carrier liable in proportion to his or her contribution to the loss, damage or delay, if the loss, damage or delay was caused by concurrent causes. This is different from the Hague-Visby Rules, which hold the carrier liable for the whole loss or damage if the carrier's failure to exercise his or her duty is a concurrent and decisive cause of the loss: see *Shipping Corp of India Ltd v Gamlen Chemical Co (A'asia) Pty Ltd* (1980) 147 CLR 142; 32 ALR 609. Under art 5(7) of the Hamburg Rules, the carrier is liable only to the extent that the loss, damage or delay is attributable to his or her (including agent's or servant's) fault or neglect. However, the onus of proof is on the carrier to establish that his or her fault or neglect has not caused the loss, damage or delay for which he or she claims not to be responsible.

Limits of carrier's liability

[4.152] The Hamburg Rules set out a higher limit of liability than the Hague-Visby Rules. Article 6(1)(a) states that the 'liability of the carrier for loss resulting from loss of or damage to goods according to the provisions of article 5 is limited to an amount equivalent to 835 units of account per package or other shipping unit or 2.5 units of account per kilogram of gross weight of the goods lost or damaged, whichever is the higher'.

Unlike the Hague-Visby Rules, the Hamburg Rules also set a limit for compensating loss arising from delay in delivery. Article 6(1)(b) provides that in case of delay in delivery, the liability of the carrier is limited to 'an amount equivalent to two and a half times the freight payable for the goods delayed, but not exceeding the total freight payable under the contract of carriage of goods by sea'. However, the maximum amount of compensation for delay in delivery, or in aggregate of liability for loss, damage and delay in delivery, is limited to 835 units of account per package or 2.5 units of account per kilogram of gross weight of the goods.

Carrier's liability and limitation of actions

[4.153] The limitation of actions is two years under the Hamburg Rules. This is set out in art 20, which states that the limitation period begins to run from the day following the day on which the carrier delivered the goods (if the goods have been delivered), or from the day following the last day on which the goods should have been delivered. The limitation period can be extended by the person against whom a claim is made, through written notice to the claimant. The limitation period is a benefit to the party against whom the claim is being made, and thus can only be extended by the express consent of that person. Similar to the Hague-Visby Rules, an action for indemnity against a third party by the person held liable is subject to the limitation period of the forum where the proceedings are instituted.

[4.154] The limitation for actions against delay in delivery is further qualified by the requirement to give notice of claim under art 19(5). The provision requires the consignee claiming compensation for delay in delivery to give written notice of the claim to the carrier within 60 days after the goods were handed over to him or her. It must be emphasised that the limitation of 60 days begins to run from the time at which the late delivery was made, rather than from the date on which the goods ought to have been delivered. Failure to comply with the requirement of art 19(5) leads to the loss of the right to claim compensation.

Loss of right to limit liability

[4.155] Under art 8 of the Hamburg Rules, the carrier and his or her agents or servants are not allowed to rely on the limit of liability if they have intentionally or recklessly caused loss, damage or delay, or have acted or failed to act with knowledge that such loss, damage or delay would probably result. The onus of proof appears to lie on the shipper or consignee alleging the existence of such intention, recklessness and knowledge.

Carrier's liability and bills of lading

Relevant provisions

[4.156] Bills of lading are regulated in arts 14–16 of the Hamburg Rules. Article 14 deals with the issue of bills of lading; art 15 deals with the contents of bills of lading; and art 16 deals with the effect of bills of lading.

Issue of a bill of lading

[4.157] Article 14 sets out the following rules for the issue of a bill of lading:

- the carrier is obliged, on the demand of the shipper, to issue a bill of lading;
- the bill of lading can be signed by the master of the ship or any person authorised by the carrier; and
- the signature on the bill can be made in any form, such as handwriting, facsimile, perforated, stamped, symbols, or any mechanical or electronic means, which is allowed by the law of the country where the bill is issued.

Contents of the bill of lading

[4.158] Article 15 requires the bill of lading to contain the following particulars:
- the nature of the goods;
- the leading marks for identification;
- the number of packages, pieces or units;
- the weight or quantity of the goods;
- the apparent condition of the goods;
- the name and principal place of business of the carrier;
- the name of the shipper;
- the name and address of the consignee, if applicable;
- the port of loading as specified in the contract of carriage;
- the date on which the goods were taken over by the carrier;
- the port of discharge as specified in the contract of carriage;
- the number of the original bill of lading, if applicable;
- the place of issuance of the bill;
- the signature of the person issuing the bill;
- the freight payable by the consignee, if relevant;
- the extra obligations undertaken by the carrier, if any;
- the statement, if applicable, that the goods shall or may be carried on deck;
- the date or the period of delivery which has been agreed by the parties; and
- the agreed higher amount of the carrier's liability, if applicable.

The carrier is obliged to exchange a house or received bill of lading for a shipped bill of lading after the shipment, but he or she has the option to indorse or amend a house or received bill and to make it into a shipped bill. It must be pointed out that a bill of lading is not invalid merely by virtue of its failure to contain the above particulars, provided that it satisfies the definition of 'bill of lading' set out in art 1(7) of the Hamburg Rules.

Effect of a bill of lading

[4.159] Under art 16(1), the carrier is obliged to state in a shipped bill of lading any inaccuracies or suspected inaccuracies in the particulars of the bill, if he or she has no reasonable means of verifying them. This is because the particulars are furnished by the shipper and the carrier is expected to verify them before incorporating them into the bill of lading. If the carrier knows that the particulars are inaccurate, or has reasonable grounds to suspect their accuracy, but has no reasonable means of verification, the carrier must state the inaccuracies, suspicions or the lack of reasonable means of checking, as the case may be, for the purpose of drawing the consignee's attention to the matter concerned.

[4.160] Under art 16(2) and (3), a shipped bill of lading is prima facie evidence of the following:
- that the goods have been shipped;

[4.160]

- the goods are shipped in good condition unless the carrier specifies otherwise in the bill;
- the receipt of the goods by the carrier; and
- that no freight or demurrage (which is a liquidated damage payable by the charterer, or another person, who fails to load or discharge goods within the time stipulated in the contract of carriage) is payable by the consignee, unless the carrier specifies otherwise in the bill.

It must be pointed out that the presumptions that the carrier has received and shipped the goods, and that the consignee is not liable for freight or demurrage, can be rebutted by the carrier providing contrary evidence. However, the presumptions cannot be rebutted if the bill of lading has been transferred to the hands of a third party, who is bona fide for value without knowledge of the inaccuracies.

Carrier's liability and notice of claim

[4.161] Article 19 sets out the rules for claims made by either a consignee or a carrier. In general, the consignee or the carrier claiming loss, damage or delay is required to give notice of the nature of the claim to the other in writing in compliance with the time requirement under art 19.

The following rules apply to notice given by a consignee or shipper under art 19:

- when damage or loss is apparent, the consignee is required to give notice of the loss and damage not later than the working date following the day when the goods were handed over to him or her;
- when damage or loss is not apparent, the consignee is required to give notice of the damage and loss within 15 consecutive days after the day when the goods were handed over to the consignee; and
- when the damage or loss is subject to a joint survey or inspection at the time of delivery, the consignee is not required to give notice for loss or damage revealed in the survey or inspection.

A carrier or actual carrier claiming damage or loss against a consignee or shipper is given a longer period. Under art 19(7), the carrier or actual carrier is required to give notice within 90 days after the occurrence of the loss or damage, or after the delivery of the goods as agreed in the contract of carriage. This requirement should be read with art 20, which sets out a limitation period of two years for any action arising under the Hamburg Rules.

Carrier's liability and freedom of contract

[4.162] While the parties are free to deal with matters falling outside the Hamburg Rules or to increase the liability of the carrier by agreement, they are not allowed to contract out the carrier's liability under the convention. This is made abundantly clear in art 23, which nullifies any clause of a contract or bill of lading which directly or indirectly derogates from the provisions of the Hamburg Rules, and results in the lessening of the carrier's liability under the Hamburg Rules. In order to enforce this principle, art 23(3) requires all contracts of carriage and bills of lading to state expressly that 'the carriage is subject to the provisions of this convention [the Hamburg Rules] which nullify any stipulation derogating therefrom to the detriment of the shipper or the consignee'.

[4.163] Article 23(4) requires the carrier to compensate the shipper or consignee who has sustained damages or losses because of a stipulation prohibited under art 23. The compensation includes not only the loss and damage arising from the carrier's failure to comply with the provisions of the Hamburg Rules, but also the costs of litigation to nullify the stipulation in question judicially. However, it is not clear whether the two-year limitation period applies to proceedings based on art 23(4).

Carrier's liabilities in comparison

[4.164] Generally speaking, the Hamburg Rules impose a much wider duty of care upon the carrier, as can be seen by the following:

- First, the carrier is liable from the time when the goods are handed over to him or her, or his or her agents or servants, to the time when the goods are handed over to the shipper, consignee or their agents under the contract. Under the Hague Rules or the Hague-Visby Rules, the carrier's liability begins when the goods pass the rail of the ship in loading and ends when the goods pass the rail of the ship in unloading, unless specified otherwise.
- Second, the carrier is liable for any loss or damage incurred when the goods are under his or her duty of care. Under the Hague Rules or the Hague-Visby Rules the carrier's liabilities are specifically limited to the extent of providing a seaworthy ship, properly supplying, equipping and staffing the ship, and carefully and adequately loading, stowing and handling the goods.
- Third, under the Hamburg Rules, the general duty of care expressly extends to the agents or servants of the carrier and the actual carrier and his or her agents or servants. Under the Hague Rules or Hague-Visby Rules, the carrier is not responsible for the intentional or negligent act or omission of master, pilot or servants committed in the navigation or management of the ship.
- Fourth, the Hamburg Rules adopt 'reasonable care' as the ground for defining the carrier's liability, rather than the test of 'due diligence' used under the Hague Rules or the Hague-Visby Rules. 'Reasonable care' appears to have a more definite content than 'due diligence', because 'reasonable care' reflects a level of care the carrier is expected to have in the circumstances concerned.
- Fifth, the Hamburg Rules clearly provide that the carrier is liable for loss or damage arising from delay in delivery. Under the Hague Rules or the Hague-Visby Rules such loss or damage may only be claimed if it relates to the seaworthiness of the ship or the staffing or supply of the ship. In other words, delay caused by an act or negligence of the ship's master or carrier's servants in navigation or management of the ship has no remedy under the Hague Rules or the Hague-Visby Rules.
- Last, but not least, the Hamburg Rules adopt a higher monetary limit on the liability of the carrier. In the event of loss or damage, the carrier's liability is limited to 835 units of account per package or other shipping unit or 2.5 units of account per kilogram of gross weight of the goods lost or damaged, whichever is the higher. In the event of

delay, the carrier's liability is limited to an amount equivalent to two-and-a-half times the freight payable for the goods delayed (assuming partial delay is possible), but not exceeding the total freight payable under the contract of carriage. These can be compared with £100 sterling per package or unit under the Hague Rules, or 666.67 units of account per package or unit or two units of account per kilogram of gross weight of the goods under the Hague-Visby Rules.

Shipper's liability under the Hamburg Rules

Shipper's general duty

[4.165] The shipper is a party to a contract of carriage. It is necessary to give redress to the carrier for any loss or damage arising from the shipper's breach of contract or fault or neglect. Both the Hague Rules and the Hague-Visby Rules deal with the shipper's responsibilities very briefly, but the Hamburg Rules stipulate much more clearly the liability of the shipper.

In general terms, a shipper is liable to the carrier only when the shipper or his or her agents or servants have been in fault or negligence. Article 12 provides that the shipper or his or her servants or agents are not liable for loss or damage sustained by the carrier or actual carrier unless the loss or damage was caused by the fault or neglect of the shipper or his or her agents or servants. Article 12 implies that a carrier or actual carrier has a separate cause of action against a shipper, or his or her servant or agent, who has intentionally or negligently caused the loss or damage in question.

Shipper's liability and dangerous goods

[4.166] The shipper is liable under art 13 to inform the carrier of the dangerous nature of the goods to be carried. This duty requires the shipper to mark or label clearly and adequately the dangerous goods as 'dangerous', and to inform the carrier or actual carrier of the dangerous nature of the goods when handing them over. The declaration of the shipper or his or her agents or servants is crucial for complying with the shipper's duty to inform. There is no presumed knowledge of the carrier or actual carrier if the shipper fails to inform. Thus the shipper's failure to inform the carrier of the dangerous nature of the goods gives rise to a cause of action to the carrier against the shipper. Like the Hague Rules and the Hague-Visby Rules, the Hamburg Rules allow the carrier to dispose, destroy or render the goods innocuous during the voyage if circumstances so require.

Shipper's liability and guarantee

[4.167] The shipper has a general liability to provide accurate and true information to the carrier for the purpose of issuing a bill of lading. Article 17(1) imposes an implied obligation upon the shipper to indemnify the carrier for any loss or damage arising from inaccurate information provided by the shipper. If a bill of lading contains any inaccurate or incorrect information, without the knowledge of the carrier, the carrier who has redress against the shipper is still liable to the holder of the bill. In such a case the carrier has to compensate the holder of the bill and later seek indemnity from the shipper.

[4.168] A letter of indemnity in the context of the bill of lading is a form of the shipper's guarantee against the carrier's loss or damage caused by the shipper's act or omission. While a genuine letter of indemnity is allowed, art 17 prohibits any arrangement based on a letter of indemnity for the purpose of defrauding a consignee or any third party. Under this provision, a letter of indemnity has the following characteristics:

- any letter of indemnity undertaken by the shipper for the purpose of issuing a clean bill of lading is void against the consignee or third party;
- any letter of indemnity undertaken by the shipper for the issuing of a clean bill of lading is unenforceable against the shipper if the carrier intentionally issued the untrue bill to defraud a third party;
- any letter of indemnity undertaken by the shipper for the issuing of a clean bill of lading is enforceable against the shipper if an inaccuracy of the bill was not a result of the carrier's intentional act or omission to defraud a third party;[119] and
- the carrier defrauding a third party, who acted in reliance on the untrue information of a bill of lading, is not entitled to rely on the benefit of the limitation of liability under the Hamburg Rules.

The above rules will certainly put *Hellenic Lines Ltd v Chemoleum Corp* [1972] 1 Lloyd's Rep 350 in a different light. It must be pointed out that defrauding any third party by issuing an untrue bill of lading is absolutely prohibited in the Hamburg Rules. Such conduct will lead not only to the loss of the carrier's right of indemnity against the shipper, but also the attraction of liability (which will not be subject to the limitations in the Hamburg Rules), for any loss or damage of the third party flowing from the bill of lading.

Arbitration under the Hamburg Rules

Right to arbitrate

[4.169] The right to arbitrate under the Hamburg Rules has three features:

- First, the parties to a contract of carriage or a bill of lading have a right to arbitrate their dispute under the provisions of the Hamburg Rules. This right can be exercised in an agreement in writing before the occurrence of the dispute. Such an agreement does not have the effect of derogating from the provisions of the Hamburg Rules as prohibited in art 23, because art 22(4) requires any arbitrator or arbitral tribunal formed for the purpose of art 22(1) to 'apply the rules of this Convention [the Hamburg Rules]'.
- Second, the parties have also a right to arbitrate their dispute under any other rules. This right must be exercised after a claim under the contract of carriage or bill of lading has arisen. This rule will certainly put *The Krasnogrosk* (1993) 31 NSWLR 18,

---

119. It must be emphasised that an intentional act or omission in this provision refers to an act or omission to defraud a third party. This means that an intentional act or omission, which was not intended to defraud a third party and which indeed did not cause any damage to the third party, is not an intentional act or omission in art 17. However, on the other hand, a carrier will lose the right of recourse against the shipper even if his or her intentional act or omission to defraud a third party did not cause any damage to the third party.

[4.169]

Appendix 2, in a totally different light. There is no express requirement that the arbitration agreement for this purpose must be made in writing under art 22(6).

- Third, in the case of any inconsistency between a charterparty bill of lading and the charterparty, the arbitration clause in the charterparty is not enforceable against the holder of the bill of lading. The holder of the bill of lading is entitled to rely on its terms if it does not expressly incorporate the arbitration clause.

Place of arbitration

[4.170] If the parties agree in writing to arbitrate any future dispute but fail to specify a place of arbitration, they must arbitrate the dispute in one of the following places:

- the principal place of business of the defendant, or in the absence thereof, the habitual residence of the defendant;
- the place where the contract was made, unless the defendant has no establishment or agency in that place;
- the port of loading;
- the port of discharge; or
- any other place expressly agreed in the arbitration agreement.

It must be pointed out the parties do have a right to choose a place of arbitration under the Hamburg Rules.

♦

[4.171] *Thyssen Canada Ltd v Mariana Maritime SA*

Decided 7 May 1999, Federal Court of Canada[1]

Enforcement of arbitration agreement

Facts: The plaintiff, Thyssen Canada, purchased 18,000 metric tonnes of hot rolled coils from Ferrostaal under CFR Windsor, Ontario, Canada. The goods which were manufactured by a Romanian mill were carried by the vessel known as the *Mariana*. Two bills of lading were issued by the master of the *Mariana* on two different dates, acknowledging the receipt of the cargo in good order and condition. A fire broke out when the vessel was in Turkey and the goods were damaged during the fire. In October 1998, the plaintiff sued the defendant carrier in the Federal Court of Canada. The defendant asked the court to refer the dispute to arbitration in London according to ss 3 and 50 of the Federal Court Act 1985 of Canada, and ss 5 and 6 of the Commercial Arbitration Act 1985 of Canada, by relying on the arbitration clause incorporated into the two bills of lading. The relevant arbitration clause actually incorporated the terms and conditions of the charterparty into the bills of lading concerned. Two charterparties were relevant to the vessel. One was a demise charterparty and another was a voyage charterparty. Both charterparties contained the identical arbitration clause. The plaintiff argued that the dispute arose from the bills of lading and that the charterparties are thus irrelevant in the present case. It also argued that the bills of lading were subject to the Hamburg Rules, which had been adopted by Romania, because the carriage started from the Romanian port. If the defendant's argument was correct, the present proceedings must be stayed under the relevant Canadian laws.

> **Decision:** Blais J of the Federal Court of Canada held that the bills of lading had incorporated the arbitration clause contained in the two charterparties and stayed the present proceedings in favour of arbitration in London. In addressing the issue of the Hamburg Rules, his Honour observed that even if the bills of lading were subject to the Hamburg Rules, Article 22 of the Hamburg Rules makes an arbitration clause enforceable in a case where a bill of lading expressly incorporates an arbitration clause.
>
> 1. Canadian Cases — available at <http://www.fja.gc.ca>.

♦

Australian Carriage of Goods by Sea Act 1991

[4.172] The Carriage of Goods by Sea Act 1991 (Cth) was passed in 1991. It appears to have three regimes of carriage of goods by sea law, because of the three schedules contained in the Act. In particular, Schedule 1 contains the Hague-Visby Rules, Schedule 1A which was inserted into the Act in 1998 contains the modified Hague-Visby Rules, and Schedule 2 contains the Hamburg Rules. Despite the existence of the three regimes, someone may argue that there are only two regimes in the Act, that is, the 'amended Hague Rules' (in the words used in the Act) and the Hamburg Rules, because of the wording of ss 7 and 10 of the Act. When the Act was passed in 1991, it indeed had two regimes, that is, the Hague-Visby Rules and the Hamburg Rules. The third regime, the modified Hague-Visby Rules, was introduced through the amendments to the Act made in 1997 and 1998 respectively. These modified rules may to some extent be described as a compromise between the Hague-Visby Rules and the Hamburg Rules. Alternatively, it can be said that the modified rules reflect the Australian perspective of what the modern Hague-Visby Rules should be. The conditions for the operation of each regime are set out in the Act.

[4.173] In terms of structure, the Carriage of Goods by Sea Act 1991 (Cth) has four parts, which consist of 22 sections, and three Schedules containing the Hague-Visby Rules, the modified Hague-Visby Rules and the Hamburg Rules. Part 1 of the Act deals with preliminary issues, such as the relationships between each part, the object of the Act and the interpretation of basic terms. Part 2 regulates the application of the amended Hague Rules which, as we will see later, refers to a combination of the Hague-Visby Rules and their modifications, with the effect that the modified Hague-Visby Rules prevail in most cases but do not totally replace the Hague-Visby Rules in Australia. Part 3 regulates the application of the Hamburg Rules in the future, which appears to be a future event with considerable uncertainty. Part 4 deals with miscellaneous issues, such as the relationships between the Act and the Trade Practices Act 1974 (Cth) and the repeal of the Sea-Carriage of Goods Act 1924 (Cth).

Generally speaking, the application of the amended Hague Rules is subject to the combined effect of Pts 1 and 2, as well as Schedule 1 and Schedule 1A; and the application of the Hamburg Rules in Australia is subject to the combined effect of Pts 1 and 3 as well as Schedule 2. The relevant provisions of the Act will be examined in the relevant subsections in this part of the book.

[4.174] In broad terms, the relationships among the said three regimes of carriage of goods by sea law are defined in s 3(2) of the Carriage of Goods by Sea Act 1991 (Cth), which provides as follows:

> The object of the Act is to be achieved by:
> (i) as a first step — replacing the Sea-Carriage of Goods Act 1924 with provisions that give effect to the Brussels Convention as amended by the Visby Protocol and the SDR Protocol, and as modified in accordance with regulations under s 7 [author's note: this refers to the modified Hague-Visby Rules contained in Schedule 1A]; and
> (ii) as a second step — replacing those provisions with provisions that give effect to the Hamburg Convention, if the Minister decides, after conducting a review, that those provisions should be so replaced.

[4.175] The above provision suggests that, if we regard the Hague-Visby Rules and their modifications as two separate regimes, the two regimes co-exist, both are exclusive to the Hamburg Rules.

Contracts for the carriage of goods by air

An introduction to the Chicago System

Structure of the Chicago System

[4.176] As we have seen in **[4.7]**, the Chicago System is based on the Chicago Convention on International Civil Aviation of 1944. It was adopted with two annexes dealing with the international air services transit and international air transport respectively, in Chicago, on 7 December 1944. But a member of the Chicago Convention has an option to decide whether or not to ratify any or all of the annexes. In 1999, the Chicago Convention had more than 185 countries and jurisdictions.

Most members opt to ratify the Transit Agreement, instead of the Transport Agreement, largely due to the fact that the Transit Agreement requires the members to undertake the obligation to provide to each other two privileges or freedoms, but the Transport Agreement promotes five privileges or freedoms (for detailed discussion, see **[4.185]**). The option to choose one of the annexed agreements under the Chicago Convention is one of the characteristics of the Chicago System. The Chicago Convention was amended in 1968 to recognise the official status of the text of the convention in French and Spanish; and in 1977 to give official status to its text in Russian. In addition, the convention was amended in 1980 by the Protocol relating to Article 83*bis*. The amendment was open for the members' approval. Many annexes dealing with technical issues and interpreting the provisions of the convention have been added to the convention by the International Civil Aviation Organisation (ICAO), which is an international organisation established in pursuance of the Chicago Convention. As far as the structure of the convention is concerned, it can be said that the Chicago Convention mainly refers to a combination of the Chicago Convention as adopted in 1944 and one of its original annexes, that is, the Transport Agreement or the Transit Agreement. It also includes the annexes adding technical details to the original provisions of the Chicago Convention as approved by the members.

[4.177] Another feature of the structure of the Chicago Convention is the establishment of ICAO. It came into existence in 1944 as the Provisional International Civil Aviation Organisation.[120] Later, in 1947, it became one of the specialised agencies of the United Nations.

The objectives of ICAO are set out in art 44 of the Chicago Convention:

> The aims and objectives of the Organisation are to develop the principles and techniques of international air navigation and to foster the planning and development of international air transport so as to:
>
> Insure the safe and orderly growth of international civil aviation throughout the world;
> Encourage the arts of aircraft design and operation for peaceful purposes;
> Encourage the development of airways, airports, and air navigation facilities for international civil aviation;
> Meet the needs of the peoples of the world for safe, regular, efficient and economical air transport;
> Prevent economic waste caused by unreasonable competition;
> Insure that the rights of contracting states are fully respected and that every contracting state has a fair opportunity to operate international airlines;
> Avoid discrimination between contracting states;
> Promote safety of flight in international air navigation;
> Promote generally the development of all aspects of international civil aeronautics.

This provision reflects the major functions of ICAO. Largely, ICAO is responsible for enforcing the Chicago Convention and coordinating the relationships between the members.

[4.178] The structure of ICAO is mainly defined in arts 43–63 of the Chicago Convention. Article 43 of the Chicago Convention provides that ICAO should be set up under the convention and that ICAO is made up of an Assembly, a Council, and such other bodies as may be necessary. Accordingly, ICAO has an assembly which consists of all members and a council which consists of 33 elected members.[121] While the assembly has regular meetings at least once every three years, the council is in fact the executive body of ICAO with permanent status. The council is responsible to the assembly and is required to submit annual reports to the assembly under art 54 of the Chicago Convention.

Under art 54, the council has power to do what is authorised by the convention, to determine its own procedural rules, to establish functional commissions, and to determine the finance of the organisation, and so on. Presently, a number of functional commissions have been established under the council. For example, there is the Air Navigation Commission, responsible for preparing amendments to the annexes of the convention and dealing with technical and safety matters of international air navigation; the Air Transport Committee, responsible for studying issues relating to economic and efficient use of air transportation; the Legal Committee, responsible for advising the council and the assembly on various legal matters arising from civil aviation; the Committee on Joint Support of Air Navigation Service, responsible for dealing with the

---

120. Diederiks-Verschoor, *An Introduction to Air Law*, 5th ed, Kluwer, Deventer, 1993, p 36.
121. The Chicago Convention, arts 48 and 50.

issues arising from the provision, maintenance and improvement of airports and other air navigation facilities; and the Financial Committee which performs the duties defined by the Financial Regulations of ICAO.[122] ICAO's functions are carried out largely by the council and the functional commissions.

Objectives of the Chicago System

[4.179] The Chicago System deals with issues of international law or public international law. In other words, it is concerned with the international relationships between countries or independent jurisdictions in the peaceful, reasonable and efficient use of airspace for the purpose of civil aviation. This is clearly set out in a number of provisions of the Chicago Convention. For example, art 1 of the Chicago Convention states that the contracting states recognise that 'every state has complete and exclusive sovereignty over the airspace above its territory'. This is one of the basic principles of international law. The preamble of the convention actually sets out the general goals of the Chicago System. It states:

> WHEREAS the future development of international civil aviation can greatly help to create and preserve friendship and understanding among the nations and peoples of the world, yet its abuse can become a threat to the general security; and
>
> WHEREAS it is desirable to avoid friction and to promote that cooperation between nations and peoples upon which the peace of the world depends;
>
> THEREFORE, the undersigned governments having agreed on certain principles and arrangements in order that international civil aviation may be developed in a safe and orderly manner and that international air transport services may be established on the basis of equality of opportunity and operated soundly and economically; ...

The above cited provisions indicate that the Chicago Convention is a treaty of public international law, as opposed to a treaty of international trade or commerce. This is why it is not necessary for us to study the Chicago System in great detail in this book.

Traffic rights promoted by the Chicago System

Traffic rights contained in the Chicago Convention

[4.180] The Chicago System advocates a number of rights, privileges or freedoms for the use of airspace for civil and commercial purposes. It purports to establish a system in which the participating countries agree to grant each other the rights, privileges or freedoms to do certain things relating to civil aviation. This task has been accomplished, as we have seen, by the creation of several regimes based on the different combinations between the Chicago Convention and its annexes or protocols. A number of basic rights, privileges and freedoms are set out in the convention itself, and more sophisticated rights, privileges and freedoms are largely set out in the Transit Agreement and Transport Agreement, although the members still retain the option to ratify any particular amendment, additional protocol or annexe made after 1944.

In this part, we will first examine the rights, privileges and freedoms included in the Chicago Convention, and later compare the relevant provisions of the Transit Agreement

---

122. Marek Zylicz, *International Air Transport Law*, Martinus Nijhoff Publishers, Dordecht, 1992, pp 83–4.

Contracts for Carriage by Sea, Air and Land [4.182]

and the Transport Agreement to find out the major differences between the two regimes co-existing within the Chicago System.

[4.181] The Chicago Convention regulates use of national airspace for the purpose of civil aviation. Flying over a national space is one of the basic issues the convention must address. Articles 5–16 regulate the flight over the territory of contracting states. The following major principles are set out in these provisions:

- the convention grants a right of non-scheduled flight to the aircraft of all members subject to the provisions of the convention on national security or prohibited areas, including the right to fly across a member's airspace for non-stop transit, or to stop for non-traffic purposes;[123]

- with approval of a member and subject to the qualifications set out in art 7 of the convention, the aircraft engaged in a non-scheduled flight has the privilege of carrying passengers, cargo or mail for remuneration within the territory of a member;[124]

- scheduled air services must be expressly authorised by the state concerned for the right to fly over or operate in the territory of the state;[125]

- a state has the right to refuse permission to aircraft of another state to engage in commercial operations within its territory, but the state is not allowed to discriminate against other members by either providing an exclusive right to or obtaining an exclusive right from another member;[126]

- a state is permitted to establish prohibited areas of airspace under the principle of non-discrimination among the members;[127]

- landing and operation of aircraft within a member's territory is subject to the regulation and control of the member;[128]

- members have an obligation to prevent the spread of disease by air navigation;[129]

- members are permitted to fix airport charges in pursuance of the provisions of the convention;[130] and

- members have the right to search and inspect each other's aircraft on landing and departure in pursuance of the relevant provisions of the convention.[131]

[4.182] The Chicago Convention also regulates the technical aspects of aircraft and civil aviation, such as nationality of aircraft, facilitation of air navigation, uniform standards for aircraft, uniform practice for air navigation, establishment of ICAO, and uniform rules for operation of airports and navigation facilities, and others. ICAO is largely responsible for enforcing the technical rules for civil aviation as agreed by the

---

123. The Chicago Convention, art 5.
124. The Chicago Convention, art 5.
125. The Chicago Convention, art 6.
126. The Chicago Convention, art 7.
127. The Chicago Convention, art 9.
128. The Chicago Convention, arts 10, 11, 12 and 13.
129. The Chicago Convention, art 14.
130. The Chicago Convention, art 15.
131. The Chicago Convention, art 16.

members. The technical rules are less sensitive than the so-called flight rights, privileges or freedoms, which are regulated in the provisions mentioned above, as well as the Transit Agreement and Transport Agreement respectively.

Traffic rights set out in the Transit Agreement

[4.183] The Transit Agreement has been approved by the majority of the members of Chicago Convention, largely because it imposes less obligations upon the members than the Transport Agreement. Article 1, section 1 of the agreement sets out the following two privileges which must be guaranteed by the members:

> Each contracting state grants to the other contracting states the following freedoms of the air in respect of scheduled international air services:
> 1. The privilege to fly across its territory without landing;
> 2. The privilege to land for non-traffic purposes.
>
> The privileges of this section shall not be applicable with respect to airports utilised for military purposes to the exclusion of any scheduled international air services. In areas of active hostilities or of military occupation, and in time of war along the supply routes leading to such areas, the exercise of such privileges shall be subject to the approval of the competent military authorities.

This provision purports to grant the so-called freedoms and privileges to scheduled international air services. As we have seen, art 5 of the Chicago Convention regulates the right to fly across and stop for non-traffic purposes of non-scheduled flights. How to differentiate them then?

According to ICAO, the scheduled international air services are a series of flights having the following characteristics:[132]

> it passes through the airspace over the territory of more than one state;
>
> it is performed by aircraft for the transport of passengers, mail or cargo for remuneration, in such a manner that each flight is open to use by members of the public; and
>
> it is operated, so as to serve traffic between the same two or more points, either according to a published time table, or with flights so regular or frequent that they constitute a recognizably systematic series.

For comparison, a flight that does not meet these requirements would be regarded as a non-scheduled flight.

[4.184] The Transit Agreement also has other provisions ensuring the implementation of the two freedoms or privileges. These provisions mainly ensure equal treatment among members, and confirm the right of members to regulate according to the principles of the Chicago Convention the scheduled international air services within their territory. The significance of the Transit Agreement to the members of the Chicago Convention can be seen by comparing the privileges or freedoms contained in the Transport Agreement.

Traffic rights set out in the Transport Agreement

[4.185] As we know, the Transport Agreement is one of the two annexes adopted together with the Chicago Convention. It provides an alternative to the members of the Chicago Convention for the scope of cooperation under the Chicago Convention. As a general rule of international law, the Transport Agreement only operates among the states

---

132. See Marek Zylicz, note 122 above, p 79.

which have ratified it. The major difference between the Transport Agreement and the Transit Agreement is that the former provides five privileges or freedoms, but the latter provides only two. Article 1, section 1 of the Transport Agreement provides five privileges in the following words:

> Each contracting state grants to the other contracting states the following freedoms of the air in respect of scheduled international air services:
> 1. The privilege to fly across its territory without landing;
> 2. The privilege to land for non-traffic purposes;
> 3. The privilege to put down passengers, mail and cargo taken on in the territory of the state whose nationality the aircraft possesses;
> 4. The privilege to take on passengers, mail and cargo destined for the territory of the state whose nationality the aircraft possesses;
> 5. The privilege to take on passengers, mail and cargo destined for the territory of any other contracting state and the privilege to put down passengers, mail and cargo coming from any such territory.

[4.186] With respect to the privileges specified under paras 3, 4 and 5 of this section, the undertaking of each contracting state relates only to through services on a route constituting a reasonably direct line out from and back to the homeland of the state whose nationality the aircraft possesses.

The privileges of this section shall not be applicable with respect to airports utilised for military purposes to the exclusion of any scheduled international air services. In areas of active hostilities or of military occupation, and in time of war along the supply routes leading to such areas, the exercise of such privileges shall be subject to the approval of the competent military authorities.

[4.187] In comparison with the Transit Agreement, the Transport Agreement has three more freedoms, which appear to be burdensome to most members of the Chicago Convention, because most members prefer to deal with these issues on a bilateral basis to ensure equality between them. This is why the Transport Agreement has been approved by only a dozen members. For the members which have ratified the Transport Agreement, the regime of international air navigation based on the combination of the Chicago Convention and the Transport Agreement operates among them. For the countries which have approved the Transit Agreement, they are bound by the regime based on the Chicago Convention and the Transit Agreement. In addition, they may extend their cooperation beyond the Transit Agreement by making bilateral treaties between any two countries.

Traffic rights developed under the Chicago System

[4.188] The Chicago Convention regulates international civil aviation largely from two perspectives: the use of national airspace and territory, and the uniformity of technical requirements for aircraft, traffic rules and airport control. The latter is easy to deal with, but the former is very sensitive because of its implications to sovereignty, national security and national economy. Nevertheless, a number of rights, privileges or freedoms have been developed within the Chicago System, largely by the efforts of ICAO. Marek

[4.188] Zylicz has identified the following rights, privileges or freedoms concerning international air aviation:[133]

> First freedom: the privilege to fly across the territory of a state without landing.
>
> Second freedom: the privilege to land for non-traffic purpose (technical landing).
>
> Third freedom: the privilege to put down passengers, mail and cargo taken on in the territory of the state whose nationality the aircraft possesses.
>
> Fourth freedom: the privilege to take on passengers, mail and cargo destined for the territory of the state whose nationality the aircraft possesses.
>
> Fifth freedom: the privilege to take on passengers, mail and cargo destined for the territory of any other third state and the privilege to put down passengers, mail and cargo coming from any such territory.
>
> Sixth freedom: the privilege to carry passengers, mail and cargo between territories of two foreign states via the territory of the home state of the aircraft.
>
> Seventh freedom: the privilege to carry passengers, mail and cargo between territories of two foreign states without transit through the home state of the aircraft.
>
> Eighth freedom: the privilege to carry passengers, mail and cargo from one place in the territory of a foreign state to another place in the same foreign state.

[4.189] From the aforesaid freedoms, we can see that the last three freedoms are actually derived from the first five freedoms, in particular, the third, fourth and fifth freedoms. As we have seen, except the first and second freedoms, the rest are largely regulated by bilateral treaties between two individual states. Variations are expected between different bilateral treaties, depending on the mutual concessions made by the countries concerned.

[4.190] The Chicago System regulates the environment in which the Warsaw System operates. In brief, the former sets out the rules of the game for operating aircraft in civil aviation, and the latter regulates the rights and obligations of the carrier and the cargo-owner during the carriage.

An introduction to the Warsaw System

Structure of the Warsaw System

[4.191] As we have seen, the Warsaw System includes the Warsaw Convention and a number of protocols amending the convention. The Warsaw Convention was adopted on 12 October 1929 and entered into force on 13 February 1933. The convention was amended in 1955 by the Hague Protocol 1955 on 28 September 1955, which entered into force on 1 August 1963. The Warsaw Convention and the 1955 Hague Protocol form the foundation of the Warsaw System, although as we can see from the following paragraphs not all members of the Warsaw Convention have ratified the Hague Protocol 1955.

[4.192] In 1995, the Warsaw Convention had 147 members: Afghanistan, Akrotiri and Dhekelia, Algeria, Argentina, Australia, Austria, Bahamas, Bangladesh, Barbados, Belgium, Benin, Bermuda, Botswana, Brazil, British Antarctic Territory, British Virgin Island, Brunei Darussalam, Bulgaria, Burkina Faso, Byelorussian Soviet Socialist Republic, Cambodia, Cameroon, Canada, Cayman Turks and Caicos Islands, Chile, China, Colombia, Congo, Costa Rica, Cote d'Ivoire, Cuba, Cyprus, Czech Republic,

---

133. Id, p 80.

Contracts for Carriage by Sea, Air and Land [4.194]

Denmark, Dominican Republic, Ecuador, Egypt, El Salvador, Equitorial Guinea, Ethiopia, Falkland Island, Fiji, Finland, France, Gabon, Gambia, Germany, Ghana, Greece, Grenada, Guatemala, Guinea, Guyana, Hong Kong, Hungary, Iceland, India, Indonesia, Iran, Iraq, Ireland, Israel, Italy, Jamaica, Japan, Jordan, Kenya, Democratic Peoples Republic of Korea, Republic of Korea, Kuwait, Laos, Lebanon, Lesotho, Liberia, Libyan Arab Jamahiriya, Liechtenstein, Luxembourg, Madagascar, Malawi, Malaysia, Mali, Malta, Mauritania, Mauritius, Mexico, Monaco, Mongolia, Montserrat, Morocco, Myanmar, Nauru, Nepal, the Netherlands, New Zealand, Niger, Nigeria, Norway, Oman, Pakistan, Papua New Guinea, Paraguay, Peru, Philippines, Poland, Portugal, Oatar, Romania, Rwanda, Samoa, Saudi Arabia, Senegal, Seychelles, Sierra Leone, Singapore, Solomon Islands, Somalia, South Africa, Spain, St Christopher Nevis and Aguilla, St Helena and Ascension, Sri Lanka, Sudan, Swaziland, Sweden, Switzerland, Syrian Arab Republic, United Republic of Tanzania, Togo, Tonga, Trinidad and Tobago, Tunisia, Turkey, Uganda, Ukrainian Soviet Socialist Republic, Union of Soviet Socialist Republic, United Arab Emirates, United Kingdom, United States, Uruguay, Vanuatu, Venezuela, Vietnam, Yemen, Yugoslavia, Republic of Zaire, Zambia and Zimbabwe.[134]

[4.193] In 1995, the Hague Protocol 1955 had 120 members: Afghanistan, Algeria, Argentina, Australia, Austria, Bahamas, Bangladesh, Belgium, Benin, Bermuda, Brazil, British Antarctic Territory, British Virgin Island, Bulgaria, Byelorussian Soviet Socialist Republic, Cameroon, Canada, Cayman Turks and Caicos Islands, Chile, China, Colombia, Congo, Costa Rica, Cote d'Ivoire, Cuba, Cyprus, Czech Republic, Denmark, Dominican Republic, Ecuador, Egypt, El Salvador, Falkland Island, Fiji, Finland, France, Gabon, Germany, Greece, Grenada, Guatemala, Guinea, Hong Kong, Hungary, Iceland, India, Iran, Iraq, Ireland, Israel, Italy, Japan, Jordan, Democratic Peoples Republic of Korea, Republic of Korea, Kuwait, Laos, Lebanon, Lesotho, Libyan Arab Jamahiriya, Liechtenstein, Luxembourg, Madagascar, Malawi, Malaysia, Mali, Mauritius, Mexico, Monaco, Montserrat, Morocco, Nauru, Nepal, the Netherlands, New Zealand, Niger, Nigeria, Norway, Oman, Pakistan, Papua New Guinea, Paraguay, Peru, Philippines, Poland, Portugal, Oatar, Romania, Samoa, Saudi Arabia, Senegal, Seychelles, Singapore, Solomon Islands, Somalia, South Africa, Spain, St Christopher Nevis and Aguilla, St Helena and Ascension, Sri Lanka, Sudan, Swaziland, Sweden, Switzerland, Syrian Arab Republic, Togo, Tonga, Trinidad and Tobago, Tunisia, Turkey, Ukrainian Soviet Socialist Republic, Union of Soviet Socialist Republic, United Kingdom, Venezuela, Vietnam, Yemen, Yugoslavia, Zambia and Zimbabwe.[135]

[4.194] The difference in the membership of the Warsaw Convention and the Hague Protocol 1955 indicates that the Warsaw Convention with the Hague Protocol 1955 and the Warsaw Convention without the said protocol are two separate regimes, although only a small number of Warsaw Convention members have not ratified the Hague Protocol 1955. As a principle of international law, the Warsaw Convention members which have not ratified the Hague Protocol 1955 are not obliged to comply with the provisions of the protocol, although they must comply with the provisions of the Warsaw

---

134. See Giemulla et al (eds), *Warsaw Convention*, Annexure 1–6, pp 1–10.
135. Ibid.

[4.194]   **International Commercial Law**

Convention. The distinction between the Warsaw Convention and the Hague Protocol 1955 without the protocol is crucial for understanding the operation of four protocols, known as the Additional Protocol No 1–4, concluded on 25 September 1975. It is also crucial for understanding the relationships between the Guadalajara Convention 1961, the Guatemala City Protocol 1971, the Additional Protocols, the Hague Protocol 1955 and the Warsaw Convention.

[4.195] Based on the diagram opposite, the structure of the Warsaw Convention can be divided into four regimes:

- The first regime of the Warsaw System consists of the Warsaw Convention, the Hague Protocol 1955, the Guatemala City Protocol 1971 and the Additional Protocol No 3. This is the most comprehensive regime of the Warsaw System in terms of the number of conventions involved.
- The second regime consists of the Warsaw Convention and the Additional Protocol No 1. This is the least comprehensive regime of the Warsaw System.
- The third regime consists of the Warsaw Convention, the Hague Protocol 1955 and the Additional Protocol No 2. This regime mainly brings a limited liability of 16,600 SDR for personal injuries into the Warsaw Convention as amended by the Hague Protocol 1955.
- The fourth regime consists of the Warsaw Convention, the Hague Protocol 1955 and the Additional Protocol No 4. This regime introduces substantial changes to the rules governing the use of air waybills, and the rights of the consignee or consignor in the Warsaw Convention as amended by the Hague Protocol 1955. This regime is perhaps most significant as far as the rights and obligations of the carrier, consignor and consignee are concerned.

[4.196] The relationships between the major international conventions under the Warsaw System can be illustrated by the following diagram:

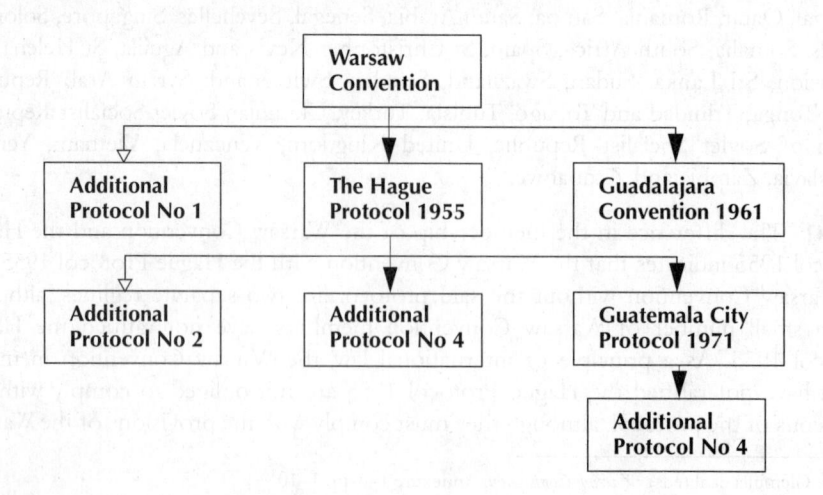

```
                          ┌──────────────┐
                          │   Warsaw     │
                          │  Convention  │
                          └──────┬───────┘
            ┌────────────────────┼────────────────────┐
            ▽                    ▽                    ▽
   ┌──────────────┐      ┌──────────────┐     ┌──────────────┐
   │  Additional  │      │  The Hague   │     │  Guadalajara │
   │ Protocol No 1│      │ Protocol 1955│     │Convention 1961│
   └──────┬───────┘      └──────┬───────┘     └──────┬───────┘
          ▽                     ▽                    ▽
   ┌──────────────┐      ┌──────────────┐     ┌──────────────┐
   │  Additional  │      │  Additional  │     │ Guatemala City│
   │ Protocol No 2│      │ Protocol No 4│     │ Protocol 1971│
   └──────────────┘      └──────────────┘     └──────┬───────┘
                                                     ▽
                                              ┌──────────────┐
                                              │  Additional  │
                                              │ Protocol No 4│
                                              └──────────────┘
```

[4.197] The Guadalajara Convention 1961 is supplementary to the Warsaw Convention in the sense that it regulates certain matters falling outside the convention. This means it is supplementary to all the four regimes set out above. Because each regime has different combinations of conventions and has different emphases on the rules of air carriage, it is difficult to state absolutely which regime is most important. In terms of practical importance, the first and the last regime have much wider implications than the other two.

[4.198] Outside the four regimes, there is also the Agreement Relating to Liability Limitations of the Warsaw Convention and the Hague Protocol (the Montreal Agreement), which was adopted on 13 May 1966. The agreement is not really an international convention in an orthodox sense, because it is basically an agreement entered into between the United States and any other country in the world. It was intended to regulate the liability of carriers for passengers, instead of carriage of goods. Thus, this agreement is not to be studied here.

Objectives of the Warsaw System

[4.199] The Warsaw System regulates carriage of goods and passengers by air. It is equivalent to the functions of the Hague Rules, the Hague-Visby Rules or the Hamburg Rules. According to art 1 of the convention, the convention applies to all international carriage of persons, luggage or goods performed by aircraft for reward. It applies equally to gratuitous carriage by aircraft performed by an air transport undertaking. This provision remains unchanged, although a number of provisions affecting the scope of application have been amended by the subsequent amendments. Generally speaking, the objectives of the Warsaw System are to regulate two types of carriage: the carriage of goods, and the carriage of passengers and luggage. In the light of art 1(1), the gratuitous carriage may also be regulated by the Warsaw Convention. In this book, only the commercial carriage of goods and carriage of passengers (including luggage) will be examined. The Warsaw System purports to provide uniform rules for determining the parties' rights and liabilities involving civil aviation, although it has in fact provided several alternative sets of rules for the regulation of parties' rights and obligations in the international carriage of goods and passengers.

[4.200] Given the existence of the four regimes within the Warsaw System, our discussion will be focusing on the most common conventions of the Warsaw System, such as the Warsaw Convention, the Hague Protocol 1955, the Additional Protocol No 4, the Guatemala City Protocol 1971 and the Additional Protocol No 3. In order to avoid confusion, each relevant convention will be examined under a separate heading in the order of the Warsaw Convention, the Warsaw Convention as amended by the Hague Protocol 1955, the Warsaw Convention as amended by the Hague Protocol 1955 and the Additional Protocol No 4, the Warsaw Convention as amended by the Hague Protocol 1955 and the Guatemala City Protocol 1971, and the Warsaw Convention as amended by the Hague Protocol 1955, the Guatemala City Protocol 1971 and the Additional Protocol No 3. When necessary, the differences between each regime or between each convention will also be examined. For the convenience of discussion, the carriage of goods and carriage of passengers will also be examined separately.

Carriage of goods under the Warsaw Convention

Application of the Warsaw Convention

[4.201] The Warsaw Convention applies to international carriage. The meaning of international carriage is defined in art 1(2) of the Warsaw Convention, which is replaced by art 1 of the Hague Protocol 1955. For the countries which have not ratified the Hague Protocol 1955, the original definition of international carriage as defined in art 1 of the Warsaw Convention still applies. For the countries which have ratified the Hague Protocol 1955, the new definition of international carriage applies. Article 1(2) of the Warsaw Convention defines international carriage as follows:

> For the purposes of this Convention the expression 'international carriage' means any carriage in which, according to the contract made by the parties, the place of departure and the place of destination, whether or not there be a break in the carriage or a transhipment, are situated either within the territories of two High Contracting Parties, or within the territory of a single High Contracting Party, if there is an agreed stopping place within a territory subject to the sovereignty, suzerainty, mandate or authority of another Power, even though that Power is not a party to this Convention. A carriage without such an agreed stopping place between territories subject to the sovereignty, suzerainty, mandate or authority of the same High Contracting Party is not deemed to be international for the purposes of this Convention.

[4.202] Sometimes, a flight can be continuous across two or more countries. Sometimes, the same goods may be carried by several successive carriers across two or more countries. Such a flight or carriage may be subject to the Warsaw Convention if part of its flight or carriage meets the definition of international carriage (as we have seen). Thus, defining successive flight or undivided carriage is necessary for the application of the Warsaw Convention. This issue is regulated in art 1(3) of the Warsaw Convention, which again is amended by art 1 of the Hague Protocol 1955. The original definition in art 1(3) of the Warsaw Convention is as follows:

> A carriage to be performed by several successive air carriers is deemed, for the purposes of this Convention, to be one undivided carriage, if it has been regarded by the parties as a single operation, whether it had been agreed upon under the form of a single contract or of a series of contracts, and it does not lose its international character merely because one contract or a series of contracts is to be performed entirely within a territory subject to the sovereignty, suzerainty, mandate or authority of the same High Contracting Party.

[4.203] The operation of art 1 is supported by art 31 of the Warsaw Convention, which deals with the issue of combined carriage. According to art 31, if a carriage is partly performed by air and partly by other modes of transport, the provisions of the Warsaw Convention apply only to the part of air carriage which satisfies the requirements of art 1. Article 31 of the Warsaw Convention is also relevant to art 18(3) of the Warsaw Convention, which defines the period of carriage by air.

[4.204] In the light of the provisions mentioned above, it can be said that the application of the Warsaw Convention is based on either the place of departure or the place of destination. This means that the convention applies only to an international carriage on three alternative grounds:

> the carriage commences from a member of the Warsaw Convention;
> the carriage ends in a member of the Warsaw Convention; and

the carriage both commences and ends in the same member of the Warsaw Convention, but has an agreed stopping place in another state.

[4.205] It follows that if a carriage begins in a non-member state and ends in a non-member state, it is not subject to the Warsaw Convention, even though the carriage may have an agreed stopping place within a member state. 'Stopping place' does not meet the definition of place of commencement or place of destination. However, it can be argued that the said carriage can be divided into two stages: the first stage starts from a non-member state and ends in the member state (the stopping place); and the second stage starts from the member state (stopping place) and ends in a non-member state. The correctness of the argument can be tested under art 1(3) of the Warsaw Convention referred to above. The meaning of successive carriage or undivided carriage then becomes relevant for consideration, as determined by the contract of carriage between the parties. If the parties to a carriage by air agree that the carriage is meant to commence and end in non-member state(s) only, the stopping place is irrelevant for determining the application of the Warsaw Convention. Thus, a carriage which is related to the contracting state of the Warsaw Convention by the place of stopover is not an international carriage covered by the Warsaw Convention.

[4.206] Some of the provisions of the Warsaw Convention are compulsory and some are optional. For example, art 32 of the convention states that any clause contained in the contract and all special agreements entered into before any damage occurring, by which the parties purport to infringe the Convention, whether by deciding the law to be applied or by altering jurisdictional rules, shall be null and void. The prohibition applies to the provisions concerning the carrier's liability.

On the other hand, art 8 of the Warsaw Convention requires that the contents of an air consignment note are compulsory only in the context of art 9 (which deprives the carrier of the right to rely on the excluded and limited liability set out in the convention). In addition, the provisions relating to the process and formality for the issue of an air consignment note appear to be flexible in the sense that variations in the process and formality may not affect the nature and functions of the air consignment note.

[4.207] The application of the Warsaw Convention is qualified by art 34, which states as follows:

> This Convention does not apply to international carriage by air performed by way of experimental trial by air navigation undertakings with the view to the establishment of a regular line of air navigation, nor does it apply to carriage performed in extraordinary circumstances outside the normal scope of an air carrier's business.

Article 34 appears to exclude non-commercial flights from the jurisdiction of the Warsaw Convention. However, the meaning of extraordinary circumstances appears also to be capable of covering some carriage which is related to commercial purposes.

[4.208] The Warsaw Convention regulates the carriage of goods, as well as the carriage of passengers and luggage. But it does not regulate all aspects of the carriages. This characteristic

[4.208] of the Warsaw Convention is noted by Lord Hope of Craighead in *Abnett v British Airways Plc (Scotland); Sidhu v British Airways Plc* in the following words:[136]

> The Convention describes itself as a 'Convention for the Unification of Certain Rules relating to International Carriage by Air'. The phrase 'Unification of Certain Rules' tells us two things. The first, the aim of the Convention is to unify the rules to which it applies. If this aim is to be achieved, exceptions to these rules should not be permitted, except where the Convention itself provides for them. Second, the Convention is concerned with certain rules only, not with all the rules relating to international carriage by air. It does not purport to provide a code which is comprehensive of all the issues that may arise. It is a partial harmonisation, directed to the particular issues with which it deals. These issues are identified in the principal chapter headings, which are those to Chapters II, III and IV — 'Documents of Carriage', 'Liability of the Carrier' and 'Provisions Relating to Combined Carriage'. Nothing is said in this Convention about the liability of passengers to the carrier, for example. Nor is anything said about the carrier's obligations of insurance, and in particular about compulsory insurance against third party risks. It is clear from the content and structure of the Convention that it is a partial harmonisation only of the rules relating to international carriage by air. That is sufficient to give content to the phrase 'Certain Rules'. I do not find in that phrase an indication that, in regard to the issues with which the Convention does purport to deal, its provisions were intended to be other than comprehensive.

[4.209] In the light of the abovementioned judgment, it is natural to expect the application of the relevant domestic law to deal with the issues which are not covered by the Warsaw Convention.[137] On the other hand, the domestic law cannot be used as a bridge to circumvent the provisions of the Warsaw Convention which purport to deny additional remedies to the consignor, the consignee or the passenger in the circumstances described by the provisions.

These two conflicting propositions can be balanced only by the court hearing a particular dispute. In *Abnett v British Airways Plc (Scotland); Sidhu v British Airways Plc*, referred to above, Lord Hope of Craighead observes that if a remedy has been excluded by the Warsaw Convention because the rules of the convention do not provide for it, the domestic court is not free to apply the remedy from its own domestic law, because so doing would distort the operation of the whole regime of the Warsaw Convention.[138]

---

136. Available at <http://www.number7.demon.co.uk> paras 38 and 39 of the judgment.
137. For example, in *Gatewhite Ltd v Iberia Lineas Aeras de Espana SA* [1990] 1 QB 326, Gatehouse J observed at 334 as follows:

> In my view the owner of goods damaged or lost by the carrier is entitled to sue in his own name and there is nothing in the Convention which deprives him of that right. As the Convention does not expressly deal with the position by excluding the owner's right of action (although it could so easily have done so) the lex fori, as it seems to me, can fill the gap. While bearing in mind the need to guard against the parochial view of the common lawyer, I see no good reason why the civil lawyers approach to the construction of the Convention, based on the importance of contract, should be of overriding importance. The fact is that the Convention is silent where it could easily have made simple and clear provision excluding the rights of the real party in interest, had that been the framer's intention.

138. Id, para 69.

[4.210] DHL International (NZ) Ltd v Richmond Ltd

[1993] 3 NZLR 10

Carriage outside the Warsaw Convention, carrier's liability based on the contract of carriage

Facts: DHL International operated an international courier service. Richmond Ltd, trading as Pacific Leathers, sold skins and hides to an Italian buyer, Conceria Bini Gastone in 1988. Under the contract of sale, Richmond Ltd was to deliver the bill of lading and drafts to an Italian bank. The bank would pass the documents to Bini upon payment of the contract price by Bini. Richmond Ltd shipped the goods as agreed. It then contracted with DHL under an airbill to deliver the documents to the Italian bank. DHL's agent misdelivered the documents to Bini, which then took delivery of the goods by presenting the bill of lading received by misdelivery without making any payment to the seller.

Bini went bankrupt soon after taking over the goods. The Italian bank claimed that it had never received the bill of lading. Richmond Ltd sued DHL for damages on the ground of breach of contract evidenced by the airbill. The High Court of New Zealand gave judgment in favour of Richmond Ltd on the ground of the existence of a fiduciary duty. DHL appealed.

Decision: The terms of the airbill excluded and limited the liability of DHL. Consequential losses were also excluded under the airbill. The relationship of the parties in the present case was based on the contract, rather than a fiduciary duty. There was no evidence that DHL was dishonest or fraudulent in misdelivery. Nor was it proven that DHL knew or ought to have known the commercial significance (or value) of the documents misdelivered. The claim of Richmond Ltd was limited, excluded or time barred by the terms of the airbill.

Differentiating the three conventions affecting air carriage documents

[4.211] It is necessary to examine the three conventions affecting the use of air consignment notes or air waybills in the Warsaw System, before discussing the rules governing the use of such air carriage documents. Since, within the Warsaw System, each convention amending the Warsaw Convention only operates between the members which have ratified it, there are three systems or three sets of rules governing the use of air carriage documents within the Warsaw System. These sets of rules are to be examined in turn.

[4.212] The Warsaw Convention regulates the use of air consignment notes in its arts 5–16. Only the expression 'air consignment note' is used throughout the convention. In detail, art 5 regulates the issue of the air consignment note and its validity; art 6 mainly describes the number of copies of the air consignment note and their different uses; art 7 gives the carrier a right to demand the consignor to fill in different air consignment notes for different packages; art 8 regulates the contents of an air consignment note; art 9 makes an air consignment note the basis for the carrier to claim limited liability under the Warsaw Convention; art 10 holds the consignor to be liable for the information provided in the air consignment note; art 11 makes the air consignment note prima facie evidence for the goods covered; art 12 deals with the consignor's right over the goods; art 13 deals with the consignee's right; art 14 permits the consignor and consignee to make claims under both art 12 and art 13; art 15 provides that the rights of the consignor and consignee under art 14 do not affect their legal relationships to each

[4.212] other outside arts 12 and 13; and art 16 holds the consignor liable for providing necessary customs information.

[4.213] The Hague Protocol 1955 amends part of the provisions of the Warsaw Convention regulating the use of air consignment notes. As the result of such amendment, both the expressions 'air consignment note', and 'air waybill', co-exist in the version of the Warsaw Convention as amended by the Hague Protocol. In fact, as far as the use of air carriage documents is concerned, the Hague Protocol 1955 only amends arts 6, 8, 9, 10 and 15. Of these amendments, amended arts 8, 9 and 15 of the Warsaw Convention (as amended by the Hague Protocol 1955) are responsible for bringing the expression 'air waybill' into the text of the Warsaw Convention. Consequently, after the amendments, arts 5, 6, 7, 10, 11, 12, 13, 15(2) and 16 of the Warsaw Convention as amended by the Hague Protocol 1955 still retain the expression 'air consignment note', but arts 8, 9 and 15(3) of the same convention adopt the expression 'air waybill'. In addition, Section III of the Warsaw Convention (as amended by the Hague Protocol 1995), which is the section covering arts 5–16, is still entitled 'Air Consignment Note'. This is why legally or theoretically both air consignment notes and air waybills are interchangeable under the Warsaw Convention (as amended by the Hague Protocol 1955).

[4.214] The Additional Protocol No 4 brings a thorough change to the Warsaw Convention (as amended by the Hague Protocol), by replacing the whole of Section III with arts 5–16 inclusive. The expression 'air waybill' has been used in the new provisions throughout, including the section title, which is now entitled Documentation Relating to Cargo.

In brief, under the Additional Protocol No 4, art 5 requires the issue of an air waybill or other similar document for the purpose of carriage; art 6 regulates the form of the air waybill and the functions of its copies; art 7 permits both the carrier and the consignor to demand separate air waybills; art 8 regulates the contents of the air waybill; art 9 provides that, in spite of the non-compliance with arts 5–8, the contract of carriage is still subject to the Warsaw Convention (as amended by the Hague Protocol 1955 and the Additional Protocol No 4); art 10 holds both the consignor and the carrier to be liable for the accuracy of the information provided by any of them; art 11 states that the air waybill is prima facie evidence of the contract of carriage and the description of the goods concerned; art 12 sets out the rights of the consignor to deal with the goods before delivery to the consignee; art 13 sets out the rights of the consignee under the contract of carriage; art 14 permits the consignor and consignee to enforce respectively all the rights under arts 12 and 13 on his or her own or for another; art 15 states that arts 12, 13 and 14 do not affect the relations between the consignor and the consignee or between any of them and another third party; and art 16 holds the consignor liable for providing the necessary documents required by customs.

[4.215] The Additional Protocol No 4 provides the most comprehensive, consistent and reasonable rules to regulate the use of air carriage documents within the Warsaw System. The relevant provisions of the Additional Protocol No 4 will be examined in detail in this chapter even though not all members of the Warsaw Convention have ratified the protocol. In addition, comparisons between different conventions will be made whenever necessary.

Air consignment note

Definition

[4.216] An 'air consignment note' is a transport document for the carriage of goods by air. As we have seen, it is also known as an 'air waybill' or airbill. The terms 'air consignment note' and 'air waybill' are adopted by the Warsaw Convention or the Warsaw Convention as amended by the Hague Protocol 1955; but the expression 'airbill' is largely a common commercial usage which does not have a formal legal status in the Warsaw Convention. Transport document is an expression adopted in the Incoterms 2000, referring to all types of documents used in the carriage of goods by sea, air, land, inland water or multimodal carriage. In this part of the discussion, the expression 'air consignment note' is preferred, because it is the term used in the Warsaw Convention.

[4.217] As a transport document, the air consignment note is equivalent to the bill of lading in carriage by sea, or the consignment note in carriage by land. It is a concept created by the Warsaw Convention and is still a valid term under the unamended Warsaw Convention. Since the Warsaw Convention has been amended several times, the legal status of air consignment notes has changed, in particular under the Additional Protocol No 4. Under the unamended Warsaw Convention, the existence of an air consignment note is the precondition for the application of the Warsaw Convention. This characteristic is seen in art 9 of the Warsaw Convention, which is set out as follows:

> If the carrier accepts goods without an air consignment note having been made out, or if the air consignment note does not contain all the particulars set out in Article 8(a) to (i) inclusive and (q), the carrier shall not be entitled to avail himself of the provisions of this Convention which exclude or limit his liability.

[4.218] This provision makes the existence of air consignment notes absolutely essential for the carrier to protect his or her interests under the convention. The special status of the air consignment note is abandoned in the Additional Protocol No 4, which has also substituted the expression 'air consignment note' with 'air waybill'. Presently, art 9 of the Warsaw Convention (as amended by the Hague Protocol 1955 and the Additional Protocol No 4) states that non-compliance with the provisions of arts 5–8: 'shall not affect the existence or the validity of the contract of carriage, which shall, none the less, be subject to the rules of this Convention including those relating to limitation of liability'.

Article 5 of the Warsaw Convention (as amended by the Hague Protocol 1955 and the Additional Protocol No 4) provides that in respect of the carriage of cargo an air waybill shall be delivered. Under the said art 5, if an air waybill is not issued, a receipt or a document evidencing the carriage by air should be issued to the consignor. However, as we have seen, art 9 subjects a contract of air carriage to the Warsaw Convention (as amended by the Hague Protocol 1955 and the Additional Protocol No 4) regardless of whether an air waybill or a similar document has been issued under art 5.

Because the Warsaw Convention adopts the expression 'air consignment note' and the Additional Protocol No 4 adopts the expression 'air waybill', we may say that under the Warsaw Convention the issue of an *air consignment note* is compulsory, but under the Warsaw Convention (as amended by the Hague Protocol and the Additional Protocol No 4), the issue of an *air waybill* is not compulsory. The difference is crucial for the interests of the parties to a carriage, in particular the carrier in the regimes of the Warsaw Convention which do not incorporate the Additional Protocol No 4. The regime consisting of the Warsaw Convention, the Hague Protocol 1955, the Guatemala City Protocol 1971 and the Additional Protocol No 3 is one of such examples.

Functions of air consignment notes

[4.219] The nature of an air consignment note is not defined in the Warsaw Convention. In the light of the relevant provisions regulating the use of air consignment notes, the functions of an air consignment note can be summarised as follows:

- an air consignment note containing the required particulars is the precondition for the carrier to rely on the excluded or limited liability provided in the Warsaw Convention;[139]

- an air consignment note is prima facie evidence of the conclusion of the contract of carriage;[140]

- an air consignment note is prima facie evidence of the conditions and terms of the contract of carriage;[141]

- an air consignment note is prima facie a receipt of the goods by the carrier;[142]

- an air consignment note is prima facie evidence of the quantity, volume or condition of the goods, only when the carrier has acknowledged in the air consignment note that he or she has checked them;[143] and

---

139. Article 9 of the Warsaw Convention states as follows:

> If the carrier accepts goods without an air consignment note having been made out, or if the air consignment note does not contain all the particulars set out in Article 8(a) to (i) inclusive and (q), the carrier shall not be entitled to avail himself of the provisions of this Convention which exclude or limit his liability.

140. Article 11(1) of the Warsaw Convention provides that 'the air consignment note is prima facie evidence of the conclusion of the contract, of the receipt of the goods and of the conditions of carriage'.

141. Article 8 of the Warsaw Convention requires a consignment note to contain the following particulars:

> ... the place and date of its execution; the place of departure and of destination; the agreed stopping places, provided that the carrier may reserve the right to alter the stopping places in case of necessity, and that if he exercises that right the alteration shall not have the effect of depriving the carriage of its international character; the name and address of the consignor; the name and address of the first carrier; the name and address of the consignee, if the case so requires; the nature of the goods; the number of the packages, the method of packing and the particular marks or numbers upon them; the weight, the quantity and the volume or dimensions of the goods; the apparent condition of the goods and of the packing; the freight, if it has been agreed upon, the date and place of payment, and the person who is to pay it; if the goods are sent for payment on delivery, the price of the goods, and, if the case so requires, the amount of the expenses incurred; the amount of the value declared in accordance with Article 22 (2); the number of parts of the air consignment note; the documents handed to the carrier to accompany the air consignment note; the time fixed for the completion of the carriage and a brief note of the route to be followed, if these matters have been agreed upon; a statement that the carriage is subject to the rules relating to liability established by this Convention.

- an air consignment note (and also an air waybill, in most cases) is not negotiable, although art 15(3) of the Warsaw Convention (as amended by the Hague Protocol) states that the convention does not prohibit the issue of a negotiable air waybill.

[4.220] Under the Warsaw Convention, an air consignment note is not a document of title, because the consignee's copy of the air consignment note will be delivered to the consignee at the time when the goods are delivered. Nor is it negotiable, because there is no document to negotiate before delivery of the goods. However, it must be pointed out that art 27 of UCP 500 treats an air consignment note as a form of air transport document for the purpose of providing credit by banks, because the air consignment note falls under the description of art 27. In such circumstances, the air consignment note is no more than evidence of the shipment and the conditions and terms of the contract of carriage.

Definition of air freight forwarder

[4.221] An air consignment note or an air waybill (examined later in this chapter), is the evidence of a contract of carriage. A contract of carriage can be made between the consignor and the carrier, or between an air freight forwarder and the carrier. An air freight forwarder is similar to a freight forwarder in a carriage by sea. The air freight forwarder may act on behalf of a cargo-owner or act in its own capacity as a carrier or contracting carrier, who receives the cargo from the owner and makes the arrangements of carriage with the actual carriers. Both the contracting carrier and the actual carrier are subject to the Guadalajara Convention 1961. When an air freight forwarder contracts a carrier to perform the carriage, the air freight forwarder is actually a consignor, who acts in the same way as a consignor under the Warsaw Convention. When an air freight forwarder performs part of the carriage and sub-contracts part of the carriage to another carrier, he or she acts as a consignor in relation to the part performed by the other carriers.

Issue of an air consignment note

[4.222] Unlike a bill of lading for the carriage of goods by sea, an air consignment note (also an air waybill) is normally made out (filled in) by the consignor (the person nominated as the consignor in an air consignment note), although sometimes the carrier (the person nominated as the carrier in an air consignment note) may complete it on behalf of the consignor with the information provided by the consignor.[144] It is given to the carrier with the goods by the consignor after filling in the details. It contains the

---

142. Article 11(2) of the Warsaw Convention provides as follows:

The statements in the air consignment note relating to the weight, dimensions and packing of the goods, as well as those relating to the number of packages, are prima facie evidence of the facts stated; those relating to the quantity, volume and condition of the goods do not constitute evidence against the carrier except so far as they both have been, and are stated in the air consignment note to have been, checked by him in the presence of the consignor, or relate to the apparent condition of the goods.

143. Ibid.

144. Article 6(5) of the Warsaw Convention provides that if at the request of the consignor, the carrier makes out the air consignment note, he or she shall be deemed, subject to proof to the contrary, to have done so on behalf of the consignor.

[4.222]

information on the delivery of the goods to the carrier and will be passed on to the consignee (the person nominated as the consignee either in the air consignment note or by the consignor expressly) of the goods. The carrier verifies the information on the air consignment note by signing the appropriate copy of it. Under art 5 of the Warsaw Convention, the carrier has a right to require the consignor to fill in an air consignment note. Similarly, the consignor has a right to require the carrier to accept the air consignment note or air waybill.[145]

[4.223] Article 6 of the Warsaw Convention requires the consignor to make out three copies of the air consignment note. The first copy should be marked 'for the carrier' and signed by the consignor. The second copy should be marked 'for the consignee' and signed by both the carrier and the consignor. This copy will be delivered to the consignee with the goods as evidence of the goods which should be received by the consignee. The third copy is to be kept by the consignor and should be signed by the carrier. This copy can be used as an air transport document for the purpose of art 27 of UCP 500.

[4.224] Article 7 of the Warsaw Convention deals with the situation where the consignor has shipped more than one package. The carrier has a right to ask the consignor to make out separate air consignment notes for each package, regardless of whether they are designated to the same consignee. However, the carrier has an option to accept one air consignment note for several packages belonging to the same consignee. On the other hand, the carrier appears to have no right to reject the air consignment notes if the consignor prefers to make out separate air consignment notes for every package belonging to the same consignee.

[4.225] Article 8 of the Warsaw Convention sets out the details of the particulars which should be contained in an air consignment note.[146] These particulars represent the necessary information about the cargo and the parties involved, such as the place the air consignment note is issued and the date of issue, the place of departure and the destination, the route of carriage, the stopping place(s) (if applicable), the name and address of the consignor, the name and address of the consignee (if applicable), the name and address of the first carrier, the nature of the cargo, the number of packages and their description, the weight or dimension of the cargo, freight and place of delivery, the statement that the carriage is subject to the liabilities under the convention, and others. Although the validity of an air consignment note will not be an issue, regardless of whether or not the above information is furnished, the lack of such information will, according to art 9 of the Warsaw Convention, lead to the loss of the carrier's right to rely on the defences of excluded or limited liability under the convention.[147] In case of a combined carriage, an air consignment note or an air transport document may incorporate a clause referring to other modes of carriage concerned. The air consignment note or air transport document is not invalid because of such reference, but the air consignment

---

145. Article 5(1) of the Warsaw Convention states that: 'Every carrier of goods has the right to require the consignor to make out and hand over to him a document called an "air consignment note"; every consignor has the right to require the carrier to accept this document.'
146. See note 141 above.

note or air transport document concerned must comply with the requirements of the Warsaw Convention to ensure the application of the convention.[148]

Rights of the consignor

[4.226] The meaning of consignor is not defined expressly in the Warsaw Convention. In the light of the relevant provisions, a consignor can be understood as a person who makes a contract of carriage by air with the carrier in pursuance of the procedures set out in the Warsaw Convention, in particular, arts 5 and 6 of the convention. Alternatively, a consignor can be defined as the person who is nominated as the consignor in an air consignment note. In case of uncertainty, the person who is nominated as the consignor in either of the copies of the air consignment note is the consignor under the Warsaw Convention. The rights of the consignor are largely set out in art 12 of the Warsaw Convention, which can be summarised as follows:

- the consignor has the right to take goods back from the carrier at the airport of departure or destination;
- the consignor has the right to stop the carriage of goods on any landing during the course of carriage; and
- the consignor has the right to direct the goods to be delivered to a person other than the consignee named in the air consignment note, before the goods have been delivered to the named consignee.

[4.227] The aforesaid right can be referred to as the consignor's right of disposition. The carrier should comply with the consignor's request under art 12. In case of impossibility, the carrier is obliged to inform the consignor of the cause or event that has made the compliance impossible. The exercise is subject to a number of restrictions under art 12 of the Warsaw Convention.

First, the performance of the consignor's liability under the contract of carriage is the precondition for him or her to exercise the right of disposition. This means that if the consignor has failed to perform his or her obligations under the contract of carriage, the carrier is entitled to refuse the consignor's request to take back the goods, to stop the carriage or to deliver the goods to a person other than the original consignee. However, if the carrier exercises such right of refusal, he or she must be responsible to the consignor for any claims of the latter which may arise from contract or in tort in relation to the goods concerned. Second, the exercise of the right of disposition by a consignor must not prejudice the interests of the carrier or other consignors. It follows that the carrier or other consignors may either refuse to comply with the request of the consignor

---

147. In *Emery Air Freight Corporation v Merck Sharpe & Dohme (Aust) Pty Ltd* [1999] NSWCA 415, the appellants sought to have their liability to the respondent reduced according to the limited liability set out in art 22 of the Warsaw Convention. The respondents argued that the airway bill relied upon by the appellants failed to provide certain particulars as required by art 8 of the Warsaw Convention, and therefore the respondents were not entitled to rely on the limited liability under art 22. The New South Wales Court of Appeal by a majority allowed the appeal, holding that the relevant airway bill had satisfied the requirements of art 8.
148. The Warsaw Convention, art 31(2).

or seek compensation from him or her if they suffer any loss because of the exercise of the right of disposition. Third, the consignor exercising the right of disposition under art 12 of the Warsaw Convention is liable for expenses occasioned by the carrier or any other person due to the exercise of the right of disposition. Lastly, it must be emphasised that the consignor's right of disposition ceases at the moment when the consignee named in the air consignment note begins to exercise his or her rights under art 13 of the Warsaw Convention.

[4.228] The exercise of the right of disposition may have implications for the interests of a third party under the air consignment note or contract of carriage or in the goods concerned. Article 12(3) of the Warsaw Convention purports to deal with some of these situations. The provision states as follows:

> If the carrier obeys the orders of the consignor for the disposition of the goods without requiring the production of the part of the air consignment note delivered to the latter, he will be liable, without prejudice to his right of recovery from the consignor, for any damage which may be caused thereby to any person who is lawfully in possession of that part of the air consignment note.

[4.229] This provision appears to deal with the interest of a party under the air consignment note only. The air consignment note is not negotiable, but it can be used as a form of security, evidence or document of title for certain commercial purposes, such as negotiation of documentary credit. For example, art 27 of the UCP 500 recognises the air consignment note as a form of air transport document. Article 12(3) of the Warsaw Convention suggests that the carrier should demand the consignor exercising the right of disposition to produce the consignor's copy of the air consignment note. In failing to do so, the carrier must be liable to the claim of a party holding the air consignment note concerned, but retains the right to seek compensation from the consignor exercising the right of disposition. Accordingly, a bank legally holding an air consignment note is entitled to seek compensation from the carrier if the bank suffers any loss because of the change of consignee. Article 12(3) does not cover any other situations involving third party interests, such as a third party's lien in the goods concerned.

Rights of the consignee

[4.230] The Warsaw Convention does not define the meaning of consignee either. Since the consignor has the right to instruct the carrier to deliver the goods to anyone who is not nominated in the air consignment note concerned, the consignee can be understood as either the person who is nominated in an air consignment note or a person who is nominated as the consignee by the consignor exercising the right of disposition. The rights of the consignee are largely regulated in art 13 of the Warsaw Convention, under which the consignee has the right to:

- demand the carrier to deliver the goods and air consignment note to him or her on the arrival of the goods at the agreed place of destination; and
- claim compensations against the carrier if the goods have been lost or have not arrived at the expiration of seven days after the scheduled date of arrival.

In order to facilitate the exercise of the right, the carrier is requested to advise the consignee as soon as possible after the goods have arrived.

[4.231] The exercise of the aforesaid rights is also subject to restrictions. First, the consignee's right to demand delivery of the goods ceases if the consignor has exercised the right of disposition. No claim against the carrier is available if the carrier is unable to deliver the goods because of the consignor's exercise of the right of disposition, unless the consignee is also the holder of the consignor's copy of the air consignment note: see **[4.241]**. Second, the consignee's right to demand delivery of the goods is subject to the payment of the charges due, and on compliance with the conditions of carriage set out in the air consignment note. This requirement may not be fair to the consignee sometimes, because theoretically, the consignee does not see the air consignment note until the goods are being delivered to him or her. However, the restriction may be necessary for the protection of the carrier.

Joint rights of the consignor and consignee

[4.232] One of the special features of the rights of the consignor and consignee under the Warsaw Convention is that they can both respectively enforce all the rights given to them by arts 12 and 13, in pursuance of art 14 of the Warsaw Convention. The consignor or the consignee can act in his or her own interest, or in the interest of another, in exercising the said rights granted by arts 12 and 13, provided that the consignor or the consignee performs his or her own obligations under the contract of carriage. In the light of art 14, there is an interesting proposition concerning the joint exercise of the said rights of the consignor or the consignee. The proposition is that if one of the parties had breached his or her contractual obligations, the other party who has complied with his or her obligations under the contract may actually exercise the right of the party having breached his or her obligations. Is this fair?

[4.233] Another interesting aspect of the rights of the consignor and consignee is that the relationships between the consignor and the consignee, or the relationships between any of them and a third party whose rights are derived from either of them, are not affected by the provisions of arts 12, 13 and 14 set out above. This means that the rights and obligations of the consignor and the consignee under a contract of sale, or in tort, if applicable, are not relevant to their rights or joint rights under the said three provisions. Similarly, arts 12, 13 and 14 cannot be used as defences in a contract or tortious dispute between the consignor (as seller) and the consignee (as buyer). The same principles apply to the rights and obligations of any third party who stands in either a contractual or tortious relationship with the consignor or the consignee. However, the abovementioned effect of art 15 can be varied by an express clause in an air consignment note.

Obligations of the consignor

[4.234] The consignor delivers the goods and makes a contract of carriage with the carrier. Filling in the air consignment note is the duty of the consignor. Thus, when the goods are delivered, the carrier has the right to require the consignor to make out an air consignment note and hand it over to him or her.[149] If several packages or parcels have been delivered, the carrier is obliged to fill in one air consignment note for each package

---

149. The Warsaw Convention, art 5.

[4.234] delivered.[150] The consignor is responsible for the correctness of the particulars and statements furnished by him or her in the air consignment note.[151] If the carrier fills in an air consignment note by relying on the information provided by the consignor, the consignor is also liable for the correctness of the information concerned. This conclusion is based on the combined effect of arts 6(5) and 10(1). Under art 6(5), a carrier who makes out the air consignment note at the request of the consignor is regarded as acting on behalf of the consignor, unless contrary evidence can be proven. Under art 10(1), the consignor is held to be liable for the accuracy of the information furnished by him or her in the air consignment note. Thus, the obligation to ensure the accuracy of the information extends to the situation where the carrier makes out an air consignment note at the request of the consignor. If the consignor fails to comply with his or her obligations to provide correct information about the goods, he or she is liable for all damages suffered by the carrier or any other person caused by the consignor's failure.

[4.235] The consignor is responsible for obtaining export, import or transit approval for customs purposes. This is set out in art 16 of the Warsaw Convention, which provides that the consignor must furnish such information and attach to the air consignment note such documents as are necessary to meet the formalities of customs and other control before the goods can be delivered to the consignee. The carrier is not obliged to ensure the accuracy and efficiency of such information or documentation. This means that if any loss of or damage to the goods is caused by the inaccuracy or deficiency of the information or documentation provided by the consignor, the carrier is not liable.[152] By the same token, the consignee or anyone else cannot hold the carrier to be responsible if any loss, damage, delay, expense or fine has been caused by the inaccuracy or deficiency of the information or documentation concerned. In any case, the consignor is liable to the carrier for any damage occasioned by the absence, insufficiency or irregularity of any such information or documents, unless the damage is due to the fault of the carrier or the carrier's agent.[153]

[4.236] The obligation of the consignor to ensure the sufficiency and accuracy of information and documentation for customs purposes has implications for the seller's obligations under Incoterms 2000. For example, if the goods are sold Ex Works and the buyer asks the seller to make arrangements for air carriage, obtaining all approval for export, import or transit is the responsibility of the buyer. If the seller is nominated as the consignor under the air consignment note, which is very likely because the seller delivers the goods to the carrier, the seller is liable to the carrier under art 16 of the Warsaw Convention for non-compliance with any necessary customs formalities.

This possibility forces the seller to make arrangements of indemnity with the buyer in case the buyer fails to perform his or her obligations under the Ex Works term. Similarly, under an FAS term, the buyer is liable for obtaining all permits for export, import or transit. The seller must consider the issue of indemnity if the buyer fails to perform his or

---

150. The Warsaw Convention, art 7.
151. The Warsaw Convention, art 10.
152. The Warsaw Convention, art 16(2).
153. The Warsaw Convention, art 16(1).

her obligations under the FAS contract. In comparison, under a CPT contract, the seller is liable for obtaining the export licence. Thus, the seller needs only to ensure his or her liability to the carrier under art 16 of the Warsaw Convention — arising from non-compliance with the import or transit customs formalities — is covered by the CPT contract concerned.

[4.237] The consignor's obligation to provide accurate information may extend to the case of misrepresentation by the consignor. In *Air Canada v Demond*,[154] the defendant, who was the end-user of a cargo of video equipment, misrepresented himself as the legal owner of a cargo to the plaintiff, who was an air carrier, and asked the plaintiff to carry the cargo from Newfoundland to Halifax. The plaintiff did as requested. The legal owner of the video equipment sued the plaintiff for misdelivery and won. The plaintiff sued the defendant to recover the loss. The court held the defendant to be liable for the loss of the plaintiff because of his misrepresentation, which amounted to a breach of the consignor's obligations under the Warsaw Convention.

Obligations of the consignee

[4.238] The obligation of the consignee is much simpler than that of the consignor. The consignee's major obligation is to pay the necessary charges to the carrier in pursuance of the air consignment note or the contract of carriage. Another obligation is to comply with the conditions set out in the air consignment note for taking delivery. These conditions are largely relevant to the formality, time and place of delivery. They may vary to some extent under different air consignment notes. Compliance with the terms of the air consignment note implies that the consignee should take over delivery as soon as possible, or alternatively expressly refuse to take delivery. If the consignee fails to do what he or she is expected to do under the air consignment note or the contract of sale, he or she will be held liable in contract to the party suffering from the breach, including the carrier and the consignor.

Liability of the carrier

Period of liability

[4.239] The meaning of carrier is not expressly defined in the Warsaw Convention. In the light of the relevant provisions, it is appropriate to define the carrier as a person who is nominated as the carrier in the air consignment note. The Warsaw Convention does not differentiate between a carrier and an actual carrier, thus giving rise to the presumption that the person who receives the goods for delivery, the person who carries the goods and the person who is named as the carrier in an air consignment note must be the same person.

Although the presumption is arguable, the Warsaw Convention does imply that the person who is named as the carrier in the air consignment note is the carrier.

---

154. Decided on 19 April 1990 by the Supreme Court of Nova Scotia, available at <http://www.admiraltylaw.com>.

[4.240] As a general characteristic of the carrier's liability under the Warsaw Convention, the period of the carrier's liability comprises the period during which the goods are in charge of the carrier.[155] This provision imposes a wide obligation upon the carrier to take care of the goods before loading and after unloading, and on board an aeroplane or outside an airport. However, it must be pointed out that the period of carriage by air does not extend to any carriage by land, sea or river performed outside an airport.[156]

The exclusion does not apply to a situation where the carriage by other means of transport is incidental to the carriage by air, that is, for the purpose of loading, delivery or transshipment of the goods carried by air.[157] Article 18 of the Warsaw Convention was tested in *Hill & Delamain (Hong Kong) Ltd v Manohar Gangaram Ahuja, Trading as Vinamito Trading House* [1994] 1 HKLR 353. In this case, the Court of Appeal of Hong Kong High Court held by a 2:1 majority that a carriage by road between the Schipol Airport and the Brussels Airport was part of the carriage by air which was meant to commence at Hong Kong and end at Brussels Airport. Accordingly, the carrier was entitled to rely on the limited liability granted by the Warsaw Convention for misdelivery at the Brussels Airport. Therefore, it can be said that the carrier is prima facie liable for any loss, damage or delay which occurs while the goods are in the process of air carriage, which extends to the period of loading, unloading, transhipment, and storage for the purpose of performing the contract of carriage.

Liability relating to the use of air consignment notes

[4.241] The liability of the carrier is largely defined in arts 17–30 of the Warsaw Convention. However, a number of carriers' liabilities can also be found in the provisions regulating the use of air consignment notes. For example, under art 5, the carrier has an obligation to accept an air consignment note submitted by the consignor with the goods. Under art 6, the consignor is obliged to sign the copies of the air consignment note to be kept by the consignor and the consignee on acceptance of the goods. Under art 11, the carrier is obliged to deliver the goods in the quantity, description and conditions as shown in the air consignment note to the consignee with the air consignment note. Under art 12(1), the carrier is obliged to follow the instructions of the consignor for stopping delivery, relieving the goods or delivering the goods to a person other than the person named as the consignee in the air consignment note. Under art 12(3), the carrier is obliged to demand the presentation of the consignor's copy of the air consignment note for changing the original terms of delivery, and is liable for the loss sustained by the legitimate holder of the consignor's copy of the air consignment note in case of his or her failure to comply with the said obligation. Under art 13(2), the carrier is obliged to inform the named consignee of the arrival of the goods promptly. Under art 13(1), the carrier is

---

155. The Warsaw Convention, art 18(2).
156. The Warsaw Convention, art 18(3).
157. The Warsaw Convention, art 18(3).

obliged to deliver the goods and the air consignment note to the named consignee at the latter's request. These obligations are largely correspondent with the obligations and rights of the consignor and the consignee.

Liability relating to the loss of or damage to goods

[4.242] The carrier's liability under arts 17–30 of the Warsaw Convention involves both the liability arising from the carriage of goods and the liability arising from the carriage of passengers, including the luggage. In this part of the book, only the carriage of goods is to be discussed. Carriage of passengers and luggage will be examined later separately.

In broad terms, the carrier is liable for the loss of or damage to the goods occurring during the carriage by air.[158] The meaning of carriage by air is defined in art 18(2) of the Warsaw Convention. As we have seen, it covers the whole period during which the carrier is in charge of the goods for the purpose of performing the contract of carriage.

Liability arising from delay

[4.243] The carrier is liable for damage arising from delay in delivery.[159] The time of delivery should be fixed by the contract of carriage or the air consignment note. Article 8 of the Warsaw Convention, which describes the contents of an air consignment note, requires an air consignment note in art 8(p) to contain detail on the time fixed for the completion of the carriage, and a brief note of the route to be followed, if the matters have been agreed. In the absence of express agreement, the intention of the parties and relevant commercial customs and usage will be considered in assessing the reasonable time for delivery.

Excluded liability

[4.244] The liability of the carrier is based on his or her fault and neglect. A lack of fault or negligence constitutes a ground for exemption. The Warsaw Convention provides the following two major grounds on which the carrier can exclude or limit his or her liability:

> The carrier is not liable if he proves that he and his servant and agents have taken all necessary measures to avoid the damage or that it was impossible for him or them to take such measures.[160]
> The carrier is not liable if he or she can prove that the damage to goods has been caused by negligent pilotage or the negligence in the handling of the aircraft or in navigation.[161]

---

158. The Warsaw Convention, art 18(1).
159. The Warsaw Convention, art 19.
160. The Warsaw Convention, art 20(1) and (2).
161. The Warsaw Convention, art 20(2).

> **[4.245]** *Canada Inc and the Prudential Assurance Co Ltd v Air Canada*
>
> Decided 4 April 1997, Federal Court of Canada[1]
>
> *Liability of the carrier, wrongful act of servants*
>
> **Facts:** The plaintiffs include the owner and the insurer of a Gamma bending machine which was damaged before it was delivered to its owner. The defendant was the carrier of the machine. The machine was carried from Milan to Mirabel Airport by the defendant. An air waybill was issued for the carriage. The plaintiffs alleged that the defendant breached its obligations under the air waybill and that the defendant's servants were negligent or reckless in damaging the machine after unloading at Mirabel Airport. The defendant relied on wrongful packaging as a defence because the machine was originally packed for the purpose of sea carriage. It was established that the machine was damaged when two ground workers tried to put it in the warehouse at the airport. The Canadian Carriage by Air Act and the Warsaw Convention applied to the dispute. Article 18 of the Warsaw Convention states as follows:
>
>> The carrier is liable for damage sustained in the event of the destruction or loss of, or of damage to, any registered baggage or any cargo, if the occurrence which caused the damage so sustained took place during the carriage by air.
>>
>> The carriage by air within the meaning of the preceding paragraph comprises the period during which the baggage or cargo is in charge of the carrier, whether in an aerodrome or on board an aircraft, or, in the case of a lading outside an aerodrome, in any place whatsoever.
>
> If the ground workers were negligent or reckless in handling the machine and causing the damage concerned, the carrier would be liable under the said provision.
>
> **Decision:** The Federal Court of Canada held the carrier to be liable for the damage concerned. The evidence of the ground workers suggesting that the packaging of the machine had resulted in the damage concerned was rejected by the court, which also stated that the defendant had failed to discharge the onus of establishing that the damage had not been attributable to its fault or had not resulted from the wrongful acts of its servants.
>
> ---
>
> 1. Canadian Cases — available at <http://www.fja-cmf.gc.ca>.

[4.246] Since the carrier and his or her agents or servants are required to take all necessary measures to prevent, reduce and mitigate the damage, the carrier may be found partially liable if the carrier or carrier's agents have not taken all necessary measures to do so. Accordingly, the carrier may be found partially liable for any damage which was initially caused by negligence in the navigation and control of the aircraft, but ought to have been reduced or mitigated had the necessary and adequate measures been taken by the carrier or the carrier's agents.

Liability of successive carriers

[4.247] The Warsaw Convention does not provide any express definition of carrier. Generally speaking, a carrier is the person who is nominated as the carrier in the relevant air transport document. Sometimes, carrier includes successive carriers who perform part of the carriage, whether or not they are adequately named as the carriers in the air transport document concerned. This is suggested in art 30(1) of the Warsaw Convention, which provides as follows:

> In the case of carriage to be performed by various successive carriers and falling within the definition set out in the third paragraph of Article 1, each carrier who accepts passengers, luggage or goods is subjected to the rules set out in this Convention, and is deemed to be one of the contracting parties to the contract of carriage in so far as the contract deals with that part of the carriage which is performed under his supervision.

[4.248] Article 30(1) suggests that a carrier who performs part of the successive carriage can be sued for the part performed by him or her as a contracting carrier, whether or not he or she is named as a contracting carrier in the contract of carriage or in the air transport document concerned. Article 1(3) of the Warsaw Convention suggests that a successive carriage can be performed under either a single contract or a series of contracts. In the case of a single contract, the carriage is compatible with the so-called through carriage by sea. In the case of a series of contracts, an air transport document is made out to cover each part of the successive carriage. The problem with a series of contracts is identifying the consignor under each successive carriage. If an agent acts on behalf of the original consignor, or the first carrier acts on behalf of the original consignor, a number of technical issues may arise from the application of the relevant provisions of the Warsaw Convention to each air transport document which is not issued to the original consignor. Actually, the Warsaw Convention appears to permit legal actions derived from the right of another person. Articles 15(1) and 24(2) are such examples.

[4.249] Article 30(3) of the Warsaw Convention sets out special rules for taking actions against successive carriers. The provision states as follows:

> As regards luggage or goods, the passenger or consignor will have a right of action against the first carrier, and the passenger or consignee who is entitled to delivery will have a right of action against the last carrier, and further, each may take action against the carrier who performed the carriage during which the destruction, loss, damage or delay took place. These carriers will be jointly and severally liable to the passenger or to the consignor or consignee.

[4.250] Article 30(3) permits the consignor to sue only the first carrier and the consignee to sue only the last carrier, but allows both the consignor and the consignee to sue the carrier directly responsible for the damage concerned. Such arrangements change the doctrine of privity of contract as commonly accepted in common law jurisdictions. The actions concerned lie in art 30(3), instead of the air transport document concerned. Article 30(1) supplements art 30(1), imposing a joint liability upon the successive carrier. However, in any particular dispute, only three carriers of all the successive carriers — the first, the last and the one actually causing the damage — are jointly liable to the consignor or consignee concerned.

[4.251] The provision on successive carriers both grants and restricts the right of the interested party to sue the carrier. Technically, only the consignor and the consignee are entitled to rely on art 30. Sometimes, a common law court may circumvent the technical requirement to permit a cargo-owner who is neither the consignor nor the consignee to sue the carrier directly. For example, in *George Straith Ltd v Air Canada* (1991) 59 BCLR (2d) 241, the plaintiff was the owner of three cartons of sweaters which were carried by air from Heathrow Airport in London to Vancouver. The consignor and the consignee

[4.251] were Rockwood International Freight Ltd in London and Vancouver respectively. The plaintiff discovered that one carton had been opened and 19 sweaters were missing. It sued the carrier directly. The carrier argued that under art 30 of the Warsaw Convention, only the consignor and the consignee are entitled to sue. The Canadian court followed the decision of the English court in *Gatewhite Ltd v Iberia Lineas Aeras de Espana SA* [1989] 1 Lloyd's Rep 160, and decided that the Warsaw Convention does not deprive the owner of the right to sue the carrier.

Limited liability

[4.252] The liability of the carrier in relation to goods is limited under the Warsaw Convention. Under art 22(2), the carrier's liability for loss of or damage to cargo is limited to the sum of 250 francs per kilogram, 'unless the consignor has made, at the time when the package was handed over to the carrier, a special declaration of the value at delivery and has paid a supplementary sum if the case so requires'. The declared sum is prima facie payable by the carrier, unless he or she proves that the sum claimed is greater than the actual value of the goods.[162] The limited liability cannot be exempted or lowered by the agreement of the parties.[163] The invalidity of a clause relieving or reducing the carrier's liability or limited liability does not necessarily affect the validity of the contract of carriage. In addition, in the light of *Saunders v Ansett Industries* (1975) 10 SASR 579 (which dealt with a similar provision under the Civil Aviation (Carrier's Liability) Act 1959 (Cth)), the limited liability only applies to damage caused by the carrier or his or her agents or servants in the course of employment.

[4.253] The limited liability of the carrier applies to all actions arising from arts 17–19 of the Warsaw Convention, unless the convention stipulates otherwise. This is set out in art 24 of the convention, which has two sub-paragraphs. Paragraph 1 purports to subject claims arising from the loss of or damage to goods and luggage, and delay in delivery under arts 18 and 19, to the provisions of the Warsaw Convention. Paragraph 2 ensures that claims arising from personal injuries from art 17 are subject to the provisions of the convention. Provisions of the convention include the provisions on limited liability and excluded liability.

[4.254] The limits of liability are not applicable if the carrier, or his or her agents or servants, intentionally or recklessly caused the loss or damage. Under art 25 of the Warsaw Convention, the carrier, or his or her agents or servants, will be deprived of the benefit of art 22 if the damage is caused by their 'wilful misconduct', or 'such default' which is considered to be equivalent to wilful misconduct. The word 'default' should include both intentional and reckless acts or omissions, and art 20 exempts the carrier from any liability only where the carrier can establish that all necessary measures have been taken by the carrier, its servants or agents, to avoid the damage and that it was impossible to avoid it. Thus, a reckless carrier cannot benefit from any 'default' or recklessness.

---

162. The Warsaw Convention, art 22(2).
163. Article 23 of the Warsaw Convention provides as follows:

>Any provision tending to relieve the carrier of liability or to fix a lower limit than that which is laid down in this Convention shall be null and void, but the nullity of any such provision does not involve the nullity of the whole contract, which shall remain subject to the provisions of this Convention.

[4.255] It must be noted that the consignor or consignee alleging the existence of wilful misconduct has the burden of proof. In *Malca-Amit Ltd v British Airways Plc*,[164] three bags of diamonds were lost during the carriage involving Antwerp, Brussels Zaventem Airport, Heathrow and Tel Aviv or Bombay. The consignor sought to deprive the carriers of the benefit of limited liability under art 25, but the court was not satisfied by the evidence of the consignor that the carrier committed wilful misconduct in causing the loss the subject of the complaint.

[4.256] The meaning of wilful misconduct is examined in *Brinks Ltd v South African Airways*.[165] In this case, Brinks Ltd, which was an insurer for air carriage, was the plaintiff and appellant. South African Airways was the carrier, the defendant and the respondent of the case. Rustenberg Platinum Mines Ltd was the consignor of 34 boxes of rhodium and palladium, both platinum metals, to be transported from Johannesburg, South Africa, to New York. When the container with the 34 boxes arrived at the John K Kennedy (JFK) International Airport in New York, six boxes were discovered missing. The value of the missing metals was allegedly US$1,789,012.67. It was agreed that the pilferage took place after the cargo was delivered to the carrier at Jan Smuts Airport in Johannesburg. Brinks Ltd paid Rustenberg US$1,777,624 in compensation, and sued the carrier as the consignee under the air waybill concerned to recover the payment. The dispute was subject to the Warsaw Convention. Article 22 of the Warsaw Convention limits the liability of the carrier to a sum of 250 francs per kilogram. Brinks Ltd sought to rely on art 25 of the Warsaw Convention, which sets out the concept of wilful misconduct, to deprive the carrier of the benefit of limited liability.

The trial court found that the boxes containing the precious metals were transported to Jan Smuts Airport by the consignor (Rustenburg) under heavy security, and then loaded into the container bound for New York at the airport under the close supervision of the consignor, the airport authority and the police. The container was sealed and padlocked after it was loaded with 34 boxes. Prior to loading, the container was placed in the high value cargo vault, which was closed and locked. The court also found that the procedures for delivering the container to Brinks Ltd at the JFK International Airport were normal. There was no evidence to suggest any abnormality on the part of the carrier during the process of carriage, and prior to the time when the six boxes were found to be missing. Under the belief that the question of wilful misconduct is a mixture of fact and law, the trial court did not find the evidence of wilful misconduct on the part of the carrier, and fixed the carrier's liability at the sum of US$1520 in pursuance of art 22 of the Warsaw Convention. The trial court referred to the English case *Rustenberg Platinum Mines Ltd v South African Airways* [1977] 1 Lloyd's Rep 564 (QB), and defined wilful misconduct as something going far beyond any negligence, even gross or culpable negligence, and involved a person doing or omitting to do that which is not only negligent but which he or she knows and appreciates is wrong, and is done or committed regardless of the consequences, not caring what the result of that carelessness may be. The trial court's decision

---

164. Decided on 28 April 1990 by QB, available at <http://www.casetrack.com>.
165. Decided on 2 July 1998 by the United States Court of Appeals for the Second Circuit, available at <http://law.touro.edu>.

was affirmed by the Court of Appeal for the Second Circuit. In light of these decisions, it can be said that under art 25 of the Warsaw Convention, wilful misconduct is an act or omission of a carrier who is reckless or careless as to the damaging consequences likely to flow from the act or omission.

[4.257] The difficulty of establishing the existence of wilful misconduct is also illustrated by an English case, *The Thomas Cook Group v Air Malta Co Ltd* [1997] 2 Lloyd's Rep 399. In this case, the goods were a consignment of banknotes, carried from London to Luqa Airport, Malta in May 1992. The plaintiffs were the consignor (the seller), the consignee (the buyer), and the security company (employed by the consignor to protect the carriage of the banknotes from the Luqa Airport to the consignee in Malta), which became a party to the plaintiffs after having paid the consignor part of the loss incurred. The security company was supposed to meet the cargo planeside in Malta. The carrier carried the cargo to Malta, but the security company was unable to enter into the airport to collect the cargo planeside.

The cargo of banknotes was placed in a room within the airport waiting for customs clearance. An armed robbery took place and the banknotes were stolen. The value of the banknotes was not declared when they were delivered to the carrier. The plaintiffs relied on several provisions of the Warsaw Convention, including arts 18(1), 20(1), 22(2) and 25, and sought to recover the full value of the banknotes from the carrier. The carrier relied on art 22 to limit its liability and alleged contributory negligence on the part of the plaintiffs. The court held that the establishment of wilful misconduct involves several steps: (1) establishing what is an expected act; (2) examining whether the carrier's act or omission can be properly regarded as misconduct; (3) determining whether the carrier's act or omission is wilful; and (4) investigating whether the wilful misconduct has caused the damage concerned. In applying the formula, Cresswell J of QB (Com Ct) concluded that the carrier's act of placing the cargo in the room for customs clearance was normal and that the presence of the security company would have probably prevented the occurrence of the armed robbery. Accordingly, the carrier was allowed to rely on art 22 to claim limited liability.

Limitation period

[4.258] The convention sets out limitation periods for the consignee to make a complaint to the carrier and to take legal action against the carrier. Article 26(2) specifies the time requirement for making a complaint as follows:

- in the case of loss of or damage to goods, a complaint must be made within seven days after receiving the goods; and
- in the case of later delivery, a complaint must be made within 14 days after the cargo has been placed at the consignee's disposal.

Compliance with these requirements is crucial. A complainant loses the right to claim compensation if he or she fails to comply with them. In the case of a latent defect or a defect which cannot be discovered by ordinary means, the existence of the alleged defect must be proven to the court dealing with the dispute.[166] If the consignee or the person entitled to receive the goods fails to make a complaint within the specified time, the absence of a complaint is prima facie evidence of the receipt of the goods by him or her in the quantity and conditions recorded in the air consignment note. However, the limitation period is not available to a carrier who has committed a fraud in causing damages to the consignor or consignee. The complaint, which is in fact a notice of claim, must be made in writing. The Warsaw Convention does not set out specific rules dealing with non-delivery. As we can see in the next paragraph, a claim based on non-delivery is covered by the maximum limitation period of two years.

[4.259] Article 29 provides a limitation period of two years for claiming damages. The time begins to run from the date of arrival at the destination, or from the date on which the aircraft ought to have arrived, or from the date on which the carriage stopped. An extension of the limitation period under domestic law is normally not allowed, although the limitation period under certain domestic law may be longer than the limitation of two years as set out in the Warsaw Convention.[167] The combined effect of arts 26 and 29 suggests that a person who has complied with the writing formality and time requirement for making a complaint may still lose his or her right of action against the carrier for the matter complained about if no formal legal action has been taken within the two-years limitation period.

A person who has not complied with the requirements for making a complaint may lose his or her right to rely on the two-years limitation period unless a fraud on the part of the carrier can be proven. There is no requirement for the formality of making a complaint in the case of non-delivery. Thus, it can be argued that in the case of non-delivery, the consignee or the consignor is not obliged to give a notice of complaint to the carrier, but must commence legal proceedings within two years from the date on which the goods concerned should have arrived.

Forum of action

[4.260] The forum of action refers to the place where the defendant may commence legal proceedings against the defendant. The Warsaw Convention restricts the plaintiff's ability to choose a forum. This is seen in art 28(1) of the Warsaw Convention, which states that an action for damage must be brought in the territory of a Warsaw Convention member and, at the option of the plaintiff, in one of the following forums:

- the carrier's ordinary residence;
- the carrier's principal place of business;
- the place the carrier's representative actually made the contract of carriage in dispute; or
- the place of destination.

---

166. In *Markham Meat Industries Supplier Inc v Air France*, decided on 9 July 1998 by the Supreme Court of Ontario, available at <http://www.admiraltylaw.com>, the consignee failed to give the carrier a written notice of claim within 14 days as required by art 26(2) of the Warsaw Convention. The defendant applied to the court for an order to dismiss the action. The court ordered a special trial to determine whether the damage complained of was concealed.

167. See *Abnett v British Airways Plc (Scotland); Sidhu v British Airways Plc*, available at <http://www.number7.demon.co.uk>.

[4.261] The above restrictions deny the plaintiff's right to sue in any country which is not a member of the Warsaw Convention. They also require that the place of action falls within the four categories described in art 28(1) above. In *Deaville v Aeroflot Russian International Airlines* [1997] 2 Lloyd's Rep 67, art 28 was examined in somewhat unusual circumstances.

In this case, an aeroplane owned by the defendant crashed near the town of Mezhdurechensk, Siberia, while en route from Moscow to Hong Kong on 22 May 1994, killing all passengers and crew on board. In 1996, a group of dependants and relatives of some of the deceased sued the carrier and the manufacturer of the aeroplane in France. Some of the plaintiffs in the French actions also commenced an action in the English court, as a precaution in case the French actions failed for lack of jurisdiction. After commencement of the English action, the defendant carrier applied to the English court for an order prohibiting the plaintiffs from further participating in the French actions, arguing art 28 of the Warsaw Convention (as amended by the Hague Protocol 1955) and the fact that France did not fall under any of the prescribed jurisdictions under art 28. On the other hand, the plaintiffs applied to the court for a stay of the proceedings in the English court. The court examined art 28 and concluded that the French court did not have jurisdiction under art 28 if the actions were brought against the carrier only. However, the court noted that the manufacturer of the aeroplane was also sued in the proceedings. Thus, the jurisdiction of the French court in such proceedings must be determined by the court itself. The court refused to issue an order to prohibit the plaintiffs from pursuing the French actions further also on the ground of international comity, while the court granted the plaintiffs' request to stay the local proceedings in the UK. This case not only confirms the exclusive jurisdictions set out in art 28, but also raises the interesting point that the exclusive jurisdictions may not apply to cases where co-defendants include someone who is not a carrier.

[4.262] It must be pointed out that the restrictions on the forum of action appear to have been based on the proposition that most actions are against the carrier. Thus, in light of art 28(1), no express reference to the consignor or the consignee has been made. If an action is to be taken by the carrier against the consignee or the consignor, it appears that the restrictions do not make much sense, except the last one — the place of destination. If the carrier is the plaintiff and the action is to be taken at the carrier's place of residence, principal business or representative office, the defendant may be in another country. It may not be easy for the plaintiff to bring the defendant to the local court, although the plaintiff may have the advantage of a default judgment if the defendant refuses to come to the court. The default judgment may, however, not be enforced in the defendant's place of business or residence because a case of procedural unfairness may be easily made out by the defendant at his or her own local court. A conflict of laws may arise from such a situation. The Warsaw Convention does not appear to have provided an adequate answer for the jurisdictional question in the cases where the carrier is the plaintiff.

[4.263] As a general principle of conflict of laws, the Warsaw Convention states that the procedures of legal actions are governed by the law of the court dealing with the case in pursuance of the relevant provisions of the Warsaw Convention.[168] The procedural issue covers the method of calculating the limitation period. Accordingly, the local law applies to the determination of the limitation period in any particular case.[169] Article 32 of the Warsaw Convention prohibits the parties from choosing the governing law or the jurisdiction in contradiction to the provisions of the convention. This prohibition does not apply to an arbitration to be held in one of the member countries of the Warsaw Convention.[170] Space does not permit discussion of other conventions modifying the Warsaw Convention.

Contracts for carriage by land

Legal framework for carriage by land

[4.264] Carriage by land consists of two specific modes: carriage by rail and carriage by road. Two major international conventions have been adopted to regulate each mode of carriage respectively. They are:

- The Convention concerning International Carriage by Rail, known as COTIF, which stands for *Convention relative aux transports internationaux ferroviaires*. COTIF incorporates the Uniform Rules concerning the Contract for International Carriage of Goods by Rail (CIM, which stands for *Convention internationale concernant le transport des marchandises par chemin de fer*) in its Appendix B. CIM was originally adopted as the 1893 International Convention concerning the Carriage of Goods by Rail and had been amended several times before being incorporated into COTIF in 1980 in Berne. The Uniform Rules concerning the Contract for International Carriage of Passengers and Luggage by Rail (CIV) is incorporated into Appendix A to COTIF. CIV will also be examined briefly in this chapter.

- The 1956 Geneva Convention on the Contract for the International Carriage of Goods by Road, known as CMR, which stands for *Convention relative au contrat de transport international des marchandises par route*. CMR was amended by the Protocol to the Convention on the Contract for International Carriage of Goods by Road on 5 July 1978, which entered into force on 28 December 1980. Only some of the CMR members have ratified the protocol.

- COTIF regulates both the carriage of goods and carriage of passengers, but CMR deals with the carriage of goods only. There is a convention dealing with the carriage of passengers by road known as the Convention on the Contract for the International Carriage of Passengers and Luggage by Road (CVR). It was concluded at Geneva on 1 March 1973, and entered into force on 12 April 1994. As at July 1999, it had six members. This convention is not examined in this chapter.

---

168. The Warsaw Convention, art 28(2).
169. The Warsaw Convention, art 29(2).
170. Article 32 of the Warsaw Convention provides that 'for the carriage of goods arbitration clauses are allowed, subject to this Convention, if the arbitration is to take place within one of the jurisdictions referred to in the first paragraph of Article 28'.

[4.265] Besides the said two major conventions there are also a number of European conventions which have various implications to the carriage by land. They are:

- the Convention on Customs Treatment of Pool Containers Used in International Transport (21 January 1994);
- the Customs Convention Concerning Spare Parts Used for Repairing European Wagons (15 January 1958);
- the International Convention for the Crossing of Frontiers for Passengers and Baggage Carried by Rail (10 January 1952);
- the Convention and Statute on Freedom of Transit (20 April 1921);
- the Customs Convention on the Temporary Importation of Commercial Road Vehicles (18 May 1956);
- the Customs Convention on the International Transport of Goods Under Cover of TIR Carnets (14 November 1975);
- the European Convention on Customs Treatment of Pallets Used in International Transport (9 December 1960);
- the Customs Convention on the Temporary Importation of Private Road Vehicles (4 June 1954);
- the Convention on Transit Trade of Land-Locked States (8 July 1965);
- the Customs Convention on the Temporary Importation for Private Use of Aircraft and Pleasure Boats (18 May 1956);
- the International Convention on the Harmonization of Frontier Controls of Goods (21 October 1982);
- the Convention Concerning Customs Facilities for Touring (4 June 1954);
- the International Convention to Facilitate the Crossing of Frontiers for Goods Carried by Rail (10 January 1952); and
- the Convention on Road Traffic Customs Convention on Containers (2 December 1972).

In addition, there is also a lesser known non-European convention: the Inter-American Convention on Contracts for the International Carriage of Goods by Road. The convention was adopted in the Inter-American Specialised Conference on Private International Law at Montevideo, Uruguay, on 15 July 1989. As we can see from the above listed conventions, all of them are regional. This is due to the feature of the carriage by land, which has geographical restrictions. As a general rule, in the absence of any international convention, the carrier by land is subject to the relevant domestic law. In this chapter, only the two major conventions will be discussed.

Carriage by rail under COTIF

An overview of COTIF

[4.266] COTIF was adopted on 9 May 1980 and entered into force on 1 May 1985. As at July 1999, COTIF had 37 members, including Albania, Algeria, Austria, Belgium,

Bosnia-Herzegovina, Bulgaria, Croatia, Czech Republic, Denmark, Finland, France, Germany, Greece, Hungary, Iran, Iraq, Ireland, Italy, Lebanon, Liechtenstein, Lithuania, Luxembourg, Monaco, Morocco, the Netherlands, Norway, Poland, Portugal, Romania, Slovak Republic, Slovenia, Spain, Sweden, Switzerland, Tunisia, Turkey and the United Kingdom. The membership suggests that COTIF is in fact a European convention.

[4.267] As an international convention, COTIF consists of three parts: the body of the main text, Appendix A (CIV), and Appendix B (CIM). The body of the main text contains 28 articles. Appendix A (CIV) contains the rules for the carriage of passengers by rail. Appendix B (CIM) contains the rules for the carriage of goods by rail. Appendix B also includes four annexes, which are Annex I (Regulations concerning the International Carriage of Dangerous Goods by Rail (RID)); Annex II (Regulations concerning the International Haulage of Private Owners Wagons by Rail); Annex III (Regulations concerning the International Carriage of Containers by Rail (RICo)); and Annex IV (Regulations concerning the International Carriage of Express Parcels by Rail (RIEx)). In addition, there is also the Protocol on the Privileges and Immunities of the Intergovernmental Organisation for International Carriage by Rail (OTIF) attached to COTIF. The main text of COTIF, CIM and CIV are to be examined below. The most essential purpose of COTIF is to bring CIV and CIM together under the same umbrella.

Main Features of COTIF

[4.268] COTIF has three major features: establishing the Intergovernmental Organisation for International Carriage by Rail (OTIF), incorporating CIV and CIM Uniform Rules into the same convention; and adopting an arbitration system for the purpose of resolving disputes between the members. The CIV and CIM are to be examined separately later in this section. Thus, only the two features — OTIF and arbitration — are to be discussed here. It needs to be noted before carrying on our discussions further that the original convention was concluded in French, and that its text has been translated into German, English, Arabic, Italian and Dutch. Thus, COTIF, CIV, CIM and OTIF are acronyms of French expressions.

[4.269] First, in order to enforce COTIF, in particular CIV and CIM, OTIF was established under art 1(2) of COTIF. Its headquarters are located in Berne. Under art 1(2) of COTIF, OTIF is an independent legal person and has the capacity to make contracts, acquire and dispose of property, and take part in legal proceedings. On the other hand, the members of OTIF have been granted diplomatic privileges and immunities necessary for them to discharge their official duties. These arrangements suggest that OTIF is not a conventional type of intergovernmental organisation. However, it is expected that the major function of OTIF is to discharge its official functions under COTIF, instead of carrying on business operations. The major function of OTIF is set out in art 2(1) of COTIF, as being responsible for establishing a uniform system of law applicable to the carriage of passengers, luggage and goods in international through traffic by rail between member states, and to facilitate the application and development of this system. OTIF consists of five major organs:[171] the General Assembly, the Administrative Committee,

---

171. COTIF, art 5.

[4.269]

the Revision Committee, the Committee of Experts for the Carriage of Dangerous Goods, and the Central Office for International Carriage by Rail (OCTI). Article 6 of COTIF regulates the operation of the General Assembly. Article 7 regulates the operation of the Administrative Committee. Article 8 regulates the operation of the Revision Committee and the Committee of Experts for the Carriage of Dangerous Goods. Article 9 regulates the operation of the Central Office for International Carriage by Rail.

[4.270] Second, a mechanism of arbitration has been adopted in the convention to resolve disputes arising from the convention. The mechanism has two distinctive characteristics: (1) being compulsory unless a member makes a reservation at the time of ratifying the convention to the contrary effect; and (2) the establishment of a panel of arbitration under OTIF.

This mechanism is meant to apply to all types of dispute relating to the application of COTIF between members. Under art 12 of COTIF, any disputes arising from COTIF between members or between a member and OTIF should be, at the request of any party, referred to an arbitration tribunal to be appointed by the disputing parties. In practice, a dispute may arise from the interpretation of the convention, or the performance of members' obligations under the convention. Under the arbitration mechanism, the members should first attempt to resolve the dispute on their own. If unsuccessful, one of the members is entitled to submit the dispute to arbitration, and the other member is obliged to accept the request of arbitration, unless it makes a reservation against all or part of art 12. The Central Office for International Carriage by Rail maintains a list of arbitrators. The disputing parties are expected to appoint one, three or five arbitrators to constitute an arbitration tribunal from the panel. If five arbitrators are appointed, each disputing party is entitled to appoint no more than one outside person to be an arbitrator. The tribunal is expected to examine the evidence provided by the parties and to interpret the provisions of COTIF independently and impartially.

[4.271] Besides these two major features, COTIF also has provisions dealing with the procedures of arbitration, enforcement of arbitral awards, enforcement of judicial decisions made by the court of a member, the decisions of the General Assembly and committees of COTIF, and others. In summary, the specific rules for the carriage by rail are set out in CIV and CIM respectively. The main text of COTIF establishes a structure under which the application of CIV, CIM and the four annexes can be adequately and effectively supervised and ensured. Due to space restrictions, only CIM will be discussed in this book.

Carriage of goods under CIM

Structure of CIM

[4.272] CIM has seven 'titles' (chapters or parts) which are set out as follows:

- Title 1 — general provisions;
- Title 2 — making and execution of the contract of carriage;
- Title 3 — modification of the contract of carriage;
- Title 4 — liability;

- Title 5 — assertion of rights;
- Title 6 — relations between railways; and
- Title 7 — exceptional provisions.

CIM has 66 articles under the seven titles. Some of these provisions are to be examined in the following subsections. As we have seen, CIM has also four annexes which regulate several aspects of carriage of goods by rail. These are:

- Annex 1 — Regulations concerning the International Carriage of Dangerous Goods by Rail (RID), which are based on arts 4 and 5 of CIM;
- Annex 2 — Regulations concerning the International Haulage of Private Owner's Wagons by Rail (RIP), which are based on art 8(1) of CIM;
- Annex 3 — Regulations concerning the International Carriage of Containers by Rail (RICo), which are based on art 8(2) of CIM; and
- Annex 4 — Regulations concerning the International Carriage of Express Parcels by Rail (RIEx), which are based on art 8(3) of CIM.

The details of these annexes are not to be studied in this subsection.

Application of CIM

[4.273] CIM applies to the carriage of goods by rail for reward, which involves more than two countries. The goods should be carried under a 'through consignment note', which is a form of transport document similar to a 'through bill of lading': see **[4.56]**. The use of a through consignment note is necessary because sometimes a cargo may be carried by carriers or railways in different countries, which, however, must be the lines and services specified or listed in COTIF. In fact, 'carrier' may not be an accurate expression in carriage by rail, because the railway accepting the goods, concluding a contract of carriage and issuing a consignment note is often unable to carry the goods for the whole route. Thus, more often than not, a particular carriage is performed by several railways or carriers. The first railway or carrier is known as the forwarding railway, which is similar to a carrier under the Hamburg Rules for carriage by sea and a contracting carrier under the Guadalajara Convention 1961 for carriage by air. The place where a carriage begins is known as the forwarding station, and the place where the carriage ends is known as the destination station.

[4.274] CIM is meant to regulate the carriage of goods by railways, which is equivalent to shipping companies in the sea carriage and airlines in the air carriage. The scope of CIM's application is defined in art 1 of CIM as follows:

§ 1. Subject to the exceptions provided for in Article 2, the Uniform Rules shall apply to all consignments of goods for carriage under a through consignment note made out for a route over the territories of at least two states and exclusively over lines or services included in the list provided for in Articles 3 and 10 of the Convention, as well as, where appropriate, to carriage treated as carriage over a line in accordance with Article 2, § 2, second subparagraph of the Convention.

§ 2. In the Uniform Rules the expression 'station' covers: railway stations, ports used by shipping services and all other establishments of transport undertakings, open to the public for the execution of the contract of carriage.

[4.275] The scope of application as defined in art 1 is qualified in art 2 to exclude a carriage which should not be regarded as international. In art 1, if a carriage passes through the territories of more than two countries, it is international and subject to the rules of CIM. However, a carriage which both starts and ends within the same territory with only a transit through the territory of another country is not subject to CIM, if (1) the lines or services over which the transit occurs are exclusively operated by a railway of the state of departure; or (2) the states or the railways concerned have agreed not to regard such carriage as international.[172]

In addition, a carriage by a regular liner service passing through stations located in more than two adjacent countries may not be subject to CIM, if the liner service is exclusively operated by a railway of one of the countries concerned and the consignment note concerned expressly chooses the internal regulations of the railway as the governing law.[173] However, the effect of such a choice of law clause in a consignment note is subject to the conflict rules of the relevant court determining the dispute.

Contract of carriage

[4.276] Like any other mode of carriage, a contract of carriage is also essential for the carriage of goods by rail. A contract of carriage by rail is made between the consignor and the forwarding railway. The detailed rules for the conclusion of a contract of carriage by rail are set out in art 11 of CIM. The contract of carriage shall come into existence as soon as the forwarding railway has accepted the goods for carriage together with the consignment note. Acceptance is established by the application to the consignment note and, where appropriate, to each additional sheet, of the stamp of the forwarding station, or accounting machine entry, showing the date of acceptance.[174]

The forwarding railway (carrier) is obliged to accept the consignment note as soon as he or she has accepted the cargo concerned, provided that the consignor pays or undertakes to pay the appropriate charges for carriage.[175] The railway shall certify receipt of the goods and the date of acceptance for carriage by affixing the date stamp to the accounting machine entry on the duplicate of the consignment note before returning the duplicate to the consignor. The duplicate shall not have effect as the consignment note accompanying the goods, nor as a bill of lading.[176] The contract of carriage should be evidenced by a consignment note, which is deemed to have been duly made once the stamp has been affixed or the accounting machine entry has been made.[177] These specific rules of art 11 suggest the differences between COTIF and international conventions for the carriage by sea and air. Indeed, CIM is meant to provide uniform rules for the practice of carriage of goods by rail.

---

172. CIM, art 2(1).
173. CIM, art 2(2).
174. CIM, art 11(1).
175. CIM, art 11(2).
176. CIM, art 11(4).
177. CIM, art 11(3).

Consignment note

[4.277] A consignment note is similar to an air waybill. It is provided by the carrier or the forwarding railway and filled out by the consignor. It should be handed over with the goods to the carrier or forwarding railway, and the contract of carriage is formed from that moment. The carrier should check the information in the consignment note and return a stamped copy to the consignor as evidence of receipt of the goods described and the conclusion of the contract of carriage. The consignment note must be printed in two or more languages, and the carrier can prescribe the type of consignment note for each type of goods.[178] A consignment note must provide sufficient information to indicate the places of departure and destination, the description of goods, and the conditions and terms of the carriage.

[4.278] A consignment note under CIM is not a document of title. Nor is it negotiable. It is handed over to the consignee with the goods at delivery, serving as evidence of the authenticity of the goods delivered. It evidences the receipt of the goods concerned by the carrier or the forwarding railway. If the goods have been loaded or packed by the consignor, 'the particulars in the consignment note relating to the mass of the goods or to the number of packages shall only be evidence against the railway when that weight or number of packages has been verified by the railway and certified in the consignment note'.[179] This means that the carrier may as well exclude his or her liability to the nature or quantity of the goods either expressly or implicitly in a consignment note if he or she is unable to verify the accuracy of the information on the goods furnished by the consignor. In addition, the delivery of the goods in apparent good order and condition or in a container with original seals intact is prima facie evidence that the carrier has performed his or her duty under CIM appropriately.[180]

[4.279] As a transport document, a consignment must contain necessary information for the carriers to perform the contract of carriage. Article 13 of CIM requires a consignment note to contain the following details:
(a) the name of the destination station;
(b) the name and address of the consignee; only one individual or legal person shall be shown as consignee;
(c) the description of the goods;
(d) the mass, or failing that, comparable information in accordance with the provisions in force at the forwarding station;
(e) the number of packages and a description of the packing in the case of consignments in less than wagon loads, and in the case of complete wagon loads, comprising one or more packages, forwarded by rail sea and requiring to be transshipped;
(f) the number of the wagon and also, for privately owned wagons, the tare, in the case of goods where the loading is the duty of the consignor;

---

178. CIM, art 12.
179. CIM, art 11(4).
180. Article 11(4) of CIM states that 'if it is obvious that there is no actual deficiency corresponding to the discrepancy between the mass or number of packages and the particulars in the consignment note, the latter shall not be evidence against the railway. This shall apply in particular when the wagon is handed over to the consignee with the original seals intact'.

[4.279]   International Commercial Law

    (g) a detailed list of the documents which are required by customs or other administrative authorities and are attached to the consignment note or shown as held at the disposal of the railway at a named station or at an office of the customs or of any other authority;

    (h) the name and address of the consignor; only one individual or legal person shall be shown as the consignor; if the provisions in force at the forwarding station so require, the consignor shall add to his name and address his written, printed or stamped signature.

[4.280] Paragraph (e) above refers to wagon load and less than wagon load. The meaning of these expressions should be defined by the carrier or the forwarding station for the whole of the route. This means that if the carriage involves several successive carriers, the first carrier who is known as the forwarding station should determine the meaning of wagon load in the consignment note concerned. The information required in art 13 is essential for a consignment note to be regarded as a transport document by a bank under art 28 of UCP 500 for the purpose of providing credits to its customers.

Rights and obligations of the consignor

[4.281] The consignor has the right to decide the route of carriage. He or she may stipulate in the consignment note the route to be followed, indicating it by reference to frontier points or frontier stations and where appropriate, to transit stations between railways. He or she may only stipulate frontier points and frontier stations which are open to traffic between the forwarding and destination places concerned.[181] In order to ensure the goods are transported through a particular route successfully, the consignor may give the forwarder routing instructions, which include: designation of stations where formalities required by the customs or other administrative authorities are to be carried out; stations where special care is required (such as feeding animals, receiving perishables); designation of the tariffs to be applied, if this is sufficient to determine the stations between which the tariffs requested are to be applied; and instructions as to the payment of the whole or a part of the charges up to a place where the tariffs of adjacent countries are to be applied.[182]

The railways are obliged to follow the consignor's routing instructions, unless deviation from them is authorised by law, or performance of the instruction is impossible. If the consignor's instructions are not consistent with each other, the railway is entitled to choose the route or tariff which appears to be the most advantageous to the consignor. The railway making a choice on behalf of the consignor, because of the said inconsistency of the instructions, is not liable for any loss or damage resulting from the choice, unless wilful misconduct or gross negligence can be proven on the part of the railway.[183]

[4.282] The consignor has the right to modify the contract of carriage by changing certain terms of the contract. For example, the consignor may withdraw the goods at the forwarding station after the conclusion of the contract; stop the goods in transit; request the railway to hold the goods for further instructions; instruct the goods to be delivered to a person who is not named as the consignee in the consignment note; change the destination station; return the goods to the forwarding station; request the goods to be

---

181. CIM, art 14(1).
182. CIM, art 14(2).
183. CIM, art 14(7).

delivered against cash payment on delivery; and attach terms of reimbursement or cash payment with the delivery of the goods to the consignee.[184] The requests or instructions of the consignor must be given expressly in compliance with the formality required by the railway concerned, that is, in the form provided by the railway. The consignor's right to change the terms of the contract ceases when the consignee has taken possession of the consignment note, has accepted the goods, has demanded delivery of the goods and consignment after the goods have arrived at the destination station, or has exercised the consignee's rights under art 31 of CIM.[185]

[4.283] The consignor's major obligations can be seen in several aspects. Generally speaking, the consignor must inform the forwarding railway truthfully of the nature of the goods to be carried. Since a carriage by railway may cross several countries and each country may have different laws and regulations which may affect the goods in transit, the railways or the carriers are entitled to refuse to accept certain articles or goods for carriage, if the carriage of the articles or goods is prohibited by the relevant domestic or international law concerned. The consignor must also disclose to the forwarding railway all the relevant information concerning the goods, because CIM has specific rules on the calculation of tariffs, carriage of privately owned wagons, carriage of dangerous goods, carriage of live animals and compliance with the customs formalities, and others.

Loading of goods can be done by either the railway or the consignor, depending on the local rules adopted by the forwarding station. If the consignor is responsible for loading the goods, he or she has an obligation to comply with the load limit. 'If different load limits are in force on the lines traversed, the lowest load limit shall be applicable to the whole route.'[186] A consignor who breaches the obligation to comply with the loading limit is liable for the loss or damage suffered by the railways or the carriers performing the contract of carriage. The consignor is also responsible for packing and marking adequately, and for providing necessary documents to comply with the administrative formalities and customs during the carriage concerned.

Rights and obligations of the consignee

[4.284] The consignee has a number of rights and obligations under CIM. The major rights of the consignee are set out in art 31 of CIM, which permits the consignee to modify the terms of the contract of carriage. The provision states as follows:

> When the consignor has not undertaken to pay the charges relating to carriage in the country of destination, and has not inserted in the consignment note the words 'Consignee not authorised to give subsequent orders', the consignee may modify the contract of carriage by giving subsequent orders:
>
> for the goods to be stopped in transit;
>
> for delivery of the goods to be delayed;
>
> for the goods to be delivered in the country of destination to a person other than the consignee shown in the consignment note;

---

184. CIM, art 30(1).
185. CIM, art 20(4).
186. CIM, art 20(2).

for the goods to be delivered in the country of destination at a station other than the destination station shown in the consignment note, subject to contrary provisions in international tariffs;

for formalities required by Customs or other administrative authorities to be carried out in accordance with Article 26, § 3.

[4.285] The rights of the consignee may be extended or varied by the supplementary provisions or the international tariffs in force between the railways participating in the carriage. However, the consignee's instructions must not in any case have the effect of splitting the consignment of the goods concerned, and the consignee's orders shall only be effective after the consignment has entered the customs territory of the country of destination.[187] Some flexibility, if not negotiability, is evidenced by such right.

[4.286] The consignee has the right to sue the railway or carrier for loss of or damage to the goods. The right to sue can be extinguished by his or her acceptance of the goods without complaint.[188] However, the acceptance may not extinguish the right to sue if the consignee has notified the railway of a partial loss or damage to the goods in pursuance of the relevant provisions of CIM, if the consignee's failure to comply with the notification procedure was caused by the fault of the railway, if the damage concerned was not apparent, if the claim is related to a delay in delivery, or if the loss or damage was caused by wilful conduct or gross negligence of the railway concerned.

[4.287] The major obligation of the consignee is to pay the relevant charges under the contract of carriage.[189] He or she is also obliged to pay the specified sum to the railway on delivery if the consignment note contains a term for cash on delivery.

Rights and obligations of the carrier

[4.288] The most important right of the carrier is to collect payments and charges for the services of carriage provided. Under CIM, it has specific rights to dispose and handle goods of a dangerous nature and character. The carrier or railway also has the right to seek compensation against the relevant consignor or the consignee if the latter has breached the contract of carriage or the provisions of CIM.

[4.289] CIM imposes a collective or joint responsibility upon the railways or carriers involved in a particular carriage. The collective responsibility is seen in three aspects: first, the railway which has accepted goods for carriage with the consignment note shall be responsible for the carriage over the entire route up to delivery;[190] and second, each 'succeeding railway, by the very act of taking over the goods with the consignment note, shall become a party to the contract of carriage in accordance with the terms of that document and shall assume the obligations arising therefrom, without prejudice to the provisions of art 55, § 3, relating to the railway of destination'.[191] Third, a railway or carrier which has paid compensation in accordance with CIM, for total or partial loss or for damage, has a right of recourse against the other railways which have taken part in the

---

187. CIM, art 31(1).
188. CIM, art 57(1).
189. CIM, art 15.
190. CIM, art 35(1).
191. CIM, art 35(2).

carriage, in accordance with the relevant provisions of art 60 of CIM. The carriers' right of recourse against each other is one of the principles of common law governing joint liability. Under the system of collective responsibility, the forwarding railway (carrier) which has accepted the goods and the consignment note is responsible for carriage over the entire route, regardless of how many carriers or railways are subsequently involved, although in practice it may be more convenient and effective for the consignee to sue the railway of destination than the forwarding railway.

[4.290] Although the railways or carriers are jointly liable for the performance of the contract of carriage, CIM has specific rules governing who can sue and whom should be sued in a particular circumstance. These rules are set out in arts 54 and 55 of CIM. Article 54 classifies actions against the railways into three categories. First, an action for the recovery of a sum paid under the contract of carriage may only be brought by the person who made the payment against the railway or the carrier which has collected that sum, or against the railway or the carrier on whose behalf the sum was collected.[192] Second, an action in respect of the cash on delivery payments provided for in art 17 may only be brought by the consignor against the forwarding railway.[193] Third, any other actions besides the category one and two arising from the contract of carriage may be brought by either the consignor or the consignee, as the case may be, against the forwarding railway, the railway of destination or the railway directly responsible for the loss or damage concerned.[194]

[4.291] It must be pointed out that the railway of destination may be sued under a contract of carriage regardless of whether it has actually received the goods or consignment note concerned. Generally speaking, such an action can be brought by the consignor unless the consignee has taken possession of the consignment note, accepted the goods, or asserted his or her rights under arts 28(4) or 31: see **[4.284]**. When a legal action is taken by the consignor, he or she must produce the duplicate of the consignment note; or alternatively, he or she must produce an authorisation from the consignee or the evidence that the consignee has refused to accept the goods concerned.[195]

On the other hand, the consignee is required to produce a consignment note to support his or her right to sue only when the consignment note has been delivered to him or her. These rules suggest that, although either the consignor or the consignee can sue, it is the consignee who exercises the right to sue in most cases; similarly, although several railways or carriers may be jointly liable, it is the railway of destination which may be sued in most cases. In addition, the rules also suggest that only one of the carriers can be sued for a particular claim. In fact, art 55(4) of CIM provides that even if the consignor or the consignee can choose between several railways or carriers, his or her right to choose shall be extinguished as soon as he or she brings an action against any one of them. The specific rules set out in arts 54 and 55 of CIM do not prohibit actions outside art 54 to be

---

192. CIM, arts 54(1) and 55(1).
193. CIM, arts 54(2) and 55(2).
194. CIM, arts 54(3) and 55(3).
195. CIM, art 54(4).

[4.291]

brought against any railways or carriers who may be liable to a person under the contract of carriage concerned.

[4.292] Under CIM, the railway or carrier shall be liable for loss or damage resulting from the total or partial loss of, or damage to, the goods between the time of acceptance for carriage and the time of delivery and for the loss or damage resulting from the transit period being exceeded. However, it may be exempt on one of the following specified grounds, as set out in art 36 of CIM:

§ 2. The railway shall be relieved of such liability if the loss or damage or the exceeding of the transit period was caused by a fault on the part of the person entitled, by an order given by the person entitled other than as a result of a fault on the part of the railway, by inherent vice of the goods (decay, wastage, etc.) or by circumstances which the railway could not avoid and the consequences of which it was unable to prevent.

§ 3. The railway shall be relieved of such liability when the loss or damage arises from the special risks inherent in one or more of the following circumstances:

carriage in open wagons under the conditions applicable thereto or under an agreement made between the consignor and the railway and referred to in the consignment note;

absence or inadequacy of packing in the case of goods which by their nature are liable to loss or damage when not packed or when not properly packed;

loading operations carried out by the consignor or unloading operations carried out by the consignee under the provisions applicable thereto or under an agreement made between the consignor and the railway and referred to in the consignment note, or under an agreement between the consignee and the railway;

defective loading, when loading has been carried out by the consignor under the provisions applicable thereto or under an agreement made between the consignor and the railway and referred to in the consignment note;

completion by the consignor, the consignee or an agent of either, of the formalities required by Customs or other administrative authorities;

the nature of certain goods which renders them inherently liable to total or partial loss or damage, especially through breakage, rust, interior and spontaneous decay, desiccation or wastage;

irregular, incorrect or incomplete description of articles not acceptable for carriage or acceptable subject to conditions, or failure on the part of the consignor to observe the prescribed precautions in respect of articles acceptable subject to conditions;

carriage of live animals;

carriage which, under the provisions applicable or under an agreement made between the consignor and the railway and referred to in the consignment note, must be accompanied by an attendant, if the loss or damage results from any risk which the attendant was intended to avert.

The burden of proving that the loss, the damage or the exceeding of the transit period was due to one of the causes specified above shall rest upon the railway or the carrier claiming the exemption.[196]

Determination of carrier's liability

[4.293] CIM has a number of provisions dealing with the limited liability of the carrier. For example, art 44 provides that 'the liability limits provided for in arts 25, 26, 30, 32, 33, 40, 42, 43, 45 and 46 shall not apply if it is proved that the loss or damage resulted from an act or omission, on the part of the railway, done with intent to cause such loss or damage, or recklessly and with knowledge that such loss or damage will probably result'. This provision deprives the carrier of the benefit of limited liability on the ground of

---

196. CIM, art 37(1).

intentional or reckless conduct. On the other hand, it suggests the complexity of the mechanism introducing the limited liability of the carrier in CIM.

[4.294] Although the limited liability of the carrier indeed varies a bit under each provision, in broad terms it can be said that art 40 is the most essential provision setting out the limited liability, because many other provisions make cross-reference to the principles set out in art 40 for the purpose of determining the carrier's liability. The detail of art 40 is set out as follows:

> § 1. In the event of total or partial loss of the goods the railway must pay, to the exclusion of all other damages, compensation calculated according to the commodity exchange quotation or, if there is no such quotation, according to the current market price, or if there is neither such quotation nor such price, according to the normal value of goods of the same kind and quality at the time and place at which the goods were accepted for carriage.
>
> § 2. Compensation shall not exceed 17 units of account per kilogramme of gross mass short.
>
> § 3. The railway shall in addition refund carriage charges, Customs duties and other amounts incurred in connection with carriage of the lost goods.

As we can see from this provision, para 1 sets out the rules for calculating the liability, and para 2 sets out the maximum monetary limit for determining the liability. Thus, it can be concluded that under CIM the carrier's liability is limited to 17 units of account per kilogram, although the methods of calculating may vary in different circumstances or for different purposes.

Limitation of action

[4.295] Limitation of action is necessary in any law granting a right of action to promote commercial stability, improve efficiency and ensure fairness and justice. The limitation period in CIM is one year, which should apply to most cases. However, a limitation period of two years should apply to:[197]

- a claim to recover a cash on delivery payment collected by the railway from the consignee;
- a claim to recover the proceeds of a sale effected by the railway;
- a claim for loss or damage resulting from an act or omission done with intent to cause such loss or damage, or recklessly and with knowledge that such loss or damage will probably result; and
- a claim arising from a contract of carriage prior to the reconsignment done under art 38(1) of CIM.

[4.296] The time when the period of limitation begins to run varies depending on the circumstances involved. Article 58(2) of CIM sets out the following rules:

> In actions for compensation for total loss, the time begins from the 30th day after the expiry of the transit period.
>
> In actions for compensation for partial loss, damage or exceeding the transit period, the period of limitation begins from the day when delivery took place.
>
> In actions for payment or refund of charges arising from the contract of carriage, the period of time begins from the date of payment if payment has been made; from the day when the goods were

---

197. CIM, art 58(1).

[4.296] accepted if payment has not been made by the consignor; or from the day when the consignee took possession of the consignment note if the payment is due from the consignee.

In actions to recover a sum to be paid under a charges note, the period of limitation begins from the day on which the railway submits to the consignor the account of charges provided for in art 15(7); if no such account has been submitted, the period in respect of sum due to the railway shall run from the 30th day following the expiry of the transit period.

In an action by the railway for recovery of a sum which has been paid by the consignee instead of by the consignor or vice versa and which the railway is required to refund to the person entitled, the period of limitation commences from the day of the claim for a refund.

In actions relating to cash on delivery as provided for in art 17, the period of limitation commences from the thirtieth day following the expiry of the transit period.

In actions to recover the proceeds of a sale, the period of limitation commences from the day of the sale.

In actions to recover additional duty demanded by the customs or other administrative authorities, the period of limitation begins from the day of the demand made by such authorities.

In all other cases, the period of limitation commences from the day when the right of action arises.

For the purpose of calculation, the day indicated for the commencement of the period of limitation shall not be included in the period. The period of limitation is suspended if a claim has been made in pursuance of the relevant provisions of CIM. Under CIM, it is possible that the limitation period for that part of the claim which has not been admitted by the party allegedly responsible will recommence from the day on which that part of the claim is rejected. As a general rule, in the absence of specific rules of the limitation of actions, the relevant domestic law should apply.

Carriage of goods under CMR

Overview of CMR

[4.297] CMR was adopted on 19 May 1956 and entered into force on 2 July 1961. As at July 1999, CMR had 43 members: Austria, Belarus, Belgium, Bosnia and Herzegovina, Bulgaria, Croatia, Czech Republic, Denmark, Estonia, Finland, France, Germany, Greece, Hungary, Iran, Ireland, Italy, Kazakhstan, Kyrgyzstan, Latvia, Lithuania, Luxembourg, Morocco, the Netherlands, Norway, Poland, Portugal, Republic of Moldova, Russian Federation, Romania, Slovakia, Slovenia, Spain, Sweden, Switzerland, Tajikistan, Macedonia, Tunisia, Turkey, Turkmenistan, United Kingdom, Uzbekistan and Yugoslavia. The composition of the memberships suggests the nature of CMR to be largely an European convention. CMR was amended by the Protocol to the Convention on the Contract for the International Carriage of Goods by Road, passed by the Inland Transport Committee of the Economic Commission for Europe on 5 July 1978. The amendment entered into force on 28 December 1980.

Unlike COTIF, CMR does not establish any international organisation under the convention. CMR is a treaty between states, which sets out uniform rules for the carriage of goods by road. The 1978 Protocol was adopted for the purpose of amending art 23 of CMR, which regulates the limited liability of the carrier. The major amendment is to introduce the use of SDR as the unit of account for the calculation of the carrier's liability. This is in line with many changes made to international conventions regulating carriage by sea or air. SDR has in fact become the prevailing unit of account for calculating payment or compensation in international treaties and conventions.

Application of CMR

[4.298] CMR applies to every contract for the carriage of goods by road for reward between two countries. This is set out in art 1 of CMR, which was examined in *Gefco UK Ltd v Mason* [1998] 2 Lloyd's Rep 585. In this case, both the plaintiff and the defendant were sub-carriers. Mason subcontracted with BOC, which was also a carrier, to perform a contract of carriage granted to BOC. Mason then contracted Gefco to perform the carriage. The Court of Appeal of the High Court of the UK affirmed the decision of the trial court and held that the contract between Gefco and Mason was a contract under art 1.

[4.299] For the application of CMR to an international carriage, one of the countries involved must be a contracting country of CMR.[198] The residence and nationality of the parties to a contract of carriage are irrelevant for the application of CMR, as is the fact that the carrier is a state enterprise or governmental institution. CMR also applies to combined carriage, such as road/sea, road/rail, or road/air or inland waterway, or a combination of these, provided that the goods are not unloaded from the vehicle during that period of time. However, CMR does not apply to carriage subject to international postal conventions, funeral consignments and furniture removal.[199] The members of CMR are not allowed to vary any provisions of CMR by special agreements, except to make it inapplicable to their frontier traffic or to authorise the use in transport operations entirely confined to their territory of consignment notes representing a title to the goods.[200]

[4.300] CMR applies to the situation where the vehicle containing the goods is carried over part of the journey by sea, rail, inland waterways or air, provided that the goods are not unloaded from the vehicle.[201] If the goods are unloaded from the vehicle in pursuance of art 14 CMR (which permits the carrier to change the terms of the contract of carriage when necessary for the purpose of performing the contract), CMR shall still apply to the whole of the carriage. When it is proven that any loss, damage or delay which occurs during the carriage by the other means of transport was not caused by an act or omission of the carrier by road, but by some reason attributable to other means of transport, the liability of the carrier by road shall be determined under the relevant law governing the mode of transport as if the carrier were a carrier under that relevant law, provided that the contract concerned satisfies the conditions of that law. If, however, the contract does not meet the conditions of the relevant law, the liability of the carrier by road in such circumstances shall be determined by CMR.[202] The same principles apply to the case of a combined carriage, where the carrier by road is also the carrier by the other means of transport, but the carrier must be regarded as if he or she were two separate persons in the different modes of transport.

---

198. CMR, art 1(1).
199. CMR, art 1(4).
200. CMR, art 1(5).
201. CMR, art 2(1).
202. CMR, art 2(1).

> **[4.301]** *Chloride Industrial Batteries Ltd v F W Freight Ltd*
>
> [1989] 2 Lloyd's Rep 274
>
> *CMR applies to international carriage only*
>
> **Facts:** The plaintiffs contracted with the defendant to carry a consignment of batteries by road from Manchester to Jersey in 1985. The batteries were lost in a fire during the journey. The plaintiffs sued the defendant for damages. One of the issues in the trial was whether the contract of carriage was subject to CMR.
>
> **Decision:** The court held that for the purpose of CMR Jersey was not a different country from the United Kingdom. CMR was thus inapplicable.

Contract of carriage and consignment note

[4.302] The carriage of goods by road is subject to the contract of carriage, which is confirmed by the issue of a consignment note.[203] The consignment note is not the contract of carriage itself. Thus the absence, irregularity or loss of the consignment note shall not affect the existence or the validity of the contract of carriage which shall remain subject to the provisions of CMR. When a contract covers many consignments or carriages and a consignment note is issued for each particular carriage or consignment, each consignment note may be regarded as evidence of the contract in so far as it relates to the particular consignment.[204]

[4.303] By definition, a consignment note is a road transport document. It is prima facie evidence of the contract of carriage and its conditions or terms.[205] It is also prima facie a receipt of the goods by the carrier. The consignee is entitled under the contract of carriage to take action against the carrier if the carrier fails to deliver the goods as agreed. In such a case, it is irrelevant whether the consignee has been given a copy of the consignment note. In the absence of specific description, the consignee is also entitled to rely on the presumption that the goods were handed over to the carrier in good condition, unless the carrier can establish the contrary.[206] But the consignment note is not a document of title; nor is it negotiable in the same way as a bill of lading.

[4.304] The use of a consignment note is similar under CIM and CMR. A consignment note is issued in three (or more) identical copies by the carrier.[207] Both the consignor (sender) and carrier must sign them. The first copy is given to the consignor as evidence of receipt of the goods in the condition stated by the carrier. The second copy is delivered with the goods to the consignee as evidence of the condition, quantity, weight or description, and so on, of the goods. The third copy is retained by the carrier for his or her record. If the goods are loaded in different vehicles or divided into different kinds or lots, either the consignor or the carrier is entitled to use separate consignment notes for each

---

203. CMR, art 4.
204. *Gefco UK Ltd v Mason* [1998] 2 Lloyd's Rep 585.
205. CMR, art 9(1).
206. CMR, art 9(2).
207. CMR, art 5.

vehicle or lot or kind of goods. The consignment note must contain certain information, such as the date and place of issue, the detail of the consignor, consignee and carrier, the places of departure and destination, the nature of the goods, the description of the goods, and a statement that the carriage is subject to CMR.

The consignment note should also contain information such as the declared value of the goods, paid and unpaid charges and insurance, if this is necessary. The consignor or the sender is obliged to inform the carrier of the dangerous nature of the goods to be carried, and is liable to the carrier for any loss, damage or expenses flowing from inaccuracies in the information furnished by him or her. The consignor or the sender is also liable to the carrier for the loss or damage caused by defective packing of the goods, unless the defect was known to the carrier at the time of delivery to the carrier and the carrier did not make any reservation in the consignment note concerning the defect.[208] On the other hand, the carrier may note any suspicion, irregularity and reservation on the condition, quantity and packaging on the consignment note. The noting by the carrier does not bind the consignor or the sender, unless the consignor or the sender expressly so agreed in the consignment note.[209]

[4.305] *Aqualon (UK) Ltd v Vallana Shipping Corp*

[1994] 1 Lloyd's Rep 669

A consignment note is prima facie evidence of the identity of the CMR carrier

Facts: Aqualon (UK) Ltd and Aqualon BV were companies in the same business group and the shippers, consignees or owners of goods damaged during carriage from Zwijndrecht, Holland to Warrington, England in 1990. Vallana Shipping Corp and the other defendants were the freight forwarders and carriers of the goods. One of the defendants was a Dutch freight forwarder, Nilsson International BV. Aqualon BV regularly sent consignments from Holland to Aqualon (UK) in England, and had been dealing with Nilsson all the time. Nilsson was always identified as the carrier in the CMR notes made out by Aqualon BV. Aqualon BV kept one copy of the notes and forwarded the other copies to Nilsson.

Unknown to Aqualon BV and Aqualon (UK), Nilsson often deleted its name as the carrier and named another carrier in the consignment notes. Nilsson also stamped the copies with the words 'as the agent only'. When the goods were damaged in 1990, Nilsson contended that it was not the CMR carrier, but the plaintiffs claimed that they were entitled to treat it as the CMR carrier.

Decision: The court held that the CMR consignment note is prima facie evidence of the contract of carriage. It is also prima facie evidence of the identity of the contracting parties. Since Nilsson's practice of substituting its name with another carrier's name had never been made known to the plaintiffs and Nilsson had knowledge that the plaintiffs believed it to be the carrier, Nilsson was not allowed to deny its responsibility as the CMR carrier.

Rights of the sender (consignor)

[4.306] The rights of the sender or the consignor are largely similar to those of the consignor in the carriage of goods by rail. They are related to the disposition of the

---

208. CMR, art 10.
209. CMR, art 8.

[4.306] goods, and to change the terms of the contract of carriage before the goods have been delivered to the consignee, or the consignee has exercised his or her rights against the goods under CMR. In particular, the consignor or the sender, who should prove his or her title by presenting his or her copy of the consignment note to the carrier, has the right to ask the carrier to stop the goods in transit, to change the place at which delivery is to take place, or to deliver the goods to a consignee other than the consignee indicated in the consignment note.[210] This right ceases to exist when the second copy of the consignment note is handed to the consignee, or when the consignee exercises his or her right under art 13(1), which grants the consignee a right to demand performance by the carrier under the contract of carriage concerned, because from that time onwards the carrier shall obey the orders of the consignee. The sender or the consignor should indemnify the carrier for any loss or damage incurred by the carrier for implementing the instructions of the consignor or the sender to change the original terms of the contract. The carrier is entitled to refuse to comply with the request of the consignor or the sender if such compliance is impossible or prejudices the interests of a third party. The carrier is also entitled to refuse to comply with the request if the request leads to a division of the consignment of the goods concerned.

[4.307] When the carrier cannot carry out the instructions received, he or she shall immediately notify the person who gave the instructions. However, a carrier who fails to carry out the instructions of the consignor or the sender to change the original terms of the contract without justification, or who has carried them out without requiring the first copy of the consignment note to be produced, shall be liable to the person entitled to make a claim for any loss or damage caused thereby.[211]

Rights of the consignee

[4.308] Rights of the consignee are also largely related to the disposition of goods. The consignor (sender) and the consignee are exclusive to each other in the contract of carriage. When the consignor is a party, the consignee is not. By corollary, when the consignee becomes a party, the consignor is out. Thus, the consignee's right and the consignor's right to dispose of the goods sometimes are in competition with each other. Consignment notes become evidence proving either the consignor's right or the consignee's right against the carrier. In *Gefco UK Ltd v Mason* [1998] 2 Lloyd's Rep 585, the Court of Appeal of the High Court of the UK, per Morritt LJ with whom Thorpe and Kennedy LJJ agreed, at 590, took the view that one of the functions of the consignment note was to enable the consignee to exercise the right to stop the goods in transit (eg, art 12) and to impose liability on a successive carrier (eg, arts 34 and 35).

Generally speaking, the consignee obtains the right to dispose of the goods after the arrival of the goods at the place designated for delivery. The consignee shall be entitled to require the carrier to deliver to him or her, against a receipt, the second copy of the consignment note and the goods.[212] The consignee obtains the right to dispose of the

---

210. CMR, art 12(1).
211. CMR, art 12(7).
212. CMR, art 13(1).

goods after he or she has paid or undertaken to pay the charges due under the contract of carriage or the consignment note. He or she may obtain the right at an earlier time when the consignment note is drawn up, provided that the consignor or the sender notes on the consignment note to this effect. Besides the right to demand delivery, the consignee may direct the carrier to deliver the goods to another person or to another place, subject to the payment of adequate charges. If the goods have not arrived after the expiry of the agreed time or a reasonable time for delivery, the consignee shall be entitled to enforce in his or her own name against the carrier any rights arising from the contract of carriage. The carrier is obliged to comply with the instructions of the consignee unless such compliance is impossible or prejudices the interests of a third party. The carrier is entitled to refuse to comply with the instruction of the consignee if the instruction results in a division of the consignment of goods. The carrier is required to inform the consignee immediately if he or she cannot comply with the instructions of the latter.

Liability of the carrier

[4.309] In general, the carrier is liable for the total or partial loss of the goods or damage or delay in delivery, which occurs from the time when he or she takes over the goods until the time of delivery. Such liability of the carrier was examined from an interesting angle in *Shell Chemicals UK Ltd v P & O Roadtanks Ltd* [1995] 1 Lloyd's Rep 297. This case involved a carriage of a tank of chemical in liquid form known as ADIP from Choques in France to Stanlow in Cheshire.

The plaintiffs were the consignor and the consignee of the goods and the defendant was the carrier. The defendant's employee collected a wrong tank from the defendant's depot and delivered it to the consignor's refinery. The tank contained detergent. The consignor ordered the carrier's employee to pump the contents of the tank into the refinery. As a result, the refinery was shut down for cleaning. The consignor suffered loss of production and certain chemicals were contaminated by the detergent. The plaintiffs sued the defendant under CMR. The defendant argued, inter alia, that CMR did not cover the situation in question. This contention was rejected by the High Court of the UK on the ground that art 17(1) of CMR does not mean to exclude the carrier's liability in any other cases which are not specified in the provision. The court also denied the defendant's argument on its right to rely on the terms of the contract to exclude or limit its liability. The defendant appealed to the Court of Appeal, which dismissed the appeal and affirmed the finding of the trial court.

[4.310] Under CMR, the carrier has a duty to exercise reasonable care and to take reasonable measures to prevent and avoid loss, damage or delay. He or she will be liable if the loss, damage or delay is caused by the defective condition of the vehicle, or wrongful act or neglect of his or her servants or agents. By the same token, the carrier is not liable if the loss, damage or delay is caused by the wrongful act or neglect of the claimant, inherent vice of the goods, insufficient packing, express acceptance of the risk by the consignor, or inherent risks in carrying livestock, and others.[213] However, the carrier is not relieved of liability by reason of the defective condition of the vehicle used by him or

---

213. CMR, art 17.

her in order to perform the carriage, or by reason of the wrongful act or neglect of the person from whom the carrier hired the vehicle or of the agents or servants of the latter. Article 17(4) of CMR sets out the special risks under which the carrier may be relieved of the liability as follows:

- use of open unsheeted vehicles, when their use has been expressly agreed and specified in the consignment note;
- the lack of, or defective condition of packing in the case of goods which, by their nature, are liable to wastage or to be damaged when not packed or when not properly packed;
- handling, loading, stowage or unloading of the goods by the sender, the consignee or persons acting on behalf of the sender or the consignee;
- the nature of certain kinds of goods which particularly exposes them to total or partial loss or to damage, especially through breakage, rust, decay, desiccation, leakage, normal wastage, or the action of moth or vermin;
- insufficiency or inadequacy of marks or numbers on the packages; and
- the carriage of livestock.

[4.311] The carrier's liability to the loss of or damage to goods shall be calculated by reference to the value of the goods at the place and time at which they were accepted for carriage.[214] The value of the goods shall be fixed according to the commodity exchange price or, if there is no such price, according to the current market price or, if there is no commodity exchange price or current market price, by reference to the normal value of goods of the same kind and quality.[215] The limit of the carrier's financial liability is fixed as 25 francs per kilogram of gross weight short. 'Franc' is defined in art 23 as referring to 'the gold franc weighing 10/31 of a gram and being of millesimal fineness 900'.

The maximum limit of liability is irrelevant to the refund of the charges, customs duties and other fees which have been paid by the consignor or consignee to the carrier. The carrier may be required to refund fully or partially the consignor or consignee for the charges paid in addition to the compensation for the consignor's or consignee's loss or damage. In case of delay in delivery, the maximum liability of the carrier is the sum of carriage charge paid under the contract of carriage. A higher sum of compensation may be claimed by the consignor or the consignee if the value of the goods or a special interest in delivery has been declared in accordance with the relevant provisions of CMR, that is, art 24 which deals with declaration of the value of the goods at a time when the contract of carriage is made, and art 26 which deals with the declaration of the special interests in ensuring the delivery on time.

[4.312] The limited liability of a carrier is amended by the 1978 Protocol. As a result of the amendment, the carrier's liability is 8.33 units of account per kilogram of gross weight short in case of loss or damage. The unit of account is SDR as determined by IMF. If a

---
214. CMR, art 23(1).
215. CMR, art 23(2).

member of CMR is not a member of IMF, the limited liability of the carrier is 25 monetary units. Each monetary unit corresponds to 10/31 of a gram of gold, millesimal fineness 900.

[4.313] The carrier is not allowed to rely on the benefit of limited liability if the damage concerned was caused by wilful misconduct of the carrier or his or her agents and servants. *Laceys Footwear (Wholesale) Ltd v Bowler International Freight Ltd* [1997] 2 Lloyd's Rep 369 is an example where wilful misconduct of the carrier's agent was established. In this case, Bowler was the carrier and forwarding agent. It contracted with Laceys Footwear to carry a consignment of shoes from Spain to the UK in 1992 for the latter. The lorry carrying the consignment was driven by a Spanish driver employed by a sub-carrier contracted by Bowler. The driver was expressly instructed to deliver the shoes at the address of Laceys Footwear, but for some strange reason the driver delivered the shoes to someone he thought to be the representative of Laceys Footwear in some place he did not know and to some unmarked truck. The trial court found the act of the driver constituted wilful misconduct under art 29 of CMR. The Court of Appeal of the High Court of the UK affirmed the finding. Thus Bowler was deprived of the right to rely on the limited liability provided by CMR. This case can be compared with *National Semiconductors (UK) Ltd v UPS* [1996] 2 Lloyd's Rep 212; **[4.314]**, where the court rejected the allegation of wilful misconduct.

[4.314] CMR imposes a joint liability upon all carriers involved in a contract of carriage. Under CMR, if carriage governed by a single contract is performed by successive road carriers, each of them shall be responsible for the performance of the whole operation, the second carrier and each succeeding carrier becoming a party to the contract of carriage, under the terms of the consignment note, by reason of his or her acceptance of the goods and the consignment note.[216] The joint liability does not mean that the consignor or the consignee is entitled to sue any carrier at his or her free will. Except in the case of a counter-claim or a set-off raised in an action concerning a claim based on the same contract of carriage, legal proceedings in respect of liability for loss, damage or delay may only be brought against the first carrier, the last carrier or the carrier who was performing that portion of the carriage during which the event causing the loss, damage or delay occurred; an action may be brought at the same time against several of these carriers.[217]

In *National Semiconductors (UK) Ltd v UPS* [1996] 2 Lloyd's Rep 212, both the first and second carriers were sued by the consignor. The goods were a load of valuable semiconductors carried by road from the UK to Milan in March 1993. UPS was the first carrier and ICT was the second carrier. The goods and the lorry carrying them were stolen in Milan while the employee of the second carrier was having a meal. The consignor sought to rely on art 29 of CMR to argue that the conduct of the employee leaving the lorry unattended constituted wilful misconduct. The High Court of the UK took the view that for establishing wilful conduct, the claimant needs to prove the existence of either an intention to do something which the actor knew to be wrong, or a reckless act in the sense that the actor was aware of the probable damage but did not care about the consequence.

---

216. CMR, art 34.
217. CMR, art 36.

[4.314]

Accordingly, the court held that the act of the second carrier's employee did not amount to wilful misconduct.

[4.315] As a consequence of the joint liability, a carrier who has compensated the consignee or the consignor under CMR is entitled to seek contribution from other carriers liable under the contract of carriage. If one of the carriers is insolvent, the share of the compensation due from him or her and unpaid by him or her shall be divided among the other carriers in proportion to the share of the payment for the carriage due to them.[218]

[4.316] *GL Cicatiello v Anglo European Shipping Services Ltd*

[1994] 1 Lloyd's Rep 678

Carrier's liability and exceptions under CMR in case of robbery

Facts: The goods (16 pallets of pickled pelts) were carried from Ayr to Salerno by a truck and were stolen in an armed robbery on the motorway between Rome and Naples. The contract of carriage was subject to CMR, which holds a carrier liable for the loss or damage to the goods carried from the time he or she takes over the goods to the time of delivery. But CMR also exempts a carrier from liability in circumstances where the loss or damage was not avoidable or preventable by him or her. The plaintiffs argued that the carrier should have fitted the truck with various security devices, such as alarms or locks, to prevent robbery. They also argued that the robbery might have been avoided if the truck had two drivers and was parked in a secure park rather than at a service station. The carrier contended that the loss was not avoidable or preventable.

Decision: The court held that there was no evidence that the proposed security devices could avoid or prevent the robbery taking place. There was no secure park for the truck driver to stop during the journey. Nor was it probable that two drivers would prevent the robbery. The carrier had taken precautions which were adequate to the nature of the goods carried. The goods were lost in circumstances in which the carrier could not have avoided or prevented the loss taking place.

Limitation period

[4.317] CMR requires a consignee claiming loss or damage to notify the carrier of the nature of the claim within seven days of delivery.[219] If the alleged loss or damage is not apparent at the time of delivery, the consignee is required to notify the carrier in writing of the nature of the claim, also within seven days of delivery. Notice to claim damage for delay in delivery must be made in writing within 21 days from the time when the goods were placed at the disposal of the consignee. The giving of notice in compliance with the time requirements is crucial for the consignee or consignor as the case may be to proceed with any claim for damage or loss. Under art 32, any action for damage or loss must be commenced within one year, unless the loss or damage was caused by wilful and intentional misconduct of the carrier.

---

218. CMR, art 38.
219. CMR, art 30(1).

[4.318] The limitation period begins to run as follows:
- when the goods have been delivered, on the day of delivery;
- in the case of total loss and the date for delivery has been agreed, from the thirtieth day after the agreed date;
- in the case of total loss and no time for delivery has been agreed, from the sixtieth day from the date on which the goods ought to be handed over to the carrier; and
- in any other case, on the expiry of a period of three months after the making of the contract of carriage.

The day on which the period of limitation begins to run is not included in the period. The extension of the limitation period and detailed rules for the calculation of the limitation period are subject to the relevant domestic law.

A written claim suspends the period of limitation until such date as the carrier rejects the claim by notification in writing and returns the documents attached thereto. If a part of the claim is admitted the period of limitation shall start to run again only in respect of that part of the claim still in dispute. The burden of proof of the receipt of the claim, or of the reply and of the return of the documents, shall rest with the party relying upon these facts. The running of the period of limitation shall not be suspended by further claims having the same object.[220] These rules of CMR are similar to those adopted in CIM: see **[4.295]–[4.296]**.

Carriage of goods by multimodal transport

What is multimodal transport?

[4.319] 'Multimodal transport' means the carriage of goods involving more than one means of transport. The need for multimodal transport is a commercial reality. The seller or the buyer may not always be located near a sea port and the buyer often prefers to make a complete arrangement for the goods to be carried from the seller's warehouse to his or her own warehouse. Otherwise, the seller or the buyer, depending on the terms of the contract of sale, such as FOB, CIF, Ex Works and C & F, and others, may have to make several arrangements for transport with different carriers engaged in different means of transport in order to move the goods physically from one place to another. Multimodal transport thus also implies that a carrier or a forwarder makes a contract of carriage with the consignor, who is often the seller, to undertake the liability of carrying the cargo through any means of transport necessary to the agreed destination. In such cases, the carrier is usually liable to the consignor or the consignee, as the case may be, for the safety of the goods during the whole process of multimodal carriage.

Legal implications of multimodal transport

[4.320] Multimodal transport has two main legal implications. First, the different modes of transport are presently subject to different international conventions. This

---
220. CMR, art 32(2).

[4.320]

means that in order to bring the carriage into the jurisdiction of each convention, a party undertaking to complete the multimodal transport has to enter into separate contracts with the carrier of each mode. In such cases, the applicability of a particular convention is subject to the specific conditions under which the convention applies. Second, when a through bill of lading or through document of transport is concluded under the present legal framework, the first carrier will be liable to the consignor under the contract of carriage in general contract law until the goods are delivered at their destination. He or she will contract directly with subsequent carriers. The consignor does not have direct redress against each subsequent carrier unless the relevant domestic law or convention permits a consignor or consignee to do so. For example, under the Warsaw Convention a sub-carrier may be sued by the consignee or consignor for the part of the service performed by the sub-carrier. If a multimodal transport includes the carriage by air, depending on the circumstances, a consignee or consignor may be able to rely on the Warsaw Convention to sue the sub-carrier if the consignee or consignor proves to be a party to the contract of air carriage.

[4.321] *Crayford Freight Services Ltd v Coral Seatel Navigation Co* [1998] FCA 263 is a case illustrating multimodal transport. Crayford Freight Services Ltd was a freight forwarder, which contracted with Carlton International PLC (shipper) to carry 255 cartons of luggage (the goods) in a 20 foot container from Enfield in the United Kingdom to Melbourne, Australia in 1996. The shipper was obliged to deliver the goods to Bradmans Stores Pty Ltd under the contract of sale. The goods were to be transported by land from Enfield in Middlesex to the Port of Tilbury on the River Thames and from Tilbury to Melbourne by sea. The shipper engaged the services of Crayford to do the job, and Crayford issued a document entitled Multimodal Transport Bill of Lading on 4 February 1996 to the shipper. The bill showed that the goods had been shipped on board in apparent good order and condition, even though they were meant to be loaded on board the sea-going vessel sometime later in the Port of Tilbury. It was more likely that the goods were carried by road or railway to Tilbury when the Multimodal Transport Bill of Lading was issued. The goods were lost during the carriage. The shipper and the consignee sued Crayford in Australia. Crayford accepted liability but sued other parties involved in the carriage, including Coral Seatel Navigation (shipowner), Lloyd Triestino Di Navigasione SPA which issued a non-negotiable sea waybill to Crayford, and Contship Containerlines Ltd which was a charterer of the vessel carrying the lost container under a time charterparty.

It was said that Contship chartered the ship concerned from the shipowner, and sublet the ship under a slot charterparty to P & O, which in turn sublet the ship to Lloyd Triestino under a slot charterparty. There was no evidence on who performed the carriage by land. The sea waybill issued by Lloyd Triestino already evidenced that the goods concerned had been loaded on board the ship concerned. Thus, the liability of the party performing the carriage by land was irrelevant in the present case. The decision of the court in this case involved certain procedural issues relating to cross-claims of Crayford, which is not a concern for our present study. However, the facts of the case demonstrate the operation of a multimodal transport bill of lading.

Through document of transport under present law

[4.322] A 'through document of transport' is a transport document issued for a carriage involving more than two modes of transport. Under such a document, the consignor only deals with one carrier, who undertakes under the contract of carriage to deliver the goods to the agreed destination even though different modes of transport have to be employed to complete the contract. A through document of transport, such as a through bill of lading (see **[4.56]**) or a through consignment note (see *Aqualon (UK) Ltd v Vallana Shipping Corp* [1994] 1 Lloyd's Rep 669; **[4.305]**), is in fact used and allowed under the present legal framework for the carriage of goods. In *Canusa Systems Ltd v The Canmar Ambassador*,[221] the freight forwarder issued a combined transport bill of lading, which stated, inter alia, that the forwarder was liable for loss of or damage to the goods occurring between the time when the forwarder took them into its charge and the time of delivery. The bill also provided exceptions. The goods were damaged. The forwarder sought to avoid its liability by arguing that it was not the carrier. The court examined the terms of the combined transport bill of lading and decided that the forwarder failed to establish that it was exempt under any of the exceptions listed in the bill.

[4.323] A through bill of lading, which may involve different modes of transport, has been used in the carriage of goods by sea.[222] It is valid under the Hague Rules and the Hague-Visby Rules, because its use is not expressly prohibited. In fact, a through bill of lading may find legal basis in art 7 of the Hague Rules and art 7 of the Hague-Visby Rules respectively (the articles are identical). This provision allows the parties to contract freely any matters which are not prohibited under the conventions. Thus the validity of a through bill of lading is not affected by the fact that only part of the carriage is governed by the conventions. The through bill of lading often contains clauses which state that the carrier acts as the agent of the shipper to arrange subsequent contracts of carriage, but is exempt from 'all liabilities' or certain risks incidental to the use of multimodal means, such as the risk in transshipment. In the absence of any international convention, the extent of the carrier's liability is defined and determined by the parties to the through bill of lading.

[4.324] A through bill of lading is expressly allowed under the Hamburg Rules. Article 1(6) stipulates that the convention applies to that part which relates to the carriage of goods by sea under a through bill of lading. Article 10 defines the responsibilities of a carrier and an actual carrier. Article 11 deals with the liabilities of the carrier and actual carrier under a through bill of lading. These provisions provide certainty and predictability in the use of the through bill of lading under the Hamburg Rules.

[4.325] The Warsaw Convention makes special provision for 'combined carriage', which means multimodal transport commencing from carriage by air. Article 31 of the convention provides that if a carriage is performed partly by air and partly by another mode, 'the provisions of this convention apply only to the carriage by air'. The parties are free to include in the consignment note, which evidences the contract of carriage by air,

---

221. 16 February 1998, No T-456-95 (FCTD), available at <http://www.admiraltylaw.com>.
222. Schmitthoff, note 32 above, pp 576–8.

[4.325] any terms and conditions in relation to other modes of transport as long as no inconsistency arises between the terms of the consignment note and the provisions of the convention.

[4.326] Multimodal transport is accepted under COTIF. For example, art 48 of CIM sets out rules for determining liability in a carriage involving 'rail–sea' traffic. It can be assumed that COTIF or CIM only applies to that part of the carriage which falls within the scope of its application.

[4.327] Multimodal transport is also anticipated in CMR. For example, art 2 deals with carriage involving other modes, such as sea, rail, inland waterway and air. Under this provision, CMR applies to the whole carriage if the goods are not unloaded from the vehicle while being carried by sea, rail, air or inland waterway. The carrier is liable for the whole carriage. If the goods must be unloaded from the vehicle for carriage by other means, the carrier must seek instruction from the consignor for making subsequent contracts of carriage. If it is impossible to seek instruction from the consignor, the carrier should act in the best interest of the consignor to make appropriate contracts of carriage. In either case, the carrier is the agent of the consignor in entering into contracts of carriage by sea, rail, air or inland waterway, as the case may be. If the goods are lost or damaged while being carried in other modes of transport, the liability of the road carrier should be determined under the relevant law (most likely the relevant international conventions) applicable to that mode of transport.

[4.328] The existing mechanism for the use of a through document of transport has shown a lack of coordination between the international conventions. Many important legal issues, such as the legal relationships between the cargo-owner and actual carrier, and redress of the parties to multimodal transport against each other, are yet to be defined. The UNCTAD/ICC Rules for Multimodal Transport Documents, which became effective on 1 January 1992, provide non-compulsory rules. They provide guidance for the parties to define their legal liabilities to each other. However, in order to be effective, the rules must be incorporated into the contract of international multimodal transport as the terms of contract. This is why international conventions, such as the 1980 United Nations Convention on International Multimodal Transport of Goods, would be more effective than non-compulsory rules.

UN Convention on International Multimodal Transport of Goods

What is the UN Convention on International Multimodal Transport of Goods?

[4.329] The UN Convention on International Multimodal Transport of Goods was passed in Geneva on 24 May 1980. Consisting of 40 articles, the convention was intended to unify the rules governing the liability of a multimodal transport operator in international carriage of goods involving at least two different modes of transport. The convention requires for its operation ratification by 30 countries. It has not come into effect as it has not been ratified by enough countries. As at July 1999, the convention had nine members. Six more countries have signed but not yet ratified the convention.

Scope of operation

[4.330] The convention applies to a multimodal transport contract, which has a place of departure or place of discharge in a member country of the convention. The convention also applies to a multimodal transport contract which is governed by the law of a member of the convention. The expression 'multimodal transport contract' refers to a contract whereby a multimodal transport operator (the person entering into the contract as the carrier) undertakes the performance of international multimodal transport.

Multimodal transport document

[4.331] A multimodal transport document (or through document of transport) must be issued by the carrier after receiving the goods. The document can, at the option of the consignor, be either negotiable or non-negotiable. A negotiable document can be made out 'to order or to bearer'. If it is made out 'to order', it is transferable by endorsement of the named person. If it is made out 'to bearer', it is transferable without endorsement. A non-negotiable document should be made out to a named consignee. The signature of the document can be made in any form, such as handwriting, stamp, or mechanical or electronic means, provided that it is allowed under the domestic law of the country where the document is issued.

[4.332] The document is prima facie evidence of the receipt of the goods by the multimodal transport operator. It should contain the conditions and terms of carriage, the condition and description of the goods, details of the multimodal transport operator, details of the consignor, negotiability of the document, place of departure and place of discharge, and a statement that the convention applies to the contract in question, and so on. The consignor is responsible for supplying accurate information to the transport operator and is liable for the operator's loss arising from the use of inaccurate information. However, art 9 also requires the operator to state in the document any reservations as to the accuracy of the information and the ground for suspicion. A multimodal transport operator who intentionally defrauds a consignee or third party by issuing the document with false information is liable for the damage of the third party and will lose the benefit of limited liability under the convention.

Liability of multimodal transport operator

[4.333] The liability of the multimodal transport operator covers the period from the time he or she takes over the goods to the time of their delivery. During this period the operator is liable for loss, damage or delay caused by his or her act or omission, as well as by an act or omission of his or her servants and agents. This means that the consignor always has redress against the operator for any loss or damage under the contract of carriage.

The multimodal transport operator is required to take reasonable care of the goods. This means that he or she is not liable for loss, damage or delay, if he or she can prove that he or she, or his or her agents, servants, or any other persons rendering services for the performance of the contract, have taken reasonable measures to avoid loss, damage or delay. If fault or neglect on the part of the operator, or his or her agents, servants or other persons is a concurrent cause of the loss, damage or delay, the operator is liable in proportion to the extent of the fault or neglect. The onus of proving the existence of other causes of the loss, damage or delay lies with the transport operator.

Limits of liability

[4.334] Like any other international convention, this convention sets out the maximum liability of the multimodal transport operator. Articles 18–20 of the convention set out the following rules for determining maximum liability:

- when the contract involves carriage by sea or inland waterways, the maximum liability of the transport operator is limited to 920 units of account per package or shipping unit, or 2.75 units of account per kilogram of gross weight of the goods lost or damaged, whichever is the higher;
- when the contract does not involve carriage by sea or inland waterways, the maximum liability is limited to 8.33 units of account per kilogram of gross weight of the goods lost or damaged;
- the maximum liability for delay is limited to an amount equivalent to two-and-a-half times the freight payable for the goods delayed in a particular mode of transport, but not exceeding the total freight payable under the multimodal transport contract;
- the aggregate liability of the carrier is limited to 920 units of account per package or shipping unit, or 2.75 units of account per kilogram of gross weight of the goods (if sea or inland waterways carriage is involved) or 8.33 units of account per kilogram of gross weight of the goods (if sea or inland waterways carriage is not involved);
- the parties cannot fix maximum limits of liability lower than those set out above, but they can increase the maximum limits by agreement; and
- the maximum limits may also be raised if any particular loss, damage or delay is governed by an international convention or domestic law which allows a higher limit.

The transport operator or his or her agents, servants or other relevant persons may lose the right to rely on the above limits if the loss, damage or delay was caused by them intentionally or recklessly or with knowledge of the probability of loss, damage or delay.

Liability of consignor

[4.335] The consignor is generally liable for any loss or damage caused by his or her fault or neglect. The consignor is also liable for loss or damage caused by the fault or neglect of his or her agents, servants or other relevant persons. The convention specifically requires the consignor to mark and label dangerous goods adequately and clearly, and to notify the operator of the dangerous nature of the goods when delivering them to the operator. Failure to do so makes the consignor liable for the loss or damage sustained by the operator. During the whole carriage, the transport operator or any actual carrier is entitled to destroy, dispose or render dangerous goods innocuous when necessary.

Notice of claim

[4.336] The convention requires the consignee claiming damage or loss to give written notice of the claim in compliance with the time requirement set out in art 24. The time requirements for giving notice are as follows:

- if the damage is apparent, the consignee should give notice to the operator not later than the working day following the day of delivery;
- if the damage is not apparent, the consignee should give notice to the operator within six days after the day of delivery;
- if the goods were subject to a joint survey or inspection at the time of delivery, the consignee is not required to notify the carrier of the loss or damage revealed during the survey or inspection;
- in the case of delay in delivery, notice should be given within 60 days after the day of delivery; and
- when the goods were not directly delivered to the consignee, notice should be given within 90 days after the occurrence of the loss or damage, or after the day of delivery, whichever is the later.

The time requirements must be complied with if the consignee intends to claim damages under the convention.

Limitation of actions

[4.337] The limitation period under the convention is two years. It can be even shorter if the consignee fails to give notice to the operator within six months after the day of delivery, or alternatively, after the contract day of delivery (if the goods have not been delivered). The limitation period in these circumstances is six months. The limitation period begins to run from the day after the day of delivery. In the case of non-delivery, it begins to run on the day after the last contract day for delivery. The limitation period can be extended by the declaration of the person (most likely the multimodal transport operator) against whom the claim is made.

Arbitration under the convention

[4.338] The convention allows the parties to submit a future dispute arising from a multimodal transport contract to arbitration by a written agreement. In the absence of an express choice in the arbitration agreement, the claimant has a right to commence arbitration in one of the specified places, including the defendant's principal place of business, the defendant's habitual residence, the place where the contract of carriage was made and where the defendant has an establishment or agent, the place of departure or the destination of the goods. An authorised arbitrator must apply the provisions of the convention. However, it can be argued that an arbitrator who received the authority to arbitrate under an agreement made after the claim relating to the contract has arisen can determine the dispute under any rules or customs. This is because art 27(5) allows the parties to submit an existing dispute to arbitration in whatever manner they prefer.

Chapter Five

Means of Payment in International Trade

Overview

[5.1] There are two basic means of payment: direct payment (or finance) between the seller and buyer; and payment (finance) through banks. In this chapter, we will examine the major methods or means of effecting payment in international sales, such as cash payment, collection and documentary credit. Special attention will be given to UCP 500, which is the most important 'international document' (note: UCP 500 is prepared by ICC and is not an international convention) for the use of documentary credit as a means of financing international sales.

[5.2] Payment is an inherent part of the process of international sales or other transactions. Generally, a process of sale involves the following aspects:

- negotiation;
- conclusion of a contract;
- carriage of goods;
- insurance of goods;
- payment of the price of the contract in exchange for documents for delivery;
- delivery of goods; and
- dispute settlement (if applicable).

The means of payment is crucial in an international sale. It is necessary to study not only the methods for effecting payment and their advantages or disadvantages, but also the rules governing their operation.

The major concerns in effecting payment in international trade

[5.3] In an international sale, the seller prefers to receive the payment from the buyer as quickly as possible, and the buyer prefers to have received the goods and to have ensured that the goods conform with the contract before making payment. These considerations affect the choice of a particular means of payment by the buyer or seller. In addition, the following considerations also affect the choice of a particular method of payment:

- exchange control regulations of a particular country;
- exchange risks;
- domestic regulation of financial transactions;
- export and import licences;
- financial credibility of the other party;
- fraud in documentation;
- reliability of the other's performance;
- effectiveness of communications; and
- effectiveness of recourse against each other.

These considerations do not include those of the banks, which will be discussed in the relevant sections: see, for example, **[5.120]–[5.125]**. A bank is mainly concerned with its liability under a method of payment and the effectiveness of the redress against a liable party for the reimbursement of its services and losses.

The basic methods of payment in international trade

[5.4] There are four basic methods of financing an international sale. The categorisation, which has no legal basis, is adopted for the convenience of study only. Although the ICC has been attempting to standardise the use of terms in international banking and finance (for example, through the use of UCP), methods of payment or their forms and terms do not currently have universal uniformity.[1] Indeed, it is doubtful that they ever will. Variations and modifications of each of the following four methods are thus to be expected in practice.

Cash in advance

[5.5] This means that the buyer transfers funds into an account accessible to the seller in advance pursuant to the contract of sale. It is difficult to define this method of payment legally, because of the infinite variations in the use of this method. Its key characteristic is 'cash in advance'. Variations arise from the interpretation of this term. For example, there could be 'cash in advance' of shipment of goods, 'cash in advance' of the manufacture of goods, or 'cash in advance' of the provision of services, and others. This method allows the seller to have cash much earlier than the other three methods of payment discussed in this chapter: see **[5.18]**.

---

1. For example, the variations in the use of terms and their legal implications are seen in Dekker (ed), *Case Studies on Documentary Credits*, ICC Publishing SA, Paris, 1989, and Dekker (ed), *More Case Studies on Documentary Credits*, ICC Publishing SA, Paris, 1991.

Open account

[5.6] This refers to an arrangement between the seller and buyer, under which the buyer undertakes to pay a sum of money into an 'open account' of the seller on a fixed date or upon the occurrence of a specified event, such as shipment or delivery of goods: see **[5.19]**.

Collection

[5.7] This refers to a process of payment in which a bank acts under the instructions of a seller to collect payment for the goods from a buyer. It usually involves the use of a bill of exchange, which is often called a 'draft'. In the process of collection, the buyer pays for the price of the contract in exchange for the documents of title over the goods with the assistance of the bank. Collection includes 'documentary collection', 'clean collection' and 'direct collection': see **[5.20]–[5.26]**.

Documentary credit

[5.8] A 'documentary credit' is also known as a 'letter of credit' (L/C). This is a method of payment under which a bank acting on behalf of an applicant (a buyer) issues a document (a letter of credit on most occasions[2]), which constitutes an undertaking that the bank will pay the price of the contract of sale on condition that the beneficiary (the seller) complies with the terms of the credit. Under this method, a bank acts as a guarantor for the buyer, and sometimes the provider of finance. There is certainty that the seller will be paid as long as compliance with the terms of credit has occurred. (A documentary credit or a letter of credit must contain the conditions and terms under which a bank undertakes the liability to pay.) The involvement of the bank provides certainty and stability in the performance of the contract of sale. The bank's guarantee is provided by the document. 'Documentary credit' will be discussed in detail in **[5.81]–[5.83]**.

International legal framework for payment in international transactions

[5.9] The legal framework for effecting payment in international trade consists of the following international conventions and ICC rules:

- the 1930 Geneva Uniform Law on Bills of Exchange and Promissory Notes (also known as the 1930 Geneva Convention providing a Uniform Law for Bills of Exchange and Promissory Notes), referred to as the 'Geneva Uniform Law' below;[3]

---

2. A bank may also issue a 'guarantee' or a substantially modified 'letter of credit' which tests the legal limits of the meaning of a 'letter of credit'. For example, art 9 of UCP 500 defines an irrevocable credit as a 'definite undertaking of the issuing bank' to honour the credit, provided that the beneficiary complies with the terms of the credit. If a bank issuing an irrevocable credit seeks to avoid any 'definite undertaking' to the beneficiary by inserting an exclusion clause into the credit, the nature and legal effect of such 'credit' are subject to debate.

- the 1931 Geneva Convention on the Unification of the Law Relating to Cheques;[4]
- the Convention on the Stamp Laws in Connection with Bills of Exchange and Promissory Notes;[5]
- the Convention on the Stamp Laws in Connection with Cheques;[6]
- the Convention for the Settlement of Certain Conflict of Laws in Connection with Bills of Exchange and Promissory Notes;[7]
- the Convention for the Settlement of Certain Conflict of Laws in Connection with Cheques;[8]
- the Collection of Bills Agreements concluded by UN members between 1952 and 1979;[9]
- the 1988 UN Convention on International Bills of Exchange and International Promissory Notes;[10]

---

3. Signed at Geneva on 7 June 1930; entered into force on 1 January 1934. In July 2002, its members were Austria, Azerbaijan, Belarus, Belgium, Brazil, Denmark, Finland, France, Germany, Greece, Hungary, Italy, Japan, Kazakhstan, Lithuania, Luxembourg, Monaco, the Netherlands, Norway, Poland, Portugal, Sweden, Switzerland, the Russian Federation and Ukraine.
4. Concluded at Geneva on 19 March 1931; entered into force on 1 January 1934. In July 2002, its members were Austria, Azerbaijan, Belgium, Brazil, Denmark, Finland, France, Germany, Greece, Hungary, Indonesia, Italy, Lithuania, Luxembourg, Japan, Malawi, Monaco, the Netherlands, Nicaragua, Norway, Poland, Portugal, Sweden and Switzerland.
5. Concluded at Geneva on 7 June 1930; came into operation on 1 January 1934. In July 2002, its members were Austria, Australia, Bahamas, Belarus, Belgium, Brazil, Cyprus, Denmark, Fiji, Finland, France, Germany, Great Britain and Northern Ireland, Hungary, Ireland, Italy, Japan, Kazakhstan, Luxembourg, Malaysia, Malta, Monaco, the Netherlands, Papau New Guinea, Norway, Poland, Portugal, Sweden, Switzerland, Tonga, the Russian Federation, Uganda and Ukraine.
6. Adopted at Geneva on 19 March 1931; came into operation on 29 November 1933. In July 2002, its members were Austria, Australia, Bahamas, Belgium, Brazil, Cyprus, Denmark, Fiji, Finland, France, Germany, Great Britain and Northern Ireland, Greece, Hungary, Indonesia, Ireland, Italy, Japan, Luxembourg, Malaysia, Malta, Monaco, the Netherlands, Nicaragua, Norway, Papua New Guinea, Poland, Portugal, Sweden, Switzerland and Tonga.
7. Signed at Geneva on 7 June 1930; came into existence on 1 January 1934. In July 2002, its members were Austria, Belarus, Belgium, Brazil, Denmark, Finland, France, Germany, Greece, Hungary, Italy, Japan, Kazakhstan, Lithuania, Luxembourg, Monaco, the Netherlands, Norway, Poland, Portugal, Sweden, Switzerland, the Russian Federation and Ukraine.
8. Concluded at Geneva at 9 March 1931; came into effect on 1 January 1934. In July 2002, its members were Austria, Belgium, Brazil, Denmark, Finland, France, Germany, Greece, Hungary, Indonesia, Italy, Japan, Lithuania, Luxembourg, Monaco, the Netherlands, Nicaragua, Norway, Poland, Portugal, Sweden and Switzerland.
9. These agreements are: the Collection of Bills Agreement signed at Brussels on 11 July 1952, which entered into force on 1 July 1953; the Collection of Bills Agreement signed at Ottawa on 3 October 1957, which entered into force on 1 April 1959; the Collection of Bills Agreement signed at Vienna on 10 July 1964, which entered into force on 1 January 1966; the Collection of Bills Agreement signed at Tokyo on 14 November 1969, which entered into force on 1 July 1971; the Collection of Bills Agreement signed at Lausanne on 5 July 1974, which entered into force on 1 January 1976 and the Collection of Bills Agreement signed at Rio de Janeiro on 26 October 1979, which entered into force on 1 July 1981.
10. Adopted on 9 December 1988, but not yet in force. Ten actions are required for the convention to enter into force. As at October 2002, only Guinea, Honduras and Mexico had ratified the convention.

[5.9]   International Commercial Law

- the UN Convention on Independent Guarantees and Standby Letters of Credit;[11]
- the 1993 ICC Uniform Customs and Practice for Documentary Credits (UCP 500);[12]
- the ICC Uniform Rules for Collections;[13]
- the ICC Uniform Rules for Contract Guarantees published in 1978;
- the ICC Uniform Rules for Demand Guarantees published in 1992;
- the ICC Uniform Rules for Contract Bonds published in 1993; and
- the ICC Uniform Rules for Bank-to-Bank Reimbursements (known as URR 525, published in 1995, entering into force 1 July 1996).

[5.10] As we can see from the conventions and laws referred to above, there is no universal regime for effecting payment in international trade. The Geneva Uniform Laws on bills of exchange or cheques have been accepted by European countries. The conventions adopted by the UN are capable of introducing uniform rules across the world. But their acceptance by world countries will take time and effort. Under the current legal framework for effecting payment in international transactions, the parties' rights and obligations in each particular transaction are largely determined by the relevant domestic law, which may or may not incorporate a particular international convention into its own system. In view of the overall development of the international commercial law governing the means of payment in international transactions, we may say that the conventions represent the future direction of the international commercial law governing the means of payment; the domestic law governs present international transactions; and the ICC rules provide practical solutions to reconcile differences between laws of different countries, which effect payment in international transactions. Under the present legal framework of international commercial law for effecting payment in international transactions, the rules of conflict of laws are crucial for determining the applicability of particular rules governing the rights and obligations of the parties to an international transaction.

[5.11] Given the present state of development of the international commercial law affecting the means of payment in international transactions, this chapter studies the law and practice from two perspectives: a domestic law perspective, and an international perspective. First, any study of domestic law must be based on the law of a particular country. Australian law, which shares the common law tradition with many other countries and jurisdictions, such as Canada, Hong Kong, New Zealand, the UK and the US, will be used for the purpose of studying domestic law governing means of payment in international transactions. References will be made to the relevant rules of ICC and practices in other common law jurisdictions whenever appropriate. Second, the emphasis in the study of international conventions is on future development. For that purpose, two documents adopted by the UN, namely, the UN Convention on International Bills of

---

11. Adopted on 11 December 1995 and entered into force on 1 January 2000. As at October 2002, six countries, Belarus, Ecuador, El Salvador, Kuwait, Panama and Tunisia, had ratified it.
12. The rules have been commonly accepted in international banking practices.
13. The Uniform Rules for Collection were first published in 1956, and amended in 1967 and 1978. The present rules were published in 1995.

Exchange and International Promissory Notes, and the UN Convention on Independent Guarantee and Standby Letters of Credit, will be examined. Comparison between the provisions of these conventions or law, and the relevant rules of Australian law will be made whenever appropriate. The UNCITRAL Model Law on International Credit Transfers deals with credit transfers between banks, and will be studied in **Chapter 6**.

Means of payment under domestic law

Australian legal framework for payment in international transactions

[5.12] Australia is not a member of any international convention governing methods of payment. The same domestic laws apply to both international and domestic transactions. Our concern is mainly on their implications to international transactions.

The following laws govern payment in international transactions in Australia:

- the Bills of Exchange Act 1909 (Cth), which was based on the Bills of Exchange Act 1882 (UK);
- the Cheques and Payment Orders Act 1986 (Cth);
- the Financial Transaction Reports Act 1988 (Cth), which may affect certain methods of payment in international sales;
- the 1993 ICC Uniform Customs and Practice for Documentary Credits (UCP 500); and
- the ICC Uniform Rules for Collections (URC), presently URC 522.[14]

The ICC rules may become the governing law of methods of payment due to the express or implied intention of the parties. They do not, however, override the express intention of the parties to vary the effect of any of their provisions.

This chapter mainly examines the Bills of Exchange Act 1909 (Cth), because this Act is most relevant to the use of the bill of exchange, which is the major financial document both in the process of collection and in the use of documentary credit (letter of credit) for effecting payment in international transactions. Other domestic laws and the ICC rules will be referred to whenever appropriate. Another reason for examining the Bills of Exchange Act 1909 (Cth) is that the domestic laws on bills of exchange are largely similar in most common law jurisdictions — they all originated from the Bills of Exchange Act 1882 (UK). In this sense, the law regulating bills of exchange is largely uniform in most common law jurisdictions.

---

14. URC was first published in 1956 by ICC, and amended in 1967 and 1978. The present URC was published in 1995, known as URC 522.

An Introduction to the Bills of Exchange Act 1909 (Cth)

[5.13] The Bills of Exchange Act 1909 (Cth) comprises five parts and 101 sections. Part I deals with the preliminary issues, such as the commencement, interpretation of terms and application of the Act. Part II regulates the use of bills of exchange and has 11 Divisions. Part III regulates the use of cheques on a banker and contains three divisions. Part IV regulates the use of promissory notes, and includes seven sections which are not broken into any divisions. Part V deals with supplementary issues, such as good faith, signature, computation of time and protest. Parts II, III and IV deserve special attention.

[5.14] Part II regulates the use of bills of exchange in 11 divisions, which are described briefly as follows:

Division 1 relates to the form and definitions of bill of exchange. This division defines the meaning of bill of exchange, and differentiates between an inland bill and a foreign bill. It deals with issues relating to the formality of the bill of exchange, such as parties to a bill, address of drawee, certainty of payee and sum payable, and the meanings of bill payable on demand or payable at a future time. Negotiability of a bill of exchange is also regulated in this division. In addition, omission of date necessary for determining the date of payment, ante-dating and post-dating, computation of time of payment, referee in case of need, optional stipulation of drawer or indorser, acceptance of bill, time for acceptance, general and qualified acceptance, inchoate instruments, and delivery are also covered in this division.

Division 2 regulates the capacity of authority of parties. It covers a number of issues, such as the capacity of parties, signature and liability, forged or unauthorised signature, procuration signature and person signing as agent or in representative capacity.

Division 3 deals with the considerations for a bill. It defines meanings of the value and holder for value, accommodation party to a bill, holder in due course and presumption of value and good faith.

Division 4 regulates negotiation of bills. Negotiability is a crucial feature of a bill of exchange. The division defines the meaning of negotiation of bill, and sets out the requisites of a valid indorsement. It deals with a number of specific issues relating to indorsement, such as conditional indorsement, indorsement in blank, special indorsement, and restrictive indorsement. It also covers the other issues concerning negotiation of bill, such as negotiation of overdue or dishonoured bill, negotiation of bill to party already liable thereon, and the right of holder. These issues affect the rights and obligations of the parties to a bill of exchange.

Division 5 concentrates on the general duties of the holder of the bill and the rules for acceptance. Issues covered in this division include circumstances where presentment of bill is necessary, time for presenting bill, rules on acceptance, meaning of non-acceptance, dishonouring a bill, notice of dishonour and the relevant rules, qualified acceptance, noting or protest of bill, and duties of holder as regards drawee and acceptor.

Division 6 regulates liabilities of parties to a bill of exchange. Issues covered in this division include funds in hands of drawee, liability of acceptor, liability of drawer or indorser, liability of stranger signing as indorser, measures of damages against parties to a dishonoured bill, and transfer by delivery.

Division 7 relates to the discharge of the bill. It deals with the payment in due course, banker paying demand draft whereon indorsement is forged, discharge of bill held by the acceptor, express waiver, cancellation of bill, and alteration of bill.

Division 8 sets out rules for acceptance and payment for honour. Issues covered in this division include acceptance for honour supra protest, liability of acceptor for honour, presentment to acceptor for honour, and payment for honour supra protest.

Division 9 deals with issues relating to the lost instruments, such as the replacement of a lost or destroyed bill and action on a lost bill.

Division 10 relates to a bill in a set. It has only one section, setting out the rules as to sets of bills.

Division 11 regulates conflict of laws and provides rules for resolving conflicts between laws of different countries, and also the rules for determining the effect of non-compliance with stamp laws in case of certain bills of exchange.

[5.15] Part III regulates the use of cheques in three divisions, which are introduced briefly as follows:

Division 1 regulates cheques generally. It provides a definition of a cheque, and sets out rules for presentment of a cheque for payment and for determining the rights of a banker as regards a stale cheque. It also deals with the issue of the revocation of a banker's authority.

Division 2 regulates the use of crossed cheques. It defines the meaning of general and special crossings. It also regulates other relevant issues, such as crossing by a drawer or after issue of the cheque, crossing a material part of a cheque, duties of banker as to crossed cheques, protection to banker and drawer where a cheque is crossed, and the effect of crossing on a holder and of cheques drawn by a bank on itself.

Division 3 relates to other provisions relating to the use of cheques, such as protection of bankers paying unendorsed or irregularly indorsed cheques or drafts, payment of unendorsed cheque or draft as evidence of receipt by payee, protection of bankers collecting payment of cheque, and rights of a banker collecting a cheque not indorsed by the payee.

[5.16] Part IV regulates the use of promissory notes in seven sections. No division is created under Part IV. The major issues covered in the seven sections include the definition of a promissory note, the delivery of a promissory note (essential), joint and several notes, note payable on demand, presentment of note for payment, liability of maker, and application of Part II to notes. It must be noted that under s 95 of the Bills of Exchange

[5.16]   *International Commercial Law*

Act 1909 (Cth), many provisions of Part II also apply to the use of promissory notes, except those provisions expressly excluded by s 95.[15]

This chapter is not intended to provide a thorough review of the Bills of Exchange Act 1909 (Cth). Instead, it only examines the major provisions relating to the use of the bill of exchange in the process of collection and in the use of documentary credit to effect payment in international transactions.

Defining terms in effecting payment

[5.17] A number of terms must be defined or explained before we discuss the rules applicable to the means of payment in international trade. The following terms, which are listed in alphabetical order, are briefly described. Their full legal meaning should be understood in the particular context where they apply.

- Accepting bank: a bank which accepts, or is authorised to accept, drafts and compliant documents under a documentary credit.
- Advising bank: a bank which advises, or is authorised to advise, a beneficiary of the availability of a credit and its terms.
- Applicant: a person who requests or instructs a bank to issue a documentary credit.
- Bearer: a person who is in possession of a negotiable instrument (for example, a bill of exchange), which is payable to a bearer. Section 4 of the Bills of Exchange Act 1909 (Cth) defines bearer as the person in possession of a bill or note which is payable to bearer.
- Beneficiary: a person in whose favour a credit is issued. Under art 2 of the UNCITRAL Model Law on International Credit Transfers, the expression 'means the person designated in the originator's payment order to receive funds as a result of the credit transfer'.
- Bill of exchange: a written document drawn by a person (drawer) to order unconditionally another person (drawee) to pay a specified sum of money to a third person (payee or bearer) or a specified person either on the person's demand or at a fixed or determinable time: see **[5.27]–[5.52]**.

---

15. Section 95 of the Bills of Exchange Act 1909 (Cth) states as follows:
    Subject to the provisions in this Part and except as by this section provided, the provisions of this Act relating to bills of exchange apply, with the necessary modifications, to promissory notes.
    In applying those provisions, the maker of a note shall be deemed to correspond with the acceptor of a bill, and the first indorser of a note shall be deemed to correspond with the drawer of an accepted bill payable to drawer's order.
    (3) The following provisions as to bills do not apply to notes, namely, provisions relating to:
        (a) presentment for acceptance:
        (b) acceptance:
        (c) acceptance supra protest:
        (d) bills in a set.
    (4) Where a foreign note is dishonoured, protest thereof is unnecessary.

- Cheque: an unconditional order in writing drawn and signed by a person for the benefit of another to direct a bank to pay a fixed sum to the named recipient or bearer of the cheque.

- Claiming bank: under art 2 of URR 525, the expression means a bank that pays, incurs a deferred payment undertaking, accepts drafts or negotiates under a credit and presents a reimbursement claim to the reimbursing bank.

- Clean collection: a particular way of carrying out collection, in which a bank (or a person) is instructed to collect payment for a draft from a buyer (or a person) who, however, does not receive the relevant commercial documents (for example, shipping documents) at the same time: see **[5.77]** and **[5.78]**. In the words of art 2(c) of UCR 522, clean collection means collection of financial documents not accompanied by commercial documents.

- Collecting bank: a bank which is authorised by the remitting bank to execute collection.

- Collection: a method of effecting payment for goods sold or services supplied, under which a seller or his or her bank, in pursuance of the seller's instructions, collects payment from the buyer by presenting drafts to the buyer with or without accompanying commercial documents: see **[5.7]**. Article 2, URC 522 defines collection as the handling by banks of documents as defined in sub-Article 2(b), in accordance with instructions received for the purposes of effecting payment or acceptance, including delivery of documents.

- Commercial documents: various documents relating to the sale of goods or services, such as documents of title of various forms, bills of lading or similar shipping documents, transport documents of various kinds, insurance contracts or policies, export and import licences, inspection certificates or certificates of origin, invoice, and others.

- Confirmation of an undertaking: according to art 6 of the UN Convention on Independent Guarantees and Standby Letters of Credit, the expression means an undertaking added to that of the guarantor/issuer, and authorised by the guarantor/issuer, providing the beneficiary with the option of demanding payment from the confirmer instead of from the guarantor/issuer, upon simple demand or upon demand accompanied by other documents, in conformity with the terms and any documentary conditions of the confirmed undertaking, without prejudice to the beneficiary's right to demand payment from the guarantor/issuer.

- Confirming bank: a bank which guarantees (confirms) the payment of a credit issued by another bank.

- Counter-guarantee: according to art 6 of the UN Convention on Independent Guarantees and Standby Letters of Credit, the expression means an undertaking given to the guarantor/issuer of another undertaking by its instructing party and providing for payment upon simple demand or upon demand accompanied by other documents, in conformity with the terms and any documentary conditions of the undertaking, indicating, or from which it is to be inferred, that payment under that other undertaking has been demanded from, or made by, the person issuing that other undertaking.

- Counter-guarantor: according to art 6 of the UN Convention on Independent Guarantees and Standby Letters of Credit, the expression means 'the person issuing a counter-guarantee'.
- Credit: in the context of 'documentary credit', 'credit' refers to any arrangement, however named (for example, credit, letter of credit or standby letter of credit), whereby a bank acting at the request of another person or on its own behalf undertakes to pay, or authorises another bank to pay or negotiate, the sum specified in the 'credit' under the terms of the 'credit'.
- Documentary collection: a particular way of performing collection in which a bank, under the seller's instructions, collects payments under a draft from the buyer who receives the relevant commercial documents for exchange. Under art 2(d) of URC 522, documentary collection has two meanings: financial documents accompanied by commercial documents, or commercial documents not accompanied by financial documents.
- Documents: includes both financial documents and commercial documents.
- Draft: a bill of exchange or a similar document.
- Drawee: a person on whom a bill of exchange is drawn. Article 5 of the UN Convention on International Bills of Exchange and International Promissory Notes defines drawee as 'a person on whom a bill is drawn and who has not accepted it'.
- Drawer: a person who draws (fills in or makes out) a bill of exchange to order the drawee to pay the sum of the bill.
- Financial documents: bills of exchange, promissory notes, cheques, payment receipts or similar instruments for obtaining the payment of money.
- Guarantor: a person (either legal or natural) who undertakes a liability to pay a certain sum of money in the event of another person's failure to keep a promise or to perform an obligation. Article 5 of the UN Convention on International Bills of Exchange and International Promissory Notes defines guarantor as 'any person who undertakes an obligation of guarantee under article 46, whether governed by paragraph 4(b) ("guaranteed") or paragraph 4(c) ("aval") of article 47'.
- Holder: a person who is in possession of a negotiable bill of exchange or a similar document. Section 4 of the Bills of Exchange Act 1909 (Cth) defines holder as the payee or indorsee of a bill or note who is in possession of it, or the bearer thereof.
- Independent guarantee: an independent guarantee may be regarded as a synonym of a standby credit in international financial transactions. In fact, the UN Convention on Independent Guarantees and Standby Letters of Credit refers to both as undertakings. Broadly speaking, an independent guarantee is a basic means of finance in international transactions. It can be used in a variety of situations, for example, to secure performance of contractual obligations, whether in a construction or supply contract, or to perform a commercial payment obligation. It can also be used to secure repayment of an advance payment; to secure a winning bidder's obligation to enter into a procurement contract; to ensure reimbursement of payment under

another undertaking; to support issuance of commercial letters of credit and insurance coverage; and to enhance creditworthiness of public and private borrowers.[16]

- Indorsee: a person who is named as the recipient or transferee of a negotiable instrument (for example, a bill of exchange).
- Indorsement: an act of signing one's name in an appropriate place on a bill of exchange for the purpose of transferring it to another, accepting it or undertaking a liability to pay, and others, as the case may be. It may also refer to the signature so made. Section 4 of the Bills of Exchange Act 1909 (Cth) defines indorsement as an indorsement completed by delivery.
- Indorser: a person who transfers a negotiable instrument to another by signing his or her name and naming another as the recipient or transferee of the negotiable instrument.
- Irrevocable credit: a credit under which the issuing bank undertakes not to revoke the credit before a specified time or event, provided that the beneficiary complies with its terms: see **[5.94]**.
- Issuing bank: the bank which issues a credit.
- Maturity: the time when the document representing a financial liability becomes payable.
- Maintenance bond: under art 2 of the ICC Uniform Rules for Contract Bonds, the expression means a bond to secure contractual obligations relating to the maintenance of works or goods following the physical completion or the provision of the goods, pursuant to a contract.
- Negotiate or negotiation: these expressions do not have precise legal definitions. They refer to a process or means of effecting a payment under a documentary credit, whereby a bank, under the instructions of another or on its own initiative, sells or purchases a draft with compliant documents at either the full price or a discounted price of the draft: see **[5.115]–[5.116]**. Sometimes making payment under a credit is also called 'negotiation'.
- Negotiating bank: the bank which sells or buys a draft and commercial documents in a process of collection, or which makes or receives payment under a documentary credit.
- Nominated bank: a bank which has been 'nominated' or instructed to perform certain functions (for example, to advise or negotiate a credit) for the purpose of effecting a payment under a documentary credit.
- Payee: a person who is named as the recipient of the payment under a bill of exchange. Article 5 of the UN Convention on International Bills of Exchange and International Promissory Notes defines payee as a person in whose favour the drawer directs payment to be made or to whom the maker promises to pay.

---

16. Explanatory note by the UNCITRAL secretariat on the Convention on Independent Guarantees and Standby Letters of Credit, para 3.

- Paying bank: a bank which makes, or is authorised to make, payment under a documentary credit (referring to an ultimate obligation to pay under a credit, as opposed to making payment to a beneficiary for the purpose of negotiation).
- Performance guarantee: as defined in art 2 of the ICC Uniform Rules for Contract Guarantees, the expression means an undertaking given by a guarantor, who can be a bank, insurance company or other party, at the request of a principal who is a supplier of goods or services or any other person, to a beneficiary whereby the guarantor undertakes in the event of default by the principal either to make payment to the beneficiary, within the limit set out in the undertaking, or to perform the underlying contract breached by the principal.
- Presenting bank: synonymous with 'collecting bank' and refers to a bank which is authorised by a remitting bank to complete a process of collection.
- Reimbursement authorisation: under art 2 of URR 525, the expression means an instruction or authorisation, independent of the credit, issued by an issuing bank to a reimbursing bank to reimburse a claiming bank, or if so requested by the issuing bank, to accept and pay a time draft drawn on the reimbursing bank.
- Reimbursement undertaking: under art 2 of URR 525, the expression means a separate irrevocable undertaking of the reimbursing bank, issued upon the authorisation or request of the issuing bank, to the claiming bank named in the reimbursement authorisation, to honour that bank's reimbursement claim, provided the terms and conditions of the reimbursement undertaking have been complied with.
- Reimbursing bank: under art 2 of URR 525, the expression means the bank instructed or authorised to provide reimbursement pursuant to a reimbursement authorisation issued by an issuing bank.
- Remitting bank: a bank (usually in the seller's country of business) which is authorised by the seller to carry out collection.
- Repayment guarantee: under art 2 of the ICC Uniform Rules for Contract Guarantees, the expression means an undertaking given by a guarantor who can be a bank, insurance company or any person at the request of the principal to the beneficiary whereby the guarantor undertakes in the event of default by the principal to repay or pay an agreed sum of money in pursuance of the terms and conditions of the contract between the principal and beneficiary.
- Retention bond: under art 2 of the ICC Uniform Rules for Contract Bonds, the expression means a bond to secure the payment of any sum paid or released to the principal by the beneficiary before the date for payment or release thereof contained in the contract.
- Revocable credit: a credit which can be revoked or withdrawn any time before it has been performed, for example, before it has been negotiated or the compliant documents have been accepted by an authorised bank: see **[5.93]**.
- Signature: Article 5 of the UN Convention on International Bills of Exchange and International Promissory Notes defines signature as a handwritten signature, its

Means of Payment in International Trade [5.19]

facsimile or an equivalent authentication effected by any other means; 'forged signature' includes a signature by the wrongful use of such means.

- 'Standby credit' or 'standby letter of credit': a documentary credit or a similar arrangement under which the issuing bank undertakes (guarantees) to make a payment in the event of another person's (applicant's) failure to honour his or her financial liability: see **[5.101]–[5.102]**. It is also a means by which a bank provides finance to its customers. See also the definition of independent guarantee.
- Tender guarantee: under art 2 of the ICC Uniform Rules for Contract Guarantee, the expression means an undertaking given by a guarantor who can be a bank, an insurance company or any person at the request of a principal who is a tender to a beneficiary who has invited tendering, whereby the guarantor undertakes in the event of default by the principal in performing his or her obligations under the tender contract to pay an agreed sum of money to the beneficiary.
- Tender bond: under art 2 of the ICC Uniform Rules for Contract Bonds, the expression means a bond in respect of a tender to secure the payment of any loss or damage suffered or incurred by the beneficiary arising out of the failure by the principal to enter into a contract or provide a performance bond or other bond pursuant to such tender.
- Transferable credit: a credit which can be transferred by the beneficiary pursuant to the terms of the credit: see **[5.107]–[5.110]**.
- Undertaking: the expression is used in the UN Convention on Independent Guarantees and Standby Letters of Credit to refer to either an independent guarantee or a standby letter of credit.

Payment by cash in advance

[5.18] This method of payment does not require the provision of credit services by a bank. The seller and buyer may in a contract of sale agree that the buyer will make payment in cash before a particular date or a particular event, such as shipment or commencement or completion of production. This method of payment is safe for the seller, but risky for the buyer. In the event of the seller's insolvency, the buyer may not be entitled to the goods or services contracted for, depending on the stage of the performance and whether the property in the goods has passed to the buyer. A seller would prefer this method if the buyer's creditworthiness is doubtful or if the goods or services involved are unique and expensive. This method of payment, compared with documentary credit, shifts part of the risk in manufacturing or transporting the goods, or in provision of services, from the seller to the buyer: see also **[5.5]**.

Payment by open account

[5.19] This is an arrangement between the buyer and seller whereby the buyer undertakes to pay a sum of money into a nominated account upon the performance of a certain act by the seller. The method is directly effected between the seller and buyer.

[5.19]   International Commercial Law

The difference between this method and 'cash in advance' is that the seller can be required to perform a substantial part of his or her contractual obligations before the payment is made. The difference between this method and 'collection' and 'documentary credit' is that the payment is effected directly by the buyer. Payment by 'open account' means that the seller agrees to perform his or her contractual obligations under the guarantee of the buyer.

In comparison with a 'documentary credit', the seller undertakes a higher risk in performing the contract of sale. Since under this method the seller often has to deliver documents of title or deliver goods to the buyer before the payment is made, the seller runs the risk of lacking effective recourse against the buyer in the case of the buyer's failure to make the payment. If the buyer fails to pay, the seller can only take action on the ground of breach of the contract of sale. This aspect of 'open account' also distinguishes this method from 'collection'. Under 'collection', a collecting bank or nominated bank seeks an undertaking or security from the buyer to pay the draft before releasing the documents of title to him or her: see also **[5.6]**.

Payment by collection

Defining 'collection'

[5.20] 'Collection' refers to an arrangement whereby a bank acts at the request or instructions of the seller (drawer) to collect payment from the buyer by presenting a draft or drafts and necessary commercial documents to the buyer after the shipment of goods. The arrangement is described as 'collection' because the seller is to collect payments from the buyer after the goods have been shipped as agreed. The buyer should pay the sum, or guarantee to pay the sum, of the draft(s) before being given the documents of title which will enable him or her to claim the goods from a carrier: see also **[5.7]**. This method can be further divided into: documentary collection, clean collection and direct collection. These forms will be examined in the relevant sections: see **[5.76]**–**[5.79]**.

[5.21] It must be noted that sometimes collection is used in a very broad sense in international trade. In almost all cases, the expression 'collection' refers to the process to effect payment outside a documentary credit, which is a totally different means of payment. However, sometimes the expression may refer to a special type of collection under a documentary credit, namely collection of a particular document or making a proportion of payment under a documentary credit, by way of collection through the banks involved in the documentary credit.

In *Harlow & Jones Ltd v American Express Bank Ltd* [1990] 2 Lloyd's Rep 343, the court held that the expression 'on collection basis' was not inconsistent with the banking practice of presenting documents under the documentary credit. In other words, in international banking practice, the use of the expression 'collection' is sometimes equivocal and flexible, creating difficulties for courts which prefer to have logical and consistent rules and guidance for international transactions. The High Court of Hong Kong was troubled by the expression 'on a collection basis' under a documentary credit in *Rudolph Robinson Steel Co v Nissho Iwai Hong Kong Corp Ltd* [1998] 1 HKLRD 966. The trial judge observed that the meaning of 'on a collection basis' or 'for collection' under a documentary credit was ambiguous and must be ascertained from the context in which it appeared.

[5.22] The process of collection can be described as follows:

- The seller (drawer), after putting the goods onto a ship (or other means of transport) pursuant to the contract of sale, delivers the shipping documents (or other transport documents) and other commercial documents and the bill of exchange (draft) to his or her bank, which is the remitting bank.
- The remitting bank forwards the documents and instructions for collection to a bank in the buyer's country, which is the collecting bank or presenting bank.
- The collecting bank then presents the shipping documents and other commercial documents and bill of exchange to the buyer (drawee) who, after examining the documents, pays, or agrees to pay, the price of the draft to the collecting bank (payee or indorsee or bearer) in order to obtain possession of the documents.
- The collecting bank then sends the money to the remitting bank usually after deducting a fee for services.
- The remitting bank ultimately makes the money available for the seller to withdraw, or pays it into an account as directed by the buyer (drawer). The remitting bank also charges for its services.
- The aforesaid process may be varied according to the agreement of the parties concerned. For example, if the seller needs cash flow urgently, he or she may sell an accepted bill of exchange at a discount to the remitting bank for cash. The bank would reserve the right of recourse against the seller in the sense that it would be entitled to deduct a sum of money equivalent to the discounted price of the bill from the account of the seller had the drawee refused to honour the bill.[17]

---

17. A similar arrangement was made between the seller and its bank in *IBBCO Trading Ltd v HIH Casualty & General Insurance Ltd* [2001] NSWSC 490.

[5.23] This process can be illustrated by the following diagram.

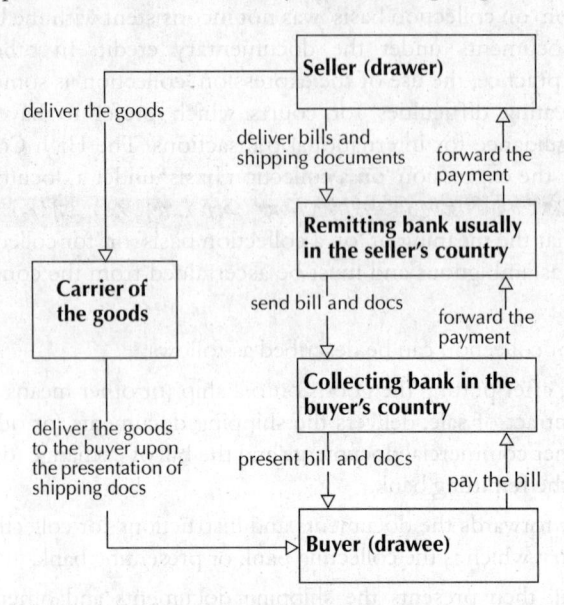

```
                           ┌─────────────────┐
                      ┌────│ Seller (drawer) │◄──────┐
    deliver the goods │    └─────────────────┘       │
                      │     deliver bills and    forward the
                      │     shipping documents    payment
                      │           │                  │
                      ▼           ▼                  │
              ┌──────────┐  ┌──────────────────────┐ │
              │Carrier of│  │ Remitting bank usually│ │
              │the goods │  │ in the seller's country│
              └──────────┘  └──────────────────────┘
                      │     send bill and docs   forward the
                      │           │               payment
                      │           ▼                  │
                      │    ┌──────────────────────┐  │
                      │    │ Collecting bank in the│ │
                      │    │ buyer's country       │ │
                      │    └──────────────────────┘
   deliver the goods        present bill and docs
   to the buyer upon              │           pay the bill
   the presentation of            ▼                  │
   shipping docs           ┌─────────────────┐       │
                      └───►│ Buyer (drawee)  │───────┘
                           └─────────────────┘
```

URC 522 sets out specific rules for carrying out a collection process. When URC 522 is incorporated in a contract of collection or collection instructions, the banks are obliged to follow the rules set out in URC 522 and are also protected by the rules.

Parties involved in a process of collection

[5.24] The parties and their roles in a process of collection are as follows:
- the seller, who is the drawer of the draft instructs his or her bank to collect the payment of the draft in accordance with specific instructions;
- the buyer, who is the drawee of the draft, pays or undertakes to pay the sum of the draft in exchange for the possession of the documents of title over the goods;
- the remitting bank, which is authorised or instructed by the drawer to collect payment from, and deliver the documents of title to, the drawee (buyer), remits the draft and documents to a collecting bank which could be a correspondent bank or the local branch of the remitting bank in the buyer's place of business (or any other place as agreed) for collection, if the remitting bank cannot collect itself; and
- the collecting bank (or presenting bank), which is authorised by the remitting bank to collect the payment from, and deliver the documents to, the drawee (buyer), completes collection as instructed.

Variations to the particular functions and tasks of the remitting bank and collecting bank can be made in practice. The process of collection may be modified in different circumstances.

[5.25] The collection process and the underlying contract of sale or services are separate. The banks in a collection process have a duty to act in good faith and exercise reasonable care in performing their obligations as specified in the collection instructions, but they are not obliged to take any action in respect of goods or services to which a documentary collection relates, including storage and insurance of the goods. The banks are not obliged to perform the instructions which require them to do something relating to the goods or services concerned, unless the banks concerned accept the instructions voluntarily. If a bank decides to take action for the protection of the goods, it assumes only reasonable liability adequate for its position in the circumstances concerned. General rules of tortious liability apply to such circumstances.

Documents involved in collection

[5.26] The documents and their functions in a process of collection are as follows:

- a draft, which is a bill of exchange in most circumstances, orders the drawee (buyer) to pay a specified sum of money to the payee (presenting or collecting bank, or any named person);
- commercial documents, which, as defined in the ICC Uniform Rules for Collection,[18] include invoices, shipping documents, documents of title, inspection certificates, insurance certificates, certificates of origin, export or import licences, and health certificates, or any other documents which do not fall under the definition of 'financial documents' (for the meaning of 'financial documents', see **[5.17]**); and
- the drawer's instructions as to how to collect the payment or to proceed with the collection will be passed on by the remitting bank (often in the form of a letter of instruction for collection from the remitting bank) to the presenting or collecting bank as the case may be.

Understanding bills of exchange

[5.27] It is necessary to study the meaning and functions of 'bill of exchange' before proceeding to the particular forms of collection, because a bill of exchange and its legal effect are a major part of the process of collection. As we have seen, a bill of exchange, generally speaking, is a 'draft' or a form of 'financial document' which is an important means of payment in international trade. Its legal definition in Australia is found in the Bills of Exchange Act 1909 (Cth): see **[5.37]**.

---

18. See Pt B of the 'General Provisions and Definition' of the Uniform Rules for Collection.

[5.28] *Korea Exchange Bank v Debenhams (Central Buying) Ltd*

[1979] 1 Lloyd's Rep 548

Whether the document is a bill of exchange

Facts: A document held by the Korea Exchange Bank (plaintiff) contained the words: 'Bill of exchange ... At 90 days D/A ...' The plaintiff and defendant disagreed as to the balance of payment under the document. The plaintiff claimed the document to be a 'bill of exchange' and the defendant contended that the parties' rights and obligations would vary depending on whether the document was a 'bill of exchange'. They asked the court to determine the nature of the document. The trial judge held that the document appeared to be a 'bill of exchange'. The defendant appealed.

Decision: The English Court of Appeal (consisting of Megaw, Waller and Eveleigh LJJ) held the document was not a 'bill of exchange' within the meaning of s 3 of the Bills of Exchange Act 1882 (UK), which is equivalent to s 8 of the Bills of Exchange Act 1909 (Cth). The decision was reached on the basis that the abbreviation 'D/A' (which was said to stand for 'documents against acceptance') did not suggest a fixed or determinable time for the maturity of the 'bill'.

Megaw LJ observed as follows:

<552> ... I have come to the conclusion that the plaintiffs have not established that those who have to handle bills of exchange from day to day in the market should be expected to understand with reasonable assurance that this unusual wording is to be interpreted as including the 'acceptance' part of the symbol 'D/A' as being part of the order to the drawee to pay. 'D/A' in commercial usage is ordinarily, at least, not any part of the order to pay directed to the drawee. If a part of the symbol is to become an essential part of the drawer's order to the drawee, this has to be made clear on the face of the instrument. In this instrument, in my judgment, it, at the best, falls short of the necessary clarity.

[5.29] It should be noted that *Korea Exchange Bank v Debenhams (Central Buying) Ltd* was not followed in a Hong Kong case, *NCNB National Bank v Gonara (HK) Ltd* [1984] HKLR 152, which involved similar facts as the former. In the Hong Kong case, the bill of exchange in question stated that the bill was to be 'payable at 120 days D/A sight'. Clough J of the High Court of Hong Kong took the view that the expression D/A (document against acceptance) was not part of the drawer's order to the payee, and should thus be eliminated from the wording, leaving the words 'payable at 120 days sight'. In this way, the judge held that the meaning of the instruction was clear and the bill was thus enforceable. The judge appears to have justified his reading of the instruction by suggesting that the instruction meant to indicate the time of payment and that D/A did not help that purpose at all. This decision can be supported by the general technique of contract interpretation. In fact, taking away D/A does not affect the meaning of the instruction. Otherwise, the party alleging a different meaning of D/A in the bill has the burden of proof.

[5.30] The expression D/A has become a common practice in the process of collection. Article 7(b) of URC 522 suggests that D/A means that commercial documents are released to the drawee against acceptance.[19] URC 522 permits the use of D/A, or D/P (document

---

19. Article 7(b) of URC 522 states that if 'a collection contains a bill of exchange payable at a future date, the collection should state whether the commercial documents are to be released to the drawee against acceptance (D/A) or against payment (D/P)'.

against payment) as part of the instructions for effecting collection. The rules do not have direct impact on the validity of a bill of exchange, which is subject to the relevant domestic law or international convention. The meaning of D/A, or D/P if relevant, as suggested in URC 522, may be considered by a court when construing the meaning of a bill of exchange which contains such expression. However, the real problem with the expression D/A or D/P is whether or not the expression is relevant for the parties or the court to determine the time of payment. It is yet to be seen whether D/A can serve such a purpose.

Usage of bill of exchange to effect payment

[5.31] A bill of exchange is a negotiable instrument used in both domestic and international transactions to effect payment. The law governing the usage of a bill of exchange in a domestic transaction and the law applicable to a bill of exchange in an international transaction may be the same, if the international transaction is not subject to any international convention. Even in the absence of an international convention, a local court may have to deal with the conflict of laws issue before applying one of the competing domestic laws to a particular transaction. This is why ss 77 and 77A of the Bills of Exchange Act 1909 (Cth) set out rules for resolving conflict of laws in the use of bills of exchange. Accordingly, it can be concluded that if an international transaction involving the use of a bill of exchange is submitted to an Australian court, and the transaction is neither subject to any international convention nor governed by a law of a foreign country, the same Bills of Exchange Act 1909 (Cth) will apply to the transaction.

[5.32] The process for the use of a bill of exchange is not regulated by the Bills of Exchange Act 1909 (Cth). In broad terms, the process for the use of a bill of exchange can be described in the following words:

- the parties agree whether or not to use a bill of exchange to effect payment;
- if using the bill of exchange, instead of any other means of payment, they need to decide to use a collection process or to use a documentary credit to effect payment;
- the bill of exchange is usually drawn by the seller (as the drawer) against the buyer, or a third party specified by the buyer as the drawee, to order the drawee to make the agreed payment to a particular person or to any person who becomes the legitimate holder of the bill;
- the drawer can make the bill either negotiable or non-negotiable;
- if negotiable, the bill can be passed through indorsement or by delivery from the seller (drawer) to a third party and continues to a fourth or fifth party, and so on;
- in the case of collection, the seller or seller's agent sends a bill of exchange (or several if necessary) with or without commercial documents to demand payment from the buyer, and the bill is usually not enforceable until acceptance by the buyer;[20]
- in the case of documentary credit, the seller will often submit the bill of exchange together with a bill of lading (or another transport document) and necessary documents

---

20. The Bills of Exchange Act 1909 (Cth) s 26(1): see **[5.61]**.

[5.32]

to the negotiation bank to negotiate payment under the credit; in which case the bill of exchange is enforceable against the negotiation bank after the acceptance by the bank;

- a bill can be dishonoured by non-acceptance,[21] or by non-payment;[22]
- if a dishonoured bill has been negotiated, the holder or indorsee is entitled to return the bill back to the indorser and to the drawer ultimately, or to take legal action against the drawee in his or her own name;
- a bill can be payable on demand, at sight or on presentation,[23] and the seller or the holder of the bill is entitled to demand payment accordingly against the acceptor, who can be either the buyer or a bank under a documentary credit; and
- the holder must follow the rules on the presentment of the bill for payment as set out in s 50 of the Bills of Exchange Act 1909 (Cth), which sets out the time and manner for demanding payment under a bill.

The above process reflects the major issues relevant to using bills of exchange. The Bills of Exchange Act 1909 (Cth) provides basic rules for dealing with these issues.

Categories of bills of exchange and their functions

[5.33] Under common law, a bill of exchange can be divided into several categories. The following categories are not mutually exclusive with other possible categorisation of bills of exchange.

[5.34] A claused bill contains additional clauses in relation to the sum or the method of payment. For example, a bill which specifies an exchange rate applicable or requires interest and bank charges, etc, is a claused bill.[24]

[5.35] A documentary bill is a bill of exchange used in a documentary collection where the payment of the bill is the condition for obtaining the bill of lading or other documents of title.[25] 'Documentary bill' is synonymous with 'financial document'.

[5.36] An avalised bill is a bill which contains a signature by a person who guarantees the payment to the holder of the bill in due course.[26] This is a guaranteed bill and the ultimate bearer of the bill is able to seek payment from the guarantor in the event that the bill is dishonoured for some reason. The use of an avalised bill is permitted by s 33 of the

---

21. This is set out in s 47 of the Bills of Exchange Act 1909 (Cth), which states that when 'a bill is duly presented for acceptance and is not accepted within the customary time, the person presenting it must treat it as dishonoured by non-acceptance. If he does not, the holder shall lose his right of recourse against the drawer and indorsers'.
22. This is set out in s 52 of the Bills of Exchange Act 1909 (Cth), which states as follows:
    (1) A bill is dishonoured by non-payment:
        (a) when it is duly presented for payment and payment is refused or cannot be obtained, or
        (b) when presentment is excused and the bill is overdue and unpaid.
    (2) Subject to the provisions of this Act, when a bill is dishonoured by non-payment, an immediate right of recourse against the drawer and indorsers accrues to the holder.
23. The Bills of Exchange Act 1909 (Cth) s 15.
24. Schmitthoff, *Schmitthoff's Export Trade*, 9th ed, London, Stevens & Sons, 1990, pp 386–9.
25. Id, p 389.
26. Id, pp 389–90.

Bills of Exchange Act 1909 (Cth), which defines the meaning of an accommodation bill and an accommodation party. Under the provision, an accommodation party to a bill is a person who has signed a bill as drawer, acceptor, or indorser, without receiving value, and for the purpose of lending his or her name to some other person; the accommodation party is liable on the bill to a holder for value; and it is immaterial whether, when such holder took the bill, he or she knew such party to be an accommodation party or not. Thus, an avalised bill can be regarded as a form of accommodation bill under the Act, although it is arguable whether or not the person has signed his or her name as a guarantor or an acceptor. *Rolfe Lubbell & Co v Keith and Greenwood* [1979] 2 QB 75 illustrates a situation where a person who indorses a bill in his or her own name on behalf of a company may incur personal liability to the holder or indorsee of the bill. In such a case, the bill is treated as if it was avalised or guaranteed by the indorser personally. In contrast, in *Maxform SpA v Mariani and Goodville Ltd* [1981] 2 Lloyd's Rep 54, the sole director who signed the bills of exchange on behalf of the company was not found to have undertaken personal liability to pay merely because of his signing of the bills, even though he was held liable for the unpaid debt of the company personally under the company law. Whether or not a person has undertaken a personal liability to guarantee the payment of a bill of exchange is regulated in s 31 of the Bills of Exchange Act 1909 (Cth): see **[5.67]**. The clarity of the words accompanying the signature of the person signing his or her name for the purpose of effecting an acceptance is crucial for determining whether the bill is an avalised bill.

Legal definitions of bill of exchange

Bills of exchange in the Bills of Exchange Act 1909 (Cth)

[5.37] Section 8 of the Bills of Exchange Act 1909 (Cth) defines a bill of exchange as follows:

(1) A bill of exchange is an unconditional order in writing, addressed by one person to another, signed by the person giving it, requiring the person to whom it is addressed to pay on demand, or at a fixed or determinable future time, a sum certain in money to or to the order of a specified person, or to bearer.

An instrument which does not comply with these conditions, or which orders any act to be done in addition to the payment of money, is not a bill of exchange.

An order to pay out of a particular fund is not unconditional within the meaning of this section; but an unqualified order to pay, coupled with:

(a) an indication of a particular fund out of which the drawee is to reimburse himself, or a particular account to be debited with the amount, or

(b) a statement of the transaction which gives rise to the bill;

is unconditional.

(4) A bill is not invalid by reason:

that it is not dated;

that it does not specify the value given, or that any value has been given therefor; or

that it does not specify the place where it is drawn, or the place where it is payable.

[5.38]

Bills of exchange in the Geneva Uniform Law

[5.38] The definition in the Bills of Exchange Act 1909 (Cth) can be compared with art 1 of the Geneva Uniform Law, which provides as follows:

A bill of exchange contains:
1. The term 'bill of exchange' inserted in the body of the instrument and expressed in the language employed in drawing up the instrument;
2. An unconditional order to pay a determinate sum of money;
3. The name of the person who is to pay (drawee);
4. A statement of the time of payment;
5. A statement of the place where payment is to be made;
6. The name of the person to whom or to whose order payment is to be made;
7. A statement of the date and of the place where the bill is issued; and
8. The signature of the person who issues the bill (drawer).

Similarities and differences can be seen in the two definitions of bill of exchange: the main ones have been summarised in the following table.

A comparison of 'bills of exchange' between the Bills of Exchange Act 1909 (Cth) and the Geneva Uniform Law (differences are *italicised*)

Bills of Exchange Act 1909 (Cth)	Geneva Uniform Law
It (the bill of exchange) is an unconditional order in writing	It (the bill of exchange) is an unconditional order
It specifies a 'sum certain in money'	It contains 'a determinate sum of money'
It is 'addressed' to the drawee	It contains the name of the drawee
It is signed by the drawer	It contains the signature of the drawer
It must indicate whether it is payable to the payee only, or to the order of a named person, or to a bearer	It must contain the name of the person to whom or to whose order payment is to be made
It directs the drawee to pay on demand or at a fixed or determinable future time a sum of money to the payee	*This is implied in the definition*
It is not invalid merely by reason that it does not specify the place where it was drawn	*In the absence of special mention, it is deemed to have been drawn in the place mentioned beside the name of the drawer*
It is not invalid merely by reason that it does not specify the place where it is payable	*In the absence of special mention, it is deemed to be payable in the place specified beside the name of the drawee, or the domicile of the drawee*
It is not invalid merely by reason that it is not dated	*It must contain the date when it was drawn*

In the absence of a specified time for payment, it is payable on demand	In the absence of a specified time for payment, it is deemed to be payable at sight
It is not invalid merely by reason that it does not specify the value given or that any value has been given	No mention of the issue
No mention of the issue	It must contain the term 'bill of exchange' in the body of the instrument and in the language employed in drawing up the instrument

The above table indicates the basic components, elements or considerations of a bill of exchange. The differences between the two definitions suggest that whether a document is a 'bill of exchange' in law is definitional, depending on the stipulation of the law governing the use of the bill. While the legal definition of a bill of exchange allows the parties to modify and vary the particulars of a bill of exchange, it also restricts the parties from altering the basic requirements for a bill.

♦

[5.39] *Rosenhain v Commonwealth Bank of Australia*

(1922) 31 CLR 46

Whether the bill satisfies s 8 of the Bills of Exchange Act 1909 (Cth)

Facts: In 1920, a 'bill of exchange' was drawn by Caravel Co in New York upon Rosenhain & Co in Melbourne. The Commonwealth Bank received the 'bill' as the ultimate indorsee after a number of transactions. The 'bill' contained the following terms: ... 60 days after sight ... pay to the order of ... 'with interest at the rate of 8 per cent, per annum until arrival of payment in London' ... Rosenhain accepted the 'bill', but refused to pay it on maturity. The bank's action against Rosenhain depended on whether the 'bill' was a 'bill of exchange' under the Bills of Exchange Act 1909 (Cth).

Decision: The High Court of Australia held that the 'bill' (or document) was not a 'bill of exchange' under s 8 of the Bills of Exchange Act 1909 (Cth). The court observed as follows:

<51> The 'sum certain' must, however, if the document is to constitute a bill of exchange, be payable on demand, or at a fixed or determinable future time. 'Certainty', as Ashhurst J said in *Carlos v Fancourt* [(1794) 5 TR 482 at 486], 'is a great object in commercial instruments; and unless they carry their own validity on the face of them, they are not negotiable'. Now, the document under consideration did <52> not fix a 'determinable future time' for payment of the sums mentioned therein, but a fixed time, namely, '60 days after sight'. Consequently, the sum must be certain at this fixed time if it is to conform to the provisions of the Bills of Exchange Acts. But clearly the sum was not certain on that date, nor could it be made certain from anything appearing on the face of the document; for interest was to run on from the time fixed for payment, namely, '60 days after sight' 'until arrival of payment in London', and it was quite uncertain, both on the face of the document and in fact, when this event would happen, or indeed whether it would happen at all.

♦

Use of bills of exchange between different legal regimes

[5.40] The Geneva system, as opposed to the system of bills of exchange in common law jurisdictions, has been accepted by about 23 countries; most of them are European countries which adopt the civil law or continental law tradition. The Geneva system is based on a number of Geneva conventions (see **[5.9]**), in particular, the Geneva Uniform Law on Bills of Exchange and Promissory Notes. Although there are differences between the Geneva Uniform Law and the common law system, the 'continental systems do not normally cause much difficulty to common law lawyers; bills are drawn on the continent and are presented, accepted and paid in the United States, Canada and Australia. The reverse also applies'.[27] Indeed, as suggested in the table of comparison (see **[5.38]**), the differences between the common law definition of a bill of exchange, as seen in s 8 of the Bills of Exchange Act 1909 (Cth) and the definition in the Geneva Uniform Law, are not substantial or material in the use of bills of exchange between the two systems.

Requirement for a bill of exchange to be unconditional and in writing

[5.41] Under both the Bills of Exchange Act 1909 (Cth) and the Geneva Uniform Law, a bill of exchange must be in writing and unconditional. The requirement is necessary because the oral form cannot serve as a transaction where three or more parties are involved. In addition, in Australia, instruments legislation (for example, s 126 of the Instruments Act 1958 (Vic) or its equivalent in other states or territories) requires that certain legal claims must be evidenced in writing in order to be enforceable. The expression 'unconditional' under s 8(2) of the Bills of Exchange Act 1909 (Cth) means that an instrument should not order 'any act to be done in addition to the payment of money', because that would make the act a condition for the payment. A bill of exchange which orders a drawee to pay a sum of money and to perform certain conduct other than the conduct of making payment would be considered to be conditional, and thus unenforceable.

Parties to a bill of exchange

[5.42] A bill of exchange normally involves three parties: it normally reflects a legal relationship between the drawer, drawee and payee (holder, bearer or indorsee) in a particular place and within a particular period of time. In a simple international sale, the 'drawer' is the person (often the seller) who draws the bill; the 'drawee' is the person (often the buyer) who makes the payment under the bill; and the payee is the person (often a bank) who receives the payment under the bill. The seller draws a bill of exchange to order the buyer to pay a specified sum (normally, the price of the goods and costs of transportation) to a specified person (or bank). The bill of exchange in such transactions is called a trade bill.

[5.43] Although a bill usually involves three parties (who are drawer, drawee and payee), the three parties in law may not always mean three different persons or companies in

---

27. Craigie, 'The Collection of Bills in International Trade', in Chinkin et al (eds), *Current Problems of International Trade Financing*, Malaya Law Review and Butterworths, Singapore, 1983, p 124.

reality. For example, under s 10 of the Bills of Exchange Act 1909 (Cth), the drawer and drawee could be the same person, as could the drawer and payee.[28] When the drawer and drawee are the same person, the bill is less likely to be used for an international sale of goods, under the Bills of Exchange Act 1909 (Cth), even though, as an indication of the future direction of the international commercial law on bills of exchange, art 11 of the UN Convention on International Bills of Exchange and International Promissory Notes expressly states that a bill may be drawn by a drawer upon him- or herself. Unlike a bill of exchange under the Bills of Exchange Act 1909 (Cth), a promissory note which is an unconditional promise to pay in writing made by one person to another may be used as a means of payment in international transactions.[29] In *McClintock v Union Bank of Australia Ltd* (1920) 20 SR(NSW) 494, a manager of a business deposited cheques payable to the business in the business's account and asked the bank to draw a bank cheque (a bank cheque can be a form of bill) to his own account which was held under a false name. The bank in this particular case would have been both the drawer and drawee, although the court was divided in this case as to whether the cheque in dispute fell under the Bills of Exchange Act 1909 (Cth). A bill of exchange may also be used as a means of finance (or lending) between a bank and its client. The bill of exchange in such a transaction is called an accommodation bill. For example, a bank may draw a bill of exchange to direct a third party to pay a sum of money to its client for the purpose of lending; and the bank's client may draw a bill of exchange upon him- or herself in favour of the bank as a means of repaying a bank's loan. However, when the drawer and payee are the same person, the transaction could be (even though this is not often the case) an international sale where the seller collects money from the buyer directly.

[5.44] Sometimes a drawer may become a payee by purchasing (negotiating) a bill of exchange from the payee or holder of the bill. This was what happened in *Jade International Steel Stahl Und Eisen GmbH & Co KG v Robert Nicholas (Steels) Ltd* [1978] 1 QB 917, where the English Court of Appeal held that a drawer who was forced to negotiate back the bill of exchange from a holder in due course has the rights of a holder in due course. 'Holder in due course' is, in brief, a legal expression often used in the law governing negotiable instruments. It means that the holder receives the bill through a legitimate transaction (due course) and thus excludes any mala fide transactions or taking possession of a bill with knowledge of the defective title of the transferor. For example, a person who obtains a bill of exchange through theft or fraud is not a holder in due course: s 34 of the Bills of Exchange Act 1909 (Cth).

[5.45] Sometimes a 'bill may be payable to two or more payees jointly, or it may be made payable in the alternative to one of two, or one of some of several payees': s 12(2) of the Bills of Exchange Act 1909 (Cth). It follows that, in certain circumstances, a bill

---

28. Section 10 of the Bills of Exchange Act 1909 (Cth) provides as follows:
    A bill may be drawn payable to, or to the order of, the drawer; or it may be drawn payable to, or to the order of, the drawee.
    Where, in a bill, drawer and drawee are the same person, or where the drawee is a fictitious person or a person not having capacity to contract, the holder may treat the instrument, at his option, either as a bill of exchange or as a promissory note.
29. 'Promissory note' is defined in s 89 of the Bills of Exchange Act 1909 (Cth).

of exchange may also involve more than three natural persons or companies. This situation arises where, for example, a seller directs a buyer to pay to two persons jointly because either the seller owes money to these persons, or the seller wants the collecting bank to keep part of the money and pay the rest to another person for business purposes. Similarly, the seller (drawer) might as well use the bill as a negotiable instrument to pay off his or her own debt to one of the debtors. Negotiability is the key for such use of the bill of exchange.

Negotiability of bills of exchange

[5.46] In brief, 'negotiable instrument' refers to a document of title which can be passed between different parties together with the benefit or entitlement conferred by the document. Most bills of exchange are negotiable. Negotiability of a bill under s 13(1) of the Bills of Exchange Act 1909 (Cth) is presumed when the bill contains neither express words nor implied intention prohibiting the transfer of the bill as a negotiable instrument.[30] The parties to the bill include the drawer, the drawee, the payee, a holder, a bearer or an indorsee, who has taken the position of the original payee through indorsement. In this context the payee is a person who is nominated as the payee or who receives payment as a payee, a 'holder' means anyone who is in possession of a bill of exchange through legal means; a 'bearer' is a person who has possession of a bill which is payable to a bearer (bearer's bill); and an 'indorsee' is a person who has been indorsed (named) by the previous indorser as the one who is entitled to the benefit of the bill.

[5.47] Although there are differences between a 'holder', a 'bearer' and an 'indorsee', in effect they are interchangeable as the bill grants the same right to each of them to claim the payment against the drawee in certain circumstances. This includes a situation where a bill indicates that it is payable alternatively to a payee, a bearer or an indorsee. However, when the bill specifies the means of transaction (for example, negotiable by indorsement only), or excludes certain means of transaction (for example, stating that the bill is not a bearer's bill[31]), the rights and liabilities of the parties vary depending on their status. While a holder or a bearer may receive a bill through delivery, an indorsee can only receive a bill through indorsement if the bill expressly states that the bill is transferable or negotiable by means of indorsement. Thus, an original payee can transfer a negotiable bill of exchange to a

---

30. Section 13 of the Bills of Exchange Act 1909 (Cth) provides as follows:
    When a bill contains words prohibiting transfer, or indicating an intention that it should not be transferable, it is valid as between the parties thereto, but is not negotiable.
    A negotiable bill may be payable either to order or to bearer.
    (3) A bill is payable to bearer which is expressed to be so payable, or on which the only or last indorsement is an indorsement in blank.
    (4) A bill is payable to order which:
       (a) is expressed to be so payable, or
       (b) is expressed to be payable to a particular person, and does not contain words prohibiting transfer or indicating an intention that it should not be transferable.
    (5) Where a bill, either originally or by indorsement, is expressed to be payable to the order of a specified person, and not to him or his order, it is nevertheless payable to him or his order at his option.
31. A bearer's bill means that anyone who has possession of the bill through a legitimate means will be a 'bearer' of the bill and will be entitled to the payment.

subsequent holder or bearer through delivery, if the bill is not required to be indorsed, but he or she must indorse the bill to pass good title to an indorsee if the bill so requires. By the same token, an indorsee who receives a bill from a previous indorser has to indorse it if the bill is to be subsequently negotiated to another person.

[5.48] A bill of exchange is prima facie negotiable unless expressly specified otherwise. The common expressions suggesting the negotiability of a bill include payable to order, payable to bearer, payable to a specified person without restrictions on the person's ability to transfer the bill, or payable to a fictitious or non-existing person. If the drawer and drawee intend to make a bill non-negotiable, they must expressly so state in the bill. A statement like payable A/C payee only,[32] or payable account payee only,[33] does not restrict the negotiability of a bill. A bill which has been expressly made non-negotiable is only enforceable between the drawer and the drawee, and the drawee and the specified payee.[34] When a bill is negotiable, it can be negotiated either by way of indorsement and delivery or by delivery only. First, if a bill is negotiable by way of indorsement and delivery, it must be indorsed by a legitimate holder (indorser) to another (indorsee). A bill containing the words payable to order is negotiable by indorsement and the delivery of the indorsed bill.[35] The indorsement can be effected by either an indorsement in blank or a special indorsement. An indorsement in blank specifies no indorsee, and a bill so indorsed becomes payable to bearer.[36] A special indorsement specifies the person to whom, or to whose order, the bill is to be payable.[37] However, when a bill has been indorsed in blank, any holder may convert the blank indorsement into a special indorsement by writing, above the indorser's signature, a direction to pay the bill to or to the order of himself or herself or some other person.[38] Second, if a bill is negotiable by delivery, it must contain the words payable to bearer. In other words, if a bill contains the words payable to bearer, it is negotiable by delivery.[39]

[5.49] The person receiving a bill legitimately from another becomes a holder of the bill. The person is also known as the holder in due course, who is defined in s 34 of the Bills of Exchange Act 1909 (Cth) as a person who has taken a bill, complete and regular on the face of it, under the following conditions, namely:
(a) That he became the holder of it before it was overdue, and without notice that it had been previously dishonoured, if such was the fact; and
(b) That he took the bill in good faith and for value, and that at the time the bill was negotiated to him he had no notice of any defect in the title of the person who negotiated it.

---

32. *Edward Wong Financial Co Ltd v Infinity Industrial Co Ltd* [1977–9] HKC 449.
33. *Wayfoong Credit Ltd v Remoco (HK) Ltd* [1983] 2 HKC 445.
34. Bills of Exchange Act 1909 (Cth) s 13(1).
35. Ibid, s 36(3).
36. Ibid, s 39(1).
37. Ibid, s 39(2).
38. Ibid, s 39(4).
39. Ibid, s 36(2).

[5.50] A holder in due course is protected by law. Generally speaking, a holder may sue on the bill in his or her own name;[40] or hold the bill free from any defect of title of prior parties, as well as from mere personal defences available to prior parties among themselves, and may enforce payment against all parties liable on the bill.[41] Thus, if a bill is dishonoured by non-acceptance or non-payment, the holder has the option of suing the drawee directly, or returning the bill to the previous indorser. Whatever action the holder takes, the holder must comply with the relevant provisions of the Bills of Exchange Act 1909 (Cth).

[5.51] As we have seen, negotiability means that the holder or bearer of a bill is able to enforce his or her title under the bill against the original drawee, provided the holder or bearer obtained the bill as a bona fide purchaser. A bona fide holder who has not given value for obtaining the bill cannot enforce the bill against a drawee if a fraud was perpetrated against the drawee; but a bona fide holder who has given value can enforce the bill against the drawee, even if a fraud was perpetrated by someone else against the drawee. The holder in the latter case is obliged to prove his or her good faith and his or her status as a purchaser of the bill.[42] This is illustrated in *Osterreichische Landerbank v S'Elite Ltd* [1980] 2 Lloyd's Rep 139, where the holder of the bill of exchange proved that it received the bill as a bona fide purchaser for value and was held to be entitled to the benefit of the bill. In this case, an Austrian company drew a bill of exchange upon S'Elite. The bill was transferred to Osterreichische Landerbank. S'Elite accepted the bill, but refused to make payment at maturity on the ground that the drawer was fraudulent or might have been fraudulent in transferring the bill. The Master of the Court ordered S'Elite to pay. This decision was affirmed by Lloyd J. S'Elite appealed to the English Court of Appeal. The court dismissed the appeal because there was no evidence that the holder of the bill was involved in or was aware of the alleged fraud at the time of transfer.

Precision in naming the drawee of a bill

[5.52] Formal indorsement of a bill is important. A bill must be indorsed by the true indorser in compliance with the requirements set out or implied in the terms of the bill. For example, in *Arab Bank Ltd v Ross* [1952] 2 QB 216, the word 'company' was omitted from the signature of the indorser. The court emphasised the crucial importance of entering a correct signature, but nevertheless recognised the effect of the promissory notes, probably because both the notes and the legal relationship which was intended by the notes were genuine.

---

40. Ibid, s 43(1)(a).
41. Ibid, s 43(1)(b).
42. For example, see *Bank fur Gemeinwirtschaft v City of London Garages* [1971] 1 WLR 149.

> **[5.53]** **_Durham Fancy Goods Ltd v Michael Jackson (Fancy Goods) Ltd_**
>
> [1968] 2 QB 839
>
> *Discrepancy between the description of the drawee's name in the bill and the full name of the intended drawee*
>
> **Facts:** Durham Fancy Goods drew a 90 days bill of exchange on Michael Jackson (Fancy Goods). The drawee was described as 'To M. Jackson (Fancy Goods) Ltd., 263 Bury New Road, Manchester'. Michael Jackson, one of the two directors of Michael Jackson (Fancy Goods), signed his name in the space provided for the drawee's signature. Michael Jackson and the other director sold their shares in Michael Jackson (Fancy Goods) and resigned from the position of directors before the bill became mature. The bill was dishonoured on maturity and Michael Jackson (Fancy Goods) was in liquidation at the time of this litigation. Durham Fancy Goods sought to hold Michael Jackson personally liable for the dishonoured bill on the basis of his signature.
>
> **Decision:** Donaldson J of the Queen's Bench Division dismissed the action. His Honour held, inter alia, that the bill was not properly addressed to the intended drawee, because the abbreviation 'M' did not clearly show that it was meant to be an abbreviation, nor did it expressly convey 'Michael'.

Sight bills and time bills

[5.54] A bill of exchange can be classed as either a 'sight bill' or a 'time bill'. A 'sight bill' is payable on demand when the bill is presented; and a 'time bill' is payable on a specified date, or a determinable future time after the bill has been presented.[43] The expression 'payable on demand' refers to a situation where a bill contains express words that the bill is payable at request, at sight or on presentation. A bill can also be treated as a sight bill under s 15 of the Bills of Exchange Act 1909 (Cth) if there is no fixed date for payment in the bill or the specified date for payment is overdue. In the latter case, the bill is deemed to be payable on demand only to the person who indorses or accepts the bill after it is overdue. While the meaning of a specified date of payment is self-evident in a time bill, the expression 'payable at a future time' refers to a situation where the bill contains express words that the bill is payable at the end of a fixed period after a particular date or after being sighted, or payable at a fixed period after the occurrence of a specified event which is certain to happen, though the time of its happening may be uncertain: s 16 Bills of Exchange Act 1909 (Cth). A 'determinable future time' must be relatively certain and ascertainable: for example, see *Korea Exchange Bank v Debenhams (Central Buying) Ltd* [1979] 1 Lloyd's Rep 548; **[5.28]**.

[5.55] The existence of the event which is certain to happen does not make the bill conditional for two reasons:
- First, the event is certain to happen. The certainty of the event appears to be a matter to be judged by a reasonable person in the same circumstances involved.

---

43. Fixed time or determinable time for payment affects the right of the holder of a bill of exchange. In *Yeoman Credit Ltd v Gregory* [1963] 1 All ER 245, a number of bills of exchange were dishonoured. The court held that several of them were not enforceable against the defendants on the ground that they were presented after the date of maturity.

- Second, the event relates merely to the time of payment and does not affect the duty to pay. A disagreement on the time to pay is different from a disagreement on the duty to pay.

Certainty in the sum of payment in a bill

[5.56] A bill of exchange must bear a sum certain in money, although it could be expressed in any currency. This requirement is necessary to avoid any dispute about the sum payable under a bill. However, the expression 'a sum certain in money' does not mean that the amount of payment must be specified and fixed in all circumstances. A bill of exchange could require a sum of payment to be made with specified interest or bank charges; or in stated instalments, with a provision that upon default in payment of any instalment the whole sum shall become due; or with a fixed or determinable rate of exchange: s 14(1) of the Bills of Exchange Act 1909 (Cth). The essence of the requirement for 'a sum certain in money' is the certainty or ascertainability of the sum. If the bill states that a sum is payable plus 'all necessary charges' or 'all the bank charges', the bill would probably be invalid because uncertainty arises from the expressions 'all necessary charges' or 'all bank charges'. In *Standard Bank of Canada v Wildey* (1919) SR (NSW) 384, the bill was regarded as invalid because the court was not able to ascertain what were 'all the bank charges' payable under the bill. The certainty in the sum payable does not affect the validity of a bill containing two specified sums of money. In such case, the lesser of the two sums will be the sum payable: s 14(2) of the Bills of Exchange Act 1909 (Cth).

Acceptance of bill of exchange

[5.57] Acceptance means the drawee or drawee's agent acknowledges the obligation to make a payment under a bill of exchange. Under s 22(2), a valid acceptance must be in writing. The drawee or his or her agent must sign his or her name. A mere signature of the person accepting the bill without additional words is sufficient for the purpose of acceptance. The acceptance cannot be subject to the condition that the acceptor will perform the obligation of the drawee by any other means than the payment of money. Signature with such condition does not constitute a valid acceptance. An acceptance can be either general or qualified. A general acceptance assents without qualification to the order of the drawer. A qualified acceptance in express terms varies the effect of the bill as drawn.[44] A qualified acceptance can take several specific forms. Under s 24(3) of the Bills of Exchange Act 1909 (Cth), an acceptance is qualified if it falls under one of the following categories:

- an acceptance is conditional, namely making payment by the acceptor dependent on the fulfilment of a condition therein stated; or
- an acceptance is partial, namely accepting to pay only part of the amount for which the bill is drawn; or
- an acceptance is local, namely accepting to pay only at a particular place;[45] or

---
44. The Bills of Exchange Act 1909 (Cth) s 24(2).

- an acceptance qualifies time, namely changing the time for payment indicated in the bill; or
- an acceptance qualifies the payees, namely undertaking to pay one or several of the drawees, but not of all of them as nominated by the drawer.

[5.58] Since a qualified acceptance changes the original terms of the bill, a holder, bearer, or indorsee of the bill has an option to accept or reject the qualified acceptance. If he or she refuses to take a qualified acceptance, he or she may treat the bill as dishonoured by non-acceptance.[46] If he or she decides to take a qualified acceptance, his or her decision does not automatically bind the drawer or an indorser, unless the latter does not reject the former's notice of such decision within a reasonable time.[47]

[5.59] Acceptance of a bill is an important part in the use of a bill of exchange, but it is not compulsory to all bills of exchange. Certain types of bill may be enforceable against the drawee without acceptance. Under s 44 of the Bills of Exchange Act 1909 (Cth), the acceptance is necessary in the following circumstances:

- Where a bill is payable after sight, presentment for acceptance is necessary in order to fix the maturity of the instrument.
- Where a bill expressly stipulates that it shall be presented for acceptance, or where a bill is drawn payable elsewhere than at the residence or place of business of the drawee, it must be presented for acceptance before it can be presented for payment.

[5.60] These conditions determining the necessity for having a bill accepted by the drawee before payment suggest that most bills used in international transactions are subject to the requirement of acceptance. The nature of international transactions decides that most bills of exchange need to be drawn payable certain days after sight, because the buyer needs time to receive the goods, or to raise his or her finance. In addition, under an arrangement of documentary credit, the place of payment is often the place of the seller's business. Thus, the second condition for requiring acceptance is also satisfied. Thus, it can be concluded that acceptance is almost a necessary part in the use of a bill of exchange to effect payment in international transactions.

[5.61] In international transactions, a bill of exchange is usually addressed to the drawee by the drawer to order the drawee to pay a fixed or ascertainable sum to the payee at a fixed or ascertainable time. Under s 44 of the Bills of Exchange Act 1909 (Cth), acceptance is thus necessary for making a bill enforceable against the drawee. Section 26(1) of the Bills of Exchange Act 1909 (Cth) provides as follows:

> Every contract on a bill, whether it be the drawer's, the acceptor's, or an indorser's, is incomplete and revocable, until delivery of the instrument in order to give effect thereto: Provided that where an acceptance is written on a bill, and the drawee gives notice to or according to the directions of the person entitled to the bill that he has accepted it, the acceptance then becomes complete and irrevocable.

---

45. This situation is qualified by s 24(4) of the Bills of Exchange Act 1909 (Cth), which provides that an 'acceptance to pay at a particular place is a general acceptance, unless it expressly states that the bill is to be paid there only, and not elsewhere'.
46. The Bills of Exchange Act 1909 (Cth) s 49(1).
47. The Bills of Exchange Act 1909 (Cth) s 49(2) and (3).

[5.61]

Section 26(1) should be read together with s 58 of the Bills of Exchange Act 1909 (Cth), which provides that a bill, of itself, does not operate as an assignment of funds in the hands of the drawee available for the payment thereof, and the drawee of a bill who does not accept as required by this Act is not liable on the instrument. The combined effect of ss 26(1) and 58 is that a bill is valid against the drawee in the circumstances as defined in s 44, which are the circumstances in which international transactions take place, only after the drawee has accepted it. A failure to comply with s 44 means that the drawer, a payee, holder, bearer or indorsee of the bill cannot enforce the bill as a valid bill of exchange against the drawee, but may use the bill as a sort of evidence to support his or her claim under the relevant contract against the drawee, or sometimes rely on the provisions applicable to the dishonoured bill under the Act against the drawee if appropriate.

[5.62] Acceptance is necessary in the situations described in s 44 of the Bills of Exchange Act 1909 (Cth). In these circumstances, the holder is obliged to present a bill of exchange to the drawee or the drawee's agent for acceptance before resorting to a court of law for assistance. Acceptance of a bill of exchange involves several issues. Besides the formality of acceptance which is discussed at the beginning of this subsection, the person capable of effecting an acceptance and the liability of acceptor are also relevant issues. The general rules for acceptance are set out in s 46 of the Bills of Exchange Act 1909 (Cth). These rules resolve the issue relating to who can or should accept a bill of exchange. Under this provision, a bill is duly presented for acceptance when it is presented in accordance with the following rules:

> The presentment must be made, by or on behalf of the holder, to the drawee or to some person authorised to accept or refuse acceptance on the drawee's behalf, such as a negotiation bank under an arrangement of documentary credit, at a reasonable hour on a business day and before the bill is overdue;
> Where a bill is addressed to two or more drawees, who are not partners, presentment must be made to them all, unless one has authority to accept for all, then presentment may be made to him or her only:
>> Where the drawee is dead, presentment may be made to his or her personal representative;
>> Where the drawee is bankrupt, presentment may be made to the drawee or his or her trustee or assignee;
>> Where authorised by agreement or usage, a presentment through the postal office is sufficient.

[5.63] Since in the circumstances described in s 44, acceptance is a prerequisite for the enforcement of a bill of exchange against the drawee, the holder of a bill has an implied obligation to present the bill of acceptance before seeking judicial assistance for enforcement. When acceptance is impossible, the right of the holder, indorser or drawer to enforce a bill becomes an issue. Section 26(2) of the Bills of Exchange Act 1909 (Cth) excuses the holder from presenting a bill for acceptance in the following circumstances:

> where the drawee is dead or bankrupt, or is a fictitious person or a person not having capacity to contract by bill;
> where, after the exercise of reasonable diligence, such presentment cannot be effected; and
> where, although the presentment has been irregular, acceptance has been refused on some other ground.

[5.64] In one of these specified situations, the bill is presumed to have been dishonoured by non-acceptance. However, the holder must prove the existence of the prescribed circumstances, and cannot merely rely on a belief that a bill will be dishonoured on presentment, as a ground to justify his or her failure to present the bill for acceptance.[48]

[5.65] The purpose of acceptance is to acknowledge a liability to honour a bill of exchange. The general liability of an acceptor is thus to pay the sum specified in a bill. The liability of an acceptor is regulated in s 59 of the Bills of Exchange Act 1909 (Cth) as follows:

> The acceptor of a bill, by accepting it:
> engages that he will pay it according to the tenor of his acceptance; and
> is precluded from denying to a holder in due course:
> the existence of the drawer, the genuineness of his signature, and his capacity and authority to draw the bill; and
> in the case of a bill payable to drawer's order, the then capacity of the drawer to indorse, but not the genuineness or validity of his indorsement; and
> in the case of a bill payable to the order of a third person, the existence of the payee and his then capacity to indorse, but not the genuineness or validity of his indorsement.

[5.66] The acceptor's liability to pay is relevant to the issue as to who is the acceptor.[49] The ascertainment of the acceptor is determined by the signature of the acceptor. One of the frequently argued questions is whether a person signing his or her name also undertakes a personal liability for the payment of the bill concerned. Sections 28 and 31 of the Bills of Exchange Act 1909 (Cth) set out four basic rules for ascertaining the acceptor's liability. First, a person is not liable as an acceptor if he or she has not signed as such.[50] Second, if a person signs a bill in a trade name or an assumed name, he or she is liable as if he or she had signed it in his or her own name.[51] Third, the signature of the name of a firm by a person representing the firm is equivalent to the signature of the names of all persons liable as partners in that firm.[52] Fourth, if a person signs a bill as an acceptor and adds words to his or her signature, indicating that he or she signs for or on behalf of a principal, or in a representative capacity, he or she is not personably liable; however, the mere addition to his or her signature of words describing him or her as an agent or as filling a representative character does not exempt him or her from personal

---

48. The Bills of Exchange Act 1909 (Cth) s 46(3).
49. The liability of acceptor is defined in s 59 of the Bills of Exchange Act 1909 (Cth), which provides as follows:
    The acceptor of a bill, by accepting it:
    (a) engages that he will pay it according to the tenor of his acceptance; and
    (b) is precluded from denying to a holder in due course:
    (i) the existence of the drawer, the genuineness of his signature, and his capacity and authority to draw the bill; and
    (ii) in the case of a bill payable to drawer's order, the then capacity of the drawer to indorse, but not the genuineness or validity of his indorsement; and
    (iii) in the case of a bill payable to the order of a third person, the existence of the payee and his then capacity to indorse, but not the genuineness or validity of his indorsement.
50. The Bills of Exchange Act 1909 (Cth) s 28(1).
51. Ibid, s 28(2).
52. Ibid, s 28(3).

[5.66]

liability.[53] The last rule emphasises the clarity of the statement to exclude the personal liability of the person signing a bill. If a personal liability is established by the signature of a person, the bill may be regarded as an avalised bill or accommodation bill: see **[5.36]**. Thus, a fine balance needs to be struck by the court of law making a determination. Section 28 was examined in *Muirhead v Commonwealth Bank of Australia* [1996] QCA 241. After analysing a number of local and foreign precedents, McPherson JA (at 246) commented on the appellant's signature as follows:

> From what has been said, it follows that in signing her name on the bills of exchange in this case, as she did and was authorised to do, the only rational conclusion is that Mrs Muirhead was intending by her own signature to confirm the words 'For and on behalf of GAR & SS Muirhead' appearing on the forms she signed. For this purpose it cannot matter whether those words were in fact printed or typed on the form of bill by the Bank before she signed it, or were placed there by Mrs Muirhead herself at the time she signed. In either event, she was adopting and authenticating those words by subscribing her own signature immediately below. In doing so, she thus 'signed' not only her own name but that of her husband GAR Muirhead. Indeed, on one view, the case seems to fall fairly within the terms of s 28(3) of the Act, which treats the signature of the name of a firm as equivalent to the signature by the person who signs the names of all the persons liable as partners of the firm. From what is said about the Muirheads in their own affidavits, it appears that they carry on business in partnership.

This case involved the signature and liability of the drawer, but the court's construction of s 28 cited above applies equally to all signatures as either a drawer or an acceptor. The appeal was dismissed in the present case.

[5.67] In *Cheung Yiu-wing v Blooming Textile Ltd* (1977) HKLR 388, the Court of Appeal of the High Court of Hong Kong was asked to determine in pursuance of s 26(1) of the Bills of Exchange Ordinance (Cap 19, HK), which is equivalent to s 31(1) of the Bills of Exchange Act 1909 (Cth), the personal liability of two directors who had signed their names without qualification on two cheques which bore the name of Sun Sang Garment Factory Ltd. The Court of Appeal affirmed the decision of the trial court and held that the name of the company printed on the cheques did not exclude the directors from personal liability to the holder of the cheques. In order to avoid such difficulties, Hong Kong has inserted s 26A into the Bills of Exchange Ordinance (Cap 19, HK), providing a clearer guidance for differentiating a corporate liability from a personal liability.[54] Under the present Australian law, a court in making a decision on the personal liability of the acceptor must refer to s 31(2) of the Bills of Exchange Act 1909 (Cth), which states that in determining whether a signature on a bill is that of the principal or that of the agent by whose hand it is written, the construction most favourable to the validity of the instrument shall be adopted. The provision requires a court to lean towards the enforcement of a bill of exchange wherever possible within the discretionary power of the court to interpret.[55]

---

53. The Bills of Exchange Act 1909 (Cth) s 31(1). Section 26(1) of the Bills of Exchange Ordinance (Cap 19 HK) is identical to s 31 of the Bills of Exchange Act 1909 (Cth). In *Kwok Wing v Maytex Trading Co* (1977) HKLR 149, the Court of Appeal of the High Court of Hong Kong held that s 26(1) did not apply to render a person personally liable where he or she affixed his or her signature on a bill of exchange as part of a composite signature of a company. As to the meaning of a composite signature of a company, the court held that when a person placed his or her name on a cheque to show that the signature was to authenticate the impression of the company's stamp, the impression and the signature together formed the composite signature of the company.

Payment under bill of exchange

[5.68] Payment of the sum by the acceptor as ordered by a bill discharges the acceptor's and the drawee's liability to pay. Thus, s 64 of the Bills of Exchange Act 1909 states that 'a bill is discharged by payment in due course by or on behalf of the drawee or acceptor'. Payment in due course means payment made at or after maturity of the bill to the holder thereof in good faith and without notice that his or her title to the bill is defective.[56] Payment in due course is the purpose of the bill. Thus, the use of a bill of exchange comes to an end when the payment has been duly made. In order to effect payment under a bill, the bill must be duly presented. The meaning of duly presenting a bill is defined in s 50 of the Bills of Exchange Act 1909 (Cth). Under the provision, a bill is duly presented for payment if it is presented in pursuance of the following rules:

> Where the bill is not payable on demand, presentment must be made on the day it falls due. This is a very important rule for international transactions. There are cases where the holder of a bill is found to have lost their right to demand payment under the bill because he or she has failed to present the bill to the relevant bank (acceptor) for payment on the date when the bill was mature.
>
> Where the bill is payable on demand, then, subject to the provisions of this Act, presentment must be made within a reasonable time after its issue, in order to render the drawer liable, and within a reasonable time after its indorsement, in order to render the indorser liable. In determining what is a reasonable time, regard shall be had to the nature of the bill, the usage of trade with regard to similar bills, and the facts of the particular case.
>
> Presentment must be made by the holder or by some person authorised to receive payment on his or her behalf, at a reasonable hour on a business day, at the proper place as defined in this section, either to the person designated by the bill as payer, or to some person authorised to pay or refuse payment on his or her behalf, if with the exercise of reasonable diligence such person can there be found.
>
> A bill is presented at the proper place:
>
> (i) where a place of payment is specified in the bill and the bill is there presented;
>
> (ii) where no place of payment is specified, but the address of the drawee or acceptor is given in the bill, and the bill is there presented;
>
> (iii) where no place of payment is specified and no address given, and the bill is presented at the drawee's or acceptor's place of business if known, and if not at his or her ordinary residence if known;

---

54. Section 26A of the Bills of Exchange Ordinance (Cap 19, HK) states as follows:

    A person who makes, accepts or indorses a bill for, in the name of, on behalf of or on account of a company shall not be liable in respect of that making, acceptance or indorsement where, on a proper construction of the bill as a whole, that making, acceptance or indorsement is a making, acceptance or indorsement of that company.

    In subsection (1), 'company' has the meaning assigned to it by s 2(1) of the Companies Ordinance (Cap 32) and includes a company to which Pt XI of that Ordinance applies.

    This section shall apply to the making, acceptance or indorsement of a bill after the commencement of the Bills of Exchange (Amendment) Ordinance 1983 (16 of 1983).

55. The application of s 31(2) may not be an easy task. In *Cheung Yiu-wing v Blooming Textile Ltd* (1977) HKLR 388, the Court of Appeal of High Court of Hong Kong observed that under s 26(1) of the Bills of Exchange Ordinance (Cap 19, HK), equivalent to s 31(1) of the Bills of Exchange Act 1909 (Cth), the court is not called upon to look at the whole of the document to find out whether it had been signed in a representative capacity. This view expressed by the Hong Kong court may reflect the Hong Kong court's attitude to the interpretation of s 26(2) of the Bills of Exchange Ordinance (Cap 19, HK), which is identical to s 31(2) of the Bills of Exchange Act 1909 (Cth).

56. The Bills of Exchange Act 1909 (Cth) s 64(1).

[5.68]

(iv) in any other case, if presented to the drawee or acceptor wherever he or she can be found, or if presented at his or her last known place of business or residence.

Where a bill is presented at the proper place, and after the exercise of reasonable diligence no person authorised to pay or refuse payment can be found there, no further presentment to the drawee or acceptor is required.

Where a bill is drawn upon or accepted by two or more persons who are not partners, and no place of payment is specified, presentment must be made to them all.

Where the drawee or acceptor of a bill is dead, and no place of payment is specified, presentment must be made to a personal representative, if such there be, and with the exercise of reasonable diligence he can be found.

Where authorised by agreement or usage, a presentment through the post office is sufficient.

[5.69] The rules set out in this provision are essential for a holder of a bill of exchange to claim payment. They certainly affect an international transaction when the bill of exchange concerned is subject to Australian law. As a general principle, a holder must comply with the formality set out in the relevant domestic law if he or she wishes to enforce the holder's right under the relevant law.

Assumption of uniformity of bills of exchange at common law

[5.70] The meaning and character of bills of exchange are more or less the same in common law countries, although it is necessary to examine the law of each country in special circumstances. If an Australian court is not satisfied that the law on bills of exchange in another common law country differs from the Australian law, it may assume similarity between the Australian law and the relevant foreign laws. For example, in *Standard Bank of Canada v Wildey* (1919) SR (NSW) 384 the parties argued as to whether the bill of exchange which ordered the drawee to pay a sum of $1288 'plus all bank charges' was a good bill. The court was of the opinion that because the plaintiff failed to prove that the bill was a good bill under the Canadian law, it could be assumed that the Canadian law is the same as the Australian law and thus the bill was not a good bill under the Bills of Exchange Act 1909 (Cth). By the same token, if a party fails to prove the content of any foreign law which is applicable to a bill of exchange, a court of law is not bound under the conflicts rules by the alleged foreign law and may choose another law which is also applicable to the bill in question.

Promissory notes

[5.71] A promissory note is a promise to pay a specified sum of money at a fixed or ascertainable date in the future, and is a means of effecting payment. It is sometimes used in international trade.

Section 89 of the Bills of Exchange Act 1909 (Cth) defines a promissory note as follows:

(1) A promissory note is an unconditional promise in writing made by one person to another, signed by the maker, engaging to pay, on demand or at a fixed or determinable future time, a sum certain in money, to or to the order of a specified person, or to bearer.

(2) An instrument in the form of a note payable to the maker's order is not a note within the meaning of this section unless and until it is endorsed by the maker.

(3) A note is not invalid by reason only that it contains also a pledge of collateral security with authority to sell or dispose thereof.

(4) A note which is, or on the face of it purports to be, both made and payable within Australia is an inland note. Any other note is a foreign note.

[5.72] A promissory note is an undertaking to pay a sum of money to a promisee. It is different from a 'documentary credit', which is more like a bank's guarantee or bank's payment in exchange of stipulated documents from the beneficiary. A promissory note may or may not depend on the fulfilment of any obligations by the named promisee or bearer. Indeed, more often than not its availability does not depend on any specific performance of the promisee. A promissory note is also often transferable without indorsement. It can be compared with a bill of exchange drawn on the drawer him- or herself to pay the sum stipulated in the bill. Article 75 of the Geneva Uniform Rules defines a promissory note in a similar way to s 89 above.

[5.73] A promissory note can be used in an international transaction: see arts 76–78 of the Geneva Uniform Rules. It can be subject to the Bills of Exchange Act or contract law. In the following case, the promissory note is governed by general contract law.

[5.74] *Export Credits Guarantee Department v Universal Oil Products Co, Procon Inc and Procon (Great Britain) Ltd*

[1983] 2 Lloyd's Rep 152

The promisor's duty to indemnify the guarantor of the dishonoured promissory notes

Facts: Export Credits Guarantee Department (ECGD) (plaintiff) was the guarantor for Universal Oil Co, Procon and Procon (Great Britain) (defendants) which issued a number of promissory notes in favour of their banks for repaying a loan advanced by the banks. The defendants designed and erected an oil refinery in Newfoundland in 1970 and took a large loan from a group of banks. The loan was to be repaid by a number of promissory notes drawn in the banks' favour at different maturity dates. ECGD was asked to provide a guarantee to the banks. A premium agreement was entered into between ECGD and the defendants, under which the defendants undertook to indemnify ECGD. The defendants went into liquidation in 1973 and left a large sum of money represented by the promissory notes unpaid. The banks called the guarantee. ECGD sought indemnity from the defendants after having paid the banks under the guarantee. The defendants intended to avoid liability on the ground that the indemnity clause in the premium agreement amounted to a penalty clause, which was prohibited in law. The trial court and appellant court gave judgment in favour of ECGD. The defendants appealed to the House of Lords.

Decisions: The court held that the defendants were obliged to indemnify ECGD and the clause in question was not a penalty clause.

Documentary collection

[5.75] 'Documentary collection' is defined in Pt B of the 'General Provisions and Definitions' of the ICC Uniform Rules for Collections as collection of commercial documents with or without financial documents enclosed. Collection of financial documents accompanied by commercial documents is the most common way of collection. The process of collection as described in **[5.22]**–**[5.25]** applies to documentary collection with financial documents. If documentary collection does not include financial documents, there must be a separate 'clean collection' (see **[5.76]–[5.77]**), either before or after the documentary collection, depending on the terms of the contract.

Clean collection

[5.76] According to the ICC Uniform Rules for Collections,[57] the expression 'clean collection' means collection of financial documents without accompanying commercial documents. This is possible if the parties to a contract of sale agree to make payment before examining the relevant commercial documents. The payment may be made even before the goods have been shipped or the seller has obtained the goods for sale. The seller may also use the method of 'clean collection' after having given the buyer commercial documents.

[5.77] The process of clean collection is almost the same as the process of documentary collection. In a process of clean collection, the seller draws a draft on the buyer for the value of the goods or services and requests his or her bank (remitting bank) to collect payment of the draft from the buyer. The remitting bank sends the draft and instructions for collection to a collecting or presenting bank in the buyer's place of business. The collecting bank presents the draft and collects payment from the buyer in pursuance of the instructions. The buyer pays the draft pursuant to the agreement between him or her and the seller. The only difference between documentary collection and clean collection is that the buyer does not receive the commercial documents at the same time as making a payment under the bill of exchange or a similar document.

Direct collection

[5.78] This refers to an arrangement whereby the seller with the permission of his or her bank (remitting bank) directly sends financial documents, commercial documents and instructions of the remitting bank to the collecting or presenting bank. This form of collection allows direct contact between the seller and the collecting bank, but the collecting bank acts as the agent of the remitting bank as if it were instructed by the remitting bank. Similarly, the remitting bank treats the act of the seller to authorise the collecting bank to carry out the collection as its own. This method of collection can be used for either documentary collection or clean collection. The difference between this arrangement and normal 'documentary collection' or 'clean collection' is that under this arrangement the remitting bank does not directly instruct the collecting bank. Instead, it allows the seller to use the bank's letter of instructions, which seeks to establish an agent–principal relationship between the remitting bank and the collecting bank, to act as the bank's agent to request the collecting bank to act on behalf of the remitting bank. This form of collection is recognised in art 3 of the ICC Uniform Rules for Collections.

---

57. See Pt B of the 'General Provisions and Definitions'.

Banks' general duties in collection

[5.79] In the process of collection, banks have contractual obligations, between the drawer and the remitting bank, as well as between the remitting bank and the collecting bank, to follow the instructions for collection. They also have a general duty to act in good faith and to exercise reasonable care: art 1 of the ICC Uniform Rules for Collections. The banks must follow the instructions for collection strictly, but do not have any obligation to examine the authenticity of the relevant documents: art 2 of the ICC Uniform Rules for Collections. Nor are banks liable for delay and damages caused by an error in communications, translation or interpretation of technical terms: art 4 of the ICC Uniform Rules for Collection. Banks are also exempt from liability arising from causes beyond their control, such as natural disasters and wars: art 5 of the ICC Uniform Rules for Collection. Although the ICC rules are not compulsory law, they represent the common practices which would be accepted in most countries.

Payment by way of documentary credit

Defining 'documentary credit'

[5.80] 'Documentary credit' has two meanings. First, it refers to a document of undertaking issued by a bank at the request of an applicant (a buyer) to pay to the beneficiary (a seller) a sum of money under specified conditions (for example, the beneficiary provides compliant documents for the purpose of transferring property in goods or possession of goods to the buyer). Second, it refers to an arrangement for effecting payment in a transaction, under which a bank acts as intermediary between the seller and buyer, a provider of finance for the applicant (if applicable) or a guarantor to the beneficiary. The expression 'documentary credit' is interchangeable with the expression 'letter of credit', but 'documentary credit' is preferred by the ICC, particularly in UCP 500. Both expressions are used in this chapter.

[5.81] The meaning of documentary credit and standby letter of credit are also defined in art 2 of UCP 500 as follows:

> For the purposes of these Articles, the expressions Documentary Credit(s); and Standby letter(s) of Credit (hereinafter referred to as Credit(s)) mean any arrangement, however named or described, whereby a bank (the Issuing Bank) acting at the request and on the instructions of a customer (the Applicant) or on its own behalf:
>
>> is to make a payment to or to the order of a third party (the Beneficiary), or is to accept and pay bills of exchange (Draft(s)) drawn by the Beneficiary; or
>>
>> authorises another bank to effect such payment, or to accept and pay such bills of exchange (Draft(s)); or
>>
>> authorises another bank to negotiate, against stipulated document(s), provided that the terms and conditions of the Credit are complied with.
>
> For the purposes of these Articles, branches of a bank in different countries are considered another bank.

The definition provided in art 2 reflects also the operation of different forms of credit arrangements and the relationships between the banks involved.

[5.82] International Commercial Law

Contracts and documentary credit

[5.82] Contracts are the foundation of the operation of a documentary credit. The mechanism of documentary credit is based on the following contractual arrangements:

- there is a contract of sale between the seller and buyer, under which the parties stipulate documentary credit as the method of payment and undertake to perform certain obligations for the purpose of effecting the documentary credit;

- there is a contract of reimbursement or similar agreement between the applicant (buyer) and issuing bank, under which the issuing bank agrees to provide a documentary credit in pursuance of the instructions of the buyer, and the applicant undertakes to reimburse the bank on performance of its obligations as agreed and compensate its loss if necessary;

- there is a contractual undertaking between the beneficiary (seller) and the issuing bank, under which the issuing bank promises or guarantees the payment to the beneficiary provided that he or she has complied with the terms of credit;

- when the issuing bank does not deal with the beneficiary directly, there would be an agent–principal arrangement between the issuing bank and a nominated bank (eg, an advising bank, a negotiating bank or a confirming bank), under which the issuing bank undertakes to reimburse and compensate the nominated bank for its services and the nominated bank undertakes to act as instructed by the issuing bank (note: the expression 'nominated bank' is preferred by the ICC); and

- if the credit is confirmed by a nominated bank, there would be a contractual undertaking between the confirming bank and the beneficiary, under which the confirming bank guarantees the payment of the credit provided that the beneficiary performs the terms of the credit.

The legal liabilities of the parties to a documentary credit are determined on the basis of these contractual arrangements. The availability of recourse is also limited by the existence of a contractual arrangement or a lack of contractual relations between the parties.[58] The same rule applies to the contractual relationships between the seller and the seller's bank, and the seller's bank and the buyer, under a letter of guarantee provided by the seller's bank to guarantee the seller's performance in relation to the payment made in advance by the buyer.[59]

---

58. For example, *JK International Pty Ltd v Standard Chartered Bank Australia Ltd* [2000] QDC 44 illustrates the contractual relationships and the use of letter of credit in international sales.

59. See *Howe Richardson Scale Co Ltd v Polimex-Cekop and National Westminster Bank Ltd* [1978] 1 Lloyd's Rep 161. In this case the seller's bank was asked by the seller to provide a letter of guarantee for the advancement of a sum of payment by the buyer. The buyer found the goods delivered did not conform with the contract description and claimed refund under the letter of guarantee against the seller's bank. The seller sought an injunction restraining its bank from making the payment. The court refused to grant an injunction on the ground that the bank has a contractual obligation towards the buyer under the guarantee and that there was no ground for restraining the bank from performing that obligation.

UCP 500 and documentary credit

[5.83] The use of documentary credit or a letter of credit is customarily 'regulated' or governed by the ICC Uniform Customs and Practice for Documentary Credits, currently UCP 500. Under art 2 of UCP 500, a credit refers either to a documentary credit or a standby letter of credit. Both can be regarded as an 'arrangement' for payment in international trade, however named or described. Under the arrangement, a bank (the issuing bank) acts, either itself or with the assistance of another bank (the advising bank), at the request, or on the instructions, of a customer (the applicant for the credit) 'to make a payment to or to the order of a third party (the "Beneficiary")', or 'to accept and pay bills of exchange (Draft(s)) drawn by the Beneficiary' upon the third party's compliance with the terms and conditions prescribed in the credit. This provision of UCP 500 may be regarded as the definition of a documentary credit.

[5.84] *Forestal Mimosa v Oriental Credit Ltd*

[1986] 1 Lloyd's Rep 329

Incorporation of ICC Uniform Customs and Practice for Documentary Credits

Facts: Forestal Mimosa sold wattle mimosa extra to Pakistani buyers. The contract of sale stipulated that the payment was to be effected by an irrevocable credit. The credit incorporated ICC Uniform Customs and Practice (UCP 400) and was confirmed by a London bank. The drafts were accepted under the credit and the payment was to be made 90 days from the day on which the bill of lading was issued. The bank later refused to make the payment on the ground, inter alia, that the buyers instructed that the drafts could be accepted only under a collection arrangement.

Decision: The English Court of Appeal (consisting of Croom Johnson and Balcombe LJJ and Sir John Megaw) held that UCP 400 governed the credit by express intention of the parties. Under UCP 400, the confirming bank or advising bank is obliged to make payment after the acceptance of the drafts.

[5.85] UCP 500 was discussed in a Hong Kong case, *Southland Rubber Co Ltd v Bank of China* [1997] HKLRD 1300. In this case, the beneficiary of an irrevocable unconfirmed letter of credit presented a bill of lading and other documents for negotiating the credit. The negotiating bank refused to accept the bill of lading under art 23(a)(i) of UCP 500,[60] alleging that the bill on its face neither indicated the name of the carrier nor bore the signature of the shipmaster or agent of the shipmaster. The letterhead of the bill showed the printed name of P T Kemah Nusasemesta. The beneficiary sued the bank for breach of UCP 500 on the ground that the letterhead indicated the name of the carrier. Pang J of the High Court of Hong Kong found in favour of the bank, observing that under

---

[60] Article 23(a)(i) of UCP 500 states as follows:

If a Credit calls for a bill of lading covering a port-to-port shipment, banks will, unless otherwise stipulated in the Credit, accept a document, however named, which:

(i) appears on its face to indicate the name of the carrier and to have been signed or otherwise authenticated by:

the carrier or a named agent for or on behalf of the carrier, or

the master or a named agent for or on behalf of the master.

[5.85] art 13a of UCP 500, the obligation placed upon the bank was not unqualified.[61] Thus, the bank's obligation was not to determine whether a document was correct, but to determine whether it on its face complied with the terms of the credit. In the view of the judge, in fulfilling the said obligation, a bank is not required to look at each set of documents presented for payment with microscopic scrutiny or as if it is embarking on a fault-finding mission; nor is the bank required to be engaged in a speculation or guessing exercise in verifying the compliance of a document. Further, his Honour held that arts 13 and 23 of UCP 500 require the name of the carrier and the signature of the shipmaster to appear in the appropriate places in the bill of lading, rejecting the beneficiary's argument that the name of the carrier was printed as the letterhead in the bill. This case interprets the meanings of arts 13(a) and 23(a)(i) of UCP 500 and illustrates the expected duties of a bank under UCP 500 in the examination of a document according to the terms of a documentary credit.

Documentary credit compared to a bill of exchange

[5.86] A documentary credit (DC) or a letter of credit (also known as L/C) is a written undertaking to a beneficiary by an issuing bank, to make a payment or payments up to a prescribed amount on certain conditions. It is provided by a bank for the benefit of the person who is named as the beneficiary of the credit. The beneficiary is entitled to claim the payment of money under the credit directly from the issuing bank, or from the confirming bank if the credit has been confirmed. A documentary credit often contains terms for payment and the beneficiary is guaranteed the payment provided that he or she complies with the terms of the credit. The terms often involve requirements for the beneficiary to present specified shipping documents or other commercial documents, such as a bill of exchange, to a specified bank for the purpose of obtaining payment under the credit.

[5.87] A bill of exchange is often drawn by the seller against the buyer, directing the buyer (or another person) to make a sum certain in a particular manner to a particular person or the holder of the bill. The bill, once accepted by the buyer (the drawee), will be enforceable in a court of law. In a collection process, acceptance of a bill of exchange is often the condition for the buyer to receive the relevant document of title, such as the bill of lading. Under a documentary credit, a bill of exchange (often known as a draft) or a similar document drawn by the beneficiary is also required for the beneficiary to claim payment. Once accepted, such a bill or draft is also enforceable by the court.

[5.88] The above discussions explain the different roles and functions played by the bill of exchange and documentary credit as means of payment in international sales. They also reflect the relationship and connection between the bill of exchange and

---

61. Article 13(a) of UCP 500 states as follows:

Banks must examine all documents stipulated in the Credit with reasonable care, to ascertain whether or not they appear, on their face, to be in compliance with the terms and conditions of the Credit. Compliance of the stipulated documents on their face with the terms and conditions of the Credit shall be determined by international standard banking practice as reflected in these Articles. Documents which appear on their face to be inconsistent with one another will be considered as not appearing on their face to be in compliance with the terms and conditions of the Credit.

documentary credit. In summary, documentary credit is a credit facility provided by a bank or financial institution to the buyer (or applicant), but the bill of exchange is an instrument drawn by the seller against the buyer (or the drawee) to ensure payment to the seller.

The operation of documentary credit

[5.89] A documentary credit is independent of the underlying contract of sale or contract of services, as the case may be. If the seller, who is often the beneficiary of a documentary credit, has satisfied the requirements of the documentary credit, but failed to perform his or her obligation satisfactorily under the underlying contract of sale, the buyer, who is often the applicant of the documentary credit, may only sue the seller for breach of contract, rather than withholding payment under the documentary credit unless a fraud can be clearly established. Similarly, if the buyer has failed to open a documentary credit as agreed, the seller would be entitled to sue the buyer under the contract of sale for a breach of contract.[62]

[5.90] The diagram illustrates a standard transaction process involving the use of a documentary credit.

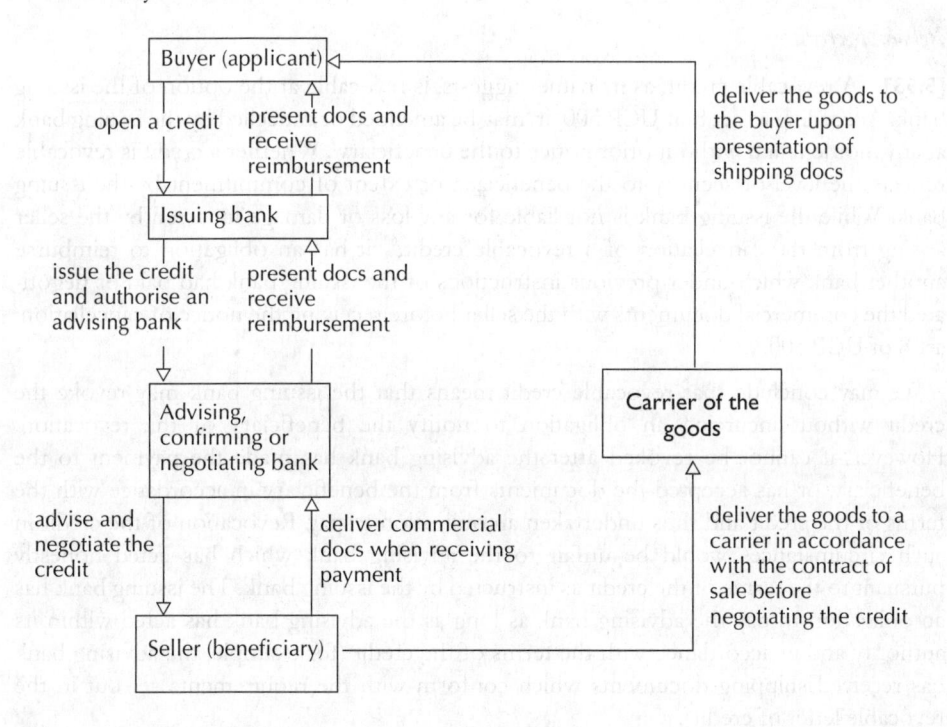

```
                    Buyer (applicant) ◄──────────────────────────┐
                         ▲  ▲                                    │
                         │  │                      deliver the goods to
       open a credit   present docs and            the buyer upon
                       receive                     presentation of
                       reimbursement               shipping docs
            ▼                                                    │
                    Issuing bank                                  │
                         ▲  ▲                                    │
                         │  │                                    │
       issue the credit  present docs and                        │
       and authorise an  receive                                 │
       advising bank     reimbursement                           │
            ▼                                                    │
                    Advising,                                    │
                    confirming or                                │
                    negotiating bank                             │
                         ▲  ▲                    Carrier of the  │
                         │  │                       goods        │
                                                      ▲          │
       advise and       deliver commercial     deliver the goods to a
       negotiate the    docs when receiving    carrier in accordance
       credit           payment                with the contract of
                                               sale before
                                               negotiating the credit
            ▼
                    Seller (beneficiary) ─────────────────────────┘
```

---

62. For example, in *Downs Investments Pty Ltd v Perwaja Steel Sdn Bhd* [2000] QSC 421, the court held the buyer to be liable under the contract of sale for its failure to open a letter of credit as agreed in the contract.

[5.91] This diagram reflects only a simple mode of transaction. It does not reflect the legal relationships between an issuing bank and an advising bank; between a beneficiary and an issuing bank; between an applicant and a beneficiary; between a seller and a carrier; and between a buyer and a carrier. The diagram should be modified accordingly when these legal relationships are involved.

Categories of documentary credits

Criteria for categorisation

[5.92] Documentary credits can be divided into various categories in accordance with different criteria. For example, according to the level of commitment by the issuing or advising bank, a credit can be revocable or irrevocable, or confirmed or unconfirmed; and in accordance with the mode of payment, a credit can be payment at sight credit, deferred payment credit, acceptance credit or negotiation credit. A credit can also be a standby letter of credit, revolving credit, packing credit, red clause credit, back-to-back and over-riding credit, or transferable credit. The categories can be identified (or defined) on the basis of either UCP 500 or common law. They are, however, neither mutually exclusive, nor wholly exhaustive. We will examine each of them in turn.

Revocable credits

[5.93] A revocable credit, as its name suggests, is revocable at the option of the issuing bank. According to art 8 of UCP 500, it 'may be amended or cancelled by the issuing bank at any moment and without prior notice to the beneficiary'. Whether a credit is revocable reflects the level of security to the beneficiary, or extent of commitment by the issuing bank. While the issuing bank is not liable for any loss or damage incurred by the seller arising from the cancellation of a revocable credit,[63] it has an obligation to reimburse another bank which under previous instructions of the issuing bank had paid or negotiated the commercial documents with the seller before receiving the notice of cancellation: art 8 of UCP 500.

We may conclude that revocable credit means that the issuing bank may revoke the credit without incurring an obligation to notify the beneficiary of the revocation. However, it cannot be revoked after the advising bank has made the payment to the beneficiary, or has accepted the documents from the beneficiary in accordance with the terms of the credit and thus undertaken an obligation to pay. Revocation of the credit in such circumstances would be unfair to the advising bank which has acted honestly pursuant to the terms of the credit as instructed by the issuing bank. The issuing bank has an obligation to pay the advising bank as long as the advising bank has acted within its authority and in accordance with the terms of the credit (for example, the advising bank has received shipping documents which conform with the requirements set out in the revocable letter of credit).

---

63. For example, *Cape Asbestos Co Ltd v Lloyd's Bank Ltd* [1921] WN 274, where the bank was held to have no legal obligation to notify the seller of the buyer's cancellation of the revocable credit.

Irrevocable credits

[5.94] In contrast to a revocable credit, an 'irrevocable Credit constitutes a definite undertaking of the Issuing Bank, provided that the stipulated documents are presented to the Nominated Bank or to the Issuing Bank and that the terms and conditions of the Credit are complied with': art 9(a) of UCP 500. Such credit is irrevocable in the sense that the issuing bank promises in the credit not to withdraw the credit, unless the seller does not comply with the terms of the credit. Neither can it be cancelled or amended without the consent of the issuing bank (when the applicant requests cancellation), the confirming bank (when the issuing bank withdraws the credit) and the beneficiary (when the credit is cancelled): art 9(d) of UCP 500.

The terms of the credit indicate the conditions or requirements for the type of shipping documents to be presented (for example, whether a clean or claused bill of lading), type of insurance cover taken by the seller (if applicable) or any certificates, reports or licences which are required in the contract of sale. Therefore, an irrevocable letter of credit indicates a contractual obligation of the issuing bank not to revoke the credit on any grounds other than those specified in the letter of credit. The 'contractual obligation' between the issuing bank and the beneficiary comes into existence through the assistance of the advising bank, which may be regarded as an agent for the issuing bank. While the law finds no difficulties in holding an issuing bank liable if it breaches the terms under a credit, there are different legal theories as to the jurisprudential basis of the contractual relationship between the issuing bank and the beneficiary; for example, whether a letter of credit should be regarded as an offer from the issuing bank, or whether the bank is estopped from denying the liability relating to what it has promised in the letter.[64]

Irrevocable straight credits

[5.95] This is a variation of an irrevocable credit. Under an irrevocable straight credit, the issuing bank only undertakes that the credit is irrevocable to the named beneficiary, provided that he or she complies with the terms of the credit. This undertaking excludes liability of the issuing bank to any person who is entitled to succeed the beneficiary under the credit. For example, banks and financial institutions may on the basis of the availability of a credit purchase a beneficiary's draft and documents at discount before the maturity of the credit, and the beneficiary may want to sell the draft and commercial documents at discount in order to speed up cash flow. The purchaser of the draft and commercial documents is entitled to act as an agent of the named beneficiary to claim the benefit of the credit. An irrevocable straight credit is intended to make an irrevocable credit revocable against any person who purchases the draft and commercial documents from the beneficiary.

However, an irrevocable straight credit usually does not expressly say that the credit is revocable against any person who derives his or her entitlement from the beneficiary. Instead, it often specifies that the credit expires at the counters of the issuing bank when the documents are presented. Alternatively, it may say that the presentation of the draft

---

64. For a detailed discussion of the relevant theories, see Penn, Shea and Arora, *The Law and Practice of International Banking*, London, Sweet & Maxwell, 1987, pp 294–303.

[5.95] and documents should be made at the office of the issuing bank on or before an expiry date.[65] By imposing restrictions on the time and location of presentation, the issuing bank intends to prevent any third party, who derived his or her title from the beneficiary, relying on the irrevocability of the credit.

Irrevocable negotiation credits

[5.96] This is an irrevocable credit of a different kind. In contrast to an irrevocable straight credit, an irrevocable negotiation credit expressly extends the irrevocability of the credit to any person who obtains the beneficiary's draft and documents through negotiation or purchase. This is usually done through the inclusion of a clause in the credit, stating that the issuing bank 'agrees with' any third party holder of the draft and documents as stipulated in the credit not to revoke the credit on or before an expiry date.[66] This arrangement is consistent with art 48 of UCP 500, which states that a credit (including an irrevocable credit) is transferable only when the issuing bank so stated expressly.

Confirmed and unconfirmed credits

[5.97] The expressions 'confirmed credit' and 'unconfirmed credit' indicate whether a credit has or has not been confirmed by a nominated bank. If the credit has been confirmed, the confirming bank undertakes a legal obligation to pay the seller provided that the seller presents the commercial documents in compliance with the terms and conditions of the credit. A credit can be confirmed by an advising bank at the request of the issuing bank, which does so under the instructions of the applicant who may be obliged to do so under the contract of sale. The beneficiary can also request the advising bank to confirm a credit as a condition for presenting commercial documents. In such a case, the advising bank will seek approval from the issuing bank, which in turn will seek authority from the applicant. Confirmation of a revocable credit normally does not arise as an issue, because an issuing bank which is prepared to authorise confirmation of a credit would have issued an irrevocable credit. However, in theory there is no barrier to a revocable credit — by agreement of the seller and buyer — being made 'irrevocable' through the confirmation of the advising bank.

[5.98] A confirmation of an irrevocable credit would give the seller double security and convenience of recourse against either the confirming bank or the issuing bank in an appropriate forum. The beneficiary is able to sue the confirming bank for non-payment provided that he or she has fulfilled his or her obligations under the terms of the credit. The confirming bank is able to seek reimbursement from the issuing bank pursuant to the agreement between them, provided that it has complied with the terms of the agreement. The liability between the confirming bank and issuing bank is based on the authority to confirm the credit given by the issuing bank.

[5.99] The liability of the confirming bank is illustrated by the case of *Hamzeh Malas & Sons v British Imex Industries Ltd* [1958] 2 QB 127. In this case, the Midland Bank in London

---

65. Busto, *ICC Guide to Documentary Credit Operations for the UCP 500*, Paris, ICC Publishing SA, 1994, p 37.
66. Id, p 39.

was instructed by the buyers (plaintiffs) of the reinforced steel rods to open two confirmed letters of credit in favour of the sellers (defendants) for two instalment deliveries of the goods. The first delivery was found unsatisfactory and the buyers sought an injunction to bar the sellers from negotiating the second letter of credit. The English Court of Appeal refused to grant an injunction on the ground that the confirmed letter of credit imposed upon the bank an absolute duty to pay. The same view was held in *Gian Singh & Co Ltd v Banque de L'Indochine* [1974] 1 WLR 1234 and *United City Merchants (Investments) Ltd v Royal Bank of Canada* [1982] 2 WLR 1039. The rationale behind these cases is that a confirmed letter of credit creates an irrevocable obligation to pay, provided that the beneficiary has fulfilled his or her obligations under the terms of the credit. If a seller (beneficiary) has breached the terms of a contract of sale, but not the terms of the credit (because the terms may be different under these documents), the confirming bank (which has legal recourse against the issuing bank) is not able to refuse to perform the obligation to pay. The buyer's remedy against the seller's breach of a contract of sale is to sue the seller under the contract of sale.

[5.100] There is a doctrine of strict compliance. This doctrine (see **[5.131]**) means that not only must the beneficiary present the commercial documents in the manner or form prescribed by the terms of the credit, but the advising bank (and issuing bank too) must also strictly enforce its terms when accepting the commercial documents from the beneficiary and making the payment under the credit. It follows that a confirming bank may refuse the payment if the documents presented appear to be inconsistent with the stipulation of the credit. By the same token, if a confirming or advising bank accepts commercial documents which apparently do not conform with the terms of the credit, the issuing bank is entitled to refuse to reimburse the bank. The doctrine of strict compliance should be read with a bank's duty of reasonable care and diligence. This means that the doctrine of strict compliance is satisfied as long as the documents concerned appear to be conforming with the terms of the credit (ostensible conformity) and the confirming or advising bank is not aware of any fraud in the documents.

Standby credits

[5.101] A standby credit (or standby letter of credit) is a particular form of documentary credit, which functions as a security or back-up to ensure the beneficiary will have remedy against the issuing bank in case the applicant fails to pay or to perform a contractual obligation.[67] This type of credit can be used in the following ways:

- the issuing bank undertakes to repay money borrowed by the applicant if the applicant fails to do so;
- the issuing bank undertakes to repay money advanced to or for the account of the applicant if the applicant fails to repay it;
- the issuing bank undertakes to be responsible for a particular debt incurred by the applicant;

---

67. The use of a standby credit is illustrated by the case of *Asian Century Holdings Inc v Fleuris Pty Ltd* [2000] WASC 169.

- the issuing bank undertakes to make a sum of money available if the applicant fails to pay it under the contract of sale; and
- the issuing bank undertakes to make a sum of money available to the beneficiary if a particular person (usually the applicant) fails to perform his or her specific obligations under a contract.[68]

[5.102] The operation of a standby credit can be described as follows:

> The standby credit is intended to protect the beneficiary in case of default of the other party to the (underlying) contract. Consequently in a standby credit the required documents need not include the transport documents but this type of credit may be activated by a document of any description, eg, a demand by the beneficiary or a statement by him that the other party is in default. The standby letter of credit is often functionally similar in effect to a bank guarantee.[69]

A standby credit is often independent of the contract of sale between the seller and buyer. The beneficiary (either a buyer or a seller) may claim payment under a standby credit without proving his or her entitlement under the underlying contract of sale as long as he or she has complied with terms of the standby credit. For example, in *Bachmann Pty Ltd v BHP Power New Zealand Ltd* [1998] VSCA 40, the letters of credit, which was meant to be a security provided by the supplier, permitted the purchaser to demand payment under the credit by furnishing a statement that the supplier had failed to perform the underlying contract. The court enforced this term and left the dispute arising from the underlying contract to be settled by an arbitrator as the parties had agreed in the underlying contract.

Revolving credits

[5.103] The expression 'revolving credits' suggests the revolving feature of this type of credit. The credit can 'revolve' continuously to maintain the credit limit at a fixed amount after each withdrawal, or remain effective for a specified time. For example, a revolving credit may state that a fixed sum of money is available for a beneficiary to withdraw every month for a period of 12 months; and the beneficiary can claim payment under the credit every time a transaction has been completed pursuant to the terms of the contract of sale. The credit will be instantly or periodically renewed after each withdrawal, depending on whether it is cumulative. This type of credit is suitable for parties who have regular business dealings. The fixed amount of the credit is the maximum sum available for the seller to withdraw in each transaction upon his or her compliance with the terms of the credit. The credit reduces the amount of paperwork for each transaction between the parties involved.

Packing credits

[5.104] A packing credit, also known as an anticipatory credit, is a variation of a negotiation credit. The 'alteration' is made in favour of the beneficiary.

---

68. Sometimes, a letter of credit can also be used for this purpose. In *Bachmann Pty Ltd v BHP Power New Zealand Ltd* [1998] VSCA 40, the supplier of equipment was requested to make two irrevocable letters of credit available to the purchaser against non-performance of the supplier. In such cases, the 'letter of credit' should probably be the 'standby credit' as an appropriate title.
69. Schmitthoff, note 24 above, pp 429–30.

The credit is payable at a time prior to the shipment of the goods, and against a document other than a transport document. The bank is instructed to pay the purchase price, or part of it, on production of, for example, a warehouse receipt (evidencing that the goods are in existence) or a forwarder's certificate of receipt (FCR) (affirming that the goods have been received for shipment or have been shipped), or an air dispatch registered post receipt.[70]

This type of credit is a means of financing the business activity of the seller to enable him or her to receive money even before delivering the goods to a carrier. The word 'packing' probably refers to the stage in the export of goods when the goods are being packed in a warehouse for the purpose of delivering them to the buyer. The credit is similar to a red clause credit. The difference between them, if any, is merely a matter of terminology.

Red clause credits

[5.105] The expression 'red clause' means the seller is in deficit in using the credit, and comes from the fact that this type of clause was originally written in red ink to draw attention to its unique nature. This type of credit allows the beneficiary (seller) to draw on the credit for the purpose of paying his or her suppliers. A red clause credit may take various forms, of which a packing credit is one. The ability of the seller to draw from the credit before delivering the shipping documents (in fact before shipping the goods) is the essential feature of the red clause credit. Thus, it is a method for the seller to finance his or her business by borrowing (or getting) money from the buyer, who may have to pay the money in order to obtain the goods or services from the seller.[71]

Back-to-back credits

[5.106] The nature of a back-to-back credit, as indicated by its name, is that the subsequent credit is issued on the basis of the previous one. In such transactions, a bank agrees to issue a credit at the request of a seller, who is the beneficiary of a credit drawn by a buyer, by taking the credit opened in the seller's favour as the security for issuing the new credit in which the seller is the applicant. For example, X (buyer) may provide a credit in favour of Y (seller), who in turn may provide a credit which is based on X's credit to Z (seller's supplier), who may in turn provide a credit identical to Y's credit to W for the goods to be ultimately sold to X. A chain of contracts of sale can be formed on the basis of the credit initially provided by X. In such a chain of contracts, a seller obtains a credit from his or her buyer both to secure the transaction with the buyer and to finance the purchase from a previous supplier. Thus, a string of contracts of sale can be entered into for the same purpose and the whole chain is virtually based on the credit provided by the ultimate buyer of the goods. This type of transaction is illustrated in *Ian Stach Ltd v Baker Bosley Ltd* [1958] 2 QB 130, where the buyers who failed to open a credit because of a failure to perform by their sub-buyers were held liable to the loss sustained by the previous sellers. The credit of the ultimate buyer is called overriding credit.

Unlike other categories of credit, a back-to-back credit does not dictate the mode and manner in which the payment is to be made. Instead, it can be provided in different terms

---

70. Id, p 431.
71. The use of red clause credit was illustrated by the case of *United Fisheries Ltd v Papasavas & Co* [2001] VSC 86, although the case was largely concerned with an action against a firm of solicitors.

[5.106] as long as the credit provided by each of the applicants is identical or compatible. A back-to-back credit implies the manner in which the legal relationships between the beneficiaries and applicants are established, rather than the method in which the payment to one of the beneficiaries is made. Back-to-back credits are also known as countervailing credits.

Transferable credits

[5.107] A transferable credit is a credit which is expressly transferable and negotiable. For example, art 48(a) of UCP 500 defines a transferable credit as follows:

> A transferable Credit is a Credit under which the Beneficiary (First Beneficiary) may request the bank authorised to pay, incur a deferred payment undertaking, accept or negotiate (the Transferring Bank), or in the case of a freely negotiable Credit, the bank specifically authorised in the Credit as a Transferring Bank, to make the Credit available in whole or in part to one or more other Beneficiary(ies) (Second Beneficiary(ies)).

[5.108] A transferable credit allows the beneficiary to transfer the benefit under the credit to another person for the purpose of, for example, financing a purchase or repaying a debt. A beneficiary under a transferable credit is able to pay the transaction with his or her supplier(s) by transferring part or the whole of the credit to them. Because credit is usually not negotiable in the same sense as a bill of exchange, art 48(b) of UCP 500 requires that a transferable credit must be expressly designated as 'transferable'. The word 'transferable' cannot be substituted by other expressions, such as 'divisible', 'fractionable', 'assignable' or 'transmissible'. These requirements must be complied with if the parties choose UCP 500 as the governing law of the credit.

[5.109] A transferable credit differs from a 'back-to-back' credit in the fact that each beneficiary under a 'back-to-back' credit has to open, in favour of his or her own supplier, a new credit which is identical to the one made in his or her own favour, but a beneficiary under a transferable credit may transfer the credit opened in his or her favour to his or her supplier(s) directly.

[5.110] *Bank Negara Indonesia 1946 v Lariza (Singapore) Private Ltd*

[1988] 1 Lloyd's Rep 407

Bank's right to refuse a request for transfer of a transferable irrevocable sight letter of credit

Facts: Lariza was the beneficiary of a transferable irrevocable sight letter of credit issued by Bank Negara in 1980. The credit was subject to UCP 400. Lariza requested the bank to transfer part of the credit to one of its own suppliers of palm oil for the purpose of fulfilling its obligations to the supplier under the relevant contract of sale. The bank refused to do so. Consequently, Lariza was ordered to pay damages to its supplier for breach of contract. Lariza sued the bank for breach of contract under the transferable credit and sought damages and indemnity against the bank. The trial judge gave judgment for Lariza. The bank appealed to the Privy Council.

Decision: The credit was subject to UCP 400, which provided that the transferability of a transferable credit was subject to the bank's consent as to the specific manner and extent of a transfer. No such consent was given in the present case. The bank was thus not liable.

Note: The compatible provision in UCP 500 is art 48(c).

Categorising credits according to instructions for payment

[5.111] Credits may also be distinguished on the basis of the instructions for payment. Four types of credit can be distinguished on this basis.

Payment at sight credits

[5.112] This means that the advising bank should pay, or make an arrangement for payment with, the beneficiary upon his or her presentation of the compliant documents. Even if the payment under a sight credit is not made immediately after the presentation of the conforming documents, the advising bank undertakes an obligation to pay at 'sight' of the documents when it accepts the documents. A payment at sight credit can be either revocable or irrevocable.

Deferred payment credits

[5.113] This means that the presentation of the stipulated commercial documents and payment of the price are not simultaneous. The advising bank is instructed to make the payment out of the credit at a 'deferred date' after a stipulated event, for example, issuing of the bill of lading, or presentation of the commercial documents to the advising bank. This mode of payment is normally agreed upon by the parties to the contract of sale and the advising bank only performs its obligation towards the issuing bank, which sets out the terms according to the instructions of the applicant (buyer). This mode of payment differs from the sight credit in that the money under a sight credit is payable as soon as the conforming documents have been presented by the beneficiary (seller). However, a deferred payment credit does not necessarily mean that the advising bank can refuse to make payment at any time before the deferred date of payment. Under UCP 500, acceptance of the required documents by a bank is usually unconditional unless the bank has accepted them under reserve or against an indemnity as permitted by art 14(d) of UCP 500. The common terms for a deferred date credit are, for example, 'payable 60 (45 or 90) days after the issue of the bill of lading', or 'payable 45 (60 or 90) days after the presentation of the commercial documents'.

Acceptance credits

[5.114] A credit may state that drafts drawn by the beneficiary on the issuing bank will be accepted and paid at their maturity. This type of credit can be called 'acceptance credit'. This means that the issuing bank undertakes a liability to pay the beneficiary as indicated in the credit. After a draft has been accepted, the beneficiary is usually able to negotiate the accepted draft with another bank or financial institution before its maturity for the purpose of receiving a cash advance, and the purchaser of the draft is entitled to claim the benefit of the draft at its maturity from the issuing bank (or a bank authorised by the issuing bank).

Negotiation credits

[5.115] A negotiation credit means that a bank is authorised under the terms of the credit to negotiate the draft and commercial documents from the beneficiary (seller) before the maturity of the credit. This is the same as saying that the credit is negotiable.

[5.115]

Under such credit, the seller wishing to obtain finance before the maturity of the credit may ask the negotiating bank to advance the money available under the credit to him or her by either discounting or transferring the relevant draft and commercial documents. A draft can be transferred (discounted) at a price lower than its face value. In addition, it is discounted if the seller pays for the bank's interest or commission (which is usually payable by the buyer — applicant of the credit), but it is purchased if the seller receives the face value of the bill and the buyer pays for the bank's interest and commission.

[5.116] Negotiation credit sometimes also means that the negotiating bank is allowed to advance money to the seller on security of a draft (bill of exchange). The essence of this type of credit is the authority from the issuing bank to allow the negotiating bank (which may or may not be an advising bank) to make an advance (if necessary) to the seller even before the seller has delivered the goods (or perhaps before he or she has purchased the goods). The negotiating bank and advising bank would be two different banks, if the seller asks his or her own bank to negotiate a bill of exchange on his or her behalf with the advising bank. A seller may use this method to finance his or her purchase.

Effect of UCP 500 and categories of credits

[5.117] The preceding categorisation of documentary credits is a legal categorisation. Contract law does not provide criteria for the categorisation of credits. The only international rules which provide some descriptions of documentary credits are UCP 500, which applies to a credit by express or implied intention of the parties. UCP 500 defines the legal effect of certain types of credits, such as revocable or irrevocable, confirmed or unconfirmed, and transferable or non-transferable. Variations are made and innovations are created by banks in the application of UCP 500. Again, it must be pointed out that UCP 500 represents the established customs and usage, and it is binding as a term of a contract or credit. Parties may override and vary the effect of the provisions of UCP 500 when such alterations are allowed under UCP 500, but UCP 500 prohibits a substantial alteration of its provisions if such alteration renders the provisions inoperative.[72] Parties have the option of not applying UCP 500 to any credit.

[5.118] Partial payment under a documentary credit may be regarded as an innovative use of the credit by the parties. Under such an arrangement, the beneficiary (seller) and the applicant (buyer) may agree that the beneficiary receives a portion, for example, 70 per cent or 80 per cent or more, of the full payment under a documentary credit and that the balance will be used as a security for the buyer to ensure the conformity of the goods delivered. Nothing is wrong about this if this is only a contractual arrangement.

---

72. Subjecting the obligation to pay under a documentary credit to the performance of a contract may be regarded as contradictory to one of the principles of the UCP500, ie, separation of the underlying contract from the operation of credit. However, the effect of such term in any given case is wholly dependent on the view of the court handling the case. In *Habib Bank Ltd v Bank of South Australia* [1977] SASC 6309, the court seemed to have upheld a term of the credit, which permitted the issuing bank to refuse to make payment to the beneficiary within 90 days of the bill of lading if the buyer gave a notice of rejection of the goods. Such a term is controversial, however, because it links up the bank's obligation to pay with the performance of the underlying contract, and thus undermines the essence of the credit by treating it merely as a documentary transaction.

However, the operation of a documentary credit is, in almost all cases, subject to UCP 500, which has set out the uniform rules for the operation of a credit. Thus, the validity of such an arrangement, or the legality of a documentary credit subject to the arrangement of partial payment, has arisen as an issue for the court of law to decide.

[5.119] Partial payment was an issue in *Harlow & Jones Ltd v American Express Bank Ltd* [1990] 2 Lloyd's Rep 343, and recently in *Rudolph Robinson Steel Co v Nissho Iwai Hong Kong Corp Ltd* [1998] HKLRD 966. In the latter case, the High Court of Hong Kong was asked to determine whether the arrangement was consistent with or valid under the established mechanism of documentary credit. In this case, Rudolph Robinson Steel Co (Rudolph) was an American company. In May 1995, Rudolph concluded a contract with Filon World Trade Company Ltd (Filon) to sell a quantity of galvanised coils to the latter. An LC was opened to effect the payment. In July 1995, Nissho Iwai Hong Kong Corp Ltd (Nissho), which was to receive a commission of 1.45 per cent of the purchase price from Filon, applied on behalf of Filon to Sanwa Bank for the issue of an LC in favour of Rudolph. The credit expressly stated that it was governed by UCP 500 and that its expiry date was 12 August 1995. On 17 August 1995, Corestates Bank intended to negotiate the credit on behalf of Rudolph and sent the relevant documents to Sanwa Bank for payment under the credit. Corestates Bank discovered a number of discrepancies in the documents and referred them to Sanwa Bank for approval. Sanwa Bank sent a notice of refusal on 23 August 1995 to Corestates Bank and advised that it was seeking instructions from Nissho Iwai. Rudolph, Nissho Iwai and Filon held a number of negotiations. On 15 September 1995, Nissho Iwai instructed Sanwa Bank to offer to Rudolph a payment of 80 per cent of the credit sum, and the balance to be paid later on a collection basis upon the receipt of a specified survey report. Sanwa Bank did so on 18 September 1995. On the same day, Filon instructed Rudolph to accept the arrangement. On 19 September 1995, Corestates Bank informed Sanwa Bank of Rudolph's acceptance of the arrangement and the payment was made accordingly. On 3 October 1995, Rudolph submitted the specified survey report and demanded payment of the balance on collection basis. On 17 October 1995, Sanwa Bank informed Corestates Bank that due to a serious quality problem in the goods delivered the balance would be settled upon solution of the problem. Rudolph subsequently sued Sanwa Bank and Nissho Iwai for the unpaid balance.

The court noted the ambiguous meaning of the expression 'on collection basis' or 'for collection', and the fact that the expression may either refer to a process outside the existing documentary credit or a process within the documentary credit. In the former sense, a discrepant document and relevant financial document may be sent to the applicant (buyer) for direct payment. In the latter sense, the expression may suggest a process of sending a discrepant document to the issuing bank for specific approval. If the expression is used in the former sense, the parties form their relationship under the collection arrangement outside the documentary credit concerned. If the expression is used in the latter sense, the parties form their contractual relationship within the frame of the credit, thus amounting to a modification to the original terms of the credit. In this case, the court took the view that the parties had formed a new contractual relationship outside the credit arrangement, and thus that Sanwa Bank was not liable to Rudolph. The court

[5.119]

examined the meaning of credit as defined in art 2 of UCP 500 (see **[5.83]**), and concluded that the partial payment arrangement or the arrangement for payment based on collection basis did not fit into the mechanics of a letter of credit transaction. The court observed (at 977) that once the documents are accepted by the bank, the shipping documents will be released to the applicant, and the bank is contractually bound to pay the beneficiary. This being the framework in which documentary credit operates, it is inherently contrary to the nature of a credit transaction to have truncated presentation of documents in which part of the price will be paid upon release of all the title documents and the balance to be paid upon presentation of a future document. Accordingly, the court (at 977) concluded that there is no evidence that letters of credit operate in this manner. Further, the court stated (at 977–8) that since Rudolph had argued that Sanwa Bank should pay the balance on collection basis under the credit, Rudolph must justify that this arrangement, which is contrary to the normal mode of operation of documentary credits, is nonetheless within the context of the letter of credit. Having determined that the expression 'on collection basis' in the present case meant an arrangement of payment outside the documentary credit, the court held that there was a contractual relationship between Rudolph and Nissho Iwai because the latter had made an offer through Sanwa Bank to the former to release the payment of the balance upon the receipt of the specified report. Accordingly, the court ordered Nissho Iwai to pay Rudolph directly a sum equivalent to the unpaid balance of the credit plus interest on the sum.

This case illustrates the dilemma in providing legal solutions to certain commercial arrangements which are made solely for the purpose of commercial expediency and convenience without any regard or concern to legal principles at all. There is not much point comparing whether it is more appropriate to enforce the plaintiff's claim in the present case within the frame of the credit, or as the court did, on the basis of a contractual relationship or a promise outside the credit. There are commercial practices, but no uniform law as the law sanctioned by a court in a common law jurisdiction or by a lawmaker in any country. UCP 500 is codified commercial usage. It is enforceable in a particular case either as part of the contractual terms of a credit or commercial usage or customs. An act inconsistent with UCP 500 may constitute a breach of contractual terms or the established commercial usage, but it is not a breach of any formal law.

Thus, whether the expression 'on collection basis' is allowed under UCP 500 is meaningful only if the parties have expressly stated that the credit concerned had the meaning of credit as defined in UCP 500. In the present case, it may as well be argued that the offer made by Sanwa Bank on 18 September 1995 was an offer to modify the terms of the documentary credit, and consequently, the balance had to be paid under the existing credit. Such modification is perfectly acceptable under art 2 of UCP 500, as long as the issuing bank expressly informs the beneficiary of the terms of credit, no matter what they are. Therefore, the court in the present case, with respect, appears to be incorrect in stating that the arrangement in question did not fit within the definition of credit under art 2 of UCP 500, or did not fit in the mechanics of credit. Article 2 does not have anything to do with the forms in which the payment is made, or the terms and conditions under which the payment or payments are paid. Since the parties can make all sorts of arrangements for the purpose of effecting payment under a documentary credit, there is hardly any mechanics of credit at all. The finding of the court in the present case did not affect the result, because either way, the beneficiary has been paid. In fact, everything is based on contract in a documentary credit and also in the present case. Only the intention of the parties to form a contract outside the credit or to modify the contractual relationship under the credit counts. In the absence of such an express intention or an implied intention supported by convincing evidence, the court of law has to do the best it can by exercising its discretion in a reasonable manner to offer a legal solution to the practical issue created by the parties. Thus, it can be argued that neither *Harlow & Jones Ltd v American Express Bank Ltd* [1990] 2 Lloyd's Rep 343, nor *Rudolph Robbinson Steel Co v Nissho Iwai Hong Kong Corp Ltd* [1998] 1 HKLRD 966, provides a convincing precedent for determining the parties' rights and liabilities in an arrangement for partial payment based on collection basis under a credit. By the end, a court has to regard a documentary credit as a contract and deal with the issues arising from a documentary credit accordingly.

Basic rules governing documentary credits

'Privity' of a documentary credit

[5.120] Given that a credit can be a contract between a beneficiary and an issuing bank, we may use the expression 'privity' to describe the relationships between the beneficiary and the issuing, or sometimes the confirming, bank. 'Privity' has two meanings:

- First, a documentary credit is independent of the contract of sale between the seller (beneficiary) and buyer (applicant), even though the terms of the contract often dictate the terms of the credit: art 3(a) of UCP 500. A dispute arising from the contract of sale cannot affect the issuing bank's obligation to pay under an irrevocable credit.[73]

- Second, a 'beneficiary can in no case avail himself of the contractual relationships existing between the banks or between the Applicant for the credit and the Issuing Bank': art 3(b) of UCP 500. If an issuing bank breaches the contract for opening a credit (other than the credit itself) entered into between a buyer and the bank, the seller cannot sue the bank directly even if the contract breached has incorporated the terms of contract of sale between the seller and the buyer. This again suggests that a documentary credit operates between only the beneficiary and issuing bank, or the beneficiary and confirming bank, as the case may be.

The privity rule suggests that the rights and obligations of the beneficiary and the banks are defined and restricted by the terms and conditions of the credit.

Liabilities of banks

[5.121] Banks' liabilities to the beneficiary: The banks concerned here are the issuing bank and advising bank. An issuing bank undertakes an obligation to pay the sum stipulated in an irrevocable credit under the condition that the beneficiary has fulfilled his or her obligations pursuant to the terms of the credit: art 9(a) of UCP 500. By the same token, a confirming bank undertakes an obligation to pay the sum prescribed in the credit under the

---

73. For example, *Discount Records Ltd v Barclays Bank Ltd* [1975] 1 WLR 315, and *Power Curber International Ltd v National Bank of Kuwait* [1981] 1 WLR 1233.

[5.121]

condition that the beneficiary has fulfilled the terms of the credit: art 9(b) of UCP 500. However, an advising bank which has not confirmed the credit does not have an obligation to pay unless it has accepted the compliant documents from the seller. The same applies to the liability of an issuing bank in relation to a revocable letter of credit. Neither the issuing bank nor the advising bank is liable to pay under a revocable credit, unless the credit has been negotiated or the stipulated documents accepted: art 8(b) of UCP 500.

[5.122] *Michael Doyle & Associates Ltd v Bank of Montreal*

(1984) 11 DLR (4th) 496

An advising bank is obliged to pay after 'acceptance'

Facts: The Bank of Montreal acted as the advising bank on behalf of a Dutch Bank. Michael Doyle, which sold frozen herring fillets to a Dutch buyer, was the beneficiary under a letter of credit. The fillets were shipped in four instalments. After the acceptance of the draft (which was payable 45 days after shipment) and commercial documents for the third delivery, the buyer became dissatisfied with the quality of the fillets and asked the issuing bank to seek a ground to stop the payment under the credit. The Dutch bank discovered that the health certificate for the third delivery did not comply with the requirement. The seller resubmitted a health certificate, but the certificate was ultimately rejected by the Dutch bank for late submission. The Dutch bank refused to pay for the third instalment. The Bank of Montreal refused to make payment to Michael Doyle, despite the draft and documents (including the non-conforming one) having been accepted by it.

Decision: The Court of Appeal of British Columbia (consisting of Carrothers, Lambert and Esson JJA) held that the bank undertook a liability to pay the draft after the acceptance.

[5.123] *Aotearoa International Ltd v Westpac Banking Corp*

[1984] 2 NZLR 34

Whether a bank which filled in a bill of exchange on behalf of a beneficiary without his or her appropriate authorisation has recourse against the beneficiary

Facts: Aotearoa International was the seller in a contract for the sale of waste paper to Harayana Paper Mills of India. Harayana asked the United Commercial Bank of New Delhi to issue an irrevocable letter of credit in favour of Aotearoa. The credit was issued in the form of a telex and addressed to the ANZ Bank in Auckland, which was instructed to advise Aotearoa of the availability of the credit. The ANZ Bank advised Aotearoa of the availability of the credit by sending it a letter of advice which, however, omitted certain terms of the credit issued by the United Commercial Bank. Two officers of Aotearoa took the letter of advice and a number of commercial documents to its own bank — the Commercial Bank of Australia (Westpac, the negotiating bank) — to negotiate the 'credit' issued by the United Commercial Bank of New Delhi. One of the officers of Aotearoa signed a blank bill of exchange in the bank, which was meant to be filled in by the bank for the purpose of negotiating the credit. An officer of the bank made a typing mistake when filling in the blank bill of exchange. He then filled in another one and had the bill signed by another officer of the bank. The bank subsequently negotiated the credit (paid Aotearoa) on the basis of the ANZ's letter of advice and sent the bill of exchange and documents directly to the issuing bank for reimbursement. The request for reimbursement was refused by the issuing bank on the grounds that the freight was not paid (although the bill of lading was stamped as 'freight prepaid') and supply of the quality certificate was late. The negotiating bank subsequently debited a sum of money from Aotearoa's account kept by it. Whether the bank had recourse against Aotearoa was at issue.

> **Decision:** Tompkins J of the High Court of New Zealand held that the bank had no recourse against Aotearoa for two reasons. First, the bill of exchange was neither signed nor authorised to be signed by Aotearoa and thus was invalid. Second, the bank, as a negotiating bank, was not entitled to seek indemnity from Aotearoa because it had neither a valid draft nor any undertaking of indemnity from Aotearoa.

♦

[5.124] Banks' liability to the applicant: While the term 'banks' here refers to both the issuing and advising bank, the 'liability' concerned is the liability of the issuing bank to the applicant for the credit — that is, the buyer in the underlying contract of sale. The main issue is whether the banks are liable to the applicant when the commercial documents or bills of exchange which appear to be consistent with the terms and conditions of the credit are not genuine. Article 13 of UCP 500 requires that banks 'must examine all documents stipulated in the Credit with reasonable care, to ascertain whether or not they appear, on their face, to be in compliance with the terms and conditions of the Credit'. The banks' responsibility is limited to the ostensible conformity of the documents. If the documents accepted by an advising bank do not appear to be consistent with the terms of credit, the advising bank is liable to the issuing bank, although the advising bank is not directly accountable to the applicant (buyer). The liability of the issuing bank to the applicant, as well as that of the advising bank to the issuing bank, is subject to the test of reasonable care and good faith, and ostensible conformity. Therefore, banks incur no liabilities to the applicant if an apparently satisfactory document turns out to be false or defective (art 15 of UCP 500), provided that the banks have acted in good faith and taken reasonable care.

[5.125] Banks are not liable to the applicant for the risk, loss or damage incurred, under the instructions of the applicant, by utilising a nominated bank's services: art 18 of UCP 500. This rule applies to the implementation of the applicant's specific instructions only. For example, if an advising bank which was nominated by the applicant did not perform its duty properly, the issuing bank is not liable to the applicant, although the issuing bank is able to minimise the loss by taking legal action under the contract against the advising bank for its misconduct, negligence or omission. This principle is probably based on the agent–principal relationship. If the agent (the issuing bank) acts within the authority of the principal (applicant), the principal is not allowed to hold the agent liable for performing the authorised act.

[5.126] Liability between the banks: Liability between the banks is twofold and consists of:

- the issuing bank's liability towards the advising bank; and
- the advising bank's liability towards the issuing bank.

The terms of credit bind both the issuing and advising banks. In the case of a revocable credit, the issuing bank is bound to reimburse the advising bank which has paid or undertaken to pay the beneficiary, who has presented the required documents in accordance with the terms of credit before the credit was cancelled.

[5.126] International Commercial Law

Similarly, if the issuing bank asks the advising bank to confirm the credit, the issuing bank is liable to reimburse the advising bank's payment to the beneficiary made under the confirmed credit. The issuing bank has a general obligation to reimburse the advising bank provided that the advising bank acts within its authority and in accordance with the terms of the credit. The advising bank also has an obligation to take reasonable care to ensure that the documents received appear on their face to be consistent with the terms of the credit.

[5.127] *Bankers Trust Co v State Bank of India*

[1991] 2 Lloyd's Rep 443

Liability between the issuing and confirming bank in case of non-conforming documents

Facts: Bankers Trust (plaintiff) was the issuing bank of an irrevocable credit, which was confirmed by the State Bank of India (defendant). The credit was issued in 1988 for the sale of steel plates from India to England and was subject to UCP 400. UCP 400 required the issuing bank to reject non-conforming documents within a reasonable time and give notice to the negotiating bank accordingly.

The State Bank of India forwarded the documents to Bankers Trust after the shipment of the goods. Bankers Trust received the documents on 21 September 1988 and discovered a number of discrepancies between the documents and the terms of the credit. It then sent the documents to the buyer for comment and ultimately informed the State Bank of India of its rejection of the non-conforming documents on 30 September 1988. The State Bank of India rejected Bankers Trust's claim and refused to reimburse Bankers Trust, which subsequently commenced legal proceedings against the State Bank of India. The validity of the Bankers Trust's claim rested on whether it had complied with the relevant requirements of UCP 400. The trial court held that Bankers Trust did not comply with the requirements of UCP 400. Bankers Trust appealed.

Decision: The English Court of Appeal held that UCP 400 required the issuing bank to examine the documents as they were and did not allow the issuing bank to send them to the buyer for the purpose of identifying the discrepancies. Bankers Trust failed to comply with the requirement to give timely notice to the negotiating bank of the alleged discrepancies and was therefore not entitled to claim reimbursement from the State Bank of India.

[5.128] The apparent conformity of the documents is a criterion used by an issuing bank to determine whether the documents remitted by an advising bank are on their face consistent with the terms of the credit. The issuing bank can reject the documents on the basis of their apparent non-conformity, even though the advising bank has paid the beneficiary. In such a case, the issuing bank will not reimburse the advising or confirming bank for the payment made upon the apparently non-conforming documents. However, if the documents are found on their face to be inconsistent with the terms of the credit, the issuing bank should notify the advising bank and the beneficiary within a reasonable time after receiving the documents: art 14(b) of UCP 500. If the documents are subsequently proved on their face to be inconsistent with the terms of the credit, the advising bank would have breached its obligation to the issuing bank.

[5.129] *Hing Yip Hing Fat Co Ltd v Daiwa Bank Ltd*

[1991] 1 HKC 383

UCP 400 (replaced by UCP 500); bank's liability; manner for rejecting documents under UCP 400

Facts: Hing Yip Hing Fat Co Ltd (Hing) sold to Cheergoal Industries Ltd (Cheergoal) 400 metric tonnes of ferrosilicon for a sum of US$376,000. Daiwa Bank opened a letter of credit in August 1988 at the request of Cheergoal in favour of Hing. The credit was subject to UCP 400. Nanyang Commercial Bank (NCB), which was the seller's bank, acted as the negotiating bank on behalf of Hing. NCB presented the relevant documents for negotiation to Daiwa Bank on 9 September 1988. Daiwa Bank refused to make payment under the credit on the ground that there were discrepancies between the documents presented and documents required. One of the discrepancies was that the credit required the presentment of 'certificate of quality/quantity', but the negotiating bank presented 'an inspection certificate of quality/quantity'.

Daiwa Bank notified NCB of the discrepancies and the rejection on 14 September 1988 by mail. NCB received the notice on 15 September 1988 and confirmed with Daiwa Bank about the ground of rejection. Hing sued Daiwa Bank for payment under the letter of credit on several grounds, including that the bank did not comply with art 16 of UCP 400 when rejecting the documents. Hing argued that the alleged discrepancies were not true and also the bank did not reject the documents in time. The bank relied on three defences: (1) the alleged discrepancies; (2) a newly alleged discrepancy that the relevant document mentioning 'Cheergoal Industrial Ltd', but the name of the buyer was 'Cheergoal Industries Ltd'; and (3) there was no sufficient evidence to show the goods certified were the goods shipped.

Decision: Kaplan J of the High Court of Hong Kong gave judgment to Hing and ordered the bank to pay US$376,000 under the L/C. His Honour's decision was based on the following major grounds:

The difference between 'industrial' and 'industries' was a typographical error, Hing's document (bill of exchange or similar document) meant 'industries';

Article 16 of the UCP 400 required the bank to inform the beneficiary clearly of the grounds on which the bank refused to make payment for the purpose of letting the beneficiary know precisely the reasons for rejection;

The inspection certificate of quality/quantity was consistent with the requirement for the certificate of quality/quantity in the L/C; and

There was sufficient evidence to establish that the inspection certificate of quality/quantity was consistent with the goods carried.

[5.130] An issuing bank also has an obligation to reimburse a paying, accepting or negotiating bank which has made the payment pursuant to the instructions or the terms of credit. The issuing bank may either directly pay the bank which made the payment, or direct another bank to pay the bank which negotiated the credit. If the bank (reimbursing bank) which was directed by the issuing bank to reimburse the paying, accepting or negotiating bank fails to do so, the issuing bank has an ultimate duty to reimburse the bank which has negotiated the credit in pursuance of its terms: art 21 of UCP 500. This is because the issuing bank is bound by the terms of the contract between it and the paying, accepting or negotiating bank. Privity of contract between the issuing bank and the reimbursing bank determines that the paying, accepting or negotiating bank has no remedy against the reimbursing bank if it fails to perform.

Doctrine of strict compliance

[5.131] The doctrine of strict compliance means that the documents presented by a beneficiary (seller) must on their face strictly comply with the terms of credit.[74] It also imposes a duty upon the negotiating bank and the issuing bank to ensure the conformity of the documents with the terms of credit.[75] It is a doctrine at common law and has been incorporated into UCP 500. The combined effect of arts 13 and 14 of UCP 500 implies that an advising bank may be held liable for breach of an authority (mandate) from an issuing bank if the issuing bank finds the documents on their face do not conform with the terms of the credit. This is why the documents presented by the beneficiary must be strictly consistent with the terms of the credit. However, it must be emphasised that the doctrine of strict compliance requires a bank to ensure only that the documents appear to be consistent with the terms of the credit (art 14 of UCP 500), and thus give rise neither to a duty to ascertain the conformity of the goods, nor an obligation to investigate an alleged fraud.[76] A beneficiary has complied with the doctrine as long as documents conforming to the terms of the credit have been presented; and an advising bank has complied with the doctrine as long as it has exercised reasonable care and the documents appear to be conforming with the terms of the credit.[77] In such a case, the beneficiary has not breached the doctrine of strict compliance even if the beneficiary (seller) might have failed to provide goods which conformed with the contract of sale. By the same token, the advising bank has not breached the duty under the doctrine even if the beneficiary had committed fraud, provided that the advising bank did not know or ought not to have known of the fraud.

[5.132] *Midland Bank v Seymour*

[1955] 2 Lloyd's Rep 147

Reasonable compliance with ambiguous instructions

Facts: The buyer did not give clear instructions as to the requirements for the documents to be presented. The seller presented a set of documents which as a whole provided sufficient information about the goods, but the bill of lading did not have sufficient detail. Whether the bank had complied with the doctrine of strict compliance arose as an issue.

Decision: Devlin J of the English High Court held that the buyer's instructions were ambiguous and that the bank had complied with the doctrine because the documents as a whole were consistent with each other and the bill of lading contained the description of the goods.

---

74. For example, in *Gian Singh & Co Ltd v Banque De L'Indochine* [1974] 2 All ER 754, the documents which appeared to be consistent with the terms and conditions of the credit were in fact forged. The court held that in ordinary circumstances a bank is only expected to have a satisfactory visual inspection. See also *Soproma SpA v Marine & Animal By-Products Corpn* [1966] 1 Lloyd's Rep 367.
75. For example, see *St George Bank Ltd v Heinz Salzberger and Norma Salzberger* [2001] NSWCA 67, where the court allowed the applicant to refuse to make payment to the issuing bank on the ground that there was a discrepancy in the documents accepted by the negotiating bank.
76. For example, *United City Merchants (Investments) Ltd v Royal Bank of Canada* [1982] 2 WLR 1039.
77. For example, see *Gian Singh v Banque de L'Indochine* [1974] 1 WLR 1234.

[5.133] There are two probable reasons for the existence of the doctrine of strict compliance:

- First, the agency and principal relationships between the issuing bank and the advising bank, and between the issuing bank and the applicant, determine that the agent must act within the scope of his, her or its authority strictly and that the principal is not liable for the acts of the agent outside the authority.

- Second, the complexity of international trade means that the banks as agents of the buyer or seller are not able to understand and appreciate all technical terms (some of which are interchangeable) or the technical differences between goods of similar functions or nature. While the seller and buyer may be able to reconcile their differences in the use of interchangeable terms or descriptions, it is not appropriate to expect a bank to undertake the task of determining whether goods with different denominations are actually the same, or whether different descriptions of the goods are in fact the same. If a bank did so without authority, it would be running the risk of breaching its authority. If a buyer allows the bank to make such judgment, the buyer runs the risk of misjudgment by the bank.

[5.134] In *J H Rayner & Oilseeds Trading Co Ltd v Hambros Bank Ltd* [1942] 2 All ER 649 the bank was allowed to refuse a bill of lading which stated the goods as being 'machine-shelled groundnut kernels' not 'Coromandel groundnuts' as described in the letter of credit, although it was later established in the court that 'machine-shelled groundnut kernels' and 'Coromandel groundnuts' were, in fact, the same thing. Similarly, in *Moralice (London) Ltd v ED & F Man* [1954] 2 Lloyd's Rep 526, the bank was entitled to reject a bill of lading which revealed a shipment to be short by three bags of sugar. The doctrine of strict compliance provides protection to both the banks and the buyer.

Tender of non-conforming documents

[5.135] Tender of non-conforming documents is an exception to the strict compliance doctrine. The doctrine of strict compliance may cause difficulties when both the seller and buyer know or agree that the differences between the documents and the terms of credit are immaterial or that the different descriptions mean the same thing. In order to facilitate international trade, an advising bank may accept non-conforming documents under the condition that the beneficiary (seller) undertakes to indemnify the advising bank if the issuing bank or the applicant (buyer) refuses to accept the documents for non-conformity. Indemnifying the advising bank in fact means that the beneficiary refunds the money received under the documentary credit and compensates the bank for the cost incurred in transferring the non-conforming documents. In order to secure compensation, an advising bank often requires the beneficiary's bank to provide a guarantee to indemnify its possible loss.

[5.136]   International Commercial Law

> [5.136] *Banque de L'Indochine ET de Suez SA v J H Rayne (Mincing Lane) Ltd*
>
> [1983] QB 711
>
> *Conditional acceptance of non-conforming documents*
>
> **Facts:** The beneficiary (Rayne) tendered documents under an irrevocable letter of credit. The advising bank (Banque de L'Indochine) discovered discrepancies between the documents and the terms of the credit. The beneficiary disagreed with the bank on the alleged discrepancies. The parties then agreed that the bank would make a payment under reserve to the beneficiary. The documents were ultimately rejected by the issuing bank. The advising bank sought reimbursement from the beneficiary, who, however, refused to reimburse the bank.
>
> **Decision:** The English Court of Appeal (consisting of Sir John Donaldson MR, Kerr LJ and Sir Sebag Shaw) held that the bank had reserved the right to have the money back when making the payment under reserve. The acceptance of the documents was conditional, depending on whether the issuing bank or the buyer would ultimately accept the disputed documents.

Short-circuiting in international trade

[5.137] 'Short-circuiting' is an exception to the privity rule. It means that the seller and buyer 'short-circuit' a documentary credit by dealing with each other directly, outside a credit payment arrangement. In common law countries, short-circuiting of a documentary credit is not normally allowed, probably because of the existing contractual liability between the buyer (applicant), the issuing bank and the seller (beneficiary). This was seen in *Soproma SpA v Marine and Animal By-Products Corp* [1966] 1 Lloyd's Rep 367. In this case, the seller intended to tender the documents directly to the buyer because the letter of credit had expired. The court held that this was not allowed because of the existence of the arrangement based on the letter of credit between the applicant, the issuing bank and the advising bank.

[5.138] In certain circumstances, in particular when the banks involved become insolvent, the courts will allow the seller to deal directly with the buyer or to make a claim directly against the buyer, provided that the seller has fulfilled his or her obligations under the contract and the terms of credit. In *E D & F Man Ltd v Nigerian Sweets & Confectionery Co Ltd* [1977] 1 Lloyd's Rep 50, the seller was allowed to make a claim for the price of the goods directly against the buyer because the issuing bank was bankrupt. Similarly, in *Sale Continuation Ltd v Austin Taylor & Co Ltd* [1967] 2 Lloyd's Rep 403, the buyer paid directly the seller of the goods (timber) for the purpose of discharging his obligation under the contract of sale. The direct dealing between the seller and the buyer in this case was upheld by the court, because the issuing bank had intentionally dishonoured the bill drawn by the seller on the bank.

[5.139] Where the issuing bank is not able to make payment, a seller is able to enforce the contract against the buyer even though the buyer had deposited the money for payment with the bank. This is illustrated in *Man v Nigerian Sweets and Confectionery* [1977] 1 Lloyd's Rep 50, where the buyer was held liable for the contract price because the issuing bank which had accepted the drafts went into liquidation. The court held that the opening of a credit is a conditional payment and the buyer's obligation to pay can be discharged either by making the payment or by express intention in the contract of sale. It was of the opinion that the buyer had not discharged his obligation to pay under the contract of sale.

[5.140] These cases suggest that a documentary credit or an arrangement for payment based on the banks' assistance may be short-circuited if it is not fair for the buyer or the seller to incur loss because of a bank's inability to honour its guarantee. Short-circuiting can be explained in terms of contract law: the buyer is obliged to pay the price of the goods under the contract of sale unless the buyer has discharged this duty successfully through the existing arrangement for payment. The privity of contract between the buyer and issuing bank, and between the beneficiary and issuing bank respectively, as existed in an arrangement based on a documentary credit, does not automatically discharge the buyer from his or her duty to pay under the underlying contract of sale.

Fraud and the bank's obligation under an irrevocable credit

[5.141] Two types of fraud may be relevant to a documentary credit: fraud in relation to the goods and fraud in relation to the documents. If an allegation of fraud in relation to goods arises before the payment is made, the issuing or confirming bank cannot withhold the payment against the beneficiary (or a third party holder in due course) who appears to have no knowledge of the fraud as long as the documents satisfy the requirements for the credit. This was established in *United City Merchants (Investments) Ltd v Royal Bank of Canada* [1983] 1 AC 168, where the House of Lords held that the bank was liable to pay the beneficiary who had presented conforming documents, even if it was established that the goods were not the same as those described in the documents. This is probably because the seller in that case neither committed nor knew of the existence of the fraud at all. By the same token, the bank may stop the payment if it has been established that the beneficiary has committed or had knowledge of the fraud.[78] Thus, in *Edward Owen Engineering Ltd v Barclays Bank International Ltd* [1978] 1 Lloyd's Rep 166; [1978] QB 159, the court held that only when the bank has notice of a clear fraud committed by the beneficiary, the court is entitled to interfere. Similarly, in *Bolivinter Oil SA v Chase Manhattan Bank NA* [1984] 1 Lloyd's Rep 251, the court took the view that when a court interferes with a transaction involving a documentary credit on the ground of fraud, the evidence of fraud must be clear, both as to the fact of fraud and as to the bank's knowledge.

---

78. For example, in *Rafsanjan Pistachio Producers Co-operative v Bank Leumi (UK) Plc* [1992] 1 Lloyd's Rep 513, the court was satisfied that the bank had established the beneficiary's involvement or knowledge of the applicant's fraud and held that the bank was entitled to refuse to make the payment. In addition, the court also held that the bank was entitled to reject the documents on the ground of non-conformity.

[5.142] *Discount Records Ltd v Barclays Bank Ltd*

[1975] 1 WLR 315

Application for an injunction to restrain banks from making payment under an irrevocable credit

Facts: Discount Records opened a confirmed irrevocable credit through Barclays Bank in favour of a French seller. The credit was made available to the beneficiary through several intermediary banks. The draft and documents were accepted by the negotiating bank in Paris. Barclays Bank debited Discount Records for the amount of the credit and put the money into an account under the joint name of Barclays Bank and Discount Records. Discount Records alleged that the cartons which were supposed to contain the goods were in fact empty or filled with rubbish and the goods not ordered. Subsequently, Discount Records asked the court to grant an interlocutory injunction.

Decision: Megarry J of the English High Court held that the injunction to restrain payment under an irrevocable credit is available only when a grave cause was established. In this case, Discount Records had not proved the existence of the alleged fraud and of the irretrievable damages from making payment by the bank under the credit. In addition, after the acceptance of the draft, the documents might have been passed to an innocent holder in due course. The use of injunction should be restricted because of the possibility of damaging the interest of an innocent holder of the draft.

[5.143] *Bank of Taiwan v Union Syndicate Corp*

[1981] HKC 205

Bank's duties and contractual obligations; fraud by a sub-beneficiary under a transferable credit

Facts: The Taiwanese buyer, Taiwan Freeway Construction Bureau, and the HK seller, the Union Syndicate Corp, entered into a contract, through their respective agents, for the sale of 10,000 metric tonnes of scrap metal located in Vietnam in CIF term Shanghai. The Bank of Taiwan issued a letter of credit at the request of the Taiwanese buyer in favour of the seller. The First National City Bank of New York was authorised by the Bank of Taiwan to make payment under the letter of credit. The Kwong On Bank of Shanghai was authorised as the advising bank to the seller. Kwong On Bank transferred part of the credit to Capricorn Seafoods (HK) Ltd, which was supposed to be the supplier for 3000 metric tonnes of the scrap metal, at the request of the seller. Capricorn negotiated the payment under the transferred credit at Ka Wah Bank, which subsequently claimed payment from the First National City Bank and sent the relevant documents to the Bank of Taiwan. It turned out later that Capricorn committed a fraud against the buyer because it did not have scrap metal to sell. The Bank of Taiwan, the buyer and its agent initiated legal proceedings against the seller and the relevant banks. The banks' liabilities to each other arose as an issue.

Held: Rhind J of the High Court of Hong Kong dismissed the action on the following grounds:
- The buyer and buyer's agent had no contractual basis to sue the banks;
- The buyer's agent could not rely on negligence to sue the banks because it failed to establish damage it had suffered;
- The buyer could not rely on negligence against the Ka Wah Bank, because the bank did not owe a duty of care to the buyer for a lack of foreseeability;
- The Bank of Taiwan and Ka Wah Bank were bound by the terms of the credit, which were subject to UCP 400;

> - Article 8 of UCP 400 required the issuing bank to notify the negotiating bank of inconsistencies in the documents accepted for negotiation of the credit within a reasonable time, which should be 48 hours in the present case; but the Bank of Taiwan rejected the documents one month after it received them; and
> - The Ka Wah Bank accepted a 'received for shipment bill' in contravention of the terms of the credit, but the Bank of Taiwan had given consent to this breach by acquiescence.

[5.144] If an allegation of fraud in relation to the commercial documents is involved, the banks are subject to the tests of reasonable care and good faith. This means that the banks must act in a reasonable manner to prevent and detect possible fraud, but are not liable to losses if the fraud cannot be revealed after the exercise of due diligence. The obligations of the banks in this situation are determined by the law governing agent–principal relationships.

[5.145] At common law, a bank, acting as the agent of another bank or for the applicant of the credit, has no obligation to ascertain the true value or authenticity of the documents. Their mandate or obligation is to make the promised payment against the documents which on their face conform with the terms of the credit: arts 13–15 of UCP 500. When an allegation of fraud cannot be substantiated or proved, the bank is bound by the promise to pay under an irrevocable or confirmed credit.[79] Nor was a bank allowed to avoid a liability to pay on a 'reasonable' assumption of fraud unless the fraud is proved.[80] In *Tukan Timber Ltd v Barclays Bank Plc* [1987] 1 Lloyd's Rep 171, Hirst J stated that the letter of credit is autonomous. The bank is not concerned in any way with the merits or demerits of the underlying transaction. The court will interfere with the bank honouring a letter of credit only in the most extremely exceptional circumstances.

Ever Eagle Co Ltd v Kincheng Banking Corp [1993] 2 HKC 157 coincides with the decision of the English court. In September 1992, a group of Hong Kong buyers opened a transferable LC in favour of a group of Japanese sellers. The buyers heard that the goods covered by the LC were stolen goods and obtained an ex parte injunction from the High Court of Hong Kong restraining the issuing bank from honouring the LC. The injunction was later discharged and the plaintiff appealed to the Court of Appeal against the order to discharge the injunction. The court dismissed the appeal. In relation to the law relating to the alleged fraud under the LC, the court stated that the alleged fraud had not been established. Interference with the operation of the LC by a court without justification destroys the autonomy of the LC and will make the seller's right to receive the payment under the LC depend on the buyer's right against the seller under the contract of sale.

[5.146] However, if a bank knew or ought to have known that the beneficiary had committed a fraud, it is not allowed to make a payment to the beneficiary even if there is

---

79. For example, *Discount Records Ltd v Barclays Bank Ltd* [1975] 1 WLR 315, *Bolivinter Oil SA v Chase Manhattan Bank N A* [1984] 1 WLR 392; and *Inflatable Toy Company Pty Ltd v State Bank of New South Wales* (1994) 34 NSWLR 243; **[5.147]**.
80. For example, in *The Society of Lloyd's v Canadian Imperial Bank of Commerce* [1993] 2 Lloyd's Rep 579, the bank relying on the defence of fraud against the beneficiary's claim under a letter of credit was required to prove the existence of the fraud, rather than merely establishing its reasonable belief in the existence of a fraud.

[5.146]

an irrevocable or confirmed letter of credit. This was established in an American case, *Sztejn v J Henry Schroder Banking Corp* (1941) 31 NYS 2nd 631, where the advising bank's claim for reimbursement from the issuing bank was denied, even though the documents retained by the advising bank on their face conformed with the terms of credit. This was because the advising bank knew of the existence of the fraud and should not have made the payment at all. Knowingly making payment to a defrauding party will make the bank an accomplice to the fraud, and negligently making payment to a defrauding party will make the bank liable to compensate the principal for breach of its duty of care.

[5.147] *Inflatable Toy Company Pty Ltd v State Bank of NSW*

(1994) 34 NSWLR 243

Bank can stop payment under an irrevocable credit only when a fraud has been established

Facts: Inflatable Toy was the buyer of a certain quantity of inflatable plastic toys from a Taiwanese seller. The State Bank of NSW was Inflatable Toy's bank, and in 1993 issued an irrevocable letter of credit for the purpose of the sale. The toys were to be delivered in instalments. On the day before the fourth shipment, the seller, after consultation with the buyer, removed certain defective toys from the container, but was unable to correct the shipping documents accordingly because of time restraints. There were discrepancies between the shipping documents, the parties' correspondence and the items actually delivered in the fourth instalment.

The buyer, however, informed the State Bank of the existence of the discrepancies and of his confidence in resolving them. The seller's bill of exchange and shipping documents were accepted by the State Bank, which subsequently obtained approval from the buyer who indorsed on the bill the words 'Discrepancies/documents acceptable'. Before the payment under the bill of exchange was due, the buyer instructed the State Bank to stop payment on the ground that the seller fraudulently and knowingly presented untrue documents. The buyer subsequently sought a court order to stop the payment.

Decision: The existence of a fraud on the part of the seller was not established. If the fraud were proved, the bank which had accepted the bill of exchange would have to stop the payment. In the present case, the buyer could not stop the payment merely because there were discrepancies between the goods delivered and the accompanying documents.

Fraud and the applicant's right under a documentary credit

[5.148] Since the documentary credit involves only transactions of documents and the bank's duty is to verify the documents (pursuant to the terms of the documentary credit, which reflect the applicant's instructions), the buyer or the applicant to the documentary credit does not have direct remedies within the documentary credit mechanism. However, as we have seen, sometimes when a fraud has been clearly established, a court may be willing to issue an injunction to restrain payment under a letter of credit. When for some technical reason an injunction is not available, the court may order the payment to be paid into a trust account held by the bank concerned (provided the bank does not object to such arrangement). The transfer of money out of the said account is subject to the direction of the court. This is what was decided in *Manzel Equipment Pty Ltd v APE Pte*

Ltd [2000] NSWSC 1172, where the buyer had established between the machine received and the machine contracted for, and asked the court to delay the payment under the letter of credit concerned. If an applicant or the buyer wishes to sue the beneficiary or the seller for an alleged fraud, he or she may have to resort to the general principles of equity, or arguably contract law, for such an action. In such cases, a court of common law jurisdiction may have difficulties in treating the documentary credit as a contract between the applicant and the beneficiary because of the doctrine of privity of contract, although the court may regard the terms of a documentary credit as evidence of the beneficiary's obligations. In any case, the court of common law jurisdiction, to deal with such cases, may invoke the equitable principle that no one should benefit from fraudulent conduct. This is illustrated in the following case.

[5.149] *Trishul (UK) Ltd v Winnie Tong t/as Winda Product*

[1987] HKLR 161

Facts: The plaintiff was a UK company providing finance for a commission to a German company which contracted with the defendant, a Hong Kong company, to buy a quantity of garments from the defendant. The plaintiff applied to a UK bank for the opening of an irrevocable letter of credit (LC) in favour of the defendant. The LC contained, inter alia, the following terms:
- Presentation of an airway bill showing the flight number, the date and the German company being the recipient of the consignment; and
- The latest date of the shipment was 30 June 1983.

The defendant negotiated the LC with a Hong Kong bank. The Hong Kong bank claimed reimbursement from the issuing bank, which in turn claimed reimbursement from the plaintiff. The German company went into liquidation and the plaintiff was unable to recover the payment from the German company. The plaintiff discovered that the copy of the airway bill sent to the German company was dated 2 July 1983, but the copy of the airway bill presented to the banks for negotiating the LC was dated 30 June 1983. In order to recover the money lost, the plaintiff sued the defendant for fraud in documentation.

Decision: Mayo J of the Hong Kong High Court held, inter alia, as follows:
- The plaintiff's claim could not succeed because the only evidence of fraud available was the actual discrepancy in the copy of the air waybills and this was insufficient.
- The fraudulent conduct on the part of the defendant would have entitled the plaintiff to pursue the rights against the defendant under the LC independently of the sale contract provided that the fraud went to the heart of the transaction.
- Even if the defendant had altered the date on the air waybill, or caused it to be altered, such conduct would not have entitled the plaintiff to pursue any rights under the L/C because the alteration would not have destroyed the whole or the essence of the air waybill and would not therefore have gone to the heart of the transaction.
- The alleged fraud must have destroyed the whole or essence of the document concerned. The alleged fraud in the present case did not change the essence of the airway bill.

Means of payment under the UN Conventions

Law affecting use of bill of exchange and promissory notes

Overview

[5.150] The UN Convention on International Bills of Exchange and International Promissory Notes is the culmination of over 15 years of work by UNCITRAL. It was adopted by the General Assembly of the United Nations under recommendation of the Sixth (Legal) Committee on 9 December 1988. The convention is not yet in force. Ten actions are required for the convention to enter into force. As at July 2002, only Guinea, Honduras and Mexico had ratified the convention.

The convention is meant to replace domestic law on bills of exchange and promissory notes. The Australian Bills of Exchange Act 1909 discussed earlier in this chapter would have been replaced had Australia ratified the convention. Unlike the said Bills of Exchange Act 1909, cheques are not regulated in the convention. The omission may perhaps reflect the civil law approach as seen in the Geneva Uniform Laws, that is, the 1930 Geneva Uniform Law on Bills of Exchange and Promissory Notes, and the 1931 Geneva Convention on the Unification of the Law Relating to Cheques, where the law regulating bills of exchange and promissory notes is separate from the law regulating cheques.

[5.151] The convention presents, for optional use in international transactions, a relatively modern and comprehensive set of rules for international bills of exchange and international promissory notes, that satisfies the convention's requirements of form. The text of the convention reflects a deliberate policy to minimise departures from the content of the two existing principal legal systems, that is, the common law and civil law tradition, preserving, where possible, the rules on which those systems concur. It was intended that where conflicts exist, requiring selection of one system's rule or a compromise solution, the convention introduces a number of novel provisions. In addition, the convention has also developed a group of new rules as the result of special efforts of UNCITRAL to meet modern commercial needs and banking and financial market practices.[81]

[5.152] The convention contains nine chapters and 90 articles. The nine chapters are described briefly as follows:

- Chapter I defines the sphere of application and form of instrument. One of the essential features of the convention is that it applies only to bills specified as international bills of exchange and notes specified as international promissory notes. The formality is a prerequisite for the application of the convention.
- Chapter II provides interpretations of basic terms and formal requirements, such as 'sum', 'instructions for payment', and 'parties to a bill'.

---

81. Explanatory Note by the UNCITRAL Secretariat on the UN Convention on International Bills of Exchange and International Promissory Notes, para 2.

- Chapter III regulates the transfer of bills, including negotiability, endorsement, holders rights, and others.
- Chapter IV sets out the rights and liabilities of the parties — who can be a holder, a protected holder, the drawer, the drawee, the acceptor, the maker, an endorser, and a guarantor.
- Chapter V deals with issues relating to presentment, dishonour by non-acceptance or non-payment, and recourse.
- Chapter VI regulates discharge, including discharging by payment and discharge by other parties.
- Chapter VII sets out rules for lost interments.
- Chapter VIII regulates the issue of limitation of time.
- Chapter IX contains final provisions, which deal with various matters of formality to give effect to the convention.

For the purpose of comparison, this section will review a number of basic aspects of bills of exchange, such as scope of application, definition, negotiability, acceptance and discharge of a bill of exchange. In addition, the meaning of promissory note will be also examined.

Scope of application

[5.153] As a distinctive characteristic of the convention, the application of the convention is based on the specified identification of words in a bill or promissory note, instead of the identity of the parties or the place of payment. The specified identification are the words 'international bill of exchange' (UNCITRAL Convention) or 'international promissory note' (UNCITRAL Convention). Under arts 1 and 2 of the convention, the words must appear as both the heading of the bill or promissory note and also in the text of the bill or note.

For example, art 1 of the convention states that the convention applies to an international bill of exchange when it contains the heading 'International bill of exchange (UNCITRAL Convention)' and also contains in its text the words 'International bill of exchange (UNCITRAL Convention)'. Similarly, art 2 states that the convention applies to an international promissory note when it contains the heading 'International promissory note (UNCITRAL Convention)' and also contains in its text the words 'International promissory note (UNCITRAL Convention)'. Accordingly, the use of an instrument governed by the convention is thus entirely optional. Ratification or accession by a state does not subject all international instruments issued in that state to the legal regime of the convention, but merely opens the door for bankers and merchants to opt for this new legal regime if they deem it preferable in their professional judgment.[82]

[5.154] The convention's practice of requiring the existence of certain distinctive words as a precondition for the application of the convention probably originates from the 1930 Geneva Uniforms Law on Bills of Exchange and Promissory Notes. For example, art 1(1)

---

82. Id, para 12.

[5.154]

of the Geneva Uniform Law, for the purpose of defining a bill of exchange, requires the term 'bill of exchange' to be inserted in the body of the bill and also expressed in the language employed in drawing up the bill. Such a requirement on the formality of a bill is not required in common law jurisdictions, where many cases have been decided on the point whether a document in question is a bill of exchange.

Definition of bill

[5.155] The convention provides its own definition of international bill of exchange and explicitly states the conditions on which a bill of exchange (or promissory note) is considered to be international. Under the convention, a bill of exchange is a written instrument containing an unconditional order whereby the drawer directs the drawee to pay a definite sum of money to the payee or to its order. It is also payable on demand or at a definite time, is dated, and is signed by the drawer.[83]

The precise meaning of an international bill of exchange is defined in arts 2(1) and 3(1) of the convention. Article 2(1) emphasises the international nature of a bill and provides as follows:

> An international bill of exchange is a bill of exchange which specifies at least two of the following places and indicates that any two so specified are situated in different states:
> (a) The place where the bill is drawn;
> (b) The place indicated next to the signature of the drawer;
> (c) The place indicated next to the name of the drawee;
> (d) The place indicated next to the name of the payee;
> (e) The place of payment,
> provided that either the place where the bill is drawn or the place of payment is specified on the bill and that such place is situated in a Contracting state.

Article 2(1) must be read together with art 3(1) which provides the basic requirements for a bill, as follows:

> A bill of exchange is a written instrument which:
> (a) Contains an unconditional order whereby the drawer directs the drawee to pay a definite sum of money to the payee or to his order;
> (b) Is payable on demand or at a definite time;
> (c) Is dated;
> (d) Is signed by the drawer.

[5.156] In comparison with the meaning of bill of exchange in a common law jurisdiction, such as Australia, Hong Kong and the UK, the meaning of an international bill of exchange under the convention is largely similar to the former, except the international nature of the bill and the requirement for the bill being dated. The compulsory requirement that an international bill must be dated appears to be a feature derived from the civil law tradition, rather than the common law tradition. For example, unlike art 3(1)(c) of the convention, s 8(4)(a) of the Bills of Exchange Act 1909 (Cth) states expressly that a bill is not invalid by reason that the bill is not dated. On the other hand, similar to art 3(1)(c) of the convention, arts 1(7) and 2 of the 1930 Geneva Uniform Law on Bills of Exchange and Promissory Notes suggest that a bill of exchange must contain a statement of the date on which the bill is issued.[84] Thus, besides the characteristic that the bill must be

---

83. Id, para 13.

international, the requirement that the bill must be dated is one of the essential differences between an international bill of exchange under the convention and a bill of exchange in common law jurisdictions.

[5.157] The requirement that an international bill of exchange must be dated is necessary under the convention for the enforcement of a number of other provisions. For example, art 8(4) of the convention states that if an instrument states that the sum is to be paid with interest, without specifying the date from which interest is to run, interest runs from the 'date of the instrument'. The date of issue is used here as the basis for calculating the interest payment, although the rationale of art 8(4) may be questioned on the ground that art 8(4) may lead to a situation where the interest begins to accrue before the drawee's or the acceptor's obligation to pay the principal under the bill has come into existence, if acceptance is a precondition of payment. This potential issue of art 8(4) may be illustrated by art 8(5) of the convention, which states that 'the time of payment of a bill payable at a fixed period after sight is determined by the date of acceptance'. Article 8(4) implies that the interest starts to accumulate before the acceptance. Another example of the importance of the date on which the bill is issued is art 51(d) of the convention. This provision states that 'a bill payable on demand or at a fixed period after sight must be presented for acceptance within one year of its date'.

Negotiability of bill

[5.158] An international bill of exchange can be either negotiable or non-negotiable, although there appears to be the same presumption that an international bill of exchange is prima facie negotiable unless stated otherwise expressly in the bill. The convention adopts the expression transfer, instead of negotiation. It appears that transfer may not have precisely the same meaning as negotiation. Article 17(1) of the convention deals with the issue of negotiability. It states that if the drawer or the maker has inserted in the instrument such words as 'not negotiable', 'not transferable', 'not to order', 'pay (X) only', or words of similar import, the instrument may not be transferred except for the purposes of collection, and any endorsement, even if it does not contain words authorising the endorsee to collect the instrument, is deemed to be an endorsement for collection. This provision appears to suggest that transfer has the implication of passing a bill from one party to another without passing the title in the bill because in the case of collection the party (or a bank) collecting payment from the drawee only acts as the agent for the drawer in taking possession of the bill concerned. The expression 'transfer' has its origin in the civil law tradition. For example, art 11 of the 1930 Geneva Uniform Law on Bills of Exchange and Promissory Notes states that every bill of exchange, even if not expressly drawn to order, may be transferred by means of indorsement. In fact, the expression 'negotiation' or 'negotiable' does not appear in the 1930 Geneva Uniform Law on Bills of Exchange and Promissory Notes.

[5.159] The convention gives the drawer, an indorser or a holder an option to stop further transfer or negotiation of a bill. Article 17(2) of the convention provides that if an

---

84. Article 1 sets out the requirements for a valid bill, and art 2 sets out a number of exceptions to the formality requirements stipulated in art 1. Omission of the date of issue is not an exception under art 2.

[5.159] endorsement contains the words 'not negotiable', 'not transferable', 'not to order', 'pay (X) only', or words of similar import, the instrument may not be transferred further except for purposes of collection, and any subsequent endorsement, even if it does not contain words authorising the indorsee to collect the instrument, is deemed to be an indorsement for collection. This provision is largely similar to art 17(1), except to the extent that it allows an indorsee or a holder a right to turn a negotiable bill into a non-negotiable bill. Article 17(2) is similar to some extent with s 40 of the Bills of Exchange Act 1909 (Cth), which regulates the so-called restrictive indorsement.[85] But, the restrictive indorsement does not really turn a negotiable bill into a non-negotiable bill.

[5.160] The means by which an international note can be transferred or negotiated are set out in art 13 of the convention. According to this provision, an instrument can be transferred either by indorsement and delivery of the instrument by the indorser to the indorsee, or by mere delivery of the instrument if the last endorsement is in blank. An indorsement in blank can be converted into a special indorsement by the holder of the bill. Inter versa, a bill transferred by a special indorsement can also be changed as an indorsement in blank by the holder.[86] The means of transfer suggest that a bearer's bill is not allowed under the convention. In fact, the convention does not allow negotiable instruments to be drawn on two or more drawees or to be issued payable to bearer. However, there is a view that neither restriction is significant in practice, because nothing prevents a payee or special indorsee from making an instrument covered by the convention payable to a bearer by indorsing it in blank under art 13, and multiple-drawee instruments have proven to be quite rare in international transactions.[87] The issue of a multiple-drawee bill of exchange is sometimes regarded as a source of confusion because of the limited function such a bill may serve. The restriction of the convention can be compared with s 11 of the Bills of Exchange Act 1909 (Cth), which states that a bill may be addressed to two or more drawees, whether they are partners or not, but an order addressed to two drawees in the alternative, or to two or more drawees successively, is not a bill of exchange. In comparison with the convention, the Bills of Exchange Act 1909 (Cth) permits the use of a bill addressing two or more drawees with a joint liability, but not for drawees under an alternative liability.

---

85. Section 40 of the Bills of Exchange Act 1909 (Cth) states as follows:
    (1) An indorsement is restrictive which prohibits the further negotiation of the bill, or which expresses that it is a mere authority to deal with the bill as thereby directed and not a transfer of the ownership thereof, as, for example, if a bill be indorsed 'Pay D. only,' or 'Pay D. for the account of X.,' or 'Pay D. or order for collection'.
    (2) A restrictive indorsement gives the indorsee the right to receive payment of the bill, and to sue any party thereto that his indorser could have sued, but gives him no power to transfer his rights as indorsee unless it expressly authorises him to do so.
    Where a restrictive indorsement authorises further transfer, all subsequent indorsees take the bill with the same rights and subject to the same liabilities as the first indorsee under the restrictive indorsement.
86. Article 16 of the convention states that the holder of a bill on which the last endorsement is in blank may further indorse it either by an indorsement in blank or by a special indorsement; on the other hand, a holder may also convert the blank indorsement into a special indorsement by indicating in the indorsement that the instrument is payable to him- or herself or to some other specified person.
87. Explanatory Note by the UNCITRAL Secretariat on the UN Convention on International Bills of Exchange and International Promissory Notes, para 17.

[5.161] Under the convention, a bill is transferable by indorsement. Under art 14 of the convention, an indorsement must be written on the instrument or on a slip affixed on it ('allonge'). It must be signed by the indorser. An indorsement can be effected either by an indorsement in blank or a special indorsement. An indorsement in blank means that an indorser signs his or her name and makes a statement to the effect that the instrument is payable to a person in possession of it. A special indorsement means that an indorser signs his or her name and also indicates the identity of the person to whom the instrument is payable. For the purpose of an indorsement in blank, a signature alone, other than that of the drawee, is an indorsement only if it is placed on the back of the instrument. In comparison with the wording of the Bills of Exchange Act 1909 (Cth), the convention is clearer and less ambiguous than the former in many aspects, including the rules on indorsement.

Concept of holder under the convention

[5.162] The convention defines the meaning of 'holder' broadly. Under arts 5 and 15 of the convention, a holder can be either a legitimate holder of an international bill of exchange (or an international promissory note), or a person who has become a holder by the fact that the bill was obtained by him or her, or any previous holder, under circumstances, including incapacity, fraud, duress or mistake of any kind, that would give rise to a claim to, or a defence against liability on, the bill. This neutral and broad definition is different from the meaning of holder in common law jurisdictions, for example, the Bills of Exchange Act 1909 (Cth), which does not expressly deal with the interest of a holder who obtains a bill of exchange by fraud or any illegitimate means directly.

[5.163] Following the adoption of a broad definition of holder, the convention creates two related concepts: holder and protected holder under arts 27–32 of the convention. Under art 29, a protected holder means the holder of a bill or note which was complete when he or she took it, or which was incomplete (para 1 of art 12 of the convention) and was completed in accordance with an authority, provided that the holder was free of fault, such as fraud or theft, or free of the knowledge of certain facts when he or she became a holder. In particular, the holder must not have any knowledge of certain defence against liability on the bill or note referred to in art 28; must not have any knowledge of a valid claim to the bill or note of any person; and must not have any knowledge of the fact that the bill or note had been dishonoured by non-acceptance or by non-payment.

In addition, a protected holder must be a person who receives the bill or note before the time limit provided by art 55 for presentment of the bill or note for payment has expired. A protected holder is protected by the convention, and on the other hand, a holder may be subject to a number of legal actions under art 28 of the convention. In other words, the rights of the protected holder are freed from the claims and defences of other persons to a greater extent than are the rights vested in the ordinary holder.[88] This is the broad difference between a holder and a protected holder. However, it must be noted that a holder is not totally unprotected from adverse claims and defences under the

---

88. Explanatory Note by the UNCITRAL Secretariat on the UN Convention on International Bills of Exchange and International Promissory Notes, para 22.

convention. In fact, it can be argued that the holder derives an appreciable degree of protection from the rules contained in the convention that allow certain types of claims or defences against the holder, only if the holder had knowledge of them or if the holder was involved in a fraud or theft concerning the instrument.[89]

[5.164] The creation of the concept of protected holder represents a compromise between the civil law and the common law tradition. For instance, the common law tradition protects an innocent and bona fide holder. So does the convention. On the other hand, under the convention, a person may be regarded as a holder even though he or she has received a bill or note under circumstances involving incapacity or fraud, duress or mistake of any kind, that may give rise to a claim to, or a defence against liability on, the bill or note. This practice resembles the civil law much more than the common law. Perhaps the most important feature of the convention on the protected holder is that a person who is in possession of a bill or note as an indorsee, or one on which the last indorsement is in blank, and on which there appears to have been an uninterrupted series of indorsements, can be regarded as a protected holder even though any indorsement appearing on the bill or note has been forged or signed by an agent without authority.[90]

Acceptance of bill

[5.165] The convention is ambiguous on the rules relating to certain aspects of acceptance. For example, art 40(1) of the convention provides expressly that 'the drawee is not liable on a bill until he accepts it'. This provision appears to make acceptance a precondition for the drawee to undertake the liability to pay under a bill. However, art 49 of the convention gives the drawer an option to decide whether acceptance is compulsory, by stating that a bill may be presented for acceptance, and that a bill must be presented for acceptance only if the drawer has so stipulated in the bill, the bill is payable at a fixed period after sight, or the bill is payable other than at the residence or place of business of the drawee, unless it is payable on demand. If art 49 prevails over art 40, the convention appears to have combined the features of both the common law and the civil law when regulating the situations for requiring acceptance. Article 49(2)(b) and (c) are similar to s 44 of the Bills of Exchange Act 1909 (Cth) (see **[5.62]**), and art 49(2)(a) is similar to art 22 of the 1930 Geneva Uniform Law on Bills of Exchange and Promissory Notes, where art 22 states that in any bill of exchange, the drawer may stipulate that it shall be presented for acceptance with or without fixing a limit of time for presentment.

[5.166] The drawee or the person accepting a bill undertakes that he or she will pay the bill in accordance with the terms of his or her acceptance to the holder of the bill.[91] Under art 41 of the convention, an acceptance must be effected by writing on either the front or the back of the bill the signature of the drawee which may or may not be accompanied by the word 'accepted' or by words of similar import. Under art 43 of the convention, an acceptance must be unqualified. An acceptance which is conditional or varies the terms

---

89. Explanatory Note by the UNCITRAL Secretariat on the UN Convention on International Bills of Exchange and International Promissory Notes, para 25.
90. Explanatory Note by the UNCITRAL Secretariat on the UN Convention on International Bills of Exchange and International Promissory Notes, para 23.
91. The convention, art 40(2).

of the bill is a qualified acceptance. An acceptance with qualifications amounts to dishonour by non-acceptance.

[5.167] If the drawee or the drawee's agent, upon due presentment, expressly refuses to accept the bill, the bill is dishonoured. So is the bill when acceptance cannot be obtained with reasonable diligence or if the holder cannot obtain the acceptance to which he or she is entitled under the convention.[92] Under art 54(2) of the convention, if a bill is dishonoured by non-acceptance, the holder may exercise an immediate right of recourse against the drawer, the indorsers and their guarantors, subject to the provisions of art 59; or sometimes, the holder may claim payment from the drawee's guarantor upon any necessary protest.

[5.168] The guarantor's liability is specifically regulated in the convention. Article 46 of the convention provides that payment of a bill or note may be guaranteed either before or after acceptance, as to the whole or part of its amount, for the account of a party, such as the drawer or an indorser, or the drawee. A guarantee may be given by any person, who may or may not already be a party. A guarantee is expressed by the words 'guaranteed', 'aval', 'good as aval' or words of similar import, accompanied by the signature of the guarantor, or effected by a signature alone on the front of the bill or note. In fact, any signature alone on the front of a bill or note, other than that of the maker, the drawer or the drawee, is a guarantee.[93] The convention is unambiguous in imposing a personal liability upon a person who has signed his or her name on the front of the bill in addition to the company's name without qualification. Since a guarantee can be provided for either the drawee or the drawee or indorser, the words by which a guarantee is expressed should be relied on for determining the nature of the obligation undertaken by the guarantor. In the absence of any notation specifying the party for whom a guarantee is given, the presumption is that the guarantee is offered for the drawee, acceptor or the maker in the case of a promissory note.

Discharge of bill

[5.169] The drawee's, acceptor's or guarantor's liability under a bill or note can be discharged by payment. Article 72(1) of the convention provides that a party is discharged of liability on the instrument when he or she pays the holder, including a party who is in possession of the instrument, by having paid the instrument or the amount due under the instrument. The party's obligation can be discharged by making the payment at or after maturity of the bill; or before maturity, upon dishonour by non-acceptance. The party who can be the drawee, an acceptor or a guarantor is regarded as having complied with his or her liability when making payment at maturity or in pursuance of the terms of the bill or note. The party who makes payment after maturity without justification or after having breached the terms of the bill or note is discharged from his or her obligations under the bill or note, but may be required to pay compensation to the holder for the breach complained of, and pay for the interest due.

---

92. The convention, art 54(1)(a).
93. Explanatory Note by the UNCITRAL Secretariat on the UN Convention on International Bills of Exchange and International Promissory Notes, para 31.

[5.170] If the person liable to pay under a bill or note has refused to make the payment due, the bill or note is dishonoured by non-payment. Under art 58(2) and (3), if a bill or note is dishonoured by non-payment, the holder may, subject to the provisions of art 59, exercise a right of recourse against the drawer, the indorsers, and their guarantors, as the case may be. Article 59 states that if an instrument is dishonoured by non-acceptance or by non-payment, the holder may exercise a right of recourse only after the instrument has been duly protested for dishonour in accordance with the relevant provisions, that is, arts 60–62 of the convention, which set out the formality for protest.

Definition of promissory note

[5.171] The meaning of an international promissory note is jointly defined in arts 2(2) and 3(2) of the convention. Article 2(2) defines the international aspect of the note covered by the convention. It states as follows:

> An international promissory note is a promissory note which specifies at least two of the following places and indicates that any two so specified are situated in different states:
> (a) The place where the note is made;
> (b) The place indicated next to the signature of the maker;
> (c) The place indicated next to the name of the payee;
> (d) The place of payment, provided that the place of payment is specified on the note and that such place is situated in a Contracting state.

In a similar manner as the definition of international bill of exchange, art 3(2) of the convention provides:

> A promissory note is a written instrument which:
> (a) Contains an unconditional promise whereby the maker undertakes to pay a definite sum of money to the payee or to his order;
> (b) Is payable on demand or at a definite time;
> (c) Is dated;
> (d) Is signed by the maker.

The definition of promissory note under the convention is similar to that adopted in common law jurisdictions, such as the one defined in s 89 of the Bills of Exchange Act 1909 (Cth) (see **[5.71]**), except the international characteristic and the requirement for being dated. However, the definition of the convention is quite similar to the definition of promissory note adopted in art 75 of the 1930 Geneva Uniform Law on Bills of Exchange and Promissory Notes. Article 75 states as follows:

> A promissory note contains:
> The term 'promissory note' inserted in the body of the instrument and expressed in the language employed in drawing up the instrument;
> An unconditional promise to pay a determinate sum of money;
> A statement of the time of payment;
> A statement of the place where payment is to be made;
> The name of the person to whom or to whose order payment is to be made;
> A statement of the date and of the place where the promissory note is issued;
> The signature of the person who issues the instrument (maker).

[5.172] The rules governing the operation of an international bill of exchange in the convention may also apply to an international promissory note except for those applicable only to the drawee.

Law affecting use of guarantee and standby credit

[5.173] The UN Convention on Independent Guarantees and Standby Letters of Credit was adopted and opened for signature by the General Assembly by its resolution 50/48 of 11 December 1995. The draft convention was prepared by UNCITRAL, in particular, the Working Group on International Contract Practices at its 13th–23rd sessions. The convention is particularly designed to facilitate the use of independent guarantees and standby credit. It also consolidates basic principles and characteristics shared by the independent guarantee and the standby credit. For convenience, the convention uses the neutral term 'undertaking' to refer to both types of instruments in the text of the convention.[94] For the time being, the use of independent guarantee and the documentary credit (or letter of credit) are regulated by the domestic law. Inconsistencies and sometimes conflicts are seen between laws of the countries which do not share the same legal tradition.

[5.174] The convention is meant to regulate the use of two types of instruments: independent guarantee and standby credit, but does not differentiate them expressly. In fact, art 2 of the convention defines both types of instruments as undertakings. Thus, broadly speaking, an independent guarantee or a standby credit is a basic means of finance in international transactions. It can be used in a variety of situations, for example, to secure performance of contractual obligations, whether in a construction or supply contract, or to perform a commercial payment obligation. It can also be used to secure repayment of an advance payment; to secure a winning bidder's obligation to enter into a procurement contract; to ensure reimbursement of payment under another undertaking; to support issuance of commercial letters of credit and insurance coverage; and to enhance creditworthiness of public and private borrowers.[95]

[5.175] It is hoped that by establishing a harmonised set of rules for the said two types of instruments, the convention will provide greater legal certainty in their use for day-to-day commercial transactions, as well as marshal credit for public borrowers. In addition, by making a single legal regime available to both independent guarantees and standby letters of credit, the convention will facilitate the issuance of both instruments in combination with each other, for example, the issuance of a standby letter of credit to support the issuance of a guarantee, or the reverse case. The convention also facilitates 'syndication' of lenders, by allowing them to combine more easily both types of instruments. Lenders participating in a syndication can spread credit risk among themselves, which enables them to extend larger volumes of credit.[96]

[5.176] The convention consists of seven chapters and 29 articles. Chapter I defines the scope of application, and the meaning of undertakings. It also explains the meaning of independence of undertaking and of internationality of undertaking. Chapter II provides

---

94. Explanatory note by the UNCITRAL secretariat on the Convention on Independent Guarantees and Standby Letters of Credit, para 2.
95. Explanatory note by the UNCITRAL secretariat on the Convention on Independent Guarantees and Standby Letters of Credit, para 3.
96. Explanatory note by the UNCITRAL secretariat on the Convention on Independent Guarantees and Standby Letters of Credit, para 4.

[5.176] International Commercial Law

interpretations, including the principles of interpretation and definitions of several basic terms. Chapter III deals with issues relating to the form and content of an undertaking, such as the issuance and amendment of an undertaking, transfer of the beneficiary's right to demand payment, assignment of proceeds, cessation of right to demand payment, and expiry of an undertaking. Chapter IV sets out rights and obligations of the parties to an undertaking, as well as defences available to them. Issues covered in this chapter include determination of rights and obligations, standard of conduct and liability of guarantor/issuer, demand for payment, examination of documents, making of payment, set-off and exception to payment obligations. Chapter V deals with the use of provisional court measures, such as injunctions and interim orders. Chapter VI sets out the rules of conflict of laws for recognising a choice of law clause and determining an applicable law. Chapter VII contains final clauses, covering incidental issues such as depository, application of the convention to territorial units, effect of declaration, reservations, entry into force and denunciation.

[5.177] The convention is meant to provide a set of rules sanctioned by its status as an international treaty. It thus gives legislative support to the autonomy of the parties to apply agreed rules of practice such as UCP 500 as formulated by the ICC, and the ICC Uniform Rules for Demand Guarantees (URDG), published in 1992 for the purpose of providing uniform rules in the use of contract guarantees or bonds. In a sense, the convention is supplementary to the operation of private rules or codified commercial practices by dealing with issues beyond the scope of such rules. For example, it sets out rules for dealing with the question of fraudulent or abusive demands for payment, and also provides judicial remedies in such instances.[97]

[5.178] A number of ICC codified rules appear to be relevant to the convention. There are the ICC Uniform Rules for Contract Bonds published in 1993, the ICC Uniform Rules for Demand Guarantees published in 1993 and the ICC Uniform Rules for Contract Guarantees published in 1978. The ICC Uniform Rules for Contract Bonds have some similarities with the present convention. However, the ICC Uniform Rules for Contract Bonds are largely intended to deal with the contract bonds or guarantees offered by any companies or individuals who may have an option either to pay a sum of money or to perform the underlying contract for which the bond has been offered,[98] while the present convention appears to place more emphasis on the independent guarantees or standby credits offered by banks, financial institutions and any other persons to pay a

---

97. Explanatory note by the UNCITRAL secretariat on the Convention on Independent Guarantees and Standby Letters of Credit, para 5.
98. The meaning of contract bond is defined in art 2 of the ICC Uniform Rules for Contract Bonds. According to this provision, a bond means any bond, guarantee or other instrument in writing, issued or executed by the guarantor in favour of the beneficiary pursuant to which the guarantor undertakes on default of another person to pay or satisfy any claim for damages or compensation up to the bond amount; or at the option of the guarantor either to pay a sum or to perform the contractual obligation of the other person.

sum of money. The ICC Uniform Rules for Demand Guarantees purport to provide uniform rules for the use of a demand guarantee, defined in art 2 of the rules as:

> ... any guarantee, bond or other payment undertaking, however named or described, by a bank, insurance company or other body or person (hereinafter called the Guarantor) given in writing for the payment of money on presentation in conformity with the terms of the undertaking of a written demand for payment and such other document(s) (for example, a certificate by an architect or engineer, a judgment or an arbitral award) as may be specified in the Guarantee.

This definition suggests that the ICC Uniform Rules for Demand Guarantees are meant to apply to similar types of transactions covered by the present convention, and also that there is certain overlapping between the ICC Uniform Rules for Demand Guarantees and the ICC Uniform Rules for Contract Bonds. The ICC Uniform Rules for Contract Guarantees are meant to apply to all types of contract guarantees. The Uniform Rules for Demand Guarantees were introduced to replace part of the role meant for the Uniform Rules for Contract Guarantees. In this sense, the Uniform Rules for Contract Guarantees are likely to be replaced gradually by other more specific rules in the future.

Chapter Six

Introduction to International Banking and Financing

Review of international banking and financing system

[6.1] The Australian Law Reform Commission in its report on *Legal Risk in International Transactions 1996* (ALRC 80) observes as follows:[1]

> Banks play a central role in virtually all international commercial transactions. The inter-bank payments systems provide a mechanism by which value can be transferred from one person in one country to a different person in a separate country. This is primarily a mechanical function but it is fundamental to effective international commerce. Banks also contribute to the management by their customers of credit, settlement and other financial risks. They do this primarily through international trade finance and through the loans and other financial services they provide for international investments. Banks play this central role partly because of the competitive advantages they have built up as institutions but partly also because of laws which, for prudential reasons, give them a virtual monopoly over the payments systems and preserve their advantages in other banking activities.

[6.2] Banks in fact play a similar role in both international and domestic markets, although they have to tailor their services to suit the needs of international trade, commerce and finance in international markets. There is not really such a thing as a truly international banking and financing system, because banks exist and operate under the laws of the relevant countries where they carry out their banking and financing business, and the law of each country does not necessarily coordinate with any other. Indeed, if there were a uniform international banking system, the Bank of Credit and Commerce International (BCCI) affair, involving a bank which took advantage of loopholes in the banking laws of different countries and scandalously carried out massive illegal activities defrauding creditors and governments, would not have progressed to such a disastrous stage.[2] While many disputes arising from the BCCI affair were settled in the courts of the UK,[3] the BCCI accident demonstrated the need for better banking supervision at an

---

1. ALRC 80, para 5.3, available at <http://www.austlii.edu.au/au/other/alrc/publications/reports/80>.
2. For discussions on the BCCI affair, see 'Symposium: International Bank Supervision Post BCCI' (1992) 26 *The International Lawyer* 943.

Introduction to International Banking and Financing [6.4]

international level.[4] We use the word 'system' merely to refer to the present state of development of international banking and financing.

[6.3] The present system of international banking and financing is based on two main forces:

- private banks and financial institutions operating internationally; and
- international financial institutions or organisations established under agreements of sovereign states (for example, the IMF and regional development banks).

The latter type of organisation is not privately owned: its funds are contributed by member countries in accordance with agreements.

Two examples of a privately organised banking system are SWIFT and CHIPS. SWIFT stands for the Society for Worldwide Interbank Financial Telecommunication, which is a non-profit cooperative society organised under Belgian law, and owned by numerous banks throughout the world. SWIFT is a central switch system linking numerous and diverse bank terminals all over the world. The central switch currently consists of two slice processors, one situated in the Netherlands and the other in the USA, each functioning as an independent and ad hoc network, linking SWIFT access points. Each country is assigned to a SWIFT access point. Interbank communication is via the SWIFT access points mediated by a slice processor. A system control processor monitors and controls functions of the system but is not involved in routing messages. Each message is validated and processed under heavy security.[5]

CHIPS stands for the Clearing House Interbank Payments Systems, which is a New York based automated private sector clearing facility for large value transfers. It is owned and operated by the New York Clearing House Association. CHIPS is a central switch communication and net settlement system where participating banks exchange same-day irrevocable payment orders over dedicated communication lines linking each onto the central computer of CHIPS. Credit risks are controlled by bilateral credit limits, net debit caps, collateral, and a loss-sharing arrangement among all participants, effectively providing for settlement finality. CHIPS settlement takes place at the end of each day's banking activity.[6]

[6.4] Each bank intending to operate or carry on banking business in a given country must satisfy the requirements of the law of that country. Many countries allow foreign banks to carry on banking business locally. Banks internationalise their operations by establishing branches or subsidiaries in foreign countries. When a country prohibits or restricts foreign banks from entering its territory (China, for example, opened its doors to foreign banking, on a restricted basis, only in 1990), a bank intending to operate in this country will

---

3. For example, *Morris v Rayners Enterprises Incorporated; Morris v Agrichemicals Ltd*, House of Lords, decided 30 October 1997; and *Malik v Bank of Credit; Mahmud v Bank of Credit*, House of Lords, decided 12 June 1997, available at <http://www.parliament.the-statione>.
4. Baxter and de Saram, 'BCCI: The Lessons for Banking Supervision' in Robert C Effros (ed), *Current Legal Issues Affecting Central Banks*, vol 4, Washington DC, IMF, 1997, pp 371–87.
5. ALRC 80, Box 5A, available at <http://www.austlii.edu.au/au/other/alrc/publications/reports/80>.
6. ALRC 80, Box 5B, available at <http://www.austlii.edu.au/au/other/alrc/publications/reports/80>.

[6.4]   **International Commercial Law**

have to invest in the existing financial institutions, if such investment is allowed, or find a cooperating local bank. In any event, the operation of an international bank in a country is solely subject to the law and jurisdiction of the country concerned. This is one of the essential features of the so-called international banking and financial system.

[6.5] International financial institutions or organisations established under international agreements play an important, though less extensive (compared with privately owned banks) role in international banking and financing. The major international financial institutions are:

- the International Monetary Fund (IMF);
- the International Bank for Reconstruction and Development (World Bank); and
- the regional development banks, such as the African Development Bank and the Asian Development Bank.

These institutions are able to provide funds to member countries pursuant to the relevant international agreements. They may invest in international financial markets in the same way as private banks do, but their main function is to facilitate and support the economic development of the member countries.[7]

[6.6] We may conclude that there is no independent system of international banking and financing as such, and banking and financing involving international elements are subject to different rules of domestic law,[8] and customs and usage accepted in international trade and international finance. Conflict of laws is thus an essential issue in international banking and financing, as are the existing international conventions or usage, such as:

- the Convention on the Unification of the Law relating to Cheques (Uniform Law on Cheques);[9]
- the UN Convention on International Bills of Exchange and International Promissory Notes;[10]
- the Unidroit Convention on International Financial Leasing;[11]
- the Unidroit Convention on International Factoring;[12]

---

7.   For relevant discussions, see Broadlow (ed), *International Borrowing*, 2nd ed, International Law Institute, Washington, 1986, pp 31–208.
8.   For example, the regulation of domestic financial institutions in the United States, EU and a number of other countries is discussed in Kumar (ed), *World Bank Discussion Paper No 362: The Regulation of Non-Bank Financial Institutions*, The World Bank, Washington DC, 1997.
9.   It was adopted on 19 March 1931 and entered into force on 1 January 1934.
10.   The convention was adopted on 9 December 1988 and is not yet in force. As at July 2002, only Guinea, Honduras, and Mexico had ratified the convention.
11.   The convention was concluded on 28 May 1988. Three ratifications are required for its operation. The Convention came into operation on 1 May 1996. As at February 2001 its membership consisted of Belarus, France, Hungary, Italy, Latvia, Nigeria, Panama, Republic of Uzbekistan, and the Russian Federation.
12.   The convention was concluded on 28 May 1988, and became operational on 1 May 1995. As at February 2001, France, Germany, Hungary, Italy, Latvia and Nigeria had ratified the Convention.

- the 1992 UNCITRAL Model Law on International Credit Transfers, which provides a model for national law governing international transfers of payment orders between banks, and can be regarded as an international document regulating international banking;[13]
- the UN Convention on the Assignment of Receivables in International Trade 2001;[14]
- the General Agreement on Trade and Services, which is part of the WTO Agreement adopted in the Uruguay negotiations, and is examined in **Chapter 10** of this book;
- ICC Uniform Rules for Bank-to-Bank Reimbursements (known as URR 525, published in 1995 and entering into force on 1 July 1996);
- acceptable customs and usage in international trade and finance; and
- the regulations of the relevant stock exchange or the rules set out by the relevant self-regulatory bodies, such as the International Capital Markets Association (ICMA), or the Australian Stock Exchange (ASX).

[6.7] The issues of international banking and financing have to be examined in a particular context: the law of a particular country or particular laws or rules which become binding because of the operation of the rules of conflict of laws. For example, the primary legal support for payments systems is the law of contract. The rights and liabilities of the payer, payee and each of the banks in the chain of transactions are primarily defined by the contracts between each of them and by agency principles. These principles are then supplemented by specific arrangements for communication of payment instructions between banks by, for example, cable or telex ('wire transfers') or through telecommunications networks such as SWIFT. They are also supplemented by clearing house arrangements. Clearing houses tend to be national systems rather than international systems like SWIFT. Thus, the USA uses Fedwire and CHIPS. Switzerland has the SIC ('Swiss Interbank Clearing'), the UK uses CHAPS, Japan uses BOJ-NET and Gaitame-Yen, and Germany uses the EIL-ZV and EAF. Some of these systems are owned and operated by a central bank. Others are owned and operated by private associations. There are a variety of legal arrangements underpinning these systems.[15]

International financial centres and international finance

[6.8] International financial centres are where international banking and financing activities are concentrated and carried out. New York, Tokyo and London are currently the three major international centres. London is the oldest of the three, and is located in an advantageous time zone which allows it to trade with Tokyo in the morning and New York in the evening. New York became important after the Second World War and Tokyo joined the league only 20 years ago as a result of the deregulation of the Japanese financial system. In terms of trading volume, the New York Stock Exchange has become

---

13. A directive of the European Parliament and of the Council of the EU based on the principles of this Model Law was issued on 27 January 1997.
14. The Convention requires a minimum of five ratifications before becoming effective. As at October 2002, only Luxembourg had signed it, but not yet ratified.
15. ALRC 80, paras 5.9, 5.10, available at <http://www.austlii.edu.au/au/other/alrc/publications/reports/80>.

[6.8]

the largest centre in recent years. It is followed by Tokyo and London. Other centres, such as Paris, Chicago, Toronto, Singapore, Hong Kong, Switzerland, Johannesburg, Amsterdam, Sydney and Kuala Lumpur, have become increasingly important.

A large number of overseas banks operate in these centres, and bring with them a large amount of foreign currency. International syndicated loans are arranged, and bonds and securities are issued, in these centres. Foreign exchange is bought and sold and different currencies are also swapped. Modern computer and electronic communications have truly globalised these centres and provided the means for international trade and commerce. Because of the high concentration of banks and financial institutions, and strong competition between them, funds are readily accessible in these centres. The presence of international banks in these centres also provides necessary expertise for international finance, particularly finance for exports or imports.

Issue of bonds and international finance

Meaning of bond

[6.9] One method of fundraising is to issue bonds on international financial markets. In legal terms, a bond is a 'formal deed whereby one person binds himself to do something to or for another, normally to pay a specified sum of money immediately or at a future date'.[16] Alternatively, an economist may describe a bond as a debt security issued by entities such as corporations, governments or their agencies.[17] More simply, a bond can also be regarded as 'a security on which interest is payable on a regular basis'.[18] These definitions suggest that a 'bond' is a written undertaking (document) provided by a borrower of money to pay the creditor (lender or holder of the bond) interest and the principal of the borrowing in the manner and sum as set out in the undertaking (document). Most bonds are unsecured debt securities.

[6.10] A number of terms in the above definitions should be explained. 'Deed' indicates the existence of certain legal relationships between the issuer and holders of a bond. In this context, 'deed' refers to all types of securities or debentures which are issued for the purpose of fundraising and which are purchased by investors in the belief that interest as specified will be paid regularly on the securities. A security is a 'type of intangible property in the form of an enforceable claim held by one person against another person'.[19] A debenture is a form of debt security issued by a company or issuer to raise funds, and is backed by the general credit of the company and issuer. In Australia, 'securities' include debentures, stocks,[20] bonds, shares or notes (where applicable), issued or proposed to be issued by a government or a body corporate or

---

16. Walker, *The Oxford Companion to Law*, Clarendon Press, Oxford, 1980, p 140.
17. County NatWest, *Dictionary of Investment Terms*, 3rd ed, Sydney, 1994.
18. Baxter, *International Banking and Finance*, Carswell, Toronto, 1989, p 95.
19. Baxt, Maxwell and Bajada, *Stock Markets and the Securities Industry*, Butterworths, Sydney, 1988, p 1.
20. 'Stock' is a generic term referring to equities, shares or bonds.

Introduction to International Banking and Financing [6.14]

unincorporated, extending to any right or option[21] in respect of any such debentures, stocks, shares, bonds, notes or a prescribed interest.[22]

[6.11] A bond has several characteristics:

- First, it evidences the existence of a debtor–creditor relationship under which the issuer (debtor) of the bond undertakes to pay the holder (creditor) of the bond a sum of money at the maturity of the bond and interest on the sum during the life of the bond.
- Second, an 'international bond' (which usually refers to a bond issued by a foreign resident in a domestic market, or a bond issued widely in international markets) is transferable or negotiable, although the negotiability of a 'domestic bond' (which usually refers to a bond issued in a domestic market by a local resident) may be restricted.
- Third, the security of the principal and interest is the major concern of investors, who expect to regain the same amount of money paid for the price of the bond at its maturity and receive the profit of interest on the bond during the term of the bond. This is perhaps the fundamental difference between investing in bonds and in shares.

[6.12] Bonds are mainly used as a means of fundraising. For an issuer of bonds, this can be an alternative way of financing its business operations, although it may issue them for different purposes, such as expanding its capital base, complying with regulations, prudent banking, internationalising its operations and prestige, and others.[23] For investors or holders of the bonds, this would appear to be an effective way of investing money because bonds should yield higher interest than bank deposits.

[6.13] Banks play an important role in international bond markets by either selling or buying bonds. They have the financial capacity and required expertise to operate in international bond markets. The major banks often act as lead managers (organisers) of the new issues. Their involvement gives the public confidence in the bonds issued.

Categorisation of international bonds

[6.14] Bonds may be divided into three types according to the market concerned: domestic, foreign and international.[24] 'A domestic bond is issued in one country by a resident of that country and denominated in the currency of the country.'[25] 'A foreign bond issue is carried out by an entity which is not incorporated in the country of the issue. The currency, however, is that of the country where the issue is effected.'[26] International bonds may be regarded as eurobonds, and may also be 'defined as an issue of bonds

---

21. 'Option' means a contract under which one party (the buyer or seller) has a right to buy or sell a specified security or asset at a stipulated price before or on a specified date. A right to buy is regarded as a 'call option', and a right to sell is called a 'put option'.
22. Securities Industry Act 1980 (Cth) s 4(1).
23. Alba, 'Tapping the Eurobond Market: the Malaysian Experience', in Pierce et al (eds), *Current Issues of International Financial Law*, Malaya Law Review/Butterworths, Singapore, 1985, p 143.
24. Roberts, *Law Relating to International Banking*, Gresham Books, Cambridge, 1998, p 96.
25. Ibid.
26. Ibid.

[6.14]   denominated in a currency which is different from that of the country of the place of issue and which are sold to investors internationally, rather than in one country'.[27] The division of bonds as suggested in this paragraph represents the approaches to the categorisation of bonds for study purposes. For the purpose of raising funds internationally, all these three types of bonds can be used because denominated currency and place of issue do not necessarily constitute restrictions on access to bonds (as far as the investors are concerned), and funds (as far as the issuers are concerned) within the world trading system based on WTO Agreements.

[6.15]   Bonds can be issued under various terms, and can be categorised into different groups on the basis of these terms. For example, according to the rate of interest, bonds can be divided into fixed rate bonds or floating rate notes; and according to the date of redemption, a bond can be a fixed term bond or a perpetual bond.

[6.16]   Watkins classed bonds into eight groups, as follows:
- those based on their redemption provisions;
- those based on their interest provisions;
- those regarded as convertible bonds;
- those called secured bonds;
- depositary receipts;
- euronotes;
- income certificates;
- those treated as subordinate issues.[28]

[6.17]   In contrast, Prime categorised bonds as follows:
- convertible bonds (convertibility of the bonds into other types of securities);
- euronotes; and
- eurocommercial paper.[29]

[6.18]   These classification systems suggest that categories of bonds are neither exclusive nor exhaustive. A bond may fall into several categories at the same time. New categories or types of bonds can be created at any time, depending on the purpose of the issue and market demand.

[6.19]   A general survey of the types of bonds available in the international bond markets is necessary in order to familiarise ourselves with the terminology of international bonds. Bearing in mind that international bond markets are undergoing constant change, innovation and expansion, any discussion on terms and categories of bonds provides only a basis for understanding the nature of various bonds issued or to be issued in international bond markets. By investigating the basic terms, we may be able to identify some

---

27.   Ibid.
28.   Watkins, 'Types of Bonds', in Pierce et al, note 23, pp 111–23.
29.   Prime, *International Bonds and Certificates of Deposit*, Butterworths, London, 1990, pp 163–229A.

essential features or elements of international bonds, which are the bases for the creation of any new types of bonds in the future.

Common terms of international bonds

Perpetual bonds

[6.20] The expression 'perpetual bonds' suggests that the bonds issued under this term do not have a maturity date. This type of bond can be issued as long as the relevant domestic law so allows. For example, s 1050 of the Australian Corporations Law (uniform throughout Australia) provides that a debenture (which includes a bond) or deed is not invalid merely because it contains a condition which makes it irredeemable or redeemable only on the happening of a contingency, however remote, or at the end of a period, however long. A perpetual bond can thus be issued in Australia provided that other requirements for a bond issue are complied with.

[6.21] Issuing bonds in perpetuity is a means of attracting investment and raising funds. Like any other terms or features of bonds, a perpetual bond appeals to some investors in certain circumstances, but may not be attractive to others. Thus, a perpetual bond may contain an option to convert it into a fixed term bond. 'Option' in this context means a contractual right to do something before or on a specified date. Examples of perpetual bonds are the National Westminster Bank issue, Citicorp issue and 'flip-flop' issues which were managed by Morgan Guaranty Ltd for Sweden, Belgium and Denmark.[30] The Citicorp issue can be sold back to the issuer two-and-a-half years after the date of the issue and 'flip-flop' issues can be converted into fixed term bonds one or two years after the date of issue, or converted back to perpetual bonds under certain conditions.[31] Similarly, certain large companies, such as BTR Nylex and Amcor, issued perpetual subordinated convertible notes which gave the holders of the notes an option to transfer the notes or to convert the debt into equity under specified conditions. These examples illustrate the variety of forms a perpetual bond can take, and the diversity of conditions which can be attached to a perpetual bond.

Extendible bonds and retractable bonds

[6.22] These terms indicate the level of flexibility in the bonds issued. For example, a bond may allow the holder to extend the term of the bond for a specified period of time before a prescribed date or to redeem (retract) the bond earlier than the fixed date. Such terms can be incorporated into any bond, whether fixed term or perpetual.

Fixed rate bonds

[6.23] This means that the interest on the bonds is payable at a fixed rate. A fixed rate can apply to either a fixed term bond or a perpetual bond, or a combination of other terms.

---

30. Watkins, note 28 above, pp 111–12.
31. Prime, note 29 above, p 170.

[6.24] International Commercial Law

Floating rate notes

[6.24] 'Floating rate notes' (FRNs) means that the interest rate on the bonds is changeable or adjustable in response to fluctuations in market rates of interest. FRNs are usually determined in accordance with, or based on, the London Inter-bank Offered Rate (LIBOR).[32] The frequency of, or interval between, interest adjustment varies from bond to bond, ranging from one month to several. The floating rate reflects a fair deal for both the issuer and bondholders and it distributes the risk in fluctuations in interest rates between the issuer and the holders. A variation on FRNs is a bond with re-fixable interest, which is something between a fixed rate and a floating rate. Re-fixable interest means that the bond has a condition which allows the issuer to review the interest rate after a certain period of time or upon the occurrence of a stipulated event. FRNs can also be subject to a capped interest rate. This means that the interest on the FRNs will not exceed a fixed sum in case the market rate is higher than the fixed amount. A capped FRN is a device for the protection of the borrower.

'Drop-lock' bonds

[6.25] This expression refers to an arrangement whereby interest on the bonds floats if the interest remains above a stipulated level, and locks (becomes fixed) if the market rate drops under the stipulated level.[33] It appears to be a protective device for the holders of the bonds and allows them to receive minimum interest on the investment. By the same token, a bond can have a floating rate for a certain period of time and a fixed rate for another period of time. Drop-lock bonds contrast with capped FRNs as the former ensure that the investor has a guarantee of the minimum interest to be received, and the latter ensure that the borrower has a guarantee of the maximum interest to be paid.

Zero coupon bonds or notes

[6.26] 'Coupon' originally referred to a voucher attached to a bond or other form of security, which could be exchanged for cash when an interest payment on the security was due. In its extended meaning, 'coupon' became a synonym of 'interest'. Therefore, the expression 'coupon securities' describes securities (bonds or notes) which pay periodic interest, and the expression 'non-coupon securities' refers to securities which do not pay periodic interest. Accordingly, 'zero coupon' bonds or notes means that there is no periodic interest payment on the bonds or notes so issued. The investor profits from this type of bond by purchasing them at a discount price (usually there is a significant margin between the nominal value of the bonds and the actual purchase price), and selling them at an appreciated value (the full price). In other words, an investor receives a lump sum payment including 'interest' (or profit) at the maturity of the securities when investing in zero coupon bonds or notes. Tax laws of both the issuer's country and the holder's country may affect the holder's (investor's) benefit under this type of bond, because interest is subject to withholding tax and gains from redemption of the bonds may be subject to income tax.

---

32. LIBOR represents the interest rate adopted by major banks in London when lending cash to each other.
33. Watkins, note 28 above, p 115.

Introduction to International Banking and Financing [6.30]

[6.27] An example of the use of zero coupon bonds is seen in the Brazilian Export Financing Programme for Aircraft, which was subject to a panel investigation under the DSU (Understanding on Rules and Procedures Governing the Settlement of Disputes) in October 1998 and April 1999. The Canadian Government complained that certain measures adopted in the Programme constituted subsidies prohibited by the relevant WTO agreements. Paragraph 2.6 of the *Report of the Panel: Brazil — Export Financing Programme for Aircraft* describes the PROEX interest equalisation payments (PROEX stands for Programa de Financiamento as Exportações) scheme in the following words:[34]

> PROEX interest equalisation payments, pursuant to the commitment, begin after the aircraft is exported and paid for by the purchaser. PROEX payments are made to the lending financial institution in the form of non-interest bearing National Treasury Bonds (Notas do Tesouro Nacional – Série I) referred to as NTN-I bonds. These are denominated in Brazilian Reais indexed to the United States dollar. The bonds are issued by the Brazilian National Treasury to its agent bank, Banco do Brasil, which then passes them on to the lending banks financing the transaction. The bonds are issued in the name of the lending bank which can decide to redeem them on a semi-annual basis for the duration of the financing or discount them for a lump sum in the market. PROEX resembles a series of zero coupon bonds which mature at six month intervals over the course of the financing period. The bonds can only be redeemed in Brazil and only in Brazilian currency at the exchange rate prevailing at the time of payment. If the lending bank is outside of Brazil, it may appoint a Brazilian bank as its agent to receive the semi-annual payments on its behalf.

[6.28] From the description above, it appears that the NTN-I bonds are a kind of financing or lending arrangement provided or guaranteed by the Brazilian Government to promote the sale of Brazilian aircraft. This is why the Panel concludes in its Report that 'PROEX interest rate equalisation payments on exports of Brazilian regional aircraft are subsidies within the meaning of Article 1 of the SCM Agreement [Agreement on Subsidies and Countervailing Measures] which are contingent upon export performance within the meaning of Article 3.1(a) of that Agreement'.[35]

Strip bonds

[6.29] A strip bond is a new product which has been seen in a number of jurisdictions, such as Canada and Hong Kong. It is similar to the zero coupon bond in the sense that it is not, generally speaking, a conventional interest-bearing debt security. A strip bond entitles the holder to a single payment of a fixed amount in the future without the payment of any interest in the interim. The expected 'payment', which is known as a 'strip bond', refers to either an amount payable on account of principal, or an amount payable on account of interest in respect of one or more 'underlying bonds' (debt securities issued or guaranteed by a government or anyone with appropriate authority).

[6.30] The purchase price or present value of a strip bond is determined by discounting the amount of the payment to be received on the payment or maturity date of the strip bond by the appropriate interest rate or yield factor. In particular, a strip bond may be purchased in several forms, for example:

> By way of 'alter-ego receipt' in the form of a deposit receipt or certificate issued by the person taking the purchase money, the receipt or certificate which represents the relevant segregated

---

34. WTO, Report of the Panel: *Brazil — Export Financing Programme for Aircraft* WT/DS46/R, 14 April 1999, available at <http://www.wto.org>.
35. Id, para 8.1.

[6.30]

underlying interest coupons or principal residues may entitle its holder to take physical delivery of the underlying coupons or residues;

By way of 'non alter-ego receipt' in the form of a deposit or certificate issued by the person taking the purchase money, the receipt or certificate which represents either an undivided interest in a pool of interest coupons or principal residues held by the person taking the purchase money, or an interest or principal payment to be made in respect of one of more underlying bonds held by the person taking the purchase money, does not entitle its holder to take physical delivery of the underlying coupons or residues unless the contract or the relevant rules stipulate otherwise; and

By any special certificate or document created by the relevant authority to serve certain functions which are not covered by alter-ego receipts or non alter-ego receipts.

[6.31] Since the strip bond is not a conventional type of bond, the terms, rights and obligations of the holder need to be defined clearly in the contract concerned. The strip bond may give the holder a certain tax advantage. However, such advantage is really artificial and must be assessed in the particular circumstances of each individual investor.

Convertible bonds

[6.32] This type of bond can be converted into equity shares of the corporation that issued them: 'The basis of a convertible issue is the issue of a bond which pays interest in the normal way. Within the rights conferred by the bond, and as part of its terms and conditions, the holder of the bond has the right, in certain circumstances, to convert the bond into shares of the issuing corporation or an associated corporation'.[36] This type of bond transcends the boundary between debt and equity, which are different means of fundraising. The right to convert is an incentive to investors who are interested in investing in the equity of the issuing company. On the other hand, a convertible bond reduces the issuer's need for cash flow at the maturity of the bond if the holder chooses to exercise the right of conversion.

[6.33] A type of bond similar to a convertible bond is a bond with warrant. Warrant means that the bond is issued under a promise that the warrant holder has an 'option of purchasing shares in the issuer at a specified price'.[37] Watkins treated this as a variation of the convertible bond.[38] The difference between a bond with warrant and a convertible bond is that the warrant can be separated and transferred independently of the bond on derivatives markets. A derivatives market is where derivatives, such as futures contracts,[39] foreign exchange swap contracts and options which are securities (or financial assets) that derive their value from another security, are traded. A bond with warrant means that while an investor holds the bond issued, he or she may sell the right to purchase shares under specified conditions to another person. The holder of the bond may make a profit from the interest on the bonds and the sale of the warrant. At the

---

36. Prime, note 29 above, p 194.
37. Id, p 196.
38. Watkins, note 28 above, pp 116–17.
39. A futures contract, in brief, is a contract to buy or sell an agreed quantity of a financial instrument at a specified date and price in the future. For example, an investor who intends to buy shares in a particular company on a future date may buy (known as 'going long') the 'share futures' (a fictional form of security created for the purpose of trading the underlying shares in the future) of the company at an agreed future price to cover the risk of an increase in the share price. At the end of the contract, the investor may sell (known as 'going short') the share futures at their prevailing price.

same time, the issuer may raise funds from two related sources — the issue of the bond and the transfer of shares.

Secured bonds

[6.34] Bonds can be secured or unsecured, although secured eurobond issues 'are something of a rarity, primarily because the eurobond market is traditionally considered as a prime borrowers' market'.[40] Whether a bond is secured or not usually depends on whether it can attract enough investors or market demand. The issue of secured bonds is a method to increase investors' confidence, but they may also be issued merely to satisfy the requirements of relevant regulations or maintain consistency of the issuer's practice. For example, the Development Finance Corp of New Zealand issued eurobonds 'pursuant to the provisions of a common trust deed' and the bonds were 'secured by a floating charge over all of the assets and undertakings of the issuer'.[41]

[6.35] A bond can be secured by using the issuer's assets as security, such as a floating or fixed charge over the assets. 'Charge' suggests a certain security interest of the chargee (creditor or holder of the charge) in the thing charged.[42] Such interest is enforceable upon the occurrence of the stipulated event against the thing charged. For example, an issuer (company) of bonds may guarantee that the creditors (investors) will be paid out of its assets if it defaults in payment of either interest or principal of the debt. The creditors may thus have a charge over the issuer's assets, which will be enforceable upon the issuer's default. A fixed charge is a charge attached to the issuer's assets and the issuer is obliged to disclose to potential creditors the existence of the fixed charge when dealing with them.

A 'floating charge' is a form of potentially fixable charge which floats over the debtor's assets, including an asset to be acquired in the future. It is a charge over the asset, not a charge attached to the asset.[43] The difference between these two types of charges is that the floating charge does not restrict the debtor's capacity to deal with assets in his or her ordinary course of business until the prescribed event occurs (that is, default of the debtor), and there is no need to disclose to the potential creditors the existence of the floating charge. The process by which the stipulated event takes place and the floating charge becomes attached to the asset(s) is called crystallisation. Where the floating charge is crystallised, the debtor cannot deal freely with the asset(s) to which the charge is attached. The legal implications of charges are mainly seen in company, securities or bankruptcy law.

[6.36] Negative pledge, which is a restriction on the issuer's power to grant security interest over its assets to other creditors (see **[6.48]**), is a device to secure the bondholders'

---

40. Walkins, note 28 above, p 118.
41. Ibid.
42. Section 9 of the Australian Corporations Law defines 'charge' as 'a charge created in any way and includes a mortgage and an agreement to give or execute a charge or mortgage, whether on demand or otherwise'.
43. Sykes, *The Law of Securities*, Law Book Co, Sydney, 1986, p 924.

interests in the bonds. It is often incorporated into the conditions and terms of the bonds and is enforceable as a contractual term.

Depositary receipts or certificates of deposit

[6.37] Depositary receipts, participation certificates or certificates of deposit are a means of short-term borrowing. They are issued by a bank for itself or on behalf of a client. A holder of the receipts or certificates is promised the face value of the securities at their maturity. Interest payment is included in the face value. In a domestic market, they are usually bearer instruments and transferable. In an international market, the terms of a depositary receipt or certificate may be qualified by the specific conditions and purpose for which it is issued. Often depositary receipts or certificates are issued to overcome various legal technicalities which prohibit or disadvantage the issue of securities in the form of bonds. Watkins summarised the following five reasons for their use:

- a prohibition on public issues under the law of the place where the issuer is located;
- a prohibition on issues in bearer form;
- the imposition of stamp duties on bond issues or on issues in bearer form;
- the imposition of an issue tax or transfer tax on bond issues; and
- the imposition of a withholding tax on bond issues or issues in bearer form.[44]

In light of the above, the depositary receipts or certificates may be regarded as a kind of scheme tailored for the purpose of maximising the benefit of bond issues under a particular domestic law, or circumventing (not quite illegally) restrictions on the issue of bonds under the governing law. For example, Venezuelan banks in the 1970s and 1980s issued depositary receipts which allowed the depositors to have undivided proprietary interest in the underlying deposit and a right to receive interest payments in proportion to their deposits. The terms of the issue were set out for the purpose of taking advantage of tax-free interest payments on short-term deposits under Venezuelan law. Under the terms of the issue, the depositary receipts were reissued every six months and interest on the deposits was paid every six months, although the maturity of the deposits was agreed to be five years.[45]

Euronotes

[6.38] 'Euronotes' refers to a special type of notes (or bonds) which are issued through the Revolving Underwriting Facility (RUF) or Note Issuance Facility (NIF). Strictly speaking, 'euronotes' (and 'eurobonds') is a misnomer, because the notes (or bonds) are neither issued exclusively in the European financial markets, nor are they issued exclusively in European currencies. Given that the word 'euro' is probably derived from the Greek meaning external, the term 'euronotes' (or 'eurobonds') was probably adopted to describe notes (or bonds) issued external to the country whose currency is the nominated currency of the issue. In any event, there is no direct or exclusive connection between euronotes and European financial markets.

---

44. Watkins, note 28 above, p 119.
45. Ibid.

[6.39] Euronotes are identified by the manner in which they are issued. They can be issued through either:

- RUF, which means that the banks involved 'agree not merely to sell the notes issued by the issuer but also to underwrite the issue of the short-term loan by agreeing to buy any which are unsold at a fixed price or to make the loan instead';[46] or

- NIF, which means that the banks involved 'agree only to endeavour to sell the short-term notes under an issue by the issuer when called to do so'.[47]

Both means suggest a direct and decisive involvement of banks in the issue. Because of the role of banks, euronotes can be regarded as a bridge between the securities market and the banks' lending market. Banks may also act as creditors in many international transactions to provide loans to exporters and importers.

Eurobonds

[6.40] Generally speaking, the eurobond is a security underwritten by an international syndicate and issued in countries other than the country of the currency in which the security is denominated. Since eurobonds are usually issued in a large quantity in different countries, they are usually issued and managed by international syndicates. Eurobonds are normally unsecured and subject to a fixed rate of interest. They usually carry a term of five to ten years, but may contain an option to redeem the bonds before their maturity.

'Eurobonds' are synonymous with 'euronotes' when we treat both as 'international bonds'.[48] But they can be differentiated — Penn, Shea and Arora distinguish 'eurobonds' from 'euronotes' as follows:

> A useful starting point is to compare the Euronote with some of the common characteristics found in the Eurobond. The principal distinctions ... are that Eurobonds are generally listed instruments (Euronotes are generally not listed); Eurobonds are generally issued in small denominations (between US$1,000 and US$10,000 each), whereas Euronotes are generally issued in large denominations (US$250,000 or more); Eurobonds generally have maturities of between three years and, say, 15 years, depending on current market conditions (Euronotes generally have maturities of up to one year); and, in view of their longer maturities, Eurobonds almost universally have extensive terms and conditions relating to their repayment and constitution. While some of the legal characteristics, such as negotiability, and some of the legal constraints, in terms of offering them for sale, are the same ...[49]

The above distinctions between eurobonds and euronotes are technical. Whether or not they are important to any particular issue is to be determined in the circumstances concerned. Generally speaking, 'notes' are used for short-term borrowing and 'bonds' are suitable for long-term borrowing.

---

46. Prime, note 29 above, p 213.
47. Id, p 212.
48. Tennekoon treats 'eurobonds' as synonymous with 'international bonds': Tennekoon, *The Law and Regulation of International Finance*, Butterworths, London, 1991, p 145.
49. Penn, Shea and Arora, *The Law and Practice of International Banking*, Sweet and Maxwell, London, 1987, p 196.

Major concerns in bond issue

[6.41] There are normally three parties — an issuer, an investor and a bank — in any issue of bonds, although more parties may be involved in the promotion of the bonds and transfer of bonds in a secondary market (a market where issued bonds are traded). Certain common concerns of the parties participating in bond markets can be identified. Some of these concerns determine the purpose for which a particular type of bond is issued, as well as the special features, conditions or terms (for example, extendible or retractable or flip-flop bonds) of the bonds issued.

[6.42] Important considerations for an issuer of bonds can be summarised as follows:
- the potential market for the issue;
- the nominated currency of the issue;
- the purpose of fundraising;
- the term of maturity and the ability to pay back on maturity;
- costs of issue;
- tax implications of the issue to the issuer and investors; and
- governing law and forum where the dispute can be resolved.

[6.43] Important considerations for an investor can be summarised as follows:
- the creditworthiness of the issuer;
- the rate of return;
- the potential capital appreciation of the bonds;
- the conditions for transfer and redemption;
- the competitiveness of the bonds;
- the tax implications of the return;
- the need to preserve the identity of the issuer or the transfer of the issuer's liability;
- the need to protect his or her ranking against the issuer's asset in case of bankruptcy;
- the need to monitor the performance of the bonds;
- payment in the nominated currency and exchange risk; and
- the law governing the bond and risks in legislative change.

[6.44] For a bank or underwriter, the following concerns are relevant:
- the credit rating of the issuer;
- the extent of financial liability to the investors;
- the extent of financial liability to the issuer;
- the rate of return;
- the feasibility of the bond in international markets; and
- the terms of the bonds and their negotiability.

[6.45] There may be conflict or congruence between the parties as regards the above considerations. For example, the anonymity of bondholders might be preferred by investors, but would make it impossible for an issuer or a bank to obtain consent from the holders to amend the terms of the bond. On the other hand, a drop-lock term in a bond provides protection to investors, and is also desirable for the issuer as this feature may increase the attraction of the bond. These concerns are dealt with by a number of common clauses or covenants usually included in a bond. These common clauses or covenants will be dealt with in the following sections.

Common clauses and covenants in bonds

Negotiability provisions

[6.46] International bonds are usually negotiable and issued in a bearer form. A bond must clearly indicate that the interest and principal are payable to its holder or bearer. This promise can be enforced by the holder against the issuer directly. International bonds often contain also a standard clause which says that the title to the bonds or notes passes to the holders on delivery for the purpose of facilitating the transactions and ensuring stability in commercial transactions.

Interest provisions

[6.47] Various arrangements and terms can be made in relation to the rate of interest, the method of payment and time of payment, such as whether interest is based on a fixed or floating rate, whether interest is payable quarterly or annually, or how to calculate interest.

Negative pledge

[6.48] A negative pledge is 'a restriction on the grant by the borrower of security interests in favour of other creditors'.[50] It means that the borrower undertakes not to provide further security over his or her assets. Alternatively, a negative pledge may refer to an undertaking by the borrower to limit any further security over his or her assets to a specified percentage figure. The purpose of this type of clause is to ensure that the ranking of the bondholder as an (often unsecured) creditor of the borrower (issuer of the bond) remains unchanged if the borrower subsequently becomes insolvent. For example, a negative pledge clause may state as follows:

> So long as any of the Bonds are outstanding the Borrower will not create or permit to subsist any mortgage, charge, pledge, lien or other encumbrance on its assets or revenues.[51]

[6.49] The enforcement of a negative pledge clause is subject to the bond's governing law dealing with the ranking of creditors. A domestic law may or may not give effect to such a clause, depending on whether it is recognised by the domestic law. If an issuer is not obliged to enforce the clause under the relevant domestic law, it may grant security interests over its assets to future creditors contrary to this clause. The holder is hence not able to enforce the clause as a contract term against the issuer to defeat the interest of a

---

50. Wood, *Law and Practice of International Finance*, Sweet & Maxwell, London, 1980, p 146.
51. Id, p 147.

subsequent and bona fide creditor, even if the issuer breached the term of the bond. The negative pledge is intended to be a device to avoid bondholders being unknowingly put in a less favourable position than any other of the issuer's creditors over the issuer's assets in the event of the issuer's bankruptcy. It is intended to impose a contractual obligation upon the issuer for the purpose of restricting and qualifying the preferential interest of third parties over the issuer's assets. Whether it can in fact defer a third party's preferential interest over the issuer's assets, or deprive a third party of that interest, is a matter to be determined under the governing domestic law.

Pari passu *clauses*

[6.50] A *pari passu* clause purports to ensure that bondholders will be in the same ranking as each other, and as any unsecured creditors, over the issuer's assets in the event of the issuer's insolvency. A standard *pari passu* clause is as follows:

> The Bonds are direct, unsecured, general and unconditional obligations of the Borrower and rank pari passu among themselves and equally with all other unsecured obligations of the Borrower.[52]

A *pari passu* clause always co-exists with a negative pledge clause to ensure the priority rule is not less favourable to bondholders in the event of the issuer's insolvency. Its enforceability is subject to the governing law of the bond. A *pari passu* clause may not be enforceable if the operation of the governing law so determines.

Maturity and redemption clauses

[6.51] A bond should indicate whether it is perpetual or fixed term. It should also indicate, where applicable, whether the issuer has an option to call or redeem the bonds and how the option is to be exercised. Where applicable, a bond should state whether the bondholders are entitled to redeem the bonds before maturity and how to exercise that right.

Remedy and limitation clauses

[6.52] There should be clauses dealing with remedies available to bondholders in the case of the issuer's default or breach of the terms of bonds, in particular a negative pledge. There may also be a limitation on the time in which a bondholder can bring an action against the issuer. These clauses may be enforced as terms of the contract in the relevant countries. They are important, given that international bonds are sold and transferred in different jurisdictions and remedies and limitations for the same breach may vary.

Choice of law clauses

[6.53] A bond should indicate its governing law and how the terms are to be construed in the event of disagreement. These clauses are important to ensure that in case of dispute a court of law will interpret the terms of the bond according to the true intention of the parties at the time of the conclusion of the contract.

---

52. Id, p 155.

Procedures for bond issue

[6.54] Particular procedures for bond issue may vary from country to country and from one type of bond to another. But there are basic procedures or steps which may exist anywhere in the international bond markets. The basic procedures for a bond issue described by Teenekoon can be summarised as follows:[53]

[6.55] Mandate: 'Mandate' is a special banking term, referring to a bank's authority to issue bonds on behalf of the issuer. A mandate is usually given on a 'pre-priced' basis, which is the price agreed upon by the issuer and the lead manager (the bank which is responsible for organising the bond issue) for the bonds to be issued. The price so determined becomes part of the mandate. A bond issue begins from the granting of a mandate.

[6.56] Launch: 'Launch' means a public announcement of the issue. In this process, the lead manager organises the team of underwriters (underwriting banks) and arranges the listing of the bonds (when necessary).

[6.57] Stabilisation: This refers to a process in which measures are taken to prevent a fall in the price of the bonds before they are formally issued. Such a fall may be caused by short selling or dumping of the bonds in the 'grey market' (where bonds which are to be issued in a future time are traded) by dealers or underwriters. The lead manager has to take counter-measures against short selling and dumping for the purpose of maintaining the intended issue price of the bonds when they are issued.

[6.58] Signing: 'Signing' means the signing of the offering circular or prospectus. The formal agreements for the issue of bonds are usually made about seven to 14 days after the launch. The formal documents to be signed include the subscription agreement, the agreement between managers, and the selling group agreement.

[6.59] Allotment: 'Allotment' refers to the process of distributing and selling bonds among banks and dealers. In this process, the lead manager allots bonds to various banks and dealers for the purpose of sale. The lead manager has discretion in determining whether to allot bonds to any dealer who has engaged in short selling. There may also be an agreement between underwriters as to the allotment between them. Allotment usually commences on the next day following the signing.

[6.60] Closing: 'Closing' refers to a process where a number of documents are signed for the purpose of administering the bonds after issue. These documents are the trust deed, paying agency agreement and fiscal agency agreement. The moneys received from sales are also transferred to the lead manager at the closing.

[6.61] 'Lock-up' period: This is a 40-day period after the closing day of the issue. In this period, the actual or definitive bonds will be printed and delivered to investors. Before the delivery of the actual bonds, the investors are given temporary global bonds (or similar documents) to prove their titles.

[6.62] The above procedures are not legally required, except those steps which may be required by the domestic law governing the issue of bonds in a particular country. They

---

53. See Tennekoon, *The Law and Regulation of International Finance*, Butterworths, London, 1991, pp 149–60.

[6.62] represent general practice and considerations in the issue of international bonds. Modifications can be made to the above procedures if necessary.

Trading of bonds at secondary market

[6.63] The 'secondary market' is the market where bonds are traded and transferred, as opposed to the market where bonds are issued or initially sold; or the 'grey market', which is where bonds whose issue has been announced are traded before the date of issue. Trading of bonds at the secondary market is carried out through the listing of bonds at stock exchanges or telecommunications networks linking financial institutions and dealers. For example, the Reuter Monitor telecommunications network, Euroclear and CEDEL (both are clearing systems for bond trading) play a crucial part in international bond markets.[54] In Australia, the trading system in stock markets is presently based on the Stock Exchange Automated Trading System (SEATS).

International syndicated loans and international finance

What is an international syndicated loan?

[6.64] A syndicated loan is not a device unique to international finance. 'This type of loan, whereby a syndicate of banks combines to make a loan to a borrower, has its roots in the United States domestic market, stimulated by the relatively small size of many banks in that country.'[55] Thus, whenever a loan is too large, or involves too much risk, to be handled by any single bank, several banks may act collectively to provide the loan. This kind of situation may arise more often in international finance than in domestic finance, because international finance usually involves a larger amount of investment and higher risks or uncertainty.

[6.65] An international syndicated loan refers to lending by a group or consortium of banks or financial institutions from various countries to a borrower who may come from any country and use the loan in any country. Internationalisation of the syndicated loan is the key feature of this form of lending. A syndicated loan is a way for banks actively to seek investment opportunity, usually long term, in the international financial markets. As in any domestic loan, the banks expect the borrower to return the loan at the end of the contract and to pay interest on the loan as stipulated in the contract.

Organisation of international syndicated loan

[6.66] An international syndicated loan is based on a contract (agreement). There are usually three parties involved in a syndicated loan:
- the borrower;
- the lead bank (agent or intermediate bank); and
- the lenders (the consortium of banks).

---

54. For discussion, see Prime, note 28 above, pp 230–7.
55. Roberts, note 24 above, p 78.

Introduction to International Banking and Financing [6.69]

[6.67] There appear to be different interpretations of the legal relationships between the borrower and the lenders. Tennekoon observed that an 'international syndicated loan is in fact a number of separate loans made by individual banks to the same borrower, which are subject to the same terms and conditions'.[56] In contrast, Baxter observed that:

> An international syndicated loan agreement must have provisions governing the relations of the members of the syndicate among themselves. If the loan contract so provides, the lead manager may have discretionary power to act for the syndicate, particularly in circumstances in which a prompt reaction on the part of the syndicate is desirable, for example, without waiting for the members of a numerous and widely dispersed syndicate to assemble for a meeting, or for the completion of a telex conference.[57]

In light of the above observations, we may say that, regardless of the form of any arrangement in which an international loan is made, the arrangement must deal clearly with the obligations between the borrower and lenders, and between the lead manager and members of the consortium: see the specimen syndicated term loan agreement between a borrower and a whole consortium found in Penn, Shea and Arora, pp 393–439.

[6.68] An international syndicated loan can be initiated either by an intending borrower authorising a particular bank to be the 'lead bank' or 'lead manager' (there may be co-lead banks if the sum of the loan is too large), or by calling for tender from interested banks.[58] The lead bank(s) will send the information memorandum (a package of information, which if accepted will form the basis of a syndicate loan contract) to potential members of the syndicate. The terms or conditions of the information memorandum should be accurate and agreed upon by the borrower and lead bank(s), because contractual liability (for example, offer and acceptance) arises from the information memorandum.[59] The terms and conditions will be negotiated and re-negotiated between the members of the syndicate, and between the syndicate and the borrower. The loan agreement is established when it is properly entered into pursuant to the agreement of the parties involved.

Management of an international syndicated loan agreement

[6.69] The loan agreement is usually managed by a lead bank which can be regarded as either an agent bank or a paying bank. While the lead bank acts as the agent for the borrower in organising the loan, it represents the syndicate in its management. In case of default by the borrower, the agent bank will distribute the borrower's security deposit to the members of the syndicate pursuant to their entitlement under the syndicate agreement. Distribution of interest payment and the security deposit in case of default are the main functions of the lead bank once the loan contract enters into force.

The agent bank acts as an intermediate bank between the borrower and the syndicate. Under a loan agreement, the borrower usually makes interest payments to the agent bank which will 'distribute the receipts *pro rata* to the lenders according to their entitlements'.[60] The agent is the manager of the loan agreement: it exercises discretion in resolving

---

56. Tennekoon, note 53 above, p 45.
57. Baxter, note 4 above, p 80.
58. Id, p 76.
59. Browne, 'The Information Memorandum: Status and Implication' in Pierce et al, note 23 above, p 209.
60. Wood, 'Sharing Clauses in Syndicated Loan Agreements' in Pierce et al, note 23 above, p 278.

various administrative and technical matters which occur from time to time in the performance of the loan agreement. For example, the agent bank has a duty or right to monitor loan covenants (covenants are those undertakings attached to the loan agreement), mainly those undertaken by the borrower.[61] It also has a duty to take appropriate measures in the occurrence of default. One of its duties is to ensure that the interests of the syndicate members are protected under the principle of *pari passu* (see **[6.50]**), which in this context means that in the event of the borrower's insolvency, the syndicate members' interests are ranked equally. However, equality in ranking does not necessarily mean an equal amount of payment, because members' contributions may be different.

Major considerations in an international syndicated loan

[6.70] There are certain matters which should be dealt with in any agreement for an international syndicated loan. These include:

- parties to the loan agreement;
- definitions of terms used in the agreement;
- the sum of the loan;
- the draw-down period (a period in which the agreed loan, or part of the loan, is transferred from the lender to the borrower);
- repayment provisions;
- interest provisions;
- changes in law provisions, which deal with the impact of changes in law to the liabilities of the parties;
- *pari passu* and negative pledge provisions;
- default and remedy;
- liabilities between the banks;
- fees and expenses;
- assignments of parties' rights and obligations;
- choice of law provisions; and
- waiver of immunity, which is necessary against a sovereign borrower.

It must be emphasised that a syndicated loan is based on contractual arrangements. Whatever the parties agree to do, they have to materialise their agreement by incorporating the matters agreed on into the terms of the contract. The terms so agreed will be enforced by a court of law, unless the enforcement of any term is prohibited by the relevant domestic law or international convention under the commonly accepted rules of conflict of laws, that is, illegality and public interest consideration. Thus, in summary, the doctrine of freedom of contract, the legality of the terms under the law or laws likely to be applicable to the contract, and the efficient use of the commonly accepted principles of conflict of laws to prove the predictability and certainty of the contract enforcement are the essential issues for the drafting of an agreement on a syndicated loan.

---

61. Tennekoon, note 53 above, p 61.

The International Monetary Fund and international finance

Why is the International Monetary Fund different?

[6.71] The International Monetary Fund (IMF) was established in a conference held in Bretton Woods, New Hampshire, the United States, between 1–22 July 1944. It came into official existence on 27 December 1945, when 29 countries signed its Articles of Agreement (its Charter) and commenced financial operations on 1 March 1947. It is a financial institution which consists of sovereign countries only.[62] As at 2002 it has 184 members.[63] The composition of the IMF determines its role as an international organisation of governments. Its main administration consists of the Board of Governors, the Interim Committee, and the Executive Board. In 2002, its Total Quotas are SDR 212 billion (which almost equals US$264 billion).[64]

The IMF's Articles of Agreement help to explain why it is different from other privately owned financial institutions. For example, the aims of the IMF are to promote international monetary cooperation, to facilitate the balanced growth of international trade, to promote stable and orderly exchange arrangements among members, and to lend money temporarily to members in order to help them correct maladjustments in their balance of payments.[65] These aims suggest that the IMF is both a forum where the members can negotiate and adjust the differences in their financial policies, and a resource where a member may seek a short-term loan for the purposes of adjusting its balance of payments. A loan agreement can be reached only between a sovereignty and the IMF. This is one of the essential differences between loans provided by the IMF and a privately owned syndicate.

The role of the IMF in international trade

[6.72] The IMF has three major roles: surveillance, financial assistance and technical assistance. These roles are to be examined below:

> Surveillance is the process by which the IMF appraises its members' exchange rate policies in the context of a comprehensive analysis of the general economic situation and the policy strategy of each member. The IMF fulfils its surveillance responsibilities through several approaches, including annual bilateral Article IV consultations with individual countries, multilateral surveillance twice a year in the context of its World Economic Outlook (WEO) exercise, and precautionary arrangements which serve to boost international confidence in a member's policies, enhanced surveillance, and program monitoring, which provide a member with close monitoring from the IMF in the absence of the use of IMF resources.

Financial assistance includes credits and loans extended by the IMF to member countries which have balance of payments problems to support their policies of adjustment

---

62. For an introduction to the IMF, see Francois P Gianviti, 'Some Specific Legal Features of the International Monetary Fund' in Effros (ed), note 4 above, pp 1–15.
63. See IMF website at <http://www.imf.org/>.
64. See IMF website at <http://www.imf.org/>.
65. Baxter, note 4 above, pp 126–7.

[6.72]

and reform. As at July 2002 the IMF had credit and loans outstanding to 88 countries for an approved amount of SDR 66 billion.[66]

Technical assistance consists of expertise and supports provided by the IMF to its members in several broad areas, including the design and implementation of fiscal and monetary policy, institution-building (such as the development of central banks or treasuries), the handling and accounting of transactions with the IMF, the collection and refinement of statistical data, training officials at the IMF Institute or through the Joint Vienna Institute, the Singapore Regional Training Institute, the Middle East Regional Training Program, and the Joint Africa Institute.

[6.73] Financial assistance is one of the essential and practical roles of the IMF. The rationale for IMF financial support to members is explained by Article I(v) of the IMF Articles of Agreement as follows:

> To give confidence to members by making the general resources of the Fund temporarily available to them under adequate safeguards, thus providing them with opportunity to correct maladjustment in their balance of payments without resorting to measures destructive of national or international prosperity.

The IMF provides the following four types of financial assistance to its members:

- First, it may assist a member to balance its payments by conditionally 'selling the currency of another member in exchange for an equivalent amount of the first member's own currency'.[67] The condition is that the member will buy back its currency in another agreed currency.

- Second, it allocates a member's 'reserve tranche' which 'is the excess of its quota (subscription) over the Fund's holdings of that member's currency (excluding holdings arising out of drawings under the Fund's special financing programs)'.[68] The reserve tranche 'is a member's reserve asset which can be used in support of its currency'.[69]

- Third, it provides 'credit tranche' to a member. Credit tranche is a form of financial assistance which allows a member to draw on the credit under the conditions and terms set out by the IMF. In this way, the IMF, like a private bank, provides a credit facility to its members. Credit tranche can be either outright or standby.[70]

- Lastly, it is also able to arrange with each member particular forms of financial assistance. Such financial assistance is possible as long as the use of the funds is consistent with the aims of the IMF.

[6.74] The role of the IMF in international trade is more or less policy-oriented. As we have seen, the IMF was established for the purpose of promoting international financial cooperation, international trade and balance of payments among its members. In rendering its assistance, the IMF imposes various conditions and terms which support these aims.

---

66. See IMF website at <http://www.imf.org/>.
67. Id, p 136.
68. Ibid.
69. Ibid.
70. Ibid.

Exchange control and international finance

Meaning of exchange control

[6.75] Exchange control means that the conversion between the local currency and a foreign currency is subject to restrictive measures of either a legal or policy nature. It is a method adopted by governments for resolving their foreign currency shortage. A country whose currency is internationally accepted would have no need to impose exchange control, whereas a country which has only limited resources of hard currencies (currencies widely accepted in international financial markets) would need to control the outflow of these currencies. Exchange control may also be imposed for policy reasons, such as maintaining the value of the national currency. Australia had exchange control before 1983, mainly because the value of the Australian dollar was artificially determined and deliberately maintained.[71] Today, exchange control has almost ceased to operate in Australia as a result of the government's policy of floating the currency. Exchange control is used in many developing countries where foreign exchange imbalance is a constant problem.

Impact of exchange control upon international finance

[6.76] Any type of international finance, bills of exchange, credit facilities, bonds, securities and syndicated loans may be subject to exchange control if the governing law restricts or prohibits the transaction purported in the document or contract concerned.[72] Thus, lawyers must be able to foresee and overcome such difficulties when formulating a syndicated loan or when entering into a contract of sale. Variations or alterations should be made to the standard terms and conditions of the contract or loan agreement.

[6.77] *Credit Lyonnais v P T Barnard & Associates Ltd*

[1976] 1 Lloyd's Rep 557

Exchange control legislation may be a relevant issue in a contract of sale

Facts: Credit Lyonnais was the holder of two bills of exchange in French drawn by a French company (seller of watches) on Barnard (buyer). The French company discounted the bills to Credit Lyonnais, which was a French bank. Credit Lyonnais sent the bills to Barnard for acceptance. Barnard's managing director signed his name and the trade name of Barnard on the bills, which were returned to Credit Lyonnais. Barnard dishonoured the bills at maturity.

---

71. For discussion on the history and implications of exchange control in Australia, see Flint, *Foreign Investment Law in Australia*, Law Book Co, Sydney, 1985, pp 265–380.
72. For example, in *Jones v Chatfield* [1993] 1 NZLR 617, the defendant buyer of certain shares in a New Zealand company sought to rely on the Fijian foreign exchange control legislation to set aside a default judgment against him for the enforcement of the contract of sale. The court held that the defendant did not establish that performance of the contract would contravene the exchange control legislation in Fiji. This suggests that had the defendant proved that the enforcement of the contract contravened the relevant Fijian law, the decision of the court might have been different.

[6.77]   International Commercial Law

> Credit Lyonnais sued Barnard for the value of the bills. Barnard contended on the ground of non est factum that its managing director was completely ignorant of the French language and that Credit Lyonnais misrepresented the bills as receipts. Barnard also relied on the ground that under the Exchange Control Act 1947 (UK), export of an accepted bill of exchange needed permission from the Treasurer, but no permission was given on the bills concerned.
>
> **Decision:** The Queen's Bench Division (Commercial Court) held that the defence of non est factum failed because Barnard did not prove that its managing director acted carefully in accepting the bills. The defence of illegality under the Exchange Control Act also failed, because the lack of permission did not render the enforcement of the dishonoured bills under the contract in England illegal.

Foreign exchange risks

Defining foreign exchange risks

[6.78] Foreign exchange risks are those risks which are associated with fluctuations in foreign exchange rates. These fluctuations affect the value of payments made by the buyer or received by the seller in terms of their own currency. Since an international sale usually involves parties in different countries, one of the parties will face foreign exchange risks if the contract nominates the other party's currency as the measure of payment. Similarly, both parties will face foreign exchange risks if the contract is based on a third country's currency. This type of risk is called 'transaction exposure' by the ICC.[73] There is also 'translation exposure', which refers to the exchange risk associated with the translation of a company's assets, liabilities and income denominated in a foreign currency into the local currency on the company's account; and 'economic exposure', which refers to the broad impact of foreign exchange rates on a company's business activities in general.[74]

Example: Exchange Clearing House Ltd (ECHO) and settlement risk[75]

[6.79] Settlement of foreign exchange (FX) trade requires the payment of one currency and the receipt of another, often in different jurisdictions and different time zones. Without an adequate settlement system there is the risk that one party to an FX transaction could pay out the currency it sold but not receive the currency it bought. Drexel, BCCI and Barings illustrate the potential problems.

[6.80] In 1990, the Drexel Burnham Lambert group (DBL) collapsed, leading to settlement problems between its UK subsidiary (which traded as principal in the FX and gold markets) and various counter-parties in these markets.

In 1991 the Bank of Credit and Commerce International (BCCI) collapsed, causing principal loss to the UK and Japanese foreign exchange counter-parties of the failed

---

73. ICC, *Managing Exchange Rate Risks*, ICC Publishing SA, Paris, 1993, p 9.
74. Id, pp 9–11.
75. This example is quoted from ALRC 80, Box 5D, available at <http://www.austlii.edu.au/au/other/alrc/publications/reports/80>.

institution. Because settlement of counter-party trades was occurring in different time zones and involved transaction queuing on the relevant automated clearing systems (CHIPS and the Foreign Exchange Yen Clearing House), the BCCI liquidator was able to freeze assets and cancel settlement payments to the detriment of the counter-parties.

The unforeseen collapse of Barings Bank in 1995 caused a problem in the ECU clearing system requiring a counter-party bank to borrow to cover an FX trade Barings Bank could not complete. Without this action by the counter-party bank the settlement of more than ECU 50 billion in payments between the 45 banks participating in the clearing on that day would have been frustrated.

[6.81] Central banks have paid close attention to settlement risk and have set out various requirements for bilateral and multilateral netting and settlement arrangements to ensure it is minimised.

ECHO provides multilateral level netting and settlement services. ECHO is a privately owned company controlled by a group of major banks which sets certain financial and other criteria for membership. To address the central bank requirements it provides details of maximum and minimum FX settlement risk twice daily to its users, it enables banks to mark limit usage so that the bank can trade its FX exposure down below its own limit, it is operational 24 hours a day, reconciles receipts in real time on the due date and does not release funds until all receipts from the previous day have been confirmed as received.

[6.82] The multilateral nature of ECHO's clearing house system inevitably creates the potential for legal issues to arise. Where an Australian payment or participant is involved those issues may or may not be determined under Australian law, taking into account (among other things) the law governing ECHO's rules. Some examples of the potential for issues to arise include:

- as ECHO is a multilateral netting arrangement, failure of one institutional participant may result in calls on other members and could expose other participants to significant financial exposure or collapse;
- if a member of ECHO is unable to meet calls on funds this could cause systemic problems with significant legal dispute over such issues as jurisdiction and liability;
- a technical payment failure within the ECHO system could lead to failure outside the ECHO system raising questions about the liability of ECHO itself as well as reflecting adversely on the reputation of ECHO's individual members; and
- as ECHO has access to bank accounts as part of its settlement arrangements with members, this may raise the possibility of exposure to fraud.

[6.83] International Commercial Law

Means of hedging foreign exchange risks[76]

Matching

[6.83] 'Matching' means that a company balances (matches) its receivables and payables in the same currency. This can be done by maintaining balance and matching two-way flow in accounts denominated in a particular currency to avoid frequent exchange between different currencies. This may also reduce bank charges for converting currencies.

Multilateral netting and netting per se

[6.84] This refers to a multinational company organising its own foreign exchange clearing system. Receivables and payables of the company in all currencies can be balanced as a whole to make payment on behalf of the company in different currencies without converting them through banks. Gradually, the concept has changed and the method can be used not only within a multinational company, but also between two different companies. According to John P Emert, there are several variations on netting.

First, in payments netting, payments between counter-parties are netted so that only one payment in each currency is made for each value date. Second, in netting by novation, a new foreign exchange transaction entered into by counter-parties for settlement on a particular value date is netted against any existing obligations to receive or deliver the currencies for such value date; new obligations to receive or deliver the currencies involved are created by contract novation. Like payment netting, only one payment per currency is made by the parties on each value date. A third method of netting is set-off. In foreign exchange options transactions, set-off of one option against another, similar option terminates in whole or part the original option. Setting off foreign exchange options is analogous to the process of netting by novation foreign exchange transaction in the cash market. A final method of netting is close-out netting. Upon the occurrence of an event of default, the non-defaulting party has the right to close-out all open transactions, converting them to the non-defaulting party's base currency, marking them to market, and netting the resulting amount, which will then become a payment owed either to or by the defaulting party.[77]

[6.85] Another example of netting is seen in para 3.2 of the International Foreign Exchange Master Agreement (IFEMA) which describes netting settlement/payment netting in the following words:

> If on any value date more than one delivery of a particular currency is to be made between a pair of settlement netting offices, then each party shall aggregate the amounts of such currency deliverable by it and only the difference between these aggregate amounts shall be delivered by the party owing the larger aggregate amount to the other party, and, if the aggregate amounts are equal, no delivery of the currency shall be made.

[6.86] IFEMA is a creation of the Foreign Exchange Committee and the British Banker's Association. A similar document was first prepared in 1985 and was amended several times since. In 1993, IFEMA came into existence. It has also been amended

---

76. This part is largely based on ICC, *Managing Exchange Rate Risks*, note 73 above, pp 15–19.
77. Emert, 'The New Foreign Exchange Master Agreements' in Effros, note 4 above, p 443.

continuously to meet the needs of commercial reality. It has become one of the standard contracts commonly used by banks.

Leading and lagging

[6.87] 'Leading' means 'accelerating', while 'lagging' means 'delaying'. A company may, by way of contract, have a right either to lead or lag payments in a foreign currency to arm's-length partners or to foreign subsidiaries in anticipation of forthcoming appreciation or depreciation of the currency. The technique is practicable for companies engaged in international transactions.

For example, in a German case decided on 8 February 1995, *Oberlandesgericht Munchen*, 7 U 1720/94,[78] an Italian buyer and a German seller concluded a contract for the sale of 11 cars for the price of DM400,000. The cars were to be delivered in August and October respectively. In October, the buyer informed the seller of its wish to cancel the contract because the extreme exchange rate fluctuations between the Lira and the Mark had made the purchase impossible. The seller claimed compensation under a bank guarantee provided by the buyer, which sued the seller in the German court to recover the payment under the bank guarantee. The court applied the CISG and the German law to determine the rights of the parties under the bank guarantee. It held that the seller was not entitled to claim the bank guarantee in the circumstances. But, on the other hand, the court found the contract of sale was still enforceable or the seller was entitled to claim damages under the contract of sale. The rationale of the court in this decision is arguable: from a common law perspective, the seller's right to claim a sum of payment under a bank guarantee wholly depends on the terms of the guarantee. However, it can be said that had the parties foreseen the exchange risk and agreed on the time of payment or the exchange rate applicable, the contract would have been easily performed and dispute avoided.

Invoicing and currency clauses

[6.88] These are arrangements whereby the parties have a contractual right to invoice or pay in one of the specified currencies, and within the exchange rates, as agreed in the contract of sale. This gives the parties flexibility to reduce foreign exchange risks and allows them to invoice or pay in an agreed currency to match their receivables and payables.

Currency futures

[6.89] This refers to trading of currency at a future date. Market participants may contract to buy or sell a currency at a future date at a fixed price. Trading of currencies in future time can be carried out in the futures markets throughout the world, such as the

---

78. Abstract of the case is available as Case 133 at <http://www.un.or.at/uncitral>.

Chicago International Monetary Market, the New York Futures Exchange, the London International Financial Futures Exchange, and the Singapore International Monetary Exchange.

Currency options

[6.90] This refers to a contractual right to buy or sell a foreign currency at an agreed price at a future date. The holder of the right is guaranteed a minimum or maximum price for a foreign currency, but he or she has to pay a higher fee to the options-writer (broker) to cover the writer's risk.[79] The International Currency Options Market (ICOM) Master Agreement aims to help parties adopt uniform and consistent practices in dealings on currency options.

Swap options

[6.91] This refers to various arrangements or schemes entered into between parties who have receivables and payables in the same currencies for the purpose of reducing their foreign exchange risks in balancing receivables and payables. Alternatively, the expression 'swap' can be understood as denoting 'a plethora of financial transactions, the core of which is the exchange of one cash flow for another'.[80] There is the International Swap Dealer's Association (ISDA) Master Agreement to provide standard terms for exercising swap options. The techniques for making swap options can be broadly classed into five categories: parallel loans, back-to-back loans, interest rate swaps, currency swaps and cross currency interest rate swaps.[81] These techniques are discussed briefly below.

[6.92] **Parallel loans:** This refers to arrangements whereby parties in different countries lend local currencies to each other in parallel in the respective countries under identical terms. The equivalent currency in each country is calculated at the prevailing exchange rate between the relevant currencies at the time of the contract. Such an arrangement allows the parties to share the loss or benefit in the fluctuations in exchange rates during the term of the contract and solve each other's need for a particular currency which can be provided by the other party. A parallel loan can be illustrated by the following diagram:

---

79. This type of transaction is illustrated by *Carragreen Currencies Corp Pty Ltd v Corporate Affairs Commission NSW* (1986) 7 NSWLR 705. In this case, Carragreen offered currency options under a 'Leverage and Indemnity Contract' (for a sample of the contract, see NSWLR at 708) to its customers. The case was brought by Carragreen for the purpose of clarifying its legal position under laws governing the operation of future industries in New South Wales.
80. Roberts, note 24 above, p 145.
81. The following discussion is based on Penn, Shea and Arora, note 49 above, pp 224–9.

Introduction to International Banking and Financing [6.93]

The following is a hypothetical parallel loan between an Australian company and a Japanese company. Both have subsidiaries in each other's country and need cash in each other's currency. The amount of the loan is based on a hypothetical exchange rate.

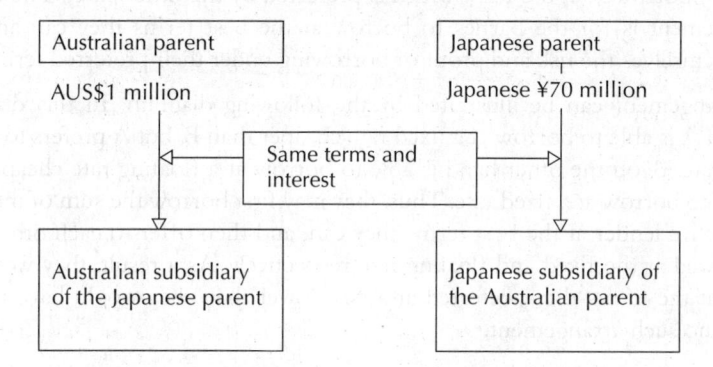

```
┌──────────────────┐                           ┌──────────────────┐
│ Australian parent│                           │  Japanese parent │
└────────┬─────────┘                           └────────┬─────────┘
    AUS$1 million                               Japanese ¥70 million
         │         ┌──────────────────┐                 │
         │◄────────│ Same terms and   │────────►│
         │         │     interest     │                 │
         │         └──────────────────┘                 │
         ▼                                              ▼
┌──────────────────────┐                   ┌──────────────────────┐
│ Australian subsidiary│                   │ Japanese subsidiary of│
│ of the Japanese parent│                  │ the Australian parent │
└──────────────────────┘                   └──────────────────────┘
```

[6.93] Back-to-back loans: This refers to an arrangement under which two parent companies lend different currencies to each other on identical terms for the purpose of supplying the relevant currency to their own subsidiary needing cash in that currency. The difference between a back-to-back loan and a parallel loan is that under a back-to-back loan the parent companies deal with each other directly as both lender and borrower under the respective loan contract, but under a parallel loan agreement the parent companies act as lenders to each other's subsidiaries under identical terms. A back-to-back loan can be illustrated as follows:

Hypothetically an Australian company and a Japanese company need cash in each other's currency for their business operation in each other's country.

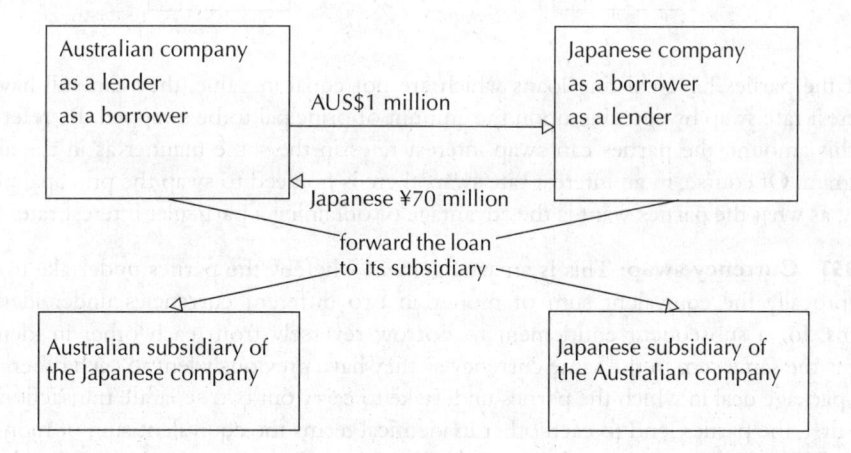

```
┌──────────────────┐                           ┌──────────────────┐
│Australian company│       AUS$1 million       │ Japanese company │
│   as a lender    │──────────────────────────►│  as a borrower   │
│   as a borrower  │◄──────────────────────────│   as a lender    │
└────────┬─────────┘      Japanese ¥70 million └────────┬─────────┘
         │              forward the loan                │
         │              to its subsidiary               │
         ▼                                              ▼
┌──────────────────────┐                   ┌──────────────────────┐
│Australian subsidiary of│                 │Japanese subsidiary of │
│ the Japanese company │                   │ the Australian company│
└──────────────────────┘                   └──────────────────────┘
```

[6.94] Interest rate swap: This refers to an arrangement in which the parties split the risk and profit in obtaining a preferable term of interest (such as fixed rate or floating rate) on funds, by borrowing at the best terms each party can, and offering to each other the funds so borrowed at the term which is preferred by the other party. The essence of this arrangement is for the parties to borrow at the best terms they can and to split between themselves the risk and profit of borrowing under their preferred terms.

This arrangement can be illustrated by the following diagram. In this diagram, we assume that A is able to borrow at a fixed rate cheaper than B, but A prefers to borrow at a floating rate. B, on the other hand is able to borrow at a floating rate cheaper than A, but prefers to borrow at a fixed rate. Thus, they may first borrow the sum of money from their respective lender at the best terms they can, and then offer to each other an equal sum borrowed at the fixed and floating rate respectively. As a result, they would obtain the funds at the terms they preferred at a cost lower than they would have to pay had there been no such arrangement.

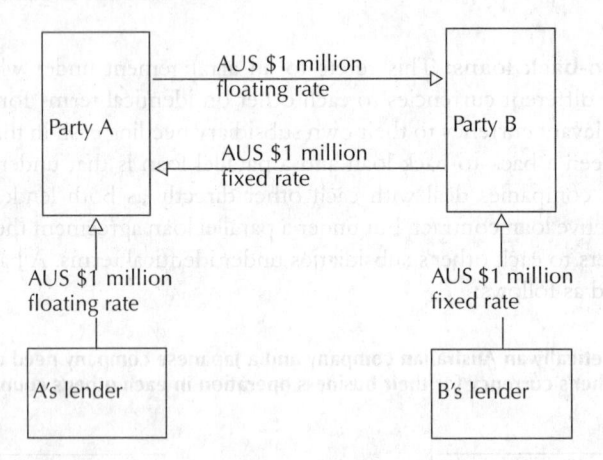

```
         AUS $1 million
         floating rate
┌─────────┐ ──────────▶ ┌─────────┐
│ Party A │              │ Party B │
│         │ ◀──────────  │         │
└─────────┘  AUS $1 million └─────────┘
              fixed rate
     ▲                         ▲
     │                         │
 AUS $1 million          AUS $1 million
 floating rate           fixed rate
     │                         │
┌─────────┐              ┌─────────┐
│A's lender│              │B's lender│
└─────────┘              └─────────┘
```

If the parties have existing loans which are not equal in value, they can still have an interest rate swap by agreeing upon the amount of principal to be swapped. By reference to this amount, the parties can swap interest rates in the same manner as in the above diagram. Of course, in an interest rate swap, there is no need to swap the principal physically, as what the parties want is the advantage of obtaining a particular interest rate.

[6.95] Currency swap: This is an arrangement whereby the parties undertake to lend reciprocally the equivalent sum of money in two different currencies under identical terms, for a subsequent entitlement to borrow reversely from each other in identical terms the same sum in the same currency as they have previously lent to each other. This is a package deal in which the parties undertake to carry out two separate transactions. In the first, the parties lend to each other in identical terms the equivalent sum of money in two different currencies. In the second transaction, the parties lend to each other in reverse in identical terms the same sum of money in the same currency as they have previously borrowed from each other. A currency swap can be illustrated as follows:

Introduction to International Banking and Financing [6.96]

First transaction

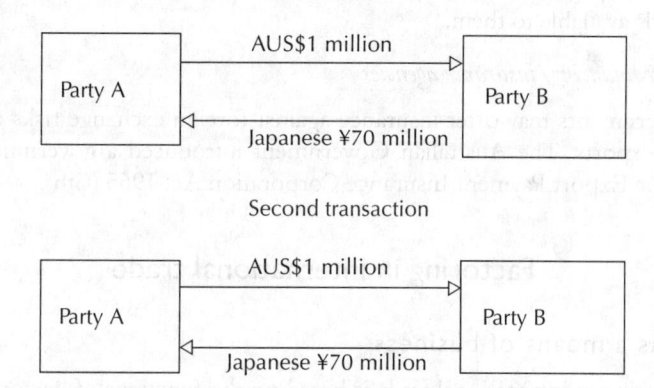

```
                AUS$1 million
    Party A  ────────────────▶  Party B
             ◀────────────────
               Japanese ¥70 million
```

Second transaction

```
                AUS$1 million
    Party A  ────────────────▶  Party B
             ◀────────────────
               Japanese ¥70 million
```

[6.96] Cross currency interest rate swap: This is an arrangement whereby both interest swap and currency swap are employed together to ensure the parties have flexibility while still being able to obtain the fund in a nominated currency at the preferable term of interest. For example, two parties may first enter into an interest rate swap agreement to enable each other to obtain the fund in a particular currency at the term they prefer. When the repayments for the loans from the respective lenders are due, they may enter into a currency swap agreement to enable each other to repay the loan borrowed under the interest rate swap agreement. As part of this currency swap agreement, the parties will lend to each other in reverse the same sum in the same currency as the initial swap. The whole arrangement can be illustrated as follows:

(1) Interest rate and currency swap

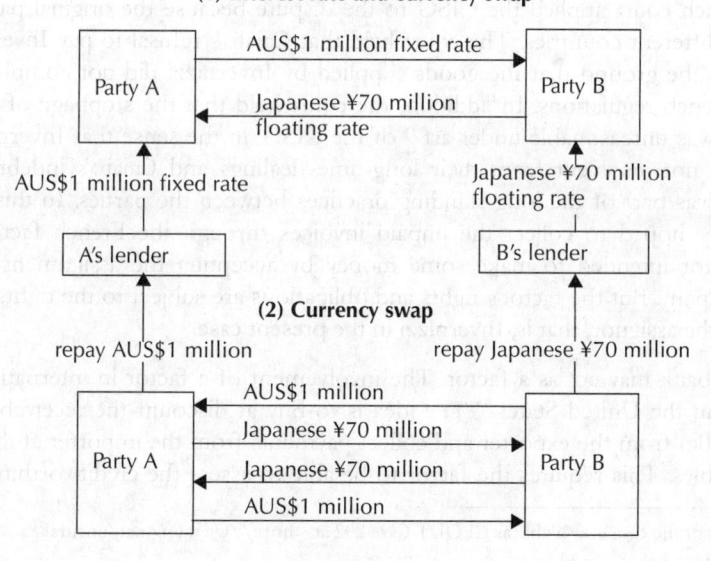

```
                    AUS$1 million fixed rate
        Party A  ────────────────────────▶  Party B
                 ◀────────────────────────
                    Japanese ¥70 million
                    floating rate
           ▲                                   ▲
           │                                   │
    AUS$1 million fixed rate          Japanese ¥70 million
                                      floating rate
       A's lender                        B's lender
```

(2) Currency swap

```
    repay AUS$1 million              repay Japanese ¥70 million
           ▲                                   ▲
           │                                   │
                      AUS$1 million
                   Japanese ¥70 million
        Party A                              Party B
                   Japanese ¥70 million
                      AUS$1 million
```

The real function of the above methods of hedging exchange risks is to distribute the risks between the parties, at the same time maximising the benefits available to each party from the funds available to them.

Official export financing/insurance agencies

[6.97] Governments may offer insurance against foreign exchange risks as a means of encouraging exports. The Australian Government introduced a government guarantee program in the Export Payment Insurance Corporation Act 1965 (Cth).

Factoring in international trade

Factoring as a means of business

[6.98] Factoring in international trade is based on the functions of 'factors' in common law countries. A factor is a merchant who buys and sells in his or her own capacity, although in a particular transaction he or she may act in the capacity of an agent for a principal; broadly speaking, a factor is similar to a broker who is engaged in the sale of goods. The role of a factor in international trade is illustrated by *Societe Francaise de Factoring International Factor France v Roger Caiato,* Court of Appeal of Grenoble (Commercial Division), decided on December 1995,[82] where a French importer, Mr Caiato, placed two orders with an Italian company, Invernizzi, for the purchase of certain goods. Invernizzi informed Caiato that Caiato needed to obtain clearance of the Ifitalia company to which Invernizzi had assigned its receivable before making the new contract. Caiato refused to pay a number of invoices and terminated its business dealings with Invernizzi. Ifitalia assigned its right to claim receivables against Caiato to a French factoring company, which sued Caiato in this case.

The French court applied the CISG to the dispute because the original parties were from two different countries. The court held that Caiato's refusal to pay Invernizzi was justified on the ground that the goods supplied by Invernizzi did not comply with the relevant French regulations. In addition, the court held that the stoppage of supply by Invernizzi was unreasonable under art 9 of the CISG, in the sense that Invernizzi knew Caiato was not insolvent from their long-time dealings and Caiato's indebtedness to Invernizzi was part of the long-standing practices between the parties. In this case, the Italian seller hoped to collect the unpaid invoices through the French factor, or the French factor intended to make some money by accepting the assignment from the Italian company. But the factor's rights and obligations are subject to the rights and obligations of the assignor, that is, Invernizzi in the present case.

[6.99] A bank may act as a factor. The involvement of a factor in international trade originated in the United States.[83] The idea is to buy at discount the receivables (documents of title) from the exporter and collect payments from the importer at the price of the receivables. This requires the factor to be able to assess the creditworthiness of the

---

82. Abstract of the case is available as CLOUT Case 202 at <http://www.un.or.at/uncitral>.
83. Baxter, note 4 above, p 40.

Introduction to International Banking and Financing [6.102]

importer and thus in practice two factors, or a factor and an agent of the factor, one in the country of the seller and the other in the country of the buyer, are often involved. The benefit to the exporter is that he or she has immediate access to the proceeds of sale and does not face the risk of the buyer defaulting in payment, although the factor shares a portion of the profit which the exporter may otherwise be entitled to. Since factoring is a means of financing or facilitating international sales, the amount of discount is normally calculated at a rate marginally higher than the overdraft rate for the same sum of money to be received from a sale. In addition, a line fee or administration charge may also be payable by a client to the factor. There are no international rules governing factoring in international trade.

[6.100] Factoring has become an important part of international transactions involving small and medium sized businesses. The Factors Chain International, which is a global network of leading factoring companies, was set up in 1968. It now has more than 90 members in about 35 countries.[84] More than 88,000 businesses throughout the world used factoring as a means of payment in international sales and the trading volume involved was more than $347 million in 1990.[85] Banks and financial institutions may act as factors because certain clients require high credit lines. The trend shows that factoring is becoming institutionalised. A factor or factoring company may by agreement with his, her, or its client buy all the export receivables of the client in an agreed market and provide the client with immediate and constant access to the proceeds from the sale of the receivables for an agreed service fee. Factoring can be useful in international transactions because sometimes it costs too much for a seller to deal with the credit risk of a buyer in a foreign country.

UNIDROIT Convention on International Factoring

Overview

[6.101] Along with the development of factoring in international trade and commerce, the need for a set of uniform rules has increased. In response to such need, UNIDROIT adopted the Convention on International Factoring on 28 May 1988. The preamble of the convention thus states that the convention has been adopted because the countries had been conscious of the fact that international factoring has a significant role to play in the development of international trade, and because of the importance of adopting uniform rules to provide a legal framework that will facilitate international factoring, while maintaining a fair balance of interests between the different parties involved in factoring transactions. The convention requires three ratifications in order to come into operation,[86] and came into effect on 1 May 1995.[87]

[6.102] The Convention on International Factoring has four chapters and 23 articles in total. Chapter I deals with the sphere of application, covering issues such as the definition

---
84. James, 'Factoring Enhances the Competitive Edge', *The Australian*, 14 April 1993.
85. Ibid.
86. The convention, art 14.
87. For its membership, see supra note 12.

of a factoring contract, international nature of the contract subject to the convention, and the principles for the interpretation of the convention. Chapter II sets out the rights and duties of the parties to a factoring contract. Chapter III regulates subsequent assignments of receivables under a factoring contract. Chapter IV contains the final clauses, such as the ratifications of the convention, entry into force, declarations, reservations and denunciations.

Definition of factoring contract

[6.103] The meaning of factoring contract is defined in art 1 of the convention in the following words:

> This Convention governs factoring contracts and assignments of receivables as described in this Chapter.
>
> For the purposes of this Convention, "factoring contract" means a contract concluded between one party (the supplier) and another party (the factor) pursuant to which:
>
> (a) the supplier may or will assign to the factor receivables arising from contracts of sale of goods made between the supplier and its customers (debtors) other than those for the sale of goods bought primarily for their personal, family or household use;
>
> (b) the factor is to perform at least two of the following functions:
> — finance for the supplier, including loans and advance payments;
> — maintenance of accounts (ledgering) relating to the receivables;
> — collection of receivables;
> — protection against default in payment by debtors;
>
> (c) notice of the assignment of the receivables is to be given to debtors.
>
> In this Convention references to "goods" and "sale of goods" shall include services and the supply of services.
>
> For the purposes of this Convention:
>
> (a) a notice in writing need not be signed but must identify the person by whom or in whose name it is given;
>
> (b) "notice in writing" includes, but is not limited to, telegrams, telex and any other telecommunication capable of being reproduced in tangible form;
>
> (c) a notice in writing is given when it is received by the addressee.

[6.104] The definition of factoring contract in art 1(2) is based on the common understanding that factoring is largely a sale of receivables for financing a commercial transaction, including international transactions. But it also includes other purposes, such as collection of receivables as agent of the seller, or provision of security against the risk of non-payment by the buyer. According to art 1(2), factoring is a contract concluded between one party, who is often the supplier, and another party, who is the factor. Under a factoring contract, the supplier may assign to the factor receivables arising from the contracts of sale or services made for commercial purposes, as opposed to personal purposes, between the supplier and its customers who are buyers or the debtors to the supplier.

Under a factoring contract, the factor may perform several functions, including finance for the supplier, that is, loans and advance payments; maintenance of accounts (ledgering) relating to receivables; collection of receivables; and protection against default in payment by the debtors. A factor must perform two of these functions in any factoring contract. When a factoring contract has been concluded, a notice of the assignment of the receivables should be given to debtors. As we have seen, the notice can be sent in an electronic form because signature is not compulsory. In this way, the notice is required largely for information purposes, instead of as evidence of the right of the factor or the obligation of the debtor or buyer of the goods.

[6.105] The definition of factoring contract in art 1 suggests that the convention covers only specified types of factoring contract or specified types of issues under a factoring contract. For example, the requirements in art 1(2)(b) that a factor must at least perform two functions specified in the provision qualifies the factoring contract falling under the definition of the convention. First, a factor who performs only one of the listed functions is not covered by the convention. Second, a factor who performs a function or functions not described in art 1(2)(b) is not subject to the convention unless he or she also performs at least two of the functions specified in art 1(2)(b). Accordingly, the convention does not cover an assignment of receivables arising from leases or from transactions involving the renting or hiring of equipment or facilities, unless the transactions are regarded as sales of goods or services. In addition, the convention does not apply to an assignment which normally does not require notification, such as block discounting or invoice discounting. However, a broad interpretation of the meaning of notice may extend the convention to certain assignments which are not normally subject to the requirement for notification. In the light of the definition in art 1, the relationships between the factor and any third party (other than the supplier or the debtor) are not covered by the convention.

Scope of application

[6.106] The scope of operation of the convention is defined in arts 2 and 3. These provisions are set out as follows:

Article 2
1. This Convention applies whenever the receivables assigned pursuant to a factoring contract arise from a contract of sale of goods between a supplier and a debtor whose places of business are in different states and:
   (a) those states and the state in which the factor has its place of business are Contracting states; or
   (b) both the contract of sale of goods and the factoring contract are governed by the law of a Contracting state.
2. A reference in this Convention to a party's place of business shall, if it has more than one place of business, mean the place of business which has the closest relationship to the relevant contract and its performance, having regard to the circumstances known to or contemplated by the parties at any time before or at the conclusion of that contract.

Article 3
1. The application of this Convention may be excluded:
   (a) by the parties to the factoring contract; or
   (b) by the parties to the contract of sale of goods, as regards receivables arising at or after the time when the factor has been given notice in writing of such exclusion.
2. Where the application of this Convention is excluded in accordance with the previous paragraph, such exclusion may be made only as regards the Convention as a whole.

The application of the convention appears to be a rather difficult task. Besides the qualifications as seen in the definition of factoring contract in art 1, arts 2 and 3 set out further conditions or qualifications on the application of the convention. First, a factoring contract which satisfies the requirements of art 1, must be based on an international

[6.106]

contract for the sale of goods or the supply of services. Second, a factoring contract relating to an international contract must also meet the requirement that parties to the factoring contract and the contract of sale or services must be from the members of the convention. Third, even if all the parties are from the members of the convention, both the contract of sale and the factoring contract must be governed by the law of a member.

[6.107] Given the limited number of convention members for the time being, the application of the convention must be very limited. It is not easy for both a contract of sale and the relating factoring contract to have been made between persons who are from the existing member countries of the convention. In addition, if either the contract of sale or the factoring contract chooses a law of a non-member as the governing law, or the relevant conflict of laws rules decides a law of a non-member should apply to one of the contracts, the convention does not apply to the factoring contract. The last reason which restricts the application of the convention is that art 3 gives the parties an option to exclude the operation of the convention. In particular, the parties to a contract of sale are entitled to exclude the application of the convention by agreement, after the notice of assignment has been given to the debtor under the contract of sale. Because of these reasons, it can be concluded that the convention has only very limited operation, if any, within the present structure of membership.

Rights and duties of the parties

Defining the parties

[6.108] Although the convention purports to regulate factoring contracts, which are made between the factor and the supplier, the meaning of parties under the convention extends to debtors to whom the factor is entitled to enforce the rights of the supplier under the relevant contract of sale or services. Thus, parties under the convention include the factor, the supplier and the debtor. It must be pointed out, however, the relationships between the supplier and the debtor under the relevant contract of sale or services are not covered by the convention, even though their rights concerning the receivables under the contract of sale or services may be affected by the provisions of the convention.[88] The rights and duties of each party will be examined in turn.

Factor's rights

[6.109] Under the relevant provisions of the convention, the factor has the following major rights:

- to receive all benefits of the supplier under the relevant contract of sale or services;[89]

---

88. For example, art 6(1) of the convention states that 'the assignment of a receivable by the supplier to the factor shall be effective notwithstanding any agreement between the supplier and the debtor prohibiting such assignment'.
89. Article 7 of the convention provides that 'a factoring contract may validly provide as between the parties thereto for the transfer, with or without a new act of transfer, of all or any of the supplier's rights deriving from the contract of sale of goods, including the benefit of any provision in the contract of sale of goods reserving to the supplier title to the goods or creating any security interest'.

- to enforce the rights of the supplier under the relevant contract of sale or services against the debtor;[90] and
- to assign the receivables assigned to him or her to a third party.[91]

Supplier's rights

[6.110] Under the relevant provisions of the convention, the supplier's major right is to assign the receivables to the factor unless the right to do so has been restricted by the relevant law, or by a contractual undertaking to the debtor.[92] In addition, it is implied that the supplier is entitled to claim payment from the factor for effecting the assignment concerned. The convention does not set out rules for any dispute affecting the supplier and the factor. Generally speaking, the general principles of contract law should apply to the factoring contract in the absence of express rules in the convention.

Debtor's rights and duties

[6.111] The debtor's rights and duties are the major concerns of the convention, because the supplier and the factor are capable of regulating their rights and obligations under the relevant factoring contract. The debtor is a third party to a factoring contract or an assignment, but must perform his or her obligations under the relevant contract of sale or services to the supplier and to the successor of the supplier's right (the factor). Thus, regulating the debtor's rights and duties under a factoring contract and in the factoring process is necessary.

---

90. Article 8 of the convention requires the debtor to pay the factor in compliance with the receivables, unless defences permitted by the convention can be established.
91. Article 11 of the convention states as follows:
    1. Where a receivable is assigned by a supplier to a factor pursuant to a factoring contract governed by this Convention:
        (a) the rules set out in Articles 5 to 10 shall, subject to sub paragraph (b) of this paragraph, apply to any subsequent assignment of the receivable by the factor or by a subsequent assignee;
        (b) the provisions of Articles 8 to 10 shall apply as if the subsequent assignee were the factor.
    2. For the purposes of this Convention, notice to the debtor of the subsequent assignment also constitutes notice of the assignment to the factor.
92. Article 6 of the convention states as follows:
    1. The assignment of a receivable by the supplier to the factor shall be effective notwithstanding any agreement between the supplier and the debtor prohibiting such assignment.
    2. However, such assignment shall not be effective against the debtor when, at the time of conclusion of the contract of sale of goods, it has its place of business in a Contracting State which has made a declaration under Article 18 of this Convention.
    3. Nothing in paragraph 1 shall affect any obligation of good faith owed by the supplier to the debtor or any liability of the supplier to the debtor in respect of an assignment made in breach of the terms of the contract of sale of goods.

[6.112] Under the relevant provisions of the convention, the debtor has the following major rights and duties:

- the debtor is obliged to pay the factor for the receivables claimed before a third party's claim under art 8 of the convention can be established;[93]
- the debtor is entitled to rely on defences under the contract of sale or services against the factor,[94] except the defences solely based on non-performance, defective goods or late performance;[95] and
- the debtor is entitled to set-off against the factor's claim by relying on the contract of sale or services concerned.[96]

[6.113] The provisions regulating the parties' rights and duties suggest that the application of the convention is also qualified by the types of rights and duties covered by the convention. Largely, it purports to set out rules governing the relationships between the factor and the debtor. Given the close connection between a contract of sale or services and a factoring contract, the convention leaves many issues to be regulated by the contract of sale or services. Consequently, the convention provides more procedural rules than substantive rules. Many issues, in particular those involving the debtor's right of recourse against the supplier under the contract of sale or services, have to be settled under the terms of the contract of sale or services.

Leasing in international trade

Leasing as a means of business

[6.114] Leasing in international trade is an extension of domestic leasing. It is used mainly as a way of providing finance to a transaction which is costly and beyond the buyer's financial capacity to pay. In a leasing agreement, a bank or financial institution may be the owner of a machine or piece of equipment, but lease the machine to a user in

---

93. Article 8 states as follows:
    1. The debtor is under a duty to pay the factor if, and only if, the debtor does not have knowledge of any other person's superior right to payment and notice in writing of the assignment:
        (a) is given to the debtor by the supplier or by the factor with the supplier's authority;
        (b) reasonably identifies the receivables which have been assigned and the factor to whom or for whose account the debtor is required to make payment; and
        (c) relates to receivables arising under a contract of sale of goods made at or before the time the notice is given.
    2. Irrespective of any other ground on which payment by the debtor to the factor discharges the debtor from liability, payment shall be effective for this purpose if made in accordance with the previous paragraph.
94. Article 9(1) states that in a claim by the factor against the debtor for payment of a receivable arising under a contract of sale of goods the debtor may set up against the factor all defences arising under that contract of which the debtor could have availed itself if such claim had been made by the supplier.
95. The convention, art 10(1). In this case, the debtor still has contractual remedies against the supplier. In practice, the difference between art 9 and art 10 is difficult to draw.
96. Article 9(2) states that 'the debtor may also assert against the factor any right of set-off in respect of claims existing against the supplier in whose favour the receivable arose and available to the debtor at the time a notice in writing of assignment conforming to Article 8(1) was given to the debtor'. See also art 10(2) of the convention.

Introduction to International Banking and Financing [6.117]

another country. The bank or financial institution may purchase goods from one country and lease the goods to a lessee in another country. A new vessel or aircraft may be bought or built under a leasing agreement purporting to provide finance for the transaction between the real supplier or builder and the user of the vessel or aircraft. So can a new plant. Such arrangements are feasible because they provide an investment opportunity to the bank or financial institution and a way to raise funds for the person who wishes to purchase an expensive piece of equipment. In addition, tax law with regard to depreciation, sale, value-added tax and customs duties varies from country to country, and provides an opportunity for the providers and borrowers of funds from different countries to take advantage of the differences.

UNDROIT Convention on International Financial Leasing

Overview

[6.115] For the purpose of removing certain legal impediments to the international financial leasing of equipment, while maintaining a fair balance of interests between different parties to the transaction, the UNDROIT Convention on International Financial Leasing was adopted on 28 May 1988. The major goal of the convention is to make international financial leasing more available and to promote the development of international commerce. Three ratifications are required for its operation. The Convention came into operation on 1 May 1996.[97]

[6.116] The convention is meant to provide a set of uniform rules for civil and commercial aspects of international leasing, which involves a triangular relationship among the lessor, lessee and supplier of equipment. It has three chapters and 25 articles. Chapter I deals with the sphere of application and the meaning of international financial leasing. Chapter II sets out the rights and duties of the parties, who are the lessor, lessee and supplier. Chapter III contains the final provisions, dealing with issues incidental to the operation of the convention, such as ratification, entry into force, declarations, reservations and denunciation. Major aspects of the convention will be discussed below.

Definition of international financial leasing

[6.117] An international financial leasing has three basic elements. First, it is international. Second, it is a leasing arrangement made for the purpose of financing a sale. Third, it is a special type of leasing arrangement. The international nature of the arrangement is set out in art 3 of the convention. The financial nature of the arrangement is defined in art 1(1) of the convention. The leasing aspect of the arrangement is defined in art 1(2) of the convention. These provisions are to be examined in turn. Article 1 will be examined here. Article 3 will be examined in **[6.119]**.

Article 1 of the convention provides as follows:
1. This Convention governs a financial leasing transaction as described in paragraph 2 in which one party (the lessor),
    (a) on the specifications of another party (the lessee), enters into an agreement (the supply agreement) with a third party (the supplier) under which the lessor acquires plant, capital

---
97. For its membership, see note 11 above.

[6.117]

goods or other equipment (the equipment) on terms approved by the lessee so far as they concern its interests, and

(b) enters into an agreement (the leasing agreement) with the lessee, granting to the lessee the right to use the equipment in return for the payment of rentals.

2. The financial leasing transaction referred to in the previous paragraph is a transaction which includes the following characteristics:

   (a) the lessee specifies the equipment and selects the supplier without relying primarily on the skill and judgment of the lessor;

   (b) the equipment is acquired by the lessor in connection with a leasing agreement which, to the knowledge of the supplier, either has been made or is to be made between the lessor and the lessee; and

   (c) the rentals payable under the leasing agreement are calculated so as to take into account in particular the amortisation of the whole or a substantial part of the cost of the equipment.

3. This Convention applies whether or not the lessee has or subsequently acquires the option to buy the equipment or to hold it on lease for a further period, and whether or not for a nominal price or rental.

4. This Convention applies to financial leasing transactions in relation to all equipment save that which is to be used primarily for the lessee's personal, family or household purposes.

[6.118] This definition suggests several essential features of financial leasing under the convention. First, the lessor has a special status in financial leasing, because he or she is the link between the lessee and the supplier. This reflects the triangular relationship of the parties to a financial leasing arrangement. Second, the arrangement involves two contracts: the leasing agreement between the lessor and the lessee and the contract of sale between the lessor and the supplier. Third, the lessor is not responsible for the technical specifications and fitness of the equipment, or goods covered by the leasing agreement, although he or she acts as the seller/lessor/owner to the lessee in the leasing agreement. Fourth, an option to purchase the leased equipment is not a mandatory feature of a financial leasing arrangement under the convention. Lastly, the financial leasing arrangement covered by the convention excludes leasing arrangements made for family or personal purposes.

Scope of application

[6.119] The scope of the convention's application is defined by arts 2–5 of the convention. Article 3 defines the international nature of the convention in the following words:

1. This Convention applies when the lessor and the lessee have their places of business in different states and:

   (a) those states and the state in which the supplier has its place of business are Contracting states; or

   (b) both the supply agreement and the leasing agreement are governed by the law of a Contracting state.

2. A reference in this Convention to a party's place of business shall, if it has more than one place of business, mean the place of business which has the closest relationship to the relevant agreement and its performance, having regard to the circumstances known to or contemplated by the parties at any time before or at the conclusion of that agreement.

This provision qualifies the operation of the convention in the same way as art 2 of the UNDROIT Convention on International Factoring qualifies the convention: see **[6.120]**.

Similarly, the application of the present convention is as difficult as for the other conventions.

[6.120] Besides art 3, arts 2, 4, and 5 of the convention affect the application of the convention from different perspectives. Article 2 deals with the sub-lease of the same equipment, and states that:

> ... the Convention applies to each transaction which is a financial leasing transaction and is otherwise subject to this Convention as if the person from whom the first lessor (as defined in paragraph 1 of the previous article) acquired the equipment were the supplier and as if the agreement under which the equipment was so acquired were the supply agreement.

Broadly speaking, this provision suggests that each subsequent leasing agreement is regarded as an independent transaction even though the equipment is the same in several sub-leasing agreements made in a chain transaction. Article 4 ensures the continuous application of the convention to the equipment which has become a fixture to or been incorporated in land since it was leased or bought last time. The provision is capable of covering a situation where the equipment has become a fixture or part of land before the first financial arrangement is made. Article 5 grants a option to the parties to an international financial leasing arrangement to exclude the application of the convention. The parties include the lessor, the lessee and the supplier.[98] In addition, art 5(2) also permits the parties, by express agreement, to amend the effect of most provisions, except for arts 8(3), 13(3)(b) and (4).[99]

Rights and duties of the parties

Defining the parties

[6.121] As suggested in art 1 of the convention, there are two separate agreements under an international financial leasing arrangement or transaction: the leasing agreement and the supply agreement. Accordingly, there are three parties, the lessor, the lessee and the supplier under an international financial leasing arrangement. The parties' rights and duties are set out in Chapter II, which includes arts 7–14. The rights and duties of each party are to be discussed separately.

Rights and duties of lessor

[6.122] The lessor is the most important person in an international financial leasing arrangement. He or she is the financier of the transaction, the seller and lessor to the real user of the equipment, and the buyer to the supplier of the equipment. Under the relevant provisions, the lessor has the following major rights:

---

98. Article 5(1) of the convention states that 'the application of this Convention may be excluded only if each of the parties to the supply agreement and each of the parties to the leasing agreement agree to exclude it'.
99. Article 5(2) of the convention states that 'where the application of this Convention has not been excluded in accordance with the previous paragraph, the parties may, in their relations with each other, derogate from or vary the effect of any of its provisions except as stated in Articles 8(3) and 13(3)(b) and (4)'.

[6.122]

the lessor's real rights in the equipment shall be valid against the lessee's trustee in bankruptcy and creditors, including creditors who have obtained an attachment or execution;[100]

except those provided by the convention or the leasing agreement, the lessor shall not incur any liability to the lessee in respect of the equipment save to the extent that the lessee has suffered loss as the result of its reliance on the lessor's skill and judgment and of the lessor's intervention in the selection of the supplier or the specifications of the equipment;[101]

the lessor shall not, in its capacity of lessor, be liable to third parties for death, personal injury or damage to property caused by the equipment;[102]

in the event of default by the lessee, the lessor may recover accrued unpaid rentals, together with interest and damages;[103] and

where the lessee's default is substantial, then subject to paragraph 5 the lessor may also require accelerated payment of the value of the future rentals, where the leasing agreement so provides, or may terminate the leasing agreement and after such termination: (a) recover possession of the equipment; and (b) recover such damages as will place the lessor in the position in which it would have been had the lessee performed the leasing agreement in accordance with its terms;[104]

the lessor may transfer or otherwise deal with all or any of its rights in the equipment or under the leasing agreement. Such a transfer shall not relieve the lessor of any of its duties under the leasing agreement or alter either the nature of the leasing agreement or its legal treatment as provided in this Convention;[105] and

the lessee may transfer the right to the use of the equipment or any other rights under the leasing agreement only with the consent of the lessor and subject to the rights of third parties.[106]

[6.123] The lessor's duties are related to his or her rights. For example, while the lessor is not liable to the third party as the lessor, he or she is liable to a third party in tort as the owner of the equipment causing the damage concerned.[107] In addition, the lessor warrants that the lessee's quiet possession will not be disturbed by a person who has a superior title or right, or who claims a superior title or right and acts under the authority of a court, where such title, right or claim is not derived from an act or omission of the lessee.[108] The other major duties of the lessor would be contractual under the two respective contracts. It must be noted that besides the special duties and rights set out in the convention, the lessor is liable as the buyer under the supply agreement with the supplier and as the lessor under the leasing agreement to the lessee. Similarly, the lessor exercises the corresponding rights under the two agreements in his or her relevant capacities: see art 13.

Rights and duties of the lessee

[6.124] The lessee is the end-user of the equipment subject to the financial leasing arrangement. The lessee exercises rights and undertakes duties under the leasing agreement

---

100. The convention, art 7(1). Under the same provision, 'trustee in bankruptcy includes a liquidator, administrator or other person appointed to administer the lessee's estate for the benefit of the general body of creditors'.
101. The convention, art 8(1)(a).
102. Ibid, art 8(1)(b).
103. Ibid, art 13(1).
104. Ibid, art 13(2).
105. Ibid, art 14(1).
106. Ibid, art 14(2).
107. Ibid, art 8(1)(c).
108. Ibid, art (2).

with the lessor. Under art 12 of the convention, the major rights of the lessee are as follows:

1. Where the equipment is not delivered or is delivered late or fails to conform to the supply agreement:
   (a) the lessee has the right as against the lessor to reject the equipment or to terminate the leasing agreement; and
   (b) the lessor has the right to remedy its failure to tender equipment in conformity with the supply agreement, as if the lessee had agreed to buy the equipment from the lessor under the same terms as those of the supply agreement.
2. A right conferred by the previous paragraph shall be exercisable in the same manner and shall be lost in the same circumstances as if the lessee had agreed to buy the equipment from the lessor under the same terms as those of the supply agreement.
3. The lessee shall be entitled to withhold rentals payable under the leasing agreement until the lessor has remedied its failure to tender equipment in conformity with the supply agreement or the lessee has lost the right to reject the equipment.
4. Where the lessee has exercised a right to terminate the leasing agreement, the lessee shall be entitled to recover any rentals and other sums paid in advance, less a reasonable sum for any benefit the lessee has derived from the equipment.
5. The lessee shall have no other claim against the lessor for non-delivery, delay in delivery or delivery of non-conforming equipment except to the extent to which this results from the act or omission of the lessor.
6. Nothing in this article shall affect the lessee's rights against the supplier under Article 10.

[6.125] In addition to art 12, art 11 also deals with the rights of the lessee. This provision states that the lessee's rights derived from the supply agreement under this convention shall not be affected by a variation of any term of the supply agreement previously approved by the lessee unless it consented to that variation. Article 11 appears to be enforcing art 10, which requires the supplier to be liable under the supply agreement to the lessee. These provisions are necessary to override the effect of the doctrine of privity of contract, because the lessee is not a contracting party to the supply agreement even though the lessee is the real user of the equipment. However, the lessee's statutory entitlement under the supply agreement does not entitle him or her to terminate the supply agreement without consent of the lessor. On the other hand, with the consent of the lessor, the lessee is entitled to rescind the supply agreement directly against the supplier.

[6.126] Under the relevant provisions of the convention, the major duties of the lessee are set out as follows:

- 'the lessee shall take proper care of the equipment, use it in a reasonable manner and keep it in the condition in which it was delivered, subject to fair wear and tear and to any modification of the equipment agreed by the parties';[109] and
- 'when the leasing agreement comes to an end the lessee, unless exercising a right to buy the equipment or to hold the equipment on lease for a further period, shall return the equipment to the lessor in the condition specified in the previous paragraph'.[110]

---

109. The convention, art 9(1).
110. The convention, art 9(2).

[6.126]

In addition, the lessee is obliged as a contracting party under the leasing agreement to the lessor to perform the terms of the agreement, in particular the terms concerning the payment and transfer of the leased equipment to a third party.

Rights and duties of the supplier

[6.127] The supplier is a party to an international financial leasing arrangement because it produces or supplies the equipment or goods concerned. As a contracting party under the supply agreement with the lessor, the supplier must perform the terms of the agreement. In addition, the supplier has imposed certain statutory obligations on the lessee. Article 10 states that the duties of the supplier under the supply agreement shall also be owed to the lessee as if it were a party to that agreement, and as if the equipment were to be supplied directly to the lessee. However, the supplier shall not be liable to both the lessor and the lessee in respect of the same damage. This provision is essential to link the interests of the supplier and the interests of the lessee, because there is no direct contractual connection between them in a financial leasing arrangement. Article 10 is a vital provision which serves the purpose of UNCITRAL to regulate the triangular relationship involving the lessor, the lessee and the supplier in an international financial leasing.

Forfaiting in international trade

[6.128] 'Forfaiting' comes from the French term 'a forfait' which implies a waiver or surrender of rights.[111] In international trade this means that the purchaser of a negotiable instrument waives the right of recourse against the seller of the instrument. Such waiver is needed for facilitating international commercial transactions. However, no party would wish to pay for documents whose value is not protected under law. Banks are thus needed to avalise the documents to provide financial security. Forfaiting means that a bank may purchase a negotiable instrument at a discount price from the bearer and sell it with its own guarantee at a higher price. Forfaiting is beneficial to the original bearer of the instrument, because many instruments are to be paid at a later date and forfaiting of them by a bank enables the bearer to have cash instantly. Forfaiting is profitable to the bank, because it purchases the instruments at a discount and receives either the full payment at maturity or a higher price at the time they are transferred to an investor. Forfaiting means banks invest in international trade and turn negotiable instruments for international trade into securities tradeable on secondary markets.[112]

[6.129] The Secretary-General of UNCITRAL examined forfaiting in the report *Possible Future Work: Legal Aspects of Receivables Financing* submitted for the 27th session of UNCITRAL held in New York between 31 May–17 June 1994, in the following words:[113]

> Forfaiting may be described as the sale of documentary receivables, that is receivables incorporated in negotiable instruments, such as bills of exchange, promissory notes, or in letters of credit and bank guarantees. However, the term 'forfaiting' may be used to indicate the sale of non-documentary

---

111. Baxter, note 4 above, p 44.
112. Id, p 45.
113. UNCITRAL, *Possible Future Work: Legal Aspects of Receivables Financing*, para 13, available at <http://www.his.com:80>.

receivables that often may be backed by a bank guarantee or a letter of credit. Any unification work on forfaiting of documentary receivables might not be desirable in view of the fact that the assignment of such documentary receivables is already regulated by uniform statutory rules (for example, the Geneva Uniform Laws on Bills of Exchange, Promissory Notes and Cheques), or uniform rules at the contractual level (for example, assignment of proceeds of letters of credit under the ICC Uniform Customs and Practice for Documentary Credits and assignment of proceeds of bank guarantees subject to the ICC Uniform Rules on Demand Guarantees), or is the subject of other ongoing unification work (for example, the UNCITRAL draft Convention on Independent Guarantees and Stand-by Letters of Credit). In addition, it should be noted that the issues arising in assignment of receivables would have to be addressed differently if documentary receivables were involved. For example, in the assignment of documentary receivables only defences based on the document incorporating the receivables could be raised by the debtor against the assignee, and priority among several assignees would have to be based on possession of the document in due course. However, future unification work could cover forfaiting of non-documentary receivables.

Model Law on transfer of credit

[6.130] The UNCITRAL Model Law on International Credit Transfers (Model Law) is meant to be a law regulating credit transfers between banks. It was adopted by UNCITRAL in 1992 as a response to a major change in the means by which fund transfers are effected internationally. This change involved two elements: the increased use of payment orders sent by electronic means rather than on paper, and the shift from the generalised use of debit transfers to the generalised use of credit transfers. The Model Law, which is a recommended model for domestic legislation of UN members, offers the opportunity to unify the law of credit transfers by enacting a domestic law that is drafted to meet the needs of modern fund transfer techniques.[114]

[6.131] Credit transfer is a type of business operation between banks. It can be used for many purposes, serving both the needs of banks' customers and the needs of banks. As noted by UNCITRAL, until the mid-1970s a person who wished to transfer funds to another country, either for the purpose of effecting payment or to move the funds to another country, had three major means to do so. First, he or she could send his or her own personal or corporate cheque to the intended recipient of the funds, but international collection of such items was both slow and expensive. Second, he or she could purchase from his or her bank a draft drawn by the bank on the bank's correspondent in the receiving country. Collection of such an international bank draft was faster than collection of a personal or corporate cheque since it was payable in the receiving country and in the funds of the receiving country. Third, payment orders, which emerged in the mid-nineteenth century were also an option for transferring funds between banks from different countries. The method involves the originator's bank sending a payment order by telegraph to its correspondent bank in the receiving country to instruct the receiving bank to pay the intended recipient of the funds. A payment order could also be transmitted by telegraph between the banks on paper. This was the common method for making fund transfers in many countries. However, it was less commonly used for international transfers, because it was relatively expensive and prone to error. When telex replaced the telegraph, the cost was reduced and accuracy improved. This led to a gradual

---

114. Explanatory Note by the UNCITRAL Secretariat on the Model Law on International Credit Transfers, para 1.

[6.131] **International Commercial Law**

movement away from the use of bank cheques for international payments. With the introduction of computer-to-computer interbank telecommunications in the mid-1970s, the cost dropped still further, while speed and accuracy improved dramatically. The extension of computer-to-computer interbank telecommunication facilities to ever increasing numbers of countries means that the use of bank cheques for international fund transfers has drastically decreased and the role of telex transfers has been significantly reduced.[115]

[6.132] Also noted by UNCITRAL, there are both similarities and differences among the existing means of fund transfer, such as the collection of bank cheques, telex transfers and the computer-to-computer transfers. One of the common characteristics among them is that value is transferred from the originator to the beneficiary by a debit to the bank account of the originator and a credit to the bank account of the beneficiary. Settlement between the banks is also accomplished by debits and credits to appropriate accounts. Those accounts may be maintained between the banks concerned or with third banks, including the central bank of one or both countries. On the other hand, one of the striking differences between them, in particular between the collection of a bank cheque (or a personal or corporate cheque) and other methods is that the cheque is transmitted to the beneficiary by mail or other means outside banking channels. Therefore, the banking process to collect the cheque is initiated by the beneficiary of the fund transfer.[116]

[6.133] The methods for transferring funds internationally can be divided into two categories according to the rights and obligations of the parties to a transfer: debit transfer and credit transfer. A fund transfer in which the beneficiary of the fund transfer initiates the banking process is more and more often called a debit transfer. Collection of a bill of exchange or a promissory note is also a debit transfer, since the beneficiary of the fund transfer initiates the fund transfer, and there are other debit transfer techniques available, including some that are based on the use of computers. In contrast to the banking process, for telex transfers and computer-to-computer transfers it is the originator of the fund transfer who begins the banking process, by issuing a payment order to its bank to debit its account and to credit the account of the beneficiary. A fund transfer in which the originator of the fund transfer initiates the banking process is often called a credit transfer.[117] The Model Law purports to regulate credit transfers by introducing a set of uniform rules among the countries adopting the Model Law. Since credit transfers are carried out and settled between banks, the Model Law purports to regulate the relationships between banks only.

[6.134] The ICC Uniform Rules for Bank-to-Bank Reimbursements (URR 525) are relevant to the operation of the Model Law in the sense that the Model Law purports to regulate credit transfers between banks and URR 525 purports to set out rules for

---

115. Explanatory Note by the UNCITRAL Secretariat on the Model Law on International Credit Transfers, paras 2 and 3.
116. Explanatory Note by the UNCITRAL Secretariat on the Model Law on International Credit Transfers, paras 4 and 5.
117. Explanatory Note by the UNCITRAL Secretariat on the Model Law on International Credit Transfers, paras 5 and 6.

reimbursement arrangements between banks. Reimbursement is a necessary part of any credit transfer. URR 525 purports to unify the rules for reimbursements. The Model Law is open for the countries to adopt. In this way, it will be sanctioned by the legislative power of each country adopting it. It may also be adopted by private parties in their private transactions. Such incorporation of the Model Law is permitted under the commonly accepted rules of conflict of laws, unless the rules so incorporated contradict the relevant rules of domestic law. The Model Law and URR 525 have a similar status (prior to the Model Law being officially adopted by any country). Both can be binding in a transaction by express agreement of the parties, unless the applicable law denies their use on the ground of illegality or public interest. In practice, the Model Law and URR 525 can be supplementary to each other, as long as their co-existence does not cause confusions or conflicts in a credit transfer.

Chapter Seven

Marine Insurance, Aviation Insurance and International Trade

Introduction

Insurance is an important aspect of international trade. In order to reduce risks in business operations, including international trade, many forms of insurance have been offered by the insurer, who carries on the business of insurance services, to the insured (or assured), who pays for the insurance services to attain some financial safety in the event that the insured risks have caused damage to the insured subject matter. In international trade, insurance policies can be offered to cover risks associated with sea carriage, air carriage, carriage by land, multimodal carriage, sale of goods, supply of services, investment projects, construction contracts and so on. This chapter deals with marine insurance and aviation insurance in international trade.

Insurance itself is a form of service covered presently by GATS (see **[9.39]**) and domestic contract law. GATS requires WTO members to liberalise their domestic service markets. Domestic laws regulate the operation of various insurance contracts, as well as rights and obligations of the contracting parties. For example, in *IBBCO Trading Pty Ltd v HIH Casualty & General Insurance Ltd* [2001] NSWSC 490, the insured was an Australian exporter of various agricultural products. The contract of insurance was made for the purpose of, inter alia, covering 'the direct loss arising from non-payment'. The insurer refused to indemnify the loss of the insured by relying on the exclusion clauses and a number of technical points. These issues are all related to contract law and the interpretation of contractual clauses. In pursuance of the relevant contract rules, the court held that the loss concerned was covered by the contract, and thus the insurer was obliged to indemnify the insured. This example illustrates the general nature of all insurance contracts, whether for marine insurance, aviation insurance or for the sale of goods. However, marine insurance law and aviation insurance law have become two distinctive branches of insurance law, largely due to their international characteristics. Special laws have been made to regulate these two types of insurance contract. This is why this chapter especially deals with these two types of insurance contract.

Explaining marine insurance

A brief history

[7.1] Marine insurance is perhaps by far the oldest form of insurance, because shipping marked the beginning of significant development for worldwide international trade. International trade, transnational trade or regional trade, whatever we call it, depending on the ancient concepts of 'state' and 'sovereign' (the key elements for the development of human society in the past several centuries), has relied heavily on the development of the shipping industry and has benefited tremendously from the improvement in the shipping capacity of mankind. Shipping has been a highly risky business for both vessel owners and cargo-owners. The need to find some way to minimise the risk for all parties involved in maritime adventures offers an opportunity and attraction for the development of marine insurance, which has become an independent industry associated closely with shipping and international trade.

[7.2] It was believed that some sort of arrangement for securing or protecting the interest of the parties involved in marine adventures was probably in place long ago when mankind began to explore trading opportunities across a vast ocean. For example, it is reported that 'general average and bottomry' were arrangements used in Rhodian times between 900–700 BC, where a shipowner could borrow money to carry out a maritime adventure, by pledging his ship as security against the borrowing — 'but neither of these methods can be described as insurance'.[1] The practice bearing some similarity to what we understand as marine insurance today did not appear until 1132, if not later, when the Danish began to reimburse those who experienced loss at sea.[2] In 1255, insurance premiums were used for the first time as the merchant-state of Venice pooled these premiums to indemnify loss due to piracy, spoilage, or pillage. The first marine insurance policy was introduced in 1384 in an attempt to cover bales of fabric travelling to Savona from Pisa, Italy. Within the next century, merchants from Lombard began the first insurance practice in London. Finally, in 1688, Lloyd's of London, named after Edward Lloyd, began the risky business of insurance underwriting, and have grown to become the largest marine insurance underwriters in the world. The Marine Insurance Act of 1906 was then proposed and initiated in an attempt to clarify and set forth the regulations and policy variables associated with marine insurance agreements.[3] Lloyd's of London has taken a lead in the development of commercial usage and customs for marine insurance since its establishment. The Marine Insurance Act 1906 (UK) formed the basis for the development of domestic marine insurance laws in the common law jurisdictions, such as Australia, Canada, Hong Kong and New Zealand, which share their legal heritage with the English common law.

---

1. O'May and Hill, *Marine Insurance: Law and Policy*, London, Sweet & Maxwell, 1993, p 1.
2. Marine Insurance, website of the College of Business of the Oregon State University, available at <http://www.acs.ucalgary.ca/MGMT/inrm/industry/marine.htm>.
3. Ibid.

A contract of indemnity

[7.3] A marine insurance contract is a contract of indemnity. Under s 7 of the Marine Insurance Act 1909 (Cth) it is a 'contract whereby the insurer undertakes to indemnify the assured, in a manner and to the extent thereby agreed, against marine losses, that is to say, the losses incident to marine adventure'.[4] Marine adventure refers to the exposure of the ship, goods or other moveables to 'maritime perils', which 'means the perils consequent on, or incidental to, the navigation of the sea, that is to say, perils of the seas, fire, war perils, pirates, rovers, thieves, captures, seizures, restraints, and detainments of princes and peoples, jettisons, barratry, and any other perils, either of the like kind, or which may be designated by the policy' (s 9 of the Act).

[7.4] The definition of 'marine insurance contract' as set out in s 7 of the Act implies the doctrine of privity of contract. It can be argued that a marine insurance contract is enforceable between the insurer and insured only, although the insurer has the right of subrogation under the contract to succeed to the right of the insured against a third party. Along with the development of modern commercial practices, variations and innovations have been seen in many insurance contracts, which impose challenges to the traditional doctrine of privity of contract. Whether or not a third party to an insurance contract is entitled to rely on a contractual clause recognising or granting certain rights to him or her rose as an issue in *Fraser River Pile & Dredge Ltd v Can-Dive Service Ltd*, decided on 27 October 1997, No CA020806 (BCCA).[5]

In this case, the insured derrick barge was lost in a storm off Little River when it was left there unattended by the charterer. The insurance policy contained two clauses affecting the interests of the charterer. One is an additional insured's clause, which gave the barge owner permission to charter the barge and make the charterer an additional insured under the policy. The other is a waiver subrogation clause which waived the action of subrogation against the charterer. The barge owner and the insurer sued the charterer for the loss of the barge. The charterer sought to rely on the clauses as defences. The trial court denied the charterer's claim on the ground of privity of contract. The British Columbia Court of Appeal allowed the appeal and held that the charterer was entitled to rely on the relevant clauses as an additional insured. This decision was affirmed by the Supreme Court of Canada, which held that the two conditions for making an exception to the doctrine of privity were made out. (The two conditions are: (1) the contracting parties must have intended to extend the benefit to the third party seeking to rely on the contractual clause; and (2) the activities performed by the third party must be the very activities contemplated by the parties in the contract concerned.[6])

[7.5] This case raises the interesting question of a third party's interest under a contract. We have seen the acceptance of a third party's right to rely on a Himalaya clause in a bill of lading in most common law jurisdictions. Whether or not there should be some exception to the privity doctrine in marine insurance contracts remains to be seen, although there appears to be a need to consider the rules affecting the third party's interests under

---

4. 'Assured' has the same meaning as 'insured'.
5. The case summary is available at <http://www.admiraltylaw.com>.
6. *Fraser River Pile & Dredge Ltd v Can-Dive Services Ltd* [1999] 2 SCR 108 (SCC).

a marine insurance contract. For example, in another Canadian case, *Demitri v General Accident Indemnity Co*, decided on 26 November 1996, NO S0301296 (BCSC),[7] the plaintiff sought to sue directly the insurer of the vessel colliding with his own vessel because he was unable to recover a judgment against the vessel owner. The insurer's defence was that the insured (owner of the vessel colliding with the plaintiff's vessel) had failed to give prompt notice of the claim as required by the terms of the policy. The court held that the insured had failed to give prompt notice as required and refused to give relief to the plaintiff. Had the insured complied with the requirement for prompt notice, would the court have permitted the plaintiff to sue the insurer directly by relying on the insurer's liability under the insurance contract to which the plaintiff was not a party? The question was not answered in this case.

Hull insurance and cargo insurance

Traditional classifications

[7.6] The purpose of marine insurance is to insure against risks incidental to the sea carriage of goods and shipping itself. Generally speaking, the risk can be divided into three categories: risk in the cargo, risk in the vessel and risk in the freight. The risk in the cargo may be borne by the cargo-owner or anyone interested in the safety of the cargo. The risk in the vessel may be borne by the vessel owner or anyone interested in the safety of the vessel. The risk in the freight is normally borne by the carrier who can be a vessel owner or a charterer, or sometimes by anyone who has some interest in the successful completion of the voyage. Different insurance policies can be offered to cover different types of risk and the risk to different types of subject matters. Broadly, insurance contracts can be classified into two categories: cargo insurance and hull insurance. At least, this is the traditional classification of insurance contracts. Since there is a close connection between the safety of the vessel and the completion of a voyage, the risk in the freight is covered as an optional subject matter under the hull insurance contract. Alternatively, by looking at the existing variations of the standard marine insurance contracts (see **[7.10]** and **[7.12]**–**[7.14]**), the classifications of marine insurance contracts can take as many forms or categories as the types of contract in use.

Hull insurance contract

[7.7] A shipowner or other person who has an insurable interest in a ship (for example, the mortgagor of the ship) may take 'hull insurance' against the general risk which may occur to the ship. This person may also insure against loss of income (freight insurance) and liability to any third parties, which may arise from marine adventure. It was argued that the oldest policy of marine insurance was a hull insurance, issued to an Italian vessel, the *Santa Clara*, for its voyage from Genoa to Majorca.[8]

---

7. The case summary is available at <http://www.admiraltylaw.com>.
8. Hayden and Balick, 'Marine Insurance: Varieties, Combinations, and Coverages' (1991) 66 *Tulane Law Review* 311, p 314.

[7.8] A hull insurance contract is an insurance policy on the safety of the vessel covered. The particular activities of the vessel and the particular risks which may occur to the vessel vary under different types of contract. For example, under the standard contract based on the Institute Time Clauses Hulls, the navigation of the vessel is covered in the following terms:

> 1.1 The vessel is covered subject to the provisions of this insurance at all times and has leave to sail or navigate with or without pilots, to go on trial trips and to assist and tow vessels or craft in distress, but it is warranted that the vessel shall not be towed, except as is customary or to the first safe port or place when in need of assistance, or undertake towage or salvage services under a contract previously arranged by the assured and/or owners and/or manager and/or charterers. This clause 1.1 shall not exclude customary towage in connection with loading and discharging.

[7.9] There are also Clauses 1.2 and 1.3 in the same clause purporting to define the insurer's liability in relation to the navigation of the vessel insured under the contract. These provisions suggest one of the basic principles of insurance contract, which is the meaning of the contract and in particular the risks covered by the contract are determined by the terms of the contract, which are presumably to be the agreements of the parties to the contract.

[7.10] The risks covered by a hull insurance contract are also defined by the contract itself, unless the relevant statute stipulated otherwise. For example, in the same standard contract entitled Institute Time Clauses Hulls (referred to above), the perils of the sea as covered by the contract include:[9]

> 6.1 This insurance covers loss or damage to the subject matter caused by
> 6.1.1 perils of the seas rivers lakes or other navigable waters;
> 6.1.2 fire, explosion;
> 6.1.3 violent theft by persons from outside the vessel;
> 6.1.4 jettison;
> 6.1.5 piracy;
> 6.1.6 breakdown of or accident to nuclear installations or reactors;
> 6.1.7 contact with aircraft or similar objects, or objects falling therefrom, land conveyance, dock or harbour equipment or installation;
> 6.1.8 earthquake volcanic eruption or lightning.
> 6.2 This insurance covers loss of or damage to the subject matter insured caused by
> 6.2.1 accidents in loading discharging or shifting cargo or fuel;
> 6.2.2 bursting of boilers breakage of shafts or any latent defect in the machinery or hull;
> 6.2.3 negligence of master officers crew or pilots;
> 6.2.4 negligence of repairers or charterers provided such repairs or charterers are not an assured hereunder;
> 6.2.5 barratry of master officers or crew; provided such loss or damage has not resulted from want of due diligence by the assured, owners or managers.
> 6.3 Master officers crew or pilots not to be considered owners within the meaning of this Clause 6 should they hold shares in the vessel.

[7.11] The above example shows that the risks covered under different types of contract may vary, depending on the intention of the parties concerned. *HIH Casualty & General Insurance Ltd v Waterwell Shipping Inc* [1998] NSWSC 436 illustrates the 'negligence

---

9. The Institute Time Clauses Hulls, para 6.

of master officers, crew or pilot' as a risk covered by a hull insurance policy.[10] By combining Clauses 1 and 6 as seen above, we have some idea about the meaning of a hull insurance contract based on the Time Clauses Hulls. The most important point concerning hull insurance is that it is a contract made against the risks which may occur to the vessel and to the persons having interests in the safety of the vessel, including the safe completion of the voyage engaged by the vessel. Thus, the activities covered, the insured subject matters and the risks covered are determined by the terms of the contract concerned. Consequently, the loss of freight can be insured as an additional risk or subject matter by the vessel owner, charterer or anyone interested in the safety of the vessel under Clause 21 of the said standard contract, which is entitled Time Clauses Hulls.

Cargo insurance contract

[7.12] A cargo insurance contract is a contract to ensure the safety of the cargo carried by a sea-going vessel. The risks and types of loss covered vary depending on the terms of contracts. For example, in the Institute Cargo Clauses (A), the risks covered are all risks of loss or damage to the subject matter insured except as provided in Clauses 4, 5, and 7 of the contract.[11] Clause 4 of the Clauses, which is entitled General Exclusion Clauses, states as follows:

4   In no case shall this insurance cover —
4.1 loss damage or expense attributable to wilful misconduct of the assured;
4.2 ordinary leakage, ordinary loss in weight or volume, or ordinary wear and tear of the subject matter insured;
4.3 loss damage or expenses caused by insufficiency or unsuitability of packing or preparation of the subject matter insured (for the purpose of this Clause 4.3 packing shall be deemed to include stowage in a container or liftvan but only when such stowage is carried out prior to attachment of this insurance or by the assured or their agents);
4.4 loss damage or expense caused by inherent vice or nature of the subject matter insured;
4.5 loss damage or expense proximately caused by delay, even though the delay be caused by a risk insured against (except expenses payable under Clause 2 above);
4.6 loss damage or expense arising from insolvency or financial default of the owners managers charterers or operators of the vessel;
4.7 loss damage or expense arising from the use of any weapon of war employing atomic or nuclear fission and/or fusion or other like reaction or radioactive force or matter.

[7.13] Clause 5, which is entitled Unseaworthiness and Unfitness Exclusions Clause, states as follows:

5.1 In no case shall this insurance cover loss damage or expenses arising from unseaworthiness of vessel or craft, unfitness of vessel craft conveyance container or liftvan for the safe carriage of the subject matter insured, where the assured or their servants are privy to such unseaworthiness or unfitness, at the time the subject matter insured is loaded therein.
5.2 The underwriters waive any breach of the implied warranties of seaworthiness of the ship and fitness of the ship to carry the subject matter insured to destination, unless the assured or their agents are privy to such unseaworthiness or unfitness.

---

10. The Court of Appeal held that there were competing proximate courses for the loss of the insured vessel — ie, the negligence of the crews to leave the starboard sea suction valves open and the corrosion of the wall of strainer box — and these courses were either risks that were covered, or not expressly excluded.
11. The Institute Cargo Clauses (A), Clause 1.

Clause 6, which is entitled War Exclusion Clause, states as follows:

6 In no case shall this insurance cover loss damage or expenses caused by —
6.1 war civil war revolution rebellion insurrection, or civil strife arising therefrom, or any hostile act by or against a belligerent power;
6.2 capture seizure arrest restraint or detainment (piracy excepted), and the consequence thereof or any attempt threat;
6.3 derelict mines torpedoes bombs or other derelict weapons of war.

[7.14] These four clauses define the scope and types of the risks covered by this particular type of contract. Because of the wording of Clause 1, the Institute Cargo Clause (A) is commonly known as 'all risks' cover. The differences between the Institute Cargo Clauses (A) and the Institute Cargo Clauses (B) are mainly seen in the types of risks covered under each contract. For comparison, the latter specifies the types of risks covered under the contract, excluding those risks which have not been specified in the relevant clauses. For example, Clause 1 of the Institute Cargo Clauses (B), which is entitled Risks Clause, states as follows:

1. This insurance covers, except as provided in Clauses 4, 5, 6 and 7 below,
1.1 loss of or damage to the subject matter insured reasonably attributable to
1.1.1 fire or explosion;
1.1.2 vessel or craft being stranded grounded sunk or capsized;
1.1.3 overturning or derailment of land conveyance;
1.1.4 collision or contact of vessel craft or conveyance with any external object other than water;
1.1.5 discharge of cargo at a port of distress;
1.1.6 earthquake volcanic eruption or lightning.
1.2 loss of or damage to the subject matter insured caused by
1.2.1 general average sacrifice;
1.2.2 jettison or washing overboard;
1.2.3 entry of sea lake or river water into vessel craft hold conveyance container liftvan or place or storage.
1.3 total loss of any package lost overboard or dropped whilst loading on to, or unloading from, vessel or craft.

[7.15] Clauses 4, 5, 6, and 7 of the Institute Cargo Clauses (B) qualify Clause 1 in the same way as Clauses 4, 5, and 6 do under the Institute Cargo Clauses (A), (set out in the preceding paragraphs). The differences between the clauses of Cargo Clauses (B) and the Cargo Clauses (A) demonstrate the differences in the risks covered by each type of contract. They and all other types of cargo insurance contract offer different options or combinations of risks to the cargo-owners or the persons who have an interest in the safety of the cargo. The differences in the types of risks covered is the key point which differentiates the Institute Cargo Classes (C) from the Cargo Clauses (A) and the Cargo Clauses (B). These Cargo Clauses illustrate the approaches and techniques employed in the cargo insurance contracts to define the risks concerned and to determine the liability of the insurer under each contract.

[7.16] In conclusion, the buyer or seller, or any persons who have an insurable interest, may take a cargo insurance against any risk which is relevant and incidental to the proposed marine adventure. Depending on the terms of the contract, a marine policy may cover the transportation of the goods by land or air which is incidental to the carriage of the goods by sea. It may also extend to temporary storage of the goods in a harbour or other place which is incidental to the carriage of goods by sea. In *United Mills Agencies Ltd v R E Harvey, Bray & Co* [1952] 1 TLR 149, the goods were insured under an open cover, but the period when the goods were in the warehouse of the packers was not included. The goods were destroyed by fire while in the packers' warehouse. The insurer was not liable for the loss. This case suggests that an insurance contract is the same as an ordinary contract, in the sense that the rights or duties of the parties are determined by the terms of the contract.

[7.17] *George Kallis (Manufactures) Ltd v Success Insurance Ltd*

[1985] 2 Lloyd's Rep 8

Connection between contract of sale and marine insurance

Facts: George Kallis was the Cyprus buyer of a cargo of denim from the Hong Kong seller — Wantex Traders. The denim was sold under the CIF term, and paid by two letters of credit. The credits expressly prohibited transhipment. Wantex Traders obtained a bill of lading stating that the goods were shipped on board the ship *Ta Shun*, but the goods were in fact not so shipped. The goods, which were supposed to have been shipped on the *Ta Shun*, were insured with Success Insurance, covering the period from warehouse to warehouse against all risks and damages caused by external causes. Wantex obtained payment under the credits by submitting a false bill of lading in August 1976. Wantex then shipped and transhipped the goods on the vessel *Intellect* to Cyprus. The *Intellect* caught fire and the goods were damaged. George Kallis claimed a total loss under the policy, but the insurers refused to pay on the ground that the goods were not carried by the ship *Ta Shun*. The Court of Appeal of Hong Kong decided in favour of the insurers. George Kallis appealed to the Judicial Committee of the Privy Council.

Decision: The Judicial Committee held in favour of the insurers. George Kallis failed because the policy covered goods to be carried by the *Ta Shun*, but the damage occurred on board the *Intellect*.

General principles for the making of a marine insurance contract

[7.18] A marine insurance contract is subject to the basic general principles of contract making, such as freedom of contract, fairness and *force majeure*, and others. The general principles of contract law do exist across the world, although people have different understandings of what constitutes general principles. The CISG is an example of the existence of universal principles of contract law. A marine insurance contract faces similar issues as an ordinary contract, such as offer and acceptance, intention of the parties, performance, remedies for breach of contract, and others. However, marine insurance is also regulated by the relevant domestic law on marine insurance, such as the Marine Insurance Act 1906 (UK), the Marine Insurance Act 1909 (Cth) and the Maritime Law 1993 (China).

Thus, a marine insurance contract is subject to both the general principles of contract law and the relevant domestic marine insurance law in most countries and jurisdictions of the world. In the case of contract construction, the court will first read the contract in the light of the specific provisions of the relevant marine insurance legislation.[12] In the absence of specific rules, the general principles of contract law should be applied.

[7.19] As we have seen, marine insurance contracts can be broadly classified into two categories: cargo insurance contracts and hull insurance contracts. Both types of marine insurance contracts are relevant to studies of international commercial law, although the cargo insurance contracts are much more common to people involved in international trade and commerce. The hull insurance contracts affect the interests of shipowners, charterers, banks and financial institutions which have financial interests in vessels, and of course the insurers, underwriters and insurance brokers. These groups of people are relatively smaller than the groups of sellers, buyers and the people who have interests in the safety of the goods carried by vessels. The general practices and rules for the making of each type of marine insurance contract are to be examined separately in the following subsections.

Making of a cargo insurance contract

[7.20] The making of a cargo insurance contract is relevant to the Incoterm adopted by the parties in a contract of sale. For example, under a CIF contract, the seller is responsible for making a cargo insurance contract to cover the goods sold. The seller transfers the cost of insurance to the buyer by quoting a CIF price to the buyer. The types of risks insured must be consistent with Item A3 of the CIF term as set out in the Incoterms 2000.[13] On the other hand, under an FOB contract, the seller is not obliged to procure a cargo insurance contract, but may do so at the request of the buyer. The buyer should bear the cost of insurance even if the seller makes a cargo insurance contract on behalf of the buyer. In most cases, the buyer makes a cargo insurance contract him- or herself. All the Incoterms 2000 have specific provisions on the duty to make a cargo insurance contract under each term. If a contract of sale is not based on the Incoterms, the parties should agree expressly on the duty to insure the goods against the marine risks and the specifications of the contract to be concluded if the seller insures the goods on the buyer's behalf.

---

12. For example, refer to the court's discussion on the meaning of 'typhoon clause' in *Neuchatel Swiss General Insurance Co Ltd v Vlasons Shipping Inc* [2001] VSCA 25.
13. Item A3 requires a seller to obtain:

    ... at his own expense cargo insurance as agreed in the contract, that the buyer, or any other person having an insurable interest in the goods, shall be entitled to claim directly from the insurer and [the seller shall] provide the buyer with the insurance policy or other evidence of insurance cover. The insurance shall be contracted with underwriters or an insurance company of good repute and, failing express agreement to the contrary, be in accordance with the minimum cover of the Institute Cargo Clauses (Institute of London Underwriters) or any similar set of clauses. The duration of insurance cover shall be in accordance with B5 and B4. When required by the buyer, the seller shall provide at the buyer's expense war, strikes, riots and civil commotion risk insurance if procurable. The minimum insurance shall cover the price provided in the contract plus ten per cent (i.e. 110%) and shall be provided in the currency of the contract.

    This clause sets out the detail of the seller's duty to conclude a cargo insurance contract under a CIF contract.

[7.21] A cargo insurance contract can be purchased by the cargo-owner, or through an agent. Most forwarding agents are able to arrange cargo insurance for the cargo-owner. If convenient, the cargo-owner can also purchase a cargo insurance contract through an insurance broker. For the purpose of making a cargo insurance contract, the agent must enter the principal's name in the contract, otherwise the principal cannot claim any loss under the policy directly. In addition, there may also be a risk of breaching the duty of utmost good faith if the agent deliberately conceals the true identity of the principal in certain circumstances where the insurer has specifically inquired about the identity of the principal, or the identity of the principal affects the decision of the insurer.[14]

[7.22] Most cargo insurance contracts are made in the form of standard contracts. The offer normally starts by the insured or his or her agent filling in the application form for a cargo insurance contract. An application form should contain the terms and conditions of the cargo insurance contract to be issued by the insurer once the application form is accepted by the insurer. Sometimes, the insurer or broker explains to a potential insured the terms and conditions of the insurance and invites the insured to fill in an application form. Even in these circumstances, the insurer or broker still retains the right to reject the application of the potential insured after the application form has been submitted. Thus, the offer still only starts by the submission of the application form. Otherwise, if a contract were concluded when the insured decided to accept the terms proposed by the insurer, the offer would have been made when the insurer or broker introduced the terms of the contract to the insured (provided that the conclusion of an insurance contract in this manner was permitted by the governing law).

[7.23] The conclusion of a marine insurance contract, including a cargo insurance contract may be regulated by the relevant domestic law. For example, s 27 of the Marine Insurance Act 1909 (Cth) states that 'a contract of marine insurance is deemed to be concluded when the proposal of the assured is accepted by the insurer, whether the policy be then issued or not; and for the purpose of showing when the proposal was accepted, reference may be made to the slip or covering note or other customary memorandum of the contract'. This means that a cargo insurance contract is made when the formal insurance policy issued by the insurer, or when any provisional documents, such as an insurance slip or covering note, is issued by the insurer to the insured to prove the conclusion of a cargo insurance contract.

---

14. For example, s 25 of the Marine Insurance Act 1909 (Cth) provides as follows:
    Subject to the provisions of the preceding section as to circumstances which need not be disclosed, where an insurance is effected for the assured by an agent, the agent must disclose to the insurer:
    - every material circumstance which is known to himself, and an agent to insure is deemed to know every circumstance which in the ordinary course of business ought to be known by, or to have been communicated to, him; and
    - every material circumstance which the assured is bound to disclose, unless it comes to his knowledge too late to communicate it to the agent.

Making of a hull insurance contract

[7.24] The making of a hull insurance contract is largely similar to the making of a cargo insurance contract. However, the hull insurance contract has its own characteristics. For example, the persons who may become insured under a hull insurance contract include not only owners, but also charterers, operators and financiers. The parties having interests in the safety of a vessel must expressly agree on the duty to insure the vessel against the potential risks which may affect the vessel. For example, the mortgage contract must expressly stipulate who is responsible for procuring a hull insurance for the vessel. This stipulation must also be made in a charterparty or similar contract. In practice, a hull insurance contract can be made for a vessel in operation as well as a vessel under construction. Furthermore, the nature of the charterparty also affects the nature of the hull insurance contract. The variety of the standard contracts offered by the Institute of London Underwriters illustrates the variety of hull insurance contracts.

[7.25] A hull insurance contract can be made directly between an insurer and an insured, or concluded through a broker or an agent. The broker who issues a policy in his or her own name without informing the insured of his or her capacity as an agent of the insurer may be held liable as an insurer. Alternatively, a broker may be held liable in negligence outside the hull insurance contract if the hull insurance contract cannot be enforced. The same principle applies to the act of a broker under a cargo insurance contract. The conclusion of a hull insurance contract is also subject to the same presumption applicable to the cargo insurance contract under s 27 of the Marine Insurance Act 1909 (Cth).

Legal framework for international marine insurance

[7.26] There is no uniform law or convention for international marine insurance. The matter is largely governed by the relevant domestic law. In those common law jurisdictions which have been strongly influenced by the common law of the UK, the marine insurance legislation of these jurisdictions are more or less consistent with each other due to their connections with the Marine Insurance Act 1906 (UK). Differences may be seen in the marine insurance laws of many countries. However, they do not differ from each other drastically, largely because shipping is an internationalised industry, and both shipping and international trade compel the world countries to adopt a marine insurance law which must meet the minimum requirements for promoting international trade and shipping. For example, China adopted a maritime law code in 1992, which entered into force on 1 July 1993. Most provisions on marine insurance are consistent with the basic rules of the Marine Insurance Act 1906 (UK), even though Chinese law is basically built on the civil law tradition. Thus, it can be argued that certain basic principles of marine insurance law, such as the principle that a marine contract cannot be used as a means of gambling, the duty of utmost good faith, the concepts of insured value, insurable interest, constructive loss, actual loss, total and partial loss, and the right of subrogation, and others, are universal, forming a basis for an international convention on marine insurance law in the future.

[7.27] Commercial customs, usage and practices in international marine insurance have played an important role in the regulation of marine insurance internationally. These customs, usage and practices are seen in the standard marine insurance clauses adopted by various non-governmental bodies of insurers, and in the model clauses recommended by UNCTAD. A number of countries have national organisations of insurers, which have their own marine insurance clauses. For example, Lloyd's SG Policy (or SG Form) and Lloyd's Marine Policy or MAR form (for example, MAR 91) are both formulated by Lloyd's of London. The former is still officially part of Schedule 2 of the Marine Insurance Act 1909 (Cth), but its use has been superseded by the latter since 1982.[15] The MAR form is much simpler and more concise than the SG Form, which has become awkward because of the attachment of many gummed slips containing additional clauses.[16]

[7.28] The Institute of London Underwriters has produced a variety of standard contracts for marine insurance. Broadly speaking, the standard contracts formulated by the Institute can be divided into two categories: the Institute Clauses and the New Institute Clauses. The Institute Clauses include the following specific forms of contract:

- the Institute Cargo Clauses (A);
- the Institute Cargo Clauses (B);
- the Institute Cargo Clauses (C);
- the Institute War Clauses (Cargo);
- the Institute Strikes Clauses (Cargo);
- the Institute Standard Conditions for Cargo Contracts;
- the Institute Classification Clause;
- the Institute Time Clauses Hulls;
- the Institute Time Clauses Freight;
- the Institute Time Clauses-Hulls-Total Loss, General Average and 3/4ths Collision Liability (Including Salvage, Salvage Charges and Sue and Labour);
- the Institute Time Clauses-Hulls-Total Loss Only (Including Salvage, Salvage Charges and Sue and Labour);
- the Institute Time Clauses-Hulls: Disbursements and Increased Value (Total Loss Only, Including Excess Liabilities);
- the Institute Time Clauses-Hulls: Excess Liabilities;
- the Institute War and Strikes Clauses (Hulls-Time);
- the Institute War and Strikes Clauses (Freight-Time);
- the Institute War and Strikes Clauses Hulls-Time Limited Conditions;
- the Institute Voyage Clauses Hulls;
- the Institute Voyage Clauses-Hulls-Total Loss, General Average and 3/4ths Collision Liability (Including Salvage, Salvage Charges and Sue and Labour);
- the Institute War and Strikes Clauses (Hulls-Voyage);
- the Institute Clauses for Builders Risks;

---

15. Butler and Duncan, *Maritime Law in Australia*, Legal Books, Sydney, 1992, p 345.
16. Ibid.

[7.28]

- the Institute War Clauses Builders Risks;
- the Institute Strikes Clauses Builders Risks; and
- the Institute Mortgagees Interest Clauses Hulls.

The New Institute Clauses consist of the following types of policy:

- the Institute Time Clauses Hulls;
- the Institute Time Clauses Hulls — Restricted Perils;
- the Institute War and Strikes Clauses Hulls — Time;
- the Institute War and Strikes Clauses Hulls — Time: Limited Conditions; and
- the Institute War and Strikes Clauses Hulls — Voyage.

In addition to these Institute Clauses, there is also the Companies Marine Policy, which is also offered by the Institute of London Underwriters.

[7.29] Besides Lloyd's of London and the Institute of London Underwriters, many other insurers have produced their own standard contracts for marine insurance. For example, there are the Rules of the Britannia Steam Ship Mutual Insurance Association Ltd (for example, the Rules of Class 3: Protection and Indemnity; and the Rules of Class 4: War Risks); the General Conditions of Hull Insurance produced by the Japanese Hull Insurers' Union, the *Police française d'assurance maritime sur corps de tous navires à l'exclusion des navires de pêche, de plaisance, des voiliers et des navires à moteur auxiliaire* (French marine hull insurance policy), the *Police française d'assurance maritime sur facultés* (French maritime insurance policy (cargo)), the *Police d'assurance maritime sur facultés* (marine insurance policy (cargo)) used by the Société nationale d'assurance (SONAS) of Zaire, the General Conditions for Cargo Insurance approved by the Associacion Mexicana de Instituciones de Seguros, the General Conditions for Cargo Insurance and Hull Insurance drafted by the National Insurance Institute of Costa Rica.[17]

The standard contracts are not law. Nor are they compulsory in most cases unless their use in certain countries is sanctioned by the relevant local law. Parties to a marine insurance contract are free to formulate their own terms and conditions of contract, even though most insurers prefer to have printed forms to improve efficiency and protect their interests.

[7.30] Marine insurance in Australia is mainly subject to the Marine Insurance Act 1909 (Cth), which is based on the Marine Insurance Act 1906 (UK). It sets out principles for dealing with marine insurance matters, but does not deal with many technical aspects of marine insurance. The English practices, such as the marine insurance clauses produced by Lloyd's and the Institute Marine Cargo Clauses, are commonly accepted in Australia. In fact, the English marine insurance clauses are the most commonly accepted clauses in the world.[18] Also available are the UNCTAD Model Clauses on Marine Cargo Insurance, which were adopted in 1987 at Geneva. Although marine insurance in Australia is governed by the principles of the Marine Insurance Act 1909 (Cth), parties are free within the limits of the Act to incorporate the English clauses, UNCTAD clauses, or any other

---

17. Cheng (ed), *Basic Documents on International Trade Law*, 2nd ed, Martinus Nijhoff, Dordrecht, 1990, p 484.
18. Ibid.

clauses in a contract of marine insurance. Indeed, the parties are free to agree upon any clauses provided that the Act so allows.

Explaining an insurable interest

[7.31] An insurable interest is defined in the Marine Insurance Act 1909 (Cth). Section 11 provides that an insurable interest means that a person is interested in a marine adventure. Whether a person is interested in a marine adventure is determined by whether the person has any legal or equitable interest in the adventure, whether he or she may benefit by the safety or due arrival of the insurable property, whether he or she may be prejudiced by the loss of or damage to the insured property, or whether he or she may incur liability as a result of the occurrence of the insured risks. This definition may be seen as a modern version of Lawrence J's statement in *Lucena v Craufurd* [1806] 2 Bos & O (NR) 269 that interest in a thing refers to 'every benefit and advantage arising out of or depending on' the existence and preservation of the thing in the circumstances concerned, including the interest which may be prejudiced by the destruction of the thing.

The definition suggests that anyone whose legal or equitable interest may be affected by their involvement in the 'insured property' — ship, goods and movables — in the marine adventure has an insurable interest.[19] In *NSW Leather v Vanguard Insurance* (1991) 25 NSWLR 699 at 707, Handley JA held that the buyer under an FOB contract 'had an insurable interest prior to loading in the profits it expected to derive from the safe arrival of the goods in Sydney'. 'Movables' means any movable or tangible property, other than the ship, and includes money, valuable securities and other documents (s 3 of the Act). This may cover a category of property on board or associated with the ship which is neither part of the ship nor part of the goods.

[7.32] *Anthony John Sharp and Roarer Investments Ltd v Sphere Drake Insurance Plc, Minster Insurance Co Ltd and EC Parker & Co Ltd (The 'Moonacre')*

[1992] 2 Lloyd's Rep 501; **[7.32]**

The true owner who was given an exclusive right to use the boat by its registered owner has an insurable interest in the boat

Facts: Sharp was the true owner of the motor yacht *Moonacre*. For taxation reasons, he arranged in 1986 for the boat to be bought by an off-the-shelf company — Roarer Investments — which became the registered owner of the boat. Roarer Investments granted Sharp an exclusive right to use and control the boat. The boat was insured under Sharp's name through the insurance brokers, EC Parker & Co. A fire broke out on board the boat in 1988, amounting to a constructive total loss of the boat. The insurers, Sphere Drake and Minster Insurance, rejected the insurance claim on a number of grounds, including breach of the terms of the insurance contract, the assured (Sharp) having no insurable interest, and misrepresentation by the assured. Sharp's insurable interest arose as an issue.

---

19. For example, Lord Brandon of Oakbrook observed in *McDermid v Nash Dredging & Reclamation Co Ltd* [1987] 2 Lloyd's Rep 201 at 209, that any person interested in the ship means 'a person having a legal or equitable interest in the ship'.

[7.32] International Commercial Law

> **Decision:** The Queen's Bench Division (Commercial Court) held that Sharp had the exclusive right to use and control the boat under the terms of power of attorney granted by the registered owner — Roarer Investments. He had an interest in the preservation and use of the boat under the power of attorney or as the bailee of the boat. He would gain and lose benefit from the use and loss of the boat. Therefore he had an insurable interest in the boat. The court also found that the assured breached the contractual term which prohibited the boat from being used as a 'houseboat', but decided that the alleged misrepresentation by the assured was not proved. The court thus held that the insurers were not liable, but the insurance brokers were because they forged the assured's signature in the insurance form and failed to advise the assured of the meaning of 'houseboat' in the contract of insurance.

◆

[7.33] Insurable interest is a crucial issue for the validity of a marine insurance policy, although it is less significant for a domestic insurance contract under the Insurance Contracts Act 1984 (Cth).[20] Schmitthoff observes that insurable interest 'is a fundamental principle of insurance law that the assured must have an insurable interest in the subject matter insured at the time of the loss'.[21] The requirement for an insurable interest is necessary for preventing speculation in marine insurance. As a general rule, a person lacking an insurable interest is not able to enforce a marine insurance contract, because for policy reasons such person is not allowed to enter into the contract and a contract so made would be void *ab initio*. However, there is an exception to the general rule. Under s 12 of the Marine Insurance Act 1909 (Cth), the parties are allowed to include a 'lost or not lost' clause which requires the assured to have an insurable interest at the time of the loss, as opposed to the time when the contract of insurance was made. Such a 'lost or not lost' clause applies to circumstances where, for example, in the case of an open or blanket cover (these terms are explained in **[7.52]**–**[7.53]**), the insurance policy is taken out to cover the risk which may occur to the prescribed type of goods to be obtained in the future.

In *NSW Leather v Vanguard Insurance* (1991) 25 NSWLR 699, the Supreme Court of New South Wales held that the 'lost or not lost' clause in the contract of insurance entitled the assured to claim indemnity pursuant to the terms of the policy, even though the property in the goods had not passed to the assured under the FOB term at the time when the alleged loss took place. The crucial requirement for the operation of the 'lost or not lost' clause is that the assured did not know or ought not to have known that the goods had been lost at the time of the contract.

[7.34] The concept of 'insurable interest' used to be subject to a stringent interpretation. In *Macaura v Northern Assurance Co Ltd* [1925] AC 619, the House of Lords held that the assured who was the sole shareholder in, and creditor of, a timber company did not have an insurable interest in the timber insured under a policy entered into by himself, because the timber belonged to the company. This case suggests that we should perhaps distinguish between the person (legal or natural) holding an insurable interest and the person (legal or natural) holding the holder of the insurable interest, although the decision

---

20. The Act replaces the common law concept of 'insurable interest' by the specified interests in property or life under ss 17 and 19.
21. Schmitthoff, *Schmitthoff's Export Trade*, 9th ed, London, Stevens & Sons, 1990, p 506.

in *Macaura v Northern Assurance Co Ltd* might be questionable on the ground of the equitable interest of a shareholder or creditor who exercised actual control over the insured property. The major legal argument in *Macaura v Northern Assurance Co Ltd* was that the company operated as an independent legal entity and the sole shareholder and creditor, Macaura, was not the company itself. This case can be compared with *The Moonacre* [1992] 2 Lloyd's Rep 501; where the true owner of the insured boat was found to have an insurable interest as the bailee or agent of the registered owner.

[7.35] Insurable interest is not limited to the established or conventional categories of legal or equitable interest. For example, in *Turner v Manx Line* [1990] 1 Lloyd's Rep 137, a case involving a hull insurance contract and a dispute between the insurers and assured as to the meaning of 'interest' in the contract, Neill LJ stated (at 143) that the word 'interest' was not limited to a legal or equitable interest. His Lordship went on to state (at 143) that 'the court is concerned to see whether there is some nexus between the liability of the assured and his interest in the vessel. The assured's interest in the vessel may be as owner or lessee or bailee, but he may also be interested in the vessel as the operator or user of it'. Neill LJ's observation suggests the possibility of giving a wider interpretation of the word 'interested' which qualifies the meaning of 'insurable interest' in marine insurance. Indeed, in this case the assured's contractual obligation to compensate a third party for any damages caused by the insured vessel was found to be within the meaning of 'interest' stipulated in the insurance policy.

In *Turner v Manx Line* [1990] 1 Lloyd's Rep 137, Ralph Gibson LJ construed the meaning of interest from a different angle. His Lordship observed (at 146) that a person has an interest in the ship where his or her interest in the ship 'can properly be regarded as one of the reasons for his becoming liable; or put another way, that included within the reasons for his becoming liable is his interest in' the ship. This observation suggests that insurable interest has a wide and flexible meaning. But the essence of insurable interest is whether the assured's rights or duties are affected or will be affected by the risks or losses sustained by the ship, goods or movables insured in the marine insurance contract concerned.

Explaining 'marine risks'

Perils of the sea in general

[7.36] The purpose of marine insurance is to protect the interests of the assured against the risks which may arise from a particular marine adventure in which the assured is involved. The risk must be associated with a marine adventure. For example, in *Hamilton, Fraser & Co v Pandorf* (1887) 12 App Cas 518, the goods were damaged by seawater entering into the hold through a pipe which had a hole gnawed in it by rats during the voyage. The court held that the accident was a peril of the sea, because the seawater entering into the vessel through some kind of damage to the vessel was a danger of marine adventure.

This decision must be read with s 61(2)(c) of the Marine Insurance Act 1909 (Cth), which expressly states that the insurer is not liable for damage caused by rats or vermin unless the policy expressly states otherwise. It can be argued that this provision refers to the damage caused directly and only by rats or vermin — for example, the gnawing of rats. This is different from water damage flowing from the gnawing of rats without the fault of the assured. Whether the ship was seaworthy at the beginning of the voyage and whether the assured had taken reasonable measures to prevent the damage are the tests for determining whether the assured was at fault.

[7.37] Marine risks also include loss caused by negligence of the assured's employees. In *Century Insurance Co of Canada v Case Existological Laboratories* [1984] 1 WWR 97, the ship sank because its storm valves were negligently left open by the crew. The court held that the sinking of the ship was caused by the ingress of seawater, which is a peril of the sea. This is so even if the ingress of the seawater was the result of the employees' negligence. This rule is incorporated into s 61(2)(a) of the Marine Insurance Act 1909 (Cth).

[7.38] *CCR Fishing Ltd v Tomenson Inc ('La Pointe')*

[1989] 2 Lloyd's Rep 537

Whether the damage is caused by perils at sea or unseaworthiness of the ship

Facts: CCR Fishing was the assured. Tomenson was the insurer. The vessel *La Pointe* was insured under a policy covering 'port risks'. The vessel was built in 1906. In 1981, a survey revealed that the vessel was unseaworthy, and it was moored in the harbour from that time onwards. The 1982 survey revealed that the vessel had been out of maintenance for more than 12 months. Between October 1981 and July 1982 the vessel was pumped several times because of water leaks. In July 1982, the vessel sank at the mooring place. The assured argued that seawater entered into the vessel through open valves on the sea suction and discharge line, which were negligently left open by its employees, and through a broken steel flange in the engine room. The insurer argued that seawater entered into the vessel because of ordinary wear and tear on the vessel. The trial judge gave judgment for the assured. The insurer appealed.

Decision: The Court of Appeal of British Columbia by a 2:1 majority allowed the appeal and found that the insurer was not liable for the loss. Macdonald J, with whom Aikins J agreed, held (at 544) that the unintentional 'ingress of sea water is more an effect than a cause'. The ingress of seawater was caused by the corroded condition of the cap screws which failed to keep the flange watertight. This cause was not a fortuitous accident of the sea and the loss was not caused by the perils of the sea.

Maritime perils under the Marine Insurance Act 1909 (Cth)

[7.39] The Marine Insurance Act 1909 (Cth) reflects general international practice. It is the governing law of any marine insurance contracts made in Australia between parties engaged in interstate or international carriage of goods by sea, or sometime in certain seagoing activities.[22] It is also applicable under the rules of conflict of laws or by the choice of the parties to any marine insurance contract. Therefore, it is necessary to examine what marine risks are under the Act.

The Act does not enumerate the types of risks which can be insured under the Act. Instead, it qualifies marine risks by defining 'marine perils' and 'insurable interest'. As already indicated, the risks which can be insured under the Act are those insurable properties and interests which are exposed to maritime perils.

[7.40] Section 9 of the Marine Insurance Act 1909 (Cth) defines 'maritime perils' as follows:

> '**Maritime perils**' means the perils consequent on, or incidental to, the navigation of the sea, that is to say, perils of the seas, fire, war perils, pirates, rovers, thieves, captures, seizures, restraints, and detainment of princes and peoples, jettisons, barratry, and any other perils, either of the like kind, or which may be designated by the policy.

As suggested by this definition, maritime perils (or risks) can be 'designated by the policy' and a clear definition of the terms used in a policy will reduce and avoid disputes. For example, in *Shell International Petroleum v Caryl Antony Vaughan Gibbs (The 'Salem')* [1981] 2 Lloyd's Rep 316, 'barratry' was argued.[23] In this case, the shipowners contemplated a scheme to import crude oil to South Africa for the purpose of breaking the embargo against shipping oil into that country. The sellers of the oil, who had no knowledge of the conspiracy, hired the service of the vessel *Salem* to carry oil from Kuwait. The sellers entered into a marine insurance contract with the defendants (insurers) under a CIF contract, before selling the oil to the buyers. The assured (buyers of the oil) bought the insured oil under a CIF contract without knowledge of the conspiracy. Most of the oil was discharged in Durban by the conspirators and the vessel was deliberately sunk after that. The assured claimed loss under the policy on the ground of barratry and taking at sea. The court held that 'barratry' does not cover the wrongful misappropriation of cargo by a shipowner, but 'taking at sea' would apply to this case. Similarly, in *Athens Maritime Enterprises Corp v Hellenic Mutual War Risks Assoc (Bermuda) Ltd (The 'Andreos Lemos')* [1983] 2 WLR 425, the court held that 'piracy' does not cover a maritime theft which does not involve force or threat. These cases suggest the importance of a uniform construction of the contract terms describing or defining the risks. It must be noted that in *Mercantile Mutual Insurance (Australia) Ltd v Gibbs* [2001] WASCA 271, the Supreme Court of Western Australia took the view that the meaning of 'sea' under the Marine Insurance Act 1909 (Cth) covers the ebb and flow of the tide. This interpretation may have implications for the operation of s 9 above.

Risks incidental to marine adventure

[7.41] The expressions 'consequent on' and 'incidental to' extend 'maritime perils' beyond the limit of the sea. Section 8 of the Marine Insurance Act 1909 (Cth) expressly states that a 'contract of marine insurance may, by its express terms, or by usage of trade, be extended so as to protect the assured against losses on inland waters or on any land risk which may be incidental to any sea voyage'. The scope of the risk is also extended

---

22. For example, in *Mercantile Mutual Insurance (Australia) Ltd v Gibbs* [2001] WASCA 271, the Supreme Court of Western Australia held that a third party liability insurance policy which covered a ski boat operating in an estuarine was a marine insurance policy.
23. For a discussion of the case, see Knox Jr, '*Shell International Petroleum Co v Gibbs*: Lloyd's SG Policy Walks the Plank' (1984) 19 *Texas International Law Journal*, p 161.

[7.41] impliedly by the Act when it defines 'marine adventure' as including 'the earning or acquisition of any freight, passage money, commission, profit, or other pecuniary benefit, or the security for any advances, loan, or disbursements', which may be endangered by the exposure of any ship, goods or movables to maritime perils. A person who may benefit from a particular marine adventure is able to insure against any possible loss or damage to the expected gains. However, the court may distinguish between a policy on goods and a policy on expected profits. This is illustrated in *NSW Leather v Vanguard Insurance* (1991) 25 NSWLR 699. In this case, Clarke and Handley JJA held that the assured had an insurable interest in the profit of the contract and safe arrival of the goods at Sydney, but this was different from an insurable interest in the stolen goods. The problem in this case was that the assured did not have an insurable interest in the goods until the property or risk in the goods passed to them, but when the property or risk passed the goods had been stolen.

Marine risks and insurable interest

[7.42] Not everyone who wants to benefit from a marine insurance policy is able to take out a policy. Section 10 of the Marine Insurance Act 1909 (Cth) prohibits a person who does not have an 'insurable interest', as defined in the Act, from entering into a marine insurance contract for the purpose of receiving benefits in case the goods, ship or movables are damaged in a particular marine adventure. In other words, no particular marine adventure, no matter how uncertain, can be used as the subject of gambling, even if the insurer and the intended assured (who does not have an insurable interest) so wish. This prohibition is based on policy considerations.

Summary of marine risks

[7.43] In summary, we may say that 'marine risks' which are insurable under Australian law are maritime perils which may cause losses or damage to the ship, goods or movables (the insurable property), whether directly, consequentially or incidentally, when the insurable property is involved in a marine adventure. This understanding of 'marine risks' is universally accepted, although this does not mean that risks which are, or can be, insured against would be the same universally. The particular forms and contents of policies offered by each insurer do vary.

Categories of marine insurance contracts

Differences in categorisation

[7.44] According to the subject matter concerned, a marine insurance contract may be either a hull insurance contract or a cargo insurance contract. There appears to be no need for an independent movable insurance contract, because movables may be covered under either a hull or a cargo insurance contract. This kind of categorisation of policies is based on the subject matter insured, as opposed to categories based on the terms of the contract.

[7.45] Marine insurance contracts are often classed by their terms. For example, Schmitthoff divides marine insurance contracts into five categories:

- valued or unvalued policies;
- voyage, time and mixed policies;
- floating policies;
- open covers; and
- blanket policies.[24]

Day adopts the first three categories, namely:

- valued and unvalued policies;
- voyage and time policies; and
- floating policies.[25]

A narrower range of categories is adopted by Tiplady,[26] and Purvis and Darvas.[27] They all distinguish marine insurance contracts or policies according to the terms of the contract. Although the terms involved are not exclusive, they do reflect the crucial nature of the contract or policy involved. We will discuss each type of marine insurance contract, as categorised by Schmitthoff, in turn.

Valued and unvalued policies

[7.46] Both a valued policy and an unvalued policy are defined in the Marine Insurance Act 1909 (Cth). Under s 33(2) of the Act, a 'valued policy is a policy which specifies the agreed value of the subject matter insured'. In contrast, an unvalued policy 'is a policy which does not specify the value of the subject matter insured, but, subject to the limit of the sum insured, leaves the insurable value to be subsequently ascertained, in the manner hereinafter specified' (s 34 of the Act). The essential difference between these two types of policies is whether the subject matter is insured for a fixed sum of money. In the case of an unvalued policy, the true value of the ship, goods or movables is usually ascertained by presenting necessary proof or documents, such as invoices, receipts, evaluation or assessment, or through any other methods agreed upon by the parties concerned.

It must be pointed out that a contract merely mentioning an amount of money may not be regarded as a valued policy, because s 33(2) of the Act requires an 'agreed value of the subject matter insured'. This is illustrated in *Ross v The Adelaide Marine Assurance Co* [1970] VR 232. In this case Stawell CJ (at 234) held that the expression 'insured the sum of freight' meant that 'the applicant was to insure 400 pounds on freight, the value afterwards to be ascertained'; and therefore the contract was an open, rather than a valued, policy. Regardless of whether the expression in question was capable of resulting in other

---

24. Schmitthoff, note 21 above, pp 492–9.
25. Day, *The Law of International Trade*, 2nd ed, Butterworths, London, 1993, pp 131–4.
26. Tiplady, *Introduction to the Law of International Trade*, BSP Professional Books, Oxford, 1989, pp 151–4.
27. Purvis and Darvas, *The Law and Practice of Commercial Letters of Credit Shipping Documents and Termination of Disputes in International Trade*, Butterworths, Sydney, 1975, pp 100–3.

[7.46]

equally convincing constructions, the case at least suggests that a valued policy must clearly and unambiguously indicate the value of the insured subject matter.

[7.47] *Randell v Atlantica Insurance Co Ltd*

(1983) 80 FLR 253

Meaning of unvalued policy

Facts: Randell was the assured, and Atlantica Insurance was the insurer. The insured subject was a 33-foot yacht *Starshine*, which was lost at sea in 1983. The assured's broker had negotiated with the insurer to increase the value of the boat to $140,000 before the occurrence of the loss. The insurer had orally agreed to increase the insured value. The broker subsequently sent a letter of confirmation to the assured. The agreed increase was not reduced to writing at the time of the loss. The insurer issued a policy after the loss, but the terms of the policy differed from the broker's confirmation. The parties disagreed as to the terms and value of the policy. The assured sued the insurer and broker. Whether the policy was a valued policy arose as an issue.

Decision: Carruthers J of the Supreme Court of New South Wales held that the policy in dispute was an unvalued policy. His Honour observed (at 281) that whether 'the policy is or is not a valued policy is a question of construction. Thus, if the policy does not specify the value of the subject matter insured, it then follows from s 33 that this is an unvalued policy'. His Honour concluded (at 283) that there is 'nothing in the document to suggest that the parties had reached agreement upon the value of the vessel'.

[7.48] In practice, valued policies are more commonly used than unvalued policies. One of the reasons, as observed by Schmitthoff, is that in an unvalued policy 'the buyer's anticipated profits cannot be included in the insurable value', but they can under a valued policy.[28] The payment under a particular policy is determined by the extent of the loss sustained by the insured. If a partial loss occurs, the insurer will only be liable for the sum of the partial loss. In *Compania Maritima Astra, SA v Archdale (The 'Armar')* [1954] Lloyd's Rep 95, the valued hull policy over the ship was $1,200,000, but the insured was allowed to claim a partial loss for the cost of repairs to the value of $816,299.

Voyage and time policies

[7.49] These policies are also defined in the Marine Insurance Act 1909 (Cth). A voyage policy, as defined in s 31 of the Act, is a contract where the subject matter is insured 'at and from', or 'from one place to another place or to other places'. A time policy is a contract where the subject matter is insured 'for a definite period of time'. As suggested by these expressions, a voyage policy is a policy based on and for a specified 'voyage'; and a time policy is effective for a specified period of time. The specified time under s 31(2) of the Act is usually less than 12 months. This provision makes a time policy exceeding 12 months invalid, unless the expiry date occurs while the voyage is incomplete. In this case, the policy extends until the completion of the voyage. The parties may also extend a time policy temporarily for a period not exceeding 30 days for the purpose of renewing or making another contract.

---

28. Schmitthoff, note 21 above, p 493.

[7.50] Under a voyage policy, an insurer is liable for loss and damage incurred when the subject matter is within the 'voyage' — that is, in the places and route of transportation as contemplated in the insurance contract. For instance, in *Industrial Waxes, Inc v Brown* [1958] Lloyd's Rep 626, the cargo insurance policy was based on the warehouse to warehouse term. The goods (wax) were stored in the warehouse after arrival for several months and were subsequently found damaged. The insured's claim under the policy failed, because the policy covered the period when the goods were in the warehouse for the purpose of transportation only. The court found that the contract was not intended to cover a period when the goods were stored in the warehouse for the purpose of storage. Under a time policy, an insurer is liable for the loss or damage to the insured subject matter when the loss arises within the period of time stipulated in the insurance contract. The place where the loss occurs may or may not be relevant, depending on the terms of the contract. Under a voyage policy, *where* the loss occurs is crucial, and under a time policy, *when* it occurs is crucial.

Floating policies

[7.51] The Marine Insurance Act 1909 (Cth) defines the meaning of floating policies. Section 35 provides that a 'floating policy is a policy which describes the insurance in general terms, and leaves the name of the ship or ships and other particulars to be defined by subsequent declaration'. A floating policy is a policy of fixed value on unascertained subject matters which fit the description of the policy. Under a floating policy, the insurer undertakes to indemnify, under the terms of the contract, any losses or damages incurred in relation to the prescribed subject matters. The assured is normally protected (insured) after he or she makes declarations, pursuant to the terms of the contract, to the insurer as to each specified voyage or transaction. The sum of compensation is restricted by the amount of the insured value available (or remaining) under the floating policy. A floating policy usually has a 'credit limit' and it offers protection to the ship or goods only to the extent that the value declared is within the remaining 'credit' (insured sum) of the policy. This is why Schmitthoff calls the floating policy 'an aggregation of voyage policies'.[29] A floating policy may be regarded as a policy under which the insurer undertakes to indemnify the assured against the risks contemplated in the contract to the amount stipulated in the insurance contract, provided that the assured declares the particulars of each consignment or transaction in accordance with the terms of the contract.

Open covers

[7.52] Open covers are not defined in the Marine Insurance Act 1909 (Cth). Schmitthoff observes that 'the open cover, like the slip, is not an insurance but is a document by which the underwriter undertakes subsequently to issue duly executed floating or specific policies within the terms of the cover'.[30] An open cover operates in a similar way to a floating policy, except that under the open cover the insurer sometimes issues a certificate of insurance which may or may not have the same effect as a contract of insurance,

---

29. Id, p 496.
30. Id, p 498.

whereas under a floating policy the insurer issues to the assured a contract of insurance. The difference between them is immaterial in most circumstances, because in 'both cases the cover [or policy] is written off, as declarations are made'.[31]

For example, in *Berger & Light Diffusers Pty Ltd v Pollock* [1973] 2 Lloyd's Rep 442, the plaintiffs sent four large steel injection moulds from Australia to England on the steamship *Paparoa*. The carrier issued a claused bill of lading stating that the goods were 'unprotected, secondhand and insufficiently packed'. The plaintiffs insured the voyage through their brokers, who had an 'open cover' with the defendant insurers. The brokers declared the shipment pursuant to the terms of the cover and stated the insured value to be £20,000. On arrival, the goods were found to have been damaged by rust caused by water entering into the hold through a broken pipe. The defendants intended to avoid their liability on the ground of non-disclosure of the claused bill of lading, the status of the moulds as secondhand goods and the fact that they were over-valued. The court held that the defendants had not proved that the non-disclosure was material to their decision under the open cover policy and they were liable for the damage. This case illustrates the procedures in which an open cover operates. It appears that the real difference, or advantage, of an open cover is that it may be open for more than 12 months or perpetually, while a floating policy is usually effective for a period of time which is less than 12 months.

Blanket policies

[7.53] According to Schmitthoff, a blanket policy is a variation of a floating or open cover. The policy covers a fixed sum of losses or damages which may occur in the separate transactions insured. Although the subject matters insured may attract different rates of premium were they insured separately, they are subject to a flat rate under the blanket policy and no separate declarations are required. This suggests that a blanket policy represents a kind of package deal between the insurer and assured. This type of policy was adopted for the benefit of avoiding burdensome paperwork or procedures when small values or short voyages are involved.

Forms of marine insurance documents

[7.54] 'Marine insurance documents' refers to the form which a policy may take. A form may not reflect the specific 'terms' of the policy, but may suggest the legal effect of the document concerned. For example, under an open cover, a certificate of insurance is a document issued by the insurer, but the certificate is not a contract of insurance. A formal policy will be issued when the assured declares the details of the shipment pursuant to the terms of the open cover. In practice, a seller often insures (sometimes with the assistance of his or her brokers) the goods under an open cover and gives the buyer a certificate of insurance which contains the general terms of insurance and the particulars of declaration as required under the open cover. This certificate will enable the buyer (or holder) to ask the insurer to issue a policy; or alternatively, to claim for losses. If

---

31. Ibid.

the certificate is used as a 'contract' for making claims, its effect depends on whether the assured has satisfied the terms set out in the open cover.

[7.55] Marine insurance documents may take various forms. A policy is a formal contract of insurance issued by the insurer. A slip or memorandum of insurance is usually prepared by a broker and presented to the insurer. It is an insurance proposal which details the policy intended. It becomes binding when accepted by the insurer who usually initials it. If initialled by the insurer, the slip operates as a temporary cover until it is replaced by a policy. There may be no difference in practical effect between an initialled slip and a policy.

[7.56] Marine insurance documents also take the form of a certificate of insurance, brokers' cover note, or letter of insurance. A certificate of insurance may be regarded as a conditional insurance contract. It is not binding if the assured has not fulfilled his or her obligations under the terms of the open cover, but it is binding once the assured has made the required declaration in accordance with the terms of the open cover. It appears that once the required declaration is made, the insurer is obliged to issue the policy or compensate for the loss regardless of who makes the demand. It is convenient for a CIF contract to be insured under an open cover with the buyer then protected by the certificate of insurance. In *A C Harper and Co Ltd v Mackechnie and Co* [1925] 2 KB 423, the buyers were ultimately protected by the certificate of insurance issued by the insurance brokers. There were discrepancies between the certificate of insurance, which was issued by the brokers tentatively to the sellers, who were liable to insure the goods under the CIF contract, and the formal policy. The certificate of insurance had been accepted by the buyers as part of the commercial documents, but the formal policy, which was issued later by the insurers, had not reached the buyers at the time when the commercial documents were handed over to them. The court found that the certificate prevailed.

[7.57] A broker's note is different from a certificate of insurance. The former is issued by the broker and advises the assured of the completion of a policy and therefore is unenforceable against the insurer. It provides legal remedies for the assured against the broker in cases where there is a discrepancy between the note and the actual policy. Similarly, a letter of insurance is a letter from the seller advising the buyer of the completion of a policy. It has no legal effect against the insurer, but can be used as evidence against the seller.

[7.58] Insurance documents are based on the principles of contract. The parties, subject to the provisions of the Marine Insurance Act 1909 (Cth), may agree on the terms and forms of insurance documents. As a general rule, a clearly defined and worded document would be beneficial to both the assured and insurer, although one of them may sometimes prefer to phrase the terms broadly to gain flexibility in their application. It is important to understand the different types of insurance documents and their legal effects. While some documents are enforceable against insurers, others may only be admissible as evidence of the existence of a marine insurance contract, or of a contractual relation between two relevant parties, for example, an assured and a broker or a seller and a buyer. Given the existence of possible alterations or modifications to forms and terms of the marine insurance documents, it is essential to remember that a document to which the insurer is a party or by which the insurer expressly undertakes a duty to indemnify the loss or damage has a better chance of being upheld by a court of law than one which the insurer is not privy to.

Assured's duty to disclose the relevant information

The doctrine of utmost good faith

[7.59] One of the fundamental duties of the assured is to disclose the relevant facts or information about the insured subject matter to the insurer, and to be honest and bona fide with the insurer. This is the doctrine of utmost good faith, or the duty of utmost good faith. It is so fundamental that a failure to disclose a material fact that may affect the decision of the insurer gives rise to a right of the insurer to avoid the contract concerned, even though the holder of the policy, who may be a transferee or consignee of the policy, is a bona fide holder. This is illustrated in *Pickersgill v London & Provincial Marine Insurance Co* [1912] 3 KB 614. In this case, the assureds were the owners of a ship yet to be built. They obtained a policy on the future ship without disclosing to the insurers that the ship was yet to be built. The policy was assigned to the builders of the ship as security. The builders' (assignees') claim on the policy was denied on the ground of non-disclosure of the material circumstances, even though the builders did not know that the shipowners had not disclosed the relevant information to the insurers.

[7.60] Section 23 of the Marine Insurance Act 1909 (Cth) provides that a 'contract of marine insurance is a contract based upon the utmost good faith, and, if the utmost good faith be not observed by either party, the contract may be avoided by the other party'. This section requires the assured to disclose all relevant information that may affect the decision of the insurer to him or her before the insurance contract is entered into. In *The Dora* [1989] 1 Lloyd's Rep 69, the assured failed to disclose to the insurers the fact that the yacht *Dora* was once arrested for carrying smuggled goods on board and that both the skipper of the yacht and the assured's representative on board had criminal records. The court held that the non-disclosure of these facts constituted dishonesty and gave rise to a right in the insurer to repudiate the contract. In addition, the court held that the statement by the assured that the assured was producing more yachts similar to the *Dora* at a rate of four vessels per year constituted a misrepresentation, which also gave rise to a right to the insurer to avoid the contract of insurance.

Similarly, in *Ionides v Pender* [1874] LR 9 QB 531 the court held that the fact that the goods of £970 in value were insured for £2800 constituted fraud and non-disclosure of the relevant information, and the insurance policy was thus not enforceable. These cases suggest that 'good faith' of the parties to a marine insurance contract has very broad implications, and any undisclosed facts which amount to 'dishonesty' or 'bad faith' on the part of the assured may give to the other party a right to repudiate the contract.

> **[7.61]** *Anthony John Sharp and Roarer Investments Ltd v Sphere Drake Insurance Pls, Minster Insurance Co Ltd and EC Parker & Co Ltd (The 'Moonacre')*
>
> [1992] 2 Lloyd's Rep 501; **[7.32]**
>
> *Determination of material facts and the broker's duty of utmost good faith*
>
> **Facts:** Sharp was the assured of a boat which was registered under the name of Roarer Investments. Sharp was the beneficial owner of the boat and was given a power of attorney to use the boat exclusively by Roarer Investments. The boat was lost in a fire. The insurers (Sphere Drake and Minster Insurance) rejected the insurance claim on the grounds, inter alia, of breach of duty of utmost good faith and misrepresentation. Sharp sued the insurers and his brokers (EC Parker).
>
> **Decision:** The Queen's Bench Division (Commercial Court) held that the assured's failure to disclose to the insurers the loss of a radio valued at £100 did not affect the decision of a prudent insurer to renew the policy in the circumstances concerned. But, the court found that the brokers' forgery of the assured's signature in the insurance form in order to meet the time deadline amounted to a breach of the brokers' utmost good faith to the insurers, even though the signature would have been approved by the assured if necessary. The court decided that the brokers were liable for the loss of the boat because they had confirmed to the assured the terms of insurance and forged the signature in the form of insurance.

The strictness of the duty of utmost good faith

[7.62] The assured's duty to make a full disclosure is 'absolute' in the sense that the assured's negligence does not exempt him or her from that duty. This is illustrated in *London General Insurance Co v General Marine Underwriters' Assoc* [1921] 1 KB 104. In this case, part of the goods which the assured intended to insure was lost by fire on board the *Vigo*. The news reached the office of Lloyd's on the night of 24 September 1918. This fact was posted on the casualty board at Lloyd's on the morning of 25 September and at the same time a casualty slip containing the same information was sent to Lloyd's subscribers, including the assured. At 10 am on 25 September 1918, the assured instructed their brokers to effect a policy over the goods in question at Lloyd's and the brokers carried out the instruction at 4 pm on the same afternoon. The assured received the casualty slip on the same day, but did not read it. Nor did the insurers, who had the same information. Thus, both the assured and insurers claimed to be equally ignorant of the loss. The court found that the assured had breached their duty of full disclosure, because in their ordinary course of business they ought to have known of the loss of the goods insured. The assured is not excused for negligence because he or she is the one who undertakes the duty of utmost good faith when filling in the form of insurance. However, the insurer may be found to have waived or to

[7.62] have been estopped from relying on the doctrine of utmost good faith in certain circumstances.[32]

[7.63] The strictness of the duty to disclose is also seen in the fact that the assured is required to disclose all the relevant information after the conclusion of the contract of insurance if the contract so requires. This was seen in *The Dora* [1989] 1 Lloyd's Rep 69, where the assured was found to have breached the duty of utmost good faith by failing to inform the insurers of events taking place after the conclusion of the contract of insurance. Similarly, in *Black King Shipping Corp v Massie (The 'Litsion Pride')* [1985] 1 Lloyd's Rep 437, the assured was also found to have breached the duty of utmost good faith. In this case, the insurance policy expressly required the assured to inform the insurers if the vessel sailed to specified waters. The vessel entered into the Gulf while Iran and Iraq were engaged in war. It was attacked and sank. The assured wrote to the insurers about the vessel entering the Gulf. But the letter reached the insurers three days after the sinking of the vessel. The English High Court held that the assured had breached the duty of utmost good faith, because the assured had had enough time to disclose the matter to the insurers earlier.

Matters not subject to disclosure

[7.64] Although the assured is generally required to disclose any material facts which 'would influence the judgment of a prudent insurer in fixing the premium, or determining whether he will take the risk' (s 24(2) of the Marine Insurance Act 1909 (Cth)), he or she does not have a duty to disclose certain information in the absence of inquiry in circumstances as prescribed in s 24 of the Act. For example, the assured has no duty to disclose any 'circumstance which diminishes the risk': s 24(3) of the Act. Similarly, the assured has no duty to disclose information which in the circumstances involved the insurer ought to have known, or which has been waived by the insurer or covered by warranty: s 24(3) of the Act. Thus, in *The Dora* [1989] 1 Lloyd's Rep 69, the court held that the fact that the yacht was still in the Lionello yard at the time of contract was a circumstance which diminished the risk and that the defendant could not rely on that fact to avoid the contract. By the same token, in *Soya GmbH v White* [1980] 1 Lloyd's Rep 491, the court held that the insurer could not avoid the contract on the basis of non-disclosure, because the agent of the assured had accurately described to the insurer the 'slightly damaged' condition of the goods which were insured. The essential test for determining whether a matter should be disclosed to the insurer is whether the matter is relevant in the sense that the insurer's decision can be influenced by its disclosure.[33]

[7.65] Sometimes, whether or not a non-disclosed fact may affect the judgment of the insurer may be hard to ascertain, and involve considerable discretion. For example, in

---

32. For instance, in *Allden v Raven* [1983] 2 QB 444, the assured argued that the insurers had waived the requirement for full disclosure because he had disclosed the fact that the boat was homemade to the broker, who, however, did not raise any objection to the fact. This argument was not accepted by the court. However, if the argument had been proved, the insurers would have been estopped from relying on the ground of non-disclosure relating to the manufacturer of the boat.

Thames & Mersey Marine Insurance Co v Gunford Shipping Co [1911] AC 529, the non-disclosure of the ship master's past records, including absence from sea for 22 years, the loss of his last ship and suspension of his certificate, was held not to have constituted non-disclosure of a material circumstance. However, the failure to disclose the fact that the ship was over-insured by several policies to the insurer constituted non-disclosure of a material fact. This case can be compared with *The Dora*, which should be regarded as representing a more recent and dominant view of the courts of law.[34]

[7.66] *Visscher Enterprises Pty Ltd v Southern Pacific Insurance Co Ltd*

[1981] Qd R 561

Determination of a material fact under s 24 of the Marine Insurance Act 1909 (Cth)

Facts: Visscher Enterprises was the assured and the owner of the fishing vessel *Illawarra Range*, which was insured by Southern Pacific Insurance. The vessel was subject to a time policy for $250,000 for the period from 20 February 1979 to 20 February 1980. The policy covered perils of sea and fire. In March 1979 the vessel caught fire and sank off the Queensland coast. The insurer rejected the assured's claim under the policy on the grounds, inter alia, that the boat was unseaworthy and that the assured failed to disclose material facts.

Connolly J of the Supreme Court of Queensland held that the fact that one of the bulkheads of the vessel had a hole in it was not a material fact which must be disclosed to the insurer under s 24 of the Marine Insurance Act 1909 (Cth), because there was no evidence that the insurer would have refused the policy if the fact were made known. Nor was his Honour satisfied that the disclosure of the said fact would lead to an increase in the premium under the policy. His Honour was of the opinion that the hole in one of the five bulkheads in the insured vessel was immaterial as most vessels insured by the insurer had only three bulkheads. His Honour held that there was no implied warranty in the time policy that the vessel must remain seaworthy during the venture, although the assured must guarantee the seaworthiness of the vessel at the beginning of the voyage. The assured was found not to have breached the contract of insurance even if there might be an alleged defect in the vessel's electrical system, which was not known to the assured. The insurer appealed.

Decision: The Full Court of the Supreme Court of Queensland dismissed the appeal on the same grounds. It also held that there was no need to determine whether the same fact would be material to a 'prudent insurer'.

---

33. For example, in *Randell v Atlantica Insurance Co Ltd* (1983) 80 FLR 253, the misrepresentation that the insured boat was licensed by the Maritime Services Board was held to be irrelevant to the decision of a prudent insurer in the circumstances involved. In *Visscher Enterprises Pty Ltd v Southern Pacific Insurance Co Ltd* [1981] Qd R 561, the fact that one of the five bulkheads of the insured vessel was defective was regarded as being immaterial because the vessel still had four good bulkheads but most vessels insured by the insurers had only three. In *Doak v Weeks* (1986) 82 FLR 334, a slight misdescription of the length of the insured vessel was considered to be immaterial to the decision of the insurer.
34. For example, in *Allden v Raven (The 'Kylie')* [1983] 2 QB 444, Parker J held that a failure to disclose the assured's previous criminal record and the fact that the boat was homemade constituted non-disclosure. Thus, the assured's claim under the policy failed.

Insurer's duties and inherent vice

[7.67] 'Inherent vice' refers to an inherent defect in the subject matter insured. As a term of insurance law, it means that damage is caused by an inherent defect in the subject matter insured, such as inadequate packing of the goods.[35] It contrasts with any risks caused by external factors, such as theft, taking at sea, fire and collision. Inherent vice is usually excluded from insurance policies. For example, the Institute Cargo Clauses, which are standard marine insurance clauses prepared by the Institute of London Underwriters, expressly exclude losses or damages caused by inherent vice. Inherent vice is a defence to the insurer's liability to pay under s 61(2)(c) of the Marine Insurance Act 1909 (Cth), but the insurer relying on the inherent vice defence must prove the existence, or the probability, of inherent vice. In *Noten (TM) BV v Harding* [1989] 2 Lloyd's Rep 527, the court disallowed reliance by the insurers on the inherent vice defence, because the damaged leather gloves were in dry condition at the time of loading and the evidence showed a probability that the damage was caused by some external sources after loading.

[7.68] Parties to a policy may agree that an inherent vice or a risk similar to inherent vice is covered under the policy.[36] This simply means that the insurer in certain circumstances is willing to take the risk of inherent vice for an appropriate sum or premium. This is possible because the risk of inherent vice varies from subject matter to subject matter.

[7.69] *Soya GmbH Kommanditgesellschaft v White*

[1982] 1 Lloyd's Rep 136

Whether the loss is caused by inherent vice

Facts: Soya GmbH, a German company, was the assured and the buyer of the soya beans in dispute. White represented the insurers — Lloyd's. Thegra was a Dutch company which sold a large quantity of soya beans to Soya GmbH. The soya beans were to be carried from Indonesia to Antwerp. Thegra took up an insurance policy with Lloyd's to cover the risk of heat, sweat and spontaneous combustion. Two shipments of the soya beans arrived at Antwerp in a heated and deteriorated condition. The insurers refused to pay under the policy on the ground, inter alia, that the damage was caused by inherent vice. The trial judge found that the risks which caused the damage were covered under the policy and that the insurers were liable. The insurers appealed.

Decision: The English Court of Appeal (consisting of Waller, Donaldson and O'Connor LJJ) dismissed the appeal. Their Lordships held that the damage was caused by an inherent vice which was covered under the policy. 'Heat, sweat, spontaneous combustion' were, in their Lordships' view, particular forms of inherent vice.

[7.70] Unseaworthiness of a vessel is a form of inherent vice in hull insurance. An assured claiming loss or damage is obliged to prove that the insured vessel was seaworthy

---

35. For example, in *Berk v Style* [1955] 3 All ER 625, the court held that the damage to the 'kieselguhr' packed in paper bags was due to the inadequate packing, which was excluded as inherent vice under the policy.
36. For example, see *Overseas Commodities Ltd v Style* [1958] 1 Lloyd's Rep 546, and *Gee & Garnham Ltd v Whittall* [1955] 2 Lloyd's Rep 562.

at the commencement of the marine adventure: see *Visscher Enterprises Pty Ltd v Southern Pacific Insurance Co Pty Ltd* [1981] Qd R 561, per Connolly J at 565. An insurer cannot avoid liability under a policy by relying on a defect that developed and led to the unseaworthiness of a vessel after the commencement of a voyage. The existence of an inherent vice — unseaworthiness of a ship, for example — is immaterial, if the loss or damage was not caused by that inherent vice.[37] Unseaworthiness of a vessel in marine insurance law may result from both mechanical defects in the vessel and the incompetence of the crew. For example, Ryan J of the Supreme Court of Queensland observed in *Doak v Weekes* (1986) FLR 334 at 339, that incompetence of 'the personnel on a vessel may render it unseaworthy'. The competence of the crew is determined by their practical skills and experience, rather than the certificates held by them. In *Doak v Weekes* (1986) FLR 334, the court held that the vessel was not unseaworthy merely because a crew member did not hold an appropriate certificate of competence.

Broker's duties to assured and insurer

[7.71] Insurance brokers may act either independently or in association with insurers. In our study, 'brokers' refers to those independent operators who act as middle-persons between an insurer and an assured.

[7.72] The legal relationship between an assured and a broker is that of principal and agent. The broker is liable to the assured as his or her agent. The broker can be sued by the assured if he or she fails to perform his or her duty adequately. By the same token, a broker can also act as the agent for an insurer and be liable to the insurer. In *Percy v West Bay Boat Builders*, decided on 28 October 1997, No CA021807 (BCCA),[38] a broker was sued for negligence in giving advice on the suitability of an insurance policy to cover a shipbuilder's liability. The shipbuilder had an insurance policy which covered product liability. The broker misrepresented to the shipbuilder that an insurance policy offered by another insurer was better and cheaper. The shipbuilder purchased the policy introduced by the broker. Later the shipbuilder had to compensate its customer for negligence in building a vessel, but discovered that it could not recover the cost under the present insurance policy because the policy did not cover product liability. The trial court and the Court of Appeal held that the broker was negligent in enticing the shipbuilder to purchase the present policy and was thus liable for the shipbuilder's loss.

[7.73] A broker has two main duties to the insurer under arts 25 and 59 of the Marine Insurance Act 1909 (Cth). The first is to disclose to the insurer 'every material circumstance' the broker knew or ought to have known (s 25 of the Act). The brokers who forged their client's signature in the proposal form were found to have breached the duty

---

37. For example, see *J J Lloyd Instruments Ltd v Northern Star Insurance Co Ltd* [1985] 1 Lloyd's Rep 264, where a yacht was damaged in brisk weather. The policy covered loss or damage arising from external causes. The insurers refused to pay part of the claim on the ground that this part arose from the faulty design of the yacht. The court held that the latent defects in design were irrelevant to the loss in question, because the loss was caused by the fortuitous action of the wind and waves. See also *Randell v Atlantica Insurance Co Ltd* (1983) 80 FLR 253.
38. The case summary is available at <http://www.admiraltylaw.com>.

[7.73] International Commercial Law

of utmost good faith to the insurers in *Anthony John Sharp and Roarer Investments Ltd v Sphere Drake Insurance Pls, Minster Insurance Co Ltd and EC Parker & Co Ltd (The 'Moonacre')* [1992] 2 Lloyd's Rep 501; [7.61]. The second is to be directly responsible to the insurer for the premium due (s 59 of the Act). These duties suggest that while a broker acts as the agent of the principal, he or she is also liable to the insurer in his or her independent capacity.

[7.74] *Trading & General Investment v Gault Armstrong & Kemble (The 'Okeanis')*

[1986] 1 Lloyd's Rep 195

Liabilities between underwriters and brokers

Facts: Trading & General was the owner of the vessel *Okeanis*. Gualt Armstrong & Kemble (GAK) were brokers for Lloyd's, who were the insurers of the *Okeanis* and were instructed to place part of the risk with Italian underwriters. GAK placed 15 per cent of the risk through Italrias (the Italian brokers) with Italian underwriters. The engine of the *Okeanis* was damaged in 1978. Two invoices representing 15 per cent of the settlement as agreed by the London underwriters were sent to Italrias for payment. Italrias informed GAK that they were unable to obtain payment from the sub-insurers. The sub-insurers stated that they had paid Italrias by way of set-off. The assured sued the insurers (GAK) for the unpaid sum.

Decision: Bingham J of the Queen's Bench Division (Commercial Court) held that Italrias acted as the agents of the Italian underwriters and as sub-brokers (agents) for GAK. The assured was entitled to claim against GAK, which could claim through Italrias against the Italian underwriters. In the absence of any concrete evidence, whether Italrias had received payments from the Italian underwriters could not be decided. However, the assured was entitled to recover the premium from GAK on the 15 per cent risk placed with the Italian underwriters, which had never been paid to the Italian underwriters.

Reinsurance and insurer's liability

[7.75] It is common for insurers to reinsure their risks of providing insurance with other insurers. Section 15 of the Marine Insurance Act 1909 (Cth) provides that the 'insurer under a contract of marine insurance has an insurable interest in his risk, and may reinsure in respect of it'. This means that in the event of a claim, the insurers are able to claim contributions from the sub-insurers and to reduce their own loss. The relationships between insurers and sub-insurers are contractual. The terms and extent of the sub-insurers' liability are defined in the contract of reinsurance. Since sub-insurers are often foreign insurers, conflicts rules are of major concern. Although it is necessary to define as clearly as possible the governing law of the contract and the forum for disputes, the effect of such clauses is ultimately dependent upon the law of the court dealing with them. The following case illustrates the complexity of actions against sub-insurers in various countries.

> **[7.76]** *Golden Ocean Assurance Ltd and World Mariner Shipping SA v Christopher Julian Martin*
>
> [1989] 2 Lloyd's Rep 390
>
> *Conflicts rules in reinsurance involving sub-insurers from various countries*
>
> **Facts:** Golden Ocean Assurance and World Marine acted as insurers for a fleet of vessels owned or chartered by the Golden Ocean Group, which had offices in London and Tokyo. Golden Ocean Group reinsured 100 per cent of the risk on the world market. The reinsurance involved more than 20 sub-insurers from England, the United States, France and Switzerland. A vessel, *Golden Mariner*, incurred salvage costs in 1984 and the insurers claimed payments under the reinsurance policies. The action commenced in London. A number of foreign sub-insurers sought to stay the proceedings on the grounds of irregular services or forum non conveniens.
>
> **Decision:** Phillips J of the Queen's Bench Division (Commercial Court) held that, inter alia, the insurers had established that they were entitled to sue all the sub-reinsurers, and that a sub-insurer could have reasonably contemplated the possibility of being sued in the English courts when undertaking the liability of reinsurance.

Burden of proof as to the cause of the loss

[7.77] The existence of insurable risks and insurable interests does not necessarily lead to the payment of indemnity when a loss occurs. This is because losses are not always caused by the risks insured against. For example, in *Compania Naviera Santi SA v Indemnity Marine Insurance Co (The Tropaiofaros)* [1960] 2 Lloyd's Rep 469, an old steamship sank in the Bay of Bengal at about 3.30 am in fine weather and a calm sea. Many of the ship's papers were missing. Neither the shipowners nor crew members could establish how and why the ship sank, except by claiming that the ship struck an unknown submerged object. The court held that the assured must prove that the loss was caused by the risks insured against when making a claim under the policy. Similarly, in *Rhesa Shipping Co SA v Edmunds (The Popi M)* [1985] 2 All ER 712, a vessel built in 1952 sank in 1976 in good weather and calm sea. The assured and insurers disagreed as to the proximate cause of the sinking. The House of Lords reversed the decisions of the lower courts and held that the assured had failed to prove the seaworthiness of the ship at the commencement of the voyage, for the purpose of establishing that the perils at sea were the proximate and probable cause of the sinking. This means that to hold the insurer liable in a given contract, the risk which has caused the loss or damage to the insured subject matter must be proved to be the one which has been insured against under the contract.[39]

---

39. In *Lamb Head Shipping Co Ltd v Jennings (The 'Marel')* [1992] 1 Lloyd's Rep 402, the ship was lost as the result of incursion of seawater into it, but the cause of incursion was not reasonably established. The Queen's Bench Division (Commercial Court) held that on the balance of probabilities the assured failed to satisfy the court that the ship was lost due to some unascertained peril of sea. The assured's claim failed.

[7.78] *Skandia Insurance v Skoljarev*

[1979] 142 CLR 375

The assured established that the loss was probably caused by the perils of sea, because of the seaworthiness of the ship

Facts: Skoljarev was the owner of a fishing vessel, *Zadar*, which was insured by Skandia. In April 1977, the vessel sank off the coast of South Australia. The specific reason for the sinking was unknown. The insurance policy covered 'perils of the seas'. The trial judge gave judgment for the assured. The Full Court of the Supreme Court of South Australia dismissed the appeal by the insurers. The insurers appealed to the Australian High Court.

Decision: The High Court (consisting of Barwick CJ, Gibbs, Stephen, Mason and Aickin JJ) dismissed the appeal. The court held that the assured had the burden of proof to establish that the loss was caused by the perils of the sea. The assured must prove the seaworthiness of the ship if the cause of the loss is uncertain. When the assured proves the seaworthiness of the ship at the commencement of the voyage, there is an inference that the loss is caused by the perils of the sea even though the particular cause was not ascertained.

[7.79] *Wood v Associated National Insurance Co Ltd*

[1984] 1 Qd R 507

The assured is not entitled to claim insurance if the loss was caused by both the perils of sea and his or her wilful misconduct

Facts: Wood and others were the assured and Associated National was the insurer. The fishing vessel *Isothel* was covered by a time policy. The vessel was damaged in a severe storm. The insurer rejected the insurance claim on the ground, inter alia, that the damage was attributable to the unseaworthiness of the vessel and the wilful misconduct of the assured.

Decision: Williams J of the Supreme Court of Queensland observed (at 532) that 'reckless conduct may amount to "wilful misconduct" for the purposes of s 61 of the Act' and held that the failure of the assured to return to the vessel and to adopt appropriate measures with the knowledge of the forthcoming storm amounted to 'reckless disregard' for the safety of the vessel. His Honour held that the assured was not entitled to claim the policy, because their wilful misconduct contributed to the damage which was in point of time caused by the perils of the sea.

Included and excluded losses

[7.80] 'Included losses' refers to those losses which are covered under an insurance contract, and excluded losses refers to those for which the insurer is not liable. These are set out in s 61 of the Marine Insurance Act 1909 (Cth).[40] Whether or not a loss is included

---

40. Section 61(1) of the Marine Insurance Act 1909 (Cth) states that 'subject to the provisions of this Act, and unless the policy otherwise provides, the insurer is liable for any loss proximately caused by a peril insured against, but, subject as aforesaid, he is not liable for any loss which is not proximately caused by a peril insured against'.

Marine Insurance, Aviation Insurance and International Trade [7.82]

or excluded should be determined in the context of the insurance contract and under the relevant provisions of law. For example, in *Strangemores Electrical Ltd v Insurance Corp of Newfoundland Ltd* [1997] ILR I-3475 (Nfld SC),[41] an insured vessel was destroyed by fire while being repaired by the insured. The vessel was owned by the president of the insured. The insurer refused to pay for the loss by relying on an exclusion clause which excluded liability for personal property in the insured's care, custody or control. The insured relied on another contractual clause stating that the exclusion did not apply to watercraft while ashore on premises which were owned or rented. The court held that the exclusion clause was overridden by the second clause and that the insurer was liable because the vessel was ashore on the insured's premises under repair.

[7.81] Similarly, in *Catherwood Towing Ltd v Commercial Union Assurance Co*, decided on 17 July 1996, No CA019997 (BCCA),[42] the insured, a tug owner, sought to claim payments for the losses sustained by the barge and the cargo towed by its tug under an insurance policy. The insured relied on an exclusion clause which excluded all liabilities in respect of cargo. The court held that the clause applied only to the cargo carried on board the tug, not the cargo carried on board the barge towed by the tug. Thus, the losses were included as losses under the contract. Also, in *Burrard Towing Co v Reed Stenhouse Ltd*, decided on 23 April 1996, No CA019659 (BCCA),[43] the insurer sought to rely on an exclusion clause excluding liability arising from any damage to the towed subject and the cargo on the towed subject. The court held that the exclusion clause applied to a towage contract, rather than a contract of carriage. The court took the view that since both the tug and the barge were owned by the insured, there was a contract of carriage between the insured and the cargo-owner. Thus, the loss of cargo carried on the barge was covered by the policy. The differences between a contract of carriage and a towage contract, as well as between the cargo carried on board the tug or on board the barge carried by the tug, were crucial for determining whether the loss was included in the present case.

[7.82] Losses can be excluded for a number of reasons. A loss can be excluded because it falls under the excluded losses stipulated in law. For instance, in *Gee & Garnham Ltd v Whittall* [1955] 2 QB 562, part of the alleged loss was found to have been caused by inadequate packing and thus fell under the exclusion of inherent vice. A loss can be excluded because of an exclusion clause of the insurance contract. For example, in *Queen Charlotte Lodge Ltd v Hiway Refrigeration Ltd*, decided on 7 January 1998, No C946385 (BCSC),[44] the relevant cargo insurance contract incorporated the Institute Frozen Meat Clauses A-24. The court held that the insurer was not liable under the insurance contract for the damage of the meat due to the use of a defective refrigeration unit. A loss can be excluded because it is not covered by the insurance contract. For example, in *Commercial Trading Co Inc v Hartford Fire Insurance Co* [1974] 1 Lloyd's Rep 179, the shipmaster misdelivered a cargo of meat to a third party in accordance with an old arrangement which had become invalid. The assured, who was the financier of the third party, was the real owner of the

---

41. The case summary is available at <http://www.admiraltylaw.com>.
42. The case summary is available at <http://www.admiraltylaw.com>.
43. The case summary is available at <http://www.admiraltylaw.com>.
44. The case summary is available at <http://www.admiraltylaw.com>.

goods and had all the required documentation for delivery under the new arrangement. The third party became bankrupt, and the assured suffered loss as the financier and claimed the insurance policy over the cargo. The policy covered barratry. The court interpreted the meaning of barratry as a criminal offence committed against the shipowners and rejected the assured's claim. These cases suggest that whether an insurer is liable for a particular loss must be determined in the circumstances involved. Thus, in *Apostolos Konstantine Ventouris v Mountain (The Italia Express) (No 2)* [1992] 2 Lloyd's Rep 281, the court held that a war risk insurance policy did not include special or general damages, such as hardship, inconvenience and mental distress.

[7.83] Another ground for excluding an insurer's liability to losses under s 61 of the Marine Insurance Act 1909 (Cth) is that 'the insurer is not liable for any loss attributable to the wilful misconduct of the assured'. A wilful misconduct must be the cause for a foreseeable loss. In *Russell v Canadian General Insurance Co*, decided on 12 January 1999, No 94-CQ-56261 (Ont Ct Gen Div),[45] an insured sailboat was declared a constructive total loss because it had been full of water after being berthed at a storage place for three years. The insurer refused to make payment on the ground of wilful misconduct on the part of the insured, arguing that the water had been accumulating in the boat for three years between 1990 and 1993 while in storage. The court rejected the argument by pointing out that the damage incurred was not foreseeable on the part of the insured and thus could not have been caused by the wilful misconduct of the insured. In addition, the court held that the insured's failure to discover the water damage during the three-year period, even if he claimed to have maintained a regular check on the state of the vessel, did not amount to wilful misconduct either.

[7.84] When alleging wilful misconduct to be the cause of a loss, the burden of proof lies upon the insurer, who makes the allegation. This is illustrated in *Slattery v Mance* [1962] 1 QB 676. In this case, the assured claimed the loss of his vessel by fire under a policy. The insurer alleged that the fire was caused by wilful misconduct of the assured. The court held that the assured was liable to prove that the loss was caused by fire, but the insurer had the onus of proving that the fire was caused or contrived by the assured. By the same token, in *Craig v Association National Insurance Co Ltd* (1983) 71 FLR 455, the Supreme Court of Queensland held that on the balance of probabilities the fire which destroyed the insured vessel was deliberately set by the assured. The court so decided because it was satisfied that the clear and cogent proof of the insurer was persuasive.

[7.85] There is a difference between the misconduct of the assured and the misconduct or negligence of the master or crew of the ship. Loss which is attributable to the misconduct or negligence of the master or crew is not excluded under a policy unless it is expressly so excluded: s 61(2)(a) of the Act. Section 61(2)(b) of the Act expressly excludes, subject to the agreement of the parties, loss caused by delay even if the delay is caused by a peril insured against. This suggests that 'delay', as a ground of exclusion, must be the direct cause of the loss in a chain of events that ultimately resulted in the loss. In addition, unless the policy so provides, losses resulting from 'ordinary wear and tear, ordinary leakage and breakage, inherent vice or nature of the subject matter insured, or for

---

45. The case summary is available at <http://www.admiraltylaw.com>.

any loss proximately caused by rats or vermin, or for any injury to machinery not proximately caused by maritime perils' are not recoverable: s 61(2)(c) of the Act.[46]

In *Laing v Boreal Pacific*, decided on 17 February 1999, No T-1713-96 (FCTD),[47] an insured excavator was declared a constructive total loss because it fell overboard the barge while in transit at sea. The insurer refused to make payment under the insurance policy on the ground that the loss had been caused by the unseaworthiness of the barge carrying the excavator. The court held that the loss had not been caused by a maritime peril, but by the unseaworthiness of the barge as the barge was overloaded for the sea conditions it was to be facing. The court held that the insured knew the unseaworthiness of the vessel and held the insurer was not liable under the policy. The risks prescribed in a statute, for example, s 61 of the Marine Insurance Act 1909 (Cth), are not implied in an ordinary policy but can be insured against expressly in any policy if both parties so agree. For example, in *Overseas Commodities Ltd v Style* [1958] 1 Lloyd's Rep 546, the inherent vice was covered by the policy that covered all risks.

Categories of losses

Losses under the Marine Insurance Act 1909 (Cth)

[7.86] Under the Marine Insurance Act 1909 (Cth), losses can be divided into several categories. For example, a loss may be either total or partial, or alternatively, actual or constructive: ss 62, 63 and 66 of the Act. A total loss means that the insured subject has been wholly destroyed. A partial loss means that the insured subject is partially damaged. An actual loss and a constructive loss are defined as follows: 'Where the subject matter insured is destroyed, or so damaged as to cease to be a thing of the kind insured, or where the assured is irretrievably deprived therefore, there is an actual loss' (s 63 of the Act); in contrast, 'there is a constructive total loss where the subject matter insured is reasonably abandoned on account of its actual total loss appearing to be unavoidable, or because it could not be preserved from actual total loss without an expenditure which would exceed its value when the expenditure had been incurred' (s 66(1) of the Act).

---

46. In *HIH Casualty & General Insurance Ltd v Waterwell Shipping Inc* [1998] NSWSC 436, the NSW Court of Appeal dismissed an appeal by the insurer on the ground that the proximate cause for the loss of the insured vessel was 'ordinary wear and tear' as excluded in s 61(2)(c), and affirmed the trial court's finding that the sinking of the vessel was caused by the negligence of the crewmen who left the starboard sea suction valves open, as well as the corrosion of the wall of strainer box. The Court of Appeal took the view that the competing proximate courses were either insured against, or not expressly excluded by the policy in dispute.
47. The case summary is available at <http://www.admiraltylaw.com>.

Constructive total loss

[7.87] Constructive total loss is defined in s 66 of the Marine Insurance Act 1909 (Cth). Section 66(1) is set out in the preceding paragraph. Section 66(2) regulates the rules for determining the existence of a constructive total loss, which is set out as follows:

> **In particular, there is a constructive total loss:**
> (a) where the assured is deprived of the possession of his ship or goods by a peril insured against, and
>   (i) it is unlikely that he can recover the ship or goods, as the case may be; or
>   (ii) the cost of recovering the ship or goods, as the case may be, would exceed their value when recovered; or
> (b) in the case of damage to a ship, where she is so damaged by a peril insured against that the cost of repairing the damage would exceed the value of the ship when repaired.
> In estimating the cost of repairs, no deduction is to be made in respect of general average contributions to those repairs payable by other interests, but account is to be taken of the expense of future salvage operations and of any future general average contribution to which the ship would be liable if repaired; or
> (c) in the case of damage to goods, where the cost of repairing the damage and forwarding the goods to their destination would exceed their value on arrival.

[7.88] It appears that there are two alternative tests for determining a constructive total loss.

- it must be established that an actual loss is unavoidable; or
- the cost or expenditure to salvage the insured subject must be greater than the insured value of the subject.

Section 66(2)(a) can be illustrated by *Polurrian Steamship v Young* [1915] All ER 116, a case involving a claim for a constructive total loss of the insured ship, which had been detained by the Greek warship as a result of the war between Greece and Turkey, was held unreasonable. The court held that it was not unlikely that the Greek authority would release the ship, and in fact the ship was released after six weeks' detention. Similarly, in *Marstrand Fishing Co Ltd v Beer (The 'Girl Pat')* (1936) 56 Ll L Rep 163, the master of a fishing boat — *Girl Pat* — took control of the boat contrary to the owners' direction, but the court found that the owners could claim neither an actual loss nor a constructive loss. The boat was eventually seized by authorities and no actual loss was caused by the hijacking of the boat alone. By comparison, s 66(2)(b) can be illustrated by *The 'Moonacre'* [1992] 2 Lloyd's Rep 501; **[7.32]** and **[7.61]**, where the insured boat caught fire and sank at its mooring place. The court allowed the assured to claim a constructive total loss against his insurance brokers because the boat was severely damaged by the fire before sinking and the costs of salvage and repairs would be greater than the boat's insured value. The cost of repair in s 66(2)(b) involves labour cost. In *Shearwater Marine Ltd v Guardian Insurance Co*, decided on 1 October 1998, No CA022988 (BCCA),[48] the Supreme Court of British Columbia decided that the normal labour charge-out rate, instead of the actual cost to the assured (which excludes a profit element), should be used for calculating the constructive total loss. The British Columbia Court of Appeal affirmed the decision.

---

48. The case summary is available at <http://www.admiraltylaw.com>.

Constructive losses and rights of insurer

[7.89] Section 67 of the Act allows an assured who suffers a constructive total loss to treat the loss either as a partial loss or a total loss. An assured claiming a partial loss is entitled to recover the remainder of the insured subject, and an assured claiming a total loss will have to pass his or her interest in the insured subject to the insurer. Section 69 of the Act provides that 'where there is a valid abandonment the insurer is entitled to take over the interest of the assured in whatever may remain of the subject matter insured, and all proprietary rights incidental thereto', including freight or remuneration which the assured may be entitled to during the insured voyage and subsequent to the incident of loss. This is what we call a right of subrogation.

Particular losses

[7.90] A 'partial loss' sometimes may include the incidental expenses incurred during the occurrence of the risk insured. The expressions 'particular average loss', 'particular charge', 'general average loss' and 'salvage charge' describe these expenses. A 'particular average loss' is a partial loss of the insured subject matter caused by the insured risk: s 70(1) of the Act. A 'particular charge' is an expense 'incurred by or on behalf of the assured for the safety or preservation of the subject matter insured, other than general average and salvage charges': s 70(2) of the Act. A 'salvage charge' is an expense incurred during the occurrence of the insured risk for the services of salvage rendered by persons other than the assured and those employed or hired by the assured. A 'general average loss' is a loss or expenditure incurred in a general average act, which refers to a situation 'where any extraordinary sacrifice or expenditure is voluntarily and reasonably made or incurred in time of peril for the purpose of preserving the property imperilled in the common adventure': s 72(2) of the Act. A general average loss can be distributed among the interested parties and the assured may recover under the relevant insurance policy his or her portion of the contribution to the general average expenditure or the total of a general average sacrifice: s 72(4) of the Act. These particular losses are incidental to the salvage act or average act which is necessary to deal with the occurrence of the risk insured under the relevant marine insurance contract.

Determination of indemnity

What is the measure of indemnity?

[7.91] A marine insurance contract is a contract of indemnity. Indemnity is an essential part of performing the contract, once the risk insured against in the contract has taken place. The Marine Insurance Act 1909 (Cth) regulates the 'measure of indemnity'. The 'measure of indemnity' is a special term, referring to 'the sum which the assured can recover in respect of a loss on a policy by which he is insured, in the case of an unvalued policy to the full extent of the insurable value, or, in the case of a valued policy to the full extent of the value fixed by the policy': s 73(1) of the Act. This is illustrated by *Goole and Hull Steam Towing Co Ltd v Ocean Marine Insurance Co Ltd* [1928] 1 KB 589. In this case there was a valued policy under which the insurer agreed to indemnify the assured to the value

[7.91]   **International Commercial Law**

of $4000. The ship was damaged in a collision. The total cost for repair was $5000. The assured recovered $2500 from the other ship which was involved in the accident. The court held that the insurer was liable only to the agreed value of $4000. Since the assured had recovered $2500, the actual liability of the insurer was limited to $1500. However, it should be borne in mind that most 'measures' specified in the Act only operate when there is no express agreement as to the measures of indemnity in the contract concerned. In most circumstances, the express agreement of the parties to a marine insurance contract takes priority over the provisions of the Act.

[7.92]   We may argue that the 'measure of indemnity' is defined in the Act by reference to both the certainty (in the sense of the insurer's financial liability under a valued or unvalued policy) of the policy, and type of loss (ie, total, partial, average loss or charges). There are three main measures of indemnity:

- First, in the case of a total loss, the assured is entitled to the sum fixed by a valued policy or the insurable value of the subject matter under an unvalued policy, unless the parties agreed otherwise.[49]
- Second, in the case of a partial loss, the measure of indemnity is basically the actual loss in proportion to the fixed value or insurable value of the subject matter.
- Third, in the case of a loss arising from a general average or salvage charge, the measure of indemnity is the actual loss as determined by the insured's liability to general average or salvage charge subject to an adjustment, if applicable, in proportion to the insured value of the subject matter.[50]

Partial losses and measures of indemnity

[7.93]   Measures of indemnity applicable to a partial loss can be further divided into three categories:

- In the case of a partial loss of a ship, the measure of indemnity is determined on the basis of the cost of the repairs,[51] actual or expected, taking into account customary

---

49. Section 74 of the Marine Insurance Act 1909 (Cth) provides as follows:

    Subject to the provisions of this Act and to any express provision in the policy, where there is a total loss of the subject matter insured:
    (a) if the policy be a valued policy, the measure of indemnity is the sum fixed by the policy:
    (b) if the policy be an unvalued policy, the measure of indemnity is the insurable value of the subject matter insured.

50. Section 79 of the Marine Insurance Act 1909 (Cth) provides as follows:

    (1) Subject to any express provision in the policy, where the assured has paid, or is liable for, any general average contribution, the measure of indemnity is the full amount of such contribution, if the subject matter liable to contribution is insured for its full contributory value; but, if such subject matter be not insured for its full contributory value, or if only part of it be insured, the indemnity payable by the insurer must be reduced in proportion to the under insurance, and where there has been a particular average loss which constitutes a deduction from the contributory value, and for which the insurer is liable, that amount must be deducted from the insured value in order to ascertain what the insurer is liable to contribute.

    (2) Where the insurer is liable for salvage charges the extent of his liability must be determined on the like principle.

51. Cost of the repairs includes the cost of towage and the cost of returning the tug. See *MacKinnon McErlane Booker Pty Ltd v P O Australia Ltd* [1988] VR 534.

deductions and depreciation of the ship.[52] However, the measure is limited to the sum insured for any one casualty or the reasonable cost of repairing the damage in question: s 75 of the Act. In *Lockwood v Moreira*, decided on 24 April 1998, No C21444 (Ont CA),[53] an insured vessel was vandalised, causing damage to its interior. The insurer arranged for the interior to be cleaned twice, but was dissatisfied with the result. The insured sought to claim a payment of $100,000 in Canadian dollars under the insurance policy for a total replacement of the interior. The trial court held that the insurer's obligation for a partial loss was to restore the vessel to substantially the same condition as it was before the vandalism, rather than to restore the vessel to the exact condition as it was before. The decision was affirmed by the Ontarian Court of Appeal.

- In the case of a partial loss of freight, the measure of indemnity is determined in proportion to the fixed sum of insurable value: s 76 of the Act.
- In the case of a partial loss of goods and merchandise, the measure of indemnity is usually determined by reference to the proportion of the actual loss and of the fixed sum or insurable value. In particular, this means that the measure of indemnity in cases where the subject matter is partially lost is calculated in accordance with the proportion of the partial loss to a constructive total loss of the subject matter. In the event where the partial loss is due to damage to the subject matter, the measure of indemnity is the difference between the gross value (the wholesale price or equivalent) and the damaged value of the subject matter in the place of the subject matter's destination: s 77 of the Act.

Insurer's duty to pay an excessive sum

[7.94] There are circumstances where the insurer may be required to pay an amount exceeding the sum insured. This may happen in two situations:

- First, 'the insurer is liable for successive losses, even though the total amount of such losses may exceed the sum insured', unless the parties agreed otherwise or the Act states otherwise: s 83 of the Act.
- Second, where 'the policy contains a suing and labouring clause, the engagement thereby entered into is deemed to be supplementary to the contract of insurance, and the assured may recover from the insurer any expenses properly incurred to the clause, notwithstanding that the insurer may have paid for a total loss': s 84 of the Act.

Suing and labouring clauses

[7.95] A suing and labouring clause (or sue and labour clause) imposes a duty on the insured to do everything possible to minimise the loss incurred. Expenses may arise from the insured's efforts to minimise the loss, but such expenses may not fall within the types of loss covered by the insurance contract concerned. In order to encourage the insured to make efforts to minimise the loss incurred and to mitigate the loss by recovering it from

---

52. This excludes any economic advantage accruing to the assured after the damaged ship has been towed to a port, even if the towage is calculated as the cost of the repairs. *MacKinnon McErlane Booker Pty Ltd v P O Australia Ltd* [1988] VR 534.
53. The case summary is available at <http://www.admiraltylaw.com>.

[7.95]

someone who is liable wholly or partially for the loss, the insurer should bear the expenses arising from the performance of a suing and labouring clause. The use of a suing and labour clause is regulated in s 84 of the Marine Insurance Act 1909 (Cth) in the following words:

(1) Where the policy contains a suing and labouring clause, the engagement thereby entered into is deemed to be supplementary to the contract of insurance, and the assured may recover from the insurer any expenses properly incurred pursuant to the clause, notwithstanding that the insurer may have paid for a total loss, or that the subject matter may have been warranted free from particular average, either wholly or under a certain percentage.

(2) General average losses and contributions and salvage charges, as defined by this Act, are not recoverable under the suing and labouring clause.

(3) Expenses incurred for the purpose of averting or diminishing any loss not covered by the policy are not recoverable under the suing and labouring clause.

(4) It is the duty of the assured and his agents, in all cases, to take such measures as may be reasonable for the purpose of averting or minimising a loss.

The provision purports to strike a balance in the use of a suing and labouring clause. It grants the insured a statutory right to claim reimbursement or compensation from the insurer for performing his or her duties under a suing and labouring clause, while setting out a general duty on the part of the insured to take reasonable measures to avert or minimise a loss.

[7.96] A suing and labouring clause in a marine insurance contract often appears as the insured's duty. For example, in the Institute Cargo Clauses (A), Clause 16, which is entitled Duty of Assured Clause, is actually a suing and labour clause. This clause states as follows:

16. It is the duty of the assured and their servants and agents in respect of loss recoverable hereunder —

16.1 to take such measures as may be reasonable for the purpose of averting or minimising such loss, and

16.2 to ensure that all rights against carriers, bailees or other third parties are properly preserved and exercised

and the underwriters will, in addition to any loss recoverable hereunder, reimburse the assured for any charge properly and reasonably incurred in pursuance of these duties.

As we can see from this clause, the wording of the clause and duty of the insured as imposed in this clause are consistent with s 84 of the Marine Insurance Act 1909 (Cth), which is identical to s 78 of the Marine Insurance Act 1906 (Cth).

[7.97] Another example of a suing and labouring clause can be seen in the American Institute Cargo Clauses. This clause is worded differently from the Institute Cargo Clauses (A) which is based on UK law, but the basic idea of a suing and labouring clause is similar, except for the part on the sharing of the expenses so incurred. Perhaps the interpretation of the reasonable expenses may help the insurer and the insured to find a fair way to share the cost for mitigating the loss, thus reducing the practical difference between the UK approach and the US approach to the enforcement of a suing and labouring clause. The said US clause states as follows:

In case of any loss or misfortune, it shall be lawful and necessary to and for the assured, his or their factors, servants and assignees, to sue, labour and travel, for in and about the defence, safeguard and recovery of the goods and merchandise, or any part thereof, without prejudice to this insurance, nor shall the acts of the assured or this Company, in recovering, saving and preserving the property insured, in case of disaster, be considered a waiver or an acceptance of abandonment. The reasonable expenses so incurred shall be borne by the Assured and the Company in proportion as the sum thereby insured bear to the whole value at risk.[54]

[7.98] Under a suing and labouring (or sue and labour) clause, the assured is able 'to recover the reasonable expenses it incurred while attempting to minimise damage suffered by the insured property'.[55] In *Integrated Container Service Inc v British Trader's Insurance Co Ltd* [1984] 1 Lloyd's Rep 154, the assured was allowed to recover under a suing and labouring clause the costs incurred as a result of suing the Official Referee's services to determine whether certain expenditure was necessary to prevent damage to the containers. A suing and labouring clause also requires the assured to take necessary measures to mitigate the loss or damage to the insured subject matter. This is ultimately for the benefit of the insurer. The duty to mitigate a loss extends, depending on the terms of the policy, to a duty to institute legal proceedings against any parties who are liable for the loss. However, non-action by the assured against other parties for a lack of cause of action does not amount to a breach of the duty to mitigate.[56] There appears to be no breach even if the assured claims insurance before taking an action against a liable third party, as long as the action against the third party is not statute-barred at the time of making the claim.[57]

Assignment of policy

[7.99] A policy can be transferred by way of indorsement or other customary manner, provided that the insured subject matter has been or is being transferred with the policy. Section 56(1) of the Marine Insurance Act 1909 (Cth) provides that a 'marine insurance is assignable unless it contains terms expressly prohibiting assignment. It may be assigned either before or after loss'. If an insured loss has taken place, a policy can be assigned to an assignee without the need to transfer the insured subject (in fact, such a transfer is not possible).[58] The effect of the assignment is that the holder (assignee) is able to claim indemnity under the policy and that the insurer can claim any defence against the assignee as if the assignee were the original assured: s 56(2) of the Act.

Insurer's right of subrogation

[7.100] Like any other insurance contract, an insurer under a marine insurance contract has the right of subrogation and of contribution after he or she has paid the assured pursuant to the policy. Under s 85 of the Marine Insurance Act 1909 (Cth) the right of subrogation enables the insurer to claim any interests, benefits or values remaining in, relating to or deriving from the losses or damages to the insured subject matter which have been indemnified by the insurer either totally or partially. The insurer's right of

---

54. Rave, Jr and Tranchina, 'Marine Cargo Insurance: an Overview' (1991) 66 *Tulane Law Review* 371, p 387.
55. Ibid.
56. *Verna Trading Pty Ltd v New India Assurance Co Ltd* (1991) 1 VR 129 at 134–5 per Beach J.
57. *Verna Trading Pty Ltd v New India Assurance Co Ltd* (1991) 1 VR 129 at 135 per Beach J.
58. *Lloyd v Fleming* [1872] LR 7 QB 299.

[7.100] subrogation is confined to the extent of the liability he or she undertakes under the underlying insurance contract. For example, in *Yorkshire Insurance Co Ltd v Nisbet Shipping Co Ltd* [1961] 2 All ER 487, the insurer indemnified the assured under a fixed value policy for a total loss of the ship. The insurer then subrogated the assured's rights in a successful action against the Canadian Government which owned the ship colliding with the assured's ship. Due to a devaluation of sterling, the conversion of Canadian dollars into sterling yielded about £127,000, exceeding the insured value of £72,000 paid to the assured. The court held that the right of subrogation allowed the insurer to recover the total amount of the indemnity paid under the policy, but the assured was allowed to retain the balance of the payment from the Canadian Government. This case suggests that an insurer's right of subrogation is restricted by the amount of indemnity made by him or her in a given circumstance.

[7.101] The right of subrogation extends to the situation where the subject matter has been insured under more than one policy or the policy was undertaken by several insurers. Under s 86 of the Marine Insurance Act 1909 (Cth), any one of the insurers involved is entitled to seek contributions from other relevant insurers in proportion to their liability under the relevant policies, if he or she paid more than his or her proportionate liability. Double insurance or insurance by a syndicate of insurers is not uncommon in international trade.

Aviation insurance

Overview

[7.102] Aviation insurance is a distinctive branch of insurance service which has a close association with international trade and commerce. In fact, aviation insurance itself is an independent form of international commerce, with insurers in one country providing insurance cover to cargoes, aircraft and passengers travelling across the airspace of various countries. Similar to marine insurance, which has been growing with the rapid development of the shipping industry, aviation insurance is the inevitable product of the continuous commercialisation of the aviation industry over the past 40–50 years. Although it was believed that Lloyd's of London began to offer aviation insurance from the beginning of the twentieth century,[59] the aviation insurance industry did not achieve any significant development until the end of the Second World War, when aircraft began to play an increasingly important role in civil and commercial aviation. The increasing use of aircraft as a practical means of transportation for both passengers and cargoes provided potential for the development of aviation insurance. The risk associated with civil aviation offered an opportunity for investors wishing to invest in the aviation insurance industry. By the early 1950s, the London market had become established as the centre of world aviation insurance.[60]

---

59. Margo, *Aviation Insurance*, 2nd ed, London, Butterworths, 1989, p 1.
60. Id, p 2.

[7.103] An aviation insurance contract is subject to the same principles of contract as any other type of insurance. In the absence of special regulations in most countries, it is also made in the same way as any other insurance contract, in the sense that the insurer makes the ultimate decision on whether to offer an insurance contract and what the terms of the contract will be. Of course, many insurers are willing to vary the standard terms and conditions to suit the needs of a particular insured whenever the modification is regarded as acceptable to the insurer. On the other hand, the insured is able to shop around to conclude an insurance contract on the best terms and conditions available to him or her in the circumstances. This reflects the principle of freedom of contract, which is one of the universally accepted principles of contracts. In addition, other basic principles of insurance law, such as the duty of utmost good faith, the requirement for the insured to have an insurable interest, the insured's duty to pay the premium and the insurer's duty to indemnify the loss of the insured pursuant to the terms and conditions of the contract, also apply to an aviation insurance contract.

[7.104] An aviation insurance contract is made between an insured and an insurer, who can be a single insurance underwriter, or a group of underwriters. The insured can be different persons depending on the nature of the subject matter insured. In a cargo insurance, the insured can be the cargo-owner, the seller, or an authorised person. In aircraft or hull insurance, the insured can be the owner, the operator or anyone who is interested in the safety of, and the legal liability incurred to, the aircraft. In a third party liability insurance, the insured is normally the operator of the aircraft and also the owner, and anyone whose interest may be affected by the third party liability incurred by the aircraft.

In passenger liability insurance, the insured should be the operator, the owner or anyone who has an interest in the safe carriage of the passengers. Similarly, the different persons may become insureds in different types of aviation insurance contracts, as long as the insured has an insurable interest in the subject matter insured. The parties to an aviation insurance contract are crucial because of the doctrine of privity of contract. In *Air Separation v Lloyd's of London* 45 F 3d 288 (9th Cir 1995),[61] the insurer made a payment to the lessee of the aircraft, under a policy for the theft of avionics equipment. However, the insurance contract was made between Air Separation and Lloyd's. The court ordered Lloyd's of London to make another payment directly to the insured (Air Separation) under the said policy.

[7.105] Insurance brokers play an important role in the facilitation of the making of insurance contracts, but a broker is an agent only. He or she neither undertakes the liability of an insurer, nor can he or she enter into a contract of insurance as an insured, unless his or her insurable interest in the insured subject matter can be established. A broker may act as the agent of the insurer to sell an aviation policy to a prospective insured. On the other hand, a broker can also act as the agent of the insured to procure a suitable insurance policy. In each case, the broker is liable as the agent to his or her principal respectively.[62] The significance of a broker is more obvious when an insured requires the broker to organise a syndicate of underwriters, or to place insurance with several insurers, to spread the risks due to the high value of the subject matter (such as an

---

61. The case is available at <http://caselaw.findlaw.com>.

aircraft), or the high liability insured against. The importance of insurance brokers or forwarders is also evident in the arrangement of cargo insurance for international sales. When a multimodal carriage is involved, a broker or forwarder is able to arrange appropriate insurance coverage for different types of transportation more efficiently than the seller or the buyer. Thus, brokers play an important role in procuring insurance coverage for carriage by air, sea and land.

[7.106] Aviation insurance is examined in this chapter because it is one of the most important forms of insurance, besides marine insurance, in international commerce. It is directly related to the safety of the cargo carried by air and the safety of aircraft engaged in international civil aviation. Aviation insurance is also relevant to the safety of the public in general as well as the safety of passengers. These matters, as we will see, are subject to international conventions. These types of aviation insurance are to be examined in this section with varying emphases.

[7.107] In this section, the legal framework for aviation insurance will be examined first to provide a basic understanding of aviation insurance from an international perspective. The general classification of aviation insurance contracts will also be reviewed to provide a general picture of the variations in aviation insurance contracts. Emphasis, however, will be placed on three types of aviation insurance contract, namely, the cargo insurance, hull insurance and passenger's liability insurance contract, which, subject to different interpretations, take more significant positions in international commerce than other types of aviation insurance contract, such as products liability insurance, airport operations liability insurance and loss of licence insurance.

Legal framework for aviation insurance

[7.108] There is no comprehensive international convention regulating the whole of aviation insurance. The Rome Convention 1952, which was formally known as the Convention on Damage Caused by Foreign Aircraft to Third Parties on the Surface, was signed at Rome on 7 October 1952. It entered into force on 4 February 1958. In 1995, its membership included Australia, Brazil, Egypt, Iraq, Italy, Kuwait, Nigeria, Pakistan, Papua New Guinea, the Russian Federation, Seychelles, Sri Lanka, United Arab Emirates, Vanuatu, and Yemen. The convention is not an international treaty on aviation insurance in general. Instead, it introduces a system of compulsory liability for aircraft owners or operators for the purpose of protecting any person who suffers a damage caused by aircraft in flight while he or she is on the surface of the earth. The convention has led to

---

62. For example, in *Agro Air Association Inc v Houston Casualty Company*, decided on 21 November 1997, No 95-5223, US Ct of App for 11th Circuit, available at <http://caselaw.findlaw.com>, the defendant was a broker who acted as the agent of the plaintiff in procuring hull and liability aviation insurance policies for the plaintiff. The broker did not follow the principal's instructions precisely and also failed to renew the original policies at a reasonable rate after the expiration of the previous policies. The principal had to engage another broker to procure insurance policies at higher costs in the London market and sued the defendant for breach of contract and fraud. The jury found in favour of the principal and the broker was ordered to pay damages to the principal. The decision of the trial court was affirmed by the court of appeal. This case illustrates the process for the procurement of hull and liability insurance policies and the relationships between the insured and the broker in general.

the creation of so-called third party liability insurance, which can be covered either in a special insurance policy or under a hull insurance. For example, the Lloyd's Aircraft Policy normally contains a third party liability clause. However, the Rome Convention 1952 has nothing to do with cargo insurance and passenger insurance. Another aspect of the Rome Convention 1952 is that the convention introduces a compulsory system of liability and grants a power in the local government to require foreign aircraft to be registered in an appropriate insurance scheme.[63] Since the Rome Convention 1952 regulates only third party liability, it has limited impact on the regulation of aviation insurance worldwide. The Rome Convention 1952 was amended by the Protocol to Amend the Convention on Damage Caused by Foreign Aircraft to Third Parties on the Surface (the Montreal Protocol 1978), signed at Montreal on 23 September 1978. The Montreal Protocol has introduced a number of amendments to the Rome Convention 1952. The most important amendments were the adoption of a higher limit of the operator's liability and the use of SDR as the unit of account to calculate the sum of liability. The Rome Convention 1952 and the Montreal Protocol 1978 will be examined further under the sub-heading on hull insurance.

[7.109] In the absence of relevant international conventions, other aspects of aviation insurance are subject to the relevant domestic law. For example, the insurance company legislation in many countries regulates the operation of the insurance industry and also certain aspects of aviation insurance contract. In fact, many domestic cases on aviation insurance contract are determined in the light of the relevant domestic law on contract, insurance company legislation and other relevant laws. Besides statute, established commercial practices and the standard contracts offered by major insurance companies, such as Lloyd's of London, the Institute of London Underwriters, Lloyd's America, and the Associated Aviation Underwriters (AAU), play an important role in the development of domestic law governing aviation insurance. For example, in *State Auto Mut Ins Co v Babcock* 220 NW 2d 717, at 721 (Mich Ct App 1974), the court held that an insurance binder is a contract of temporary insurance which is only effective until a formal policy is drafted and issued. It is not a complete contract in a sense, but is evidence of the existence of a contractual obligation to be expressed in complete written form at a later date. This observation was based on the commercial practice concerning the use of the insurance binder in insurance services in the United States.

Classification of aviation insurance contracts

[7.110] Aviation insurance contracts can be classified in different ways, depending on the nature of risk or of the subject matter concerned. For example, according to the nature of the risk or type of risk insured against, aviation insurance contracts can be divided into the following categories:

---

63. For example, art 15(1) of the Rome Convention 1952 provides that any 'Contracting State may require that the operator of an aircraft registered in another Contracting State shall be insured in respect of his liability for damage sustained in its territory for which a right to compensation exists under Article 1 by means of insurance up to the limits applicable according to the provisions of Article 11'.

[7.110]

- third party liability insurance;
- passenger liability insurance;
- travel accident insurance;
- product liability insurance;
- loss of licence insurance;
- personal accident and life insurance;
- war and hijacking insurance;
- aircraft excess liability insurance; and
- aircraft consequential loss insurance.

For comparison, according to the subject matter insured, aviation insurance contracts can be classified into the following groups:

- hull insurance;
- cargo insurance;
- airport owners' and operators' liability insurance;
- hovercraft insurance;
- spacecraft insurance; and
- commercial aircraft insurance.

[7.111] The variations of insurance policy are not exhaustible, because insurance policy is designed to meet the need of commercial reality, which is constantly changing. Policies with different combinations or a standard policy incorporating an additional term may constitute a new type of policy, depending on the criteria for categorisation. Therefore, the classification of aviation insurance in our discussion demonstrates certain aspects of international aviation insurance today. For example, in *North American Speciality Insurance Co v Shirley Myers*, 1997 Fed App 0133p (6th Cir),[64] the insurance in dispute was known as a liability and hull insurance, which covered, inter alia, hull insurance, third party liability insurance, and passenger liability insurance. It was meant for a small aircraft for commercial use.

[7.112] Most aviation insurers specialise in hull insurance, third party liability insurance, passenger liability insurance, product liability insurance and any insurance which is directly related to the aircraft, aircraft owner, operators or financiers. Cargo insurance is a small part of the world aviation insurance industry. This is the inevitable consequence of commercial reality, because cargo shipping is less important than passenger carriage in civil aviation operation. However, insuring cargoes against risk of carriage is not a problem at all. Many insurers offer all types of insurance to cover many risks associated with international carriage of goods by air, sea or land, although each of them may have specialities in emphasising one or several types of insurance policies.

---

64. The case is available at <http://caselaw.findlaw.com>.

Cargo insurance

[7.113] In the absence of specific international convention and domestic legislation, cargo insurance is subject to the general principles of contract law. In particular, the insurer's liability is determined by the terms and conditions of the contract under the doctrine of freedom of contract. For example, the Institute Cargo Clauses (Air) of the Institute of London Underwriters, which do not apply to the carriage of postal items by air, defines the risks covered in the following terms:

Risks covered
1. This insurance covers all risks of loss or damage to the subject matter insured except as provided in Clauses 2, 3, and 4 below.

Exclusions
2. In no case shall this insurance cover:
2.1 loss damage or expense attributable to wilful misconduct of the assured;
2.2 ordinary leakage, ordinary loss in weight or volume, or ordinary wear and tear of the subject matter insured;
2.3 loss damage or expenses caused by insufficiency or unsuitability of packing or preparation of the subject matter insured (for the purpose of this Clause 2.3 packing shall be deemed to include stowage in a container or liftvan but only when such stowage is carried out prior to attachment of this insurance or by the assured or their agents);
2.4 loss damage or expense caused by inherent vice or nature of the subject matter insured;
2.5 loss damage or expense arising from unfitness of aircraft conveyance containers or liftvan for the safe carriage of the subject matter insured, where the assured or their servants are privy to such unfitness at the time the subject matter is loaded therein;
2.6 loss damage or expense proximately caused by delay, even though the delay be caused by a risk insured against;
2.7 loss damage or expense arising from insolvency or financial default of the owners managers charterers or operators of the aircraft;
2.8 loss damage or expense arising from the use of any weapon of war employing atomic or nuclear fission and/or fusion or other like reaction or radioactive force or matter.
3. In no case shall this insurance cover loss damage or expenses caused by
3.1 war civil war revolution rebellion insurrection, or civil strife arising therefrom, or any hostile act by or against a belligerent power;
3.2 capture seizure arrest restraint or detainment (piracy excepted), and the consequence thereof or any attempt thereat;
3.3 derelict mines torpedoes bombs or other derelict weapons of war.
4. In no case shall this insurance cover loss damage or expenses
4.1 caused by strikes, locked-out workmen, or persons taking part in labour disturbances, riots or civil commotion;
4.2 resulting from strikes, lock-outs, labour disturbances, riots or civil commotion;
4.3 caused by any terrorist or any person acting from a political motive.

[7.114] These four clauses define the scope of risks covered by the policy. There is no uniform law on what should be covered and what should be excluded. But commercial usage and customs dictate some sort of uniformity in the standard of cargo insurance offered by the insurers in a particular market, and to a large extent there is some sort of minimum risk an aviation cargo insurance policy should cover. The similarities between the Institute Cargo Clauses (Air) and the Institute Cargo Clauses (A) for marine cargo insurance (see **[7.12]–[7.16]**) demonstrate the types of common risks which should be covered by most insurers in international carriage of goods.

[7.115] A cargo insurance policy should expressly stipulate the value insured and procedures for claiming indemnity under the policy. It should also define the duration of the policy to indicate the period of time and the part of carriage covered by it to avoid disagreement. A cargo insurance policy must contain a choice of law clause to ensure the validity of the contract, because a policy valid under one particular law may be void under another domestic law. A choice of forum clause in a cargo insurance policy may not be useful, because many courts may refuse to enforce it due to the impossibility, inconvenience or unfairness of forcing an insured to sue the insurer in a particular court.

Third party liability insurance

[7.116] A third party liability insurance can be procured either as an independent insurance policy or as a clause of a hull or aircraft insurance contract. The essence of the third party liability in aviation is that the operator of an aircraft is liable to any damage caused by the aircraft in the air or for anything falling from the aircraft to any person on the surface of the earth. This liability is based on the Rome Convention 1952. Article 1 of the Rome Convention 1952, which is one of the major provisions imposing third party liability, sets out the basis of liability and defines the meaning of an aircraft in flight. It states as follows:

1. Any person who suffers damage on the surface shall, upon proof only that the damage was caused by an aircraft in flight or by any person or thing falling therefrom, be entitled to compensation as provided by this Convention. Nevertheless there shall be no right to compensation if the damage is not a direct consequence of the incident giving rise thereto, or if the damage results from the mere fact of passage of the aircraft through the airspace in conformity with existing air traffic regulations.
2. For the purpose of this Convention, an aircraft is considered to be in flight from the moment when power is applied for the purpose of actual take-off until the moment when the landing run ends. In the case of an aircraft lighter than air, the expression "in flight" relates to the period from the moment when it becomes detached from the surface until it becomes again attached thereto.

The Rome Convention 1952 imposes a compulsory third party liability upon certain persons controlling the aircraft which has caused damage to a person on the surface. The persons who are held liable under the convention are defined in art 2(2) and (3), which provides as follows:

2.(2) (a) For the purposes of this Convention the term "operator" shall mean the person who was making use of the aircraft at the time the damage was caused, provided that if control of the navigation of the aircraft was retained by the person from whom the right to make use of the aircraft was deprived, whether directly or indirectly, that person shall be considered an operator.
 (b) A person shall be considered to be making use of an aircraft when he is using it personally or when his servants or agents are using the aircraft in the course of their employment, whether or not within the scope of their authority.
3. The registered owner of the aircraft shall be presumed to be the operator and shall be liable as such unless, in the proceedings for the determination of his liability, he proves that some other person was the operator and, in so far as legal procedures permit, takes appropriate measures to make that other person a party in the proceedings.

[7.117] In the light of arts 1 and 2 above, an operator, an owner and anyone in control of an aircraft may be held liable under the convention if any damage as described in art 1 has been caused by the aircraft controlled by such person. The Rome Convention sets out the limits of third party liability under art 1(1), which is set out as follows:

1. Subject to the provisions of Article 12, the liability for damage giving a right to compensation under Article 1, for each aircraft and incident, in respect of all persons liable under this Convention, shall not exceed:

    500 000 francs for aircraft weighing 1000 kilograms or less;

    500 000 francs plus 400 francs per kilogram over 1000 kilograms for aircraft weighing more than 1000 but not exceeding 6000 kilograms;

    2 500 000 francs plus 250 francs per kilogram over 6000 kilograms for aircraft weighing more than 6000 but not exceeding 20 000 kilograms;

    6 000 000 francs plus 150 francs per kilogram over 20 000 kilograms for aircraft weighing more than 20 000 but not exceeding 50 000 kilograms;

    10 500 000 francs plus 100 francs per kilogram over 50 000 kilograms for aircraft weighing more than 50 000 kilograms.

2. The liability in respect of loss of life or personal injury shall not exceed 500 000 francs per person killed or injured.

3. "Weight" means the maximum weight of the aircraft authorised by the certificate of airworthiness for take-off, excluding the effect of lifting gas when used.

[7.118] Article 12 of the convention deprives a person liable under the convention of the right to rely on the limited liability as set out in art 1(1) on the ground of intentional or wilful misconduct. Article 12(1) states that if 'the person who suffers damage proves that it was caused by a deliberate act or omission of the operator, his servants or agents, done with intent to cause damage, the liability of the operator shall be unlimited; provided that in the case of such act or omission of such servant or agent, it is also proved that he was acting in the course of his employment and within the scope of his authority'. Similarly, under art 12(2), if 'a person wrongfully takes and makes use of an aircraft without the consent of the person entitled to use it, his liability shall be unlimited'. The major difference between these two provisions is that art 12(1) applies to an operator, and art 12(2) applies to anyone in control of the aircraft by exercising a de facto right of operator. The latter category of person may be regarded as an illegal operator.

[7.119] The limits of the liability in art 12 are amended by the Montreal Protocol 1978. Besides the adoption of SDR as the units of account, the limits of the operator's liability have been increased. Article 3 of the Montreal Protocol 1978 amends the limits of liability as follows:

1. Subject to the provisions of Article 12, the liability for damage giving a right to compensation under Article 1, for each aircraft and incident, in respect of all persons liable under this Convention shall not exceed:
    (a) 300,000 Special Drawing Rights for aircraft weighing 2000 kilograms or less;
    (b) 300,000 Special Drawing Rights plus 175 Special Drawing Rights per kilogram over 2000 kilograms for aircraft weighing more than 2000 but not exceeding 6000 kilograms;
    (c) 1,000,000 Special Drawing Rights plus 62.5 Special Drawing Rights per kilogram over 6000 kilograms for aircraft weighing more than 6,000 but not exceeding 30,000 kilograms;
    (d) 2,500,000 Special Drawing Rights plus 65 Special Drawing Rights per kilogram over 30,000 kilograms for aircraft weighing more than 30,000 kilograms.
2. The liability in respect of loss of life or personal injury shall not exceed 125 000 Special Drawing Rights per person killed or injured.

3. "Weight" means the maximum weight of the aircraft authorised by the certificate of airworthiness for take-off, excluding the effect of lifting gas when used.

[7.120] Unamended art 1(1) of the Rome Convention 1952 and amended art 1(1) constitute two different regimes of liability. Each operates among the countries which have ratified the particular convention. In other words, the Montreal Protocol 1978 operates only among the convention members which have ratified the protocol. Any third party liability insurance policy entered into by an aircraft operator or an owner must comply with the relevant regime of limited liability as requested by the relevant countries visited by the aircraft.

Hull insurance

[7.121] Hull insurance, which is also known as aircraft insurance, is largely an insurance contract to insure against risks which may take place to an aircraft itself, for example, physical damage caused to the body of an aircraft. But, a hull insurance policy may incorporate other clauses concerning risks which do not directly cause damage to the aircraft. For example, third party liability and loss of freight can be insured under a hull insurance policy. So is the risk of extortion or hijack. The Aircraft Hull and Liability Insurance offered by the Associated Aviation Underwriters combines the traditional hull insurance and liability insurance, such as medical expenses, bodily injury and property damages. The general rule is that the insured to a hull insurance policy is the owner, operator or anyone who has an insurable interest in the safety and operation of an aircraft, and thus any risks which affect interests of the insured may be incorporated into the same insurance contract, provided that both the insurer and insured so agree. This rule explains why different combinations of risks can be seen in different standard contracts offered by different insurers.

[7.122] A hull insurance policy must stipulate the types of risks and liabilities covered. For example, the W F&D Commercial Aircraft Policy states that 'the insurers will pay for or make good accidental loss of or damage to the aircraft or any equipment or accessories whilst thereon from whatsoever cause arising except wear and tear, gradual deterioration, mechanical breakage or breakdown but including direct loss or damage caused thereby'. This section shall include loss or damage arising out of taxi-ing by licensed and authorised ground staff, other than for the purpose of flight. On the other hand, another clause sets out general exclusions as follows:

This policy does not cover —
1. Loss, damage or liability arising from:
    (a) war, riots, strikes, civil commotion, or military or usurped power, or confiscation or requisition by any government or public authority;
    (b) the use of the aircraft for racing, pace making, aerobatics or attempts, or any purposes other than as described in Schedule II or use outside the geographical limits named, unless due to force majeure;
2. Any loss, damage, or liability which is insured by or would, but for the existence of this policy, be insured by any other existing policy or policies except in respect of any excess beyond the amount which would have been payable under such other policy or policies had this policy not been affected;
3. Liability assumed by the assured by agreement under any contract unless such liability would have attached to the assured even in the absence of such agreement;

4. (a) Loss or destruction of or damage to any property whatsoever or any loss or expenses whatsoever resulting or arising therefrom or any consequential loss; or
    (b) Any legal liability of whatsoever nature directly or indirectly caused by or contributed to by or arising from radiation or contamination by radioactivity from any nuclear fuel or from any nuclear waste from the combustion of nuclear fuel.

[7.123] The above two clauses define the scope of the insurer's liability under the contract. The damage or loss falling under the included risks should be borne by the insurer, and those falling within the excluded risks, by the insured. Any uncertainty or ambiguity should be resolved by agreement of the parties, or by a court of law if the parties fail to resolve their differences. In most cases, a dispute arising from an insurance contract ends at the court of law because insurance companies have a natural tendency to minimise their liability in any insurance contract.[65] On the other hand, the exclusions and qualifications which purport to limit the insurer's liability must be complied with by the insured. In *North American Speciality Insurance Co v Shirley Myers*, 1997 Fed App 0133p (6th Cir),[66] the insurance binder, which was regarded as evidence of the terms and conditions of the liability and hull insurance to be issued by North American Speciality Insurance, contained a requirement that the insureds had piloting experience. The two insureds were killed in an accident, and there was a high probability that they violated the said requirement. Both the trial court and the court of appeal found the insurer not liable under the policy concerned.

Similarly to marine insurance and any other insurance, excluded risks can be insured against as special or additional risks, subject to the payment of a higher premium, and other restrictions as the insurer considers appropriate. For example, an insurer may offer a special policy based on war risks, or alternatively, a clause of war risks may be offered as an optional clause for an insured, who may decide whether to incorporate it into the hull or aircraft policy between the insured and the insurer.

---

65. Sometimes the construction of a clause appears to be a difficult task. In *American Eagle Insurance Co v John H Thompson*, decided on 28 May 1996, No 95-2672, US Court of Appeals for the 8th Circuit, available at <http://caselaw.findlaw.com>, the insurance policy covered liability incurred by the employee of the insured. However, the insurer and insured disagreed on the coverage for Thompson (who took a casual job, on an hourly basis, and on his first time as a pilot, his airplane (the insured's) collided with another airplane mid-air). The trial court held that Thompson was covered by the language of the policy. The Court of Appeals reversed the decision and remanded the case for a new trial.
66. The case is available at <http://caselaw.findlaw.com>.

Chapter Eight

Foreign Investment Law

Introduction

[8.1] Foreign investment began to form a significant area of international commercial activity after the Second World War, when many countries which gained independence at the end of the war drastically needed foreign capital, technology, and managerial skills to develop their own economies. As a result of foreign investment, many local companies and industries fell into the hands of foreign investors. Economic conflicts inevitably arose between foreign investors and local workers as well as governments, because in any given circumstances, the more one side earned, the less was left for the other. Thus, whenever there was a tension between foreign employers and local workers, or between foreign investors and local governments, taking over control of the economy from the hands of foreign investors always appeared to be the best solution for the locals. Thus, nationalisation and appropriation by local governments became a common practice in the 1950s and early 1960s in many host countries; in particular, in many newly independent countries in Africa, Asia and Latin America. This led to the conclusion of the Washington Convention on the Settlement of Investment Disputes 1965. The International Centre for Settlement of Foreign Investment Disputes (ICSID) was established to deal with disputes arising from nationalisation or appropriation of foreign investment by local government. Foreign investment continued to develop at a stable pace throughout the 1970s and 1980s.

[8.2] World politics experienced dramatic changes in the 1980s. Foreign investment became a powerful vehicle to develop the new market of the former socialist countries. The United Nations Conference on Trade and Development estimated in its *World Investment Report* 2001 that FDI inflows reached US$1.3 trillion in 2000.[1] This represented a sharp increase from direct foreign investment of US$50 billion in 1980.[2]

---

1. See page 9 of the Report.
2. *The Economist Yearbook 1993*, The Economist Newspaper Ltd, London, 1993, p 195.

The popularity of foreign investment in the twentieth century is probably attributable to three decisive factors:

- the comparative advantages of countries in their natural, human and financial resources;[3]
- the continuous and insurmountable existence of barriers of trade protectionism; and
- the increased activities of transnational (or multinational) corporations.[4]

[8.3] The existence of comparative advantages between countries naturally leads to the utilisation and exploitation of these advantages. The existence of limited but nevertheless insuperable barriers of trade restrictions in many countries forces capital-rich countries to seek an alternative way of infiltrating foreign markets and utilising their financial resources. Indeed, a large amount of foreign investment in the world today is based on the strategic considerations of infiltrating and controlling foreign markets, rather than merely the consideration of comparative advantages.

[8.4] Foreign investment has grown rapidly in the 1990s, in particular after 1995 when the WTO came into operation. The dismantlement of the Eastern Block and the adoption of the economic reforms by the Chinese Government have offered tremendous opportunities for foreign investors from industrialised countries. In addition, within the framework of the WTO, the members are obliged to abolish the use of the trade related investment measures (TRIMs), opening more opportunities for foreign investment within the WTO. For example, foreign direct investment (FDI):

> ... by firms into and from OECD countries set a new record in 1998. Inward investment into OECD countries reached $465 billion, representing a 71 per cent increase over 1997. Outflows also reached an unprecedented $566 billion. Growth in OECD FDI flows was driven by a number of large-scale cross-border mergers and acquisitions, particularly between American and European — often British — firms. The enthusiasm for cross-border mega-mergers among firms based in OECD countries overshadowed FDI in developing countries which continued to grow in spite of the crisis.[5]

[8.5] The rapid development of foreign investment activities across the world demands the development of an adequate set of rules governing international foreign investment. A number of international organisations, such as the OECD, UNCTAD, the IMF, MIGA and the WTO have been active in developing universal rules for foreign investment or the basic principles which provide a foundation for the future development of international investment law. OECD proposed a draft Multilateral Agreement on Investment (MAI) in 1997, which has been subject to consultation and amendments since.[6] A number of non-OECD countries have also participated in the drafting of the MAI. In May 1999, the IMF and OECD completed the Report on the Survey of Implementation of Methodological Standards for Direct Investment

---

3. For discussion, see Kreinin, *International Economics A Policy Approach*, 6th ed, Harcourt Brace Jovanovich, New York, 1992, pp 244–70.
4. For discussion, see Folsom, Gordon and Spanogle, *International Business Transactions in a Nutshell*, 4th ed, West, St Paul, Minn, 1992, pp 27–32.
5. OECD website, at <http://www.oecd.org/daf/cmis/fdi/fdi.htm>.
6. For relevant discussions, see eg G Kelley, 'Multilateral Investment Treaties: A Balanced Approach to Multinational Corporations' (2001) 39 *Colum J Transnat'l L* 483.

[8.5]   International Commercial Law

(SIMSDI),[7] which involved data from 114 counties. UNCTAD has done a number of studies on foreign investment. One of such recent examples is the Comprehensive Study of the Interrelationship between Foreign Direct Investment (FDI) and Foreign Portfolio Investment (FPI), completed on 23 June 1996.[8] In addition, the WTO has kept a constant review of its members' foreign investment law and policies under the Agreement on Trade Related Investment Measures, which is to be examined later in this chapter: see **[8.73]–[8.82]**.

[8.6] This chapter purports to provide a broad introduction to the current state and development of foreign investment in the world. It will first examine a number of theoretical issues affecting the foundation of the foreign investment law. Then, it will investigate more recent developments in the international regulation of foreign investment, by examining the draft Multinational Investment Agreement and the Agreement on Trade Related Investment Measures. The efforts of a number of international organisations, such as the OECD, IMF and UNCTAD, to develop international rules of foreign investment law, will also be reviewed.

Explaining foreign investment

[8.7] Foreign investment is commonly classified into two categories: foreign direct investment (FDI) or foreign portfolio investment (FPI). At least this is the popular classification adopted by world countries today. FDI (which may also be referred to as DFI, or direct foreign investment) is defined by UNCTAD as a:

> category of international investment in which a resident entity in one economy obtains a lasting interest in an enterprise resident in another. A lasting interest implies the existence of a long-term relationship between the direct investor and the enterprise and a significant degree of influence by the investor on the management of the enterprise.[9]

This definition is similar to what was adopted by the International Monetary Fund (IMF) in the 1970s, when IMF defined a foreign investment as an 'investment that is made to acquire a lasting interest in an enterprise operating in an economy other than that of the investor, the investor's purpose being to have an effective voice in the management of the enterprise'.[10] FPI can be understood as including 'a variety of instruments which are *traded (or tradeable)* in organised and other financial markets: bonds, equities and money market instruments. The IMF even includes derivatives or secondary instruments, such as options, in the category of FPI.'[11] Thus, FPI can be broadly defined as an investment activity carried out in the stockmarket or other financial markets for the purpose of making profits from share transactions or the share holding itself, rather than obtaining a lasting interest in the issuer of the shares or instruments traded on the market. Following

---

7. The text of the report is available at <http://www.oecd.org/daf/cmis/fdi/method.htm>.
8. The text of the report is available at <http://www.unctad.org/en/special/special.htm>.
9. UNCTAD, 'Foreign Portfolio Investment (FPI) and Foreign Direct Investment (FDI): Characteristics, similarities, and complementarities and differences, policy implications and development impact', 15 April 1999, para 5, available at <http://www.unctad.org/en/special/special.htm>.
10. IMF, *Balance of Payment Manual*, 1977, p 136.
11. UNCTAD, note 9 above, para 6.

this definition, technically, an FPI activity may become an FDI activity if the investor exercises certain options granted in the instruments to become a shareholder of the issuer to hold voting power, for example, by way of merger and acquisition. The differences between FDI and FPI for the time being have academic implications only. Their technical differences in law are yet to be developed, if this is necessary for the development of a uniform foreign investment law across the world.

[8.8] 'Foreign investment' in international commercial law refers to FDI and FPI as well as any other form, such as transfer of technology or countertrade, which has not amounted to the control of any lasting interest in the local enterprise, made by a foreign person, either natural or legal, within the territory of a host country.

There are two essential features of a foreign investment:

- First, the investor is not a citizen of the country where the investment is made.
- Second, the investment activity is not a mere act of sale of goods, or supply of services, between parties from different countries, although an international sale may be part of a foreign investment activity. A foreign investment must involve ongoing operations, in the form of either FDI or FPI, in a foreign country.

[8.9] In summary, foreign investment means a foreigner investing in, or carrying on, a business within a host country and competing with local industries or local investors in either the domestic or international markets. In a broader sense, foreign investment also extends to an investment made by nationals of the host country in a foreign country. The concept of foreign investment itself is based on the identity of the investor or the origin of the capital or technology used as the 'investment' (if the investor is unknown). Identity is largely decided by the nationality of the investor. There are many instances where a person has to acquire a local nationality to meet the legal requirement for merging with or taking over a local company before the merger or takeover can be approved by the relevant government authority.

Relationships between foreign investment and host country

[8.10] Foreign investment is a complicated form of international commerce. Foreign investment law is thus a complex area of international commercial law. It involves conflict of interests between host states and local industries (local party) on the one hand, and the foreign investors and foreign governments (foreign party) on the other, because of the disparity between the economic powers of the foreign party and the local party as well as inevitable struggles between them to gain the power to control local economies in order to increase security for their own future. No doubt, local economies need injection of foreign capital and technology, and human society needs international cooperation by way of investment to gain the highest possible speed of economic development. On the other hand, undeniably, foreign investment is capable of destroying a local economy in a situation where a sacrifice of the other is the price for its own survival. Most Asian countries which suffered badly in the 1997 Asian financial crisis have blamed foreign speculators (investors) for manipulating and attacking local financial systems. Indeed, the notion of free market hangs on a very fine balance of local restrictions on foreign investment within the context of foreign investment. No country has offered totally free or totally unrestricted access to foreign investors, who are capable of destroying, manipulating or controlling a local economy as much as they are capable of building or strengthening a local economy. No politician will place the fate of a country at the mercy of powerful foreign investors. There is an inherent dilemma in the love–hate relationship that exists between foreign investors and the local government.

[8.11] The policy of trade protectionism is, in most circumstances, based on concern for the growth of local industries and employment, although sometimes a government protects a local industry merely for strategic considerations, whether economic, political or military. The 'national security' consideration in Japanese foreign investment law is an example. The importation of foreign products may destroy certain local industries and consequently reduce the level of employment. However, the 'import' of foreign capital, which is not readily available in the domestic market, into local industries often does not directly reduce the level of local employment, unless a rationalisation immediately follows the foreign takeover of the target company. In addition, the 'import' of foreign capital is usually accompanied by the importation of advanced foreign technology and skills which are not readily available in the domestic market. The advantages of foreign investment are the rational bases for a host country to accept foreign investment.

[8.12] Foreign investment also has detrimental effects on a local economy. Because foreign investment is a vehicle for infiltrating local markets, a foreign investor often succeeds at the expense of a local competitor. This may eventually result in partial or total control of a local market by foreign investors, a consequence which would be desperately avoided by independent countries for political and economic reasons. Thus, foreign investment is both welcome and restricted in all countries, although the levels of restrictions vary depending on the individual need for foreign investment.

[8.13] The relationships between foreign investment and a host country can be summed up as follows:
- foreign investment is a means of overcoming trade barriers existing between the investing and invested countries;
- foreign investment often provides finance and advanced technology urgently needed by the host country, which may have to take the risk of allowing foreign control of certain domestic industries;
- foreign investment may improve a local industry's international competitiveness by injecting foreign capital and technology, but may also destroy local competition in the domestic market by using its financial and technological advantages;
- foreign investment may strengthen local industries and increase local employment, but may also take control of local economies, which would be regarded as a risk by most countries for strategic and political reasons; and
- foreign investment may make positive contributions to a local economy, but may also put the future of the local economy in doubt by remitting large profits overseas and manipulating the local market in accordance with its needs, a point which has been made constantly by nationalists against foreign control of the local economy.

[8.14] Both international foreign investment law and domestic foreign investment law in each country are developed on the basis of the abovementioned considerations. These laws reflect the balance and compromise operating between the different interests. On the one hand, a foreign investor seeks legal protection and guarantee in local law when investing in a particular country; on the other, a host government seeks control of the foreign investment to the extent it regards appropriate.

Forms of foreign investment

Defining the forms of foreign investment

[8.15] Forms of foreign investment can be classified under different criteria. For example, an investment can be either a portfolio or a direct investment, depending on whether the investor controls the business operation of the invested company. By reference to the parties involved, an investment can also be classed as either a joint venture or a solely foreign owned venture, depending on whether the foreign investor has a legal right to carry on the business in his or her own right. By reference to the particular method by which an investment is introduced into a host country, a foreign investment can be regarded as either a proposal to establish a new business or a proposal to take or acquire interests in an existing business. Classifications may also be made by referring to the legal relationships between a foreign investor and a local company, for example, a franchising agreement or a parent–subsidiary relationship; or by referring to the legal status of a particular company — a 'foreign company' means a company established under a foreign law and a 'foreign-controlled Australian company' is a company established under Australian law but controlled by foreign investments.

[8.16] 'Forms of foreign investment' in this chapter means the forms or vehicles by which a foreign investment is carried out or made.[12] The forms so identified are not meant to be exclusive or exhaustive and may overlap with each other in certain circumstances. The forms of foreign investment are intended to be a survey of the basic means of effecting foreign investment, and an introduction to the terminology describing these means, which we are likely to encounter in dealing with the issues of foreign investment law.

Multinational corporations

[8.17] The expressions 'multinational corporations', 'multinational companies', 'transnational companies or corporations' or 'multinational enterprises' are synonymous. They refer to 'all enterprises which control assets — factories, mines, sales offices and the like — in two or more countries'.[13] The key indicator of a multinational corporation is its ability to control its subsidiaries in various countries. If a company is able to control, either directly or indirectly, its subsidiaries in different countries, it can be regarded as a

---

12. For a comprehensive description of 'investment', see art II.2 of draft MAI (as of 24 April 1998), available at <http://www.oecd.org/>.
13. Ryan, *International Trade Law*, Law Book Co, Sydney, 1975, p 364.

[8.17]

multinational company. Direct control is when the overseas subsidiaries do not have autonomy or independent decision-making power. Indirect control of a local company by a multinational company is when the local company exists in its own right but is wholly or substantially controlled by the multinational company. The multinational company's liability can be restricted to the assets of the local company. The expression 'multinational corporation' indicates a controlling relationship between a parent company and its subsidiaries, branches or controlled companies.[14] In comparison, the OECD defines 'multinational enterprises' as 'companies or other entities established in more than one country and so linked that they may co-ordinate their operations in various ways. While one or more of these entities may be able to exercise a significant influence over the objectives of others, their degree of autonomy within the enterprise may vary widely from one multinational enterprise to another'.[15] This definition emphasises the connection, rather than the control, between different national operations or establishments of the same multinational enterprise.

[8.18] The multinational company is a popular form of foreign investment because of the advantages deriving from this type of business operation. In 2001, the total number of transnational corporations (TNCs) 'exceeded 60,000, with more than 800,000 foreign affiliates'.[16] Bearing in mind that two important purposes of foreign investment are to infiltrate foreign markets and utilise foreign resources, a multinational company is an ideal vehicle for such purposes. This is because, first, a multinational company is able to provide the much needed capital and technology to establish a competitive position in a given market; and second, a multinational company is able to rationalise the use of any given market by its established global marketing power. In addition, a multinational corporation is also capable of utilising most efficiently its capital or resources (to take advantage of taxation law or hedge foreign exchange risks, for example) by moving them to a country where the foreign investment climate is more favourable for its current or future goals. Thus, it is no surprise that the multinational company has become a dominant form of foreign investment today.[17]

Joint ventures

[8.19] 'Joint venture' refers to a particular form of foreign investment, although the term is also used in domestic investment. In the context of foreign investment, it means that the invested project is jointly owned by foreign and local investors. It 'connotes an association of persons for the purposes of particular trading, commercial, mining or financial undertaking or endeavour with a view to mutual benefit',[18] with each participant contributing to the venture in the form of money, property, skill or technology. A joint

---

14. There are no universal definitions of 'subsidiary' and 'controlled company', and the two concepts may overlap with each other in certain circumstances.
15. See OECD, *The OECD Guidelines for Multinational Enterprises (Revision 2000)*, pp 17–18, available at <http://www.oecd.org/>.
16. United Nations Conference on Trade and Development, *World Investment Report 2001*, p 1, available at <http://www.unctad.org/>.
17. See Folsom, Gordon and Spanogle, note 4 above, pp 27–32, and id, pp 11–17.
18. *United Dominions Corp Ltd v Brian Pty Ltd* (1985) 157 CLR 1 at 10 per Mason, Brennan and Deane JJ.

venture may take a suitable business form, such as a company, a partnership, a trust or a cooperative contract,[19] depending on the intention of the parties and the relevant domestic law. It is usually used as a device by which the host government can restrict the proportion of foreign ownership and avoid foreign control of the invested project. Sometimes it is used as a safeguard for both foreign and local investors (including the host government) in order to minimise the investment risks associated with a particular project, such as projects in exploring or for the exploitation of natural resources.

[8.20] The ownership of a joint venture in the international (rather than purely domestic) context is shared by both local and foreign investors. A venture whose ownership is jointly held by several foreign investors is regarded as a 'sole foreign investment' by the host country if there is no local interest — 'joint' refers not to the fact that there is more than one owner, but that there is local and foreign participation in the venture. Whether a foreign investor is able to control a particular venture depends on the law applicable. For example, under Australia's Foreign Investment Policy (1992), acquisitions of interests in developed non-residential commercial real estate involving more than $5 million are subject to what is called 'a fair opportunity test'.[20] Under this test, a 'foreign interest'[21] is able to acquire interests in, or control, a joint venture in the sector of developed non-residential commercial real estate, provided that the real estate has been actively marketed for at least three months or is sold by public auction or open tender. A joint venture in China, in comparison, can be controlled by a foreign investor as long as there is some amount (no minimum requirement is set out) of Chinese investment in the venture.

[8.21] 'Joint venture' and 'multinational company' may be overlapping concepts. A joint venture can be controlled by a multinational company. 'Control' is a broad concept, referring not only to direct control of voting shares, but also to the power to control a legal or natural person who holds voting shares. For example, s 10 of the Foreign Acquisitions and Takeovers Act 1975 (Cth) determines a 'subsidiary' of a corporation by the following three tests:

- if company A is in a position to control more than 50 per cent voting power in company B, company B is a subsidiary of company A;

- if company A holds more than 50 per cent voting shares in company B, company B is a subsidiary of company A; and

- if company C is a subsidiary of company B and company B is a subsidiary of company A, company C is also a subsidiary of company A.

[8.22] Since a joint venture allows the host country to have better control of foreign investment, it is favoured by developing countries, particularly in areas where national

---

19. For example, see the relevant discussions in *Balmedie Pty Ltd v Nicola Russo* [1997] FCA 467.
20. Dept of Treasury, *Australia's Foreign Investment Policy*, AGPS, Canberra, 1992, p 10.
21. *Australia's Foreign Investment Policy* (p 1) defines the expression 'foreign interest' as follows:

    ... a natural person not ordinarily resident in Australia; or any corporation, business or trust in which there is a substantial foreign interest, regardless of whether the corporation, business or trust is foreign controlled ('substantial foreign interest' refers to any holding of 15% or more by a single foreigner or any holding of 40% or more in aggregate by two or more foreigners).

security, natural resources and local living standards are major concerns. Even in a developed country like Australia, the government imposes strict controls over foreign investment in real estate, presumably in the interests of local living standards (that is, home ownership).

[8.23] In Australia, the term 'joint venture' is not exclusively used to refer to foreign investment. For example, in *United Dominions Corp Ltd v Brian Pty Ltd* (1984–85) 157 CLR 1, parties to a joint venture disagreed as to the construction of the terms of the venture. Brian sued UDC for breach of its fiduciary duty. Mason, Brennan and Deane JJ (at 10) described a 'joint venture' in the following words:

> The term 'joint venture' is not a technical one with a settled common law meaning. As a matter of ordinary language, it connotes an association of persons for the purposes of a particular trading, commercial, mining or other financial undertaking or endeavour with a view to mutual profit, with each participant usually (but not necessarily) contributing money, property or skill. Such a joint venture (or, under Scots' law, 'adventure') will often be a partnership. The term is, however, apposite to refer to a joint undertaking or activity carried out through a medium other than a partnership: such as a company, a trust, an agency or joint ownership. The borderline between what can properly be described as a 'joint venture' and what should more properly be seen as no more than a simple contractual relationship may on occasion be blurred. Thus, where one party contributes only money or other property, it may sometimes be difficult to determine whether a relationship is a joint venture in which both parties are entitled to a share of profits or a simple contract of loan or a lease under which the interest or rent payable to the party providing the money or property is determined by reference to the profits made by the other.

In Australia, in the absence of express legislative intention, what their Honours stated above is relevant for determining the existence of a joint venture. At an international level, in particular in many developing countries, the meaning of 'joint venture' is defined by domestic laws.

Sole foreign ventures

[8.24] 'Sole foreign venture' and 'wholly foreign-owned enterprise' refer to the same thing. A sole foreign venture (or enterprise), as opposed to a joint venture, is a form of foreign investment in which one or several foreign investors are allowed to carry out the invested project in their own right. The concept was created in developing countries where the right of foreigners to carry on business alone is deemed to be a privilege or a concession made by the host countries. A sole foreign venture means that a host government waives the requirement for local participation in the venture concerned. A sole foreign venture can be controlled by a multinational company.

[8.25] Since a foreign investor is allowed to carry on a business operation in his or her own right in developed countries, except in certain restricted sectors of the economy, 'sole foreign venture' as a means of foreign investment is significant only in developing countries. In these countries only can the advantages of a sole foreign venture be exploited. For example, a sole foreign venture's right to make independent business decisions in a state-controlled economy appears to be a luxury which a foreign participant in a joint venture may not have. However, a sole foreign venture in a developing country may also be excluded from certain privileges available only to a joint venture. For example, a sole foreign venture in China enjoys fewer privileges and concessions (such as a foreign exchange subsidy) than a joint venture operating in the same sector of the economy. This is because a sole foreign venture, in theory, implies a larger risk of foreign domination in a local economy than a joint venture, even if a joint venture in China may well be controlled by foreign investors.

Licensing agreements and countertrade

[8.26] Licensing agreements and countertrade are independent categories of foreign investment, but none of them has acquired a precise definition in law. Licensing in international commerce is an arrangement under which the lessee is authorised to use or develop certain intellectual property of the lessor for commercial purposes. Countertrade is an arrangement which either enables one party to fulfil his or her obligations to the other by the provision of specific goods or permits both the contracting parties to set off against each other's contractual obligations by mutual supply of goods and technology.

Countertrade has different meanings in the context of international trade or in the context of foreign investment. Both licensing agreement and countertrade can be means of international trade, if the purpose of the agreement is to sell an industrial property right or the like. Both are regarded as forms of foreign investment if the holder of the industrial property right uses the right as an investment. A contractual relationship is the basis of both the licensing agreement and countertrade. The legal distinction between them is meaningful only when the host country has provided privileges, such as tax benefits or concessions in the use of infrastructure, exclusively to one of them. When an industrial property right is sold as a form of 'goods', the seller receives payment, either in cash or products, for the right so sold. When the right is *invested* in a foreign country, the investor shares the profits from the invested project, also either in the form of cash or products. The same result can be achieved by way of either a licensing or countertrade arrangement.

[8.27] Investment made under a licensing agreement is different from investment by way of a multinational company. A licensing agreement differs from both a joint and a sole foreign venture in that the investor investing in the industrial property right normally does not have control over the operation of the company which receives the right. In terms of control, a licensing agreement made for the purpose of effecting a foreign investment is similar to a 'portfolio investment'. A licensing agreement also differs from a countertrade agreement, in that the profit in an invested project under a licensing agreement may be shared on a cash basis, although a share of products is possible. In contrast, a countertrade agreement usually means that an investor granting the industrial property right receives his or her shares from the venture in the form of products manufactured by the venture.

[8.28] A countertrade agreement is a feasible form of foreign investment, because it enables the holder of an industrial property to invest his or her right in a joint venture as a partner to the venture. It allows the holder to have better control of the right within the terms of the agreement. There is a similarity between a countertrade agreement for the purpose of sale and a countertrade agreement for the purpose of investment. In either case, the investor is paid in the form of manufactured products and goods. In most countries, a sale of industrial property rights is subject to contract law, but an investment of

[8.28]   **International Commercial Law**

the same right is subject to foreign investment law or the law governing joint ventures. The two sets of law may render substantially different privileges and benefits to the provider of the industrial property rights in certain countries. The UNCITRAL Legal Guide on International Countertrade Transactions is the only international document intended to set out uniform rules for international trading activities based on countertrade arrangements, although it is not meant to deal with the use of countertrade as a means of foreign investment specifically: see **[8.58]–[8.61]**.

Build-Operate-Transfer (BOT) projects

[8.29]   BOT is the acronym for build-operate-transfer; the former is better known worldwide than the latter. BOT is a common form of investment project and is also a concept involving project financing. BOT, as its name suggests, involves a series of activities or arrangements, comprising roughly three stages: investment, recoupment of investment and transfer of the investment project to another party. BOT is a contractual arrangement by nature. In most cases, one party to a BOT project is the government and the other is a consortium of investors. Sometimes, one party can be a private party which has acquired a specific concession or privilege to carry on a large project from a government, and the other party is the consortium. The drafting of the contract in such cases may take a lot of time because non-commercial risk in such a contract is too high. If the first party can rely on the general rules of *force majeure* to avoid liability in case of government intervention, the latter will be in a position worse than in a contract made directly with a government.

[8.30]   UNCITRAL defines BOT as follows:[22]

> BOT is essentially a form of project financing whereby a Government awards to a group of investors (hereafter referred to as 'project consortium') a concession for the development, operation, management and commercial exploitation of a particular project. The project consortium, or a company established by the project consortium (hereafter referred to as 'concessionaire', in turn, undertakes to develop the project and operate the concession in accordance with the agreement between the Government and the concessionaire (hereafter referred to as 'project agreement'). While the generic term used for this type of project is 'build-operate-transfer' (BOT), the following expressions may also be used to describe this form of project financing: 'build-own-operate' (BOO), 'build-own-operate-transfer' (BOOT), 'build-own-lease-transfer' (BOLT) and 'build-rent-transfer' (BRT). Despite the varying denomination, all these different arrangements consist of project financing schemes by which a government grants a concession to private entities undertaking to finance, carry out and manage a particular project. Similar arrangements are sometimes also used between a private licensor and a project developer.

In this arrangement, the repayments of any loans or returns on the investments made on the project is not guaranteed by the government, but depends on the revenue generated by the project. Since direct funds from the public budget are not required, the government of a country will thus experience reduced pressure of public borrowing, while allowing the transfer of the industrial risks and also of new technologies to the private sector. Furthermore, since the project is built and, during the concession period,

---

22. UNCITRAL, *Possible Future Works: Build-Operate-Transfer Projects* (Notes by the Secretariat), available at <http://www.uncitral.org/en-index.htm>.

operated by the consortium, the government gains the benefit of private sector expertise in these areas.

[8.31] BOT is commonly used for large-sized infrastructure projects, such as building highways, harbours, bridges, telecommunications networks and other public facilities. It can also be used to build smaller projects, such as a power plant or factory construction. There is no inherent prohibition, within the concept of BOT itself, against its usage for accomplishing small projects. The real problem is practicality, namely, whether it is beneficial for both parties to resort to BOT for small projects.

[8.32] The future non-commercial risk is a serious problem for a BOT project. As we have seen, BOT involves project financing. It may take a long time for the investors to recover their investment in a project. The commercial risk lies on the part of the investors, but the government must provide assurance which is free of political risks — the major concern of investors engaged in BOT projects. Assistance from MIGA may therefore be necessary in circumstances where some uncertainty exists as to the future of the project concerned. MIGA as an international authority is in a better position to deal with a government than a consortium of investors or financiers in the case of an investment dispute involving a large sum of capital.

[8.33] Presently, a BOT project is subject to the relevant domestic law, or the Washington Convention on the Settlement of Investment Disputes 1965, if the convention is applicable. The major issues relating to BOT involve the obligation of the relevant government to perform a BOT contract. Many countries are not prepared to give up their sovereignty and immunity formally in an international convention. This is true, in particular, in BOT projects which are often involved in construction and control of large infrastructures which may have strategic or national security implications to local governments. This issue is the major concern of any international regulation of BOT projects in the future.

Foreign takeovers or acquisitions

[8.34] The expression 'foreign takeover or acquisition' means that foreign investors take over or acquire interests in local companies, which have been owned or controlled by either local or foreign interests. A foreign investor may take over the whole company, or acquire only part of the shares. If a multinational company obtains control of a local company, the local company is likely to become part of the multinational company. If a foreign investor does not take over the whole company, his or her power to control the company depends on the quantity of shares acquired and the constitution (articles) of the company. The Foreign Takeovers and Acquisitions Act 1975 (Cth) applies to foreign investments made by acquiring interests in Australian companies — that is, companies established under Australian law regardless of whether or not they are controlled by Australian interests.

Foreign direct investment and portfolio investment

[8.35] The distinction between these two forms of investment is drawn by the control test. If a foreign investor obtains control of the target company as a result of the investment, the investment is a direct investment. If the investor invests only in preference shares, the investment would be regarded as a portfolio investment. 'Portfolio investment' in this context refers to the investment in the preference shares. It may also refer to investment in ordinary shares, which, however, is too small to exercise any control over the company. The boundary between a portfolio and a direct investment is often blurred. For example, several portfolio investments in ordinary shares may in aggregate enable the investor to obtain control of the invested company. A direct investment under which a foreign investor holds a controlling interest may become a portfolio investment if the investor loses the controlling power, for example, as a result of an acquisition by another shareholder or the issue of new shares in the company. A host country normally does not restrict foreign portfolio investments (particularly in non-voting preference shares), but is likely to impose various restrictions on direct foreign investments.

International legal framework for foreign investment

International efforts to regulate foreign investment

[8.36] Foreign investment, in particular foreign investment carried out in the form of multinational enterprises (MNEs) or transnational corporations (TNCs), has increasingly attracted world attention.[23]

The major legal issues arising from the operation of this type of foreign investment are as follows:

- a host country may feel the need to regulate the conduct of multinational corporations; but
- a capital-exporting country may feel the need to protect its nationals' interests for the purpose of promoting its overseas investment and trade.

The different preferences of the host country and the investing country, as well as the industrialised country and the developing country, are fully reflected in the draft MAI, which contains numerous footnotes recording diversifying views of the participating countries on almost every provision of the draft.

[8.37] A number of regulatory efforts have been made by the OECD, and certain UN or non-UN bodies, such as the IMF, UNCTAD, International Labour Organisation (ILO) and the United Nations Economic and Social Council (UNECOSCO), the International Chamber of Commerce (ICC) and the World Bank, and recently by the WTO. The major documents representing these efforts are as follows:[24]

- ICC International Code of Fair Treatment for Foreign Investments, 1949;

---

23. For example, United Nations Department of Economic and Social Development, *World Investment Report 1992: Transnational Corporations as Engines of Growth* and *Formulation and Implementation of Foreign Investment Policies*, United Nations, New York, 1992; OECD, *Structure and Organisation of Multinational Enterprises* (1987) and *The OECD Declaration and Decisions on International Investment and Multinational Enterprises: 1991 Review* (1992), OECD, Paris.
24. For discussion, see Tschofen, 'Multilateral Approaches to the Treatment of Foreign Investment' in Shihata, *Legal Treatment of Foreign Investment*, Martinus Nijhoff, Dordrecht, 1993, pp 268–9.

- ICC Guidelines for International Investments, 1972;
- OECD Declaration and Guidelines for Multinational Enterprises, 2000;
- ILO Tripartite Declaration of Principles concerning Multinational Enterprises and Social Policy, 2000;
- OECD Declaration on International Investment and Multinational Enterprises 2000;
- OECD Guidelines for Multinational Enterprises 2000, which are technically an annex to the OECD Declaration on International Investment and Multinational Enterprises but can be regarded as an independent document because of their direct impact on the activity of multinational companies;
- Convention Establishing the Multinational Investment Guarantee Agency 1985;[25]
- World Bank Draft Guidelines on the Treatment of Foreign Direct Investment, 1992;
- UNCITRAL Legal Guide on International Countertrade Transactions, published by UNCITRAL in 1993;[26]
- GATT Agreement on Trade-Related Investment Measures (TRIMs), 1993; and
- OECD draft Multilateral Agreement on Investment, distributed for consultation on 13 January 1998.[27]

Most of these documents are 'guidelines', which are accepted and voluntarily applied by the parties. However, the Agreement on Trade-Related Investment Measures, established by the GATT members in the 1993 Uruguay Round negotiations, is binding between the members of the WTO. The Agreement on TRIMs is to be discussed later in this chapter: see **[8.73]–[8.82]**.

The OECD Declaration

Structure of the OECD Declaration

[8.38] The Organisation for Economic Cooperation and Development (OECD) presently has 29 members, including Australia, Austria, Belgium, Canada, the Czech Republic, Denmark, Finland, France, Germany, Greece, Hungary, Iceland, Ireland, Italy, Japan, Korea, Luxembourg, Mexico, the Netherlands, New Zealand, Norway, Poland, Portugal, Spain, Sweden, Switzerland, Turkey, the United Kingdom and the United States. It was established in 1960 for the purpose of promoting policies designed to achieve the highest sustainable economic growth and employment and a rising standard of living of the population. This goal of OECD is set out in art 1 of the convention establishing OECD. In comparison with any other international organisation, OECD has been the leader in the regulation of foreign investment through

---

25. As June 2000, MIGA had 157 members, including 22 industralised countries and 135 developing countries. In addition, 12 countries were in the process of fulfilling membership requirements.
26. The legal guide was adopted by UNCITRAL in its 25th session between 4–22 May 1992 in New York. It is not a treaty or a model law. Instead, the goal of UNCITRAL is to have the legal guide endorsed by the General Assembly of UN and to promote its use by private parties in UN members.
27. This is the first comprehensive effort to regulate foreign investment at an international level. The Agreement on TRIMs, as we will see, regulates only limited aspects of foreign investment law and policy of a WTO member.

[8.38]

international cooperation between countries. It has also been a pioneer in testing feasible approaches to the regulation of foreign investment at an international level.

[8.39] The OECD Declaration on International Investment and Multinational Enterprises was first adopted in 1976. The present version of the Declaration was adopted on 27 June 2000.[28] It has so far been the only formally adopted international instrument on multinational enterprises which has some impact on MNEs. Presently, the Declaration consists of two major parts: the declaration and two annexes; and the Decisions of the OECD Council. The first part is the Declaration itself, which includes two annexes: the Guidelines for Multinational Enterprises and the General Considerations and Practical Approaches concerning Conflicting Requirements Imposed on Multinational Enterprises. The second part is composed of various decisions concerning procedural issues, implementing rules and interpretations of specific concepts of the Declaration. The Council's decisions which constitute part of the OECD Declaration currently include decisions in four areas: guidelines for multinational enterprises, national treatment, conflicting requirements, and international investment incentives and disincentives.

[8.40] The rationale for adopting the OECD Declaration is set out in the preamble of the OECD Declaration. The increasing importance of foreign investment to the development of national economies of the OECD countries; the crucial role played by multinational enterprises in this investment process; the need to strengthen cooperation between the members for the purpose of improving the foreign investment climate, encouraging the positive contributions of the multinational enterprises to economic and social progress, minimising and resolving difficulties arising from various operations of multinational enterprises, are the major considerations underlying the adoption of the declaration.[29] In addition, the adhering governments of the Declaration have hoped that continuing endeavours to regulate foreign investment and to intensify the cooperation between them for the purpose of regulating foreign investment and MNEs would lead to further international arrangements and agreements in the field of foreign investment. These considerations led to the creation of the OECD Declaration.

[8.41] A 'declaration' in international law is different from an international treaty or agreement, in that it may or may not impose legal obligations upon the parties to the declaration. Generally speaking, a declaration is often used to declare principles, rather than specified rules, governing a particular matter. It imposes broadly legal or moral obligations upon the parties and declares the parties' intention to deal with a particular matter in accordance with the principles of the declaration. It has binding force if the parties state so expressly. It may also give the parties an option as to whether or not to accept the principles so declared.[30] The OECD Declaration may be binding if the members so choose. For example, the adhering governments have undertaken to accord national treatment to MNEs operating within their territories (art II of the OECD Declaration).

---

28. Besides 29 OECD members, Argentina, Brazil, Chile and the Slovak Republic are also members of the Declaration.
29. Preamble to the OECD Declaration.
30. For example, see Brownlie, 'Legal Effects of Codes of Conduct for MNEs: Commentary' in Horn (ed), *Legal Problems of Codes of Conduct for Multinational Enterprises*, Kluwer, Deventer, 1980, pp 39–43.

This obligation has been reinforced by the 1991 OECD Decision on National Treatment, under which OECD members undertake to be bound by certain procedures to ensure the implementation of national treatment. The Guidelines for MNEs which are attached to the declaration are not binding, and are implemented voluntarily.

Principles of the OECD Declaration

[8.42] The OECD Declaration itself is a fairly simple statement, which contains six articles. Each article has a different emphasis and part of the articles contain sub-provisions. The OECD Declaration declares a number of principles as follows:[31]

I. Guidelines for multinational enterprises: The adhering governments jointly recommend to multinational enterprises operating in their territories the observance of the Guidelines as set forth in Annex 1 hereto having regard to the considerations and understandings which introduce the Guidelines and are an integral part of them.

II. National treatment:

1. The adhering governments should, consistent with their needs to maintain public order, to protect their essential security interests and to fulfil commitments relating to international peace and security, accord to enterprises operating in their territories and owned or controlled directly or indirectly by nationals of another member country (hereinafter referred to as 'Foreign-Controlled Enterprises') treatment under their laws, regulations and administrative practices, consistent with international law and no less favourable than that accorded in like situations to domestic enterprises (hereinafter referred to as 'National Treatment');
2. The adhering governments will consider applying 'National Treatment' in respect of countries other than adhering governments;
3. The members will endeavour to ensure that their territorial subdivisions apply 'National Treatment';
4. This Declaration does not deal with the right of members to regulate the entry of foreign investment or the conditions of establishment of foreign enterprises.

III. Conflicting requirements: The members will co-operate with a view to avoiding or minimising the imposition of conflicting requirements on multinational enterprises and that they will take into account the general considerations and practical approaches as set forth in Annex 2 hereto;

IV. International investment incentives and disincentives:

1. The adhering governments recognise the need to strengthen their co-operation in the field of international direct investment;
2. The adhering governments thus recognise the need to give due weight to the interests of members affected by specific laws, regulations and administrative practices in this field (hereinafter called 'measures') providing official incentives and disincentives to international direct investment;
3. The adhering governments will endeavour to make such measures as transparent as possible, so that their importance and purpose can be ascertained and that information on them can be readily available.

V. Consultation Procedures: The adhering governments are prepared to consult one another on the above matters in conformity with the relevant Decisions of the Council.

VI. Review: The adhering governments agree to review the above matters periodically with a view to improving the effectiveness of international economic co-operation among adhering governments on issues relating to international investment and multinational enterprises.

[8.43] The OECD Declaration can be construed as follows:

- First, its existence suggests that the member countries agreed that legal issues arising from foreign investment between them need to be dealt with collectively.

---

31. The following is an edited version of the articles of the Declaration.

[8.43]   **International Commercial Law**

- Second, it sets out national treatment, subject to national interest considerations, as the basis of regulating foreign investment within each member.

- Third, it implies that a preferable method for controlling foreign investment within each country is the use of incentives and disincentives. This can be compared with direct restrictions on foreign investment based on the nationality of the investors.

- Fourth, it emphasises that conflicts between capital-importing and capital-exporting countries and further regulation of foreign investment at an international level should be resolved by a consultation approach, suggesting the acceptance of the collective approach as the preferable means of regulating foreign investment.

- Last, but not least, it recommends a 'guideline' (code of conduct) to be used to regulate MNEs operating within member countries. This is very important, because these guidelines represent a uniform law or set of principles governing foreign investment among member countries. Self-regulation by MNEs in pursuance of the guidelines also represents an alternative approach to the regulation of foreign investment.

The OECD Guidelines for Multinational Enterprises

[8.44] The present OECD Guidelines for Multinational Enterprises were adopted in June 2000. They recommend a number of measures or principles to be adopted by MNEs operating within the territories of members of the Declaration (see **[8.38]–[8.43]**). The major obligations of the Guidelines can be summarised as follows:

- **General policy:** The Guidelines require MNEs to take fully into account the established policies of the countries in which they operate, and to consider the views of other stakeholders. Eleven broad categories of obligation, such as contributions to sustainable development, respect for human rights, practice of good corporate governance principles and abstaining from improper involvement in local policitical activities, are imposed to ensure an MNE respects and cooperates with the law and policy of a host country.

- **Disclosure of information:** The Guidelines require MNEs to disclose to a host country the information required to be disclosed under the national law of the host country. In addition, MNEs are expected to apply high quality standards for disclosure, accounting and audit to ensure full disclosure. This obligation, if accepted, means that an MNE should take an active role in facilitating communications between its offices and the general public of a host country. The obligation is necessary because an MNE can easily take advantage of its multinational operation to circumvent local laws and regulations which require disclosure of certain information.

- **Employment and industrial relations:** The Guidelines require MNEs to comply with host countries' employment and labour laws and to improve labour relations with local employees. MNEs are also required to adopt adequate training programs for their local employees.

- **Environmental protection:** The Guidelines require MNEs to comply with local environmental legislation and to take an active role in minimising and reducing environmental risks in their business operations.

- **Combating bribery:** The Guidelines require MNEs not to directly or indirectly offer, promise, give or demand a bribe or other undue advantage in their business operations.

- **Consumer interests:** The Guidelines require MNEs to act in accordance with fair business, marketing and advertising practices, and to take all reasonable steps to ensure the safety and quality of the goods and services they provide when dealing with consumers.

- **Science and technology:** The Guidelines require MNEs to comply with host countries' policies on scientific and technological developments. They encourage MNEs to transfer their technology to local companies wherever possible.

- **Competition:** The Guidelines require MNEs operating in OECD countries to undertake not to breach or circumvent the competition law (for example, restrictive trade practices law) of host countries.

- **Taxation:** The Guidelines require MNEs to cooperate with the tax laws of host countries. There is at least a moral obligation on an MNE not to circumvent local tax laws by taking advantage of its status.

The Guidelines represent the principles which the adhering governments hope MNEs will comply with. They do not impose any concrete obligations upon MNEs, nor are they enforceable at a court of law, but they convey the expected standards for MNEs' operations. They have made some contribution to the development of foreign investment within the OECD.[32]

The general considerations and practical approaches

[8.45] The General Considerations and Practical Approaches Concerning Conflicting Requirements Imposed On Multinational Enterprises comprises annex 2 to the OECD Declaration. It provides guidelines for the members of the Declaration to avoid conflicts between laws made for the purpose of implementing the Declaration and regulating multinational enterprises in their domestic law. The so-called general considerations are the principles a member is expected to follow when regulating foreign investment in its law. The following general considerations have been set out in the document:

> In contemplating new legislation, action under existing legislation or other exercise of jurisdiction which may conflict with the legal requirements or established policies of another member and lead to conflicting requirements being imposed on multinational enterprises, the member concerned should:
>
> (a) Have regard to relevant principles of international law;
>
> (b) Endeavour to avoid or minimise such conflicts and the problems to which they give rise by following an approach of moderation and restraint, respecting and accommodating the interests of other members;

---

32. For discussions on the regulation and development of foreign investment within the OECD, see, for example, OECD, *The OECD Guidelines in a Globalising World*, distributed on 17 February 1999; *The Recent Experience with Capital Flows to Emerging Market Economies* (Economics Department Working Papers No 211); *Foreign Direct Investment and the Environment: An Overview of the Literature* (Dec 1997); and *The OECD Guidelines for Multinational Enterprises* (Discussion Paper, Dec 1997); available at <http://www.oecd.org>.

(c) Take fully into account the sovereignty and legitimate economic, law enforcement and other interests of other members;

(d) Bear in mind the importance of permitting the observance of contractual obligations and the possible adverse impact of measures having a retroactive effect.

Members should endeavour to promote co-operation as an alternative to unilateral action to avoid or minimise conflicting requirements and problems arising therefrom. Members should on request consult one another and endeavour to arrive at mutually acceptable solutions to such problems.

[8.46] The general considerations are meant to improve cooperation between the members and avoid multinational enterprises being placed under conflicting requirements imposed by different members, which make the operation of the enterprises impossible. In order to implement these general considerations, the members have agreed on a number of practical approaches, which are in fact the agreed methods or techniques for resolving any conflicts or potential conflicts between the members. These approaches are set out as follows:

Members recognise that in the majority of circumstances, effective co-operation may best be pursued on a bilateral basis. On the other hand, there may be cases where the multilateral approach could be more effective.

Members should therefore be prepared to:

(a) Develop mutually beneficial, practical and appropriately safeguarded bilateral arrangements, formal or informal, for notification to and consultation with other members;

(b) Give prompt and sympathetic consideration to requests for notification and bilateral consultation on an ad hoc basis made by any member which considers that its interests may be affected by a measure of the type referred to under paragraph 1 above, taken by another member country with which it does not have such bilateral arrangements;

(c) Inform the other concerned members as soon as practicable of new legislation or regulations proposed by their governments for adoption which have significant potential for conflict with the legal requirements or established policies of other members and for giving rise to conflicting requirements being imposed on multinational enterprises;

(d) Give prompt and sympathetic consideration to requests by other members for consultation in the Committee on International Investment and Multinational Enterprises or through other mutually acceptable arrangements. Such consultations would be facilitated by notification at the earliest stage practicable;

(e) Give prompt and full consideration to proposals which may be made by other members in any such consultations that would lessen or eliminate conflicts.

By signing the OECD Declaration, a member is obliged to comply with all requirements set out in the Declaration. The General Considerations and Practical Approaches discussed in this subsection are part of the Declaration and must be implemented by the members. In order to avoid confusion or conflicts between the different obligations, members have agreed that the General Considerations and Practical Approaches do not apply to those aspects of restrictive business practices or other matters which are the subject of existing OECD arrangements.

Decisions of the Council

[8.47] The Decisions of the Council presently consist of four decisions: the decision on national contact points; the decision on national treatment; the decision on conflicting requirements; and the decision on international investment incentives and disincentives. The four decisions are directly related to the OECD Declaration and its annexes. For example, national contact points are needed to co-ordinate the implementation of the

Guidelines. National treatment is the principle set out in art II of the Declaration. The international investment incentives and disincentives are set out in art IV of the Declaration. The conflicting requirements are set out in art III of the Declaration and annex 2 to the Declaration. These show clearly the connections between the Declaration and the decisions. The four decisions are examined briefly below.

[8.48] The role of National Contact Points is to further the effectiveness of the Guidelines. The Decision on National Contact Points (NCP) requires members of the Declaration to make institutional arrangements for the operation of the NCP. Generally speaking, NCPs should operate in accordance with core criteria of visibility, accessibility, transparency and accountability to further the objective of functional equivalence. NCPs are obliged to provide information on the Guidelines and facilitate discussions on various issues concerning the implementation of the Guidelines.

[8.49] The Decision on National Treatment sets out a number of procedural requirements or rules for the purpose of implementing national treatment in foreign investment matters. First, there is a notification requirement, which requires a member to notify the Council of any exceptions to the national treatment principle in its domestic law. Second, there is an examination process under which the Council has power to examine the exceptions lodged by a member to see whether it is justified and reasonable. Third, a member is entitled to report to the Council about any measures adopted by another member, which, in the view of the former, is discriminatory or inconsistent with the principle of national treatment. These three rules ensure that the Council is able to monitor a member's sufficient compliance with the principle of national treatment.

[8.50] The decision on conflicting requirements is intended to implement principles for the avoidance and resolution of conflicting requirements, which may be imposed upon MNEs by the members the Declaration. The decision requires the members to consult with each other and also to consult with the Committee on International Investment and Multinational Enterprises to avoid, minimise and resolve conflicts. In fact, the decision sets out two procedures for avoiding or resolving conflicts between the requirements of the members: first, consultation between the members; second, consultation through the committee. In formally adopting the procedures, the members of the Declaration hope that inconsistencies and conflicts between their laws and policies on foreign investment can be avoided, minimised and resolved.

[8.51] The Decision on International Investment Incentives and Disincentives is meant to control the procedural aspects for the use of incentives and disincentives, which are the permissible means for the control of foreign investment within the members of the Declaration. The obligation of the members is to make these measures transparent. The decision requires the members to consult with each other when the use of a particular measure may affect the interest of another member and to provide necessary information to each other for the members to assess the impact of a measure or measures adopted by another member. The committee also plays a consultative role in the coordinating matters relating to the use of incentives and disincentives.

[8.52] We can see from the discussions above that the decisions are actually the agreed approaches, methods, techniques and procedures for the members of the Declaration to follow to ensure the implementation of the Declaration. Most of them are designed to promote communications between the members, and all of them are related to the Committee on International Investment and Multinational Enterprises, which has played an important role in the development of new ideas and principles for the regulation and promotion of foreign investment within the OECD. The members have an obligation to follow the stipulated procedures for dealing with issues falling within the scope of the four decisions.

The Multilateral Agreement on Investment

[8.53] The draft Multinational Agreement on Investment (MAI) was distributed on 13 January 1997 for consultation among OECD members and a number of non-members. Another draft was finalised on 22 April 1998. This draft contains more than 140 pages, covering a wide range of issues relating to foreign investment, such as treatment of foreign investors and investments, investment protection and dispute settlement. Records of the negotiation group suggest difficulties in the negotiation of an agreement of such a nature.[33]

The purpose of establishing the MAI is to ensure uniformity, fairness, transparency and predictability in the regulation of foreign investment. Setting out any universal standards for regulating foreign investment is a highly controversial task if the standards impose certain obligations upon the contracting countries to grant foreign investment specific rights or concessions. On the other hand, transparency does not directly impose much obligation upon the contracting countries to grant any particular privilege or concession, but requires the contracting countries to make their investment laws and policies accessible to the public. The transparency requirement places a pressure on a government which practises certain measures which are not consistent with the basic principles for regulating foreign investment as agreed by the contracting countries. Thus, transparency may be an alternative approach for the countries to agree on certain highly controversial issues arising from the regulation of foreign investment.

[8.54] The draft MAI as completed in April 1998 appears to be a comprehensive document, covering a wide range of aspects of foreign investment law. The draft includes both the consolidated text of the MAI and commentary made by OECD members and non-member countries. The structure of the MAI as suggested by the 1998 draft can be described as follows:

- There are general provisions dealing with various preliminary matters, such as scope and application of the MAI; and definitions of the relevant concepts, such as 'investor',[34] and 'investment'.[35]

---

33. See the website of the OECD for relevant information, at <http://www.oecd.org/>.
34. Under the draft MAI, an investor can be either a natural or a legal person established under a law of a contracting country.
35. Under the draft MAI, investment refers to every kind of asset owned by or controlled directly or indirectly by an investor, including, for example, an enterprise or business, shares, stocks, bonds or derivatives arising from them, contractual rights, claims to money or performance, intellectual property rights, concessions or privileges, and any other tangible or intangible property.

- There are basic principles for the treatment of foreign investment. The basic principles are national treatment, most favoured national treatment (MFN), and transparency of law and policy. There are also provisions concerning employment requirements, performance requirements, privatisation, investment incentives and environment protection.
- There are special provisions for regulating financial services. For example, prudential measures may be allowed as requirements for the operation of financial services. The principle of national treatment demands the same prudential measures apply to both foreign and local investments, unless an exception to the principle can be justified. Key personnel of foreign investment companies may be given special considerations and privileges in the MAI to facilitate the operation of MNEs.
- There may be provisions regulating the corporate practices of MNEs. These provisions may have implications to domestic company laws and are not easy to formulate.
- There are provisions on investment protection, largely dealing with the general principles for treating foreign investment, which overlap with the basic principles mentioned earlier, and the issues of expropriation and compensation which are the traditional issues of foreign investment law. The right to transfer currency across national borders was regarded as a protection to the investors. Certain other rights, such as the right of subrogation in insurance matters and the rights of a foreign investor based on other international agreements may be covered by the MAI.
- There are special provisions on dispute settlement. Generally speaking, disputes can be divided into two types: state–state, and investor–state. For the first type, the contracting countries are encouraged to resolve their disputes by way of consultation, conciliation, mediation, and arbitration. For the second type, litigation at a domestic court and arbitration were recommended. Of course, the parties can always resolve their differences by way of negotiation and mediation.
- There are provisions on exceptions and safeguards. Such provisions are necessary in most international conventions to accommodate the special needs of members.
- There are provisions regulating the taxation of foreign investment. These provisions set out a number of principles when taxation of foreign investment arises as an issue of foreign investment law in a contracting country.
- There are also provisions dealing with the relationships between the proposed MAI and other relevant international conventions. Such provisions are necessary to avoid conflicts between the international obligations of a member.
- There are final provisions to deal with various incidental issues, such as signature, ratification, accession and denunciation of the convention by the members.
- There are a number of annexes attached to the MAI. They contain specific proposals from negotiating countries and the chair of the negotiating group on various issues covered by the draft.

[8.55] The regulation of foreign investment at an international level is a difficult and controversial task. First, it is difficult to decide what should be regulated. For example, freedom to transfer money internationally is not an issue for most industrialised countries

[8.55] which have adopted the policy of free economy, but is a serious problem in the developing countries and less developed countries which rely heavily on the administrative control of transfer of funds to stabilise the local economy. Similarly, company and taxation matters should not be covered in an international convention on foreign investment if national treatment is one of the basic principles of the agreement. Under the principle of national treatment, such matters should be subject to the relevant domestic law. Second, it is also difficult to have a consensus on how to regulate. Negotiating countries may expect or favour different standards in the regulation and protection of foreign investment. The commentary and annexes attached to the 1998 draft of the MAI represent such differences and difficulties.

[8.56] Should the MAI impose specific obligations upon the contracting parties to satisfy the minimum standards for foreign investment, or should it only set out certain procedural requirements to ensure the transparency of the domestic law on foreign investment? If the minimum standards are preferred, what are the minimum standards then? Can foreign investment be regulated in the same way as the import and export of goods under GATT by setting out specific rules of control? Obtaining consensus on these issues is very difficult because the interests of foreign investors and capital exporting countries on one hand, and the interests of local investors and host countries on the other, are in competition with each and the balance between them is constantly changing. It is very difficult to regulate such matters in a law which is supposed to be more stable and transparent than policy. The difficulties in the regulation of foreign investment at an international level can be seen in the commentary of the participating countries attached to the 1998 draft MAI. These difficulties have resulted in the slow progress in the drafting of the MAI since 1997.

[8.57] The OECD's efforts provide valuable experiences for world countries, in particular WTO members. Given the sensitivity and complexity of the issues, it is more likely that an international convention setting out a number of general principles for the protection and promotion of foreign investment worldwide will be made before a comprehensive code setting out rules for many specific issues can be accepted by most countries of the world.

The Legal Guide on International Countertrade Transactions

[8.58] The UNCITRAL Legal Guide on International Countertrade Transactions was adopted by UNCITRAL in May 1992 and published by UNCITRAL in 1993. The legal guide does not have any binding effect, but provides guiding principles for parties engaged in countertrade transactions, which are given a very broad meaning in the legal guide. For example, an excerpt of the legal guide prepared by UNCITRAL states as follows:[36]

> Countertrade transactions covered by the Legal Guide are those transactions in which one party supplies goods, services, technology or other economic value to the second party, and, in return, the first party purchases from the second party an agreed amount of goods, services, technology or

---

36. See Chapter I. Scope and terminology of the Legal Guide, the information is available at <http://www.uncitral.org/en-index.htm>.

other economic value. A distinctive feature of these transactions is the existence of a link between the supply contracts in the two directions in that the conclusion of the supply contract or contracts in one direction is conditioned upon the conclusion of the supply contract or contracts in the other direction (paragraph 1). The discussion in the Guide on goods is generally applicable also to services, and can be used as a broad guidance also for transactions involving technology and investment (paragraph 2). The focus of the Guide is on countertrade transactions in which the goods are delivered across national boundaries (paragraph 3).

[8.59] Countertrade transactions in the legal guide are understood largely as a flexible concept capable of including a range of trade and investment activity. As a common feature of all types of countertrade transactions, one or both parties may fulfil their obligations to the other party by way of complex contractual arrangements under which most obligations are not settled by cash. Alternatively, it can be argued that whatever forms countertrade may take, the obligations of the parties do not fit squarely in the traditional type of relationships between the buyer and seller although the transactions between them may sometimes involve the exchange between cash and goods. In a sense perhaps, countertrade transactions are the extended forms for sale of goods or services. Foreign investment by way of countertrade where an investor invests in capital and technology but receives profits in goods can be covered by the description referred to above because the expression 'economic value' can be anything, including cash and other forms of investment.

[8.60] The legal guide is not an international convention. Nor was it drafted in a manner similar to the international convention. The structure of the legal guide includes 14 chapters and an introduction. The nature and operation of the legal guide are suggested by its structure. It appears to be a set of rules of conduct which may be adopted wholly or partially at the option of the parties. In a sense, it is similar to the commercial customs and usage codified or developed by ICC, which are meant to be guidance for the parties and will become binding as clauses of the contract if the parties expressly have incorporated them in the contract.

[8.61] In fact, the definitions and rules of the legal guide are all flexible. Since the guide has no legal force of its own, the parties are free to change any part of the rules or definitions, unless all provisions of the guide have obtained the status of law in a particular country or jurisdiction. In this case, the private parties to a transaction may be bound by the guide because it is part of the governing law of the transaction. Similarly, if a country only adopts part or some of the rules of the guide, only those sanctioned by local law become binding upon the parties subject to the local law.

Multilateral Investment Guarantee Agency

Status of MIGA

[8.62] MIGA is an international authority established under the Convention Establishing the Multilateral Investment Guarantee Agency. It is also a financial institution specialising in foreign investment insurance. It was established in 1988 as a member of the World Bank Group. Its function is to encourage FDI in developing countries by providing investment guarantees or insurance to investors against the political risks of transfer restriction, expropriation, breach of contract and war and civil disturbance in the

[8.62] host country; and by providing technical assistance to host countries on means to enhance their ability to attract foreign direct investment. Thus, technically, MIGA does not provide insurance to foreign portfolio investment. Since its establishment, MIGA has issued more than 500 guarantees for projects in 78 developing countries. As of June 2001, total coverage issued by MIGA exceeded US$9 billion.[37]

[8.63] MIGA's status and nature are defined in art 1 of the Convention Establishing the Multilateral Investment Guarantee Agency, which grants MIGA a full juridical personality and capacity to make contracts, to acquire and dispose of property and to institute legal proceedings. Thus, MIGA is an international authority with commercial functions. It was created to supplement national and private agencies which support FDI through their own investment insurance programs. Its special feature is to provide viable alternatives in investment insurance against non-commercial risks in developing countries thereby creating investment opportunities in those countries. MIGA's multilateral character and joint sponsorship by developed and developing countries were seen as enhancing confidence among investors with different nationalities seeking to invest jointly in an investment project in a developing country.

[8.64] MIGA's membership is open to all World Bank members. In 2002, its membership stood at 157 countries,[38] which have subscribed certain shares of MIGA's authorised capital. According to art 5 of the convention the authorised capital of MIGA is 1 billion SDR, which is further divided into 100,000 shares of 10,000 SDR each. In March 1999, the Council of Governors of MIGA adopted a resolution to increase the capital of MIGA by approximately US$850 million. In addition, the World Bank has transferred US$150 million to MIGA as operating capital. MIGA only provides insurance guarantees to individuals and companies from a member.

Operation of MIGA

[8.65] MIGA specialises in the provision of insurance against non-commercial risks, which are divided into four categories: transfer restriction, expropriation, breach of contract, and war and civil disturbance. These four categories of risks are explained by MIGA as follows:[39]

> **Transfer restriction:** This type of insurance protects against losses arising from an investor's inability to convert local currency (capital, interest, principal, profits, royalties and other remittances) into foreign exchange for transfer outside the host country. The coverage insures against excessive delays in acquiring foreign exchange caused by host government action or failure to act, by adverse changes in exchange control laws or regulations, and by deterioration in conditions governing the conversion and transfer of local currency. However, currency devaluation is not covered. When the insured risk takes place, MIGA pays compensation in the currency of its contract of guarantee on receipt of the blocked local currency from an investor.
>
> **Expropriation:** This type of insurance protects against loss of the insured investment as a result of acts by the host government that may reduce or eliminate ownership of, control over, or rights to the insured investment. In addition to outright nationalisation and confiscation, 'creeping' expropriation which refers to a series of acts that, over time, have an expropriatory effect is also covered.

---

37. See MIGA website at <http://www.miga.org/>.
38. See MIGA website at <http://www.miga.org/>.
39. MIGA, Overview of MIGA's Investment Guarantee Services, available at <http://www.miga.org/screens/services/guarant/guarant.htm>.

Coverage is available on a limited basis for partial expropriation (for example, confiscation of funds or tangible assets). However, bona fide, non-discriminatory measures by the host government in the exercise of legitimate regulatory authority are not covered. When the insured risk has resulted in total expropriation of equity investments, MIGA pays the net book value of the insured investment. When the insured risk has resulted in expropriation of funds, MIGA pays the insured portion of the blocked funds. For loans and loan guaranties, MIGA insures the outstanding principal and any accrued and unpaid interest. Compensation will be paid upon assignment of the investor's interest in the expropriated investment (for example, equity shares or interest in a loan agreement) to MIGA.

Breach of contract: This type of insurance protects against losses arising from the host government's breach or repudiation of a contract with the investor. In the event of an alleged breach or repudiation, the investor must be able to invoke a dispute resolution mechanism (for example, arbitration) in the underlying contract and obtain an award for damages. If, after a specified period of time, the investor has not received payment or if the dispute resolution mechanism fails to function because of actions taken by the host government, MIGA will pay compensation. MIGA may sometime make a provisional payment pending the outcome of the dispute resolution mechanism.

War and civil disturbance: This type of insurance protects against loss from damage to, or the destruction or disappearance of, tangible assets caused by politically motivated acts of war or civil disturbance in the host country, including revolution, insurrection, coupe d'état, sabotage, and terrorism. For equity investments, MIGA will pay the investor's share of the least of the book value of the assets, of their replacement cost, or of the cost of repair of damaged assets. For loans and loan guaranties, MIGA will pay the insured portion of the principal and interest payments in default as a direct result of damage to the assets of the project caused by war and civil disturbance. War and civil disturbance coverage also extends to events that, for a period of one year, result in an interruption of project operations essential to overall financial viability. This type of business interruption is effective when the investment is considered a total loss; at that point, MIGA will pay the book value of the total insured equity investment. For loans and loan guaranties, MIGA pays the insured portion of the principal and interest payments in default as a result of business interruption caused by covered events.

[8.66] MIGA is an insurance service available to its members only. It is provided to investments originating from one member and destined for a developing member. The investor must be a national of a member country other than the country in which the investment is made. Companies or financial institutions are qualified to apply for the guarantees if they are incorporated in and have their principal place of business in a member country, or if they are majority owned by nationals of member countries. The duration of guarantee is normally 15 years. The maximum term is 20 years. MIGA may cover up to 90 per cent of the principal or investment contribution in most transactions. The maximum coverage at present is US$200 million for a single project. As an insurer, MIGA examines the application for insurance before offering a cover and charges premiums and fees for the services offered. Due to the special status of MIGA, it must acquire approval of the relevant host country before issuing a contract of guarantee (insurance cover) to any investor. When necessary, MIGA may offer an insurance cover to certain projects jointly with private or national insurers to split the risk.

[8.67]   International Commercial Law

The WTO and foreign investment

Foreign investment as an issue of the WTO

[8.67] The WTO Agreement includes the Agreement on TRIMs. This is the first time that foreign investment is covered by an international agreement which has wide international implications. As we know, the WTO comes from GATT, but GATT had not dealt with foreign investment until the Uruguay Round negotiation (1986–93), because it was initially intended to be an agreement on tariffs and trade, and foreign investment is not a traditional form of trade. Tariffs and trade become relevant to foreign investment when a host country applies trade-related measures to foreign investment, such as requiring a foreign investor to purchase certain local products in conjunction, either directly or indirectly, with an invested project, for the purpose of restricting or controlling foreign investment. For example, under the Canadian Foreign Investment Review Act (1985), Gannett had to agree to sell the products of the invested Canadian company to its US companies, and Apple Computer had to purchase Canadian-made parts for its Canadian operation.[40] These controlling measures are not made for the purpose of restricting trade, but may offend the principles underlying GATT 1994.[41]

[8.68] In 1986 TRIMs were listed as one of the issues to be negotiated in the Uruguay Round. The United States has played a crucial role in pushing TRIMs into the GATT agenda. It took more than 10 years for the United States to convince GATT members that countries' foreign investment law and policies are related to trade in goods covered by GATT. The link between foreign investment law and policy and the trade in goods gives GATT the right to deal with the issue, but the scope of negotiation is limited to the impact of investment law and policy upon trade in goods only. The 1986 Ministerial Declaration of GATT mandating the special negotiating group on TRIMs authorised the group to elaborate provisions to avoid the restrictive, distorting and adverse effects of investment measures on trade in goods only.

    The United States promoted the notion of TRIMs actively during the negotiations. It approached the issue by identifying a number of areas which had distorting or prohibitive effects on foreign investment, such as local content requirements, export performance requirements, trade balancing requirements, requirements for supplying specified markets, domestic sale requirements, restrictions on local manufacturing, technology transfer requirements, requirements for transfer by licensing only, remittance restrictions, local equity requirements, exchange restrictions, and incentives based on the acceptance of other TRIMs.[42] This approach stepped beyond the scope of GATT in that some measures, such as technology transfer requirements, remittance restrictions and local equity requirements, were not necessarily related to trade in goods. This broad approach was

---

40. Christy, 'Negotiating Investment in the GATT: a Call for Functionalism' (1991) 12 *Michigan Journal of International Law* 743, pp 789–90.
41. GATT as amended in the Uruguay Round is known as GATT 1994, and GATT prior to the amendment is referred to as GATT 1947.
42. See id, pp 779–80; and K E Maskus and D R Eby, 'Developing New Rules and Disciplines on Trade-Related Investment Measures' in Stein (ed) *The Multilateral Trading System*, Harvester Wheatsheaf, New York, 1993, pp 453–4.

opposed by many industrialised and developing countries alike, because these countries do apply various restrictions on FDI to protect local industries and local economies.[43] The negotiating group on TRIMs was split by three separate opinions in 1990. The majority argued that investment measures discriminating and restricting trade in goods should be prohibited or discouraged. The United States insisted that investment measures which do not directly relate to trade in goods should also be prohibited. Certain developing countries preferred to restrict only those investment measures directly related to GATT principles, thus opposing any approach exceeding the scope of GATT.[44]

The group reached consensus in 1991, adopting the present Agreement on TRIMs.[45] The Agreement expressly states in art 1 that it 'applies to investment measures related to trade in goods only', thus limiting the scope of its application to GATT principles. This provision is reinforced by art 2, which restricts the operation of the Agreement on TRIMs to issues that are covered by arts III and XI of GATT. In other words, an investment measure prohibited by the Agreement on TRIMs must have a restrictive, adverse or distorting effect on trade in goods under arts III and XI. Any battle as to whether or not a particular investment measure violates the agreement must be fought within the existing legal framework of GATT. This is an essential characteristic of the Agreement on TRIMs, which has brought FDI issues into the regime of GATT with qualifications.

[8.69] As we have seen, foreign investment, like any other form of international trade and commerce, inherently involves conflicting interests between the investing and invested parties. Foreign investment will not be adopted as a means of international trade and commerce if investors do not receive competitive benefits (or comparative advantages) for the investment made overseas: at the same time, it will not be accepted by a host country if that country does not receive benefits which are a direct result of the foreign investment. These considerations are the grounds for any negotiation directed at restricting the host country's power to restrict and regulate foreign investment in that country. The Agreement on Trade-Related Investment Measures (Agreement on TRIMs) was eventually concluded in the Uruguay Round. This agreement prohibits the use of TRIMs, which are inconsistent with the principles of GATT 1994, as a means of restricting foreign investment. Certain investment measures may be permitted under the Agreement on TRIMs if they are not inconsistent with the principles of GATT.

[8.70] In the Doha Conference held in November 2001, the WTO members adopted the Ministerial Declaration 2001,[46] which promised to liberalise trade further within the WTO and to promote various work programs for the implementation and improvement

---

43. For example, certain EU countries have restrictions on FDI in automobile industries to restrict the invasion of the Japanese car industry into Europe. Similarly, Australia has requirements for local equity in certain sectors when the FDI exceeds fixed monetary thresholds. Many developing countries, such as India, Brazil and Bangladesh, impose various restrictions to protect local industries, even though they do need foreign capital and technology to develop their economies.
44. Xiaotian Wang and Shen Yu (eds), *GATT and China's Economy* (in Chinese) China Foreign Economy and Trade Relations Press, Beijing, 1993, pp 282–3.
45. Id, p 284.
46. The Ministerial Declaration was adopted on 14 November 2001, document number: WT/MIN(01)/DEC/1, available at <http://www.wto.org/>.

[8.70] International Commercial Law

of WTO agreeements. The interests of lesser-developed countries; the need to protect human, animal or plant life and health; environmental protection; and fair competion issues, among others, were noted by the WTO members. These issues have direct or indirect implications for the regulation of foreign investment in WTO members. Specifically, the WTO ministers agreed to develop a multilateral framework to secure transparent, stable and predictable conditions for long-term cross-border investment, particularly FDI. In principle, the WTO ministers agreed that any framework should reflect, in a balanced manner, the interests of home and host countries, and take due account of the development policies and objectives of host governments, as well as their rights to regulate FDI in the public interest.[47] These principles are largely similar to those discussed and adopted in the MAI as discussed earlier in this chapter.

Defining the Trade-Related Investment Measures

[8.71] A TRIM 'is any requirement which affects trade applied by a government as a condition to the making or operation of an investment'.[48] In other words, TRIMs are any measures or policies affecting foreign investment which fall under the scope of the Agreement on TRIMs. The term serves the purpose of 'legitimising' certain aspects of foreign investment as a concern of the WTO — foreign investment may otherwise fall outside the concept of 'tariffs' and 'trade'. Although countries are capable of reaching a more general agreement on foreign investment and a new legal framework for foreign investment, TRIMs allow WTO members to deal with certain aspects of foreign investment within the existing framework of the WTO.

[8.72] 'TRIMs' are not defined in specific detail. Any trade-related measures and policies which affect foreign investment directly or indirectly fall into the category of TRIMs. For example, the proposal made by the United States and the European Community for the Uruguay negotiation identified the following measures.

Import restrictions
1. 'Local content requirements' force the investor to purchase or to use input from local sources in some absolute amount or as a percentage of production value or quantity.
2. 'Domestic manufacturing requirements' oblige an investor to manufacture some percentage or fixed amount of production or input in the host country.
3. 'Trade balance requirements' restrict an investor from importing products or using imported products to an amount corresponding in some way to the amount of its exports.
4. 'Exchange restrictions' limit an investor's access to foreign exchange generally or to that earned from exports.

Export restrictions
5. 'Domestic sales requirements' require the sale of a certain percentage of output or a minimum quantity or value of production in the host country market.

Export requirements
6. 'Export performance requirements' oblige an investor to export a specified percentage or amount of production quantity or value.
7. 'Product mandating' requires an investor to grant the investment exclusive rights to specified export markets, or requires the investor to export to certain foreign markets or regions.

---

47. According to the Ministerial Declaration 2001, these issues and the framework for foreign investment would be further discussed in the 5th Ministerial Conference to be held in Mexico in 2003.
48. Christy, note 40 above, p 779.

566

Non-trade specific TRIMs

8. 'Technology transfer requirements' require an investor to include specified technology in its production process or to conduct some minimum level of research and development in the host country.
9. 'Local equity requirements' require local investors to hold or control a minimum percentage of equity in an investment.
10. 'Licensing requirements' oblige an investor to license the production and use, or to sell some product or technology, to domestic companies.
11. 'Manufacturing restrictions' prevent an investor from manufacturing certain products.
12. 'Remittance restrictions' limit an investor's transfer of profits, earnings, or capital to the home country.
13. 'Incentives' include measures which force foreign investors to accept certain TRIMs, while also offering some benefit or advantage to the investor.[49]

The above list identifies many sensitive areas where restrictions, requirements and preconditions have been imposed by countries receiving foreign investment. It is difficult to ask a host country to give up most of these measures, because they ensure that it will receive maximum benefits from a foreign investment. The Agreement on TRIMs does not expressly define the concept of TRIMs and permits WTO members to determine whether there are any TRIMs which are inconsistent with art III (national treatment) and art XI (quantitative restrictions) of GATT 1994. There is flexibility in the construction of the term 'TRIMs' and in the interpretation of the relationships between a TRIM and any other relevant provisions of GATT 1994.

The Agreement on Trade-Related Investment Measures

Overview

[8.73] The Agreement on TRIMs was adopted by the GATT members as one of the integral documents of the WTO Agreement in the 1993 Uruguay Round. The agreement entered into force in January 1995. It applies to investment measures related to trade in goods only (art 1 of the Agreement on TRIMs). Its application is subject to two qualifications: trade-related measures, and measures relating to foreign investment. It is not meant to be a general agreement on foreign investment.[50]

The Agreement on TRIMs is a fairly short agreement, containing only nine articles and an annex which contains an illustrative list indicating what are regarded as TRIMs. Article 1 sets out the scope of operation. Article 2 states the principle of national treatment and the principle prohibiting the use of quantitative restrictions. Article 3 makes the relevant GATT exceptions applicable under the Agreement on TRIMs. Article 4 provides rules for developing countries. Article 5 regulates notification and transitional arrangements. Article 6 requires transparency of law and policies. Article 7 establishes the Committee on Trade-Related Investment Measures. Article 8 deals with consultation and dispute settlement. Article 9 sets out rules for review of the operation of the Agreement on TRIMs by the Council for Trade in Goods. The application of the Agreement on TRIMs is closely

---

49. Id, pp 779–80.
50. For further discussions of the Agreement on TRIMs, see Mo, 'China, the World Trade Organisation, and the Agreement on TRIMs' (1996) 30 *Journal of World Trade* 89–113.

related to the operation of arts III and XI of GATT. In fact, the GATT provisions need to be relied on in most circumstances to decide whether or not a TRIM is prohibited under the Agreement on TRIMs.

This section of the book examines the theoretical basis of the Agreement on TRIMs and the relationships between GATT 1994 and the Agreement on TRIMs. In addition, the major principles of international trade as set out in the Agreement on TRIMs will also be reviewed.

The Agreement on TRIMs and the effects test

[8.74] The Agreement on TRIMs applies, as suggested in art 1, to investment measures related to trade in goods only. Article 1 has two alternative meanings: first, the Agreement covers those investment measures which are directly applicable to trade in goods; and second, the Agreement governs the measures which have distorting and adverse effects on trade in goods. If the first meaning prevails, an investment measure which does not directly apply to trade in goods but has a negative effect on trade in goods falls outside the scope of the Agreement on TRIMs. If the second is preferred, any measure which has the effect of distorting or restricting trade in goods will be covered, whether or not it is directly related to trade in goods. The two constructions lead to different scopes of operation of the Agreement on TRIMs.

[8.75] The second meaning referred to above is consistent with the effects test proposed by the United States in the Uruguay Round to create a broad concept of TRIMs. The measures, such as technology transfer requirements and local equity requirements, were accordingly identified by the United States as TRIMs.[51] The US approach appears to be largely consistent with the position of the GATT ministers during the negotiations. For example, the relevant part of the 1986 Ministerial Declaration states as follows:

> Following an examination of the operation of GATT articles related to the trade restrictive and distorting effects of investment measures, negotiations should elaborate, as appropriate, further provisions that may be necessary to avoid such adverse effects on trade.[52]

This statement twice mentions the word 'effects'. Indeed, in the Mid-Term Review Agreements reached in April 1989, the ministers agreed that further identification of the trade restrictive and distorting 'effects' of investment measures should be carried out.[53] Though the effects test gives rise to a wide application of TRIMs, interestingly enough, it appears to have been accepted by India which vigorously opposed the broad approach to TRIMs as adopted by the United States in the Uruguay Round.[54] It seems that the Agreement on TRIMs has adopted the 'effects test' and that the Agreement applies to all investment measures which have restrictive and distorting effects to trade in goods.

---

51. For example, see Christy, note 40 above, p 784.
52. Reprinted in Petersmann and Hilf (eds), *The New GATT Round of Multilateral Trade Negotiations*, Kluwer Law, Deventer, 1991, p 587.
53. *GATT Documents*, MTN.TNC/11. Reprinted in Petersmann and Hilf, id, p 609.
54. Christy, note 40 above, pp 785–6.

[8.76] The wording of the Agreement on TRIMs suggests a victory of the 'effects test'. As we have seen, the application of the Agreement is qualified by both art 2 which limits the TRIMs to arts III and XI of GATT 1994 and the Illustrative List which illustrates (non-exclusively) what are regarded as TRIMs under arts III:4 and XI:1 of GATT 1994. This approach implies that any investment measures which have distorting and adverse effects to any provisions of arts III and XI of GATT 1994 are prohibited. But when a violation of arts III:4 or XI:1 is alleged, the Illustrative List should be followed to establish the existence of the TRIM. While the effects test appears to be self-evident, its application may lead to ambiguities and confusions. This possibility was seen in the Uruguay Round negotiations where the United States justified its broad approach to TRIMs by applying the effects test. However, it is interesting to note that the test remains in the Agreement on TRIMs, but the broad approach was refused by the negotiating group. The potential difficulties which may arise from the operation of the 'effects test' in the Agreement on TRIMs will be investigated in the subsequent sections.

GATT and TRIMs

[8.77] The TRIMs are meant to be those investment measures which contravene the principles of arts III and XI of GATT 1994. There is thus a need to read arts III and XI thoroughly to ascertain the meaning and scope of the TRIMs. Article III of GATT 1994 deals with national treatment on internal taxation and regulation and art XI deals with general elimination of quantitative restrictions. Both provisions are concerned with the use of the said means to discriminate against imported goods, to prohibit international trade or to protect local products. Article III is directly and expressly related to imported 'products' or domestic products. Article XI eliminates the use of any quantitative restrictions, which are barriers to the development of international trade, subject to the exceptions made in the provision. A careful reading of art III seems to lead to the conclusion that it is intended to prohibit or eliminate the taxes, charges, laws, regulations and quantitative measures which purport either to disadvantage foreign products or to protect local products.[55] The taxes, charges, laws, regulations and quantitative restrictions which have the effect of prohibiting international trade or protecting local products also fall under art III. The TRIMs are linked to art III on the ground that the measures have distorting and adverse effects to trade in goods. This is how the TRIMs were brought in the legal framework of GATT 1994.

[8.78] Although the link between GATT 1994 and TRIMs was accepted by the GATT ministers as a last minute compromise in September 1986 when the Uruguay Round was launched,[56] the compromise did not make the link more logical than what it was. It can be argued that art III of GATT 1994 prohibits the members from deviating from national treatment when applying internal taxes, charges, laws, regulations and requirements to the manufacturing, sale, transportation, distribution, or use of domestic or

---

55. For example, art III:1 provides that taxes, charges, laws, regulations and requirements 'should not be applied to imported or domestic products *so as to afford protection to domestic production*' (emphasis added). Similarly, arts III:5 and 7 state that the quantitative regulation cannot be applied to compel the use of local or overseas content in local industries or consumption.
56. Christy, note 40 above, p 778.

[8.78]

imported products. Three major elements can be identified in the provisions: national treatment; the use of internal taxes, charges, laws, regulations and requirements; and products. A country violates this provision when its use of the said means to the products amounts to a contravention of national treatment.[57] Accordingly, a country breaches art III when the application of the said means by it has the effect of deviating from national treatment. This is different from saying that a measure falls under art III if it has a distorting or adverse effect on trade in goods. It can be argued, at least, that a measure having a restrictive or adverse effect on trade in goods may not necessarily contravene national treatment, thus being subject to art III. This is why it can be argued that the link between art III and TRIMs is not logical. The potential inconsistency or discrepancy between art III and TRIMs may lead to ambiguities and confusions in the application of the Agreement on TRIMs.

[8.79] Article XI of GATT 1994 may render the TRIMs a more reliable and unambiguous support than art III. Article XI non-discriminatorily eliminates the use of quantitative restrictions, unless the restrictions fall under the exceptions of the provision. The TRIMs which exist in the form of quantitative restrictions are subject to art XI, without a need to prove their distorting or adverse effects on trade in goods. The difficulty with the TRIMs under art XI of GATT 1994 lies in the meaning of quantitative restrictions. Article XI defines the quantitative measures as 'quotas, import or export licences or other measures'. How far can the meaning of 'other measures' extend? Can the expression 'other measures' cover any measure which is alleged to be a TRIM, regardless of whether it satisfies the description (whatever it is) of art XI:1? If not, what then is a quantitative restriction under art XI:1? Difficulties may arise from the application of art XI under the Agreement on TRIMs.

Exceptions to the obligation of not applying prohibited TRIMs

[8.80] Article 3 of the Agreement on TRIMs permits a member to rely on all exceptions under GATT 1994 which may affect its obligation to accord national treatment and to eliminate the use of quantitative restrictions. This means that the Agreement on TRIMs does not impose extra obligations upon the member countries of the WTO, which they are not obliged to take under arts III and XI of GATT 1994. The function of the Agreement on TRIMs is to make TRIMs expressly a form of trade which is examinable under arts III and XI.

Article 4 of the Agreement on TRIMs permits a developing country to deviate temporarily from the obligation of not applying the prohibited TRIMs. This exception is made for the purpose of enabling the developing country to maintain its balance-of-payments. It is permissible only for this purpose and must be exercised in the manner described in art XVIII of GATT 1994, the Understanding on the Balance-of-Payments Provisions of GATT 1994 and the Declaration on Trade Measures Taken for Balance-of-Payments Purposes adopted on 28 November 1979, which permits a GATT member to deviate from the provisions of arts III and XI of GATT 1994 in certain circumstances.

---

57. This proposition is supported by the title of art III, which is National Treatment on Internal Taxation and Regulation.

Elimination of the prohibited TRIMs and the transitional period

[8.81] Article 5 of the Agreement on TRIMs requires its members to notify the Council for Trade in Goods of their TRIMs which are inconsistent with art 2 of the Agreement. It also requires members to phase out the prohibited TRIMs within two years from the date on which the WTO Agreement enters into force. The detail of art 5 is as follows:

- a member is obliged to notify the Council for Trade in Goods of all TRIMs which are inconsistent with the Agreement on TRIMs within 90 days after the WTO Agreement enters into force;
- a member which is a developed country is obliged to eliminate all TRIMs prohibited under the Agreement on TRIMs within two years of the date on which the WTO Agreement enters into force;
- a member which is a developing country is obliged to eliminate all TRIMs prohibited under the Agreement on TRIMs within five years of the date on which the WTO Agreement enters into force;
- a member which is a least-developed country is obliged to eliminate all TRIMs prohibited under the Agreement on TRIMs within seven years of the date on which the WTO Agreement enters into force;
- the transitional periods for phasing out the TRIMs can be extended by the Council for Trade in Goods in the cases of developing or least-developed countries;
- members are not permitted to increase the degree of inconsistency within the transitional periods; and
- a member may, during the transitional period, apply the same TRIM to a new investment which is similar to the existing enterprises already restricted by the TRIM for the purpose of maintaining a fair competition between the new investment and the existing enterprises.

Determination of a TRIM under the Agreement on TRIMs

[8.82] As we have seen, the effects test has been adopted in the Agreement on TRIMs. In addition, the Annex to the Agreement on TRIMs provides illustrative examples of what are regarded as TRIMs which are inconsistent with the principles of GATT 1994. It provides the criteria for determining whether a TRIM is prohibited under the Agreement on TRIMs. The criteria can be summarised as follows:

- a measure is mandatory or enforceable under domestic law or administrative rulings;
- the measure is compulsory in that compliance with it is a prerequisite for a foreign investor to obtain an advantage or benefit;
- the measure requires the purchase or use by an enterprise of products of domestic origin or from any domestic source in the terms of a specified product, specified volume or value of products, or a proportion of local production;
- the measure requires the purchase or use of imported products by an enterprise be limited to an amount related to the volume or value of local products that it exports;

- the measure restricts the importation by an enterprise of products to an amount related to the volume or value of local production that it exports;
- the measure controls the importation by an enterprise of products by restricting its access to foreign exchange to an amount related to the foreign exchange inflows attributable to the enterprise; and
- the measure restricts the exportation or sale for export by an enterprise of products, whether specified in terms of particular products, volume or value of products or a proportion of volume or value of its local production.

This list can be compared with the TRIMs identified in the proposal made by the United States and the European Community. The criteria for determining TRIMs under the Agreement on TRIMs appear to be narrower than those adopted in the US and EC proposal. Again, it must be pointed out that the Agreement on TRIMs permits its members to determine whether a particular TRIM is inconsistent with the principles of GATT 1994. In the case of disagreement, the matter can be reported to the Council for Trade in Goods and also may be submitted for the panel proceedings within WTO.[58] However, the precise scope of the prohibited TRIMs is yet to be ascertained and developed.

Selected issues for the regulation of foreign investment

Voluntary regulation and compulsory rules

[8.83] 'Voluntary regulation' and 'compulsory rules' represent two different approaches. The OECD Guidelines represent the voluntary regulation approach of MNEs, although it must be pointed out that there is so far no international convention or treaty imposing compulsory rules of conduct upon MNEs. In addition to the OECD effort, the International Labour Organisation adopted the Tripartite Declaration of Principles concerning Multinational Enterprises and Social Policy in 1977 and the United Nations Economic and Social Council adopted the Transnational Corporations Code of Conduct in 1979. While both provide more detailed rules of conduct, neither of them imposes strict legal obligations upon MNEs. This is because it is arguable whether any international organisation or international treaty is capable of regulating MNEs directly. There appears to be a jurisprudential issue. Any law directly enforceable against any MNE must be made by a sovereign state, because the state has the effective means and power of enforcement. Although we cannot exclude the possibility of the conduct of MNEs

---

58. For example, in 1996, the EU, Japan and the US complained individually that Indonesian measures concerning exemption from customs duties and luxury taxes on imports of 'national vehicles' and components thereof were in violation of Indonesia's obligations under GATT 1994, the TRIMs Agreement and the SCM Agreement. In 1997, a panel was established to hear these disputes. In July 1998, the panel found that Indonesia was in violation of arts I and II:2 of GATT 1994, art 2 of the TRIMs Agreement, art 5(c) of the SCM Agreement. At its meeting on 23 July 1998, the DSB adopted the panel report. See WT/DS54, WT/DS55, WT/DS59 and WT/DS64; *Indonesia — Certain Measures Affecting the Automobile Industry*, Update of WTO Dispute Settlement Cases, WT/DS/OV/12, 7 April 2003, available at <http://www.wto.org>.

being regulated directly by the United Nations or a group of countries (in this case the force of law may be derived from the submission of sovereign power by the countries concerned), the enforcement of any such law still relies on the domestic law of each contracting party. This is the main difficulty of compulsory regulation by a supranational body.

[8.84] Although each sovereign state is able to regulate the conduct of foreign and local companies within its territory, there are, however, difficulties in regulating an MNE which is a local company but carries on substantial business overseas. One of the difficulties is the fact that a sovereign state may be reluctant to regulate an MNE to another country's benefit and its own disadvantage. International regulation of MNEs for the purpose of coordinating the policy of sovereign states is thus preferable, because uniform regulations would probably bring mutual benefits to all the countries involved.

[8.85] Compulsory regulation may, however, be difficult to achieve in an international forum. It is virtually impossible to reconcile all the conflicting interests of capital-exporting and capital-importing countries in any code of conduct which is intended to accord particular rights and impose specified obligations upon MNEs. Such regulation has a wide impact upon the relevant laws of the countries, such as company law, takeovers, taxation, securities, competition law,[59] and others. Such extensive cooperation between states does not appear to be feasible in the foreseeable future. Thus, a voluntary or semi-voluntary approach, either by states or MNEs, to the regulation of MNEs in the area of foreign investment, may continue to prevail.

Protectionism and sovereignty

[8.86] Protectionism may refer to the protectionism of a host country against foreign investment, as well as the protectionism of a home country against the restrictions of a foreign country on investment by the home country. Sovereignty means that a host country has sovereignty to regulate and restrict foreign investment within its territory, and that a home country has sovereignty to protect the interests and to regulate the conduct of its nationals investing overseas. Protectionism and sovereignty are the essential issues concerning the regulation of foreign investment at the international level.

Under a policy of protectionism, a host country would restrict the conduct of foreign investors for the benefit of local industries (national interest). Similarly, a home country has the responsibility and authority to protect the interests of its nationals investing overseas by whatever means for its best interest. Thus, it is very difficult to produce a universal code of conduct for MNEs.

These are the basic issues which have to be dealt with in any international attempt to regulate foreign investment. Given the existence of conflicting sovereignty and interests, any code of conduct or regulation of foreign investment must be a compromise between the capital-exporting and importing countries, as is seen in many bilateral

---

59. For discussions on the relationship between FDI and competition, see eg KC Kennedy, 'Symposium: Global Trade Issues in the New Millennium: Foreign Direct Investment and Competition Policy at the World Trade Organisation' (2001) 33 *Geo Wash Int'l L Rev* 585.

foreign investment protection treaties. The main theme of this type of treaty is that, while the investments from both countries are subject to the respective local laws in the place where the investment is made, the countries promise to each other that they will treat an investment from the other in a non-discriminatory and reciprocal manner. Any successful attempt at regulating foreign investment must be a compromise between conflicting interests, or a reciprocal concession made by the sovereign states involved.

Principles in domestic regulation of foreign investment

[8.87] The World Bank conducted a study of national codes on foreign investment in 1991 and identified the following principles which are common to most domestic laws:[60]

- foreign investments are admitted in conformity with the economic priorities of the country;
- foreign investments are usually, but not always, granted national treatment;
- foreign investors are allowed to transfer capital abroad under the law of host countries, specifically foreign exchange control regulations;
- foreign investments should only be expropriated for public interest and in accordance with laws which accord fair procedures and equitable compensation; and
- disputes arising from foreign investment are usually subject to the jurisdiction of local courts, but may be arbitrated if the law so permits.

These principles are very broad, representing the general position of capital-importing countries. Particular measures and policies vary from country to country depending on the economic priorities of the country. Thus, many countries' investment codes may provide incentives from time to time to attract particular forms of foreign investment, or foreign investment in a particular sector of the economy.[61]

Means for protection of foreign investment

[8.88] Protection of foreign investment is an issue of international law. While any sovereign government has power to expropriate or requisition property of its own nationals and foreign nationals pursuant to the relevant law (such as constitutional law), foreign nationals may be disadvantaged in reality even if the doctrine of national treatment is followed and the principle of non-discrimination appears to have been complied with. This is because in certain circumstances, particularly in developing countries, foreign investment or MNEs are often the controlling or dominating forces in a particular sector of the economy. When the host country decides to expropriate, requisition or nationalise a particular type of industry where foreign investors are the sole or major operators, it will disadvantage foreign nationals (as the major or sole owners of the industry) rather than its own nationals. In addition, most decisions to expropriate or

---

60. Parra, 'Principles Governing Foreign Investment, as Reflected in National Investment Codes' in Shihata, note 24 please insert, pp 311–35.
61. For example, see United Nations Department of Economic and Social Development, *Formulation and Implementation of Foreign Investment Policies*, United Nations, New York, 1992, pp 51–76.

nationalise are politically motivated. Thus, a home country needs to use whatever diplomatic means it can to protect the investments of its nationals overseas.

[8.89] *AGIP v Congo*

(1993) ICSID Reports 306

Nationalisation of a foreign company in breach of contract

Facts: AGIP was an Italian company. It established an oil distribution company named AGIP (Brazzaville) SA in the People's Republic of Congo in 1968. AGIP owned 90 per cent of the shares and Hydrocarbons, a Swiss company, owned 10 per cent of the shares. In 1974, the Congolese Government nationalised the entire oil distribution industry, but allowed AGIP to keep 50 per cent of the shares in AGIP (Brazzaville) SA under a contract which allowed the government to take over 50 per cent of the shares free of charge. The government was also obliged to take over 50 per cent liability as the guarantor of the investment made in the company. The government failed to undertake 50 per cent liability as agreed. In 1975, the government nationalised AGIP (Brazzaville) SA by passing a decree without compensation. AGIP commenced arbitration proceedings against the Congolese Government under art 38 of the ICSID Convention.

Decision: The arbitral tribunal decided that the Congolese Government had breached the contract and granted damages against it.

[8.90] There are three main means of protecting foreign investment in a particular country:

- First, two countries can agree upon the principles, measures and compensation for expropriating or nationalising the investment from the other party through a bilateral treaty.[62] As at May 1994, 744 bilateral investment treaties had been entered into worldwide, of which 488 were in force.[63] The Australia–China Investment Protection Treaty is an example.[64]

- Second, countries may agree upon the principles and measures for protection of foreign investment through a multinational treaty. As at May 1994, seven multinational investment treaties had been made worldwide, all of which were in force.[65] The Washington Convention on the Settlement of Investment Disputes 1965, under which the International Centre for Settlement of Foreign Investment Disputes (ICSID) was established, is an example.[66] ICSID will be discussed further in **Chapter 12**.

- Third, any host country which is eager to attract foreign investment would have to provide a legal guarantee for fair and equal treatment of foreign investment. This

---

62. For a recent review of bilateral foreign investment treaties, see Siqueiros, 'Bilateral Treaties on the Reciprocal Protection of Foreign Investment' (1994) 24 *California Western International Law Journal* 255.
63. See 33 ILM 833 (1994).
64. For a discussion of this treaty, see Mo, 'Some Aspects of the Australia-China Investment Protection Treaty' (1991) 25 *Journal of World Trade* 43.
65. See 33 ILM 833 (1994).
66. For example, see *AGIP v Congo* (1993) ICSID Reports 306; **[8.89]**; *Adriano Gardella SpA v The Government of the Republic of the Ivory Coast* (1993) ICSID Reports 283; and *Amco Asia Corp v The Republic of Indonesia* (1993) ICSID Reports 377.

[8.90]

often involves a promise that foreign investment is not to be nationalised unless in exceptional circumstances and will be adequately compensated pursuant to international law if the exceptional circumstances arise. Such guarantees provide legal remedy for foreign investors in cases where the legal procedures for appropriation are not followed, or compensation is not made pursuant to the acceptable international legal principles.[67]

International Court of Justice and foreign investment

[8.91] The International Court of Justice (ICJ) has been used as a forum for international dispute settlement since its inauguration in 1946. The court has been asked to deal with territorial disputes, such as the one between France and the United Kingdom in relation to certain Channel islets, where the court found in 1953 that the islets were under British sovereignty. It has also dealt with disputes relating to the law of the seas, such as the one between the United States and Canada in relation to the continental shelf and fisheries zones in the Gulf of Maine in 1981; disputes relating to the interpretation of international treaties; prohibition of nuclear tests (for example *Australia and New Zealand v France* in 1973); diplomatic protection and hostage crises (for example, *The United States v Iran* in 1979); violation of sovereignty (for example, *Nicaragua v The United States* in 1984); and compensation claims between sovereign states (for example, *Nauru v Australia* pending decision). However, the ICJ has not been frequently used for resolving international trade and commercial disputes.

[8.92] *Elettronica Sicula SpA ('ELSI')* (1989) ICJ 15; 28 ILM 1109, between the United States and Italy, is one of the few cases in relation to foreign investment disputes heard by the ICJ.[68] The dispute involved the requisition of ELSI, which was fully controlled by a US company, Raytheon, in 1968. Raytheon entered into a licensing and technical assistance agreement with ELSI in 1952 and obtained full control of ELSI in 1967. Between 1956 and 1967, Raytheon invested about 7.42 billion lire in ELSI.[69] ELSI manufactured sophisticated electronic components and equipment throughout the world, and in 1965–1966 its sales exceeded 8 billion lire.[70] However, ELSI had not been able to offset its debts and had accumulated losses. In 1968, Raytheon decided to close the operation. This would result in not only a loss of local employment, but also a loss of revenue to the government.

In 1968, the Mayor of Palermo issued an order requisitioning ELSI for six months. The order was to prevent the rise of unemployment and the potential impact to the stability of

---

67. For example, in *AGIP v Congo* (1993) ICSID Reports 306; **[8.89]**, the Congolese Government undertook in the 1974 Agreement with AGIP not to alter unilaterally the juridical status of AGIP (Brazzaville) SA. The tribunal held that this agreement formed part of the Congolese law and was enforceable against the government.
68. There is at least one other case which may fall under the sphere of international trade and commerce. *Barcelona Traction, Light and Power Company; Belgium v Spain* [1970] ICJR 4 involved the requisition by a country of the shares held by its own nationals in a foreign corporation.
69. Murphy, 'The *ELSI* case: an Investment Dispute at the International Court of Justice' (1991) 16 *Yale Journal of International Law* 391, p 399.
70. Ibid.

the regional economy. The matter was subsequently heard in the District Court of Palermo, the Court of Appeal of Palermo and the Italian Supreme Court of Appeals. The US party was not satisfied with the amount of damages awarded by the courts. The requisition was governed by the Treaty of Friendship, Commerce and Navigation (FCN Treaty) between the United States and Italy, and the parties disagreed as to the reason and amount of compensation for the requisition.[71] Between 1974 and 1979, the US and Italian governments negotiated the matter through diplomatic channels unsuccessfully and eventually agreed to seek a third party settlement. Between 1981 and 1985 the United States proposed to submit the dispute to an arbitral body, but in 1985 the parties agreed that the matter should be submitted to the ICJ.[72] The matter was submitted to the ICJ in 1987, and the court delivered its decision in 1989, holding that no violation of the FCN Treaty had occurred.

[8.93] The rationale behind the ICJ's decision and the technical aspects of the case are not our concern in this chapter. The fact that the ICJ was used as a forum for settling an international trade and commercial dispute is more important than the decision itself. Generally speaking, the court can only make decisions which are based on law. In this case, the court examined the terms of the FCN Treaty and found that the treaty was not violated. Given the variety of sources of international commercial law (such as conventions, treaties, domestic law and customs), we may wonder whether the court will take into account the less formal forms of international commercial law, such as customs and domestic law, in dealing with international commercial disputes. Although it is doubtful that the ICJ can be as active as a national court in setting out precedents for international commercial law, it is certain that the ICJ is able to deal with international commercial disputes arising from international conventions and treaties, provided that at least one of the parties is a state. The *ELSI* case may suggest a potentially significant function of the ICJ which is yet to be explored.

---

71. Id, p 401 and Mann, 'Foreign Investment in the International Court of Justice: the ELSI Case', vol 86 *The American Journal of International Law* 92–102.
72. Murphy, note 69 above, pp 405–6.

Chapter Nine

The World Trade Organisation

Introduction

[9.1] The World Trade Organisation (WTO) is the most important development in the history of international trade. It came into operation on 1 January 1995 and its headquarters are in Geneva, Switzerland. It is the only international body dealing with the rules of trade between nations or independent customs territories. The WTO has three main objectives: to help trade flow as freely as possible, to achieve further liberalisation gradually through negotiation, and to set up an impartial and effective means of dispute settlement. The WTO is the continuation of GATT, but it is much more powerful and covers more areas of international trade and commerce than GATT, which is now one of the trade agreements included under the WTO Agreement.

The phrase 'Multilateral Trade Organisation' (MTO) was initially used in all documents and agreements reached in the Uruguay Round negotiation. The participants of the Uruguay Round agreed on 15 December 1993 that references to 'Multilateral Trade Organisation' or MTO should be replaced by 'World Trade Organisation' or WTO throughout all the agreements reached in the Uruguay Round.

This chapter provides a broad review of the WTO, its organisation, its major functions, agreements under the umbrella of the WTO Agreement, roles of major commissions and committees, and the major principles adopted by GATT, GATS, TRIPs Agreement and a number of other important agreements.

A brief history of the WTO

[9.2] The WTO was created as the result of the Uruguay Round of GATT negotiations (1986–93). GATT was a forum for trade negotiations among its members and seven rounds of GATT negotiation had been carried out prior to the Uruguay Round. Negotiations were a permanent feature of GATT through which the members reached consensus and agreements on amendments and improvements to GATT. The events leading to the creation of the WTO began in 1982 when the ministerial meeting of GATT members decided to set up a preparatory committee for the purpose of considering the next round of GATT negotiations. The committee came into existence in 1985. It entered into operation immediately and called for proposals from members to prepare the agenda of negotiation. Some countries wished to widen the scope of the negotiation; others preferred to maintain the traditional sphere of discussion. These differences were not resolved and the committee could not reach any decision in June 1986 when the ministerial declaration for the next round was scheduled for announcement. The final meeting of members' representatives took place in September 1986 at Punta del Este, Uruguay and the countries wishing to expand the scope of negotiation succeeded. Consequently, many new areas, such as services, intellectual property rights and investment were included in the agenda of discussion.

Negotiations were lengthy and difficult and lasted from 1986–93, carried out by 14 negotiating groups consisting of countries which had interests in the matters concerned. The Trade Negotiation Committee supervised and monitored the activities of each group. The 14 groups were rationalised and consolidated in 1990. As a result, seven new groups were formed. These were agriculture; textiles and clothing; services; rule-making and TRIMs; TRIPs; Institutions; and market access. The results of these negotiations are seen in the agreements or decisions attached in the WTO Agreement.

In 1992 and 1993, negotiations reached a stage where the United States and the EU could not compromise on a number of trade terms, in particular on subsidised farm products. In January 1993, Clinton became the President of the United States. In June 1993, the US Congress granted a new 'fast track' negotiating authority (which means an authority to negotiate a trade agreement at a fast speed) to President Clinton. The authority required Clinton to notify Congress by 15 December 1993 of his intention to sign a Uruguay Round accord and to submit a final deal for approval to the Congress by 16 April 1994. This forced the United States to give its consent to the WTO Agreement on 15 December 1993 subject to the condition that the expression 'WTO' is used to replace 'MTO' (Multilateral Trade Organisation). This was accepted by other countries and the Final Act Embodying the Result of the Uruguay Round of Multilateral Trade Negotiations was signed on 15 December 1993. This was the end of the Uruguay Round negotiations.

On 15 April 1994, 124 countries and the EU approved the WTO Agreement in the Ministerial Meeting held in Marrakesh, Morocco. The WTO Agreement came into effect on 1 January 1995. As at April 2003, WTO had 146 members.

Major functions of the WTO

[9.3] The functions of the WTO are set out in art 3 of the WTO Agreement. This article has five provisions (subsections). Each of them represents a particular task or group of tasks to be accomplished by the WTO.

The first task of the WTO is to implement and administer the WTO Agreement and annexes. The WTO must also provide a framework to implement and administer the Plurilateral Trade Agreements (PTAs) among the countries which have ratified them. The PTAs, which presently include two agreements,[1] are not compulsory agreements. In order to perform this task, the WTO may have to set up mechanisms for each of the PTAs, as contracting countries to each of them can be different. There is certainly a connection between the functions of the WTO and its structure.

The second task is to provide a forum of negotiation for members to discuss issues of concern; the WTO must provide a forum for members to negotiate issues arising from the operation and implementation of the WTO Agreement. It is also obliged to provide a forum or establish a mechanism to deal with any trade issues arising from international trade within the WTO, or to be decided by the Ministerial Conference of WTO members.

The third task is to provide a dispute settlement mechanism pursuant to the Understanding on Rules and Procedures Governing the Settlement of Disputes (DSU). The WTO must enforce agreement on the establishment of the WTO dispute settlement mechanism and ensure the effective operation of the mechanism. This task is subject to the first and second tasks in that if there is any problem arising from the enforcement of the agreement on dispute settlement, the WTO must provide an adequate forum and take appropriate measures to ensure the problem can be dealt with effectively. In fact, the dispute settlement mechanism appears to be working well and productively. As at July 2002, 261 disputes had been submitted to the dispute settlement mechanism for consultation, mediation, panel proceedings and arbitration. More than 80 disputes have been submitted to panel proceedings, which in a sense can be regarded as rule-based proceedings.[2]

The fourth task is to administer the Trade Policy Review Mechanism (TPRM) established under Annex 3. The TPRM is a monitoring body which observes, collects and reviews data and information on members' trade policies. It does not have power to determine whether or not a policy is consistent with the WTO Agreement, and provides assistance for the evaluation of the relevant policy by the Ministerial Conference.

The last task is to cooperate with the International Monetary Fund (IMF) and the International Bank for Reconstruction and Development (IBRD). The IMF was set up under the Bretton Woods Agreement of 1944, which was also the basis for the IBRD. The IMF came into existence in 1945 and began operation in 1947. It makes funds available to its member countries to enable them to maintain balance of payments. The IBRD is an intergovernmental financial institution and membership is open to IMF members only.

---

1. There were originally four PTAs: Agreement on Trade in Civil Aircraft; Agreement on Government Procurement; International Dairy Agreement; and International Bovine Meat Agreement. In 1997, the WTO members agreed to terminate the International Dairy Agreement and International Bovine Meat Agreement.
2. For relevant discussions, see J Waincymer, 'International Economic Law: Transparency of Dispute Settlement Within the World Trade Organisation' (2000) 24 *Melbourne ULR* 797.

The WTO Agreement and its annexes

[9.4] The WTO Agreement establishes the WTO as the organisation regulating and controlling international trade between contracting countries. It consists of the Final Act Embodying the Results of the Uruguay Round of Multilateral Trade Negations, the Marrakesh Agreement Establishing the World Trade Organisation and six annexes: Annex 1A, Annex 1B, Annex 1C, Annex 2, Annex 3 and Annex 4. The details of the annexes are as follows:

- Annex 1A is entitled the Multilateral Agreements on Trade in Goods. It consists of the following agreements:
  - the General Agreement on Tariffs and Trade 1994 (GATT 1994) which defines the meaning of GATT 1994 and contains the amendments to GATT made during the Uruguay negotiations, in particular: Understanding on the Interpretation of Article II:1(b) of GATT 1994; Understanding on the Interpretation of Article XVII of GATT 1994; Understanding on Balance-of-Payments Provisions of GATT 1994; Understanding on the Interpretation of Article XXIV of GATT 1994; Understanding in Respect of Waivers of Obligations under GATT 1994; Understanding on the Interpretation of Article XXVIII of GATT 1994; and Marrakesh Protocol to GATT 1994;
  - Agreement on Agriculture;
  - Agreement on the Application of Sanitary and Phytosanitary Measures;
  - Agreement on Textiles and Clothing;
  - Agreement on Technical Barriers to Trade;
  - Agreement on Trade-Related Investment Measures;
  - Agreement on Implementation of Article VI of GATT 1994;
  - Agreement on Implementation of Article VII of GATT 1994;
  - Agreement on Preshipment Inspection;
  - Agreement on Rules of Origin;
  - Agreement on Import Licensing Procedures;
  - Agreement on Subsidies and Countervailing Measures; and
  - Agreement on Safeguards.
- Annex 1B is entitled General Agreement on Trade in Services.
- Annex 1C is entitled Agreement on Trade-Related Aspects of Intellectual Property Rights.
- Annex 2 is entitled Understanding on Rules and Procedures Governing the Settlement of Disputes.
- Annex 3 is entitled Trade Policy Review Mechanism.

[9.4]   International Commercial Law

- Annex 4 is entitled Plurilateral Trade Agreements, and includes two agreements:[3]
  - Annex 4(a): Agreement on Trade in Civil Aircraft;
  - Annex 4(b): Agreement on Government Procurement.

The agreements reflect the results of the negotiations carried out within the special groups. The annexes to the WTO Agreement are divided into two categories: integral agreements and optional agreements. Annexes 1A, 1B, 1C, 2 and 3 are integral agreements of the WTO Agreement, and a WTO member must unconditionally approve them when joining. Annex 4 is optional, and a WTO member can decide whether or not to approve any agreements covered by Annex 4. It follows that any of the agreements under Annex 4 operate only between those WTO members who have approved it.

Structure of the WTO

Status of the WTO

[9.5] The WTO is an international organisation. It has legal personality, and has been accorded by each of its members such legal capacity as may be necessary for the exercise of its functions. It has also been accorded by each of its members such privileges and immunities as are necessary for the exercise of its functions.[4] As an international organisation, the WTO is fundamentally different from GATT, which did not have any formal organisational structure. In other words, the organisational structure adopted by GATT did not have any legal basis in GATT 1947. The lack of structural rule within GATT was due to the fact that GATT was not meant to be a treaty establishing an international trade organisation.

The official structure of the WTO is set out in art 4 of the WTO Agreement, which describes the status and functions of the major authorities within the WTO. According to art 4, the highest authority within the WTO is the Ministerial Conference, which is followed by the General Council. Under the General Council, there are several councils and committees in charge of implementation of specific agreements. Committees are also set up under each council to perform particular tasks of that council. The Secretariat is the administrative organ of the WTO. The general structure of the WTO is illustrated by the diagram on p 583. (This is a copy of the organisational chart published by WTO, available at <http://www.wto.org/>.)

---

3. See note 1 above.
4. WTO Agreement, art VIII.

The World Trade Organisation [9.5]

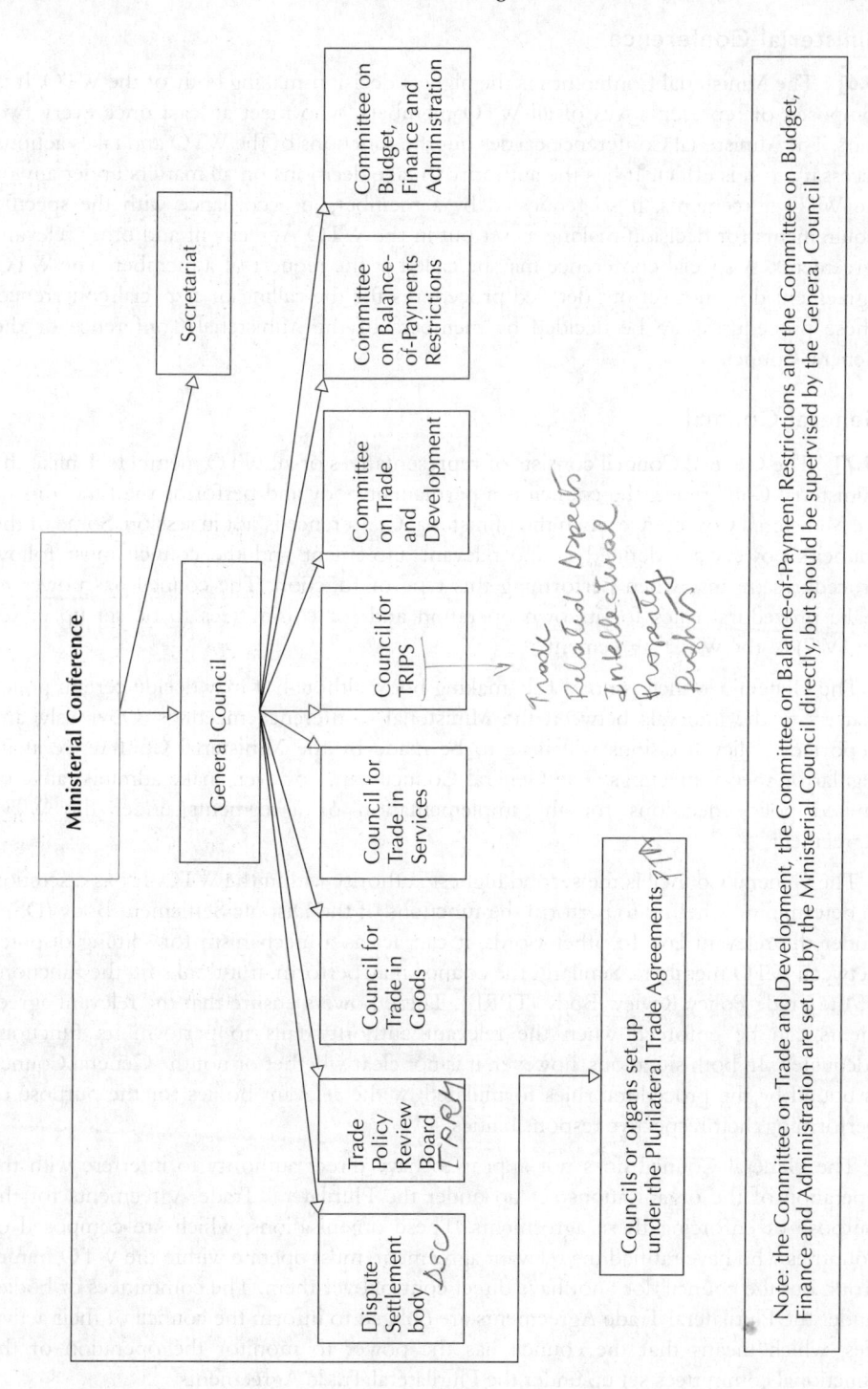

```
Ministerial Conference
    │
    ├──────────────► Secretariat
    │
    ▼
General Council ──────► Committee on Budget, Finance and Administration
    │         ──────► Committee on Balance-of-Payments Restrictions
    │         ──────► Committee on Trade and Development
    │         ──────► Council for TRIPS
    │         ──────► Council for Trade in Services
    │         ──────► Council for Trade in Goods
    │         ──────► Trade Policy Review Board (TPRM)
    │         ──────► Dispute Settlement body (DSU)
    │
    └──────► Councils or organs set up under the Plurilateral Trade Agreements (PTA)
```

TRIPS → Trade Related aspects Intellectual Property Rights

Note: the Committee on Trade and Development, the Committee on Balance-of-Payment Restrictions and the Committee on Budget, Finance and Administration are set up by the Ministerial Council directly, but should be supervised by the General Council.

583

Ministerial Conference

[9.6] The Ministerial Conference is the highest decision-making body of the WTO. It is composed of representatives of all WTO members, who meet at least once every two years. The Ministerial Conference carries out the functions of the WTO and takes actions necessary to this effect. It has the authority to take decisions on all matters under any of the WTO agreements, if so requested by a member, in accordance with the specific requirements for decision-making as set out in the WTO Agreement and other relevant agreements. A special conference may be called at the request of a member. The WTO Agreement does not set out detailed procedures for the calling of a special conference. These procedures can be decided by members of the Ministerial Conference or the General Council.

General Council

[9.7] The General Council consists of representatives of all WTO members. Unlike the Ministerial Conference, the council is a permanent body and performs the functions of the Ministerial Conference when the Ministerial Conference is not in session. Some of the council's powers are defined in the relevant agreement and the council must follow procedures (if any) when performing this type of function. The council has power to make procedural rules for its own operation and for committees to be set up under art IV(7) of the WTO Agreement.

The General Council is not a rule-making body, although it may decide certain policy matters in the intervals between the Ministerial Conference meetings. Obviously, any important policy decisions will have to be made by the Ministerial Conference at its regular or special meetings. The General Council can, however, make administrative or limited policy decisions for the implementation of agreements under the WTO Agreement.

The General Council is the second highest authority within the WTO. It has discretion in determining whether to perform the functions of the Dispute Settlement Body (DSB) under the relevant law. In other words, it can act as a mechanism for settling disputes between WTO members. Similarly, the council may perform, if it thinks fit, the functions of the Trade Policy Review Body (TPRB). These powers ensure that the relevant agreements can be enforced when the relevant authority fails to perform its functions adequately. In both situations, however, it is not clear whether or not the General Council is bound by the procedural rules formulated by the relevant bodies for the purpose of performing their respective responsibilities.

The General Council does not appear to have direct authority to interfere with the operation of the organisations set up under the Plurilateral Trade Agreements for the purpose of enforcing these agreements. These organisations, which are composed of countries who have ratified the relevant agreement, must operate within the WTO framework, but the council does not have direct control over them. The committees or bodies under the Plurilateral Trade Agreements are obliged to inform the council of their activities, which means that the council has the power to monitor the operation of the functional committees set up under the Plurilateral Trade Agreements.

Council for Trade in Goods

[9.8] The Council for Trade in Goods is set up under arts IV(5) and (6) of the WTO Agreement. It consists of representatives of all members and is responsible for administering the operation of 14 agreements contained in Annex 1A. All these agreements are concerned with trade in goods. The council is subject to the supervision of the General Council. It has power to make its own procedural rules, subject to the approval of the General Council. It can also set up subsidiary bodies when necessary.

Council for Trade in Services

[9.9] The Council for Trade in Services administers the operation of the General Agreement on Trade in Services (GATS). It also consists of representatives of all members. Trade in services forms a particular category of trading activities and is regulated by GATT for the first time in the Uruguay Round. Like the Council for Trade in Goods, the Council for Trade in Services can make its own procedural rules, which must, however, be approved by the General Council. The council can set up subsidiary bodies.

Council for Trade-Related Aspects of Intellectual Property Rights

[9.10] The Council for TRIPs oversees the operation of the Agreement on Trade-Related Aspects of Intellectual Property Rights (TRIPs Agreement). Membership is open to all WTO members. Intellectual property rights are dealt with by GATT for the first time in the Uruguay Round. The council acts as the WTO's representative to enforce the agreement. Its procedural rules must be approved by the General Council. Various functional bodies may be established by the council for the purpose of enforcing the TRIPs Agreement.

Dispute Settlement Body

[9.11] The Dispute Settlement Body (DSB) is an authority set up under art IV of the WTO Agreement and the Understanding on Rules and Procedures Governing the Settlement of Disputes (referred to as the DSU). It is responsible for enforcing the DSU. It may have its own chairperson and formulate procedural rules for the purpose of implementing the DSU. It is theoretically subordinate to the General Council, but in fact has the same membership.

The dispute settlement mechanism of the WTO is based on the DSU, which provides means and procedures for the settlement of certain disputes between members. Not all disputes arising from the WTO Agreement and its annexes are subject to the procedures of the DSU. According to Appendix 1 to the DSU, disputes arising from the WTO Agreement, GATT 1994, GATS, the TRIPs Agreement, the DSU, and the Plurilateral Trade Agreements are subject to the procedures of the DSU. Disputes arising from Annex 3 are not subject to the DSU (Annex 3 regulates the Trade Policy Review Mechanism, which may not be directly related to disputes between WTO members).

The DSB provides general procedures or rules for settling disputes. In broad terms, the dispute settlement procedures are: consultations, good offices, conciliation or mediation,

[9.11]   and panel proceedings. Panel proceedings are different from arbitration proceedings. The jurisdiction of a panel proceeding is compulsory, in the sense that a respondent does not have the power or the right to block the proceeding once the DSB has accepted an applicant's request for setting up a panel. In comparison, an arbitration proceeding, in most cases, will be based on an agreement of the parties, unless a dispute is referred to arbitration pursuant to arts 21(3) or 22(6) of the DSU.[5] The panel makes reports, containing findings and recommendations, to the DSB, which will make a decision on whether to accept the panel report only when the parties do not indicate an intention to appeal against the panel finding. Otherwise, the matter should go to the appeal process of the panel proceeding. The DSU also sets out procedures for dealing with multiple complainants and the interests of third parties. Basic rules for the operation of the panel, such as the power to collect information and the issue of confidentiality, are set out in the DSU (see **[9.68]**) and the Rules of Conduct for the Understanding on Rules and Procedures Governing the Settlement of Disputes.

The DSB is responsible for setting up the Appellate Body at the request of the disputants. The Appellate Body has power to hear appeals against the panel's findings on points of law only. Procedures for appeal are decided by the Appellate Body in consultation with the DSB and relevant authorities. Like the panel report, the Appellate Body's report does not have force until it is accepted by the DSB. The parties, however, do not have the right to challenge the report, no matter what the DSB's decision is. The DSB is under time restraints, and has to resolve a dispute within nine months (when the panel report is not challenged) or 12 months (when an appeal is made to the Appellate Body). The DSB has power to supervise the implementation of the report of the panel or the Appellate Body, as the case may be.

The DSB supervises the operation of the dispute settlement mechanism, based on a range of ADR methods such as negotiation, mediation, good offices, and panel proceedings. Panel proceedings differ from mediation in that recommendations are made to the DSB, rather than to the parties; they differ from arbitration in that the panel is only an adviser to the DSB and has no power to make a decision.

Secretariat

[9.12]   The Secretariat of the WTO is set up under art VI of the WTO Agreement. The head of the Secretariat is the Director-General appointed by the Ministerial Conference. The Director-General has the power to select the staff members of the Secretariat and to define their functions and duties. The Secretariat's staff must be neutral in discharging their duties and must consult the governments which are affected by their acts.

---

5. Article 21(3) requires the use of arbitration to determine the length of a reasonable time to implement a binding panel report. If the parties cannot agree on the appointment of arbitration, the Director-General of the DSB can appoint one for them. Article 22(6) of the DSU requires the adequacy and appropriateness of a decision to suspend benefits or concessions against a non-compliant member to be arbitrated by a tribunal.

The power, functions and duties of the Director-General are determined by the Ministerial Conference, which can change the terms if necessary. The Secretariat administers the routine operation of the WTO: it is its bureaucratic side.

Trade Policy Review Body

[9.13] The Trade Policy Review Body (TPRB) is established under art IV of the WTO Agreement and the agreement entitled 'Trade Policy Review Mechanism'. It is a body in charge of periodic review of members' trade policies and practice. It does not have any decision-making power. However, its reports on the members' policies will be published and its findings may thus affect the decisions of the Ministerial Conference with regard to particular matters. The function of the TPRB is to collect information, assess the trade policies of members, publish reports and submit reports to the Ministerial Conference.

Various functional bodies and committees

[9.14] In order to implement all the agreements of the WTO, many subsidiary bodies may be set up under the supervision of the General Council. For example, art IV(7) establishes the Committee on Trade and Development, the Committee on Balance-of-Payments Restrictions and the Committee on Budget, Finance and Administration. More committees or bodies will be set up as necessary, with their functions and tasks determined by the General Council.

Admission procedure

[9.15] There are two ways to become a WTO member. When the WTO came into operation in 1995, only members of GATT 1947 were eligible to become original members of the WTO Agreement. Article 5 of the Final Act Embodying the Results of the Uruguay Round of Multilateral Trade Negotiations provides that before accepting the WTO Agreement, countries which 'are not contracting parties to GATT 1947 must first have concluded negotiations for their accession to GATT 1947 and become contracting parties thereto'. A member of GATT 1947 could become a member of the WTO Agreement by accepting the WTO Agreement pursuant to arts XI, XII and XIV. For any country which is not a member of GATT, the admission procedure is governed by art XII of the WTO Agreement, which states that any 'state or separate customs territory possessing full autonomy in the conduct of its external commercial relations and of the other matters provided for in this Agreement and the Multilateral Trade Agreements may accede to this Agreement, on terms to be agreed between it and the WTO'. The WTO follows the GATT practice of consensus for admission of new members. This means that a prospective member needs to negotiate with all existing members who have expressed special interest in its application for admission. Interested countries may form an interest group to exchange their views of the admission matter. The purpose of negotiation is to ensure that enough support will be received when the application is put for a vote in the Ministerial Conference, which 'shall approve the agreement on the terms of accession by a two-thirds majority of the Members of the WTO'.[6]

---

6. WTO Agreement, art XII.

General Agreement on Tariffs and Trade

Historical review of GATT

[9.16] The General Agreement on Tariffs and Trade was drafted in 1947 and entered into force in 1948 under the Protocol of Provisional Application of the General Agreement on Tariffs and Trade. It was intended to be a multilateral treaty based on reciprocity and was adopted for the purpose of overcoming trade barriers, which had detrimentally affected trading and commercial relationships between countries. The Preamble of GATT 1947 states that for the purpose of increasing living standards and the world economy and fully developing world resources the contracting countries agreed to enter into 'reciprocal and mutual advantageous arrangements directed to the substantial reduction of tariffs and other barriers to trade and to the elimination of discriminatory treatment in international commerce'.[7]

The history of trade protectionism is as old as the history of international trade itself, and the use of bilateral (or multilateral) treaties to resolve various conflicts between trade and commercial policies of states was by no means a new discovery in 1947.[8] However, the worldwide depression after the Second World War and the indisputable domination of the United States over world affairs at the end of the war were perhaps what made GATT a feasible means of adjusting trade and commercial relationships between countries which were endeavouring to improve their economies. The contracting parties to GATT in 1947 agreed to be bound by it, to treat the other contracting parties on an equal and reciprocal basis and, above all, to curb or restrain protectionism within the sphere of GATT.

[9.17] An episode which had implications for GATT was the failure of the intended International Trade Organisation (ITO) to come into existence at all. The ITO, as its name suggested, was meant to be an international organisation in charge of international trade and commerce. The draft of the ITO was proposed by the United States in 1946 and the final version of the charter of the ITO (known as the Havana Charter) was completed in Havana in 1948.[9] However, the ITO did not enter into operation at all, mainly because the Congress of the United States refused to approve the charter, probably on the technical ground that the President had no power to enter into an agreement on an international organisation.[10] The failure of the ITO contrasts sharply with the success of GATT. The United States was crucial in the establishment of GATT; the final form of GATT was developed on the basis of US experience in resolving international trade disputes since 1934. As at 1945, the United States had entered into 32 bilateral

---

7. GATT Preamble.
8. For example, as early as 1271 England entered into its first commercial treaty with Norway. See Nwogugu, *The Legal Problems of Foreign Investment in Developing Countries*, Manchester University Press, Manchester, 1965, p 121. Similarly, the Romans used international treaties as a means of protecting their commercial interests outside the Empire.
9. Jackson, *Restructuring the GATT System*, Printer Publishers, London, 1990, p 10.
10. Id, p 12.

treaties reducing tariffs.[11] In the light of these historical facts, we may draw at least two conclusions:

- The United States was the decisive force for the initiation and establishment of GATT 1947.
- GATT 1947 was not initially intended to be an international organisation — the US President had constitutional difficulty in 'making' GATT 1947 an international organisation. Also, the ITO was meant to be the international trade organisation; its role, however, was de facto replaced by GATT 1947 until 1995 when the WTO came into existence.

GATT grew rapidly from its establishment in 1947, when there were only 23 founding members to the agreement (organisation). During the 1960s, GATT expanded rapidly. In 1970, it had 77 members, of which 52 were developing countries. Along with the growth in the number of developing members, conflicts between developed and developing members intensified. The developing countries formed a significant force to defend their interests within GATT, whilst a number of developed countries began to deviate from GATT's principles and spirit in order to protect their economic interests. Both forces were testing ground within the GATT framework, and the 1960s saw the authority of GATT principles seriously challenged by both developed and developing countries.

During the 1970s, GATT members began to search for a compromise within the GATT system, probably because economic interdependence forced them to do so. The Tokyo Round was held from 1973–79, during which time a number of significant and detailed multilateral trade negotiation codes were produced. The Anti-dumping Code and dispute settlement proceedings were developed in the 1970s.

In the 1980s, GATT's membership grew to about 120. While many disputes were resolved within the system, more and more countries, in particular developed countries, felt that the GATT system was not effective in protecting their economic interests. This was due to the fact that compromises were expected in resolving any GATT disputes and the means of enforcement were not as effective as domestic means. A number of developed countries adopted unilateral practices to address the issue of trade imbalance and to protect their own interests. This led to a number of inquiries into the trade policies of the developed countries, such as the United States and Canada. There was a strong demand from the developed countries to make GATT powerful and extensive. The Uruguay Round negotiations commenced in such circumstances.

In the 1990s, GATT moved into a new era of development. The WTO was established in 1995 as an umbrella for various international trade agreements and an exclusive world trade organisation to deal with issues of international trade. This decade is probably marked by the end of GATT 1947, under which GATT functioned as a forum for negotiations. This decade has certainly been characterised by the birth of the WTO, which has succeeded GATT as the organisation regulating international trade.

---

11. Id, p 9.

Defining GATT 1947 and GATT 1994

[9.18] 'GATT 1947' refers to GATT as adopted in 1947 and its subsequent amendments prior to the 1993 Uruguay Round (from 1986–93). 'GATT 1994' refers to GATT 1947 as amended in the Uruguay Round, during which a number of amendments to GATT and new treaties on international trade were adopted. The WTO was established under the Agreement Establishing the Multilateral Trade Organisation (note: 'Multilateral Trade Organisation' in the documents adopted in the Uruguay Round has been replaced by 'World Trade Organisation' throughout).

The major differences between GATT 1947 and GATT 1994 can be summarised as follows:

- GATT 1947 is an independent code of conduct governing world trade relationships, but GATT 1994 operates as one of the integral parts (documents) of the WTO Agreement;
- GATT 1994 represents a new era in GATT, in which the multilevel-structured WTO coordinates world trade relationships; and
- GATT 1947 and GATT 1994 are two different treaties, and members of GATT 1947 must expressly ratify or accept GATT 1994 and withdraw from GATT 1947 in order to participate in the new trade system based on the WTO.

GATT Agreement

Nature of GATT 1947

[9.19] GATT 1947 was not meant to be an international organisation. Jackson comments as follows:

> GATT — the General Agreement on Tariffs and Trade — is generally recognised as the principal international organisation and rule system governing most of the world's international trade. Yet this organisation is a curious institution, to say the least. The basic treaty comprising GATT has never come into force, being applied through a 1947 'Protocol of Provisional Application'. After 40 years of 'provisional application', one might think that the world was ready for something more than 'provisional'! In addition, at its origin, GATT was not intended as an international organisation. Yet today, as it actually operates, it clearly falls well within any reasonable definition of 'international organisation'.[12]

The US Subcommittee to Study the Organisation for Trade Cooperation of the Committee on International Trade and Investment observed in 1957 that 'GATT is not an agreement setting up an international organisation. It is rather a substantive agreement, dealing with trade policy on tariffs, quotas, restrictions and similar devices affecting the free flow of international trade'.[13] Although it is true that GATT 1947 acted as an international organisation for the purpose of coordinating trade and commercial relationships between the contracting countries, it is important to note that it was not originally intended to be a code for an international trade organisation.

---

12. Id, p 1.
13. Ebb (ed) *Regulations and Protection of International Business — Cases, Comments and Materials*, West, St Paul, 1964, p 690.

Practical status of GATT 1947

[9.20] The proposition that GATT 1947 functioned as an international organisation is supported by the manner in which a country could become a contracting party to the agreement. An outside country should be allowed to negotiate with existing contracting countries to become a party to the agreement. However, 'negotiation' under GATT 1947 involved a formal application by a country and the approval of the application by two-thirds of existing GATT members. This made joining the agreement a process similar to the joining of an organisation. Alternatively, a newly independent country could become a contracting party upon sponsorship by the parent country. The implications of this rule were twofold. On the one hand, it reflected the world situation after the Second World War, where a number of trustee territories were under the temporary care and administration of other states before they became independent. Papua New Guinea, which was administered by Australia before independence, was an example. On the other hand, it was a remnant of colonialism which diminished greatly since the Second World War. GATT 1947, whatever the original intention of its development, operated as an informal international trade organisation (or union or community) which controlled and 'regulated' four-fifths of world trade before 1995.

GATT 1947 was an agreement, and amendments to it were made by way of negotiations. There have been eight rounds of GATT negotiation since 1947. The first round was held in 1947 in Geneva, the second in Annecy in 1949, and the third in Torquay in 1950. The fourth was back to Geneva in 1956. The fifth lasted for two years (1960–61) in Dillion. The sixth lasted for five years (1962–67) in Kennedy. The seventh was held in Tokyo from 1973–79. The most recent negotiation, the Uruguay Round, began in 1986 and was completed in December 1993. These dates show that the rounds of negotiation became longer and longer. This can be explained by the increase in the number of contracting parties (particularly developing countries) and the extension of the agreement to many sensitive areas which had traditionally been subject to extensive protection by the contracting governments. For example, the Uruguay Round dealt with banking, insurance, construction, maritime transport, professional services, telecommunications, films and other forms of tradeable services, as well as the protection of foreign investment and intellectual property. GATT ceased to be a de facto international organisation in 1995 when the WTO came into operation.

Principle of most favoured nation treatment

General meaning of MFN treatment

[9.21] Accordingly to one commentator, 'the most-favoured-nation (MFN) clause has figured as one of the central provisions in commercial treaties over the past 300 years'.[14] MFN means that one contracting country agrees to treat another contracting country as the most favoured nation within the territory of the first contracting country. In particular, it means that the promisee (the country which has been granted the status of most favoured nation) will be given all the benefits, privileges, advantages, favour and treatment

---
14. Ryan, *International Trade Law*, Law Book Co, Sydney, 1975, p 3.

[9.21]

which have been, and will be, offered to any third country by the promisor (the country granting MFN treatment) within the promisor's territory. Usually the other contracting country reciprocally undertakes the same obligation towards the first country. The term 'most favoured nation' represents an international obligation undertaken by one country ('grantor') towards another ('grantee'), usually reciprocally. It also reflects the status of one country (grantee) within the territory of another (grantor). However, MFN status was in the past offered without reciprocity under what might be called 'unequal treaties'. For example, the colonial powers in the eighteenth and nineteenth centuries often enjoyed MFN status in colonised countries without undertaking the same obligation towards the colony.

The expression 'most favoured nation' does not really mean the 'most' favoured nation at all. No country is prepared to treat all countries in the same manner and offer them exactly the same benefits or privileges, which is perhaps why the expression 'most favoured nation' was created to distinguish this type of obligation from other types of obligation, such as national treatment. A country often offers MFN status to another country for the sake of courtesy, or formality perhaps, at the same time qualifying and restricting the accorded privileges as it thinks necessary. For example, Garrett J in *John T Bill Co v United States* 104 F. 2d 67, 27 CCPA (Customs) 26 (1939) observed as follows:

> The traditional policy of the United States in respect to most-favoured-nation treatment was developed on the theory that privileges and concessions in the field of duties on imports or exports should be granted only in return for privileges and concessions reciprocally accorded. Thus there was almost uniformly written into the treaties to which we became a party the provision that most-favoured-nation treatment should be conditional. The benefit of concessions or reductions of duties made to third states by either contracting power should accrue to the other contracting power freely, if freely made to the third state, but only in return for an equivalent if made to the third state for a reciprocal concession or reduction.[15]

The conditional nature of most favoured nation status leads to some absurdities: if qualified or restricted treatment is supposed to be 'most favoured nation' treatment, is unqualified privileged treatment then 'most most favoured nation' treatment? Even the 'most most favoured nation' treatment could be overshadowed by 'most most most favoured nation' treatment if there is a third country which receives extra benefits or preferential treatment not offered to the country receiving the 'most most favoured nation' treatment! The notion of MFN implies equal treatment of all foreign countries within the territory of the host country, subject to special concessions or preferential treatment granted to a particular foreign country.

MFN in GATT

[9.22] The MFN principle is one of the essential principles of GATT, which promotes it among contracting parties in matters not related to domestic tax legislation. It requires members to accept this principle, subject to the exceptions in art I(2)(3)(4), art III and art XXIV of GATT, as the basis for dealing with trade and commercial relationships between them. But a contracting party is allowed to provide certain preferential treatment to countries which have special relationships with it. Subject to this exception, a contracting party offering a particular privilege or right to any of the contracting parties is

---

15. Ebb, note 13 above, p 687.

obliged to grant the same privilege to other contracting parties trading with it in the same circumstances. The MFN principle applies not only to tariffs, taxes and customs, but also to policies affecting trade and commercial activities of the contracting parties. MFN status in GATT is granted to goods or products imported to a contracting party. The MFN principle is expressly set out in art I, and implied in arts II (concessions), V (freedom of transit), VIII (fees and formalities), IX (marks of origin), XI (quantitative restrictions), etc.

Article I(1) of GATT provides as follows:

With respect to customs duties and charges of any kind imposed on or in connection with importation or exportation or imposed on the international transfer of payment for imports or exports, and with respect to the methods of levying such duties and charges, and with respect to all rules and formalities in connection with importation and exportation, and with respect to all matters referred to in paragraphs 2 and 4 of Article III, and advantage, favour, privilege or immunity granted by any contracting party to any product originating in or destined for any other country shall be accorded immediately and unconditionally to the like product originally in or destined for the territories of all other contracting parties.

The meaning of the MFN principle in GATT can be summarised as follows:

- Measures or policies subject to the principles include: customs duties; imported or exported charges; fees relating to the payment for imports or exports of goods; method of levying the charges and fees; measures relating to export or import control; laws, regulations and policies relating to internal sales, purchase, transportation, distribution or use of goods.
- Privilege, advantage, favour or immunity under the provisions includes: all forms of right or benefit relating to export or import of goods, such as a right to apply for an import permit, privilege of having market access, advantage resulting from simplified import or export procedures, a favour to be exempt from a fee or procedural requirement or immunity from a tariff or inspection, etc.
- The recipient of MFN treatment is the 'product' of a GATT member, but the product must be sold between GATT members.
- A distinction is made between a product sold between GATT members (grantor and grantee) and any like product originating from or destined for any GATT member (ie the other party is not necessarily a GATT member). But, it is rare for a GATT member to treat a non-member more favourably than other GATT members.
- Immediately and unconditionally in art I means that a member must do so in circumstances which are not covered by the exceptions under GATT.

Principle of national treatment

General meaning of national treatment

[9.23] National treatment is another popular term in international commercial treaties. It means that one country undertakes to treat the nationals of another country in the same way or manner as it treats its own nationals. Even if the treatment is based on reciprocity, it may be too idealistic to exist in reality. Why should a sovereign state grant the citizens of another sovereign state exactly the same benefits, access, rights, privileges and

[9.23]   **International Commercial Law**

entitlements which are available to its own nationals? In Australia, for example, if a resident moves from one state to another, the government of the second state, which is not even a sovereign state in international law, will require that resident to replace his or her original driver's licence with one issued by that state. Indeed, it does not make sense for a foreigner to be entitled to the same social benefits and privileges as a local resident, if that foreigner has not contributed as much, if anything, to the taxation and revenue of the country as the locals. National treatment in fact means qualified national treatment, which allows the nationals of a country that has been granted this treatment to be subject to the same set of rules or to be entitled to the same rights and benefits as the nationals of the host country to the extent, or in relation to the matters, stipulated in the relevant agreement. National treatment is qualified by the treaty which accords this privilege.

National treatment in GATT

[9.24] GATT requires contracting parties to accord national treatment to other contracting parties when domestic tax law is involved. Article III provides that, subject to the exceptions under the same provision, domestic law should not be used to impose higher taxes or internal quantitative restrictions in relation to the composition or process of a particular product on imported goods from other contracting countries for the purpose of protecting domestic production. The key issue is the purpose of the higher tax or the internal quantitative restriction. The principle of national treatment is violated only when the tax, charge or internal quantitative restriction is used as a protective measure against imported goods from another contracting party. National treatment is an undertaking not to discriminate between a contracting party's own nationals and another contracting party's nationals.

GATT upholds the principle of national treatment in an effort to reduce tariffs among the contracting parties. Article III(1) provides as follows:

> The contracting parties recognise that internal taxes and other internal charges, and laws, regulations and requirements affecting the internal sale, offering for sale, purchase, transportation, distribution or use of products, and internal quantitative regulations requiring the mixture, processing or use of products in specified amounts or proportions, should not be applied to imported or domestic products so as to afford protection to domestic production.

Article III(4) further states that:

> The products of the territory of any contracting party imported into the territory of any other contracting party shall be accorded treatment no less favourable than that accorded to like products of national origin in respect of all law, regulations and requirements affecting their internal sale, offering for sale, purchase, transportation, distribution or use. The provisions of this paragraph shall not prevent the application of differential internal transportation charges which are based exclusively on the economic operation of the means of transport and not on the nationality of the product.

The combined effect of art III(1) and (4) is that a contracting party is not allowed to use taxes, charges, laws, regulations and policies to create protection for domestic products, or to discriminate against products of other contracting parties on the basis of their nationality. (Note: the emphasis here is discrimination on the *basis of nationality*.) However, the effect of art III should not be viewed in too romantic a light, because under GATT a contracting state has the power to restrict or impose quotas on the sale of another contracting state's products within its territory.

In summary, 'national treatment' requires one contracting country to treat the nationals and products of another contracting country in the same manner as its own nationals or products to the extent, or in relation to the matters, specified or agreed upon by the parties in the agreement. It is a qualified privilege, or obligation (depending on the status of the country), because equality and non-discrimination between the nationals or products of the contracting parties are achieved only within the limits set out and defined in the international agreement or treaty concerned.

Principle of non-discrimination

Meaning of non-discrimination in international commerce

[9.25] Non-discrimination is a popular notion in international commercial treaties. Most favoured nation treatment implies that there should be no discrimination against countries which have been granted most favoured nation status by the host, recipient or importing country. National treatment implies that in relation to the matters specified in the agreement, the host, recipient or importing country should not impose any restrictive laws, regulations or policies which create inequality between its own and prescribed foreign nationals, thus resulting in discrimination against the nationals and products of the country which has been granted national treatment. For example, art XIII of GATT imposes a duty of non-discriminatory administration of quantitative restrictions upon contracting countries, which simply means that contracting countries are not allowed to impose quantitative restrictions upon the products of other contracting countries on the basis of the nationality of the products. A country can in fact impose quantitative restrictions under art XIII, provided that the restrictions are not directly based on nationality of any particular goods.

Sub-Committee I of the International Committee on Legal Aspects of a New International Economic Order (NIEO) suggested that the notion of non-discrimination means that equal cases should be treated equally and unequal cases, unequally.[16] The determination of equal or unequal cases involves the exercise of subjective criteria, which may be 'objective criteria' selected subjectively by the person making the determination. There is no uniform rule for the application of the non-discrimination principle. The purposes of the treaty, nature of the right, function of the benefit, and reciprocal obligations of the contracting parties under the different measures of treatment which have been alleged to be discriminatory, must be taken into account.

Non-discrimination in GATT

[9.26] Non-discrimination is required in the administration of quantitative restrictions. Quantitative restrictions are quotas on the quantity of certain imported (or exported) products or raw materials. Article XIII provides that a contracting party should not discriminate against any other contracting party in imposing import or export quantitative restrictions. The key factor here is non-discrimination among contracting parties. The 'legality' of imposing quantitative restrictions is not an issue under this provision as long

---

16. Draft Report of Sub-Committee on Legal Aspects of a NIEO: Exporting and Evolving Principles and Norms of International Law Relating to a New International Economic Order, p 18.

[9.26]   **International Commercial Law**

as the country is not discriminating against any other country when imposing quantitative restrictions on either imports or exports.

The principle of non-discrimination in art XIII of GATT should be examined. Article XIII has a rather interesting title: non-discriminatory administration of quantitative restrictions. As a general rule, quantitative restrictions are not allowed, unless exceptions under GATT apply. This is what art XI says. Article XIII is consistent with art XI. Article XIII broadly states that the exceptions must be applied on a non-discriminatory basis. In most circumstances, the principle of non-discrimination applies to the operation of the measures on imports, but it is capable of applying to the measures on exports.

The non-discrimination principle appears to be redundant in circumstances where either the MFN principle or the principle of national treatment applies. For example, art XIII(1) prohibits the use of restrictions on imports or exports, 'unless the importation of the like product of all third countries or the exportation of the like product to all third countries is similarly prohibited or restricted'. This provision indicates that the MFN principle is applied to justify the application of a discriminatory measure or policy. On the same basis, we can say that if the MFN principle applies, discrimination between foreign and local products is allowed as long as all foreign countries which have been given MFN status are treated equally. Article XIII(5) provides that the principle of non-discrimination applies to the use of tariff quotas and to the regulation of exports. GATT members are obliged to follow the principles of national treatment in the application of internal taxation and regulation. When a country cannot apply internal taxes or regulations to afford protection to domestic production, it is certainly not allowed to discriminate between foreign and local products.

Principle of eliminating quantitative restrictions

[9.27]   GATT does not define the meaning of quantitative restrictions. It is an expression capable of covering any form of restriction, except for those in the form of duties, taxes or charges. For example, various import or export quotas, licences, permits, requirements or formalities are regarded as quantitative restrictions under GATT. However, necessary administrative requirements for export and import control are not regarded as quantitative restrictions. Whether or not a requirement is of an administrative nature should be determined on the basis of commonsense and by comparison with acceptable international practices. So far countries have been able to avoid trivial disputes on requirements or formalities under art XI.

As a general principle, all forms of quantitative restriction are prohibited under art XI(1). This provision states as follows:

> No prohibitions or restrictions other than duties, taxes or other charges, whether made effective through quotas, import or export licences or other measures, shall be instituted or maintained by any contracting party on the importation of any products of the territory of any other contracting party or on the exportation or sale for export of any product destined for the territory of any other contracting party.

Like any other principles of GATT, exceptions to the obligation to eliminate quantitative restrictions are made under art XI.

Anti-dumping

Meaning of dumping

[9.28] Dumping can be described as the sale of imported merchandise at less than its prevailing market or wholesale price in the country of production, or 'the act whereby an exporter sells goods to an export market at a price below that charged for comparable goods in the exporter's home market'.[17] This definition is important, as there is a tendency for dumping to be confused with ordinary low-price sales, price-cutting and severe competition of a legitimate sort, as well as certain other trade practices which are generally considered unfairly competitive.[18]

Although dumping may be determined by referring to whether the price of a product is lower than the prevailing market price or the wholesale price of the same or like product in the exporting country, price is not the only test for determining dumping prohibited under GATT. Cheap goods enable consumers of the importing country to receive better value for their money (indeed, 'the revival of the British tin plate industry was largely credited to the dumping of cheap steel in the British Island')[19] — and it is only when undervalued sales cause damage to local industry and the local economy that it becomes an issue of local concern.

GATT does not directly define dumping. Article VI(1) provides as follows:

> The contracting parties recognise that dumping, by which products of one country are introduced into the commerce of another country at less than the normal value of the products, is to be condemned if it causes or threatens material injury to an established industry in the territory of a contracting party or materially retards the establishment of a domestic industry.

This definition of dumping has several basic characteristics:

- dumping involves an international sale of products or goods;
- dumping refers to the export of goods or products under their normal value, which is the market value or the commercial price of the goods or products concerned;
- the cheap or undervalued goods or products concerned must have caused or threatened to cause material injury to any established industry or to the establishment of a domestic industry in the territory of a GATT member;
- the injured industry can be the one which is in existence or an industry to be established in the future;
- dumping can be established when injury is done or will be done to the importing country or to any third country; this means that a country can in fact impose an anti-dumping measure on the imported products or goods for the sake of protecting an established industry in another GATT member.

---

17. Stewart (ed), *The GATT Uruguay Round: A Negotiating History*, Kluwer Law and Taxation Publishers, Deventer, 1993, p 1389.
18. US Tariff Commission Report, 1919, on Dumping and Unfair Foreign Competition in the United States, see Ebb, note 13 above, p 836.
19. Ibid.

A brief history of dumping

[9.29] Dumping has been an international trade practice for a hundred years. At the end of the nineteenth century, Germany was known for dumping its products in the United States. The real issue is competition between imported products and local products. In order to expand markets, some countries encourage their businesses to sell at very low prices to foreign markets. The industries in importing countries regard this practice as unfair, because (1) they are not subject to the same production environment as the industries which sell undervalued goods, and (2) the imported goods are sold at prices lower than their domestic prices. In the end of the nineteenth and beginning of the twentieth century, a number of Western countries, such as the United States, Canada, New Zealand, Australia and England, adopted anti-dumping measures. This anti-dumping war was largely carried out between Western countries which had sufficient capacity to manufacture cheap products and had the markets to consume them. Japan adopted anti-dumping measures in the 1920s when it began to industrialise its economy.

The United States pioneered the development of anti-dumping legislation. In 1919 the US Tariff Commission observed that:

[f]or many years the tariff laws of the United States have regularly provided for the imposition of countervailing duties equal to the net amount of any grants or bounties allowed by any foreign government in aid of the exportation of merchandise to this country.[20]

In fact, the United States adopted legislation on countervailing duties as early as 1894 'to restrict the dumping of sugar, the production of which had been stimulated by government bounties';[21] and prior to that legislation, it had dealt with the problem of dumping in its Tariff Act of 1816.[22] The earlier anti-dumping legislation purported to countervail mainly foreign governments' subsidies in dumped goods. It is no surprise that anti-dumping was incorporated into art VI of GATT, which bears distinctive marks of US influence.

'Anti-dumping' describes the government act of imposing tariffs or duties upon imported goods which are regarded as dumped goods, for the purpose of offsetting the detrimental effect of the dumped goods. The duties imposed are regarded as 'dumping duties'. Anti-dumping measures impose discriminatory duties or tariffs upon the dumped goods to prevent damage to local industries and the economy that may otherwise flow from the import and sale of the dumped goods: they offset the price advantage of cheap foreign goods which are sold under their 'normal value'. Such discriminatory duties are 'legitimate' under GATT as dumping falls under art VI of GATT.

Many disputes on anti-dumping arose within GATT. In the 1964 Kennedy Round, anti-dumping and countervailing duties were raised as an issue and the possibility of concluding an anti-dumping code was discussed. As a result of the Kennedy Round, the Agreement on the Implementation of Article VI came into existence in 1968. The Anti-Dumping Code was established under the 1968 agreement. The code was an independent agreement operating between those GATT members who ratified it. The code

---
20. Ibid.
21. Ibid.
22. Taussig, *The Tariff History of the United States*, Johnson Reprint, New York, 1966, p 68.

was further discussed in the Tokyo Round in 1973–79. A number of technical issues were discussed: such as how to determine 'sale at a loss', how to determine cost of a product, how to determine price, how to determine material injury and how to make concessions to developing countries. A new anti-dumping code entitled 'Agreement on Implementation of Article VI of the General Agreement on Tariffs and Trade' came into operation in 1980. Anti-dumping was discussed again in the Uruguay Round. The Agreement on Implementation of Article VI of GATT 1994 was concluded as an integral part of the WTO Agreement. This is the new anti-dumping code. But it differs from the previous Anti-dumping Code, which was an independent document, as it is now part of the WTO Agreement, which operates between all WTO members. As at July 2002, about 19 anti-dumping disputes had been submitted to WTO panel proceedings for settlement.[23]

Tests for determining normal value of goods

[9.30] A crucial aspect of dumping is the sale under normal value. When a normal price has been determined, whether or not the product has been exported at a price lower than its normal value can then be determined. Article VI of GATT sets out the following tests for determining the normal value of an allegedly dumped product:

- if the price of the imported goods is lower than the comparable price of the like product determined when the product is sold in the ordinary course of trade in the exporting country;

- when there is no comparable price available in the exporting country, the normal value can be determined by examining the highest comparable price of the like product for export to any third country in the ordinary course of trade; or

- in the absence of information for determining any of the prices above, the normal value is decided by referring to the cost of production of the product in the country of origin plus a reasonable addition for selling cost and profit.

The same test is adopted in art 2 of the Agreement on Implementation of Article VI of GATT 1994, a special agreement made for the purpose of implementing the anti-dumping provision of GATT 1994. The provision states that:

> for the purpose of this agreement, a product is to be considered as being dumped, i.e. introduced into the commerce of another country at less than its normal value, if the export price of the product exported from one country to another is less than the comparable price, in the ordinary course of trade, for the like product when destined for consumption in the exporting country.

The Agreement on Implementation of Article VI of GATT 1994 supplements art VI by providing specific rules for the determination of normal value in pursuance of art VI.

---

23. For details, see *Update of the WTO Dispute Settlement Cases*, WT/DS/OV/7, at <http://www.wto.org/>.

Use of anti-dumping measures

[9.31] Anti-dumping measures are permitted under GATT as a means of protecting a national economy against unfair competition. They are not a vehicle for trade protection. Thus, art 1 of the Agreement on Implementation of Article VI of GATT 1994, which is part of Annex 1A to the WTO Agreement, states that:

> [an] anti-dumping measure shall be applied only under the circumstances provided for in Article VI of GATT 1994 and pursuant to investigations initiated[24] and conducted in accordance with the provisions of this Agreement.

Article VI of GATT does not itself provide specific rules for the application of the three tests for the determination of normal value set out above. GATT has instead formulated a special code of rules for making a determination. Currently, art 2 of the Agreement on Implementation of Article VI of GATT 1994 does not address equally each of the three situations described in art VI. It emphasises the rules applicable to the second and third situations, while providing some rules for determination in the first situation. The specific rules in art 2 of the Agreement on Implementation of Article VI of the GATT 1994 have the following features.

First, in the three tests specified in art VI of GATT (see **[9.28]**), the first and second are based on the concept of like product, while the third is based on the product itself. Determination of 'like product' thus arises as an issue. Under art 2.6 of the Agreement on Implementation of Article VI of GATT 1994, the term 'like product' ('*produit similaire*'):

> shall be interpreted to mean a product which is identical, i.e. alike in all respects to the product under consideration, or in the absence of such a product, another product which, although not alike in all respects, has characteristics closely resembling those of the product under consideration.

Second, when determining the normal value of imported goods by referring to the like product sold for local consumption in the exporting country, sales of the like product shall normally be considered a sufficient quantity for the determination of the normal value if such sales constitute 5 per cent or more of the sales of the product under consideration to the importing country, provided that a lower ratio should be acceptable where the evidence demonstrates that domestic sales at such lower ratio are nonetheless of sufficient magnitude to provide for a proper comparison.[25] This rule sets out a specific ratio relating to quantity of domestic sale for determining whether the sample is reasonable.

Third, when there is no sale of the like product in the ordinary course of trade in the domestic market of the exporting country or when, because of the particular market situation or the low volume of sales in the domestic market of the exporting country, the margin of dumping shall be determined by comparison with a comparable price of a like product when exported to an appropriate third country, provided that this price is representative, or with the cost of production in the country of origin plus a reasonable amount for administrative, selling and general costs, as well as profits.[26]

---

24. The term 'initiated' as used in this Agreement means the procedural action by which a member formally commences an investigation as provided in Article 5.
25. The Agreement on Implementation of Article VI of GATT 1994, footnote 5.
26. The Agreement on Implementation of Article VI of GATT 1994, art 2.2.

Fourth, when comparing prices, the comparison shall be made at the same level of trade, normally at the ex-factory level, and in respect of sales made at as nearly as possible the same time. Due allowance shall be made in each case, on its merits, for differences which affect price comparability, including differences in conditions and terms of sale, taxation, levels of trade, quantities, physical characteristics, and any other differences which are also demonstrated to affect price comparability. Allowances for costs include duties and taxes incurred between importation and resale. Appropriate allowance for profits should be made in determining the comparable price.

Fifth, the price ascertained by applying the stipulated methods sometimes may not reflect the true normal value of the goods concerned because of other factors which affect sales. Thus, art 2.2.1 of the Agreement on Implementation of Article VI of GATT 1994 states that sales of 'the like product in the domestic market of the exporting country or sales to a third country at prices below per unit (fixed and variable) costs of production plus administrative, selling and general costs may be treated as not being in the ordinary course of trade by reason of price and may be disregarded in determining normal value' only if the authorities determine that such sales are made within an extended period of time, which should normally be one year but shall in no case be less than six months, in substantial quantities,[27] and are at prices which do not provide for the recovery of all costs within a reasonable period of time. If prices which are below per unit costs at the time of sale are above weighted average per unit costs for the period of investigation, such prices shall be considered to provide for recovery of costs within a reasonable period of time.

Last, in cases where there is no export price or where it appears to the authorities concerned that the export price is unreliable because of association or a compensatory arrangement between the exporter and the importer or a third party, the export price may be constructed on the basis of the price at which the imported products are first resold to an independent buyer, or if the products are not resold to an independent buyer, or not resold in the condition as imported, on such reasonable basis as the authorities may determine.[28]

There are also specific rules on the collection of information and evidence for the purpose of making the determination. These rules are set out in art 6 of the Agreement on Implementation of Article VI of GATT 1994.

---

27. Sales below per unit costs are made in substantial quantities when the authorities establish that the weighted average selling price of the transactions under consideration for the determination of the normal value is below the weighted average per unit costs, or that the volume of sales below per unit costs represents not less than 20 per cent of the volume sold in transactions under consideration for the determination of the normal value.
28. The Agreement on Implementation of Article VI of GATT 1994, art 2.3.

> **[9.32]** *Rocklea Spinning Mills Pty Ltd v Anti-Dumping Authority*
>
> (1995) 129 ALR 401
>
> *Domestic anti-dumping legislation should be construed in the light of the relevant provisions of GATT*
>
> **Facts:** Rocklea was an Australian company and manufacturer of cotton products. It alleged in 1993 that cotton yarn imported to Australia from Pakistan had been subsidised or given financial assistance by the Pakistan Government, and applied to the Comptroller-General of Customs for the issue of a countervailing duty notice under s 269TJ of the Customs Act 1901 (Cth). The allegation was based on the fact that the Pakistan Government set compulsory export prices for Pakistan cotton yarn. The Comptroller-General was not satisfied that a case of dumping had been established by Rocklea, which subsequently applied to the Anti-Dumping Authority (ADA) for a review of the Comptroller-General's decision. The ADA upheld the decision and found that the allegedly subsidised import, if proved, did not cause any material injury to the Australian yarn-producing industry. Rocklea appealed to the Federal Court, which found the decision of the ADA was reasonable. Rocklea then appealed to the Full Court of the Federal Court.
>
> **Decision:** The court (Spender, Einfeld and Tamberlin JJ) dismissed the appeal. It held (at 411), inter alia, that:
>
>> ... in considering provisions such as s 269TJ, where the meaning is not clear, the courts can have regard to the international agreements and codes to which Australia is a signatory. These include what was known at the relevant time as the General Agreement on Tariffs and Trade (GATT) and the Countervailing Code: see *Atlas Air Australia Pty Ltd v Anti-Dumping Authority* (1990) 26 FCR 456 at 469; 99 ALR 29. These agreements embody the international rights and obligations of the parties in relation to international trade and the extent to which and circumstances in which governments may subsidise export goods and the action which can be taken in relation to goods exported to states which are subsidised in the country of origin.

Committee on Anti-Dumping Practices

[9.33] The Agreement on Implementation of Article VI of GATT 1994 establishes the Committee on Anti-Dumping Practices to enforce the relevant provisions of GATT on anti-dumping. The committee is composed of representatives from each WTO member. It elects its own chairperson and meets not less than twice a year and otherwise as envisaged by relevant provisions of the Agreement on Implementation of Article VI of GATT 1994 at the request of any member. The committee carries out responsibilities as assigned to it under the agreement or by the members and it affords members the opportunity of consulting on any matters relating to the operation of the agreement or the furtherance of its objectives. The WTO Secretariat acts as secretariat to the committee.[29]

The committee may set up sub-committees as necessary. In carrying out their functions, the committee and any subsidiary bodies may consult with and seek information from any source they deem appropriate. However, before the committee or a subsidiary body seeks such information from a source within the jurisdiction of a member, it shall inform the member involved. It shall obtain the consent of the member and any firm to be consulted.[30]

---

29. The Agreement on Implementation of Article VI of GATT 1994, art 16.1.
30. The Agreement on Implementation of Article VI of GATT 1994, art 16.3.

The committee supervises the compliance of WTO members with the relevant provisions. Members are obliged to report to the committee all preliminary or final anti-dumping actions taken. Such reports shall be available in the secretariat for inspection by other members. Members shall also submit, on a semi-annual basis, reports of any anti-dumping actions taken within the preceding six months. The semi-annual reports shall be submitted on an agreed standard form.[31]

Broadly speaking, the committee is more of a mentor than an authority with enforcement power. In the case of disputes between WTO members, the DSB should be resorted to. But the committee provides a forum for consultation and exchange of information. Its existence improves the transparency of and access to domestic measures affecting anti-dumping.

Countervailing duty under GATT

Concept of countervailing duty

[9.34] According to art VI(3) of GATT, a countervailing duty 'shall be understood to mean a special duty levied for the purpose of offsetting any bounty or subsidy bestowed, directly or indirectly, upon the manufacture, production or export of any merchandise'. This statement refers to a subsidy, which, as defined in art 1 of the Agreement on Subsidies and Countervailing Measures, exists in the following forms if a benefit has been conferred by:

a financial contribution by a government or any public body within the territory of a member where:

(i) government practice involves a direct transfer of funds (eg grants, loans, and equity infusion), potential direct transfers of funds or liabilities (eg loan guarantees);

(ii) government revenue that is otherwise due is foregone or not collected (eg fiscal incentives such as tax credits);[32]

(iii) a government provides goods or services other than general infrastructure, or purchases goods;

(iv) a government makes payments to a funding mechanism, or entrusts or directs a private body to carry out one or more of the type of functions illustrated in (i) to (iii) above which would normally be vested in the government and the practice, in no real sense, differs from practices normally followed by governments; or

there is any form of income or price support in the sense of Article XVI of GATT 1994.

A countervailing duty can be imposed upon subsidised goods. No special test for determining governmental subsidies is set out in GATT. The relevant rules are provided in the special code made for the purpose of implementing art VI. The Tokyo Round produced the Agreement on Subsidies and Countervailing Duties, which applied to imported goods receiving governmental subsidies from the exporting countries. The Agreement on Subsidies and Countervailing Measures was made in the Uruguay Round, which is also an

---

31. The Agreement on Implementation of Article VI of GATT 1994, art 16.4.
32. In accordance with the provisions of Article XVI of GATT 1994 (Note to Article XVI) and the provisions of Annexes I through III of this Agreement, the exemption of an exported product from duties or taxes borne by the like product when destined for domestic consumption, or the remission of such duties or taxes in amounts not in excess of those which have accrued, shall not be deemed to be a subsidy.

[9.34]

integral part of the WTO Agreement. This agreement forms the current regime for the use of countervailing duties within the WTO. Whether or not a product has received governmental subsidies is an issue of fact, even though WTO members have shown considerable differences in their understandings of the meaning of subsidies.[33] Differences can be seen when comparing the cost analysis of the imported goods and the goods of the same or comparable nature imported under normal market conditions.

Actionable and non-actionable subsidies

[9.35] Use of subsidies per se is not normally prohibited under the WTO. There must be evidence of injury or damage to the importing countries. Subsidies are thus classified into actionable subsidies and non-actionable subsidies under the Agreement on Subsidies and Countervailing Measures. An actionable subsidy is one which has an adverse effect on the interests of another WTO member. An export subsidy falls within the category of actionable subsidy because it has a direct and adverse effect on the competing products of the importing country. The Agreement on Subsidies and Countervailing Measures regards export subsidies as a special category of subsidy, not necessarily to be judged by the criteria for determining actionable or non-actionable subsidies. An adverse effect can be any of the following:[34]

- injury to the domestic industry of another member;
- nullification or impairment of benefits accruing directly or indirectly to other members under GATT 1994, in particular, the benefits of concessions bound under art II of GATT 1994; or
- serious prejudice to the interests of another member (the meaning of 'serious prejudice' is defined in art 6 of the Agreement on Subsidies and Countervailing Measures).

A non-actionable subsidy is one falling outside the definition of actionable subsidy. Article 8.2 of the Agreement on Subsidies and Countervailing Measures provides a definition of non-actionable subsidy to exempt a number of subsidies from countervailing duties. Briefly, the following subsidies are exempt form countervailing measures notwithstanding whether or not they may be caught by other provisions of the agreement:

- assistance for certain research activities conducted by firms or by higher education or research establishments;
- assistance to disadvantaged regions within the territory of a member given pursuant to a general framework of regional development[35] subject to the qualifications set out in art 8.2(b) of the Agreement on Subsidies and Countervailing Measures;

---

33. As at June 2002, more than four cases concerning countervailing duties had been submitted to the WTO panel proceedings for settlement, for example, see *United States — Measures Treating Export Restraints as Subsidies*, decided on 29 June 2001, case number: WT/DS194, available at <http://www.wto.org/>.
34. Agreement on Subsidies and Countervailing Measures, art 5.
35. A 'general framework of regional development' means that regional subsidy programs are part of an internally consistent and generally applicable regional development policy and that regional development subsidies are not granted in isolated geographical points having no, or virtually no, influence on the development of a region.

- assistance to promote adaptation of existing facilities[36] to new environmental requirements imposed by law and/or regulations which result in greater constraints and financial burden on firms in the circumstances as described in art 8.2(c).

The Agreement on Subsidies and Countervailing Measures permits WTO members to impose countervailing duties upon subsidised goods in pursuance of the principles of art VI of GATT. However, members are required to follow the procedures and rules set out in the agreement for the investigation of the existence of actionable subsidies and the imposition of the countervailing duties on the subsidised goods.

Committee on Subsidies and Countervailing Measures

[9.36] The Committee on Subsidies and Countervailing Measures is set out under the Agreement on Subsidies and Countervailing Measures. It consists of representatives from WTO members. Like the Committee on Anti-Dumping Practices, this committee elects its own chairperson and meets not less than twice a year and otherwise as envisaged by relevant provisions of the Agreement on Subsidies and Countervailing Measures at the request of any member. The committee carries out responsibilities as assigned to it under the agreement or by the members and it affords members the opportunity of consulting on any matter relating to the operation of the agreement or the furtherance of its objectives. The WTO Secretariat acts as the secretariat to the committee.[37]

One of the special features of the committee is the expert group established under it. Under art 24.3 of the Agreement on Subsidies and Countervailing Measures, the committee establishes a Permanent Group of Experts (PGE) composed of five independent persons, highly qualified in the fields of subsidies and trade relations. The experts will be elected by the committee and one of them will be replaced every year. The PGE may be requested to assist a panel to discharge its functions. The PGE may be consulted by any member and may give advisory opinions on the nature of any subsidy proposed to be introduced or currently maintained by that member. The committee has also the functions of collecting the relevant information on the use of countervailing measures in member countries.

Rules concerning customs valuation

[9.37] Valuation of imported goods for customs purposes is important in GATT, because valuation is the basis for imposing tariffs and related restrictions on imports. Article VII of GATT provides that the value of the imported goods for customs purposes should be based on their actual value in the importing country, which refers to the price sold or offered for sale in the ordinary course of trade under fully competitive conditions, rather than their value in the exporting country. This provision allows the importing country to evaluate the imported goods in the context of domestic law and the domestic market, and impose customs duties on that basis. This provision gives the importing country certain discretion to offset the negative impacts of certain imported

---

36. The term 'existing facilities' means facilities that have been in operation for at least two years at the time when new environmental requirements are imposed.
37. Agreement on Subsidies and Countervailing Measures art 24.1.

[9.37]

cheap goods, because duties so imposed should affect the market price of the imported goods. The provision also requires an importing country to review its laws and regulations in relation to valuation at the request of another contracting party. This will prevent a country from abusing the power of valuation to 'legalise' discriminatory measures which are inconsistent with the principles of GATT. The valuation of imported goods in accordance with local law does not resolve the problem of dumping. The value for customs purposes of imported merchandise is based on the actual value of the imported merchandise, or of like merchandise, rather than the value of merchandise of national origin or arbitrary or fictitious values. In justifying the assessment of any 'actual value' of the allegedly 'dumped goods', a contracting party's discretion under art VII is supported by art VI of GATT. The Agreement on Implementation of Article VII of GATT 1994 which is part of Annex 1A to the WTO Agreement provides detailed rules for the operation of art VII of GATT.

Rules governing exchange control

[9.38] Exchange control has two main functions in international trade — maintaining a balance between a country's foreign exchange income and expenditure, and restricting import of certain foreign goods or services. It may indirectly affect international trade through government restrictions on methods of payment, conversion of currency and repatriation of currency overseas. GATT does not deal directly with issues of exchange control among contracting parties. Article XV provides that contracting parties should form their foreign exchange policy in consultation with the International Monetary Fund. This provision brings the IMF into the operation of GATT and imposes upon contracting parties a broad duty to consult the IMF in forming their national laws and regulations relating to exchange control.

Exchange control became a significant issue in international trade after the Second World War. The Cold War, the disparate economic capacities of the industrialised and developing countries and the use of artificial exchange rates in many industrialised countries contributed to the extensive use of exchange control as a means of controlling international trade. Exchange control is less of an issue today due to the relative stability of world politics, political and economic reforms in most communist and socialist countries, abandonment of artificial exchange rates by many industrialised countries, and an increasing economic interdependence between countries. In international trade today most countries do not use exchange control simply as a barrier to international trade, and a great number of trading and commercial activities are carried out without the involvement of direct cash payments. Bearing in mind the flexibility of the language of art XV, exchange control is prohibited under GATT only when a contracting party, without consulting the IMF, uses exchange control as a sole means of trade protection. For example, art XV prohibits a country which does not have a foreign exchange imbalance problem from imposing measures of exchange control.

General Agreement on Trade in Services (GATS)

Service trade and making of GATS

[9.39] Service trade is one of the major forms of international trading activities today. Presently, services account for over 60 per cent of global production and employment, even though they usually represent about 20 per cent of total trade (BOP basis) annually.[38] According to the statistics provided by the WTO, the total value of all commercial services within the WTO amounted to US$1435 billion in 2000,[39] of which transportation services acounted for US$330 billion, travel services accounted for US$465 and other services accounted for US$640. It was also reported by the WTO that in 2001, the total value of merchandise trade within the WTO was US$5990 billion and the total value of service trade within the WTO was US$1440 billion.[40] These statistics suggest that service trade has become more and more important as a major trading form within the WTO.

[9.40] Depending on definitions, the term 'services' in international trade law refers to more than 600 different types of commercial services in various professions and sectors of the economy.[41] The major service sectors or professions are transportation, travel, wholesale and retail operations, advertising, banking, insurance, communications, construction, franchising, architecture, accounting, education, engineering, health, medical and legal services. Schedules of Specific Commitments made by each WTO member when joining the WTO illustrate the diversity and variety of service sectors and categories recognised by GATS. It is said that the Schedule divides services into about 150 different categories.[42]

The world economy has become highly integrated largely due to increasing economic interdependence between countries and rapid developments in modern technology, such as communications and computers. Political changes, such as the end of communism in Eastern Europe, China's open door policy and the integration of the EU, have also contributed, as have large immigration flows and the movement of labour throughout the world. Trade in services has become an important area of international trade and commercial law in the last 20 years as a result. In the 1980s, service exports were the dominant form of trade in services. In the 1990s, trade in services has moved to an investment-based form, which means that an exporting country invests in service industries in another country for the purpose of gaining access to the domestic market and earning foreign income.

Trade in services showed an impressive growth between the 1970s and 1990s. Internationally it grew at an annual rate of 19 per cent between 1970 and 1980. In 1980, the estimated value of international services exports was about US$350 bn, and transportation (carriage of goods by sea, land and air), travel and tourism were the major sectors for service exports. In 1980, the first 10 largest service exporters were the United States, the

---

38. See WTO document, 'The General Agreement on Trade in Services (GATS): Objectives, Coverage and Disciplines', available at <http://www.wto.org/>.
39. WTO, *International Trade Statistics 2001*, available at <http://www.wto.org/>.
40. See WTO, *Annual Report 2002*, available at <http://www.wto.org/>.
41. See Reference List of Sectors, GATT Doc. No. MTN.GNS/w/50 (13 April 1989).
42. See WTO Secretariat, *An Introduction to the GATS*, available at <http://www.wto.org/>.

[9.40]

United Kingdom, France, Germany, Italy, Japan, Netherlands, Belgium, Spain and Austria.[43] In 1990, the value of service industries counted for more than 50 per cent of gross domestic product in most industrialised countries, such as the United States, Japan, Germany, France, Canada, Australia, and a number of developing countries, such as India, Brazil, Mexico and Argentina.

At the beginning of the Uruguay Round, a number of industrialised countries, such as the United States, Australia, Austria, Canada, the EU and Japan, suggested that services should be included in the Uruguay Round. A number of developing countries, such as Brazil, India and Sri Lanka, argued that GATT did not have the legal basis to deal with trade in services. Several other countries, including Argentina, Egypt, the United Kingdom, Jamaica, Nigeria and Uruguay, believed that more information was necessary to decide whether services should be negotiated in the GATT negotiations. Those in favour of negotiating services in the Uruguay Round won and a special group on trade in services was set up.

There were two different views on the scope of GATS. A majority of countries, most of them developed countries who are exporters of services and investors of service-related projects, preferred a wide coverage for negotiation. Some less developed countries, such as the Latin American and Caribbean countries, also supported wide coverage to balance the interests of different countries, whose interests might be disadvantaged as the result of more select coverage. A number of developing countries, on the other hand, wanted to take a sectoral approach to negotiation in order to protect their local markets. This sectoral approach argued that countries should be allowed to determine which of their services would be open for discussion, and which would not. After seven years of negotiation, the countries agreed that GATS should cover all sectors of services except services supplied in the exercise of governmental authority. This leaves the possibility for a country to close off a particular sector of service to foreign countries by exercising governmental authority in that sector.

Further liberalisation of service trade is one of the major tasks promulgated by the Ministerial Declaration 2001 adopted on 14 November 2001 in Doha. The WTO ministers declared that the negotiation on trade in services should be conducted with a view to promoting the economic growth of all WTO members with a special emphasis on the development of developing and least-developed countries. For such purposes, WTO members agreed to submit their initial requests for specific commitments (suggestions and amendments) by 30 June 2002 and initial offers by 31 March 2003.[44] These requests and offers will form grounds for further negotiations on the liberalisation of service trade under GATS.

Structure of GATS

[9.41] GATS is contained in Annex 1B of the WTO Agreement. It has 32 articles. Three of them are marked 'bis' (meaning second time).[45] These provisions cover a wide range of issues and principles concerning trade in services, including, for example, modes

---

43. Stewart, note 17 above, p 2350.
44. See Doha Declaration, WT/Min(01)/DEC/1, available at <http://www.wto.org/>.

of international service trade, the meaning of services covered by GATS, the MFN principle, the NT principle, market access, and transparency requirements. They set out the legal framework for international trade in services within the WTO. GATS has eight annexes, which deal with the following issues:

- exemptions under art II: most favoured nation clause;
- movement of natural persons supplying services under the agreement;
- air transport services;
- financial services (two annexes dealing with financial services);
- maritime transport services;
- telecommunications; and
- basic communications.

Meaning of services under GATS

[9.42] Defining the meaning of services is not an easy task. In general terms, any trade or trading activity based on the one party's supply of labour, skill or knowledge can be regarded as a sale or supply of services. Accordingly, any business operation meeting such criterion can be regarded as a type of service.

[9.43] GATS has adopted a broad approach to the definition of services. Given the reality that it is impossible to define exclusively the meaning of services, art I(3)(b) of GATS states that services 'includes any service in any sector except services supplied in the exercise of governmental authority'. This is a very broad definition of services, which works by indicating what is not regarded as 'services' under GATS. The provision allows a country to exclude the application of GATS in any particular sector of services on the ground that the service is supplied in the exercise of governmental authority; that is, 'any service which is supplied neither on a commercial basis, nor in competition with one or more service suppliers'.[46] The two criteria for differentiating services included and services excluded by GATS are concurrent and supplementary to each other. Only when both criteria have been satisfied, a particular sector of economy can be closed to services and service suppliers from other WTO members.

[9.44] About 150 categories of services are listed in the Schedule of Specific Commitments attached to GATS. Each WTO member must make specific commitments in the Schedule to undertake specific liabilities for granting market access to foreign service products and service suppliers to enter its local market. The Schedule of Specific Commitment also contains a specific undertaking on NT (or any other benefits), which should be offered to foreign service products and suppliers under GATS. The Schedule of Specific Commitment is an illustrative list of the meaning of services under GATS.

---

45. Formally, there are 29 articles in GATS. However, there are three additional articles marked as 'bis', ie, art IIIbis, art Vbis and art XIVbis. Thus, there are actually 32 articles in GATS.
46. GATS art I(3)(c).

Modes of international trade in services

[9.45] GATS applies only to international trade in services. Therefore, internationalisation is the essential feature of services covered by GATS, which has accordingly identified four modes of international trade in services.[47] These four modes are set out as follows:

- **Cross-border supply:** This mode covers service flows from the territory of one WTO member into the territory of another. Advice or education received via telecommunication, internet or mail from a source situated outside the recipient's own territory is one such example.
- **Consumption abroad:** This mode covers services provided within the supplier's territory to foreign consumers. Services offered to foreign tourists fall under such mode.
- **Commercial presence:** This mode covers any forms of services offered by a foreign supplier in another member's territory through the establishment of local subsidies or local companies. Establishment of local branches by foreign banks, managing of local hotels by foreign companies under contract, and taking over local companies providing services by foreign companies are such examples.
- **Presence of natural persons:** This mode covers the situation where a national of one WTO member enters into the territory of another member to offer services. Services by foreign lawyers, accountants and seafarers are such examples.

[9.46] The importance of the modes of services is seen in art XVI(1) of GATS, which imposes the duty to guarantee market access. This provision states that with 'respect to market access through the modes of supply identified in Article I, each Member shall accord services and service suppliers of any other Member treatment no less favourable than that provided for under the terms, limitations and conditions agreed and specified in its schedule'.

'Most favoured nation' treatment

[9.47] Article II(1) of GATS requires that 'each Member shall accord immediately and unconditionally to services and service suppliers of any other Member, treatment no less favourable than that it accords to like services and service suppliers of any other country'. The essence of 'most favoured nation' (MFN) treatment is to treat the country which has been granted this treatment the best terms which have been, or will be, provided to any third country. If an undertaking country (the country which undertakes to provide the MFN treatment) grants another country MFN treatment, it undertakes a liability to treat that country in the same way as any third country which has received, or will receive, the most favoured trading conditions and privileges, from the undertaking country. An undertaking country is not obliged to satisfy any request of the grantee of the treatment, if the request contains conditions and privileges which have not been granted to any other country. An undertaking country does not breach its duty under GATS if it closes a particular sector of services non-discriminatorily to all the countries in pursuance of the specified exceptions under art II(3) of GATS: see **[9.48]**.

---

47. GATS, art I(2).

[9.48] Two exceptions are specified in arts II(2) and (3) of GATS to release a member from the duty of MFN. These are as follows:

- a member may apply to the Council for Trade in Services for an exemption pursuant to the Annex on Article II Exemptions; and
- a member is not required to accord to another member the special privileges or advantages available to 'adjacent countries in order to facilitate exchanges limited to contiguous frontier zones of services that are both locally produced and consumed'.

The second exception appears to apply to certain regional economic arrangements, such as the EU, ASEAN and the CER, or part of the arrangements. The privileges under this exception are qualified by the phrase 'that are both locally produced and consumed'. This qualification suggests that if any privilege is accorded with respect to 'services' that are either not produced within the 'contiguous frontier zones' (which are yet to be defined) or are not consumed within the 'contiguous frontier zones', the privilege does not fall under the exception. The precise contour of this exception is yet to be determined.

Transparency

[9.49] Article III of GATS requires members to make their laws, regulations and measures for the implementation of GATS transparent. This requirement includes the following obligations:

- a member should as soon as practicable publish its rules, policies, measures and any international agreements relating to GATS;
- if publication is not practicable, such information should be publicly accessible;
- a member must inform the Council for Trade in Services promptly of any changes in its laws, regulations and policies which significantly affect the performance of its obligations under GATS;
- a member is obliged to provide information requested by another member with respect to laws, regulations, policies and agreements which should be published under GATS; and
- a member is entitled to report to the Council for Trade in Services on any measure taken by another member if it considers the measure to be inconsistent with the provisions of GATS.

The duty to make laws, regulations and policies transparent is a duty to provide adequate information to the public and member countries and to guarantee access to general information relating to the operation of GATS in a particular country. This requirement applies equally to industrialised and developing countries, although the transparency of laws, regulations and policies normally causes more concern to foreign services industries operating in developing countries than in industrialised countries.

Market access

Defining market access

[9.50] 'Market access' in GATS means an obligation under which a member undertakes to provide market access, through 'modes of services' as defined in art I(2) of GATS, to another member, in a manner appropriate to the undertaking agreed by the member (art XVI of GATS). For example, if a member undertakes to allow a supply of insurance services from its territory to another member's territory and the cross-border movement of capital is an essential part of the services, the member also undertakes to allow such movement of capital. By the same token, if a member undertakes to allow a foreign insurance company to operate within its territory, it is obliged to allow the company to transfer capital which is necessary for the operation into its territory. 'Market access' includes an obligation to guarantee the exercise and enjoyment of the market access by other members within the territory of any member.[48]

Restrictions on market access

[9.51] Under art XVI(2) of GATS, a member is allowed to make specified restrictions pursuant to art XVI of GATS on the market access of foreign services industries. These restrictions can be summarised as follows:

- limitations on the number of service suppliers or service operations in a country;
- limitations on the total value of service transactions or assets;
- limitations on the total number of employees in a particular sector, for example, the insurance sector, or one of the segments of the sector;
- requirements for the specific type of legal entity to carry on a particular service; and
- limitation on the quantity of foreign investment or foreign control in a particular service.

These restrictions should be read with the members' obligation to accord to each other 'most favoured nation' treatment. Any restriction must apply equally to all members, unless an exception is allowed under GATS.

Specific commitments and market access

[9.52] Market access is guaranteed by art XVI of GATS, which states that 'each Member shall accord services and service suppliers of any other Member treatment no less favourable than that provided for under the terms, limitations and conditions agreed and specified in its Schedule'. This provision means that the actual market access granted by a WTO member to service products and suppliers of other WTO members is subject to the contents of Specific Commitments as agreed by all WTO members in the Schedule attached to GATS. The Schedule of Specific Commitments on Services is one of the essential documents which is discussed and approved by other WTO members when a country or customs territory becomes a WTO member. For example, China made

---

48. For relevant discussions, see John Mo, 'Mystery of Market Access' Vol 3: No 2 (2000) *The Journal of World Intellectual Property* 225–47.

detailed undertakings as to the liberalisation of its service market in the Schedule of Specific Commitments when it became a WTO member in 2001. The close connection between market access as a right or principle under GATS and the Schedule of Specific Commitments illustrates the nature of market access. It also suggests that market access must be read together with Specific Commitments made by each WTO member in the relevant Schedule.

In each Schedule of Specific Commitments, market access to each particular sector of service market or service industry must be decided under the specific undertakings (commitments) made by the relevant WTO member against each mode of service as defined in art I(1) of GATS: see **[9.45]**. For example, a WTO member may not have any restriction on the mode of cross-border supply, but may restrict the foreign ownership in the local banking or insurance industry. Similarly, a WTO member may allow foreign accountants to provide services in any modes, but refuse to allow foreign lawyers to provide legal services on local law. Therefore, whenever an issue of market access arises under GATS, it is essential to read the relevant Schedule of Specific Commitments to ascertain the rights and obligations of the WTO members concerned.[49] It must be noted that specific commitments contained in a schedule may be modified or withdrawn pursuant to the procedures set out in art XXI of GATS.

National treatment

[9.53] The expression 'national treatment' means that a member is obliged to treat nationals of another WTO member and their products in the same way as its own nationals and products. While the principle of 'most-favoured-nation treatment' emphasises equality between two foreign parties or products within the territory of a member, the principle of 'national treatment' emphasises equality between a foreign party and a local party, or between a foreign product and local product. Article XVII of GATS requires a member to accord national treatment to nationals of another member and their products in pursuance of the terms and conditions set out in the relevant Schedule of Specific Commitments. A member is obliged to treat nationals of another member and their products equally as its own nationals and products in all respects unless restrictions and exemptions have been made in the Schedule of Specific Commitments. This means that a member is allowed to treat foreign nationals and products differently from its own nationals and products only within the scope of the restrictions as approved in the Schedule of Specific Commitments attached to GATS.

TRIPs Agreement

Introduction

[9.54] TRIPs stands for trade-related intellectual property rights. Intellectual property (IP) broadly includes copyrighted materials, patents, trademarks, industrial designs, trade

---

49. For relevant discussions, see WTO Secretariat, *An Introduction to the GATS*, Section 1.4 'How to read a GATS Schedule', available at <http://www.wto.org/>.

names and know-how. Computer software and integrated circuits are regarded as forms of intellectual property. All forms of IPs can be divided into two broad categories: copyright and rights related to copyright; and industrial property. Copyright is the author's right in literary and artistic works, such as books, writings, music, paintings, sculpture, computer programs and films. The rights related to copyright are also known as neighbouring rights, referring to the rights of performers (such as actors, singers and musicians), and producers of phonograms and broadcasting organisations. The industrial property mainly refers to patent, trademarks, geographical indications, industrial designs, know-how and trade secrets. The IPs which are related to international trade in goods and services are regulated and protected by WTO.

IP was not covered under GATT 1947. The 1883 Paris Convention for the Protection of Industrial Property covers industrial property, such as patents, trademarks, industrial designs and trade names. The 1886 Berne Convention for the Protection of Literary and Artistic Works covers copyright. The World Intellectual Property Organisation (WIPO) was set up in 1967 under the Convention Establishing the World Intellectual Property Organisation as a specialised UN agency to coordinate the protection of intellectual property worldwide. The increasing transfer of technology in international trade from developed countries to developing countries has made the building of an adequate legal framework for protection of intellectual property one of the major concerns of international trade regulation.

Protection of intellectual property in international trade is an important issue. In the 1970s, trade in counterfeit goods became a serious issue and caused world concern. Control of counterfeiters was not enough to eliminate trade in counterfeited goods. Attention turned to control of trade in counterfeited goods. Countries were asked not to trade in counterfeited goods for the purpose of discouraging their production. The Anti-dumping and Counterfeiting Code was drafted by a number of countries at the end of the 1970s, but it failed to obtain support from most GATT members. In 1986, GATT members agreed to put trade in counterfeited goods on the agenda for negotiations, and a negotiating group was set up to deal with the issue.

Protection of intellectual property requires commitment from GATT members to adopt adequate domestic laws. Many developing countries were worried that they would lose access to modern technology as a result of adopting strict rules for the protection of intellectual property in domestic laws. In 1989, intellectual property was one of the areas where GATT members could not reach agreement. In 1991, the differences between countries were narrowed to several specific issues, such as collective licensing (an arrangement under which fees for use of intellectual property are paid into a fund which will compensate authors according to rules) and rental rights (a right to prohibit rental shops from renting one's intellectual property, such as a CD or VCD, within a specific period of time). The final draft was concluded in 1991, and was a compromise between the interests of different countries. The present TRIPs Agreement contains 73 articles and a Preface. With GATT (and associated agreements), GATS, the TRIPs Agreement represents one of the three pillars of the WTO trading system. However, it should be noted that if counting the dispute settlement mechanism of WTO, there should be four pillars in the WTO trading system.

IPs protected by the TRIPs Agreement

[9.55] IP under the TRIPs Agreement refers to the following categories of intellectual property:

- copyright which extends to computer programs, data and expressions, but excludes ideas, procedures, methods of operation or mathematical concepts;
- trademarks;
- geographical indications which contribute to the reputation and quality of a product;
- industrial designs;
- patents;
- layout-designs (topographies) of integrated circuits (design for hardware); and
- undisclosed information, such as trade secrets or data on experiments.

There is some difference between intellectual property in a general sense and intellectual property under the agreement. For example, a business name is not protected under the agreement unless it is a trademark or geographical indication. Similarly, know-how must be a trade secret or layout-design to be eligible for protection under the TRIPs Agreement.

TRIPs Agreement and existing international conventions

[9.56] Article 2 of the TRIPs Agreement clearly states that the agreement does not affect the operation of existing international conventions on protection of intellectual property, such as the Paris Convention and the Berne Convention. Article 9 of the TRIPs Agreement requires WTO members to comply with arts 1 through 21 of the Bern Convention (1971). Article 35 of the TRIPs Agreement refers to the Treaty on Intellectual Property in respect of Integrated Circuits. In the light of these provisions, it can be said that the following four IP conventions have been incorporated into the TRIPs Agreement:

- Paris Convention for the Protection of Industrial Property (1967);
- Berne Convention for the Protection of Literary and Artistic Works (1971);
- International Convention for the Protection of Performers, Producers of Phonograms and Broadcasting Organisations (the Rome Convention) (1961); and
- Treaty on Intellectual Property in Respect of Integrated Circuits (1989).

National treatment

[9.57] Article 3(1) of the TRIPs Agreement grants national treatment to all WTO members. Under this principle, a WTO member is obliged to treat foreign nationals and its own nationals equally in pursuance of the relevant WTO agreement, such as the TRIPs Agreement. But the operation of the national treatment principle under the TRIPs Agreement is subject to exceptions provided in the existing international conventions. Article 3(1) states as follows:

> Each Member shall accord to the nationals of other Members treatment no less favourable than that it accords to its own nationals with regard to the protection of intellectual property, subject to

the exceptions already provided in, respectively, the Paris Convention (1967), the Berne Convention (1971), the Rome Convention or the Treaty on Intellectual Property in Respect of Integrated Circuits.

The exception is necessary because, as we have seen, the TRIPs Agreement co-exists with a number of existing international conventions on IPs. In case of any potential conflicts, the operation of NT under the TRIPs Agreement must be reconciled with the relevant provisions in the aforesaid conventions. Further, the exception is also necessary, because not all WTO members have joined the aforesaid conventions. Therefore, the said exceptions only operate between the WTO members who are members of the three conventions.

MFN treatment

[9.58] Article 4 of the TRIPs Agreement applies the MFN principle by stating that with regard to 'the protection of intellectual property, any advantage, favour, privilege or immunity granted by a Member to the nationals of any other country shall be accorded immediately and unconditionally to the nationals of all other Members'. The general purpose of the MFN principle is to ensure that all nationals of WTO members are treated equally by any individual WTO member. The operation of this principle under the agreement is, however, subject to the following exceptions:

- if a privilege is derived from international agreement on judicial assistance or law enforcement of a general nature;
- if a privilege is granted under the relevant international conventions (ie, Berne Convention and Rome Convention);
- if a privilege relates to the rights of performers, producers of phonograms and broadcasting organisations which are not covered by the TRIPs Agreement;
- if a privilege is derived from an international agreement made prior to the entry of force of the TRIPs Agreement provided that the agreement is consistent with the WTO Agreement.

The purpose of setting out exceptions is to ensure effective operation of the MFN principle in the TRIPs Agreement. Exceptions to general rules are necessary in most cases in the regulation of international trade and commerce.

Rental rights

[9.59] Rental rights are defined in art 11 of the TRIPs Agreement as follows:

In respect of at least computer programs and cinematographic works, a Member shall provide authors and their successors in title the right to authorise or to prohibit the commercial rental to the public of originals or copies of their copyright works. A Member shall be excepted from this obligation in respect of cinematographic works unless such rental has led to widespread copying of such works which is materially impairing the exclusive right of reproduction conferred in that Member on authors and their successors in title. In respect of computer programs, this obligation does not apply to rentals where the program itself is not the essential object of the rental.

Accordingly, the author of a computer program, CD, VCD or film is entitled to prohibit the unauthorised commercial rental to the public of his or her works. However, a country is entitled to make an exception to the author's right if rental of a cinematographic work does not lead to widespread copy of the work and will not materially damage the rights of the author. A country may also ignore the author's right if a computer program itself is not the essential object of the rental. This provision shows a compromise between different positions on rental rights.

Transitional arrangements

[9.60] Transitional arrangements deal with periods of time in which a WTO member is expected to comply with the provisions of the TRIPs Agreement. Article 65 sets out the following rules for the implementation of the agreement:

- a developed country should start to implement the provisions of the TRIPs Agreement from 1 January 1996;
- a developing country or a country transforming from a centrally planned economy to a market economy is entitled to have four additional years from the completion date applicable to a developed country;
- a developing country is entitled to have an additional five years to comply with the provisions on patent protection, if the protection is needed in an area which was not protectable when the country became a WTO member; and
- the least-developed countries have 10 years to comply with the TRIPs Agreement from 1 January 1996.

This provision reflects a general practice of GATT and the WTO Agreement, whereby countries with different economic status are given different periods of time to comply with the agreements.

Dispute settlement within the WTO

Dispute settlement mechanism

[9.61] Renato Ruggiero, the former Secretary-General of the WTO, called the WTO dispute settlement procedure its most significant contribution to the stability of the global economy. According to the WTO, between 1 January 1995 and 21 June 2002, a total of 260 disputes had been submitted to the dispute settlement mechanism for consultation, which is a compulsory stage for WTO members to resolve their disputes within the WTO. About one-third of these disputes had actually been submitted to panel proceedings for settlement. Cases submitted to panel proceedings involved many specific issues of WTO agreements, such as quantitative restrictions, anti-dumping, countervailing duties, subsidies, safeguards, customs duties, health standards, taxation, IP protection, customs evaluation, and so on. The statistics demonstrate that the Dispute Settlement Body (DSB) has been very active in providing assistance to WTO members for dispute settlement.

The dispute settlement mechanism of the WTO is based on the DSU. It consists of the DSB, which is set up under art 2 of the DSU, and a number of means of dispute settlement, such as consultation, good offices, conciliation, mediation, panel proceedings and

[9.61]

arbitration. The DSB is an important part of the dispute settlement mechanism. The operation of the DSB and each different procedure for dispute settlement are discussed below.

Functions of the DSB

[9.62] The Dispute Settlement Body or DSB is the authority in charge of dispute settlement within the WTO. It has the same membership as the General Council. This means that every WTO member is also a member of the DSB. According to the overall design of the WTO, many agreements refer disputes arising from them to the DSB, which is therefore responsible for enforcing not only the DSU, but also all agreements that grant it the power to settle their disputes. Technically, the DSB is established under art 2 of the DSU to administer DSU rules and procedures, including procedures based on consultation, good offices, mediation, arbitration and panel proceedings. Under the DSU, the DSB has the authority to establish panels, adopt panel and Appellate Body reports, maintain surveillance of implementation of rulings and recommendations, and authorise suspension of concessions and other obligations under the relevant agreements. In practice, the DSB is a council of all members which makes ultimate decisions in pursuance of the relevant rules to resolve disputes arising from all WTO agreements.

The notion of a general council of all WTO members must be qualified in the case of a Plurilateral Trade Agreement. Under the current WTO structure, the Plurilateral Trade Agreements are optional. When a dispute arises from any of the Plurilateral Trade Agreements, only those WTO members which have ratified that particular Plurilateral Trade Agreement are entitled to constitute the DSB for resolving a dispute arising from the agreement concerned. In such cases, the DSB is the general council of all WTO members which have ratified the agreement in dispute.

The DSB's functions are largely defined in the DSU. Depending on the procedure involved, the DSB's function varies. For example, in case of consultation under art 4 of the DSU (see **[9.64]**), the role of the DSB is to supervise the implementation of art 4, ensuring that the disputing members comply with the procedures set out in art 4. If disputing countries choose to resort to the assistance of good offices and mediation under art 5 (see **[9.65]**), the role of the DSB is also largely supervisory. However, if the parties decide to resort to panel proceedings under arts 6–21 of the DSU (see **[9.67]**–**[9.72]**), the role of the DSB is more than supervisory; it is actually part of the decision-making process. It is not only responsible for organising the panels, but also makes decisions in pursuance of the relevant provisions of the DSU on whether to endorse or reject a panel report. The DSB's decision in such cases forms part of the panel proceedings. The panel proceeding is the most important dispute settlement mechanism under the WTO. Arbitration proceedings are also available under the DSU. The DSB provides assistance to parties who wish to resort to arbitration under the DSU.

General procedures of dispute settlement under the DSU

[9.63] The DSU provides a range of alternative means of dispute settlement. As a general principle, the parties are encouraged to resolve their differences and disputes by consultation or negotiation first. If unsuccessful, the parties are encouraged to consider the use of good offices, conciliation and mediation. After that, panel proceedings and arbitration should be considered. The general process for dispute settlement under the DSU is divided into two major stages by the WTO.[50]

The first stage involves consultation, in which the parties have up to 60 days to resolve their dispute. Before taking any other action the countries in dispute have to talk to each other to see if they can settle their differences by themselves. If that fails, they can also ask the WTO Director-General to mediate or try to help in any other way.

The second stage involves panel proceedings, during which a panel must be appointed within 45 days from the date of application, and the panel has six months to complete its report. If consultations fail, the complaining country can ask for a panel to be appointed. The country 'in the dock' can block the creation of a panel once, but when the DSB meets for a second time, the appointment can no longer be blocked unless there is a consensus against appointing the panel. Officially, the panel is helping the DSB make rulings or recommendations. But because the panel's report can only be rejected by consensus in the DSB, its findings and conclusions are difficult to overturn.

The description of dispute settlement procedures by the WTO as a two-stage process is largely based on the compulsory requirements of the DSU. It is implied in the relevant provisions of the DSU that disputing parties should attempt consultation first, before resorting to panel proceedings. But there are no compulsory requirements for the use of good offices, mediation, conciliation and arbitration, unless the time for implementing a binding panel report is referred to arbitration under art 21(3) or a matter concerning compensation or suspension of concession as described in art 22 is referred to arbitration by the DSB in pursuance of art 22(6).

Consultation under the DSU

[9.64] Article 4 of the DSU requires WTO members to resolve their disputes by consultation or negotiation. Article 4(2) of the DSU requires members to accord sympathetic consideration to and afford adequate opportunity for consultation regarding any representations made by another member concerning measures affecting the operation of any WTO agreement. Accordingly, if a request for consultation is made pursuant to a WTO agreement, the member to which the request is made shall, unless otherwise mutually agreed, reply to the request within 10 days after the date of its receipt and shall enter into consultations in good faith within a period of no more than 30 days after the date of receipt of the request, with a view to reaching a mutually satisfactory solution. If the member does not respond within 10 days after the date of receipt of the request, or does not enter into consultations within a period of no more than 30 days, or a period otherwise mutually agreed, after the date of receipt of the request, then the member that requested the holding of consultations may proceed directly to request the establishment of a panel.[51] This means that a WTO member has an obligation to resort to consultation for resolving a dispute. But if the other party fails to respond to the request for consultation within a

---
50. The information is available at <http://www.wto.org/wto/about/dispute1.htm>.
51. DSU art 4(3).

[9.64]

reasonable time as set out in art 4 of the DSU, the first party is entitled to resort to panel proceedings which can compel the other party to respond.

In order to enable the DSB to monitor the process of consultation, the parties are required to notify the DSB and the relevant council or committee of the WTO of all requests for consultations, which should be made in writing and should give the reasons for the request, including identification of the measures at issue and an indication of the legal basis for the complaint.[52] The process of consultation is confidential and does not prejudice the rights of the parties in other proceedings. This means that any information, admission or concession made by any party during consultation cannot be used by the other as evidence against the maker in other proceedings, in particular panel proceedings and arbitration. A third party may join a consultation process in pursuance of art 4(11) of the DSU where justifications under the relevant agreements must be given.

The process of consultation is not subject to any procedural requirement if the other party fails to respond to the request of the party seeking consultation. However, if both parties have commenced consultation, neither can resort to other means, particularly panel proceeding, unless 60 days have passed since the receipt of the request for consultation by the responding party. This means that if consultations fail to settle a dispute within 60 days after the date of receipt of the request for consultations, the complaining party may proceed to request the establishment of a panel. However, the complaining party may request a panel during the 60-day period if the consulting parties jointly consider that consultations have failed to settle the dispute.[53] The compulsory period of consultation may be reduced in cases of urgency, including the case of perishable goods, where members shall enter into consultations within a period of no more than 10 days after the date of receipt of the request. If the consultations have failed to settle the dispute within a period of 20 days after the date of receipt of the request, the complaining party may request the establishment of a panel.[54]

Good offices and mediation under the DSU

[9.65] There is no definition of good offices, conciliation or mediation in the DSU. It used to be a popular term in international law, referring to a process similar to mediation or conciliation in which a third party who is probably a high official or a head of foreign government, or an international organisation, offers his or her assistance in searching for a peaceful solution to a dispute between two governments. The WTO is an international organisation, and its agreements are international treaties. Thus, the use of good offices to resolve disputes arising from treaties is similar to the use of good offices in international law. Conciliation and mediation are similar processes in which a third party who can be either a foreign government or an individual acts as a mediator or conciliator to help the disputing parties to reach a settlement. Under art 5(6) of the DSU, the Director-General of the WTO may, acting in an ex officio capacity, offer good offices, conciliation or mediation with the view to assisting members to settle a dispute. Mediation and

---

52. DSU art 4(4).
53. DSU art 4(7).
54. DSU art 4(8).

conciliation are also known as methods of alternative dispute resolution (ADR) in the domestic law context.

The use of good offices, conciliation and mediation is set out in art 5 of the DSU, which does not, however, make them a compulsory stage after the failure of consultation. In fact, good offices, conciliation or mediation may be requested at any time by any party to a dispute. They may begin at any time and be terminated at any time.[55] Once procedures for good offices, conciliation or mediation are terminated, a complaining party may then proceed with a request for the establishment of a panel. Arrangements on the use of good offices, conciliation or mediation are interesting. There is no obligation to go from consultation to good offices, conciliation or mediation, because under art 4(3) and (7) a party may go directly from consultation to panel proceedings if consultation cannot commerce or cannot be completed within the stipulated time. But once a process of good offices, conciliation or mediation has begun, the parties are bound by certain procedural requirements on time. In particular, when good offices, conciliation or mediation are entered into within 60 days after the date of receipt of a request for consultation, the complaining party must allow a period of 60 days after the date of receipt of the request for consultations before requesting the establishment of a panel. The complaining party may request the establishment of a panel during the 60-day period if the parties to the dispute jointly consider that the good offices, conciliation or mediation process has failed to settle the dispute.[56]

This procedure is largely voluntary. It is confidential and without prejudice to the rights of any party in any other proceedings. A unique feature of good offices, conciliation or mediation under the DSU, is that the procedure may continue between parties who have submitted their dispute to panel proceedings under the DSU.

Panel proceedings under the DSU

Two-tier structure

[9.66] Panel proceedings under the DSU are based on a two-tier structure. When one or both parties resort to panel proceedings, a panel will be appointed in pursuance of the relevant rules of the DSU. The panel must complete its report within the timeframe as set out by the DSU and submit its report to the DSB. Any disputing party is entitled to lodge an appeal against the report within 60 days after the date of circulating the report to the members. At such a request, the DSB must allow the parties to pursue the appeal process in accordance with the DSU. The Appellate Body must complete the appeal review within the time limit of 60–90 days. When the report of the Appellate Body has been submitted to the DSB, according to art 17(14) of the DSU, the report shall be adopted by the DSB and unconditionally accepted by the parties to the dispute unless the DSB decides by consensus not to adopt it within 30 days following its circulation to the members.[57] This adoption procedure is without prejudice to the right of members to

---

55. DSU art 5(3).
56. DSU art 5(4).
57. If a meeting of the DSB is not scheduled during this period, such a meeting of the DSB shall be held for this purpose.

[9.66] express their views on an Appellate Body report. Panel proceedings end with the decision of the DSB on the report provided by the Appellate Body.

The organisational structures of the panel and of the Appellate Body are different. The panel is not a permanent tribunal. The DSB maintains a list of panel members and panel members for each panel should normally be appointed from this list. Article 8(4) of the DSU provides that in order to:

> assist in the selection of panellists, the Secretariat shall maintain an indicative list of governmental and non-governmental individuals possessing the qualifications outlined in paragraph 1, from which panellists may be drawn as appropriate. That list shall include the roster of non-governmental panellists established on 30 November 1984 (BISD 31S/9), and other rosters and indicative lists established under any of the covered agreements, and shall retain the names of persons on those rosters and indicative lists at the time of entry into force of the WTO Agreement. Members may periodically suggest names of governmental and non-governmental individuals for inclusion on the indicative list, providing relevant information on their knowledge of international trade and of the sectors or subject matter of the covered agreements, and those names shall be added to the list upon approval by the DSB. For each of the individuals on the list, the list shall indicate specific areas of experience or expertise of the individuals in the sectors or subject matter of the covered agreements.

The Appellate Body is a permanent tribunal. It is established in pursuance of art 17(1), which states that a standing Appellate Body which consists of seven permanent members shall be established by the DSB:

> The DSB shall appoint persons to serve on the Appellate Body for a four-year term, and each person may be reappointed once. However, the terms of three of the seven persons appointed immediately after the entry into force of the WTO Agreement shall expire at the end of two years, to be determined by lot. Vacancies shall be filled as they arise. A person appointed to replace a person whose term of office has not expired shall hold office for the remainder of the predecessor's term.[58]

> The Appellate Body shall comprise persons of recognised authority, with demonstrated expertise in law, international trade and the subject matter of the covered agreements generally. They shall be unaffiliated with any government. The Appellate Body membership shall be broadly representative of membership in the WTO. All persons serving on the Appellate Body shall be available at all times and on short notice, and shall stay abreast of dispute settlement activities and other relevant activities of the WTO. They shall not participate in the consideration of any disputes that would create a direct or indirect conflict of interest.[59]

Commencement of panel proceedings

[9.67] A request for panel proceedings under the DSU should be made to the DSB. If a party so requests, a panel shall be established at the latest at the DSB meeting following that at which the request first appears as an item on the DSB's agenda, unless at that meeting the DSB decides by consensus not to establish a panel.[60] The request for the establishment of a panel shall be made in writing. It shall indicate whether consultations were held, identify the specific measures at issue and provide a brief summary of the legal basis of the complaint sufficient to present the problem clearly. In case the applicant requests the establishment of a panel with other than standard terms of reference as set

---

58. DSU art 17(2).
59. DSU art 17(3).
60. DSU art 6(1).

out in art 7 of the DSU, the written request shall include the proposed text of special terms of reference for endorsement by the DSB.[61]

A panel should normally have three panellists, who are normally chosen by the DSB from the panel list maintained by the DSB. With the agreement of the disputing parties, an unlisted person may be appointed as a panel member. Similarly, the constitution of a panel can also be extended to five members. Persons listed as panellists by the DSB must be well-qualified governmental and/or non-governmental individuals, including persons who have served on or presented a case to a panel, served as a representative of a member or of a contracting party to GATT 1947 or as a representative to the council or committee of any WTO agreement or its predecessor agreement, or in the Secretariat, taught or published on international trade law or policy, or served as a senior trade policy official of a member.[62] General speaking, citizens of the disputing parties should not be appointed as panellists in the dispute. However, this restriction can be waived by agreement of the parties. The Secretariat shall propose nominations for the panel to the parties to the dispute. The parties to the dispute shall not oppose nominations except for compelling reasons.[63]

If there is no agreement on the panellists within 20 days after the date of the establishment of a panel, at the request of either party, the Director-General, in consultation with the chairperson of the DSB and the chairperson of the relevant council or committee, shall determine the composition of the panel by appointing panellists whom the Director-General considers most appropriate in accordance with any relevant special or additional rules or procedures of the covered agreement or covered agreements which are at issue in the dispute, after consulting with the parties to the dispute. The chairperson of the DSB shall inform the members of the composition of the panel thus formed no later than 10 days after the date the chairperson receives such a request.[64]

Panel members are independent and serve in their individual capacities and not as government representatives, nor as representatives of any organisation. WTO members shall not give them instructions nor seek to influence them as individuals with regard to matters before a panel.[65]

In the case of multiple complaints, whenever feasible a single panel may be established to examine these complaints, taking into account the rights of all members concerned. If more than one panel is established to examine complaints related to the same matter, to the greatest extent possible the same persons shall serve as panellists on each of the separate panels and the timetable for the panel process in such disputes shall be harmonised.[66]

---

61. DSU art 6(2).
62. DSU art 8(1).
63. DSU art 8(6).
64. DSU art 8(7).
65. DSU art 8(9).
66. DSU art 9.

Panel procedures

[9.68] Efficiency is one of the major considerations of panel proceedings. Thus, a panel is required to comply with the timeframe set out in the DSU in dealing with a dispute. Detailed working procedures of panel proceedings are set out in Annex 3 to the DSU, which provide general rules for the conduct of proceedings. A proposed timetable for panel proceedings is set out in the working procedures. Generally speaking, a panel should complete its investigation and submit its report within a timeframe of six months. This is required by art 12(8) of the DSU. When necessary, the time may be extended to eight months as suggested by the working procedures included in Annex 3.

The panel should receive written submissions from the parties about the matter in dispute. There is no formal procedure for the submission of 'complaint' and 'defence' from both parties. They can be submitted together or in any order the parties wish, because the matter in dispute has been well argued between the parties before it reaches the panel. In this regard, panel proceedings within the WTO are different from ordinary arbitration proceedings, where the parties see each other's arguments formally during the proceedings. The panel should fix a firm deadline for the parties to submit further evidence and argument after the submission of the initial complaint and defence.

The panel may have closed sessions to investigate the matter in dispute. Both parties should be given opportunities to speak during the meeting. There are no detailed rules on how to conduct a session. Nor are there rules of evidence. In most cases, there should be two sessions; the first for presenting different views and the second for arguing major issues in dispute. On both occasions, the complainant should be asked to speak first. One of the essential functions of the panel is to investigate. This is stated in art 11 of the DSU, which provides that:

> a panel should make an objective assessment of the matter before it, including an objective assessment of the facts of the case and the applicability of and conformity with the relevant covered agreements, and make such other findings as will assist the DSB in making the recommendations or in giving the rulings provided for in the covered agreements.

Therefore, during proceedings a panel should consult regularly with the parties to the dispute and give them adequate opportunity to develop a mutually satisfactory solution, including speaking to each other during closed sessions.

A third party is permitted to join the panel proceedings. This is one of the special features of the WTO dispute settlement mechanism. Even for consultation, art 4(11) of the DSU permits a third party to join the consultation in pursuance of the relevant rules. Article 10(2) states that any third party having a substantial interest in a matter before a panel and having notified its interest to the DSB shall have the opportunity to be heard by the panel and to make written submissions to the panel. These submissions shall also be given to the parties to the dispute and shall be reflected in the panel report. If a third party considers that a measure pending in a panel proceeding nullifies or impairs benefits accruing to it under WTO agreements, the party is entitled to refer its complaint to the original panel wherever possible.[67] This means that a third party may join an ongoing panel process as a joint complainant.

---

67. DSU art 10(4).

The rule of confidentiality applies to panel proceedings. Panel deliberations shall be confidential and the reports of panels shall be drafted without the presence of the parties to the dispute, but only in the light of the information provided and the statements made. In addition, opinions expressed in the panel report by individual panellists shall be anonymous to ensure confidentiality.[68]

Making of panel report

[9.69] The making of a panel report may involve three stages: drafting of the section on facts; drafting of the interim report on the dispute; and submission of the final report. First, following the consideration of rebuttal submissions and oral arguments, the panel issues the descriptive (factual and argument) sections of its draft report to the parties to the dispute for comments. Within a period of time set by the panel, the parties submit their comments in writing.[69] This process reduces disagreement on the relevant facts and minimises the possibility of appeal by the disputing parties.

Second, following the expiration of the set period of time for receipt of comments from the parties, the panel issues an interim report to them, including both the descriptive sections and the panel's findings and conclusions. Within the period of time set by the panel, a party may submit a written request for the panel to review specific aspects of the interim report prior to circulation of the final report to members of the DSB. At the request of a party, the panel shall hold a further meeting with the parties on the issues identified by the parties. If no comments are received from any party within the comment period, the interim report shall be considered the final panel report and circulated promptly to DSB members.[70]

Third, a panel may either submit the interim report as the final report if no objection from the parties has been heard within the time limit, or redraft the final report by incorporating the parties' comments on the interim report. When relevant, the findings of the final panel report shall include a discussion of the arguments made at the interim review stage. The final report should be submitted to the DSB within the time framework allowed by the DSU.

Effect of the panel report

[9.70] Since the panel does not make any decision, a panel report cannot be enforced without the endorsement of the DSB. Generally speaking, one of four things may happen to a final report:

- A disputing party lodges an objection to the report in writing in pursuance of art 6(4) of the DSU, which provides that within 60 days 'after the date of circulation of a panel report to the Members, the report shall be adopted at a DSB meeting, unless a party to the dispute formally notifies the DSB of its decision to appeal or the DSB decides by consensus not to adopt the report'. When necessary, a special meeting of the DSB shall be held for the purpose of implementing art 16 of the DSU. If a party

---

68. DSU art 14.
69. DSU art 15(1).
70. DSU art 15(2).

[9.70]

has notified its decision to appeal, the report concerned shall not be considered for adoption by the DSB until after completion of the appeal. This adoption procedure is without prejudice to the right of members to express their views on a panel report.
- Second, a WTO member who is not a disputing party may lodge a written objection to the report in pursuance of art 16(2) of the DSU at least 10 days prior to the scheduled DSB meeting. The objection must be supported by reasons, and is meant for DSB members' consideration of the report.
- Third, in the absence of an appeal from the disputing parties, the DSB may decide to adopt the report. By adopting the report, the DSB endorses the findings and the recommendations made by the report.
- Lastly, in the absence of an appeal, the DSB may decide to reject the report. In such cases, the findings and recommendations of the report do not have any legal effect. In order to ensure that DSB members have been appropriately informed, art 16(1) of the DSU requires that there are at least 20 days between the distribution of the report and the meeting in which a decision on the adoption of the report is to be made.

Appeal process

[9.71] A disputing party has a right of appeal under art 16(4) of the DSU. A third party may lodge an objection to a panel report under art 16(2) of the DSU, but does not have the right of appeal against a report. However, a third party who is unhappy about a report may resort to art 10(2) of the DSU, which permits a third party to claim a right to be heard by a panel, including the Appellate Body, by notifying the DSB in writing of its substantial interest in the dispute.[71] This right to be heard is available when there is an ongoing proceeding. This means that if none of the disputing parties wishes to lodge an appeal, no third party can initiate an appeal process on its own with the Appellate Body.

In most cases, a panel of the Appellate Body has three members. The proceedings of the appeal shall not exceed 60 days from the date a party to the dispute formally notifies its decision to appeal to the date the Appellate Body circulates its report. In fixing its timetable the Appellate Body shall take into account the provisions of paragraph 9 of art 4, if relevant. When the Appellate Body considers that it cannot provide its report within 60 days, it shall inform the DSB in writing of the reasons for the delay together with an estimate of the period within which it will submit its report. In no case shall the proceedings exceed 90 days.[72] An appeal is limited to issues of law covered in the panel report and legal interpretations developed by the panel.[73] Working procedures for appeal were drawn up by the Appellate Body (WT/AB/WP/3) on 28 February 1997 in consultation with the chairman of the DSB and the Director-General.

Like panel proceedings, proceedings of the Appellate Body must be confidential and comply with the time requirements. In exceptional circumstances, where strict adherence to a time period set out in these rules would result in a manifest unfairness, a party to the dispute, a participant, a third party or a third participant may request that a division

---

71. DSU art 17(4).
72. DSU art 17(5).
73. DSU art 17(6).

modify a time period set out in these rules for the filing of documents or the date set out in the working schedule for the oral hearing. Where such a request is granted by a division, any modification of time shall be notified to the parties to the dispute, participants, third parties and third participants in a revised working schedule.[74]

Generally speaking, the appellant should within 10 days after the date of the filing of the notice of appeal, file with the Secretariat a written submission prepared in accordance with the relevant rules and serve a copy of the submission on the other parties to the dispute and the third party. Any party to the dispute that wishes to respond to allegations raised in an appellant's submission may, within 25 days after the date of the filing of the notice of appeal, file with the Secretariat a written submission and serve a copy of the submission on the appellant and other parties to the dispute. An appeal panel of the Appellate Body (known as a 'division') shall hold an oral hearing, as a general rule, 30 days after the date of the filing of the notice of appeal. At any time during the appellate proceeding, including, in particular, during the oral hearing, the Appellate Body may address questions orally or in writing to, or request additional memoranda from, any participant or third participant, and specify the time periods by which written responses or memoranda shall be received.

The appeal process is completed when the appeal panel of the Appellate Body submits its report to the DSB. The reports of the Appellate Body shall be drafted without the presence of the parties to the dispute and in the light of the information provided and the statements made.[75] The views of the members of the Appellate Body are also anonymous.

Effect of the Appellate Body's report

[9.72] The report of the Appellate Body should make recommendations as to the matter in dispute. It may have legal effect automatically. An Appellate Body report can be adopted by the DSB, in which case the disputing party must accept it unconditionally. However, the DSB has the power to decide by consensus not to adopt the Appellate Body report within 30 days following its circulation to DSB members.[76] Accordingly, under the DSU, a report of the Appellate Body becomes binding upon the parties 30 days after its distribution unless the DSB unanimously rejects it. The process for the adoption of the Appellate Body's report suggests that in most cases a report of the Appellate Body should be final after the 30-day period.

Members are expected to implement the recommendations of the panel or the Appellate Body, as the case may be, promptly and effectively. Therefore, at a DSB meeting held within 30 days after the date of adoption of the panel or Appellate Body report, the party concerned is required to inform the DSB of its intentions in respect of implementation of the recommendations and rulings of the DSB. If it is impracticable to comply immediately with the recommendations and rulings, the party should be given a reasonable period of time to do so.[77] The length of a reasonable time is determined in pursuance of

---

74. Working Procedures of Appellate Body art II(2).
75. DSU art 17(10).
76. DSU art 17(14).

[9.72]

the rules set out in art 21 of the DSU. If the party concerned fails to act within a reasonable period of time, it has to enter into negotiations with the complaining party in order to determine mutually acceptable compensation, such as tariff reductions in areas of particular interest to the complaining side. If after 20 days no satisfactory compensation is agreed, the complaining side may ask the DSB for permission to impose limited trade sanctions, for example, to suspend concessions or obligations against the party liable. The DSB should grant this authorisation within 30 days of the expiry of the 'reasonable period of time' unless there is a consensus against the request.

Arbitration under the DSU

[9.73] Arbitration is one of the alternative means of dispute settlement within the WTO. There is no special panel for arbitration under the DSU or within the DSB. The general rules of arbitration law apply. For example, art 25(2) provides that except:

> as otherwise provided in this Understanding, resort to arbitration shall be subject to mutual agreement of the parties which shall agree on the procedures to be followed. Agreements to resort to arbitration shall be notified to all Members sufficiently in advance of the actual commencement of the arbitration process.

The WTO and competition law

Origin of the term 'anti-trust'

[9.74] Anti-trust, which is another term for prohibition of unfair competition in international commercial law, is a lesser issue than anti-dumping. Anti-trust law, like anti-dumping law, originated in the United States. The expression 'anti-trust' is predominantly American: other countries adopt the same expression (certain European countries, for example), or use the term 'restrictive trade practices' (Australia, for example) to deal with the same issues. The Foreign Proceedings (Excess of Jurisdiction) Act 1984 (Cth) defines 'anti-trust' as:

> any law of a kind commonly known as an antitrust law and includes any law having as its purpose, or as its dominant purpose, the preservation of competition between manufacturing, commercial or other business enterprises or the prevention or repression of monopolies or restrictive practices in trade or commerce.

Anti-trust became an issue of international trade and commerce mainly because of the extra-territorial effect of the anti-trust legislation of the United States and certain European countries. This unilaterally enforced extra-territorial operation of the anti-trust law, in particular by US courts, has received furious criticism and strong resistance from many countries. An example of its operation occurred in 1910, when a German law controlling the mining of potash in Germany resulted in an increase in the purchase price of potash paid by Americans. American importers now had to pay twice as much as they had before the law came into operation. The Attorney-General of the United States was of the opinion that the German law was likely to violate the provisions of the Sherman anti-trust

---

77. DSU art 21(3).

law.[78] Similarly, the US court in the *Westinghouse* cases[79] found a violation of anti-trust law by four Australian companies. As a response to this finding, the Australian Parliament passed the Foreign Antitrust Judgements (Restriction of Enforcement) Act 1979 (Cth) to prohibit the enforcement of certain anti-trust judgments in Australia.

Purpose of anti-trust legislation

[9.75] The restrictive trade practices legislation in most countries contains provisions similar to those adopted in the anti-trust law of the United States. The purpose of these laws is to prevent unfair competition and market monopoly based on arrangements between foreign and local companies. Anti-trust in a broader sense (an act against restrictive trade practices) raises international concern because many foreign companies intend to achieve market dominance in a particular country by entering into exclusive licensing, patent or transferring agreements, arrangements or contracts with local companies either within or outside that country. Those same activities are prohibited in Australia under the Trade Practices Act 1974 (Cth). The only difference between restrictive trade practices prohibited in local law and anti-trust legislation is that 'anti-trust' has become a special term referring to restrictive international trade practices that, though carried out by a foreign company overseas, have a detrimental effect on the local market.

Relationships between anti-trust and anti-dumping laws

[9.76] The major differences between anti-dumping and anti-trust laws are as follows:

- dumping is directly related to international trade and a direct result (or even a form) of trading activity, but unfair business practices may not directly involve the import or export of goods or products between countries, though a licensing or patent agreement may result in the sale of 'foreign goods';
- dumping is the detrimental sale of goods under normal value, but a 'trust' is the creation of or engagement in restrictive trade practices by way of 'trust' arrangements;
- anti-dumping is dealt with under the WTO, but competition law is only an area which has been studied by the WTO.

The common feature of dumping and trust is that both of them are detrimental to the local economy. But they have different emphases. Anti-trust law or competition law is made for the purpose of ensuring fair competition in a domestic market. Anti-dumping law is made for the purpose of offsetting the unfair advantage of imported goods created

---

78. Ebb, note 13 above, pp 583–6.
79. The *Westinghouse* cases took place in the United States in 1976. Westinghouse was an American manufacturer of uranium-powered electrical generators. It was sued for having failed to perform its contracts with a number of its customers due to a sharp rise in the price of uranium in the world market. It then commenced actions in the United States against a number of uranium producers from Australia, Canada and the UK, claiming the existence of a cartel controlling the price of the uranium market. The actions resulted in the uranium producers being requested to provide a number of confidential documents for the purpose of discovery. The three relevant countries, Australia, Canada and the UK, responded to the requests by passing so-called 'blocking' legislation. The legislation effectively stated that US laws had no applications to acts outside the US by persons who could not in any sense be described as US residents, or citizens. This allowed the producers to refuse production of the documents.

by a sale under normal value. It is meant to protect local industries. Sometimes, they may overlap as both are related to the notion of fairness in the market. But the underlying purposes of the two types of law are different. The exclusion of 'anti-trust' or competition law from the WTO was probably due to the fact that the competition laws and policies of various countries are difficult to reconcile. Uniformity in competition laws and policies would require WTO members to make further commitments which are beyond the scope of the current WTO agreements. If the WTO did attempt to bring a uniform competition law into its framework, the use of anti-dumping measures would have to be assessed in the light of market competition. This would mean many countries would lose the privilege of imposing anti-dumping duties, which may partly explain why anti-trust or competition matters are not presently covered by the WTO agreements.

In 1996, a working group on competition policy was set up. The working group examined a number of specific trade issues concerning competition policy and trade, since WTO members had not reached any consensus on the inclusion of competition issues into the negotiation agenda. There has been no substantial development on the regulation of competition issues within the WTO.

The WTO and other international trade organisations

[9.77] Members of the WTO are obliged to perform their obligations under the various agreements under the WTO Agreement. Existing agreements which are inconsistent with members' obligations under the WTO Agreement may be overridden, unless the WTO Agreement permits the members to make reservations in relation to a particular obligation: see art XIII of the WTO Agreement. Presently, a WTO member may join any other regional trade organisation provided that its obligations under the regional organisation are consistent with its WTO obligations. Since the WTO agreements do not cover all issues of international trade and commerce and the level of trade liberalisation within WTO is still modest, there is still a need and scope for the existence of regional trade organisations. Such a need will continue to exist as long as there are considerable differences or imbalances in the economic status of WTO members, particularly between members of different regions.

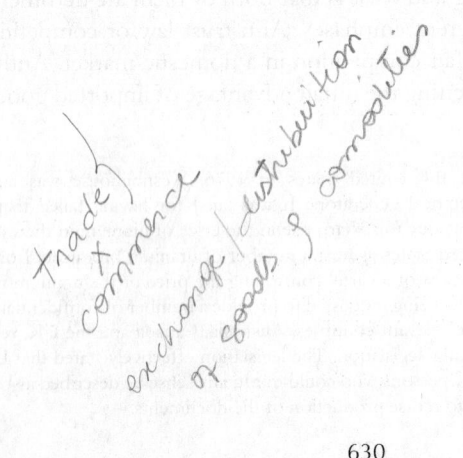

Chapter Ten

Regional Trade Organisations

Introduction

[10.1] A regional trade organisation can be understood as an international organisation established between countries in a particular region for the purpose of fostering and strengthening economic and commercial relationships among them. The common bond between members of a regional trade organisation is their geographical connections and the possibility of a relatively high flow of cross-border trade. Regional trade organisations form an important part of international commercial law and there are many regional trade and economic organisations in existence. As at June 2002, more than 200 regional trade agreements (RTAs) had been notified to WTO, and more than 170 of them were in force.[1] These agreements either build free trade areas (also known as customs unions) or make special arrangements to facilitate trading activities between contracting parties. In this chapter, several major regional organisations or arrangements will be reviewed: the EU, APEC, ASEAN, NAFTA and Australia New Zealand Closer Economic Relations (a treaty purporting to establish special economic cooperation between the two countries). NAFTA and Australia New Zealand Closer Economic Relations are better defined as arrangements than organisations. The structure and operation of these organisations provide valuable insight into the regulation of international trade and commerce.

The European Union

Historical review

[10.2] 'EU' stands for the European Union. It currently consists of 15 countries: Austria, Belgium, Denmark, Finland, France, Germany, Greece, Ireland, Italy, Luxembourg, Netherlands, Portugal, Spain, Sweden, and the United Kingdom. It is the most powerful and organised regional trade organisation existing today. The EU is of course

---

1. See the relevant information under the heading of 'Regionalism', in WTO website, available at <http://www.wto.org/>.

much smaller than the WTO, but the WTO is classified as an international trade organisation, while the EU is a regional trade organisation, although it is also 'international'.

The history of the EU can be traced back to the 1950s. After the Second World War, the notion of establishing some form of economic cooperation between European countries was welcomed by most Western European countries, including the United Kingdom. In 1951, the European Coal and Steel Community Treaty (ECSC) was concluded between six countries: Belgium, France, Germany, Italy, Luxembourg and the Netherlands.[2] The United Kingdom refused to sign the treaty. The purpose of the community was to coordinate the policies and practices of the members in relation to the sale of coal and steel between them. The ECSC Treaty came into existence in 1952 and the community was established in the same year. In 1957, the same six countries made the European Economic Community Treaty (EEU Treaty) and the European Atomic Energy Community Treaty (Euratom Treaty). Both treaties are also known as the Treaties of Rome. The United Kingdom again refused to sign the treaties. They became effective in 1958 and thus three separate communities existed between the same six countries. The communities shared the European Court of Justice set up under the EEU Treaty.

The EU went into its second stage of development in the 1960s. Acknowledging the need for uniform policies in various areas of trade between members, the three communities merged in 1965 under the Merger Treaty and became the EEC. The EEU Treaty has been the most important legislation for the development of the EU. In the 1970s and 1980s, the EEC grew bigger. Denmark, Ireland and the United Kingdom joined in 1973; Greece became a member in 1979; Portugal and Spain were accepted as members in 1985. In 1987, the Single European Act was concluded, which promotes the notion of the European Union for wider cooperation among the members.

The EU entered into a third stage of development in the 1990s. On 7 February 1992, the Treaty on European Union (TEU Treaty or Masstricht Treaty) was concluded, and entered into force on 1 November 1993.[3] It strengthens integration within the EU and streamlines its legal framework. The EEC subsequently became the EC, when the word 'economic' was dropped from its name to indicate the expanded scope of cooperation between members. This cooperation extended to monetary and fiscal policies. The EC is moving towards coordination of national policies on many political, social and economic issues. The 'European Community' then became the 'European Union'. A number of other European countries, such as Cyprus, the Czech Republic, Estonia, Hungary, Malta, Poland, Slovenia, Switzerland and Turkey, have applied for EU membership.

The EU may enter its fourth stage in the twenty-first century. A political agreement on Agenda 2000, covering the period 2000–2006, was reached by EU leaders on 26 March 1999 at the end of a special European Council meeting held in Berlin. The agreement paves the way for the enlargement of the EU to a first wave of countries from Central and Eastern Europe. It provides basic policies and measures for the EU to deal with major challenges expected during this period, such as how to strengthen and reform the EU's common agricultural policy and social and economic cohesion policy; how to prepare

---

2. This treaty expired on 23 July 2002.
3. 11:9 *EC News*, October/November 1993, p 1.

Central and Eastern European countries for the EU; and how to put in place a new financial framework. Agenda 2000 is a strategy for strengthening growth, competitiveness and employment, for modernising key policies and for extending the EU's borders as far eastwards as the Ukraine, Belarus and Moldova.[4] Bulgaria, Romania, Latvia, Lithuania and Slovakia are expected to join the EU during the period covered by Agenda 2000. In April 2003, the Czech Republic, Cyprus, Estonia, Latvia, Lithuania, Hungary, Malta, Poland, Slovenia and Slovakia signed the Treaty of Accession with the EU. These countries will become members of EU on 1 May 2004. The EU will then have 25 members.

The ultimate goal of the EU is to establish an ever closer union between the peoples of Europe. It aims to promote balanced and sustainable economic and social progress, assert itself on the international scene and introduce European citizenship for the nationals of the EU members. It is not only a regional trade organisation, but meant ultimately to be a European federation or organisation for economic, political and social cooperation.

The legal framework of the EU

[10.3] The EU has its own law and regulations. Several organisations within the EU, such as the council, the parliament and the court, have law-making power. The nature of the power exercised by each organisation is different, but all of them are based on the EU Treaty. In broad terms the legal framework of the EU consists of the following treaties and instruments:

- the Treaty on European Union (the Maastricht Treaty);
- the European Community Treaty (formerly the EEC Treaty);
- the European Atomic Energy Community Treaty (EAEC);
- regulations, which are directly applied within the EU without the need for national measures to implement them;
- directives, which bind member states as to the objectives to be achieved while leaving national authorities the power to choose the form and means of their implementation;
- decisions, which may be addressed to any or all member states, enterprises or individuals, and are binding in all their aspects upon those to whom they are addressed; and
- recommendations and opinions, which are not binding.

The Treaty on European Union is 'in large measure a statement of political intent, containing relatively few legally specific commitments'.[5] It extends the cooperation of the EU to certain new areas not covered by the EEC Treaty. For example, the treaty purports to establish a common foreign and social policy within the EU and to deal with areas involving justice and home affairs. These extensions caused concern among certain members and led to Denmark's initial rejection of the treaty on 2 June 1992.[6] Following the ratification of the Maastricht Treaty by all EC members, the EU has come into a new era.

---

4. EU, *2000 Agenda*, available at <http://europa.eu.int/comm/agenda2000/overview/en/agenda.htm>.
5. Weatherill and Beaumont, *EC Law*, Penguin Books, London, 1993, p 9.
6. For discussion on Denmark and the Maastricht Treaty, see Bierman, Kolari and Pustay, 'Denmark and the Maastricht Treaty: A Market Analysis' (1992) 3 *Duke Journal of Comparative & International Law* 147.

[10.3]   **International Commercial Law**

Its success presents a model for regional economic development in the future. The differences between each type of legislation are crucial for EU members and private parties operating within the EU. As we can see, most legislation in the EU is administrative in nature. The EU Parliament's legislative power is qualified by the EU Treaty, which appears to have given wider law-making power to the EU Commission than to the EU Parliament.

Structure of the EU

[10.4] The structure of the EU is based on the Treaty Establishing the European Community (EU Treaty), which is the continuation of the 1957 EEU Treaty. If the EU were a federal state, the amended EEU Treaty would be its constitution. Part V of the EU Treaty deals with the organisational structure of the EU. It creates a number of bodies and organisations within the EU. The organs of the EU are:

- The Council of the European Union (EU Council): see **[10.5]–[10.6]**.
- The European Commission: see **[10.7]**.
- The European Parliament: see **[10.8]**.
- The European Court of Justice: see **[10.9]**.
- The Court of Auditors (arts 188a–188c) is regarded as the taxpayers' representative, responsible for checking that the EU spends its money according to its budgetary rules and regulations and for the purposes for which it is intended. The Court of Auditors has 15 members chosen from 15 countries, but the auditors act independently. It has power to examine all accounts of the revenue and expenditure of the EU.
- The Economic and Social Committee (arts 193–198) advises the Commission, the Council and the European Parliament on various economic and social matters. The opinions which it delivers (either in response to a referral or on its own initiative) are drawn up by representatives of the various categories of economic and social activity in the EU. Membership quotas are set according to the size of each country, but members act in an independent capacity.
- The Committee of the Regions (arts 198a–198c) is the EU's youngest institution, whose birth reflects member states' strong desire not only to respect regional and local identities and prerogatives, but also to involve them in the development and implementation of EU policies. It consists of representatives of regional and local bodies. Quotas for membership are set for each country and committee members act in an independent capacity.
- The European Investment Bank (arts 198d and 198e) is the EU's financing institution. It provides loans for capital investment and promotes balanced economic development and integration. Membership consists of the 15 EU countries.

Other institutions include the European System of Central Banks (ESCB), the European Central Bank (ECB) (as regulated by the Protocol on the Statute of the European System of Central Banks and the European Central Bank), the European Monetary Institute (EMI) as regulated by the Protocol on the Institute of the European Monetary Institute, the Committee of Inquiry and Ombudsman under the Parliament, and the Conciliation Committee for the Council and Parliament. The functions and roles of these institutions are defined in the EU Treaty and other relevant treaties and regulations.

Regional Trade Organisations [10.4]

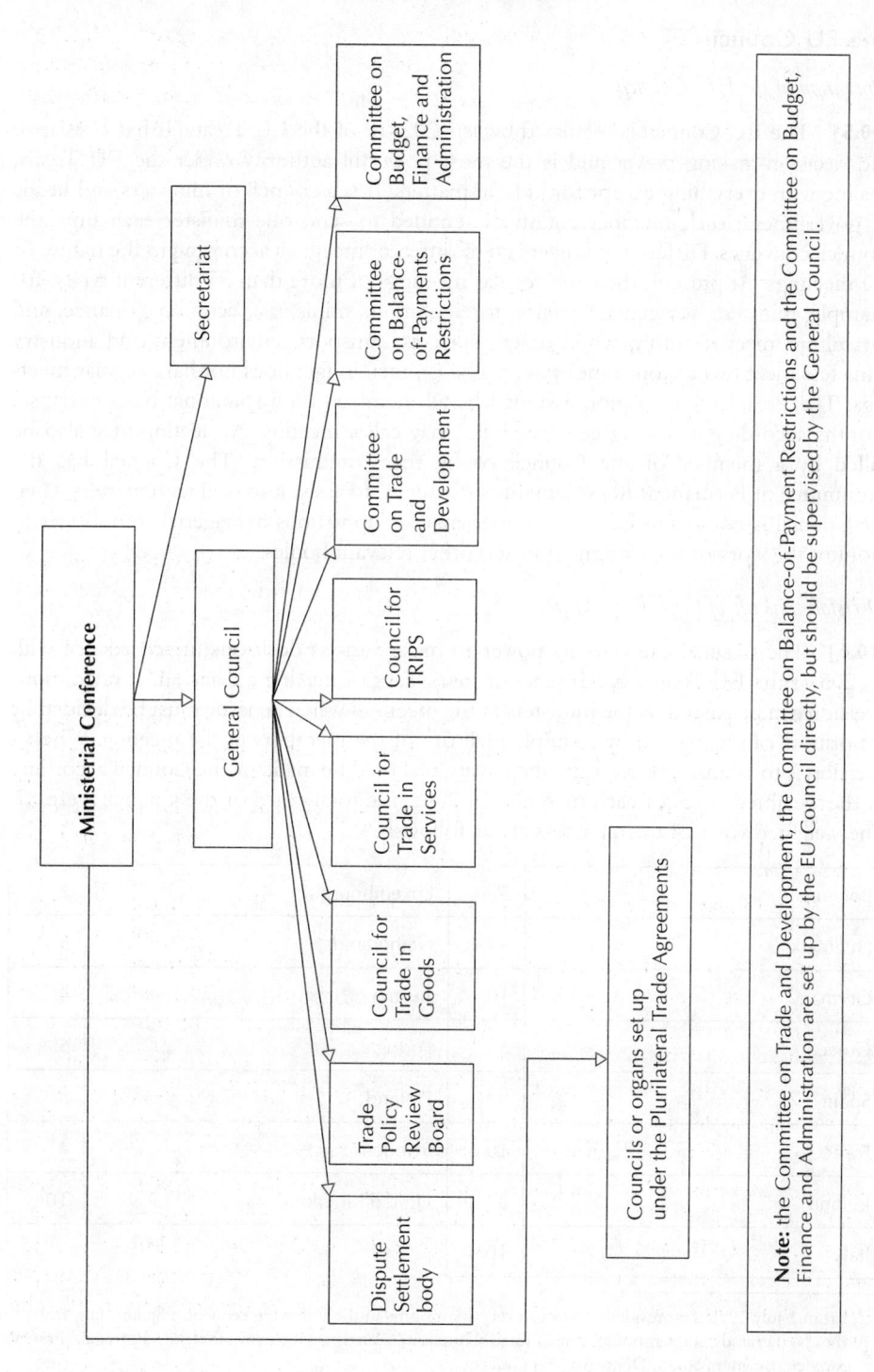

```
Ministerial Conference
    │
    ├──────────────► Secretariat
    │
    ▼
General Council ──► Committee on Budget, Finance and Administration
    ├──► Committee on Balance-of-Payments Restrictions
    ├──► Committee on Trade and Development
    ├──► Council for TRIPS
    ├──► Council for Trade in Services
    ├──► Council for Trade in Goods
    ├──► Trade Policy Review Board
    └──► Dispute Settlement body
              │
              ▼
    Councils or organs set up under the Plurilateral Trade Agreements
```

Note: the Committee on Trade and Development, the Committee on Balance-of-Payment Restrictions and the Committee on Budget, Finance and Administration are set up by the EU Council directly, but should be supervised by the General Council.

635

The EU Council

Operation of the EU Council

[10.5] The EU Council is regulated by arts 202–10 of the EU Treaty. It has legislative and decision-making power and is the most powerful authority under the EU Treaty, dealing with everything except for judicial matters. It is a council of ministers and heads of government: each member country is entitled to send one minister each time the Council convenes. Different ministers go to different meetings according to the nature of the meetings. At present, there are regular meetings of more than 25 different types: for example, ministers for general affairs (foreign affairs ministers), economy, finance, and agriculture meet monthly, while others such as transport, environment and industry ministers meet two to four times a year. The Council in fact does not have regular meetings. The President, a position assumed by all members on a rotational basis every six months according to the agreed schedule,[7] may call a meeting. A meeting may also be called by a member of the Council or by the Commission. The Council has the Committee of Permanent Representatives (Coreper) to assist it to deal with matters when the Council is not in session. The Council may set up various managerial committees to monitor the work of the Commission and other relevant bodies.

Decision-making of the EU Council

[10.6] The Council exercises its power to make various decisions in accordance with art 205 of the EU Treaty, which sets out three ways of making a decision. A unanimous decision can be passed by the ministers at the meeting. When an issue must be decided by majority, it can be passed by a simple majority of the members in the meeting. When a decision is to be made by a qualified majority, it should be made by the Council according to the weighted votes of each member. In 2002, the total votes of the Council were 87. The weighted votes of the members are as follows:

Belgium	5	Luxembourg	2
Denmark	3	Netherlands	5
Germany	10	Austria	4
Greece	5	Portugal	5
Spain	8	Finland	3
France	10	Sweden	4
Ireland	3	United Kingdom	10
Italy	10		

---

7. From 1 July 1995 the presidency rotates every six months in the following sequence: Spain, Italy, Ireland, the Netherlands, Luxembourg, the United Kingdom, Austria, Germany, Finland, Portugal, France, Sweden, Belgium, Spain, Denmark, and Greece.

Voting is divided into two types: unanimous vote and qualified majority vote. The policy areas in Pillar One are subject to unanimity: Pillar One covers a wide range of community policies (such as agriculture, transport, environment, energy, research and development) designed and implemented according to a well-proven decision-making process which begins with a Commission proposal. Following a detailed examination by experts and also at the political level, the Council can either adopt the Commission proposal, amend it or ignore it. Presently, Pillar One areas include taxation, industry, culture, regional and social funds and the framework program for research and technology development.

For the other two pillars created by the EU Treaty — Common Foreign and Security Policy (Pillar Two) and cooperation in the fields of Justice and Home Affairs (Pillar Three), the Council is the decision-maker as well as the promoter of initiatives. Unanimity is the rule in both pillars, except for the implementing of a joint action which can be decided by qualified majority. The objectives of the Common Foreign and Security Policy are to define and implement an external policy covering all foreign and security areas. Cooperation in Justice and Home Affairs aims to achieve the free movement of persons inside the EU, promote measures of common interest in the fields of external border control, asylum policy and immigration policy, and fight against terrorism, drug trafficking and other serious forms of international crime.[8]

The qualified majority is subject to two further qualifications: when the Council considers a proposal from the Commission in pursuance of the EU Treaty, it needs 62 votes in favour to adopt the proposal; when the Council considers any other matters, it needs 10 countries whose total votes amount to 62 votes in favour to make a decision. In practice, the Council tries to reach the widest possible consensus before taking a decision. Consequently, only about 14 per cent of the legislation adopted by the Council in 1994 was subject to negative votes and abstentions. The Council is required under the Treaty to consult with various bodies before making certain decisions. This includes consultation with the Parliament when making certain regulations and rules. When the EU Treaty requires the Council to act at the proposal of the Commission or a special body, the Council must follow procedural requirements.

The European Commission

[10.7] The European Commission is regulated by arts 211–219 of the EU Treaty. It exercises specified functions as designated to it by the treaty, or by the power delegated to it by the Council. It administers the operation of the EU Treaty, and has specified decision-making power. The combination of both administrative and decision-making functions distinguishes the Commission from the General Council of the WTO.

The Commission has 20 commissioners who are nationals of EU members. The procedure for appointing commissioners is set out in arts 213–216 of the EU Treaty. Generally speaking, names of potential commissioners and president of the Commission are provided by each member. The Council may appoint commissioners on the basis of their

---

8. The Council of the EU, available at <http://europa.eu.int/inst/en/cl.htm#function>.

individual merits. The appointment needs to be approved by the Parliament. Article 213 of the EU Treaty requires a country to have a minimum of one appointee and a maximum of two. Currently, five large countries — France, Germany, Italy, Spain and the United Kingdom — have two commissioners each in the Commission. Commissioners are required to act independently in the interests of the EU, rather than in the interest of their own countries.

The major functions of the Commission as set out in art 211 of the EU Treaty are as follows:

- Enforcer of EU laws and regulations: the Commission ensures the enforcement of the EU Treaty and the laws, regulations and policies of the EU, and has power to prosecute breaching countries or institutions failing to abide by the laws and regulations.
- Initiator of legislation: the Commission makes recommendations as to various matters regulated by the EU Treaty, or proposes legislative changes in accordance with the EU Treaty or on its own initiative.
- Decision-maker: the Commission exercises independent decision-making power under the relevant provisions of the EU Treaty, and may also be involved in the law-making process conducted by the Council and the Parliament.
- Holder of delegated power: the Commission can exercise authority delegated to it by the Council and also enforce rules made by the Council.

The Commission operates at the very heart of the EU. Its role as the source of policy initiatives is unique, yet this role is not always clearly understood. The Commission has used its right of initiative to transform the framework provided by the EU's founding treaties into today's integrated structures. The benefits for citizens and companies throughout the EU have been considerable: there is more freedom to travel and trade, increased prosperity and much less red tape.[9]

Although it has the right of initiative, the Commission does not make the main decisions on EU policies and priorities. This is the responsibility of the Council, whose members are ministers from member governments and (in many instances) of the European Parliament as well. The belief that the Commission has wide law-making power under the EU Treaty is a misconception which the Commission believes greatly exaggerates its power. The Commission has few powers of coercion, although its neutral role and the depth of specialised knowledge it has acquired over the years give it plenty of scope for persuasion.[10] Its power or powerful image comes from its knowledge and experience, and the Commission has often been called upon to play the honest broker in conflicts between member states. Its impartiality and commitment to the common interest make it a mediator accepted by all sides.[11] Despite these arguments, the fact that the present EU legislation consists largely of regulations, directives and decisions of the Commission speaks for itself. The power to make these regulations, decisions and directives has made the Commission a powerful authority at least to the individuals residing within the EU.

---

9. EU Commission, available at <http://europa.eu.int/comm/presentation_en.htm#1>.
10. EU Commission, ibid.
11. EU Commission, ibid.

The European Parliament

[10.8] The European Parliament is regulated by arts 189–201 of the EU Treaty. It represents about 374 million people. Since 1957 the Parliament's powers have gradually grown, particularly since the signing of the Single European Act (1986) and of the EU Treaty (1992). The Parliament is involved in adopting community legislation and the EC budget. It supervises the activities of the Commission and the Council and exercises power to appoint the European Ombudsman. It also represents the interests of the citizen, through the Committee on Petitions. The first direct elections to the European Parliament took place in June 1979 among citizens of nine European nations. Now parliamentarians are elected directly from the 15 member countries.

However, the European Parliament is not a real legislative body as we understand in a domestic context. It is not in fact the highest law-making body of the EU: the EU Council is. Article 189 of the EU Treaty states that the Parliament consists of the representatives of EU members and exercises 'the powers conferred upon it' by the Treaty, which is made by the governments of the EU. Although the Parliament shares legislative power with the EU Council, the functions of the Parliament are largely advisory, consultative and supervisory in nature. As we have seen, it may exercise check-balance power against the power of the Council. It may also be involved in the legislative process conducted by the Council. There are special procedural requirements to deal with disagreements between the Council and Parliament. The Council sometimes has to establish a conciliation committee to negotiate with the Parliament if the EU Treaty so states. The Parliament also has the power to supervise the work of the Commission under arts 197 and 200 of the EU Treaty, under which the Parliament may set up committees of inquiry to investigate violation of EC laws and regulations. It can also appoint an Ombudsman under art 191 to deal with various complaints from EU countries in relation to EU laws and regulations.

Parliamentarians are elected directly from the EU countries. In 2002, the Parliament had 626 members. The quotas of parliamentarians for each country are as follows:

Belgium	25	Luxembourg	6
Denmark	16	Netherlands	31
Germany	99	Austria	21
Greece	25	Portugal	25
Spain	64	Finland	16
France	87	Sweden	22
Ireland	15	United Kingdom	87
Italy	87		

[10.8]   International Commercial Law

The European Parliament has been given wider powers of involvement in the legislative process within the EU. However, there is an inherent limit on how much it can participate in the legislative process under the notion of the EU, which is not meant to be a federal nation. The Council consists of ministers of EU countries and thus the government of each EU country has better control over EU affairs through the Council. If the European Parliament were given complete legislative power, EU governments would lose their ability to control the EU. No country is prepared to leave its future in the hands of 626 ordinary Europeans, most of whom do not understand other countries as well as they know their own. It should be noted that under the present arrangement, out of the total 626 members, the largest share of the votes by single country belongs to Germany (99 votes) and the smallest share belongs to Luxembourg (6 votes). Any reasonable person can see the risks of allowing the European Parliament to make laws for all the people of the EU, even though the lack of legislative power in the Parliament may be seen as a sign of a democratic defect in the EU.[12]

The European Court of Justice

[10.9] The European Court of Justice is regulated by arts 220–245 of the EU Treaty. It interprets and enforces the EU Treaty and the laws and regulations of the EU. It consists of 15 judges and nine Advocates-General. Both judges and Advocates-General act independently in the interests of the EU. The judges are appointed from nominees from each EU member, and every EU country has a judge in the court. The Advocates-General are not based on the practice of one appointee for each country, probably because there is no need to appoint several appointees who are from the same legal tradition. The function of the Advocates-General is to assist the court to understand the particular national law concerned. This is necessary as the 15 EU countries have individual legal systems although some of them may belong to the same legal tradition.

The court may hear complaints about breach of EU laws and regulations by a country or by an institution within the EU. It has the power to deal with alleged breaches of the EU Treaty by the Council, the Commission and the Parliament. This arrangement reflects the principle of check and balance. The Court has power to make rulings and to enforce them. Articles 164–188 deal with the functions, power and composition of the Court. Since it was set up in 1952, more than 8600 cases have been brought before it. There were already 200 new cases a year by 1978, and 1985 saw more than 400 cases brought.[13] To cope with that influx while still dealing with cases with reasonable despatch, the Court of Justice amended its Rules of Procedure to enable it to deal with cases more rapidly and requested the Council to set up a new judicial body.

Article 170 requires a dispute between two EU countries to be heard by the Commission first. The Commission is required to deliver its opinion within three months from the date on which the dispute was brought to it. If a party is dissatisfied with the Commission's opinion, it can take the matter to the Court. If a party fails to implement the opinion of the Commission, the other party may also bring the dispute to the Court.

---

12. Foster, *Swot EC Law*, Blackstone Press Ltd, London, 1993, p 50.
13. EU Court, available at <http://curia.eu.int/en/pres/jeu.htm>.

A Court of First Instance was set up in 1989 to strengthen the judicial safeguards available to individuals by introducing a second tier of judicial authority and enabling the Court of Justice to concentrate on its essential task, the uniform interpretation of community law. The function of the Court of First Instance is to hear a specified class of case as determined by the Council under the EU Treaty. The Court of First Instance has 15 members and has no special Advocates-General. A member may act as an Advocate-General when necessary. The Court of First Instance was formally incorporated into the court system in 1992 and has dealt with complaints against EU institutions. The Council has power to extend the Court's jurisdiction to other areas of law except for matters covered in the EU Treaty.

Areas of cooperation within the EU

General areas

[10.10] Articles 2 and 3 of the EU Treaty set out the following areas of cooperation for EU members:

- development of a common market;
- elimination of customs duties and quantitative restrictions;
- development of common commercial policies;
- establishment of an internal market based on free movement of goods, persons, services and capital;
- development of a common policy on agriculture and fisheries;
- development of a common policy on transport;
- development of a common policy on competition;
- development of a common policy on the European Social Fund;
- development of a common policy on environment;
- promotion of research and new technology;
- development of trans-European networks;
- attainment of a high level of health protection;
- cooperation in education, training and cultural exchange;
- development of economic relationships with other countries;
- consumer protection; and
- cooperation in the areas of energy, civil protection and tourism.

These suggest that EU countries have a wider area of cooperation than WTO members. With the adoption of a single currency, the EU looks more like a federation than a trade organisation. Whether or not countries can enter into a federation on the basis of close economic ties is an issue yet to be seen in Europe.

Free movement within the EU

[10.11] The EU creates a single market among its members. To that end, EU countries uphold the notion of free movement of goods and services and free movement of workers. This requires that trade barriers within the EU be eliminated and the governments' policies and laws affecting the operation of the single market be consistent and unified. In other words, member countries must cooperate with each other and make commitments and sacrifices to promote and facilitate the operation of the single market.

[10.12] Free movement of goods and services has the following meanings:

- Member countries undertake to reduce gradually, and eventually to abolish, the existing tariffs on imports and exports within the EU. This includes an undertaking to offer member countries the lowest tariffs offered to any non-EU country, if there are still any tariffs existing in any member countries.[14] In addition, any charge which has the same effect as a tariff or customs duty is prohibited under the Maastricht Treaty. Thus, the European Court of Justice found the Belgian Government's compulsory storage charge, incurred when goods are examined for customs purposes, to be inconsistent with its obligation to abolish customs and tariffs and not to impose any new customs and tariffs within the EU.[15]

- Members undertake not to impose taxes upon products of other members which are higher than domestic taxes on the same products or which are imposed for the purpose of indirect protection of domestic products.[16]

- Members undertake to abolish quantitative control of imports and exports within the EU, unless the restrictions are necessary for the national interest, environmental protection or protection of cultural heritage.[17]

- Members undertake to abolish gradually restrictions on free movement of services within the EU.[18]

- Members undertake to abolish gradually restrictions on the freedom of establishment by nationals of member countries within the EU.[19] This undertaking is necessary for both the free movement of goods and services and the free movement of workers within the EU, because establishment refers to business establishment for any business purposes and activities. Companies established within the EU should be treated the same throughout the EU,[20] including their capacity to set up establishments and supply goods and services.

[10.13] Free movement of workers also has several meanings, as follows:

- Members undertake to adopt the same definition of, or test for determining, a worker. The European Court of Justice has decided that 'the determining characteristic of a

---

14. EEC Treaty, arts 9, 12, 13, 16, 32 and 33.
15. Case 132/82 *Commission v Belgium* [1983] ECR 1649.
16. EEC Treaty, art 95.
17. EEC Treaty, arts 30, 34, 36 and 115.
18. EEC Treaty, arts 59–63.
19. EEC Treaty, arts 52–57.
20. EEC Treaty, art 58.

"worker" is that he or she performs services of some economic value for or under the direction of another person, in return for which he or she receives remuneration'.[21]

- Members undertake to provide equal treatment in accordance with the EEC Treaty to workers of member countries within the EU.[22] This includes non-discrimination on the basis of nationality. For example, the European Court has decided on several occasions that a national employment law which accorded different treatment to its own and foreign nationals in the same circumstances was discriminatory,[23] but procedural requirements for immigration purposes that do not restrict the free movement of workers are not discriminatory.[24]

- Members undertake to accord freedom of establishment to nationals of member countries within the EU in order to facilitate free movement of workers.

As we have seen, the main function of the EU is to create and manage a single European market. The existence and operation of the single market require, inter alia, free movement of goods and workers, free supply of services, no restrictions on the establishment of business, no discrimination on the ground of nationality, fair competition throughout the EU and consistent or uniform trade policies and customs or tariffs.[25]

Relationship between the EU and the WTO

[10.14] The EU came into existence before the WTO was created in 1995. Prior to the WTO's creation, the EU co-existed with its predecessor, GATT, as an international economic organisation outside GATT. The co-existence of the EU and GATT was not inconsistent with GATT principles, because GATT allowed contracting parties to establish customs unions. The preferential treatment available within such a union was not discriminatory against other contracting parties who were not union members, because contracting parties to GATT agreed that they were not required to extend preferential treatment within a customs union to other non-union contracting parties.

The relationships between the EU and the WTO is regulated by art XI of the WTO Agreement, which provides as follows:

> The contracting parties to GATT 1947 as of the date of entry into force of this Agreement and the European Communities which accept this Agreement and the Multilateral Trade Agreements and for which Schedules of Concessions and Commitments are annexed to GATT 1994 and for which Schedules of Specific Commitments are annexed to the General Agreement on Trade in Services in Annex 1B shall become original Members of the WTO.

This provision appears to suggest that the EU can join the WTO as a separate entity. However, each member of the EU is qualified to join the WTO as a contracting party to GATT 1947. There appears to be some 'constitutional difficulty' within the EU as to its power to represent its members in certain areas of trade and commerce. For the time

---

21. Plender, Plender and Usher's *Cases and Materials on the Law of the European Communities*, 2nd ed, Butterworths, London, 1990, p 287.
22. EEC Treaty, art 48(2).
23. Case 15/69 *WŸrttembergische Milchverwertung-SŸdmilch-AG v Salvatore Ugliola* [1969] ECR 363.
24. Case 118/75 *Lynne Watson and Alessandro Belmann* [1976] ECR 1185, and Case 13/76 *Gaetano Don'v Mario Mantero* [1976] ECR 1333.
25. EEC Treaty, arts 8A, 9, 10, 18, 19, 23 and 24.

[10.14] being, it appears that the EU can either act as a block for some matters or in the capacity of each EU country for other matters within the WTO.

Asia Pacific Economic Cooperation (APEC)

A brief history

[10.15] APEC was established in 1989 in response to the growing economic interdependence between Asia–Pacific economies. In that year, officials of the governments of the 12 founding members of APEC (Australia, Brunei Darussalam, Canada, Indonesia, Japan, Republic of Korea, Malaysia, New Zealand, Republic of the Philippines, Singapore, Thailand and the United States) held an informal dialogue to discuss various economic issues of interest to them. The earliest attempt to set up a regional organisation in the Asia–Pacific region began in 1968 when an annual meeting to discuss the notion of a Pacific Free Trade Area commenced after Japanese initiatives. At about the same time, business people organised the Pacific Basin Economic Council which has held annual meetings since. In the 1970s, the Pacific Economic Cooperation Council was set up at the initiative of the Japanese Government. It appears, however, that Australia initiated the idea of establishing some sort of economic cooperation in the Asia–Pacific Region in the 1980s. The People's Republic of China, Hong Kong and Chinese Taipei became members of APEC in 1991. Mexico and Papua New Guinea were accepted as members in 1993. Chile became a member in 1994. Peru, Russia and Vietnam became the latest members of the APEC community at the 10th APEC Ministerial Meeting, held on 14–15 November 1998 in Kuala Lumpur, Malaysia. Presently, APEC has 21 members which are either sovereign states or jurisdictions without independent international legal status.

APEC has developed steadily since 1989. The annual meeting of APEC members has been an essential feature of APEC. There are two types of meetings: the ministerial meeting and the economic leaders' meeting (the meeting of the government heads of APEC members). The initial years of APEC were focused largely on the exchanges of views and project-based initiatives. The concerns were simply to advance the process of APEC and to promote a positive conclusion to the Uruguay Round of GATT negotiations. Graudally, APEC has evolved into a forum of greater substance and higher purpose, namely to build the Asia–Pacific community, and to achieve higher economic growth and equitable development through trade and economic cooperation.

APEC members

[10.16] APEC has 21 members: Australia, Brunei, Canada, Chile, the PRC, Hong Kong, Indonesia, Japan, South Korea, Malaysia, Mexico, New Zealand, Papua New Guinea, the Philippines, Singapore, Taiwan, Thailand, the United States, Peru, Russia and Vietnam. These countries or jurisdictions have different legal systems, cultural traditions and economic status. Some of them are developed economies; some are less developed and some are least-developed countries. However, the spirit and intention to seek some form of cooperation among them is high and positive. In 2000, the combined GDP of the APEC economies amounted to US$17,921 billion, accounting for 46.76 per cent of the world trade for the year.[26]

APEC has become the primary regional vehicle for promoting open trade and economic cooperation in the Asia–Pacific region. Its goal is to advance Asia–Pacific economic dynamism and sense of community. Despite the financial instability of 1997–98, the Asia–Pacific remains one of the fastest growing regions in the world. It is a major contributor to global prosperity and stability. APEC may become the most powerful regional trading block in the future.

Nature of APEC

[10.17] APEC is not yet an international organisation as some APEC members have been unwilling to make those commitments necessary to build an international organisation. Submission of part of a country's sovereignty and the willingness to accept the superiority of an international organisation by a jurisdiction or economy is essential: without this commitment from all its members, APEC remains, at least for the time being, merely a forum for discussing issues of concern to its members. The cooperation between members is rather loose. The nature of APEC is illustrated by its developments since 1989, particularly those taking place after 1993.

APEC entered an important new era in November 1993 when the government heads of APEC members met for the first time for informal discussions at Blake Island near Seattle. They envisioned a community of Asia–Pacific economies based on the spirit of openness and partnership, and of cooperative efforts to solve economic issues. They also promoted the ideas of free exchange of goods, services and investment, broadly based economic growth, higher living and educational standards, and sustainable growth that respects the natural environment.

In subsequent annual meetings, APEC members further refined the vision and launched mechanisms to translate the vision into action. In the 1994 Jakarta meeting held in Borgor, Indonesia, APEC members agreed upon a number of particular tasks to be accomplished. They undertook to cooperate in a number of areas, such as the improvement of public and commercial infrastructure, trade and investment data collection, trade promotion, the development of industrial science and technology, human resources development, energy industries, marine resources conservation, telecommunications, fisheries, transportation and tourism. In particular, they project the vision of free investment in the Asia–Pacific by 2010 for developed member economies and 2020 for developing ones.

In the 1995 Osaka meeting, the Osaka Action Agenda was adopted. The plan firmly established the three pillars of APEC activities: trade and investment liberalisation, business facilitation and economic and technical cooperation. APEC members agreed to cooperate in the areas of human resources development, industrial science and technology, policy relating to small and medium enterprises, infrastructure, energy development, transportation, telecommunications, tourism, trade and investment data

---

26. See APEC website, at <http://www.apecsec.org.sg/>.

collection, trade promotion, marine resource conservation, fisheries, agricultural technology and finance.

In 1996, the Manila Action Plan Agenda for APEC (MAPA), which included collective and individual plans, was adopted. It compiled members' initial individual action plans to achieve the objectives outlined in Bogor. APEC members agreed that serious attention should be given to the following six areas of economic and technical cooperation:

- developing human capital;
- fostering safe and efficient capital markets;
- strengthening economic infrastructure;
- harnessing technologies of the future;
- promoting environmentally sustainable growth; and
- encouraging the growth of small and medium-sized enterprises.

Further developments were achieved in Vancouver in 1997, when APEC members recognised members' efforts to improve the commitments in their Individual Action Plans and reaffirmed their intention to update them annually. The government heads of APEC members endorsed their ministers' agreement that action should be taken with respect to early voluntary sectoral liberalisation (EVSL) in 15 sectors, with nine to be advanced throughout 1998 and implementation to begin in 1999. The members reviewed their action plans and undertook to cooperate further in trade and investment liberalisation. Emphases were placed on better business environments for small and medium-sized enterprises, cooperation between the government and business/private sector, simplified customs clearance procedures, and better information on government procurement and investment regimes.

In 1998 in Kuala Lumpur, the APEC leaders agreed to cooperate to end the financial crisis. They also agreed to make efforts to strengthen social safety nets, financial systems, trade and investment flows, the scientific and technological base, human resources development, economic infrastructure and business and commercial links.

In 1999 in Auckland, the APEC leaders pledged to strengthen markets and improve the international framework for trade and investment. In addition, they also agreed that business and private sector involvement in APEC activities should be encouraged.

The APEC leaders met in 2000 in Bandar Seri Begawan. In this meeting, the leaders agreed to strengthen multilateral trading systems and to improve their cooperation further. Environment protection, market structure, institution and infrastructure investment, technology development and human capacity building were the focuses for discussion.

The APEC leaders met in Shanghai in 2001. The leaders undertook to combat terrorism, to promote sustainable economic growth, to share the benefits of economic globalisation, and to promote open and free trade. These goals were detailed in a document known as the Shanghai Accord attached to the Ministerial Declaration. Specific rules, policies, and measures in various areas of cooperation are set out in the Shanghai Accord, which represents a substantial progress in the APEC cooperation.

Although APEC members have made considerable efforts to strengthen their cooperation, they are yet to undertake many concrete obligations for the purpose of regional trade cooperation. APEC is still essentially an organisation for coordinating members' economic policies, rather than imposing any obligations upon them in the form of a uniform trade policy or tariff. In addition, no power to regulate and control the conduct of APEC members has been given to APEC. Therefore, it may take a long time for APEC to progress into a real regional trade organisation.

Structure of APEC[27]

[10.18] APEC is not an international organisation. Nor does it have the structure of an organisation. Its administration is performed by the Secretariat, but the Secretariat does not have any decision-making power. Decisions are made in the members' meetings — the economic leaders' meeting (the meeting of the heads of APEC members' governments) and the ministers' meeting (the meeting of responsible ministers from APEC members, also known as ministerial and senior officials' meetings) — and are made by consensus. In 1991, APEC members committed themselves to conducting their activities and work programs on the basis of open dialogue with equal respect for the views of all participants. There are a number of committees within APEC to deal with certain technical matters, and to formulate or implement policies in particular areas. These include the APEC Business Advisory Council, Ad Hoc Policy Level Group on Small and Medium Enterprises (PLG-SME); Budget and Administrative Committee (BAC); Committee on Trade and Investment (CTI); Economic Committee (EC); and Sub-Committee on Economic and Technical Cooperation. There are also a number of advisory committees, and working groups and expert groups to advise APEC and the relevant governments of relevant policy issues: these include the APEC Advisory Council (ABAC), Eminent Persons Group (APG), and Pacific Business Forum (PBF). These committees or groups are fora provided for the purpose of facilitating the exchange of views among APEC members.[28]

The APEC leaders' meeting is held annually to provide a forum where the government heads of all APEC members can exchange their views on various matters affecting economic cooperation within APEC. This is in fact the highest authority of APEC. The authority of the leaders' meeting is based on the basic principles of international law, which allow government heads to act on behalf of their respective governments in making treaties and undertaking obligations of international law. The declarations, action plan and any other documents are sanctioned by the general principles of international law. None of the declarations and instruments produced by the leaders' meetings imposes any specific obligations in law upon APEC members. Thus, only very broad principles of international law are relevant to APEC and the decisions of its leaders.

Ministerial and senior officials' meetings are the fora where negotiations among APEC members take place and decisions are made. The annual ministerial meeting of foreign and economic ministers is held by the APEC Chair, which rotates annually among

---
27. Information is available at <http://www.apecsec.org.sg/97brochure/97organize.html>.
28. For an organisational chart of APEC, see the APEC website at <http://www.apecsec.org.sg/>.

[10.18]

members. At the 1989 Canberra Ministerial Meeting, it was agreed that it would be appropriate that every alternate ministerial meeting be held in an ASEAN economy. Senior Officials Meetings (SOMs) are held regularly prior to every ministerial meeting. APEC senior officials make recommendations to the ministers and carry out their decisions. They oversee and coordinate, with approval from ministers, the budgets and work programs of the APEC fora. APEC member economies have hosted a number of other ministerial meetings for ministers of education, energy, environment and sustainable development, finance, human resources development, regional science and technology cooperation, small and medium enterprises, telecommunications and information industry, trade, and transportation.

The APEC Business Advisory Council (APAC) was established in 1995 by APEC Economic Leaders as a permanent organisation within APEC. It is composed of up to three senior business people from each member economy. The major role of the council is to provide advice on the implementation of APEC action plans and on other specific business sector priorities. Chairmanship of ABAC rotates each year according to which economy chairs APEC. APEC's major sub-committees are an ad hoc policy level group, 10 working groups and other APEC fora. (Details can be found at the website <http://www.apecsec.org.sg>.)

APEC as a model of trade regulation

[10.19] Most of APEC's areas of cooperation are economic in nature, which is one of the major differences between APEC and the EU, as well as between APEC and ASEAN. Both the EU and ASEAN have extended their cooperation to areas of political cooperation, regional security and foreign relations. In addition, cooperation of APEC members has so far been largely voluntary. Member economies are still exploring the most efficient ways of achieving cooperation and development within the framework of APEC, without sacrificing too much of their sovereignty or autonomy. This characteristic also separates APEC from the WTO. The fact is that APEC members have so far not undertaken any substantial obligations in terms of developing economic cooperation between them. APEC presents a model of its own for the regulation of international trade. The fact that APEC members are enthusiastic in engaging in various discussions, communications and experiments suggests that they may be able to create a unique model of trade cooperation which suits the economic needs of the Asia–Pacific economies, characterised by such huge diversity in their political and legal systems, cultural traditions and economic capacity.

Association of South East Asian Nations (ASEAN)

A brief history[29]

[10.20] ASEAN was established by Indonesia, Malaysia, the Philippines, Singapore and Thailand in 1967 for the purpose of promoting peace, stability, progress and prosperity in

---

29. Information is available from ASEAN homepage at <http://www.aseansec.org>.

South-east Asia. In the 1960s, Asia was a poor area. For example, in 1960 East and South East Asian countries produced about 10 per cent of the world's gross national product. For the same year, North America counted for 36 per cent of the world's gross national product and Western Europe counted for about 23 per cent of the world's gross national product.[30] Finding an effective way to improve national economies was the major concern of the South East Asian countries. In the ASEAN Declaration unveiled in Bangkok on 8 August 1967, the ASEAN countries spelled out three aims and purposes of ASEAN as follows:

- to accelerate the economic growth, social progress and cultural development in the region through joint endeavours in the spirit of equality and partnership in order to strengthen the foundation for a prosperous and peaceful community of South East Asian nations;
- to promote regional peace and stability through abiding respect for justice and the rule of law in the relationship among countries of the region and adherence to the principles of the United Nations Charter; and
- to promote active collaboration and mutual assistance on matters of common interest in the economic, social, cultural, technical, scientific and administrative fields.

The ASEAN Declaration made clear that 'the Association is open for participation to all states in the South-East Asian Region subscribing to the aforementioned aims, principles and purposes'. It further stated that 'the Association represents the collective will of the nations of South-East Asia to bind themselves together in friendship and cooperation and, through joint efforts and sacrifices, secure for their peoples and for posterity the blessings of peace, freedom and prosperity'.

During the late 1960s and early 1970s, Cambodia, Laos and South Vietnam attended some of the ASEAN ministerial meetings as observers. On 7 January 1984, Brunei Darussalam was admitted as a member, one week after the country gained independence from the British. On 28 July 1995, Vietnam was accepted as the 7th member of ASEAN. At the 5th ASEAN Summit in Bangkok in mid-December 1995, the ASEAN heads of government met their counterparts from Cambodia, Laos and Myanmar for the first time. Cambodia, Laos and Myanmar submitted their respective applications for ASEAN membership in 1996. Subsequently, Laos and Myanmar became ASEAN members on 23 July 1997. Cambodia was admitted into ASEAN on 30 April 1999. Presently, ASEAN has 10 members: Brunei Darussalam, Cambodia, Indonesia, Laos, Myanmar, Malaysia, the Philippines, Singapore, Thailand and Vietnam. In 2001, the total GDP from ASEAN countries reached US$737 billion and total trade reached US$720 billion, making ASEAN one of the important economic forces in international trade.

---

30. Victor Li, 'Introduction' in Martin (ed) *The ASEAN Success Story*, East-West Centre, Honolulu, p xv.

[10.21]   International Commercial Law

Structure of ASEAN

Overall structure

[10.21] ASEAN is a regional trade organisation with specified functions. It is not as well organised as the EU, but much more organised than APEC. Its organisational structure is largely decided by the functions it is meant to carry out. Meetings and committees have been organised to implement the agreements reached by the governments of ASEAN. This means that the structure of ASEAN can be modified and changed any time by agreement of the parties if such necessity arises in the future.

The structure of ASEAN is based on three divisions, or three types of organisation: the government meetings, the functional committees and the Secretariat. Its model is less organic, independent and powerful than the WTO. It is something between a forum like APEC and a modern trade organisation like the WTO or EU. Decisions are made by various meetings at the government level, and are implemented by the committees and the Secretariat. Disputes between members do not have formal status: this means that there are no disputes between ASEAN members, or that all disputes are settled through various meetings at government level at closed sessions. ASEAN thus provides another model for the regulation of international trade. The three divisions of the ASEAN organisation are examined below.[31]

Government meetings

[10.22] The government meetings are fora where important decisions can be made and are similar to any diplomatic meeting. Officials from ASEAN countries meet to make decisions for their countries. These meetings can be divided into three levels according to the nature of the decision-making power and the effect of the decisions made at each level. At the highest level is the meeting of the government heads of ASEAN members; next are the meetings of foreign ministers and economic ministers; at the lowest level are the meetings of various other ministers.

The highest power of ASEAN lies in the hands of the ASEAN governments. Thus, the highest authority of ASEAN is the meeting of the ASEAN heads of government, known as the ASEAN Summit. In 1992, the 4th ASEAN Summit in Singapore decided that the ASEAN heads of government would meet formally every three years and informally at least once in between to lay down directions and initiatives for ASEAN activities. The arrangement was confirmed formally in the 5th ASEAN Summit in Bangkok. Consequently, the heads of ASEAN governments should meet at intervals of about one and half years. Informal summits were held in Jakarta in December 1996 and in Kuala Lumpur in December 1997 respectively. The 6th ASEAN Summit was held in Hanoi in December 1998. The 7th Summit was held in Bandar Seri Begawan in November 2001. China, Japan and Korea also participated in the Summit as observers or potential partners. ASEAN showed strong interests in strengthening trade relations with the three countries, in particular China.

---

31. Information is available at the ASEAN homepage at <http://www.aseansec.org>.

Functional committees

[10.23] A number of functional committees have been established within ASEAN. These are accountable to the relevant government meetings. They are set up for implementing specific decisions of ASEAN members. There is no hierarchical connection between the functional committees.[32] Details can be found at the website <http://www.aseansec.org>.

ASEAN Secretariat

[10.24] The ASEAN Secretariat was established by an agreement signed by ASEAN foreign ministers during the 1976 Bali Summit to enhance coordination and implementation of policies, projects and activities of the various ASEAN bodies. The 1992 Singapore Summit agreed to strengthen the ASEAN Secretariat so that it would effectively support the Summit's initiatives. The Protocol Amending the Agreement on the Establishment of the ASEAN Secretariat, signed at the 25th AMM in Manila in 1992, provided the Secretariat with a new structure. The protocol vested the Secretariat with an expanded set of functions and responsibilities to initiate, advise, coordinate and implement ASEAN activities. The Special Meeting of the ASEAN Foreign Ministers in Kuala Lumpur in May 1997 agreed to the creation of an additional post of Deputy Secretary-General at the ASEAN Secretariat. One Deputy Secretary-General will assist the Secretary-General on AFTA and Economic Cooperation while the other will assist in Functional Cooperation, ASEAN Cooperation and Dialogue Relations and Administration, Finance and Personnel. The Deputy Secretaries-General are appointed based on nominations by the governments of ASEAN member countries. Staffing of the Secretariat has moved from national nomination to open recruitment. A total of 35 professional staff have been recruited, more than double the size of the previous professional staff of 14 before the reorganisation.

Areas of cooperation

[10.25] ASEAN is not merely an economic organisation. Its members also intend to cooperate in the areas of regional security and stability, as well as relationships between ASEAN and other countries or international organisations. ASEAN is meant to be both a regional trade organisation and a political organisation with limited commitment from its members. It is not as wide as the EU in terms of the areas in which the members undertake to cooperate, nor is it as serious as the WTO in terms of the scope of its proposed economic cooperation. ASEAN's areas of cooperation are: economic cooperation, political and security cooperation, and foreign affairs cooperation.[33]

ASEAN as a model of trade regulation

[10.26] ASEAN is a regional trade organisation. It has its own structure, system and principles. The close cultural connections between ASEAN countries have contributed to its development. The principles and the spirit of cooperation adopted by ASEAN are

---

32. For detail, see note 27.
33. Discussion is based on the information provided at the ASEAN homepage at <http:// www.aseansec.org>.

[10.26] also related to the cultural traditions of the ASEAN countries. The level of cooperation between ASEAN members is lower than within the EU, but higher than APEC. Its areas of cooperation are broader than those of the WTO, but less sophisticated and strict in terms of the obligations imposed in the area of economic cooperation. The purpose of any regional economic or trade cooperation is to facilitate regional development and achieve efficiency in the national development of the countries concerned. The members have to decide the format and scope of cooperation. As long as cooperation is productive and fair, it is beneficial to the countries concerned. ASEAN provides a unique model for regional trade organisation.

North America Free Trade Agreement (NAFTA)

Overview

[10.27] The North America Free Trade Agreement established the North America Free Trade Zone between Canada, Mexico and the United States. It was concluded in December 1992 and entered into force on 1 January 1994. NAFTA is a comprehensive document, containing specific rules on various aspects of the free trade zone. It is allowed under art XXIV of GATT, which deals with customs unions within the GATT. NAFTA is consistent with the WTO as long as the three NAFTA countries comply with their obligations under the WTO agreements. Unlike the EU or ASEAN, NAFTA is a trade agreement, rather than an organisation. It covers cross-border sale of goods and services between the members, fair competition within the free trade area, protection of investment within the area and protection of intellectual property within the area. The members have also agreed to extend the areas of cooperation between them in the future.

Organisational structure

Features of NAFTA

[10.28] NAFTA is not an organisation and therefore does not have the same structure as an organisation. For the purposes of administration, NAFTA has the Free Trade Commission (FTC) and the Secretariat to administer and enforce it. There are also various functional committees or groups established in pursuance of the relevant provisions of NAFTA to implement specific tasks. However, there is no council or ministerial conference to make specific decisions, even though the FTC consists of official representatives of the three governments. As it is not an organisation, arrangements are made for the purpose of implementing the agreement and to ensure the operation of the free trade zone only.

Free Trade Commission

[10.29] The FTC is established in pursuance of art 2001 of NAFTA. It is comprised of cabinet-level representatives of the three countries and their designees, and thus appears to be a sort of ministerial committee under a regional trade organisation. It has the following major roles:

- to supervise the implementation of NAFTA;
- to oversee its further elaboration;
- to resolve disputes that may arise regarding its interpretation or application;
- to supervise the work of all committees and working groups established under NAFTA, referred to in Annex 2001.2; and
- to consider any other matter that may affect the operation of NAFTA.

In order to discharge its functions, the FTC is entitled to establish and delegate its responsibilities to any ad hoc or standing committee, working group or expert group. It may seek the advice of non-governmental persons or groups, and take such other action as authorised by the governments of Canada, Mexico and the United States. Under art 2001(4) of NAFTA, the FTC establishes its rules and procedures. As a general rule, all decisions should be taken by consensus, unless the FTC agrees otherwise. This rule reflects the fact that the FTC is an authority whose power is equally shared by all representatives of the three countries. Generally, the FTC convenes at least once a year in regular session, which is chaired successively by each country of NAFTA. It appears that the FTC is a sort of joint ministerial conference of Canada, Mexico and the United States, which makes unanimous decisions and is run on an equal basis by all three countries.

The NAFTA Secretariat[34]

[10.30] The NAFTA Secretariat was established by the FTC in pursuance of art 2002 of NAFTA for the purpose of overseeing NAFTA's operation. It consists of the Canadian, United States and Mexican sections. It is a unique organisation and is responsible for the administration of the dispute settlement provisions of NAFTA. The mandate of the Secretariat also includes the provision of assistance to the FTC and support for various committees and working groups. More specifically, the NAFTA Secretariat administers the NAFTA dispute resolution processes under Chapters 14, 19 and 20 of NAFTA and has certain responsibilities related to Chapter 11 dispute settlement provisions. Each national section maintains a court-like registry relating to panel, committee and tribunal proceedings.

The NAFTA Secretariat bears some resemblance to a similar administrative body, the Binational Secretariat, which had existed under the Canada–United States Free Trade Agreement (FTA). In 1994, pursuant to the parties' obligation under NAFTA to establish a permanent national section office in each country, the Binational Secretariat, Canadian and United States national sections became the NAFTA Canadian and United States national sections. The Mexican section was created simultaneously. The national sections, which are mirror images of each other, are located in Ottawa, Washington and Mexico City and are headed by the Canadian, the United States and Mexican Secretaries.

---

34. Information is available at the NAFTA homepage at <http://www.nafta-sec-alena.org>.

Major principles of NAFTA

Objectives of NAFTA

[10.31] NAFTA's objectives are set out in art 102:

    as elaborated more specifically through its principles and rules, including national treatment, most-favoured-nation treatment and transparency, are to:

    a)   eliminate barriers to trade in, and facilitate the cross-border movement of, goods and services between the territories of the Parties;

    b)   promote conditions of fair competition in the free trade area;

    c)   increase substantially investment opportunities in the territories of the Parties;

    d)   provide adequate and effective protection and enforcement of intellectual property rights in each Party's territory;

    e)   create effective procedures for the implementation and application of this Agreement, for its joint administration and for the resolution of disputes; and

    f)   establish a framework for further trilateral, regional and multilateral cooperation to expand and enhance the benefits of this Agreement.

The statement above refers to three fundamental principles of international trade: national treatment, most-favoured-nation treatment and transparency of trade laws and policies. These are the most important principles of NAFTA for building the free trade zone concerned and guide the establishment and operation of the free trade zone, which applies largely to trade in goods, services and investment. A number of incidental issues are also covered by NAFTA: for example, government procurement (which is covered by an optional agreement under the WTO), protection of intellectual property, and dispute settlement. NAFTA is freer and wider in all aspects of economic cooperation than agreements under the WTO.

National treatment principle

[10.32] The national treatment principle applies to almost all aspects of NAFTA to ensure market access for, and equal protection of, goods, services and investment. For example, in relation to trade in goods, art 301.1 states that each party shall accord national treatment to the goods of another party in accordance with art III of GATT. In relation to trade in services, art 1202.1 provides that each party 'shall accord to service providers of another Party treatment no less favourable than that it accords, in like circumstances, to its own service providers'. In relation to investment, art 1102 states each party shall accord to investors and investments of another party treatment 'no less favourable than it accords, in like circumstances, to its own' investors and investments. In addition, national treatment is also adopted in art 1003.1 to regulate government procurement. The provision requires each party in carrying on government procurement to accord to goods of another party, to the suppliers of such goods and to service suppliers of another party, treatment no less favourable than the most favourable treatment that the party accords to its own goods and suppliers, or goods and suppliers of another party. This provision combines the principle of national treatment and MFN in the same clause. National treatment is also incorporated into art 1703 to regulate the protection of intellectual property. This provision states that each party 'shall accord to nationals of another Party treatment no less favourable than that it accords to its own nationals with regard to the protection and enforcement of all intellectual property rights'. These provisions suggest that national treatment is indeed one of the major principles of NAFTA.

MFN principle

[10.33] The MFN principle requires the NAFTA countries to offer to each other most favourable treatment: any deals, privileges, benefits or concessions between any two countries must be made available to the third country. The enforcement of the MFN principle is relatively easy; it is similar to the principle of non-discrimination in the context of NAFTA. However, in certain provisions of NAFTA, the MFN principle applies to the privileges and benefits granted by a contracting party to a non-contracting party. This is seen in art 1103, which requires that each party accords to investors and investments of another party treatment no less favourable than that it accords, in like circumstances, to investors or investments of any other party or of a non-party with respect to the establishment, acquisition, expansion, management, conduct, operation, and sale or other disposition of investments.

Transparency of law and regulations

[10.34] Transparency of law and regulations is one of the basic principles of international trade today. It is a very broad principle. Access to information is one of the examples of the obligations imposed by this principle. Often the principle is implied in an international treaty. In fact, national treatment, MFN treatment, non-discrimination, enforcement of parties' obligations and implementation of a treaty, etc, cannot be assessed without transparency in the law-making and management of the government concerned. The principle of transparency in law and regulations is adopted in art 1306, which states that each party 'shall make publicly available its measures relating to access to and use of public telecommunications transport networks or services'. Similarly, transparency is expressly required in art 1411, which states that each party shall, 'to the extent practicable, provide in advance to all interested persons any measure of general application that the Party proposes to adopt in order to allow an opportunity for such persons to comment on the measure'. The principle of transparency in law and regulations does not set out standards for the substance of the law and regulations concerned. However, the requirement for transparency forces the relevant country to consider its law, regulations and policies carefully to ensure consistency with its obligations under NAFTA.

Dispute settlement mechanism of NAFTA[35]

[10.35] The dispute settlement mechanism of NAFTA has its unique features. It is based on a number of interrelated arrangements under NAFTA. The principal dispute settlement mechanism of NAFTA is found in Chapters 11, 4, 19 and 20, and involves the use of panel proceedings, the Secretariat and other available means of dispute settlement. Disputes are classified into different categories according to the provisions under which they arise, although the major types of disputes, which require the assistance of NAFTA for settlement, appear to arise from investment and the use of anti-dumping or

---

35. Information is available from the NAFTA homepage at <http://www.nafta-sec-alena.org>.

countervailing duties. Different approaches may be taken for disputes arising from different provisions of NAFTA. Disputes relating to the investment provisions of Chapter 11 may be referred to dispute settlement mechanisms. Chapter 19 provides for bi-national panel review of final determinations of a national government on anti-dumping duties, countervailing duties and related injuries. Under Chapter 19, panels may also review amendments made by Canada, Mexico, or the United States to their anti-dumping or countervailing duties law. The dispute settlement provisions of Chapter 20 are applicable to disputes which arise from the interpretation or application of NAFTA, including disputes relating to the financial services provisions of Chapter 14.

NAFTA has special arrangements for the settlement of disputes arising from the imposition of anti-dumping or countervailing duties. The use of such duties has been subject to the determination of the governments of the three members. In Canada, final determinations on anti-dumping and countervailing duties are made by Revenue Canada or Customs and Excise, and final injury determinations are made by the Canadian International Trade Tribunal (CITT); an appeal can be made to the Federal Court of Appeal or, for some Revenue Canada decisions, to the Canadian International Trade Tribunal (CITT). In the US final determinations on anti-dumping and countervailing duties are made by the Department of Commerce and final injury determinations are made by the US International Trade Commission; an appeal against the determination can be made to the Court of International Trade. In Mexico final determinations on anti-dumping and countervailing duties and related injuries are made by the Secretaría de Comercio y Fomento Industrial (SECOFI); an appeal can be made to the Tribunal Fiscal de la Federación. NAFTA does not interfere with these, but certain measures have been adopted to ensure the contracting parties comply with their obligations under NAFTA in the use of anti-dumping and countervailing duties. Article 1903 provides that a party may request that an amendment to the other party's anti-dumping or countervailing duty statute be referred to a panel for a declaratory opinion on whether the amendment is consistent with GATT and NAFTA. Article 1904 provides for the establishment of panels relating to the review of anti-dumping and countervailing duties and injury final determinations. In addition, art 1904 offers bi-national panel review involving the countries in dispute as an alternative to judicial review or appeal to the relevant national authority for the review of anti-dumping or countervailing decisions.

NAFTA sets out procedures for the settlement of investment disputes in Chapter 11, which establishes a mechanism to assure both equal treatment among investors of the parties in accordance with the principle of international reciprocity and due process before an impartial tribunal. Under Chapter 11, a NAFTA investor who alleges that a host government has breached its investment obligations under NAFTA may, at its option, have recourse to one of the following arbitral mechanisms:

- the World Bank's International Center for the Settlement of Investment Disputes (ICSID);
- ICSID's Additional Facility Rules;
- the rules of the United Nations Commission for International Trade law (UNCITRAL rules).

Alternatively, the investor may choose the remedies available in the host country's domestic courts. An important feature of the Chapter 11 arbitral provisions is the enforceability in domestic courts of final awards by the arbitration tribunals.

As a safeguard against impropriety or gross-panel error that could threaten the integrity of the process, art 1904 provides for an 'extraordinary challenge procedure'. In defined circumstances, a participating party can appeal a panel's decision to a three-member committee of judges or former judges. The committee would make a prompt decision to affirm, vacate or remand the panel's decision. Similarly, art 1905 also provides a mechanism for safeguarding the panel review system. Under this article, a three-member special committee may be established to review allegations of one party that the application of another party's domestic law has interfered with the proper functioning of the panel system. These rules ensure effective and fair operation of the panels under NAFTA.

NAFTA as a model of trade regulation

[10.36] NAFTA is not meant to be an organisation. It operates on the basis of the conventional obligations of international law undertaken by the contracting countries. In other words, it imposes treaty obligations upon the parties who must comply with what the obligations require. The obligations of the parties have been expressly decided by the treaty. If an amendment is made to any of the existing obligations, the parties have to negotiate the change. This is one of the major differences between an organisation like the WTO or the EU and NAFTA. Under the WTO or the EU, new obligations may be created through the agreed process of decision-making, which is certainly less formal than the process of treaty-making. Consequently, the WTO may make certain decisions by majority to bind the minority who do not necessarily agree with the decisions. However, in a process of treaty-making or treaty-amendment, the country which disagrees with the treaty or amendment reserves the right not to ratify the treaty. NAFTA is a model for trade regulation for specific purposes. It may work for the NAFTA countries, who are prepared to make firm commitments to build a free trade zone.

Australia–New Zealand Closer Economic Relations

Major principles

[10.37] The Australia–New Zealand Closer Economic Relations Trade Agreement was entered into in 1983. The agreement is a bilateral treaty between Australia and New Zealand for the purpose of establishing a free trade area between them.[36] The idea was developed on the basis of the Australia–New Zealand Free Trade Agreement of 1965. One of its goals is 'to eliminate barriers to trade between Australia and New Zealand in a gradual and progressive manner under an agreed timetable and with a minimum of disruption'.[37]

---

36. The Australia–New Zealand Closer Economic Relations Trade Agreement, art 2.
37. The Australia–New Zealand Closer Economic Relations Trade Agreement, art 1(c).

[10.37]   **International Commercial Law**

The agreement consists of 26 articles and a number of schedules, agreements or arrangements in particular areas of trade. The major features of the agreement are as follows:

- a general reduction of tariffs in the free trade area on the goods originating in the territory of the contracting country, gradually phasing out the tariffs on goods originated and sold within the free trade area (art 4(1)–(4));
- in the process of a gradual reduction of tariffs within the free trade area, the parties undertake to grant each other MFN treatment in relation to any goods as compared with the same goods from a third country (art 4(9) and (10));
- before phasing out the tariffs between the contracting parties, the parties agree that on one hand either party may adopt the lowest tariff for protection of local industries, on the other, they should always give the other party a preferential rate of tariff which is at least 5 per cent less than the general rate on the same products from a third party (art 4(11) and (12));
- a gradual phasing out of the quantitative import restrictions and tariff quotas within the free trade area (art 5);
- a gradual phasing out of quantitative export restrictions within the free trade area (art 8);
- a gradual phasing out of export subsidies and incentives to goods originated and sold within the free trade area (art 9);
- the governments undertake not to discriminate against sellers or suppliers from the other contracting party when making government purchases (art 11);
- the governments undertake to coordinate their policies when taking anti-dumping actions against dumped goods originated and sold within the free trade area (art 15);
- the governments undertake to impose countervailing duties on dumped goods originating from the other contracting party only as a measure of necessity and in a manner consistent with GATT and the agreement (art 16);
- agreement allows the parties to take necessary measures which may otherwise be inconsistent with the agreement, provided that specific grounds, such as national security, public morale, protection of human, animal or plant life, protection of industrial property, protection of limited natural resources and enforcement of domestic laws or International Commodity Agreements, are established (art 18);
- cooperation and unification of customs practices (art 21); and
- disputes arising from the application of the agreement should be resolved through consultation between ministers of the two countries (art 22).

The Australia–New Zealand Closer Economic Relations Trade Agreement is a fairly comprehensive agreement. It covers most traditional trade and commercial activities between the two countries, although services, industrial property, investment and labour management are not included. The agreement definitely liberalises trade and commercial activities between the two countries. However, it has only a limited impact on the national economy of both countries, because both economies are largely dependent upon imports from, and exports to, other countries.

Australia–New Zealand Closer Economic Relations as model of trade regulation

[10.38] The Australia–New Zealand Closer Economic Relations Trade Agreement was allowed under GATT 1947. Article XXIV of GATT allows contracting parties to set up customs unions or free trade areas between them. In this case, the parties to the proposed customs union or free trade area have no obligation to extend the same preferential treatment available within the union or area to other contracting parties of GATT. This explains why special trade arrangements, such as the EU, the Australia–New Zealand Closer Economic Relations Trade Agreement and NAFTA, can exist within the legal framework of the WTO. The Australia–New Zealand Closer Economic Relations agreement is a sort of declaration made by the countries concerned; it does not have an efficient mechanism of enforcement, and the treaty establishing it has not had a significant impact upon the two countries. However, it is a model of trade regulation for countries who are not only similar to each other in many ways but also highly interdependent economically.

Chapter Eleven

International Commercial Litigation and Conflict of Laws

Defining international trade and commercial disputes

[11.1] International trade and commercial disputes arise from international trade and commerce. For our purposes, they are disputes arising from or relating to international sales of goods; carriage of goods by sea, air or land; international financing and banking; marine insurance and provision of international insurance services; tariffs and trade restrictions under the GATT and WTO Agreement; regional economic cooperation; foreign investment; operations of MNEs; franchising; licensing; distribution agreements; transfer of technology; enforcement of international trade and commercial treaties; and any other matters which fall into the category of international trade and commerce.[1] Although international trade and commercial disputes may arise from all forms of trade and commerce, most commercial disputes in fact come from the areas of international sales of goods, contracts for the carriage of goods, international banking and financing, insurance contracts, international licensing or distribution agreements, international supply of services, international construction of work and foreign investment.

[11.2] International trade and commercial disputes can perhaps be divided into three categories: disputes between governments, disputes between a government (or an international organisation) and a private person, and disputes between two private persons (either natural or legal). The disputes between governments are often covered by the relevant international treaty or convention on international trade and commerce. For example, WTO members may take each other to the panel proceedings of WTO for the purpose of resolving their disputes. Disputes between a government and a private party are largely governed by domestic law, except in the case of foreign investment disputes

---

1. The UNCITRAL Model Law describes international commerce as all relationships of a commercial nature, in particular, 'any trade transaction for the supply or exchange of goods or services; distribution agreement; commercial representation or agency; factoring; leasing; construction of works; consulting; engineering; licensing; investment; financing; banking; insurance; exploitation agreement or concession; joint venture and other forms of industrial or business cooperation; carriage of goods or passengers by air, sea, rail or road'. See note 2, the Model Law.

under the Washington Convention of 1965. Even when a person alleges a WTO government has breached its obligations under a WTO agreement and wishes to take a legal action in the territory of the government concerned, the person would have to resort to the relevant domestic rules for the commencement of such action. Otherwise, the person would have to turn to his or her own government for assistance in the hope that his or her government would be able to raise the issue with the WTO govenrment concerned. Sovereign immunity is always an issue relating to disputes between a government party and a private party in the sense that many governments today are still reluctant to waive sovereign immunity in certain civil and commercial disputes. Disputes between private parties are subject to domestic laws, which have incorporated various international treaties ratified by the countries concerned. In this chapter, international commercial disputes are to be classified into two broad categories: disputes between governments, and disputes involving only one government party or between two private parties.

Resolving disputes between governments

[11.3] Disputes between governments can be further divided into two groups: those taking place within an international trade organisation and those arising outside a trade organisation. The two groups of disputes are categorised according to whether or not a dispute between two governments falls within the scope of any international trade organisation to which the disputing parties are members. If a dispute falls within the scope of a trade organisation, it should be resolved according to the mechanism adopted by the organisation concerned. For example, the WTO, the EU, ASEAN, and NAFTA have their own mechanisms for dispute settlement. Methods adopted for resolving such disputes have shown a considerable diversity. The EU has its own court to enforce EU law and regulations: see **[10.9]**. The WTO has special panel proceedings, aided by consultation, mediation, good offices and arbitration: see **[9.61]–[9.73]**. ASEAN does not have any formal dispute settlement arrangements and the conflict is resolved through friendly dialogue and negotiation between the governments. NAFTA's dispute settlement mechanism is largely based on its own panel system, which is aided by domestic proceedings, negotiation among the three members and arbitration proceedings: see **[10.35]**.

[11.4] If a dispute falls outside a trade organisation, it should be resolved by the governments in pursuance of the relevant international trade or commercial treaty (if any) between them. At present, most countries have negotiated bilateral trade and commercial treaties to deal with specific issues which are not covered by any multilateral trade and commercial treaties. For example, a bilateral treaty is a common means for two countries to resolve their differences arising from tax matters or investment disputes. In the absence of any agreement, the general principle of international trade law requires negotiation. The relevant parties have to find a mutually acceptable way to resolve their trade dispute, if they wish to maintain their normal trading relations. In special circumstances, where both parties have submitted to the compulsory jurisdiction of the court, disputing governments may refer their disputes to the ICJ, which is capable of adjudicating certain commercial disputes between governments: see, for example, **[8.91]–[8.93]**. Settlement of disputes by negotiation probably means the making of a new treaty to resolve a dispute

[11.4]   **International Commercial Law**

not covered by any treaties. These are the basic approaches through which commercial disputes between two governments can be resolved peacefully and effectively today. The settlement of this type of dispute is examined in Chapters 9 and 10, when discussing the WTO and regional trade organisations. Unless stated otherwise in this chapter, this type of dispute will not be examined here.

Resolving disputes involving private parties

[11.5] Commercial disputes involving private parties are divided into two groups: disputes between a government and a private party; and disputes between two private parties. The disputes between a government and a private party are largely subject to domestic law, because of the prevalence of restrictive immunity doctrine, which requires a government to be liable in the same way as a private party in commercial transactions, in most countries of the world. This means that in most commercial disputes the fact that one party is a government is irrelevant for determining the means of dispute settlement. Of course, this general rule is qualified by the principles of conflict of laws, under which the court may apply different rules if the country of the court practises absolute sovereign immunity. In addition, certain foreign investment disputes arising from the Washington Convention of 1965 are subject to the special procedures set out in the convention. This means that such disputes are handled by ICSID (see **[12.19]–[12.30]**), which is in fact an arbitration proceeding. For commercial disputes between two private parties, the means of dispute settlement are largely based on domestic law and conflict of laws rules. This chapter largely focuses on this type of commercial dispute. It must be pointed out that, unless specified otherwise, the expression 'international commercial disputes' in this chapter refers to commercial disputes between two private parties or between a private party and a government.

Defining the means of dispute settlement

[11.6] International commercial and trade disputes are settled through three major means: litigation, arbitration and consultation. Conciliation (or mediation) is sometimes also used: see **[12.108]–[12.109]**. Occasionally, countries resort to economic sanctions or 'trade war' (involving measures and counter-measures of an economic nature) as a means of settling their differences. The use of military force as a means of resolving a commercial dispute is rarely seen today.

[11.7] Litigation is the traditional means of dispute settlement. It involves the use of a court of law as the referee (judge) for settling a dispute. It is characterised by the power of the court to enforce its decisions and the formality of the procedures under which the court conducts its business. Although 'international commercial litigation' is not an established branch of law in any country, because there is 'no such subject as international commercial litigation',[2] for the sake of convenience we use this expression to refer to the settlement of international commercial disputes by a domestic or international court of

---

2.   Cromie, *International Commercial Litigation*, Butterworths, London, 1990, p v.

law. 'Settlement' in this context includes the whole process of settling an international commercial dispute, extending to the enforcement of a foreign judicial decision.

[11.8] Arbitration involves the use of an impartial and competent person (or persons) as the referee (or referees) to arbitrate a dispute. It is characterised by the freedom of the disputing parties to choose the forum, rules and arbitrators. The main features of arbitration are as follows:

- First, the parties have the option to choose the place and time for arbitration.
- Second, the parties have the option, subject to restrictions of law, to decide whether to be bound by procedural rules; and by what particular rules, if they choose to be bound.
- Third, the parties have the option to choose the arbitrator or arbitrators regardless of the place, time and procedural rules of arbitration, although in the case of institutional arbitration the choice of arbitrators may be confined to the institute's list, such as the institutional arbitration practised in China.

[11.9] Consultation, which is synonymous with 'negotiation', is not only the most natural process, but also an inherent part of any dispute settlement. In a process of consultation parties resolve their dispute by direct contact and exchange of opinions. Consultation may lead either to a settlement of the dispute or to the preparation and submission of the dispute to a third party. Consultation, as a means of dispute resolution, should be emphasised, because from time to time the parties may dogmatically refuse to accept the potential for a consultative approach, in preference for the familiarity or formality of adversarial litigation, and to some extent, arbitration.

[11.10] Every means of dispute settlement has its advantages as well as disadvantages. Parties to a dispute should choose the one which appears to be the most suitable for their purposes. Normally, there is no need to obtain the consent of the other party (except, perhaps, when submitting a dispute to the International Court of Justice, or asking a court of law to adjudicate on a point of law only) for submitting a dispute to a court of law. The court would exercise its power to require the presence (or appearance) of the other party for the purpose of dispute settlement. This is perhaps one of the advantages of commercial litigation. The process of litigation can be relatively slow (this is expected in most court proceedings), costly and detrimental to business relationships between the parties. Arbitration is promoted as an alternative to litigation. In comparison with litigation, arbitration is flexible in that the parties are able to choose the place of arbitration, the appointment of arbitrator(s), and the procedural rules (if any) for arbitration. This effectively removes, reduces or prevents possible disadvantage to a party who has to appear in front of a foreign court and be judged under a set of foreign laws. For these reasons, an arbitration clause is almost a 'must' in all contracts of international trade and commerce. Consultation is different from either litigation or arbitration. It is a process initiated and controlled by the parties themselves. The process is based on cooperation between the parties, who will benefit from the continuing cooperation between them and also from possible savings of money and time. However, without the backing (availability) of judicial and semi-judicial force (arbitration), consultation may sometimes become futile or time-consuming, particularly in cases where one or both parties lack sincerity.

Defining international commercial litigation

[11.11] The whole process of international commercial litigation involves a choice of forum, commencement of proceedings, service outside jurisdiction (if applicable), the seeking of interlocutory relief (if applicable), discovery and gathering of evidence outside the jurisdiction (if applicable), the trial and enforcement of judgment. These matters are dealt with under the civil procedural rules or rules of court in each jurisdiction.

[11.12] The whole process of international commercial litigation includes three stages:
- choice of forum and commencement of proceedings;
- carrying out the proceedings under the rules of the court; and
- enforcement of judgments.

[11.13] The procedural rules of a court, including the conflicts rules, are most relevant to the process. Because of the enormous amount of information relating to rules of courts in various jurisdictions, it is not possible for us to deal with the procedural rules of various countries here. Instead, we deal briefly with the general conflicts rules for the determination of a proper law or governing law of a dispute, as well as the general rules governing the enforcement of a foreign judgment. For the convenience of discussion, Australian law, Hong Kong law and the law of any other jurisdictions (when applicable) will be referred to as examples of domestic laws governing such matters.

[11.14] The conflicts rules dealing with international commercial litigation can be divided into two categories — those relating to the determination of a court's jurisdiction, and those relating to the determination of the governing law of the dispute. It must be emphasised that the determination of a governing law or proper law is different from the determination of an appropriate jurisdiction. The determination of a proper law or governing law is a process by which the court decides which of the competing laws should govern the rights and obligations of the disputing parties. In contrast, the determination of an appropriate jurisdiction is a process by which the court decides which of the competing courts has better jurisdiction to hear the dispute. We will briefly examine here certain conflicts rules relating to the determination of the substantive law, which governs the rights and obligations of the parties to a particular international commercial dispute. However, it must be noted that sometimes the same conflicts rule may apply to the determination of both the choice of jurisdiction and the choice of a proper law, according to the intention of the parties.

For example, in *Akai Pty Ltd v The People's Insurance Comp Ltd*, decided on 23 December 1996 by the High Court of Australia,[3] the High Court was asked to determine whether the choice of law clause in the insurance contract concerned should be enforced. The majority of the court looked at the possibility that if the matter were moved to a court in the UK, the English court would not apply the Insurance Act 1984 (Cth) as part of the *lex causae*. That possibility weighed in favour of the majority's decision that the action in Australia should continue in order to ensure the implementation of the Insurance Act. In this case, the jurisdiction and governing law were intermingled issues.

---

3. The case is available at <http://www.austlii.edu.au>.

Domestic courts and international commercial litigation

[11.15] Litigation is mainly based on domestic judicial systems. Domestic judicial systems are not ideal forums for settling international commercial disputes, but they are established, convenient and powerful forums where a dispute can be heard and where an effective remedy can be sought. A domestic court of law becomes a forum for resolving international commercial disputes merely because there is no other effective supranational judicial system where a dispute can be adjudicated and a claim be enforced. This does not mean, however, that the European Court of Justice and the International Court of Justice are irrelevant. These courts have a limited role in resolving international commercial disputes. Restricted by the instruments under which they were created, the courts can only deal with specific types of cases, such as disputes within the EU or disputes where a state is a party.

[11.16] While a domestic court must follow the law of the forum, it may also under its conflicts rules take into account relevant foreign law and international laws (treaties or customs). 'International' commercial law may be enforced by a domestic court of law either because an international convention has been incorporated into the relevant domestic law, such as the CISG in Australia or the United States, or because the international commercial customs, such as Incoterms 2000 (see **[1.12]–[1.34]**), have been accepted expressly or impliedly by the parties to the dispute.[4] There is no inconsistency between the use of a domestic court and the application of international commercial law. The body of international commercial law also includes the rules of domestic law governing certain international transactions, such as international sales, carriage of goods, international banking, marine insurance and foreign investment. This explains why domestic courts should be used as a forum for international litigation. Further, the sovereignty of a country dictates that a dispute arising from, or relating to, that country's law or jurisdiction can be submitted to its courts, although the courts may later refer the dispute to another jurisdiction under their conflicts rules.

[11.17] *Voth v Manildra Flour Mills*

(1990) 171 CLR 538; 97 ALR 124

The Australian court refers a matter to a foreign court

Facts: The plaintiffs and respondents, Manildra Flour Mills (MFM, the first plaintiff and first respondent) and Honan Investments Pty Ltd (the second plaintiff and second respondent, the holding company of MFM), were incorporated under New South Wales law. MFM sold starches and starch products between 1976–83 to Manildra Milling Corporation (MMC), which was a subsidiary of Honan Investments and incorporated under the law of the state of Kansas (USA).

---

4. In the case of an implied acceptance of a custom or usage, the courts will have to make a determination. The High Court of Australia in *Con-Stan Industries of Australia Pty Ltd v Norwich Winterthur Insurance (Australia) Ltd* set out tests for determining whether a usage of trade or custom should be implied into a contract: the existence of a usage that imports a term into a contract is a matter of fact; the usage must be evidently well known to, and relied upon by, the contracting parties; the usage should not be inconsistent with the express terms of the contract and a notorious usage binds on the party who is reasonably expected to know it: (1986) 64 ALR 481 at 485–6 per Gibbs, CJ, Mason, Wilson, Brennan and Dawson JJ.

[11.17]

Voth, the defendant and appellant, was a practising accountant in Missouri, the United States. He had allegedly provided negligent advice on tax matters to MMC, affecting MFM. Under the laws of the United States, MFM was liable to pay withholding tax on the interest received from MMC, which became indebted to MFM as the result of the transactions between them. MMC was liable to deduct the withholding tax from the payments of interest to MFM. MMC did not deduct the tax during the period 1976–83. Nor did MFM pay tax to the US Government during that period. All were allegedly the results of Voth's negligence. In 1984, MFM and MMC realised that the backdated tax payments and a penalty for MMC's failure to comply with the US law were payable to the Inland Revenue Services of the United States. MFM and Honan Investments sued Voth in New South Wales for professional negligence. Voth's application for a stay of proceedings in New South Wales was denied by the Supreme Court of New South Wales, and an appeal to the Court of Appeal of the Supreme Court of New South Wales failed. Voth thus appealed to the Australian High Court on the ground that the NSW court was not the appropriate forum for the dispute.

Issues: Whether the proceedings in New South Wales should be stayed, given the existence of the following circumstances:
- the alleged negligence (omission or misrepresentation) was committed in Missouri;
- the damages flowing from the alleged negligence occurred in New South Wales (MFM) and US (MMC);
- Voth was resident in Missouri; and
- MFM and Honan Investments were resident in New South Wales.

Decision: The majority of the High Court was determined to clarify the uncertainty arising from the divergent tests adopted by the majority judges in *Oceanic Sun* for determining the appropriateness of an Australian court's jurisdiction in such cases. Five judges (Mason CJ, Brennan, Deane, Dawson, and Gaudron JJ) agreed that the 'clearly inappropriate forum' test should be adopted in Australia. One judge (Toohey J) insisted that the *'forum non conveniens'* doctrine should be the test in Australia. While the five judges were united (although maybe conditionally, as Brennan J, as his Honour then was, accepted the majority's test for the sake of unity) in reinforcing the test of 'clearly inappropriate forum', they differed in the interpretation and application of the test. Four judges (Mason CJ, Deane, Dawson and Gaudron JJ) found that New South Wales was clearly an inappropriate forum under the test, but Brennan J found New South Wales was not a clearly inappropriate forum under the same test. Toohey J found Missouri was a more appropriate forum under the *'forum non conveniens'* doctrine.

At the end, five judges (Mason CJ, Deane, Dawson, Toohey and Gaudron JJ) held that:
- the alleged tort was committed in Missouri and the liability should be determined by the law of Missouri; and
- the action should be stayed either because New South Wales is clearly an inappropriate forum (by the joint judgment) or because Missouri is a more appropriate forum (by Toohey J).

The dissenting judge (Brennan J) found that the alleged negligence was initiated in Missouri but completed in New South Wales, the principal damage occurred in New South Wales, and New South Wales was not clearly an inappropriate forum.

◆

Functions of the courts in international commercial litigation

[11.18] In international commercial litigation, a court has two main functions:
- to adjudicate the dispute; and
- to enforce a foreign judicial or arbitral judgment.

[11.19] 'Adjudicating a dispute' refers to a process where the court of law first determines whether it has jurisdiction over the dispute, and then proceeds to resolve the dispute if it is satisfied that its jurisdiction is competent and appropriate. This process involves the exercise of the judicial power to interpret the conflict of laws rules, to ascertain the relevant facts, and to apply the governing law. In this process, the court is bound by domestic law, established international usage and customs and international conventions or treaties which are enforceable in the country of the court.

[11.20] Enforcement of a foreign judicial or arbitral decision occurs when a domestic court is asked by a party, either foreign or local, to enforce a decision of a foreign judicial or arbitral body. It is a necessary part of international commercial litigation, because a dispute is not really solved and the interests of the innocent party are not effectively protected until the decision of the judicial or arbitral body is enforced. A domestic court does not have a general obligation to enforce a foreign judgment or award, unless an obligation to do so arises from a domestic law or an international treaty to which the country of the court is a signatory. The enforcement of foreign judgments or awards under a domestic law, for example, Australian law, is discussed in **[11.67]–[11.79]**.

Contract disputes and conflict of laws

Application of conflicts rules to contracts

[11.21] In adjudicating an international commercial contract dispute, a court of law usually has first to determine its jurisdiction over the matter, and then determine the governing law of the contract. The two steps are sometimes inseparable. For example, a court of law may assume its jurisdiction on the ground of an action in personam, that is, an action based on a claim against the defendant in person. In such an action, the court may compel the defendant to do or not to do certain things, such as to perform a contract or pay damages. We may argue that when the court determines whether it has jurisdiction over the matter in dispute, it evaluates the matter in the context of substantive law — the legality of the claim against the defendant in person, which is seen in the context of a legal relationship, such as contract, tort or fiduciary relationship. This means that the court examines the substantive law under which the legal relationship exists, when determining whether it has jurisdiction over the matter. However, the determination of a governing law or proper law of a contract is the concern of this chapter.

[11.22] The rules of *lex loci contractus* and *lex loci solutionis* are often referred to in contractual disputes. The former points to the law of the place where the contract is entered into, and the latter refers to the law of the place where the contract, or part of the contract, is performed. Both are relevant to the determination of the proper law of a contract. However, the 'proper law' of the contract, which 'is a shorthand reference to the law, selected in accordance with the forum's choice of law rule, which governs most of the substantive aspects of a contract',[5] is not always easy to determine. While the 'proper law' could be the one governing 'the formation, essential validity and discharge

---
5. Skyes and Pryles, *Australian Private International Law*, Law Book Co, Sydney, 1991, p 584.

[11.22]

of a contract',[6] it is no more than a 'convenient and succinct expression',[7] 'which the English or other court is to apply in determining the obligations under the contract'.[8] Therefore, in the determination of a proper law, *lex loci contractus* and *lex loci solutionis* are no more than two possible considerations which may be taken into account by the court of law in reaching a decision.

Determination of governing law of a contract

Basic rules

[11.23] The determination of a governing law (or a proper law) of a contract is a process of balancing conflicting interests. Given the transnational elements in an international commercial contract, it is possible that the laws of two or more countries may be regarded as the proper laws at the same time.[9] It is neither necessary nor practicable for a book on international commercial law to deal with conflict of laws in great detail. Thus, we will only deal with the relevant conflicts rules from two broad perspectives:

- certain particular connections or determining factors which may be taken into account for ascertaining a proper law; and
- the basic approaches which may be adopted by a court of law for balancing the conflicting interests based on the competing laws.

[11.24] The general rule affecting the determination of the governing law of a contract is largely twofold: first, the governing law can be determined by referring to the express intention of the contracting parties; and second, the governing law can be decided by referring to the closest, real or most significant connection between a contract and a law (the connection test). The second approach applies in the absence of an express choice by the parties. Sometimes, there is another approach which lies between these two — by referring to the implied intention of the parties. English courts often take this approach for the determination of a governing law. When determining the implied intention of the parties, the court is in fact guessing the 'intention' of the parties by looking at signposts, evidence and indicators, which are often inseparable from what we would otherwise call 'connections'. Thus, ascertainment of the so-called implied intention is in fact the determination of intention by a court.

[11.25] This is, in turn, a determination of the governing law by presenting the choice of the court as the implied choice or intended choice of the parties, even though both the 'implied intention' and the 'connections' are decided by referring to the same facts, indicators and signposts. Presenting something which can be regarded as the 'connection' (justification for linking a law and a dispute), or as the 'implied intention' of the parties, implies discretion and sometimes manipulation. Therefore, a twofold approach, leaving the implied intention approach aside, appears to be more rational. This book favours

---

6. Ibid.
7. North, *Cheshire's Private International Law*, 9th ed, Butterworths, London, 1974, p 201.
8. *Mount Albert Borough Council v Australasian Temperance and General Mutual Life Assurance Society* [1937] 4 All ER 206 at 214.
9. For discussions of cases, see Skyes and Pryles, note 5 above, pp 584–9.

such a twofold approach, but acknowledges the practice of the implied intention test in certain courts.

[11.26] If there is an express choice of law clause, the task of the court is to ascertain whether or not a choice was indeed made willingly by the parties concerned. In the absence of the express choice, the court considers a number of relevant factors, which, depending on the particular circumstances, may be any factors and elements which suggest the nature, scope and level of connection between a contract and a law. In the practices of common law jurisdictions, residence of the parties, language of the contract, terminology of the contract, place of performance, place of contract, and others, have been taken into account for the determination of the real connection between a law and a contract, which leads to the determination of the governing law or applicable law of the contract.

[11.27] *Bank of India v Gobindram Naraindas Sadhwani*

[1988] 2 HKLR 262

Indicators suggesting connections

Facts: The plaintiff was an Indian bank, having a branch in Osaka, Japan. The first and second defendant who were resident in Hong Kong were co-guarantors for a credit facility issued to an Indian family company operating in Japan. The plaintiff had a branch in Hong Kong. The defendants also managed the company in Japan. The plaintiff sued the defendants in Hong Kong and argued that the governing law of the guarantee was Indian law. The defendants argued that the governing law was the Japanese law. The defendants presented evidence on Japanese law. The plaintiff did not present evidence on Indian law and asked the court to apply Hong Kong law. How to determine the governing law was one of the major issues concerned.

Decision: Zazareth J of the High Court of Hong Kong made the following points:
- Japanese law was the governing law of the contract, because the contract was performed in Japan, two of the co-guarantors resided in Japan. In addition, the negotiation to provide the guarantee was conducted in Japan and the currency account under the contract was Japanese yen.
- Under Japanese law, the plaintiff's claim was unsustainable.
- Under Japanese law, the court had discretion to decline jurisdiction in the circumstances concerned. It exercised this discretion and dismissed the plaintiff's claim.
- Even under HK law, which was preferred by the plaintiff, the guarantee was unenforceable because the defendants were discharged by the misconduct of the plaintiff who had failed to inform the defendants of the principal debtor's repudiation of the principal contract before declining to accept that repudiation.

Intention of the parties

[11.28] Intention of the parties to the contract is a decisive factor in determining the governing law.[10] This has been accepted in a number of Australian cases. For example, in *John Kaldor Fabricmaker Pty Ltd v Mitchell Cotts Freight (Australia) Ltd* (1989) 18 NSWLR 172;

---

10. North, note 7 above, p 202.

90 ALR 244, the Supreme Court of New South Wales held that the proper law of the contract should be decided by the intention of the parties, and the intention can be determined by express or implied words or by the nature of the contract.[11] If no intention can be ascertained, there would be an assumed intention that the parties intended to apply the law which has the closest and most real connection with the transaction.[12]

[11.29] However, the intention of the parties in entering into the contract may be denied on the ground of illegality under local law or public policy consideration in certain cases. For example, in *Green v Australian Industrial Investment Ltd* (1989) 25 FCR 532; 90 ALR 500, the parties agreed in the agreement for the sale of shares, which was concluded in England, that the agreement should be construed and governed by English law; but the Federal Court of Australia decided that the express intention of the contracting parties did not prevent the Australian courts from hearing the dispute under the TPA.

[11.30] A similar decision was reached in *Golden Acres Ltd v Queensland Estates Pty Ltd* [1969] Qd R 378. These precedents suggest that while the intention of the parties may be regarded as decisive in normal circumstances, courts of law may neglect intention in special circumstances in the interests of the parties and of justice. 'In the interests of justice' is a convenient expression allowing the exercise of wide discretion by courts of law: the discretion of the courts is integral to the judicial system, which is the ultimate 'arbiter' of justice and fairness in a given society. In *Akai Pty Ltd v The People's Insurance Comp Ltd*, decided on 23 December 1996 by the High Court of Australia,[13] the High Court by a 3:2 majority allowed an appeal against the ruling of the Supreme Court of New South Wales, which had enforced a choice of law clause despite the argument that the enforcement of the clause may lead to the circumvention of the Insurance Act 1984 (Cth). The majority judges of the High Court appeared to believe that the choice of law clause should not be used to circumvent the local law in the present case.

◆

[11.31] *John Kaldor Fabricmaker Pty Ltd v Mitchell Cotts Freight (Aust) Pty Ltd*

(1989) 18 NSWLR 172; 90 ALR 244

Relationships between the intention of the parties and proper law of a contract

Facts: John Kaldor sued Mitchell Cotts for negligence in acting as its agent. Mitchell Cotts cross-claimed against Through Transit Insurance Association Ltd (Association), which was the insurer of Mitchell Cotts. The Association sought to stay the proceedings under the arbitration clause in the insurance contract. Mitchell Cotts argued that the governing law of the insurance contract was the law of New South Wales and the arbitration clause was void under s 43(1) of the Insurance Contract Act 1984 (Cth). The Association argued that the governing law of the insurance contract was either English law or the law of Bermuda. The insurance contract contained an arbitration clause stating expressly that the contract was subject to English law.

---

11. See also *Trustees, Executors & Agency Co Ltd v Margottini* [1960] VR 417.
12. *John Kaldor Fabricmaker Pty Ltd v Mitchell Cotts Freight (Australia) Ltd* (1989) 18 NSWLR 172; 90 ALR 244.
13. The case is available at <http://www.austlii.edu.au>.

Decision: Brownie J of the Supreme Court of New South Wales held that English law was the proper law of the contract and the proceedings against the Association should be stayed in favour of the arbitration clause. His Honour set out the steps for determining the proper law of a contract as follows:
- an express intention of the parties determines the proper law;
- in the absence of an express intention, the intention should be inferred from the terms and nature of the contract and the general circumstances of the case; and
- when neither an express nor an implied intention can be established, the contract is governed by the system of law with which the transaction has its closet and most real connection.

♦

Formation of a contract and governing law

[11.32] Formation of a contract is a relevant consideration for determining the existence of a connection, although it is not always determinative: the 'term "formation" embraces issues relating to the fact and reality of agreement and the requirement of consideration'.[14] The process of determining the formation of a contract is to identify or ascertain the connection between the facts which suggest the existence of the contract and the law which gives effect to the contract. In *The Parouth* [1982] 2 Lloyd's Rep 351, 'the English Court of Appeal endorsed the view that the formation of a contract is governed by the law which would be the proper law of the contract if the contract was validly concluded'.[15]

[11.33] In other words, formation of a contract is the application of the *lex loci contractus* rule. For example, in *Elders IXL Ltd v Lindgren* (1987) 79 ALR 411, the Federal Court of Australia held that the application by the respondent to join Gunze Ltd, a Japanese company, as a cross-respondent to the applicant's claim that the respondent had sold defective goods to the applicant should be dismissed, because the contract of sale between the respondent and Gunze Ltd, which was alleged to be the source of the defective goods, was formed in Japan and thus the proper law for that contract was Japanese law. In this case, the determination of proper law and the determination of the court's jurisdiction were blended into one process, and the court refused to hear the claim because the contract from which the claim arose was governed by Japanese law.

[11.34] In some circumstances, a court may use its own law (*lex fori*) to judge the validity of a contract. This view was held by Brennan and Gaudron JJ in *Oceanic Sun Line Special Shipping v Fay* (1988) 165 CLR 197; 79 ALR 9. Despite criticism of the view that the formation and terms of a contract are governed by the *lex fori*,[16] it is likely that the abovementioned view only reflects a practice (or intention) of the court to displace the *lex loci contractus* by other law which is regarded as fair and just in the circumstances concerned. In *Green v Australian Industrial Investment Ltd* (1989) 25 FCR 532; 90 ALR 500, the Federal Court of Australia decided, inter alia, that a bona fide claim under the Trade Practices Act

---

14. Skyes and Pryles, note 5 above, p 611.
15. Id, p 612.
16. For example, see Pryles, 'Judicial Darkness on the Oceanic Sun' (1988) 62 *ALJ* 744.

1974 (Cth) would make the local court's jurisdiction appropriate and local law applicable to the contract concerned, despite the fact that the contract was entered into and performed substantially in England and that the contract was then subject to proceedings in the English Companies Court. These cases suggest that while courts of law have considered the law governing the formation of a contract to be essential for determining the governing law in some cases, they have declined its application in others. Sometimes it is, perhaps, appropriate to consider the connection between a contract (or the matter concerned) and other relevant laws for the sake of fairness and justice.

[11.35] *Euro-Diam v Bathurst*

[1988] 2 All ER 23; 1 Lloyd's Rep 228

An insurance contract made under the local law but substantially performed overseas

Facts: Euro-Diam delivered diamonds on 'sale or return' terms (see **[1.53]**) to a dealer in Germany. Euro-Diam insured its business with Bathurst. The policy covered business risks both in and outside England. The policy required the insured to comply with local laws where the diamonds were kept. Euro-Diam entered the correct value of the diamonds sent to the German dealer in its register, but issued understated invoices at the request of the dealer, who intended to avoid import duties on some of the diamonds. A large number of unsold diamonds were stolen in Germany. Euro-Diam claimed loss against the policy. Bathurst denied liability on the basis of Euro-Diam's contravention of the German customs law.

Decision: Kerr and Russel LJJ and Sir Denys Buckley of the English Court of Appeal held that Bathurst was liable for the loss. Kerr LJ observed (at 813) that the 'understated invoice also involved no deception of the insurers, since the true value of the diamonds was recorded in Euro-Diam's register and the correct premium was paid'. His Lordship was of the view that the public policy did not require that Euro-Diam's claim in the circumstances be rejected. Thus, only English law was held to be material in this case.

Performance of contract and proper law

[11.36] Performance of a contract is another relevant factor, although it may be less determinative than the *lex loci contractus*.[17] This is the '*lex loci solutionis* rule'. Performance can be carried out in any manner as required in the contract. The law of the place where a contract is performed is important, because an international commercial contract is often concluded in one country but performed in another. The rule of *lex loci solutionis* may amount to a decisive consideration in cases where the performance of the contract is the issue in dispute.

---

17. North is of the opinion that this rule has limited operation, covering only 'the mode and manner of performance': North, note 7 above, p 243.

[11.37] *The Ship 'Mercury Bell' v Amosin*

(1986) 27 DLR (4th) 641

Choice between the law of the flag state or the law of forum

Facts: The 'Mercury Bell' was a cargo ship. The plaintiffs, who were nationals of the Philippines, were crew members of the ship. The ship was registered under the law of Liberia. The plaintiffs were employed on the basis of individual contracts. They later discovered that their wages were lower than the minimum wages set out in a collective agreement between the shipowners and an international union. The plaintiffs commenced an action in rem at the Federal Court of Canada to recover the difference between their wages and the minimum wages specified in the collective agreement. The trial judge held that the plaintiffs were entitled to make the claim. The shipowners appealed.

Decision: Marceau, Hugessen and Lacombe JJ of the Canadian Federal Court of Appeal dismissed the appeal. The court held that the rights of the seamen were usually governed by the law of the flag state. But, in the present case, there was no proof of the Liberian law. The law of the forum thus applied. Accordingly, the court found that the plaintiffs were entitled to rely on the Canadian law which gave effect to the collective agreement.

Location of property

[11.38] *Lex situs* may be a relevant consideration in a contract relating to real property, or sometimes movable property. In an international commercial contract, particularly a foreign investment in real estate, the governing law would be the law of the place where the real estate is located, unless the parties stipulate otherwise.[18] This is not only because the performance of the contract relating to real estate is governed by *lex situs*, but also because that remedy can be effectively sought only when the judgment so made, regardless of whether it is made by a local court or not, is consistent with the *lex situs* where the judgment is to be enforced. A court of law may refuse to enforce a foreign judicial or arbitral decision if the decision is contrary to local law.

[11.39] *Lindsay v Miller*

[1949] VLR 13

In the absence of an express intention, the proper law of the deed is where the trust property is located

Facts: A trust deed was prepared in Scotland. It contained certain provisions which may not be valid under English or Victorian law. The settlor was resident in England, but had domicile in Scotland. The trust property, mainly shares, was located in Australia, mainly in Victoria. The trustees were living in China and Australia when the deed was executed. The deed did not expressly state its governing law.

---

18. Skyes and Pryles, note 5 above, p 618.

[11.39] International Commercial Law

Decision: Lowe J of the Supreme Court of Victoria held that the proper law of a trust deed is determined by the same tests as are applicable to the determination of the proper law of a contract. His Honour observed that (at 15) the 'deed contains no express intention to apply Scots law nor can I see any necessary intendment to that end'. His Honour also rejected the argument that English law was intended to be the governing law. The law of Victoria, where the property was located, was held to be the proper law of the deed.

◆

Discretion of courts and governing law

[11.40] The application and use of the abovementioned considerations are subject to the court's jurisdiction. The practice of the courts has not suggested any definite, consistent and unambiguous approach, which indicates clearly how the court has balanced the conflicting interests and determined the governing law in particular circumstances. However, there are some common considerations which may affect the exercise of judicial discretion in determining the governing law. These can be summarised as follows:

- First, the court of law may uphold a law chosen expressly or impliedly by the parties concerned to be the governing law of the contract, provided that this does not result in illegality under the local law, and violation of public interest.[19]

- Second, no matter what rules are involved — *lex loci contractus* or *lex loci solutionis* — the court of law will not allow a party to use any rules for illegal, unjust, unconscionable and unfair purposes, or to benefit from his or her fraud, dishonesty or illegal activities.[20] This means if any of the basic rules of conflict of laws results in an illegal, unjust or unfair consequence, it may be overruled by another rule which leads to a fair and just outcome.

◆

[11.41] *The KH Enterprise (Cargo Owners) v The Pioneer Container (Vessel Owners)*

[1994] 2 HKLR 134

Determination of the governing law, parties to a choice of law or choice of jurisdiction clause

Facts: The cargo-owners were the plaintiffs, who sued the vessel owners in Hong Kong for the goods lost near the Taiwanese 'territorial waters'. The defendant vessel owners argued that the goods were lost while being carried by the vessel owned by someone else, who had issued a bill of lading which chose Taiwan as the forum for settling disputes.

---

19. For example, in *Hellenics Steel Co v Svolamar Shipping Co Ltd* [1990] 1 Lloyd's Rep 541, the Queen's Bench Division (Commercial Court) held that Greek law was intended to be the governing law of the contract and the defendants would be liable for breach of contract and tortious liability under the English law. See also *Vita Food Products Inc v Unus Shippings Co* [1939] AC 277.
20. *Green v Australian Industrial Investment Ltd* (1989) 25 FCR 532; 90 ALR 500. By the same token, in *Euro-Diam Ltd v Bathurst* [1988] 2 All ER 23; 1 Lloyd's Rep 228, the English Court of Appeal refused to allow the insurers to avoid liability (to benefit from the transaction), on the ground that the insured issued understated invoices which were used by another person to circumvent the German customs law.

> The defendants contended that under the law of Taiwan, the action was time-barred. The cargo-owners argued that the bill of lading which contained the choice of forum clause did not bind them, because it was a contract between the defendants and the sub-carriers. Whether or not the present dispute was subject to the law of Taiwan became an issue. The Court of Appeal of Hong Kong granted a stay. The cargo-owners appealed to the Privy Council.
>
> **Decision:** The Privy Council held that the dispute between the cargo-owners and vessel owners was subject to the law of Taiwan, because of the choice of jurisdiction in the bill of lading for the sub-carriage. The cargo-owners had agreed that the vessel owners had a right to sub-bail the goods to someone else, and thus were bound by the contractual terms of such sub-bailment. The appeal was dismissed.

♦

Tortious disputes and conflict of laws

Tortious disputes and international commerce

[11.42] At common law, the governing law of a tort is usually the law where the tortious act is committed. Because the purpose of our discussion is to study commercial dispute resolution, conflicts rules applicable to non-commercial disputes, such as a tortious claim arising from a motor vehicle accident,[21] or a claim arising from defamation,[22] will be largely ignored. A tortious dispute can arise from international commercial transactions. For example, in *Voth v Manildra Flour Mills* (1990) 171 CLR 538; 96 ALR 124, the plaintiffs alleged that the defendant had breached his duty of care in giving negligent advice as to the tax matters of the plaintiffs' subsidiary in the United States. The alleged breach was relevant to international commerce, because the advice was given to the subsidiary and business partner of the Australian companies with regard to international transactions between the subsidiary and the plaintiffs. In this case, the majority of the High Court of Australia held that New South Wales was a clearly inappropriate forum for determining the dispute, because the alleged negligent conduct was governed by the law of Missouri.

[11.43] It must also be pointed out that a tortious action in international commerce and trade usually refers to a tortious act committed by a person outside the territory of the country of the alleged victim. A tort committed by a foreign person within the territory of the country of the victim is usually, without a real conflict, governed by the *lex fori* (assuming the action is taken in the victim's own country).

General rules for tortious disputes

[11.44] The general rules adopted in most common law jurisdictions in relation to torts committed outside the forum of the court are described by Willes J in *Phillips v Eyre* (1870) LR 6 QB 1 at 28–9, as follows:

> As a general rule, in order to found a suit in England for a wrong alleged to have been committed abroad, two conditions must be fulfilled. First, the wrong must be of such a character that it would

---
21. For example, *Breavington v Godleman* (1988) 80 ALR 362.
22. For example, *Lazarus v Deutsche Lufthansa AG* (1985) 1 NSWLR 188.

[11.44]

have been actionable if committed in England; therefore, in *The Halley* [(1868) LR 2 PC 193], the Judicial Committee pronounced against a suit in the Admiralty founded upon a liability by the law of Belgium for collision caused by the act of a pilot whom the shipowner was compelled by that law to employ, and for whom, therefore, as not being his agent, he was not responsible by English law. Secondly, the act must not have been justifiable by the law of the place where it was done.

[11.45] This is the 'double actionability' rule. In light of Willes J's observation, the following two rules or tests can be identified:

- First, a court in a common law country may entertain a tortious action originated overseas only when the action is allowed under its own law.
- Second, the *lex fori* will not override the effect of *lex loci delicti commissi* in circumstances where the *lex loci delicti commissi* excuses the alleged tortious act, even though the act is actionable under the *lex fori*. This means that a defendant is entitled to rely on the defences available under the law where the alleged tort was committed.

[11.46] The 'double actionability' rule does not provide answers to all legal issues which may arise from an international tort. This rule was subsequently modified in *Chaplin v Boys* [1971] AC 356. In this case, the court decided that although the tort was still actionable under the foreign law where the tort was committed, the compensation or the heads of compensation could be subject to the local law to allow the victim to claim higher compensation. Commentators and courts may have different understandings on the significance of *Chaplin v Boys* [1971] AC 356. It appears that the latter case simply suggests that in a grey area which is not expressly addressed by *Phillips v Eyre* (1870) LR 6 QB 1, the court has discretion in determining which of the competing or conflicting laws should apply. Such a practice can be either regarded as a departure or deviation from the original rule or an enrichment of the original rule. The two extreme propositions are available for anyone to pursue, depending on one's construction of the meaning of *Phillips v Eyre*. Indeed, the Privy Council took some liberty in developing and enriching the 'double actionability' rule in *Red Sea Insurance Co Ltd v Bouygues SA* [1994] 2 HKC 35 by upholding the right of subrogation of the insurer who had not indemnified the insured at the time of the legal proceedings: see **[11.48]**.

[11.47] The general principle of *Phillips v Eyre* (1870) LR 6 QB 1 appears to have been accepted by the Australian courts.[23] For example, in *McKain v R W Miller & Co (South Australia) Pty Ltd* (1991) 174 CLR 1, the High Court of Australia held, inter alia, that an action to enforce a civil liability claim arising from a tortious act committed outside the court's jurisdiction can be commenced in the court when the laws of both the forum of trial and the place where the tort was allegedly committed allow such action.

---

23. For example, *Breavington v Godleman* (1988) 80 ALR 362; and *Hodge v Club Motor Insurance Agency Pty Ltd and Australian Associated Motor Insurers Ltd* (1974) 2 ALR 421.

[11.48] *Red Sea Insurance Co Ltd v Bouygues SA*

[1994] 2 HKC 35

Extension of the Phillips v Eyre *rule*

Facts: Bouygues and others were the insured. Red Sea Insurance was the insurer. The insured sued the insurer under an insurance policy issued by the insurer in relation to a construction project in Saudi Arabia. The insurer counter-claimed against the insured on the ground that the insured breached its duty to the other insured, and thus the insurer could subrogate the other insured's rights against the insured. The counter-claim was struck out in the Hong Kong courts on the ground that the right of subrogation arises only after the insurer has paid to the insured under the relevant policy, and that the right of subrogation can only be brought in the name of the insured. Red Sea Insurance relied on the Saudi Arabian law which allowed an insurer to sue another directly by way of subrogation to amend the proceedings. The application was refused on the ground that the law of Saudi Arabia could not be relied on alone to determine a liability in torts in a Hong Kong court. Red Sea Insurance appealed. The Court of Appeal held that the insurer had the right to prove under the Saudi Arabian law that it was entitled to sue the insured directly by way of subrogation, but refused the insurer the right to sue the insured in its own name solely under the law of Saudi Arabia as the *lex loci delicti*, because of the court's previous decision in *The Adhiguna Meranti* [1987] 2 HKC 126. Red Sea Insurance appealed to the Privy Council on the point of law as to whether or not it was entitled to sue the insured directly by way of subrogation under the Saudi Arabian law.

Decision: The Privy Council allowed the appeal and gave, inter alia, the following reasons:
- *The Adhiguna Meranti* [1987] 2 HKC 126 was overruled.
- *Boys v Chaplin* is in favour of *lex fori*, but the majority of the court in that case recognised a need for flexibility in giving priority to *lex fori*.
- The consideration that a foreign law gives a remedy which is not available in the *lex fori* is important for the court to decide whether to make an exception.
- In the present case, all the relevant factors supported overwhelmingly the use of *lex loci delicti*, and thus the Saudi Arabian law should apply.

Certain exceptions

[11.49] Although the jurisdiction of a forum is wide enough to apply to a foreign defendant in most circumstances,[24] a court of law may, sometimes, decline jurisdiction over a dispute on the ground that it does not have jurisdiction over a foreign defendant (on the ground of *lex domicilli* perhaps), who has allegedly committed civil wrong against the plaintiff. In *National Commercial Bank v Wimborne* (1979) 11 NSWLR 156, the National Commercial Bank (NCB) of Saudi Arabia was the plaintiff, claiming a debt owed to it by the defendants in New South Wales under a bank guarantee provided by the NCB for the defendants to secure a loan from the Swiss Bank Corporation. The defendants cross-claimed, inter alia, damages for conversion of a wheat bagging plant and aggravated damages for wrongful imprisonment. But the claims were not defences to the plaintiff's action. The Supreme Court of New South Wales declined to entertain the cross-claims. It held, inter alia, that the NCB had not been present (not carrying on

---

24. For example, *Razelos v Razelos (No 2)* [1970] 1 WLR 392.

[11.49] any business) in New South Wales, and that the NCB as a foreign party had not submitted itself to the jurisdiction of the court over the matters raised in the cross-claims. This means that in certain circumstances, a court will not impose its jurisdiction upon a foreign party who has allegedly committed a tortious act unless the foreign party submits him- or herself to the jurisdiction of the court.[25] The crucial factor for the New South Wales defendants' failure in this case is that the cross-claims were not defences to the allegation made by the plaintiff and thus were irrelevant to the proceedings commenced by the plaintiff.

[11.50] The abovementioned cases suggest that, in bringing an action for international commercial tort, a plaintiff should not only consider the two general rules as set out by Willes J in *Phillips v Eyre* (1870) LR 6 QB 1, but also other relevant factors which give rise to exceptions or modifications to the general rules. The other relevant factors are the notion of fairness and justice, convenience of the parties (not in the sense of *forum non conveniens*), jurisdiction of the courts over the defendant and relevant legislation which has substituted the rules of common law in a given circumstance.[26]

Disputes relating to real estate and conflict of laws

[11.51] In order to avoid unsettled disputes as to the distinction between movables and immovables,[27] we will divide property into real estate and personal property. Any other forms of 'property', such as securities, choses in action and equitable interests in property, should be examined in the light of the governing law. It must be pointed out that we are not dealing with issues of property law, and the categorisation is adopted only for the purpose of finding a less ambiguous way of identifying the rules of conflict of laws in circumstances where property is the main concern of the party.

[11.52] *Lex situs* is the basic law for resolving disputes relating to real property. North observes that an English court 'has no jurisdiction to adjudicate upon the right of property in, or the right to possession of, foreign immovables, even though the parties may be resident or domiciled in England'.[28] This is 'based upon the practical consideration that only the court of the *situs* can make an effective decree with regard to land'.[29] The *lex situs* applies to the purchase of land, houses or other forms of real property, extending to disputes relating to legal or equitable interests derived from the transfer of real property. To some extent, contract, torts and real property overlap. For example, while a dispute arising from a contract for the sale of land is a contractual dispute, it is also a dispute

---

25. The same rule may not be applicable to a contractual dispute if the court finds that the parties have intended to choose the local law as the governing law of the contract. If the court finds that the governing law of a contract is a foreign law, it would be likely to refer the matter to the relevant foreign court for determination.
26. For example, in *Bankinvest AG v Seabrook* (1988) 14 NSWLR 711, the doctrine of *forum non conveniens* was regarded as inapplicable because of the operation of the relevant legislation, that is, the Jurisdiction of Courts (Cross-vesting) Act 1987 (Cth).
27. North, note 7 above, for example, pp 487–92.
28. Id, p 493.
29. Ibid.

relating to real estate. In such cases, the *lex situs* prevails.[30] Similarly, a trespass to a land is a tortious wrong, but it is also an act committed against the land. We may perhaps say that *lex situs* is a governing rule in all cases involving real property, except in circumstances where the notion of justice and fairness or the operation of law results in the prevalence of other rules.

Disputes relating to chattels personal and conflict of laws

[11.53] Chattels personal are important in international commercial law, because the majority of goods sold under international sale contracts are chattels personal.[31] However, chattels personal relating to international sales of goods do not form an independent category of dispute in most circumstances. The *lex loci contractus* and *lex loci solutionis* are thus always relevant. In other words, disputes relating to chattels personal in international commercial disputes can normally be regarded as contractual disputes.

[11.54] Chattels personal, as a form of property, have the characteristics of property. The proprietary nature of chattels personal demands the operation of other relevant rules, such as actions *in rem*, in certain circumstances.

[11.55] The definition of property in international commercial litigation is twofold:

- First, property as a legal title is created and protected by law and thus, laws are in conflict when a title created under one law is denied by another.
- Second, it is an object whose remedy in most circumstances is practically decided by the fact of whether a court is able to enforce its order effectively against the very object.

Thus, the common law courts recognise action *in rem*. The action can be brought against a ship, a cargo or a thing associated with the ship or cargo. The fact that the ship, cargo or thing may fall under the category of either real property or chattels personal is irrelevant in an action *in rem*.

[11.56] A classic example of the complexity of the sale of chattels personal internationally is *Cammell v Sewell* (1858) 157 ER 615. In this case, a Russian seller sold timber to an English buyer. The timber was shipped by a Prussian vessel which sank close to Norwegian coasts. The timber was then auctioned in Norway. The insurers of the timber, after having paid the buyer for the loss under the insurance contract, took an action in the Norwegian court to stop the auction. But the action failed. The purchaser of the timber later shipped the goods from Norway to England. The insurers brought an action against the timber (*in rem*) at the English court, and again the action failed. The English court was of the opinion that if 'personal property is disposed of in a manner binding according to the law of the country where it is that disposition is binding everywhere': (1860) 5 H&N 728 at 745 per Crompton J. The position of the English court can be explained by the rules of *lex situs*, action *in rem* and *lex loci actus*, because the Norwegian law may govern the auction of the timber in Norway on one of the three

---

30. For example, see *Merwin Pastoral Co Pty Ltd v Moolpa Pastoral Co Pty Ltd* (1933) 48 CLR 565.
31. There is, perhaps, disagreement as to the meaning of 'goods'.

grounds. By giving effect to disposition under a foreign law, the English court intends to avoid a conflict of laws arising from the legal title in the chattels personal. This case suggests that although a court of law may have jurisdiction over a dispute relating to chattels personal, it would be likely, either on the basis of international comity or for a practical consideration of avoiding conflict of laws, to take into account the whole transaction and give effect to the existing legal relationships created under a foreign law. This proposition may be subject to the general rule that no injustice and unfairness should arise from the operation of the foreign law.

[11.57] There is no absolute rule in conflict of laws. The conclusion in the previous paragraphs is subject to general considerations affecting the court's efforts to balance conflicting interests and maintain the justice of law. An obvious reason for a court to decline to support a claim based on a foreign law is that the foreign law is used as a cloak for a fraud or misconduct. The rules of conflict of laws enable a court of law to strike a balance, or to have an opportunity to redress injustice, by determining whether it has jurisdiction over the matter in question.

♦

[11.58] *Confecciones Del Atlantico v Lamont Shipping Inc*

[1982] HKLR 393

Action in personam, chattel personal

Facts: This was an admiralty action *in personam* brought by cargo-owners on the ground of short delivery. The case was tried at the High Court of Hong Kong. There were three defendants. The first defendant was the registered owner of the vessel in question. The second and third defendants were the charterers of the vessel. On the reverse of the bill of lading concerned, there was a clause naming either the second or the third defendant as the 'carrier' depending on who was operating the vessel. The bill of lading also stated that if the second defendant were sued, the court in Venezuela should have the exclusive jurisdiction, and if the third defendant were sued, the court in Colombia should have the exclusive jurisdiction. It also stated that when the second or the third defendant were sued, the Hague Rules as enacted in the defendants' countries should apply. On the face of the same bill of lading, the words 'Subject to the Hong Kong Carriage of Goods by Sea Ordinance 1964' which incorporated the Hague Rules were found. The 1964 Ordinance was repealed in 1980 by the Carriage of Goods by Sea (Hong Kong) Order. Under rule 6 of the Hague Rules, the plaintiff was time-barred at the time of litigation. The second defendant admitted that it was the operator of the vessel concerned at the time of the accident, but applied to the court for a stay of the proceeding.

Held: Fuad J of the High Court dismissed the application for a stay of the proceeding, and gave the following reasons:

> In considering an application for a stay of proceeding, the court may take into account the circumstances, in particular, the country in which the evidence was available;
>
> There was nothing in the bill of lading concerned to suggest that the action was time-barred and that the plaintiff could not sue the three defendants together;

> The plaintiff was not irresponsible in suing the three defendants in the light of the knowledge possessed by the legal advisor of the plaintiff, and the plaintiff had shown a strong case that the choice of jurisdiction clause in the bill of lading should be overridden.

Enforcement of foreign judgment

Rationale for enforcement

[11.59] According to the vested right theory, a foreign judgment should be enforced by the local court because the right of the party seeking enforcement has been granted by another law. According to the theory of comity, a foreign judgment should be enforced, because a local court should respect the decision of a foreign court out of courtesy. However, in reality, a local court may be reluctant to enforce a foreign judgment because of the conflict between the foreign judgment and the jurisdiction of the local court. For example, a divorce case is pending the decision of a local court, but the respondent has obtained a foreign judgment on the same matter. If the local court enforces the foreign judgment without any question, the local court's jurisdiction will be undermined. If the local court refuses to enforce the foreign judgment, the above-said theories are challenged. This is a dilemma in the study of conflict of laws.

[11.60] The major issue of conflict of laws as far as the enforcement of foreign judgments is concerned is the means of enforcement. Should the local court re-try or re-examine the case? Should the local court simply enforce the judgment made by the foreign court? Or should there be a neutral means that does not offend the sovereignty of the local court, while maintaining due respect for the foreign court's decision?

Enforcement of foreign judgments at common law

Basic common law rules for enforcement

[11.61] According to the common law tradition, a foreign judgment can be enforced by two alternative ways. First, the party seeking enforcement may commence a local proceeding for the same cause decided by the foreign judgment. Second, the party seeking enforcement may commence a local proceeding for the enforcement of a debt against the other party. In the first case, the foreign judgment may be considered as evidence of the applicant's rights under the relevant foreign law, and the interpretation of the relevant foreign law by the foreign court is the evidence for the local court to try the same cause of action. In some sense, the first method is a new litigation supported by the evidence of a foreign judgment. In the second case, the foreign judgment is the evidence of the applicant's right to collect a debt against the other party, and thus, the foreign judgment is recognised as the evidence of a foreign legal right. In the second means, the local court avoids answering the difficult issue of whether or not the enforcement of the foreign judgment may undermine the sovereignty of the local court.

[11.62] At common law, an enforceable judgment must satisfy three requirements: the foreign court has jurisdiction; the judgment must be final; and the judgment must be for a fixed sum. First, the court may obtain jurisdiction on any basis which has been recognised as one of the grounds for a court to exercise jurisdiction, such as personal law, *lex situs*, admiralty law, agreement of the parties and voluntary submission of the defendant. However, the location of the property against which a foreign judgment is to be enforced is the key consideration for a local court to examine. Second, the judgment must be final, meaning that the judgment to be enforced is neither an interim decision, nor a decision subject to appeal. Third, for a judgment to be enforced, it must be for a fixed sum. At common law, a party has the right to ask the court to enforce a foreign judgment as a debt. Otherwise, the party may commence a local action for the same cause determined by the foreign judgment. The requirement that a foreign judgment must be for a fixed sum partially came from the practice of enforcing a foreign judgment as a debt. In addition, as a general rule for policy considerations probably, a local court does not want to enforce a foreign judgment which requires a party to perform a specific act, to restrain from doing a specific act or perform a non-monetary obligation.

[11.63] *Schibsby v Westenholz*

(1870) LR 6 QB 155

A lack of jurisdiction in the court making a judgment

Facts: The plaintiff was a Dane resident in France. The defendants were Danes, resident in London. They made a written contract in London for the sale of Swedish oats by the defendants. The plaintiff sued the defendants for short delivery in a French court. The writ was served on the defendants in London, but the defendants did not appear in the French court. The plaintiff obtained a judgment in default against the defendants and wanted to enforce it in London. The defendants argued that they were not resident in France, that they had no knowledge of the pending proceedings and that they did not submit to the jurisdiction of the French court.

Decision: The court held that the French judgment did not bind the English residents. Since the defendants did not submit to the jurisdiction of the French court and were not residents of France, the judgment could not be enforced against them.

[11.64] *Vogel v R and A Kohnstamm Ltd*

[1973] QB 133

Submission to the jurisdiction of the foreign court must be definite

Facts: The plaintiff was a leather merchant in Tel Aviv, Israel. The defendant was an English company which had no place of business in Israel. The defendant authorised an Israeli resident to elicit orders from customers only. The contract of sale would subsequently be made by the defendant and customers directly.

Two contracts were made between the plaintiff and the defendant. The plaintiff was not happy about the quality of the suede skins supplied by the defendant, and commenced legal action against the defendant in an Israeli court. The writ was served upon the defendant in London. The defendant wrote to the Israeli court to challenge the jurisdiction of the court. The Israeli court gave a judgment in default against the defendants. The plaintiff sought to enforce the judgment in London.

Decision: The court decided that the defendants did not have a place of business in Israel, and thus, the Israeli court did not have jurisdiction over them. Nor did the defendants submit to the jurisdiction of the Israeli court by submitting the letter of protest, because submission to a foreign court's jurisdiction must be express. Therefore, the judgment could not be enforced as a debt in England.

Basic common law rules for refusing to enforce a foreign judgment

[11.65] When a party asks the court to enforce a foreign judgment, the other party may ask the court to refuse to enforce it on a number of grounds. The major grounds for the refusal to enforce a foreign judgment are as follows:

- a foreign judgment can be refused for a lack of jurisdiction;
- a foreign judgment can be refused, if it is not final;
- a foreign judgment can be refused, if it does not have a fixed sum;
- a foreign judgment can be refused on the ground of fraud;
- a foreign judgment cannot be refused on its merits even if the foreign court has misinterpreted the local law; and
- a foreign judgment cannot be refused merely because the foreign court has mistaken or misapplied its own procedures.

[11.66] *WFM Motors Pty Ltd v Maydwell*

[1996] 1 HKC 444

Refusal on ground of fraud

Facts: WFM Motors Pty Ltd was an Australian company. Maydwell was the guarantor of a debt owed to WFM by Skink Ltd which was a HK company. Skink had a distribution agreement with WFM's subsidiary, ATD, for the sale of cordless telephones in Australia. Skink became indebted to ATD. Maydwell provided a guarantee to WFM. Under the guarantee, ATD was entitled to demand payment from Maydwell if Skink became insolvent. WFM commenced proceedings in Australia to enforce the agreement of the guarantee. Skink filed a defence in Australia claiming that the guarantee was void, because WFM's false representations led to the making of the guarantee agreement. WFM was granted a summary judgment by the Australian court and registered the judgment in Hong Kong. Findlay J set aside the registration of the judgment on the ground of fraud. WFM appealed to the Court of Appeal.

> **Decision:** The Court of Appeal of Hong Kong allowed the appeal and set out the following principles for determining fraud in a foreign judgment:
>
> If a party alleges fraud in a foreign judgment, the court may examine the evidence presented to the foreign court to see whether a fraud existed in the foreign trial. Both the evidence considered and the evidence dismissed by the foreign court can be reviewed by the local court.
>
> The fraud proved must meet the gravity of the fraud alleged to justify the refusal to enforce the foreign judgment. In this case, it had not been established that WFM had obtained the judgment by fraud.

♦

Enforcement of foreign judgments in Australia

Legal framework for the enforcement of foreign judgments

[11.67] The enforcement of foreign judicial judgments in Australia is based on both the federal and state legislation. But the relationships between the relevant federal and state legislation are rather obscure. For example, s 6(3) of the Foreign Judgments Act 1991 (Cth) ambiguously states that the Supreme Court of a state or territory, or the Federal Court, is to order a judgment to be registered only when the Foreign Judgments Act 1991 (Cth) and the applicable rules of the relevant court so allow. This suggests that a state's Supreme Court may refuse to register a foreign judgment under its rules, regardless of whether the same judgment is registrable under the federal law. On the other hand, s 17 of the Act provides that the power of a state Supreme Court to make rules of the court is subject to the proviso that the exercise of the power is not 'inconsistent with this Act or any regulations made under this Act'. If we read ss 6(3) and 17 together, we may assume that s 6 is meant to say that any judgment which is registrable under the federal Act must be registrable in any state. The enforcement of foreign judgments in all Australian states but Queensland is still regulated by statutes of parliaments, rather than the rules of Supreme Courts. This is the case, even though the Foreign Judgments Act 1991 (Cth) requires the Supreme Courts of the states and territories to adopt the same position as the federal Act.

[11.68] The equivocal relationships between the federal and state laws in the area of enforcement of foreign judgments can probably be traced back to the Australian Constitution. Since the enforcement of foreign judgments within a state or territory does not expressly fall under any specified head of legislative power of the Commonwealth, the matter has been legislated by the Commonwealth, states and territories individually. Bearing in mind this unsettled constitutional puzzle, we may argue that the present legal framework for the enforcement of foreign judgments in Australia consists of the following federal and state legislation:

- the Service and Execution of Process Act 1992 (Cth);
- the Foreign Judgments Act 1991 (Cth);
- the Foreign Proceedings (Excess of Jurisdiction) Act 1984 (Cth);
- the Foreign Judgments Act 1973 (NSW);

- the Foreign Judgments Act 1962 (Vic);
- the Supreme Court (Foreign Judgments) Rules Order 1993 (Qld), giving effect to the Foreign Judgments Act 1991 (Cth) in Queensland;
- the Foreign Judgments (Reciprocal Enforcement) Act 1963 (WA);
- the Foreign Judgments Act 1971 (SA);
- the Foreign Judgments (Reciprocal Enforcement) Act 1962 (Tas);
- the Foreign Judgments (Reciprocal Enforcement) Act 1980 (NT); and
- the Foreign Judgments (Reciprocal Enforcement) Ordinance 1954 (ACT).

[11.69] The Foreign Judgments Act 1991 (Cth) deals with the registration of foreign judgments in Australia. It is binding on the Federal Court. It also grants a power upon the state Supreme Courts to register foreign judgments under the Act, but the power is exercisable subject to 'proof of the matters prescribed by the applicable Rules of court' (s 6(3) of the Foreign Judgments Act 1991 (Cth)). This suggests that a state Supreme Court does not have to enforce the Act if there is no 'proof of the matters prescribed by the applicable Rules of court'. This suggestion becomes a probability in view of the fact that a Supreme Court of a state is subject to the constitution of the state, which may have direct or indirect impacts upon the rules of the court. However, the flexible language of the federal legislation accommodates the co-existence of federal and state enforcement legislation. There should be no substantial difference between the enforcement legislation of each state and territory, because most of them are based on the Foreign Judgment (Reciprocal Enforcement) Act 1933 (UK). It must be noted that Queensland is so far the only Australian state that has responded to the call of the Foreign Judgments Act 1991 (Cth) to make rules of court in pursuance of the Act. Leaving aside the issue of constitutional implications, Queensland's practice signifies a solution to the currently duplicated and cumbersome system of enforcement in Australia.

[11.70] The framework for the enforcement of foreign judgments also includes a number of federal statutes concerning judicial assistance and arbitration. The Service and Execution of Process Act 1992 (Cth) replaced the 1901 Act. The Act enables the enforcement throughout Australia of judgments rendered or registered in any Australian jurisdiction. This means that once a foreign judgment is registered in any Australian jurisdiction, it should be enforceable in any other Australian jurisdiction (s 6(8) of the Foreign Judgments Act 1991 (Cth)). The Foreign Proceedings (Excess of Jurisdiction) Act 1984 (Cth) deals with the provision of evidence in foreign proceedings under an anti-trust law and the enforcement of a foreign judgment made under a foreign anti-trust law. This Act is relevant to international trade when an Australian party is involved in foreign proceedings under a foreign anti-trust law. In addition, there is also the International Arbitration Act 1974 (Cth) which gives effect to the Convention on the Recognition and Enforcement of Foreign Arbitral Awards adopted in New York on 10 June 1958 (the New York Convention).[32] The Act is discussed in **Chapter 12**.

---

32. The Convention entered into force on 7 June 1959. It was reprinted in (1968) ILM 1046 and incorporated into Schedule 1 of the International Arbitration Act 1974 (Cth).

Registration of foreign judgments

[11.71] Registration of a foreign judgment is crucial under any enforcement legislation in Australia. For example, s 6 of the Foreign Judgments Act 1991 (Cth) provides that a holder of a foreign judgment (a judgment creditor) may apply to an appropriate court for registration of the judgment. Once the judgment is registered in a state Supreme Court, it is regarded as the judgment of the court registering it and is registrable in other states and territories. Similarly, state legislation, such as s 6 of the Foreign Judgments Act 1973 (NSW), also allows a judgment creditor to apply for registration under the state law; and the judgment so registered has the same effect as a judgment originally granted by the court registering it. These provisions suggest that the enforcement of foreign judgments is based on the system of registration, which conveys recognition of the foreign judgment by the local court.

[11.72] Reciprocity is another fundamental principle adopted by the Australian enforcement legislation. The principle is embedded in both the federal and state legislation. For example, s 5(1) of the Foreign Judgments Act 1991 (Cth) provides that the Governor-General may allow the judgments of a foreign country to be registered under the Act if he or she is satisfied that the country would reciprocally enforce Australian judgments in similar circumstances. Similarly, s 5(3) of the Foreign Judgments Act 1973 (NSW) states that the Governor may decide whether judgments of a foreign country can be registered under the Act on the ground of reciprocity. Because the legislation only grants the privilege of applying for registration to the judgments of foreign countries which have been approved by the Governor-General or Governors on the ground of reciprocity, there is a list of approved countries, in the form of regulations, orders or schedules, attached to the federal and state legislation.

[11.73] *Re Word Publishing Co Ltd*

[1992] 2 Qd R 336

A court may refuse to register a foreign judgment if there is a sufficient ground that the registration will be set aside in a subsequent legal challenge

Facts: Word Publishing Company Ltd sued Denis Reinhardt in the National Court of Justice of Papua New Guinea. The court delivered a default judgment in favour of Word Publishing, which later sought to register the judgment with the Supreme Court of Queensland. Section 5 of the Reciprocal Enforcement of Judgment Act 1959 (Qld) allowed a court to refuse an application for registration on the ground that the court making the judgment had no jurisdiction over the matter decided.

Decision: The Supreme Court of Queensland held that the default judgment was based on an action *in personam*. A foreign court's jurisdiction over such an action was set out in s 7 of the Reciprocal Enforcement of Judgment Act 1959 (Qld). The default judgment in the present case did not satisfy the requirements of s 7. The court was of the opinion that it may refuse to register a foreign judgment if it is satisfied that a subsequent action to set aside the registration would inevitably succeed. The application was refused.

Grounds for refusing or setting aside registration

[11.74] Under ss 5 and 6 of the Foreign Judgments Act 1991 (Cth), the Federal Court or a Supreme Court of a state or territory may refuse to register a foreign judgment on the following major grounds:

- it is made in a country which has not been approved by the Governor-General as being eligible for the benefit of the Act under the reciprocal principle;
- it is of a kind (for example, a non-money judgment) which has not been approved by the Governor-General as being registrable under the Act under the reciprocal principle;
- it has been made more than six years from the date for the application for registration; and
- it is contrary to any provisions of the Act or the rules of the court which hears the application.

[11.75] Under s 7 of the Foreign Judgments Act 1991 (Cth), the Federal Court or the Supreme Court of a state or territory may set aside a registered foreign judgment on one of the following grounds:

- it is not, or has ceased to be, a judgment to which the Act applies;
- it was registered for an amount greater than the amount payable under it at the date of registration;
- its registration contravened the provisions of the Act;
- it was originally rendered by a court which had no jurisdiction in the circumstances concerned (whether the original court has an appropriate jurisdiction in an action *in personam* or action *in rem*, or whether the judgment debtor has submitted to the jurisdiction of the original court);
- the judgment debtor was not given sufficient time to defend the original proceedings and thus did not appear;
- it was obtained by fraud;
- it has been reversed or set aside in the original country;
- the applicant for registration did not have rights to do so under the registered judgment;
- it has been discharged or satisfied;
- its enforcement is contrary to public policy (inapplicable to a judgment enforcing a payment of New Zealand tax); and
- it is proved that the matter concerned had been decided by a competent court before the original court made the registered judgment.

[11.76] Under s 8 of the Foreign Judgments Act 1991 (Cth), the Federal Court or the Supreme Court of a state or territory may stay enforcement of a registered judgment on one of the following grounds:

- it is subject to appeal in the original country; or
- the judgment debtor has been granted an appeal in the original country.

[11.77] *Re Dooney*

[1993] 2 Qd R 362

Setting aside or suspending the enforcement of a registered judgment
(Note: Queensland gave effect to the Foreign Judgments Act 1991 (Cth) by the Supreme Court
(Foreign Judgments) Rules Order 1993)

Facts: The case involved the registration of a judgment made by the High Court of New Zealand against Dooney in the Supreme Court of Queensland. After the registration of the judgment, Dooney applied to the court to set aside the registration or suspend its enforcement on the ground that the judgment was a default judgment and that action had been taken in New Zealand to set the judgment aside.

Decision: The Supreme Court of Queensland held that a default judgment was capable of registration, and that Dooney had failed to establish that he had reasonable grounds to apply to the High Court of New Zealand to set aside the default judgment. Dooney's application failed.

[11.78] Identical grounds for refusing registration of a foreign judgment, for setting aside a registered judgment, and for a stay of the enforcement of a registered judgment are adopted in the state legislation. For instance, s 12 of the Foreign Judgments Act 1973 (NSW) allows the Governor, under the reciprocal principle, to decide that judgments of a particular country are not enforceable under the Act. Similarly, s 6 of the Foreign Judgments Act 1973 (NSW) allows the Supreme Court to refuse the application for registration if the application is not made within six years after the date of the judgment. In addition, the Supreme Court may also, under s 8 of the Foreign Judgments Act 1973 (NSW), set aside a registered judgment on the grounds of, inter alia, the registration contravening the Act, the original court lacking jurisdiction in delivering the judgment, the registered judgment being obtained by fraud, or enforcement being contrary to public policy. There is no need to examine the enforcement legislation of each state and territory individually, because the foreign judgments laws in Australian states and territories are largely uniform and the Foreign Judgments Act 1991 (Cth) is consistent with the relevant state Acts. This is particularly true in Queensland.

[11.79] Keele v Findley

(1990) 21 NSWLR 444

Fraud and setting aside a registered judgment

Facts: Keele and another party (plaintiffs) obtained a judgment against Findley and another party (defendants) in the Superior Court of Arizona for the County of La Paz. The plaintiffs sought to enforce the judgment under the Foreign Judgments Act 1973 (NSW). The defendants asked the court to refuse the application on the ground that the judgment was obtained by fraud.

Decision: The Supreme Court of New South Wales held that the alleged fraud was based on procedural issues. The same test for setting aside a local judgment applies to the application for setting aside a foreign judgment. The defendants in the present case did not establish that the foreign judgment must be set aside under the test.

Chapter Twelve

Alternative Means of Settling International Commercial Disputes

Defining alternative means

[12.1] 'Alternative means' refers to non-judicial methods of dispute resolution, which are alternatives to international commercial litigation. Although any methods which do not fall within the formal judicial means of dispute resolution may be regarded as alternatives to litigation, 'alternative means' in this chapter refers to arbitration, consultation (negotiation) and conciliation (mediation). International arbitration is a commonly used alternative to litigation for settling international commercial disputes.[1] Consultation is always a necessary step in the settlement of a dispute. Conciliation is somewhere between arbitration and consultation, because it is conducted by a third party (conciliator) who does not, however, have any decision-making power (that is, makes recommendations only).

Defining international commercial arbitration

Meaning of arbitration

Arbitration in historical perspective

[12.2] Arbitration is one of the traditional means of dispute resolution. The method was used by the Ancient Greeks in the Middle Ages: for example, arbitration clauses were found in a treaty in relation to the Peloponnesian war between Athens and Sparta in 445 BC.[2] Similar evidence has been found throughout the history of international relations. For example, 'Henry II in 1177 arbitrated between the kings of Castille and Navarre; Louis IX of France in 1264 arbitrated between Henry III and his barons; and Edward I in

---

1. For discussion, see Vibhute, 'Settlement of International Trade Disputes through Litigation and Arbitration: a Comparative Evaluation' (1995) 14 *The Arbitrator* pp 53–64.
2. Sohn, 'International Arbitration in Historical Perspective: Past and Present', in Soons (ed), *International Arbitration: Past and Prospects*, Martinus Nijhoff, Dordrecht, 1990, p 10.

1291 arbitrated between the thirteen competitors to the throne of Scotland'.[3] There was also a treaty between:

> the King of Bohemia, the German Princes and the Duke of Brabant where Philippe de Valois in 1334 was to act as a "judge, traiteur et amiable compositeur". Louis XI acted as umpire in many disputes, between the Kings of Castile and Aragon in 1463, between Sigismund of Austria and the Helvetic Republic in 1475, in which same year he submitted himself to the assembly of bishops in order to decide a dispute between himself and the King of England, Edward VI.[4]

There was also an arbitration clause in the 1907 Hague Convention Respecting the Limitation of the Employment of Force for the Recovery of Contract Debts.[5] Today, arbitration has been promoted and regulated in many international treaties and conventions, such as the European Convention on International Commercial Arbitration,[6] the Washington Convention of 1965 which creates the International Centre for the Settlement of Investment Disputes (ICSID),[7] and the UNCITRAL Model Law on International Commercial Arbitration.[8]

The need for a uniform definition

[12.3] It seems to be taken for granted today, in a period when arbitration is a popular means of dispute resolution, that 'arbitration' is a self-explanatory concept. Books dealing with arbitration, particularly international arbitration, commercial or non-commercial, do not define its meaning.[9] The lack of any universal definition of arbitration does not affect the use of arbitration as a means of dispute resolution in practice. However, a clear understanding of its meaning will certainly be beneficial for our studies of international commercial arbitration.

Basic features of arbitration

[12.4] Arbitration has the following basic features:

- First, arbitration is a means of dispute resolution.

- Second, it is a means of third party dispute resolution, as opposed to the settlement of disputes by the parties themselves, such as consultation.

- Third, it is a semi-judicial process of dispute resolution (or at least it is meant to be semi-judicial, even if sometimes a domestic arbitral body may exercise an authority similar to a judicial power), as opposed to litigation or conciliation. Thus, the procedural rules of arbitration should not be as rigid as judicial proceedings.

---

3. Hutton, 'Arbitration — Some Historical Aspects' (1994) 13 *The Arbitrator* p 51.
4. Lachs, 'Arbitration and International Adjudication', in Soons, note 2 above, p 38.
5. Sohn, note 2 above, p 10.
6. Made in Geneva in April 1961, see *United Nations Treaty Series* (1963–1974), vol 484, no 7041.
7. See *United Nations Treaty Series* (1966) vol 575, no 8359.
8. Adopted on 21 June 1985, incorporated into schedule 2 of International Arbitration Act 1974 (Cth).
9. No definition of arbitration is found in several new books on international arbitration, eg, Redfern and Hunter, *Law and Practice of International Commercial Arbitration*, 2nd ed, Sweet & Maxwell, London, 1991; Toope, *Mixed International Arbitration*, Crotius Publications, Cambridge, 1990; Rubino-Sammartano, *International Arbitration Law*, Kluwer, Deventer, 1990; Dorter and Widmer, *Arbitration (Commercial) in Australia*, Law Book Co, Sydney, 1979; and Soons (ed), *International Arbitration: Past and Prospects*, Martinus Nijhoff, Dordrecht, 1990.

[12.4]   International Commercial Law

- Fourth, it is a semi-autonomous process of third party dispute resolution, as opposed to the non-autonomy of parties in a court proceeding or the full autonomy of conciliation or consultation. The meaning of semi-autonomy is explained in **[12.5]**.

- Lastly, an arbitral award is enforceable in law, unless the parties expressly agree otherwise in pursuance of the governing law of the agreement. The United Nations Convention on Recognition and Enforcement of Foreign Arbitral Awards (New York Convention 1958) deals with the enforcement of foreign arbitral awards.

Meaning of semi-autonomy in arbitration

[12.5] The semi-autonomous position of parties in a process of arbitration is evidenced as follows:

- submission to international arbitration is entirely based on the agreement of the parties, although a court of law may sometimes under the relevant statutes refer a matter to arbitration or conciliation;[10]

- the parties are entitled to choose where to arbitrate a dispute, but once an agreement is made, it may be enforced by the court if one of the parties refuses to comply with it;

- the parties have the liberty to choose the arbitrators, but the arbitrators chosen by the parties will impose an arbitral award upon the parties often against the will of one party or (sometimes) to the disappointment of both parties;

- the parties can often decide which or what rules of arbitration to use, but once the rules have been decided the parties are bound by them;

- overall, the parties have autonomy to decide whether, where and how to arbitrate; once the agreement is reached, the parties' autonomy is limited by the relevant law giving effect to the agreement.

Defining arbitration

[12.6] We may conclude that arbitration is a means of third party dispute resolution, in which the parties to a dispute have freedom, subject to the relevant laws, to determine whether, when and where to use this method, to appoint an arbitrator (or arbitrators) and to choose procedural rules (if applicable) for arbitration. The decision of an arbitral body is binding and enforceable unless an exception is made under the relevant laws. Arbitration can be pursued either on an institutional basis or on an ad hoc basis.

Defining commercial arbitration

[12.7] 'Commercial' is defined in the UNCITRAL Model Law on International Commercial Arbitration as a wide term capable of covering:

> ... matters arising from all relationships of a commercial nature, whether contractual or not. Relationships of a commercial nature include, but are not limited to, the following transactions: any trade transaction for the supply or exchange of goods or services; distribution agreement; commercial representation or agency; factoring; leasing; construction of works; consulting; engineering; licensing; investment; financing; banking; insurance; exploitation agreement or concession; joint

---

10. For example, under the uniform Arbitration Act of each Australian state and territory, a court may refer a matter described by the legislation to arbitration before adjudicating it.

venture and other forms of industrial or business co-operation; carriage of goods or passengers by air, sea, rail or road.[11]

Accepting the meaning of 'commercial' as defined above, we may say that commercial arbitration is a type of arbitration used for the purpose of arbitrating disputes or disagreements arising from all relationships, whether contractual or not, of a commercial nature, thus excluding disputes of a non-commercial nature, such as personal injury claims arising from non-commercial activities, neighbourhood disputes, disputes on administrative decisions, family disputes, etc.

Meaning of international commercial arbitration

[12.8] 'International commercial arbitration' is commercial arbitration carried out at an international level. Its commercial nature distinguishes it from other forms of international arbitration, such as those used in resolving political, territorial or diplomatic disputes between states or between states and individuals. International commercial arbitration has developed rapidly over the last two decades.[12]

[12.9] Its international nature is the most salient feature of international commercial arbitration. Parties to a dispute often come from different countries, and arbitrators are frequently foreigners to them. It is also possible that neither the parties nor the arbitrators have any connection with the procedural rules adopted in the process of arbitration. More often than not, an arbitrator is chosen from the nationals of a third country which is expected to be impartial to the parties involved. In international commercial arbitration the matters in dispute, the parties to the dispute, the arbitrators of the dispute and the rules for settling the dispute may arise, relate to or come from different countries. Indeed, there is no domestic law that automatically governs the process of international commercial arbitration unless the parties so agree.

Legal framework for international commercial arbitration

Internationalisation of commercial arbitration

[12.10] At an international level, the arbitral rules of any particular country represent the jurisdiction of that country in the sense that the arbitral award made under the rules is to be recognised under the local law first before it can be enforced locally or in another country under the New York Convention 1958. A party to a dispute would naturally avoid the application of the arbitration rules of the other disputing party for fear of possible partiality or prejudice against him or her. In fact, a party may be disadvantaged by lack of knowledge and understanding of foreign arbitration rules. In addition, most countries regard the choosing of local arbitration rules as a submission to the local law and jurisdiction, because the local arbitration rules are part of the local 'law' or the local arbitration rules often apply local law. It follows that a local court may subsequently be capable of assuming a jurisdiction over the foreign party, which it does

---
11. UNCITRAL Model Law, footnote 2.
12. For discussion, see Pryles, 'Institutional International Arbitrations' (1991) 10 *The Arbitrator* pp 127–45.

[12.10]   International Commercial Law

not otherwise have. Referring to an arbitration clause as a signpost for determining the connection between a law and a contract is one of the commonly practised rules of conflict of laws. For these reasons, parties to an international commercial dispute may prefer to use international conventions, the UNCITRAL Model Law on International Arbitration, or the arbitration rules of a third country which appears to be neutral to both disputing parties. Sometimes, parties may also prefer to submit a potential or existing dispute to arbitration in a third country which has its own arbitration rules for the sake of neutrality. However, often for the considerations of practicality, in particular, cost considerations, the parties have to make some compromise and submit their disputes to a place where the interests of the parties can be balanced best.

Major conventions and arbitral rules

[12.11] The legal framework for international commercial arbitration consists of conventions, arbitration rules and arbitral institutions. The major international arbitral institutions or bodies are examined in **[12.45]–[12.61]**. The major conventions and arbitration rules which do not have the same binding force as conventions can be summarised as follows:

- the 1958 New York Convention on the Recognition and Enforcement of Foreign Arbitral Awards;
- the 1961 European Convention on International Commercial Arbitration;
- the 1962 Paris Agreement relating to the Application of the European Conventions on International Community Arbitration;
- the UNCITRAL Arbitration Rules 1976;
- the UNCITRAL Model Law on International Commercial Arbitration;
- the UNCITRAL Notes on Organising Arbitral Proceedings 1996;
- the 1965 Washington Convention on the Settlement of Investment Disputes between States and Nationals of Other States; and
- the arbitration rules of each individual international arbitral body, such as the ICC Rules of Conciliation and Arbitration, the London Court of Arbitration Rules, the International Arbitration Rules of the American Arbitration Association and the Arbitration Rules of China International Economic and Trade Arbitration Commission.

Of the abovementioned conventions and rules, the New York Convention, the UNCITRAL Model Law on International Commercial Arbitration, and the Washington Convention are the most important conventions on international commercial arbitration. These conventions will be examined in turn.

New York Convention

Functions of the New York Convention

[12.12] The full title of the New York Convention is the New York Convention on the Recognition and Enforcement of Arbitral Awards of 1958. As its title suggests, the New York Convention is not about the procedural rules of international arbitration, but relates to the enforcement of the international arbitral awards made by various arbitral bodies, whether domestic or international. Its functions are to promote cooperation between the contracting states and to unify their practice of enforcing foreign arbitral awards. It is considered to be 'the most important international treaty relating to international commercial arbitration',[13] for the certainty and efficiency it offers in the enforcement of international arbitral decisions. As at October 2002, the New York Convention had 132 members.[14]

Application of the New York Convention

[12.13] The New York Convention governs the recognition and enforcement of foreign arbitral awards within the territory of a contracting party. A 'foreign arbitral award' is an arbitral award made outside the jurisdiction of a contracting party, in whose territory the award is to be recognised and enforced. This broad concept includes any arbitral awards made outside the country enforcing them. It may also extend to any award which is not regarded as a 'domestic award' under the law of the country where the enforcement is sought. This arguably opens a possibility for a country by its own law to classify an award made within its territory to be a 'foreign award' for the purpose of enforcement.[15] Thus, a foreign arbitral award is any arbitral award whose effect is not based on the domestic law of the country where the award is to be recognised and enforced.

[12.14] The broad meaning of 'foreign arbitral award' suggests a broad obligation of the contracting parties to the New York Convention. Under this obligation, a contracting party may be obliged to enforce an arbitral award made under the law of a country which refuses to accept the New York Convention. This consequence is inconsistent with the notion of reciprocity, which forms the basis of most international conventions and treaties. In order to avoid this consequence, art I(3) of the New York Convention permits a contracting party to declare the convention valid only between it and another contracting country, thus excluding arbitral awards made under the laws of non-contracting parties from the scope of 'foreign arbitral awards'. A contracting party is also permitted to declare that enforceable awards are limited to those relating to commercial relationships as recognised in its law.

Obligations under the New York Convention

[12.15] Contracting parties under the New York Convention have four major obligations:

- under art II, a contracting party is obliged to recognise a written arbitration agreement, which can be made in the form of an arbitration clause, a separate agreement, or an exchange of letters or telegrams;

---

13. Redfern and Hunter, note 9 above, p 478.
14. UNCITRAL, *Status of Conventions and Model Laws*, updated on 15 October 2002, available at <http://www.uncitral.org/>.
15. Such possibility is meaningful in a country consisting of several regimes of law, such as the relationship between Mainland China and Hong Kong or Macau under 'One Country Two Systems' principle. However, a country will be probably reluctant to accept such an interpretation of the New York Convention to avoid controversies in international politics. This is why China has chosen to make a reciprocal arrangement for mutual enforcement of arbitral awards between it and Hong Kong or Macau.

- under art II, a contracting party is obliged, at the request of one of the parties to an arbitration agreement, to refer the parties to arbitration;
- under art III, a contracting party is obliged to recognise and enforce foreign arbitral awards in accordance with its own law; and
- under art III, a contracting party is obliged not to impose substantially more onerous conditions or higher fees or charges on the recognition or enforcement of foreign arbitral awards than are imposed on the recognition or enforcement of domestic arbitral awards.

Exceptions to the obligations

[12.16] Article V of the convention makes exceptions to the fulfilment of the above obligations. Article IV also provides a ground for refusal of recognition and enforcement, if the party applying for the recognition and enforcement of an arbitral award fails to comply with this provision. A contracting party may, upon proof provided by the party requesting refusal, refuse to recognise and enforce a foreign arbitration award on the following grounds:

- one or both parties to the arbitration agreement, under which the award was made, were incapable of entering into the arbitration agreement under the chosen law of the agreement, or in the absence of the chosen law, under the law of the country where the award was made;
- the arbitration agreement, under which the award was made, was invalid under the chosen law of the agreement, or in the absence of the agreement, under the law of the country where the award was made;
- there was procedural unfairness to the party against whom the award is invoked, in particular when there was no adequate notice of the appointment of the arbitrator or of the arbitration proceedings, or the party was unable to present his or her case;
- the award exceeds the terms of the arbitration agreement (however, if part of the award, which is severable from the rest of the award, falls under the terms of the award, the complying part should be enforced);
- the composition of the arbitral authority is inconsistent with the agreement of the parties, or in the absence of such an agreement, with the law of the country where the award was made;
- the actual procedures contravene the agreement of the parties, or in the absence of such an agreement, the law of the country where the award was made;
- the award is not binding under the law of the country where the award was made;
- the award has been set aside or suspended by a competent authority in the country where the award was made;
- the matter covered in the award is not capable of settlement by arbitration under the law of the country where the award is to be enforced;
- recognition and enforcement of the award is contrary to the public policy of the country where the enforcement is sought; and

- the party applying for recognition and enforcement of an award fails to comply with art IV to provide appropriate documents.

In addition, art VII, which excludes the operation of the provisions of the convention from areas covered by multilateral or bilateral agreements concerning the recognition and enforcement of arbitral awards, may also provide grounds for a court to refuse to enforce an arbitral award in certain circumstances.

The Washington Convention of 1965

An overview of the convention

[12.17] The full title of the Washington Convention is the Convention on the Settlement of International Investment Disputes between States and Nationals of Other States of 1965. The convention is incorporated into Schedule 3 of the International Arbitration Act 1974 (Cth). It was formulated by the International Bank for Reconstruction and Development (the World Bank), adopted by the member states of the World Bank on 18 March 1965 and entered into force on 14 October 1966.[16] The Washington Convention created the International Centre for Settlement of Investment Disputes, and is also known as the ICSID Convention. In September 2002, 153 countries had ratified the Washington Convention.[17]

[12.18] The Washington Convention sets out rules for conciliation and arbitration.[18] It was designed for dealing with the thorny issues arising from investment disputes between a sovereign state and foreign investors investing in that state. It purports to provide effective remedies to individual investors against the decisions or commercial activities of a sovereign state in the area of foreign investment, although it also aims to strike a balance between the interests of the investors and the interests of the host countries, as well as between developing and developed countries.[19] Arbitration under the Washington Convention is characterised by 'a special mechanism for identifying the law governing the investment contract; the waiving of diplomatic protection on the part of the investor's national state *vis-á-vis* the host State, thus ensuring execution of awards rendered by arbitral tribunals instituted by ICSID; the guarantee that the arbitral awards will have the same force as a national judgment in all member States of the Washington Convention; an international system to review the validity of the arbitral awards';[20] and the procedural rules for establishing and conducting an arbitral tribunal under the Washington Convention.

Structure of ICSID

[12.19] ICSID is an autonomous international organisation. However, it has close links with the World Bank. All of ICSID's members are also members of the Bank. The ICSID

---

16. Id, p 47.
17. See ICSID, at <http://www.worldbank.org/icsid/constate/c-states-en.htm>.
18. Washington Convention, arts 28–55.
19. Toope, note 9 above, p 219.
20. Giardina, 'The International Centre for Settlement of Investment Disputes between States and Nationals of Other States (ICSID)', in Sarcevic (ed), *Essays on International Commercial Arbitration,* Graham & Trotman, London, 1989, pp 214–15.

is managed by the Administrative Council, which is composed of one representative of each member. The expenses of the ICSID Secretariat are financed out of the Bank's budget, although the costs of individual proceedings are borne by the parties involved.[21]

Articles 1–24 of the Washington Convention deal with the establishment, structure, financing and status of ICSID. The Centre is located in Washington. Its administrative structure consists of the following organisations.

[12.20] The Administrative Council is composed of representatives of the contracting states. The president of the IBRD is *ex officio* Chairman of the Administrative Council. The council is the highest power within the Centre. It exercises a number of specified powers under art 6 of the convention to administer and regulate the activities of the Centre.

[12.21] The Secretariat is the executive body of the Centre. It is headed by the Secretary-General who is elected by the Administrative Council by a majority of two-thirds of the members of the Administrative Council.

[12.22] The Panels: there are two panels within the Centre: the Panel of Conciliators and the Panel of Arbitrators. Panel members are nominated by the contracting states and the Chairman of the Administrative Council in accordance with art 13. Panel members represent various legal systems and cultures. A person can be listed in both panels.

[12.23] Article 18 of the convention provides that ICSID has full international legal personality, including a capacity to enter into a contract, to acquire and dispose of property and to institute legal proceedings. The Centre and its officials enjoy the immunities and privileges which are necessary for the performance of their functions.

Jurisdiction of ICSID

[12.24] Article 25 of the convention defines the jurisdiction of the Centre as follows:

> The jurisdiction of the Centre shall extend to any legal dispute arising directly out of an investment, between a Contracting State (or any constituent subdivision or agency of a Contracting State designated to the Centre by the State) and a national of another Contracting State, which the parties to the dispute consent in writing to submit to the Centre. When the parties have given their consent, no party may withdraw its consent unilaterally.

[12.25] This provision suggests that the jurisdiction of the Centre is characterised by two features:

- the Centre has jurisdiction over investment disputes only; and
- the disputes must be those which involve a contracting state and a national of another contracting state (a dispute between two contracting states should be submitted to the International Court of Justice, art 64 of the convention).

Arbitration under the Washington Convention

[12.26] Arbitration proceedings in ICSID are set out in arts 36–54 of the Washington Convention. Any contracting state or national of a contracting state may request the Secretary-General to provide arbitration. The Secretary-General makes a decision either

---

21. ICSID homepage at <http://www.worldbank.org/icsid/about/main.htm>.

Alternative Means of Settling International Commercial Disputes [12.30]

to register or to refuse the request. If registered, the state party cannot withdraw its consent unilaterally to avoid the proceedings.

[12.27] An arbitral tribunal will be formed under arts 37–40. The parties may appoint an arbitrator or arbitrators by agreement. If the parties fail to appoint the arbitrator(s) within 90 days after the Secretary-General dispatches the notice of registration, the Chairman of the Administrative Council should appoint the arbitrator(s). The majority of arbitrators in a tribunal should not be nationals of a state which is a party to the proceedings. Arbitrators may be appointed from outside the Panel of Arbitrators.

[12.28] The powers and functions of the tribunal are defined in arts 41–47. Article 42 of the convention states that the tribunal 'shall decide a dispute in accordance with such rules of law as may be agreed by the parties'. If the parties have not reached any agreement as to the procedural rules, the tribunal may apply the law of the state and the relevant international law applicable in the circumstances. The tribunal has power to call evidence or make inquiries, unless the parties expressly agree otherwise. The tribunal also has power, at the request of a party, to make an award in default after the other party fails or refuses without justification to attend the proceedings.

[12.29] The award of the arbitrator should be made in writing and is binding and final. This is expressly stated in art 53 of the convention, which provides that the award shall not be subject to any appeal or to any other remedy except those provided for in the convention. A contracting state is obliged to recognise and enforce the award as if the award were a final judgment of its own court. An arbitral award of ICSID is not subject to the New York Convention in the territory of a state which is a member of both the Washington Convention and the New York Convention.

[12.30] *Amco Asia Corp v The Republic of Indonesia*

(1993) ICSID Report 377

Arbitration of foreign investment disputes by ICSID

Facts: Amco Asia Corporation (Amco) was a company incorporated in Delaware, United States. In 1968 it entered into a lease of management with PT Wisman Kartika (Wisman), an Indonesian company, for the development of a hotel and office block in Indonesia. Wisman was wholly owned by Inkopad, which was incorporated under Indonesian law for the welfare of Indonesian army personnel and accountable to the Indonesian Government.

Amco obtained approval from the Indonesian Foreign Investment Board for the establishment of PT Amco Indonesia (PT Amco) for the purpose of taking advantage of benefits and tax concessions available under the Indonesian Foreign Capital Investment Law. Amco's interests in the lease were transferred to PT Amco. In 1972, PT Amco obtained approval from the Indonesian authorities to transfer part of its interests in the lease to Pan American Development Ltd (Pan American), allegedly for the purpose of honouring a 1968 agreement between Pan American and Amco made in Hong Kong. In 1969 PT Amco exercised its rights under the lease with Wisman and sub-leased the project to a consortium.

[12.30]

In 1978 Inkopad took over the management of the hotel. In the same year, Wisman entered into a profit-sharing agreement with PT Amco, which took over the management. In 1980 Wisman took over the hotel forcefully from PT Amco because of a dispute on profit-sharing. It alleged that PT Amco failed to fulfil its obligations under the original lease between Amco and Wisman to invest US$4 million as agreed. Consequently, the Indonesian Capital Investment Coordinating Board revoked PT Amco's investment licence without offering PT Amco an opportunity to defend itself. Wisman commenced proceedings for breach of contract in the Indonesian courts. The courts annulled the lease and awarded damages to Wisman. Amco, Pan American and PT Amco requested arbitration by ICSID pursuant to the Washington Convention.

Decision: The first arbitration took place in September 1983. The tribunal found in favour of Amco in 1984 on a number of grounds, including, inter alia, unlawful revocation of the investment licence, unlawful taking over of management of the hotel by Wisman, and the Indonesian Government's failure to protect the interests of foreign investors according to Indonesian law and international law. In 1986 Indonesia sought to annul the award pursuant to art 52(3) of the Washington Convention in front of an ad hoc committee. The committee annulled the award, but did not annul the initial finding that Wisman's taking over of the management was illegal. The matter was resubmitted to ICSID for arbitration in 1987. A new tribunal decided in 1990 that, inter alia, Indonesian law must be consistent with the standards of international law, and PT Amco's damages claim should be limited to the loss of the right to manage the hotel because PT Amco was not deprived of the right to share profits by Wisman's taking over of the management. In 1990 Amco resubmitted the case for rectification on the ground that the tribunal failed to consider a number of issues, such as the rate of exchange and construction of the 1978 profit-sharing agreement, etc. Most of the allegations were subsequently rejected by the tribunal.

♦

The UNCITRAL Model Law

What is the UNCITRAL Model Law?

[12.31] The full title of the UNCITRAL Model Law is the United Nations Commission on International Trade Law Model Law on International Commercial Arbitration, which is included in Schedule 2 of the International Arbitration Act 1974 (Cth). It was adopted by the United Nations Commission on International Trade Law on 21 June 1985, and by the United Nations General Assembly on 11 December 1985 'without a vote Resolution 40/72 recommending "that all States give due consideration to the Model Law on International Commercial Arbitration, in view of the desirability of uniformity of the law of arbitral procedures and the specific needs of international commercial arbitration practice"'.[22] The Model Law is an international instrument, but is not an international convention in that it is not binding until it has been incorporated into the national law of each member of the United Nations. There is no mechanism for the administration of the Model Law. Nor is there a need to ratify or accept it. A UN member has only a moral obligation to implement the Model Law through its domestic legislation.

---

22. Broches, *Commentary on the UNCITRAL Model Law on International Commercial Arbitration*, Kluwer, Deventer, 1990, p IX.

Alternative Means of Settling International Commercial Disputes [12.34]

[12.32] The Model Law has the following basic features:

- First, it is a 'recommended model' for the formulation of a national law of arbitration.
- Second, it was intended to apply to international commercial disputes, which have been defined widely in footnote 2 of the Model Law: see **[12.7]**. But UNICITRAL intended that the contracting states should have liberty in applying the Model Law to their domestic commercial arbitration.[23]
- Third, it was intended for the settlement of international commercial disputes. This distinguishes it from other rules for international arbitration, such as the Hague Conventions, which were intended to apply to non-commercial disputes, in particular disputes arising under the 'public international law', between contracting states. Because of the wide interpretation of the word 'commercial', the Model Law and the Washington Convention may overlap where a foreign investment dispute is involved.
- Lastly, it represents the most recent international effort in the codification of rules for international commercial arbitration. Being a 'model', the Model Law reflects the flexibility of international commercial arbitration as a means of dispute resolution at international level.

Meaning of 'arbitration agreement' in the Model Law

[12.33] Article 7(1) of the Model Law states as follows:

'Arbitration agreement' is an agreement by the parties to submit to arbitration all or certain disputes which have arisen or which may arise between them in respect of a defined legal relationship, whether contractual or not. An arbitration agreement may be in the form of an arbitration clause in a contract or in the form of a separate agreement.

Under the Model Law, an arbitration agreement must be made in written form. In fact, art 7(2) of the Model Law recognises any written 'arbitration agreement', which evidences the intention or agreement of the parties to submit a dispute to arbitration.

Arbitration agreement and obligation of the court

[12.34] Under art 8(1) of the Model Law, a court of law is obliged, at the request of a party to the agreement, to refer the matter to arbitration pursuant to the written agreement of the parties. When a written agreement to arbitrate is established and one of the parties requests the court to enforce the agreement, the court must refer the dispute to arbitration in accordance with the agreement. The request for arbitration must be made before the parties make first submission on the substance of the dispute (defence or counter-claim) to the court. If a court is satisfied that the agreement is null, void, inoperative or incapable of being performed, it may refuse to enforce it.

---

23. Broches, note 22 above, p 2.

> **[12.35]** *Tanning Research Laboratories Inc v O'Brien*
>
> (1990) 169 CLR 332; 91 ALR 180; 1 ACSR 510
>
> *Court refers a matter to arbitration pursuant to the arbitration agreement in a contract*
>
> **Facts:** O'Brien was the liquidator of Hawaiian Tropic Pty Ltd (Hawaiian). Tanning Research Laboratories Inc (Tanning) was a Florida corporation, which claimed the price of goods sold to Hawaiian under an exclusive licence to manufacture, distribute and sell certain suntan products within Australia and New Zealand. O'Brien rejected the proof for the claim. Tanning obtained a court order to direct O'Brien to accept the proof of a specified sum. This order was set aside by the Court of Appeal of New South Wales on the ground that the liability of the debt or the sum of the debt should be arbitrated in accordance with an arbitration clause in the licence. Section 7(2) of the Arbitration (Foreign Awards and Agreements) Act 1974 (Cth), which is now known as the International Arbitration Act 1974 (Cth), allows a court, at the request of a party, to refer a matter to arbitration in pursuance of an arbitration agreement. Tanning appealed to the High Court of Australia.
>
> **Decision:** The High Court by majority dismissed the appeal. The minority judges allowed the appeal in part. However, the whole court was unanimous in upholding the New South Wales court's decision to refer the matter to arbitration.

Arbitral tribunal and arbitrators

[12.36] The composition of an arbitral tribunal and the choice of arbitrators are regulated in arts 10–15 of the Model Law. Under art 10, the parties are free to determine the total number of arbitrators in a tribunal. In the absence of any agreement, a tribunal consists of three arbitrators. The parties are free to agree upon the procedures for appointing arbitrators. If the parties fail to reach an agreement, the arbitrators should be appointed in accordance with art 11. An arbitrator must be impartial and have no conflict of interests with respect to the matter or parties in dispute. Articles 12 and 13 allow the parties to challenge the suitability of any arbitrator during the proceedings of arbitration.

Jurisdiction of arbitral tribunal

[12.37] As a general rule, the jurisdiction of an arbitral tribunal and its power are defined by the agreement submitting the matter to arbitration. Article 16 of the Model Law permits a tribunal to determine whether it has jurisdiction under the relevant arbitration agreement and whether the arbitration agreement is valid.

Proceedings of arbitral tribunal

[12.38] Parties to arbitration generally have autonomy to decide the procedures of arbitration. This includes the determination of various matters relating to the conduct of the proceedings. Articles 18–32 set out the principles for conducting arbitral proceedings as follows:

- equality between the parties should be maintained;
- a party should have a full opportunity to present his or her case;
- in the absence of the parties' agreement, the tribunal has discretion in determining procedural issues;

- in the absence of the parties' choice, the tribunal has discretion in choosing the location of the proceedings;
- in the absence of agreement otherwise, the proceedings are deemed to begin from the date on which the notice of arbitration is received by the respondent;
- in the absence of the parties' choice, the tribunal determines the language to be used in the proceedings;
- there should be statements of claim and defence;
- the parties' right to request an oral hearing, in the absence of any agreement, is subject to the tribunal's discretion;
- unless agreed otherwise by the parties, the tribunal may make a default award;
- unless agreed otherwise by the parties, the tribunal may call expert witnesses;
- the parties are entitled to settle the dispute during the proceedings; and
- the award should be made under the governing law of the dispute as chosen by the parties; and in the absence of agreement, the tribunal has discretion in choosing the governing law under the rules of conflict of laws as it thinks fit.

Effect of the award

[12.39] Article 31 requires an award to be made in writing and signed by the arbitrator or arbitrators. Unless the parties agree otherwise, an award shall contain the reasons for which the award was made. Under art 33, a party has the right to request the tribunal to correct technical errors in the award, or to interpret the award. The request must be made within 30 days after the party receives a copy of the award. The tribunal must respond to the request within 30 days of receipt of the request. A party may also request the tribunal to make an additional award within 30 days of receipt of the award and the tribunal is obliged to make the additional award within 60 days of receipt of the request only when it considers the request to be justified.

[12.40] Article 34 provides the following grounds for setting aside an arbitral award by a court of law:
- a party to the arbitration agreement is legally incapable of entering into the agreement;
- the arbitration agreement was invalid under the law expressly chosen to be the governing law of the agreement, or in the absence of such governing law, under the law of the state where arbitration takes place;
- the award exceeds the authority of the agreement, but if the part of the award that exceeded the authority can be separated from the part falling within the authority, the conforming part is enforceable;
- the composition of the tribunal was inconsistent with the agreement, which is consistent with the provisions of the Model Law;
- the composition of the tribunal contravened the Model Law;
- the subject matter of the dispute is not capable of being arbitrated under the law of the state where arbitration took place; and
- the award is contrary to the public policy of the state where arbitration took place.

[12.41] An application for setting aside an award must be made within three months from the date on which the applicant received the award, or three months from the date on which the request for correction, interpretation or additional award was disposed of by the tribunal.

[12.42] An award which is not challengeable under the provisions of the Model Law is binding and enforceable by a court of law. Article 35 of the Model Law provides that an 'arbitral award, irrespective of the country in which it was made, shall be recognised as binding and, upon application in writing to the competent court, shall be enforceable subject to the provisions of this article and of article 36'. This provision purports to give an award the same effect as is given in the New York Convention. Articles 35 and 36 to some extent overlap with provisions of the New York Convention: art 36 sets out similar grounds for a court to refuse to enforce a foreign arbitral award as art V of the New York Convention: see **[12.95]–[12.105]**. The difference between them is that the Model Law binds only states which incorporate the Model Law into their own national law, but the New York Convention binds a contracting country as soon as it ratifies or accedes to the convention.

The Hague Conventions

[12.43] The Hague Conventions should be reviewed briefly, although they are not conventions on commercial arbitration. The Hague Conventions are the Hague Convention for the Pacific Settlement of International Disputes of 1899 and the Hague Convention for the Pacific Settlement of International Disputes of 1907. Both are the result of peace conferences held in 1899 and 1907 respectively. The 1899 conference was convened by the Czar of All Russians, resulting in the agreement on the use of good offices, mediation and voluntary arbitration as the means of preventing armed conflicts between nations.[24] The Permanent Court of Arbitration was established in the Peace Palace at The Hague in the 1899 Conference, although an attempt to establish a Judicial Arbitration Court in the 1907 Conference failed.[25] The Permanent Court of Arbitration maintains a list of arbitrators who may be chosen by disputing parties as arbitrators. The same method has been adopted by many arbitral institutes today. At the time, however, the creation of the Permanent Court of Arbitration in 1899 was deemed rebellious by those who preferred the dogmatic and dignified formality of judicial proceedings. A participant in the 1899 Conference was reported to have said that 'the Convention of 1899 only created the phantom of a Court, an impalpable ghost, or, to speak more plainly, it created a clerk's office with a list'.[26]

[12.44] The Hague Conventions have their historical importance in shaping the modern foundation and structure of international arbitration. In particular, they represent an internationally cooperative effort to codify the rules of arbitration. This was acknowledged by

---

24. Kooijmans, 'International Arbitration in Historical Perspective: Past and Present' in Soons, note 9 above, p 23.
25. Redfern and Hunter, note 9 above, p 476.
26. Kooijmans, note 24 above, p 23.

Alternative Means of Settling International Commercial Disputes [12.47]

the International Law Commission in 1949, when the Chairman of the Commission (Judge Manley O Hudson) commented that the question of arbitral procedure 'had been amply dealt with in The Hague Conventions of 1899 and 1907 on the Pacific Settlement of International Disputes. Since that time the rules of arbitral procedure had been frequently applied'.[27] However, the Permanent Court of Arbitration has rarely been used because of the availability of many other more sophisticated and flexible arbitral facilities.

Major international arbitral institutions and their functions

Defining an international arbitral institution

[12.45] An 'international arbitral institution' is an arbitral body which provides arbitral services for settling international disputes. International arbitral institutions may be established under an international treaty, such as the Permanent Court of Arbitration in the Peace Palace of The Hague, ICSID, and the Iran–US Claims Tribunal, or as a private organisation or body under the governing domestic law where the institute is situated, such as the American Arbitration Association (AAA), the London Court of International Arbitration (LCIA), China International Economic and Trade Arbitration Commission (CIETAC) and the Institute of Arbitrators Australia. An official arbitral body can be established under an international treaty, and a non-official and private arbitral institute exists on its own reputation and voluntary acceptance by the parties to a dispute. While the former provides a forum for international arbitration, the latter provides 'services' of international arbitration. For the latter, international arbitration is more like a commercial service, although the rules of the relevant institute can be binding through voluntary acceptance by the parties. Thus, an international arbitral institute is either an official or a non-governmental body established for the purpose of providing arbitral services to parties involved in an international dispute. Its power is based on either the relevant treaty (if applicable), or the voluntary submission of the parties. Its awards can be enforced under the New York Convention or the relevant domestic law, whichever is applicable.

Major governmental international arbitral bodies

[12.46] 'Governmental' arbitral institutes are those international arbitral bodies established under international treaties. These are presently the Permanent Court of Arbitration, the Inter-American Commercial Arbitration Commission, ICSID and the Iran–US Claims Tribunal. These bodies will be examined in turn.

[12.47] The Permanent Court of Arbitration is located in the Peace Palace, The Hague. The administrative body of the court is the bureau which has a list of arbitrators who may constitute a tribunal at the choice of the parties in a given dispute. The tribunal arbitrates a dispute 'on the basis of respect of law'.[28] This makes the proceedings of the court as rigid as judicial proceedings and thus discourages its use in international disputes.

---

27. *Yearbook of the International Law Commission* 1949, p 237.
28. Kooijmans, note 24 above, p 24.

[12.47]

Between 1918 and 1938 only six disputes were submitted to the court and between 1945 to 1990 only one case was arbitrated by it.[29] It appears that the Permanent Court of Arbitration does not have any practical implication for international arbitration, in particular international commercial arbitration, today.

[12.48] The Inter-American Commercial Arbitration Commission was established under the Inter-American Convention on International Commercial Arbitration (the Panama Convention). The member countries of the convention are Chile, Columbia, Costa Rica, El Salvador, Guatemala, Honduras, Mexico, Panama, Paraguay, Peru, Uruguay, Venezuela and the United States.[30] The Panama Convention was based on the New York Convention 1958 and the Commission has adopted the UNCITRAL Arbitration Rules,[31] which were adopted by Resolution 31/98 of the UN General Assembly on 15 December 1976. The rules of the commission are basically consistent with the major international conventions on international arbitration.

[12.49] ICSID provides conciliation and arbitration services to the contracting parties and their nationals. However, it deals only with disputes arising directly out of an investment between a contracting state or its agency and a national of another contracting party.[32] The jurisdiction of ICSID is as follows:

- First, the dispute must be relevant to an investment, whether direct or portfolio, including an investment by a licensing agreement, but excluding disputes from other types of commercial relationships (as defined in the UNCITRAL Model Law, see **[12.32]**).

- Second, the dispute must arise between a government authority or agent and a national of another contracting party, thus excluding disputes between two contracting states or between the nationals of different contracting parties.

ICSID (the Centre) is located at the principal office of the World Bank in Washington.[33] It is managed by an Administrative Council and a Secretariat with a Panel of Conciliators and a Panel of Arbitrators.[34] The Administrative Council, which usually meets once a year, or more if necessary, consists of representatives of the contracting parties on the basis of one representative from each country. The President of the World Bank is *ex officio* Chairman of the council, who does not, however, have voting power.[35] The Secretariat, which consists of a Secretariat-General and one or more Deputy Secretariat-General, are elected by two-thirds votes of the Administrative Council for a term not exceeding six years.[36] Although the Panel of Conciliators is separate from the Panel of Arbitrators, the members of both panels are subject to the same requirements. For example, each contracting country may nominate four persons, who

---

29. Id, p 25.
30. Redfern and Hunter, note 9 above, p 467.
31. Id, pp 65 and 468.
32. Washington Convention, art 25.
33. Washington Convention, art 2.
34. Washington Convention, art 3.
35. Washington Convention, arts 4, 5 and 7.
36. Washington Convention, arts 9 and 10.

may be nationals of any countries, to either panel.[37] The Chairman of the Administrative Council may also appoint 10 persons, who must be from different contracting countries and preferably from the principal legal systems, to each panel.[38] The panel members should be 'persons of high moral character and recognised competence in the field of law, commerce, industry or finance, who may be relied upon to exercise independent judgment. Competence in the field of law shall be of particular importance in the case of persons on the Panel of Arbitrators'.[39] The term of service for both panels is six years per term. The appointment can be renewed and a person may serve on both panels.[40]

[12.50] The Iran–US Claims Tribunal is a special body established for dealing with disputes between Iran and the United States. It suggests a particular model of international arbitration for resolving commercial and non-commercial disputes. In this particular instance, the tribunal has replaced litigation proceedings, which were initiated by US nationals against the Iranian Government following the Iranian Revolution in 1979. The tribunal was set up under the Algeria Declaration,[41] which was the result of mediation by the government of Algeria in 1981.[42] The immediate effect of the declaration was the release of American hostages by the Iranian Government and the release of Iranian assets held in American banks. This was followed by arrangements (Claims Settlement Declarations) for settling claims of the nationals of one party against the other party, mainly commercial claims made by US nationals against the Iranian Government.[43] The tribunal is located in The Hague with nine arbitrators, three from each country and three from other countries.[44] The UNCITRAL Arbitration Rules have been adopted by the tribunal.[45]

Major non-governmental international arbitral institutions

Arbitration as a service

[12.51] Non-governmental international arbitral institutions have thrived in recent years. Given that the fundamental principle of arbitration is the parties' freedom to choose the forum, the rules and the arbitrators, the popularity of any private-based arbitral institutes in the world today can only be explained by their credibility, reliability and convenience. That is not to say that the economic power of the countries where the major non-governmental international arbitral bodies are situated is not a factor in the reputation of the arbitral institutes concerned. The American Arbitration Association and the London Court of International Arbitration are examples. The services of international arbitral institutions include the provision of the forum for arbitration and the provision

---

37. Washington Convention, art 13(1).
38. Washington Convention, arts 13(2) & 14(2).
39. Washington Convention, art 14(1).
40. Washington Convention, arts 15 & 16.
41. The declaration is reproduced in *Yearbook of Commercial Arbitration* 1982, vol VII, pp 256–60.
42. Toope, note 9 above, p 265.
43. Id, p 266.
44. For discussion, see Rubino-Sammartano, note 9 above, pp 65–86.
45. Redfern and Hunter, note 9 above, p 51.

[12.51] of the rules of arbitration. The major non-governmental international arbitral institutions will be reviewed below.

The International Chamber of Commerce

[12.52] The ICC's International Court of Arbitration was established in Paris in 1923, initially under the name of the Court of Arbitration.[46] The court provides conciliation and arbitration services under its own rules. Since 1999, it has handled more than 500 requests for arbitration per year. By 2002, the court had been involved in the settlement of more than 11,500 international commercial disputes since its establishment.[47] Under the new ICC's Rules of Arbitration which came into operation on 1 January 1998, the court is a permanent arbitral institution with a Chairman, eight Vice-Chairmen, a Secretary-General and a number of Technical Advisers appointed by the Council of the ICC.[48] The other main features of the court are as follows:

- The court 'does not itself settle disputes': art 2(1).
- The actual arbitral tribunal consists of either one or three arbitrators, appointed by either the disputing parties or the court pursuant to its rules.
- The disputing parties' written agreement to submit the dispute to the court is the prerequisite for the court's jurisdiction.
- Arbitral proceedings under the court commence from the date on which the written request is received by the Secretariat of the court.
- Although there are rules governing the statement of defence and counter-claim, there are no specific rules on evidence, hearings, amendment of claim and legal representation.
- The power of each tribunal in a given case is defined by the agreement of the parties, and the tribunal has discretion in determining procedural issues within its power.
- The tribunal has power to determine the costs of arbitration and its awards are final.

These facts suggest that the court is an administrative body for providing conciliation and arbitration services and that its rules represent a flexible process of arbitration in which the disputing parties have relatively wide autonomy and control.

Besides arbitration, the ICC International Court of Arbitration also offers other means of dispute settlement, including the ICC's Rules of Optional Conciliation, which facilitate the amicable settlement of disputes, and the ICC's Rules for Expertise, administered by the ICC's International Centre for Expertise. For nearly 20 years, the Centre has been a world leader in finding and appointing neutral experts able to assist in resolving technical and financial disputes. The ICC's innovative Pre-Arbitral Reference Procedure complements these rules. It was introduced in 1990 to provide parties with an alternative to courts of law in obtaining urgent interim relief in connection with international commercial disputes.[49]

---

46. Id, p 15.
47. ICC International Court of Arbitration homepage at <http://www.iccwbo.org>.
48. ICC Rules of Arbitration (1998), art 1.
49. ICC International Court of Arbitration, available at <http://www.iccwbo.org/arb/4.htm>.

The American Arbitration Association

[12.53] The American Arbitration Association (AAA), situated in New York, provides arbitral services under its International Arbitration Rules. Under these rules, the parties to an international commercial dispute (although the application of these rules is not expressly limited to commercial disputes) should agree in writing to arbitrate the dispute before invoking the rules.[50] Under art 2 of the rules, a party is able to initiate arbitral proceedings by giving written notice to the association and the other party. The other party is required to file a statement of defence and counter-claim (if applicable) within a prescribed number of days (eg, 45 days) after the commencement of the proceeding: art 3. The claim or defence may be amended pursuant to art 4 of the rules. The parties to the dispute should appoint one or more arbitrators pursuant to art 6, or the administrator of the association may appoint either one or three arbitrators pursuant to art 5 of the rules. The rules governing the proceeding are fairly detailed and relatively formal, such as the rules relating to the challenge to the appointment of an arbitrator under arts 7, 8 and 9; the rules concerning the replacement of an arbitrator under arts 10 and 11; and the rules governing the place of arbitration, legal representation, language, jurisdiction of the arbitral tribunal, evidence, hearings, forms and effect of awards or costs under arts 12–35. These suggest that arbitral proceedings under the AAA Rules are indeed of semi-judicial nature.

The London Court of International Arbitration

[12.54] The London Court of International Arbitration (LCIA) is a non-governmental arbitral institute for international arbitration, which combines characteristics of the ICC's International Court of Arbitration and the AAA. Its name includes the word 'court' (like the ICC's 'court'), but it has adopted a set of arbitral rules which are semi-judicial, like the AAA International Arbitration Rules. It does not arbitrate disputes directly, but accepts disputes on the basis of the parties' written agreement to arbitration and assists them to appoint the arbitrator or arbitrators who constitute the arbitral tribunal: LCIA Rules, arts 1 and 3. There are specific rules relating to defences by the other party (art 2), the submission of written documents (art 6), the language of the proceedings, legal representation, hearings, witnesses, awards and costs for arbitration: arts 7–18. The rigidity of these procedural rules suggests that the LCIA is a semi-judicial body, although its jurisdiction is based merely on voluntary acceptance by the parties. LCIA does not retain a closed list of individual arbitrators, or a closed list of nationalities. When a request for arbitration is made, LCIA will search through its own database or the relevant networks for the appointment of qualified arbitrators.

The Netherlands Arbitration Institute

[12.55] The Netherlands Arbitration Institute (NAI), established in 1949, 'is a non-profit organisation in the form of a foundation (*stichting*) under Dutch law'.[51] It is administered by the Secretary of the Governing Board of the Institute, who is referred to as the Administrator under the NAI Arbitration Rules: art 1. The institute maintains a list of

---

50. AAA International Arbitration Rules, art 1.
51. NAI Arbitration Rules, Introduction and Purpose NAI, para 1.1.

[12.55] arbitrators. The arbitrators chosen by the parties or the Administrator pursuant to the rules constitute an arbitral tribunal which must consist of an odd number.[52] Like any other arbitration rules, the agreement to arbitrate is the basis of the institute's jurisdiction: art 6. The rules set out detailed procedural requirements for conducting arbitration proceedings, including legal representation, claims, counter-claims, defences, hearing, evidence, witnesses, amendment of claims, language, joint parties, types and forms of award, and costs for arbitration: arts 20–62. The NAI Arbitration Rules may be the lengthiest institutional arbitral rules, totalling about 80 articles including the introduction.

The Arbitration Institute of the Stockholm Chamber of Commerce

[12.56] The Arbitration Institute of the Stockholm Chamber of Commerce 'is an organ within the Stockholm Chamber of Commerce ("the Chamber") for dealing with matters of arbitration'.[53] The institute is administered by a board with a list of arbitrators: arts 2 and 5. Its rules require the existence of an arbitration agreement as the precondition for arbitration, and the proceedings are initiated by the written request of a party to a dispute: art 9. The procedural rules of the institute are relatively simple, including rules on language, statement of defence, amendment to claim or defence, oral hearing, evidence, awards and costs: arts 17–31. It appears that the arbitration services provided by the institute are more flexible than those offered by the NAI.

The China International Economic and Trade Arbitraion Commission

[12.57] The CIETAC was initially established as the Foreign Trade Arbitration Commission in 1954 within the China Council for the Promotion of International Trade (CCPIT). The Foreign Trade Arbitration Commission was renamed in 1980 as the Foreign Economic and Trade Arbitration Commission, which was renamed again in 1988 as the CIETAC.

The CIETAC was established as an arbitration institution specialising in foreign trade disputes. However, today it has become an arbitration institution handling both foreign-related and domestic disputes. This has been reflected in its Arbitration Rules, which were amended in October 2000. In addition, the CIETAC is the authorised institution to deal with disputes arising from bond transactions and the registration of internet names in China.

The administrative structure of the CIETAC is broadly regulated by arts 8, 9, and 11 of its Arbitration Rules. Under art 8 of the Arbitration Rules, the CIETAC has an Honorary Chairman and several advisers as honorary appointments to strengthen the management of the commission. Under art 9 of the Arbitration Rules, the management of the CIETAC is composed of one Chairman, several Vice-Chairmen and a number of Commissioners. The honorary appointees and the persons appointed under art 9 constitute the membership of CIETAC. When a decision of the CIETAC is required, these people should make a collective decision on behalf of the CIETAC.

---

52. NAI Arbitration Rules, Introduction and Purpose NAI, para 8 and section 3.
53. The Stockholm Chamber of Commerce Arbitration Rules, art 1.

The headquarters of the CIETAC are located in Beijing. It has two local offices outside Beijing. The Shenzhen Office of the CIETAC was established in 1989 and the Shanghai Office was established in 1990. Parties can submit their dispute to any of the three offices. However, a mere reference to the CIETAC without indicating which of the three offices has been chosen is sufficient enough to trigger the jurisdiction of the CIETAC. In such cases, the applicant has a right to choose which of the three offices hears the dispute. In recent years, the CIETAC has handled around 700–800 cases per year. This has made the CIETAC the busiest arbitration institution in the world in terms of the caseload alone.[54]

Commercial arbitration in Australia

The Institute of Arbitrators Australia (IAA)

[12.58] The Institute of Arbitrators Australia was established in 1975 in Canberra as an independent institution to promote arbitration and other means of alternative dispute resolution.[55] The institute's headquarters are presently located in Melbourne. It has branches in each state and territory. The institute has a list of arbitrators and conciliators, who come from business, the building industry, the legal profession and other sectors of society with specialised knowledge. It is so far mainly a domestic arbitral institute, but may provide international arbitration services on request. It has published its own Rules for the Conduct of Commercial Arbitration with supporting Notes to the Rules. The rules contain detailed procedural requirements and are of a more or less semi-judicial nature. The institution has played and will continue to play a crucial role in the promotion of arbitration in Australia.[56]

The Australian Centre for International Commercial Arbitration (ACICA)

[12.59] The ACICA was established in 1985 in Melbourne with the support of the Institute of Arbitrators Australia and the Victorian Government.[57] The centre maintains a panel of international arbitrators drawn from various countries, such as Australia, the United Kingdom, the United States, France, Italy, Norway, Germany, Denmark, Japan, China, Malaysia and Singapore.[58] Its services include arbitration, mediation, conciliation and other methods of alternative dispute resolution. Its headquarters are located in Melbourne, but there is also an ACICA (NT) office in Darwin. The ACICA does not have its own arbitration rules. It recommends the use of the UNCITRAL Arbitration Rules, but will accept any other arbitration rules if the parties so desire. The centre has adopted a practice of concluding cooperation agreements with other international arbitration institutions to facilitate international commercial arbitration in Australia.

---

54. For a detailed study of arbitration in China, see John Mo, *Arbitration Law in China*, Hong Kong, Sweet & Maxwell Asia, 2001.
55. IAA, *The Institute of Arbitrators Australia Information*, IAA Brochure, Melbourne, p 1.
56. For discussion, see James, 'The Institute of Arbitrators Australia: the Future' (1995) 14 *The Arbitrator* pp 106–23.
57. ACICA, *Australian Centre for International Commercial Arbitration* (Melbourne, ACICA brochure) p 4.
58. Id, p 6.

[12.60] **International Commercial Law**

The Australian Commercial Dispute Centre (ACDC)

[12.60] The ACDC was established in 1986 as a non-government and non-profit organisation providing alternative dispute resolution (ADR) services for settling commercial disputes. It is located in Sydney, but provides ADR services nation-wide. The centre has a list of mediators, experts and arbitrators drawn from various areas of commerce and law. The methods of dispute resolution recommended by the centre include: mediation, expert appraisal, expert determination, expert recommendation, board of dispute avoidance and arbitration.[59] The application of these methods is based on the voluntary submission of the parties to the authority of the mediator, expert or arbitrator. Thus, the centre recommends the parties to adopt standard ACDC Dispute Resolution Clauses in the relevant commercial contracts. However, there is no reason for the ACDC's services not to be available if the disputing parties fail to adopt the standard clause in the first instance. After all, flexibility is one of the advantages of arbitration over litigation. The ACDC services are available to both domestic and international commercial disputes.

SMART

[12.61] SMART stands for Sydney Maritime Arbitration Rules and Terms, which is not an arbitral institution like the ACDC. It was published on 7 March 1991 for the purpose of facilitating the settlement of maritime disputes in Australia.[60] SMART is a set of arbitral rules and terms which can be adopted by disputing parties voluntarily and will bind the parties once adopted. The institutional framework in support of SMART is yet to be developed and there does not appear to be any permanent body in charge of the administration of SMART, although a SMART committee does exist.[61] Nor is there any panel of arbitrators in Australia who are especially affiliated with SMART. An adequate supporting facility will certainly improve the public accessibility of SMART both domestically and internationally.

Major procedural issues in international commercial arbitration

Defining procedural issues

[12.62] International commercial arbitration is a process of third party dispute settlement which involves two uncompromising disputants and one or more neutral and impartial arbitrators acting as referee(s). Certain fundamental issues are essential for the performance of an arbitrator's functions, for maintaining the fairness of the arbitral process and for ensuring the impartiality of an arbitral award. These issues must be clearly

---

59. For a description of these methods, see ACDC, *Dispute Resolution Clauses for Commercial Contracts and Employment Agreements*, ACDC, Sydney, 1995, pp 6–7. In brief, 'expert appraisal', 'expert determination' and 'expert recommendation' involve the use of an expert to appraise or determine a dispute or to recommend a solution; and 'board of dispute avoidance' means that the parties' representatives constitute a board to resolve the dispute.
60. Levingston, 'The Development of Arbitration and Mediation as Alternative Dispute Resolution Procedures for Resolving Maritime Disputes in Australia' (1995) 6 *ADRJ* 127, p 145.
61. Id, p 146.

addressed, defined and agreed upon by the disputing parties or the applicable rules of arbitration in any proceedings.

[12.63] 'Procedural issues' is a term borrowed from litigation. In judicial proceedings, the parties are bound by the court rules, which are designed to strike a balance between the interests of the parties and the interests of justice, and to defend and protect fairness and justice in any democratic society.[62] Procedural issues in international commercial arbitration are concerned with the jurisdiction of an arbitral tribunal, the rules relating to documentation, rights and obligations of the disputing parties, rules relating to the effect of evidence or witnesses, the effect of an arbitral award and costs of the proceedings. Given that arbitral proceedings are not meant to be as stringent as court proceedings and that the actual proceedings under the international conventions and institutional rules vary, we will, for the purpose of discussion, divide procedural issues into three categories: the constitution and jurisdiction of an arbitral tribunal; conduct of proceedings; and the effect of an arbitral award. These categories will be examined in turn.

The constitution and jurisdiction of an arbitral tribunal

Freedom to arbitrate

[12.64] The jurisprudential basis for any international commercial arbitration is the parties' voluntary submission to the arbitral body. Without the prior consent of the disputing parties, no arbitral tribunal is able to assume jurisdiction over the parties and the matter in dispute (unless a statute authorises otherwise). Consent of a state party can be given in an international convention or treaty, where the contracting parties are obliged to accept the tribunal's jurisdiction over the matters stipulated in the treaty ratified or accepted by them. The Iran–US Claim Tribunal is an example, where the individual complainant may submit his or her complaint to the tribunal on a voluntary basis but the Iranian Government and the US Government are bound to enforce the decisions of the tribunal under their obligations. Similarly, a contracting state to the Washington Convention is obliged to accept ICSID's jurisdiction when a national of another contracting state submits a complaint against it pursuant to the ICSID Rules of Procedure for the Institution of Conciliation and Arbitration Proceedings (ICSID Rules). Consent of the private parties to the jurisdiction of any particular arbitral institution, body or tribunal is evidenced by their written agreement made prior to arbitration. The existence of a written agreement for arbitration, either in the form of a separate agreement or an arbitration clause, is required in the arbitration rules formulated by major international arbitral institutions. Even the UNCITRAL Model Law requires the parties to reach an arbitration agreement before submitting their dispute to an arbitral tribunal. Therefore, we may conclude that the parties to an international commercial dispute have the

---

62. Here 'interests of justice' means the interests of the administration of (the court of) law: the 'public at large has delegated its decision-making in this sphere to its microcosm, the jury and judge': *A-G v Times Newspapers* [1974] AC 273 at 320 per Lord Simon of Glaisdale. Nevertheless, as Lord Cross of Chelsea observed in the same case at 325, 'often the answer which the law gives to some problem is regarded by many people as unjust'.

[12.64]

freedom to decide whether to arbitrate, unless a state party has waived such freedom by undertaking a treaty obligation.

Freedom to choose the rules for arbitration

[12.65] The disputing parties are at liberty to choose arbitral rules before submitting a dispute to arbitration, unless a state has undertaken a treaty obligation to be bound by specific rules. The right to choose arbitration rules is implied in, but not limited to, the fact that the disputing parties are able to decide the place of arbitration. It is often implied that the arbitration rules of the chosen arbitral institute should apply, unless the parties have expressly chosen another set of arbitration rules, provided that the rules of the chosen arbitral institute allow the adoption of other arbitration rules or the variation of its own arbitration rules.[63] The parties may also choose the arbitration rules before choosing a forum of arbitration. The UNCITRAL Model Law was designed for this purpose. It follows that when the arbitration rules, rather than the place of arbitration, are the major concern of the party, a process of international arbitration can even be conducted in a domestic forum.

[12.66] *Union of India v McDonnell Douglas Corp*

[1993] 2 Lloyd's Rep 48

Determination of the procedural rules when the arbitration agreement chose a place of arbitration but specified a foreign law as the governing law

Facts: Union of India was the plaintiff. McDonnell Douglas Corporation was the defendant. The dispute arose from a contract made in 1987 for the launch of a space satellite. The contract contained an arbitration clause which provided that the seat of arbitration proceedings was London, but the proceedings should be conducted in accordance with the Indian Arbitration Act 1940. The parties agreed to submit the dispute to arbitration in 1993, but disagreed as to the governing law of the proceedings. Union of India argued that the proceedings should be governed by the Indian Arbitration Act, but McDonnell insisted that the proceedings were to be governed by English law because London was the chosen forum for arbitration. The parties applied to the court for clarification.

Decision: Saville J of the Queen's Bench Division (Commercial Court) set out, inter alia, the following general principles:
- the choosing of Indian law as the proper law of the arbitration agreement does not necessarily lead to Indian law being the governing law of the proceedings, unless the arbitration agreement expressly or impliedly so provided;
- English law allows, at least theoretically, the conducting of arbitration proceedings in one country under the procedural rules of another, but the jurisdiction of English courts under arbitration legislation cannot be excluded by any agreement choosing foreign law unless the English legislation so permits;

---

63. For example, art 11 of the ICC Rules of Arbitration provides that the 'rules governing the proceeding before the arbitrator shall be those resulting from these Rules and, where these Rules are silent, any rules which the parties (or, failing them, the arbitrator) may settle, and whether or not reference is thereby made to a municipal procedural law to be applied to the arbitration'. Similarly, art 5.1 of the LCIA Rules states that 'parties may agree on the arbitral procedures, and are encouraged to do so'.

- choosing of London as the place of arbitration implied that the proceedings were potentially subject to both Indian law and English law; and
- the correct interpretation of the arbitration clause meant that the procedure of the arbitration proceedings could be conducted in pursuance of Indian law which is not inconsistent with the relevant English law, but the English courts have supervisory jurisdiction over the proceedings.

♦

Freedom to choose arbitrators

[12.67] Disputing parties are at liberty to decide the appointment of an arbitrator. This is very important, because by electing an arbitrator the disputing parties entrust the power to arbitrate (to judge or assess) the merits of their case, and to decide their crucial financial or economic interests, to a stranger, who is deemed to be impartial, fair and knowledgeable of the matters in dispute. The nationality and qualifications of an arbitrator are, therefore, relevant issues.

[12.68] The nationality of the arbitrator is relevant to the issue of impartiality, because impartiality requires the arbitrator to be unconnected to, dissociated from and not sympathetic to any of the disputing parties in any way. An arbitrator is often chosen from a national of a third country under the understanding that neither the arbitrator nor the country of the arbitrator has any direct or indirect interest in the matter to be arbitrated. It is appreciated that the impartiality of the arbitrator can be endangered either by the involvement of the country or the personal connection of the arbitrator. For the sake of impartiality, where more than three arbitrators are appointed the appointments are to be made on an equal basis or in a balanced manner. This involves both parties appointing an equal number of arbitrators respectively, with the rest to be appointed jointly by the parties or by the appointed arbitrators; or alternatively, by the administrator of the arbitral institute.

[12.69] An arbitrator's qualifications are crucial to the fairness and reasonableness of an arbitral award, which may dramatically affect the interests of the parties. A fair and reasonable award can be made only by a reasonable and impartial person who has the necessary knowledge to appreciate the nature and circumstances of the dispute. This is why all arbitral institutions maintain a list of experts who have special experience and knowledge in various business, industrial and legal fields. The parties must be given the liberty or autonomy to choose the most suitable candidate for arbitrating a dispute.

Constitution of an arbitral tribunal

[12.70] The establishment of a tribunal's jurisdiction and determination of the tribunal's composition are simultaneous steps for commencing actual arbitration proceedings, although a process of arbitration is usually deemed to 'commence' from the receipt of a party's request for arbitration by the chosen institute.[64] For our purposes we regard the establishment, or granting, of a tribunal's jurisdiction and the actual constitution of the tribunal as the first step of arbitration. The jurisdiction of the tribunal and the actual constitution of the tribunal are inseparable. This is because the jurisdiction of the tribunal, the very reason for which the tribunal exists, must be decided or

[12.70]

granted before the tribunal can be set up, and the parties have to accept the jurisdiction of the tribunal which is yet to be established before proceeding to appoint the members of the tribunal. Thus the availability of potential appointees for a tribunal may be a consideration for the parties in deciding whether to grant jurisdiction to a particular tribunal yet to be constituted.

[12.71] The 'constitution of an arbitral tribunal' means the appointment of an arbitrator or arbitrators to constitute the tribunal. None of the international arbitral institutes, except the Iran–US Claims Tribunal, has a permanent tribunal consisting of fixed members. This is because arbitration itself is based on the autonomy of the disputing parties to choose suitable referees. We may argue that all matters arising before the constitution of a tribunal are preliminary and the actual arbitration proceedings begin when the tribunal exercising the power granted by the disputing parties is duly constituted pursuant to the relevant rules of arbitration.

Procedures for conducting arbitration proceedings

Claims, defences and counter-claims

[12.72] Although arbitration should not be subject to the same rules as judicial proceedings, certain minimum procedural requirements are necessary for the purpose of facilitating effective communications between the parties, and between the parties and the tribunal. This is why all arbitration rules deal with a number of common issues, such as the procedures for requesting arbitration, submission of defences, making of a counter-claim, and amendment of a claim, although they deal with them to different degrees. For example, art 3 of the UNCITRAL Arbitration Rules sets out the details of the request for arbitration, but there is no provision in the rules dealing directly with the formality of defences, counter-claims or amendment of claims, except art 15 of the rules broadly states that 'the arbitral tribunal may conduct the arbitration in such manner as it considers appropriate, provided that the parties are treated with equity and that at any stage of the proceedings each party is given a full opportunity of presenting his case'. By contrast, the AAA International Arbitration Rules require the notice requesting arbitration to be consistent with the requirements of art 2, the statement of defence to be filed pursuant to art 3, and the tribunal to exercise discretion under art 4 in determining whether an amendment to claims and defences can be made. The arbitration rules of other arbitral institutions are structured more or less along the same lines as the AAA International Arbitration Rules, although they may be more flexible or rigid than the AAA Rules. The parties have more flexibility in controlling proceedings under the UNCITRAL Arbitration Rules than under the AAA Rules.[64]

---

64. For example, art 2(2) of the AAA International Arbitration Rules states that arbitration proceedings 'shall be deemed to commence on the date on which the notice of arbitration is received by the administrator' of the association. Similarly, art 3 of the ICC Rules of Arbitration provides that the 'date when the request is received by the Secretary of the Court shall, for all purposes, be deemed to be the date of commencement of the arbitral proceedings'.

Legal representation

[12.73] Legal representation poses a dilemma to arbitration. On the one hand, the introduction of arbitration into international commerce (or other types of disputes) as an alternative to legal proceedings implies that the arbitration proceedings must be less formal than judicial proceedings. On the other, the fact that an arbitral award has the same effect as a judicial decision implies that legal representation may be necessary for ensuring the fairness and justice of the award. Different philosophical preferences are seen in the rules of the arbitral institutes. Some rules clearly deal with the issue of legal representation, such as art 21 of the NAI Arbitration Rules,[65] some do not.[66] There is no clear-cut argument as to the desirability of legal representation. The choice is in the hands of the disputing parties, who may either choose the rules providing legal representation or add legal representation to the applicable rules pursuant to their relevant provisions, if legal representation is deemed to be necessary.

Evidence, witnesses and hearings

[12.74] Although evidence, witnesses and hearings form a crucial part of the judicial proceedings, they are not universally regarded as an integral part of commercial arbitration proceedings. Again, diversity is seen in the arbitral rules of the existing arbitral institutions. For example, art 20 of the AAA International Arbitration Rules provides that each 'party shall have the burden of proving the facts relied on to support its claim or defence'; and art 21 sets out specifically the number of days required for the tribunal to notify the parties of the hearing, the number of days for the parties to submit a list of the witnesses and the rules governing the witnesses and evidence presented in the hearing. These detailed requirements resemble court-like proceedings. By contrast, there is no specified time requirement for the tribunal to conduct its proceedings under the ICC Rules of Arbitration, and matters relating to hearings, witnesses and evidence are dealt with in broad language and a flexible manner.[67]

[12.75] A number of procedural issues may arise from evidence, witnesses or hearings in arbitration. For example, a tribunal may have to decide whether a particular piece of evidence is admissible, who has the burden of proof, who can be admitted as a witness or how to conduct a hearing. Most arbitration rules deal expressly with the issue of admissibility of evidence. For instance, art 34 of the ICSID Rules provides that the 'Tribunal shall be the judge of the admissibility of any evidence'.[68] A few of them even clearly address the issue of burden of proof.[69] Similarly, most arbitration rules also expressly deal with the rules of witnesses one way or another: for example, art 11 of the LCIA Rules

---

65. Article 21 of the NAI Arbitration Rules provides that the 'parties may appear before the arbitral tribunal in person, be represented by a practising lawyer or be represented by any other person expressly authorised in writing for this purpose'.
66. For example, there is no legal representation provision in the ICC Rules for Conciliation and Arbitration, in the ICSID Rules, or in the UNCITRAL Arbitration Rules.
67. For example, art 14 of the ICC Rules of Arbitration provides that the 'arbitrator shall proceed as short a time as possible to establish the facts of the case by all appropriate means'. Article 15 provides that the arbitrator may summon the parties to appear before him or her at the request of any party, and art 16 states that the parties may bring any new claims or counter-claims as long as the matters raised fall under the granted power of the tribunal.

gives the tribunal discretion in allowing the appearance of witnesses, art 35 of the ICSID Rules requires witnesses to take an oath before giving evidence, and art 29 of the NAI Rules allows the tribunal to determine the procedural rules governing witnesses. As to the rules of hearings, most arbitration rules appear to prefer a wide discretion in the tribunal, rather than setting out any specified time requirement for conducting the proceedings. For example, art 10 of the LCIA Rules allows the tribunal to decide a date of hearing without being subject to a fixed time frame. A similar provision is seen in art 26 of the NAI Arbitration Rules, art 20 of the Stockholm Chamber of Commerce Arbitration Rules, and art 25 of the UNCITRAL Arbitration Rules. These facts suggest that most arbitration rules do impose certain requirements for the production of evidence, calling for witnesses and conduct of hearings, although some may be more flexible than others.

Privacy and confidentiality of arbitration proceedings

[12.76] Privacy and confidentiality are not the same thing,[70] although they may overlap to some extent in a process of arbitration. The distinction between them is immaterial if both disputing parties agree that arbitration should be conducted in a private and confidential manner. This may explain the existence of the general presumption that arbitration proceedings are private and confidential.[71] Such a presumed characteristic has been marketed as one of the advantages of arbitration over litigation, and indeed, has been accepted with little qualification by English courts in *Dolling-Baker v Merrett* [1990] 1 WLR 1205 and *Hassneh Insurance v Mew* [1993] 2 Lloyd's Rep 243. While this presumption is generally correct, its legal parameter in Australia had not been tested until the case of *Esso Australia Resources v Plowman* (1995) 128 ALR 391. In this case, the parties disagreed as to the exact meaning of privacy and confidentiality and the party (Plowman) relying on the exceptions to privacy and confidentiality of arbitration argued about the distinction between them. The case suggests that there is no absolute privacy and confidentiality of arbitration proceedings in Australia.

---

68. The same provision is also seen in art 21 of the AAA International Arbitration Rules, art 27 of the NAI Arbitration Rules, art 21 of the Stockholm Chamber of Commerce Arbitration Rules, and art 25 of the UNCITRAL Arbitration Rules.
69. Burden of proof is imposed upon the party presenting the evidence in art 24 of the UNCITRAL Arbitration Rules, art 21 of the Stockholm Chamber of Commerce Arbitration Rules, and art 20 of the AAA International Arbitration Rules.
70. Johnstone, 'Private and Confidential' (1992) 11 *The Arbitrator* pp 153–6; and *Esso Australia Resources v Plowman* (1995) 128 ALR 391, per Mason CJ at 401.
71. For example, Pryles, 'Institutional International Arbitration' (1991) 10 *The Arbitrator* p 129.

[12.77] *Esso Australia Resources v Plowman*

(1995) 128 ALR 391

Exceptions to the privacy and confidentiality of arbitration proceedings in Australia

Facts: The appellants were Esso and BHP, two major producers of petroleum products in Australia. The respondents were the Minister for Manufacturing and Industry Development of Victoria (the Minister), the Gas and Fuel Corporation of Victoria (GFC) and the State Electricity Commission of Victoria (SEC). Esso and BHP sold natural gas to GFC and SEC under a number of agreements. In 1991, they sought to increase the price of gas under the agreements, but GFC and SEC refused the request. Esso and BHP referred the matter to arbitration in pursuance of the sale agreements. In 1992, the Minister sought a court declaration that the information supplied by Esso and BHP during the course of arbitration was not subject to the duty of confidentiality. GFC and SEC cross-claimed against Esso and BHP for the same declaration. Esso and BHP applied, by way of counter-claim, for a declaration that the arbitration proceedings be conducted in private and the information disclosed in arbitration be treated in confidence. Esso and BHP specifically refused the Minister's request for detailed information on how the price of gas was calculated. The trial judge decided in favour of the Minister, GFC and SEC. The appeal to the Full Court of the Supreme Court of Victoria by Esso and BHP succeeded in part, but the court denied the existence of absolute confidentiality in relation to the information disclosed in the arbitration proceedings. Esso and BHP appealed to the High Court of Australia.

Decision: The court dismissed the appeal by majority and directed the Supreme Court of Victoria to reformulate its order in accordance with the majority's decision. The majority (Mason CJ, Brennan, Dawson and McHugh JJ) held that there is not a duty of absolute confidentiality of arbitration proceedings. The major qualifications imposed on the privacy and confidentiality of arbitration are as follows:

- privacy of arbitration inheres in the *subject matter* of the arbitration agreement, rather than an implied term of the agreement;
- confidentiality is not an essential attribute of a private arbitration in Australia and thus no obligation of confidentiality inheres in private arbitration;
- information disclosed in arbitration proceedings is subject to public interest exceptions, such as freedom of information, open government and the public's interest in disseminating the information, etc;
- information provided in arbitration proceedings can be disclosed under compulsion by law; and
- disclosure of confidential information can be justified by the party's legitimate interests.

This case suggests that if the parties intend that arbitration proceedings be conducted in privacy and confidence, they must expressly state so in their arbitration agreement. However, the intention of the parties cannot override a statute which compels the disclosure of the information concerned. *Esso Australia Resources v Plowan* indicates that the Australian courts will not accept the existence of absolute privacy and confidentiality of arbitration, but has not unambiguously demarcated the boundary of privacy and confidentiality of arbitration proceedings in Australia.

Arbitral awards and costs for arbitration

Two aspects of a decision

[12.78] The decision of a tribunal includes two major parts: the arbitral award and the decision on costs for arbitration. An arbitral award presents a solution to the dispute concerned, and the decision on costs allocates the expenses incurred from the operation of the tribunal and the conduct of the proceedings. Both are regarded as the last step of the proceedings.

Meanings and effect of an award

[12.79] An arbitral award is a decision of an arbitral tribunal, made for the purpose of resolving the dispute or answering the question which has been submitted to the tribunal by the disputing parties. In relation to international commercial arbitration, the expression 'arbitral awards' 'shall include not only awards made by arbitrators appointed for each case but also those made by permanent arbitral bodies to which the parties have submitted'.[72] An international commercial arbitral award is the decision of a tribunal authorised by the disputing parties to deal with a dispute arising from international commercial relationships, regardless of whether the tribunal is ad hoc or permanent.

[12.80] An international commercial arbitral award has several characteristics:

- First, it is usually final, unless the governing arbitration rules specify otherwise. For example, while most arbitration rules state that a final award, as opposed to an interim or partial award, is 'final' (for example, art 32 of the UNCITRAL Arbitration Rules, art 16.8 of the LCIA Rules, art 24 of the ICC Rules of Arbitration and art 28 of the AAA International Arbitration Rules), certain arbitration rules, such as the ICSID Rules[73] and UNCITRAL Model Law,[74] allow the disputing parties to apply for a review of the award pursuant to relevant arbitration rules or under the governing domestic law.[75]

- Second, it may also be partial, interlocutory or interim.[76] A partial award states a decision on part of the dispute or questions submitted to the tribunal. For example, art 27 of the Stockholm Chamber of Commerce Arbitration Rules provides that a 'separate issue or part of the matter in dispute between the parties may, at the request of a party, be decided by a separate award'. If an award is partial, it may not be final in certain circumstances not only because 'partial' and 'interim' are sometimes interchangeable in international commercial arbitration,[77] but also because there is a possible connection between the partial award and the part of dispute yet to be resolved. An interlocutory award and interim award appear to be the same thing — a temporary relief to the disputing parties in cases where a temporary solution is needed

---

72. New York Convention, art 1(2).
73. For example, arts 49 and 50–55.
74. For example, art 34.
75. In the common law countries and certain civil law countries, eg, Switzerland, an arbitral award can be reviewed on points of law by a court of law. See Redfern and Hunter, note 9 above, pp 420–1.
76. For example, art 44 of the NAI Arbitration Rules, art 28 of the AAA International Arbitration Rules, and art 32 of the UNCITRAL Arbitration Rules.
77. Redfern and Hunter, note 9 above, p 380.

before a final award is made. For example, in a dispute involving an Italian supplier and the South Korean buyer, the arbitrator of the ICC made a preliminary (interim) award for the purpose of deciding whether the Italian complainant which had merged with the original supplier to the Korean buyer had a right to take action and whether an agreement made in 1976 was enforceable under Korean law.[78] Such an award is often used in cases where measures for mitigating losses are needed before a final award can be made.

- Third, an award may be made in default. For example, art 24 of the AAA International Arbitration Rules allows the tribunal to proceed with the arbitration in the event where one party without justification fails to file a defence, to appear at the tribunal or to provide evidence. A similar rule is found in art 23 of the Stockholm Chamber of Commerce Arbitration Rules and art 28 of the UNCITRAL Arbitration Rules. Such an award might be subject to close scrutiny of the domestic court where the award is to be enforced.

- Last but not least, the enforcement of an arbitral award relies on the assistance of the relevant domestic courts. At present, an award made by an international commercial arbitral institute may be enforced on two grounds: the New York Convention and the domestic law. Contracting countries to the New York Convention undertake to enforce arbitral awards made in another contracting country and there is an international obligation for the contracting countries to assist the enforcement of arbitral awards falling under the New York Convention. Alternatively, an award is enforceable directly under the domestic law where it is to be enforced. A court of law may have power to review an award on points of law.

Meanings of costs

[12.81] Costs are an important part of judicial proceedings, by which a court of law allocates financial liabilities arising from or associated with the litigation between the parties. Sometimes a court of law may also use costs as a means of penalising the party which is unreasonably conducting, or prolonging, the litigation, or the court may compensate the innocent party, forced to unreasonably incur the expenses of litigation. The term 'costs' in proceedings of international commercial arbitration has the same meaning, although it must be pointed out that parties are allowed under certain arbitration rules to make a cost-sharing agreement to take the power of awarding costs from the tribunal. For example, art 18.2 of the LCIA Rules states that unless 'the parties shall agree otherwise, the Tribunal shall determine the proportions in which the parties shall pay all or part' of the costs to the court. The UNCITRAL Model Law does not deal with the issue of costs at all. However, certain arbitration rules do expressly impose costs upon the losing party or allocate the costs in proportion to the 'fault' of the parties. For example, art 61(2) of the NAI Arbitration Rules and art 29 of the Stockholm Chamber of Commerce Arbitration Rules provide that the losing party should be condemned or ordered to pay the costs; and art 61(2) of the NAI Arbitration Rules and art 32 of the AAA International Arbitration Rules state that if both parties have lost in part, the tribunal may apportion the costs

---

78. Jarvin and Derains (eds), *Collection of ICC Arbitral Awards 1974–1985*, Kluwer, Deventer, 1990, p 164, Preliminary Award of September 22, 1983, case no 4132.

[12.81] between them as it thinks reasonable. These facts suggest the parties should consult more flexible rules if they intend to avoid the unexpected financial burden of costs at the end of arbitral proceedings.

[12.82] What are covered under 'costs' is another relevant issue. Given that costs are essentially expenses arising from arbitration proceedings, the term can be defined in two ways. Broadly speaking, the 'costs of the arbitration include the costs which, in the opinion of the arbitral tribunal, were necessarily incurred in the arbitration as well as the administration costs and the fees and disbursement of the arbitrator(s)'.[79] More specifically, 'costs' can be itemised as follows:

(a) the fees of the arbitral tribunal to be stated separately as to each arbitrator and to be fixed by the tribunal;
(b) travel and other expenses incurred by the arbitrators;
(c) the costs of expert advice and of other assistance required by the tribunal;
(d) travel and other expenses of witnesses to the extent such expenses are approved by the tribunal;
(e) the costs of legal representation and assistance of the successful party if such costs were claimed during the arbitral proceedings, and only to the extent that the tribunal determines that the amount of such costs is reasonable; and
(f) any fees and expenses of the appointing authority as well as the expenses of the Secretary-General of the Permanent Court of Arbitration at The Hague.[80]

The costs rules of most arbitral institutions are more or less structured in a manner similar to the above itemised costs. It is necessary to examine the particular provisions to ascertain the scope of the costs under the particular rules, because the items included under each set of rules may vary.

The New York Convention and international commercial arbitration

Meaning of foreign awards

[12.83] We have examined the New York Convention briefly in **[12.12]**–**[12.16]**. In this section, we discuss in detail some aspects of the convention which are important to international commercial arbitration.

[12.84] The New York Convention was made for the purpose of unifying the rules for the recognition and enforcement of international arbitral awards. The convention uses the term 'foreign arbitral awards' rather than 'international arbitral awards'. However, the arbitral awards referred to in the convention are undoubtedly international, not only because 'foreign' and 'international' are sometimes interchangeable, but also because art 1 of the convention excludes from its application an arbitral award that is regarded as a

---

79. NAI Arbitration Rules, art 56.
80. UNCITRAL Arbitration Rules, art 38.

'domestic award' under the law of the state where the award is to be recognised or enforced. Article I of the convention provides as follows:

> This Convention shall apply to the recognition and enforcement of arbitral awards made in the territory of a State other than the State where the recognition and enforcement of such awards are sought, and arising out of differences between persons, whether physical or legal. It shall also apply to arbitral awards not considered as domestic awards in the State where their recognition and enforcement are sought.

[12.85] This provision suggests that a foreign arbitral award under the convention is determined by two tests:

- First, the award is usually made outside the territory of the state where the award is to be recognised or enforced. This clearly suggests the international nature of the award.

- Second, the award must also be one which is not classified as a domestic award under the law of the forum where the award is to be recognised or enforced, regardless of where the award was made. This category of awards, in the language of art I, is capable of including an award which, although made within the territory of the state where it is to be recognised or enforced, does not fall under the definition of domestic award (if there is such definition in the relevant domestic law). This type of 'foreign awards' probably refers to an arbitral decision made by a permanent international arbitral institution, which is more likely to be an arbitral institution established under an international treaty,[81] situated within the territory of the state where the award is sought to be recognised or enforced. For example, an award of the Permanent Court of Arbitration, or of the Iran–US Claims Tribunal, both located in The Hague, could be a 'foreign award' under the New York Convention if the recognition and enforcement are sought in the Netherlands and Dutch law does not regard it as a 'domestic award'. By the same token, an arbitral award of ICSID made within the United States could be regarded as a 'foreign award' in the United States, provided that the United States law does not regard it as a domestic award. If a 'foreign award' is actually made within the territory of the state where the award is to be recognised or enforced, it appears to be more logical to call it an 'international arbitral award', rather than a 'foreign arbitral award'.

Distinguishing 'recognition' from 'enforcement'

[12.86] The function of the New York Convention is to give effect to international arbitral awards (or foreign awards) as defined in the convention, in particular to recognise and to enforce these awards. 'Recognition' may be different from 'enforcement' in their legal meanings in that the recognition of an award is the first step to its enforcement. In theory, although the purpose of recognition is to enforce an award, recognition does not necessarily result in enforcement, depending on the intention of the parties. For example, recognition of an award by a local court of law under the convention would be sufficient

---

81. This proposition is supported by art I(2) of the New York Convention, which provides that an 'arbitral award' also includes the award made by permanent arbitral bodies to which the parties have submitted. Given that the arbitral tribunals formed under the arbitral rules of any non-governmental arbitral institution are all of ad hoc nature, 'permanent arbitral bodies' could only be those established under the relevant international treaties.

Uniformity of rules

[12.87] It can also be argued that the function of the New York Convention is to unify the rules on recognition and enforcement of international arbitral awards. This function is perhaps the most important feature of the convention. Traditionally, the recognition and enforcement of a foreign arbitral award are subject to the law of the country where the arbitral award is to be recognised or enforced. The rules governing recognition and enforcement are inevitably divergent and even conflicting, because different legal traditions exist. Disputes inevitably arise from the conflict of laws. The unification of the rules for recognition and enforcement of foreign arbitral awards was attempted in 1927, when the Geneva Convention on the Execution of Foreign Arbitral Awards was adopted. However, the Geneva Convention achieved only a limited operation, because its member countries were largely limited to the continental states of Europe.[82] The New York Convention has completed what the Geneva Convention was not able to and has indeed unified the rules for recognition and enforcement of international arbitral awards among its large number of members from different legal traditions (there were 92 members to the convention as at October 1992[83]). The convention can thus be described as representing 'a vital stage in the shaping of modern international commercial arbitration'.[84]

Conditions for recognising and enforcing an international arbitral award

Implied conditions

[12.88] The convention does not expressly state the conditions for the recognition and enforcement of an international arbitral award. However, the language of the convention implies that an arbitral award can be enforced in a contracting country only when the two conditions or tests (validity of the arbitration agreement and validity of the arbitral award) are satisfied. These conditions are examined below.

Validity of an arbitral agreement

[12.89] There must be a valid written arbitration agreement, either independently or as part of the contract from which the dispute arises. Article II of the New York Convention provides as follows:

> Each contracting State shall recognise an agreement in writing under which the parties undertake to submit to arbitration all or any differences which have arisen or which may arise between them in respect of a defined legal relationship, whether contractual or not, concerning a subject-matter capable of settlement by arbitration.

---

82. Toope, note 9 above, p 109.
83. Hunter et al, *The Freshfields Guide to Arbitration and ADR*, Kluwer, Deventer, 1993, pp 101–3.
84. Redfern and Hunter, note 9 above, p 64; similar comments are found in Toope, note 9 above, pp 108–9.

[12.90] The proposition that a written arbitration agreement should be a condition for the recognition or enforcement of an international arbitral award is supported by two arguments:

- First, if there is not a valid arbitral agreement, a domestic court of law is not bound by the provisions of the New York Convention: art III of the convention requires the party applying for the recognition or enforcement of an international arbitral award under the convention to provide the 'original agreement referred to in article II or a duly certificated copy thereof'. Failure by the applicant to provide an authenticated copy of the agreement may lead to a court of law rejecting his or her application.

- Second, a valid agreement is subject to the governing domestic law, because under art II of the convention a domestic court of law has only an obligation to recognise an agreement which deals with matters 'capable of settlement by arbitration'. If a matter referred to arbitration under an agreement is not allowed to be arbitrated, for whatever reasons, under the domestic law, the court concerned has power to refuse to recognise and enforce the arbitral award in question.

Thus, the existence of a valid arbitration agreement, which must also be valid under the law of the state where the recognition and enforcement are sought, is a precondition for recognising and enforcing an international arbitral award under the New York Convention.

[12.91] The existence of a valid arbitration agreement may prevent a court of law from adjudicating the matter referred to in the agreement, unless the court finds that the said agreement is null and void, inoperative or incapable of being performed.[85] Under the convention, a court has an obligation to refer a matter stipulated in an arbitration agreement to arbitration only when one of the parties so requests. If both parties choose to ignore the existence of an arbitration clause, a court of law has no obligation to refer the matter to an arbitration tribunal under the convention. However, a domestic law (such as the Arbitration Act (NSW)) may require a court to refer a matter to arbitration before adjudicating it.

[12.92] *Furness Withy (Aust) Pty Ltd v Metal Distributors (UK) Ltd (The 'Amazonia')*

[1990] 1 Lloyd's Rep 236

Arbitration clause in a bill of lading is invalid for contravention of statute

Facts: Furness Withy (Aust) (Furness) was the disponent owner of the *Amazonia*, who chartered the vessel from the registered owners. Metal Distributors chartered the vessel from Furness to carry a cargo of zinc concentrates from Port Pirie in South Australia to Visakhapatnam and Cochin in India. Metal Distributors alleged short delivery in Cochin. The charterparty contained two inconsistent clauses. One clause stated that the charter was subject to the Sea Carriage of Goods Act 1924 (Cth). Another clause stated that any disputes arising from the charter should be arbitrated in London. Section 9 of the Sea Carriage of Goods Act 1924 (Cth) gave exclusive jurisdiction to the Australian courts over any disputes arising from bills of lading or similar documents involving the carriage of goods from a place in Australia to a place outside Australia. The parties disagreed as to the construction of the clauses.

---

85. New York Convention, art II(3).

> **Decision**: Dillon, Staughton and Mann LJJ of the English Court of Appeal held the arbitration clause invalid because the charterparty was subject to s 9 of the Sea Carriage of Goods Act 1924 (Cth).

Validity of an international arbitral award

[12.93] The existence of a valid arbitral award is another condition for a court of law to recognise and enforce an award. Article III of the convention provides as follows:

> Each Contracting State shall recognise arbitral awards as binding and enforce them in accordance with the rules of procedure of the territory where the award is relied upon, under the conditions laid down in the following articles. There shall not be imposed substantially more onerous conditions or higher fees or charges on the recognition or enforcement of arbitral awards to which this Convention applies than are imposed on the recognition or enforcement of domestic arbitral awards.

[12.94] This provision implies a condition that the award to be enforced must be valid under the law of the country where the award is to be recognised and enforced. This proposition is supported by two arguments:

- First, a court of law is required to recognise and enforce an international arbitral award 'in accordance with the rules of procedure of the territory where the award is relied upon'. In the language of art III, it is not clear what the 'territory where the award is relied upon' is; and thus, the 'territory' may be either the place where the making of the award 'is relied on' or the place where the enforcement of the award 'is relied on'. However, this uncertainty is immaterial for the purpose of art III, because the act of recognition and enforcement is qualified by the conditions laid down in the following articles. Provisions following art III may be used to deal with the grounds for denying the recognition or enforcement of an international arbitral award by a domestic court. In any event, a local court may determine the validity of an arbitral award by the governing domestic law and only recognise and enforce those which are recognisable or enforceable under the governing domestic law.

- Second, a court of law has an obligation not to impose 'substantially more onerous conditions' for the recognition and enforcement of an international arbitral award than those imposed on a domestic arbitral award. This means that a court may refuse to recognise the validity of an international arbitral award under the same conditions as, or slightly more onerous conditions than, those applicable to a domestic arbitral award. If the international arbitral award fails to meet these conditions, the court is not liable to enforce it.

Article III is another precondition for an international arbitral award to gain recognition and enforcement in a contracting state.

Grounds for refusal of international arbitral awards

Article V as the main grounds

[12.95] While the provisions (arts II, III and IV) dealing with the preconditions for the recognition and enforcement of an international arbitral award are also the grounds for refusing an international arbitral award, the major grounds which provide uniform rules for a contracting state to refuse to recognise or enforce an international arbitral award are set out in art V of the New York Convention. Article V provides the follows grounds for denying the validity and enforcement of an international arbitral award.

Invalidity of the arbitration agreement

[12.96] A domestic court may refuse to recognise or enforce an international arbitral award if the underlying arbitration agreement is invalid. The validity of the agreement can be determined on several grounds. For example, under art V(1)(a) of the New York Convention, if one or both of the contracting parties are legally incapable of entering into the arbitration agreement under the law governing the validity of the agreement, the agreement is invalid. The governing law of the agreement is either chosen by the parties, or determined under the conflict of laws rules. For example, art V(1)(a) provides that if no governing law is established by the parties, a court of law may refer to the 'law of the country where the award was made'.

Procedural fairness

[12.97] Procedural fairness is sometimes a synonym of natural justice, which requires a tribunal or a decision-maker whose decision may substantially or significantly affect the interests of a legal or natural person to give the person a fair opportunity of hearing before making the decision. Although the principles of natural justice may allow a reviewing body also to examine the basis of a decision (which must be free of bias), the New York Convention expressly sets out procedural fairness as a ground for invalidating an international arbitral award. An award may be set aside if 'the party against whom the award is invoked was not given proper notice of the appointment of the arbitrator or of the arbitration proceedings or was otherwise unable to present his case'.[86]

[12.98] The principle of procedural fairness under the New York Convention has two particular requirements.

- First, the party which was deprived of procedural fairness must be 'the party against whom the award is invoked'.
- Second, procedural fairness is limited to three particular instances:
  - lack of proper notice of the appointment of the arbitrator;
  - lack of proper notice of the hearings in the arbitration proceedings; and
  - lack of a fair opportunity to present one's case.

These particular requirements suggest that a party intending to revoke an international arbitral award must prove procedural unfairness on one of the three specified grounds.

Lack of authority to make the award

[12.99] International arbitration, whether commercial or non-commercial, is usually based on the parties' voluntary submission. The power of an arbitral tribunal is also delimited or defined by the parties who submit the dispute. An award which deals with matters which have not been submitted for arbitration is not enforceable because it

---

86. New York Convention, art V(1)(b).

[12.99] exceeds the authority of the tribunal. An award exceeding the authority given by the disputing parties amounts to an abuse of arbitral power. Such an award should not be enforced by a court of law. This is why art V(1)(c) allows a domestic court to deny the validity of an award which exceeds the authority of the tribunal.

[12.100] There are two particular instances in which an international arbitral award can be set aside under the New York Convention:

- First, the award dealt with a point or issue which was not contemplated in the arbitration agreement, or fell outside the terms of submission by the parties. This obviously exceeds the power granted by the tribunal.

- Second, if an award decides on not only the matter submitted for arbitration, but also those matters which are not expressly provided for in the submission, it may be regarded as exceeding the arbitral power of the tribunal. However, the power of a court to deny an arbitral award under art V(1)(c) may be limited to the extent to which the authority has been exceeded, because art V1(c) also states that 'if the decisions on matters submitted to arbitration can be separated from those not so submitted, that part of the award which contains decisions on matters submitted to arbitration may be recognised and enforced'.

Lack of authority to conduct arbitral proceedings

[12.101] Article V(1)(d) of the New York Convention provides that if the 'composition of the arbitral authority or the arbitral procedure was not in accordance with the agreement of the parties, or, failing such agreement, was not in accordance with the law of the country where the arbitration took place', the award concerned may be set aside. This ground for setting aside an award is more or less based on the authority or the granted power of a tribunal to conduct arbitration. As we have seen, the arbitration rules of all the arbitration institutions, except perhaps the Iran–US Claims Tribunal, allow the parties to a dispute to participate in the constitution of a tribunal. Failure to follow the parties' agreement in the constitution of a tribunal is a denial of the parties' rights, and thus a decision made by a tribunal so constituted should not be enforced. Similarly, certain arbitration rules allow the parties to decide upon the procedural rules for conducting arbitration proceedings. If a tribunal fails to follow the rules, it breaches its authority and violates the governing arbitration rules. An award so made should not be enforced. Alternatively, in the absence of the parties' agreement, whether a tribunal is constituted legally or whether the arbitration proceedings have been conducted legally, are decided by reference to the law of the country where the arbitration took place. It may be argued that while a failure to follow the parties' agreement amounts to a breach of authority or violation of the parties' right, a failure to follow the law amounts to a violation of law. Both grounds may allow a court to set an award aside.

Lack of legal effect in the award

[12.102] Article V(1)(e) of the convention states that a court of law may refuse to enforce an arbitral award if the 'award has not yet become binding on the parties, or has been set aside or suspended by a competent authority of the country in which, or under the law of which, that award was made'. It follows that only an arbitral award which is valid under the law of the country where the award was made may be recognised or enforced by another country. The country where the award is to be recognised or enforced has no legal obligation to make an invalid award valid by virtue of its recognition and enforcement.

Illegality of the award under local law

[12.103] Article V(2)(a) allows a local court to set aside an international arbitral award if the 'subject-matter of the difference is not capable of settlement by arbitration under the law of that country'. This ground of refusal may be based on the sovereignty of the refusing country: the country should not be compelled to enforce an international arbitral award whose enforcement endangers the integrity of that country's legal system.

Violation of public policy

[12.104] Article V(2)(b) allows a court to reject an international arbitral award on the ground of public policy. 'Public policy' is a very broad and uncertain concept, which is affected by contemporary political, economic, moral and cultural values. It is a catch-all provision universally accepted by all legal traditions for the purposes of maintaining the integrity of a given legal system, striking a balance between conflicting social values and, idealistically perhaps, defending the notion of fairness and justice in a given society. Article V(2)(b) of the New York Convention simply says that a court of law may refuse to recognise or enforce an international arbitral award, if such recognition and enforcement are inconsistent with public policy (however defined) of the country where the court is located.

[12.105] These are the major grounds under the New York Convention on which an international arbitral award, whether commercial or non-commercial, can be set aside by a court of the contracting country. The most significant feature of the convention is the unification of the rules for recognition and enforcement of international arbitral awards. Such unification provides a certainty to and guarantee of the enforcement of international arbitral awards and, subsequently, greatly promotes the use of international arbitration as a means of resolving international commercial disputes.

International commercial arbitration and the CISG

[12.106] It can be assumed that disputes arising from the interpretation of the CISG would be dealt with under the relevant domestic law, because the Convention operates in each contracting country as part of that country's own law. This inevitably results in each country construing the Convention in the light of its own legal principles and institutions. A diversity in the interpretation of the Convention is, thus, reasonably anticipated. The diversity so created hinders the development of international commerce and trade, which the CISG purports to facilitate. However, it must be admitted that a state has sovereignty to decide how to implement its international obligations as long as it complies with the obligations.

[12.107] International commercial arbitration is able to provide a more effective means of reaching a uniform and consistent construction of the CISG, thus offering an opportunity to exploit the potential of the Convention and to preserve its spirit. There are at least three reasons for applying arbitration to disputes arising from the CISG:

- First, arbitration is flexible. This flexibility allows practical interpretation and application of many provisions of the Convention, which were designed for the preservation and promotion of contracts and commercial relationships between the contracting parties.
- Second, arbitration is international. The internationalisation of commercial arbitration means that the inherent disadvantages of litigating in an unfamiliar legal system are not present in arbitration proceedings. Although an arbitrator has to deal with the law of a particular country which governs the particular legal relationship created under the CISG, the arbitrator, who is usually a national of a third country, is capable of approaching the legal issues as an ordinary and reasonable person would in the same circumstances. Both the disputing parties and the arbitrator are given equal access to the governing law, which may be strange to one or all of the disputing parties. This means not only that the arbitrator would construe the governing law in a more equitable manner, but also that the difference in the understanding of the law between the arbitrator and the disputing parties would be smaller than it would have been between a court of law and one or all of the disputing parties.
- Third, arbitration is autonomous. The autonomy of the parties to a dispute in a process of international commercial arbitration means that they are able to control the scope of the dispute as they wish. In addition, the parties have autonomy to choose the arbitrators, the place of arbitration and the rules of arbitration.

These factors all facilitate cooperation between the parties to a commercial relationship. Parties often do have to settle differences between them in order to carry on their commercial relationships. Bearing in mind that the notion of contract preservation and promotion is the underlining principle of the CISG, we may argue that international commercial arbitration may well serve that notion by providing solutions which are flexible, practical, controlled and allow for compromises to parties whose legal relationships are based on the CISG.

Other alternative methods of settling international commercial disputes

[12.108] The other alternative methods are consultation and conciliation (mediation). Consultation refers to direct negotiation between the parties to a dispute. Unlike third party dispute resolution, consultation does not require the assistance of a third party or referee. The method has been promoted as a technique of alternative dispute resolution both in Australia and overseas, in particular the United States. Although there are no formal rules governing consultation, it should not be ignored in the settlement of international commercial disputes.

[12.109] Conciliation and mediation are interchangeable terms. Both refer to a process of third party dispute settlement, where procedural rules are very flexible or do not exist at all. A crucial distinction between conciliation and arbitration is that a conciliator is not empowered to make a decision. Instead, a conciliator may either endeavour to assist the parties to reach a settlement or make a recommendation or report at the end of a conciliation process. It is a useful means for settling disputes between parties which have long-term commercial relationships or when the amount of dispute is relatively small. The ICC has formulated Rules for Optional Conciliation.

Index

references are to paragraphs

African Development Bank, 6.5
Agency agreements
  distribution agreements, and, 3.30
Agents *see also* **Carriers**
  acts of, carrier's duty, and, 4.145–4.147
  carrier's agents, liability, 4.115
Agreement Concerning the International Registration of Marks 1891 (Madrid Agreement) *see* **Madrid Agreement**
Agreement Relating to Liability Limitations of the Warsaw Convention and Hague Protocol 1966 (Montreal Agreement), 4.198
Agreement on Trade-Related Aspects of Intellectual Property Rights (TRIPS), 3.2
  existing international conventions, and, 9.56
  intellectual property
    meaning, 3.2, 9.54
    protected by, 9.55
  licensing agreements, 3.23
  most favoured nation (MFN) treatment, 9.58
  national treatment, 9.57
  rental rights, 9.59
  technology transfer agreements, 3.38
  trade in counterfeit goods, 9.54
  transitional arrangements, 9.60
Agreement on Trade-Related Investment Measures (TRIMs)
  foreign investment, 8.6, 8.37
    determination of TRIM, 8.82
    effects test, 8.74–8.76
    exceptions to the obligation of not applying prohibited TRIMs, 8.80
  GATT and TRIMs, 8.77–8.79
  overview, 8.73
  prohibited TRIMs and the transition period, elimination, 8.81
Air consignment note
  carriage of goods by air, 4.216–4.225
American Arbitration Association, 12.53
Animals
  carrier's duty, and, 4.150
Anti-dumping
  anti-dumping measures, use of, 9.31
  anti-trust and anti-dumping laws, 9.76

Committee on Anti-Dumping Practices, 9.33
  domestic anti-dumping legislation, 9.32
  dumping, meaning, 9.28
  history of dumping, 9.29
  normal value of goods, tests for, 9.30
Anti-trust
  anti-trust and anti-dumping laws, 9.76
  anti-trust legislation, purpose, 9.75
  origin of term, 9.74
Arbitral tribunal, *see* **International commercial arbitration**
Arbitration *see also* **International commercial arbitration**
  dispute settlement, means of, 11.6, 11.8, 11.10
  Hamburg Rules, under
    arbitration agreement, enforcement, 4.171
    place of arbitration, 4.170
    right to arbitrate, 4.169
  UN Convention on International Multimodal Transport of Goods
    arbitration under, 4.338
Arbitration Institute of the Stockholm Chamber of Commerce, 12.56
Arbitrators *see* **International commercial arbitration**
Asia Pacific Economic Cooperation (APEC)
  annual meeting of members, 10.15
  APEC members, 10.16
  Asia-Pacific region, trade and economic cooperation, 10.15
  history, 10.15
  model of trade regulation, as, 10.19
  nature of, 10.17
    economic policies, coordinating, 10.17
  structure of, 10.18
    APEC Business Advisory Council (ABAC), 10.18
    committees, 10.18
    Ministerial Meetings, 10.18
Asian Development Bank, 6.5
Assignment
  marine insurance policy, 7.99
Associated Aviation Underwriters, 7.109

Association of South East Asian Nations (ASEAN)
  areas of cooperation, 10.25
  dispute settlement, 11.3
  history, 10.20
  model of trade regulation, as, 10.26
  structure
    ASEAN Secretariat, 10.24
    functional committees, 10.23
    government meetings, 10.22
    overall structure, 10.21
Australia, commercial arbitration in
  Australian Centre for International Commercial Arbitration (ACICA), 12.59
  Australian Commercial Dispute Centre (ACDC), 12.60
  Institute of Arbitrators Australia (IAA), 12.58
  Sydney Maritime Arbitration Rules and Terms (SMART), 12.61
Australian Centre for International Commercial Arbitration (ACICA), 12.59
Australian Commercial Dispute Centre (ACDC), 12.60
Australian Constitution
  international sale of goods
    state sale of goods legislation, and, 1.41
Australian domestic law *see* **Domestic law**
Australia-New Zealand Closer Economic Relations
  Australia-New Zealand Free Trade Agreement 1965, 10.37
  major principles, 10.37
  model of trade regulation, as, 10.38
Australian Law Reform Commission
  report on *Legal Risk in International Transactions*, 6.1
Aviation insurance in international trade
  aviation insurance contract, 7.103
    doctrine of privity of contract, 7.104
    insured and insurer, 7.104
  aviation insurance contracts, classification
    aircraft consequential loss insurance, 7.110
    aircraft excess liability insurance, 7.110
    airport owners and operators insurance, 7.110
    cargo insurance, 7.110
    commercial aircraft insurance, 7.110
    hovercraft insurance, 7.110
    hull insurance, 7.110, 7.112
    loss of licence insurance, 7.110
    nature of risk, 7.112
    passenger liability insurance, 7.110, 7.112
    personal accident and life insurance, 7.110
    product liability insurance, 7.110
    third party liability insurance, 7.110, 7.112
    travel accident insurance, 7.110
    variations, 7.111
  cargo insurance, 7.106, 7.113
    Institute of London Underwriters, 7.113
    procedures for claiming indemnity, 7.115
    risks covered, 7.114
    uniformity, 7.114
    value insured, 7.115
  hull insurance, 7.110
    aircraft hull and liability insurance, 7.121
    aircraft insurance, 7.121
    exclusions, 7.122
    hull insurance policy, 7.121
    risks and liabilities covered, 7.122
    scope of insurer's liability, 7.122, 7.123
  insurance brokers, 7.105
  international commerce, 7.102
  legal framework, 7.107
    Associated Aviation Underwriters (AAU), 7.109
    domestic law, 7.109
    Institute of London Underwriters, 7.109
    Lloyd's Aircraft Policy, 7.108
    Lloyd's America, 7.109
    Lloyd's of London, 7.109
    Montreal Protocol 1978, 7.108
    Rome Convention 1952, 7.108
    third party liability, 7.108
  passenger liability insurance, 7.104
  public and passenger safety, 7.106
  third party liability insurance
    hull or aircraft insurance, clauses in, 7.116
    independent insurance policy, 7.116
    limited liability, 7.118
    limits of liability amended
      Montreal Protocol 1978, by, 7.119, 7.120
    regimes of liability, 7.120
    Rome Convention 1952, 7.116, 7.117, 7.120

Banking and financing, *see* **International banking and financing**
Banks
  documentary credits
    banks, definition, 5.17
    conformity of documents, 5.128, 5.129
    issuing bank's obligation, 5.130
    liabilities to beneficiaries, 5.121, 5.122, 5.123
    liability to applicant, 5.124–5.125
    liability between banks, 5.126, 5.127
    privity, meaning, 5.120
  international banking and financing system, 6.2, *see also* International banking and financing
  international bond market, and, 6.13
Beneficiaries, 5.17
  bank's liabilities to, 5.121, 5.122, 5.123

Index

Berne Convention for the Protection of Literary and Artistic Work 1886, 3.38

Bills of exchange
acceptance of, 5.57
  acceptor's liability to pay, 5.66
  Bills of Exchange Act 1909 (Cth), 5.61–5.65
  conditions, 5.60
  enforceable without acceptance, 5.59
  Hong Kong case, 5.67
  purpose of, 5.65
  qualified acceptance, 5.58
categories and functions of, 5.33
  avalised bill, 5.36
  claused bill, 5.34
  documentary bill, 5.35
certainty in sum of payment, 5.56
documentary credit, compared with, 5.86–5.88
legal definitions, 5.17
  Bills of Exchange Act 1909 (Cth), 5.37, 5.39
  comparisons of definitions, 5.38
  Geneva Uniform Law, 5.38
  legal regimes, use between different, 5.40
negotiability, 5.46
  enforcement of title under bill, 5.51
  holder of bill, 5.49
    protection by law, 5.50
  indorsement and delivery, 5.48
  negotiable instrument, 5.46
  rights to claim payment, 5.47
parties to, 5.42–5.45
payment under, 5.68, 5.69
precision in naming drawee, 5.52, 5.53
process for use of, 5.32
regulation of, 5.14
sight bills, 5.54, 5.55
time bills, 5.54, 5.55
UN Conventions, means of payment under
  acceptance of bill, 5.165–5.168
  concept of holder under convention, 5.162–5.164
  definition of bill, 5.155–5.157
  discharge of bill, 5.167–5.168
  negotiability of bill, 5.158–5.161
  overview, 5.150–5.152
  scope of application, 5.153–5.154
unconditional, to be, 5.41
understanding, 5.27, 5.28, 5.29–5.30
uniformity at common law, assumption of, 5.70
usage of, to effect payment, 5.31, 5.32
writing, to be in, 5.41

Bills of Exchange Act 1909 (Cth) (Aus), 5.13, *see also* **Bills of exchange**
acceptance of bill, 5.165
bill of exchange, definition, 5.37, 5.38, 5.39

Geneva Uniform Law, and
  comparison of bills of exchange between, 5.38
parties involved, 5.43–5.45
process for use of bills, 5.32
promissory notes, definition, 5.71
regulation for use of
  bills of exchange, 5.32
  cheques, 5.15
  promissory notes, 5.16

Bills of lading
carrier's liability and, 4.157– 4.164, *see also* Carriers
characteristics and functions of, 4.38, 4.39
charterparty, and, 4.60
  Hague Rules, 4.62
  Hague-Visby Rules, 4.62
  Hamburg Rules, 4.62
  letter of indemnity by charterers, 4.63
  types of charterparty, 4.61
classification of, 4.47
  charterparty bills 4.54
  clean or claused bills, 4.52
  damage caused by sub-carrier under through bill, 4.57
  electronic bills, 4.59
  forwarder's bill, 4.48
  house bill or ocean bill, distinction, 4.51
  house or received bills, 4.49
  liner bills, 4.58
  negotiable or non-negotiable bills, 4.53
  non-negotiable sea waybills, 4.55
  shipped or ocean bills, 4.50
  through bills of lading, 4.56
definition, 4.35–4.37
  Hamburg Rules, under, 4.36
delivery orders, and, 4.66
  differences between, 4.67
  ship's delivery orders issued, 4.68
fraud, and, 4.69–4.72
Hague-Visby Rules, under, 4.41, 4.42
Hamburg Rules, under, 4.43
historical perspective, 4.40
issuance of, 4.44–4.46
mate's receipt, and, 4.64
  discrepancy between, 4.65

Bonds
bond issue, concerns in, 6.41–6.45
  bank or underwriter, considerations, 6.44
  conflict between parties, 6.45
  investor, considerations for, 6.43
  issuer, considerations for, 6.42
bond, meaning, 6.9–6.13
  characteristics of bond, 6.11
  debenture, meaning, 6.10

references are to paragraph numbers

Bonds — *cont'd*
  deed, meaning, 6.10
  fundraising, for, 6.12
  international bond market, 6.13
  security, meaning, 6.10
  common clauses and covenants in bonds, 6.46–6.53
    choice of law clauses, 6.53
    interest provisions, 6.47
    maturity and redemption clauses, 6.51
    negative pledge, 6.48, 6.49
    negotiability provisions, 6.46
    pari passu clauses, 6.50
    remedy and limitation clauses, 6.52
  common terms of international bonds, 6.20–6.40
    certificates of deposit, 6.37
    convertible bonds, 6.32–6.33
      bond with warrant, 6.33
    depository receipts, 6.37
    'drop-lock' bonds, 6.25
    eurobonds, 6.40
    euronotes, 6.38–6.39
    extendible and retractable bonds, 6.22
    fixed rate bonds, 6.23
    floating rate notes, 6.24
    perpetual bonds, 6.20, 6.21
      'flip-flop' issues, 6.21
      option, 6.21
    secured bonds, 6.34–6.36
      charge, 6.35
      floating charge, 6.35
      negative pledge, 6.36
    strip bonds, 6.29–6.31
    zero coupon bonds or notes, 6.26–6.28
  international bonds, categorisation, 6.14–6.18
    classification systems, 6.16–6.18
    domestic bond, 6.14
    foreign bond, 6.14
    international bond, 6.14
    issue, terms of, 6.15
    types of, 6.19
  procedures for bond issue, 6.54
    allotment, 6.59
    closing, 6.60
    launch, 6.56
    'lock–up' period, 6.61, 6.62
    mandate, 6.55
    signing, 6.58
    stabilisation, 6.57
  trading of bonds on secondary market, 6.63

Brokers
  aviation insurance, *see* Aviation insurance in international trade
  marine insurance, *see also* Marine insurance in international trade
    broker's duties to assured and insurer, 7.71–7.74

Brussels International Convention for the Unification of Certain Rules relating to Bills of Lading (Hague Rules) 1924 *see* **Hague Rules**

Brussels Protocol Amending the Hague Rules Relating to Bills of Lading 1968 (the Hague-Visby Rules) *see* **Hague-Visby Rules**

Build-Operate-Transfer (BOT) projects
  foreign investment project, 8.29
    domestic law, 8.33
    large-size infrastructure project, 8.31
    non-commercial risk, 8.32
  UNCITRAL definition of BOT, 8.30

Buyers
  foreign party, as. 1.1
  international sale of goods
    CISG, under, *see* United Nations Convention on Contracts for the International Sale of Goods 1980 (CISG)
    Incoterms, responsibilities under terms, 1.16–1.18, 1.21–1.30, *see also* Incoterms 2000
  sale of goods legislation, Australia
  buyer's remedies, rights, 1.89–1.95

California law
  Californian Franchise Investment Law
    franchising, definition, 3.5
  franchising regulation, 3.10

Cargo insurance
  aviation insurance, 7.106–7.115, *see also* Aviation insurance in international trade
  marine insurance, 7.6, 7.12–7.22, *see also* Marine insurance in international trade

Carriage of goods *see also* **Carriage of goods by air; Carriage of goods by land; Carriage of goods by sea**
  international commercial litigation, *see* International commercial litigation
  modes of international transport
    carriage of goods by air, 4.4
    carriage of goods by inland waters, 4.4
    carriage of goods by land, 4.4
    carriage of goods by sea, 4.4
    complexity of, 4.3
    Incoterms 1990
    multimodal transport, 4.1, 4.2
    responsibilities of parties, 4.3
    unimodal transport, 4.1, 4.3
  multimodal transport, carriage by, 4.319, *see also* Multimodal means of carriage

Index

Carriage of goods by air
  air carriage documents, conventions affecting, 4.211
    Additional Protocol No 4, 4.214, 4.215
    Hague Protocol 1955, 4.213
    Warsaw Convention, 4.212
  air consignment note
    air freight forwarder, definition, 4.221
    definition, 4.216–4.218
    functions of, 4.219, 4.220
    issue of, 4.222–4.225
  carrier's liability, 4.239, *see also* Carriers
  Chicago System, 4.6, 4.7, 4.9, 4.176–4.190, *see also* Chicago System
  consignee
    consignor, and, joint rights of, 4.232, 4.233
    obligations of, 4.238
    rights of, 4.230–4.231
  consignor
    consignee, and, joint rights of, 4.232, 4.233
    meaning of consignor, 4,226
    obligations of, 4.234–4.237
    rights of, 4.226–4.229
    right of disposition, 4.227, 4.228
  forum of action, 4.260
    procedures of legal action, 4.263
    restrictions on, 4.261, 4.262
  legal framework
    Chicago System, 4.6, 4.7, 4.9
    Warsaw System, 4.6, 4.8, 4.9
  Warsaw Convention, carriage of goods under, 4.191–4.209, *see also* Warsaw Convention
  Warsaw System, 4.8, 4.9, 4.191–4.200, *see also* Warsaw System

Carriage of goods by land
  CIM, carriage of goods under, 4.10, 4.272–4.288, *see also* Uniform Rules concerning Contract for International Carriage of Goods by Rail (CIM)

CMR, carriage of goods under, 4.10, 4.297–4.318, *see also* **Geneva Convention on Contract for International Carriage of Goods by Road (CMR)**
  COTIF, carriage by rail under, 4.10, 4.266–4.271, *see also* Convention concerning International Carriage by Rail (COTIF)
  legal framework
    Convention concerning International Carriage by Rail (COTIF), 4.10, 4.264
    European conventions, 4.265
    Geneva Convention on Contract for the International Carriage of Goods by Road 1956 (CMR), 4.10, 4.264
    Uniform Rules concerning Contract for International Carriage of Goods by Rail (CIM), 4.10, 4.264
    Uniform Rules concerning Contract for International Carriage of Passengers and Luggage by Rail (CIV), 4.10, 4.264

Carriage of goods by rail *see* **Carriage of goods by land**

Carriage of goods by sea
  arbitration under Hamburg Rules
    arbitration agreement, enforcement, 4.171
    place of arbitration, 4.170
    right to arbitrate, 4.169
  bills of lading, 4.35, *see also* Bills of lading
  Carriage of Goods by Sea Act 1991 (Cth) (Aus), 4.18, 4.172–4.175
  carriers, *see also* Carriers
    liabilities under Hague-Visby Rules, 4.73–4.122
      liability and bills of lading, 4.157–4.163
      liability under Hamburg Rules, 4.138–4.155
    meaning, 4.20
  consignee, meaning, 4.31, 4.32
  consignor, 4.33
  contract of, definition, 4.16
    Carriage of Goods by Sea Act 1991 (Cth), 4.18
    meaning, flexibility in, 4.19
    orally or in writing, 4.18
    safe conveyance of goods, 4.17
  fault or negligence of chipper, liability arising, 4.133
  freight, liability to pay, 4.134, 4.235
    back freight, liability to pay, 4.136, 4.137
  Hague Rules, 4.5, 4.13
  Hague-Visby Rules, 4.5, 4.14
  Hamburg Rules, 4.5, 4.15
  indorsee, 4.34
  indorser, 4.34
  legal framework for
    Hague Rules, 4.5
    Hague-Visby Rules, 4.5
    Hamburg Rules, 4.5
    international conventions, 4.5
  modes of international transport, 4.4
  shippers, *see also* Shippers
    liability under Hague-Visby Rules or Hague Rules, 4.123–4.132
    liability under Hamburg Rules, 4.165–4.168
    meaning, 4.27–4.30

Carriage of Goods by Sea Act 1991 (Cth) (Aus), 4.18, 4.172–4.175

Carriers
  carriage by air, liability,
    air consignment notes, use of, 4.241
    delay, liability arising from, 4.243

Carriers — *cont'd*
- excluded liability, 4.244, 4.245
- limitation period, 4.258–4.259
- limited liability, 4.252–4.257
- loss of or damage to, goods, 4.242
- period of liability, 4.239, 4.240
- successive carriers, 4.247–4.251
- wrongful act of servants, 4.246

meaning of carrier
- actual carrier and carrier, 4.26
- definition in contract, 4.25
- general meaning, 4.20
  - Carriage of Goods Act 1979 (NZ), 4.21, 4.22
  - Carriage of Goods by Sea Act 1991 (Cth), 4.21
  - Chinese Maritime Law, 4.21
  - Hague-Visby Rules, 4.21
- Hague-Visby Rules, under, 4.23
  - domestic laws, 4.24

liabilities under Hague-Visby Rules
- Art 3, liabilities under, 4.79–4.85
  - duty of due diligence, 4.79–4.83
  - issue of bill of lading, 4.85
  - properly and carefully looking after goods, 4.84
- Art 4, exceptions under, 4.92–4.108
  - carriage of goods, alteration of liability, 4.108
  - carrier's right of indemnity, 4.97, 4.98
  - financial liability, limits to, 4.102–4.105
  - fixing a lower ceiling of liability, illegality, 4.106
  - general exceptions, 4.92–4.96
  - loss of benefit of limitation, 4.107
  - necessary or reasonable deviation, 4.99, 4.100, 4.101
- carriage of goods, meaning, 4.73, 4.74–4.78
  - contract clause exempting carrier, 4.75
  - exclusion of liability, 4.78
  - period of carriage, 4.76
- dangerous goods, obligations, 4.126–4.132
- deliver goods, liability to, 4.86, 4.87–4.91
  - exclusion clause and liability, 4.88–4.91
  - freedom to contract outside carriage of goods, 4.109–4.111
- limitation of time, and, 4.113, 4.114
- notice of loss, and, 4.112
- servants and agents of carrier, liabilities, 4.115–4.122

liability and bills of lading
- comparison of carrier's liabilities, 4.164
- contents of bill of lading, 4.158
- effect of bill of lading, 4.159, 4.160
- freedom of contract, 4.162, 4.163
- issue of bill of lading, 4.157
- notice of claim, 4.161
- relevant provisions, 4.156
- liability, determination under CIM, 4.293–4.295
- liability under CMR, 4.309–4.315, 4.316
- liability under Hamburg Rules
  - acts of actual carrier, and, 4.145–4.147
  - acts of agents and carrier's duty, 4.144
  - basic liability, 4.138, 4.139
  - carrier's breach as concurrent cause, 4.151
  - deliver goods on time, duty to, 4.142
  - limitation of actions, and, 4.153, 4.154
  - limits of liability, 5.152
  - live animals, and, 4.150
  - loss of right to limit liability, 4.155
  - period of carrier's liability, 4.148, 4.149
  - take care of goods, duty to, 4.140
- rights and obligations, under CIM, 4.288–4.292

Celebrity licence agreements, 3.26

Character licence agreements, 3.26

Charterparty
- bills of lading, and, 4.60
- chain transaction, 4.63
- Hague Rules, Hague-Visby Rules or Hamburg Rules, 4.62
- types of charterparty, 4.61

Charterparty bills of lading, 4.54

Chattels personal
- conflict of laws, and, 11.53–11.58

Cheques 5.17, *see also* **Payment in international trade**

Chicago Convention on International Civil Aviation 1944 (Chicago Convention) *see* **(Chicago System)**

Chicago System
- carriage of goods by air, 4.6, 4.7, 4.9
- conventions contained in, 4.7
- International Civil Aviation Organisation (ICAO), 4.177, 4.178
- objectives, 4.179
- structure, 4.176
- traffic rights promoted by
  - Chicago Convention, contained in, 4.180–4.182
  - Chicago System, developed under, 4.188–4.190
  - Transit Agreement, in, 4.183, 4.184
  - Transport Agreement, in, 4.185–4.187

China International Economic and Trade Arbitration Commission (CIETAC), 12.57

Chinese Code of Contract Law 1999, 1.9
- contract of sale, under
  - capacity to contract, 1.97
  - cases, 1.100, 1.101
  - legal persons, 1.99
  - natural persons, 1.98

Index

other organizations, 1.102
international sales, applicability, 1.96
negotiation of contract, 1.103
  forms of communication, 1.105
  oral contract, 1.104
  offers and invitations, 1.106
  resolving inconsistencies, 1.108
  revocation of offers, 1.107
  validity of contract, 1.109
operation of Code, 1.137
performance of contracts
  conformity of goods, 1.114–1.116
  delivery, 1.117
  payment of price, 1.118–1.119
  transfer of property, 1.110
  transfer of risk, 1.111–1.113
remedies for breach of contract
  damages, 1.129–1.132
  specific performance, 1.133–1.136
  suspension of contract, 1.120–1.122
  termination of contract, 1.123–1.128
technology transfer agreements, 3.41

Chinese domestic law
Code of Contract Law 1999, 1.9, *see also* Chinese Code of Contract Law 1999
international sale of goods
  Australian and Chinese law, 1.4
marine insurance, 7.26
  marine insurance contracts
  Maritime Law 1993 (China), 7.18
maritime law
  carrier, meaning, 4.21, 4.22
technology transfers, domestic regulation, 3.41
  Code of Contract Law, 3.41
  legal issues, 3.43

CIM *see* **Uniform Rules concerning the Contract for International Carriage of Goods by Rail (CIM)**

CISG *see* **United Nations Convention on Contracts for the International Sale of Goods (1980) (CISG)**

Clean or claused bills, 4.52

Clearing House Interbank Payments Systems (CHIPS), 6.3, 6.7

CMR *see* **Geneva Convention on the Contract for the International Carriage of Goods by Road (CMR)**

Collection
payment by, 5.20–5.26

Commercial customs *see also* **Incoterms 2000**
effect of, 1.7
ICC rules, 1.3, 1.7
Incoterms 2000, 1.7

Commercial law, *see also* **International commercial law**
commercial licensing, 3.21
licensing in commercial transactions, 3.21

Commercial litigation, *see* **International commercial litigation**

Competition law
distribution agreements, 3.34
franchising agreements, 3.18
licensing agreements, 3.29
World Trade Organisation, and
  anti-trust and anti-dumping law
    relations between, 9.76
  anti-trust legislation, purpose of, 9.75
  anti-trust, origin of term, 9.74

Conciliation
international commercial disputes, 12.1, 12.108, 12.109

Conflict of laws *see also* **International commercial litigation**
chattels personal disputes, and, 11.53
  action *in personam*, chattel personal, 11.58
  actions *in rem*, 11.54
  definition of property, 11.55
  form of property, 11.54
  sale of chattels personal internationally, 11.56, 11.57
conflicts rules, 11.13, 11.14
contract disputes, and
  conflicts rules, application to, 11.21
    lex loci contractus, 11.22
    lex loci solutionis, 11.22
  governing law of contract, determining
    basic rules, 11.23–11.26, 11.27
    discretion of courts, and, 11.40, 11.41
    formation of contract, and, 11.32–11.34, 11.35
    intention of parties, 11.28–11.30, 11.31
    location of property, 11.38, 11.39
    performance of contract and proper law, 11.26, 11.37
real estate disputes, and
  lex situs, governing rule, 11.52
  personal property, 11.51
  property main concern of party, where, 11.51
  real estate, 11.51
tortious disputes, and
  exceptions, 11.49, 11.50
  general rules for tortious disputes, 11.44
    double actionability rule, 11.44–11.47, 11.48
    rules or tests, 11.45
  tortious disputes and international commerce, 11.42

Consignees
carriage of goods by air
consignor and, joint rights of, 4.232, 4.233
obligations of, 4.238
rights of, 4.230–4.231
carriage of good under CIM
rights and obligations, 4.281–4.283
carriage of goods under CMR
rights, 4.308
carriage of goods by rail under COTIF
rights and obligations, 4.284–4.287
carriage of goods by sea
meaning of consignee, 4.31–4.32

Consignment note
carriage of goods by land, 4.277–4.280
contract of carriage, and, 4.302–4.304, 4.305

Consignors
carriage of goods by air
consignor and, joint rights of, 4.232, 4.233
obligations of, 4.234–4.237
rights, 4.226–4.229
carriage of goods by multimodal transport
liability, 4.335
carriage of goods by rail under COTIF
rights and obligations, 4.281–4.283
carriage of goods by sea
meaning of consignor, 4.33
carriage of good under CIM
rights and obligations of, 4.281–4.283
carriage of goods under CMR
rights, 4.206–4.307

Consultation
dispute settlement, means of, 11.6, 11.9, 11.10, 12.108

Contract law *see also* **Contracts**
distribution agreements, 3.34, 3.35
franchising agreements, 3.17
international sale of goods, and, 1.35–1.39, *see also* International sale of goods
licensing agreements, 3.28
technology transfer agreements, 3.37, 3.43

Contracts
breach of contract, *see* United Nations Convention for the International Sale of Goods (CISG)
carriage of goods by air, *see* Carriage of goods by air
carriage of goods by land, *see* Carriage of goods by land
carriage of goods by sea, *see* Carriage of goods by sea
contract disputes and conflict of laws, 11.21–11.41, *see also* Conflict of laws
conflict rules, application, 11.21, 11.22
documentary credit, and, 5.82
intellectual property, *see* Intellectual property contracts
international sale of goods
CISG, under, *see* United Nations Convention on Contracts for the International Sale of Goods 1980 (CISG)
marine insurance contracts, *see* Marine insurance and international trade

Convention concerning International Carriage by Rail 1980 (COTIF), 4.10
carriage of goods by land, 4.10
main features of COTIF, 4.268–4.271
overview of COTIF, 4.266, 4.267

Convention Establishing World Intellectual Property Organisation 1967, 3.38

Convention for the Unification of Certain Rules relating to International Carriage by Air 1929 (Warsaw Convention) *see* **Warsaw Convention; Warsaw System**

Convention on Damage Caused by Foreign Aircraft to Third Parties on the Surface 1952 (Rome Convention) *see* **Rome Convention**

Convention on the Carriage of Goods by Sea 1978 (Hamburg Rules), 1.6

Convention on the Contract for the International Carriage of Passengers and Luggage by Road 1973 (CVR), 4.10

Convention on the Settlement of International Investment Disputes between States and Nationals of Other States 1965 (Washington Convention) *see* **Washington Convention**

Copyright, 3.2
licensing, 3.26
TRIPS, protected by, 9.54, 9.55

COTIF *see* **Convention concerning International Carriage by Rail 1980 (COTIF)**

Council for Trade in Goods, WTO, 9.8

Council for Trade in Services, WTO, 9.9

Council for Trade-Related Aspects of Intellectual Property Rights, WTO, 9.10

Countertrade agreements
foreign investment, 8.26–8.28

Countervailing duty under GATT
actionable and non-actionable subsidies, 9.35
Committee on Subsidies and Countervailing Measures, 9.36
countervailing duty, concept, 9.34
customs valuation, rules concerning, 9.37

Index

Customs *see* **Commercial customs**

Dangerous goods
shippers' liability, 4.126–4.132, 4.166

Datacasting Charge (Imposition) Act 1998 (Cth) (Aus), 3.50

Delivery orders
bills of lading, and, 4.66, 4.67, 4.68

Designs, 3.2
licensing, 3.26
TRIPS, protection by, 9.54, 9.55

Dispute settlement *see also* **International commercial disputes; International commercial litigation**
defining means of dispute settlement
international commercial litigation, in, 11.6
    arbitration, 11.6, 11.8, 11.10
    consultation, 11.6, 11.9, 11.10
    International Court of Justice, 11.10
    litigation, 11.6, 11.7, 11.10
international commercial litigation, defining, 11.11
    conflicts rules, 11.13, 11.14
    domestic courts, and, 11.15, 11.16, 11.17
    procedural rules, 11.13
    stages, 11.12
international trade and commercial disputes, 11.1, 11.2
    disputes between government, resolving, 11.3, 11.4
    disputes between private parties, resolving, 11.5
NAFTA, dispute settlement mechanism, 10.35

Dispute settlement (WTO)
Dispute Settlement Body, 9.11
    functions, 9.66
mechanism for, 9.61
Understanding on Rules and Procedures Governing the Settlement of Disputes (DSU), 9.11
    arbitration under, 9.73
    consultation under, 9.64
    general procedures, 9.63
    good offices and mediation under, 9.65
    panel proceedings
        commencement of proceedings, 9.67
        panel procedures, 9.68
        panel report, making, 9.69
        two-tiered structure, 9.66
    panel report, effect, 9.70
        appeal process, 9.71
        Appellate Body's report, effect, 9.72

Distribution agreements
definition, 3.30
    agency agreements, and, 3.30
    franchising agreement, and, 3.30
    Spanish law, under, 3.30
forms of distribution agreements
    exclusive purchase agreements, 3.33
    exclusive versus non-exclusive distribution agreement, 3.31
    exclusive versus sole distribution agreement, 3.32
legal framework for distribution agreements
    domestic law, 3.34
    EU Treaty, 3.34
    WTO Agreement, 3.34
legal issues of distribution agreements, 3.35
    competition law, 3.35
    contract law, 3.35
    exclusive and sole distributor, case, 3.36
    matters to be covered, 3.35
technology transfer agreements, 3.37, 3.43

Doctrine of strict compliance
documentary credits, 5.131, 5.132, 5.133, 5.134

Documentary credit
bills of exchange compared to, 5.86–5.88
categories of
    back-to-back credits, 5.106
    confirmed and non-confirmed credits, 5.97
        confirmation, 5.98
        doctrine of strict compliance, 5.100
        liability of confirming bank, 5.99
    criteria for categorisation, 5.92
    irrevocable credits, 5.94
    irrevocable negotiation credits, 5.96
    irrevocable straight credits, 5.95
    packing credits, 5.104
    'red clause' credits, 5.105
    revocable credits, 5.93
    revolving credits, 5.103
    standby credits, 5.101
        operation of, 5.102
    transferable credits, 5.107–5.109, 5.110
        UCP 500, effect of, and, 5.117–5.119
        partial payment, 5.118, 5.119
categorising according to instructions for payment, 5.111
    acceptance credits, 5.114
    deferred payment credits, 5.113
    negotiation credits, 5.115, 5.116
    payment at sight credits, 5.112
contracts, and, 5.82
definition, 5.80, 5.81
doctrine of strict compliance, 5.131–5.134
    reasonable compliance, 5.132
    reasons for existence of, 5.133
fraud and applicant's right under, 5.148, 5.149

International Commercial Law

Documentary credit — *cont'd*
  fraud and bank's obligation under irrevocable credit, 5.141
    application for injunction, 5.142
    bank as agent of another bank, 5.145
    bank can stop payment, 5.147
    beneficiary commits fraud, 5.146
    commercial documents, fraud alleged, 5.144
    sub-beneficiary under transferable credit, 5.143
  non-conforming documents, tender of, 5.135
    conditional acceptance, 5.136
  operation of, 5.89
    process of use, 5.90–5.91
  rules governing
    liabilities of banks, 5.121
      acceptance, payment after, 5.122
      applicants, to, 5.124, 5.125
      beneficiaries to, 5.121, 5.123
      issuing bank's obligations, 5.130
      liability between banks, 5.126, 5.127
      non-conforming documents, 5.128, 5.129
    privity of documentary credit, 5.120
      short-circuiting in international trade, 5.137–5.140
  UCP 500, and, 5.83, 5.84, 5.85

Domestic law
  aviation insurance, 7.109
  cargo insurance contract, 7.23
  carrier, meaning under Hague-Visby Rules, 4.24
  Chinese domestic law, and, 1.4, *see also* Chinese domestic law
  conflict of laws, and, 11.5
  distribution agreements, 3.35
  foreign investment project, 8.33
  franchising, regulation by, 3.11
  international commercial litigation, 11.2, 11.15, *see also* International commercial litigation
  international sale of goods, 1.1, 1.3
    CISG, 1.8
  international sale of car
    case, 1.10
  other overseas jurisdictions, 1.9
  relevance of, 1.8
  sale of goods legislation, 1.8
  licensing agreements, 3.24
    Australian case, 3.25
  marine insurance, 7.26
  payment in international transactions, 5.12–5.16
  technology transfer agreements, 3.41

DSU
  arbitration under, 9.73
  consultation under, 9.64
  general procedures under, 9.63
  good offices and mediation under, 9.65
  panel proceedings under, 9.66–9.69
  panel report, 9.70–9.72

E-commerce
  defining e-commerce, 3.44
    electronic commerce, 3.45
    European Commission, Policy Paper, 1997, 3.45
    WTO, 3.45
  legal issues arising from e-commerce
    contractual liabilities, 3.46
    duty of care, 3.46
    intellectual property protection, 3.46
    privacy issues, 3.46
    reliability of data, 3.46
    WTO's Seminar on Electronic Commerce and Development, 3.47
  recent development of e-commerce
    EU's Policy Paper, 3.46
    jurisdiction issues, 3.46
    OECD countries, 3.46
  regulation, domestic efforts, 3.50
    Australia, in, 3.50
    Californian Civil Code, 4.50
  regulation, international efforts
    Declaration on Global Electronic Commerce, 3.48
    developments in regulation of e-commerce, 3.48
    UNCITRAL Model Law on Electronic Commerce, 3.49

Electronic bills of lading, 4.59

Electronic commerce *see* **E-commerce**

English law
  franchising, definition, 3.4

EU Commission *see* **European Commission**

EU Regulation on Technology Transfer Agreements 1996, 3.39
  technology transfer agreements, 3.40
    legal issues, 3.43

Eurobonds, 6.40

Euronotes
  identification, 6.39
  Note Issuance Facility (NIF), 6.38, 6.39
  Revolving Underwriting Facility (RUF), 6.38, 6.39

European Agreement on Important International Combined Transport Lines and Related Installations 1991 (AGTC), 4.11

European Commission
  distribution agreements
    legal framework, 3.34
  EU Treaty, regulation by, 10.7

Index

exclusive purchase agreements, 3.33
functions, 10.7
Policy Paper 1997
   e-commerce, defining, 3.45
   recent development of e-commerce, 3.46

European conventions
carriage of goods by land, 4.265

European Convention on International Commercial Arbitration, 12.2

European Council, 10.5–10.6

European Court of Justice, 10.9

European Franchise Federation (EFF)
franchising
   definition, 3.8
   self-regulation, 3.11

European Parliament, 10.8

European Patent Convention 1973, 3.38

European Union (EU)
areas of cooperation within
   general areas, 10.10
Block Exemption Regulation of the EU
   franchising, definition, 3.6
   master franchising agreement, definition, 3.14
dispute settlement, 11.3
EU Council
   decision-making of, 10.6
      EU Treaty, 10.6
   operation, 10.5
European Commission, 10.7
   functions, 10.7
European Court of Justice, 10.9
European Parliament, 10.8
   powers, 10.8
free movement within the EU, 10.11
   goods and services, 10.12
   workers, 10.13
historical review, 10.2
legal framework, 10.3
   treaties and instruments, 10.3
structure of, 10.4
   bodies and organisations, 10.4
WTO, and, relationship between, 10.14

Exchange Clearing House Ltd (ECHO)
settlement risk, and
   bilateral and multilateral netting, 6.81
   international banks, collapse of, 6.80
   legal issues, 6.82
   multilateral nature of, 6.82
   settlement of foreign exchange trade, 6.79

Exchange control and international finance
exchange control legislation, 6.77
exchange control, meaning, 6.75
impact on international finance, 6.76

Factoring in international trade
factoring as a means of business, 6.98–6.100
   bank may act as factor, 6.99
   Factors Chain International, 6.100
rights and duties of parties
   debtor's rights and duties, 6.111–6.113
   factor's rights, 6.109
   parties, definition, 6.108
   supplier's rights, 6.110
UNIDROIT Convention on International Factoring
   factoring contract, definition, 6.103–6.105
   overview, 6.101–6.102
   scope of application, 6.106–6.107

Foreign exchange risks
definition, 6.78
Exchange Clearing House Ltd (ECHO) and settlement risk example, 6.79–6.82
hedging foreign exchange risks, means of
   currency futures, 6.89
   currency options, 6.90
   invoices and currency clauses, 6.88
   leading and lagging, 6.87
   matching, 6.83
   multilateral netting and netting per se, 6.84–6.86
      International Foreign Exchange Master Agreement (IFEMA), 6.85
   official export financing/insurance agencies, 6.97
   swap options, 6.91–6.96
      back-to-back loans, 6.93
      cross currency interest rate swap, 6.96
      currency swap, 6.95
      interest rate swap, 6.94
      parallel loans, 6.92

Foreign investment law
Agreement on Trade Related Investment Measures, 8.6
comparative advantages between countries, 8.3
economic conflicts, 8.1
foreign investment, definition, 8.7–8.9
   concept of, 8.9
   features of, 8.8
   foreign direct investment (FDI), 8.7, 8.8
   foreign portfolio investment (FPI), 8.7, 8.8
   IMF, 8.7
   UNCTAD, 8.7
forms of foreign investment
   Build-Operate-Transfer (BOT) projects, 8.29
   domestic law, 8.33
   future non-commercial risk, 8.32

references are to paragraph numbers

International Commercial Law

Foreign investment law — *cont'd*
    large-size infrastructure projects, 8.31
    UNCITRAL, definition under, 8.30
  countertrade
    agreement, 8.28
    feasible form of foreign investment, 8.28
    meaning, 8.26
    UNCITRAL Legal Guide on International Countertrade Transactions, 8.28
  defining, 8.15, 8.16
  foreign direct investment and portfolio investment, 8.35
  foreign takeovers or acquisitions, 8.34
  joint ventures, 8.19
    Australia, in, 8.23
    control of foreign investment, 8.22
    multinational company, and, 8.21
    ownership of, 8.20
  licensing agreements, 8.26
    investments made under, 8.27
  multinational corporations, 8.17
    advantages of, 8.18
    transnational corporations, 8.18
  sole foreign ventures, 8.24, 8.25
  growth of, 8.4
  host country, and, relationships between
    international commercial law, 8.10
    international foreign investment law
    domestic foreign investment law, and, 8.14
    local economy, effects on, 8.12
    summary of relationships, 8.13
    trade protectionism, policy of, 8.11
  International Centre for Settlement of Foreign Investment Disputes (ICSID), 8.1
  international commercial activity, 8.1
  International Court of Justice and foreign investment, 8.91–8.93
  international legal framework
    decisions of the Council, 8.47–8.52
    general considerations and practical approaches, 8.45–8.46
    international efforts to regulate, 8.36
    international organisations, 8.37
    Legal Guide on International Countertrade Transactions, 8.58–8.61
    Multilateral Investment Guarantee Agency (MIGA)
      operation of, 8.65–8.66
      status, 8.62–8.64
    OECD Declaration
      principles of, 8.42–8.43
      structure of, 8.38–8.41
    OECD Guidelines for Multinational Enterprises (MNEs), 8.44
  International Monetary Fund, 8.5–8.7, 8.37
  international organisations, 8.5, 8.6
  Multilateral Agreement on Investment (MAI), 8.5, 8.6
  Multilateral Investment Guarantee Agency (MIGA), 8.62–8.66
  OECD, 8.5
  protection of foreign investment, means of, 8.88, 8.89, 8.90
  regulation of foreign investment, issues for
    compulsory rules, 8.83–8.85
    domestic regulation, principles in, 8.87
    protectionism, 8.86
    sovereignty, 8.86
    voluntary regulation, 8.83–8.85
  rules governing, 8.5
  UNCTAD, 8.2, 8.5, 8.6
  Washington Convention on the Settlement of Investment Disputes 1965, 8.1
  WTO, 8.4, 8.5
    Agreement on Trade-Related Investment Measures (TRIMs)
    determination of a TRIM under, 8.82
    effects test, and, 8.74–8.76
      prohibited TRIMs and transitional period, elimination, 8.81
    exceptions to obligations of not applying prohibited TRIMs, 8.80
    GATT, and, 8.77–8.79
    overview, 8.73
    foreign investment as issue of WTO, 8.67–8.70
    Agreement on TRIMs, 8.67, 8.68, 8.69
    Uruguay Round of GATT, 8.67, 8.68, 8.69
    Trade-Related Investment Measures, defining, 8.71–8.72

Foreign Judgments Act 1991 (Cth) (Aus)
  legal framework for enforcement, 11.69–7–11.70
  registration, grounds for refusal, 11.75, 11.76

Foreign judgments, enforcement
  Australia, in
    grounds for refusing or setting aside registration, 11.74
    Foreign Judgments Act 1991, (Cth), 11.75, 11.76
    fraud and setting aside judgment, 11.79
    setting aside or suspending enforcement, 11.77
    state legislation, 11.78
  legal framework for enforcement, 11.67
    federal and state legislation, 11.68
    Foreign Judgments Act 1991 (Cth), 11.67, 11.68, 11.69, 11.70
    judicial assistance and arbitration, federal statutes, 11.70
  registration of foreign judgments, 11.71

Index

reciprocity, 11.72
refusal to register, 11.73
common law, at
common law rules for enforcement, 11.61, 11.62
lack of jurisdiction in court making judgment, 11.63
submission to jurisdiction of foreign court, 11.64
means of enforcement, 11.60
rationale for, 11.59
refusal to enforce, common law rules for, 11.65, 11.66

Foreign takeovers or acquisitions
foreign investment, 8.34

Forfaiting in international trade
forfaiting, meaning, 6.128, 6.129
UNCITRAL Model Law on International Credit Transfers, 6.130–6.134

Forwarder's bills, 4.48

Franchising agreements, 3.1
distribution agreements, and, 3.30
format of franchising arrangements
classification of formats, problems, 3.12
direct franchising, 3.13
joint venture agreements, 3.15
major considerations of, 3.16
master franchising, 3.14
franchising, definitions
Block Exemption Regulation of the EU, 3.6
Californian law, 3.5
early English legal definition, 3.4
European Franchise Federation (EFF), definition, 3.8
International Franchise Association (IFA), definition, 3.7
summarising definitions of franchising, 3.10
universal definition, lack of, 3.3
international commercial activities or arrangements, 3.1
international commercial litigation, *see* International commercial litigation
legal framework for franchising
domestic law, regulation by, 3.10
self-regulation, 3.11
European Franchise Federation, 3.11
Hong Kong, in, 3.11
World Franchise Association, 3.11
legal issues of franchising
competition law, 3.18
contract law, 3.17
intellectual property law, 3.20
tax law, 3.19
technology transfer agreements, 3.37, 3.43

Fraud
bills of lading, and, 4.69, 4.70
determination on issue of, 4.72
intent, 4.71
documentary credits
applicant's right under, 5.148, 5.149
bank's obligation under irrevocable credit, 5.141, 5.142, 5.143
bank as agent of another bank, 5.145
commercial documents, 5.144
payment to defrauding party, 5.146
stopping payment, 5.147

Free Trade Commission, NAFTA, 10.29

Freight
liability to pay, 4.134
back freight, 4.136, 4.137
Hague-Visby Rules, 4.135

GATS *see* **General Agreement on Trade in Service 1993 (GATS)**

GATT *see* **General Agreement on Tariffs and Trade (GATT)**

GATT Agreement on Trade-Related Aspects of Intellectual Property Rights (TRIPS) *see* **Agreement on Trade-Related Aspects of Intellectual Property Rights (TRIPS)**

GATT Agreement on Trade-Related Investment Measures (TRIMs) *see* **Agreement on Trade-Related Investment Measures (TRIMs)**

General Agreement on Tariffs and Trade (GATT) *see also* **Uruguay Round of GATT Negotiations 1993**
anti-dumping
anti-dumping measures, use of, 9.31
Committee on Anti-Dumping Practices, 9.33
domestic anti-dumping measures, 9.32
dumping, meaning, 9.28
history of dumping, 9.29
normal value of goods, tests for determining, 9.30
countervailing duty under GATT
actionable and non-actionable subsidies, 9.35
Committee on Subsidies and Countervailing Measures, 9.36
countervailing duty, concept, 9.34
customs valuation, rules concerning, 9.37
exchange control, rules governing, 9.38
expansion of, 9.17
GATS, *see* General Agreement on Trade in Service (GATS)
GATT 1947, 9.17
intellectual property contracts, 3.1

General Agreement on Tariffs and Trade (GATT) — cont'd
international banking and financing, 6.6
nature of, 9.19
practical status of, 9.20
GATT 1947 and GATT 1994
defining, 9.18
major differences between, 9.18
historical review, 9.16
international commercial litigation, *see* International commercial litigation
International Trade Organisation, failure of, 9.17
most favoured nation (MFN) treatment, principle of
general meaning, 9.21
MFN in GATT, 9.22
national treatment, principle of
general meaning, 9.23
national treatment in GATT, 9.24
non-discrimination, principle of
eliminating quantitative restrictions, principle of, 9.27
international commerce, meaning in, 9.25
non-discrimination in GATT, 9.26
TRIMs, *see* Agreement on Trade-Related Investment Measures (TRIMs)
TRIPS, *see* Agreement on Trade-Related Aspects of Intellectual Property Rights (TRIPS)

General Agreement on Trade in Service 1993 (GATS)
GATS and the Uruguay Round, 9.40
modes of international trade in services, 9.45
commercial presence, 9.45
consumption abroad, 9.45
cross-border supply, 9.45
importance, 9.46
presence of natural persons, 9.45
market access
definitions, 9.50
restrictions on, 9.51
specific commitments, and, 9.52
most favoured nation treatment, 9.47
exceptions, 9.48
national treatment, 9.53
service trade and making of GATS, 9.39
services, meaning, 9.40
trade in services, 9.40
services, meaning under, 9.42
broad approach, 9.43
categories of services, 9.44
structure, 9.41
transparency, 9.49

General Council, WTO, 9.7

Geneva Convention on Contract for the International Carriage of Goods by Road 1956 (CMR), 4.10, 4.264
carriage of goods by land, 4.10
application of CMR, 4.298–4.300
international carriage, 4.301
carrier, liability of, 4.309–4.315
robbery, in case of, 4.316
consignment note, contract of carriage, and, 4.302–4.304
evidence of identity of carrier, 4.305
consignee, rights of, 4.308
consignor, rights of, 4.306, 4.307
limitation period, 4.317, 4.318
overview of CMR, 4.297

Geneva Uniform Law on Bills of Exchange and Promissory Notes (Geneva Uniform Law), 5.9–5.11
acceptance of bill, 5.165
bill of exchange, definition, 5.38
Bills of Exchange Act 1909 (Cth), and, comparison of bills of exchange between, 5.38
international banking and financing, 6.6
promissory notes, definition, 5.72, 5.73

Goods *see also* **Dangerous goods**
carriers' liability, 4.140, *see also* Carriers
international sale of goods, *see* International sale of goods
meanings under different laws, 1.11
sale of goods *see* Sales of goods legislation, Australia

Guadalajara Convention 1961, 4.196, 4.197
Guatemala City Protocol 1971, 4.195, 4.196

Hague Convention for the Pacific Settlement of International Disputes 1899, 12.43

Hague Convention for the Pacific Settlement of International Disputes 1907, 12.43

Hague Convention on Uniform Laws on International Sales 1969, 1.5

Hague Conventions, 2.1
international commercial arbitration, on, 1899 and 1907, 12.43, 12.44
Permanent Court of Arbitration, 12.43, 12.45, 12.47
rules of arbitration, 12.44

Hague Protocol 1955, 4.8, 4.191–4.196, 4.213

Hague Rules, 4.5
carriage of goods by sea, 4.5, 4.13, *see also* Carriage of goods by sea
shipper's liability under, 4.123
accurate information, obligation to provide, 4.124, 4.125

Index

dangerous goods, obligations, 4.126–4.132
Hague-Visby Rules, 4.5
  bills of lading, under, 4.41, 4.42
  carriage of goods by sea, 4.5, 4.14, *see also* Carriage of goods by sea
  carrier's liabilities under Hague-Visby Rules, 4.73–4.122, *see also* Carriers
    carriage of goods, meaning, 4.73
  carriers, meaning under, 4.21, 4.23
  shipper, meaning under, 4.27
  shipper's liability under, 4.123
    accurate information, obligation to provide, 4.124, 4.125
    dangerous goods, obligations, 4.126–4.132
Hamburg Rules, 4.5
  arbitration under
    arbitration agreement, enforcement, 4.171
    place of arbitration, 4.170
    right to arbitrate, 4.169
  bills of lading, under, 4.36, 4.38, 4.43
  carriage of goods by sea, 4.5, 4.15, *see also* Carriage of goods by sea
  carrier's liability under, 4.138–4.155, *see also* Carriers
  shipper, meaning under, 4.28, 4.29–4.30
  shipper's liability under
    dangerous goods, and, 4.166
    general duty, 4.165
    guarantee, and, 4.167, 4.168
Hedging foreign exchange risks, 6.84, *see also* Foreign exchange risks
Himalaya clause
  liability of independent contractors, and, 4.116, 4.117
  limited or excluded liability, extension, 4.121
  NZ case, 4.119
  OTT Convention, 4.122
  protection of third party, 4.120
  validity of clause, 4.118
House bills, 4.49
Hull insurance, *see also* **Aviation insurance in international trade; Marine insurance in international trade**
  aviation insurance, 7.110, 7.121–7.123
  marine insurance, 7.6–7.11, 7.24, 7.25

ICC *see* **International Chamber of Commerce (ICC)**
Incoterms 2000, 1.4
  application in international sales
    conformity rules, 1.80
    C-terms, Main carriage paid, 1.14

CFR — Cost and Freight (C&F), 1.22
CIF — Cost, Insurance and Freight, 1.23, 1.55
CIP — Carriage and Insurance Paid to, 1.25
CPT — Carriage Paid to, 1.24
definition, 1.12
D-terms, Arrival, 1.13, 1.14
  DAF — Delivered at Frontier, 1.26
  DDE — Delivered Duty Unpaid, 1.29
  DDP — Delivered Duty Paid, 1.30
  DEQ — Delivered Ex Quay, 1.28
  DES — Delivered Ex Ship, 1.27
E-term, Departure, 1.13, 1.14
  EXW — Ex works, 1.15, 1.16
F-terms, Main carriage unpaid, 1.14
  FAS — Free Alongside Ship, 1.12, 1.18, 1.19, 1.20
  FCA — Free Carrier, 1.17
  FOB — Free on Board, 1.21, 1.55
groups in, 1.13
ICC, compiled by, 1.12
seller and buyer, rights and liabilities, 1.13
summary of Incoterms, 1.31
terms for mode of transport, 1.13
trade terms for carriage or delivery of goods, 1.12
transfer of risk, 1.59
buyers' remedies, 1.95
buyers' responsibilities under, 1.16–1.30
contracts for international sale of goods
  incorporation into, 1.38, 1039
implied condition
  goods conform with sample, 1.79
international transport of goods, 4.1
rules governing international sales contracts, 1.7
sellers' remedies, 1.88
sellers' responsibilities under, 1.16–1.30
Independent contractors
  liability of, Himalaya clause, and, 4.116, 4.117
    limited or excluded liability, extension, 4.121
    NZ case, 4.119
    OTT Convention, 4.122
    protection of third party, 4.120
    validity of clause, 4.118
Indorsee, 4.34
Indorsor, 4.34
Industrial property *see* **Intellectual property contracts; Agreement on Trade-Related Aspects of Intellectual property (TRIPS)**
Inherent vice, 7.67–7.69
Institute of Arbitrators Australia (IAA), 12.58

references are to paragraph numbers

International Commercial Law

Institute of London Underwriters, 7.28, 7.29, 8.23

Insurance in international trade
  aviation insurance, 7.102, *see also* Aviation insurance in international trade
  marine insurance, 7.1, *see also* Marine insurance in international trade

Intellectual property contracts
  Agreement on TRIPS, 3.2
  confidential information, 3.2
  copyright, 3.2
  designs, 3.2
  distribution agreements, 3.30, *see also* Distribution agreements
  E-commerce, 3.44, *see also* E-commerce
  franchising agreements, 3.3, *see also* Franchising agreements
  GATT, 3.1
  intellectual property, meaning, 3.2
  international commercial activities or arrangements, 3.1
  licensing agreements, 3.21, *see also* Licensing agreements
  patents, 3.2
  technology transfer agreements, 3.37, *see also* Technology transfer agreements
  trademarks, 3.2
  trade names, 3.2
  World Trade Organisation Agreement, 3.1

Intellectual property law
  franchising agreements, 3.20

Inter-American Commercial Arbitration Commission, 12.46, 12.48

International arbitral institutions *see also* **International commercial arbitration**
  definition, 12.45
  government international arbitral bodies, 12.46
    China International Economic and Trade Arbitration Commission (CIETAC), 12.45
    ICSID, 12.45, 12.49
    Inter-American Commercial Arbitration Commission, 12.45, 12.48
    Iran-US Claims Tribunal, 12.45, 12.50
    Permanent Court of Arbitration, 12.46, 12.47
  non-governmental international arbitral institutions
    American Arbitration Association, 12.53
    arbitration as service, 12.51
    Arbitration Institute of the Stockholm Chamber of Commerce, 12.56
    China International Economic and Trade Arbitration Commission (CIETAC), 12.57
    International Chamber of Commerce, 12.52
    London Court of International Arbitration, 12.54
    Netherlands Arbitration Institute, 12.55

International Bank for Reconstruction and Development (World Bank) *see* **World Bank**

International banking and financing
  bonds and international finance, issue of, *see also* Bonds
    bond issue, concerns in, 6.41–6.45
    bond, meaning, 6.9–6.13
    categorising international bonds, 6.14–6.19
    common clauses and covenants in bonds, 6.46–6.53
    common terms of international bonds, 6.20–6.40
    procedures for bond issue, 6.54–6.62
    trading of bonds on secondary market, 6.63
  exchange control and international finance
    exchange control legislation, 6.77
    exchange control, meaning, 6.75
    impact on international finance, 6.76
  factoring in international trade
    factoring as a means of business, 6.98–6.100
    rights and duties of parties, 6.108–6.113
    UNIDROIT Convention on International Factoring, 6.101–6.107
  foreign exchange risks, *see also* Foreign exchange risks
    definition, 6.78
    Exchange Clearing House Ltd (ECHO) and settlement risk, 6.79–6.82
    hedging foreign exchange risks, means of, 6.83–6.97
  forfaiting in international trade
    forfaiting, meaning, 6.128, 6.129
    Model Law on transfer of credit, 6.131–6.135
  international commercial litigation, *see* International commercial litigation
  international financial centres and international finance, 6.8
  International Monetary Fund (IMF) and international finance
    difference in IMF, 6.71
    role of IMF in international trade, 6.72–6.74
  international syndicated loans and international finance
    international syndicated loan, 6.64, 6.65
    major considerations, 6.70
    organisation, 6.66–6.68
    international syndicated loan agreement management, 6.69
  leasing in international trade, *see also* Leasing in international trade
    leasing as means of business, 6.114

Index

rights and duties of parties, 6.121–6.126
supplier, rights and duties, 6.127
UNIDROIT Convention on International Financial Leasing, 6.115–6.120
review of international banking and financing system
   Australian Law Reform Commission report, 6.1
   banks in international and domestic markets, 6.2
   laws of particular countries, examination of issues, 6.7
   international conventions, 6.6
   international financial institutions
      agreements of sovereign states, under, 6.3
      International Bank for Reconstruction and Development (World Bank), 6.5
      International Monetary Fund (IMF), 6.5
      regional development banks, 6.5
   private banks and financial institutions, 6.3
      Clearing House Interbank Payments Systems (CHIPS), 6.3
      laws of the country, 6.4
      Society for Worldwide Interbank Financial Telecommunication (SWIFT), 6.3

International bonds *see* **Bonds; International banking and financing**

International Centre for Settlement of Foreign Investment Disputes (ICSID), 8.1, 11.5
arbitration proceedings, 12.26, 12.30
arbitral tribunal, 12.18, 12.27
award of arbitrator, 12.29
powers and functions, 12.28
   government international arbitral bodies, 12.46, 12.49
   international arbitral institution, defining, 12.45
jurisdiction of, 12.24
   investment disputes over, 12.25
structure of, 12.19
   Administrative Council, 12.20
   full international legal personality, 12.23
   Panels, 12.22
   Secretariat, 12.21
Washington Convention, created by, 12.2, 12.17
World Bank, and, 12.19

International Chamber of Commerce (ICC)
foreign investment, regulation, 8.37
Incoterms 2000, *see* Incoterms 2000
International Court of Arbitration, 12.52
UCP 500, 5.1

International Chamber of Commerce rules, 1.3, 1.7
payment in international trade, 5.9, 5.12

International Chamber of Commerce Uniform Customs and Practice for Documentary Credits (UCP 500), 5.1, 5.85, 5.86
documentary credit, 5.83, 5.85
   effect of UCP 500 and categories of, 5.117–5.119
   Hong Kong case, 5.85
   incorporation of ICC UCP 500, 5.84
   rules governing, 5.120–5.130
   transferable credits, 5.107, 5.108
payment of international transactions, 5.12
standby letter of credit, 5.83

International Chamber of Commerce Uniform Rules for Bank-to-Bank Reimbursements (URR 525), 5.9
Model law on transfer of credit, 6.134

International Chamber of Commerce Uniform Rules for Collection (URC 522), 5.9, 5.12, 5.76–5.77
collection process, 5.23, 5.130
commercial documents, 5.26

International Civil Aviation Organisation (ICAO), 4.177, 4.178

International Code of Conduct on the Transfer of Technology (TOT Code) 1980, 3.38
international transfer of technology
   definition of technology transfer, 3.39
   international collation, 3.39
   international institutional machinery, 3.39
   principles of national regulation, 3.39
   provisions for developing countries, 3.39
   restrictive trade practices, 3.39
   rights and obligations of parties, 3.39
   settlement of disputes, 3.39
legal issues of transfer of technology, 3.43

International commercial arbitration *see also* **Arbitration**
arbitration, meaning
   basic features of arbitration, 12.4
   definition, 12.6
   historical perspective, in, 12.2
   semi-autonomy in arbitration, meaning, 12.5
   uniform definition, need for, 12.3
commercial arbitration, definition
   commercial, definition, 12.7
CSIG, and
   disputes arising from interpretation of, 12.106
   diversity in interpretation, 12.106
   reasons for applying arbitration to disputes, 12.107
international arbitral institutions and functions
   commercial arbitration in Australia

International Commercial Law

International commercial arbitration — *cont'd*
    Australia Centre for International Commercial Arbitration (ACICA), 12.59
    Australian Commercial Dispute Centre (ACDC), 1.60
    Institute of Arbitrators Australia (IAA), 12.58
    SMART, 12.61
  government international arbitral bodies, 12.46
    ICSID, 12.46, 12.49
    Inter-American Commercial Arbitration Commission, 12.46, 12.48
    Iran-US Claims Tribunal, 12.46, 12.50
    Permanent Court of Arbitration, 12.46, 12.47
  international arbitral institution, definition, 12.45
  international commercial disputes *see* International commercial disputes
  non-governmental international arbitral institutions
    American Arbitration Association, 12.53
    arbitration as a service, 12.51
    Arbitration Institute of the Stockholm Chamber of Commerce, 12.56
    China International Economic and Trade Arbitration Commission, 12.57
    International Chamber of Commerce, 12.52
    London Court of International Arbitration, 12.54
    Netherlands Arbitration Institute, 12.55
  legal framework for
    arbitral rules, 12.11
    conventions, 12.11
    Hague Conventions, 12.43, 12.44
    internationalisation of commercial arbitration, 12.10
    New York Convention, 12.11
      application of, 12.13
      exceptions to obligations, 12.16
      foreign arbitral awards, 12.14
      functions, 12.12
      obligations under, 12.15
    UNCITAL Model Law, 12.31
      arbitral tribunal and arbitrators, 12.36
      arbitration agreement and obligation of court, 12.34, 12.25
      arbitration agreement, meaning in, 12.33
      effect of award, 12.39–12.42
      features of, 12.32
      jurisdiction of arbitral tribunal, 12.37
      proceedings of arbitral tribunal, 12.38
    Washington Convention 1965
      arbitration of foreign disputes by ICSID, 12.30
      arbitration under, 12.26–12.29
      ICSID, creation of, 12.17
      jurisdiction of ICSID, 12.24, 12.25
      overview of convention, 12.17
      rules for conciliation and arbitration, 12.18
      structure of the ICSID, 12.19–12.23
  meaning of
    commercial nature of, 12.8
    international nature of, 12.9
  New York Convention, and, *see also* New York Convention on Recognition and Enforcement of Arbitral awards 1958
    distinguishing recognition from enforcement, 12.86
    foreign awards, meaning, 12.83–12.85
    recognising and enforcing, conditions for, 12.88–12.93
    refusal of international arbitral awards, grounds for, 12.95–12.105
    uniformity of rules, 12.87
  procedural issues in
    arbitral awards and costs for arbitration
      characteristics, 12.80
      costs, meanings, 12.81
      covered under costs, 12.82
      meanings and affect of award, 12.79
      two aspects of decision, 12.78
    arbitral tribunal, constitution and jurisdiction, 12.64
      constitution of, 12.70–12.71
      determination of procedural rules, 12.66
      freedom to arbitrate, 12.64
      freedom to choose arbitrators, 12.67–12.69
      freedom to choose rules for arbitration, 12.65, 12.66
    arbitration proceedings, procedures for conducting
      claims, defences and counter-claims, 12.72
      evidence, witnesses and hearings, 12.74, 12.75
      legal representation, 12.73
      privacy and confidentiality, 12.76, 12.77
    procedural issues, definition, 12.62, 12.63

International commercial disputes *see also* **International commercial litigation**
  alternative means of settling
    alternative means, definition, 12.1
    arbitration, 12.1
    conciliation, 12.1, 12.108, 12.109
    consultation, 12.1, 12.108
    mediation, 12.108, 12.109
  international commercial arbitration, 12.2, *see also* International commercial arbitration

Index

International commercial law
  licensing, meaning, 3.21
  substance of, 1.2, *see also* International sale of goods

International commercial litigation
  contract disputes and conflict of laws, 1.21, *see also* Conflicts of laws
  courts in, functions, 11.18
    adjudicate dispute, 11.18, 11.19
    enforce foreign judicial or arbitral judgment, 11.18, 11.20
  defining, 11.11
    choice of forum, 11.12
    commencement of proceedings, 11.12
    conflicts rules, 11.13, 11.14
    enforcement of judgments, 11.12
    procedural rules of court, 11.13
    stages in, 11.12
  dispute settlement, means, defining
    arbitration, 11.6, 11.8, 11.10
    conciliation, 11.6
    consultation, 11.6, 11.9, 11.10
    International Court of Justice, 11.10
    litigation, 11.6, 11.7, 11.10
    parties to dispute, choice of, 11.10
  domestic courts, and, 11.15
    foreign law and international law, 11.16
    international commercial law, 11.16
    matter referred from Australian court to foreign court, 11.17
  foreign judgment, enforcement, *see also* Foreign judgments, enforcement
    Australia, enforcement in
      grounds for refusing or setting aside registration, 11.74–11.79
      legal framework for enforcement, 11.67–11.70
      registration of foreign judgments, 11.71–11.73
    common law, at, 11.61–11.64
    means of enforcement, 11.60
    rationale for, 11.59
    refusal to enforce, common law rules for, 11.65, 11.66
  governments, disputes between, 11.2
    resolving, 11.3
  international trade organisations, outside, 11.3, 11.4
  international trade organisations, within, 11.3
  international trade and commercial disputes
    defining, 11.1
      government and private person, between, 11.2
      governments, between, 11.2
      private persons, between, 11.2
    governments and private parties, disputes between, 11.2
      domestic laws and conflict of laws, 11.5
      resolving, 11.5
    private parties, disputes between, 11.2
      domestic laws and conflict of laws, 11.5
      resolving, 11.5
    tortious disputes and conflict of laws, 11.42, *see also* Conflict of laws

International commercial terms *see* **Incoterms 1990**

International construction contracts, 3.1

International Convention concerning the Carriage of Passengers and Luggage by Rail 1980 (CIV), 4.10

International Convention for the Protection of Performers, Producers of Phonograms and Broadcasting Organisations (Rome Convention) 1961, 3.38

International Convention for the Unification of Certain Rules of Law Relating to Bills of Lading 1924 (Hague Rules), 4.5, *see also* **Hague Rules**

International Convention to Facilitate the Crossing of Frontiers for Goods Carried by Rail 1953, 4.10

International conventions, 1.2, 1.3
  carriage of goods by air, 4.6–4.9
  carriage of goods by land, 4.10
  carriage of goods by multimodal means, 4.11
  carriage of goods by sea, 4.5
  international banking and financing, 6.6
  international sale of goods, 1.5, 1.6
  payment in international transactions, 5.9–5.11
  Uniform Law on International Sale of Goods 1964, 1.5
  Uniform Law on the Formation of Contracts for International Sale of Goods 1964, 1.5

International countertrade agreements, 3.1

International Court of Arbitration, 12.52

International Court of Justice
  foreign investment, and
    international dispute settlement, 8.91–8.93

International financial centres, 6.8

International financial institutions
  agreements of sovereign states, under, 6.3
  International Bank for Reconstruction and Development (World Bank), 6.5
  International Monetary Fund (IMF), 6.5
  regional development banks, 6.5

references are to paragraph numbers

International Commercial Law

International Foreign Exchange Master Agreement (IFEMA), 6.85
International foreign investment *see* Foreign investment law
International Franchise Association (IFA)
  franchising, definition, 3.7
International mineral development agreements, 3.1
International Monetary Fund (IMF)
  foreign investment, 8.5, 8.6, 8.7
    regulation of, 8.37
  international banking and financing, 6.3, 6.5
  International Monetary Fund (IMF) and international finance
    difference in IMF, 6.71
    role of IMF in international trade, 6.72–6.74
      financial assistance, 6.72, 6.73
      policy oriented, 6.74
      surveillance, 6.72
      technical assistance, 6.72
International oil and gas exploration and exploitation contracts, 3.1
International sale of goods
  Australian domestic law and Chinese domestic law, 1.4
  Australian sale of goods legislation, *see also* Sale of goods legislation, Australia
    buyer's remedies, rights, 1.89–1.95
    conformity of goods under, implied conditions, 1.73–1.80
    constitutional implications, 1.41
    delivery of goods under, rules, 1.60–1.72
    formation of contract under, 1.42, 1.43
    passing of property under, 1.44–1.55
    seller's remedies under, rights, 1.81–1.88
    transfer of risk under, 1.56–1.59
    uniformity of legislation, 1.40
  CISG, under, *see* United Nations Convention on Contracts for the International Sale of Goods 1980 (CISG)
  customs in regions and trades, 1.2, 1.3
    effect of, 1.7
    ICC rules, 1.3, 1.7
    Incoterms 2000, 1.7
  domestic law, subject to, 1.1, 1.3, 1.8–1.10
  elements in
    goods, meaning, 1.11
    international level, effect at, 1.11
    sale, 1.11
    subject matter of sale is goods, 1.11
  general contract law, and, 1.35
    Australia, in, 1.37
    contract of sale, 1.36
    Incoterms, incorporation into contracts, 1.38, 1.39
    international conventions, 1.37
    oral contract, 1.36
    parties to contract, rights and obligations, 1.38
  Incoterms 2000, application, *see* Incoterms 2000
  international commercial litigation, *see* International commercial litigation
  international conventions, 1.2, 1.3, 1.4, *see also* International conventions
  legal framework, Australia in
    contract construction, 1.34
    goods, meaning, 1.32
    Incoterms and sale of goods legislation, application
      case, 1.33
      remedy, adequacy of, in international sale, 1.34
  legal issues, 1.4
  meaning of, 1.4
International syndicated loans and international finance
  international syndicated loan, 6.64, 6.65
    major considerations, 6.70
    organisation, 6.66–6.68
  international syndicated loan agreement management, 6.69
International trade and commercial disputes, *see* International commercial litigation
International trade organisations *see also* Regional trade organisations
  World Trade Organisation, and, 9.77
International trade, payment *see* Payment in international trade
International transport of goods *see* Carriage of goods; Carriage of goods by air; Carriage of goods by land; Carriage of goods by sea
Iran-US Claims Tribunal, 12.46, 12.50

Joint ventures
  agreement for the purpose of franchising, 3.15
  foreign investment, 8.19
    Australia, in, 8.23
    controls over, 8.22
    multinational company and joint venture, 8.21
    ownership of joint venture, 8.20

Know how
  licensing, 3.26
  TRIPS, protection by, 9.54

Index

Leasing in international trade
  international commercial litigation, *see* International commercial litigation
  leasing as means of business, 6.114
  rights and duties of parties
    lessee, rights and duties, 6.124–6.126
    lessor, rights and duties, 6.122–6.123
    parties, definition, 6.121
  supplier, rights and duties, 6.127
  UNIDROIT Convention on International Financial Leasing
    international financial leasing, definition, 6.117–6.118
    overview, 6.115–6.116
    scope of application, 6.119–6.120

Licensing agreements, 3.1
  foreign investment, 9.26
    investment made under, 9.27
  forms of licensing agreements
    celebrity licensing agreements, 3.26
    character licensing agreements, 3.26
    technology transfer agreements, 3.26
    trademark licensing agreements, 3.26
  international commercial litigation, *see* International commercial litigation
  legal framework for licensing
    domestic law, 3.24
      Australian case, 3.25
    international convention, 3.23
  legal issues of licensing agreements
    competition law, 3.29
    contract law, 3.28
    protection of intellectual property, 3.27
  licensing, meaning
    commercial licensing, 3.21
    international commercial licensing, 3.21
  licensing agreement, definition, 3.22
  technology transfer agreements, 3.37, 3.43

Licensing Guide for Developing Countries
  technology, definition, 3.37

Limited liability
  carriers, 4.353–4.257

Liner bills of lading, 4.58

Litigation *see* **International commercial litigation**

Lloyd's of America, 7.109

Lloyd's of London, 7.2, 7.27, 7.29

London Court of International Arbitration, 12.54

Madrid Agreement concerning International Registration of Marks, 3.38

Marine Insurance Act 1906 (UK), 7.2, 7.18, 7.26, 7.30

Marine Insurance Act 1909 (Cth) (Aus)
  assignment of policy, 7.99
  broker's duties, 7.72
  contract of indemnity, 7.3
  insurable interest, 7.31
  insurer's duties and inherent vice, 7.67
  international marine insurance, 7.30
  losses, included and excluded, 7.80
  losses under, 7.86–7.90
  marine insurance contract, 7.4, 7.18, 7.23, 7.46, 7.49, 7.51, 7.52, 7.58
    doctrine of utmost good faith, 7.60
    matter not subject to disclosure, 7.64
  marine risks, 7.36–7.42
  measure of indemnity, 7.91
  reinsurance and insurer's liability, 7.75
  subrogation, insurer's right, 7.100

Marine insurance in international trade
  assignment of policy, 7.99
  assured's duty to disclose information
    doctrine of utmost good faith, 7.59, 7.60, 7.61
      strictness of, 7.62
    matter not subject to disclosure, 7.64, 7.65, 7.66
    strictness of duty to disclose, 7.63
  broker's duties to asssured and insurer, 7.71
    legal relationship, 7.72
    liabilities between underwriter and brokers, 7.74
    main duties to insurer, 7.73
  burden of proof as to cause of loss, 7.77, 7.78, 7.79
  cargo insurance, 7.6
  cargo insurance contract, 7.12
    cargo owner or agent, purchased by, 7.21
    CIF contract, 7.20
    contract of sale and marine insurance, 7.17
    domestic law, regulated by, 7.23
    FOB contract, 7.20
    form of, 7.22
    general exclusion clauses, 7.12
    Incoterm, 7.20
    Institute cargo clauses, 7.12, 7.14, 7.15
    risks covered by, 7.12–7.14, 7.15
    terms of contract, 7.16
    unseaworthiness and unfitness exclusions, 7.13
    war exclusion clause, 7.13
  contract of indemnity, 7.3
    marine insurance contract, definition, 7.4
    third party's interest under contract, 7.5
  history of, 7.1–7.2
  hull insurance and cargo insurance
    traditional classifications, 7.6

references are to paragraph numbers

Marine insurance in international trade — *cont'd*
  hull insurance contract, 7.7
    broker and agent, between, 7.25
    characteristics, 7.24
    Institute Time Clauses Hulls, 7.10, 7.11
    insurance policy, 7.8
    insurer and insured, between, 7.25
    insurer's liability, 7.9
    risks covered by, 7.10, 7.11
    variety of, 7.24
  indemnity, determination of
    insurer's duty to pay excessive sum, 7.94
    measure of indemnity, 7.91
      definition, 7.92
      partial losses, and, 7.93
    suing and labouring clauses, 7.95
      American Institute Cargo Clauses, 7.97
      Institute Cargo Clauses, 7.96
      recovery of reasonable expenses, 7.98
  insurable interest, 7.31–7.35
    concept of interpretation, 7.34
    definition, 7.31, 7.32
  interest, meaning, 7.35
  marine risks, and, 7.42
    validity of marine insurance policy, 7.33
  insurer's duties and inherent vice
    cover in policy, 7.68
    inherent vice, meaning, 7.67, 7.69
    unseaworthiness, 7.70
  legal framework for
    commercial customs usages and practices, 7.27
    domestic law, governed by, 7.26
    Institute of London Underwriters
      Institute Clauses, 7.28
      New Institute Clauses, 7.28
      standard contracts, 7.28
    Lloyd's of London, 7.29
    Marine Insurance Act 1909 (Cth), 7.30
    standard contracts, 7.29
    UNCTAD Model Clauses on Marine Cargo Insurance 1987, 7.30
  losses, categories of
    constructive losses and rights of insurer, 7.89
    constructive total loss, 7.87
      alternative tests, 7.88
    marine Insurance Act 1909 (Cth), under, 7.86
    particular losses, 7.90
  losses, included and excluded
    exclusion clauses, 7.80, 7.81
    grounds for excluding, 7.83
    included losses, 7.80
    misconduct or negligence, 7.85
    reasons for exclusion, 7.82
    wilful misconduct, 7.84
  marine insurance contract
    cargo insurance contracts, 7.19
    general principles, 7.18
      contract law, 7.18
      domestic marine insurance law, 7.18
    hull insurance contracts, 7.19
  marine insurance contracts, categories of
    blanket policies, 7.53
    classified by terms, 7.45
    floating policies, 7.51
    hull insurance or cargo insurance contract, 7.44
    open cover, 7.52
    subject-matter insured, 7.44
    valued and unvalued policies, 7.46, 7.47, 7.48
    voyage and time policies, 7.49, 7.50
  marine insurance documents, forms of
    broker's cover note, 7.56, 7.57
    certificate of insurance, 7.56
    form of policy, 7.54
    letter of insurance, 7.56
    policy, 7.55
    principles of contract, based on, 7.58
    slip or memorandum of insurance, 7.55
  marine risks
    insurable interest, and, 7.42
    marine adventure, risks incidental to , 7.41
    maritime perils under Marine Insurance Act 1909 (Cth), 7.39
      maritime perils, definition, 7.40
    perils of sea in general, 7.36, 7.38
      negligence of employees, 7.37
    summary of, 7.43
  reinsurance and insurer's liability, 7.75, 7.76
  subrogation, insurer's right of, 7.100, 7.101

Mate's receipts
  bills of lading, and, 4.64, 4.65

Mediation, 12.1, 12.108, 12.109

Ministerial Conference, WTO, 9.6

Montreal Protocol 1978
  aviation insurance
  legal framework, 7.108
  third party liability insurance, 7.119, 7.120

Most favoured nation (MFN) treatment
  GATS, 9.47
  GATT
    general meaning of MFN treatment, 9.21
    MFN in GATT, 9.22
  NAFTA, 10.33
  TRIPS Agreement, 9.58

Multilateral Agreement on Investment (MAI), 8.53–8.57
  draft MAI, 8.54
  foreign investment, regulation, 8.55
  obligations on parties, 8.56

Index

provisions, 8.54
purpose, 8.53
structure, 8.54
Multilateral Investment Guarantee Agency (MIGA)
operation of, 8.65
  breach of contract, 8.65
  expropriation, 8.65
  insurance service available to members, 8.66
  transfer restriction, 8.65
  war and civil disturbance, 8.65
status of, 8.62, 8.63
  membership, 8.64
Multilateral Trade Organisation (MTO), 9.1
Multimodal means of carriage
legal framework
  Liability of Operators of Transport Terminals in International Trade 1991, 4.12
  United Nations Convention on International Multimodal Transport of Goods 1980, 4.11
multimodal transport, carriage of goods by
  legal implications, 4.320, 4.321
  multimodal transport, meaning, 4.319
  through document of transport, present law, 4.322–4.328
  UN Convention on International Multimodal Transport of Goods
    arbitration under convention, 4.338
    consignor, liability, 4.335
    limitation of actions, 4.337
    limits of liability, 4.334
    meaning, 4.329
    multimodal transport document, 4.331, 4.332
    multimodal transport operator, liability, 4.333
    notice of claim, 4.336
    scope of operation, 4.330
Multinational enterprises (MNEs)
foreign investment
  advantages, 8.18
  control of subsidiaries, 8.17
  decisions of the Council, 8.47–8.52
  form of foreign investment, 8.18
  general considerations and practical approaches, 8.47
  OECD Guidelines for, 8.44
Multinational Investment Agreement, 8.6

National treatment
GATS, 9.53
GATT
  general meaning, 9.23
  national treatment in GATT, 9.24
NAFTA, 10.32
TRIPS Agreement, 9.57
Negative pledge, 6.36
negative pledge clause, 6.48, 6.49
Negligence
shipper, liability arising from, 4.133
Negotiable or non-negotiable bills, 4.53
Netherlands Arbitration Institute, 12.55
New York Convention on the Recognition and Enforcement of Arbitral Awards 1958
application of, 12.13
  foreign arbitral award, 12.13, 12.14
arbitral rules, 12.11
commercial arbitration, internationalisation, 12.10
  functions of, 12.12
  international commercial arbitration, and foreign awards, meaning, 12.83
foreign arbitral awards, 12.84
  tests, 12.85
international arbitral awards, validity, 12.93–12.94
  recognising and enforcing award, conditions
    arbitral agreement, validity of, 12.89–12.92
    recognition distinguished from enforcement, 12.86
  refusal of international arbitral awards, grounds for, 12.95–12.105
    arbitration agreement, invalidity, 12.96
    Article V as main grounds, 12.95
    authority to conduct arbitral proceedings, lack of, 12.101
    authority to make award, lack of, 12.99–12.100
    illegality of award under local law, 12.103
    legal effect in award, lack of, 12.102
  procedural fairness, 12.97–12.98
  public policy, violation of, 12.105
uniformity of rules, 12.87
  obligations under, 12.15
    contracting parties, obligations, 12.15
    exceptions to obligations, 12.16
Non-discrimination
GATT, principle of
  eliminating quantitative restrictions, 9.27
  international commerce, meaning in, 9.25
  non-discrimination in GATT, 9.26
Non-negotiable sea waybills, 4.55
North America Free Trade Agreement (NAFTA)
dispute settlement mechanism, 10.35, 11.3
major principles of
  MFN principle, 10.33
  national treatment principle, 10.32

references are to paragraph numbers

International Commercial Law

North America Free Trade Agreement (NAFTA) — *cont'd*
    objectives of NAFTA, 10.31
    transparency of law and regulations, 10.34
    model of trade regulation, as, 10.36
    organisational structure
        features of NAFTA, 10.28
        Free Trade Commission, 10.29
        NAFTA Secretariat, 10.30
    overview, 10.27

Organisation for Economic Cooperation and Development (OECD)
    e-commerce, recent developments, 3.46
    foreign investment, 8.5
    decisions of the Council, 8.47–8.52
        conflicting requirements, 8.47, 8.50
        international investment incentives and disincentives, 8.47, 8.51
        national contact points, 8.47, 8.48
        national treatment, 8.47, 8.49
    general considerations and practical approaches, 8.45, 8.46
    Legal Guide on International Countertrade Transactions, 8.58
    definitions and rules flexible, 8.61
    structure of, 8.60
    trade and investment activity, 8.59
    Multilateral Agreement on Investment (MAI), 8.53
    draft MAI, 8.54
    obligations or requirements, 8.56
    regulation of foreign investment, 8.55
    structure of, 8.54
    WTO members, 8.57
    Multilateral Investment Guarantee Agency (MIGA)
        operation of, 8.65–8.66
        status of, 8.62–8.64
    regulation, 8.37
    OECD Declaration
        principles of, 8.42
        conflicting requirements, 8.42
        construed as, 8.43
        consultation procedures, 8.42
        international enterprises incentives and disincentives, 8.42
    review, 8.42
        national treatment, 8.42
    structure, 8.38–8.41
        adoption, 8.39
        members, 8.38
        rationale, 8.40

OECD Guidelines for Multinational Enterprises, 9.44

***Pari Passu* clauses**, 6.50
Paris Convention for the Protection of Industry Property 1883, 3.38
Passenger liability insurance, 7.104, 7.110, 7.112
Passing of property
    sale of goods legislation, Australia, 1.44–1.55
        delivery on approval, 1.53
        implied intention, 1.46, 1.47
        intention ascertained, 1.45, 1.48
        unconditional contract, 1.50
Passing of risk
    Chinese Code of Contact Law, 1.110
    CSIG, under, 2.277, *see also* United Nations Convention for the International Sale of Goods (CISG)
    sale of goods legislation, Australia, 1.56–1.59
        CISG provisions, 1.58
        Incoterm, incorporation, 1.59
        liability for costs, losses or damages in delay, 1.57
        risk and property pass together, 1.57
Patent Cooperation Treaty 1970, 3.38
Patents, 3.2
    rights, licensing of, 3.26
    TRIPS, protection by, 9.54, 9.55
Payment in international trade
    cash in advance, payment by, 5.18
    collection, payment by, 5.1
        banks' general duties in collection, 5.879
        bills of exchange, 5.27–5.70, 5.26–5.70, *see also* Bills of exchange
        broad sense of term, 5.21
        clean collection, 5.76, 5.77
        collection, definition, 5.20
        direct collection, 5.76
        documentary collection, 5.75
        documents involved in, 5.26
        parties involved in process, 5.24, 5.25
        process of collection, 5.22, 5.23
        promissory notes, 5.16, 5.71, *see also* Promissory notes
    concerns in effecting payment, 5.3
    definitions of terms in effecting payment, 5.17
    direct payment between seller and buyer, 5.1
    documentary credit, payment by, 5.1, 5.8, 5.80–5.149, *see also* Documentary credit
        bill of exchange, compared to, 5.86–5.88
        categories of, 5.90–5.107
        UCP 500, effect, and, 5.117–5.119

Index

categorising according to instruction for payment, 5.111–5.116
contracts, and, 5.82
definition, 5.80, 5.81
doctrine of strict compliance, 5.131–5.134
fraud and applicant's right under, 5.148, 5.149
irrevocable credit
    fraud and bank' obligation under, 5.141–5.147
non-conforming documents, tender of, 5.135, 5.136
operation of, 5.89–5.91
rules governing, 5.120–5.130
short-circuiting in international trade, 5.137–5.140
UCP 500, and, 5.83, 5.84, 5.85
domestic law, means of payment under
    Australian legal framework, 5.12
    Bills of Exchange Act 1909 (Cth), 5.12, 5.13
        bills of exchange, regulation of use, 5.14
        cheques, regulation of use, 5.15
        promissory notes, regulation of use, 5.16
international legal framework for payment
    domestic law, 5.11
    Geneva Uniform Law on Bills of Exchange and Promissory Notes, 5.9, 5.10
    ICC rules, 5.9
    international commercial law, 5.11
    international conventions, 5.9
means of payment, 5.2
methods of payment, 5.4
    cash in advance, 5.5
    collection, 5.7
    documentary credit, 5.8
    open account, 5.6
open account, payment by, 5.19
payment through banks, 5.1
process of international sale, 5.2
UN Conventions, means of payment under
    bill of exchange, law affecting
        acceptance of bill, 5.165–5.168
        bill, definition, 5.155, 5.157
        concept of holder under Convention, 5.162–5.164
        discharge of bill, 5.169
        negotiability of bill, 5.158–5.161
        overview, 5.150–5.152
        scope of application, 5.153
    guarantee and standby credit, law affecting, 5.173–5.178
    promissory note, law affecting, 5.150, 5.151
        definition, 5.171, 5.172

Privity of contract, doctrine of, 7.104
Privity rule
    documentary credit, 5.120
Product liability insurance, 7.110
Promissory notes
    Bills of Exchange Act 1909 (Cth), 5.71, 5.74
    definition, 5.71 5.72
    guarantor, indemnity, 5.74
    international transactions, 5.73
    regulation, 5.16
    UN Conventions, means of payment under definition, 5.171–5.172
Protectionism
    foreign investment, regulation, 8.86
Protocol to Amend the Convention on Damage Caused by Foreign Aircraft to Third Parties on the Surface 1978 (Montreal Protocol) *see* **Montreal Protocol**
Purchase agreements
    exclusive purchase agreements
        distribution agreements, 3.33

Real estate disputes
    conflict of laws, and, 11.51, 11.52
Regional trade organisations
    Asia Pacific Economic Cooperation (APEC), 10.1, 10.15, *see also* Asia Pacific Economic Cooperation (APEC)
    Association of South East Asian Nations (ASEAN), 10.1, 10.20, *see also* Association of South East Asian Nations (ASEAN)
    Australia-New Zealand Closer Economic Relations, 10.1, 10.37, *see also* Australia-New Zealand Closer Economic Relations
    European Union (EU), 10.1, 10.2, *see also* European Union (EU)
    geographical connections, 10.1
    North America Free Trade Agreement (NAFTA), 10.1, 10.27, *see also* North America Free Trade Agreement (NAFTA)
Remedies
    international sale of goods
        buyers and sellers
            CISG, under, *see* United Nations Convention on Contracts for the International sale of Goods 1980 (CISG)
    sale of goods legislation, Australia
        buyers, 1.89–1.95
        sellers, 1.81–1.88
Rental rights
    TRIPS Agreement, 9.59

references are to paragraph numbers

Report on the Economic and Social Impacts of Electronic Commerce: Preliminary Findings and Research Agenda 1999, 3.46

Rome Convention
aviation insurance
  legal framework, 7.108
  third party liability insurance, 7.116, 7.117, 7.120

Sale of Goods Act 1923 (NSW)
goods, meaning, 1.11

Sale of goods legislation, Australia
buyer's remedies, under, 1.89
  claim damages for breach of warranty, to, 1.92
  claim damages for non-delivery, to, 1.91
  claim interest or special damages, to, 1.93
  Incoterms 2000, 1.95
  remedies, application, 1.79
  terminate contract where breach, 1.90
conformity of goods under, implied conditions, 1.73
  conformity rules, application, 1.79
  consumer protection, 1.79
  goods are merchantable, 1.76
  goods conform with contract description, 1.75
  goods conform with sample, 1.78
  goods fit for purpose acquired, 1.77
  Incoterms 2000, 1.80
  seller has title to sell, 1.74
consignee, definition, 4.32
constitutional implications, 1.41
delivery of goods under, rules, 1.60
  acceptance of delivery, 1.70
  adequate contract of carriage by seller, 1.68
  delivery of wrong quantity, 1.66
  delivery rules, application, 1.72
  general rule, 1.61
  goods in third party's possession, 1.64
  goods readiness for insurance, notification, 1.69
  incidental costs for delivery, 1.65
  instalment deliveries, 1.67
  presumed place of delivery, 1.62
  rejected goods, buyer's duty, 1.71
  time for delivery, 1.63
formation of contract under, 1.42
  letter of confirmation, 1.43
passing of property under, 1.44
  application of rule, 1.55
  delivery on approval, 1.53
  express intention, 1.44
  implied intention, 1.46, 1.47
  Incoterms, use of, 1.55
  intention to be ascertained, 1.45, 1.48
  specific goods, deliverable state, 1.51, 1.52
  time and manner to be ascertained, 1.49
  unascertained goods, 1.54
  unconditional contract, 1.50
seller's remedies under, rights, 1.81
  claim damages, to, 1.85
  claim interest or special damages, to, 1.86–1.88
  Incoterms, application, 1.88
  remedies, application, 1.87
  stop goods in transit, to, 1.83
  sue for unpaid price of goods, to, 1.84
  withhold delivery, to, 1.82
transfer of risk under, 1.56
  CISG provisions, 1.58
  Incoterm, incorporation, 1.59
  liability for costs, losses or damages in delay, 1.57
  risk and property pass together, 1.57
uniformity of legislation, 1.40

Secretariat
ASEAN, 10.24
NAFTA, 10.28
WTO, 9.12

Sellers
foreign party, as, 1.1
international sale of goods
  CISG, *see* United Nations Convention on Contracts for the International Sale of Goods 1980 (CISG)
  Incoterms, responsibilities under terms, 1.16–1.18, 1.21–1.30, *see also* Incoterms 2000
  sale of goods legislation, Australia
  seller's remedies under, rights, 1.81–1.88

Shipped or ocean bills, 4.50, 4.51

Shippers
meaning of shipper
  Hague-Visby Rules, under, 4.27
  Hamburg Rules, under, 4.28, 4.29
  intention of parties in contract, 4.30
shipper's liability under Hague-Visby Rules or Hague Rules, 4.123
  accurate information, obligation to provide, 4.124, 4.125
  dangerous goods, obligations, 4.126–4.132
  fault or negligence of, 4.133
  freight, liability to pay, 4.134
shipper's liability under Hamburg Rules
  dangerous goods, and, 4.166
  general duty, 4.165
  guarantee, and, 4.167, 4.168

Society for Worldwide Interbank Financial Telecommunication (SWIFT), 6.3, 6.7

Sole foreign ventures
foreign investment, 8.24, 8.25

Index

Sovereignty
  foreign investment, regulation, 8.86
Strasbourg Convention on the Unification of Certain Points of Substantive Patent Law 1971, 3.38
Subrogation
  insurer's right of
    marine insurance, 7.100, 7.101
Swap options, 6.91–6.96
  back-to-back loans, 6.93
  cross currency interest rate swap, 6.96
  currency swap, 6.95
  interest rate swap, 6.94
  parallel loans, 6.92
Sydney Maritime Arbitration Rules and Terms (SMART), 12.61

Taxation law
  franchising agreements, 3.19
Technology transfer agreements, 3.1, 3.26
  defining technology transfer agreements
    Licensing Guide for Developing Countries, 3.37
    technology, definition, 3.37
  forms of technology transfer, 3.42
  legal framework for international transfer of technology
    domestic regulation of technology transfers, 3.41
      Chinese Code of Contract Law, 3.41
      EU Regulation on Technology Transfer Agreements, 3.40
      International Code of Conduct on Transfer of Technology
      international collation, 3.39
    national regulation, principles, 3.39
    restrictive trade practices, 3.39
    rights and obligations of parties, 3.39
    settlement of disputes, 3.39
    special provisions for developing countries, 3.39
    technology transfer, definition, 3.39
    international legal framework
      conventions and instruments, 3.38
    legal issues of technology transfer, 3.43
      Chinese Code of Contracts Law, 3.43
      distribution agreements, 3.43
      EU Regulation for Technology Transfer Agreements, 3.43
      franchising agreements, 3.43
      licensing agreements, 3.43
      TOT Code, 3.43

Through bills of lading, 4.56, 4.57
Through document of transport, 4.322–4.328
Tortious disputes
  conflict of laws, and
    exceptions, 11.49, 11.50
    general rules for tortious disputes, 11.44–11.47, 11.48
    international commerce, 11.42, 11.43
Trade Facilitation Information Exchange (TraFix), 3.48
Trademark licence agreements, 3.26
Trade organisations *see* International trade organisations; Regional trade organisations
Trade Policy Review Body (TPRB), **WTO**, 9.13
Trade Practices Act 1974 (Cth)
  consumer protection, 1.79
  goods, meaning, 1.11
  licensing agreements, 3.28
Trade regulation, model of
  APEC, as, 10.19
  ASEAN, as, 10.26
  Australia-New Zealand Closer Economic Relations, as, 10.38
  NAFTA, as, 10.36
Trade secrets
  licensing, 3.26
  TRIPS, protection by, 9.55
Transnational corporations, 8.18
Treaty on Intellectual Property in Respect of Integrated Circuits 1989, 3.38
TRIMs *see* Agreement on Trade-Related Investment Measures (TRIMs)
TRIPs *see* Agreement on Trade-Related Aspects of Intellectual Property Rights (TRIPs)

UNCITRAL
  Build-Operate-Transfer (BOT) project
    definition, 8.30
UNCITRAL Legal Guide on International Countertrade Transactions, 8.37, 8.58
  concept, 8.59
  definitions and rules, flexible, 8.61
  structure of, 8.60
UNCITRAL Model Law on Electronic Commerce 1996, 3.48, 3.49
UNCITRAL Model Law on Electronic Signatures, 3.48
UNCITRAL Model Law on International Commercial Arbitration 1985, 12.2, 12.31
  arbitral award
    binding and enforceable, 12.42

International Commercial Law

UNCITRAL Model Law on International Commercial Arbitration 1985 — *cont'd*
   effect, 12.39
   setting aside, grounds for, 12.40
      application for, 12.41
   arbitral rules, 12.11
   arbitral tribunal
      arbitrators, and, 12.36
      jurisdiction of, 12.37
      proceedings of, 12.38
   arbitration agreement
      meaning, 12.33
      obligation of court, and, 12.34, 12.35
   commercial arbitration
      commercial, definition, 12.7
      internationalisation of, 12.10
   features, 12.32
   international commercial arbitration practice, 12.31
   law of arbitral procedures, uniformity, 12.31

UNCITRAL Model Law on International Credit Transfers of 1992, 1.6, 5.11, 5.17, 6.6
   forfaiting in international trade, 6.128
      means of fund transfers, 6.132
      methods for transferring funds internationally, 6.133
   regulation of credit transfers, 6.130

UNCITRAL Model Law on Procurement of Goods, Construction and Services 1994, 1.6

UNCITRAL Recommendations on the Legal Value of Computer Records 1985, 3.48

UNCITRAL Uniform Rules on Electronic Signature 1999, 3.48

UNCTAD
   foreign investment, 8.5, 8.7
      regulation of, 8.37

UNCTAD Model Clauses on Marine Cargo Insurance 1987, 7.27, 7.30

Understanding on Rules and Procedures Governing the Settlement of Disputes *see* DSU

UNIDROIT Convention on Agency in the International Sale of Goods 1983, 1.6

UNIDROIT Convention on International Factoring, 6.6
   factoring contract, definition, 6.103–6.105
   overview, 6.101–6.102
   scope of application, 6.106–6.107

UNIDROIT Convention on International Financial Leasing, 6.6
   international financial leasing, definition, 6.117–6.118
   overview, 6.115–6.116

   scope of application, 6.119–6.120

UNIDROIT Convention on International Financing
   factoring contract, definition, 6.103–6.105
   overview, 6.101–6.102
   scope of application, 6.106–6.107

Uniform Law on International Sale of Goods 1964, 1.5, 2.1

Uniform Law on the Formation of Contracts for International Sale of Goods 1964, 1.5, 2.1

Uniform Rules concerning Contract for International Carriage of Goods by Rail (CIM), 4.10, 4.264
   carriage of goods by land, 4.10
   application of CIM, 4.273–4.275
   carrier, rights and obligations, 4.288–4.292
   carrier's liability, determination of, 4.293, 4.294
   consignment note, 4.277–4.280
   consignee, rights and obligations, 4.284–4.287
   consignor, rights and obligations, 4.281–4.283
   contract of carriage, 4.276
   limitation of action, 4.295, 4.296
   structure of CIM, 4.272

United Nations Commission on International Trade Law, *see* UNCITRAL

United Nations Convention on Contracts for the International Sale of Goods 1988 (CISG)
   Australian law, incorporating, 2.309
   buyer's duty in relation to rejected goods, 1.71
   Chinese Code of Contract Law, and, *see* Chinese Code of Contract Law
   conformity of goods, 1.79
   contracts of sale under, 2.1
      application, 2.4
         criteria, 2.4
         compulsory application of Convention, 2.6
         conflict of laws rule, 2.5
         country contracting must be member, 2.6
         franchise agreements, 2.8–2.10
         legal tradition of country, affecting application, 2.7
         severable part of contract, application to, 2.9
   buyer's remedies
      additional period of time for performance, 2.228–2.231
      avoid contract and restitution, 2.247–2.252
      avoid contract, anticipated fundamental breach, 2.264–2.266
      avoid contracts in general, right to, 2.237–2.247
      categories of remedies, 2.219–2.222
      damages claim and foreseeability, 2.268–2.269

Index

damages claim and instalment deliveries, 2.267
damages claim and market price, 2.273
damages claim and purchase of substitute goods, 2.270–2.272
damages, right to claim, 2.220
interest, right to claim, 2.275–2.276
mitigation of loss, and, 2.274
performance, right to require, 2.224–2.227
proviso of no-fault, right and, 2.223
reduce price, right to, 2.253–2.256
refuse delivery, limited right to, 2.257–2.259
set-off, 2.221–2.222
specific performance, and, 2.236
substitute goods and restitution, right to request, 2.232–2.235
suspend contract, right to, 2.260–2.263
constitutional implications of Convention, 2.315, 2.316
contracting countries, 2.2, 2.3
modification and interpretation, potential use of Convention
  domestic parol evidence rule, 2.307
  fundamental issues, 2.302
  legal tradition of country, 2.308
  principles for interpretation, 2.304, 2.305, 2.308
  provisions construed in broad context, 2.304
  provisions, modification and variation, 2.303
modifying or varying effect of provisions
  exclusions, 2.23, 2.26, 2.27
  express agreement, by, 2.23
  international sale, 2.28
  legal traditions, same or similar, 2.24
  procedural requirements, 2.28
  provisions allowing, 2.21–2.28
  reservations to provisions, 2.22
operation of Convention, rules governing, 2.15–2.17
passing of property in goods, 1.44
passing of risk under
  absence of rules governing, 2.278
  buyer's duty to pay price, 2.279, 2.280
  delivery, through, 2.288
  goods sold in transit, 2.285, 2.287
  goods to be transported by carrier, 2.282–2.283
  issue in sale of goods, 2.277
  seller's fundamental breach, 2.289, 2.290
  unascertained goods, 2.284
place of business
  application of Convention, relevant for, 2.13
  court, determination by, 2.14
  international nature of contract, 2.12
  rules for determining, 2.11

preservation of goods under
  buyer's duty and right, 2.395–2.397
  preservation of goods, provisions, 2.291
  sale of goods, 2.399–2.301
  seller's duty and right, 2.292–2.294
  third party, by, 2.398
restrictions on application, 2.18
  contract of consultation, 2.19
  controversial provisions, 2.20
  sale of report and ideas, distinction, 2.19
  sales where not applicable, 2.18
seller's remedies under
  additional period for performance, right to fix, 2.176–2.180
  avoid a contract in general, right to, 2.182–2.187
  avoid contract and instalment deliveries, right to, 2.199–2.203
  avoid contract on ground of anticipated fundamental breach, 2.196–2.198
  categories of seller's remedies, 2.172
  claim and mitigation of loss, 2.214–2.215
  claim damages and foreseeability, right to, 2.204–2.207
  damages claim and market price of goods, 2.211–2.213
  damages claim and resale of goods, 2.208–2.210
  interest, right to claim, 2.216–2.218
  proviso of non-fault, right and, 2.173
  request performance, right to, 2.174–2.175
  sale of goods legislation, 1.87
  specific performance, right to, 2.181
  specifications, right to supply, 2.188–2.190
  stop delivery after suspension, 2.194–2.195
  suspend contract, right to, 2.191–2.193
domestic law, 1.8, 1.9
Ex Works in the context of, 1.15
formation of contract of sale under
  acceptance, meaning under, 2.45
    German case, 2.48
    manner of, 2.57, 2.46, 2.47
    time of acceptance, 2.45, 2.48, 2.49
    withdrawal of acceptance, 2.50
  conclusion of contract, 2.59–2.60
  counter-offer and modified acceptance, 2.54–2.55
  effective offer, meaning, 2.33–2.39
  effective rejection, 2.44
  formality of contract, 2.29
    oral contract, 2.31
    reservation to provision, 2.32–2.34
    written formality, 2.30
  late acceptance, effect of, 2.56
    delayed by errors, 2.57, 2.58

references are to paragraph numbers

International Commercial Law

United Nations Convention on Contracts for the International Sale of Goods 1988 (CISG)
— cont'd
  modification or termination of contract
    commercial transactions, 2.61
    mere agreement, 2.62, 2.63
    regulation of the formality of, 2.64
  offer, meaning of, 2.35
    description of goods, 2.35, 2.36
    offer and invitation, distinction, 2.37
    price or determinable price, 2.35, 2.36
    quantity or determinable quantity, 2.35, 2.36
  rejection of offer, 2.43
  revocation of offer, 2.40
    general rule, 2.41
    irrevocable offer, 2.41, 2.42
  rules for calculating time for acceptance, 2.51
    holidays or non-business days, 2.53
    instantaneous communication, 2.51
    letter or telegram, 2.51, 2.52
  fundamental breach of contract under
    Article 25, under, 2.66
      foreseeability, 2.72–2.75
      fundamental breach, definition, 2.67–2.69
      reasonable person test, and, 2.73, 2.74
    Article 25, history, 2.70
      detriment, 2.71
      fundamental obligation, 2.70
      substantial detriment, 2.71
    definition, 2.71, 2.72
  fundamental breach, flexible meaning, 2.65
  Hague Conventions, replacing, 2.1
  international commercial arbitration, and, 12.106–12.107
  international sale of goods contracts, 1.35–1.39
    marine insurance contract, 7.18
  member countries, 2.2–2.3
  performance of contract of sale under
    buyer's obligations, performance of
      buyer's obligations, definition, 2.151
      delivery, to take, 2.151, 2.164–2.168
      determination of price, 2.154–2.156
      exemptions, 2.169–2.171
      pay price of goods, 2.151, 2.152–2.153
      place of payment, 2.157–2.159
      time of payment, 2.160–2.163
    defining performance, 2.76
      buyers and sellers from two countries, 2.78
      mixed contractual relationships, 2.76
    seller's obligations, performance
      breach of title, limitation of action based on, 2.101–2.102
      buyer's right of examination, 2.129–2.133
      conformity after delivery, to ensure, 2.127–2.128
      conformity of goods, meaning under Convention, 2.103–2.107
      conformity of goods with contract, 2.79
      conformity of goods with sample, 2.118–2.119
      contract of carriage, to enter, 2.89, 2.90
      delivery in accordance with contract, 2.79
      documents, to deliver, 2.93–2.97
      exemptions, 2.147–2.150
      fitness for purpose, 2.108–2.110
      implied terms, provisos relating to, 2.122–2.124
      insurance, to facilitate, 2.91, 2.92
      intellectual property, title to sell, 2.299
      latent defect, 2.125–2.126
      limitation period under Convention, 2.136–2.138
      merchantability of goods, 2.111–2.117
      non-conformity, notice of, 2.134–2.135
      notice on consignment of goods, 2.87–2.88
      packaging, reasonable manner of, 2.120–2.121
      place of delivery, 2.81–2.82
      self-cure remedy after date of delivery, 2.144–2.146
      self-cure remedy before date of delivery, 2.139–2.143
      time for delivery, 2.83–2.86
      title to sell in general, 2.98
  sale of goods, meaning, 1.11

United Nations Convention on Independent Guarantees and Stand-by Letters of Credit 1995, 1.6

United Nations Convention on International Bills of Exchange and International Promissory Notes 1988, 1.6, 6.6
  means of payment of international trade
    bills of exchange and promissory notes
      acceptance of bill, 5.165–5.168
      concept of holder under convention, 5.162–5.164
      definition of bill, 5.155–5.157
      definition of promissory note, 5.171–5.172
      discharge of bill, 5.169–5.170
      negotiability of bill, 5.158–5.161
      overview, 5.150–5152
      scope of application, 5.153–5.154
    guarantee and standby credit, law affecting, 5.173–5.178

United Nations Convention on International Multimodal Transport of Goods 1980, 1.5, 4.11
  arbitration under, 4.338
  consignor, liability of, 4.335

Index

limitation of action, 4.337
limits of liability, 4.334
meaning of, 4.329
multimodal transport document, 4.331, 4.332
multimodal transport operator, liability of, 4.333
notice of claim, 4.336
scope of operation, 4.330

United Nations Convention on the Carriage of Goods by Sea 1978 (Hamburg Rules) *see* **Hamburg Rules**

United Nations Convention on the Liability of Operators of Transport Terminals in International Trade 1991 (OTT Convention), 4.5, 4.122

United Nations Convention on the Limitation Period in the International Sale of Goods 1974, 1.6

United Nations Economic and Social Council (UNECOSCO)
foreign investment, regulation, 8.37

United Nations Rules for Electronic Data Interchange for Administration, Commerce and Transport (UN/EDIFACT Standards), 3.48

Universal Copyright Convention 1952, 3.38

Uruguay Round of GATT Negotiations 1993
foreign investment, regulation, 8.67, 8.68, 8.69
GATS, and, 9.40 *see also* General Agreement on Trade and Service 1993 (GATS)
intellectual property, 3.2
World Trade Organisation (WTO), *see* World Trade Organisation (WTO) 1995

Warsaw Convention, 4.8, 4.191, *see also* **Warsaw System**
carriage of goods under
application of Convention, 4.201–4.209
carriage outside, carrier's liability, 4.210
Hague Protocol, and, 4.191
members, 4.192

Warsaw System, 4.192
carriage of goods by air, 4.8, 4.9
conventions contained in, 4.8
Hague Protocol, 4.8, 4.191–4.196
members of, 4.192
objectives of, 4.199, 4.200
structure, 4.191–4.198
Guadalajara Convention, 4.197
international conventions, 4.195, 4.196
Montreal Agreement, 4.198
regimes of, 4.196

Washington Convention 1965
arbitration under
arbitral tribunal, 12.27
award of arbitrator, 12.29
powers and functions, 12.28
arbitration proceedings, 12.26
ICSID
arbitration proceedings, 12.26–12.29, 12.30
creation of, 12.2, 12.17
jurisdiction of, 12.24, 12.25
structure of, 12.19–12.23
international commercial arbitration, 12.2
arbitral rules, 12.11
overview of Convention, 12.17
rules for conciliation and arbitration, 12.18

World Bank
foreign investment, regulation, 8.37
ICSID, and, 12.19
international banking and financing, 6.5

World Franchise Association
franchising, self-regulation, 3.11

World Intellectual Property Organisation
Licensing Guide for Developing Countries
technology, definition, 3.37

World Trade Organisation (WTO) 1995
Agreement and annexes, 9.4
Agreement on TRIPS, 9.1, 9.54, *see also* Agreement on Trade-Related Aspects of Intellectual Property Rights
competition law
anti-trust and anti-dumping laws
relationship between, 9.76
anti-trust legislation, purpose of, 9.75
anti-trust, origin of term, 9.74
Declaration on Global Electronic Commerce 1998, 3.48
dispute settlement within WTO
Dispute Settlement Body (DSB)
functions, 9.62
dispute settlement mechanism, 9.61
Understanding on Rules and Procedures Governing the Settlement of Disputes (DSU), 9.11
arbitration under, 9.73
consultation under, 9.64
general procedures under, 9.63
good offices and mediation under, 9.65
panel proceedings under, 9.66–9.69
panel report, effect, 9.70
appeal process, 9.71
Appellate Body's report, effect, 9.72
Dispute Settlement Body (DSB), 9.11
distribution agreements, 3.34
e-commerce

references are to paragraph numbers

World Trade Organisation (WTO) 1995 — *cont'd*
   defining, 3.45
   Electronic Commerce and Development Seminar
      legal issues arising from e-commerce, 3.47
      international efforts to regulate, 3.48
   European Union, and, relationship, 10.14
   foreign investment, 8.4, 8.5
      Agreement on Trade-Related Investment Measures, 8.67
         determination of a TRIM under, 8.82
         effects test, and, 8.74–8.76
         exceptions to obligation of not applying prohibited TRIMs, 8.80
         GATT, and, 8.77–8.79
         overview, 8.73
         prohibited TRIMs and transitional period, elimination, 8.81
      issue of, as, 8.67
      regulation of, 8.37
      TRIMs, definition, 8.71
         export requirements, 8,.72
         export restrictions, 8.72
         import restrictions, 8.71
         non-trade specific TRIMS, 8.72
   functions of, 9.3
   WTO Agreement and annexes, 9.3
   General Agreement on Tariffs and Trade (GATT), 9.1, 9.16, *see also* General Agreement on Tariffs and Trade (GATT)
   General Agreement on Trade in Service (GATS), 9.1, 9.39, *see also* General Agreement on Trade in Service (GATS)
   history of, 9.2
   intellectual property contracts, 3.1
   international commercial litigation, *see* International commercial litigation
   international trade organisations, and, 9.77
   licensing agreements, 3.23
   Multilateral Trade Organisation (MTO), 9.1
   regional trade agreements, 10.1
   regional trade organisations
      APEC, *see* Asia Pacific Economic Cooperation (APEC)
      ASEAN, *see* Association of South East Asian nations(AASEAN)
      Australia-New Zealand Closer Economic Relations, *see* Australia-New Zealand Closer Economic Relations
      NAFTA, *see* North America Free Trade Agreement
   rules of trade between nations, 9.1
   structure, 9.5–9.15
      admission procedure, 9.15
      Council for Trade in Goods, 9.8
      Council for Trade in Service, 9.9
      Council for Trade-Related Aspects on Intellectual Property Rights, 9.10
      Dispute Settlement Body, 9.11
      functional bodies and committees, 9.14
      General Council, 9.7
      Ministerial Conference. 9.6
      Secretariat, 9.12
      status of, 9.5
      Trade Policy Review Body, 9.13
WTO *see* World Trade Organisation (WTO) 1995
WTO Ministerial Declaration on Trade in Information Technology Products 1996, 3.38